W9-BZA-931

The expanded Laudon & Laudon Companion Web site features new Electronic Commerce Projects and Software Application Exercises for every chapter. Interactive Web exercises, Student Study Guide, International Resources, monthly Technology Updates, and PowerPoint presentations are also included.

www.prenhall.com/laudon

Available as a stand-alone item or in a PH Value Pack, this interactive student CD-ROM includes "bullet" text to assist students in their understanding of the material in the text, audio and video tours, and links to the student's Web site exercises and study guide so users can continually check their progress in mastering the material.

Essentials of
Management
Information
Systems

Organization and Technology in the Networked Enterprise

Fourth Edition

Kenneth C. Laudon

New York University

Jane P. Laudon

Azimuth Information Systems

Prentice
Hall

Upper Saddle River, New Jersey 07458

Senior Acquisitions Editor: David Alexander
Editor-in-Chief: Mickey Cox
Development Editor: Rebecca Johnson
Associate Editors: Kyle Hannon and Lori Cardillo
Editorial Assistant: Erika Rusnak
Director Strategic Marketing: Nancy Evans
Sales Director: Jason Dodge
Senior Marketing Manager: Kris King
Senior Production Editor: Anne Graydon
Managing Editor/Production: Sondra Greenfield
Manufacturing Buyer: Lisa DiMaulo Babin
Senior Manufacturing Supervisor: Paul Smolenski
Associate Director, Manufacturing: Vincent Scelta
Senior Designer: Cheryl Asherman
Design Director: Pat Smythe
Interior Design: Jill Little
Cover Design: Jill Little
Cover Illustrations: Michael Hite
Production and Composition: Carlisle Communications, Inc.
Photo Research: Shirley Webster
Photo Permissions Editor: Charles Morris
Photo Permissions Supervisor: Kay Dellosa
Photo and screen capture credits appear following the indexes.

© 2001, 1999, 1997, 1995 by Prentice-Hall, Inc.
Upper Saddle River, New Jersey 07458

All rights reserved. No part of this book may be reproduced, in any form, or by any means, without permission in writing from the Publisher.

Microsoft and Windows are registered trademarks of the Microsoft Corporation in the U.S.A. and other countries. Microsoft screen shots and icons reprinted with permission from the Microsoft Corporation. This book is not sponsored or endorsed by or affiliated with the Microsoft Corporation.

Library of Congress Cataloging-in-Publication Data
Laudon, Kenneth C.
    Essentials of management information systems : organization and technology in the networked enterprise / Kenneth C. Laudon, Jane P. Laudon—4th ed.
        p. cm.
    Includes bibliographical references and index.
    ISBN 0-13-019323-2
    1. Management information systems. I. Laudon, Jane Price. II. Title.

T58.6. L3753 2001
658.4'038'011—dc 21   00-041676

Printed in the United States of America
10   9   8   7   6   5   4   3   2

Prentice-Hall International (UK) Limited, *London*
Prentice-Hall of Australia Pty. Limited, *Sydney*
Prentice-Hall Canada, Inc., *Toronto*
Prentice-Hall Hispanoamericana, S.A., *Mexico*
Prentice-Hall of India Private Limited, *New Delhi*
Prentice-Hall of Japan, Inc., *Tokyo*
Prentice-Hall (*Singapore*) Pte. Ltd.
Editora Prentice-Hall do Brasil, Ltda., *Rio de Janeiro*

For

Erica and Elisabeth

About the
Authors

Kenneth C. Laudon is a Professor of Information Systems at New York University's Stern School of Business. He holds a B.A. in Economics from Stanford and a Ph.D. from Columbia University. He has authored eleven books dealing with information systems, organizations, and society. Professor Laudon has also written over forty articles concerned with the social, organizational, and management impacts of information systems, privacy, ethics, and multimedia technology.

Professor Laudon's current research is on the planning and management of large-scale information systems and digital learning environments. He has received grants from the National Science Foundation to study the evolution of national information systems at the Social Security Administration, the IRS, and the FBI. A part of this research is concerned with computer-related organizational and occupational changes in large organizations, changes in management ideology, changes in public policy, and understanding productivity change in the knowledge sector.

Ken Laudon has testified as an expert before the United States Congress. He has been a researcher and consultant to the Office of Technology Assessment (United States Congress) and to the Office of the President, several executive branch agencies, and Congressional Committees. Professor Laudon also acts as an in-house educator for several consulting firms and as a consultant on systems planning and strategy to several Fortune 500 firms. Ken works with the Concours Group to provide advice to firms developing enterprise systems.

Ken Laudon's hobby is sailing.

Jane Price Laudon is a management consultant in the information systems area and the author of seven books. Her special interests include systems analysis, data management, MIS auditing, software evaluation, and teaching business professionals how to design and use information systems.

Jane received her Ph.D. from Columbia University, her M.A. from Harvard University, and her B.A. from Barnard College. She has taught at Columbia University and the New York University Graduate School of Business. She maintains a lifelong interest in Oriental languages and civilizations.

The Laudons have two daughters, Erica and Elisabeth.

Essentials of Management Information Systems: Organization and Technology in the Networked Enterprise reflects a deep understanding of MIS research and teaching as well as practical experience designing and building real world systems.

Management Decision Problems

Hands-on Application Exercises Found on the Companion Web Site (www.prenhall.com/laudon)

Brief Contents

Table of Contents

ix

Preface

Essentials of Management Information Systems: Organization and Technology in the Networked Enterprise (Fourth Edition) is based on the premise that it is difficult, if not impossible, to manage a modern organization without at least some knowledge of information systems—what they are, how they affect the organization and its employees, and how they can make businesses more competitive and efficient. Information systems have become essential for creating competitive firms, managing global corporations, and providing useful products and services to customers. This book provides an introduction to management information systems that undergraduate and MBA students will find vital to their professional success.

The Information Revolution in Business and Management: The New Role of Information Systems

The growth of the Internet, globalization of trade, and the emergence of information economies, have recast the role of information systems in business and management. The Internet is becoming the foundation for new business models, new business processes, and new ways of distributing knowledge. Traditional firms are finding they can use the Internet to organize suppliers, manage production, and deliver to customers. Internally, companies can use the Internet and networking technology to conduct more of their work electronically, seamlessly linking factories, offices, and sales forces around the globe. Companies such as Coca-Cola, Dell Computer, and Procter & Gamble are extending these networks to suppliers, customers, and other groups outside the organization so they can react instantly to customer demands and market shifts. When Coca-Cola corporate managers use information systems to examine their daily operations, they are able to find out exactly which bottling plant and which channels were used to sell Cola-Cola in a 500 milliliter bottle in any supermarket throughout the world. This digital integration both within the firm and without, from the warehouse to the executive suite, from suppliers to customers, is changing how we organize and manage a business firm. Accordingly, we have changed the subtitle of this text to *Organization and Technology in the Networked Enterprise.*

New to the Fourth Edition

The Internet has created a universal platform for buying and selling goods. Its technology also provides powerful capabilities for driving important business processes inside the company and for linking such processes electronically to those of other organizations. This edition more fully explores the electronic business uses of the Internet for the management of the firm as well as the Internet's growing role in electronic commerce. It includes detailed treatment of enterprise resource planning (ERP) systems and related technology for creating extended enterprises that electronically link the firm to suppliers and other industry partners. The text provides a complete set of tools for integrating the Internet and multimedia technology into the

MIS course and for promoting interactive problem solving. The following features and content reflect this new direction:

DETAILED COVERAGE OF ENTERPRISE RESOURCE PLANNING SYSTEMS AND EXTENDED ENTERPRISES

We introduce enterprise resource planning systems in Chapter 3 and provide descriptions, discussions, and case studies of enterprise systems throughout the text. We detail the management organization, and technology issues surrounding the implementation of enterprise systems and the use of these systems, the Internet, and other technologies to link with other organizations in industry-wide networks and global supply chains.

MORE ACTIVE HANDS-ON LEARNING

This edition contains several new features to help students make text concepts more meaningful by applying them in active hands-on learning projects.

New Management Decision Problems

We have added a Management Decision Problem to each chapter to encourage students to apply what they have learned to a real-world management decision-making scenario. These problems can be used for practical group or individual learning both in and outside of the classroom. The problems require students to use quantitative data to make decisions based on real-world MIS issues such as:

- Reducing operating costs (Chapter 3)
- Measuring the effectiveness of Web advertising (Chapter 8)
- Monitoring how much time employees spend on the Web (Chapter 14)

New Hands-on Application Exercises

Each chapter now features a hands-on Application Exercise where students can develop a solution using spreadsheet, database, expert system, CASE, or electronic presentation software. Some of these exercises require students to use these application software tools in conjunction with Web activities. The Application Exercises give students the opportunity to apply their software skills and text concepts in management problem solving. The complete Application Exercises along with required data files can be found at the Laudon and Laudon Web site. The Application Exercises include business problems such as:

- Developing a Web page for a small business
- Developing a hotel reservation database and management reporting system
- Developing a spreadsheet application for information technology risk assessment

INCREASED COVERAGE OF ELECTRONIC COMMERCE AND ELECTRONIC BUSINESS

The Internet, electronic commerce, and electronic business are introduced in Chapter 1 and integrated throughout the text and the entire learning package. A full chapter, entitled The Internet: Electronic Commerce and Electronic Business (Chapter 8), describes the underlying technology, capabilities, and benefits of the Internet, with expanded treatment of electronic commerce, Internet business models, and the use of intranets for the internal management of the firm. Every chapter contains a Window On box or case study devoted to electronic commerce or electronic business, as well as in-text descriptions of how the Internet is changing a particular aspect of information systems.

ENHANCED COMPANION WEB SITE

The Laudon & Laudon Web site has been enhanced to provide a wide array of capabilities for interactive learning and management problem solving that have been carefully prepared for use with the text. They include:

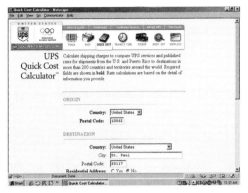

Students are presented with a problem to develop a budget for annual shipping costs. To obtain the information required for the solution, they can input data on-line and use the interactive software at this Web site to perform the required calculations or analysis.

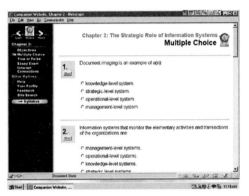

Student responses to questions are automatically graded and can be e-mailed to the instructor.

Internet Connections direct students to Web-based exercises on the Laudon Web site. Students can e-mail their work to their professors.

Electronic Commerce Projects for Every Chapter

On the Web site are Web-based Electronic Commerce exercises for each chapter. Students can use interactive software at various company Web sites to solve specific problems related to chapter concepts.

Two of these Electronic Commerce projects are longer and more comprehensive than the others. The first asks students to explore various Internet business models on the Web and develop an Internet strategy for a new business. The second asks students to research and analyze technology, design, training, and other cost components of a new Web site and calculate its Total Cost of Ownership (TCO).

Interactive Study Guide and Internet Connections for Each Chapter

For each chapter of the text, the Web site features an Interactive Study Guide and Internet Connection exercise.

- The on-line Interactive Study Guide helps students review and test their mastery of chapter concepts with a series of multiple-choice, true-false, and essay questions.

- Internet Connections noted by marginal icons in the chapter direct students to exercises and projects on the Laudon Web site related to organizations and concepts in that chapter.

Hands-on Application Exercise for Every Chapter

The Laudon Web site contains the complete description of the hands-on application software exercise for each chapter with data files required for the projects and links to relevant Web sites.

Message Boards and Chat Rooms

The Message Board allows users to post messages and check back periodically for responses. Chat Rooms allow users to discuss course topics in real-time and enable professors to host online classes.

Additional Case Studies

The Web site contains additional case studies with hyperlinks to the Web sites of the organizations they discuss.

Technology Updates
The Web site provides monthly technology updates to keep instructors and students abreast of leading-edge technology changes.

International Resources
Links to Web sites of non-U.S. companies are provided for users interested in more international material.

Unique Features of This Text

Essentials of Management Information Systems: Organization and Technology in the Networked Enterprise (Fourth Edition) has many unique features designed to create an active, dynamic learning environment.

TECHNOLOGY INTEGRATED WITH CONTENT

An interactive CD-ROM multimedia version of the text can be purchased as an optional item. In addition to the full text and bullet text summaries by chapter, the CD-ROM features interactive exercises, simulations, audio/video overviews explaining key concepts, on-line quizzes, hyperlinks to the exercises on the Laudon Web site, technology updates, and more. Students can use the CD-ROM as an interactive supplement or as an alternative to the traditional text.

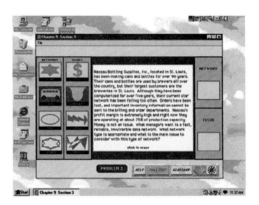

Students can reinforce and extend their knowledge of chapter concepts with interactive exercises on the CD-ROM.

TOOLS FOR INTERACTIVE LEARNING

A Tools for Interactive Learning section concluding each chapter shows students how they can extend their knowledge of each chapter with projects and exercises on the Laudon Web site and the optional CD-ROM multimedia edition.

Students and instructors can see at a glance exactly how Internet Connections, Electronic Commerce projects, and hands-on Application Exercises can be used to enhance student learning for each chapter. Students can also see immediately how the chapter can be used in conjunction with the optional CD-ROM.

Tools for Interactive Learning

○ Internet Connection

The Internet Connection for this chapter will take you to the United Parcel Service (UPS) Web site where you can complete an exercise to evaluate how UPS uses the Web and other information technology in its daily operations. You can also use the Interactive Study Guide to test your knowledge of the topics in this chapter and get instant feedback where you need more practice.

○ Electronic Commerce Project

At the Laudon Web site for Chapter 1, you will find an Electronic Commerce project that will use the interactive software at the UPS Web site to help a company calculate and budget for its shipping costs.

○ CD-ROM

If you purchase and use the Multimedia Edition CD-ROM with this chapter, you will find a simulation showing you how the Internet works, a video clip illustrating UPS's package tracking system, an audio overview of the major themes of this chapter, and bullet text summarizing the key points of the chapter.

○ Application Exercise

At the Laudon Web site, you can find a spreadsheet Application Exercise for this chapter where you can analyze investments in electronic retailing.

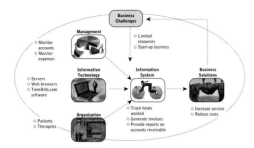

A special diagram accompanying each chapter-opening vignette graphically illustrates how management, organization, and technology elements work together to create an information system solution to the business challenges discussed in the vignette.

Each chapter opens with a vignette illustrating the themes of the chapter by showing how a real-world organization meets a business challenge using information systems.

INTEGRATED FRAMEWORK FOR DESCRIBING AND ANALYZING INFORMATION SYSTEMS

An integrated framework portrays information systems as being composed of management, organization, and technology elements. This framework is used throughout the text to describe and analyze information systems and information system problems.

REAL-WORLD EXAMPLES

Real-world examples drawn from business and public organizations are used throughout to illustrate text concepts. More than 100 companies in the United States and nearly 100 organizations in Canada, Europe, Australia, Asia, and Africa are discussed.

Each chapter contains three Window-On boxes (Window on Management, Window on Organizations, Window on Technology) that present real-world examples illustrating the management, organization, and technology issues in the chapter. Each Window-On box concludes with a section called To Think About containing questions for students to apply chapter concepts to management problem solving. The themes for each box are:

Window on Management
Management problems raised by systems and their solution; management strategies and plans; careers and experiences of managers using systems.

Window on Technology
Hardware, software, telecommunications, data storage, standards, and systems-building methodologies.

Window on Organizations
Activities of private and public organizations using information systems; experiences of people working with systems.

Management Wrap-Up provides a quick overview of the key issues in each chapter, reinforcing the authors' management, organization, and technology framework.

 MANAGEMENT WRAP-UP

Management

Management is responsible for developing the control structure and quality standards for the organization. Key management decisions include establishing standards for systems accuracy and reliability, determining an appropriate level of control for organizational functions, and establishing a disaster recovery plan.

Organization

The characteristics of the organization play a large role in determining its approach to quality assurance and control issues. Some organizations are more quality and control conscious than others. Their cultures and business processes support high standards of quality and performance. Creating high levels of security and quality in information systems can entail a lengthy process of organizational change.

Technology

A number of technologies and methodologies are available for promoting system quality and security. Technologies such as antivirus and data security software, firewalls, and programmed procedures can be used to create a control environment, whereas software metrics, systems development methodologies, and automated tools for systems development can be used to improve software quality. Organizational discipline is required to use these technologies effectively.

For Discussion

1. It has been said that controls and security should be among the first areas to be addressed in the design of an information system. Do you agree? Why or why not?

2. How much software testing is "enough"? What management, organization, and technology issues should you consider in answering this question?

MANAGEMENT WRAP-UP OVERVIEWS OF KEY ISSUES

Management Wrap-Up sections at the end of each chapter summarize key issues using the authors' management, organization, and technology framework for analyzing information systems.

A TRULY INTERNATIONAL PERSPECTIVE

In addition to a full chapter on managing international information systems (Chapter 15), all chapters of the text are illustrated with real-world examples from nearly one hundred corporations in Canada, Europe, Asia, Latin America, Africa, Australia, and the Middle East. Each chapter contains at least one Window-On box, case study, or opening vignette drawn from a non-U.S. firm, and often more. The text concludes with five major international case studies contributed by leading MIS experts in Canada, Europe, Singapore, and Australia—Len Fertuck, University of Toronto (Canada); Gerhard Schwabe, University of Koblenz (Germany); Andrew Boynton, Donald Marchand, and Janet Shaner, International Institute for Management Development (Switzerland); Boon Siong Neo and Christina Soh, Nanyang Technological University (Singapore); and Joel B. Barolsky, Paul Richardson, and Peter Weill, University of Melbourne, (Australia).

ATTENTION TO SMALL BUSINESSES AND ENTREPRENEURS

A blue diamond-shaped symbol identifies in-text discussions and specially designated chapter-opening vignettes, Window-On boxes, and ending case studies that highlight the experiences and challenges of small businesses and entrepreneurs using information systems.

PEDAGOGY TO PROMOTE ACTIVE LEARNING AND MANAGEMENT PROBLEM SOLVING

In addition to the new Management Decision Problems and hands-on Application Exercises, the text contains many other features that encourage students to learn actively and to engage in management problem solving.

Group Projects

At the end of each chapter is a group project that encourages students to develop teamwork and oral and written presentation skills. The group projects have been enhanced in this edition to make even better use of the Internet. For instance, students might be asked to work in small groups to evaluate the Web sites of two competing businesses or to develop a corporate ethics code on privacy that considers e-mail privacy and the monitoring of employees using networks.

Management Challenges Section
Each chapter begins with several challenges relating to the chapter topic that managers are likely to encounter. These challenges are multifaceted and sometimes pose dilemmas. They make excellent springboards for class discussion. Some of these Management Challenges are: finding the right Internet business model; overcoming the organizational obstacles to building a database environment; and agreeing on quality standards for information systems.

Case Studies
Each chapter concludes with a case study based on a real-world organization. These cases help students synthesize chapter concepts and apply this new knowledge to concrete problems and scenarios. Major international case studies and electronic case studies at the Laudon & Laudon Web site provide additional opportunities for management problem solving.

Book Overview
Part One is concerned with the organizational foundations of systems and their emerging strategic role. It provides an extensive introduction to real-world systems, focusing on their relationship to organizations, management, and business processes.

Part Two provides the technical foundation for understanding information systems, describing the hardware, software, storage, and telecommunications technologies that comprise the organization's information technology (IT) infrastructure. Part Two concludes by describing how all of these information technologies work together through the Internet to create a new infrastructure for electronic commerce and electronic business.

Part Three focuses on the process of redesigning organizations using information systems, including reengineering of critical business processes. We see systems analysis and design as an exercise in organizational design, one that requires great sensitivity to the right tools and techniques, quality assurance, and change management.

Part Four describes the role of information systems in capturing and distributing organizational knowledge and in enhancing management decision making. It shows how knowledge management, work group collaboration, and individual and group decision making can be supported by the use of knowledge work, group collaboration, artificial intelligence, decision support, and executive support systems.

Part Five concludes the text by examining the special management challenges and opportunities created by the pervasiveness and power of contemporary information systems and the global connectivity of the Internet: ensuring security and control, understanding the ethical and social consequences of systems, and developing global systems. Throughout the text, emphasis is placed on using information technology to redesign the organization's products, services, procedures, jobs, and management structures; numerous examples are drawn from multinational systems and global business environments.

CHAPTER OUTLINE

Each chapter contains the following:

- A detailed outline at the beginning to provide an overview
- A diagram analyzing the opening vignette in terms of the management, organization, and technology model used throughout the text
- An opening vignette describing a real-world organization to establish the theme and importance of the chapter
- A list of learning objectives
- Management Challenges related to the chapter theme
- Marginal glosses of key terms in the text

- An Internet Connection icon directing students to related material on the Internet
- A Management Decision Problem presenting a real-world management decision scenario
- A Management Wrap-Up tying together the key management, organization, and technology issues for the chapter, with questions for discussion
- A chapter summary keyed to the learning objectives
- A list of key terms that the student can use to review concepts
- Review questions for students to test their comprehension of chapter material
- A group project to develop teamwork and presentation skills
- A Tools for Interactive Learning section showing specifically how the chapter can be integrated with the Laudon Web site and the optional CD-ROM edition of the text
- A chapter-ending case study that illustrates important themes

Instructional Support Materials

INSTRUCTOR'S RESOURCE CD-ROM (0-13-027933-1)

Most of the support materials described below are now conveniently provided for adopters on the Instructor's Resource CD-ROM. The CD includes the Instructor's Resource Manual, Test Item File, Windows PH Test Manager, PowerPoint slides, and the helpful lecture tool "Image Library."

IMAGE LIBRARY

The Image Library is a wonderful resource to help instructors create vibrant lecture presentations. Just about every figure and photo found in the text is provided and organized by chapter for your convenience. A complete listing of the images and their copyright information are also provided. These images and lecture notes can be easily imported into Microsoft PowerPoint to create new presentations or to add to existing sets.

INSTRUCTOR'S MANUAL (0-13-027931-5)

The Instructor's Manual, written by Dr. Glenn Bottoms of Gardner-Webb University, features not only answers to review, discussion, case study, and group project questions, but also an in-depth lecture outline, teaching objectives, key terms, teaching suggestions, and Internet resources. This supplement can be downloaded from the secure faculty section of the Laudon & Laudon Web site, and is also available on the Instructor's Resource CD-ROM.

TEST ITEM FILE (0-13-027935-8)

The Test Item File is a comprehensive collection of true-false, multiple-choice, fill-in-the-blank, and essay questions, written by Dr. Lisa Miller of the University of Central Oklahoma. The questions are rated by difficulty level and answers are referenced by section. An electronic version of the Test Item File is available as the **Windows PH Test Manager** on the Instructor's Resource CD-ROM.

POWERPOINT SLIDES (ON WEB AND INSTRUCTOR'S CD-ROM)

Over one-hundred electronic color slides created by Dr. Edward Fisher of Central Michigan University are available in Microsoft PowerPoint, Version 97. The slides illuminate and build upon key concepts in the text. In addition, they contain hyperlinks to the Laudon Web site within each chapter. The PowerPoints can be downloaded from the Web site and are available on the Instructor's Resource CD-ROM within Image Library.

VIDEOS

Prentice Hall MIS Video, Volume I (0-13-027199-3)

The first video in the Prentice Hall MIS Video Library includes custom clips created exclusively for Prentice Hall featuring real companies such as Andersen Consulting, Land's End, Lotus Development Corporation, Oracle Corporation, and Pillsbury Company.

Prentice Hall MIS Video, Volume 2 (0-13-027929-3)
Video clips are provided to adopters to enhance class discussion and projects. These clips highlight real-world corporations and organizations and illustrate key concepts found in the text.

WEB SITE

The Laudon & Laudon text is once again supported by an excellent Web site at **http://www.prenhall.com/laudon** that truly reinforces and enhances text material with Electronic Commerce Projects, hands-on Application Exercises, Internet Exercises, an Interactive Study Guide, International Resources, and PowerPoint slides. The Web site also features a secure password-protected faculty area from which instructors can download the Instructor's Manual, MIS Video Guides, and suggested answers to the Internet Connections and E-Commerce Projects. Please see its complete description found earlier in this preface.

ON-LINE COURSE

The *Essentials of Management Information Systems: Organization and Technology in the Networked Enterprise (Fourth Edition)* On-line Course can help you create and implement a high-quality distance learning course with relative ease. The course allows you to customize the Laudon & Laudon course content and integrate your own custom materials.

The course features: lecture notes with discussion questions, Internet Exercises, off-line activities that offer directions to integrate the text and Multimedia CD-ROM, on-line quizzes (auto-scored and recorded), test item database and test preparation tools (auto-scored and recorded), glossary, e-mail accounts for students and instructors, and a bulletin board.

A wizard program guides you through the initial stages of course development, including the creation of a password-protected course home page. The *Course Management* feature automatically grades on-line tests and records scores in your electronic grade book. The *Progress Tracking* feature lets you monitor individual and overall student progress. The *Content Tracking* feature tells you how often and for how long each and every student visits.

TUTORIAL SOFTWARE

For instructors looking for Application Software support to use with this text, Prentice Hall is pleased to offer CBT CD-ROMs for Microsoft Office 2000. These exciting tutorial CDs are fully certified up to the expert level of the Microsoft Office User Specialist (MOUS) Certification Program. They are not available as stand-alone items but can be packaged with the Laudon & Laudon text at an additional charge. Please contact your local Prentice Hall representative for more details.

Acknowledgments

The production of any book involves many valuable contributions from a number of people. We would like to thank all of our editors for encouragement, insight, and strong support for many years. Our editor David Alexander continues to do an outstanding job in guiding the development of our texts, and we feel very fortunate to work with him. We remain grateful to Mickey Cox, Jim Boyd, and Sandy Steiner for their support of this project. We thank Nancy Evans, Director of Strategic Marketing, for her superb marketing work and her continuing contributions to our texts. Thanks go as well to CIS Senior Marketing Manager Kris King and to CIS Sales Directors Matt Denham, Vanessa Juenger, Jonathan Ahlbrand, and Dana Simmons for their suggestions for improving this edition and their support to the reps and faculty. We would like to thank Rebecca Johnson, who as development editor, made many thoughtful contributions to the text. We commend Lori Cerreto and Kyle Hannon for directing the preparation of ancillary materials and Anne Graydon, Lisa DiMaulo Babin, and Paul Smolenski for production of this text under an extraordinarily ambitious schedule. We thank Shirley Webster for her energetic photo research work and Nancy Welcher for her work as Media Project Manager.

Our special thanks go to Dr. Lisa Miller of Central Oklahoma University for developing the hands-on Application Exercises for this edition and the testing systems that accompany our text. Thank you to Barbara J. Ellestad, who contributed tremendously to the On-line

Course. We also want to thank Professor Beverly Amer of Arizona State University for her assistance in reviewing the Management Decision Problems and other text features as well as Dr. Glenn Bottoms of Gardner-Webb University and Dr. Edward Fisher of Central Michigan University for their work on supporting materials.

We remain deeply indebted to Marshall R. Kaplan for his invaluable assistance in the preparation of the text. Todd Traver of IBM Global Services provided additional suggestions for improvement.

The Stern School of Business at New York University and the Information Systems Department provided a very special learning environment, one in which we and others could rethink the MIS field. Special thanks to Professors Edward Stohr, Jon Turner, Vasant Dhar, Alex Tuzhilin, and Roy Radner for providing critical feedback and support where deserved. Professor William H. Starbuck of the Management Department at NYU provided valuable comments and insights in our joint graduate seminar on organization theory.

The Concours Group has provided stimulation, insight, and new research on enterprise systems and industrial networks. We remain especially grateful to Dr. Edward Roche for his contributions and to Jim Ware, Walt Dulaney, Vaughn Merlyn, and Peter Boggis of the Concours Group for ideas and feedback.

Professor Gordon Everest of the University of Minnesota, Professors Al Croker and Michael Palley of Baruch College and NYU, Professor Lisa Friedrichsen of the Keller Graduate School of Management, and Professor Kenneth Marr provided additional suggestions for improvement. We continue to remember the late Professor James Clifford of the Stern School as a wonderful friend and colleague who also made valuable recommendations for improving our discussion of files and databases.

One of our goals was to write a book that was authoritative, synthesized diverse views in the MIS literature, and helped define a common academic field. A large number of leading scholars in the field were contacted and assisted us in this effort. Reviewers and consultants for *Essentials of Management Information Systems: Organization and Technology in the Networked Enterprise* are listed in the back endpapers of the book. We thank them for their contributions. Consultants for this new edition include:

Beverley Amer
Northern Arizona University

Roy Alvarez
Cornell University

William B. Fredenberger
Valdosta State University

Albert M. Hayashi
Loyola Marymount University

Robert W. Key
University of Phoenix

Teresita Leyell
Washburn University

Carl Longnecker
Loyola University

Gary Margot
Ashland University

Lisa Miller
University of Central Oklahoma

Denise Nitterhouse
DePaul University

Sasan Rahmatian
California State University, Fresno

Joko W. Saputro
University of Wisconsin—Madison

Werner Schenk
University of Rochester

Rod Sink
Northern Illinois University

Bee K. Yew
Arkansas Tech University

It is our hope that this group endeavor contributes to a shared vision and understanding of the MIS field.

—K.C.L.
—J.P.L.

Essentials of
Management
Information
Systems
Organization and
Technology in the
Networked Enterprise

The Information Systems Revolution:

Transforming Business and Management

Learning
Objectives

After completing this chapter, you will be able to:

1. Define an information system.

2. Distinguish between computer literacy and information systems literacy.

3. Explain why information systems are so important today and how they are transforming organizations and management.

4. Compare electronic commerce and electronic business and analyze their relationship to the Internet and digital technology.

5. Identify the major management challenges to building and using information systems in organizations.

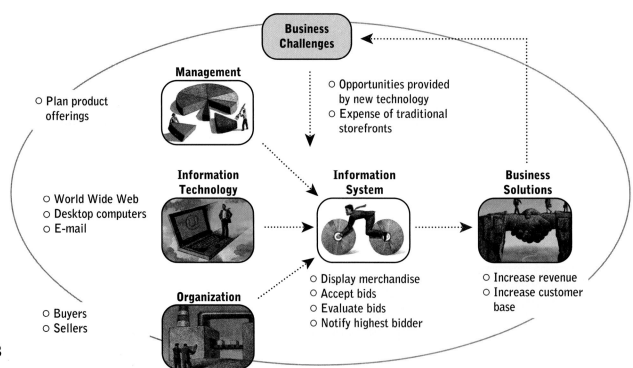

Business Challenges

Management

- Plan product offerings

- Opportunities provided by new technology
- Expense of traditional storefronts

Information Technology

- World Wide Web
- Desktop computers
- E-mail

Information System

Business Solutions

- Display merchandise
- Accept bids
- Evaluate bids
- Notify highest bidder

- Increase revenue
- Increase customer base

Organization

- Buyers
- Sellers

Web Auctions Create a New Breed of E-Merchants

For eight years, Fred Parks tried to eke out a living selling all sorts of antiques and collectibles from a series of stores in downtown Baltimore. When he closed his last store in 1998, he didn't go out of business. Instead, he began selling ceramics—art nouveau, art deco, and arts and crafts styles—to interested collectors using eBay, the leading Web auction site. eBay connects sellers of collectibles such as antiques, sports memorabilia, toys, and coins with buyers who bid for them in auctions conducted over the Internet.

Founded in September 1995 by Pierre Omidyar to help his fiancée trade Pez candy dispensers, eBay has become a major retailing force, listing 4 million items for sale each day. Many people use eBay occasionally as a virtual "garage sale" to get rid of an old VCR or Lionel train set, but small businesses and entrepreneurs such as Parks are increasingly using this Web auction site as their principal place of business. Parks now works out of his home and a small studio he rents for $100 per month. By selling through eBay auctions, he has lowered expenses while increasing prices and profits because he can reach more buyers through the Internet than through a traditional bricks-and-mortar storefront. On a good day, Parks' Baltimore store might draw in 35 people, but his "virtual store" on the Internet draws in thousands.

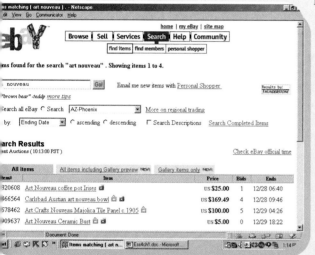

Sellers such as Parks pay a fee ranging from $.25 to $2 (for high-ticket items such as cars and real estate) to post an item on the eBay Web site. If the item is sold, the seller pays a commission on a sliding scale starting at 5 percent of any item less than $25 to 1.25 percent of a sale of $1,000 or more. Buyers usually pay the cost of shipping their purchases. Because eBay makes it so easy for buyers and sellers to locate each other and complete a sale, the transaction costs of doing business are very low—for many types of goods, much lower than placing advertisements or selling through a physical storefront.

Buyers can examine the descriptions of items for sale (which often include photos) on eBay's Web site and enter their bids directly into their computers. eBay's information system accepts the bids, evaluates them, and identifies the highest bidder. eBay's e-mail system automatically notifies high bidders when they have been outbid and notifies winners when the auctions are over. Sellers and auction winners are required to contact each other within three days and make their

CHAPTER OUTLINE

3

own arrangements for payment. Buyers and sellers can contact each other via e-mail using the eBay Web site, and potential buyers can contact sellers by e-mail if they want additional information while an auction is still ongoing.

The Web site displays sellers and buyers' comments about their transaction for all to see. This self-policing feature of the eBay Web site helps other buyers and sellers find out who is reputable or dishonest. Many small businesses have found eBay's Web site so useful that they do not need to set up their own Web site or marketing program—the eBay auctions are their virtual storefront.

Sources: Danny Rimer, "Keeping Their Day Jobs," *The Industry Standard,* January 3, 2000; Roy Furchgott, "Betting the Farm on the Virtual Store," *The New York Times,* September 9, 1999; Denise Caruso, "Success Stories from eBay," *The New York Times,* May 24, 1999; and Chuck Lenatti, "Auction Mania," *Upside,* July 1999.

Bay's innovative use of the Internet illustrates just one of the many new business opportunities that have been created with this technology. Both small and large companies can use information systems and networks to conduct more of their business electronically to make them more efficient and competitive. In today's global business environment, information systems, the Internet, and other global networks are creating new opportunities for organizational coordination and innovation. Information systems can help companies extend their reach to faraway locations, offer new products and services, reshape jobs and work flows, and perhaps profoundly change the way they conduct business. This chapter starts our investigation of information systems and organizations by describing information systems from both technical and behavioral perspectives and by surveying the changes they are bringing to organizations and management.

1.1 Why Information Systems?

Until recently, information itself was not considered an important asset for a firm. The management process was considered a face-to-face, personal art and not a far-flung, global coordination process. Today it is widely recognized that understanding information systems is essential for managers because most organizations need information systems to survive and prosper.

THE COMPETITIVE BUSINESS ENVIRONMENT

Three powerful worldwide changes have altered the business environment. The first change is the emergence and strengthening of the global economy. The second change is the transformation of industrial economies and societies into knowledge- and information-based service economies. The third is the transformation of the business enterprise. These changes in the business environment and climate, summarized in Table 1-1, pose a number of new challenges to business firms and their management.

Emergence of the Global Economy

A growing percentage of the American economy—and other advanced industrial economies in Europe and Asia—depends on imports and exports. Foreign trade, both exports and imports, accounts for a little more than 25 percent of the goods and services produced in the United States, and even more in countries like Japan and Germany. The success of firms today and in the future depends on their ability to operate globally.

Globalization of the world's industrial economies greatly enhances the value of information to the firm and offers new opportunities to businesses. Today, information systems provide the communication and analytic power that firms need for conducting trade and managing busi-

Table 1-1 The Changing Contemporary Business Environment

Globalization

Management and control in a global marketplace

Competition in world markets

Global work groups

Global delivery systems

Transformation of Industrial Economies

Knowledge- and information-based economies

Productivity

New products and services

Knowledge: A central productive and strategic asset

Time-based competition

Shorter product life

Turbulent environment

Limited employee knowledge base

Transformation of the Enterprise

Flattening

Decentralization

Flexibility

Location independence

Low transaction and coordination costs

Empowerment

Collaborative work and teamwork

nesses on a global scale. Controlling the far-flung global corporation—communicating with distributors and suppliers, operating 24 hours a day in different national environments, servicing local and international reporting needs—is a major business challenge that requires powerful information system responses.

Globalization and information technology also bring new threats to domestic business firms: Because of global communication and management systems, customers now can shop in a worldwide marketplace, obtaining price and quality information reliably, 24 hours a day. This phenomenon heightens competition and forces firms to play in open, unprotected worldwide markets. To become effective and profitable participants in international markets, firms need powerful information and communication systems.

Transformation of Industrial Economies

The United States, Japan, Germany, and other major industrial powers are being transformed from industrial economies to knowledge- and information-based service economies, whereas manufacturing has been moving to low-wage countries. In a knowledge- and information-based economy, knowledge and information are key ingredients in creating wealth.

The knowledge and information revolution began at the turn of the twentieth century and has gradually accelerated. By 1976 the number of white-collar workers employed in offices surpassed the number of farm workers, service workers, and blue-collar workers employed in manufacturing (see Figure 1-1). Today, most people no longer work on farms or in factories but instead are found in sales, education, healthcare, banks, insurance firms, and law firms; they also provide business services like copying, computer programming, or making deliveries. These

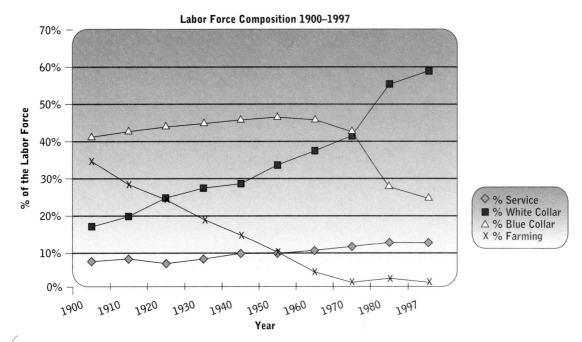

Labor Force Composition 1900–1997

◇ % Service
■ % White Collar
△ % Blue Collar
X % Farming

FIGURE 1-1 The growth of the information economy. Since the beginning of the twentieth century, the United States has experienced a steady decline in the number of farm workers and blue-collar workers who are employed in factories. At the same time, the country is experiencing a rise in the number of white-collar workers who produce economic value using knowledge and information.
Sources: U.S. Department of Commerce, Bureau of the Census, *Statistical Abstract of the United States*, 1998, Table 672: 1900–1970; and *Historical Statistics of the United States, Colonial Times to 1970*, Vol. 1, Series D 182–232.

knowledge- and information-intense products Products that require a great deal of learning and knowledge to produce.

jobs primarily involve working with, distributing, or creating new knowledge and information. In fact, knowledge and information work now account for a significant 60 percent of the American gross national product and nearly 55 percent of the labor force.

Knowledge and information are becoming the foundation for many new services and products. **Knowledge- and information-intense products** such as computer games require a great deal of knowledge to produce. Entire new information-based services have sprung up, such as Lexis, Dow Jones News Service, and America Online. These fields are employing millions of people.

Knowledge is used more intensively in the production of traditional products as well. This trend is readily seen throughout the automobile industry where both design and production now rely heavily on knowledge and information technology. During the past 15 years, the automobile producers have hired more computer specialists, engineers, and designers while reducing the number of blue-collar production workers.

New kinds of knowledge- and information-intense organizations have emerged that are devoted entirely to the production, processing, and distribution of information. For instance, environmental engineering firms, which specialize in preparing environmental impact statements for municipalities and private contractors, simply did not exist 30 years ago.

In a knowledge- and information-based economy, information technology and systems take on great importance. Knowledge-based products and services of great economic value, such as credit cards, overnight package delivery, and worldwide reservation systems, are based on new information technologies. Information technology constitutes more than 70 percent of the invested capital in service industries like finance, insurance, and real estate.

Across all industries, information and the technology that delivers it have become critical, strategic assets for business firms and their managers (Leonard-Barton, 1995). Information systems are needed to optimize the flow of information and knowledge within the organization and to help management maximize the firm's knowledge resources. Because employees' productivity will depend on the quality of the systems serving them, management decisions about information technology are critically important to the firm's prosperity and survival.

Transformation of the Business Enterprise

The third major change in the business environment has been a transformation in the possibilities for organizing and managing. Some firms have begun to take advantage of these new possibilities.

The traditional business firm was—and still is—a hierarchical, centralized, structured arrangement of specialists that typically relies on a fixed set of standard operating procedures to deliver a mass-produced product (or service). The new style of business firm is a flattened (less hierarchical), decentralized, flexible arrangement of generalists who rely on nearly instant information to deliver mass-customized products and services uniquely suited to specific markets or customers. This new organization style is not yet firmly entrenched; it is still evolving. Nevertheless, the new direction is clear and would be unthinkable without information technology.

The traditional management group relied—and still does—on formal plans, a rigid division of labor, and formal rules. It appeals to loyalty to ensure the proper operation of a firm. The new manager relies on informal commitments and networks to establish goals (rather than formal planning), a flexible arrangement of teams and individuals working in task forces, and a customer orientation to achieve coordination among employees. The new manager appeals to professionalism and knowledge to ensure proper operation of the firm. Once again, information technology makes this style of management possible.

Information technology is bringing about changes in organization that make the firm even more dependent than in the past on the knowledge, learning, and decision making of individual employees. Throughout this book, we describe the role that information technology is now playing in the transformation of the business enterprise.

WHAT IS AN INFORMATION SYSTEM?

An **information system** can be defined technically as a set of interrelated components that collect (or retrieve), process, store, and distribute information to support decision making, coordination, and control in an organization. In addition to supporting decision making, coordination, and control, information systems may also help managers and workers analyze problems, visualize complex subjects, and create new products.

Information systems contain information about significant people, places, and things within the organization or in the environment surrounding it. By **information** we mean data that have been shaped into a form that is meaningful and useful to human beings. **Data,** in contrast, are streams of raw facts representing events occurring in organizations or the physical environment before they have been organized and arranged into a form that people can understand and use.

A brief example contrasting information and data may prove useful. Supermarket checkout counters ring up millions of pieces of data such as product identification numbers or the cost of each item sold. Such pieces of data can be totaled and analyzed to provide meaningful information such as the total number of bottles of dish detergent sold at a particular store, which brands of dish detergent were selling the most rapidly at that store or sales territory, or the total amount spent on that brand of dish detergent at that store or sales region (see Figure 1-2).

Three activities in an information system produce the information that organizations need to make decisions, control operations, analyze problems, and create new products or services. These activities are input, processing, and output (see Figure 1-3). **Input** captures or collects raw data from within the organization or from its external environment. **Processing** converts this raw input into a more meaningful form. **Output** transfers the processed information to the people who will use it or to the activities for which it will be used. Information systems also require **feedback,** which is output that is returned to appropriate members of the organization to help them evaluate or correct the input stage.

In eBay's information system for running an on-line auction for a business such as Fred Parks', the raw input consists of a buyer identification name or number and the amount of each bid from prospective buyers. (Sellers also input their identification number and a description of each item for auction.) The computer processes these data into reports of bids for each item up for auction, which become the output. The system thus provides meaningful information such as the highest bid amount, identity of the highest bidder, number of bidders, and other bidders for the item. The eBay system must respond to

information system Interrelated components working together to collect, process, store, and disseminate information to support decision making, coordination, control, analysis, and visualization in an organization.

information Data that have been shaped into a form that is meaningful and useful to human beings.

data Streams of raw facts representing events occurring in organizations or the physical environment before they have been organized and arranged into a form that people can understand and use.

input The capture or collection of raw data from within the organization or from its external environment for processing in an information system.

processing The conversion, manipulation, and analysis of raw input into a form that is more meaningful to humans.

output The distribution of processed information to the people who will use it or to the activities for which it will be used.

feedback Output that is returned to the appropriate members of the organization to help them evaluate or correct input.

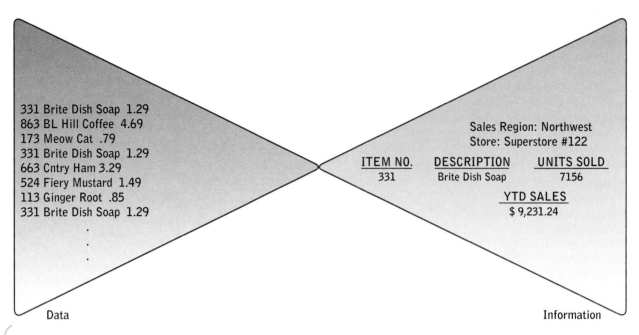

ITEM NO.	DESCRIPTION	UNITS SOLD

Sales Region: Northwest
Store: Superstore #122

331 Brite Dish Soap 1.29
863 BL Hill Coffee 4.69
173 Meow Cat .79
331 Brite Dish Soap 1.29
663 Cntry Ham 3.29
524 Fiery Mustard 1.49
113 Ginger Root .85
331 Brite Dish Soap 1.29
.
.
.

Data

Information

331   Brite Dish Soap   7156

YTD SALES
$ 9,231.24

FIGURE I-2 Data and information. Raw data from a supermarket checkout counter can be processed and organized in order to produce meaningful information such as the total unit sales of dish detergent or the total sales revenue from dish detergent for a specific store or sales territory.

computer-based information systems (CBIS) Information systems that rely on computer hardware and software for processing and disseminating information.

formal system System resting on accepted and fixed definitions of data and procedures, operating with predefined rules.

an environment of many buyers and sellers and federal and state regulations concerning on-line auctions.

Our interest in this book is in formal, organizational **computer-based information systems (CBIS)** like those designed and used by eBay and its customers. **Formal systems** rest on accepted and fixed definitions of data and procedures for collecting, storing, processing, disseminating, and using these data. The formal systems we describe in this text are structured; that is, they operate in conformity with predefined rules that are relatively fixed and not easily changed. For instance, eBay's auction system requires that all bids contain a name or identification number for the bidder and the amount of the bid.

Informal information systems (such as office gossip networks) rely, by contrast, on unstated rules of behavior. There is no agreement on what is information or on how it will be

FIGURE I-3 Functions of an information system. An information system contains information about an organization and its surrounding environment. Three basic activities—input, processing, and output—produce the information organizations need. Feedback is output returned to appropriate people or activities in the organization to evaluate and refine the input. Environmental actors such as customers, suppliers, competitors, stockholders, and regulatory agencies interact with the organization and its information systems.

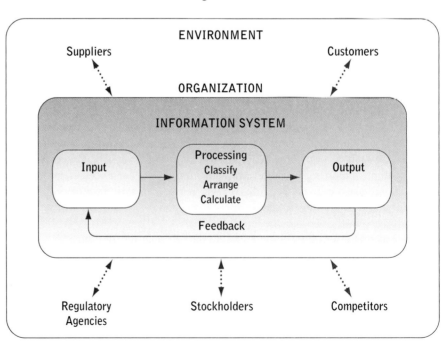

stored and processed. Such systems are essential for the life of an organization, but an analysis of their qualities is beyond the scope of this text.

Formal information systems can be either computer-based or manual. Manual systems use paper-and-pencil technology. These manual systems serve important needs, but they too are not the subject of this text. Computer-based information systems, in contrast, rely on computer hardware and software technology to process and disseminate information. From this point on, when we use the term *information systems,* we are referring to computer-based information systems— formal organizational systems that rely on computer technology. The Window on Technology describes some of the typical technologies used in computer-based information systems today.

Although computer-based information systems use computer technology to process raw data into meaningful information, there is a sharp distinction between a computer and a computer program on the one hand, and an information system on the other. Electronic computers and related software programs are the technical foundation, the tools and materials, of modern information systems. Computers provide the equipment for storing and processing information. Computer programs, or software, are sets of operating instructions that direct and control computer processing. Knowing how computers and computer programs work is important in designing solutions to organizational problems, but computers are only part of an information system. A house is an appropriate analogy. Houses are built with hammers, nails, and wood, but these do not make a house. The architecture, design, setting, landscaping, and all of the decisions that lead to the creation of these features are part of the house and are crucial for solving the problem of putting a roof over one's head. Computers and programs are the hammers, nails, and lumber of CBIS, but alone they cannot produce the information a particular organization needs. To understand information systems, one must understand the problems they are designed to solve, their architectural and design elements, and the organizational processes that lead to these solutions.

A BUSINESS PERSPECTIVE ON INFORMATION SYSTEMS

From a business perspective, an information system is an organizational and management solution, based on information technology, to a challenge posed by the environment. Examine this definition closely because it emphasizes the organizational and managerial nature of information systems: To fully understand information systems, a manager must understand the broader organization, management, and information technology dimensions of systems (see Figure 1-4) and their power to provide solutions to challenges and problems in the business environment. We refer to this broader understanding of information systems, which encompasses

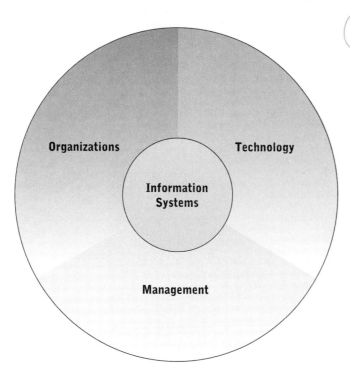

FIGURE 1-4 Information systems are more than computers. Using information systems effectively requires an understanding of the organization, management, and information technology shaping the systems. All information systems can be described as organizational and management solutions to challenges posed by the environment.

UPS COMPETES GLOBALLY USING INFORMATION TECHNOLOGY

United Parcel Service (UPS), the world's largest air and ground package-distribution company, started out in 1907 in a closet-size basement office. Jim Casey and Claude Ryan—two teenagers from Seattle with two bicycles and one phone—promised the "best service and lowest rates." UPS has used this formula successfully for more than 90 years.

UPS still lives up to that promise today, delivering more than 3 billion parcels and documents each year to the United States and to more than 200 other countries and territories. The firm has been able to maintain its leadership in small-package delivery services in the face of stiff competition from Federal Express and Airborne Express by investing heavily in advanced information technology. During the past decade, UPS has poured more than $11 billion into technology to boost customer service while keeping costs low and streamlining its overall operations.

Using a handheld computer called a Delivery Information Acquisition Device (DIAD), UPS drivers automatically capture customers' signatures along with pickup, delivery, and time-card information. The drivers then place the DIAD into their truck's vehicle adapter, an information-transmitting device that is connected to the cellular telephone network. (Drivers may also transmit and receive information using an internal radio in the DIAD.) Package tracking information is transmitted to UPS's computer network for storage and processing in UPS's main computers in Mahwah, New Jersey, and Alpharetta, Georgia. From there, the information can be accessed worldwide to provide proof of delivery to the customer or respond to customer queries.

Through its automated package tracking system, UPS can monitor packages throughout the delivery process. At various points along the route from sender to receiver, a bar code device scans shipping information on the package label; the information is fed into the central computer. Customer service representatives can check the status of any package from desktop computers linked to the central computers and are able to respond immediately to inquiries from customers. UPS customers can also access this information directly from their own computers, using either the World Wide Web of the Internet or special package tracking software supplied by UPS.

Anyone with a package to ship can access the UPS Web site to track packages, check delivery routes, calculate shipping rates, determine time in transit, and schedule a pickup. Businesses anywhere can use the Web site to arrange UPS shipments and bill the shipments to the company's UPS account number or to a credit card. The data collected at the UPS Web site are transmitted to the UPS central computer and then back to the customer after processing. UPS also provide tools that enable its customers to embed UPS functions, such as tracking and cost calculation, into their own Web sites and information systems. For example, customers of Marshall Industries can use Marshall's Web site to access UPS tracking information and find out about the status of their orders. UPS started a new service called UPS Document Exchange to deliver business documents electronically using the Internet. The service provides a high level of security for these important documents as well as document tracking.

UPS is enhancing its information system capabilities so that it can guarantee that a particular package, or group of packages, will arrive at a destination at a specified time. If requested by the customer, UPS can intercept a package prior to delivery and have it returned or rerouted.

TO THINK ABOUT: What are the inputs, processing, and outputs of UPS's package tracking system? What technologies are used? How are these technologies related to UPS's business strategy? What would happen if these technologies were not available?

Sources: Kelly Barron, "Logistics in Brown," **Forbes**, January 10, 2000; Art Jahnke, "Deliverance," **CIO Web Business Magazine**, July 1, 1999; David Baum, "UPS: Keeping Track," **Oracle Magazine**, May/June 1999; Carol Sliwa, "FedEx, UPS Seek Online Shipping Market Share," **Computerworld**, April 19, 1999; and "On-the-Spot Tracking," **Round UPS**, Summer 1999.

an understanding of the management and organizational dimensions of systems as well as the technical dimensions of systems as **information systems literacy.** Information systems literacy includes a behavioral as well as a technical approach to studying information systems. **Computer literacy,** in contrast, focuses primarily on knowledge of information technology.

Review the diagram at the beginning of the chapter, which reflects this expanded definition of an information system. The diagram shows how eBay's information system solves the business challenges of trying to overcome the high expenses of locating customers for collectible ceramics, the owner's limited financial resources, and trying to take advantage of opportunities new technology creates—in this case, the Internet. The diagram also illustrates how management, technology, and organization elements work together to create the system. Each chapter of this text begins with a diagram like this one to help you analyze the opening case. You can use this diagram as a starting point for analyzing any information system or information system problem you encounter.

Organizations

Information systems are an integral part of organizations. Indeed, for some companies, such as credit reporting firms, without the information system there would be no business. The key elements of an organization are its people, structure, operating procedures, politics, and culture. We introduce these components of organizations here and describe them in greater detail in Chapter 3. Organizations are composed of different levels and specialties. Their structures reveal a clear-cut division of labor. Experts are employed and trained for different functions. The major **business functions,** or specialized tasks performed by business organizations, consist of sales and marketing, manufacturing and production, finance, accounting, and human resources (see Table 1-2). Chapter 2 provides more detail on these business functions and the ways in which they are supported by information systems.

An organization coordinates work through a structured hierarchy and formal, standard operating procedures. The hierarchy arranges people in a pyramid structure of rising authority and responsibility. The upper levels of the hierarchy consist of managerial, professional, and technical employees, whereas the lower levels consist of operational personnel.

Standard operating procedures (SOPs) are formal rules that have been developed over a long time for accomplishing tasks. These rules guide employees in a variety of procedures, from writing an invoice to responding to customer complaints. Most procedures are formalized and written down, but others are informal work practices, such as a requirement to return telephone calls from co-workers or customers, that are not formally documented. Many of a firm's SOPs are incorporated into information systems, such as how to pay a supplier or how to correct an erroneous bill.

Organizations require many different kinds of skills and people. In addition to managers, **knowledge workers** (such as engineers, architects, or scientists) design products or services and create new knowledge and **data workers** (such as secretaries, bookkeepers, or clerks)

information systems literacy Broad-based understanding of information systems that includes behavioral knowledge about organizations and individuals using information systems as well as technical knowledge about computers.

computer literacy Knowledge about information technology, focusing on an understanding of how computer-based technologies work.

business functions Specialized tasks performed in a business organization, including manufacturing and production, sales and marketing, finance, accounting, and human resources.

standard operating procedures (SOPs) Formal rules for accomplishing tasks that have been developed to cope with expected situations.

knowledge workers People such as engineers or architects who design products or services and create knowledge for the organization.

data workers People such as secretaries or bookkeepers who process the organization's paperwork.

Table 1-2 Major Business Functions

Function	Purpose
Sales and marketing	Selling the organization's products and services
Manufacturing and production	Producing products and services
Finance	Managing the organization's financial assets (cash, stocks, bonds, etc.)
Accounting	Maintaining the organization's financial records (receipts, disbursements, paychecks, etc.); accounting for the flow of funds
Human resources	Attracting, developing, and maintaining the organization's labor force; maintaining employee records

production or service workers People who actually produce the products or services of the organization.

process the organization's paperwork. **Production or service workers** (such as machinists, assemblers, or packers) actually produce the organization's products or services.

Each organization has a unique culture, or fundamental set of assumptions, values, and ways of doing things, that has been accepted by most of its members. Parts of an organization's culture can always be found embedded in its information systems. For instance, the United Parcel Service's concern with placing service to the customer first is an aspect of its organizational culture that can be found in the company's package tracking systems.

Different levels and specialties in an organization create different interests and points of view. These views often conflict. Conflict is the basis for organizational politics. Information systems come out of this cauldron of differing perspectives, conflicts, compromises, and agreements that are a natural part of all organizations. In Chapter 3 we examine these features of organizations in greater detail.

senior managers People occupying the topmost hierarchy in an organization who are responsible for making long-range decisions.

middle managers People in the middle of the organizational hierarchy who are responsible for carrying out the plans and goals of senior management.

operational managers People who monitor the day-to-day activities of the organization.

Management

Managers perceive business challenges in the environment; they set the organizational strategy for responding and allocate the human and financial resources to achieve the strategy and coordinate the work. Throughout, they must exercise responsible leadership. Management's job is to "make sense" out of the many situations faced by organizations and formulate action plans to solve organizational problems. The business information systems described in this book reflect the hopes, dreams, and realities of real-world managers.

But managers must do more than manage what already exists. They must also create new products and services and even re-create the organization from time to time. A substantial part of management responsibility is creative work driven by new knowledge and information. Information technology can play a powerful role in redirecting and redesigning the organization. Chapter 3 describes managers' activities and management decision making in detail.

It is important to note that managerial roles and decisions vary at different levels of the organization. **Senior managers** make long-range strategic decisions about products and services to produce. **Middle managers** carry out the programs and plans of senior management. **Operational managers** are responsible for monitoring the firm's daily activities. All levels of management are expected to be creative and to develop novel solutions to a broad range of problems. Each level of management has different information needs and information system requirements.

computer hardware Physical equipment used for input, processing, and output activities in an information system.

computer software Detailed, preprogrammed instructions that control and coordinate the work of computer hardware components in an information system.

storage technology Physical media and software governing the storage and organization of data for use in an information system.

communications technology Physical devices and software that link various computer hardware components and transfer data from one physical location to another.

network Two or more computers linked to share data or resources such as a printer.

information technology (IT) infrastructure Computer hardware, software, data and storage technology, and networks providing a portfolio of shared information technology resources for the organization.

Technology

Information technology is one of many tools managers use to cope with change. **Computer hardware** is the physical equipment used for input, processing, and output activities in an information system. It consists of the computer processing unit; various input, output, and storage devices; and physical media to link these devices together. Chapter 4 describes computer hardware in greater detail.

Computer software consists of the detailed preprogrammed instructions that control and coordinate the computer hardware components in an information system. Chapter 5 explains the importance of computer software in information systems.

Storage technology includes both the physical media for storing data, such as magnetic or optical disk or tape, and the software governing the organization of data on these physical media. More detail on physical storage media can be found in Chapter 4, whereas Chapter 6 covers data organization and access methods.

Communications technology, consisting of both physical devices and software, links the various pieces of hardware and transfers data from one physical location to another. Computers and communications equipment can be connected in networks for sharing voice, data, images, sound, or even video. A **network** links two or more computers to share data or resources such as a printer. Chapters 7 and 8 provide more details on communications and networking technology and issues.

All of these technologies represent resources that can be shared throughout the organization and constitute the firm's **information technology (IT) infrastructure.** The information technology (IT) infrastructure provides the foundation or platform on which the firm can build its specific information systems. Each organization must carefully design and manage its information technology infrastructure so that it has the set of technology services it needs for the work it wants to accomplish with information systems. Chapters 4 through 8 of this text examine each major technology component of information technology infrastructure and show how they all work together to create the technology platform for the organization.

Let us return to UPS's package tracking system in the Window on Technology and identify the organization, management, and technology elements. The organization element anchors the package tracking system in UPS's sales and production functions (the main product of UPS is a service—package delivery). It specifies the required procedures for identifying packages with both sender and recipient information, taking inventory, tracking the packages en route, and providing package status reports for UPS customers and customer service representatives. The system must also provide information to satisfy the needs of managers and workers. UPS drivers need to be trained in both package pickup and delivery procedures and in how to use the package tracking system so that they can work efficiently and effectively. UPS customers may need some training to use UPS in-house package tracking software or the UPS World Wide Web site. UPS's management is responsible for monitoring service levels and costs and for promoting the company's strategy of combining low cost and superior service. Management decided to use automation to increase the ease of sending a package via UPS and of checking its delivery status, thereby reducing delivery costs and increasing sales revenues. The technology supporting this system consists of handheld computers, bar code scanners, wired and wireless communications networks, desktop computers, UPS's central computer, storage technology for the package delivery data, UPS's in-house package tracking software, and software to access the World Wide Web. The result is an information system solution to the business challenge of providing a high level of service with low prices in the face of mounting competition.

1.2 Contemporary Approaches to Information Systems

Multiple perspectives on information systems show that the study of information systems is a multidisciplinary field. No single theory or perspective dominates. Figure 1-5 illustrates the major disciplines that contribute problems, issues, and solutions in the study of information systems. In general, the field can be divided into technical and behavioral approaches. Information systems are sociotechnical systems. Though they are composed of machines, devices, and "hard" physical technology, they require substantial social, organizational, and intellectual investments to make them work properly.

TECHNICAL APPROACH

The technical approach to information systems emphasizes mathematically based models to study information systems, as well as the physical technology and formal capabilities of these systems. The disciplines that contribute to the technical approach are computer science, management science, and operations research. Computer science is concerned with establishing

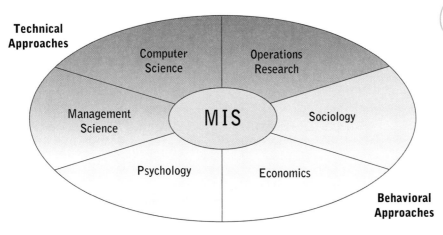

FIGURE 1-5 Contemporary approaches to information systems. The study of information systems deals with issues and insights contributed from technical and behavioral disciplines.

theories of computability, methods of computation, and methods of efficient data storage and access. Management science emphasizes the development of models for decision-making and management practices. Operations research focuses on mathematical techniques for optimizing selected parameters of organizations such as transportation, inventory control, and transaction costs.

BEHAVIORAL APPROACH

An important part of the information systems field is concerned with behavioral issues that arise in the development and long-term maintenance of information systems. Issues such as strategic business integration, design, implementation, utilization, and management cannot be explored usefully with the models used in the technical approach. Other behavioral disciplines contribute important concepts and methods. For instance, sociologists study information systems with an eye toward how groups and organizations shape the development of systems and also how systems affect individuals, groups, and organizations. Psychologists study information systems with an interest in how human decision makers perceive and use formal information. Economists study information systems with an interest in what impact systems have on control and cost structures within the firm and within markets.

The behavioral approach does not ignore technology. Indeed, information systems technology is often the stimulus for a behavioral problem or issue. But the focus of this approach is generally not on technical solutions. Instead it concentrates on changes in attitudes, management and organizational policy, and behavior (Kling and Dutton, 1982).

APPROACH OF THIS TEXT: SOCIOTECHNICAL SYSTEMS

management information systems (MIS) The study of information systems focusing on their use in business and management.

The study of **management information systems (MIS)** arose in the 1970s to focus on computer-based information systems aimed at managers (Davis and Olson, 1985). MIS combines the theoretical work of computer science, management science, and operations research with a practical orientation toward building systems and applications. It also pays attention to behavioral issues raised by sociology, economics, and psychology.

Our experience as academics and practitioners leads us to believe that no single perspective effectively captures the reality of information systems. Problems with systems—and their solutions—are rarely all technical or all behavioral. Our best advice to students is to understand the perspectives of all disciplines. Indeed, the challenge and excitement of the information systems field is that it requires an appreciation and tolerance of many different approaches.

Adopting a sociotechnical systems perspective helps to avoid a purely technological approach to information systems. For instance, the fact that information technology is rapidly declining in cost and growing in power does not necessarily or easily translate into productivity enhancement or bottom-line profits.

In this book, we stress the need to optimize the system's performance as a whole. Both the technical and behavioral components need attention. This means that technology must be changed and designed in such a way as to fit organizational and individual needs. At times, the

FIGURE 1-6 A sociotechnical perspective on information systems. In a sociotechnical perspective, the performance of a system is optimized when both the technology and the organization mutually adjust to one another until a satisfactory fit is obtained.

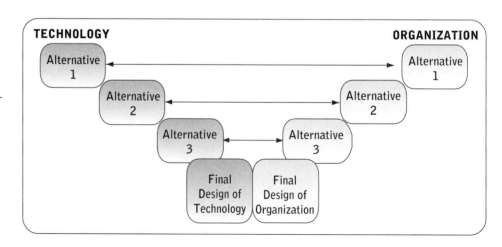

technology may have to be "de-optimized" to accomplish this fit. Organizations and individuals must also be changed through training, learning, and planned organizational change in order to allow the technology to operate and prosper (see, for example, Liker et al., 1987). People and organizations change to take advantage of new information technology. Figure 1-6 illustrates this process of mutual adjustment in a sociotechnical system.

1.3 The New Role of Information Systems in Organizations

Managers cannot ignore information systems because they play such a critical role in contemporary organizations. Digital technology is transforming business organizations. The entire cash flow of most Fortune 500 companies is linked to information systems. Today's systems directly affect how managers decide, how senior managers plan, and in many cases what products and services are produced (and how). They play a strategic role in the life of the firm. Responsibility for information systems cannot be delegated to technical decision makers.

THE WIDENING SCOPE OF INFORMATION SYSTEMS

Figure 1-7 illustrates the new relationship between organizations and information systems. There is a growing interdependence between business strategy, rules, and procedures on the one hand, and information systems software, hardware, databases, and telecommunications on the other. A change in any of these components often requires changes in other components. This relationship becomes critical when management plans for the future. What a business would like to do in five years often depends on what its systems will be able to do. Increasing market share, becoming the high-quality or low-cost producer, developing new products, and increasing employee productivity depend more and more on the kinds and quality of information systems in the organization.

A second change in the relationship between information systems and organizations results from the growing complexity and scope of system projects and applications. Building systems today involves a much larger part of the organization than it did in the past (see

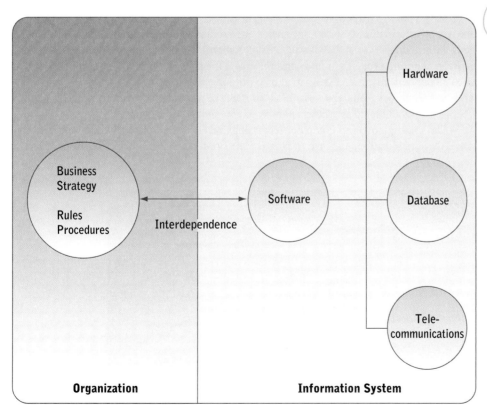

FIGURE 1-7 The interdependence between organizations and information systems. In contemporary systems there is a growing interdependence between organizational business strategy, rules, and procedures and the organization's information systems. Changes in strategy, rules, and procedures increasingly require changes in hardware, software, databases, and telecommunications. Existing systems can act as a constraint on organizations. Often, what the organization would like to do depends on what its systems will permit it to do.

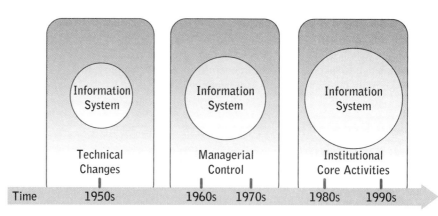

FIGURE 1-8 The widening scope of information systems. Over time, information systems have come to play a larger role in the life of organizations. Early systems brought about largely technical changes that were relatively easy to accomplish. Later systems affected managerial control and behavior; ultimately systems influenced "core" institutional activities concerning products, markets, suppliers, and customers.

Figure 1-8). Whereas early systems produced largely technical changes that affected few people, contemporary systems bring about managerial changes (who has what information about whom, when, and how often) and institutional "core" changes (what products and services are produced, under what conditions, and by whom).

In the 1950s, employees in the treasurer's office, a few part-time programmers, a single program, a single machine, and a few clerks might have used a computerized payroll system. The change from a manual to a computer system was largely technical: The computer system simply automated a clerical procedure such as check processing. In contrast, today's integrated human resources system (which includes payroll processing) may involve all major corporate divisions, the human resources department, dozens of full-time programmers, a flock of external consultants, multiple machines (or remote computers linked by telecommunications networks), and perhaps hundreds of end users in the organization who use payroll data to make calculations about benefits and pensions and to answer a host of other questions. The data, instead of being located in and controlled by the treasurer's office, are now available to hundreds of employees via desktop computers, each of which is as powerful as the large computers of the mid-1980s. This contemporary system embodies both managerial and institutional changes.

THE NETWORK REVOLUTION AND THE INTERNET

One reason information systems play such a large role in organizations and affect so many people is the soaring power and declining cost of computer technology. Computing power, which has been doubling every 18 months, has improved the performance of microprocessors 25,000 times since their invention 30 years ago. With powerful, easy-to-use software, the computer can crunch numbers, analyze vast pools of data, or simulate complex physical and logical processes with animated drawings, sounds, and even tactile feedback.

The soaring power of computer technology has spawned powerful communication networks that organizations can use to access vast storehouses of information from around the

The Internet. This global network of networks provides a highly flexible platform for information-sharing. Digital information can be distributed at almost no cost to millions of people throughout the world.

Table 1-3 What You Can Do on the Internet

Function	Description
Communicate and collaborate	Send electronic mail messages; transmit documents and data; participate in electronic conferences
Access information	Search for documents, databases, and library card catalogs; read electronic brochures, manuals, books, and advertisements
Participate in discussions	Join interactive discussion groups; conduct voice transmission
Supply information	Transfer computer files of text, computer programs, graphics, animations, sound, or videos
Find entertainment	Play interactive video games; view short video clips; listen to sound and music clips; read illustrated and even animated magazines and books
Exchange business transactions	Advertise, sell, and purchase goods and services

world and to coordinate activities across space and time. These networks are transforming the shape and form of business enterprises and even our society.

The world's largest and most widely used network is the **Internet.** The Internet is an international network of networks that are both commercial and publicly owned. The Internet connects hundreds of thousands of different networks from more than 200 countries around the world. More than 300 million people working in science, education, government, and business use the Internet to exchange information or perform business transactions with other organizations around the globe. The number of Internet users is expected to surpass 500 million by the year 2003.

The Internet is extremely elastic. If networks are added or removed or failures occur in parts of the system, the rest of the Internet continues to operate. Through special communication and technology standards, any computer can communicate with virtually any other computer linked to the Internet using ordinary telephone lines. Companies and private individuals can use the Internet to exchange business transactions, text messages, graphic images, and even video and sound, whether they are located next door or on the other side of the globe. Table 1-3 describes some of the Internet's capabilities.

The Internet is creating a new "universal" technology platform on which to build all sorts of new products, services, strategies, and organizations. It is reshaping the way information systems are used in business and daily life. By eliminating many technical, geographic, and cost barriers obstructing the global flow of information, the Internet is accelerating the information revolution, inspiring new uses of information systems and new business models. The Window on Management provides some examples.

Internet International network of networks that is a collection of hundreds of thousands of private and public networks.

Window on Management

GLOBAL NETREPRENEURS

A new breed of entrepreneurs is rapidly setting up businesses on the Internet. Wang Zhidong and Fernando Espuelas are two examples of "netrepreneurs" who launched new Internet-based businesses for Asia and Latin America.

In China, free-market enterprise is still very young, and only 1 in 1,000 residents uses the Internet. Wang was trained as an electrical engineer but set up a software company in Beijing called Stone Rich Sight (SRS), which received $6.5 million in U.S. venture capital in 1997 from Walden International Group and Robertson Stephens. More than one million pages on SRS's Web site were viewed each day, making it one of the most popular Chinese language sites in the world.

In November 1998, SRS merged with Sinanet.com, based in Cupertino, California, which was the most popular portal for "global," or nonmainland Chinese. (A portal is a Web site or other service offering a broad array of resources or services such as e-mail, on-line shopping, discussion forums and tools for locating information.) The combined sites are now know as Sina.com and have become the most heavily trafficked Web sites in the Chinese language market. To avoid clashes over content restrictions with the Chinese government, Sina.com currently maintains separate portals for mainland Chinese, Taiwanese, Hong Kong, and U.S. markets.

The company is implementing locally oriented, full-service, Chinese language portals that combine content, services, and capabilities for searching for information on the Web. For example, Sina's U.S. portal provides news, Dow Jones stock quotes, advertising, shopping, electronic mail (e-mail), links to other Chinese language sites, and tools for searching for information. To provide content for the China site, Wang negotiated with mainland newspapers, magazines, television stations, and other media. The bulk of Sina's revenue currently comes from advertising, primarily from U.S. and Taiwan operations. But Sina.com hopes eventually to charge subscription fees for access and to add electronic commerce and Internet telephone capabilities to its Web sites.

Fernando Espuelas had already risen to become AT&T's youngest managing director, but he wanted to create his own company where he could make a difference. While vacationing in Nepal, he came up with an idea: Why not create a Latin American Web site with news, e-mail, classified advertisements, games, and capabilities for chatting with other users on-line that could bond all Latin American countries. Espuelas believes Latin Americans are searching for a sense of community that transcends national borders.

In 1996, Espuelas joined with his longtime friend Jack Chen to create a Web site that offers localized content and services to a Latin American audience with an American flair. He chose StarMedia—an English name—for the company because Latin Americans are attracted to U.S. brands, yet the name translates well into both Spanish and Portuguese. Espuelas hopes that StarMedia can re-create the plaza—the traditional Latin American community square—on the Internet.

Today, StarMedia attracts about two million visitors each month. It has offices in 19 countries and is well positioned to attract the growing number of Latin American Internet users. Although only 1 or 2 percent of Latin American households own personal computers, about 34 million people use the Internet and their number is rapidly growing. Moreover, 72 percent of Latin American Internet users are between the ages of 18 and 34, an attractive demographic group for advertisers. International Data Corporation, a Framingham, Massachusetts research firm, predicts that Latin Americans will spend more than $8 billion online by 2003. StarMedia has also developed content for the Hispanic market in the United Sates. StarMedia's revenue comes from advertising from multinational companies with interests in Latin America and from electronic commerce transactions. StarMedia hopes to sell subscriptions for "value-added bundles" of content and services such as a financial data source, a Web site presence, and an e-mail service packaged together for small businesses.

TO THINK ABOUT: How essential is the Internet in the strategy and operation of these businesses? Explain your answer.

Sources: Andrea Petersen, "E-Commerce Apostles Target Latin America, but It's a Tough Sell," **The Wall Street Journal**, January 25, 2000; Leslie Chang, "Sina.com Bends to Beijing to Get Nasdaq Listing," **The Wall Street Journal**, March 29, 2000; Harold Goldberg, "Star Media: Porta Rica," **The Industry Standard**, March 1, 1999; and James Ryan, "China.com," **The Industry Standard**, January 15, 1999.

World Wide Web A system with universally accepted standards for storing, retrieving, formatting, and displaying information in a networked environment.

Because it offers so many new possibilities for doing business, the Internet capability known as the **World Wide Web** is of special interest to organizations and managers. The World Wide Web is a system with universally accepted standards for storing, retrieving, formatting, and displaying information in a networked environment. Information is stored and displayed as electronic "pages" that can contain text, graphics, animations, sound, and video. These Web pages can be linked electronically to other Web pages, regardless of where they are located, and viewed by any type of computer. By clicking on highlighted words or buttons on a Web page, one can link to related pages to find additional information, software programs, or still more links to other points on the Web. The Web serves as the foundation for new kinds of information systems such as eBay's Web-based information system to create a global auction place.

All of the Web pages maintained by an organization or individual are called a **Web site.** (The chapter opening vignette illustrates a page from eBay's Web site.) Businesses are creating Web sites with stylish typography, colorful graphics, push-button interactivity, and often sound and video to disseminate product information widely, to "broadcast" advertising and messages to customers, to collect electronic orders and customer data, and increasingly to coordinate far-flung sales forces and organizations on a global scale.

Web site All of the World Wide Web pages maintained by an organization or an individual.

In Chapter 8 we describe the Web and other Internet capabilities in greater detail. We also discuss relevant features of the Internet in every chapter of the text because the Internet affects so many aspects of information systems in organizations.

NEW OPTIONS FOR ORGANIZATIONAL DESIGN: THE NETWORKED ENTERPRISE

The explosive growth in computing power and networks, including the Internet, is turning organizations into networked enterprises, allowing information to be instantly distributed within and beyond the organization. This capability can be used to redesign and reshape organizations, transforming their structure, scope of operations, reporting and control mechanisms, work practices, work flows, products, and services. New ways of conducting business electronically have emerged.

Flattening Organizations

Large, bureaucratic organizations, which primarily developed before the computer age, are often inefficient, slow to change, and less competitive than newly created organizations. Some of these large organizations have downsized, reducing the number of employees and the number of levels in their organizational hierarchies. For example, by 1994 heavy-equipment manufacturer Caterpillar, Inc., was producing the same level of output as it did 15 years earlier, but with 40,000 fewer employees. Financial services firm Charles Schwab & Co. can serve 600,000 European customers with only two branch offices and European securities trading volumes are growing 25 percent a month (Field, 2000).

Flatter organizations have fewer levels of management, with lower level employees being given greater decision-making authority (see Figure 1-9). Those employees are empowered to make more decisions than in the past; they no longer work standard 9-to-5 hours, and they no longer necessarily work in an office. Moreover, such employees may be scattered geographically, sometimes working half a world away from the manager.

Contemporary information technology has made such changes possible. It can make more information available to line workers so they can make decisions that previously had been made by managers. Networked computers have made it possible for employees to work together as a team, another feature of flatter organizations. With the emergence of global networks such as the Internet, team members can collaborate closely even from distant locations. These changes mean that the management span of control has also been broadened, allowing high-level managers to manage and control more workers spread over greater distances. Many companies have eliminated thousands of middle managers as a result of these changes. AT&T, IBM, and General Motors are just a few of the organizations that have eliminated more than 30,000 middle managers in one fell swoop.

Separating Work from Location

It is now possible to organize globally while working locally: Information technologies such as e-mail, the Internet, and video conferencing to the desktop permit tight coordination of geographically dispersed workers across time zones and cultures. Entire parts of organizations can disappear: Inventory, and the warehouses to store it, can be eliminated as suppliers tie into the firm's computer systems and deliver just what is needed and just in time.

Communications technology has eliminated distance as a factor for many types of work in many situations. Salespersons can spend more time in the field with customers and have more up-to-date information with them while carrying much less paper. Many employees can work remotely from their homes or cars, and companies can reserve space at smaller central offices for meeting clients or other employees.

FIGURE I-9 Flattening organizations. Information systems can reduce the number of levels in an organization by providing managers with information to supervise larger numbers of workers and by giving lower level employees more decision-making authority.

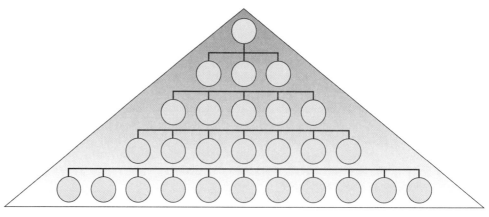

A traditional hierarchical organization with many levels of management

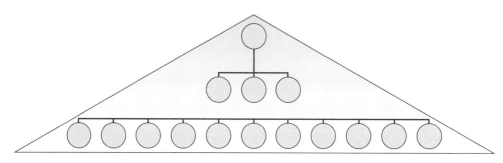

An organization that has been "flattened" by removing layers of management

Collaborative teamwork across thousands of miles has become a reality as designers work on a new product together even if they are located on different continents. Ford Motor Co. has adopted a cross-continent collaborative model to design its automobiles. Supported by high-capacity communications networks and computer-aided design (CAD) software, Ford designers launched the Mustang design in Dunton, England. The design was worked on simultaneously by designers at Dearborn, Michigan, and Dunton, with some input from designers in Japan and Australia. Once the design was completed, Ford engineers in Turin, Italy, used it to produce a full-size physical model. Ford now designs other models this way and is starting to use Web technology for global collaboration (see Chapter 11).

Companies are not limited to physical locations or their own organizational boundaries for providing products and services. Networked information systems are allowing companies to coordinate their geographically distributed capabilities and even coordinate with other organizations as **virtual organizations,** sometimes called virtual corporations or networked organizations. Virtual organizations use networks to link people, assets, and ideas, allying with suppliers and customers, and sometimes even competitors, to create and distribute new products and services without being limited by traditional organizational boundaries or physical location. One company can take advantage of the capabilities of another company without actually physically linking to that company. Each company contributes its core competencies, the capabilities that it does the best. For example, one company might be responsible for product design, another for assembly and manufacturing, and another for administration and sales. These virtual organizations last as long as the opportunity remains profitable. Figure 1-10 illustrates the concept of a virtual organization.

Calyx and Corolla, which has its headquarters in San Francisco, created a networked virtual organization to sell fresh flowers directly to customers, bypassing the traditional flower shop. The company takes orders via a toll-free telephone number or from its Web site and enters them into a central computer, which transmits them directly to grower farms. Farmers pick the flowers and place them in waiting Federal Express refrigerated vans. Calyx and Corolla flowers are delivered within a day or two to their final destination. They are weeks fresher than flowers provided by traditional florists.

virtual organization Organization using networks linking people, assets, and ideas to create and distribute products and services without being limited by traditional organizational boundaries or physical location.

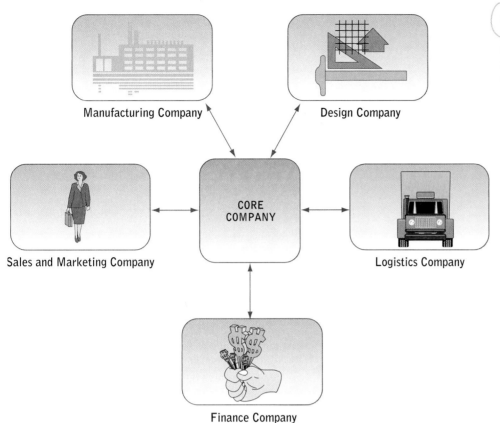

Manufacturing Company

Design Company

Sales and Marketing Company

CORE COMPANY

Logistics Company

Finance Company

Although most organizations will not become fully virtual organizations, some of their key business activities may have "virtual" features, such as using networks and the Internet to outsource the development of products and components, to leverage knowledge and expertise located inside and outside the firm, and to help customers experience products and services remotely (Venkatraman and Henderson, 1998).

Reorganizing Work Flows

Information systems have been progressively replacing manual work procedures with automated work procedures, work flows, and work processes. Electronic work flows have reduced the cost of operations in many companies by displacing paper and the manual routines that accompany it. Improved work flow management has enabled many corporations not only to cut costs significantly but also to improve customer service at the same time. For instance, insurance companies can reduce processing of applications for new insurance from weeks to days (see Figure 1-11).

Redesigned work flows can have a profound impact on organizational efficiency and can even lead to new organizational structures, products, and services. We discuss the impact of restructured work flows on organizational design in greater detail in Chapters 3 and 9.

Increasing Flexibility of Organizations

Companies can use communications technology to organize in more flexible ways, increasing their ability to respond to changes in the marketplace and to take advantage of new opportunities. Information systems can give both large and small organizations additional flexibility to overcome some of the limitations posed by their size. Table 1-4 describes some of the ways in which information technology can help small companies act "big" and help big companies act "small." Small organizations can use information systems to acquire some of the muscle and reach of larger organizations. They can perform coordinating activities, such as processing bids or keeping track of inventory, and many manufacturing tasks with very few managers, clerks, or production workers. For example, Beamscope Canada, a Toronto distributor of electronic

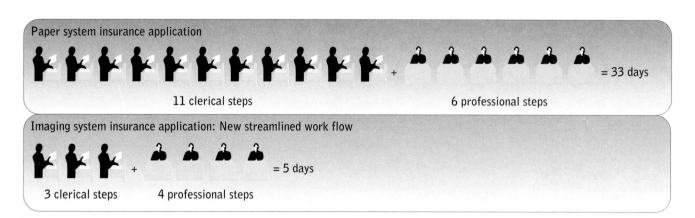

FIGURE 1-11 Redesigned work flow for insurance underwriting. An application requiring 33 days in a paper system would only take 5 days using computers, networks, and a streamlined work flow.

and computer parts, competes effectively against global giants such as Ingram Micro Inc. and Merisel Inc. Its Beamscope Online system offers customers on-line service and 24-hour ordering capabilities (Engler, 1999).

Information can be easily distributed down the ranks of the organization to empower lower level employees and work groups to solve problems. Large organizations can use information technology to achieve some of the agility and responsiveness of small organizations. One aspect of this phenomenon is **mass customization,** where software and computer networks are used to link the plant floor tightly with orders, design, and purchasing and to finely control production machines. The result is a dynamically responsive environment in which products can be turned out in greater variety and easily customized with no added cost for small production runs. For example, Levi Strauss has equipped its stores with an option called Personal Pair, which allows customers to design jeans to their own specifications, rather than picking them off the rack. Customers enter their measurements into a personal computer, which transmits the customer's specifications over a network to Levi's plants. The company is able to produce the custom jeans on the same lines that manufacture its standard items. There are almost no extra production costs because the process does not require additional production overruns and inventories.

mass customization Use of software and computer networks to finely control production so that products can be easily customized with no added cost for small production runs.

Table 1-4 **How Information Technology Increases Organizational Flexibility**

Small Companies

Desktop machines, inexpensive computer-aided design (CAD) software, and computer-controlled machine tools provide the precision, speed, and quality of giant manufacturers.

Information immediately accessed by telephone and communications links eliminates the need for research staff and business libraries.

Managers can easily obtain the information they need to manage large numbers of employees in widely scattered locations.

Large Companies

Custom manufacturing systems allow large factories to offer customized products in small quantities.

Massive databases of customer purchasing records can be analyzed so that large companies know their customers' needs and preferences as easily as local merchants.

Information can be easily distributed down the ranks of the organization to empower lower level employees and work groups to solve problems.

A related trend is micromarketing, in which information systems help companies pinpoint tiny target markets for these finely customized products and services—as small as individualized "markets of one." We discuss micromarketing in more detail in Chapter 2.

The Changing Management Process

Information technology is recasting the management process, providing powerful new capabilities to help managers plan, organize, lead, and control. For instance, it is now possible for managers to obtain information on organizational performance down to the level of specific transactions from just about anywhere in the organization at any time. Product managers at Frito-Lay Corporation, the world's largest manufacturer of salty snack foods, can know within hours precisely how many bags of Fritos have sold on any street in America at its customers' stores, how much they sold for, and what the competition's sales volumes and prices are. This greater availability and detail of information makes possible far more precise planning, forecasting, and monitoring than ever before.

Information technology has also opened new possibilities for leading. By distributing information through electronic networks, the new manager can effectively communicate frequently with thousands of employees and even manage far-flung task forces and teams—tasks that would be impossible in face-to-face organizations.

Redefining Organizational Boundaries

Networked information systems can enable transactions such as payments and purchase orders to be exchanged electronically among different companies, thereby reducing the cost of obtaining products and services from outside the firm. Organizations can also share business data, catalogs, or mail messages through such systems. These networked information systems can create new efficiencies and new relationships between an organization, its customers, and suppliers, redefining their organizational boundaries. For example, the Chrysler Corporation is networked to suppliers, such as the Budd Company of Rochester, Michigan. Through this electronic link, the Budd Company monitors Chrysler production and ships sheet metal parts exactly when needed, preceded by an electronic shipping notice. Chrysler and its suppliers have thus become linked business partners with mutually shared responsibilities.

The information system linking Chrysler and its suppliers is called an interorganizational information system. Systems linking a company to its customers, distributors, or suppliers are termed **interorganizational systems** because they automate the flow of information across organizational boundaries (Barrett, 1986–1987; Johnston and Vitale, 1988). Such systems allow information or processing capabilities of one organization to improve the performance of another or to improve relationships among organizations.

interorganizational systems Information systems that automate the flow of information across organizational boundaries and link a company to its customers, distributors, or suppliers.

ELECTRONIC COMMERCE AND ELECTRONIC BUSINESS

The changes we have just described are creating new ways of conducting business electronically both inside and outside the firm. Increasingly, the Internet is providing the underlying technology for these changes. The Internet can link thousands of organizations into a single network, creating the foundation for a vast electronic marketplace. An **electronic market** is an information system that links together many buyers and sellers to exchange information, products, services, and payments. Through computers and networks, these systems function like electronic intermediaries, with lowered costs for typical marketplace transactions such as selecting suppliers, establishing prices, ordering goods, and paying bills (Malone, Yates, and Benjamin, 1987). Buyers and sellers can complete purchase and sale transactions digitally, regardless of their location.

electronic market A marketplace that is created by computer and communication technologies that link many buyers and sellers.

A vast array of goods and services are being advertised, bought, and exchanged worldwide using the Internet as a global marketplace. Companies are furiously creating eye-catching electronic brochures, advertisements, product manuals, and order forms on the World Wide Web. All kinds of products and services are available on the Web, including fresh flowers, books, real estate, musical recordings, electronics, and steaks.

Many retailers maintain their own sites on the Web, such as Wine.com, an on-line source of wine and food items. Others offer their products through electronic shopping malls, such as ShopNow.com. Customers can locate products on this mall either by retailer, if they

INTERNET TRADING HEATS UP

When people wanted to trade stocks, they used to call a traditional full-service broker and pay a hefty commission for placing the trade. Today, thanks to the Internet, they are buying and selling stocks, bonds, and mutual funds directly from their desktops using one of a new crop of on-line discount trading services.

These discount Internet trading services offer low-cost trades because they do not have to pay for large research departments, retail offices, or personnel to make the trades. People who actively trade stocks have flocked to these discount brokers because they make their own decisions and only need a broker to enter trades. Using their networked computer, they can bypass brokers and enter their trades electronically on their own. And they pay much less for making those trades. Internet brokerage firms such as E*Trade and Datek Online charge commissions of between $5 and $15 for most trades of any size. In comparison, full-service brokers such as Merrill Lynch, who provide stock selection advice, might charge more than $100 for trades of 200 stock shares. Recognizing the Web's convenience and popularity, Merrill Lynch, Paine Webber, and other full-service companies are starting to offer on-line trading capabilities for their clients.

The Web sites maintained by Internet brokerage companies allow customers to access their account data over the Internet. They are open 24 hours a day, so customers can enter their trades any time of the day or night and any day of the year. Internet brokerage sites offer links to other sites at which the investor can obtain stock quotes, charts, investment news, historical data, and all kinds of advice online. Some even offer free up-to-the-minute stock quotes and stock graphs with capabilities to make users' home computers look like the same flashy terminals used by high-powered Wall Street traders.

Internet trading is growing rapidly, with on-line firms averaging 15,000 new accounts each day. About 40% of all retail trading is now conducted online. Although there are many Internet brokerage companies, Charles Schwab, E*Trade, Datek Online, and Toronto Dominion Bank are emerging as the leaders.

Charles Schwab & Co., Inc., has been the number 1 discount brokerage firm in the United States for 2 years, with 30 percent of the market share of on-line trading. Internet trading accounts for over half of the company's trades. Its main domestic competitor, in the minds of many, is E*Trade, a young entrepreneurial company that was a pioneer in Internet-based, on-line trading. However, Schwab's most serious opposition may come from a very large and venerated bank, Toronto Dominion Bank, which is the fifth-largest bank in Canada.

Toronto Dominion has several obvious advantages. First, it has available all the large resources one would expect from a bank. Second, Toronto Dominion is a rare North American bank with real stock brokerage experience—it is not a newcomer to the field. U.S. banks were forbidden to participate in stock brokerage until recently; however, Canadian banks were given permission years earlier. Toronto Dominion ventured into on-line trading in 1992 when it established a dial-up trading system. In 1996 Toronto Dominion acquired Waterhouse Securities, Inc., a U.S. stock brokerage firm, which is now the third largest in the country in on-line trading.

Toronto Dominion's Waterhouse has already achieved virtually the same foreign brokerage expansion as has Schwab. Both, for example, are in the United Kingdom and Hong Kong, two of the largest financial markets in the world. Toronto Dominion's strategy involves opening physical offices in other parts of the world using a discount brokerage named GreenLine Investor Services. Combining GreenLine and Waterhouse offices abroad, Toronto Dominion seems to be well ahead of Schwab.

In contrast, E*Trade, the vigorous entrepreneurial company, is not moving to open new offices abroad. Instead, it has 32 licensing agreements to give on-line access to E*Trade through local trading firms in foreign countries. Which approach will win out? Only time will tell, but more and more people are moving to Internet trading every day.

TO THINK ABOUT: How has the Internet changed the brokerage business? In what ways can using electronic marketplaces on the Internet affect other organizations?

Sources: Peter Cohan, "The Dilemma of the 'Innovator's Dilemma'," The Industry Standard, January 3, 2000; Tom Field, "Trade Secrets," CIO Magazine, February 2000; Kimberly Weisul and Kevin Jones, "Online Trading Heats Up Abroad: Move Over, Charles Schwab," Inter@ctive Week, January 6, 1999; Leah Nathans Spiro with Edward C. Baig, "Who Needs a Broker?" Business Week, February 22, 1999; and "Industry Spotlight: Online Trading," The Industry Standard, February 15, 1999.

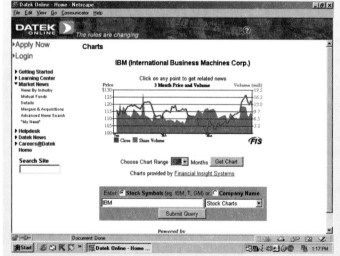

MANAGEMENT DECISION PROBLEM

PLANNING A NEW INTERNET BUSINESS

You would like to create a new business on the Web that provides cat and dog owners with advice on animal health, behavior, and nutrition and sells products such as pet beds, carriers, dishes, toys, flea treatments, and grooming aids. Your Web site would also have capabilities for pet owners to exchange electronic messages about their pets and pet care with other pet owners.

In researching the U.S. market for your business, you have found the following statistics from the U.S. Commerce Department's Statistical Abstract of the United States.

1. What are the implications of this information for starting this business on the Internet?

2. What additional information might be useful to help you decide whether such a business could be profitable and what type and price range of products to sell?

Household Pet Ownership by Income Level:

Annual Income	Dog Owners	Cat Owners
Less than $12,500	14%	15%
$12,500-$24,999	20%	20%
$25,000 to $39,999	24%	23%
$40,000 to $59,999	22%	22%
Over $60,000	20%	20%
Total	100%	100%

Internet Usage by Income Level

Annual Income	Percent Using the Internet
Less than $20,000	5%
$20,000 to $49,999	26%
$50,000 to $74,999	28%
$75,000 and over	41%
Total	100%

know what they want, or by product type, and then order the products directly. Even electronic financial trading has arrived on the Web for stocks, bonds, mutual funds, and other financial instruments (see the Window on Organizations).

Increasingly the Web is being used for business-to-business transactions as well. For example, airlines can use the Boeing Corporation's Web site to order parts electronically and check the status of their orders.

The global availability of the Internet for the exchange of transactions between buyers and sellers is fueling the growth of electronic commerce. **Electronic commerce** is the process of buying and selling goods and services electronically with computerized business transactions using the Internet, networks, and other digital technologies. It also encompasses activities supporting those market transactions, such as advertising, marketing, customer support, delivery, and payment. By replacing manual and paper-based procedures with electronic alternatives and by using information flows in new and dynamic ways, electronic commerce can accelerate ordering, delivery, and payment for goods and services while reducing companies' operating and inventory costs.

> **electronic commerce** The process of buying and selling goods and services electronically involving transactions using the Internet, networks, and other digital technologies.

The Internet is emerging as the primary technology platform for electronic commerce. Equally important, Internet technology is starting to facilitate the management of the rest of the business—publishing employee personnel policies, reviewing account balances and production plans, scheduling plant repairs and maintenance, and revising design documents. Companies are taking advantage of the connectivity and ease of use of Internet technology to create internal corporate networks called **intranets** that are based on Internet technology. The number of these private intranets for organizational communication, collaboration, and coordination is soaring. In this text, we use the term **electronic business** to distinguish these uses of Internet and digital technology for the management and coordination of other business processes from electronic commerce.

> **intranet** An internal network based on Internet and World Wide Web technology and standards.

By distributing information through electronic networks, electronic business extends the reach of existing management. Managers can use e-mail, Web documents, and work-group software to effectively communicate frequently with thousands of employees, and even to manage far-flung task forces and teams. These tasks would be impossible in face-to-face traditional organizations. Table 1-5 lists some examples of electronic commerce and electronic business.

> **electronic business** The use of the Internet and other digital technology for organizational communication and coordination and the management of the firm.

At the Drugstore.com Web site, customers can make online purchases of prescription medicine and over-the-counter health, beauty, and wellness products. The World Wide Web is fueling the growth of electronic commerce.

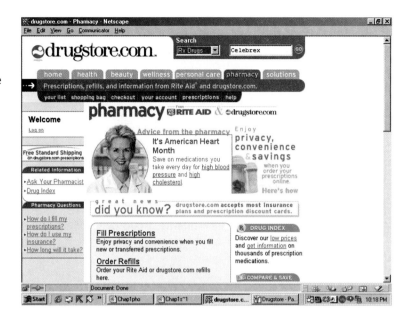

Figure 1-12 illustrates an enterprise making intensive use of Internet and digital technology for electronic commerce and electronic business. Information flows seamlessly among different parts of the company and between the company and external entities—its customers, suppliers, and business partners. Organizations are moving toward this vision as they increasingly use the Internet and networks to manage their internal processes and their relationships with customers, suppliers, and other external entities.

Both electronic commerce and electronic business can fundamentally change the way business is conducted. To use the Internet and other digital technologies successfully for elec-

---

Table 1-5   Examples of Electronic Commerce and Electronic Business

Electronic Commerce

Drugstore.com operates a virtual pharmacy on the Internet selling prescription medicine and over-the-counter health, beauty, and wellness products. Customers can input their orders via Drugstore.com's Web site and have their purchases shipped to them.

Travelocity provides a Web site that can be used by consumers for travel and vacation planning. Visitors find information on airlines, hotels, vacation packages, and other travel and leisure topics, and they can make airline and hotel reservations on-line through the Web site.

Gilbarco Inc. created an order management system based on Internet technology that allows its distributors to submit purchase orders on-line for gas pumps, pump controllers, and other gas station supplies. Distributors can order parts, check on an order's status, and look up equipment training data and technical documentation.

Electronic Business

Roche Bioscience scientists worldwide use an intranet to share research results and discuss findings. The intranet also provides a company telephone directory and newsletter.

EDS Corporation uses an intranet to provide 70,000 employees with access to personalized health benefits information based on location, age, salary, and family status. Employees can compare benefits of different medical plans before enrolling.

Dream Works SKG uses an intranet to check the daily status of projects, including animation objects, and to coordinate movie scenes.

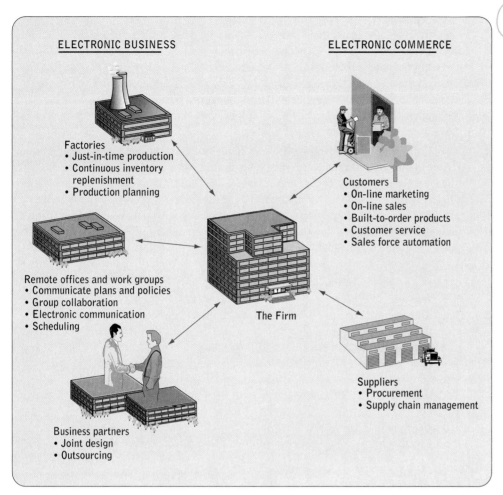

ELECTRONIC BUSINESS

Factories
- Just-in-time production
- Continuous inventory replenishment
- Production planning

Remote offices and work groups
- Communicate plans and policies
- Group collaboration
- Electronic communication
- Scheduling

The Firm

Business partners
- Joint design
- Outsourcing

ELECTRONIC COMMERCE

Customers
- On-line marketing
- On-line sales
- Built-to-order products
- Customer service
- Sales force automation

Suppliers
- Procurement
- Supply chain management

FIGURE 1-12 Electronic commerce and electronic business in the networked enterprise. Electronic commerce uses Internet and digital technology to conduct transactions with customers and suppliers, whereas electronic business uses these technologies for the management of the rest of the business.

tronic commerce and electronic business, organizations may have to redefine their business models, reinvent business processes, change corporate cultures, and develop closer relationships with customers and suppliers. We discuss these issues in greater detail in later chapters.

1.4 Learning to Use Information Systems: New Opportunities with Technology

Although information systems are creating many exciting opportunities for both businesses and individuals, they are also a source of new problems, issues, and challenges for managers. In this course, you will learn about the challenges and opportunities information systems pose, and you will be able to use information technology to enrich your learning experience.

THE CHALLENGE OF INFORMATION SYSTEMS: KEY MANAGEMENT ISSUES

Although information technology is advancing at a blinding pace, there is nothing easy or mechanical about building and using information systems. There are five key challenges confronting managers:

1. **The Strategic Business Challenge: How can businesses use information technology to design organizations that are competitive and effective?** Investment in information technology amounts to more than half of the annual capital expenditures of most large service-sector firms. Yet despite these heavy investments, many organizations are not obtaining significant business benefits. The power of computer hardware and software has grown much more rapidly than the ability of organizations to apply and use

this technology. To stay competitive or realize genuine productivity benefits from information technology, many organizations actually need to be redesigned. They will have to make fundamental changes in organizational behavior, develop new business models, and eliminate the inefficiencies of outmoded organizational structures. If organizations merely automate what they are doing today, they are largely missing the potential of information technology. To fully benefit from information technology, including the opportunities the Internet provides, organizations need to rethink and redesign the way they design, produce, deliver, and maintain goods and services.

2. **The Globalization Challenge: How can firms understand the business and system requirements of a global economic environment?** The rapid growth in international trade and the emergence of a global economy call for information systems that can support both producing and selling goods in many different countries. In the past, each regional office of a multinational corporation focused on solving its own unique information problems. Given language, cultural, and political differences among countries, this focus frequently resulted in chaos and the failure of central management controls. To develop integrated, multinational information systems, businesses must develop global hardware, software, and communications standards and create cross-cultural accounting and reporting structures (Roche, 1992).

3. **The Information Architecture and Infrastructure Challenge: How can organizations develop an information architecture and information technology infrastructure that supports their business goals?** Creating a new system now means much more than installing a new machine in the basement. Today, this process typically places thousands of personal computers on the desks of employees who have little experience with them, connecting the devices to powerful communications networks, rearranging social relations in the office and work locations, changing reporting patterns, and redefining business goals. Briefly, new systems today often require redesigning the organization and building a new information architecture and information technology (IT) infrastructure.

information architecture The particular design that information technology takes in a specific organization to achieve selected goals or functions.

Information architecture is the particular form that information technology takes in an organization to achieve selected goals or functions. It is a design for the business application systems that serve each functional specialty and level of the organization and the specific way that they are used by each organization. Because managers and employees directly interact with these systems, it is critical for organizational success that the information architecture meet business requirements now and in the future.

Figure 1-13 illustrates the major elements of information architecture that managers need to develop. At each level of the organization, the architecture shows the firm's business application systems for each of the major functional areas, including sales and marketing, manufacturing, finance, accounting, and human resources. The firm's information technology (IT) infrastructure provides the technology platform for this architecture. Computer hardware, software, data and storage technology, networks, and human resources required to operate the equipment constitute the shared IT resources of the firm and are available to all of its applications. Although this technology platform is typically operated by technical personnel, general management must decide how to allocate the resources it has assigned to hardware, software, data storage, and telecommunications networks to make sound information technology investments (Weill and Broadbent, 1997; 1998).

Typical questions regarding information architecture and IT infrastructure facing today's managers include: Should the corporate sales data and function be distributed to each corporate remote site, or should they be centralized at headquarters? Should the organization purchase stand-alone personal computers or build a more powerful, centralized mainframe environment within an integrated communications network? Should the organization build systems to connect the entire enterprise or separate islands of applications? There is no one right answer to these questions (see Allen and Boynton, 1991). Moreover, business needs are constantly changing, which requires the architecture to be reassessed continually (Feeny and Willcocks, 1998).

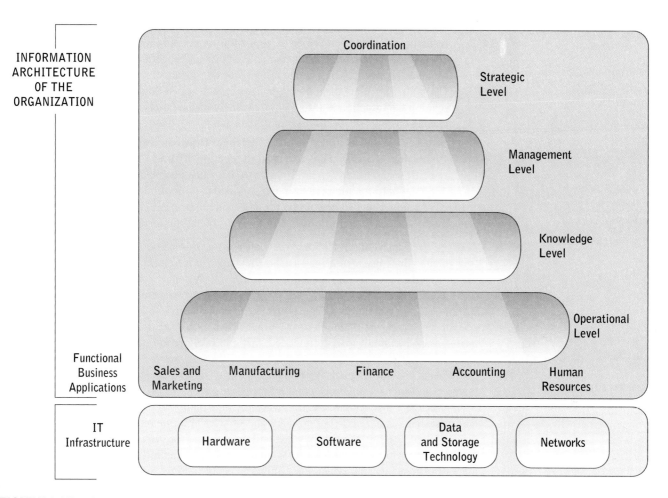

FIGURE I-I 3 Information architecture and information technology (IT) infrastructure. Today's managers must know how to arrange and coordinate the various computer technologies and business system applications to meet the information needs of each level of the organization and the needs of the organization as a whole.

Even under the best of circumstances, combining knowledge of systems and the organization is itself a demanding task. For many organizations, the task is even more formidable because they are crippled by fragmented and incompatible computer hardware, software, telecommunications networks, and information systems. Although Internet standards have solved some of these connectivity problems, integration of diverse computing platforms is rarely as seamless as promised. Many organizations are still struggling to integrate islands of information and technology into a coherent architecture. Chapters 3 through 8 provide more detail on information architecture and IT infrastructure issues.

4. **The Information Systems Investment Challenge: How can organizations determine the business value of information systems?** A major problem raised by the development of powerful, inexpensive computers involves not technology but management and organizations. It's one thing to use information technology to design, produce, deliver, and maintain new products. It's another thing to make money doing it. How can organizations obtain a sizable payoff from their investment in information systems?

Engineering massive organizational and system changes in the hope of positioning a firm strategically is complicated and expensive. Is this an investment that pays off?

How can you tell? Senior management can be expected to ask these questions: Are we receiving the kind of return on investment from our systems that we should be? Do our competitors get more? Understanding the costs and benefits of building a single system is difficult enough; it is daunting to consider whether the entire systems effort is "worth it." Imagine, then, how a senior executive must think when presented with a major transformation in information architecture—a bold venture in organizational change costing tens of millions of dollars and taking many years.

5. The Responsibility and Control Challenge: How can organizations ensure that their information systems are used in an ethically and socially responsible manner? How can we design information systems that people can control and understand? Although information systems have provided enormous benefits and efficiencies, they have also introduced new problems and challenges of which managers should be aware. Table 1-6 describes some of these problems and challenges.

Many chapters of this text describe scenarios that raise these ethical issues and Chapter 14 is devoted to this topic. A major management challenge is to make informed decisions that are sensitive to the negative consequences of information systems as well as to the positive ones.

Managers will also be faced with ongoing problems of security and control. Information systems are so essential to business, government, and daily life that organizations must take special steps to ensure that they are accurate, reliable, and secure. A firm invites disaster if it uses systems that don't work as intended, that don't deliver information in a form that people can interpret correctly and use, or that have control rooms where controls don't work or where instruments give false signals. Information systems must be designed so that they function as intended and so that humans can control the process.

Managers will need to ask: Can we apply high quality assurance standards to our information systems as well as to our products and services? Can we build information systems that respect people's rights of privacy while still pursuing our organization's goals? Should information systems monitor employees? What do we do when an information system designed to increase efficiency and productivity eliminates people's jobs?

This text is designed to provide future managers with the knowledge and understanding required to deal with these challenges. To further this objective, each succeeding chapter begins with a Management Challenges box that outlines the key issues of which managers should be aware.

Table 1-6 Positive and Negative Impacts of Information Systems

Benefits of Information Systems	Negative Impact
Information systems can perform calculations or process paperwork much faster than people.	By automating activities that were previously performed by people, information systems may eliminate jobs.
Information systems can help companies learn more about the purchase patterns and preferences of their customers.	Information systems may allow organizations to collect personal details about people that violate their privacy.
Information systems provide new efficiencies through services such as automated teller machines (ATMs), telephone systems, or computer-controlled airplanes and air terminals.	Information systems are used in so many aspects of everyday life that system outages can cause shutdowns of businesses or transportation services, paralyzing communities.
Information systems have made possible new medical advances in surgery, radiology, and patient monitoring.	Heavy users of information systems may suffer repetitive stress injury, technostress, and other health problems.
The Internet distributes information instantly to millions of people across the world.	The Internet can be used to distribute illegal copies of software, books, articles, and other intellectual property.

INTEGRATING TEXT WITH TECHNOLOGY: NEW OPPORTUNITIES FOR LEARNING

In addition to the changes in business and management that we have just described, we believe that information technology creates new opportunities for learning that can make the MIS course more meaningful and exciting. We have provided a Web site and an interactive multimedia CD-ROM for integrating the text with leading-edge technology.

As you read each chapter of the text, you can visit the Prentice Hall Laudon Web site and use the Internet for interactive learning and management problem-solving. The Internet Connection icon in the chapter directs you to Web sites for which we have provided additional exercises and projects related to the concepts and organizations described in that chapter. For each chapter, you will also find an Electronic Commerce project where you can use interactive software at various company Web sites to solve specific problems. Two of these Electronic Commerce projects are longer comprehensive projects. A graded on-line Interactive Study Guide contains questions to help you review what you have learned in each chapter and test your mastery of chapter concepts. You can also use the Laudon Web site to find links to additional on-line case studies, international resources, technology updates, and discussion boards and chat rooms.

An interactive CD-ROM multimedia version of the text can be purchased as an optional item. The Multimedia Edition CD-ROM features interactive exercises, simulations, audio/video overviews explaining key concepts, on-line quizzes, hyperlinks to the exercises on the Laudon Web site, technology updates, and more. You can use the CD-ROM as an interactive study guide or as an alternative to the traditional text.

We have added Application Exercises for each chapter that require students to use spreadsheet, database, and other application software in hands-on projects related to chapter concepts. Students can apply the application software skills they have learned in other courses to real-world business problems. You will find these exercises and their data files on the Laudon Web site.

You will find a Tools for Interactive Learning section, with the icon shown in the margin here, concluding every chapter to show how you can use the Web and interactive multimedia to enrich your learning experience.

MANAGEMENT WRAP-UP

Managers are problem-solvers who are responsible for analyzing the many challenges confronting organizations and for developing strategies and action plans. Information systems are one of their tools, delivering the information required for solutions. Information systems both reflect management decisions and serve as instruments for changing the management process.

Management

Information systems are rooted in organizations, an outcome of organizational structure, culture, politics, work flows, and standard operating procedures. They are instruments for organizational change, making it possible to recast these organizational elements into new business models and redraw organizational boundaries. Advances in information systems are accelerating the trend toward globalized, knowledge-driven economies and flattened, flexible, decentralized organizations.

Organization

A network revolution is under way. Information systems technology is no longer limited to computers but consists of an array of technologies that enable computers to be networked together to exchange information across great distances and organizational boundaries. The Internet provides global connectivity and a flexible platform for information-sharing, creating new uses for information systems and revolutionizing the role of information systems in organizations.

Technology

For Discussion

1. Information systems are too important to be left to computer specialists. Do you agree? Why or why not?

2. As computers become faster and cheaper and the Internet becomes more widely used, most of the problems we have with information systems will disappear. Do you agree? Why or why not?

SUMMARY

1. Define an information system. The purpose of a CBIS is to collect, store, and disseminate information from an organization's environment and internal operations to support organizational functions and decision making, communication, coordination, control, analysis, and visualization. Information systems transform raw data into useful information through three basic activities: input, processing, and output.

2. Distinguish between computer literacy and information systems literacy. Computer literacy focuses on how computer-based technologies work. Information systems literacy requires an understanding of the organizational and management dimensions of information systems as well as the technical dimensions addressed by computer literacy. Information systems literacy draws on both technical and behavioral approaches to studying information systems. Both perspectives can be combined into a sociotechnical approach to systems.

3. Explain why information systems are so important today and how they are transforming organizations and management. The kinds of systems built today are very important for the organization's overall performance, especially in today's highly globalized and information-based economy. Information systems are driving both daily operations and organizational strategy. Powerful computers, software, and networks, including the Internet, have helped organizations become more flexible, eliminate layers of management, separate work from location, and restructure work flows, giving new powers to both line workers and management. Information technology provides managers with tools for more precise planning, forecasting, and monitoring of the business. To maximize the advantages of information technology, there is a much greater need to plan the organization's information architecture and IT infrastructure.

4. Compare electronic commerce and electronic business and analyze their relationship to the Internet and digital technology. The Internet and other networks have made it possible for businesses to replace manual and paper-based processes with the electronic flow of information. In electronic commerce, businesses can exchange electronic purchase and sale transactions with each other and with individual customers. Electronic business uses the Internet and digital technology to expedite the exchange of information to facilitate communication and coordination both inside the organization and between the organization and its business partners.

5. Identify the major management challenges to building and using information systems in organizations. There are five key management challenges in building and using information systems: (1) designing systems that are competitive and efficient; (2) understanding the system requirements of a global business environment; (3) creating an information architecture and information technology infrastructure that support the organization's goals; (4) determining the business value of information systems; and (5) designing systems that people can control, understand, and use in a socially and ethically responsible manner.

KEY TERMS

REVIEW QUESTIONS

1. Why are information systems so important in business today?

2. What is an information system? Distinguish between a computer, a computer program, and an information system. What is the difference between data and information?

3. What activities convert raw data to usable information in information systems? What is their relationship to feedback?

4. What is information systems literacy? How does it differ from computer literacy?

5. What are the organization, management, and technology dimensions of information systems?

6. Distinguish between a behavioral and a technical approach to information systems in terms of the questions asked and the answers provided.

7. What major disciplines contribute to an understanding of information systems?

8. What is the relationship between an organization and its information systems? How is this relationship changing over time?

9. What are the Internet and the World Wide Web? How have they changed the role played by information systems in organizations?

10. Describe some of the major changes that information systems are bringing to organizations.

11. How are information systems changing the management process?

12. What is the relationship between the network revolution, electronic commerce, and electronic business?

13. What do we mean by information architecture and IT infrastructure? Why are they important concerns for managers?

14. What are the key management challenges involved in building, operating, and maintaining information systems today?

GROUP PROJECT

In a group with three or four classmates, find a description in a computer or business magazine of an information system used by an organization. Look for information about the company on the Web to gain further insight into the company and prepare a brief description of the business. Describe the system you have selected in terms of its inputs, processes, and outputs, and in terms of its organization, management, and technology features and the importance of the system to the company. Present your analysis to the class.

Tools for Interactive Learning

○ Internet Connection

The Internet Connection for this chapter will take you to the United Parcel Service (UPS) Web site where you can complete an exercise to evaluate how UPS uses the Web and other information technology in its daily operations. You can also use the Interactive Study Guide to test your knowledge of the topics in this chapter and get instant feedback where you need more practice.

○ Electronic Commerce Project

At the Laudon Web site for Chapter 1, you will find an Electronic Commerce project that will use the interactive software at the UPS Web site to help a company calculate and budget for its shipping costs.

○ CD-ROM

If you purchase and use the Multimedia Edition CD-ROM with this chapter, you will find a simulation showing you how the Internet works, a video clip illustrating UPS's package tracking system, an audio overview of the major themes of this chapter, and bullet text summarizing the key points of the chapter.

○ Application Exercise

At the Laudon Web site, you can find a spreadsheet Application Exercise for this chapter where you can analyze investments in electronic retailing.

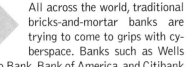

All across the world, traditional bricks-and-mortar banks are trying to come to grips with cyberspace. Banks such as Wells Fargo Bank, Bank of America, and Citibank now offer banking services over the Internet. Customers can access their accounts through the World Wide Web and check account balances or make transfers of funds between different accounts. Internet-only banks such as Net.Bank, Telebank, Security First Network Bank, and CompuBank that exist only on-line are springing up. The technology to set up an Internet bank is inexpensive and easily available. A Norcross, Georgia company called Nfront Inc. offers services to build a full-service "Internet branch" for any bank for about $50,000. Even retailers such as Nordstrom and Virgin Direct are offering financial services on the Web.

BancOne doesn't want to be left out. John B. McCoy, BancOne's former CEO, didn't want any competing Internet bank to take away business. McCoy decided that the best way to combat its Internet competition was to join it, even at the risk of cutting into BancOne's own business. BancOne launched an entirely new Internet-only bank called WingspanBank.com on June 24, 1999. BancOne's management believes that if Internet-only banks attract a large portion of the banking market, only a few can survive. As the fifth-largest bank in the United States in terms of assets, BancOne has much deeper pockets than its Internet-only competitors and can spend much more on marketing—close to $100 million in 1999 alone.

BancOne sees advantages in starting an entirely new Internet bank, in addition to setting up an Internet branch of its existing brick-and-mortar bank. Wingspan didn't have to spend months trying to figure out how to tie into BancOne's massive computer system. Wingspan can assume whatever identity it wants without regard to the brand image of BancOne. It can make fresh decisions without being saddled by bricks-and-mortar thinking. "If your bank could start over, this is what it would be," claims WingspanBank.com's advertisements. In addition, BancOne can use WingspanBank.com to find out whether customers prefer the higher rates and lower costs of Internet-only banks or the security of banks that have a physical as well as on-line presence.

Wingspan has its own advisory board that includes a software programmer, a college student, and a stay-at-home mother. Members of this "iBoard" meet on-line as well as face-to-face. It uses an ultrafast computer system that can process account transactions immediately. (BancOne and many other traditional banks use older systems that wait to update customer records overnight.) Although BancOne's Web site only sells the bank's products, Wingspan offers a large array of financial services, including 7,000 mutual funds, as well as mortgage and insurance from other companies. A special search capability surfs the Internet for the lowest mortgage rate and e-mails the customer when it is found, even if it is not through BancOne. Customers can shop the Net for five different kinds of insurance. For some types of loans, customers can apply on-line and find out if they are approved in less than a minute. Wingspan customers can even trade stocks on-line using an Internet discount brokerage service. Certificates of deposit at Wingspan have interest rates that are at least half a percentage point higher than those available at BancOne's traditional branches.

The downside is that this virtual bank can't deliver cash and customers must mail in their deposits, which can be a very slow process. Customers must be persuaded to change their recordkeeping habits. For example, Wingspan customers do not automatically receive copies of their cancelled checks nor are the checks themselves returned to them.

Wingspan customers can use BancOne ATMs to get cash, but BancOne does not have branches in most states. If a customer wants to use another bank's ATM, Wingspan will reimburse up to $5 per month for the ATM fees incurred.

Many other banks have concluded that they can benefit from the Internet without starting an entirely new bank. Wells Fargo & Co., for example, is merely adding an Internet branch to its existing bricks-and-mortar banking operation. Wells Fargo sees the Internet as merely another way to deliver bank services to traditional banking customers. These customers can still go into a bank branch or use an ATM, but they have the additional option of managing their accounts over the Web. Wells isn't rushing to convert customers to Internet banking and charges customers up to $5 per month to use the Internet for bill-paying as a way of recouping some of its costs.

James Hance, Jr., Chief Financial Officer for Bank of America, believes that banks must have physical branches because people still want face-to-face service and a way to withdraw their money.

Banking analysts worry that ventures such as Wingspan could encourage customers to repeatedly move their money among different banks to get the best interest rates of the moment, thereby shrinking profit margins and pushing banks into price wars. Net.Bank is already attracting customers by offering interest rates that are higher than Wingspan's.

Wingspan management figures that market share for Internet banking will be claimed quickly, so they need to grab it in the most assertive way possible. When the Internet-only banking business reaches maturity, there will be a shakeout, leaving only a few major players left to reap the rewards. Wingspan is using customer feedback to improve its Web site and product offerings.

To date, Internet-only banks have attracted only 225,000 customers representing 2 percent of the 9.5 million customers who manage their accounts on-line using Internet banking Web sites. Many people who have signed up for on-line banking have discontinued because they were unhappy with the quality of customer service.

Wingspan expected 500,000 customers by mid-2000 but only had 107,000 customer accounts by December 1999. McCoy said the size of its early customer base was less important than quickly establishing dominance in Internet banking. BancOne projected that Wingspan would reduce its earnings in the first year by roughly $60 million and did not expect to turn a profit until well into 2000.

Other banks are looking at BancOne's Internet venture very closely. Citigroup, the largest bank in the United States, has launched an Internet-only retail bank and brokerage company called Citi f/i. Other competitors such as Wells Fargo could easily create Internet-only banks if Wingspan takes off.

To survive, Wingspan may have to modify its business model and incorporate some traditional banking features. For example, it might have to build ATMs in areas where BancOne doesn't have any. And if ATMs are not enough to deliver all the services people want, Wingspan might even have to open bricks-and-mortar branches in some places.

Sources: Paul Beckett and Nikhil Deogun, "BankOne Hires Morgan Stanley to Help Explore Potential Sales of Web Bank Unit," **The Wall Street Journal**, March 22, 2000; Carrick Mollenkamp, "Old-time Banks Advance in Bricks vs. Clicks Battle," **The Wall Street Journal**, January 21, 2000; Candee Wilde, "WingspanBank.com Reinvents Online Model," **Information Week**, October 18, 1999; Rick Brooks, "BancOne's Strategy as Competition Grows: New, Online Institution," **The Wall Street Journal**, August 25, 1999; Thomas Hoffman, "WingspanBank.com Counts on Simplicity," **Computerworld**, August 23, 1999; and Jackie Cohen, "Everybody's a Banker," **The Industry Standard**, March 15, 1999.

CASE STUDY QUESTIONS

1. How does WingspanBank.com use the Internet for electronic commerce?

2. What management, organization, and technology issues did BancOne have to address in creating an Internet-only bank?

3. What are the advantages and disadvantages of using an Internet-only bank?

4. Do you think Wingspan Bank will succeed? Why or why not?

CHAPTER 2

The Strategic Role of Information Systems

Learning
Objectives

After completing this chapter, you will be able to:

1. Analyze the role played by the six major types of information systems in organizations and their relationship to each other.

2. Describe the types of information systems supporting the major functional areas of business.

3. Examine how the competitive forces and value chain models can be used to identify opportunities for strategic information systems.

4. Explain why strategic information systems are difficult to build and to sustain.

5. Describe how organizations can use information systems to enhance quality in their operations, products, and services.

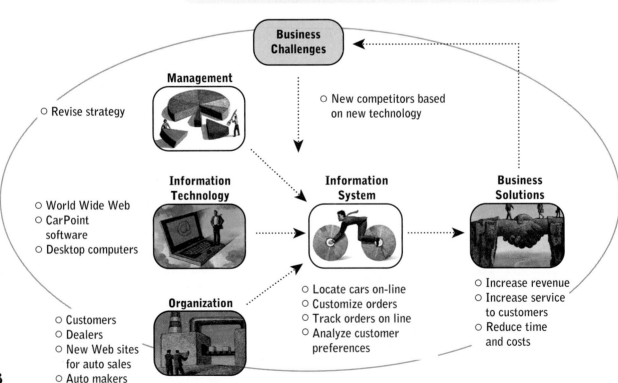

Business Challenges

Management
○ Revise strategy

○ New competitors based on new technology

Information Technology
○ World Wide Web
○ CarPoint software
○ Desktop computers

Information System
○ Locate cars on-line
○ Customize orders
○ Track orders on line
○ Analyze customer preferences

Business Solutions
○ Increase revenue
○ Increase service to customers
○ Reduce time and costs

Organization
○ Customers
○ Dealers
○ New Web sites for auto sales
○ Auto makers

Ford Fights Back on the Web

Ford Motor Company, headquartered in Dearborn, Michigan, has been manufacturing and selling cars for nearly a century. With operations spanning 200 countries, it is the world's largest truck maker and is second only to General Motors in car manufacturing. For many years, Ford's competitors have been other U.S. and Japanese automakers, but its greatest threat today may be coming from the Internet.

Traditionally, automakers competed by offering new models of cars and trucks and by streamlining their manufacturing and product development processes to bring new models to market quickly. The Internet and networking technology have changed the basis of competition by providing new capabilities for cutting costs, reducing inventory, and widening access to customers. A host of Web sites are challenging the traditional relationship between the automakers, franchised dealers, and customers. AutoNation Inc. sells several brands of cars through dealer groups that are not bound by dealership franchise laws, which prohibit automakers from selling cars directly to the public in competition with their dealerships. Customers can purchase vehicles at the AutoNation Web site and pick up their cars at one of AutoNation's affiliated dealers. CarsDirect.com allows consumers to research and purchase new cars on-line without talking to or visiting a dealer.

Ford is fighting back. In September 1999 the company announced a joint venture with Microsoft Corporation to use Microsoft's CarPoint Web site to help consumers find the specific car they want from dealer inventory or have it quickly built to order. The Web site links directly to Ford's order entry and materials-management systems as well as to factories and dealers. After an order is placed, buyers will be able to track it on-line and receive periodic updates on its status via e-mail. Although consumers can order cars directly through CarPoint, any sale will still be finalized through a franchised Ford dealer. Consumers can also link to Ford's build-to-order capability through Ford's other Web sites such as Ford.com and BuyerConnection.

The CarPoint system will also collect data on customer purchase patterns and preferences, which can help Ford fine-tune its products to include the features that consumers want the most. Traditionally, only about 10 percent of all new cars are built to order. Most automakers build and equip cars in standard configurations

CHAPTER OUTLINE

37

that are often based on outdated information. If Ford could build only the cars that consumers have actually ordered, it could realize significant savings in manufacturing and inventory costs.

Ford dealers' reactions are mixed. Some are welcoming CarPoint because it could attract new business, capitalizing on the growing number of car buyers who like to use the Internet. But others worry that by providing more information about product availability, pricing, and options, Ford's new Web site may shift power from the dealer to the customer and eventually lower profit margins.

Sources: Fara Warner, "Racing for Slice of a $350 Billion Pie, Online Auto-Sale's Sites Retool," *The Wall Street Journal,* January 24, 2000; Fred Andrews, "Dell, It Turns Out, Has a Better Idea than Ford," *The New York Times,* January 26, 2000; Bob Wallace and Aaron Ricadela, "Drive to the Web," *Information Week,* September 27, 1999; Fara Warner and David Bank, "Ford May Soon Receive Orders Online in an Expected Alliance with Microsoft," *The Wall Street Journal,* September 20, 1999; and John Markoff, "A Web-Researched Ford in Microsoft's Future," *The New York Times,* September 21, 1999.

MANAGEMENT CHALLENGES

Ford's use of the Web illustrates how critical information systems have become for supporting organizational goals and for enabling firms to stay ahead of the competition. Ford has temporarily gained a market advantage over its competitors by offering a service others cannot and by using information gathered from its Web site to fine-tune its products to customer needs. But something more than a single technological leap is required to sustain this competitive edge over many years. Specifically, managers need to address the following challenges:

1. **Integration:** Although it is necessary to design different systems serving different levels and functions in the firm, more and more firms are finding advantages in integrating systems. However, integrating systems for different organizational levels and functions to freely exchange information can be technologically difficult and costly. Managers need to determine what level of systems integration is required and how much it is worth in dollars.

2. **Sustainability of competitive advantage:** The competitive advantages strategic systems confer do not necessarily last long enough to ensure long-term profits. Because competitors can retaliate and copy strategic systems, competitive advantage isn't always sustainable. Market conditions change. The business and economic environment changes. Technology and customers' expectations change. The Internet can make competitive advantage for some companies disappear very quickly (Yoffie and Cusumano, 1999). The classic strategic information systems—American Airlines' SABRE computerized reservation system, Citibank's ATM system, and Federal Express' package tracking system—benefited by being the first in their respective industries. But then rival systems emerged. Information systems alone cannot provide an enduring business advantage (Mata et al., 1995; Kettinger et al., 1994; Hopper, 1990). Systems originally intended to be strategic frequently become tools for survival, something every firm has in order to stay in business, or they may even inhibit organizations from making the strategic changes required for future success (Eardley, Avison, and Powell, 1997).

In this chapter we examine the role of the various types of information systems in organizations. We then look at the problems firms face from competition and the ways in which information systems can provide competitive advantage. And because quality has become so important in today's competitive environment, we describe the various ways that information systems can contribute to the firm's quality goals.

2.1 Key System Applications in the Organization

Because there are different interests, specialties, and levels in an organization, there are different kinds of systems. No single system can provide all the information an organization needs. Figure 2-1 illustrates one way to depict the kinds of systems found in an organization. In the illustration, the organization is divided into strategic, management, knowledge, and operational levels and then is further divided into functional areas such as sales and marketing, manufacturing, finance, accounting, and human resources. Systems are built to serve these different organizational interests (Anthony, 1965).

DIFFERENT KINDS OF SYSTEMS

Four main types of information systems serve different organizational levels: operational-level systems, knowledge-level systems, management-level systems, and strategic-level systems. **Operational-level systems** support operational managers by keeping track of the elementary activities and transactions of the organization, such as sales, receipts, cash deposits, payroll,

operational-level systems
Information systems that monitor the elementary activities and transactions of the organization.

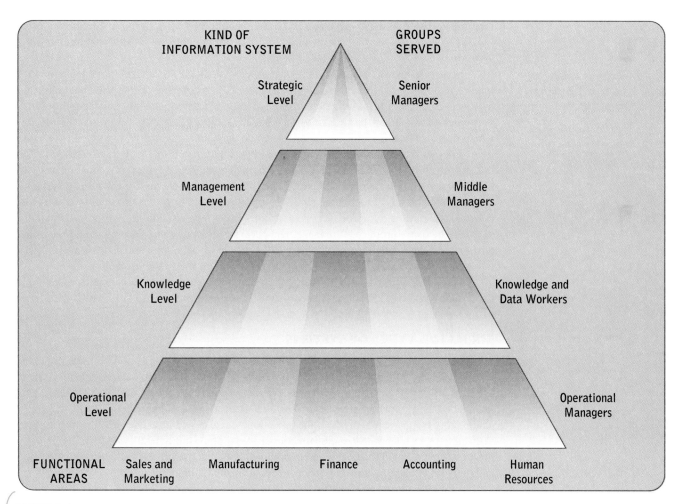

FIGURE 2-1 Types of information systems. Organizations can be divided into strategic, management, knowledge, and operational levels and into five major functional areas: sales and marketing, manufacturing, finance, accounting, and human resources. Information systems serve each of these levels and functions.

credit decisions, and the flow of materials in a factory. The principal purpose of systems at this level is to answer routine questions and to track the flow of transactions through the organization. How many parts are in inventory? What happened to Mr. Williams's payment? To answer these kinds of questions, information generally must be easily available, current, and accurate. Examples of operational-level systems include a system to record bank deposits from ATMs or one that tracks the number of hours worked each day by employees on a factory floor.

knowledge-level systems
Information systems that support knowledge and data workers in an organization.

Knowledge-level systems support the organization's knowledge and data workers. The purpose of knowledge-level systems is to help the business firm integrate new knowledge into the business and to help the organization control the flow of paperwork. Knowledge-level systems, especially in the form of workstations and office systems, are among the fastest-growing applications in business today.

management-level systems
Information systems that support the monitoring, controlling, decision-making, and administrative activities of middle managers.

Management-level systems serve the monitoring, controlling, decision-making, and administrative activities of middle managers. The principal question addressed by such systems is: Are things working well? Management-level systems typically provide periodic reports rather than instant information on operations. An example is a relocation control system that reports on the total moving, house-hunting, and home financing costs for employees in all company divisions, noting wherever actual costs exceed budgets.

Some management-level systems support nonroutine decision making (Keen and Morton, 1978). They tend to focus on less-structured decisions for which information requirements are not always clear. These systems often answer "what if" questions: What would be the impact on production schedules if we were to double sales in the month of December? What would happen to our return on investment if a factory schedule were delayed for six months? Answers to these questions frequently require new data from outside the organization, as well as data from inside that cannot be easily drawn from existing operational-level systems.

strategic-level systems
Information systems that support the long-range planning activities of senior management.

Strategic-level systems help senior management tackle and address strategic issues and long-term trends, both in the firm and in the external environment. Their principal concern is matching changes in the external environment with existing organizational capability. What will employment levels be in five years? What are the long-term industry cost trends, and where does our firm fit in? What products should we be making in five years?

Information systems also serve the major business functions, such as sales and marketing, manufacturing, finance, accounting, and human resources. A typical organization has each kind of system (operational, management, knowledge, and strategic) for each functional area. For example, the sales function generally has a sales system on the operational level to record daily sales figures and to process orders. A knowledge-level system designs promotional displays for the firm's products. A management-level system tracks monthly sales figures by sales territory and reports on territories where sales exceed or fall below anticipated levels. A system to forecast sales trends over a five-year period serves the strategic level.

We first describe the specific categories of systems serving each organizational level and their value to the organization. Then we show how organizations use these systems for each major business function.

SIX MAJOR TYPES OF SYSTEMS

Figure 2-2 shows the specific types of information systems that correspond to each organizational level. The organization has executive support systems (ESS) at the strategic level; management information systems (MIS) and decision-support systems (DSS) at the management level; knowledge work systems (KWS) and office systems at the knowledge level; and transaction processing systems (TPS) at the operational level. Systems at each level in turn are specialized to serve each of the major functional areas. Thus, the typical systems found in organizations are designed to assist workers or managers at each level and in the functions of sales and marketing, manufacturing, finance, accounting, and human resources.

Table 2-1 summarizes the features of the six types of information systems. It should be noted that each of the different kinds of systems may have components that are used by organizational levels and groups other than their main constituencies. A secretary may find information on an MIS, or a middle manager may need to extract data from a TPS.

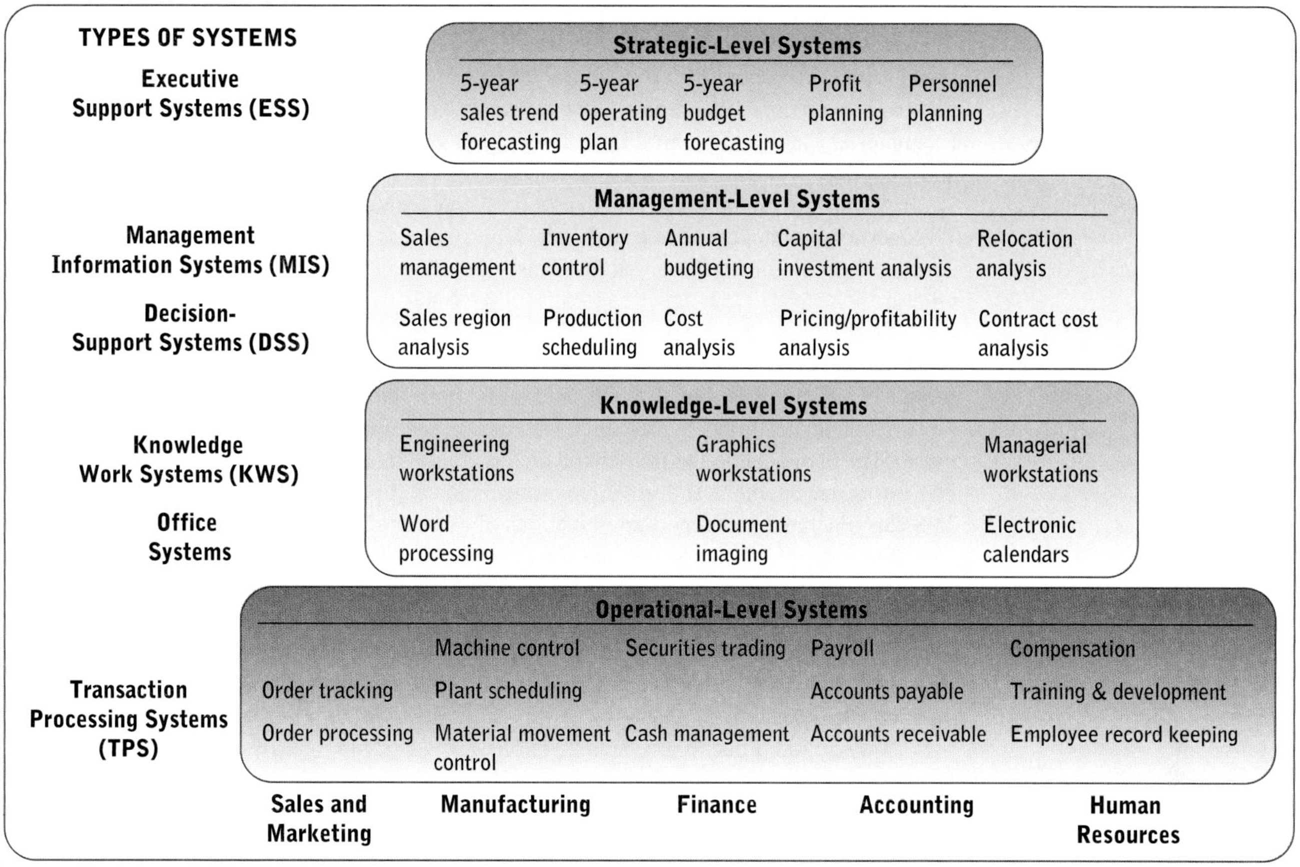

TYPES OF SYSTEMS

Executive Support Systems (ESS)	**Strategic-Level Systems**				
	5-year sales trend forecasting	5-year operating plan	5-year budget forecasting	Profit planning	Personnel planning

Management Information Systems (MIS)	**Management-Level Systems**				
	Sales management	Inventory control	Annual budgeting	Capital investment analysis	Relocation analysis
Decision-Support Systems (DSS)	Sales region analysis	Production scheduling	Cost analysis	Pricing/profitability analysis	Contract cost analysis

Knowledge Work Systems (KWS)	**Knowledge-Level Systems**			
	Engineering workstations	Graphics workstations		Managerial workstations
Office Systems	Word processing	Document imaging		Electronic calendars

Transaction Processing Systems (TPS)	**Operational-Level Systems**				
		Machine control	Securities trading	Payroll	Compensation
	Order tracking	Plant scheduling		Accounts payable	Training & development
	Order processing	Material movement control	Cash management	Accounts receivable	Employee record keeping
	Sales and Marketing	**Manufacturing**	**Finance**	**Accounting**	**Human Resources**

FIGURE 2-2 The six major types of information systems. This figure provides examples of TPS, office systems, KWS, DSS, MIS, and ESS, showing the level of the organization and business function that each supports.

Table 2-1 Characteristics of Information Processing Systems

Type of System	Information Inputs	Processing	Information Outputs	Users
ESS	Aggregate data; external, internal	Graphics; simulations; interactive	Projections; responses to queries	Senior managers
DSS	Low-volume data or massive databases optimized for data analysis; analytic models and data analysis tools	Interactive; simulations; analysis	Special reports; decision analyses; responses to queries	Professionals; staff managers
MIS	Summary transaction data; high-volume data; simple models	Routine reports; simple models; low-level analysis	Summary and exception reports	Middle managers
KWS	Design specifications; knowledge base	Modeling; simulations	Models; graphics	Professionals; technical staff
Office systems	Documents; schedules	Document management; scheduling; communication	Documents; schedules; mail	Clerical workers
TPS	Transactions; events	Sorting; listing; merging; updating	Detailed reports; lists; summaries	Operations personnel; supervisors

Transaction Processing Systems

transaction processing systems (TPS) Computerized systems that perform and record the daily routine transactions necessary to conduct the business; they serve the organization's operational level.

Transaction processing systems (TPS) are the basic business systems that serve the operational level of the organization. A transaction processing system is a computerized system that performs and records the daily routine transactions necessary to the conduct of the business. Examples are sales order entry, hotel reservation systems, payroll, employee record keeping, and shipping.

At the operational level, tasks, resources, and goals are predefined and highly structured. The decision to grant credit to a customer, for instance, is made by a lower level supervisor according to predefined criteria. All that must be determined is whether the customer meets the criteria.

Figure 2-3 depicts a payroll TPS, which is a typical accounting transaction processing system found in most firms. A payroll system keeps track of the money paid to employees. The master file is composed of discrete pieces of information (such as a name, address, or employee number) called data elements. Data are keyed into the system, updating the data elements. The elements on the master file are combined in different ways to make up reports of interest to management and government agencies and paychecks sent to employees. These TPS can generate other report combinations of existing data elements.

Other typical TPS applications are identified in Figure 2-4. The figure shows that there are five functional categories of TPS: sales/marketing, manufacturing/production, finance/accounting, human resources, and other types of TPS that are unique to a particular industry. The UPS package tracking system described in Chapter 1 is an example of a manufacturing TPS. UPS sells package delivery services; the system keeps track of all of its package shipment transactions.

Transaction processing systems are often so central to a business that TPS failure for a few hours can spell a firm's demise and perhaps other firms linked to it. Imagine what would happen to UPS if its package tracking system were not working! What would the airlines do without their computerized reservation systems?

Managers need TPS to monitor the status of internal operations and the firm's relations with the external environment. TPS are also major producers of information for the other types

FIGURE 2-3 A symbolic representation for a payroll TPS.

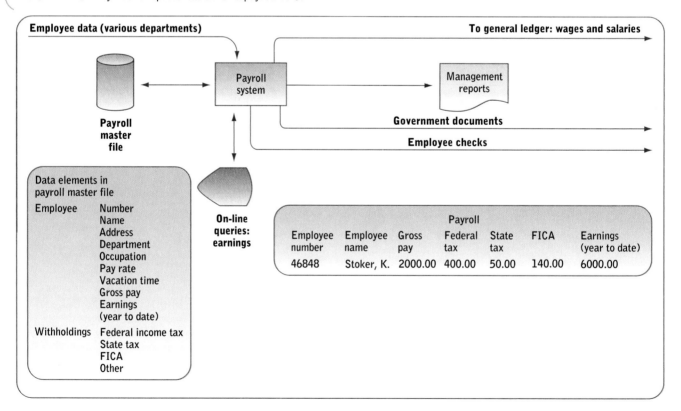

TYPE OF TPS SYSTEM				
Sales/ marketing systems	Manufacturing/ production systems	Finance/ accounting systems	Human resources systems	Other types (e.g., university)

	Sales/ marketing systems	Manufacturing/ production systems	Finance/ accounting systems	Human resources systems	Other types (e.g., university)
Major functions of system	Sales management	Scheduling	Budgeting	Personnel records	Admissions
	Market research	Purchasing	General ledger	Benefits	Grade records
	Promotion	Shipping/receiving	Billing	Compensation	Course records
	Pricing	Engineering	Cost accounting	Labor relations	Alumni
	New products	Operations		Training	
Major application systems	Sales order information system	Materials resource planning systems	General ledger	Payroll	Registration system
	Market research system	Purchase order control systems	Accounts receivable/payable	Employee records	Student transcript system
	Pricing system	Engineering systems	Budgeting	Benefit systems	Curriculum class control systems
		Quality control systems	Funds management systems	Career path systems	Alumni benefactor system

FIGURE 2-4 Typical applications of TPS. There are five functional categories of TPS: sales/marketing, manufacturing/production, finance/accounting, human resources, and other types of systems specific to a particular industry. Within each of these major functions are subfunctions. For each of these subfunctions (e.g., sales management) there is a major application system.

of systems. (For example, the payroll system illustrated in Figure 2-3, along with other accounting TPS, supplies data to the company's general ledger system, which is responsible for maintaining records of the firm's income and expenses and for producing reports such as income statements and balance sheets.)

Knowledge Work and Office Systems

Knowledge work systems (KWS) and **office systems** serve the information needs at the knowledge level of the organization. Knowledge work systems aid knowledge workers, whereas office systems primarily aid data workers (although they are also used extensively by knowledge workers).

In general, *knowledge workers* are people who hold formal university degrees and who are often members of a recognized profession, like engineers, doctors, lawyers, and scientists. Their jobs consist primarily of creating new information and knowledge. Knowledge work systems (KWS), such as scientific or engineering design workstations, promote the creation of new knowledge and ensure that new knowledge and technical expertise are properly integrated into the business. *Data workers* typically have less formal, advanced educational degrees and tend to process rather than create information. They consist primarily of secretaries, bookkeepers, filing clerks, or managers whose jobs are principally to use, manipulate, or disseminate information. Office systems are information technology applications designed to increase data workers' productivity by supporting the coordinating and communicating activities of the typical office. Office systems coordinate diverse information workers, geographic units, and functional areas: The systems communicate with customers, suppliers, and other organizations outside the firm and serve as a clearinghouse for information and knowledge flows.

Typical office systems handle and manage documents (through word processing, desktop publishing, document imaging, and digital filing), scheduling (through electronic calendars), and communication (through electronic mail, voice mail, or videoconferencing). **Word processing** refers to the software and hardware that creates, edits, formats, stores, and prints documents (see Chapter 5). Word processing systems represent the single most common application

knowledge work systems (KWS) Information systems that aid knowledge workers in the creation and integration of new knowledge in the organization.

office systems Computer systems, such as word processing, electronic mail systems, and scheduling systems, that are designed to increase the productivity of data workers in the office.

word processing Hardware and software technology that facilitates the creation of documents through computerized text editing, formatting, storing, and printing.

Graphics designers use desktop publishing software to design a page for "La Opinion." Desktop publishing software enables users to control all aspects of the design and layout process for professional-looking publications.

desktop publishing Technology that produces professional-quality documents combining output from word processors with design, graphics, and special layout features

document imaging systems Systems that convert documents and images into digital form so that they can be stored and accessed by the computer.

management information systems (MIS) Information systems at the management level of an organization that serve the functions of planning, controlling, and decision making by providing routine summary and exception reports.

decision-support systems (DSS) Information systems at the organization's management level that combine data and sophisticated analytical models or data analysis tools to support nonroutine decision making.

of information technology to office work, in part because producing documents is what offices are all about. **Desktop publishing** produces professional publishing-quality documents by combining output from word processing software with design elements, graphics, and special layout features. Companies are now starting to publish documents in the form of Web pages for easier access and distribution. We describe Web publishing in more detail in Chapter 11.

Document imaging systems are another widely used knowledge application. Document imaging systems convert documents and images into digital form so that they can be stored and accessed by the computer. The Window on Organizations describes how a document imaging system works and the benefits it can provide to organizations.

Management Information Systems

In Chapter 1, we defined management information systems as the study of information systems in business and management. The term *management information systems (MIS)* also designates a specific category of information systems serving management-level functions. **Management information systems (MIS)** serve the management level of the organization, providing managers with reports or with on-line access to the organization's current performance and historical records. Typically, they are oriented almost exclusively to internal, not environmental or external, events. MIS primarily serve the functions of planning, controlling, and decision making at the management level. Generally, they depend on underlying transaction processing systems for their data.

MIS summarize and report on the company's basic operations. The basic transaction data from TPS are compressed and are usually presented in long reports that are produced on a regular schedule. Figure 2-5 shows how a typical MIS transforms transaction level data from inventory, production, and accounting into MIS files that are used to provide managers with reports. Figure 2-6 shows a sample report from this system.

MIS usually serve managers interested in weekly, monthly, and yearly results—not day-to-day activities. MIS generally provide answers to routine questions that have been specified in advance and have a predefined procedure for answering them. For instance, MIS reports might list the total pounds of lettuce used this quarter by a fast-food chain or, as illustrated in Figure 2-6, compare total annual sales figures for specific products to planned targets. These systems are generally not flexible and have little analytical capability. Most MIS use simple routines such as summaries and comparisons, as opposed to sophisticated mathematical models or statistical techniques.

Decision-Support Systems

Decision-support systems (DSS) also serve the management level of the organization. DSS help managers make decisions that are unique, rapidly changing, and not easily specified in

IMPROVING MERCANTILE MUTUAL'S CUSTOMER IMAGE

When customers call the company that manages their money, they expect quick, accurate answers. After all, it's their money they are calling about. Recently, executives in the Retail Funds Management Division of Australia's $17.5 billion (Australian) Mercantile Mutual concluded their division was responding too slowly to customer inquiries. Worse yet, Retail Funds' customers knew it. "Customers would do business with us and another two companies," Retail Funds' project manager Bruce Appleton explained, "and were easily able to determine if one company was offering slightly better service." Mercantile Mutual offers insurance, banking, and investment services.

The reason customer service was slow was obvious. Almost all customer records were still stored as paper. Moreover, these records were not centralized but rather were scattered among various company sites. As a result customer inquiries almost always required callbacks because the customer service staff first had to locate and pull the relevant documents before being able to answer a customer's questions.

To solve the problem, Retail Funds needed to make the documents instantly available to all customer service personnel at any site. The only answer was a document imaging and work flow system that scans paper documents and stores them on the computer where they can be accessed by many different people at the same time if required. The new system, Imagic, stores documents in color because color is more accurate than black and white, enabling the customer service staff to see exactly what the customer was seeing. Now, when a customer calls, the customer service staff can retrieve the document instantly and immediately address the customer's question. Newly created outgoing documents such as monthly statements are scanned and stored prior to being mailed to the customers so that they will already be

accessible when the telephone calls begin. The division even images approximately 3,000 pieces of mail it receives daily from its customers so that they too are easily available to customer service personnel when needed. Now most customer's questions can be answered without delay.

The work flow side of Imagic also helps customers. Retail Funds' staff can view, access, and work on documents from desktop computers anywhere in the company, and they can do it simultaneously. No longer is a document passed from person to person to be worked on in the traditional time-consuming serial fashion. Instead multiple employees are able to act on the document simultaneously, thereby completing the processing of a customer's request much more quickly.

Imagic has done more than just improve customer relations for Retail Funds. First, the system actually saves the company money and has already paid back the $1.5 million (Australian) Mercantile invested in the system. Retrieving documents manually was slow, requiring a lot of expensive staff time. Moreover, storing the documents required a lot of space that the company is now using for more productive purposes. The system has also become a benefit to marketing. According to Appleton, the new system is now a major selling point in pursuing "new business opportunities." Because the system has won several quality and technology awards, marketing uses Imagic with potential customers as an example of what Mercantile can do for them.

TO THINK ABOUT: How did Mercantile Mutual's document imaging system change the way the company conducted business? What benefits does the system provide for Mercantile Mutual?

Sources: "It's a Colorful World," **Strategic Vision**, Summer 1999; and http://www.mercantilemutual.com.au/, February 2, 2000.

---

advance. They address problems where the procedure for arriving at a solution may not be fully predefined. Although DSS use internal information from TPS and MIS, they often bring in information from external sources, such as current stock prices or product prices of competitors.

Clearly, by design, DSS have more analytical power than other systems. They are built explicitly with a variety of models to analyze data, or they condense large amounts of data into a form where they can be analyzed by decision makers. DSS are designed so that users can work with them directly; these systems explicitly include user-friendly software. DSS are interactive; the user can change assumptions, ask new questions, and include new data.

An interesting, small, but powerful DSS is the voyage-estimating system of a subsidiary of a large American metals company that exists primarily to carry bulk cargoes of coal, oil, ores, and finished products for its parent company. The firm owns some vessels, charters others, and bids for shipping contracts in the open market to carry general cargo. A voyage-estimating system calculates financial and technical voyage details. Financial calculations include ship/time costs (fuel, labor, capital), freight rates for various types of cargo, and port

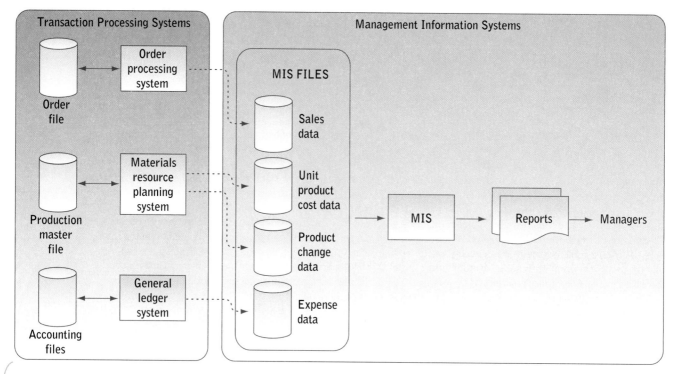

FIGURE 2-5 How management information systems obtain their data from the organization's TPS. In the system illustrated by this diagram, three TPS supply summarized transaction data at the end of the time period to the MIS reporting system. Managers gain access to the organizational data through the MIS, which provides them with the appropriate reports.

expenses. Technical details include myriad factors such as ship cargo capacity, speed, port distances, fuel and water consumption, and loading patterns (location of cargo for different ports). The system can answer questions such as the following: Given a customer delivery schedule and an offered freight rate, which vessel should be assigned at what rate to maximize profits? What is the optimum speed at which a particular vessel can optimize its profit and still meet its delivery schedule? What is the optimal loading pattern for a ship bound for the U.S. West Coast from Malaysia? Figure 2-7 illustrates the DSS built for this company. The system operates on a powerful desktop personal computer, providing a system of menus that makes it easy for users to enter data or obtain information. We describe other types of DSS in Chapter 12.

FIGURE 2-6 A sample report that might be produced by the MIS in Figure 2-5.

Consolidated Consumer Products Corporation
Sales by Product and Sales Region: 2000

PRODUCT CODE	PRODUCT DESCRIPTION	SALES REGION	ACTUAL SALES	PLANNED	ACTUAL VS. PLANNED
4469	Carpet Cleaner	Northeast	4,066,700	4,800,000	0.85
		South	3,778,112	3,750,000	1.01
		Midwest	4,867,001	4,600,000	1.06
		West	4,003,440	4,400,000	0.91
	TOTAL		16,715,253	17,550,000	0.95
5674	Room Freshener	Northeast	3,676,700	3,900,000	0.94
		South	5,608,112	4,700,000	1.19
		Midwest	4,711,001	4,200,000	1.12
		West	4,563,440	4,900,000	0.93
	TOTAL		18,559,253	17,700,000	1.05

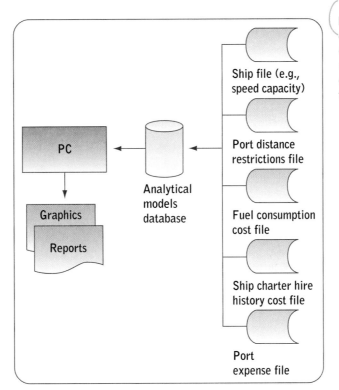

FIGURE 2-7 Voyage estimating decision-support system. This DSS operates on a powerful PC. It is used daily by managers who must develop bids on shipping contracts.

Executive Support Systems

Senior managers use **executive support systems (ESS)** to make decisions. ESS serve the strategic level of the organization. They address nonroutine decisions requiring judgement, evaluation, and insight because there is no agreed-on procedure for arriving at a solution. ESS create a generalized computing and communications environment rather than providing any fixed application or specific capability. ESS are designed to incorporate data about external events such as new tax laws or competitors, but they also draw summarized information from internal MIS and DSS. They filter, compress, and track critical data, emphasizing the reduction of time and effort required to obtain information useful to executives. ESS employ the most advanced graphics software and can deliver graphs and data from many sources immediately to a senior executive's office or to a boardroom.

> **executive support systems (ESS)** Information systems at the organization's strategic level designed to address unstructured decision making through advanced graphics and communications.

Unlike the other types of information systems, ESS are not designed primarily to solve specific problems. Instead, ESS provide a generalized computing and communications capacity that can be applied to a changing array of problems. Whereas many DSS are designed to be highly analytical, ESS tend to make less use of analytical models.

Questions ESS assist in answering include the following: What business should we be in? What are the competitors doing? What new acquisitions would protect us from cyclical business swings? Which units should we sell to raise cash for acquisitions (Rockart and Treacy, 1982)? Figure 2-8 illustrates a model of an ESS. It consists of workstations with menus, interactive graphics, and communications capabilities that can access historical and competitive data from internal corporate systems and external sources such as Dow Jones News/Retrieval or Internet news services. Because ESS are designed to be used by senior managers who often have little, if any, direct contact or experience with computer-based information systems, they incorporate easy-to-use graphic interfaces. More details on leading-edge applications of DSS and ESS can be found in Chapter 12.

RELATIONSHIP OF SYSTEMS TO ONE ANOTHER: INTEGRATION

Figure 2-9 illustrates how the systems serving different levels in the organization are related to one another. TPS are typically a major source of data for other systems, whereas ESS are primarily a recipient of data from lower level systems. The other types of systems may exchange data with each other as well. Data may also be exchanged among systems serving

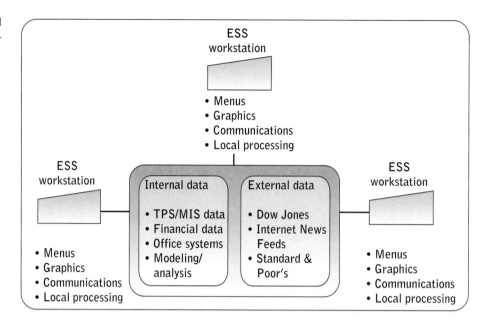

FIGURE 2-8 Model of a typical executive support system. This system pools data from diverse internal and external sources and makes them available to executives in an easy-to-use form.

different functional areas. For example, an order captured by a sales system may be transmitted to a manufacturing system as a transaction for producing or delivering the product specified in the order.

It is definitely advantageous to have some measure of integration among these systems so that information can flow easily among different parts of the organization. But integration costs money, and integrating many different systems is extremely time consuming and complex. Each organization must weigh its needs for integrating systems against the difficulties of mounting a large-scale systems integration effort. There is no "one right level" of integration or centralization (Allen and Boynton, 1991; King, 1984). Chapter 3 addresses the issue of integrating information across the company in greater detail.

FIGURE 2-9
Interrelationships among systems. The various types of systems in the organization have interdependencies. TPS are a major producer of information that is required by the other systems, which, in turn, produce information for other systems. These different types of systems are only loosely coupled in most organizations.

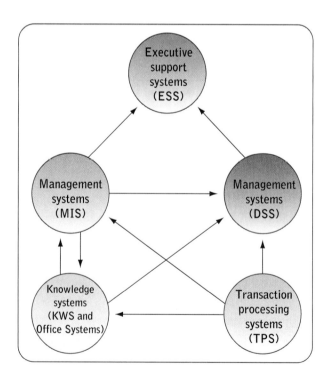

SYSTEMS FROM A FUNCTIONAL PERSPECTIVE

Information systems can be classified by the specific organizational function they serve as well as by organizational level. We now describe typical information systems that support each of the major business functions and provide examples of functional applications for each organizational level.

Sales and Marketing Systems

The sales and marketing function is responsible for selling the organization's product or services. Marketing is concerned with identifying the customers for the firm's products or services, determining what they need or want, planning and developing products and services to meet their needs, and advertising and promoting these products and services. Sales is concerned with contacting customers, selling the products and services, taking orders, and following up on purchases. **Sales and marketing information systems** support these activities.

Table 2-2 shows that information systems are used in sales and marketing in a number of ways. At the strategic level, sales and marketing systems monitor trends affecting new products and sales opportunities, support planning for new products and services, and monitor the performance of competitors. At the management level, sales and marketing systems support advertising and promotional campaigns and pricing decisions. They analyze sales performance and the performance of the sales staff. Knowledge-level sales and marketing systems support market research and marketing analysis workstations. At the operational level, sales and marketing systems assist in locating and contacting prospective customers, tracking sales, processing orders, and providing customer service support.

Review Figure 2-6. It shows the output of a typical sales information system at the management level. The system consolidates data about each item sold (such as the product code, product description, and price) for further management analysis. Company managers examine these sales data to monitor sales activity and buying trends.

sales and marketing information systems Systems that help the firm identify customers for the firm's products or services, develop products and services to meet their needs, promote these products and services, sell the products and services, and provide ongoing customer support.

Manufacturing and Production Systems

The manufacturing and production function is responsible for actually producing the firm's goods and services. Manufacturing and production systems deal with the planning, development, and maintenance of production facilities; the establishment of production goals; the acquisition, storage, and availability of production materials; and the scheduling of equipment, facilities, materials, and labor required to fashion finished products. **Manufacturing and production information systems** support these activities.

Table 2-3 shows some typical manufacturing and production information systems arranged by organizational level. Strategic-level manufacturing and production systems deal with the firm's long-term manufacturing goals, such as where to locate new plants or whether to invest in new manufacturing technology. At the management level, manufacturing and production systems analyze and monitor manufacturing and production costs and resources.

manufacturing and production information systems Systems that deal with the planning, development, and production of products and services and with controlling the flow of production.

Table 2-2 Examples of Sales and Marketing Information Systems

System	Description	Organizational Level
Order processing	Enter, process, and track orders	Operational
Market analysis	Identify customers and markets using data on demographics, markets, consumer behavior, and trends	Knowledge
Pricing analysis	Determine prices for products and services	Management
Sales trend forecasting	Prepare five-year sales forecasts	Strategic

Table 2-3

Examples of Manufacturing and Production Information Systems

System	Description	Organizational Level
Machine control	Control the actions of machines and equipment	Operational
Computer-aided design (CAD)	Design new products using the computer	Knowledge
Production planning	Decide when and how many products should be produced	Management
Facilities location	Decide where to locate new production facilities	Strategic

Knowledge manufacturing and production systems create and distribute design knowledge or expertise to drive the production process, and operational manufacturing and production systems deal with the status of production tasks.

Most manufacturing and production systems use some sort of inventory system, illustrated in Figure 2-10. Data about each item in inventory, such as the number of units depleted because of a shipment or purchase or the number of units replenished by reordering or returns are either scanned or keyed into the system. The inventory master file contains basic data about each item, including the unique identification code for each item, the description of the item, the number of units on hand, the number of units on order, and the reorder point (the number of units in inventory that triggers a decision to reorder to prevent a stockout). Companies can estimate the number of items to reorder or they can use a formula for calculating the least ex-

FIGURE 2-10 Overview of an inventory system. This system provides information about the number of items available in inventory to support manufacturing and production activities.

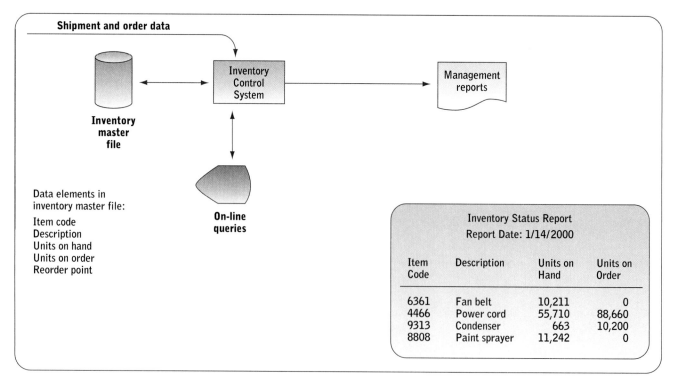

pensive quantity to reorder called the *economic order quantity.* The system produces reports such as the number of each item available in inventory, the number of units of each item to reorder, or items in inventory that must be replenished.

Finance and Accounting Systems

The finance function is responsible for managing the firm's financial assets, such as cash, stocks, bonds, and other investments in order to maximize the return on these financial assets. The finance function is also in charge of managing the capitalization of the firm (finding new financial assets in stocks, bonds, or other forms of debt). In order to determine whether the firm is getting the best return on its investments, the finance function must obtain a considerable amount of information from sources external to the firm.

The accounting function is responsible for maintaining and managing the firm's financial records—receipts, disbursements, depreciation, payroll—to account for the flow of funds in a firm. Finance and accounting share related problems—how to keep track of a firm's financial assets and fund flows. They provide answers to questions such as these: What is the current inventory of financial assets? What records exist for disbursements, receipts, payroll, and other fund flows?

Table 2-4 shows some of the typical **finance and accounting information systems** found in large organizations. Strategic-level systems for the finance and accounting function establish long-term investment goals for the firm and provide long-range forecasts of the firm's financial performance. At the management level, information systems help managers oversee and control the firm's financial resources. Knowledge systems support finance and accounting by providing analytical tools and workstations for designing the right mix of investments to maximize returns for the firm. Operational systems in finance and accounting track the flow of funds in the firm through transactions such as paychecks, payments to vendors, securities reports, and receipts.

> **finance and accounting information systems** Systems that keep track of the firm's financial assets and fund flows.

Review Figure 2-3, which illustrates a payroll system, a typical accounting TPS found in all businesses with employees.

Human Resources Systems

The human resources function is responsible for attracting, developing, and maintaining the firm's workforce. **Human resources information systems** support activities such as identifying potential employees, maintaining complete records on existing employees, and creating programs to develop employees' talents and skills.

Strategic-level human resources systems identify the employee requirements (skills, educational level, types of positions, number of positions, and cost) for meeting the firm's long-term business plans. At the management level, human resources systems help managers monitor and analyze the recruitment, allocation, and compensation of employees. Knowledge systems for human resources support analysis activities related to job design, training, and the modeling of employee career paths and reporting relationships. Human resources operational systems track the recruitment and placement of the firm's employees (see Table 2-5).

> **human resources information systems** Systems that maintain employee records; track employee skills, job performance, and training; and support planning for employee compensation and career development.

Figure 2-11 illustrates a typical human resources TPS for employee record keeping. It maintains basic employee data, such as the employee's name, age, sex, marital status, address,

---

Table 2-4 **Examples of Finance and Accounting Information Systems**

System	Description	Organizational Level
Accounts receivable	Track money owed the firm	Operational
Portfolio analysis	Design the firm's portfolio of investments	Knowledge
Budgeting	Prepare short-term budgets	Management
Profit planning	Plan long-term profits	Strategic

Table 2-5 Examples of Human Resources Information Systems

System	Description	Organizational Level
Training and development	Track employee training, skills, and performance appraisals	Operational
Career pathing	Design career paths for employees	Knowledge
Compensation analysis	Monitor the range and distribution of employee wages, salaries, and benefits	Management
Human resources planning	Plan the long-term labor force needs of the organization	Strategic

educational background, salary, job title, date of hire, and date of termination. The system can produce a variety of reports, such as lists of newly hired employees, employees who are terminated or on leaves of absence, employees classified by job type or educational level, or employee job performance evaluations. Such systems are typically designed to provide data that can satisfy federal and state record keeping requirements for Equal Employment Opportunity (EEO) and other purposes.

Because no two organizations have exactly the same objectives, structures, or interests, these differences will be reflected in their information systems. The information systems of two different organizations for the same functional area are not likely to be identical. Every organization does the job somewhat differently.

2.2 The Strategic Role of Information Systems

Each of the major types of information systems described previously is valuable for helping organizations solve an important problem. In the past few decades, some of these systems have

FIGURE 2-11 An employee recordkeeping system. This system maintains data on the firm's employees to support the human resources function.

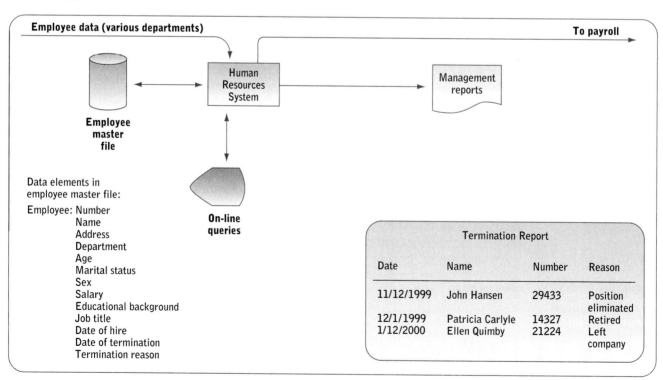

become especially critical to firms' long-term prosperity and survival. Such systems, which are powerful tools for staying ahead of the competition, are called strategic information systems.

WHAT IS A STRATEGIC INFORMATION SYSTEM?

Strategic information systems change the goals, operations, products, services, or environmental relationships of organizations to help them gain an edge over competitors. Systems that have these effects may even change the business of organizations. For instance, State Street Bank and Trust Co. of Boston transformed its core business from traditional banking services, such as customer checking and savings accounts and loans, to electronic recordkeeping, providing data processing services for securities and mutual funds, and services for pension funds to monitor their money managers (Rebello, 1995).

Strategic information systems should be distinguished from strategic-level systems for senior managers that focus on long-term, decision-making problems. Strategic information systems can be used at all organizational levels and are more far reaching and deep rooted than the other kinds of systems we have described. Strategic information systems profoundly alter the way a firm conducts its business or the very business of the firm itself.

In order to use information systems as competitive weapons, one must first understand where strategic opportunities for businesses are likely to be found. Two models of a firm and its environment have been used to identify areas of the business where information systems can provide advantages over competitors. These are the competitive forces model and the value chain model.

COUNTERING COMPETITIVE FORCES

In the **competitive forces model,** which is illustrated in Figure 2-12 (Porter, 1980), a firm faces a number of external threats and opportunities. These threats and opportunities include the threat of new entrants into its market, the pressure from substitute products or services, customers' bargaining power, suppliers' bargaining power, and the positioning of traditional industry competitors.

Competitive advantage can be achieved by enhancing the firm's ability to deal with customers, suppliers, substitute products and services, and new entrants to its market, which in turn may change the balance of power between a firm and other competitors in the industry in the firm's favor. Businesses can use four basic competitive strategies to deal with these competitive forces: product differentiation, focused differentiation, developing tight linkages to customers and suppliers, and becoming the low-cost producer. A firm may achieve competitive advantage by pursuing one of these strategies or by pursuing several strategies simultaneously.

strategic information systems Computer systems at any level of the organization that change goals, operations, products, services, or environmental relationships to help the organization gain a competitive advantage.

competitive forces model Model used to describe the interaction of external influences, specifically threats and opportunities, that affect an organization's strategy and ability to compete.

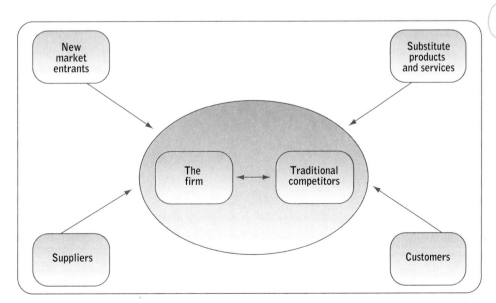

FIGURE 2-12 The competitive forces model. There are various forces that affect an organization's ability to compete and, therefore, greatly influence a firm's business strategy. There are threats from new market entrants and from substitute products and services. Customers and suppliers wield bargaining power. Traditional competitors constantly adapt their strategies to maintain their market position.

For instance, Art.com operates a Web site where customers can select online from more than 100,000 prints and arrange to have them framed, at a price that is 20 to 50 percent lower than a traditional bricks-and-mortar art or frame shop. Art.com thus competes through product differentiation and low cost. We now describe how information systems can support these competitive strategies.

Product Differentiation

Firms can develop brand loyalty by **product differentiation**—creating unique new products and services that can easily be distinguished from those of competitors, and that existing competitors or potential new competitors can't duplicate.

Many of these information-technology-based products and services have been created by financial institutions. Citibank developed automatic teller machines (ATMs) and bank debit cards in 1977. As a leader in this area, Citibank became at one time the largest bank in the United States. Citibank ATMs were so successful that other banks were forced to counterstrike with their own ATM systems. Citibank, Wells Fargo bank, and others have continued to innovate by providing on-line banking services so that customers can do most of their banking transactions with home computers linked to proprietary networks or the Internet. Some companies such as WingspanBank.com, described in the Chapter 1 Case Study, have used the Web to set up "virtual banks" offering a full array of banking services without any physical branches. Customers mail in their deposits.

Manufacturers and retailers are also using information systems to create products and services that are custom-tailored to fit individual customers' precise specifications. Dell Computer Corporation sells directly to customers using build-to-order manufacturing. Individuals, businesses, and governments can purchase computers directly from Dell customized with exactly the features and components they need. They can place their orders directly using a toll-free telephone line or through Dell's Web site. Once the Dell factory receives an order, it assembles the computer based on the configuration specified by the customer. International Case Study 5 provides more detail on Dell's business model. Chapter 1 described other instances in which information technology is creating customized products and services while retaining the cost efficiencies of mass production techniques.

Focused Differentiation

Businesses can create new market niches by **focused differentiation**—identifying a specific target for a product or service that it can serve in a superior manner. A firm can provide a specialized product or service that serves this narrow target market better than existing competitors and that discourages potential new competitors.

product differentiation
Competitive strategy for creating brand loyalty by developing new and unique products and services that are not easily duplicated by competitors.

focused differentiation
Competitive strategy for developing new market niches for specialized products or services where a business can compete in the target area better than its competitors.

At Dell Computer Corporation's Web site, customers can select the options they want and order their computer custom-built to these specifications. Dell's build-to-order system is a major source of competitive advantage.

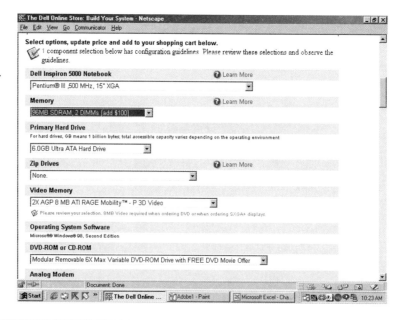

An information system can give companies a competitive advantage by producing data to improve their sales and marketing techniques. Such systems treat existing information as a resource that the organization can "mine" to increase profitability and market penetration. Information systems enable companies to finely analyze customer buying patterns, tastes, and preferences so that the companies can efficiently pitch advertising and marketing campaigns to smaller and smaller target markets.

Sophisticated **datamining** software tools find patterns in large pools of data and infer rules from them that can be used to guide decision making. For example, mining data about purchases at supermarkets might reveal that when potato chips are purchased, soda is also purchased 65 percent of the time. When there is a promotion, soda is purchased 85 percent of the time people purchase potato chips. Table 2-6 describes how some organizations are benefiting from datamining.

The data come from a range of sources—credit card transactions, purchase data from checkout counters, demographic data, and, now, information collected from visitors to Web sites. Datamining helps companies engage in one-to-one marketing where personal or individualized messages can be created based on individualized preferences. The level of fine-grained customization provided by these datamining systems parallels that for mass customization described in Chapter 1.

The cost of acquiring a new customer has been estimated at five times greater than that of retaining an existing customer. By carefully examining transactions of customer purchases and activities, firms can identify profitable customers and win more of their business. Likewise, companies can use these data to identify nonprofitable customers (Clemons and Weber, 1994).

Datamining is both a powerful and profitable tool, but it poses challenges to the protection of individual privacy. Datamining technology can combine information from many diverse sources to create a detailed "data image" about each of us—our income, our driving habits, our hobbies, our families, and our political interests. The question of whether companies should be allowed to collect such detailed information about individuals is explored in Chapter 14.

datamining Analysis of large pools of data to find patterns and rules that can be used to guide decision making and predict future behavior.

Developing Tight Linkages to Customers and Suppliers

Firms can create ties to customers and suppliers that "lock" customers into the firm's products and that tie suppliers into a delivery timetable and price structure shaped by the purchasing

Table 2-6 **How Businesses Use Datamining**

Organization	Datamining Application
Canadian Imperial Bank of Commerce (CIBC)	Customer profitability system helps the bank identify its most profitable customers so that it can offer them special sales and services.
Stein Roe Investors	Analyzes data generated by visitors to its Web site to create profiles of existing and prospective customers. The company can use these profiles to target potential customers with content, advertising and incentives geared to their interests, such as retirement planning.
American Express	Analyzes data from hundreds of billions of credit card purchases to create "one-to-one" marketing campaigns. Customers receive personalized messages promoting goods and services in which they have shown interest along with their credit card bills.
U.S. West Communications	Analyzed data from billing operations and external sources to derive customer trends and needs based on household characteristics such as family size, median ages of family members, types of spending patterns, and location. Its findings helped the company increase customer service and reduce the number of lost customers by 45 percent.

ANALYZING CUSTOMER ACQUISITION COSTS

Companies that sell products directly to consumers over the Web need to measure the effectiveness of their Web site as a sales channel. Web sites are often expensive to build and maintain and firms want to know if they are getting a good return on their investment. One way of measuring Web site effectiveness is by analyzing new customer acquisition costs. In other words, how much must the company spend in advertising, marketing, or promotional discounts to turn an online browser into an online buyer? Are the firm's customer acquisition costs higher or lower than for other companies selling online? (The average new customer acquisition cost for companies that only sell online is $42 per customer although such costs may be higher or lower for certain types of businesses.) If new customer acquisition costs continue to rise, this could be an indicator that the company is facing higher marketing costs because of increased competition. Below is the information on quarterly new customer acquisition costs for four different Web companies:

New Customer Acquisition Costs: July 1, 1999 to July 1, 2000

Company	Q3'99	Q4'99	Q1'00	Q2'00
Internet Software City	81.82	84.70	92.98	142.65
Online Garage Sale	8.79	9.22	10.60	7.73
Books and More Books	24.77	26.88	31.20	36.17
Online Travel and Vacation	5.11	5.14	5.98	5.61

1. Are any of these companies experiencing customer acquisition problems? Explain your answer.
2. What can companies facing competitive pressure do to lower their customer acquisition costs and compete more effectively in a virtual environment?

---

switching costs The expense a customer or company incurs in lost time and expenditure of resources when changing from one supplier or system to a competing supplier or system.

firm. This raises **switching costs** (the cost for customers to switch to competitors' products and services) and reduces customers' and suppliers' bargaining power.

Baxter Healthcare International, Inc., has developed a "stockless inventory" and ordering system to prevent customers from switching to competitors. Participating hospitals become unwilling to switch to another supplier because of the system's convenience and low cost. Baxter supplies nearly two-thirds of all products used by U.S. hospitals. Terminals tied to Baxter's own computers are installed in hospitals. When hospitals want to place an order, they do not need to call a salesperson or send a purchase order—they simply use a Baxter computer terminal on-site to order from the full Baxter supply catalog. The system generates shipping, billing, invoicing, and inventory information, and the hospital terminals provide customers with an estimated delivery date. With more than 80 distribution centers in the United States, Baxter can make daily deliveries of its products often within hours of receiving an order.

This system is similar to the just-in-time delivery systems developed in Japan and now being used in the American automobile industry. In these systems, automobile manufacturers such as General Motors or Chrysler enter the quantity and delivery schedules of specific automobile components into their own information systems. Then these requirements are automatically transmitted to a supplier's order entry information system. The supplier must respond with an agreement to deliver the materials at the time specified. Thus, automobile companies can reduce the cost of warehousing components or materials and construction time.

Baxter has even gone one step further. Delivery personnel no longer drop off their cartons at a loading dock to be placed in a hospital storeroom. Instead, they deliver orders directly to the hospital corridors, dropping them at nursing stations, operating rooms, and stock supply closets. This has created, in effect, a "stockless inventory," with Baxter serving as the hospitals' warehouse (Caldwell, 1991). Figure 2-13 compares stockless inventory with the just-in-time supply method and traditional inventory practices.

Whereas just-in-time inventory allows customers to reduce their inventories, stockless inventory allows them to eliminate their inventories entirely. All inventory responsibilities shift to the distributor, who manages the supply flow. The stockless inventory is a powerful instrument for binding customers, giving the supplier a decided competitive advantage.

Strategic systems aimed at suppliers are designed to maximize a firm's purchasing power (and minimize costs) by having suppliers interact with its information system to satisfy the firm's precise business needs. Suppliers who are unwilling to go along with this system may lose business to other suppliers who can meet these demands.

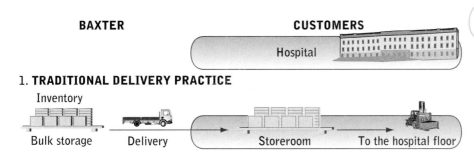

BAXTER

CUSTOMERS

Hospital

1. TRADITIONAL DELIVERY PRACTICE

Inventory

Bulk storage — Delivery — Storeroom — To the hospital floor

2. JUST-IN-TIME SUPPLY METHOD

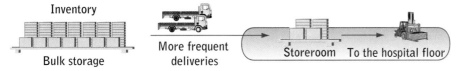

Inventory

Bulk storage — More frequent deliveries — Storeroom — To the hospital floor

3. STOCKLESS INVENTORY METHOD

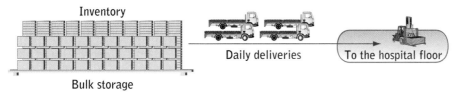

Inventory

Bulk storage — Daily deliveries — To the hospital floor

FIGURE 2-13 Stockless inventory compared to traditional and just-in-time supply methods. The just-in-time supply method reduces inventory requirements of the customer whereas stockless inventory allows the customer to eliminate inventories entirely. Deliveries are made daily, sometimes directly to the departments that need supplies.

Becoming the Low-Cost Producer

To prevent new competitors from entering their markets, businesses can produce goods and services at a lower price than competitors. Some strategic information systems help firms significantly lower their internal costs, allowing them to deliver products and services at a lower price (and sometimes with higher quality) than their competitors can provide.

By keeping prices low and shelves well-stocked, Wal-Mart has become the leading retail business in the United States. Wal-Mart uses a legendary inventory replenishment system triggered by point-of-sale purchases that is considered the best in the industry. The "continuous replenishment system" sends orders for new merchandise directly to suppliers as soon as

Wal-Mart's continuous inventory replenishment system uses sales data captured at the checkout counter to transmit orders to restock merchandise directly to its suppliers. The system enables Wal-Mart to keep costs low while fine-tuning its merchandise to meet customer demands.

consumers pay for their purchases at the cash register. Point-of-sale terminals record the bar code of each item passing the checkout counter and send a purchase transaction directly to a central computer at Wal-Mart headquarters. The computer collects the orders from all of the Wal-Mart stores and transmits them to suppliers. Because the system can replenish inventory with lightning speed, Wal-Mart does not need to spend much money on maintaining large inventories of goods in its own warehouses. The system also allows Wal-Mart to adjust purchases of store items to meet customer demands. Competitors such as Sears spend nearly 30 percent of each dollar in sales to pay for overhead (that is, expenses for salaries, advertising, warehousing, and building upkeep). Kmart spends 21 percent of sales on overhead. But by using systems to keep operating costs low, Wal-Mart pays only 15 percent of sales revenue for overhead.

supply chain management
Integration of supplier, distributor, and customer logistics requirements into one cohesive process.

supply chain A collection of entities, such as manufacturing plants, distribution centers, retail outlets, people, and information, which are linked together into processes supplying goods or services from source through consumption.

Both Baxter and Wal-Mart systems are examples of automated supply chain management. **Supply chain management** integrates supplier, distributor, and customer logistics requirements into one cohesive process. The **supply chain** is a collection of entities, such as manufacturing plants, distribution centers, conveyances, retail outlets, people, and information, that are linked through processes such as procurement or logistics to supply goods and services from source through consumption. Goods or services start out as raw materials and move through the company's logistics and production systems until they reach customers. To manage the supply chain, a company tries to eliminate delays and cut the amount of resources tied up along the way. Information systems make supply chain management more efficient by integrating demand planning, forecasting, materials requisition, order processing, inventory allocation, order fulfillment, transportation services, receiving, invoicing, and payment. Supply chain management can not only lower inventory costs but also can create efficient customer response systems that deliver the product or service more rapidly to the customer.

Table 2-7 shows how the Internet can be used to support each of the competitive strategies.

LEVERAGING TECHNOLOGY IN THE VALUE CHAIN

value chain model Model that highlights the primary or support activities that add a margin of value to a firm's products or services where information systems can best be applied to achieve a competitive advantage.

The **value chain model** highlights specific business activities where competitive strategies can be best applied (Porter, 1985) and where information systems are most likely to have a strategic impact. The value chain model can supplement the competitive forces model by identifying specific, critical leverage points where a firm can use information technology most effectively to enhance its competitive position. Exactly where can it obtain the greatest benefit from strategic information systems—what specific activities can be used to create new products and services, enhance market penetration, lock in customers and suppliers, and lower operational costs? This model views the firm as a series or "chain" of basic activities that add a margin of value to a firm's products or services. These activities can be categorized as either primary activities or support activities.

Table 2-7 **Strategic Uses of the Internet**

Strategy	Internet Application
Product differentiation	Iprint.com allows customers to design and order their own stationery, business cards, and brochures on-line through its Web site.
Focused differentiation	Hyatt Hotels can track the activities of visitors to the TravelWeb site, which provides electronic information on participating hotels. It can analyze these usage patterns to tailor hospitality-related products more closely to customer preferences.
Links to customers and suppliers	J.B. Hunt Transport Services manages the transportation logistics for J.C. Penney. Penney employees can access Hunt's Web site to check the status of any shipment.
Low-cost producer	Reliant Energy uses Internet technology to deliver operational data to more than 12,000 employees in Texas and California, saving more than $2 million.

Primary activities are most directly related to the production and distribution of the firm's products and services that create value for the customer. Primary activities include inbound logistics, operations, outbound logistics, sales and marketing, and service. Inbound logistics include receiving and storing materials for distribution to production. Operations transforms inputs into finished products. Outbound logistics entail storing and distributing products. Marketing and sales includes promoting and selling the firm's products. The service activity includes maintenance and repair of the firm's goods and services. **Support activities** make the delivery of the primary activities possible and consist of organization infrastructure (administration and management), human resources (employee recruiting, hiring, and training), technology (improving products and the production process), and procurement (purchasing input).

Organizations have a competitive advantage when they provide more value to their customers or when they provide the same value to customers at a lower price. An information system could have strategic impact if it helped the firm provide products or services at a lower cost than competitors or if it provided products and services at the same cost as competitors but with greater value. Ford's system, described earlier, creates value by both raising the level of customer service and potentially lowering marketing and sales costs. The value activities that add the most value to products and services depend on the features of each particular firm. Businesses should try to develop strategic information systems for the value activities that add the most value to their particular firm. Figure 2-14 illustrates the activities of the value chain, showing examples of strategic information systems that could be developed to make each of the value activities more cost effective.

For instance, a firm such as Wal-Mart could save money in the inbound logistics activity by having suppliers make daily deliveries of goods to its stores, thereby lowering the costs of warehousing and inventory. A computer-aided design system might support the technology activity, helping a firm to reduce costs and perhaps to design higher quality products than the competition produces.

IMPLICATIONS FOR MANAGERS AND ORGANIZATIONS

Strategic information systems often change the organization as well as its products, services, internal procedures, and relationships with other firms in its industry, driving the organization into new behavior patterns. Such changes often require a new workforce, a much closer relationship with customers and suppliers, and changes in management thinking.

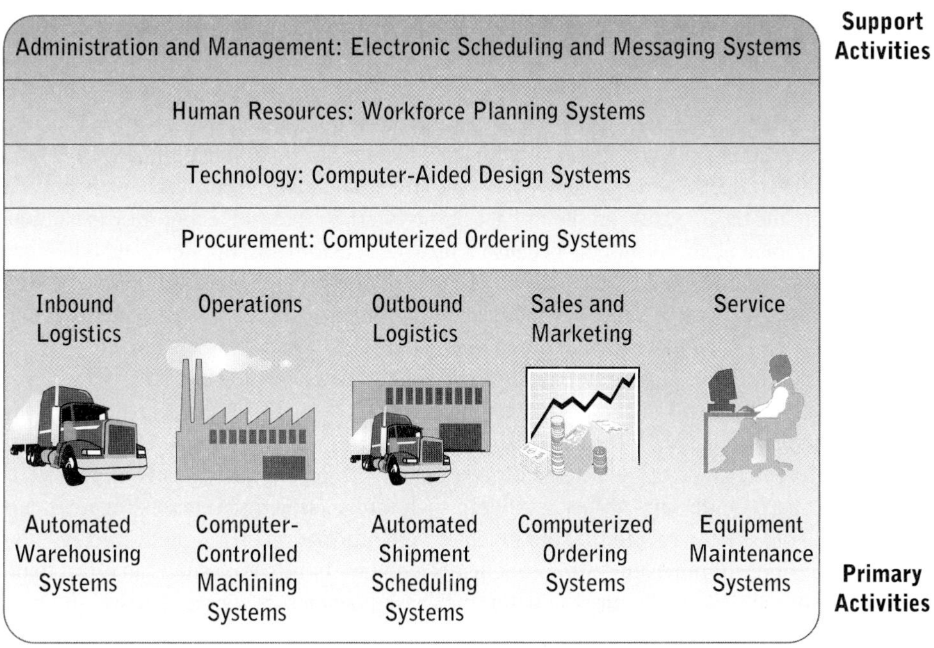

primary activities Activities most directly related to the production and distribution of a firm's products or services.

support activities Activities that make the delivery of a firm's primary activities possible. They consist of the organization's infrastructure, human resources, technology, and procurement.

Support Activities

| Administration and Management: Electronic Scheduling and Messaging Systems |
| Human Resources: Workforce Planning Systems |
| Technology: Computer-Aided Design Systems |
| Procurement: Computerized Ordering Systems |

| Inbound Logistics | Operations | Outbound Logistics | Sales and Marketing | Service |

| Automated Warehousing Systems | Computer-Controlled Machining Systems | Automated Shipment Scheduling Systems | Computerized Ordering Systems | Equipment Maintenance Systems |

Primary Activities

FIGURE 2-14 Activities of the value chain. Various examples of strategic information systems for the primary and support activities of a firm that would add a margin of value to a firm's products or services.

Strategic Alliances and Information Partnerships

Companies are increasingly using information systems for strategic advantage by entering into strategic alliances with other companies in which both firms cooperate by sharing resources or services. Such alliances are often **information partnerships** in which two or more firms share data for mutual advantage (Konsynski and McFarlan, 1990). They can join forces without actually merging. American Airlines has an arrangement with Citibank to award one mile in its frequent flier program for every dollar spent using Citibank credit cards. American benefits from increased customer loyalty, whereas Citibank gains new credit card subscribers and a highly creditworthy customer base for cross-marketing. Northwest Airlines has a similar arrangement with U.S. Bank. American and Northwest have also allied with MCI, awarding frequent flier miles for each dollar of long-distance billing. The Window on Management describes another information partnership among British consumer companies.

Looking Beyond the Business: Strategic Systems at the Industry Level

The Jigsaw Consortium described in the Window on Management shows that firms may obtain benefits by cooperating with other members of their industry or firms in related industries, even if they are competitors. Firms can cooperate by working together to build customer awareness, to develop industry standards that will increase the efficiency of all firms in the industry, and to collectively encourage suppliers to lower costs (Shapiro and Varian, 1999). Companies can also use information systems to create industry-wide consortia to coordinate their activities relating to government agencies or foreign competition. For instance, the OASIS System is a series of Web sites for electrical utility companies that have formed regional power pool groups to sell their surplus electrical power. Wholesale electric customers can use the OASIS sites to locate and purchase the surplus power and to arrange to move the electricity over competing power grids from its source to destination.

Managing Strategic Transitions and the Impact of the Internet

Adopting the kinds of systems described in this chapter generally requires changes in business goals, relationships with customers and suppliers, internal operations, and information architecture. These sociotechnical changes, affecting both social and technical elements of the organization, can be considered **strategic transitions**—a movement between levels of sociotechnical systems. Managers struggling to boost competitiveness will need to redesign various organizational processes to make effective use of leading-edge information systems technology and perhaps look beyond the firm to cooperate with others in the industry. They will require new mechanisms for coordinating their firms' activities with those of customers and suppliers (Kambil and Short, 1994). Such changes often entail blurring of organizational boundaries, both external and internal. Suppliers and customers may become intimately linked and may share each other's responsibilities. For instance, in Baxter International's stockless inventory system, Baxter has assumed responsibility for managing its customers' inventories (Johnston and Vitale, 1988). Over time, Baxter has redesigned its work processes numerous times to continually improve its overall service level and business relationship with customers (Short and Venkatraman, 1992).

To remain competitive, companies may face strategic transitions that are much more far-ranging than in the past because of the impact of the Internet. Internet technology is challenging many traditional business models because it provides customers, suppliers, and others with rich new sources of information. Customers can use the Internet to locate alternative products more easily and even obtain products by directly communicating with suppliers. New competitors can develop businesses that exploit the most profitable parts of the value chain (Evans and Wurster, 2000). The chapter-opening vignette about Ford Motor Company illustrates these forces at work. In the past, consumers had to purchase cars through automobile dealers, which were their primary source of information about models, prices, and options. The dealers held inventory, offered test drives, and helped locate financing for the purchase. Competitive advantage was based on dealers' ability to bundle such information and services together. Now customers can use the Internet to find out much of this information on their own and even purchase a car on-line without even setting foot in a dealership. Ford's Web site is an effort to provide more customer value to counter new Internet-based businesses for comparison shopping, auto financing, and auto purchasing.

---

information partnership
Cooperative alliance formed between two or more corporations for the purpose of sharing information to gain strategic advantage.

strategic transitions A movement from one level of sociotechnical system to another. Often required when adopting strategic systems that demand changes in the social and technical elements of an organization.

BRITISH CONSUMER COMPANIES POOL THEIR DATA

It used to be easy for British consumer goods manufacturers to reach their customers. With only five television channels, they could merely run an advertisement on the daytime soap operas on U.K. television and be assured they were reaching a large percentage of British housewives. Now more than 200 channels plus PCs and the Internet compete for viewers, and many more women are working outside the home, making consumers very difficult to locate.

Unilever, the parent company of Lever Brothers and Birds Eye, with dual headquarters in London and Rotterdam, wanted to make sure that its marketing budget of £3.6 billion (approximately U.S. $6 billion) was not being squandered in hit or miss campaigns to find elusive consumers and it wanted to focus on its hottest-selling brands. After highly publicized product failures such as Persil Power, a laundry detergent that was so powerful that it ate right through some fabrics, the company wanted to avoid losing touch with its customers.

In January 1997 Unilever's management decided to share customer data with Kimberly-Clark, Cadbury-Schweppes, and Bass Brewers, three noncompeting consumer goods companies. These companies realized that they probably had a similar set of customers and could benefit by grouping their products together in joint promotions. They formed the Consumer Needs Consortium, which was subsequently renamed the Jigsaw Consortium, and started testing the feasibility of creating a national consumer database.

Major retailers such as supermarket chains have data on purchase transactions that they collect at checkout counters, but their wide range of stock makes it difficult to track and analyze customer data with the level of specificity required for targeted marketing campaigns. Before forming the consortium, each member company had collected its own data from promotions, calls to customer service centers, and paper-based surveys. Unilever had a database of 1.5 million U.K. households; Kimberly-Clark had collected data on new mothers for marketing its Huggies diapers, and Bass had begun to build a regional database of beer drinkers. Cadbury did not yet have a database but was eager to collaborate. All of these companies realized they could benefit by sharing their customer data and by cooperating on the acquisition and analysis of consumer data for the United Kingdom.

The consortium members pooled their data on customers in one region of England and started testing different types of coupon mailings to see if multibrand offers would be more effective than single-brand offers. The results of the pilot confirmed that large households with children tend to consume disproportionate amounts of detergent, chocolate, soap, and diapers. This knowledge of what kinds of households are the most likely to purchase their products helped the consortium members target their direct mail campaigns. Tests of mailings targeted to specific households showed a coupon redemption rate that was up to 10 times better than random mailings, providing further proof that pooling customer data would provide a favorable return on investment.

Puzzling findings also emerged. The consortium learned that empty nesters are exceptionally heavy consumers of tea, soup, chocolate, and ice cream and that 18- to 24-year-old men did not purchase much of the other consortium members' brands. Bass dropped out of the consortium as a result but continued cross-marketing with the consortium on its Web site for Carling beer.

Consodata, based in Paris, built the final database, which consolidated data from consortium members and supplied additional data gathered from surveys. The new system can provide fine-tuned analyses such as how many Huggies users have two children, a pet, read the **Times**, and have annual incomes of £40,000. Then it can cross-tabulate the information to determine what other products this set of consumers might want. Armed with more precise information, consortium members can develop more efficient marketing promotions.

TO THINK ABOUT: What are the management benefits of forming a consortium to share customer data with other companies? Are there any drawbacks?

Sources: Sarah Ellison, "Unilever, Microsoft in European Net Deal," **The Wall Street Journal**, February 2, 2000; Alice Dragoon, "Looking for Mr. Candybar," **CIO Enterprise Magazine**, January 15, 1999; and Deborah Orr, "A Giant Reawakens," **Forbes Magazine**, January 25, 1999.

What Managers Can Do

Managers must take the initiative to identify the types of systems that would provide a strategic advantage to the firm. Some of the important questions managers should ask are:

○ How is the industry currently using information systems? Which organizations are the industry leaders in the application of information systems technology? How is the industry changing? Should the firm be looking at new ways of doing business or forming alliances with other industry members? What impact is the Internet having on the industry?

○ Can significant strategic opportunities be gained by introducing new information systems technology? Where would new information systems provide the greatest value to the firm?

○ What is the current business strategic plan, and how does that plan mesh with the current strategy for information systems?

○ Does the firm have the technology and capital required to develop a strategic information systems initiative? (Kettinger et al., 1994)

2.3 How Information Systems Promote Quality

Global competition is forcing companies to focus more than ever on using quality in their competitive strategies. There are many ways in which information systems can help organizations achieve higher levels of quality in their products, services, and operations.

WHAT IS QUALITY?

quality Conformance to producer specifications and satisfaction of customer criteria such as quality of physical product, quality of service, and psychological aspects.

Quality can be defined from both producer and customer perspectives. From the perspective of the producer, **quality** signifies conformance to specifications (or the absence of variation from those specifications). A wristwatch manufacturer, for example, might include a specification for reliability that requires that 99.995 percent of the watches will neither gain nor lose more than one second per month. Simple tests enable the manufacturer to measure precisely against these specifications.

A customer definition of quality is much broader. First, customers are concerned with the quality of the physical product—its durability, safety, ease of use, and installation. Second, customers are concerned with the quality of service, by which they mean the accuracy and truthfulness of advertising, responsiveness to warranties, and ongoing product support. Finally, customer concepts of quality include psychological aspects: the company's knowledge of its products, the courtesy and sensitivity of sales and support staff, and the product's reputation.

total quality management (TQM) A concept that makes quality control a responsibility to be shared by all people in an organization.

Today more and more businesses are turning to an idea known as total quality management. **Total quality management (TQM)** is a concept that makes quality the responsibility of all people within an organization. TQM holds that the achievement of quality control is an end in itself. Everyone is expected to contribute to the overall improvement of quality—the engineer who avoids design errors, the production worker who spots defects, the sales representative who presents the product properly to potential customers, and even the secretary who avoids typing mistakes. Total quality management encompasses all of the functions within an organization.

TQM derives from quality management concepts developed by American quality experts such as W. Edwards Deming and Joseph Juran, but it was popularized by the Japanese. Japanese management adopted the goal of zero defects, focusing on improving their product or service prior to shipment rather than correcting them after they have been delivered. Japanese companies often give the responsibility for quality consistency to the workers who actually make the product or service, as opposed to a quality control department. Studies have repeatedly shown that the earlier in the business cycle a problem is eliminated, the less it costs the company. Thus the Japanese quality approach not only brought a shift in focus to the workers and an increased respect for product and service quality, but it also lowered costs.

HOW INFORMATION SYSTEMS CONTRIBUTE TO TOTAL QUALITY MANAGEMENT

Information systems can help firms achieve their quality goals by helping them simplify products or processes, meet benchmarking standards, make improvements based on customer demands, reduce cycle time, and increase the quality and precision of design and production.

Simplifying the Product, the Production Process, or Both

Quality programs usually have a "fewer is better" philosophy—the fewer steps in a process, the less time and opportunity for an error to occur. The Carrier Corporation, the Syracuse, New York, manufacturing giant, was faced with an eroding market share. One reason: a 70 percent error rate in using its manual order entry system, which was used to match customers and products when ordering Carrier's commercial air conditioning units. The system required so many steps to process an order that mistakes were all but inevitable. Errors sometimes went undetected until the end of the manufacturing line, where workers might discover a wrong coil or some other similar problem. Big mistakes occasionally affected customers. The company finally instituted a TQM program in which information technology played a large role. Carrier now coordinates everything from sales to manufacturing by using an artificial intelligence system (LaPlante, 1992). When information systems helped reduce the number of steps, the number of errors dropped dramatically, manufacturing costs dropped, and Carrier found itself with happier customers.

Benchmark

Many companies have been effective in achieving quality by setting strict standards for products, services, and other activities, and then measuring performance against those standards. This procedure is called **benchmarking.** Companies may use external industry standards, standards set by other companies, internally developed high standards, or some combination of the three. L.L. Bean, Inc., the Freeport, Maine, mail order clothing company, uses benchmarking to achieve an order shipping accuracy of 99.9 percent.

> **benchmarking** Setting strict standards for products, services, or activities and measuring organizational performance against those standards.

To provide better information for benchmarking, information systems specialists can work with business specialists either to design new systems or to analyze quality-related data in existing systems. For instance, L.L. Bean carefully designed its information systems so it could analyze the data embedded in customer return transactions. Bean's return forms require customers to supply "reason codes" explaining why each item was returned. A report from these systems showing return transaction frequency and dollar value summarized by week or month and broken down by the reason for the returns helps management target areas where mistakes are being made.

Use Customer Demands as a Guide to Improving Products and Services

Improving customer service, making customer service the number one priority, will both improve the quality of the product and strengthen the company's relationship with customers. Customer relationships and high-quality customer service have become even more important sources of strategic advantage in today's global Internet-fueled economy because companies find it increasingly difficult to differentiate themselves on the basis of products and prices. The Window on Technology shows how companies are using new kinds of information systems to improve customer service.

Reduce Cycle Time

Experience indicates that the single best way to address quality problems is to reduce the amount of time from the beginning of a process to its end (cycle time). Reducing cycle time usually results in fewer steps. Shorter cycles mean that errors are often caught earlier in production (or logistics or design or whatever the function), often before the process is complete,

A group of Chrysler Corporation engineers examines a new automobile design using a computer-aided design (CAD) tool. CAD systems improve the quality and precision of product design by performing much of the design and testing work on the computer.

Window on Technology

CUSTOMER SERVICE TECHNOLOGY TO THE RESCUE

Quality customer service is defined differently by each company. "Customer service," says Roger Green, CIO of excimer laser producer Cymer Inc., "is about building trust between a company and its customers." One question for Cymer is how to use software and hardware to help build that trust. For Green it has meant making its system repository of repair problems encountered by field service engineers available to its technicians remotely. Now technicians working in the field with customers have the information necessary to solve customers' problems on the spot, and customers have more trust that when something goes wrong, Cymer will fix it.

Each organization must also find its own way to apply technology as part of the customer service solution. For example, potential customers of Mortgage.com, an on-line mortgage broker headquartered in Plantation, Florida, use the Web to apply for loans and receive an answer. To differentiate itself and to better serve its customers, the company promised 24-hour loan approvals. However, this approach quickly backfired. "A request came in at 8 on a Saturday night," according to Mortgage.com executive vice president Larry Lewis, "and by Monday morning the borrower had been in [to the Web site] three times expecting that the loan should have been approved." In this case the company had to respond by not only clarifying its policies but also by building a link between its consumer communications and its customer service and lead-tracking systems. In the future, the company hopes not to disappoint customers again.

A recent study showed that the Internet has become important for customer service to large companies as well: 57 percent now use the Net in customer service, and another 24 percent plan to do so in the near future. According to Hank Stringer, president of Hire.com, an online recruiting service, "everything in e-commerce goes back to relationships." Customer service and support staff are in high demand today because they are so important in creating good relationships with customers. Scudder Investor Services Inc., the financial management company managing $280 billion in assets, allows its customers to use many channels to contact the company, including the telephone and the

Internet. Customers can use the Scudder Web site to track their accounts on-line and to transfer funds. Because many different units across Scudder share customer data, Scudder wanted to make customer contact information available regardless of what channel the customer used to contact the company. To accomplish this, Scudder built a new system that linked all customer channels, thereby integrating its Web site with other systems. As a result customers can have confidence that however they choose to contact Scudder, their information will go to wherever it is needed.

Airlines are known for using technology to schedule airplanes and to reserve and ticket passengers, and Delta Airlines Inc. has added another dimension: customer service. "No one ever looked at it from the customer's point of view," says Delta CIO Charlie Feld. "If the customer gets lucky, they get a good trip." But not all are so lucky. Twenty percent of Delta's customers experience problems and delays, and Feld wanted to apply technology to help. One aid is a customer-care system Delta has installed at its gates. For each flight, the airplane seating chart, reservations, check-in information, and boarding data are now all linked in a central data repository. Airline personnel can track which passengers are on board regardless of where they checked in. The system is particularly useful when mechanical problems or bad weather delay a flight. Delta's new system will identify which passengers are going to miss connecting flights. Armed with this information in advance, Delta agents often can find empty seats on another flight and get the passengers to their destination on time, sometimes by a different route.

TO THINK ABOUT: How did these technological solutions to customer service problems affect each company's organization and the way it conducts business? How much strategic value do these solutions provide? Explain your response.

Sources: Lisa Hamm-Greenawalt, "Labor Crunch," *Internet World*, January 1, 2000; Emily Kay, "www.where'smyorder.com," *Computerworld*, July 19, 1999; Jeff Sweat, "Customer Centricity in the Post-Y2K Era," *Information Week Online*, May 17, 1999.

---

eliminating many hidden costs. Iomega Corporation in Roy, Utah, a manufacturer of disk drives, was spending $20 million a year to fix defective drives at the end of its 28-day production cycle. Reengineering the production process allowed the firm to reduce cycle time to a day and a half, eliminating this problem and winning the prestigious Shingo Prize for Excellence in American Manufacturing in the process.

Improve the Quality and Precision of the Design

Quality and precision in design will eliminate many production problems. Computer-aided design (CAD) software has made dramatic quality improvements possible in a wide range of businesses from aircraft manufacturing to production of razor blades. Alan R. Burns, head of the Airboss Company in Perth, Australia, was able to use CAD to invent and design a new tire product. His concept was a modular tire made up of a series of replaceable modules or segments so that if one segment were damaged, only that segment, not the whole tire, would need replacing. Burns established quality performance measurements for such key tire characteristics as load, temperature, speed, wear life, and traction. He then entered these data into a CAD software package, which he used to design the modules. Using the software he was able iteratively to design and test until he was satisfied with the results. He did not need to develop an actual working model until the iterative design process was almost complete. Because of the speed and accuracy of the CAD software, the product he produced was of much higher quality than would have been possible through manual design and testing.

Increase the Precision of Production

For many products, one key way to achieve quality is to make the production process more precise and decrease the variation from one part or component to another. CAD software often includes a facility to translate design specifications into specifications both for production tooling and for the production process itself. In this way, products with more precise designs can also be produced more efficiently. Once his tire segment design was completed, Burns used the CAD software to design his manufacturing process. He was able to design a shorter production cycle, improving quality while increasing his ability to meet customer demand more quickly.

GE Medical Systems performed a rigorous quality analysis to improve the reliability and durability of its Lightspeed diagnostic scanner. It broke the processes of designing and producing the scanner into many distinct steps and established optimum specifications for each component part. By understanding these processes more precisely, engineers learned that a few simple changes would significantly improve the product's reliability and durability (Deutsch, 1998).

MANAGEMENT WRAP-UP

Management is responsible for developing the strategy and quality standards for the organization. Key management decisions include identifying the competitive strategies and the points in the value chain where information systems can provide the greatest benefit, as well as the principal areas for quality improvement.

Management

There are many types of information systems in an organization that serve different purposes, from transaction processing to knowledge management and management decision making. Each type of system can contribute a strategic edge. Systems that significantly promote competitive advantage and TQM often require extensive organizational change.

Organization

Information technology can be used to differentiate existing products, create new products and services, raise customer and supplier switching costs, and reduce operating costs. Selecting an appropriate technology for the firm's competitive strategy is a key decision.

Technology

For Discussion

1. Several information systems experts have claimed that there is no such thing as a sustainable strategic advantage. Do you agree? Why or why not?

2. How can using information systems to promote quality provide a strategic advantage?

SUMMARY

1. Analyze the role played by the six major types of information systems in organizations and their relationship to each other. There are six major types of information systems in contemporary organizations that are designed for different purposes and different audiences. Operational-level systems are transaction processing systems (TPS), such as payroll or order processing, that track the flow of the daily routine transactions that are necessary to conduct business. Knowledge-level systems support clerical, managerial, and professional workers. They consist of office systems for increasing data workers' productivity and knowledge work systems (KWS) for enhancing knowledge workers' productivity. Management-level systems (MIS and DSS) provide the management control level with reports and access to the organization's current performance and historical records. Most MIS reports condense information from TPS and are not highly analytical. Decision-support systems (DSS) support management decisions when these decisions are unique, rapidly changing, and not specified easily in advance. They have more advanced analytical models and data analysis capabilities than MIS and often draw on information from external as well as internal sources.

Executive support systems (ESS) support the strategic level by providing a generalized computing and communications environment to assist senior management's decision making. They have limited analytical capabilities but can draw on sophisticated graphics software and many sources of internal and external information.

The various types of systems in the organization exchange data with one another. TPS are a major source of data for other systems, especially MIS and DSS. ESS primarily receives data from lower level systems. However, the different systems in an organization are only loosely integrated. The information needs of the various functional areas and organizational levels are too specialized to be served by a single system.

2. Describe the types of information systems supporting the major functional areas of business. At each level of the organization there are information systems supporting the major functional areas of business. Sales and marketing systems help the firm identify customers for the firm's products or services, develop products and services to meet their needs, promote these products and services, sell the products and services, and provide ongoing customer support. Manufacturing and produc-

tion systems deal with the planning, development, and production of products and services, and controlling the flow of production. Finance and accounting systems keep track of the firm's financial assets and fund flows. Human resources systems maintain employee records, track employee skills, job performance, and training, and support planning for employee compensation and career development.

3. Examine how the competitive forces and value chain models can be used to identify opportunities for strategic information systems. The competitive forces and value chain models can help identify areas of a business where information systems can supply a strategic advantage. The competitive forces model describes a number of external threats and opportunities confronting firms that they must counter with competitive strategies. Information systems can be developed to help cope with the threat of new entrants into the market, the pressure from substitute products, buyers' bargaining power, suppliers' bargaining power, and the positioning of traditional industry competitors. Companies can also achieve competitive advantage at the industry level by creating communities for sharing information or coordinating activities with other firms in the industry. The value chain model highlights specific activities in the business where competitive strategies can best be applied and where information systems are most likely to have a strategic impact. This model views the firm as a series or "chain" of basic activities that add a margin of value to the firm's products or services. Information systems can have a strategic impact on the activities that add the most value to the firm.

4. Explain why strategic information systems are difficult to build and to sustain. Not all strategic systems make a profit; they can be expensive and risky to build. Strategic advantage is not always sustainable because other firms can easily copy many strategic information systems. Implementing strategic systems often requires extensive organizational change and a transition from one sociotechnical level to another. Such strategic transitions are often difficult and painful to achieve.

5. Describe how organizations can use information systems to enhance quality in their operations, products, and services. Information systems can help organizations simplify their products and the production process, meet benchmarking standards, improve customer service, reduce production cycle time, and improve the quality and precision of design and production.

KEY TERMS

Benchmarking, 63

Competitive forces model, 53

Datamining, 55

Decision-support systems (DSS), 44

Desktop publishing, 44

Document imaging systems, 44

Executive support systems (ESS), 47

Finance and accounting information systems, 51

Focused differentiation, 54

Human resources information systems, 51

Information partnership, 60

Knowledge-level systems, 40

Knowledge work systems (KWS), 43

Management information systems (MIS), 44

Management-level systems, 40

Manufacturing and production information systems, 49

Office systems, 43

Operational-level systems, 39

Primary activities, 59

Product differentiation, 54

Quality, 62

Sales and marketing information systems, 49

Strategic information systems, 53

Strategic-level systems, 40

Strategic transitions, 60

Supply chain, 58

Supply chain management, 58

Support activities, 59

Switching costs, 56

Total quality management (TQM), 62

Transaction processing systems (TPS), 42

Value chain model, 58

Word processing, 43

REVIEW QUESTIONS

1. Identify and describe the four levels of the organizational hierarchy. What types of information systems serve each level?

2. List and briefly describe the major types of systems in organizations. How are they related to one another?

3. What are the five types of TPS in business organizations? What functions do they perform? Give examples of each.

4. Describe the functions performed by knowledge work and office systems and some typical applications of each.

5. What are the characteristics of MIS? How do MIS differ from TPS? From DSS?

6. What are the characteristics of DSS? How do they differ from those of ESS?

7. List and describe the information systems serving each of the major functional areas of a business.

8. What is a strategic information system? What is the difference between a strategic information system and a strategic-level system?

9. Define and compare the competitive forces and value chain models for identifying opportunities for strategic systems.

10. What are the four basic competitive strategies? How can information systems help firms pursue each of these strategies?

11. Why are strategic information systems difficult to build?

12. Explain the advantages of an information partnership and of cooperating with other firms in an industry.

13. How can managers find strategic applications in their firm?

14. What is total quality management?

15. How can companies use information systems to promote total quality management?

GROUP PROJECT

Form a group with two or three classmates. Research a business using annual reports or business publications such as *Fortune, Business Week,* and *The Wall Street Journal.* Visit the company Web site to gain further insights into the company. Analyze the business using the competitive forces and value chain models, including a description of the firm and its business strategies. Suggest strategic information systems for that particular business including those using the Internet, if appropriate. Present your findings to the class.

Tools for Interactive Learning

○ Internet Connection

The Internet Connection for this chapter will take you to the WingspanBank.com Web site where you can see how one company used the Internet to create an entirely new type of business. You can complete an exercise for analyzing this Web site's capabilities and its strategic benefits. You can also use the Interactive Study Guide to test your knowledge of the topics in this chapter and get instant feedback where you need more practice.

○ Electronic Commerce Project

At the Laudon Web site for Chapter 2, you will find an Electronic Commerce project that will use the interactive software at the Web sites for Ford and for other Internet auto sale companies to analyze competitive auto pricing.

○ CD-ROM

If you purchase and use the Multimedia Edition CD-ROM with this chapter, you can complete two interactive exercises. The first asks you to match various types of information systems described in the chapter to user information needs. The second asks you to perform a value chain analysis for a business. You can also find a video clip illustrating the strategic use of Lands' End's information systems, interactive exercises, an audio overview of the major themes of this chapter, and bullet text summarizing the key points of the chapter.

○ Application Exercise

At the Laudon Web site, you can find a database Application Exercise for this chapter where you can develop a hotel reservation transaction processing system (TPS) and management reporting system.

Sears, Roebuck used to be the largest retailer in the United States, with sales representing 1 to 2 percent of the U.S. gross national product for almost 40 years after World War II. Its legendary Big Book catalog was considered the primary (and sometimes the only) source for everything from wrenches to bathtubs to underwear. During the 1980s, Sears moved into other businesses, hoping to provide middle-class consumers with almost every type of banking, investment, and real estate service in addition to selling appliances, hardware, clothes, and other goods.

This diversification tore Sears away from its core business, retail sales. Sears has steadily lost ground in retailing, moving from the number one position to number three behind discounters Wal-Mart Stores, Inc., and Kmart Corporation. Sears had been slow to remodel stores, trim costs, and keep pace with current trends in selling and merchandising. Sears could not keep up with the discounters and with specialty retailers such as Toys R Us, Home Depot, Inc., and Circuit City Stores, Inc., that focus on a wide selection of low-price merchandise in a single category. Nor could Sears compete with trendsetting department stores.

Yet Sears has been heavily computerized. At one time it spent more on information technology and networking than all other noncomputer firms in the United States except the Boeing Corporation. It was noted for its extensive customer databases of 60 million past and present Sears credit card holders, which it used to target groups such as appliance buyers, tool buyers, gardening enthusiasts, and mothers-to-be with special promotions. For example, Sears would mail customers who purchased a washer and dryer a maintenance contract and follow up with annual contract renewal forms.

Why hasn't this translated into competitive advantage? One big problem is Sears' high cost of operations. Nearly 30 percent of each dollar in sales is required to cover overhead (e.g., expenses for salaries, maintenance, and advertising) compared to 15 percent for Wal-Mart and about 21 percent for Kmart.

In 1991, retail operations contributed to 38 percent of the corporate bottom line. The rest of the merchandising group's profits came from the lucrative Sears credit card. Strategies that worked well for competitors fizzled at Sears. J.C. Penney successfully refocused its business to emphasize moderately priced apparel. Everyday low pricing, the pricing strategy used by Wal-Mart and other retailers, bombed at Sears because the firm's cost structure, one of the highest in the industry, did not allow for rock-bottom prices. Everyday low pricing has become "everyday fair pricing" supplemented by frequent sales.

Sears' catalog sales also stagnated. Although the Sears Big Book catalog, founded in 1887, had the largest revenues of any mail-order business, sales had not been profitable for 20 years, and the catalog had lost ground to specialty catalogs such as those of L.L. Bean and Lands' End. On January 25, 1993, Sears stopped issuing its famous Big Book catalogs, closed 113 of its stores, and eliminated 50,000 jobs. In order to return to its core business and recapture its leadership in retailing, the company also disposed of its Dean Witter securities, Discover credit card, Coldwell Banker real estate, and Allstate insurance subsidiaries.

To help turn Sears around and refocus on retailing, CEO Edward A. Brennan hired executive Arthur C. Martinez away from Saks Fifth Avenue in September 1992, naming Martinez his successor as Sears Chairman and Chief Executive Officer two years later. Martinez ordered the company to combine its half-dozen disparate customer databases to find out who was really shopping at Sears. It turned out that Sears' biggest shoppers were not men looking for Craftsmen tool belts but women age 25 to 55 with average family incomes of $40,000 who were in the market for everything from skirts to appliances.

Under Martinez, Sears stopped trying to sell everything and started focusing on six core types of merchandise—men's, women's, and children's clothing; home furnishings; home improvement; automotive services and supplies; appliances; and consumer electronics. The company is rearranging its merchandise displays to resemble those of more upscale department stores, with more attention to women's apparel, which is considered a highly profitable segment of merchandising. Sears is also offering special merchandise in each store geared to its local customer base. And it is relieving managers and clerks of some reporting and administrative tasks so they have more time to actually sell. Beginning in 1996 every employee's compensation included a measurement for customer service. Sears realized that it could not compete with discounters such as Wal-Mart on price alone and focused on building a competitive edge through superior service.

Sears embarked on a $4 billion five-year store renovation program to make Sears stores more efficient, attractive, and convenient by bringing all transactions closer to the sales floor and centralizing every store's general offices, cashiers, customer services, and credit functions. New point-of-sale (POS) terminals allow sales staff to issue new charge cards, accept charge card payments, issue gift certificates, and report account information to cardholders. The POS devices provide information such as the status of orders and availability of products, allowing associates to order out-of-stock goods directly from the sales floor.

Some stores have installed ATMs to give customers cash advances against their Sears Discover credit cards. Telephone kiosks have been installed throughout the Sears retail network. Customers can use them to inquire about service, parts, and credit, check the status of their car in the tire and auto center, or call the manager.

Customer service desks have been largely eliminated. Sales personnel are authorized to handle refunds and returns, eliminating the need for two separate staffs. If a customer forgets his or her charge card, he or she can obtain immediate credit by telling the cashier his or her name and address and presenting identification. Streamlining of patterns of work in back rooms and loading docks also trimmed staff and created savings. These changes also increased the ratio of selling space to nonselling space at Sears so an additional 6 million square feet of space could be used to generate revenues.

Sears has been moving its suppliers to an electronic ordering system similar to that described for Baxter Healthcare. By linking its computerized ordering system directly to that of each supplier, Sears plans to eliminate paper throughout the order process and hopes to expedite the flow of goods into its stores.

Sears further tightened its grip over the business by building an even larger database for its Sears Credit and Home Services businesses. It consolidates information on 90 million households, 31 million Sears Card users, transaction records, credit status, and related data. Sears hopes to use this information to provide even more finely targeted database marketing. The database houses Sears' Strategic Performance Reporting System (SPRS), which helps the company manage pricing and merchandising for its 1,950 North American stores.

Until a few years ago, Sears merchandise buyers lacked reliable information on precisely what customers were buying at each store. They could not view anything more specific than each division's daily performance. Management relied on 18 separate systems that often contained conflicting and redundant pricing information. Today, any authorized Sears employee can use SPRS to look up any sales figure by store, by area, by item, right down to the size and color of a sweater. Sales can be analyzed by item or product category, by individual store or company wide. Sales of items advertised in newspapers for a specific day can be tallied so that Sears' 1,000 buyers and managers know what hot-selling merchandise to replenish right away. Buyers can compare current performance of merchandise with that of the previous week or the previous year. The data can be displayed in a number of different ways, including pie charts or graphs.

The Sears charge card, with more than 32 million accounts, is the fourth-largest credit card operation in the United States, serving nearly half the households in the United States. Sears' credit card business generates almost half of corporate profits. About half of all purchases made in Sears stores are made with the Sears credit card. Starting in 1993, Sears aggressively courted new credit card customers, doubling the rate at which it issued new credit cards to more than 6 million per year. The increase in credit helped fuel Sears' rising store sales. Although Martinez claims that Sears did not reduce its standards for determining creditworthy customers, Sears

attracted too many high-risk customers, and many of its new credit card customers defaulted on paying their bills. Steve Goldstein, who took charge of Sears credit in 1996, invested in technology to bring Sears' risk-management systems up to the level of leading-edge credit card issuers such as Citicorp.

Troubles mounted in early 1997. Some cardholders in Massachusetts sued Sears over the intimidating methods it used to persuade bankrupt customers to pay their credit card balance, and Sears wound up paying $475 million to settle lawsuits in all 50 states. Later that year, bad-debt charge-offs for uncollectible credit card accounts skyrocketed to more than 8 percent of Sears receivables, twice the level of two years earlier. Goldstein's group could not properly analyze the delinquent accounts. Although teams of people worked day and night, Sears computer systems still weren't state of the art and analysis that should have taken a few hours took weeks. Goldstein resigned in December 1997.

To stem the rising loan losses, Sears cut back on new credit accounts to 4.2 million. But as the credit business was reined in, retail sales flattened out. Sales at Sears stores open at least one year only rose 1.1 percent during 1998, when the retail climate was very strong and competitors posted an average sales increase of 4.4 percent.

Martinez has realized that the Internet could play an important role in Sears' turnaround. Sears' campus in Hoffman Estates, Illinois, now has an Internet division with 50 employees. The mission of this Internet group is to make Sears' Web site the "definitive online source for the home." Sears started out by selling appliances, tools, and parts on its Web site along with Web access to its Wishbook catalog. Later on, the Web site added lawn and garden accessories, home furnishings, consumer electronics, and capabilities for customers to arrange for repair service online.

One way Sears hopes to jumpstart its online business is by partnering with America Online (AOL). In March 2000, both companies announced a multiyear, multimillion-dollar marketing alliance in which AOL would customize a version of its Internet access service specifically for Sears customers. Sears hopes the alliance will make the company more visible to AOL's base of 21 million customers so that

they will go to the Sears.com Web site when they need products for the home. Sears will develop content for AOL on subjects such as how to build a deck, tips on home decorating, and other home improvement topics. AOL will also develop special electronic communication capabilities for Sears customers so that they can exchange messages electronically with Sears customer service representatives when they are having trouble with their Sears appliances. To promote the service, areas within Sears' 858 department stores will have demostration stations where consumers can try out the service. Consumers can sign up for AOL service at Sears and pay for it using their Sears credit cards.

However, an arrangement with AOL is not exclusive to Sears. Wal-Mart, Sears' biggest competitor, also has a marketing alliance with AOL and a deal to provide customized Internet access to Wal-Mart customers at a discount. AOL also has deals with Crate & Barrel, the Gap, Macy's, and J.C. Penney.

Sears is using Internet technology to develop a system that will let suppliers check the status of their invoices. Sears wants to give vendors access to SPRS so that they can check the sales of their products and provide just-in-time inventory service. It is also working with Sun Microsystems and other technology companies to create home appliances and services that use the Internet.

Can the Internet help Sears to turn around? Will Sears be able to prosper without easy credit? Since Martinez arrived, Sears has had a measure of success in lowering its margins and increasing same-store sales. The question is whether Sears can sustain this momentum. Its operating expenses are still high compared with industry leaders. Market research indicates that Sears continues to be the destination of choice for lawn mowers, wrenches, washing machines, and other "hard" goods—and its tools and appliance businesses are posting large sales gains. But Sears has not yet secured itself as a place for fashionable women's clothing. Some critics believe that future earnings growth will flag once the company completes its remodeling program and that Sears remains vulnerable to aggressive discounters. Can Sears' reinvention keep the company competitive now and in the future?

Sources: Bernhard Warner, "Sears Has AOL," **The Industry Standard,** March 14, 2000; "Sears, Sun Microsystems Working on Internet-Connected Home," Sears Public Relations, January 6, 2000; Eryn Brown, "The E-volution of Big Business," **Fortune,** November 8, 1999; Joseph P. Cahill, "Sears's Credit Business May Have Helped Hide Larger Retailing Woes," **The Wall Street Journal,** July 6, 1999; Julia King and Thomas Hoffman, "Sears Launches Do-It-Yourself Site," **Computerworld,** April 19, 1999; Gene Koprowski, "The Harder Side of Sears," **Software Magazine,** January 15, 1998; Patricia Sellers, "Sears' Big Turnaround Runs into Big Trouble," **Fortune,** February 16, 1998; Daniel Gross, "Remodeling Sears," **CIO Magazine,** December 1, 1996; "Yes, He's Revived Sears. But Can He Reinvent It?" **The New York Times,** January 7, 1996; John Foley, "Sears' Data Store Grows," Information Week, June 24, 1996; Susan Chandler, "Sears' Turnaround Is for Real—For Now," **Business Week,** August 15, 1994; and Stephanie Strom, "Sears Eliminating Its Catalogues and 50,000 Jobs," **The New York Times,** January 26, 1993.

CASE STUDY QUESTIONS

1. Evaluate Sears using the competitive forces and value chain models.

2. What management, organization, and technology factors were responsible for Sears' poor performance?

3. Evaluate Sears' new business strategy under Martinez. What management, organization, and technology issues are addressed by this strategy?

4. How successful is Sears' new strategy? What role does information systems play in that strategy?

5. To what extent have information systems provided competitive advantage for Sears? Explain.

6. How important is the Web in Sears' strategy?

CHAPTER 3

Information Systems, Organizations, and Management:
Business Processes and Enterprise Systems

Learning
Objectives

After completing this chapter, you will be able to:

1. Identify the salient characteristics of organizations.

2. Analyze the relationship between information systems and organizations.

3. Assess the organizational and information technology (IT) infrastructure implications of enterprise systems, industrial networks, and mergers and acquisitions.

4. Contrast the classical and contemporary models of managerial activities and roles.

5. Describe how managers make decisions in organizations.

6. Assess the implications of the relationship between information systems, organizations, and management decision making for the design and implementation of information systems.

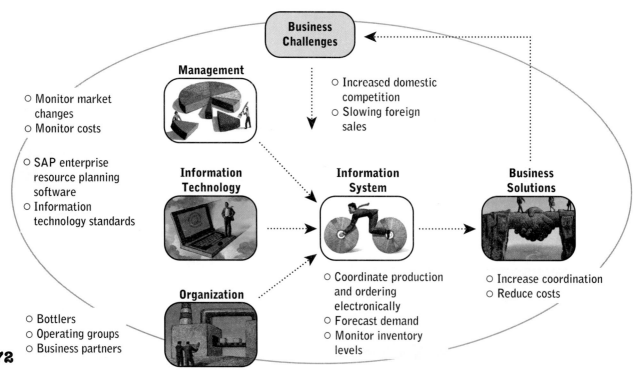

Business Challenges

Management
- Monitor market changes
- Monitor costs

- Increased domestic competition
- Slowing foreign sales

Information Technology
- SAP enterprise resource planning software
- Information technology standards

Information System
- Coordinate production and ordering electronically
- Forecast demand
- Monitor inventory levels

Business Solutions
- Increase coordination
- Reduce costs

Organization
- Bottlers
- Operating groups
- Business partners

Coca-Cola Creates an Extended Enterprise

Coca-Cola is one of the most recognized companies on Earth, with a soft drink empire in nearly 200 countries. Although it dominates most world markets, the company faces very tough business challenges. Coca-Cola today derives more than half of its revenue from countries outside North America. Sales growth has slowed abroad, as consumers turn to local beverages whose flavors or brand names are not in the Coca-Cola lineup. Coke faces competition domestically from new sources such as bottled waters and health drinks. Pepsico Inc., the company's main rival, recently restructured its North American business to take away some of Coke's market share.

Coke is counting on a major information systems initiative to stay competitive. It is implementing enterprise resource planning software from SAP within its own organization and extending this system to other companies, such as its bottling partners. The new system will link Coke and its suppliers together into an extended enterprise where they can pool resources, share best practices, and leverage their combined size to obtain lower raw materials cost. Another goal is to share sales information and increase communication with partners so they can react rapidly to market changes and deploy products efficiently to the places where they are most likely to sell.

Creating an interconnected enterprise requires a standard information architecture that will allow all participants to share data and provide a standard view of the business in terms of brands, customers, and packages. Once completed, Coke should be able to answer questions such as what bottling plant and what channel were used to sell Coca-Cola in a 500 milliliter plastic bottle in a Singapore supermarket and achieve better control over its supply chain. Improved forecasting and production planning will also help Coca-Cola and its partners reduce the costs of making and shipping products. Coke and its partners will be able to exchange electronic purchase orders and key inventory information.

The system will capture detailed sales and promotional data for each of Coke's five major operating groups in North America, Europe, the Middle East, and Asia and will integrate this information with details from manufacturing, finance, and procurement. To make data flow seamlessly, Coca-Cola established

CHAPTER OUTLINE

73

standards for software running on desktop and larger computers, network services, document technology, security, and applications.

Coca-Cola's bottlers are independent companies, and Coke had to make special efforts to convince them to participate in the enterprise resource planning (ERP) system. All of the company's 11 anchor bottlers (major partners in which Coke has a controlling stake) are rolling out the ERP applications at their own pace. Coke hopes that many more of the 1,000 other bottlers it uses around the world will eventually switch to the new system as well.

Coke is now working on establishing electronic links to customers such as Burger King, McDonald's, Wal-Mart, and other business partners such as Alcoa, Reynolds Metals, and Archer Daniels Midland. Coke's electronic integration internally and externally should prove to be a powerful weapon.

Sources: Constance L. Hays, "Learning to Think Smaller at Coke," *The New York Times,* February 6, 2000; Bob Violino, "Extended Enterprise," *Information Week,* March 22, 1999; and Constance L. Hays, "Pulp Friction," *The New York Times,* May 19, 1999.

MANAGEMENT CHALLENGES

Coca-Cola's experience illustrates the interdependence of business environments, organizational culture, management strategy, and the development of information systems. Coca-Cola developed a new enterprise system to link with bottlers and suppliers in response to changes in competitive pressures from its surrounding environment, but its systems effort could not succeed without a significant amount of organizational and management change. The new information system is changing the way Coke and its bottlers run their business and make management decisions. Coca-Cola's story raises the following management challenges:

1. **The difficulties of managing change.** Bringing about change through the development of information technology and information systems is slowed considerably by the natural inertia of organizations. (For example, Coke's bottlers were initially hesitant to participate in the new enterprise system.) This is especially true of large system-building efforts, such as implementing enterprise systems, where massive changes to jobs, business processes, management thinking, and reporting relationships are often required to get different parts of the organization to work toward a common goal. Of course, organizations do change, and powerful leaders are often required to bring about these changes. Nevertheless, the process, as leaders eventually discover, is more complicated and much slower than typically anticipated.

2. **Fitting technology to the organization (or vice versa).** On the one hand, it is important to align information technology to the business plan, to the firm's business processes, and to senior management's strategic business plans. Information technology is, after all, supposed to be the servant of the organization. On the other hand, these business plans, processes, and management strategy all may be very outdated or incompatible with the envisioned technology. In such instances, managers will need to change the organization to fit the technology or to adjust both the organization and the technology to achieve an optimal "fit."

his chapter explores the complex relationships between organizations, management, and information systems. We introduce the features of organizations that you will need to understand when you design, build, and operate information systems. We describe the changing role of information systems in organizations and the new arrangements of organization and technology required by enterprise systems, industrial networks, and mergers and acquisitions. We also scrutinize the manager's role and try to identify areas where information systems can enhance managerial effectiveness. The chapter concludes by examining the management decision-making process.

3.1 Organizations and Information Systems

Information systems and organizations influence one another. Information systems must be aligned with the organization to provide information that important groups within the organization need. At the same time, the organization must be aware of and open itself to the influences of information systems in order to benefit from new technologies.

The interaction between information technology and organizations is very complex and is influenced by a great many mediating factors, including the organization's structure, standard operating procedures, politics, culture, surrounding environment, and management decisions (see Figure 3-1). Managers must be aware that information systems can markedly alter life in the organization. They cannot successfully design new systems or understand existing systems without understanding organizations. Managers decide what systems will be built, what they will do, how they will be implemented, and so forth. Sometimes, however, the outcomes are the result of pure chance and of both good and bad luck.

WHAT IS AN ORGANIZATION?

An **organization** is a stable, formal, social structure that takes resources from the environment and processes them to produce outputs. This technical definition focuses on three elements of an organization. Capital and labor are primary production factors provided by the environment. The organization (the firm) transforms these inputs into products and services in a production function. The products and services are consumed by environments in return for supply inputs (see Figure 3-2). An organization is more stable than an informal group (such as a group of friends that meets every Friday for lunch) in terms of longevity and routineness. Organizations are formal legal entities, with internal rules and procedures, that must abide by laws. Organizations are also social structures because they are a collection of social elements, much as a machine has a structure—a particular arrangement of valves, cams, shafts, and other parts.

This definition of organizations is powerful and simple, but it is not very descriptive or even predictive of real-world organizations. A more realistic behavioral definition of an **organization** is that it is a collection of rights, privileges, obligations, and responsibilities that are delicately balanced over a period of time through conflict and conflict resolution (see Figure 3-3). In this behavioral view of the firm, people who work in organizations develop customary ways of working; they gain attachments to existing relationships; and they make arrangements with

organization (technical definition) A stable, formal, social structure that takes resources from the environment and processes them to produce outputs.

organization (behavioral definition) A collection of rights, privileges, obligations, and responsibilities that are delicately balanced over a period of time through conflict and conflict resolution.

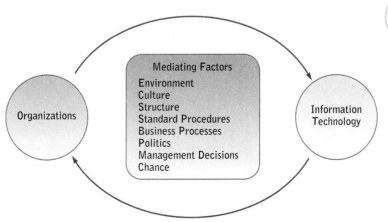

FIGURE 3-1 The two-way relationship between organizations and information technology. This complex two-way relationship is mediated by many factors, not the least of which are the decisions made—or not made—by managers. Other factors mediating the relationship include the organizational culture, bureaucracy, politics, business fashion, and pure chance.

FIGURE 3-2 The technical microeconomic definition of the organization. In the microeconomic definition of organizations, capital and labor (the primary production factors provided by the environment) are transformed by the firm through the production process into products and services (outputs to the environment). The products and services are consumed by the environment, which supplies additional capital and labor as inputs in the feedback loop.

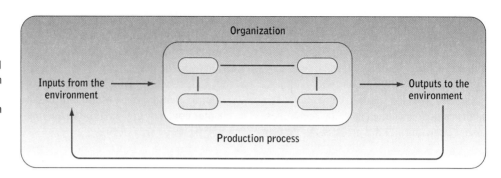

subordinates and superiors about how the work will be done, how much work will be done, and under what conditions. Most of these arrangements and feelings are not discussed in any formal rule book.

How do these definitions of organizations relate to information system technology? A technical view of organizations encourages us to focus on the way inputs are combined into outputs when technology changes are introduced into the company. The firm is seen as infinitely malleable, with capital and labor substituting for each other quite easily. But the more realistic behavioral definition of an organization suggests that building new information systems or rebuilding old ones involves much more than a technical rearrangement of machines or workers—that some information systems change the organizational balance of rights, privileges, obligations, responsibilities, and feelings that have been established over a long period of time.

Technological change requires changes in who owns and controls information, who has the right to access and update that information, and who makes decisions about whom, when, and how. For instance, Coca-Cola's new enterprise system provides central managers with more information to make production decisions affecting bottlers and distributors. This more complex view forces us to look at the way work is designed and the procedures used to achieve outputs.

The technical and behavioral definitions of organizations are not contradictory. Indeed, they complement each other: The technical definition tells us how thousands of firms in competitive markets combine capital, labor, and information technology, whereas the behavioral model takes us inside the individual firm to see how that technology affects the organization's inner workings. Section 3.2 describes how each of these definitions of organizations helps explain the relationships between information systems and organizations.

Some features of organizations are common to all organizations; others distinguish one organization from another. Let us look first at the features common to all organizations.

COMMON FEATURES OF ORGANIZATIONS

bureaucracy Formal organization with a clear-cut division of labor, abstract rules and procedures, and impartial decision making that uses technical qualifications and professionalism as a basis for promoting employees.

You might not think that Apple Computer, United Airlines, and the Aspen, Colorado, police department have much in common, but they do. In some respects, all modern organizations are alike because they share the characteristics that are listed in Table 3-1. A German sociologist, Max Weber, was the first to describe these "ideal-typical" characteristics of organizations in 1911. He called organizations **bureaucracies** that have certain "structural" features.

FIGURE 3-3 The behavioral view of organizations. The behavioral view of organizations emphasizes group relationships, values, and structures.

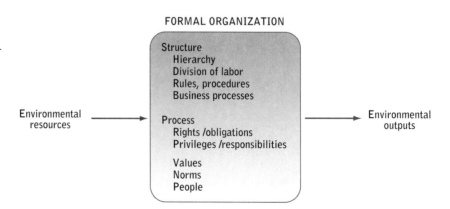

Table 3-1	**Structural Characteristics of All Organizations**

Clear division of labor

Hierarchy

Explicit rules and procedures

Impartial judgments

Technical qualifications for positions

Maximum organizational efficiency

According to Weber, all modern bureaucracies have a clear-cut division of labor and specialization. Organizations arrange specialists in a hierarchy of authority in which everyone is accountable to someone and authority is limited to specific actions. Authority and action are further limited by abstract rules or procedures (standard operating procedures, or SOPs) that are interpreted and applied to specific cases. These rules create a system of impartial and universalistic decision making; everyone is treated equally. Organizations try to hire and promote employees on the basis of technical qualifications and professionalism (not personal connections). The organization is devoted to the principle of efficiency: maximizing output using limited inputs.

According to Weber, bureaucracies are prevalent because they are the most efficient form of organization. Other scholars have supplemented Weber, identifying additional features of organizations. All organizations develop standard operating procedures, politics, and cultures.

Standard Operating Procedures

Organizations that survive over time become very efficient, producing a limited number of products and services by following standard routines. These standard routines become codified into reasonably precise rules, procedures, and practices called **standard operating procedures (SOPs)** that are developed to cope with virtually all expected situations. Some of these rules and procedures are written, formal procedures. Most are "rules of thumb" to be followed in selected situations.

standard operating procedures (SOPs) Precise rules, procedures, and practices developed by organizations to cope with virtually all expected situations.

These standard operating procedures have a great deal to do with the efficiency that modern organizations attain. For instance, in the assembly of a car, managers and workers develop complex standard procedures to handle the thousands of motions in a precise fashion, permitting the finished product to roll off the assembly line. Any change in SOPs requires an enormous organizational effort. Indeed, the organization may need to halt the entire production process before the old SOPs can be retired.

Difficulty in changing standard operating procedures is one reason Detroit automakers were slow to adopt Japanese mass production methods. For many years, U.S. automakers followed Henry Ford's mass production principles. Ford believed that the cheapest way to build a car was to churn out the largest number of autos by having workers repeatedly perform a simple task. By contrast, Japanese automakers have emphasized "lean production" methods whereby a smaller number of workers, each performing several tasks, can produce cars with less inventory, less investment, and fewer mistakes. Workers have multiple job responsibilities and are encouraged to stop production in order to correct a problem.

Organizational Politics

People in organizations occupy different positions with different specialties, concerns, and perspectives. As a result, they naturally have divergent viewpoints about how resources, rewards, and punishments should be distributed. These differences matter to both managers and employees, and they result in political struggle, competition, and conflict within every organization. Political resistance is one of the great difficulties of bringing about organizational change—especially the development of new information systems. Virtually all information systems that bring about significant changes in goals, procedures, productivity, and personnel are politically charged and will elicit serious political opposition. The chapter opening vignette described how Cola-Cola made special efforts to persuade its bottlers to participate in its new enterprise system to prevent such resistance from occurring.

Organizational Culture

All organizations have bedrock, unassailable, unquestioned (by the members) assumptions that define their goals and products. **Organizational culture** is this set of fundamental assumptions about what products the organization should produce, how it should produce them, where, and for whom. Generally, these cultural assumptions are taken totally for granted and are rarely publicly announced or spoken about (Schein, 1985).

organizational culture The set of fundamental assumptions about what products the organization should produce, how and where it should produce them, and for whom they should be produced.

You can see organizational culture at work by looking around your university or college. Some bedrock assumptions of university life are that professors know more than students, the reason students attend college is to learn, and classes follow a regular schedule. Organizational culture is a powerful unifying force that restrains political conflict and promotes common understanding, agreement on procedures, and common practices. If we all share the same basic cultural assumptions, then agreement on other matters is more likely.

At the same time, organizational culture is a powerful restraint on change, especially technological change. Most organizations will do almost anything to avoid making changes in basic assumptions. Any technological change that threatens commonly held cultural assumptions usually meets a great deal of resistance. For instance, one key longstanding assumption of U.S. automakers is that management should be very authoritarian and not listen to workers' opinions, and this is another reason these automakers have been slow to switch to "lean production."

An organization's culture is thus a powerful force shaping its information systems. The Window on Organizations explains how organizational culture affected government systems in Australia.

However, there are times when the only sensible way is to employ a new technology that directly opposes an existing organizational culture. When this occurs, the technology is often stalled while the culture slowly adjusts.

UNIQUE FEATURES OF ORGANIZATIONS

Although all organizations have common characteristics, no two organizations are identical. Organizations have different structures, goals, constituencies, leadership styles, tasks, and surrounding environments.

Different Organizational Types

One important way in which organizations differ is in their structure or shape. The differences among organizational structures are characterized in many ways. Mintzberg's classification, described in Table 3-2, identifies five basic kinds of organizations (Mintzberg, 1979).

Organizations and Environments

Organizations reside in environments from which they draw resources and to which they supply goods and services. Organizations and environments have a reciprocal relationship. On the one hand, organizations are open to, and dependent on, the social and physical environment that surrounds them. Without financial and human resources—people willing to work reliably and consistently for a set wage or revenue from customers—organizations could not exist. Organizations must respond to legislative and other requirements imposed by government, as well as the actions of customers and competitors. On the other hand, organizations can influence their environments. Organizations form alliances with others to influence the political process; they advertise to influence customer acceptance of their products.

Figure 3-4 shows that information systems play an important role in helping organizations perceive changes in their environments, and also in helping organizations act on their environments. Information systems are key instruments for *environmental scanning*, helping managers identify external changes that might require an organizational response.

Environments generally change much faster than organizations. The main reasons for organizational failure are an inability to adapt to a rapidly changing environment and a lack of resources—particularly among young firms—to sustain even short periods of troubled times (Freeman et al., 1983). New technologies, new products, and changing public tastes and val-

AUSTRALIA'S SYSTEMS SERVE THE PEOPLE

National culture profoundly affects what systems governments develop and the interfaces of those systems. Australians have a closer relationship with their governments than do most Americans, and as a result Australians expect and receive more from the state. However, Australians are willing to pay high income taxes to support social welfare programs. The Australian Prime Minister, John Howard, mandated that all appropriate federal, state, and local services be on-line by 2001, and the country has made massive strides in that direction. As a result, citizens are finding themselves better served.

The state of Victoria has 4.6 million people, or nearly one-quarter of Australia's population, and is a leader in electronic government. Victoria offers its residents a diversity of services that citizens can obtain by telephone, interactive kiosks, and the Web. By the end of 1999 residents were able to apply for liquor licenses, pay for parking tickets, renew vehicle and voter registration, pay utility bills, and execute at least 30 other transactions quickly and conveniently using its new Maxi information system. The system can be accessed at 45 strategically placed kiosks, as well as through the Internet (including an interactive voice response system) and by telephone from anywhere in the country. Moreover, residents will be able to pay any charges using their credit cards. By early 1999 Maxi was already logging 40,000 transactions monthly and growing. And no wonder—these transactions are typically completed in as little as five minutes. The system cost about A$15 million (US$10 million) and was paid for by computer giant NEC rather than by taxpayers.

Brisbane, Queensland, illustrates success at the local level. With 1.5 million residents, the city council decided in 1995 that it was time to improve the service to its "customers." James Brown, the manager of information and knowledge for the city council, described resident dealings with the city in 1995 as "a nightmare." Even finding whom to contact was a trial given the 650 government organizations listed (from libraries to construction units), each with a separate telephone number. On an average day, 30 percent of outside calls were not even answered, and one-third of the rest resulted in the caller being transferred from department to department. To solve the problem, Brisbane developed a 24-hour call center. Now residents no longer have to search for the telephone number because all the government organizations are reached through one city number. By 1999 the system was handling 50,000 calls per week, with 90 percent being answered within 20 seconds. Moreover, because of the city's new Web-based call center computer system, the agent receiving the call was able to resolve the problem without transferring the caller at all. By autumn 1999 Brisbane had installed a network of public kiosks, enabling residents to handle many of their problems themselves.

Brisbane's promise of customer service has been fulfilled in another way also. If a resident sees a dangerous situation or a problem, that person can contact the call center or register the problem using a kiosk. The call center immediately notifies the appropriate agency such as the police (who all carry wireless notebook computers in their vehicles). When residents do report such problems through the call center, the call center will contact the caller as soon as the problem is resolved. The Brisbane government even guarantees pothole repairs within 48 hours after receiving a report.

TO THINK ABOUT: Why are customer-friendly information systems being mandated in Australia but not in the United States? What organizational and managerial factors are involved?

Sources: Howard Baldwin, "Thunder Down Under," **CIO Magazine**, June 1, 1999; Howard Baldwin, "Small World Big Business," **CIO Magazine**, June 1, 1999; Polly Schneider, "Politically Direct," **CIO Magazine**, June 1, 1999; and "Australian Post Jumps into e-Bill Market," **Global Technology Business**, December 1999.

ues (many of which result in new government regulations) put strains on any organization's culture, politics, and people. Most organizations do not cope well with large environmental shifts. The inertia built into an organization's standard operating procedures, the political conflict raised by changes to the existing order, and the threat to closely held cultural values typically inhibit organizations from making significant changes. It is not surprising that only 10 percent of the Fortune 500 companies in 1919 still exist today.

Other Differences Among Organizations

Organizations have different shapes or structures for many other reasons also. They differ in their ultimate goals and the types of power used to achieve them. Some organizations have coercive goals (e.g., prisons); others have utilitarian goals (e.g., businesses); still others have normative goals (universities, religious groups). Organizations also serve different groups or have different constituencies, some primarily benefiting their members, others benefiting clients, stockholders, or the public. The nature of leadership differs greatly from one organization to

Table 3-2　Organizational Structures

Organizational Type	Description	Example
Entrepreneurial structure	Young, small firm in a fast-changing environment. It has a simple structure and is managed by an entrepreneur serving as its single chief executive officer.	Small start-up business
Machine bureaucracy	Large bureaucracy existing in a slowly changing environment, producing standard products. It is dominated by a centralized management team and centralized decision making.	Midsize manufacturing
Divisionalized bureaucracy	Combination of multiple machine bureaucracies, each producing a different product or service, all topped by one central headquarters.	Fortune 500 firms such as General Motors
Professional bureaucracy	Knowledge-based organization where goods and services depend on the expertise and knowledge of professionals. Dominated by department heads with weak centralized authority.	Law firms, school systems, hospitals
Adhocracy	"Task force" organization that must respond to rapidly changing environments. Consists of large groups of specialists organized into short-lived multidisciplinary teams with weak central management.	Consulting firms such as the Rand Corporation

another—some organizations may be more democratic or authoritarian than others. Another way organizations differ is by the tasks they perform and the technology they use. Some organizations perform primarily routine tasks that could be reduced to formal rules that require little judgment (such as manufacturing auto parts), whereas others (such as consulting firms) work primarily with nonroutine tasks.

BUSINESS PROCESSES

business processes The unique ways in which organizations coordinate and organize work activities, information, and knowledge to produce a product or service.

Business processes refer to the manner in which work is organized, coordinated, and focused to produce a valuable product or service. On the one hand, business processes are concrete work flows of material, information, and knowledge—sets of activities. But business processes also refer to the unique ways in which organizations coordinate work, information, and knowledge, and the ways in which management chooses to coordinate work.

The current interest in business processes stems from the recognition that strategic success ultimately depends on how well firms execute their primary mission of delivering the lowest cost, highest quality goods and services to customers. Examples of processes are new-product develop-

FIGURE 3-4 Environments and organizations have a reciprocal relationship. Environments shape what organizations can do, but organizations can influence their environments and decide to change environments altogether. Information technology plays a critical role in helping organizations perceive environmental change and in helping organizations act on their environment. Information systems act as a filter between organizations and their environments. They do not necessarily reflect reality, but instead refract environmental change through a number of built-in biases.

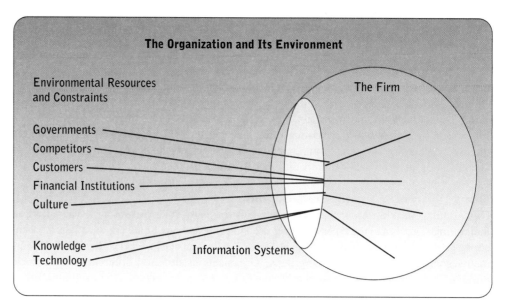

Keying data from tax returns into the Internal Revenue Service computer system is an important activity in the tax collection process. Business processes coordinate work, information, and knowledge.

ment, which turns an idea into a manufacturable prototype, or order fulfillment, which begins with the receipt of an order and ends when the customer has received and paid for the product.

Business processes, by nature, are generally cross-functional, transcending the boundaries between sales, marketing, manufacturing, and research and development. Processes cut across the traditional organizational structure, grouping employees from different functional specialties to complete a piece of work. For example, the order fulfillment process at many companies requires cooperation among the sales function (receiving the order, entering the order), the accounting function (credit checking and billing for the order), and the manufacturing function (assembling and shipping the order). Some organizations have built information systems to support these cross-functional processes, such as product development, order fulfillment, or customer support, in addition to their systems for separate business functions, such as those described in the previous chapter. Objectives for processes are more external and more focused on meeting customer and market demands than those for the traditional functional approach.

Figure 3-5 depicts the traditional paper-based income tax collection process at the U.S. Internal Revenue Service. Taxpayers mail their income tax returns (and payment checks) to the IRS (Step 1) where they are first sorted by type of return, by whether checks are enclosed, and other criteria (Step 2). IRS examiners look over the paper returns for mistakes, making sure all schedules are attached (Step 3). Thousands of people key only the most important pieces of information from each return into the IRS computer system (Step 4). The computers check the calculations and data on the returns, generating a report of returns with errors (Step 5). The paper returns are filed in cabinets (Step 6). The IRS sends out refunds, bills for additional payments, and letters to taxpayers informing them of errors on their returns (Step 7).

Information systems can help organizations achieve great efficiencies by automating parts of these processes or by helping organizations rethink and streamline these processes through the development of work-flow software. For example, experts have pointed out that

FIGURE 3-5 The Internal Revenue Service tax collection process. Collecting U.S. federal income taxes is a multistep process with many activities to coordinate.

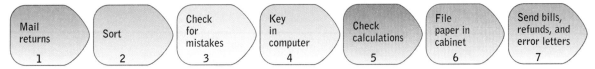

Mail returns	Sort	Check for mistakes	Key in computer	Check calculations	File paper in cabinet	Send bills, refunds, and error letters
1	2	3	4	5	6	7

the IRS tax collection process for returns that are not filed electronically could be made more efficient—and taxpayer information more easily accessible—by eliminating some of the manual and paper-based activities. Instead of entering limited pieces of data from the returns into the computer system, the entire tax return could be scanned into the computer, with all of its information available for instant access. The computer could perform all of the returns examination and error checking instead of having people make preliminary examinations of the returns (Johnston, 1998). Chapter 9 treats this subject in greater detail because it is fundamental to systems analysis and design.

Automating business processes requires careful analysis and planning. When systems are used to strengthen the wrong business model or business processes, the business can become more efficient at doing what it should not do. As a result, the firm becomes vulnerable to competitors who may have discovered the right business model. Therefore, one of the most important strategic decisions that a firm can make is not deciding how to use computers to improve business processes, but instead to first understand what business processes need improvement (Keen, 1997). The choice of which business process to improve is critical.

As you can see in Table 3-3, the list of unique features of organizations is longer than the common features list. It stands to reason that information systems will have different impacts on different types of organizations. Different organizations in different circumstances will experience different effects from the same technology. Only by close analysis of a specific organization can a manager effectively design and manage information systems.

3.2 The Changing Role of Information Systems in Organizations

Information systems have become integral, on-line, interactive tools deeply involved in the minute-to-minute operations and decision making of large organizations. We now describe the changing role of systems in organizations and how it has been shaped by the interaction of organizations and information technology.

THE EVOLUTION OF INFORMATION TECHNOLOGY (IT) INFRASTRUCTURE

One way that organizations can influence how information technology (IT) will be used is through decisions about the technical and organizational configuration of systems. Chapters 1 and 2 also described the ever-widening role of information systems in organizations. Supporting this widening role have been changes in information technology (IT) infrastructure, which are illustrated in Figure 3-6. In Chapter 1, we defined IT infrastructure as the set of hardware, software, data storage, and network technologies constituting a portfolio of

Table 3-3 Summary of Salient Features of Organizations

Common Features	Unique Features
Formal structure	Organizational type
Standard operating procedures (SOPs)	Environments
Politics	Goals
Culture	Power
	Constituencies
	Function
	Leadership
	Tasks
	Technology
	Business processes

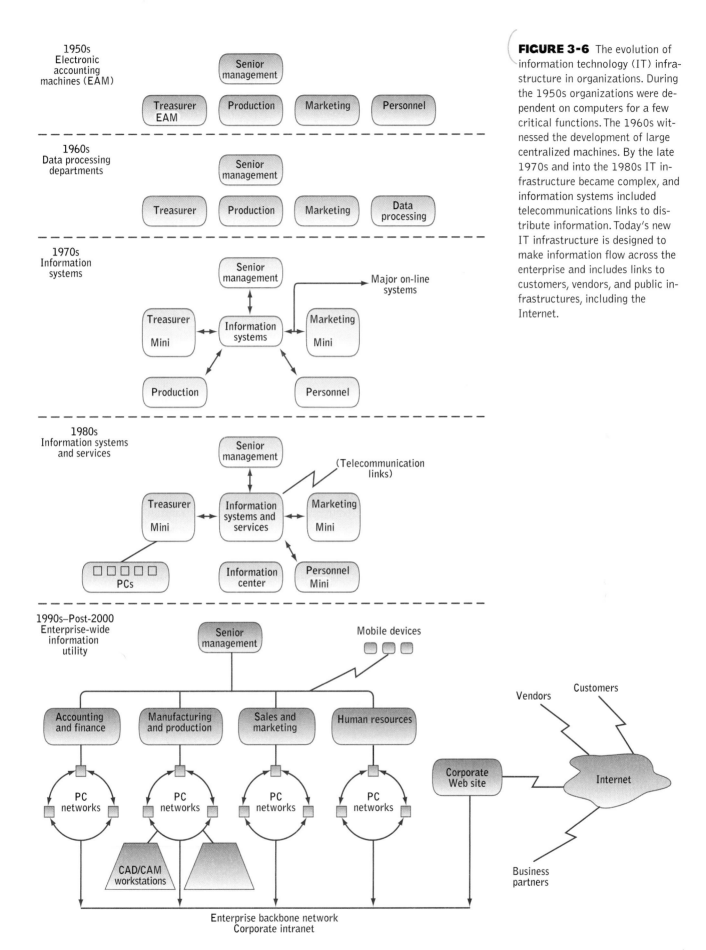

FIGURE 3-6 The evolution of information technology (IT) infrastructure in organizations. During the 1950s organizations were dependent on computers for a few critical functions. The 1960s witnessed the development of large centralized machines. By the late 1970s and into the 1980s IT infrastructure became complex, and information systems included telecommunications links to distribute information. Today's new IT infrastructure is designed to make information flow across the enterprise and includes links to customers, vendors, and public infrastructures, including the Internet.

shared resources for the organization. The earliest IT infrastructure in the 1950s consisted of isolated "electronic accounting machines" that were only used for a few business functions such as processing the company's payroll. In the 1960s IT infrastructure was based on large, centralized mainframe computers that served corporate headquarters and a few remote sites. In the 1970s, midsize minicomputers located in individual departments or divisions of the organization were networked to large, centralized computers. Desktop PCs first were used independently and then were linked to minicomputers and large computers in the 1980s.

During the past five years, a new IT infrastructure for a fully networked organization has emerged. In this new enterprise-wide infrastructure, computers coordinate information flowing among desktops and larger computers and perhaps among hundreds of smaller local networks. These networks can be connected into a network linking the entire enterprise or linking to external networks of customers, vendors, and business partners. The "new infrastructure" for companies today incorporates public network services, including the Internet and computing devices such as portable PCs, programmable mobile phones, and pagers used by the company's mobile workforce.

INFORMATION TECHNOLOGY SERVICES

Another way that organizations have affected information technology is through decisions about who will design, build, and operate the technology within the organization. These decisions determine how information technology services will be delivered.

The formal organizational unit or function responsible for technology services is called the **information systems department.** The information systems department is responsible for maintaining the hardware, software, data storage technology, and networks that comprise the firm's information technology (IT) infrastructure.

The information systems department consists of specialists such as programmers, systems analysts, project leaders, and information systems managers (see Figure 3-7). **Programmers** are highly trained technical specialists who write the software instructions for the computer. **Systems analysts** constitute the principal liaison between the information systems group and the rest of the organization. It is the systems analyst's job to translate business problems and requirements into information requirements and systems. **Information systems managers** are leaders of teams of programmers and analysts, project managers, physical facility managers, telecommunications managers, and heads of office system groups. They are also managers of computer operations and data entry staff. Also external specialists, such as hardware vendors and manufacturers, software firms, and consultants, frequently participate in the day-to-day operations and long-term planning of information systems.

information systems department The formal organizational unit that is responsible for the information systems function in the organization.

programmers Highly trained technical specialists who write computer software instructions.

systems analysts Specialists who translate business problems and requirements into information requirements and systems; they act as liaisons between the information systems department and the rest of the organization.

information systems managers Leaders of the various specialists in the information systems department.

FIGURE 3-7 Information technology services. Many types of specialists and groups are responsible for the design and management of the organization's information technology (IT) infrastructure.

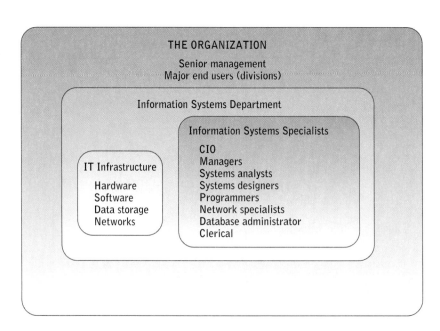

In many companies, the information systems department is headed by a **chief informa-tion officer (CIO).** The CIO is a senior management position to oversee the use of informa-tion technology in the firm.

End users are representatives of departments outside of the information systems group for whom applications are developed. These users are playing an increasingly larger role in the design and development of information systems.

In the early years, the information systems group was composed mostly of programmers and performed very highly specialized but limited technical functions. Today a growing propor-tion of staff members are systems analysts and network specialists, with the information systems department acting as a powerful change agent in the organization. The information systems de-partment suggests new business strategies and new information-based products and services and coordinates both the development of the technology and the planned changes in the organization.

In the past, firms generally built their own software and managed their own computing facilities. Today, many firms are turning to external vendors to provide these services (see Chapters 5 and 10) and using their information systems departments to manage these service providers.

HOW INFORMATION SYSTEMS AFFECT ORGANIZATIONS

How have changes in information technology affected organizations? To find answers, we draw on research and theory based on both economic and behavioral approaches.

Economic Theories

From an economic standpoint, information technology can be viewed as a factor of produc-tion that can be freely substituted for capital and labor. As the cost of information technology falls, it is substituted for labor, which historically has been a rising cost. Hence, in the **microeconomic model of the firm,** information technology should result in a decline in the number of middle managers and clerical workers as information technology substitutes for their labor.

Information technology also helps firms contract in size because it can reduce transac-tion costs—the costs incurred when a firm buys on the marketplace what it cannot make itself. According to **transaction cost theory,** firms and individuals seek to economize on transaction costs much as they do on production costs. Using markets is expensive (Williamson, 1985) be-cause of coordination costs such as locating and communicating with distant suppliers, mon-itoring contract compliance, buying insurance, obtaining information on products, and so forth. Traditionally, firms have tried to reduce transaction costs by getting bigger, hiring more employees, or buying their own suppliers and distributors, as General Motors used to do.

Information technology, especially the use of networks, can help firms lower the cost of market participation (transaction costs) making it worthwhile for firms to contract with exter-nal suppliers instead of using internal sources. For example, by using computer links to exter-nal suppliers, the Chrysler Corporation can achieve economies by obtaining more than 70 per-cent of its parts from the outside. Figure 3-8 shows that as transaction costs decrease, firm size (the number of employees) should shrink because it becomes easier and cheaper for the firm to contract the purchase of goods and services in the marketplace rather than to make the prod-uct or service itself. Firm size can stay constant or contract even if the company increases its revenues. (For example, General Electric reduced its workforce from about 400,000 people in the early 1980s to about 230,000 while increasing revenues 150 percent.)

Information technology also can reduce internal management costs. According to **agency theory,** the firm is viewed as a "nexus of contracts" among self-interested individuals rather than as a unified, profit-maximizing entity (Jensen and Mekling, 1976). A principal (owner) employs "agents" (employees) to perform work on his or her behalf. However, agents need constant supervision and management because they otherwise will tend to pursue their own interests rather than those of the owners. As firms grow in size and scope, agency costs or coordination costs rise because owners must expend more and more effort supervising and managing employees.

Information technology, by reducing the costs of acquiring and analyzing information, permits organizations to reduce agency costs because it becomes easier for managers to oversee

chief information officer (CIO) Senior manager in charge of the information systems function in the firm.

end users Representatives of de-partments outside the information systems group for whom applica-tions are developed.

microeconomic model of the firm Model of the firm that views information technology as a factor of production that can be freely sub-stituted for capital and labor.

transaction cost theory Economic theory stating that firms grow larger because they can con-duct marketplace transactions inter-nally more cheaply than they can with external firms in the market-place.

agency theory Economic theory that views the firm as a nexus of contracts among self-interested in-dividuals who must be supervised and managed.

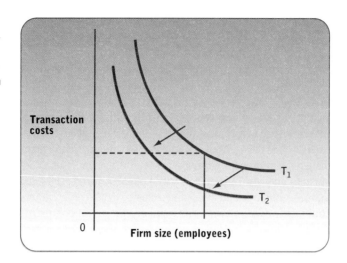

FIGURE 3-8 The transaction cost theory of the impact of information technology on the organization. Firms traditionally grew in size in order to reduce transaction costs. IT potentially reduces the costs for a given size, shifting the transaction cost curve inward, opening up the possibility of revenue growth without increasing size, or even revenue growth accompanied by shrinking size.

a greater number of employees. Figure 3-9 shows that by reducing overall management costs, information technology allows firms to increase revenues while shrinking the numbers of middle management and clerical workers. We have seen examples in earlier chapters where information technology expanded the power and scope of small organizations by allowing them to perform coordinating activities such as processing orders or keeping track of inventory with very few clerks and managers.

Behavioral Theories

While economic theories try to explain how large numbers of firms act in the marketplace, behavioral theories from sociology, psychology, and political science are more useful for describing the behavior of individual firms. Behavioral research has found little evidence that information systems automatically transform organizations, although the systems may be instrumental in accomplishing this goal once senior management decides to pursue this end.

Behavioral researchers have theorized that information technology could change the hierarchy of decision making in organizations by lowering the costs of information acquisition and broadening the distribution of information (Malone, 1997). Information technology could bring information directly from operating units to senior managers, thereby eliminating middle managers and their clerical support workers. Information technology could permit senior managers to contact lower level operating units directly using networked telecommunications and computers, thereby eliminating middle management intermediaries. Alternatively, information technology could be used to distribute information directly to lower level workers, who could then make their own decisions based on their own knowledge and information without any

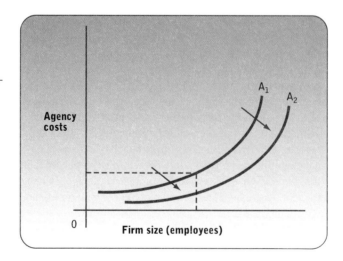

FIGURE 3-9 The agency cost theory of the impact of information technology on the organization. As firms grow in size and complexity, traditionally they experience rising agency costs. IT shifts the agency cost curve down and to the right, allowing firms to increase size while lowering agency costs.

management intervention. Some research even suggests that computerization increases the information given to middle managers, empowering them to make more important decisions than in the past, thus reducing the need for large numbers of lower level workers (Shore, 1983).

In postindustrial societies, authority increasingly relies on knowledge and competence, and not on mere formal position. Hence, the shape of organizations should "flatten" because professional workers tend to be self-managing, and decision making should become more decentralized as knowledge and information become more widespread throughout (Drucker, 1988). Information technology may encourage "task force" networked organizations in which groups of professionals come together—face-to-face or electronically—for short periods of time to accomplish a specific task (e.g., designing a new automobile); once the task is accomplished, the individuals join other task forces. More firms may operate as virtual organizations where work no longer is tied to geographic location.

Who makes sure that self-managed teams do not head off in the wrong direction? Who decides which person works on what team and for how long? How can managers judge the performance of someone who is constantly rotating from team to team? How do people know where their careers are headed? New approaches for evaluating, organizing, and informing workers are required, and not all companies can make virtual work effective (Davenport and Pearlson, 1998).

No one knows the answers to these questions, and it is not clear that all modern organizations will undergo this transformation. General Motors, for example, may have many self-managed knowledge workers in certain divisions, but it still will have a manufacturing division structured as a large, traditional bureaucracy. In general, the shape of organizations historically changes with the business cycle and with the latest management styles. When times are good and profits are high, firms hire large numbers of supervisory personnel; when times are tough, they let go many of these same people (Mintzberg, 1979).

Another behavioral approach views information systems as the outcome of political competition between organizational subgroups for influence over the organization's policies, procedures, and resources (Laudon, 1974; Keen, 1981; Kling, 1980; Laudon, 1986). Information systems inevitably become bound up in organizational politics because they influence access to a key resource—namely, information. Information systems can affect who does what to whom, when, where, and how in an organization. For instance, a major study of FBI efforts to develop a national computerized criminal history system (a single national listing of the criminal histories, arrests, and convictions of more than 36 million individuals in the United States) found that the state governments strongly resisted the FBI's efforts. This information would enable the federal government, and the FBI in particular, to monitor how states use criminal histories. The states resisted the development of this national system quite successfully (Laudon, 1986).

Because information systems potentially change an organization's structure, culture, politics, and work, there is often considerable resistance to them when they are introduced. There are several ways to visualize organizational resistance. Leavitt (1965) used a diamond shape to illustrate the interrelated and mutually adjusting character of technology and organization (see Figure 3-10). Here, changes in technology are absorbed, deflected, and defeated by

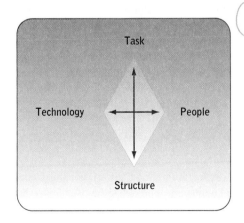

FIGURE 3-10 Organizational resistance and the mutually adjusting relationship between technology and the organization. Implementing information systems has consequences for task arrangements, structures, and people. According to this model, in order to implement change, all four components must be changed simultaneously.
Source: Leavitt, 1965.

REDUCING AGENCY COSTS

Your company has 3,000 employees and is looking for ways to reduce some of its operating costs. You have prepared the following list of operating expenses.

Telephone costs	$750,000 per year
Employee policy handbooks	$8.75 per handbook for printing and distribution
Employee benefits counseling	$80 per hour meeting

You are hoping you can reduce some of these costs by using Internet technology to build an intranet for the firm. The intranet would do the following:

- Provide e-mail communication among employees worldwide.
- Provide employee handbooks that could be published and revised electronically and accessed from each employee's desktop computer.
- Enable employees to select and revise their medical and life insurance plans on-line through their computers.

You believe that employees could use e-mail to accomplish 40 percent of the communication that is taking place over the telephone.

All employees are required to review their health benefits and re-enroll in their benefits plans once per year.

New employee handbooks are distributed to each employee once a year.

The intranet would cost $600,000 to develop and $100,000 annually to maintain. No new hardware or networking infrastructure would be required since all employees already use networked desktop PCs.

1. How would the intranet make the management process more efficient?

2. How much would the intranet reduce agency costs? Is the intranet worthwhile to build?

3. Are there any other benefits that could be produced by the intranet? Are there any disadvantages to using the intranet?

---

organizational task arrangements, structures, and people. In this model, the only way to bring about change is to change the technology, tasks, structure, and people simultaneously. Other authors have spoken about the need to "unfreeze" organizations before introducing an innovation, quickly implementing it, and "refreezing" or institutionalizing the change (Kolb, 1970; Alter and Ginzberg, 1978).

THE INTERNET AND ORGANIZATIONS

The Internet, especially the World Wide Web, is beginning to have an important impact on the relationships between firms and external entities, and even on the organization of business processes inside a firm. The Internet increases the accessibility, storage, and distribution of information and knowledge for organizations. In essence, the Internet is capable of dramatically lowering the transaction and agency costs facing most organizations. For instance, brokerage firms and banks in New York can now "deliver" their internal-operations procedures manuals to their employees at distant locations by posting them on their corporate Web site, saving millions of dollars in distribution costs. A global sales force can receive nearly instant price and product information updates via the Web or instructions from management via e-mail. Vendors of some large retailers can access retailers' internal Web sites directly for up-to-the-minute sales information and initiate replenishment orders instantly.

Businesses are rapidly rebuilding some of their key business processes based on Internet technology and making this technology a key component of their information technology (IT) infrastructures. If prior networking is any guide, one result will be simpler business processes, fewer employees, and much flatter organizations than in the past.

IMPLICATIONS FOR THE DESIGN AND UNDERSTANDING OF INFORMATION SYSTEMS

One cannot take a narrow view of organizations and their relationship to information systems. Experienced systems observers and managers approach systems change very cautiously. In order to reap the benefits of technology, changes in organizational culture, values, norms, and interest-group alignments must be managed with as much planning and effort as the technology changes. In our experience, the central organizational factors to consider when planning a new system are as follows:

- The environment in which the organization must function.
- The structure of the organization: hierarchy, specialization, standard operating procedures.
- The organization's culture and politics.
- The type of organization.
- The nature and style of leadership.
- The extent of top management's support and understanding.
- The principal interest groups affected by the system.
- The kinds of tasks, decisions, and business processes that the information system is designed to assist.
- The sentiments and attitudes of workers in the organization who will be using the information system.
- The history of the organization: past investments in information technology, existing skills, important programs, and human resources.

3.3 Integrating Systems and Business Processes: Enterprise Systems, Industrial Networks, and Mergers and Acquisitions

Many firms are using the changes in information technology we have described to reduce transaction and agency costs by coordinating activities and decisions across entire firms and even entire industries. Companies are building systems that integrate key business processes spanning the firm and that link the firm's business processes to those of other companies in its industry. Companies are also trying to achieve new economies and efficiencies by merging with other companies and integrating their systems and information technology infrastructures.

ENTERPRISE SYSTEMS

The new IT infrastructure we have described provides a set of technologies that can be used to coordinate activities and decisions across entire firms and even entire industries. A large organization typically has many different kinds of information systems that support different functions, organizational levels, and business processes. Most of these systems that are built around different functions, business units, and business processes do not "talk" to each other, and managers might have a hard time assembling the data they would need for a comprehensive, overall picture of the organization's operations. For instance, sales personnel might not be able to tell at the time they placed an order whether the items that were ordered were in inventory; customers could not track their orders; and manufacturing could not communicate easily with finance to plan for new production. This fragmentation of data in hundreds of separate systems could thus have a negative impact on organizational efficiency and business performance. Figure 3-11 illustrates the traditional arrangement of information systems.

Many organizations are now building **enterprise systems,** or enterprise resource planning (ERP) systems, to solve this problem. Enterprise software models and automates many business processes, such as filling an order or scheduling a shipment, with the goal of integrating information across the company and eliminating complex, expensive links between computer systems in different areas of the business. Information that was previously fragmented in different systems can seamlessly flow throughout the firm so that it can be shared by business processes in manufacturing, accounting, human resources, and other areas of the

enterprise systems Firmwide information systems that integrate key business processes so that information can flow freely between different parts of the firm.

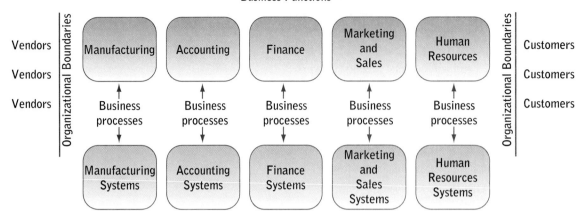

Business Functions

FIGURE 3-11 Traditional view of systems. In most organizations today, separate systems built over a long period of time support discrete business processes and discrete functions. The organization's systems rarely included vendors and customers.

business. Discrete business processes from sales, production, finance, and logistics can be integrated into company-wide business processes that flow across organizational levels and functions. An enterprise-wide technical platform serves all processes and levels. Figure 3-12 illustrates how enterprise systems work.

The enterprise system collects data from various key business processes and stores the data in a single comprehensive data repository where they can be used by other parts of

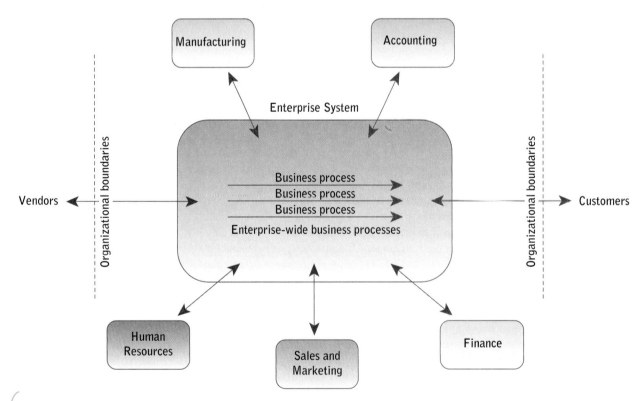

FIGURE 3-12 Enterprise systems. Enterprise systems can integrate the key business processes of an entire firm into a single software system that allows information to flow seamlessly throughout the organization. These systems may include transactions with customers and vendors.

the business. Managers emerge with precise and timely information for coordinating the daily operations of the business and a firmwide view of business processes and information flows.

Iowa Spring Manufacturing Inc., which makes coil springs for form and construction machines, automobiles, garage doors, furniture, and major appliances, installed an enterprise system to help it stay ahead in a fiercely competitive industry by providing fast and responsive customer service. ERP software from Time Critical Manufacturing handles Iowa Spring's accounting, order processing, purchasing and receiving, inventory management, shop floor routing and control, and bills of material, which list the part number of components used in a finished product. When a clerk enters an incoming order for a spring into the system, the ERP software automatically checks the bill of materials for the spring to see what parts are needed. The system automatically determines whether enough material is on hand to produce the ordered spring. If not, the system sets up a procedure to purchase the material. Other parts of the system determine what machines will be needed to make the spring, check the speeds and gear combinations to run on those machines, and arrange machine scheduling. Finally, the system creates a work order telling the machine operators to make the spring. When workers complete the job, the system automatically creates an invoice.

Using PCs on the shop floor to scan bar codes printed on each work order, factory workers register the time they start and finish their portion of the job. The enterprise system stores this information, and it can be accessed by customer service representatives to track the progress of an order through every step of the manufacturing process. If a customer wants to know about the status of an order, the system lets managers see what's happening on the shop floor at any time. Before implementing the enterprise system, if a customer inquired about the status of an order, Iowa Spring had to send a runner out to its plant to find out how much work had been done on the order. Such detailed information also helps Iowa Spring price its jobs much more accurately than in the past. Through the ERP system, managers learned which jobs were the most and least profitable. They eliminated the most unprofitable jobs, which helped Iowa Spring raise profits 10 percent (Zygmont, 1998).

Although enterprise systems can improve organizational coordination, efficiency, and decision making, they have proven very difficult to build. Companies will need to rework their business processes to make information flow smoothly between them. Employees will have to take on new job functions and responsibilities. Enterprise systems require complex pieces of software and large investments of time, money, and expertise. Chapter 9 provides more detail on the organizational and technical challenges of enterprise system implementation.

INDUSTRIAL NETWORKS

Some companies are extending their enterprise systems beyond the boundaries of the firm to share information and coordinate business processes with other firms in their industry. **Industrial networks,** which are sometimes called *extended enterprises,* link together the enterprise systems of firms in an entire industry (see Figure 3-13). For instance, Procter & Gamble (P&G), the world's largest consumer goods company, has been developing an integrated industry-wide system that coordinates the grocery store point-of-sale systems with grocery store warehouses, shippers, its own manufacturing facilities, and its suppliers of raw materials. This single industry-spanning system effectively allows P&G to monitor the movement of all its products from raw materials to customer purchase.

There are two kinds of industrial networks (see Figure 3-13). *Vertically organized industrial networks,* such as Coca-Cola's extended enterprise described in the chapter opening vignette, integrate the operations of the firm with its suppliers and can be used for supply chain management. *Horizontally organized industrial networks* link firms across an entire industry. An example would be the OASIS network of utility industry firms, which uses the Web to help members sell surplus electrical power. A few industrial networks coordinate the activities of competitors. For example, General Motors, Ford and DaimlerChrysler created a common Internet purchasing system to help them obtain parts and other goods on-line from suppliers. They expect to reduce costs and save time from their cooperation (Bradsher, 2000).

industrial networks Networks linking systems of multiple firms in an industry. Also called extended enterprises.

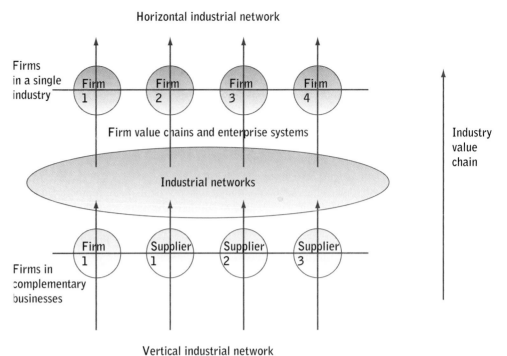

FIGURE 3-1 3 Industrial networks. Industrial networks link the enterprise systems of firms in an entire industry into an industry-wide system. Horizontal industrial networks link firms in the same industry, including competitors, while vertical industrial networks link a firm with suppliers in the same industry.

Most industrial networks today are vertical and do not link together competitors in the same industry.

Internet technology has fueled the growth of industrial networks because it provides a platform where systems from different companies can seamlessly exchange information. The Window on Technology describes how Procter & Gamble's industrial network benefits from Internet and related network technologies. We provide more detail on industrial networks in Chapter 8.

MERGERS AND ACQUISITIONS: SYSTEM AND INFRASTRUCTURE IMPLICATIONS

The relationships between organizations and information technology that we have described influence what happens when companies decide to combine. Mergers and acquisitions (M&As) are deeply affected by the organizational characteristics of the merging companies as well as by their information technology (IT) infrastructures.

Mergers and acquisitions have been proliferating because they are a major growth engine for businesses. In 1998 the value of global mergers and acquisitions was approximately $1.9 trillion (compared to $400 billion in 1992). The reasons behind mergers and acquisitions are economies of scale, scope, knowledge, and time. Potentially, firms can cut costs significantly by merging with competitors, reduce risks by expanding into different industries (e.g., conglomerating), and create a larger pool of competitive knowledge and expertise by joining forces with other players. There are also economies of time: A firm can gain market share and expertise very quickly through acquisition rather than by building on its own for the long term. Some firms—like General Electric—are quite successful in carrying out mergers and acquisitions. But in general, research has found that more than 70 percent of all M&As result in a decline in shareholder value, and often lead to divestiture at a later time (Braxton Associates, 1997; *Economist,* 1997).

One reason mergers and acquisitions fail is because of the difficulty of integrating the systems of different companies. Without a successful systems integration, the intended economies cannot be realized, or, worse, the merged entity cannot execute its business processes and it loses customers. IT plays a significant role in achieving M&A economies, but

Window on Technology

PROCTER & GAMBLE'S INDUSTRIAL NETWORK NETS MANY BENEFITS

Procter & Gamble Co., the 163 year old consumer goods giant, has traditionally aimed at doubling its sales every decade and has usually succeeded—until recently. During the last five years, annual sales growth has slowed from 5% to 2.6%. Durk Jager, P&G's new CEO, is trying to revitalize the company to make faster and better decisions, cut red tape, wring costs out of systems and procedures, and fuel innovation. According to Tod Garrett, the company's CIO, if P&G doesn't change, "we won't be around in the next 160 years."

A key component in P&G's ambitious change program is the use of Internet and other technology to streamline its business processes and its supply chain. Taking a cue from Wal-Mart, one of its largest customers, P&G built a system that uses data collected from point-of-sale terminals and triggers shipments to retailers of items that customers have purchased and that need restocking. P&G also has electronic links to suppliers, so that it can order materials from them when its inventories are low. The system helps P&G reduce its inventory by allowing the company to produce products as they are demanded by retailers.

To make better use of Internet technology, P&G started work on an Ultimate Supply System that would replace a private network with 4000 electronic links to suppliers and retailers with a more cost-effective system using the Web. The system would use Internet technology to link retailers and suppliers to P&G's private corporate intranet. By making it easier—and less expensive—for retailers and suppliers to integrate their systems with P&G's systems, P&G hopes to reduce product cycle time by half, inventory costs by $4.5 billion, and systems costs by $5 billion.

P&G's volume of business with small and midsize retailers had not been large enough to justify the cost of linking these firms to P&G's inventory replenishment system over a private network. These companies were still placing orders manually to P&G. P&G created a special Key Account Replenishment System (Kars) running on a PC that these smaller retailers can use to generate orders to P&G based on their customer demand. Kars automatically transmits retailers' orders from their point-of-sale or inventory systems to P&G's billing system via the Web. P&G's Web based systems for both large and small retailers are more efficient than the systems they replaced because even the older networked systems often required some degree of manual work.

Retailers can use the new system to feed information about their category-management needs to P&G. P&G in return can feed information back to retailers about shopper purchases and market position. P&G can analyze this information and then use it to help retailers figure out, for instance, the mix of various shampoos that sell best at a particular store location. The information could also be used to provide P&G's suppliers with more precise information about what items and materials need replenishment.

TO THINK ABOUT: How did P&G benefit from using Web technology in its industrial network? Why is Web technology so useful in creating industrial networks?

Sources: Marianne Kolbasuk McGee, "Lessons from a Cultural Revolution," *Information Week*, October 25, 1999 and Nikhil Deogun and Emily Nelson, "P&G Is on the Move; Before Drug Talks, It Approached Gillette," *The Wall Street Journal*, January 24, 2000.

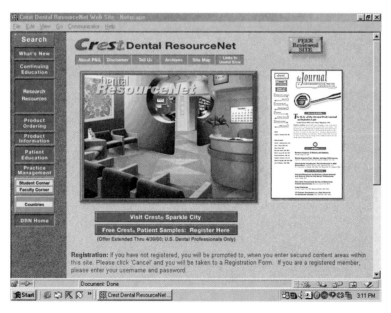

Dentists can order Crest toothpaste, toothbrushes, and dental products directly from Procter & Gamble via the Web. P&G has used Web technology to expand its industrial network with its suppliers and customers.

it can also act as an impediment to organizational performance and corporate infrastructure development. In failed M&A situations, firms become a hodgepodge of inherited legacy systems built by aggregating the systems of one firm after another with little time or resources devoted to integrating systems or shedding complexity.

When a company targeted for acquisition has been identified, information systems managers can identify the realistic costs of integration; the estimated benefits of economies of operation, scope, knowledge, and time; and any problematic systems that might require major investments to integrate. In addition, IT managers can critically estimate any likely costs required to upgrade IT infrastructures or make major system improvements to support the merged companies.

3.4 Managers, Decision Making, and Information Systems

To determine how information systems can benefit managers, we must first examine what managers do and what information they need for decision making and their other functions. We must also understand how decisions are made and what kinds of decisions can be supported by formal information systems.

THE ROLE OF MANAGERS IN ORGANIZATIONS

Managers play a key role in organizations. Their responsibilities range from making decisions, to writing reports, to attending meetings, to arranging birthday parties. We can better understand managerial functions and roles by examining classical and contemporary models of managerial behavior.

Classical Descriptions of Management

The **classical model of management,** which describes what managers do, was largely unquestioned for the more than 70 years since the 1920s. Henri Fayol and other early writers first described the five classical functions of managers as planning, organizing, coordinating, deciding, and controlling. This description of management activities dominated management thought for a long time, and it is still popular today.

But these terms actually describe formal managerial functions and are unsatisfactory as a description of what managers actually do. The terms do not address what managers do when they plan, decide things, and control the work of others. We need a more fine-grained understanding of how managers actually behave.

Behavioral Models

Contemporary behavioral scientists have observed that managers do not behave as the classical model of management led us to believe. Kotter (1982), for example, describes the morning activities of the president of an investment management firm.

> 7:35 A.M. Richardson arrives at work, unpacks her briefcase, gets some coffee, and begins making a list of activities for the day.
>
> 7:45 A.M. Bradshaw (a subordinate) and Richardson converse about a number of topics and exchange pictures recently taken on summer vacations.
>
> 8:00 A.M. They talk about a schedule of priorities for the day.
>
> 8:20 A.M. Wilson (a subordinate) and Richardson talk about some personnel problems, cracking jokes in the process.
>
> 8:45 A.M. Richardson's secretary arrives, and they discuss her new apartment and arrangements for a meeting later in the morning.
>
> 8:55 A.M. Richardson goes to a morning meeting run by one of her subordinates. Thirty people are there, and Richardson reads during the meeting.
>
> 11:05 A.M. Richardson and her subordinates return to the office and discuss a difficult problem. They try to define the problem and outline possible alternatives. She lets the discussion roam away from and back to the topic again and again. Finally, they agree on a next step.

classical model of management Traditional description of management that focused on its formal functions of planning, organizing, coordinating, deciding, and controlling.

A corporate chief executive learns how to use a computer. Many senior managers lack computer knowledge or experience and require systems that are extremely easy to use.

In this example, it is difficult to determine which activities constitute Richardson's planning, coordinating, and decision making. **Behavioral models** state that the actual behavior of managers appears to be less systematic, more informal, less reflective, more reactive, less organized, and much more frivolous than students of information systems and decision making generally expect it to be.

behavioral models Descriptions of management based on behavioral scientists' observations of what managers actually do in their jobs.

Observers find that managerial behavior actually has five attributes that differ greatly from the classical description: First, managers perform a great deal of work at an unrelenting pace; studies have found that managers engage in more than 600 different activities each day, without breaking their pace. Second, managerial activities are fragmented; most activities take less than 9 minutes; only 10 percent of the activities exceed 1 hour in duration. Third, managers prefer speculation, hearsay, gossip; they want current, specific, and ad hoc information (printed information often will be too old). Fourth, they prefer oral forms of communication to written forms because oral media provide greater flexibility, require less effort, and bring a faster response. Fifth, managers give high priority to maintaining a diverse and complex web of contacts that acts as an informal information system.

From his real-world observations, Kotter argues that effective managers are actually involved in only three critical activities:

1. General managers spend significant time establishing personal agendas and both short- and long-term goals.

2. Perhaps most important, effective managers spend a great deal of time building an interpersonal network composed of people at virtually all organizational levels, from warehouse staff to clerical support personnel to other managers and senior management.

3. Managers use their networks to execute personal agendas to accomplish their own goals.

Analyzing managers' day-to-day behavior, Mintzberg found that it could be classified into 10 managerial roles. **Managerial roles** are expectations of the activities that managers should perform in an organization (Mintzberg, 1971 and 1973). Mintzberg found that these managerial roles fell into three categories: interpersonal, informational, and decisional.

managerial roles Expectations of the activities that managers should perform in an organization.

Interpersonal Roles Managers act as figureheads for the organization when they represent their companies to the outside world and perform symbolic duties such as giving out employee awards. Managers act as leaders attempting to motivate, counsel, and support subordinates. Managers also act as a liaison between various organizational levels; within each of these levels, they serve as a liaison among the members of the management team. Managers provide time and favors, which they expect to be returned.

interpersonal roles Mintzberg's classification for managerial roles where managers act as figureheads and leaders for the organization.

Window on Management

MANAGERS TURN TO THE INTERNET

The insurance industry today is extraordinarily competitive, requiring firms to react instantly to events in the marketplace. Superior National Insurance is pursuing a strategy of maintaining low rates by reducing costs yet improving customer service. When Superior acquired two competitors, the magnitude of this challenge increased.

Members of Superior's Claims Compliance team used to travel to the company's remote offices to ensure compliance with all requirements of the company and the state, stopping at more than 40 offices nationwide. Superior could not afford to have managers spending one to two days traveling to each site to manage the process in person. The company decided to try WebEx, a Web-based service where companies can share documents, presentations, and applications to conduct on-line meetings. Up to five people can communicate with each other using standard Web browser software. The WebEx document sharing and document viewing services are free, but the cost for up to 3 users per meeting to work together on an application over the Web is $9.95.

The Claims Compliance team uses WebEx to conduct two weekly meetings with remote offices. Hal Fedora, vice president of Claims Compliance, uses WebEx to transmit electronic presentations and share applications and documents with staff anywhere in the country. By using manager and employee time more efficiently, Superior has boosted productivity and profits.

Managers at other companies have found ways to benefit from the Internet as well. Millipore, a multinational company specializing in filtration and purification technology based in Bedford, Massachusetts, built an intranet to provide information that would help managers and employees work more efficiently. The intranet provides managers and interested employees with daily business briefings about customers and competitors. Managers can use the intranet to arrange a meeting, file an expense report, or post a job opening.

Nike Inc.'s footwear division uses a Global Product Information Network (GPIN) based on Internet technology to improve global collaboration and make its footware development process more efficient. Marketing managers can enter their production forecasts, which then flow to corporate forecasting. Designers can scan their design sketches into the system and send them electronically to managers for review. Merchandisers can review information about product lines sorted by color, price, and target audience. Senior executives can view confidential reports on the top selling items for a specific season. Ellen Devlin, product creation director for Nike's branded athletic wear, uses GPIN to show designs quickly to European and Asian partners, reducing the need for face-to-face meetings. Devlin's overseas colleagues can use GPIN to make suggestions for changes, so that face-to-face meetings are used primarily to finalize plans.

TO THINK ABOUT: How has the Internet helped these managers manage? What managerial roles do the systems described here support?

Sources: "WebEx Provides Web-based Collaboration Services for eWork Exchange," *WebEx Public Relations*, January 28, 2000; Sari Kalin, "SneakerNet," **CIO Web Business Magazine**, August 1, 1999; Natalie Engler, "Share Via the Web," **Information Week**, February 8, 1999; Mary Ryan Garcia, "Intranets Boost Productivity," **Beyond Computing**, April 1999.

---

informational roles
Mintzberg's classification for managerial roles where managers act as the nerve centers of their organizations, receiving and disseminating critical information.

decisional roles Mintzberg's classification for managerial roles where managers initiate activities, handle disturbances, allocate resources, and negotiate conflicts.

Informational Roles Managers act as the nerve centers of their organization, receiving the most concrete, up-to-date information and redistributing it to those who need to be aware of it. Managers are, therefore, information disseminators and spokespersons for their organization.

Decisional Roles Managers make decisions. They act as entrepreneurs by initiating new kinds of activities, they handle disturbances arising in the organization, they allocate resources to staff members who need them, and they negotiate conflicts and mediate between conflicting groups in the organization.

The Window on Management describes some of the ways that the Internet can support these managerial roles.

Table 3-4, based on Mintzberg's role classifications, shows where systems can and cannot help managers. The table shows that information systems do not yet contribute a great deal to important areas of management life. These areas will provide great opportunities for future systems efforts.

WebEx is a Web-based service where companies can share documents, presentations, and applications to conduct on-line meetings. Such tools can help managers broaden their span of control.

MANAGERS AND DECISION MAKING

Decision making is often a manager's most challenging role. Information systems have helped managers communicate and distribute information; however, they have provided only limited assistance for management decision making. Because decision making is an area that system designers have sought most of all to affect (with mixed success), we now turn our attention to this issue.

The Process of Decision Making

Decision making can be classified by organizational level, corresponding to the strategic, management, knowledge, and operational levels of the organization introduced in Chapter 2.

Table 3-4 **Managerial Roles and Supporting Information Systems**

Role	Behavior	Support Systems
Interpersonal Roles		
Figurehead		None exist
Leader	Interpersonal	None exist
Liaison		Electronic communication systems
Informational Roles		
Nerve center		Management information systems
Disseminator	Information	Mail, office systems
Spokesperson	processing	Office and professional systems, workstations
Decisional Roles		
Entrepreneur		None exist
Disturbance handler	Decision	None exist
Resource allocator	making	DSS systems
Negotiator		None exist

Source: Kenneth C. Laudon and Jane P. Laudon; and Mintzberg, 1971.

strategic decision making
Determining the long-term objectives, resources, and policies of an organization.

management control
Monitoring how efficiently or effectively resources are used and how well operational units are performing.

operational control Deciding how to carry out tasks specified by upper and middle management and establishing criteria for completion and resource allocation.

knowledge-level decision making Evaluating new ideas for products, services, ways to communicate new knowledge, and ways to distribute information throughout the organization.

unstructured decisions
Nonroutine decisions in which the decision maker must provide judgment, evaluation, and insights into the problem definition; there is no agreed-on procedure for making such decisions.

Strategic decision making determines the objectives, resources, and policies of the organization. Decision making for **management control** is principally concerned with how efficiently and effectively resources are used and how well operational units are performing. **Operational control** decision making determines how to carry out the specific tasks set forth by strategic and middle-management decision makers. **Knowledge-level decision making** deals with evaluating new ideas for products and services, ways to communicate new knowledge, and ways to distribute information throughout the organization.

Within each of these levels of decision making, researchers classify decisions as structured and unstructured. **Unstructured decisions** are those in which the decision maker must provide judgment, evaluation, and insights into the problem definition. Each of these decisions are novel, important, and nonroutine, and there is no well-understood or agreed-on procedure for making them (Gorry and Scott Morton, 1971). **Structured decisions,** by contrast, are repetitive and routine and involve a definite procedure for making them so that they do not have to be treated each time as if they were new. Some decisions are semistructured; in such cases, only part of the problem has a clear-cut answer provided by an accepted procedure.

Combining these two views of decision making produces the grid shown in Figure 3-14. In general, operational control personnel face fairly well-structured problems. In contrast, strategic planners tackle highly unstructured problems. Many of the problems knowledge workers encounter are fairly unstructured as well. Nevertheless, each level of the organization contains both structured and unstructured problems.

Stages of Decision Making

Making decisions consists of several different activities. Simon (1960) described four stages in decision making: intelligence, design, choice, and implementation.

Intelligence consists of identifying and understanding the problems occurring in the organization—why the problem, where, and with what effects. Traditional MIS systems that deliver a wide variety of detailed information can help identify problems, especially if the systems report exceptions.

FIGURE 3-14 Different kinds of information systems at the various organization levels support different types of decisions.
Source: G. Anthony Gorry and Michael Scott Morton, "A Framework for Management Information Systems," Sloan Management Review 13, No. 1 (Fall 1971).

	ORGANIZATIONAL LEVEL			
TYPE OF DECISION	Operational	Knowledge	Management	Strategic
Structured	Accounts receivable — TPS	Electronic scheduling — Office systems	Production cost overruns — MIS	
Semi-structured	Project scheduling		Budget preparation — DSS	Production facility location
Unstructured		KWS — Product design		ESS — New products New markets

Key:
TPS = Transaction processing system
KWS = Knowledge work system
MIS = Management information system
DSS = Decision-support system
ESS = Executive support system

During solution **design,** possible resolutions to the problems are developed. Smaller DSS systems are ideal in this stage of decision making because they operate on simple models, can be developed quickly, and can be operated with limited data.

Choice consists of selecting from among solution alternatives. Here the decision maker might need a larger DSS system to develop more extensive data on a variety of alternatives and complex models or data analysis tools to account for all of the costs, consequences, and opportunities.

During solution **implementation,** when the decision is put into effect, managers can use a reporting system that delivers routine reports on the progress of a specific solution. Support systems can range from full-blown MIS systems to much smaller systems, as well as project-planning software operating on personal computers.

The stages of decision making do not necessarily follow a linear path. Think again about the decision you made to attend a specific college. At any point in the decision-making process, you may have to loop back to a previous stage (see Figure 3-15). For instance, one can often devise several designs but may not be certain if a specific design meets the requirements for the particular problem. This situation requires additional intelligence work. Alternatively, one can be in the process of implementing a decision, only to discover that it is not working. In such a case, one is forced to repeat the design or choice stage.

Individual Models of Decision Making

A number of models attempt to describe how people make decisions. Some of these models focus on individual decision making, whereas others focus on group decision making.

The basic assumption behind individual models of decision making is that human beings are in some sense rational. The **rational model** of human behavior is built on the idea that people engage in basically consistent, rational, value-maximizing calculations. Using this model, an individual identifies goals, ranks all possible alternative actions by their contributions to those goals, and chooses the alternative that contributes most to those goals.

Criticisms of this model show that in fact people cannot specify all of the alternatives, and that most individuals do not have singular goals and so are unable to rank all alternatives

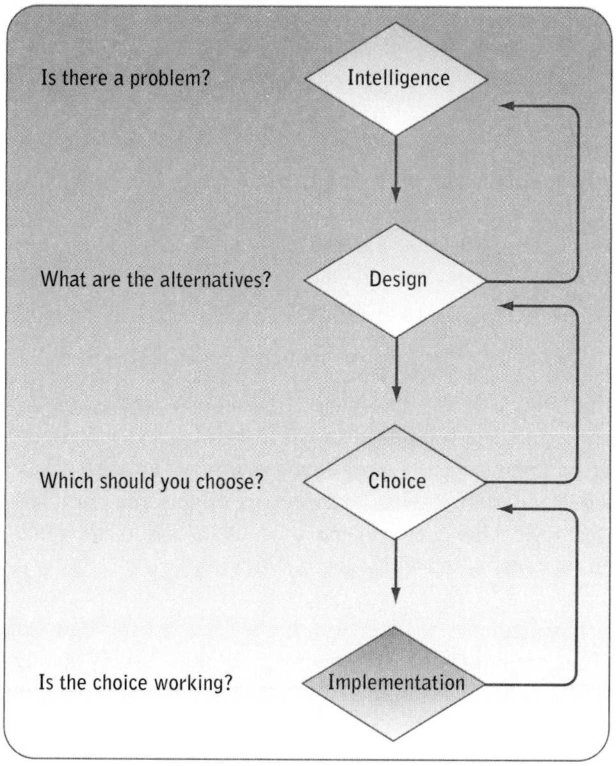

structured decisions Decisions that are repetitive, routine, and have a definite procedure for handling them.

intelligence The first of Simon's four stages of decision making, when the individual collects information to identify problems occurring in the organization.

design Simon's second stage of decision making, when the individual conceives of possible alternative solutions to a problem.

choice Simon's third stage of decision making, when the individual selects among the various solution alternatives.

implementation Simon's final stage of decision making, when the individual puts the decision into effect and reports on the progress of the solution.

rational model Model of human behavior based on the belief that people, organizations, and nations engage in basically consistent, value-maximizing calculations or adaptations within certain constraints.

FIGURE 3-15 The decision-making process. Decisions are often arrived at after a series of iterations and evaluations at each stage in the process. The decision maker often must loop back through one or more of the stages before completing the process.

and consequences. Many decisions are so complex that calculating the choice (even if done by computer) is virtually impossible. One modification to the rational model states that instead of searching through all alternatives, people actually choose the first available alternative that moves them toward their ultimate goal. Another modification to the rational model suggests that in making policy decisions people choose policies most like the previous policy (Lindblom, 1959). Finally, some scholars point out that decision making is a continuous process in which final decisions are always being modified.

Modern psychology has further qualified the rational model by research that finds that humans differ in how they maximize their values and in the frames of reference they use to interpret information and make choices. **Cognitive style** describes underlying personality dispositions toward the treatment of information, the selection of alternatives, and the evaluation of consequences. McKenney and Keen (1974) described two decision-making cognitive styles: systematic and intuitive types. **Systematic decision makers** approach a problem by structuring it in terms of some formal method. They evaluate and gather information in terms of their structured method. **Intuitive decision makers** approach a problem with multiple methods, using trial and error to find a solution. They tend not to structure information gathering or evaluation. Neither style is considered superior to the other and some people use either style, depending on the nature of the decision situation (Sauter, 1999). There are different ways of being rational. More recent psychological research shows that humans have built-in biases that can distort decision making. People can be manipulated into choosing alternatives that they might otherwise reject simply by changing the frame of reference (Tversky and Kahneman, 1981).

Organizational Models of Decision Making

Decision making often is not performed by a single individual but by entire groups or organizations. **Organizational models of decision making** take into account the structural and political characteristics of an organization. Bureaucratic, political, and even "garbage can" models have been proposed to describe how decision making takes place in organizations. We now consider each of these models.

Bureaucratic Models According to **bureaucratic models of decision making,** an organization's most important goal is the preservation of the organization itself. The reduction of uncertainty is another major goal. Policy tends to be incremental, only marginally different from the past, because radical policy departures involve too much uncertainty. These models depict organizations generally as not "choosing" or "deciding" in a rational sense. Rather, according to bureaucratic models, whatever organizations do is the result of standard operating procedures (SOPs) honed during years of active use.

Organizations rarely change these SOPs because they may have to change personnel and incur risks (who knows if the new techniques will work better than the old ones?). Although senior management and leaders are hired to coordinate and lead the organization, they are effectively trapped by the organization's standard solutions. Some organizations do, of course, change; they learn new ways of behaving, and they can be led. But all of these changes require a long time. Look around and you will find many organizations doing pretty much what they did 10, 20, or even 30 years ago.

Political Models of Organizational Choice Power in organizations is shared; even the lowest level workers have some power. In **political models of decision making,** what an organization does is a result of political bargains struck among key leaders and interest groups. Organizations do not come up with "solutions" that are "chosen" to solve some "problem." They come up with compromises that reflect the conflicts, the major stakeholders, the diverse interests, the unequal power, and the confusion that constitute politics.

"Garbage Can" Model A more recent theory of decision making, called the **"garbage can" model,** states that organizations are not rational. Decision making is largely accidental and is the product of a stream of solutions, problems, and situations that are randomly associated.

cognitive style Underlying personality dispositions toward the treatment of information, selection of alternatives, and evaluation of consequences.

systematic decision makers Cognitive style that describes people who approach a problem by structuring it in terms of some formal method.

intuitive decision makers Cognitive style that describes people who approach a problem with multiple methods in an unstructured manner, using trial and error to find a solution.

organizational models of decision making Models of decision making that take into account the structural and political characteristics of an organization.

bureaucratic models of decision making Models of decision making where decisions are shaped by the organization's standard operating procedures (SOPs).

political models of decision making Models of decision making where decisions result from competition and bargaining among the organization's interest groups and key leaders.

"garbage can" model Model of decision making that states that organizations are not rational and that decisions are solutions that become attached to problems for accidental reasons.

If this model is correct, it should not be surprising that the wrong solutions are applied to the wrong problems in an organization or that, over time, a large number of organizations make critical mistakes that lead to their demise. The Exxon Corporation's delayed response to the 1989 Alaska oil spill is an example. Within an hour after the Exxon tanker *Valdez* ran aground in Alaska's Prince William Sound on March 29, 1989, workers were preparing emergency equipment; however, the aid was not dispatched. Instead of sending out emergency crews, the Alyeska Pipeline Service Company (which was responsible for initially responding to oil spill emergencies) sent the crews home. The first full emergency crew did not arrive at the spill site until at least 14 hours after the shipwreck, by which time the oil had spread beyond effective control. Yet enough equipment and personnel had been available to respond effectively. Much of the 10 million gallons of oil fouling the Alaska shoreline in the worst tanker spill in American history could have been confined had Alyeska acted more decisively (Malcolm, 1989).

IMPLICATIONS FOR SYSTEM DESIGN

The research on decision making shows that it is not a simple process even in the rational individual model. Decision situations differ from one another in terms of the clarity of goals, the types of decision makers present, the amount of agreement among them, and the frames of reference brought to a decision-making situation. Information systems do not make the decision for humans but rather support the decision-making process. How this is done will depend on the types of decisions, decision makers, and frames of reference.

Research on organizational decision making should alert students of information systems to the fact that decision making in a business is a group and organizational process. Systems must be built to support group and organizational decision making. As a general rule, research on decision making indicates that information systems designers should design systems that have the following characteristics:

- ○ They are flexible and provide many options for handling data and evaluating information.
- ○ They are capable of supporting a variety of styles, skills, and knowledge.
- ○ They are powerful in the sense of having multiple analytical and intuitive models for the evaluation of data and the ability to keep track of many alternatives and consequences.
- ○ They reflect understanding of group and organizational processes of decision making.
- ○ They are sensitive to the bureaucratic and political requirements of systems.

MANAGEMENT WRAP-UP ◀ ·········

Information technology provides tools for managers to carry out both their traditional and newer roles, allowing them to monitor, plan, and forecast with more precision and speed than ever before and to respond more rapidly to the changing business environment. To use information technology, including the Internet, effectively, however, changes in management thinking may be required. For example, enterprise systems and industrial networks require management to take a firmwide and industry-wide view of business processes and information flows.

Management

Each organization has a unique constellation of information systems that result from its interaction with information technology. Contemporary information technology can lead to major organizational changes—and efficiencies—by reducing transaction and agency costs, but extensive changes in organizational structure, job design, and business processes often encounter resistance.

Organization

Technology

Information technology offers new ways of organizing work and information, including enterprise systems, that can promote organizational survival and prosperity. Firms must have an IT infrastructure that can support changes in structure, business processes, and information flows. Enterprise systems and industrial networks require major technology investments and planning.

For Discussion

1. It has been said that implementation of a new information system is always more difficult than anticipated. As an example, discuss some of the difficulties that might arise in developing a corporate Internet application that allows customers to order products directly instead of working through the direct sales force or the retailers who traditionally carry your products.

2. How has the Internet changed the management process?

SUMMARY

1. Identify the salient characteristics of organizations. All modern organizations are hierarchical, specialized, and impartial. They use explicit standard operating procedures to maximize efficiency. All organizations have their own culture and politics arising from differences in interest groups. Organizations differ in goals, groups served, social roles, leadership styles, incentives, surrounding environments, and business processes. Business processes are unique ways in which organizations coordinate and organize work, information, and knowledge. These differences create varying types of organizational structures.

2. Analyze the relationship between information systems and organizations. Information systems and the organizations in which they are used mutually interact with and influence each other. The introduction of a new information system will affect organizational structure, goals, work design, values, competition between interest groups, decision making, and day-to-day behavior. At the same time, information systems must be designed to serve the needs of important organizational groups and will be shaped by the organization's structure, tasks, goals, culture, politics, and management. The power of information systems to transform organizations radically by flattening organizational hierarchies has not yet been demonstrated for all types of organizations but information technology can reduce transaction and agency costs. The Internet has a potentially large impact on organizational structure and business processes because it can dramatically reduce transaction and agency costs.

3. Assess the organizational and information technology (IT) infrastructure implications of enterprise systems, industrial networks, and mergers and acquisitions. Enterprise systems integrate the key business processes of a firm into a single software system so that information can flow seamlessly throughout the organization, improving coordination, efficiency, and decision making. Industrial networks link other organizations in the same industry in a single industry-wide system. Changes in IT infrastructure are usually required to make information flow smoothly among different business processes and parts of the organization as well as between different organizations in the industry. Mergers and acquisitions are deeply affected by the organizational characteristics of the merging companies, including their underlying information systems and IT infrastructures. To implement enterprise systems, industrial networks, and systems integrations for merging companies, managers need to take a firm- and industry-wide view of problems and carefully orchestrate organizational change.

4. Contrast the classical and contemporary models of managerial activities and roles. Early classical models of management stressed the functions of planning, organizing, coordinating, deciding, and controlling. Contemporary research has examined the actual behavior of managers to show how managers get things done.

Mintzberg found that managers' real activities are highly fragmented, variegated, and brief in duration, with managers moving rapidly and intensely from one issue to another. Other behavioral research has found that managers spend considerable time pursuing personal agendas and goals and that contemporary managers shy away from making grand, sweeping policy decisions.

5. Describe how managers make decisions in organizations. Decisions can be structured, semistructured, or unstructured, with structured decisions clustering at the operational level of the organization and unstructured decisions at the strategic planning level. The nature and level of decision making are important factors in building information systems for managers.

Decision making itself is a complex activity at both the individual and the organizational level. Individual models of decision making assume that human beings can accurately choose alternatives and consequences based on the priority of their objectives and goals. The rigorous rational model of individual decision making has been modified by behavioral research that suggests that rationality is limited. People select alternatives biased by their cognitive style and frame of reference. Organizational models of decision making illustrate that real decision making in organizations takes place in arenas where many psychological, political, and bureaucratic forces are at work. Thus, organizational decision making may not necessarily be rational.

6. Assess the implications of the relationship between information systems, organizations, and management decision making for the design and implementation of information systems. Salient features of organizations that must be addressed by information systems include organizational structures, types of tasks and decisions, the nature of management support, and the sentiments and attitudes of workers who will be using the system. The organization's history and external environment must be considered as well.

Implementation of a new information system is often more difficult than anticipated because of organizational change requirements. Because information systems potentially change important organizational dimensions, including the structure, culture, power relationships, and work activities, there is often considerable resistance to new systems.

If information systems are built properly, they can support individual and organizational decision making. Up to now, information systems have been most helpful to managers for performing informational and decisional roles; the same systems have been of very limited value for managers' interpersonal roles. Information systems that are less formal and highly flexible will be more useful than large, formal systems at higher levels of the organization.

KEY TERMS

Agency theory, 85

Behavioral models, 95

Bureaucracy, 76

Bureaucratic models of decision making, 100

Business processes, 80

Chief information officer (CIO), 85

Choice, 99

Classical model of management, 94

Cognitive style, 100

Decisional roles, 96

Design, 99

End users, 85

Enterprise systems, 89

"Garbage can" model, 100

Implementation, 99

Industrial networks, 91

Information systems department, 84

Information systems managers, 84

Informational roles, 96

Intelligence, 99

Interpersonal roles, 95

Intuitive decision makers, 100

Knowledge-level decision making, 98

Management control, 98

Managerial roles, 95

Microeconomic model of the firm, 85

Operational control, 98

Organization, 75

Organizational culture, 78

Organizational models of decision making, 100

Political models of decision making, 100

Programmers, 84

Rational model, 99

Standard operating procedures (SOPs), 77

Strategic decision making, 98

Structured decisions, 99

Systematic decision makers, 100

Systems analysts, 84

Transaction cost theory, 85

Unstructured decisions, 98

REVIEW QUESTIONS

1. What is an organization? Compare the technical definition of organizations with the behavioral definition.

2. What features do all organizations have in common?

3. In what ways can organizations differ?

4. What is a business process? Give two views and two examples.

5. How has information technology (IT) infrastructure in organizations evolved over time?

6. How are information technology services delivered in organizations? Describe the role played by programmers, systems analysts, information systems managers, and the chief information officer (CIO).

7. Describe the major economic theories that help explain how information systems affect organizations.

8. Describe the major behavioral theories that help explain how information systems affect organizations.

9. Why is there considerable organizational resistance to the introduction of information systems?

10. What are enterprise systems and industrial networks? How do they change the flow of information in organizations?

11. What role do information systems and IT infrastructure play in mergers and acquisitions?

12. Compare the descriptions of managerial behavior in the classical and behavioral models.

13. What specific managerial roles can information systems support? Where are information systems particularly strong in supporting managers, and where are they weak?

14. Define structured and unstructured decisions. Give three examples of each.

15. What are the four stages of decision making described by Simon?

16. Describe each of the organizational models of decision making. How would the design of systems be affected by the choice of model employed?

17. What is the impact of the Internet on organizations and the process of management?

GROUP PROJECT

With a group of three or four students, select a company described in *The Wall Street Journal, Forbes,* or another business publication. Visit the company's Web site to find out additional information about that company and to see how the firm is using the Web. On the basis of this information, describe some of the organization's features, such as important business processes, culture, structure, and environment. Assess the impact of this Web site on the organization. Is the Web site helping the company reduce transaction costs? What impact is it having, if any, on the firm's business processes? Present your findings to the class.

Tools for Interactive Learning

○ Internet Connection

The Internet Connection for this chapter will take you to a Web site where you can view an interactive demonstration of an intranet. You can complete an exercise to evaluate how companies can use intranets to reduce agency costs and make the management process more efficient. You can also use the Interactive Study Guide to test your knowledge of the topics in this chapter and get instant feedback when you need more practice.

○ Electronic Commerce Project

At the Laudon Web site for Chapter 3, you will find an Electronic Commerce project that will use the interactive software at the Travel Web site to help a company with sales planning.

○ CD-ROM

If you purchase and use the Multimedia Edition CD-ROM with this chapter, you will find an interactive exercise asking you to apply the correct model of organizational decision making to solve a series of problems. You can also find a video clip illustrating the role of information systems management at the Pillsbury Company, an audio overview of the major themes of this chapter, and bullet text summarizing the key points of the chapter.

○ Application Exercise

At the Laudon Web site, you can find a spreadsheet Application Exercise for this chapter where you can analyze alternative financing options for a small business.

The financial world was shaken on April 5, 1998, when Citicorp and the Travelers Group announced they would merge to form Citigroup. The merger was one of the largest in history, with combined assets of $700 billion, net revenues of nearly $50 billion, a combined equity of more than $44 billion, an operating income of approximately $7.5 billion, about 150,000 employees, and more than 100 million customers. Citigroup is the largest financial services company in the world.

By combining two different types of financial businesses, Citigroup can operate as a powerhouse in traditional banking, consumer finance (including home mortgages), credit cards, savings and IRA plans, investment banking, securities brokerage, asset management, and property, casualty, and life insurance. The merger provides Citigroup with a dramatically enlarged client base and extensive domestic and international distribution channels.

Until recently, a financial company embracing such a broad business spectrum was illegal in the United States. The Glass-Steagall Act, passed in 1932, prohibited commercial banks, insurance companies, and securities firms from entering each others' businesses. The Citigroup merger went into effect in October 1998, anticipating the congressional repeal of the Glass-Steagall Act on November 4, 1999.

THE MERGING COMPANIES: CITICORP AND TRAVELERS

Citicorp is one of the largest banks in the world and is the world's largest issuer of bankcards with more than 60 million active cards in 1998. It has a major global reach, with more than 1,000 bank locations in more than 40 countries around the world, plus banking services in about 60 other countries. The bank also specializes in transaction and funding services both for global corporations and for growth companies in emerging market areas.

The Travelers Group is best known as an insurance company, but it is much more. Among its subsidiaries is Salomon Smith Barney, a major Wall Street brokerage firm. It is also the parent of Salomon Smith Barney Asset Management, Travelers Life & Annuity, Primerica Financial Services, and Travelers Property Casualty Corp. The

Travelers Group specializes in investment services, asset management, consumer lending, life insurance, and property casualty insurance.

A STUDY IN CONTRASTS

Citicorp and Travelers have two fundamental principles in common: First, both have a core commitment to customer service; second, in this age of globalization both companies have a desire for a major global reach. However, their differences are numerous.

○ Global reach: Citicorp is a leader in electronic commerce, using it as a basic underpinning of its strategy to offer round-the-clock service all over the globe. However, Travelers has a relatively limited reach globally.
○ Domestic reach: Despite Citicorp's great international product and service distribution systems, within the United States Citicorp is just another important bank that falls far short of achieving nationwide coverage. Travelers, however, has 80,000 people selling its products in homes and offices throughout the United States.
○ Customer base: Citicorp has a younger, less affluent customer base, whereas Travelers' customer base is older and more affluent.
○ Sales channels: Citicorp is strong at mail, telephone, bankcards, and branches, whereas Travelers' strength is in personal, often home, sales staff selling.
○ Product offerings: Although both corporations are part of the financial industry, they offer very different products, with little overlap.
○ Customer asset management: Although Citicorp is a bank, it is weak in asset management, whereas Travelers is a major asset manager, with more than $200 billion in mutual funds.
○ Technology: Citicorp stresses the development and use of advanced, innovative technology and is a leader in electronic banking services. Travelers, however, has a decided preference for low-cost, no-frills systems.

○ Centralization and standardization: Finally, although both companies are working toward centralized information systems, Travelers, particularly Salomon Smith Barney, is much more advanced in standardizing and integrating its systems than is Citicorp.

WHY THE MERGER?

The basic concept driving Citigroup is as a one-stop financial supermarket. It will be a customer-centered organization that offers a wide variety of product lines that can be cross-marketed and cross-sold to its customers.

Most people purchase different financial services from different companies. A person will bank with one company, buy life insurance elsewhere, handle investments with a third company, and may even have a home mortgage with a fourth company. As the two firms become integrated, Travelers' agents will be able to offer a whole set of Citicorp products to their current customers, and Citicorp employees likewise will have a new set of Travelers products to offer. For example, Travelers' agents could sell mutual funds and auto and life insurance to Citicorp customers, and Citicorp could sell home equity loans and bankcards to Travelers customers. Travelers gains globalization, and Citicorp secures an expanded presence in the United States.

Both companies believe that as a single company they will be able to expand dramatically their customer base. In April 1998 Citicorp executive vice president, Edward Horowitz, announced a goal of 1 billion customers worldwide for Citigroup by 2010, a 10-fold increase. They will rely heavily on electronic connections such as online banking and electronic commerce services.

Management also sees opportunities for cost savings through improved and efficient customer service, and reduced overhead and distribution costs. Citicorp claims its Asia-Pacific credit and bankcard costs per transaction have fallen dramatically through centralized backroom processing. Some also see vast savings by standardizing and integrating their information technology. Diogo Teixeira, president of Tower Group, estimates that the combined organizations can save about $700 million annually in IT costs. He believes the one-time cost of the IT merger will be about $100 million, thus leaving vast funds available for new IT investment.

WILL CROSS-SELLING BE A SUCCESSFUL BUSINESS STRATEGY?

Critics of the merger point to repeated past cross-selling failures, including attempts in the 1980s by Sears and American Express. Studies indicate that only about 20 percent of all financial services customers bundle their services with one provider.

Today the opportunities for cross-selling may be more limited than ever before because customer choices have multiplied. The Internet is now making comparison shopping for financial services quick and easy. Potential customers shop on-line from the comfort of home, comparing services and costs, making decisions, and even entering transactions. On-line banks are beginning to appear (see the Chapter 1 Case Study), and brokerage houses with on-line facilities, such as Charles Schwab and E*Trade, are taking business from traditional brokerage houses. The question analysts ask is, why would most people buy their financial products from one place when they can easily do better by selecting the best products for themselves?

MERGING TWO CULTURES

Cultural differences are fundamental and must be addressed if the merger is to succeed. Citicorp and Travelers concepts and practices regarding pay structure are quite different. Citicorp compensates its bank officers and executives much as other banks do. It has about 1,100 corporate calling officers of whom only three earned more than $1 million in 1997. Citicorp uses grants of restricted Citicorp stock to reward and hold onto its high-level people. In addition, Citicorp does not require its officers and board members to be significant shareholders. As a result the officers and directors combined owned less than one-half of 1 percent of the company's stock, giving them only a minimal financial stake in the future success of the company. Travelers views compensation very differently. First, Salomon Smith Barney, its brokerage and investment banking company, has about 1,000 investment bankers of whom about 150 were paid more than $1 million in 1997. In addition, Travelers offers bountiful stock option grants and binds its executives' fortunes tightly to that of the company by including stringent restrictions on their right to sell their stock. Travelers CEO Sanford Weill personally owned 1.3 percent of Travelers' shares, and the other officers and directors combined owned another 1.1 percent.

The two companies also differ on compensation for back-office operations. Back-office pay traditionally is high in investment banking firms like Salomon because the staff works on sophisticated, highly speculative, derivative products. At Citicorp the back-office pay is much lower because they work on less intricate products such as check processing.

Many analysts fear that such different pay structures will destroy the morale of many employees, and they believe it is essential to achieve a unified approach. But this may not be possible. Travelers cannot cut its investment banking salaries and stock options and still compete in hiring and retaining top employees. Yet Citicorp CEO John Reed argues that stock options are not appropriate for a global organization with many foreign senior managers because options are strange to most foreigners.

Risk-taking is another area of sharp cultural contrast. Citicorp has been much more risk-averse than Travelers. Citicorp trades stocks, bonds, and currencies for its clients but not for its own account, whereas Salomon takes large trading positions for its own account.

OTHER NONTECHNICAL MERGER PROBLEMS

Still other problems exist. History at both companies shows that their business units have been unwilling to share proprietary customer data for cross-selling even within their own companies. This has made integration of each business's own units very difficult. For instance, although Travelers acquired Shearson Lehman Brothers in 1993 and Salomon Brothers in 1997, the two units continue to operate separately. Citicorp also has struggled for years to integrate its disparate financial systems in order to develop cross-selling opportunities. Bankers on both sides of the merger appear concerned about sharing customers in case the merger does not work out.

INTEGRATING INFORMATION TECHNOLOGY INFRASTRUCTURE

Some analysts even say that success or failure of the financial services supermarket will depend on how well the two companies' information technology infrastructures and information architectures can be integrated. Creating a financial services supermarket requires integrating information systems, customer databases, product lines, and multiple transaction types. Yet both Citicorp and Travelers have very different information architectures, with applications, databases, and processes that are based on very different business models.

Over the years, Citicorp built up a very decentralized information architecture by allowing its business units to have a great deal of local autonomy. Many of its information systems are fragmented, with traders and their offices spread worldwide using different computers and applications. Citicorp's information technology infrastructure has about 20,000 different pieces of technology throughout the world. Salomon Smith Barney's systems are somewhat more integrated and centrally managed, although they are smaller and locally based.

Experts point out two ways of handling the information technology issues associated with the merger. One is to emulate Morgan Stanley and Dean Witter, which did not integrate their business and services when they merged, keeping two primary dealers, sales forces, and trading desks. The other alternative is to integrate both companies as tightly as possible. The question is whether Citigroup could cross-sell products and become a financial supermarket without this full IT integration.

All financial service organizations are information-dependent because they generate and store immense quantities of data that have been described as "the jewels of the company." Such data are vital not only for customer sharing, but also for data-mining to create tailored marketing and sales efforts. By pooling customer data from all of its business units, Citigroup could target banking customers who, for example, might be interested in insurance or investment services.

In 1997, combined Travelers and Citicorp IT spending amounted to $6.8 billion, an enormous expense. The payoffs from integration could be significant. For instance, once the systems are merged, future development costs for Internet-based marketing and transaction systems or other capabilities would be shared. In addition to product-related systems, it is likely the two companies could combine other systems, such as accounting and billing systems, marketing and sales, to achieve even greater savings.

Citicorp has been trying to centralize many of its systems for years and only now is achieving some success. For example, the bank has succeeded only recently in centralizing the processing of bankcards in Asia-Pacific after many years of effort. (See International Case Study 4.) Citicorp finally consolidated its numerous wide area networks into one centrally managed network. It recently had to resort to outside help, signing a five-year, $750 million contract with AT&T to outsource its networking in 98 countries worldwide. Travelers is further along with integrating its systems.

Citigroup could opt for total systems integration, creating common hardware and software platforms, risk management software, and back-office operations. But building a standard IT infrastructure serving all of its organizations would require both massive expenditures and organizational changes. Alternatively, it could keep separate IT infrastructures but create a central data repository for customer information that could be used for cross-selling. The data repository would be populated with customer data from both Travelers and Citicorp units, but both organizations could continue with their own systems and business processes. This is more expedient and less disruptive to the organization, but analysts suggest that complete system integration would be required to realize the full range of benefits of a financial supermarket with efficient risk management.

The two companies use technologically disparate trading systems. Citicorp uses Reuters' Triarch 2000, whereas Salomon Smith Barney relies primarily on TIB (Tibco Finance) systems (also owned by Reuters but operated independently). Salomon also makes some use of Triarch as well as FS Partner, a mixture that is the result of the 1997 Salomon-Smith Barney merger. Other systems at both companies are based on disparate hardware and software standards and cannot be integrated easily. Questions being asked include: Do the various units have the short run will to move to a single technology in order to bring about major long run cost savings? If so, how much money are the two companies willing to spend on the transition? Can both companies overcome cultural differences relating to centralization and the use of cutting-edge technology?

If the two companies do move to standardize their systems, power struggles and personnel problems will surely emerge. The dynamic between the IT department's desire to standardize and the desire of the business groups to customize is complex and difficult to deal with. IT personnel problems also are a real possibility because of a fear of layoffs. Both companies announced massive layoffs just a month prior to their legal merger and more are being planned. Many are wondering whether an IT merger can or should ever take place.

Sources: Paul Beckett, "Banks Still Seek Big Payoff in Online Services," **The Wall Street Journal**, January 21, 2000; Joseph Kahn, "Financial Services Industry Faces a New World," **The New York Times**, October 23, 1999; Tara Siegel, "Citigroup Is Ready to Realize Benefits of Cross-Selling," **The Wall Street Journal**, March 15, 1999; Paul Beckett and Thomas Hoffman, "Citigroup Cuts to Pinch IT Support Staff," **Computerworld**, December 21, 1998; Erik Helland, "Can Citigroup Reign in Citicorp's Decentralized Strategy," **Wall Street and Technology**, July 1998; Robert Sales, "A Battle Brews on Citigroup Trading Floor," **The Wall Street and Technology**, July 1998; Ivy Schmerken, "The Big Gamble: Mergers and Technology," **Wall Street and Technology**, July 1998; Saul Hansell, "Clash of Technologies in Merger," **The New York Times**, April 13, 1998, and "Citibank Sets New On-Line Bank System," **The New York Times**, October 5, 1998; Michael Schrage, "IT and the Citigroup Gamble," **Computerworld**, April 27, 1998; Thomas Hoffman and Kim S. Nash, "Titanic Tangle," **Computerworld**, April 13, 1998; Lawrence Quinn, "If the Systems Fit, So Must the Corporate Cultures," **Wall Street and Technology**, July 1998; Beth Davis and Rich Levin, "Bank Shot," **Information Week**, April 20, 1998; Stephen E. Frank, Anita Raghavan, and Matt Murray, "Travelers and Citicorp Agree to Join Forces in $83 Billion Merger," **The Wall Street Journal**, April 7, 1998; Mary Kelleher, Anita Raghavan, and Stephen E. Frank, "Making Oil and Water (Citicorp, Travelers Group) Mix," **The Wall Street Journal**, April 17, 1998; Richard W. Stevenson, "In Largest Deal Ever, Citicorp Plans Merger with Travelers Group," **The New York Times**, April 7, 1998; and "Travelers and Citicorp Plan to Cut Jobs," **The New York Times**, September 18, 1998.

CASE STUDY QUESTIONS

1. What is the business strategy of Citigroup? How is the merger of Citicorp and Travelers related to this business strategy?

2. How is information technology vital to the success of Citigroup's strategy?

3. What management, organization, and technology issues must be addressed by the Citigroup merger?

4. List each of the factors that will be key to a successful integration of Citicorp and Travelers. Explain why each is so important.

CHAPTER 4

Computers and Information Processing

Learning Objectives

After completing this chapter, you will be able to:

1. Identify the hardware components in a typical computer system.

2. Describe how information is represented and processed in a computer system.

3. Describe the principal media for storing data and programs in a computer system.

4. Describe the major input and output devices, approaches to input and processing, and interactive multimedia.

5. Contrast the capabilities of mainframes, midrange computers, PCs, workstations, servers, and supercomputers.

6. Compare different arrangements of computer processing, including the use of client/server computing and network computers.

7. Analyze important hardware technology trends.

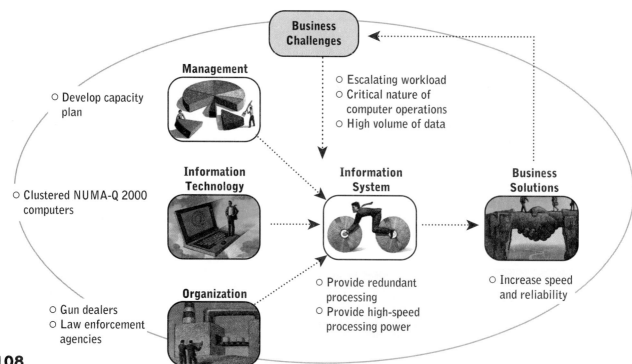

Business Challenges

Management
- Develop capacity plan

○ Escalating workload
○ Critical nature of computer operations
○ High volume of data

Information Technology
- Clustered NUMA-Q 2000 computers

Information System
○ Provide redundant processing
○ Provide high-speed processing power

Business Solutions
○ Increase speed and reliability

Organization
○ Gun dealers
○ Law enforcement agencies

Which Computer Is Right for the California Department of Justice?

The California Department of Justice (CDJ) had to make a major decision about its computer systems. In late 1997, the department realized it needed a larger, faster computer to accommodate its growing workload. With so many different computers to choose from, which was the best one to buy?

The CDJ computers ran several critical systems for law enforcement, including the state's Consolidated Firearms Information System, which gun dealers use to screen and approve customers wishing to purchase guns. The CDJ's

computer had to provide high-speed processing for large amounts of data, and it also had to be up and running all the time. Could the CDJ find a computer with the raw processing horsepower and reliability it needed?

The CDJ considered both a parallel processing system and a system using multiple computers clustered together. Both provide processing speed, but with trade-offs. Clustered computers are connected in a group in a way that allows them to work as a single, continuously available system. For additional cost, clustering provides a high level of availability of processing resources by providing duplicate processors, interconnections, storage, and controllers. This redundancy enables processing work to continue if one or more components in the cluster fail.

A parallel processing system with symmetric multiprocessing, in contrast, uses multiple processors housed in a single physical cabinet. Parallel systems provide more processing power than single processor systems or single processor computers that are clustered but do not have the built-in redundancy of clustered computers. If one of their components fails, the entire system can go down. However, parallel systems are more appropriate for very large computing tasks where a lot of horsepower is required.

The California Department of Justice resolved its dilemma by creating clusters of multiple parallel processing systems. (Some parallel systems can be clustered together.) The agency installed a clustered pair of Sequent NUMA-Q 2000 systems from IBM. NUMA (Non-Uniform Memory Access) technology can support up to 64 Intel central processing units (CPUs) functioning as one system without degrading performance. Each of these systems has four Pentium microprocessors. If one computer fails, work is automatically routed to the other computer to continue processing.

Sources: John Edwards, "Speedy Systems Become a Blur," *CIO Magazine*, August 1, 1999 and Martin J. Garvey and Eileen Collin with Tanvi Chveda, "IBM Acquires Sequent," *Information Week*, July 19, 1999.

CHAPTER OUTLINE

By shifting to clustered parallel processing computers, the California Department of Justice was able to provide more computing power for its operations. To select the right computer, the CDJ's management needed to understand how much computer processing capacity its business processes required and how to evaluate the price and performance of various types of computers. Management also had to plan for future processing requirements and understand how the computer worked with related storage, input/output, and communications technology in its IT infrastructure. Selecting appropriate computer hardware raises the following management challenges:

1. The centralization vs. decentralization debate. A long-standing issue among information system managers and CEOs has been the question of how much to centralize or distribute computing resources. Should processing power and data be distributed to departments and divisions, or should they be concentrated at a single location using a large central computer? Client/server computing facilitates decentralization, but network computers and mainframes support a centralized model. Which is the best for the organization? Each organization will have a different answer based on its own needs. Managers need to make sure that the computing model they select is compatible with organizational goals.

2. Making wise technology purchasing decisions. Soon after making an investment in information technology, managers often find the completed system obsolete and too expensive, given the power and lower cost of newer technology. In this environment it is difficult to keep one's own systems up to date. A considerable amount of time must be spent anticipating and planning for technological change.

Successful use of information systems to support an organization's business goals requires an understanding of computer processing power and the capabilities of hardware devices. By understanding the role of hardware technology in the firm's information technology (IT) infrastructure, managers ensure their firms have the processing capability they need to accomplish the work of the firm and to meet future business challenges.

In this chapter we describe the typical hardware configuration of a computer system, explaining how a computer works and how computer processing power and storage capacity are measured. We then compare the capabilities of various types of computers and related input, output, and storage devices.

4.1 What Is a Computer System?

A contemporary computer system consists of a central processing unit (CPU), primary storage, secondary storage, input devices, output devices, and communications devices (see Figure 4-1). The central processing unit manipulates raw data into a useful form and controls the other parts of the computer system. Primary storage temporarily stores data and program instructions during processing, whereas secondary storage devices (magnetic and optical disks and magnetic tape) store data and programs when they are not being used in processing. Input devices, such as a keyboard or mouse, convert data and instructions into electronic form for input into the computer. Output devices, such as printers and video display terminals, convert electronic data produced by the computer system and display them in a form that people can

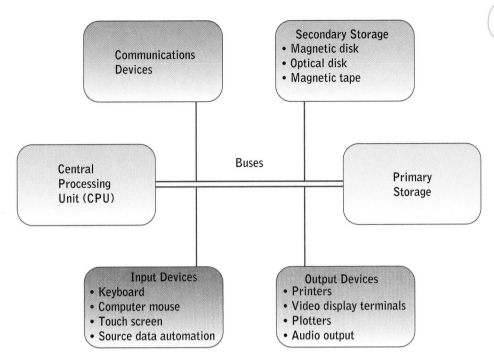

FIGURE 4-1 Hardware components of a computer system. A contemporary computer system can be categorized into six major components. The central processing unit manipulates data and controls the other parts of the computer system; primary storage temporarily stores data and program instructions during processing; secondary storage feeds data and instructions into the central processor and stores data for future use; input devices convert data and instructions for processing in the computer; output devices present data in a form that people can understand; and communications devices control the passing of information to and from communications networks.

understand. Communications devices provide connections between the computer and communications networks. Buses are circuitry paths for transmitting data and signals among the parts of the computer system.

HOW COMPUTERS REPRESENT DATA

In order for information to flow through a computer system in a form suitable for processing, all symbols, pictures, or words must be reduced to a string of binary digits. A binary digit is called a **bit** and represents either a 0 or a 1. In the computer, the presence of an electronic or magnetic signal means one, and its absence signifies zero. Digital computers operate directly with binary digits, either singly or strung together to form bytes. A string of eight bits that the computer stores as a unit is called a **byte.** Each byte can be used to store a decimal number, a symbol, a character, or part of a picture (see Figure 4-2).

bit A binary digit representing the smallest unit of data in a computer system. It can only have one of two states, representing 0 or 1.

byte A string of bits, usually eight, used to store one number or character in a computer system.

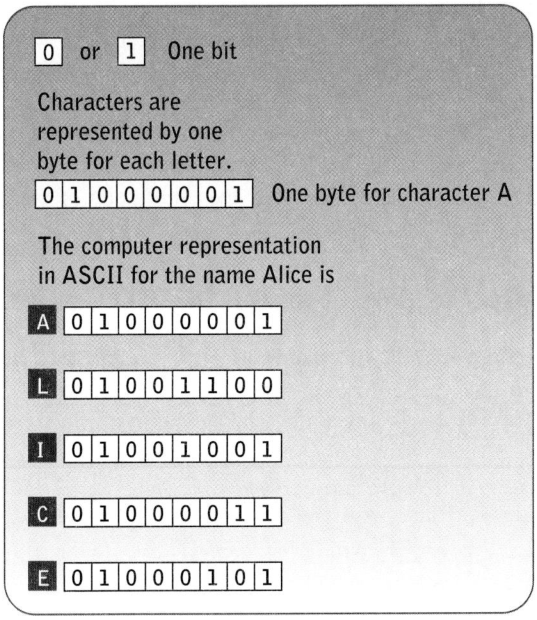

FIGURE 4-2 Bits and bytes. Bits are represented by either a 0 or 1. A string of eight bits constitutes a byte, which represents a character here. The computer's representation for the word "ALICE" is a series of five bytes, where each byte represents one character (or letter) in the name.

FIGURE 4-3 The binary number system. Each decimal number has a certain value that can be expressed as a binary number. The binary number system can express any number as a power of the number 2.

10100, which is equal to:

$$0 \times 2^0 = 0$$
$$0 \times 2^1 = 0$$
$$1 \times 2^2 = 4$$
$$0 \times 2^3 = 0$$
$$1 \times 2^4 = \underline{16}$$
$$20$$

Place	5	4	3	2	1
Power of 2	2^4	2^3	2^2	2^1	2^0
Decimal value	16	8	4	2	1

EBCDIC (Extended Binary Coded Decimal Interchange Code) Binary code representing every number, alphabetic character, or special character with eight bits, used primarily in IBM and other mainframe computers.

ASCII (American Standard Code for Information Interchange) A seven- or eight-bit binary code used in data transmission, PCs, and some large computers.

pixel The smallest unit of data for defining an image in the computer. The computer reduces a picture to a grid of pixels. The term pixel comes from picture element.

central processing unit (CPU) Area of the computer system that manipulates symbols, numbers, and letters, and controls the other parts of the computer system.

Figure 4-3 shows how decimal numbers are represented using binary digits. Each position in a decimal number has a certain value. Any number in the decimal system (base 10) can be reduced to a binary number. The binary number system (base 2) can express any number as a power of the number 2. The table at the bottom of the figure shows how the translation from binary to decimal works. Using a binary number system a computer can express all numbers as groups of zeroes and ones. In addition to representing numbers, a computer must represent alphabetic characters and many other symbols used in natural language, such as $ and &. Manufacturers of computer hardware have developed standard binary codes for this purpose.

Two common codes are EBCDIC and ASCII. The **Extended Binary Coded Decimal Interchange Code (EBCDIC**—pronounced ib-si-dick) was developed by IBM in the 1950s, and it represents every number, alphabetic character, or special character with eight bits. **ASCII,** which stands for the **American Standard Code for Information Interchange,** was developed by the American National Standards Institute (ANSI) to provide a standard code that could be used by many different manufacturers in order to make machinery compatible. ASCII was originally designed as a seven-bit code, but most computers use eight-bit versions. EBCDIC is used in IBM and other mainframe computers, whereas ASCII is used in data transmission, PCs, and some larger computers. Table 4-1 shows how some letters and numbers would be represented using EBCDIC and ASCII. Other coding systems are being developed to represent a wide array of foreign languages.

How can a computer represent a picture? The computer stores a picture by creating a grid overlay of the picture. Each single point in this grid, or matrix, is called a **pixel** (picture element) and consists of a number of bits, which the computer stores on each pixel. A high-resolution computer display monitor has a 1024×768 SVGA (supervideo graphics array) standard grid, creating more than 700,000 pixels. Whether processing pictures or text, modern computers operate by reducing such data into bits and bytes.

THE CPU AND PRIMARY STORAGE

The **central processing unit** (CPU) is the part of the computer system where the manipulation of symbols, numbers, and letters occurs, and it controls the other parts of the computer

Table 4-1 Examples of ASCII and EBCDIC Codes

Character or Number	ASCII-8 Binary	EBCDIC Binary
A	01000001	11000001
E	01000101	11000101
Z	01011010	11101001
0	00110000	11110000
1	00110001	11110001
5	00110101	11110101

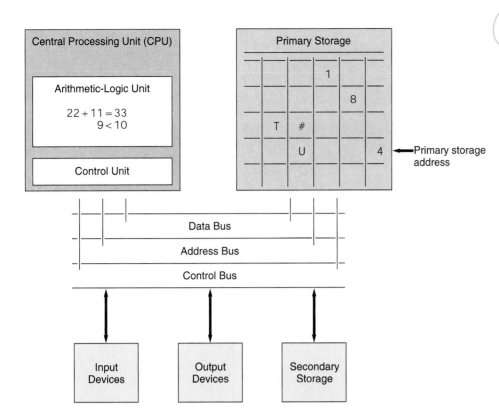

FIGURE 4-4 The CPU and primary storage. The CPU contains an arithmetic-logic unit and a control unit. Data and instructions are stored in unique addresses in primary storage that the CPU can access during processing. The data bus, address bus, and control bus transmit signals between the CPU, primary storage, and other devices in the computer system.

system (see Figure 4-4). Located near the CPU is **primary storage** (sometimes called primary memory or main memory) where data and program instructions are stored temporarily during processing. Three kinds of buses link the CPU, primary storage, and the other devices in the computer system. The data bus moves data to and from primary storage. The address bus transmits signals for locating a given address in primary storage indicating where data should be placed. The control bus transmits signals specifying whether to read or write data to or from a given primary storage address, input device, or output device. The characteristics of the CPU and primary storage are very important in determining a computer's speed and capabilities.

primary storage Part of the computer that temporarily stores program instructions and data being used by the instructions.

The Arithmetic-Logic Unit and Control Unit

Figure 4-4 also shows that the CPU consists of an arithmetic-logic unit and a control unit. The **arithmetic-logic unit (ALU)** performs the computer's principal logical and arithmetical operations. It adds, subtracts, multiplies, divides, and determines whether a number is positive, negative, or zero. In addition to performing arithmetical functions, an ALU must be able to determine when one quantity is greater than or less than another and when two quantities are equal. The ALU performs logic operations on the binary codes for letters as well as numbers.

The **control unit** coordinates and controls the other parts of the computer system. It reads a stored program one instruction at a time and directs other components of the computer system to perform the program's required tasks. The series of operations required to process a single machine instruction is called the **machine cycle.** As illustrated in Figure 4-5, the machine cycle has two parts: an instruction cycle and an execution cycle.

During the instruction cycle, the control unit retrieves one program instruction from primary storage and decodes it so the CPU can understand what to do. It places the part of the instruction telling the ALU what to do next in a special instruction register and places the part specifying the address of the data to be used in the operation into an address register. A **register** is a special temporary storage location in the ALU or control unit that acts like a high-speed staging area for program instructions or data being transferred from primary storage to the CPU for processing.

During the execution cycle, the control unit locates the required data in primary storage, places it in a storage register, instructs the ALU to perform the desired operation, temporarily

arithmetic-logic unit (ALU) Component of the CPU that performs the computer's principal logical and arithmetical operations.

control unit Component of the CPU that controls and coordinates the other parts of the computer system.

machine cycle Series of operations required to process a single machine instruction.

register Temporary storage location in the ALU or control unit where small amounts of data and instructions reside just before use.

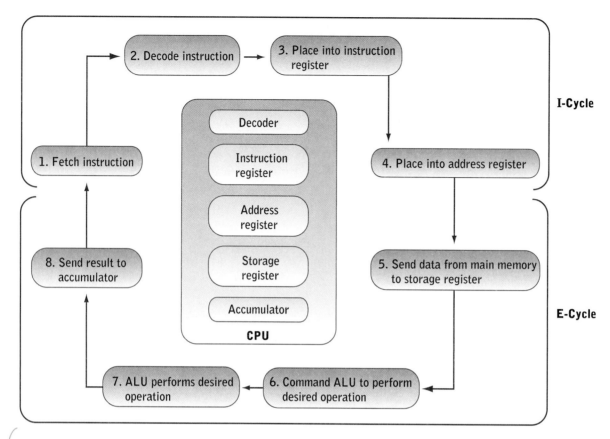

FIGURE 4-5 The various steps in the machine cycle. The machine cycle has two main stages of operation: the instruction cycle (I-cycle) and the execution cycle (E-cycle). There are several steps within each cycle required to process a single machine instruction in the CPU.

stores the result of the operation in an accumulator, and finally places the result in primary memory. As each instruction is completed, the control unit advances to and reads the next instruction of the program.

microsecond One-millionth of a second.

Older computers and PCs have machine cycle times measured in **microseconds** (one-millionth of a second). More powerful machines have machine cycle times measured in **nanoseconds** (billionths of a second) or picoseconds (trillionths of a second). Another measure of machine cycle time is by MIPS (millions of instructions per second).

nanosecond One-billionth of a second.

Primary Storage

Primary storage has three functions: (1) It stores all or part of the program that is being executed. (2) It stores the operating system programs that manage the operation of the computer. (These programs are discussed in Chapter 5.) And (3) it holds data that the program is using. Data and programs are placed in primary storage before processing, between processing steps, and after processing has ended prior to being returned to secondary storage or released as output.

Figure 4-5 illustrates primary storage in an electronic digital computer. Internal primary storage is often called **RAM,** or **random access memory,** because it can directly access any randomly chosen location in the same amount of time.

RAM (random access memory) Primary storage of data or program instructions that can directly access any randomly chosen location in the same amount of time.

Figure 4-6 shows that primary memory is divided into storage locations called bytes. Each location contains a set of eight binary switches or devices, each of which can store one bit of information. The set of eight bits found in each storage location is sufficient to store one letter, one digit, or one special symbol (such as $) using either EBCDIC or ASCII. Each byte has a unique address, similar to a mailbox, indicating where it is located in RAM. The computer remembers where the data in all of the bytes are located simply by keeping track of these addresses.

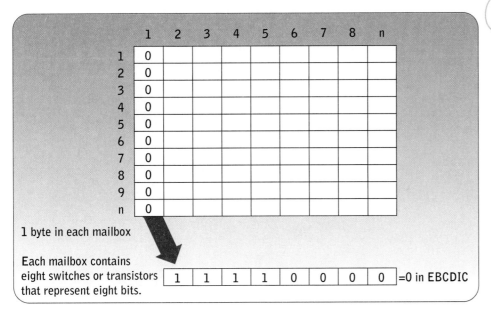

FIGURE 4-6 Primary storage in the computer. Primary storage can be visualized as a matrix. Each byte represents a mailbox with a unique address. In this example, mailbox [n,1] contains eight bits representing the number 0 (as coded in EBCDIC).

Computer storage capacity is measured in bytes. Table 4-2 lists computer storage capacity measurements. One thousand bytes (actually 1,024 storage positions) is called a **kilobyte.** One million bytes is called a **megabyte** and one billion bytes is called a **gigabyte.**

Most of the information used by a computer application is stored on secondary storage devices, such as disks and tapes, located outside of the primary storage area. In order for the computer to work on information, information must be transferred into primary memory for processing. Therefore, data are continually being read into and written out of the primary storage area while a program executes.

Primary storage is composed of semiconductors. A **semiconductor** is an integrated circuit made by printing thousands and often millions of tiny transistors on a small silicon chip. There are several different kinds of semiconductor memory used in primary storage. RAM is used for short-term storage of data or program instructions. RAM is volatile: Its contents will be lost when the computer's electric supply is disrupted by a power outage or when the computer is turned off. **ROM,** or **read-only memory,** can only be read from; it cannot be written to. ROM chips come from the manufacturer with programs already burned in, or stored. ROM is used in general-purpose computers to store important or frequently used programs, such as computing routines for calculating the square roots of numbers.

MICROPROCESSORS AND PROCESSING POWER

Contemporary CPUs also use semiconductor chips called **microprocessors,** which integrate all of the memory, logic, and control circuits for an entire CPU on a single chip. The speed and performance of a computer's microprocessors help determine a computer's processing power. Some popular microprocessors are listed in Table 4-3. You may have heard of chips labeled 16-bit, 32-bit, or 64-bit devices. These labels refer to the **word length,** or the number of bits that the computer can process at one time. A 16-bit chip can process 16 bits, or 2 bytes, of

kilobyte One thousand bytes (actually 1,024 storage positions).

megabyte Approximately one million bytes. Unit of computer storage capacity.

gigabyte Approximately one billion bytes. Unit of computer storage capacity.

semiconductor An integrated circuit made by printing thousands and often millions of tiny transistors on a small silicon chip.

ROM (read-only memory) Semiconductor memory chips that contain program instructions. These chips can only be read from; they cannot be written to.

microprocessor Very large scale circuit technology that integrates the computer's memory, logic, and control on a single chip.

word length The number of bits that the computer can process at one time. The larger the word length, the greater the computer's speed.

Table 4-2 Computer Storage Capacity

Byte	String of eight bits
Kilobyte	1000 bytes*
Megabyte	1,000,000 bytes
Gigabyte	1,000,000,000 bytes
Terabyte	1,000,000,000,000 bytes

*Actually 1,024 storage positions

The Pentium III microprocessor contains more than nine million transistors and provides mainframe and supercomputer-like processing capabilities.

information in a single machine cycle. A 32-bit chip can process 32 bits or 4 bytes in a single cycle and a 64-bit chip can process 64 bits or 8 bytes in a single cycle. The larger the word length, the greater the computer's speed.

A second factor affecting chip speed is cycle speed. Every event in a computer must be sequenced so that one step logically follows another. The control unit sets a beat for the chip. This beat is established by an internal clock and is measured in **megahertz** (abbreviated MHz, which stands for millions of cycles per second). The Intel 8088 chip, for instance, originally had a clock speed of 4.47 megahertz, whereas the Intel Pentium III chip has a clock speed that ranges from 450 to over 800 megahertz.

A third factor affecting speed is the **data bus width.** The data bus acts as a highway between the CPU, primary storage, and other devices to determine how much data can be moved at one time. The 8088 chip used in the original IBM personal computer, for example, had a 16-bit word length but only an 8-bit data bus width. This meant that data were processed within

megahertz A measure of cycle speed, or the pacing of events in a computer; one megahertz equals one million cycles per second.

data bus width The number of bits that can be moved at one time between the CPU, primary storage, and the other devices of a computer.

Table 4-3 **Examples of Microprocessors**

Name	Microprocessor Manufacturer	Word Length	Data Bus Width	Clock Speed (MHz)	Used In
Pentium	Intel	32	64	75–200	IBM and other PCs
Pentium II	Intel	32	64	233–450	PCs
Pentium III	Intel	32	64	800+	High-end PCs, servers, and workstations
PowerPC	Motorola, IBM, Apple	32 or 64	64	100–400	PCs and workstations
Alpha 21364	Compaq	64	64	1,000+	Compaq workstations and servers
AMD Athlon	Advanced Micro Devices	32	64	600–1000	High-end PCs and workstations.

the CPU chip itself in 16-bit chunks but could only be moved 8 bits at a time between the CPU, primary storage, and external devices. However, the Alpha chip has both a 64-bit word length and a 64-bit data bus width. To have a computer execute more instructions per second and work through programs or handle users expeditiously, it is necessary to increase the processor's word length, the data bus width, the cycle speed—or all three.

Microprocessors can be made faster by using **reduced instruction set computing (RISC)** in their design. Some instructions that a computer uses to process data are actually embedded in the chip circuitry. Conventional chips, based on complex instruction set computing, have several hundred or more instructions hard-wired into their circuitry, and they may take several clock cycles to execute a single instruction. In many instances, only 20 percent of these instructions are needed for 80 percent of the computer's tasks. If instructions that are not used often are eliminated, the remaining instructions execute much faster.

RISC computers have only the most frequently used instructions embedded in them. A RISC CPU can execute most instructions in a single machine cycle and sometimes multiple instructions at the same time. RISC is most appropriate for scientific and workstation computing, where there are repetitive arithmetical and logical operations on data or applications calling for three-dimensional image rendering.

However, software written for conventional processors cannot be automatically transferred to RISC machines; new software is required. Many RISC suppliers are adding more instructions to appeal to a greater number of customers, and designers of conventional microprocessors are streamlining their chips to execute instructions more rapidly.

Microprocessors optimized for multimedia and graphics improve processing of visually intensive applications. Recent Intel, AMD, and other microprocessors include a set of additional instructions called **MMX (MultiMedia eXtension)** to increase performance in many applications featuring graphics and sound. Multimedia applications such as games and video using MMX run more smoothly, with more colors, and perform more tasks simultaneously than other microprocessors if software can take advantage of MMX instructions. For example, multiple channels of audio, high-quality video or animation, and Internet communication could all be running in the same application. Intel's Pentium III chip also has special capabilities for speech recognition, imaging, video, and the Internet.

MULTIPLE PROCESSORS AND PARALLEL PROCESSING

Many computers use multiple processors to perform their processing work. For example, PCs often use a **coprocessor** to speed processing by performing specific tasks such as mathematical calculations or graphics processing so the CPU is free for other processing tasks.

Processing can also be sped up by linking several processors to work simultaneously on the same task. Figure 4-7 compares serial or sequential processing to parallel processing. In **parallel processing,** multiple processing units (CPUs) break down a problem into smaller parts and work on it simultaneously. Getting several processors to attack the same problem at once requires both rethinking the problem and using special software to divide the problem among different processors in the most efficient way possible, providing the needed data, and reassembling the many subtasks to reach an appropriate solution.

Massively parallel computers have huge networks of hundreds or even thousands of processor chips interwoven in complex and flexible ways to attack large computing problems. As opposed to parallel processing, where small numbers of powerful but expensive specialized chips are linked together, massively parallel machines chain hundreds or even thousands of inexpensive, commonly used chips to break problems into many small pieces and solve them. For instance, Wal-Mart uses a massively parallel machine to sift through an inventory and sales trend database with 24 trillion bytes of data.

4.2 Secondary Storage

In addition to primary storage, where information and programs are stored for immediate processing, modern computer systems use other types of storage in order to accomplish tasks. Information systems need to store information outside of the computer in a nonvolatile state (one that does not require electrical power) and to store volumes of data too large to fit into a

reduced instruction set computing (RISC) Technology used to enhance the speed of microprocessors by embedding only the most frequently used instructions on a chip.

MMX (MultiMedia eXtension) A set of instructions built into a microprocessor to improve processing of multimedia applications.

coprocessor Additional processor that enhances performance by performing specific tasks to free the CPU for other processing activities.

parallel processing Type of processing in which more than one instruction can be processed at a time by breaking down a problem into smaller parts and processing them simultaneously with multiple processors.

massively parallel computers Computers that use hundreds or thousands of processing chips to attack large computing problems simultaneously.

FIGURE 4-7 Sequential and parallel processing. During sequential processing, each task is assigned to one CPU that processes one instruction at a time. In parallel processing, multiple tasks are assigned to multiple processing units to expedite the result.

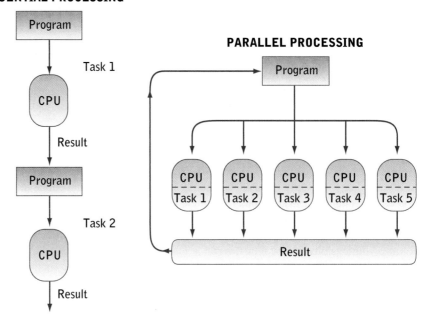

secondary storage Relatively long term, nonvolatile storage of data outside the CPU and primary storage.

computer of any size today (such as a large payroll or the U.S. census). The relatively long-term storage of data outside the CPU and primary storage is called **secondary storage.**

Primary storage is where the fastest, most expensive storage technology is used. Access to information stored in primary memory is electronic and occurs almost at the speed of light. Secondary storage is nonvolatile and retains data even when the computer is turned off. There are many kinds of secondary storage; the most common are magnetic disk, optical disk, and magnetic tape. These media can transfer large bodies of data rapidly to the CPU. However, secondary storage requires mechanical movement to gain access to the data, so in contrast to primary storage, it is relatively slow.

MAGNETIC DISK

magnetic disk A secondary storage medium in which data are stored by means of magnetized spots on a hard or floppy disk.

hard disk Magnetic disk resembling a thin metallic platter used in large computer systems and in most PCs.

RAID (Redundant Array of Inexpensive Disks) Disk storage technology to boost disk performance by packaging more than 100 smaller disk drives with a controller chip and specialized software in a single large unit to deliver data over multiple paths simultaneously.

floppy disk Removable magnetic disk storage primarily used with PCs.

The most widely used secondary-storage medium today is **magnetic disk.** There are two kinds of magnetic disks: floppy disks (used in PCs) and **hard disks** (used on commercial disk drives and PCs).

Hard disks are thin metallic platters. A hard disk drive contains one or more hard disks mounted on a vertical shaft. Read/write heads attached to access arms move across the spinning disk or disks to read or write data on concentric, circular tracks. Large mainframe or midrange computer systems have multiple disk drives because they require immense disk storage capacity. Removable disk drives such as those manufactured by Iomega and Syquest are becoming popular as sources of backup storage capacity for PC systems.

Disk drive performance can be enhanced by using a disk technology called **RAID (Redundant Array of Inexpensive Disks).** RAID devices package more than a hundred disk drives, a controller chip, and specialized software into a single, large unit. Traditional disk drives deliver data from the disk drive along a single path, but RAID delivers data over multiple paths simultaneously, accelerating disk access time. Small RAID systems provide 10 to 20 gigabytes of storage capacity, whereas larger systems provide more than 15 terabytes. RAID is potentially more reliable than standard disk drives because other drives are available to deliver data if one drive fails.

PCs usually contain hard disks, which can store between 4 and 40 gigabytes. PCs also use removable **floppy disks,** which are flat, 3.5-inch disks of polyester film with a magnetic coating. These disks have a storage capacity ranging from 360 kilobytes to 2.8 megabytes and a much slower access rate than hard disks.

Magnetic disks on both large and small computers permit direct access to individual records. Each record can be given a precise physical address on the disk, and the read/write head can be directed to go directly to that address to access the information. The computer system does not have to search the entire file, as in a sequential tape file, in order to find the record. Disk storage is often referred to as a **direct access storage device (DASD).**

For on-line systems requiring direct access, disk technology provides the only practical means of storage today. DASD is, however, more expensive than magnetic tape. Updating information stored on a disk destroys the old information because the old data on the disk are written over if changes are made. The disk drives themselves are susceptible to environmental disturbances. Even smoke particles can disrupt the movement of read/write heads over the disk surface, which is why disk drives are sealed from the environment.

OPTICAL DISKS

Optical disks, also called compact disks or laser optical disks, store data at densities many times greater than those of magnetic disks and are available for both PCs and large computers. Data are recorded on optical disks when a laser device burns microscopic pits in the reflective layer of a spiral track. Binary information is encoded by the length of these pits and the space between them. Optical disks can store massive quantities of data, including not only text but also pictures, sound, and full-motion video, in a highly compact form. The optical disk is read by having a low-power laser beam from an optical head scan the disk.

The most common optical disk system used with PCs is called **CD-ROM (compact disk read-only memory).** A 4.75-inch compact disk for PCs can store up to 660 megabytes, nearly 300 times more than a high-density floppy disk. CD-ROM storage is most appropriate for applications where enormous quantities of unchanging data must be stored compactly for easy retrieval or for storing graphic images and sound. A CD-ROM is also less vulnerable than floppy disks to magnetism, dirt, or rough handling.

CD-ROM is read-only storage. No new data can be written to it; it can only be read. CD-ROM has been most widely used for reference materials with massive amounts of data, such as encyclopedias and directories, and for storing multimedia applications that combine text, sound, and images (see Section 4.3). For example, U.S. census demographic data and financial databases from Dow Jones or Dun and Bradstreet are available on CD-ROM.

WORM (write once/read many) and **CD-R (compact disk-recordable)** optical disk systems allow users to record data only once on an optical disk. Once written, the data cannot be erased but can be read indefinitely. CD-R technology allows individuals and organizations to create their own CD-ROMs at low cost using a special CD-R recording device. New CD-RW (CD-ReWritable) technology has been developed to allow users to create rewritable optical disks. (Magneto-optical technology was developed earlier for this purpose.) Rewritable optical disk drives are not yet competitive with magnetic disk storage for most applications. Their access speed is slower than that of magnetic disks, and they are more expensive than magnetic media. Rewritable optical disks are useful primarily for applications requiring large volumes of storage where the information is only occasionally updated or for making a backup copy of the data in a computer system.

CD-ROM storage is likely to become more popular and more powerful in years to come, and access speeds will improve. **Digital video disks (DVDs),** also called digital versatile disks, are optical disks that are the same size as CD-ROMs but of even higher capacity. They can hold a minimum of 4.7 gigabytes of data, enough to store a full-length, high-quality motion picture. DVDs are initially being used to store movies and multimedia applications using large amounts of video and graphics, but they may replace CD-ROMs because they can store such large amounts of digitized text, graphics, audio, and video data.

MAGNETIC TAPE

Magnetic tape is an older storage technology that still is employed for secondary storage of large volumes of information. It is still used in mainframe batch applications and for archiving data. (PCs and some midrange computers use small tape cartridges resembling home audiocassettes to store information.) However, more and more organizations are moving away from using the old reel-to-reel magnetic tapes and instead are using mass storage tape

direct access storage device (DASD) Magnetic disk technology that permits the CPU to locate a record directly.

CD-ROM (compact disk read-only memory) Read-only optical disk storage used for imaging, reference, and applications with massive amounts of unchanging data and for multimedia.

WORM (write once/read many) Optical disk system that allows users to record data only once; data cannot be erased but can be read indefinitely.

CD-R (compact disk-recordable) Optical disk system that allows individuals and organizations to record their own CD-ROMs.

digital video disk (DVD) High-capacity, optical storage medium that can store full-length videos and large amounts of data.

magnetic tape Inexpensive, older secondary-storage medium in which large volumes of information are stored sequentially by means of magnetized and nonmagnetized spots on tape.

Secondary storage devices such as floppy disks, optical disks, and hard disks are used to store large quantities of data outside the CPU and primary storage. They provide direct access to data for easy retrieval.

cartridges that hold far more data (up to 35 gigabytes) than the old magnetic tapes. Moreover, today, these cartridges are part of automated systems that store hundreds of such cartridges and select and mount them automatically using sophisticated robotics technology. Contemporary magnetic tape systems are used for archiving data and for storing data that are needed rapidly but not instantly. These systems, dubbed *near-line,* can locate and access a record stored somewhere within a bank of cartridges in about 20 seconds or less. Such inexpensive speed is useful in many industries and is used extensively in such fields as banking, broadcasting (replacing videotapes), and healthcare (for example, to store X-rays and other medical images).

The principal advantages of magnetic tape are that it is very inexpensive, it is relatively stable, and it can store very large quantities of information. Magnetic tape also can be reused many times.

The principal disadvantages of magnetic tape are that it stores data sequentially and is relatively slow compared to the speed of other secondary storage media. In order to find an individual record stored on magnetic tape, such as an employment record, the tape must be read from the beginning up to the location of the desired record. Tape also ages over time and older type storage devices are labor intensive to mount and dismount. Although magnetic tape is not good for data that need to be accessed in a second or less, it can be very useful if a few extra seconds are not a problem.

STORAGE REQUIREMENTS FOR ELECTRONIC COMMERCE

Companies today need to store vast quantities of data for data-intensive applications, such as videos, graphics, or electronic commerce transactions. Although electronic commerce may reduce the use of paper as data of all types (such as orders, invoices, and inventories) can be transmitted and stored electronically, all these data now must be stored and also be available whenever they are needed. Electronic commerce has put new strategic emphasis on technologies that can store vast quantities of transaction data and make them immediately available online as needed. The Window on Organizations describes how some companies are grappling with this issue.

storage area network (SAN)
A high-speed network dedicated to storage, which connects different kinds of storage devices, such as tape libraries and disk arrays.

With conventional storage systems overflowing, companies are turning to storage area networks (SANs) to deal with mushrooming storage requirements. A **storage area network (SAN)** is a high-speed network dedicated to storage, which connects different kinds of storage devices, such as tape libraries and disk arrays. Many companies are storing vital information on servers at many different locations, and SANs can be shared by all users regardless of location. The SAN creates a large central pool of storage that can be shared by multiple servers so that users can rapidly share data across the SAN. Figure 4-8 illustrates how a SAN works. The SAN storage devices are located on their own network and connected using a high-transmission technology such as Fibre Channel. The SAN supports communication between any server and the storage unit as well as between different storage devices in the network. A typical SAN consists of a server, storage devices, and networking devices and is used strictly for storage. The storage devices connect to the server independently, providing a dedicated path to the computer.

Window on Organizations

STORAGE BECOMES STRATEGIC IN E-COMMERCE

Customers and suppliers doing business electronically no longer expect transactions to occur only during the traditional nine-to-five business day. They want to place orders, check accounts, and do research at any hour of the day, and so they demand 24-hour availability. For business to occur 24 hours a day anywhere in our electronic world, all possibly relevant data must be stored on-line.

Even e-mail is falling into this special category as it becomes ever more tightly integrated into business transactions. Of course, all these data also must be backed up. Thanks to the Internet, the business world is forced to focus not only on data and but also on ways to store these data. Storage has become an essential component of the information technology (IT) infrastructure for electronic commerce.

Planning for data storage can be very difficult because, at this early stage in the development of e-commerce, storage needs are usually unpredictable. Storage needs are growing so rapidly that many no longer view computer storage like traditional hardware. Instead storage is viewed much like the model of a utility, such as electricity or water. With utilities, we use what we need and pay for what we use. Thus, building meters measure the amount of electricity used, and building owners or tenants only pay for the amount they use. Following the utility model, some companies are no longer providing their own data storage. Instead, they store their data elsewhere. "Eventually, you'll rent a storage locker, the storage will appear local and attached to your server," explains Nora Denzel, senior vice president of Legato Systems. "You rent storage space somewhere, you pay per gigabyte, you pay as you go."

Let us consider two examples of spiraling data storage needs caused by the explosion of e-commerce. On-line banking is one of a number of e-commerce areas that has become very important at Chase Manhattan Bank, forcing Chase to change its check-handling method. Until recently the bank stored its 12 million daily checks on microfilm and microfiche, which could not be available on-line. Now Chase creates a digital image of each check that is stored on-line for 45 days, after which it is archived to a fast tape system. Customers can now view any recent check within one to two seconds. How much storage is needed? Each check requires about 40,000 bytes, so they need more than 20 gigabytes at current levels in a business that is expanding fast.

Charles Schwab has also seen its business change because of e-commerce. The securities business was once designed to be batch oriented. According to Fred Matteson, Schwab's executive vice president of information technology, "You traded all day, you compared your trades all night." However, customers today no longer want to wait until tomorrow to see the results of today's activities. Moreover, Matteson continues, "As you internationalized, the market notion that you trade from 9:30 A.M. EST to 4 P.M. . . . goes away. Our systems are accessible 24 hours a day." As a result Schwab has been forced to move much of its data from batch to on-line, requiring a major increase in demand for on-line data storage capacity.

TO THINK ABOUT: Why is storage management an important business issue? What might be the organizational impact of the explosion of data storage needs?

Sources: Rivka Tadjer, "Storage Unlimited," **Internet Storage**, CMP Media Inc., April 1999; Mitch Wagner, "High Availability Rules," **Internet Storage**, CMP Media Inc., April 1999; and Nate Zelnick, "Solutions for Storage-Starved Sites," **Internet World**, May 17, 1999.

4.3 Input and Output Devices

Human beings interact with computer systems largely through input and output devices. Advances in information systems rely not only on the speed and capacity of the CPU but also on the speed, capacity, and design of the input and output devices. Input/output devices are often called *peripheral devices.*

INPUT DEVICES

Keyboards remain the principal method of data entry for entering text and numerical data into a computer. However, pointing devices, such as the computer mouse and touch screens, are becoming popular for issuing commands and making selections in today's highly graphic computing environment.

Pointing Devices

The point-and-click actions of the **computer mouse** have made it an increasingly popular alternative to keyboard and text-based commands. A mouse is a handheld device that is usually

computer mouse Handheld input device whose movement on the desktop controls the position of the cursor on the computer display screen.

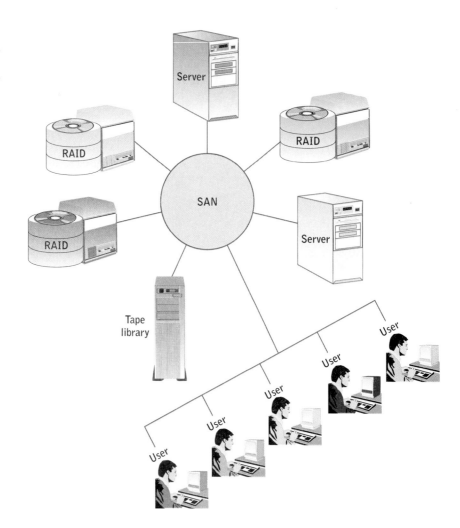

FIGURE 4-8 A storage area network (SAN). The SAN stores data on many different types of storage devices. Users can share data across the SAN.

touch screen Input device technology that permits the entering or selecting of commands and data by touching the surface of a sensitized video display monitor with a finger or a pointer.

source data automation Input technology that captures data in computer-readable form at the time and place the data are created.

optical character recognition (OCR) Form of source data automation in which optical scanning devices read specially designed data off source documents and translate the data into digital form for the computer.

bar code Form of OCR technology widely used in supermarkets and retail stores in which identification data are coded into a series of bars.

connected to the computer by a cable. The computer user moves the mouse around on a desktop to control the cursor's position on a computer display screen. Once the cursor is in the desired position, the user can push a button on the mouse to select a command. The mouse also can be used to "draw" images on the screen. Trackballs and touch pads often are used in place of the mouse as pointing devices on laptop PCs.

Touch screens are easy to use and appeal to people who have difficulty using traditional keyboards. Users can enter limited amounts of data by touching the surface of a sensitized video display monitor with a finger or a pointer. With colorful graphics, sound, and simple menus, touch screens often are found in information kiosks in retail stores, restaurants, and shopping malls.

Source Data Automation

Source data automation technology captures data in computer-readable form at the time and place they are created. Point-of-sale systems, optical bar code scanners used in supermarkets, and other optical character recognition devices are examples of source data automation. One advantage of source data automation is that the many errors that occur when people use keyboards to enter data are almost eliminated. Bar code scanners make fewer than 1 error in 10,000 transactions, whereas skilled keypunchers make about 1 error for every 1,000 keystrokes. The principal source data automation technologies are optical character recognition, magnetic ink character recognition, pen-based input, digital scanners, voice input, and sensors.

Optical character recognition (OCR) devices translate specially designed marks, characters, and codes into digital form. The most widely used optical code is the **bar code,** which is used in point-of-sale systems in supermarkets and retail stores. Bar codes also are used in hospitals, libraries, military operations, and transportation facilities. The codes can in-

Touch screens allow users to enter small amounts of data by touching words, numbers, or specific points on the screen.

clude time, date, and location data in addition to identification data. The information makes them useful for analyzing the movement of items and determining what has happened to the items during production or other processes. (The discussion of the United Parcel Service in Chapter 1 shows how valuable bar codes can be for this purpose.)

Magnetic ink character recognition (MICR) technology is used primarily in check processing for the banking industry. The bottom portion of a typical check contains characters identifying the bank, checking account, and check number that are preprinted using a special magnetic ink. An MICR reader translates these characters into digital form for the computer.

Handwriting-recognition devices such as pen-based tablets, notebooks, and notepads are promising new input technologies, especially for people working in the sales or service areas or for those who have traditionally shunned computer keyboards. These **pen-based input devices** usually consist of a flat-screen display tablet and a penlike stylus.

With pen-based input, users print directly onto the tablet-size screen. The screen is fitted with a transparent grid of fine wires that detect the presence of the special stylus, which emits a faint signal from its tip. As users write letters and numbers on the tablet, they are translated into digital form, where they can be stored or processed and analyzed. For instance, the United Parcel Service replaced its drivers' familiar clipboard with a battery-powered Delivery Information Acquisition Device (DIAD) to capture signatures (see the Chapter 1 Window on Technology) along with other information required for pickup and delivery. This technology requires special pattern-recognition software to accept pen-based input instead of keyboard input. Most pen-based systems still cannot recognize freehand writing very well.

Digital scanners translate images such as pictures or documents into digital form and are an essential component of image-processing systems. **Voice input devices** convert spoken words into digital form for processing by the computer. Voice recognition devices allow people to enter data into the computer without using their hands, making them useful for inspecting and sorting items in manufacturing and shipping and for dictation. (Documents can be created by speaking words into a computer rather than keying them.) Microphones and tape cassette players can serve as input devices for music and other sounds.

Sensors are devices that collect data directly from the environment for input into a computer system. For instance, today's farmers can use sensors on their tractors to monitor speed

magnetic ink character recognition (MICR) Input technology that translates characters written in magnetic ink into digital codes for processing.

pen-based input devices Input devices such as tablets, notebooks, and notepads consisting of a flat-screen display tablet and a penlike stylus that digitizes handwriting.

digital scanners Input devices that translate images such as pictures or documents into digital form for processing.

voice input devices Technology that converts the spoken word into digital form for processing.

sensors Devices that collect data directly from the environment for input into a computer system.

batch processing A method of collecting and processing data in which transactions are accumulated and stored until a specified time when it is convenient or necessary to process them as a group.

on-line processing A method of collecting and processing data in which transactions are entered directly into the computer system and processed immediately.

transaction file In batch systems, a file in which all transactions are accumulated to await processing.

master file A file that contains all permanent information and is updated during processing by transaction data.

and adjust the amount of fertilizer or pesticide sprayed on soil. Sensor-equipped combines can monitor, calculate, and record each field's yield as the combines harvest crops (Feder, 1998).

BATCH AND ON-LINE INPUT AND PROCESSING

The manner in which data are input into the computer affects how the data can be processed. Information systems collect and process information in one of two ways: through batch or on-line processing. In **batch processing,** transactions such as orders or payroll time cards are accumulated and stored in a group or batch until it is efficient or necessary to process them because of some reporting cycle. This was the only method of processing until the early 1960s, and it is still used today in older systems or in some systems with massive amounts of transactions. In **on-line processing,** which is now very common, the user enters transactions into a device (such as a data entry keyboard or bar code reader) that is directly connected to the computer system. The transactions usually are processed immediately.

The demands of the business determine the type of processing. If the user needs periodic or occasional reports or output, as in payroll or end-of-year reports, batch processing is most efficient. If the user needs immediate information and processing, as in an airline or hotel reservation system, then the system should use on-line processing.

Figure 4-9 compares batch and on-line processing. Batch systems often use tape as a storage medium, whereas on-line processing systems use disk storage, which permits immediate access to specific items. In batch systems, transactions are accumulated in a **transaction file,** which contains all the transactions for a particular time period. Periodically this file is used to update a **master file,** which contains permanent information on entities. (An example is a payroll master file with employee earnings and deduction data. It is updated with weekly time-

FIGURE 4-9 A comparison of batch and on-line processing. In batch processing, transactions are accumulated and stored in a group. Because batches are processed on a regular interval basis, such as daily, weekly, or monthly, information in the system will not always be up to date. A typical batch-processing job is payroll preparation. In on-line processing, transactions are input immediately and usually processed immediately. Information in the system is generally up to date. A typical on-line application is an airline reservation system.

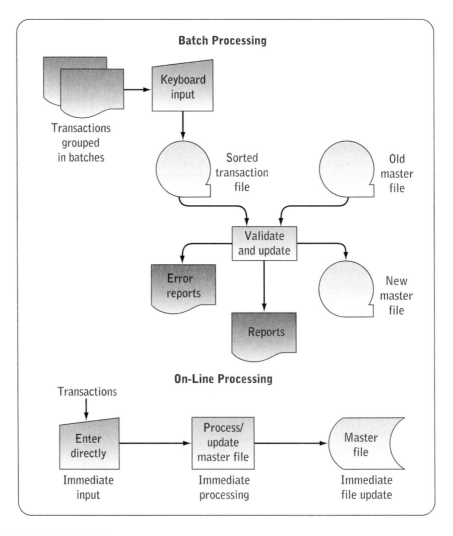

card transactions.) Adding the transaction data to the existing master file creates a new master file. In on-line processing, transactions are entered into the system immediately using a keyboard, pointing device, or source data automation, and the system usually responds immediately. The master file is updated continually. In on-line processing, there is a direct connection to the computer for input and output.

OUTPUT DEVICES

The major data output devices are cathode ray tube terminals, sometimes called video display terminals or VDTs, and printers.

The **cathode ray tube (CRT)** is probably the most popular output device in modern computer systems. It works much like a television picture tube, with an electronic gun shooting a beam of electrons to illuminate the pixels on the screen. The more pixels per screen, the higher the resolution, or clarity, of the image on the screen. Special-purpose graphics terminals used in CAD/CAM (computer-aided design/computer-aided manufacturing) and commercial art have very high resolution capabilities (1,280 × 1,024 pixels). Laptop computers use flat panel displays, which are less bulky than CRT monitors.

cathode ray tube (CRT) A screen, also referred to as a video display terminal (VDT), that provides a visual image of both user input and computer output.

Printers and Plotters

Printers produce a printed hard copy of information output. They include impact printers (such as a dot matrix printer) and nonimpact printers (laser, inkjet, and thermal transfer printers). Most printers print one character at a time, but some commercial printers print an entire line or page at a time. In general, impact printers are slower than nonimpact printers.

High-quality graphics documents can be created using **plotters** with multicolored pens to draw (rather than print) computer output. Plotters are much slower than printers, but are useful for outputting large-size charts, maps, or drawings.

printer A computer output device that provides paper hard-copy output in the form of text or graphics.

plotter Output device using multicolored pens to draw high-quality graphic documents.

Other Output Devices

A **voice output device** converts digital output data back into intelligible speech. For instance, when you call for information on the telephone, you may hear a computerized voice respond with the telephone number you requested.

Audio output such as music and other sounds can be delivered by speakers connected to the computer. In addition to audio output, multimedia applications, including those on the Web, also can produce graphics or video as visual output. Microfilm and microfiche have been used to store large quantities of output as microscopic film documents, but they are being replaced by optical disk technology.

voice output device A converter of digital output data into spoken words.

INTERACTIVE MULTIMEDIA

The processing, input, output, and storage technologies we have just described can be used to create interactive multimedia applications that integrate sound and full-motion video, or animation with graphics and text. **Multimedia** technologies facilitate the integration of two or more types of media, such as text, graphics, sound, voice, full-motion video, still video, or animation, into a computer-based application. Multimedia is becoming the foundation of new consumer products and services, such as electronic books and newspapers, electronic classroom-presentation technologies, full-motion video conferencing, imaging, graphics design tools, and computer games. Many Web sites use multimedia.

PCs today come with built-in multimedia capabilities, including a high-resolution color monitor, a CD-ROM drive or DVD drive to store video, audio, and graphic data, and stereo speakers for amplifying audio output.

The most difficult element to incorporate into multimedia information systems has been full-motion video, because so much data must be brought under the digital control of the computer. The massive amounts of data in each video image must be digitally encoded, stored, and manipulated electronically using techniques that compress the digital data.

The possibilities this technology offers are endless, but multimedia seems especially well suited for training and presentations. For training, multimedia is appealing because it is interactive and permits two-way communication. People can use multimedia training sessions any time of the day, at their own pace (Hardaway and Will, 1997). Instructors easily can integrate

multimedia The integration of two or more types of media such as text, graphics, sound, voice, full-motion video, or animation into a computer-based application.

Multimedia combines text, graphics, sound, and video into a computer-based experience that permits two-way communication. Many organizations use this technology for interactive training.

words, sounds, pictures, and both live and animated video to produce lessons that capture students' imaginations. For example, Duracell, the $2.6 billion battery manufacturer, used an interactive multimedia program to teach new employees at its Chinese manufacturing facility how to use battery-making machinery. Workers use computer simulations to "stop," "start," and control equipment (Kay, 1997).

Interactive Web pages replete with graphics, sound, animations, and full-motion video have made multimedia popular on the Internet. For example, visitors to the CNN Interactive Web site can access news stories from CNN, photos, on-air transcripts, video clips, and audio clips. The video and audio clips are made available using **streaming technology,** which allows audio and video data to be processed as a steady and continuous stream as they are downloaded from the Web. (RealAudio and RealVideo are widely used streaming technology products on the Web.) Table 4-4 lists examples of other multimedia Web sites. If Internet transmission capacity and streaming technology continue to improve, Web sites could provide broadcast functions that compete with television along with new two-way interactivity.

Multimedia Web sites are also being used to sell digital products, such as digitized music clips. A compression standard known as **MP3,** also called MPEG3, which stands for Motion Picture Experts Group, audio layer 3, can compress audio files down to one-tenth or one-twelfth of their original size with virtually no loss in quality. Visitors to Web sites such as MP3.com can download free MP3 music clips over the Internet and play them on their own computers.

streaming technology
Technology for transferring data so that they can be processed as a steady and continuous stream.

MP3 (MPEG3) Compression standard that can compress audio files for transfer over the Internet with virtually no loss in quality.

Table 4-4	Examples of Multimedia Web Sites

Web Site	Description
TerraQuest	Provides interactive tours of exotic destinations including maps, film clips, photos, and on-line discussions.
Newsworld Online	Provides news from Canada, including live video, 24 hours a day.
Lands' End	Allows shoppers to create a "personal model" allowing them to "try on" clothes from their computer screens.
VideoSonicNet	Provides streaming music videos on demand as well as music, news, reviews, and radio broadcasts.

VideoSonicNet is a multimedia company produced by the MTVi Group that provides streaming music videos on demand as well as music, news, reviews, and radio broadcasts. Web sites can incorporate multimedia elements such as graphics, sound, animation, and full-motion video.

4.4 Types of Computers and Computer Systems

Computers represent and process data the same way, but there are different classifications. We can use size and processing speed to categorize contemporary computers as mainframes, midrange computers, PCs, workstations, and supercomputers. Managers need to understand the capabilities of each of these types of computers, and why some are more appropriate for certain processing work than others. They also need to work with information systems specialists on hardware capacity planning to make sure that the firm has enough computing power for its current and future needs.

CATEGORIES OF COMPUTERS

The **mainframe** is the largest computer, a powerhouse with extensive memory and extremely rapid processing power. It is used for very large business, scientific, or military applications where a computer must handle massive amounts of data or many complicated processes. A **midrange computer** is less powerful, less expensive, and smaller than a mainframe but capable of supporting the computing needs of smaller organizations or of managing networks of other computers. Midrange computers can be **minicomputers,** which are used in systems for universities, factories, or research laboratories or they can be **servers,** which are used for managing internal company networks or Web sites. Server computers are specifically optimized to support a computer network, enabling users to share files, software, peripheral devices such as printers, or other network resources. Servers have large memory and disk-storage capacity, high-speed communications capabilities, and powerful CPUs. Organizations with heavy electronic commerce requirements and massive Web sites are running their Web and e-commerce applications on multiple servers in **server farms** in computing centers run by commercial vendors such as IBM.

A **personal computer (PC),** which is sometimes referred to as a microcomputer, can be placed on a desktop or carried from place to place. Small laptop PCs are often used as portable desktops on the road. PCs are used for personal business as well as in organizations. A **workstation** also fits on a desktop but has more powerful mathematical and graphics-processing capability than a PC and can perform more complicated tasks than a PC in the same amount of time. Workstations are used for scientific, engineering, and design work that requires powerful graphics or computational capabilities. A **supercomputer** is a highly sophisticated and powerful machine that is used for tasks requiring extremely rapid and complex calculations with hundreds of thousands of variable factors. Supercomputers traditionally have been used for scientific and military work, such as classified weapons research, weather forecasting, and petroleum and engineering applications, all of which use complex mathematical models and

mainframe Largest category of computer, used for major business processing.

midrange computer Middle-size computer that is capable of supporting the computing needs of smaller organizations or of managing networks of other computers.

minicomputer Middle-range computer used in systems for universities, factories, or research laboratories.

server Computer specifically optimized to provide software and other resources to other computers over a network.

server farm Large group of servers maintained by a commercial vendor and made available to subscribers for electronic commerce and other activities requiring heavy use of servers.

personal computer (PC) Small desktop or portable computer.

workstation Desktop computer with powerful graphics and mathematical capabilities and the ability to perform several complicated tasks at once.

supercomputer Highly sophisticated and powerful computer that can perform very complex computations extremely rapidly.

HARDWARE CAPACITY PLANNING FOR ELECTRONIC COMMERCE

Your company recently implemented its own electronic commerce site using its own hardware and software, and business is growing rapidly. The company Web site has not experienced any outages and customers always have requests for information answered promptly and purchase transactions processed rapidly. Your Information Systems Department continuously monitors key indicators of system usage that affect processing capacity and response time. The following report illustrates two of those indicators: daily CPU usage and daily I/O usage for the system. I/O usage measures the number of times a disk has been read.

Your server supports primarily U.S. customers who access the Web site during the day and early evening. I/O usage should be kept below 70% if the CPU is very busy so that the CPU does not waste machine cycles looking for data. I/O usage is high between 1 and 6 A.M. because the firm backs up its data stored on disk when the CPU is not busy.

CPU and I/O Usage

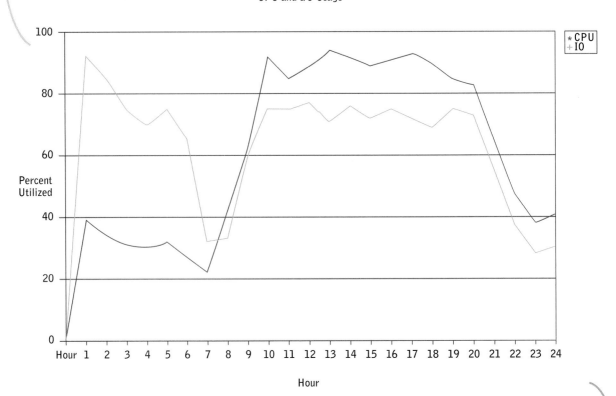

Daily CPU and I/O usage (Hours are for U.S. Eastern Standard Time.)

1. Anticipated increases in your e-commerce business during the next year are expected to increase CPU usage and I/O usage by 20 percent between 1:00 P.M. and 9:00 P.M. and by 10 percent during the rest of the day. Does your company have enough processing capacity to handle this increased load?

2. What would happen if your organization did not pay attention to capacity issues?

simulations. They are also used in business for datamining and the manipulation of vast quantities of data. Supercomputers can perform hundreds of billions of calculations per second—many times faster than the largest mainframes. Some supercomputers perform more than a trillion mathematical calculations each second—a teraflop. (The term *teraflop* comes from the Greek *teras,* which for mathematicians means one trillion, and *flop,* an acronym for floating point operations per second. A floating point operation is a basic computer arithmetic operation, such as addition, on numbers that include a decimal point.)

The problem with this classification scheme is that the capacity of the machines changes so rapidly. Powerful PCs have sophisticated graphics and processing capabilities similar to workstations. PCs still cannot perform as many tasks at once as mainframes, minicomputers, or workstations (see the discussion of operating systems in Chapter 5); nor can they be used by as many people simultaneously as the larger machines. Even these distinctions will become less pronounced in the future. The most powerful workstations have some of the capabilities of older mainframes and supercomputers.

Servers have become important components of firms' information technology (IT) infrastructure because they provide the hardware platform for electronic commerce. By adding special software, they can be customized to deliver Web pages, process purchase and sale transactions, or exchange data with systems inside the company. As companies' electronic commerce activities expand, they must carefully review their servers and other infrastructure components to ensure they can handle increasing numbers of transactions while maintaining a high level of performance and availability. IT infrastructures need to be scalable so that they have the capacity to grow with the business. **Scalability** refers to the ability of a computer, product, or system to expand to serve a larger number of users without breaking down. The Window on Management discusses the importance of providing a scalable IT infrastructure for electronic commerce.

scalability The ability of a computer, product, or system to expand to serve a larger number of users without breaking down.

COMPUTER NETWORKS AND CLIENT/SERVER COMPUTING

Today, stand-alone computers have been replaced by computers in networks for most processing tasks. The use of multiple computers linked by a communications network for processing is called **distributed processing.** In contrast with **centralized processing,** in which all processing is accomplished by one large central computer, distributed processing distributes the processing work among PCs, midrange computers, and mainframes linked together.

distributed processing Multiple computers linked by a communications network for processing work.

centralized processing Processing that is accomplished by one large central computer.

One widely used form of distributed processing is **client/server computing.** Client/server computing splits processing between "clients" and "servers." Both are on the network, but each machine is assigned functions it is best suited to perform. The **client** is the user point-of-entry for the required function and is normally a desktop computer, workstation, or laptop computer. The user generally interacts directly only with the client portion of the application, often to input data or retrieve data for further analysis. The *server* provides the client with services. The server could be a mainframe or another desktop computer, but specialized server computers are often used in this role. Servers store and process shared data and also perform back-end functions not visible to users, such as managing network activities. Figure 4-10 illustrates the client/server computing concept. Computing on the Internet uses the client/server model (see Chapter 8).

client/server computing A model for computing that splits processing between "clients" and "servers" on a network, assigning functions to the machine most able to perform the function.

client The user point-of-entry for the required function in client/server computing. Normally a desktop computer, workstation, or laptop computer.

Figure 4-11 illustrates five different ways that the components of an application could be partitioned between the client and the server. The interface component is essentially the application interface—how the application appears visually to the user. The application logic component consists of the processing logic, which is shaped by the organization's business rules. (An example might be that a salaried employee is to be paid monthly.) The data management component consists of the storage and management of the data used by the application.

The exact division of tasks depends on the requirements of each application, including its processing needs, the number of users, and the available resources. For example, client

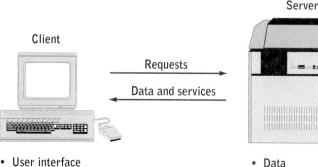

Client

Server

Requests →

← Data and services

- User interface
- Application function

- Data
- Application function
- Network resources

FIGURE 4-10 Client/server computing. In client/server computing, computer processing is split between client machines and server machines linked by a network. Users interface with the client machines.

SCALING FOR E-COMMERCE

Many electronic commerce sites present a friendly, welcoming screen to visitors inviting them to enter, explore, and make a purchase with a few clicks of the mouse any time of day. The Web sites are friendly, easy to use, and always available. But behind the friendly facade are sophisticated systems for maintaining peak performance of the Web site no matter now many people are accessing it at the same time. Outages and slow response times translate into lost customers and lost revenue.

Large e-commerce sites such as Amazon.com, Dell Online, or Schwab.com are based on huge server farms with sophisticated capabilities of balancing computer loads and handling millions of purchases, inquiries, and other transactions through a maze of networks, processors, and data storage devices. The raw performance of these servers, which house Web sites and business applications, is the key to customer satisfaction. The servers need to provide the processing power to keep e-commerce up and running as the business grows. Slow response times frustrate users and can slow the flow of commerce transactions through the pipeline. Delivering large Web pages with graphics and multimedia to users over the Internet often creates performance bottlenecks.

If e-commerce continues to mushroom, how can companies make sure they have enough processing power to maintain peak performance yet allow for future growth? It's a bit of an art, experts claim. Companies can't just deal with computer hardware in isolation. They must examine the e-commerce system as a whole and look at how processing, data storage, and software all work together.

Send.com is an on-line gift company in Waltham, Massachusetts, which specializes in corporate gift purchases such as wine or golf outings for important clients. The company took in almost $1 million in the 1998 holiday season alone. It anticipated an even greater burst of on-line shopping for the 1999 holiday season. Whenever it ran radio ads, business spiked 200 percent. For Christmas 1999, Send.com spent $20 million in an extensive television campaign, and the company expected national TV exposure to dwarf that amount of activity with up to 500 Web page requests per second during the holiday rush. To find out if its system could handle the load, Send.com's IT staff tried to push the system to its limits. Send.com sent a server home with every employee. Those servers were then set up to re-

quest a one-kilobyte Web page over and over again until something blew up. Send.com tested Compaq Computer Corporation 1850R servers with dual CPUs against servers with single CPUs. The servers with the dual CPUs won hands down. Tests showed that the dual-CPU servers could handle the anticipated page-request load, and the slowest transactions ran an acceptable 5 to 7 seconds. Management then arranged to use 20 of these servers at NaviSite, Inc., an Andover, Massachusetts-based provider of application services, which actually runs the hardware and software for Send.com's systems.

With 300 to 4,000 shoppers simultaneously visiting its on-line store at peak hours, Dell Online had to make sure its system could keep processing customer transactions even if there were some system failures. Dell Online's e-commerce site uses more than 75 Dell PowerEdge servers, each with one or two processors and 256 megabytes to 2 gigabytes of RAM. When visitors enter Dell Online, they usually hit several servers and the connection information needs to be shared from server to server. Dell's front-end servers store information about each customer's session on the Web site. Although the size of Dell's Web pages impacts performance, using leading-edge fast hardware gives Dell Online a competitive edge.

When the Kansas City Southern Railway decided to provide customers with real-time access to information over the Web, it decided to upgrade its mainframe so that the mainframe could host the customer Web site. The company believed that the mainframe would provide a stable, secure environment based on trustworthy technology and could handle 3 to 4 times more Web traffic than its current volume as well as its core transaction processing systems.

TO THINK ABOUT: Why is scalability such an important management decision in e-commerce? What factors should companies consider when selecting the servers for their e-commerce applications?

Sources: Peter Ruber, "Choosing a Server that Suits Your Business," Beyond Computing, January/February 2000; Jason Levitt, "Built to Scale," Information Week, August 23, 1999; Steve Ulfelder, "IT Gets Stress-Tested Days before Web Debut," Computerworld, November 8, 1999; and David Passmore, "Scaling Large E-Commerce Infrastructures," Packet Magazine, Third Quarter 1999.

tasks for a large corporate payroll might include inputting data (such as enrolling new employees and recording hours worked), submitting data queries to the server, analyzing the retrieved data, and displaying results on the screen or on a printer. The server portion fetches the entered data and processes the payroll. It also controls access so that only authorized users can view or update the data.

In some firms client/server networks with PCs have actually replaced mainframes and minicomputers. The process of transferring applications from large computers to smaller ones is called **downsizing.** Downsizing has many advantages. Memory and processing power on a

downsizing The process of transferring applications from large computers to smaller ones.

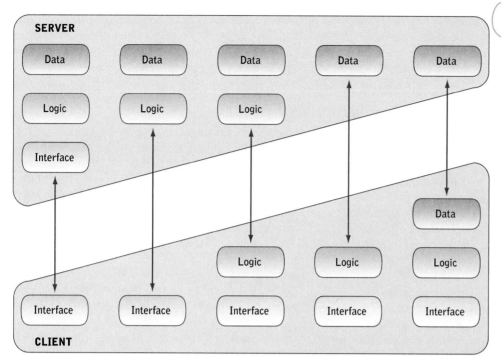

FIGURE 4-1 I Types of client/server computing. There are various ways in which an application's interface, logic, and data management components can be divided among the clients and servers in a network.

PC cost a fraction of their equivalent on a mainframe. The decision to downsize involves many factors in addition to the cost of computer hardware, including the need for new software, training, and perhaps new organizational procedures.

NETWORK COMPUTERS AND TOTAL COST OF OWNERSHIP

In one form of client/server computing, client processing and storage capabilities are so minimal that the bulk of computer processing occurs on the server. The term *thin client* is sometimes used to refer to the client in this arrangement. Thin clients with minimal memory, storage, and processor power that are designed to work on networks are called **network computers (NCs).** Users download whatever software or data they need from a central computer over the Internet or an organization's internal network. The central computer saves information for the user and makes it available for later retrieval, effectively eliminating the need for secondary storage devices such as hard disks, floppy disks, CD-ROMs, and their drives. A network computer may consist of little more than a stripped-down PC, a monitor, a keyboard, and a network connection.

If managed properly, both network computers and client/server computing can reduce the total cost of ownership of information technology resources. **Total cost of ownership (TCO)** is a popular term that describes the cost of owning technology resources including the original cost of the computer and software, hardware and software upgrades, maintenance, technical support, and training. Proponents of network computers believe NCs can reduce TCO because they are less expensive to purchase than PCs with local processing and storage and because they can be administered and updated from a central network server. Software programs and applications would not have to be purchased, installed, and upgraded for each user because software would be delivered and maintained from one central point. Network computers thus could increase management control over the organization's computing function. So much data and information are being delivered through the Web that computers do not necessarily need to store their own content. Network computers are finding additional uses as application software that can be rented over the Web becomes widely available (see Chapter 5).

Not everyone agrees that network computers will bring benefits. Some researchers believe that centralizing control of computing would stifle worker initiative and creativity. PCs have become so cheap and plentiful ($500 and even less if Internet services are purchased with the machine) that many question whether the savings promised by network computers will actually be realized. If a network failure occurs, hundreds or thousands of employees would not

network computer (NC) Simplified desktop computer that does not store software programs or data permanently. Users download whatever software or data they need from a central computer over the Internet or an organization's own internal network.

total cost of ownership (TCO) Designates the total cost of owning technology resources, including initial purchase costs, the cost of hardware and software upgrades, maintenance, technical support, and training.

be able to use their computers, whereas people could keep on working if they had full-function PCs. Full-function PCs are more appropriate for situations where end users have varied application needs that require local processing. Companies should closely examine how network computers fit into their information technology infrastructure.

4.5 Hardware Technology Trends

During the past 30 years, each decade has seen computing costs drop by a factor of 10 and capacity increase by a factor of at least 100. Today's microprocessors can put mainframe processing power on a desktop, in a briefcase, and even in a shirt pocket. As computers become progressively smaller, more powerful, and easier to use, computer intelligence is being incorporated into more aspects of daily life. Computers and related information technologies will increasingly blend data, images, and sound, sending them coursing through vast networks that process all of them with equal ease. We can see how this is possible through the use of superchips, microminiaturization, information appliances, and social interfaces.

SUPERCHIPS

Microprocessors perform faster by improving their design and by shrinking the distance between transistors. This process gives the electrical current less distance to travel. The narrower the lines forming transistors, the larger the number of transistors that can be squeezed onto a single chip, and the faster these circuits will operate. The Pentium III microprocessor, for example, squeezes more than 9 million transistors on a postage-stamp-size silicon pad. Intel is now working on a 64-bit microprocessor known as the IA-64 or the Itanium, which contains more than 10 million transistors.

Researchers already have created semiconductors with circuits as small as .10 microns. Figure 4-12 shows the number of transistors on some prominent microprocessors and memory chips. Both the number of transistors that can fit economically onto a single silicon chip and the speed of microprocessors have been doubling every 18 months. There are physical limits to this approach that soon may be reached, but researchers are experimenting with new materials to increase microprocessor speed. For example, researchers in molecular electronics are trying to use chemical processes to build integrated circuits with switches as small as one mol-

FIGURE 4-12 The shrinking size and growth in number of transistors.

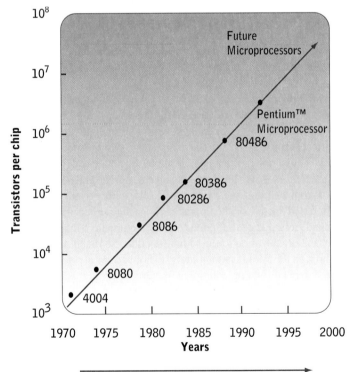

ecule. If they succeed, they will be able to make future microprocessors and memory components several orders of magnitude tinier than today's transistors and computers that are equally more powerful (Markoff, 1999).

Intel's IA-64 microprocessor introduces a new style of processing, known as explicitly parallel instruction computing (EPIC), to high-performance computing. An EPIC processor can execute many different instructions at once inside a single processor using software to sort instructions to decide which ones can be run simultaneously. The Itanium is designed to push parallel computing into the mainstream. In the future, computers will increasingly use such powerful microprocessors in applications requiring parallel processing and massively parallel processing to blend voice, images, and huge pools of data from diverse sources using artificial intelligence and intricate mathematical models. New advances in computer memory, input, output, and storage technology will be required to keep pace with these gains in computer processing performance (Messina et al., 1998).

MICROMINIATURIZATION AND INFORMATION APPLIANCES

Microprocessor technology has fueled a growing movement toward microminiaturization—the proliferation of computers that are so small, fast, and cheap that they have become ubiquitous. For instance, many of the intelligent features that have made automobiles, stereos, toys, watches, cameras, and other equipment easier to use are based on microprocessors. The future will see even more intelligence built into everyday devices, with mainframe and perhaps even supercomputer-like computing power packed in a pocket- or notebook-size computer.

More computing work will be performed by small handheld computers and information appliances. Unlike a PC, which is a general-purpose device capable of performing many different kinds of tasks, an **information appliance** is customized to perform only a few specialized tasks very well with a minimum of effort. Such information appliances include mobile phones with e-mail and Internet access, fixed-screen telephones that can browse the Web and exchange e-mail, wireless handheld devices for transmitting messages, and television set-top boxes to access the Web and provide e-mail and home shopping services. Chapter 7 describes the capabilities of these information appliances in greater detail. These specialized computing devices are less expensive and less difficult to use than PCs, and they provide enough capabilities for communication or accessing the Web to meet many peoples' computing needs. PCs will play a smaller role in both personal and corporate computing as information appliances become more widely used.

> **information appliance** A computing device customized to perform only a few specialized tasks very well with a minimum of effort.

Microminiaturization is making possible the use of smart cards for many everyday transactions. A **smart card** is a plastic card the size of a credit card that contains a small amount of storage and a tiny microprocessor instead of a magnetic strip. The embedded chip can carry information, such as one's health records, identification data, or telephone numbers, and the cards can serve as "electronic purses" in place of cash. For example, New York City Transit Authority smart cards can be used as alternatives to subway and bus tokens and for paying tolls on highways and bridges. Although smart cards are not as popular in the United States as in Europe, they are very versatile and their uses are growing.

> **smart card** A credit card-size plastic card containing embedded storage and a microprocessor.

SOCIAL INTERFACES

Potentially, computer technology could become so powerful and integrated into daily experiences that it would appear essentially invisible to the user (Weiser, 1993). More information and knowledge will be represented visually through graphics (Lieberman, 1996). Social interfaces are being developed that model the interaction between people and computers using familiar human behavior. People increasingly will interact with the computer in more intuitive and effortless ways—through writing, speech, touch, eye movement, and other gestures (Selker, 1996).

Voice-recognition technology is moving closer to natural speech. Until recently, voice recognition only could be used for accepting simple commands. Voice-recognition devices had small vocabularies and could identify individual words. Now continuous-speech voice recognition is possible using a type of artificial intelligence called natural language processing to identify phrases and sentences. Commercial, continuous-speech, voice-recognition products have vocabularies large enough for general business use (see the Window on Technology).

COMPUTERS LEARN TO LISTEN

"Computers are getting smaller and smaller, and they're going to be very pervasive," claims W. S. Osborne, general manager of IBM speech and pen systems. "So," he adds, "how are you going to interface with these devices? You're not going to carry a keyboard around with you." With these words he is making a clear case for the development of voice-recognition input.

Advances in this technology are occurring rapidly. Voice-recognition systems now respond accurately more than 90 percent of the time. IBM has developed a system that is handling more than 250,000 names and, in theory, is capable of handling twice that number. Moreover, the systems are becoming more sophisticated. For example, in the past voice recognition always required the speaker to repeat a whole sentence if it could not decipher a word, but newer systems will ask the speaker to repeat only the word that was unclear. Systems also are being developed that will recognize the voice of the speaker, a system that is 99.9 percent accurate when the individual speaks her or his account number and identification. Thus, these systems also are becoming useful for security purposes. One other advantage of these systems is that they are relatively inexpensive. For example, a system that must recognize only 2,000 to 3,000 names costs only $5,000 and can handle several thousand phone calls daily.

One problem this technology hasn't solved is the public reaction to what many feel is a cold and impersonal experience when talking to a computer. Despite this one problem, however, the many improvements have resulted in more companies beginning to rely on voice-recognition products. The main reasons for the recent dramatic growth in voice recognition have been a drive to improve customer service and to do so without raising costs. Let us look at a few of the applications.

Hewlett Packard (HP) is turning to voice-recognition technology because of its low cost compared to the cost of hiring employees to answer help line telephones. According to Lyle Hurst, general manager of HP's product-support division, he is turning to voice recognition software because

"We want to solve customers' problems, and we want to solve them quickly." He expects speech technology to be able to answer the most common questions asked by customers who have purchased low-margin products such as scanners and printers.

The securities industry is also finding a role for voice-recognition technology. Prudential Securities began using the technology in 1998 to cover telephone calls at night. By early 1999 the software was handling about 15 percent of Prudential's 2,000 daily calls.

United Airlines uses speech recognition to handle customer and employee flight status calls. Callers can use the flight number, but if they do not have it, they can speak the cities of origin and destination and the flight time into the telephone and get the information they need. The system is capable of pulling key information out of their speech regardless of how many words are in the caller's sentences or in what order the information is given. American Airlines is also using speech recognition to improve customer service. Its most valued frequent fliers, members of its AAdvantage Executive Platinum frequent flier club, expressed annoyance at having to punch their long identification numbers into the telephone. Now they can simply speak the number into the telephone. If the system misunderstands the number, it will ask the customer to repeat it. If it is still unclear, the individual is immediately connected to a customer service agent.

TO THINK ABOUT: What are the business benefits of using voice-recognition technology?

Sources: John Rossheim, "Giving Voice to Customer Service," **Datamation**, November 1999; Mary E. Thyfault, "Vendors Plan Speech Applications," **Information Week**, February 22, 1999, and "Voice Gets Reliable," **Information Week**, February 22, 1999; Nancy Weil, "IBM, Nokia Join on Speech Recognition," **Computerworld**, October 27, 1999, and "IBM, Partners Offer Glimpse of Speech Tech's Potential," **Computerworld**, June 14, 1999.

Continuous-speech recognition with a familiar voice on powerful PCs can be as much as 98 percent accurate today. Computers increasingly are able to understand what is said to them and to talk back.

MANAGEMENT WRAP-UP

Management

Selecting computer hardware technology for the organization is a key business decision, and it should not be left to technical specialists alone. General managers should understand the capabilities of various computer processing, input, output, and storage options, as well as price/performance relationships. They should be involved in hardware-capacity planning and decisions to distribute computing, to downsize, or to use network computers.

Computer hardware technology can either enhance or impede organizational performance. Computer hardware selection should consider how well the technology meshes with the organization's culture and structure as well as its information-processing requirements.

Organization

Information technology today is not limited to computers but must be viewed as an array of digital devices networked together. Organizations have many computer processing options to choose from, including mainframes, workstations, PCs, and network computers, and many different ways of configuring hardware components to create systems.

Technology

For Discussion

1. What factors would you consider in deciding whether to switch from centralized processing on a mainframe to client/server processing?

2. A firm would like to introduce computers into its order entry process but feels that it should wait for a new generation of machines to be developed. After all, any machine bought now will be quickly out of date and less expensive a few years from now. Do you agree? Why or why not?

SUMMARY

1. Identify the hardware components in a typical computer system. The modern computer system has six major components: a central processing unit (CPU), primary storage, input devices, output devices, secondary storage, and communications devices.

2. Describe how information is represented and processed in a computer system. Digital computers store and process information in the form of binary digits called bits. A string of eight bits is called a byte. There are several coding schemes for arranging binary digits into characters. The most common are EBCDIC and ASCII. The CPU is the part of the computer where the manipulation of symbols, numbers, and letters occurs. The CPU has two components: an arithmetic-logic unit and a control unit. The arithmetic-logic unit performs arithmetical and logical operations on data, whereas the control unit controls and coordinates the computer's other components.

The CPU is closely tied to primary memory, or primary storage, which stores data and program instructions temporarily before and after processing. Several different kinds of semiconductor memory chips are used with primary storage: RAM (random access memory) is used for short-term storage of data and program instructions; ROM (read-only memory) permanently stores important program instructions.

Computer processing power depends in part on the speed of microprocessors, which integrate the computer's logic and control on a single chip. Microprocessors' capabilities can be gauged by their word length, data bus width, and cycle speed. Most conventional computers process one instruction at a time, but computers with parallel processing can process multiple instructions simultaneously.

3. Describe the principal media for storing data and programs in a computer system. The principal forms of secondary storage are magnetic tape, magnetic disk, and optical disk. Tape stores records in sequence and only can be used in batch processing. Disk permits direct access to specific records and is much faster than tape. Disk technology is used in on-line processing. Optical disks can store vast amounts of data compactly. CD-ROM systems can only be read from, but rewritable optical disk systems are becoming available.

4. Describe the major input and output devices, approaches to input and processing, and interactive multimedia. The principal input devices are keyboards, computer mice, touch screens, magnetic ink, optical character recognition, pen-based instruments, digital scanners, sensors, and voice input. The principal output devices are video display terminals, printers, plotters, voice output devices, microfilm, and microfiche. In batch processing, transactions are accumulated and stored in a group until it is efficient or necessary to process them. In on-line processing, the user enters transactions into a device that is directly connected to the computer system. The transactions are usually processed immediately. Multimedia integrates two or more types of media, such as text, graphics, sound, voice, full-motion video, still video, and/or animation into a computer-based application.

5. Contrast the capabilities of mainframes, midrange computers, PCs, workstations, servers, and supercomputers. Depending on their size and processing power, computers are categorized as mainframes, midrange computers, PCs, workstations, servers, or supercomputers. Mainframes are the largest computers; midrange computers can be minicomputers used in factory, university, or research lab systems or servers providing software and other resources to computers on a network. PCs are desktop or laptop machines; workstations are desktop machines with powerful mathematical and graphic capabilities; and supercomputers are sophisticated, powerful computers that can perform massive and complex computations rapidly. Because of continuing advances in microprocessor technology, the distinctions between these types of computers are constantly changing.

6. Compare different arrangements of computer processing, including the use of client/server computing and network computers. Computers can be networked together to distribute processing among different machines. In the client/server model of computing, computer processing is split between "clients" and "servers" connected via a network. Each function of an application is assigned to the machine best suited to perform that function. The exact division of tasks between client and server depends on the application.

Network computers are pared-down desktop machines with minimal or no local storage and processing capacity. They obtain most or all of their software and data from a central network server. Network computers help organizations maintain central control over computing. If they are managed properly, both network computers and client/server computing can reduce the total cost of ownership (TCO) of information technology resources.

7. Analyze important hardware technology trends. The future will see faster chips that can package large amounts of computing power in very small spaces. Microminiaturization will embed intelligence in more everyday devices, including information appliances and smart cards. More computing tasks will be performed by specialized information appliances instead of PCs. Computers using massively parallel processing will be used more widely, and computers and related information technologies will be able to blend data, images, and sound. Social interfaces will make using computers more intuitive and natural.

KEY TERMS

Arithmetic-logic unit (ALU), 113

ASCII (American Standard Code for Information Interchange), 112

Bar code, 122

Batch processing, 124

Bit, 111

Byte, 111

Cathode ray tube (CRT), 125

CD-R (compact disk-recordable), 119

CD-ROM (compact disk read-only memory), 119

Central processing unit (CPU), 112

Centralized processing, 129

Client, 129

Client/server computing, 129

Computer mouse, 121

Control unit, 113

Coprocessor, 117

Data bus width, 116

Digital scanners, 123

Digital video disk (DVD), 119

Direct access storage device (DASD), 119

Distributed processing, 129

Downsizing, 130

EBCDIC (Extended Binary Coded Decimal Interchange Code), 112

Floppy disk, 118

Gigabyte, 115

Hard disk, 118

Information appliance, 133

Kilobyte, 115

Machine cycle, 113

Magnetic disk, 118

Magnetic ink character recognition (MICR), 123

Magnetic tape, 119

Mainframe, 127

Massively parallel computers, 117

Master file, 124

Megabyte, 115

Megahertz, 116

Microprocessor, 115

Microsecond, 114

Midrange computer, 127

Minicomputer, 127

MMX (MultiMedia eXtension), 117

MP3 (MPEG3), 126

Multimedia, 125

Nanosecond, 114

Network computer (NC), 131

On-line processing, 124

Optical character recognition (OCR), 122

Parallel processing, 117

Pen-based input device, 123

Personal computer (PC), 127

Pixel, 112

Plotter, 125

Primary storage, 113

Printer, 125

RAID (Redundant Array of Inexpensive Disks), 118

RAM (random access memory), 114

Reduced instruction set computing (RISC), 117

Register, 113

ROM (read-only memory), 115

Scalability, 129

Secondary storage, 118

Semiconductor, 115

Sensors, 123

Server, 127

Server farm, 127

Smart card, 133

Source data automation, 122

Storage area network (SAN), 120

Streaming technology, 126

Supercomputer, 127

Total cost of ownership (TCO), 131

Touch screen, 122

Transaction file, 124

Voice input device, 123

Voice output device, 125

Word length, 115

Workstation, 127

WORM (write once/read many), 119

REVIEW QUESTIONS

1. What are the components of a contemporary computer system?

2. Distinguish between a bit and a byte.

3. What are ASCII and EBCDIC, and why are they used?

4. Name the major components of the CPU, and describe the function of each.

5. Describe how information is stored in primary memory.

6. What are the different types of semiconductor memory, and when are they used?

7. Name and describe the factors affecting a microprocessor's speed and performance.

8. Distinguish between serial, parallel, and massively parallel processing.

9. List the most important secondary storage media. What are the strengths and limitations of each?

10. List and describe the major input devices.

11. What is the difference between batch and on-line processing? Diagram the difference.

12. List and describe the major output devices.

13. What is multimedia? What technologies are involved?

14. What is the difference between a mainframe, a minicomputer, a server, and a PC? Between a PC and a workstation?

15. What are downsizing and client/server processing?

16. What is a network computer? How does it differ from a conventional PC?

17. Name three hardware technology trends and explain their implications for business organizations.

GROUP PROJECT

Experts predict that notebook computers soon will have 10 times the power of a current personal computer, with a touch-sensitive color screen that one can write on or draw on with a stylus or type on when a program displays a keyboard. Each will have a small, compact, rewritable, removable CD-ROM that can store the equivalent of an encyclopedia set. In addition, the computers will have voice-recognition capabilities, including the ability to record sound and give voice responses to questions. The computers will be able to carry on a dialogue using voice, graphics, typed words, and displayed video graphics.

Thus, affordable computers will be about the size of a thick pad of paper and just as portable and convenient but with the intelligence of a computer and the multimedia capabilities of a television set.

Form a group with three or four of your classmates and develop an analysis of the impacts such developments would have on one of these areas: university education, corporate sales and marketing, manufacturing, or management consulting. Explain why you think the impact will or will not occur.

Tools for Interactive Learning

○ Internet Connection

The Internet Connection for this chapter will direct you to a series of Web sites where you can complete an exercise to survey the products and services of major computer hardware vendors and the use of Web sites in the computer hardware industry. You can also use the Interactive Study Guide to test your knowledge of the topics in this chapter and get instant feedback where you need more practice.

○ Electronic Commerce Project

At the Laudon Web site for Chapter 4, you will find an Electronic Commerce project for buying and financing a house purchase.

○ CD-ROM

If you purchase and use the Multimedia Edition CD-ROM with this chapter, you can complete an interactive exercise testing your knowledge of the machine cycle and view a simulation of a program executing on a computer. You can also find a video clip by Intel showing the evolution of computer hardware, an audio overview of the major themes of this chapter, and bullet text summarizing the key points of the chapter.

○ Application Exercise

At the Laudon Web site, you can find a spreadsheet and presentation software Application Exercise for this chapter where you can analyze requirements for personal computer hardware.

If you could reduce the total cost of owning your PCs, servers, and other computer hardware by 20 percent, would you do it? According to studies done by Tom Oleson of International Data Corp., management can do precisely that simply by employing known asset management techniques. The savings can be significant, and if the organization is large enough they can amount to hundreds of thousands or even millions of dollars annually. Let us look at several companies' programs for information technology asset management.

Willis Corroon, based in London, is one of the world's largest insurance and reinsurance brokers. In addition to selling insurance, Willis Corroon provides consulting services to help clients manage, finance, and control risk. With 300 offices in 93 countries, the company can provide personal, local service all over the world.

Much of the company's recent growth resulted from the 1991 merger of the firms of Willis Faber and Corroon & Black. The merger provided many benefits, but it also left the company with an inconsistent IT infrastructure.

For example, Willis has about 100 local offices in North America. Their payroll and general ledger systems were centralized and ran on a mainframe in Willis's North American headquarters in Nashville, Tennessee. However, local offices had been allowed to acquire their own technology resources. These offices maintained a hodgepodge of PC and server systems, ranging from PCs with obsolete 80486 microprocessors to new, leading-edge models with state-of-the art technology. Different offices were using different versions of word processing and office automation software and each local office had its own support person.

The flow of information between offices suffered. One Willis office could not read the documents created by another Willis office using different hardware or software. Local offices, the head office in the United States, and the home office in London could not communicate easily.

Such inconsistent hardware and software configurations prevented Willis from realizing company-wide efficiencies and raised the total cost of ownership (TCO) of its desktop and server environment. According to Greg Linder, Willis's director of operations support, the company spent $2.5 million in annual salary, benefits, and administrative costs for 53 local desktop and server administrators who spent part of their time performing redundant tasks. Productivity losses among information system specialists and end users amounted to tens of thousands of dollars annually.

In late 1998, Willis embarked on an aggressive technology asset management program to standardize technology in its offices, increase productivity, and lower administrative and support costs. Willis selected Dell OptiPlex GX1 desktop PCs and Dell Latitude Cpi laptops and Compaq ProLiant 800, 1600, 3000, and 5500 servers for all of its offices. The company purchased 4,350 PCs, 50 central servers, and 150 distributed servers altogether. Willis selected standard software for use with all of its offices, including Microsoft Office software for word processing and other desktop productivity applications.

Benefits have been greater than originally anticipated. Willis originally estimated that it would cost $6 million to implement the systems management technology over a 5-year period, saving $3 million during that time. Linder reported that the company had realized $2 million in tangible savings in 1999 alone and projected that savings for the 5-year period will well exceed the target. Because Willis has company-wide standards for hardware and software, new applications or updates to existing software are less expensive to install and use. Linder reported that every time Willis rolled out a new software application, it saved $20 per hardware device. "A rollout to every desktop translates into $87,000 in savings," he says. With centralized hardware and software standards, the company can install new software rapidly as well. When the company faced a serious new computer virus outbreak, it was able to quickly deploy Network Associates' McAfee VirusScan antivirus software, and no computer processing time was lost to the outbreak.

Standardizing hardware and software assets reduced the need for desktop and server administrators in Willis offices. Willis reduced the number of administrators from 53 to 14, moving former administrators to sales-related jobs. Company expenditures on local consulting fees shrunk as well, saving more than $100,000 in 1999 alone.

UnitedHealth Group of Minneapolis, Minnesota, has about 29,000 employees scattered among 216 sites. Until recently no company-wide asset management policy or process existed. When Tony Abate, director of technology acquisitions, decided to do an inventory, he found that the company owned 11,000 more PCs, many of which were obsolete, than it had employees. The company has since reduced the number of PCs to one per employee, a major savings in hardware costs. But that is only the beginning of the savings.

By inventorying all the hardware, Abate found too many hardware and software platforms and brands, which created major incompatibilities. In addition, the company lost the benefit of coordinated national purchasing contracts that would have been the result of buying in quantity. Of course, all the extra PCs had software installed, just like all the others, which was an immense and unnecessary expense. Then there was the problem of maintenance. For the hardware, that meant extra repairs and upgrades, and for the installed software, it meant extra upgrades and installations.

The one problem was selling management on the project. As with many projects, costs are up front and savings are in the future. The up-front costs included $1.2 million just for the original manual physical inventory (including travel to the many sites). However, management eventually agreed, and UnitedHealth now estimates that it has saved $1.5 million in maintenance costs alone. Today, using an asset management system and knowing what is needed around the company, management is able to negotiate contracts at lower prices. One very nice extra saving was the elimination of millions of dollars in excess purchase billings because of the centralized management process. Finally, with asset management software installed on all the PCs, the company no longer needs to count all the PCs in order to take inventory. That is done automatically and almost instantly. Altogether UnitedHealth estimates total savings amounted to $11 billion for the first few years.

Sources: Ed Trapasso, "Managing Assets Helps Manage Costs," **Beyond Computing,** October 1999; Oliver Rist, "Managed PC Care," **Information Week,** May 31, 1999; David Essex, "Cover Your Assets," **Computerworld,** June 21, 1999; and www.williscorroon.com.

CASE STUDY QUESTIONS

1. What problems did Willis Corroon and UnitedHealth have with their IT infrastructure? Why?

2. How were the business processes at both companies affected by their problems with hardware resources?

3. How did Willis and UnitedHealth reduce the TCO of their information technology assets?

4. What management, organization, and technology issues should be considered when selecting computer hardware?

5. It has been said that asset management requires an organization to change the way it does business. Do you agree? Why or why not?

CHAPTER 5

The Role of Software in the Information Technology (IT) Infrastructure

Learning Objectives

After completing this chapter, you will be able to:

1. Describe the major types of software.

2. Examine the functions of system software and compare leading PC operating systems.

3. Explain how software has evolved and how it will continue to develop.

4. Analyze the strengths and limitations of the major application programming languages and software tools.

5. Describe new approaches to software development.

6. Identify important issues in the management of organizational software assets.

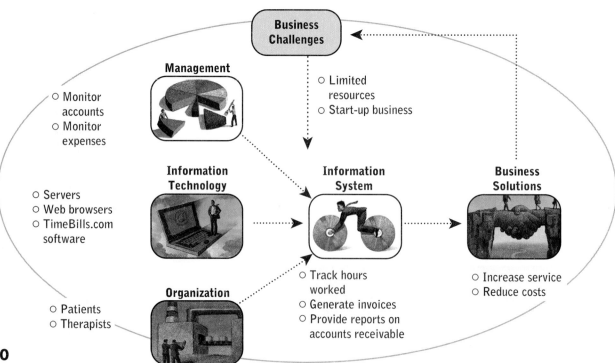

Business Challenges

Management
- Monitor accounts
- Monitor expenses

- Limited resources
- Start-up business

Information Technology
- Servers
- Web browsers
- TimeBills.com software

Information System

Business Solutions

Organization
- Patients
- Therapists

- Track hours worked
- Generate invoices
- Provide reports on accounts receivable

- Increase service
- Reduce costs

Renting Software on the Web:
A Lifeline for Small Businesses

Phoenix Therapeutic Counseling Services in Chilliwac, British Columbia, started out on a shoestring. April Canning, the firm's owner, did all the invoicing to patients by hand using receipt books purchased at the local stationary store. But as the business grew, the old paper-based system became too time consuming to use. It was impossible for Canning to obtain a quick, accurate picture of her company's financial status. One day she threw up her hands crying, "There's no way we can go on doing it this way."

Canning first turned to an accountant and specialized accounting software to solve her problem. After spending hundreds of dollars, she was still unhappy. She then started using TimeBills.com, which provides Web-based software for small businesses and self-employed people. The software runs on the Web and provides individuals or groups working in different locations with capabilities to track time and expenses. The software then uses this information to generate invoices. Users can enter the amount of time worked, hourly billing rates, and related expense data into the system using standard Web browser software for accessing the Web. The system stores their data on TimeBills.com's servers, where they are protected so that they can only be accessed by an authorized TimeBills.com member. Using their Web browsers and the software on the TimeBills.com Web site, business professionals can generate invoices in less than a minute and send them directly to clients via e-mail, fax, or conventional mail. Managers can use the service to evaluate employee performance and plan projects more accurately.

Unlike high-priced software that might be very complicated to learn or too time-consuming to use, TimeBills' software focuses on performing a handful of essential tasks easily and efficiently. By providing the software over the Web, the TimeBills.com service eliminates the need for companies to purchase, install, and maintain complex software on their own. TimeBills is especially well suited for companies with fewer than 20 employees that cannot afford traditional accounting software. Businesses with up to five users can use TimeBills.com for free. Each additional user costs only $3.95 per month.

Entrepreneurs and start-up companies waste an average of 3.5 hours per day filling out timesheets, billing, and organizing receipts and records. Besides saving employee time, TimeBills.com can help companies cut down on administrative overhead by as much as 40 percent. By renting software from TimeBills.com, April Canning has saved on accountant fees and can instantly see how much money her company will be taking in from clients that have been billed.

Sources: "Managers Go Online to Automate Payroll and Analyze Employee Time with TimeBills.com Suite of Integrated Business Services," CBS Market Watch, February 15, 2000; Megan Santarus, "Time Is Money," *Web Business* Magazine, January 2000; and David Haskin, "Get Top Billing," *Small Business and Office Computing,* December, 1999.

MANAGEMENT CHALLENGES

Many businesses like Phoenix Therapeutic Counseling Services that derive most of their revenue from billing for services have access to computer hardware and outside accounting help. What prevented April Canning from reducing the time and cost to prepare bills for clients was the lack of appropriate software. To find the software it needed, Phoenix Therapeutic Counseling Services had to know the capabilities of various types of software, and it had to select invoicing and billing software that met its specific business requirements and was affordable and easy to use. Selecting and developing the right software can improve organizational performance, but it raises the following management challenges:

1. Increasing complexity and software errors. Although some software for desktop systems and for some Internet applications can be rapidly generated, a great deal of what software will be asked to do remains far-reaching and sophisticated, requiring programs that are large and complex. Citibank's automatic teller machine application required 780,000 lines of program code, written by hundreds of people, each working on small portions of the program. Large and complex systems tend to be error-prone, and software errors or "bugs" may not be revealed for years after exhaustive testing and actual use. Researchers do not know if the number of bugs grows exponentially or proportionately to the number of lines of code, nor can they tell for certain whether all segments of a complex piece of software will always work in total harmony. The process of designing and testing software that is reliable and bug-free is a serious quality control and management issue (see Chapter 13).

2. The application backlog. Advances in computer software have not kept pace with the breathtaking productivity gains in computer hardware. Developing software has become a major preoccupation for organizations. A great deal of software must be intricately crafted. Moreover, the software itself is only one component of a complete information system that must be carefully designed and coordinated with other people, as well as with organizational and hardware components. Managerial, procedural, and policy issues must be carefully researched and evaluated apart from the actual coding. The "software crisis" is actually part of a larger systems analysis, design, and implementation issue, which will be treated in detail later. Despite the gains from fourth-generation languages, personal desktop software tools, object-oriented programming, and software tools for the World Wide Web, many businesses continue to face a backlog of two to three years in developing the information systems they need, or they may not be able to develop them at all.

To play a useful role in the firm's information technology (IT) infrastructure, computer hardware requires instructions provided by computer software. This chapter shows how software turns computer hardware into useful information systems, describes major software types, and presents new approaches to software development and acquisition. It also introduces some key issues for managing software as an organizational asset in the information technology infrastructure.

5.1 What Is Software?

Software is the detailed instructions that control the operation of a computer system. Without software, computer hardware could not perform the tasks we associate with computers. The functions of software are to (1) manage the computer resources of the organization, (2) provide tools for human beings to take advantage of these resources, and (3) act as an intermediary between organizations and stored information. Selecting appropriate software for the organization is a key management decision.

software The detailed instructions that control the operation of a computer system.

SOFTWARE PROGRAMS

A software **program** is a series of statements or instructions to the computer. The process of writing or coding programs is termed *programming,* and individuals who specialize in this task are called *programmers.*

program A series of statements or instructions to the computer.

The **stored program concept** means that a program must be stored in the computer's primary storage along with the required data in order to execute, or have its instructions performed by the computer. Once a program has finished executing, the computer hardware can be used for another task when a new program is loaded into its memory.

stored program concept The idea that a program cannot be executed unless it is stored in a computer's primary storage along with required data.

MAJOR TYPES OF SOFTWARE

There are two major types of software: system software and application software. Each kind performs a different function. **System software** is a set of generalized programs that manages the computer's resources, such as the central processor, communications links, and peripheral devices. Programmers who write system software are called system programmers.

system software Generalized programs that manage the computer's resources, such as the central processor, communications links, and peripheral devices.

Application software describes the programs that are written for or by users to apply the computer to a specific task. Software for processing an order or generating a mailing list is application software. Programmers who write application software are called application programmers.

application software Programs written for a specific application to perform functions specified by end users.

The types of software are interrelated and can be thought of as a set of nested boxes, each of which must interact closely with the other boxes surrounding it. Figure 5-1 illustrates this relationship. The system software surrounds and controls access to the hardware. Application software must work through the system software in order to operate. End users work primarily with application software. Each type of software must be specially designed for a specific machine to ensure its compatibility.

5.2 System Software

System software coordinates the various parts of the computer system and mediates between application software and computer hardware. The system software that manages and controls the computer's activities is called the **operating system.** Other system software consists of computer language translation programs, which convert programming languages into machine language, and utility programs, which perform common processing tasks.

operating system The system software that manages and controls the activities of the computer.

FUNCTIONS OF THE OPERATING SYSTEM

One way to look at the operating system is as the system's chief manager. Operating system software decides which computer resources will be used, which programs will be run, and the order in which activities will take place.

An operating system performs three functions. It allocates and assigns system resources, it schedules the use of computer resources and computer jobs, and it monitors computer system activities.

FIGURE 5-1 The major types of software. The relationship between the system software, application software, and users can be illustrated by a series of nested boxes. System software—consisting of operating systems, language translators, and utility programs—controls access to the hardware. Application software, such as the programming languages and fourth-generation languages, must work through the system software to operate. The user interacts primarily with the application software.

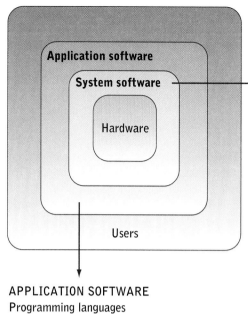

SYSTEM SOFTWARE

Operating Systems
Schedules computer events
Allocates computer resources
Monitors events

Language Translators
Interpreters
Compilers

Utility Programs
Routine operations (e.g., sort, list, print)
Manage data (e.g., create files, merge files)

APPLICATION SOFTWARE
Programming languages
Assembly language
FORTRAN
COBOL
BASIC
PASCAL
C
Fourth-generation languages and PC software tools

Allocation and Assignment

The operating system allocates resources to the application jobs in the execution queue. It provides locations in primary memory for data and programs, and controls the input and output devices, such as printers, terminals, and telecommunication links.

Scheduling

Thousands of pieces of work can be going on in a computer simultaneously. The operating system decides when to schedule the jobs that have been submitted and how to coordinate the scheduling in various areas of the computer so that different parts of different jobs can be worked on at the same time. For instance, while a program is executing, the operating system is scheduling the use of input and output devices. Not all jobs are performed in the order they are submitted; the operating system schedules jobs according to organizational priorities. On-line order processing may have priority over a job to generate mailing lists and labels.

Monitoring

The operating system monitors the activities of the computer system. It keeps track of each computer job and may also keep track of who is using the system, of what programs have been run, and of any unauthorized attempts to access the system. Information system security is discussed in detail in Chapter 13.

MULTIPROGRAMMING, VIRTUAL STORAGE, TIME SHARING, AND MULTIPROCESSING

How is it possible for 1,000 or more users sitting at remote terminals to use a computer information system simultaneously if, as we stated in the previous chapter, most computers can execute only one instruction from one program at a time? How can computers run thousands of programs? The answer is that the computer has a series of specialized operating system capabilities.

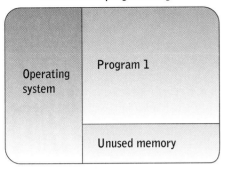

Traditional system
with no multiprogramming

Multiprogramming
environment

FIGURE 5-2 Single-program execution versus multiprogramming. In multiprogramming, the computer can be used much more efficiently because a number of programs can be executing concurrently. Several complete programs are loaded into memory. This memory management aspect of the operating system greatly increases throughput by better management of high-speed memory and input/output devices.

Multiprogramming

The most important operating system capability for sharing computer resources is **multiprogramming.** Multiprogramming permits multiple programs to share a computer system's resources at any one time through concurrent use of a CPU. By concurrent use, we mean that only one program is actually using the CPU at any given moment but that the input/output needs of other programs can be serviced at the same time. Two or more programs are active at the same time, but they do not use the same computer resources simultaneously. With multiprogramming, a group of programs takes turns using the processor.

Figure 5-2 shows how three programs in a multiprogramming environment can be stored in primary storage. The first program executes until an input/output event is read in the program. The operating system then directs a channel (a small processor limited to input and output functions) to read the input and move the output to an output device. The CPU moves to the second program until an input/output statement occurs. At this point, the CPU switches to the execution of the third program, and so forth, until eventually all three programs have been executed. In this manner, many different programs can be executing at the same time, although different resources within the CPU are actually being used.

The first operating systems executed only one program at a time. Before multiprogramming, when a program read data off a tape or disk or wrote data to a printer, the entire CPU came to a stop. This was a very inefficient way to use the computer. With multiprogramming, the CPU utilization rate is much higher.

multiprogramming A method of executing two or more programs concurrently using the same computer. The CPU executes only one program but can service the input/output needs of others at the same time.

Multitasking

Multitasking refers to multiprogramming on single-user operating systems such as those in older personal computers. One person can run two or more programs or program tasks concurrently on a single computer. For example, a sales representative could write a letter to prospective clients with a word processing program while simultaneously using a database program to search for all sales contacts in a particular city or geographic area. Instead of terminating the session with the word processing program, returning to the operating system, and then initiating a session with the database program, multitasking allows the sales representative to display both programs on the computer screen and work with them at the same time.

multitasking The multiprogramming capability of primarily single-user operating systems, such as those for older PCs.

Virtual Storage

Virtual storage handles programs more efficiently because the computer divides the programs into small fixed- or variable-length portions, storing only a small portion of the program in primary memory at one time. If only two or three large programs can be read into memory, a certain part of the main memory generally remains underused because the programs add up to less than the total amount of primary storage space available. Given the limited size of primary memory, only a small number of programs can reside in primary storage at any given time.

Only a few statements of a program actually execute at any given moment. Virtual storage breaks a program into a number of fixed-length portions called pages or into variable-length

virtual storage Handling programs more efficiently by dividing the programs into small fixed- or variable-length portions with only a small portion stored in primary memory at one time.

portions called segments. Each of these portions is relatively small (a page is approximately two to four kilobytes). This permits a very large number of programs to reside in primary memory, inasmuch as only one page of each program is actually located there (see Figure 5-3).

All other program pages are stored on a peripheral disk unit until they are ready for execution. Virtual storage provides a number of advantages. First, the central processor is used more fully. Many more programs can be in primary storage because only one page of each program actually resides there. Second, programmers no longer have to worry about the size of the primary storage area. With virtual storage, programs can be of infinite length and small machines can execute a program of any size (admittedly, small machines will take longer than big machines to execute a large program).

Time Sharing

time sharing The sharing of computer resources by many users simultaneously by having the CPU spend a fixed amount of time on each user's program before proceeding to the next.

Time sharing is an operating system capability that allows many users to share computer processing resources simultaneously. It differs from multiprogramming in that the CPU spends a fixed amount of time on one program before moving on to another. In a time-sharing environment, thousands of users are each allocated a tiny slice of computer time. In this time slot, each user is free to perform any required operations; at the end of this period, another user is given a tiny slice of CPU time. This arrangement permits many users to be connected to a CPU simultaneously, with each receiving only a tiny amount of CPU time. But because the CPU is operating at the nanosecond level, a CPU can accomplish a great deal of work in several thousandths of a second.

Multiprocessing

multiprocessing An operating system feature for executing two or more instructions simultaneously in a single computer system by using multiple CPUs.

Multiprocessing is an operating system capability that links together two or more CPUs to work in parallel in a single computer system. The operating system can assign multiple CPUs to execute different instructions from the same program or from different programs simultaneously, dividing the work between the CPUs. Whereas multiprogramming uses concurrent processing with one CPU, multiprocessing uses simultaneous processing with multiple CPUs.

LANGUAGE TRANSLATION AND UTILITY SOFTWARE

When computers execute programs written in languages such as COBOL, FORTRAN, or C, the computer must convert these humanly readable instructions into a form it can understand. System software includes special language translator programs that translate high-level language programs written in programming languages such as BASIC, COBOL, and FORTRAN into machine language that the computer can execute. This type of system software is called a compiler or interpreter. The program in the high-level language before translation into machine

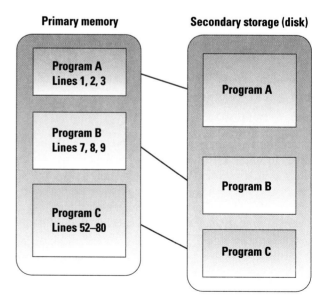

FIGURE 5-3 Virtual storage. Virtual storage is based on the fact that, in general, only a few statements in a program can actually be used at any given moment. In virtual storage, programs are broken down into small sections called pages. Individual program pages are read into memory only when needed. The rest of the program is stored on disk until it is required. In this way, very large programs can be executed by small machines, or a large number of programs can be executed concurrently by a single machine.

language is called **source code. A compiler** translates source code into machine code called **object code.** Just before execution by the computer, the object code modules are joined with other object code modules in a process called linkage editing. The resulting load module is what is actually executed by the computer. Figure 5-4 illustrates the language translation process.

Some programming languages such as BASIC do not use a compiler but an **interpreter,** which translates each source code statement one at a time into machine code and executes it. Interpreter languages such as BASIC provide immediate feedback to the programmer if a mistake is made, but they are very slow to execute because they are translated one statement at a time. An assembler is similar to a compiler, but it is used to translate only assembly language (see Section 5.3) into machine code.

System software includes **utility programs** for routine, repetitive tasks, such as copying, clearing primary storage, computing a square root, or sorting. If you have worked on a computer and have performed such functions as setting up new files, deleting old files, or formatting diskettes, you have worked with utility programs. Utility programs are prewritten programs that are stored so that they can be shared by all users of a computer system and can be used rapidly in many different information system applications when requested.

GRAPHICAL USER INTERFACES

When users interact with a computer, even a PC, the interaction is controlled by an operating system. The user interface is the part of an information system with which users interact. Users communicate with an operating system through the user interface of that operating system. Early PC operating systems were command-driven, but the **graphical user interface,** often called a **GUI,** makes extensive use of icons, buttons, bars, and boxes to perform the same task. It has become the dominant model for the user interface of PC operating systems and for many types of application software.

Older PC operating systems such as DOS, described in the following section, are command-driven, requiring the user to type in text-based commands using a keyboard. For example, to perform a task such as deleting a file named DATAFILE, the user must type in a

source code Program instructions written in a high-level language that must be translated into machine language to be executed by the computer.

compiler Special system software that translates a high-level language into machine language for execution by the computer.

object code Program instructions that have been translated into machine language so that they can be executed by the computer.

interpreter A special translator of source code into machine code that translates each source code statement into machine code and executes them, one at a time.

utility program System software consisting of programs for routine, repetitive tasks, which can be shared by many users.

graphical user interface (GUI) The part of an operating system users interact with that uses graphic icons and the computer mouse to issue commands and make selections.

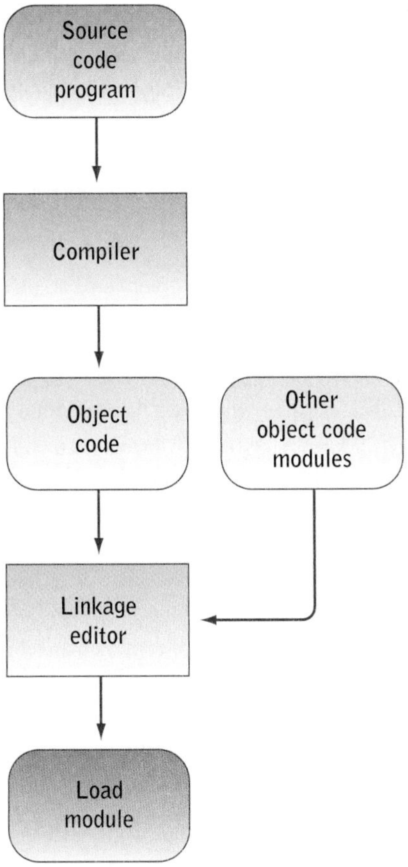

FIGURE 5-4 The language translation process. The source code in a high-level language program is translated by the compiler into object code so that the instructions can be "understood" by the machine. These are grouped into modules. Prior to execution, the object code modules are joined together by the linkage editor to create the load module. It is the load module that is actually executed by the computer.

command such as DELETE C:\DATAFILE. Users need to remember these commands and their syntax to work with the computer effectively. An operating system with a graphical user interface uses graphic symbols called icons to depict programs, files, and activities. Commands can be activated by rolling a mouse to move a cursor about the screen and clicking a button on the mouse to make selections. Icons are symbolic pictures, and they are also used in GUIs to represent programs and files. For example, a file could be deleted by moving the cursor to a trash icon. Many graphical user interfaces use a system of pull-down menus to help users select commands and pop-up boxes to help users select among command options. Windowing features allow users to create, stack, size, and move around boxes of information.

Proponents of graphical user interfaces claim that they save learning time because computing novices do not have to learn different arcane commands for each application. Common functions such as getting help, saving files, or printing output are performed the same way. A complex series of commands can be issued simply by linking icons. However, GUIs may not always simplify complex tasks if the user has to spend too much time first pointing to icons and then selecting operations to perform on those icons or if the GUI is poorly designed (Morse and Reynolds, 1993). Users may be more productive if the interface is less generic and more customized to specific tasks (Satzinger and Olfman, 1998).

PC OPERATING SYSTEMS

Like any other software, PC software is based on specific operating systems and computer hardware. A software package written for one PC operating system generally cannot run on another. Table 5-1 compares the leading PC operating systems: Windows 98 and Windows 95, Windows 2000, Windows CE, OS/2, Unix, Linux, the Macintosh operating system, and DOS.

DOS was the most widely used operating system for 16-bit PCs, which were popular in the late 1980s. It is used today only with older PCs based on the IBM PC standard because so much available application software was written for systems using DOS. (PC-DOS is used exclusively with IBM PCs. MS-DOS, developed by Microsoft, is used with other 16-bit PCs that function like the IBM PC.) DOS itself does not support multitasking and limits the size of a program in memory to 640 kilobytes.

DOS is command-driven, but it can present a graphical user interface by using Microsoft **Windows,** a highly popular graphical user interface shell that runs in conjunction with the DOS operating system. Windows supports limited forms of multitasking and networking but

DOS Operating system for older 16-bit PCs based on the IBM personal computer standard.

Windows A graphical user interface shell that runs in conjunction with the DOS PC operating system. Supports multitasking and some forms of networking.

Table 5-1 Leading PC Operating Systems

Operating System	Features
Windows Me, Windows 98, and Windows 95	32-bit operating system for personal computing with a streamlined graphical user interface. Has multitasking and powerful networking capabilities and can be integrated with the information resources of the Web.
Windows 2000 (Windows NT)	32-bit operating system for PCs, workstations, and network servers. Supports multitasking, multiprocessing, intensive networking, and Internet services for corporate computing.
Windows CE	Pared-down version of the Windows operating system for handheld computers and wireless communication devices.
OS/2	Operating system for IBM PCs that can take advantage of the 32-bit microprocessor. Supports multitasking and networking.
Unix	Used for powerful PCs, workstations, and midrange computers. Supports multitasking, multi-user processing, and networking. Is portable to different models of computer hardware.
Linux	Free, reliable alternative to Unix and Windows 2000 that runs on many different types of computer hardware and provides source code that can be modified by software developers.
Mac OS	Operating system for the Macintosh computer. Supports networking and multitasking and has powerful multimedia capabilities. Supports connecting to and publishing on the Internet.
DOS	Operating system for older IBM (PC-DOS) and IBM-compatible (MS-DOS) PCs. Limits program use of memory to 640 kilobytes.

Microsoft's Windows 98 is a powerful operating system with a graphical user interface and capabilities to integrate the user's desktop with the information resources of the Internet.

shares the memory limitations of DOS. Early versions of Windows had some problems with application crashes when multiple programs competed for the same memory space.

Microsoft's **Windows 98** and **Windows 95** are genuine 32-bit operating systems. A 32-bit operating system can address data in 32-bit chunks (and thus run faster than DOS, which could only address data in 16-bit chunks). Both Windows 98 and Windows 95 provide a streamlined graphical user interface that arranges icons to provide instant access to common tasks. They can support software written for DOS but can also run programs that take up more than 640 kilobytes of memory. Windows 98 and 95 feature multitasking, multithreading (the ability to manage multiple independent tasks simultaneously), and powerful networking capabilities, including the capability to integrate fax, e-mail, and scheduling programs.

Windows 98 is faster and more integrated with the Internet than Windows 95; it includes support for new hardware technologies such as MMX, DVD (see Chapter 4), videoconferencing cameras, scanners, TV tuner-adapter cards, and joysticks. It provides capabilities for optimizing hardware performance and file management on the hard disk and enhanced three-dimensional graphics. The most visible feature of Windows 98 is the integration of the operating system with Web browser software. Users can work with the traditional Windows interface or use the Web browser interface to display information. The user's hard disk can be considered an extension of the World Wide Web, so that a document residing on the hard disk or on the Web can be accessed the same way. Small applet programs (see the discussion of Java in Section 5.4) on the Windows desktop can automatically retrieve information from specific Web sites whenever the user logs onto the Internet. These applets can automatically update the desktop with the latest news, stock quotes, or weather. Windows 98 also includes a group collaboration tool called NetMeeting (see Section 5.3) and a tool for creating and storing Web pages called Front Page Express.

Microsoft is providing an enhanced Windows operating system for consumer users called **Windows Millennium Edition (Windows Me.)** It features tools to let users edit video recordings and put them up on the Web and tools to simplify home networking of two or more PCs. A media player bundled with Windows Me can record, store, and play CDs, digital songs downloaded from the Internet, and video.

Windows 2000 is another 32-bit operating system developed by Microsoft with features that make it appropriate for applications in networked business organizations. Earlier versions of this operating system were known as Windows NT (for New Technology). It is used as an operating system for high-performance desktop and laptop computers and network servers. Windows 2000 shares the same graphical user interface as the other Windows operating systems, but it has more powerful networking, multitasking, and memory-management capabilities. Windows 2000 can support some of the software written for Windows, and it can

Windows 98 Version of the Windows operating system that is more closely integrated with the Internet and that supports hardware technologies such as MMX, digital video disk, videoconferencing cameras, scanners, TV tuner-adapter cards, and joysticks.

Windows 95 A 32-bit operating system with a streamlined graphical user interface and multitasking, multithreading, and networking capabilities.

Windows Millennium Edition (Windows Me) Recent release of the Windows operating system for personal computing.

Windows 2000 Powerful operating system developed by Microsoft for use with 32-bit PCs, workstations, and network servers. Supports networking, multitasking, multiprocessing, and Internet services.

provide mainframelike computing power for new applications with massive memory and file requirements. It can even support multiprocessing with multiple CPUs.

There are two basic versions of Windows 2000—a Professional version for users of stand-alone or client desktop and laptop computers and several server versions designed to run on network servers and provide network management functions, including tools for creating and operating Web sites and other Internet services. An Active Directory allows server computers to manage user identities and access to resources across computer networks.

Windows CE has some of the capabilities of Windows, including its graphical user interface, but it is designed to run on small handheld computers, personal digital assistants, or wireless communication devices such as pagers and cellular phones. It is a portable and compact operating system requiring very little memory. Information appliances and consumer devices can use this operating system to share information with Windows-based PCs and to connect to the Internet.

OS/2 is a robust 32-bit operating system for powerful IBM or IBM-compatible PCs with Intel microprocessors. OS/2 is used for complex, memory-intensive applications or those that require networking, multitasking, or large programs. OS/2 provides powerful desktop computers with mainframe-operating-system capabilities, such as multitasking and supporting multiple users in networks; it also supports networked multimedia and pen-computing applications.

OS/2 supports applications that run under Windows and DOS and has its own graphical user interface. There are now two versions of OS/2. OS/2 Warp is for personal use. It accepts voice-input commands and runs Java applications without a Web browser (see Sections 5.3 and 5.4). OS/2 Warp Server has capabilities similar to Windows 2000 for supporting networking, systems management, and Internet access.

Unix is an interactive, multiuser, multitasking operating system developed by Bell Laboratories in 1969 to help scientific researchers share data. Many people can use Unix simultaneously to perform the same kind of task, or one user can run many tasks on Unix concurrently. Unix was developed to connect various machines together and is highly supportive of communications and networking. Unix is often used on workstations and servers, and it provides the reliability and scalability for running large systems on high-end servers. Unix can run on many different kinds of computers and can be customized easily. Application programs that run under Unix can be ported from one computer to run on a different computer with little modification. Unix also can store and manage a large number of files.

Unix is considered powerful but very complex, with a legion of commands. Graphical user interfaces have been developed for Unix. Unix does not respond well to problems caused by the overuse of system resources such as jobs or disk space. Unix also poses some security problems because multiple jobs and users can access the same file simultaneously. Vendors have developed different versions of Unix that are incompatible, thereby limiting software portability.

Linux is a Unixlike operating system that runs on Intel, AMD, Motorola, Digital Alpha, SPARC, and Mips processors. Linux can be downloaded from the Internet free of charge or purchased for a small fee from companies that provide additional tools for the software. Because it is free, reliable, compactly designed, and capable of running on many different hardware platforms, it has become popular during the past few years among sophisticated computer users and businesses as an alternative to Unix and Windows 2000 as an operating system for Web servers. Major application software vendors are starting to provide versions that can run on Linux. The source code for Linux is available along with the operating system software, so it can be modified by software developers to fit their particular needs.

Linux is an example of **open-source software,** which provides all computer users with free access to its source code so they can fix errors or make improvements. Open-source software such as Linux is not owned by any company or individual. A global network of programmers and users manages and modifies the software, usually without being paid to do so. The Window on Organizations describes how organizations are starting to benefit from this new operating system.

Mac OS, the operating system for the Macintosh computer, features multitasking, powerful multimedia and networking capabilities, and a mouse-driven graphical user interface. New features of this operating system allow users to connect to, explore, and publish on the Internet and World Wide Web; use Java software (see Section 5.4); and load Chinese, Japanese, Korean, Indian, Hebrew, and Arabic fonts for use in Web browser software (see

Windows CE Portable and compact operating system designed to run on small handheld computers, personal digital assistants, or wireless communication devices.

OS/2 Powerful operating system used with 32-bit IBM/PCs or workstations that supports multitasking, networking, and more memory-intensive applications than DOS.

Unix Operating system for all types of computers that is machine independent and supports multiuser processing, multitasking, and networking. Used in high-end workstations and servers.

Linux Reliable and compactly designed operating system that is an offshoot of Unix, which can run on many different hardware platforms and is available free or at very low cost. Used as alternative to Unix and Windows 2000.

open-source software Software that provides free access to its program code, allowing users to modify the program code to make improvements or fix errors.

Mac OS Operating system for the Macintosh computer that supports multitasking, has access to the Internet, and has powerful graphics and multimedia capabilities.

SHOULD BUSINESSES SWITCH TO LINUX?

Burlington Coat Factory, the $1.8 billion clothing discounter based in Burlington, New Jersey, decided to take the plunge with Linux and is installing this new operating system on 1,150 computers in its 250 stores. Why would such a large company opt for a new shareware operating system that can be downloaded free from the Internet?

According to Mike Prince, Burlington's CIO, Linux was attractive both for its price and its performance. It's free and "runs like the wind." Prince also believes Linux is more stable than Windows 2000 and will be less costly to support. Burlington is known as a company that has been comfortable embracing new technology, including network computers and Java as well as Linux. The company also has used Unix for many years and was using Linux on development workstations for about a year before installing it in its stores.

Burlington's previous in-store systems were based on aging technology—Sun Microsystems' SPARC workstations running the SunOS 4.1 operating system. Its client computers for back-office and inventory applications were either radio-frequency, handheld scanners or dumb terminals. Burlington's point-of-sale system, which will not change, uses old PCs running MS-DOS. Prince is replacing the dumb terminals with Pentium PCs but hasn't made up his mind about whether to scrap the SPARC workstations entirely or install Linux on them. When Burlington completes its upgrade, the new hardware should cost between $1.15 million and $1.8 million, but the cost of Linux will only be a few hundred dollars. Burlington expects to save thousands of dollars in each store by not buying a commercial operating system.

The low cost, fast performance, and reliability of Linux also made it attractive to Jay Jacobs, Inc., another retailer based in Seattle, which is installing Linux servers in all of its 120 stores. The Linux servers will be tracking purchases by customer as well as by item. Bill Lawrence, the firm's chief financial officer, thinks that Linux will provide fast, Unixlike performance for less cost than the slower Windows 2000 environment. By using Linux instead of another operating system, the company is saving $666 per store, amounting to a total of $80,000.

However, both Burlington and Jay Jacobs are not relying solely on Linux. Jay Jacobs is using the more established Unix and Windows 2000 operating systems at its corporate headquarters. Burlington is keeping Windows 2000 for desktop productivity applications such as Microsoft Excel and Word. Burlington is sticking with Unix servers from Sequent Computer Systems to house and manipulate its corporate data. Other retailers have primarily selected Windows 2000 when upgrading the operating systems for their stores.

Until more kinds of applications are developed for Linux, this operating system is being used primarily on specialized departmental servers providing Web, e-mail, or printing services or to run custom applications that only require a simple interface. Retailers such as Burlington, which run very few third-party applications, are in a stronger position to select more obscure software platforms. Businesses are also waiting for computer hardware vendors to provide more services and software so that Linux can run easily on their machines and for Linux to acquire stronger graphics, animation, and sound capabilities.

Burlington is using Red Hat Software's version of Linux, an inexpensive commercial version available on CD-ROM that offers technical support. Red Hat's version is the market leader, but it represents only one of a number of different versions of Linux that are currently in use. Because Linux has no single owner, the software is updated by a large group of programmers around the globe. Unlike Windows, which is controlled by Microsoft, anyone can find errors and make changes to Linux code, increasing the risk that Linux could splinter into many slightly different versions as did Unix. The Linux Standards Base is working on rules to keep different Linux versions compatible. Different versions of Linux would discourage its widespread adoption in business.

TO THINK ABOUT: Should a company select Linux as its operating system for its major business applications? Under what conditions? What management, organization, and technology factors would have to be addressed when making that decision?

Sources: Annalee Nemitz, "Is It Time for Linux?" **The Industry Standard,** February 14, 2000; David Orenstein, "Burlington Commits to Linux in 250 Stores," **Computerworld,** February 15, 1999; "Retailer Bets Big on Linux," **Computerworld,** February 8, 1999; and Alex Lash, "Standardizing Linux," **The Industry Standard,** March 8, 1999.

Section 5.3). A new search capability called Sherlock provides a standard interface for efficiently searching for files on the Internet as well as on the user's own hard drive.

5.3 Application Software

Application software is primarily concerned with accomplishing the tasks of end users. Many different languages can be used to develop application software. Each has different strengths and drawbacks.

GENERATIONS OF PROGRAMMING LANGUAGES

machine language A programming language consisting of the 1s and 0s of binary code.

To provide instructions for the first generation of computers, specialized programmers wrote programs in **machine language**—the 0s and 1s of binary code. Programming in 0s and 1s (reducing all statements such as add, subtract, and divide into a series of 0s and 1s) made early programming a slow, labor-intensive process.

As computer hardware improved and processing speed and memory size increased, computer languages changed from machine language to languages that were easier for humans to understand. Figure 5-5 shows the development of programming languages during the past 50 years as hardware capabilities have increased. The major trend is to increase the ease with which users can interact with hardware and software.

Machine language was the first-generation programming language. The second generation of programming languages occurred in the early 1950s with the development of assembly language. Instead of using 0s and 1s, programmers could substitute languagelike acronyms and words such as add, sub (subtract), and load in programming statements. A language translator called a compiler converted the Englishlike statements into machine language.

high-level language

Programming languages in which each source code statement generates multiple statements at the machine-language level.

From the mid-1950s to the mid-1970s, the third generation of programming languages emerged. These languages, such as FORTRAN, COBOL, and BASIC, allowed programs to be written with regular words using sentencelike statements. These languages are called **high-level languages** because each statement generates multiple statements when it is translated into machine language. Programs became easier to create and became widely used for scientific and business problems.

Beginning in the late 1970s, fourth-generation languages and tools were created. These languages dramatically reduced programming time and made software tasks so easy that many could be performed by nontechnical computer users without the help of professional programmers. Software such as word processing, spreadsheets, data management, and Web browsers became popular productivity tools for end users.

FIGURE 5-5 Generations of programming languages. As the capabilities of hardware increased, programming languages developed from the first generation of machine and second generation of assembly languages of the 1950s to 1960s, through the third-generation, high-level languages such as FORTRAN and COBOL developed in the 1960s and 1970s, to today's fourth-generation languages and tools.

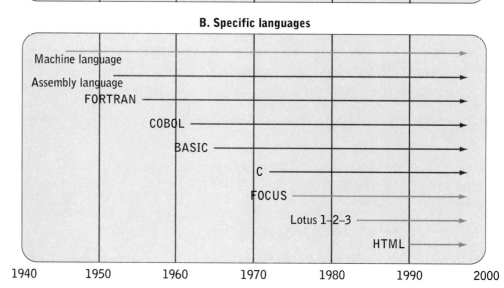

POPULAR PROGRAMMING LANGUAGES

Most managers need not be expert programmers, but they should understand how to evaluate software applications and be able to select programming languages that are appropriate for their organization's objectives. We now briefly describe the more popular high-level languages.

Assembly Language

Like machine language, **assembly language** (Figure 5-6) is designed for a specific machine and specific microprocessors. Each operation in assembly language corresponds to a machine operation. Assembly language makes use of certain mnemonics (e.g., load, sum) and assigns addresses and storage locations automatically. Although assembly language gives programmers great control, it is costly in terms of programmer time; it is also difficult to read, debug, and learn. Assembly language is used primarily today in system software.

assembly language A programming language developed in the 1950s that resembles machine language but substitutes mnemonics for numeric codes.

FORTRAN

FORTRAN (FORmula TRANslator) (Figure 5-7) was developed in 1956 to provide an easy way of writing scientific and engineering applications. FORTRAN is especially useful in processing numeric data. Many kinds of business applications can be written in FORTRAN, and contemporary versions provide sophisticated structures for controlling program logic. FORTRAN is not very good at providing input/output efficiency or in printing and working with lists. The syntax is very strict and keying errors are common, making the programs difficult to debug.

FORTRAN (FORmula TRANslator) A programming language developed in 1956 for scientific and mathematical applications.

COBOL

COBOL (COmmon Business Oriented Language) (Figure 5-8) came into use in the early 1960s. It was developed by a committee representing both government and industry. Rear Admiral Grace M. Hopper was a key committee member who played a major role in COBOL development. COBOL was designed with business administration in mind, for processing large data files with alphanumeric characters (mixed alphabetic and numeric data), and for performing repetitive tasks such as payroll. It is not good at complex mathematical calculations. Also, there are many versions of COBOL, and not all are compatible with each other.

COBOL (COmmon Business Oriented Language) Major programming language for business applications because it can process large data files with alphanumeric characters.

```
AR 5, 3
```

FIGURE 5-6 Assembly language. This sample assembly language command adds the contents of register 3 to register 5 and stores the result in register 5.

```
READ (5,100) ID, QUANT, PRICE
TOTAL = QUANT * PRICE
```

FIGURE 5-7 FORTRAN. This sample FORTRAN program code is part of a program to compute sales figures for a particular item.

```
MULTIPLY QUANT-SOLD BY UNIT-PRICE GIVING SALES-TOTAL.
```

FIGURE 5-8 COBOL. This sample COBOL program code is part of a routine to compute total sales figures for a particular item.

BASIC

BASIC (Beginners All-purpose Symbolic Instruction Code) was developed in 1964 by John Kemeny and Thomas Kurtz to teach students at Dartmouth College how to use computers. Today it is a popular programming language on college campuses and for PCs. BASIC can do almost all computer processing tasks from inventory to mathematical calculations. It is easy to use, demonstrates computer capabilities well, and requires only a limited interpretation. The weakness of BASIC is that it does few tasks well even though it does them all. Different versions of BASIC exist.

Pascal

Named after Blaise Pascal, the seventeenth-century mathematician and philosopher, **Pascal** was developed by the Swiss computer science professor Niklaus Wirth of Zurich in the late 1960s. Pascal programs can be compiled using minimal computer memory, so they can be used on PCs. With sophisticated structures to control program logic and a simple, powerful set of commands, Pascal is used primarily in computer science courses to teach sound programming practices. The language is weak at file handling and input/output and is not easy for beginners to use.

C and C++

C is a powerful and efficient language developed at AT&T's Bell Labs in the early 1970s. It combines machine portability with tight control and efficient use of computer resources, and it can work on a variety of different computers. It is used primarily by professional programmers to create operating system and application software, especially for PCs.

C++ is a newer version of C that is object-oriented (see Section 5.4). It has all the capabilities of C plus additional features for working with software objects. C++ is used for developing application software.

FOURTH-GENERATION LANGUAGES AND PC SOFTWARE TOOLS

Fourth-generation languages consist of a variety of software tools that enable end users to develop software applications with minimal or no technical assistance or that enhance professional programmers' productivity. Fourth-generation languages tend to be nonprocedural or less procedural than conventional programming languages. Procedural languages require the specification of the sequence of steps, or procedures, that tell the computer what to do and how to do it. Nonprocedural languages need only specify what has to be accomplished rather than provide details about how to carry out the task. Thus, a nonprocedural language can accomplish the same task with fewer steps and fewer lines of program code than a procedural language.

There are seven categories of fourth-generation languages: query languages, report generators, graphics languages, application generators, very high-level programming languages, application software packages, and PC tools. Figure 5-9 illustrates the spectrum of these tools and some commercially available products in each category.

BASIC (Beginners All-purpose Symbolic Instruction Code) A general-purpose programming language used with PCs and for teaching programming.

Pascal A programming language used on PCs and used to teach sound programming practices in computer science courses.

C A powerful programming language with tight control and efficiency of execution; it is portable across different microprocessors and is used primarily with PCs.

C++ Object-oriented version of the C programming language.

fourth-generation language A programming language that can be employed directly by end users or less-skilled programmers to develop computer applications more rapidly than conventional programming languages.

FIGURE 5-9 Fourth-generation languages. The spectrum of major categories of fourth-generation languages; commercially available products in each category are illustrated. Tools range from those that are simple and designated primarily for end users to complex tools designed for information systems professionals.

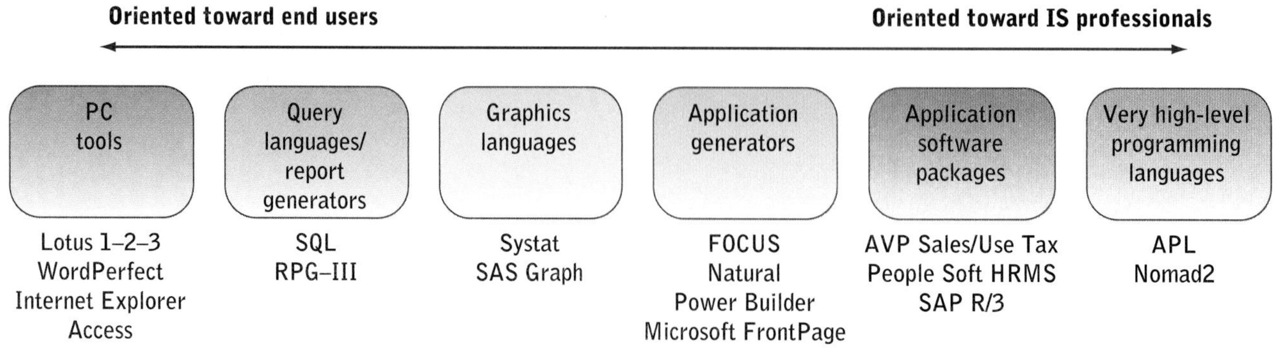

Oriented toward end users ← → **Oriented toward IS professionals**

PC tools	Query languages/ report generators	Graphics languages	Application generators	Application software packages	Very high-level programming languages
Lotus 1–2–3 WordPerfect Internet Explorer Access	SQL RPG–III	Systat SAS Graph	FOCUS Natural Power Builder Microsoft FrontPage	AVP Sales/Use Tax People Soft HRMS SAP R/3	APL Nomad2

Query Languages

Query languages are high-level languages for retrieving data stored in databases or files. They are usually interactive, on-line, and capable of supporting requests for information that are not predefined. They are often tied to database management systems (see Chapter 6) or some of the PC software tools described later in this section. For instance, the query

SELECT ALL WHERE age >40 AND name = "Wilson"

requests all records where the name is "Wilson" and the age is more than 40. Chapter 6 provides more detail on Structured Query Language (SQL), which has become a standard query language.

Available query tools have different kinds of syntax and structure; some are closer to natural language than others (Vassiliou, 1984–1985). **Natural language** software allows users to communicate with the computer using conversational commands that resemble human speech. Natural language development is one of the concerns of artificial intelligence (see Chapter 11). Some consider the movement toward natural language as the next generation in software development.

query language A high-level computer language used to retrieve specific information from databases or files.

natural language Programming language that is very close to human language.

Report Generators

Report generators are software for creating customized reports. They extract data from files or databases and create reports in many formats. Report generators generally provide more control over the way data are formatted, organized, and displayed than query languages. The more powerful report generators can manipulate data with complex calculations and logic before they are output. Some report generators are extensions of database or query languages.

report generator Software that creates customized reports in a wide range of formats that are not routinely produced by an information system.

Graphics Languages

Graphics languages retrieve data from files or databases and display them in graphic format. Users can ask for data and specify how they are to be charted. Some graphics software can perform arithmetical or logical operations on data as well. SAS and Systat are examples of powerful analytical graphics software.

graphics language A computer language that displays in graphic format data from files or databases.

Application Generators

Application generators contain preprogrammed modules that can generate entire applications, greatly speeding development. A user can specify what needs to be done, and the application generator will create the appropriate code for input, validation, update, processing, and reporting. Most full-function application generators consist of a comprehensive, integrated set of development tools including a query language, screen painter, graphics generator, report generator, decision support/modeling tools, security facilities, high-level programming language, and tools for defining and organizing data. Application generators now include tools for developing full-function Web sites.

application generator Software that can generate entire information system applications; the user needs only to specify what must be done, and the application generator creates the appropriate program code.

Very High-Level Programming Languages

Very high-level programming languages are designed to generate program code with fewer instructions than conventional languages such as COBOL or FORTRAN. Programs and applications based on these languages can be developed in short periods of time. End users can employ simple features of these languages. However, these languages are designed primarily as productivity tools for professional programmers. APL and Nomad2 are examples of these languages.

very high-level programming language A programming language that uses fewer instructions than conventional languages. Used primarily as a professional programmer productivity tool.

Application Software Packages

A **software package** is a prewritten, precoded, commercially available set of programs that eliminates the need for individuals or organizations to write their own software programs for certain functions. There are software packages for system software, but the vast majority of package software is application software. These packages are available for major business applications on mainframes, midrange computers, and PCs. Although application packages for large complex systems must be installed by technical specialists, many application packages, especially those for PCs, are marketed directly to end users. Systems development based on application packages is discussed in Chapter 10.

software package A prewritten, precoded, commercially available set of programs that eliminates the need to write software programs for certain functions.

PC Software Tools

Some of the most popular and productivity-promoting software tools are the general-purpose application packages that have been developed for PCs, especially word processing, spreadsheet, data management, presentation graphics, integrated software packages, e-mail, Web browsers, and groupware.

word processing software
Software that handles electronic storage, editing, formatting, and printing of documents.

Word processing software   **Word processing software** stores text data electronically as a computer file rather than on paper. The word processing software allows the user to make changes in the document electronically in memory. This eliminates the need to retype an entire page to incorporate corrections. The software has formatting options to make changes in line spacing, margins, character size, and column width. Microsoft Word and WordPerfect are popular word processing packages. Figure 5-10 illustrates a Microsoft Word screen displaying text, with the spelling and grammar check and major menu options showing.

Most word processing software has advanced features that automate other writing tasks, such as spell checkers, style checkers (to analyze grammar and punctuation), thesaurus programs, and mail merge programs, which link letters or other text documents with names and addresses in a mailing list. The newest versions of this software can create and access Web pages.

Although today's word processing programs can turn out very polished-looking documents, businesses that need to create highly professional-looking brochures, manuals, or books will likely use desktop publishing software. **Desktop publishing software** provides more control over the placement of text, graphics, and photos in the layout of a page than does word processing software. Users of this software can produce finished documents that look like those created by professional print shops by designing the layout; determining spacing between letters, words, and lines; reducing or enlarging graphics; or rearranging blocks of text and graphics. Adobe Pagemaker and QuarkXpress are two popular desktop publishing packages.

desktop publishing software
Software that produces professional-quality documents with design, graphics, and special layout features.

Spreadsheets   Electronic **spreadsheet** software provides computerized versions of traditional financial modeling tools such as the accountant's columnar pad, pencil, and calculator. An electronic spreadsheet is organized into a grid of columns and rows. The power of the electronic spreadsheet is evident when one changes a value or values and all related values on the spreadsheet are automatically recomputed.

Spreadsheets are valuable for applications in which numerous calculations of data must be related to each other. Spreadsheets also are useful for applications that require modeling and what-if analysis. After the user has constructed a set of mathematical relationships, the spreadsheet can be recalculated instantly using a different set of assumptions. Alternatives easily can be

spreadsheet   Software displaying data in a grid of columns and rows, with the capability of easily recalculating numerical data.

FIGURE 5-10 Text and the spell-checking option in Microsoft Word. Word processing software provides many easy-to-use options to create and output a text document to meet a user's specifications.
Source: Courtesy of Microsoft.

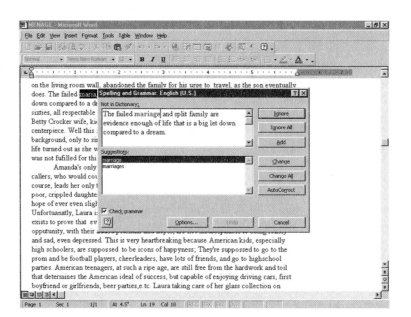

evaluated by changing one or two pieces of data without having to rekey in the rest of the worksheet. Spreadsheet packages include graphics functions that can present data in the form of line graphs, bar graphs, or pie charts. The most popular spreadsheet packages are Microsoft Excel and Lotus 1-2-3. The newest versions of this software can read and write Web files.

Figure 5-11 illustrates the output from a spreadsheet for a breakeven analysis and its accompanying graph.

Data management software   Although spreadsheet programs are powerful tools for manipulating quantitative data, **data management software** is more suitable for creating and manipulating lists and for combining information from different files. PC database management packages have programming features and easy-to-learn menus that enable nonspecialists to build small information systems.

Data management software typically has facilities for creating files and databases and for storing, modifying, and manipulating data for reports and queries. A detailed treatment of

data management software
Software used for creating and manipulating lists, creating files and databases to store data, and combining information for reports.

Total fixed cost	19,000.00
Variable cost per unit	3.00
Average sales price	17.00
Contribution margin	14.00
Breakeven point	1,357

FIGURE 5-11 Spreadsheet software. Spreadsheet software organizes data into columns and rows for analysis and manipulation. Contemporary spreadsheet software provides graphing abilities for clear visual representation of the data in the spreadsheets. This sample breakeven analysis is represented as numbers in a spreadsheet as well as a line graph for easy interpretation.

Custom Neckties Pro Forma Income Statement				
Units sold	0.00	679	1,357	2,036	2,714
Revenue	0	11,536	23,071	34,607	46,143
Fixed cost	19,000	19,000	19,000	19,000	19,000
Variable cost	0	2,036	4,071	6,107	8,143
Total cost	19,000	21,036	23,071	25,107	27,143
Profit/Loss	(19,000)	(9,500)	0	9,500	19,000

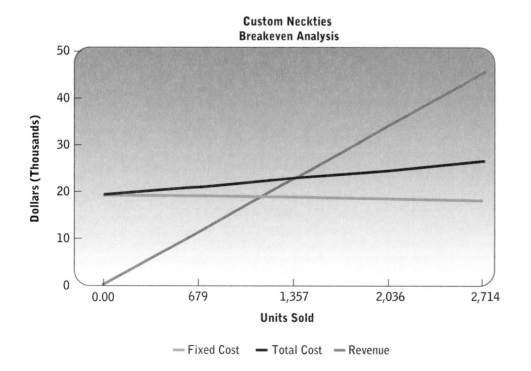

data management software and database management systems can be found in Chapter 6. Popular database management software for personal computers includes Microsoft Access, which has been enhanced to publish data on the Web. Figure 5-12 shows a screen from Microsoft Access illustrating some of its capabilities.

presentation graphics
Software used to create professional-quality, graphics presentations that can incorporate charts, sound, animation, photos, and video clips.

Presentation graphics   **Presentation graphics** software allows users to create professional-quality graphics presentations. This software can convert numeric data into charts and other types of graphics and can include multimedia displays of sound, animation, photos, and video clips. The leading presentation graphics packages include capabilities for computer-generated slide shows and translating content for the Web. Microsoft PowerPoint, Lotus Freelance Graphics, and Aldus Persuasion are popular presentation graphics packages.

integrated software package
A software package that combines two or more applications, such as word processing and spreadsheets, providing for easy transfer of data between them.

Integrated software packages and software suites   **Integrated software packages** combine the functions of the most important PC software packages, such as word processing, spreadsheets, presentation graphics, and data management. This integration provides a general-purpose software tool and eliminates redundant data entry and data maintenance. For example, the breakeven analysis spreadsheet illustrated in Figure 5-11 could be reformatted into a polished report with word processing software without separately keying or copying the data. Integrated packages are a compromise. Although they can do many things well, they generally do not have the same power and depth as single-purpose packages.

Integrated software packages should be distinguished from software suites, which are collections of applications software sold as a unit. Microsoft Office is an example. This software suite contains Word word processing software, Excel spreadsheet software, Access database software, PowerPoint presentation graphics software, and Outlook (tools for e-mail, scheduling, and contact management). Office 2000 contains additional capabilities to support collaborative work on the Web, including on-line discussions about documents and the ability to automatically notify others about changes to documents. Documents created with Office tools can be viewed with a Web browser and published on a Web server. Software suites have some features of integrated packages, such as the ability to share data among different applications, but they consist of full-featured versions of each type of software.

FIGURE 5-1 2 Data management software. This screen from Microsoft Access illustrates some of its powerful capabilities for managing and organizing information.

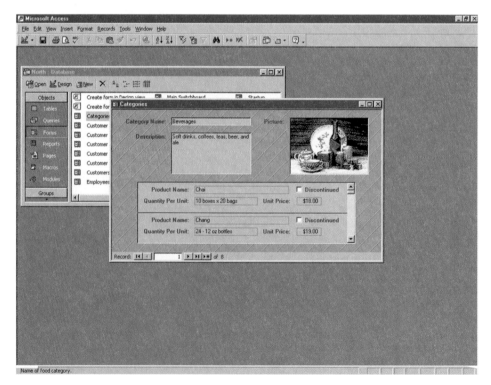

E-mail software Electronic mail (e-mail) is used for the computer-to-computer exchange of messages and is an important tool for communication and collaborative work. A person can use a networked computer to send notes or lengthier documents to a recipient on the same network or on a different network. Many organizations operate their own e-mail systems, but communications companies such as MCI and AT&T offer these services, as do commercial on-line information services such as America Online and Prodigy, and public networks on the Internet.

Web browsers and the PC software suites have e-mail capabilities, but specialized e-mail software packages such as Eudora are also available for use on the Internet. In addition to providing electronic messaging, many e-mail software packages have capabilities for routing messages to multiple recipients, message forwarding, and attaching text documents or multimedia to messages.

Web browsers Web browsers are easy-to-use software tools for displaying Web pages and for accessing the Web and other Internet resources. Web browser software features a point-and-click graphical user interface that can be used throughout the Internet to access and display information stored on computers at other Internet sites. Browsers can display or present graphics, audio, and video information as well as traditional text, and they allow you to click on-screen buttons or highlighted words to link to related Web sites. Web browsers have become the primary interface for accessing the Internet or for using networked systems based on Internet technology. Examples of Web browser software displaying Web pages are illustrated in each chapter of this text.

The two leading commercial Web browsers are Microsoft's Internet Explorer and Netscape Navigator, which is also available as part of the Netscape Communicator software suite. They include capabilities for e-mail, file transfer, on-line discussion groups and bulletin boards, along with other Internet services. Newer versions of these browsers contain support for Web publishing and workgroup computing. (See the following discussion of groupware.)

Groupware Groupware provides functions and services to support the collaborative activities of work groups. Groupware includes software for information-sharing, electronic meetings, scheduling, and e-mail as well as a network to connect the members of the group as they work on their own desktop computers, often in widely scattered locations. Table 5-2 lists groupware capabilities.

Groupware enhances collaboration by allowing the exchange of ideas electronically. All the messages on a topic can be saved in a group and stamped with the date, time, and author. The messages can be followed in a **thread** to see how a discussion evolved. (A thread is a series of messages in an on-line discussion that have been posted as replies to each other.) Any group member can review the ideas of others at any time and add to them, or individuals can post a document for others to comment on or edit. Members can post requests for help. If a group so chooses, its members can store their work notes on the groupware so that everyone in the group can see what progress has been made, what problems occurred, and what activities are planned. The leading commercial groupware product has been Lotus Notes from the Lotus Development Corporation. The Internet is rich in capabilities to support collaborative work. Recent versions of Microsoft Internet Explorer and Netscape Communicator include

electronic mail (e-mail) The computer-to-computer exchange of messages.

Web browser An easy-to-use software tool for accessing the World Wide Web and the Internet.

groupware Software that provides functions and services that support the collaborative activities of work groups.

thread A series of messages in on-line discussions on a specified topic that have been posted as replies to each other. Each message in a thread can be read to see how a discussion has evolved.

Table 5-2 Groupware Capabilities

Group writing and commenting

E-mail distribution

Scheduling meetings and appointments

Shared files and databases

Shared timelines and plans

Electronic meetings and conferences

groupware functions, such as e-mail, electronic scheduling and calendaring, audio and data conferencing, and electronic discussion groups and databases (see Chapters 8 and 11). Microsoft's Office 2000 software suite includes groupware features using Web technology. Powerful Web-based groupware features can also be found in products such as Opentext's Livelink.

5.4 New Software Tools and Approaches

A growing backlog of software projects and the need for businesses to fashion systems that are flexible or that can run over the Internet have stimulated new approaches to software development with object-oriented programming tools and new programming languages such as Java, hypertext markup language (HTML), and Extensible Markup Language (XML).

OBJECT-ORIENTED PROGRAMMING

Traditional software development methods have treated data and procedures as independent components. A separate programming procedure must be written every time someone wants to take an action on a particular piece of data. The procedures act on data that the program passes to them.

What Makes Object-Oriented Programming Different?

object-oriented programming An approach to software development that combines data and procedures into a single object.

Object-oriented programming combines data and the specific procedures that operate on those data into one object. The object combines data and program code. Instead of passing data to procedures, programs send a message for an object to perform a procedure that is already embedded in it. (Procedures are termed methods in object-oriented languages.) The same message may be sent to many different objects, but each will implement the message differently.

For example, an object-oriented financial application might have Customer objects sending debit and credit messages to Account objects. The Account objects in turn might maintain Cash-on-Hand, Accounts-Payable, and Accounts-Receivable objects.

An object's data are hidden from other parts of the program and can only be manipulated from inside the object. The method for manipulating the object's data can be changed internally without affecting other parts of the program. Programmers can focus on what they want an object to do, and the object decides how to do it.

An object's data are encapsulated from other parts of the system, so each object is an independent software building block that can be used in many different systems without changing the program code. Thus, object-oriented programming can reduce the time and cost of writing software by producing reusable program code or software chips that can be reused in other

Groupware facilitates collaboration by enabling members of a group to share documents, schedule meetings, and discuss activities, events, and issues. Illustrated are capabilities for following a threaded discussion.

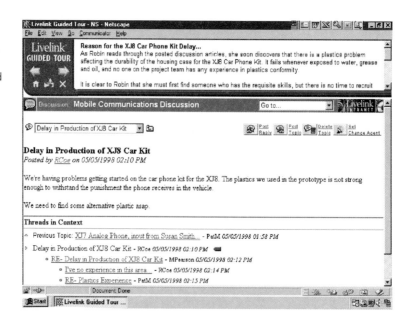

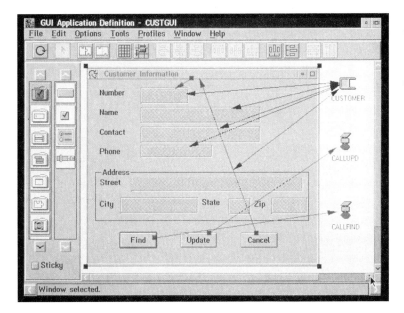

With visual programming tools such as IBM's Visual Age Generator, working software programs can be created by drawing, pointing, and clicking instead of writing program code.

related systems. Future software work could draw on a library of reusable objects, and productivity gains from object-oriented technology could be magnified if objects were stored in reusable software libraries and explicitly designed for reuse (Fayad and Cline, 1996). However, such benefits are unlikely to be realized unless organizations develop appropriate standards and procedures for reuse (Kim and Stohr, 1998).

Object-oriented programming has spawned a new programming technology known as **visual programming** for which programmers do not write code. Rather, they use a mouse to select and move around programming objects, copying an object from a library into a specific location in a program, or drawing a line to connect two or more objects. Visual Basic is a popular visual programming tool for creating applications that run in Microsoft Windows.

visual programming The construction of software programs by selecting and arranging programming objects rather than by writing program code.

Object-Oriented Programming Concepts

Object-oriented programming is based on the concepts of class and inheritance. Program code is not written separately for every object but for classes, or general categories, of similar objects. Objects belonging to a certain class have the features of that class. Classes of objects in turn can inherit the structure and behaviors of a more general class and then add variables and behaviors unique to each object. New classes of objects are created by choosing an existing class and specifying how the new class differs from the existing class, instead of starting from scratch each time.

Classes are organized hierarchically into superclasses and subclasses. For example, a car class might have a vehicle class as its superclass, so the car class would inherit all the methods and data previously defined for vehicle. The design of the car class would only need to describe how cars differ from vehicles. A banking application could define a Savings-Account object that is very much like a Bank-Account object with a few minor differences. Savings-Account inherits all the Bank-Account's state and methods and then adds a few extras.

class The feature of object-oriented programming in which all objects in a specific class have all of the features of that class.

We can see how class and **inheritance** work in Figure 5-13, which illustrates a tree of classes concerning employees and how they are paid. Employee is the common ancestor of the other four classes. Nonsalaried and Salaried are subclasses of Employee, whereas Temporary and Permanent are subclasses of Nonsalaried. The variables for the class are in the top of the box, and the methods are in the bottom. Dark-shaded items in each box are inherited from some ancestor class. (For example, by following the tree upward, we can see that Name and ID in the Nonsalaried, Salaried, Temporary, and Permanent subclasses are inherited from the Employee superclass [ancestor class].) Lighter-shaded methods, or class variables, are unique to a specific class and they override, or redefine, existing methods. When a subclass overrides an inherited method, its object still responds to the same message, but it executes its definition of the method rather than its ancestor's. Whereas Pay is a method inherited from some superclass, the method Pay-OVERRIDE is specific to the Temporary, Permanent, and Salaried classes.

inheritance The feature of object-oriented programming in which a specific class of objects receives the features of a more general class.

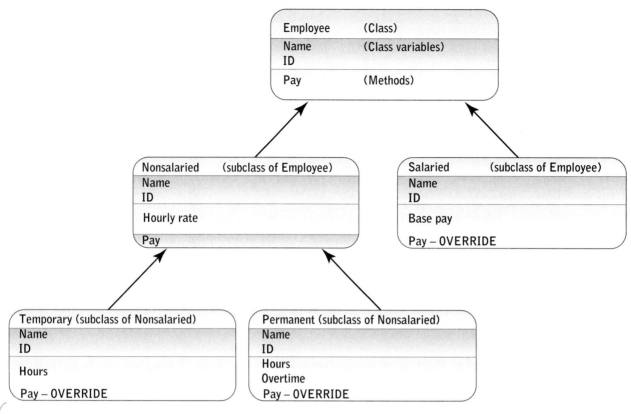

FIGURE 5-13 Class, subclasses, and overriding. This figure illustrates how a message's method can come from the class itself or from an ancestor class. Class variables and methods are shaded when they are inherited from above.

Object-oriented software can be custom-programmed or it can be developed with rapid-application development tools, which can potentially cost 30 percent to 50 percent less than traditional program development methods. Some of these tools provide visual programming environments in which developers can create ready-to-use program code by "snapping" together prebuilt objects. Other tools generate program code that can be compiled to run on a variety of computing platforms.

JAVA

Java Programming language that can deliver only the software functionality needed for a particular task as a small applet downloaded from a network; can run on any computer and operating system.

Java is a programming language named after the many cups of coffee its Sun Microsystems developers drank along the way. It is an object-oriented language, combining data with the functions for processing the data, and it is platform-independent. Java software is designed to run on any computer or computing device, regardless of the specific microprocessor or operating system it uses. A Macintosh Apple, an IBM personal computer running Windows, a Compaq server running Unix, and even a smart cellular phone or personal digital assistant can share the same Java application.

Java can be used to create miniature programs called "applets" designed to reside on centralized network servers. The network delivers only the applets required for a specific function. With Java applets residing on a network, a user can download only the software functions and data that he or she needs to perform a particular task, such as analyzing the revenue from one sales territory. The user does not need to maintain large software programs or data files on his or her desktop machine. When the user is finished with processing, the data can be saved through the network. Java can be used with network computers because it allows all processing software and data to be stored on a network server, downloaded via a network as needed, and then placed back on the network server.

Java is also a very robust language that can handle text, data, graphics, sound, and video, all within one program if needed. Java applets often are used to provide interactive capabilities for Web pages. For example, Java applets can be used to create animated cartoons or real-time news tickers for a Web site, or to add a capability to a Web page to calculate a loan payment schedule on-line in response to financial data input by the user. (Microsoft's **ActiveX** sometimes is used as an alternative to Java for creating interactivity on a Web page. ActiveX is a set of controls that enables programs or other objects such as charts, tables, or animations to be embedded within a Web page. However, ActiveX lacks Java's machine independence and was designed for a Windows environment.)

Java also can be used to create more extensive applications that can run over the Internet or over a company's private network. Java lets PC users manipulate data on networked systems using Web browsers, reducing the need to write specialized software. Table 5-3 describes how businesses are benefiting from Java's capabilities.

To run Java software, a computer needs an operating system containing a Java Virtual Machine (JVM). (A JVM is incorporated into Web browser software such as Netscape Navigator or Microsoft Internet Explorer.) The JVM is a compact program that enables the computer to run Java applications. The JVM lets the computer simulate an ideal standardized Java computer, complete with its own representation of a CPU and its own instruction set. The JVM executes Java programs by interpreting their commands one by one and commanding the underlying computer to perform all the tasks specified by each command.

Management and Organizational Benefits of Java

Companies are starting to develop more applications in Java because such applications can potentially run in Windows, Unix, IBM mainframe, Macintosh, and other environments without having to be rewritten for each computing platform. Sun Microsystems terms this phenomenon "write once, run anywhere." Java also could allow more software to be distributed and used through networks. Functionality could be stored with data on the network and downloaded only as needed. Companies might not need to purchase thousands of copies of commercial software to run on individual computers; instead users could download applets over a network and use network computers.

Java is similar to C++ but it is considered easier to use. Java program code can be written more quickly than with other languages. Sun claims that no Java program can penetrate the user's computer, making it safe from viruses and other types of damage that might occur when downloading more conventional programs off a network.

Despite these benefits, Java has not yet fulfilled its early promise to revolutionize software development and use. Programs written in current versions of Java tend to run slower than "native" programs, which are written for a particular operating system, because they first must be interpreted by the Java Virtual Machine. Vendors such as Microsoft are supporting alternative versions of Java that include subtle differences in their Virtual Machines that affect Java's performance in different pieces of hardware and operating systems. Without a standard version of Java, true platform independence cannot be achieved.

ActiveX A set of controls for the Windows software environment that enables programs or other objects such as charts, tables, or animations to be embedded within a Web page.

Table 5-3	**How Businesses Are Using Java**

Organization	Java Application
Sprint PCS	Java application allows its employees to use Web browsers to analyze business data and send reports to colleagues via e-mail on an internal network.
Home Depot	Uses Java to write new applications such as one that automatically sends an application for employment to all of its 840 stores because it can roll out the software easily on more than 50,000 computing devices throughout the company.
Lincoln National Reassurance	Uses Java to extend its business systems to clients; LincStar application lets insurers use their Web browsers to access information on whether Lincoln National will assume additional risk on a particular individual.
General Motors	Uses Java applets on its Web site to help visitors select vehicles they might want to purchase.

HYPERTEXT MARKUP LANGUAGE (HTML) AND XML

hypertext markup language (HTML) Page description language for creating Web pages and other hypermedia documents.

Web server Software that manages user requests for HTML documents stored on a computer and that delivers the document to the user's computer.

XML (eXtensible Markup Language) General-purpose language that describes the structure of a document and supports links to multiple documents, allowing data to be manipulated by the computer. Used for both Web and non-Web applications.

Hypertext markup language (HTML) is a page description language for creating hypertext or hypermedia documents such as Web pages. (See the discussions of hypermedia in Chapter 6 and of Web pages in Chapter 8.) HTML uses instructions called tags (see Figure 5-14) to specify how text, graphics, video, and sound are placed on a document and to create dynamic links to other documents and objects stored in the same or remote computers. These links allow a user to simply point at a highlighted key word or graphic, click on it, and immediately be transported to another document. **Web server** software manages the requests for these HTML documents on the computer where they are stored and delivers the HTML document to the user's computer.

HTML programs can be custom written, but they also can be created using the HTML authoring capabilities of Web browsers or of popular word processing, spreadsheet, data management, and presentation graphics software packages. HTML editors such as Claris Home Page and Adobe PageMill are powerful HTML authoring tool programs for creating Web pages.

An extension to HTML called Dynamic HTML enables Web pages to react to user input without having to send additional requests to the Web server. Web pages using Dynamic HTML appear less static and more like active and alive applications.

XML

XML, which stands for **eXtensible Markup Language,** is a new specification originally designed to improve the usefulness of Web documents. It is actually a further development of HTML. Whereas HTML only determines how text and images should be displayed on a Web document, XML describes what the data in these documents mean. XML makes the information in documents usable in computer programs. Any piece of information on a document or Web page can be given an XML tag to describe what the data mean. In XML, a number is not just a number; the XML tag specifies whether the number represents a price, a piece of data, or a ZIP code.

For example, an HTML tag to highlight the price of a sweater in bold on a Web page would look like this: <b>$39</b. The number has no context. But an XML tag could designate that $39 is a price by labeling it with a tag such as <price>$39<price>. XML can also describe the meaning of nonnumerical data, such as the sweater's color or style, for instance. Figure 5-15 illustrates the differences between HTML and XML

By tagging selected elements of the content of documents for their meanings, XML makes it possible for computers to automatically manipulate and interpret data in documents and perform operations on the data without human intervention. The XML tags and the stan-

FIGURE 5-14 Sample of the HTML code used to create the NASA Web page displayed here.

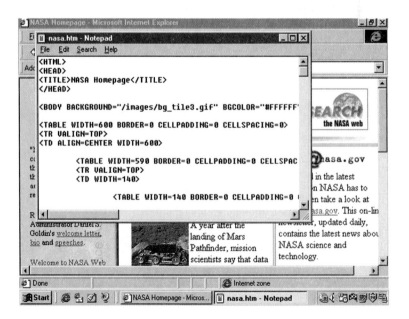

Plain English	HTML	XML
Sport utility vehicle	`<TITLE> Automobile</TITLE>`	`<AUTOMOBILE TYPE="Sport utility vehicle">`
ABC Gremlin 300X SUV	`<BODY>`	`<MANUFACTURER>ABC</MANUFACTURER>`
	`<UL>`	`<LINE>Gremlin</LINE>`
	`<LI>ABC Gremlin 300X SUV`	`<MODEL>300X SUV</MODEL>`
4 passenger	`<LI>4 passenger`	`<PASSENGER UNIT="PASS">4</PASSENGER>`
145 maximum speed	`<LI>145 maximum speed`	`<SPEED UNIT="MPH">145</SPEED>`
$19,280	`<LI>$19,280`	`<PRICE CURRENCY="USD">19,280</PRICE>`
	`</UL></BODY>`	

FIGURE 5-1 5 HTML as compared to XML. HTML is used to display a Web page and tells where words should be placed and which words should be bold or italic. XML describes what the words mean.
Source: From "Putting it all in Context," from **Computerworld,** November 23, 1999. Copyright © 1999 COMPUTERWORLD, Inc. Reprinted with permermission of Computerworld Magazine.

dardized procedures for interpreting them accompany the information wherever it goes. Web browsers and computer programs such as order processing or ERP software can follow programmed rules for applying and displaying the data.

For example, documents or Web pages describing the price of the sweater could be easily accessed by buyers searching for a sweater that costs $39 or less. Data on Web pages describing new automobiles being offered for sale such as the brand, price, number of doors, color, and engine power could be tagged so that someone could use these data to submit a purchase order for a new car and have the data located automatically by a computer program to process the order. The Window on Technology describes how some businesses are benefiting from using XML.

XML is already becoming a serious technology for Web-based applications and could open the way for a whole new class of Internet software and services. Wider use of XML could conceivably speed up the response time for using the Web to process information. Right now, computing devices connected to the Web can basically obtain a form, fill it out, and then swap it back and forth with a company's Web server. XML adds meaning and structural information that will allow computing devices linked to the Web to do a great deal of processing on the spot, taking the load off Web servers and reducing network traffic (Bosak and Bray, 1999).

The key to XML is the setting of standards (or vocabulary) that enable data to be identified very easily. The impact of XML will be felt more strongly over time as more and more industries develop their own widely accepted standards. Each standard is contained in an XML Document Type Definition (DTD), usually simply called a dictionary. For example, RosettaNet is an XML dictionary developed by 34 leading companies within the PC industry. It defines all properties of a personal computer, such as modems, monitors, and cache memory. As a result the entire PC industry is now able to speak the same language. The entire supply chain of the industry is linked now easily. XML is supported by the latest versions of Microsoft and Netscape Internet browsers, making Web site data more usable.

The impact of XML extends far beyond the Web, facilitating the integration of different system applications within the organization. Companies can use XML to exchange data between different systems merely by assigning each piece of data an XML name. XML has strategic impacts as well. Companies can now give their suppliers and customers access to their own data without high application development costs, thus better integrating their operations. However, XML may be making some strategies more difficult to pursue. Once an industry has published an XML dictionary, companies will find it more difficult to raise their customers' "switching costs" (see Chapter 2) because customers will have the software to easily exchange data with new vendors and suppliers.

5.5 Managing Software Assets

Software costs are one of the largest information technology expenditures in most firms, amounting to more than double the expenditures for computer hardware, and thus software represents a major asset. At many points in their careers, managers will be required to make important decisions concerning the selection, purchase, and use of their organization's software assets. Here are some important software issues of which they should be aware.

XML PROVIDES NEW BUSINESS SOLUTIONS

Although XML is a relatively new programming language, it is already having a major impact. One early adopter, Dun & Bradstreet Corp. (D&B) of Murray Hill, New Jersey, the venerable credit rating agency, wanted to change its relationship with its customers, so it turned to XML. In the past D&B reports had been well organized and formatted, making them easy for people to read. However, computers had no way to read these same reports. Beginning in early 1999, customers were able to obtain these same reports with XML tags via the Internet. D&B's customers can feed the reports into their computer applications immediately. As Laura Keating, manager of D&B's XML project, explained, "If we want to be part of our customers' systems, we have to deliver the data so they can put it directly into their applications."

D&B is using XML to solve another problem as well, that of creating a common interface for a wide range of computers used in its offices around the world. To accomplish this, the company used software called B2B Developer, from WebMethods, Inc., to automate the exchange of data from the company's internal systems into XML data so that D&B's enterprise resource planning, EDI, and other applications can access them without expensive application development.

NuSkin Enterprises, a beauty products firm in Provo, Utah, is using XML to integrate its Enterprise Resource Planning (ERP) system with other applications. By converting record formats to XML, the company can move data between systems without having to convert the record formats to work with each individual system.

iVendor Inc. of Redwood City, California, is another major user of XML. E-commerce consultant Tony Hill and database expert Dr. Kee Ong founded the company in late 1998 to provide huge quantities of wholesale product data to e-commerce retailers. The first key problem XML solved for them was to enable iVendor to organize and manipulate all the product data it collected from wholesalers. Hill explains that it then "offers the flexibility to allow merchants to get access to the suppliers' data very quickly, very easily, on a real-time basis."

Matthew Bender and Co. Inc. of New York City first turned to XML to eliminate a major cut-and-paste operation in Web publishing. Freelance writers were sending this legal publishing giant weekly summaries of bankruptcy case decisions, highlighting three or four key legal points. Bender staff then quickly edited them and made them available to customers via the Web and e-mail. The company wanted to issue a monthly report on the Web that recompiled the information by legal points, a cut-and-paste task that required 60 hours. By developing an XML template with tags for elements such as judge and jurisdiction, Bender was able to automate the compilation process. The freelance writers now use the template in developing their weekly summaries, enabling the editors to create the monthly summaries simply by running a script program using XML tags. Developing the automated system took only about a month and cost less than $15,000.

TO THINK ABOUT: In each of these cases, how was the adoption of XML technology related to the business strategy of the company?

Sources: Alan Radding, "The Rush to XML," *Information Week*, January 3, 2000; Susan E. Fisher, "The X Files," *CIO WebBusiness Magazine*, June 1, 1999; Dan Orzech, "XML Is Here to Stay," *Datamation*, July 1999; and Charles Waltner, "XML's Legacy," *Information Week*, August 9, 1999.

SOFTWARE TRENDS

A number of key software trends are of special interest to managers. As computer hardware costs drop, concern with machine efficiency is being replaced with efforts to create software that provides more natural, seamless relationships between people and information systems—through graphical interfaces, natural language, voice recognition, touch, or other gestures (see Section 5 of Chapter 4).

Technology expenditures will increasingly focus on ways to use software to cut down on "people" costs, as opposed to computer hardware costs, by increasing the ease with which users can interact with the hardware and software. More organizations are using software packages, fourth-generation languages, object-oriented tools, or the services of other companies to run their software because such software lowers "people" costs by reducing the need for custom-crafted software written by skilled computer programmers. Renting software and software services from other companies can lower some of these "people" costs even more.

Application Service Providers (ASPs)

Chapter 4 described hardware capabilities for providing data and software programs to desktop computers and over networks. On-line **application service providers** (**ASP**s) are spring-

application service provider (ASP) Company providing software that can be rented by other companies over the Web or a private network.

ing up to provide these software services over the Web and over private networks. These application software services can run applications for other companies at their own computer center, and subscribers can access their systems from the application service provider's computer center over the Web or a private network. Instead of buying and installing software programs, companies can rent these functions from the services. For example, companies can pay $5 per month per user (plus a one-time start-up fee of $5,000) to rent travel and entertainment (T&E) expense reporting software from ExpensAble.com instead of buying and installing T&E programs on their computers.

Some services such as Desktop.com, which provides Web-based programs for word processing, news feeds, electronic calendars, and e-mail services, are available for free on the Web. This service provides a "virtual desktop" where consumers can access the applications they use every day anywhere, anytime, through the Web. Each person's data are stored on Desktop.com's servers. Many other Web-based software services allow users to store their data on their own local machines.

The "time sharing" services of the 1970s, which ran applications such as payroll on their computers for other companies, were an earlier version of this application hosting. Today's ASPs run a wider array of applications than those earlier services and deliver many of the software services over the Web. At many Web-based services, servers perform the bulk of the processing and the only essential program needed by users is their Web browser. Table 5-4 lists examples of ASPs. Large- and medium-size businesses are using these services for enterprise systems, sales force automation, or financial management, whereas small businesses are using them for functions such as invoicing, tax calculations, electronic calendars, and accounting. TimeBills.com, described in the chapter opening vignette, is an ASP providing software for time accounting and billing for small businesses.

Companies are turning to this "software utility" model as an alternative to developing their own software. Some companies will find it easier to "rent" software from another firm and avoid the expense and difficulty of installing, operating, and maintaining complex systems, such as enterprise resource planning (ERP). The ASP contracts guarantee a level of service and support to ensure the software is available and working at all times. For example, Telecomputing ASA charges $349 per seat per month for a 3-to-5-year contract that includes a guarantee of a 99.7 percent service level. Today's Internet-driven business environment is changing so rapidly that getting a system up and running in three months instead of six could make the difference between success and failure. Application service providers also enable small and medium-size companies to use applications that they otherwise could not afford. More detail on application service providers can be found in the chapter ending case study and in Chapter 10.

Software components or objects that can be assembled into complete systems may also be available through networks. These network-based software services should lead to further software economies for firms.

Table 5-4 Examples of Application Service Providers

Application Service Provider	Service	Customer Access
Oracle Business Online	Provides Oracle applications for financials, manufacturing, distribution, and human resources for small and medium-size companies using hardware and technical services from Hewlett Packard Co. and Sun Microsystems.	Web, private networks
Telecomputing ASA (Norway)	Offers complete suite of desktop applications such as Microsoft Office, e-mail, and Web access; also provides enterprise system, e-commerce, and custom applications.	Private networks
Corio Inc.	Hosts enterprise resource planning (ERP) applications from PeopleSoft, focusing primarily on midsize companies.	Web
Salesforce.com	Provides software on the Web to help sales representatives track leads, manage contacts, create reports, and measure their performance to other sales reps in the company.	Web

EVALUATING AN APPLICATION SERVICE PROVIDER

Your company has grown from 40 to 200 employees in the past 2 years. All of your human resources recordkeeping, such as processing hired and terminated employees, documenting promotions, and enrolling employees in medical and dental insurance plans used to be performed manually, but your two-person Human Resources Department is swamped with paperwork. You are looking at two options to automate these functions. One is to purchase a client/server human resources package to run on the company's midrange computer. The other is to use an application service provider that runs human resources software over the Web. The company's Human Resource Department has PCs with Web browser software and Internet access. Your information systems staff consists of two people.

The human resources software package that best fits your needs costs $9,500 to purchase. One information systems specialist with an annual salary of $65,000 would have to spend 4 hours per 40-hour work week supporting the program and applying upgrades as they became available. Upgrades cost $1,000 each, and the vendor provides 1 upgrade every year after the first year the package is purchased.

The application service provider you have identified charges $1,500 to set up the system initially and $5.00 per month for each employee in the firm. You do not need to purchase any additional hardware to run the system, and the vendor is responsible for supporting the system.

1. What are the costs of each option in the first year?
2. Which option is less expensive over a three-year period?
3. Which option would you select? Why? What factors would you use in making a decision? What are the risks of each approach?

Enterprise Systems and Middleware

Another major software trend is the development of integrated programs such as enterprise resource planning systems (ERP) that support organizational needs for communication and control (see Chapter 3). Such systems require the development of very large, sophisticated programs to manage data for the organization as a whole, to prepare data for end users, to integrate parts of the organization, and to permit precise control and coordination of organizational decision making. These very large systems integrate what once were separate systems (e.g., accounts receivable and order processing) operated by separate departments (e.g., accounting and sales). Chapter 9 provides more detail on technical and organizational issues that must be addressed when implementing ERP software.

Most firms cannot jettison all of their existing systems and create such systems from scratch. Many legacy mainframe applications are essential to daily operations and very risky to change, but they can be made more useful if their information can be integrated with other applications (Noffsinger, Niedbalski, Blanks, and Emmart, 1998). One way to integrate various legacy applications is to use special software called **middleware** to create an interface or bridge between two different systems. Middleware is software that connects two otherwise separate applications to pass data between them and may consist of custom software written in-house or a software package (see Figure 5-16).

Middleware is used to link client and server machines in client/server computing and, increasingly, to link a Web server to data stored on another computer. This allows users to request data from the computer in which they are stored using forms displayed on a Web browser, and it enables the Web server to return dynamic Web pages based on information requested by users. Using middleware to integrate applications is becoming another important software trend.

middleware Software that allows two different applications to exchange data.

SOFTWARE MAINTENANCE

After software has been created for the organization, it usually has to be modified over time to incorporate new information requirements. Because of the way software is currently designed,

FIGURE 5-16 Middleware. Middleware is software that can be used to pass data between two disparate applications so that they can work together.

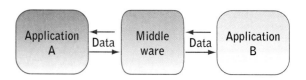

this maintenance process is very costly, time-consuming, and challenging to manage. In most information systems departments more than 50 percent of staff time is spent maintaining the software for existing systems.

At the end of the millennium, an even larger maintenance problem called the year 2000 problem emerged. The **Year 2000 problem,** sometimes referred to as the millennium bug or the **Y2K** problem, was the inability of software programs to handle any dates other than those of the twentieth century—years that begin with "19." Many older computer programs (and even some recent PC programs) stored dates as six digits, two digits each for the day, month, and year (MM–DD–YY). Programs were written this way for decades because it saved data entry time and storage space if the century number "19" did not have to be entered.

With dates represented this way, computers could interpret the year following 1999 as 1900 rather than 2000, creating errors in any software that was time-sensitive. The year 2000 problem affected organizations of all sizes—business, nonprofit, and government alike—and the Window on Management explains what happened to some information systems when January 1, 2000, arrived.

To solve the problem before 2000 arrived, organizations combed through their programs to locate all coding in which dates were used. Many companies have computer programs with millions of lines of code, making correcting date processing problems a daunting task. It is estimated that organizations spent $400 billion to $600 billion worldwide to fix this problem.

Year 2000 problem (Y2K)
Inability of software programs to handle dates other than those of the twentieth century, which begin with "19," because the software represents years with only two digits. Presented a massive maintenance problem for most organizations.

SELECTING SOFTWARE FOR THE ORGANIZATION

Although managers need not become programming specialists, they should be able to use clear criteria in selecting application and system software for the organization. The most important criteria are as follows.

Appropriateness

Some languages are general-purpose languages that can be used on a variety of problems, whereas others are special-purpose languages suitable for only limited tasks. Special-purpose graphics programs, for example, may not work well at routine processing of transactions. COBOL is excellent for business data processing but not for mathematical calculations. Language selection involves identifying the organizational use for the software and the users. Application software should also be easy to maintain and change, and it should be flexible enough so that it can grow with the organization. These organizational considerations have direct long-term cost implications.

Efficiency

Although less important than in the past, the efficiency with which a language compiles and executes remains a consideration when purchasing software. Some programming languages are more efficient in the use of machine time than others, and there are instances where such considerations outweigh personnel costs. Languages with slow compilers or interpreters like BASIC or Java or fourth-generation languages may prove too slow and expensive in terms of machine time for high-speed transaction systems, which must handle many thousands of transactions per second (see Chapter 10).

Compatibility

Application software must be able to run on the firm's hardware and operating system platform. Likewise, the firm's operating system software must be compatible with the software required by the firm's mainstream business applications. Mission-critical applications typically have large volumes of transactions to process and require robust operating systems that can handle large complex software programs and massive files.

Support

In order to be effective, a programming language must be easy for the firm's programming staff to learn, and the staff should have sufficient knowledge of that software to provide ongoing support for all of the systems based on that software. It is also important to purchase package software that has widespread use in other organizations and that is supported by many

Window on Management

THE AFTERMATH OF Y2K

In the last few years before the new millennium, the Year 2000 Problem was called "the biggest business problem in human history." Some experts believed 10 to 15 million software applications would be affected. The Gartner Group, a Stamford, Connecticut, consulting firm, estimated that the worldwide cost for fixing the Y2K problem would run between $1 to $2 trillion, representing as much as $300 for every person on this planet.

In addition to software programs in computers, experts worried that Year 2000 bugs were lurking in programmed computer chips that have been built into electronic equipment, such as industrial machinery, traffic lights, elevators, security alarms, automobiles, and microwave ovens. Inability to process the date rollover in these embedded systems would create problems with electrical power, telephones, or transportation systems. Experts also worried about Y2K problems in military systems, including malfunctioning weapons systems that could trigger a military crisis.

The global costs of scanning millions of computer systems and identifying and fixing the trouble spots were enormous, totaling over $600 billion. For example, to fix the problem, business and government organizations spent $32.4 billion in the United Kingdom, over $100 billion in the United States, and $500 million in Russia, which is much less computer-dependent than other advanced countries.

Besides modifying parts of software programs affected by date processing, all changes had to be thoroughly tested, a massive job. In addition, all links to other programs had to be tested so that wrong data were neither sent to nor received from other programs and systems. Warnings abounded that Russia and many developing countries had not made the necessary preparations.

When January 1, 2000, actually arrived, most of the predicted computer disasters failed to materialize. Essential services were maintained in the developed and even the developing world. A few glitches were reported. Japan experienced problems with data transmission at nuclear plants, but none affected safety or production. Ticketing machines jammed on some Australian buses. France's Syracuse II military satellite system lost the ability to detect equipment failures but remained functional. Equipment for interpreting electrocardiogram data at some Swedish hospitals shut down on New Year's Day, but patients were never endangered. Only a few minor Y2K mishaps occurred in the United States, even among small businesses that did not have the time and resources to attack software date problems.

With no major Y2K outages occurring worldwide, was the Y2K problem overstated? Did businesses and governments overspend on a problem that was exaggerated? Most computer experts and business managers say no. They believe that had they not made the enormous investments in modernizing their software, the impact of Y2K would have been much more catastrophic. Experts may have also overestimated the dependence on computer technology in many parts of the world. Y2K may have primarily posed problems for large complex organizations.

Fixing the Y2K program provided other long-term benefits. Many organizations used the millennium bug as an opportunity to modernize their information technology infrastructures, replacing outdated systems or installing Y2K-compliant enterprise systems that could provide new business efficiencies. Y2K projects also provided many organizations with improved software asset management, stronger contingency plans for dealing with system emergencies, and stronger communication among disparate business units.

TO THINK ABOUT: Why was the Year 2000 Problem a serious management issue? It has been said that if information systems were all thoroughly object oriented, the Year 2000 Problem would probably be a minor annoyance. Do you agree or disagree? Why?

Sources: Thomas Hoffman and Julia King, "Execs Back Y2K Spending All the Way," Information Week, January 10, 2000; Rodney Ho, Jeffrey A. Tannenbaum, and Dan Morse, "Remember Y2K Threat at Small Firms? Forget It," The Wall Street Journal, January 4, 2000; "World-Wide the Bug Had Little Bite," The Wall Street Journal, January 3, 2000; Jared Sandberg, "Why Y2K Won't Die," Newsweek, January 10, 2000; Peter de Jager, "Y2K: So Many Bugs . . . So Little Time," Scientific American, January 1999.

consulting firms and services. Another kind of support is the availability of software editing, debugging, and development aids.

MANAGEMENT WRAP-UP

Management

Managers should know how to select and manage the organization's software assets in the firm's IT infrastructure. They should understand the advantages and disadvantages of building and owning these assets or of renting them from outside services. Managers should also be aware of the strengths and weaknesses of business software tools, the tasks for which they are best suited, and whether these tools fit into the firm's long-term business strategy and IT infrastructure. Trade-offs between efficiency, ease of use, and flexibility should be carefully analyzed. These organizational considerations have long-term cost implications.

Software can either enhance or impede organizational performance depending on the software tools and services selected and how they are used. Organizational needs should drive software selection. Software tools selected should be easy for the firm's IS staff to learn and maintain and be flexible enough to grow with the organization. Software for non-IS specialists should have easy-to-use interfaces and be compatible with the firm's other software tools. Software services provided by outside vendors should fit into organizational computing plans.

Organization

A range of system and application software technologies is available to organizations. Key technology decisions include the appropriateness of the software tool for the problem to be addressed; compatibility with the firm's hardware and other components of the IT infrastructure; the efficiency of the software for performing specific tasks; vendor support of software packages and software services; and capabilities for debugging, documentation, and reuse.

Technology

For Discussion

1. Why is selecting both system and application software for the organization an important management decision?

2. Should organizations develop all of their systems with fourth-generation tools? Why or why not?

SUMMARY

1. Describe the major types of software. The major types of software are system software and application software. Each serves a different purpose. System software manages the computer resources and mediates between application software and computer hardware. Application software is used by application programmers and some end users to develop specific business applications. Application software works through system software, which controls access to computer hardware.

2. Examine the functions of system software and compare leading PC operating systems. System software coordinates the various parts of the computer system and mediates between application software and computer hardware. The system software that manages and controls the activities of the computer is called the operating system. Other system software includes computer-language translation programs, which convert programming languages into machine language, and utility programs, which perform common processing tasks.

The operating system acts as the chief manager of the information system, allocating, assigning, and scheduling system resources and monitoring the use of the computer. Multiprogramming, multitasking, virtual storage, time sharing, and multiprocessing enable system resources to be used more efficiently, allowing the computer to attack many problems at the same time.

Multiprogramming (multitasking in PC environments) allows multiple programs to use the computer's resources concurrently. Virtual storage splits up programs into small portions so that the main memory can be used more efficiently. Time sharing enables many users to share computer resources simultaneously by allocating each user a tiny slice of computing time. Multiprocessing is the use of two or more CPUs linked together working in tandem to perform a task.

In order to be executed by the computer, a software program must be translated into machine language via special language-translation software—a compiler, an assembler, or an interpreter.

PC operating systems have developed sophisticated capabilities such as multitasking and support for multiple users on networks. Leading PC operating systems include Windows Me, Windows 98 and 95, Windows CE, Windows 2000, OS/2, Unix, Linux, Mac OS, and DOS. PC operating systems with graphical user interfaces have gained popularity over command-driven operating systems.

3. Explain how software has evolved and how it will continue to develop. Software has evolved along with hardware. The general trend is toward user-friendly, high-level languages that both increase professional programmer productivity and make it possible for amateurs to use information systems. There have been four generations of software development: (1) machine language; (2) symbolic languages such as assembly language; (3) high-level languages such as FORTRAN and COBOL; and (4) fourth-generation languages, which are less procedural and closer to natural language than earlier generations of software. Software is starting to incorporate both sound and graphics and to support multimedia applications.

4. Analyze the strengths and limitations of the major application programming languages and software tools. The most popular conventional programming languages are assembly language, FORTRAN, COBOL, BASIC, Pascal, and C. Conventional programming languages make more efficient use of computer resources than fourth-generation languages, and each is designed to solve specific types of problems.

Fourth-generation languages include query languages, report generators, graphics languages, application generators, very high-level programming languages, application software packages, and PC software tools. They are less procedural than conventional programming languages and enable end users to perform many software tasks that previously required technical specialists. Popular PC software tools include word processing, spreadsheet, data management, presentation graphics, and e-mail software along with Web browsers and groupware.

5. Describe new approaches to software development. Object-oriented programming combines data and procedures into one object, which can act as an independent software building block. Each object can be used in many different systems without changing program code.

Java is an object-oriented programming language designed to operate on the Internet. It can deliver precisely the software functionality needed for a particular task as a small applet that is downloaded from a network. Java can run on any computer. HTML is a page description language for creating Web pages. XML is a language for creating structured documents in which data are tagged for meanings. The tagged data in XML documents can be manipulated and used by other computer systems.

6. Identify important issues in the management of organizational software assets. Software represents a major organizational asset that should be carefully managed. The growing use of "people-friendly" software, software on networks, application service providers, middleware, and large, complex programs integrating many different organizational functions and processes are important trends that managers should follow closely. Maintenance can account for more than 50 percent of information system costs. Criteria such as efficiency, compatibility with the organization's technology platform, support, and whether the software language or tool is appropriate for the problems and tasks of the organization should govern software selection.

KEY TERMS

ActiveX, 163

Application generator, 155

Application service provider (ASP), 166

Application software, 143

Assembly language, 153

BASIC (Beginners All-purpose Symbolic Instruction Code), 154

C, 154

C++, 154

Class, 161

COBOL (COmmon Business Oriented Language), 153

Compiler, 147

Data management software, 157

Desktop publishing software, 156

DOS, 148

Electronic mail (e-mail), 159

FORTRAN (FORmula TRANslator), 153

Fourth-generation language, 154

Graphical user interface (GUI), 147

Graphics language, 155

Groupware, 159

High-level languages, 152

Hypertext markup language (HTML), 164

Inheritance, 161

Integrated software package, 158

Interpreter, 147

Java, 162

Linux, 150

Machine language, 152

Mac OS, 150

Middleware, 168

Multiprocessing, 146

Multiprogramming, 145

Multitasking, 145

Natural language, 155

Object code, 147

Object-oriented programming, 160

Open-source software, 150

Operating system, 143

OS/2, 150

Pascal, 154

Presentation graphics, 158

Program, 143

Query language, 155

Report generator, 155

Software, 143

Software package, 155

Source code, 147

Spreadsheet, 156

Stored program concept, 143

System software, 143

Thread, 159

Time sharing, 146

Unix, 150

Utility program, 147

Very high-level programming language, 155

Virtual storage, 145

Visual programming, 161

Web browser, 159

Web server, 164

Windows, 148

Windows CE, 150

Windows 95, 149

Windows 98, 149

Windows Millennium Edition (Windows Me), 149

Windows 2000, 149

Word processing software, 156

XML (eXtensible Markup Language), 164

Year 2000 problem (Y2K), 169

REVIEW QUESTIONS

1. What are the major types of software? How do they differ in terms of users and uses?

2. What is the operating system of a computer? What does it do?

3. Describe multiprogramming, virtual storage, time sharing, and multiprocessing. Why are they important for the operation of an information system?

4. What is the difference between an assembler, a compiler, and an interpreter?

5. Define and explain the significance of graphical user interfaces.

6. Compare the major PC operating systems.

7. What are the major generations of software, and approximately when were they developed?

8. What is a high-level language? Name three high-level languages. Describe their strengths and weaknesses.

9. Define fourth-generation languages, and list the seven categories of fourth-generation tools.

10. What is the difference between fourth-generation languages and conventional programming languages?

11. What is the difference between an application generator and an application software package? Between a report generator and a query language?

12. Name and describe the most important PC software tools.

13. What is object-oriented programming? How does it differ from conventional software development?

14. What is Java? How could it change the way software is created and used?

15. What are HTML and XML? Compare their capabilities. Why are they important?

16. What are application service providers? Why are they becoming important?

17. Name and describe three issues in managing software assets.

18. What criteria should be used when selecting software for the organization?

GROUP PROJECT

Which is the better Internet software tool, Internet Explorer or Netscape Communicator? Your instructor will divide the class into two groups to research this question. Each group will present their findings to the class. To prepare your analysis, use articles from computer magazines and the Web, and examine the software's features and capabilities.

Tools for Interactive Learning

○ Internet Connection

The Internet Connection for this chapter will direct you to a series of Web sites of various computer software vendors where you can complete an exercise to compare the capabilities of various PC software suites. You can also use the Interactive Study Guide to test your knowledge of the topics in this chapter and get instant feedback where you need more practice.

○ Electronic Commerce Project

At the Laudon Web site for Chapter 5, you will find an Electronic Commerce project that will use the interactive software at the Mapquest Website for logistics planning.

○ CD-ROM

If you purchase and use the Multimedia Edition CD-ROM with this chapter, you can complete an interactive exercise asking you to select the appropriate programming language or application software for a series of business problems. You can also find a video clip illustrating the capabilities of geographic information system (GIS) software, an audio overview of the major themes of this chapter, and bullet text summarizing the key points of the chapter.

○ Application Exercise

At the Laudon Web site, you can find an Application Exercise for this chapter, in which you can use the Netscape Page Wizard to develop a Web page.

Sunburst Hotels International Turns to an Application Service Provider

When Sunburst Hotels International Inc. was spun off in late 1997, the company had no IT infrastructure, and CIO Charles Warczak had to create it. Sunburst earned about $114 million in 1997 by owning and operating 87 hotels in 27 states, including some Comfort Inns and EconoLodges. He knew his company could not perform all the many complex functions required without the support of application packages. Choice Hotels International Corp., Sunburst's former parent company, was using an enterprise resource planning (ERP) system from PeopleSoft, and Warczak wanted to use the same system. The major problems he faced involved costs. Warczak calculated that to acquire and install the ERP package he wanted, the company would have had to spend $1.5 million on capital expenses (mainly computer hardware and software) up front, a hefty cost for the small, newly independent company. And that was only the beginning of his projected costs. In this case study we examine his problem and the method he selected to solve it.

Installing a new ERP system can be very expensive, particularly for a start-up or a new spin-off which may also lack information systems staff with the technical expertise for such projects. In Sunburst's case, Warczak met with both IS and finance personnel at Choice to determine Sunburst's needs and costs. They ultimately concluded that Sunburst needed to spend well over $1 million up front on hardware and software, including both computers and networking. In addition Sunburst would need to purchase a $500,000 Oracle database to support the PeopleSoft ERP system. And these were only some of the costs.

Complex computer systems require highly skilled staffs to run and maintain them, and Warczak estimated that the cost of such a staff for his small corporation would be about $500,000. However, the immediate problem was even tougher: locating and hiring such a staff in the first place. Skilled technicians are in short supply and finding and hiring them was a challenge. Warczak would need staff skilled in PeopleSoft software, and the competition for experienced ERP technicians was fierce everywhere but particularly so in the greater Washington, DC, area. (Sunburst headquarters are in Silver Springs, Maryland, a Washington suburb.) Networking experts were also difficult to locate and hire. However, hiring such a skilled staff would not be the end of the problem: Warczak would also face the challenge of keeping employees who are in such high demand. "We'd have a real tough time holding on to people who are experts in, say, the accounts payable module," said Warczak. And, thinking about long-range costs, he added, "There's a lot of cost with high turnover."

Being bottom-line oriented, Warczak believed that "Everything at the corporate office including IT is an overhead [expense]." However, the company had another major concern. ERP software is extremely complex, and its successful implementation can be a long and arduous process. Based on implementations at other corporations, Sunburst anticipated a minimum implementation period of six to eight months. However, Sunburst could look to an example of a challenging implementation program close to home. Choice faced the same problem a year earlier (prior to the Sunburst spin-off) when it installed PeopleSoft. Although they were ultimately pleased with the software, the implementation "was a disaster," according to Warczak. "There were lots of cost overruns." He added that once the implementation was completed, "functionality was terrible" because of technical problems, and there was a long learning curve for creating an infrastructure.

With all this information and experience, the decision was not difficult. Warczak opted to outsource his ERP system. However, he did not want to give the computer system and all the vital ongoing tasks the hotel used on a daily basis to outsiders, so he chose a route that had only recently become available, an application service provider (ASP). ASPs are different because they own and operate the computer hardware and software and rent usage on the computer application to customers. The customer, in this case Sunburst, pays the ASP and uses the system as if it owned it, but the ASP actually operates and maintains both the software and hardware.

Companies have been renting software in this way since 1997, and software renters include PeopleSoft, J.D. Edwards & Co., Great Plains Software Inc., and Oracle Corp. Sunburst selected a less-known ASP, USinternetworking Inc. (USi) of Annapolis, Maryland, and signed a five-year contract that began on April 1, 1999. Let us consider some of the benefits Sunburst realized by going this route.

The fundamental change, out of which every other benefit flows, is that Sunburst did not have to purchase and own computers (except for PCs or network computers). The company also did not have to buy the PeopleSoft and Oracle software. In addition, the costs of building and maintaining a network were eliminated because Sunburst accesses its ERP via the Web. The only Sunburst costs, in addition to the monthly rental, are for PCs, Web browsers, and telephone lines to connect to the Web. Thus, most of Sunburst's infrastructure start-up costs were eliminated. The company did have the normal personnel costs associated with converting from the old system to the new one and learning the new system. Although Sunburst has not released the amount of its monthly fee, USi says its charges range from $50,000 to $200,000, depending on the number of PeopleSoft modules the customer uses. Some ASPs charge not by the module but by the number of users, typically charging $3 to $500 per user per month. This approach enables small companies to pay less; their costs grow only as their companies grow.

Staff costs were all but eliminated by going to an ASP because PeopleSoft software is owned and supported by USi. However, customers of ASPs usually assign one or more persons as full-time supervisors of the system to ensure that it is running properly and that the staff of the renting company is using it properly. This same person (or group) usually is assigned as liaison to the ASP. By using an ASP, Sunburst also eliminated the other staffing problem. The company did not have to face the fierce competition for skilled technicians—that was USi's problem and it already had its staff in place.

Even the implementation was much quicker than it would otherwise have been. The software was already working, ready for the Sunburst staff to access it. Sunburst's PeopleSoft ERP system was up and running in only 3 months and went live in April 1999.

Using an ASP has another benefit for many organizations. Companies are able to move slowly into using an ASP's software, trying out one function of the software package at a time. In that way they can find out whether the particular package is right for them without major upfront costs (a benefit Sunburst did not need because they learned the package when they were part of Choice, and they knew it was a good fit).

Using an ASP does present risks. Some companies are concerned because this type of service is so new. Companies that are risk averse may want to wait a year or two until ASPs have a longer track record. Security is a risk in the minds of many, particularly when a company has to access its sensitive data via the Internet. Dick Lefebvre, the vice president of information technology at auto parts producer Simpson Industries Inc. in Plymouth, Michigan, had precisely that concern. He wanted to use J.D. Edwards ERP system through IBM Global Services, a company also in the ASP business. To solve the problem, he decided not to use the Web, but instead to connect to IBM Global Services through a private line. Leasing a private line is expensive, however, and his communication costs were perhaps 10 times the cost of using the Web. Lefebvre was willing to pay the price in order to be certain that competitors could not capture vital information about the parts that his company produces. However, other companies feel very secure using the Internet. Typically they use multiple firewalls and encryption to protect their data.

One other fear common to all companies that outsource is that they will be locked into the outside vendor, placing them at the vendor's mercy. Only time will tell if this becomes the case, but using an ASP is an alternative, and risk may be reduced more than with traditional outsourcing. The main difference is that the software the company is using (PeopleSoft in the case of Sunburst) usually does not belong exclusively to the ASP (USi in this example). Sunburst is able to leave USi and take their business to another ASP that is running PeopleSoft's ERP. And ultimately, if the company (Sunburst) cannot make it work with any ASP, it can travel the original road, purchasing the software and hardware itself, bringing the whole operation inside.

Sources: Jenny C. McCune, "ASPs @ Your Service," **Beyond Computing,** January/February 2000; Peter Fabris, "Network Computer Revival?" and "A New Lease," **CIO Web Business Magazine,** May 1, 1999; Lee Gomes, "Somebody Else's Problem," **The Wall Street Journal,** November 15, 1999; and Paul Keegan, "Is This the Death of Packaged Software?" **Upside,** October 1999.

CASE STUDY QUESTIONS

1. Why was a complex ERP system so vital to Sunburst?

2. Describe the problems that caused Sunburst to decide to use an outside ASP. What other reasons might they have had for making that decision?

3. What management, organizational, and technical issues did Warczak have to consider when installing an ERP?

4. What management, organizational, and technical issues did Warczak have to consider when planning to outsource the ERP to an ASP?

CHAPTER 6

Managing (Data) Resources

After completing this chapter, you will be able to:

1. Compare traditional file organization and management techniques.

2. Explain the problems of the traditional file environment.

3. Describe how a database management system organizes information.

4. Identify the principal types of databases and some principles of database design.

5. Discuss new database trends.

6. Analyze the managerial and organizational requirements for creating a database environment.

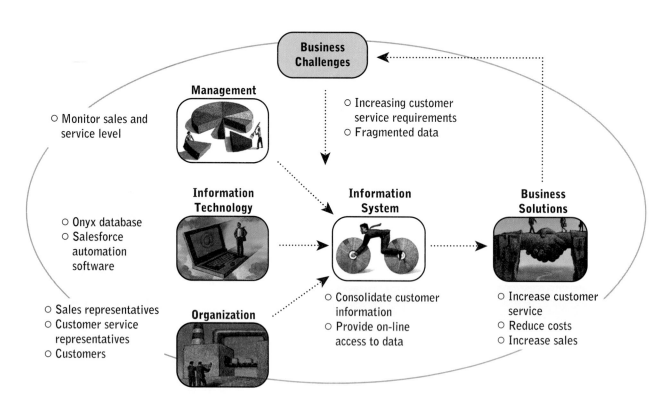

Business Challenges

Management
- Monitor sales and service level

- Increasing customer service requirements
- Fragmented data

Information Technology
- Onyx database
- Salesforce automation software

Information System
- Consolidate customer information
- Provide on-line access to data

Business Solutions
- Increase customer service
- Reduce costs
- Increase sales

Organization
- Sales representatives
- Customer service representatives
- Customers

Connecting Customer Files Creates New Business Opportunities

Community Playthings is a community-based business that manufactures toys, playground equipment, and furniture for both able-bodied and disabled children. It has 6 locations in the northeastern United States and two in England. Community Playthings found that unconnected customer files can lead to missed business opportunities. Its sales and customer service processes had become disorganized because data about customers were stored in several different systems. For example, the company's billing and order entry functions were handled by different systems that did not communicate with each other. When a representative made a sale, the customer data had to be entered separately into both systems. If the sale was made to an existing customer, there was no way to use the data the company 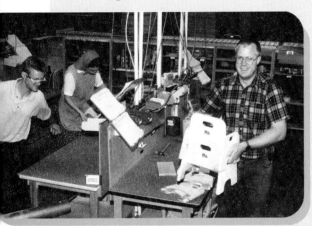 had already collected on that customer. The customer information had to be entered again, creating multiple records for the same customer, often with slight variations in the customer's name. Sales representatives kept records of their contacts in their own personal files on departmental servers. Without the access to each others' records, they could not determine who had been in contact with various customers and the results of those contacts. In short, Community Playthings' data were in a state of chaos.

In 1995 several key Community Playthings managers started working on a solution that required a system that could integrate telephone sales, order entry, customer service, and collection data. The system, called the Customer Center, uses salesforce automation software from Onyx Software and a database that combines order and accounts receivable data with data from the sales reps' customer records. The system can display all sales and ordering activity for a specific customer from a single screen, enabling sales reps to quickly identify the most profitable customers and focus on their needs. (Community Playthings' best sales prospects are existing customers and the referrals they provide.)

Customer service representatives now instantly locate information about returns and account activity, a process that used to take hours and even days before the new system was installed. The system can track complex links between

CHAPTER OUTLINE

customers, products, and purchase records. If a customer doesn't have a purchase order number, for example, the representative can instantly pull up an existing order using other criteria such as the customer's name. With the new system and database, sales and customer service staff know precisely what is going on with every customer.

After the new system was installed, company sales increased 12 percent in 1998. More precise customer information helped Community Playthings reduce costs as well. Before creating the new system, the company mass-mailed 200,000 catalogs. Much of the $600,000 spent on this effort was wasted because many recipients ignored the mailings. By using Customer Center, the company needed to mail only 60,000 catalogs to target existing customers and develop them as sources of new leads. Sales staff no longer try to sell customers inappropriate or previously purchased products, so the entire sales process is much more efficient. By marketing to a more targeted audience, the sales force has become more productive. Community Playthings has seen a 10% growth in business using the same number of people.

Sources: Samuel Greengard, "360-Degree Database Views: Know Your Customer," *Beyond Computing,* May 1999; and Onyx Software Corporation, "Community Playthings," 1999.

MANAGEMENT CHALLENGES

Community Playthings' system illustrates how much the effective use of information depends on how data are stored, organized, and accessed. Proper delivery of information not only depends on the capabilities of computer hardware and software but also on the organization's ability to manage data as an important resource. Community Playthings' fragmented sales data led to disorganized sales and customer service processes that impaired organizational performance. It has been very difficult for organizations to manage their data effectively. Two challenges stand out.

1. **Organizational obstacles to a database environment.** Implementing a database requires widespread organizational change in the role of information (and information managers), the allocation of power at senior levels, the ownership and sharing of information, and patterns of organizational agreement. A database management system (DBMS) challenges the existing power arrangements in an organization and for that reason often generates political resistance. In a traditional file environment, each department constructed files and programs to fulfill its specific needs. Now, with a database, files and programs must be built that take into account the full organization's interest in data. Although the organization has spent the money on hardware and software for a database environment, it may not reap the benefits it should because it is unwilling to make the requisite organizational changes.

2. **Cost/benefit considerations.** The costs of moving to a database environment are tangible, up front, and large in the short term (three years). Most firms buy a commercial DBMS package and related hardware. The software alone can cost a half million dollars for a full-function package with all options. New hardware may cost an additional $1 million to $2 million annually. It soon becomes apparent to senior management that a database system is a huge investment.

Unfortunately, the benefits of the DBMS are often intangible, back loaded, and long term (five years). Several million dollars have been spent over the years designing and maintaining existing systems. People in the organization understand the existing system after long periods of training and socialization. For these reasons, and despite the clear advantages of the DBMS, the short-term costs of developing a DBMS often appear to be as great as the benefits. When the short-term political costs are added to the equation, it is convenient for senior management to defer the database investment. Managers, especially those unfamiliar with (and perhaps unfriendly to) information systems, tend to severely discount the obvious long-term benefits of the DBMS. Moreover, it may not always be cost effective to build organization-wide databases that integrate all the organization's data (Goodhue et al., September 1992).

This chapter examines the managerial and organizational requirements as well as the technologies for managing data as a resource. First, we describe the traditional file management technologies that have been used for arranging and accessing data on physical storage media and the problems they have created for organizations. Then we describe the technology of database management systems, which can overcome many of the drawbacks of traditional file management. We end the chapter with a discussion of the managerial and organizational requirements for successfully implementing database management systems.

6.1 Organizing Data in a Traditional File Environment

An effective information system provides users with timely, accurate, and relevant information. This information is stored in computer files. When the files are properly arranged and maintained, users can easily access and retrieve the information they need.

You can appreciate the importance of file management if you have ever written a term paper using three-by-five-inch index cards. No matter how efficient your storage device (a metal box or a rubber band), if you organize the cards randomly your term paper will have little or no organization. Given enough time, you could put the cards in order, but your system would be more efficient if you set up your organizational scheme early. If your scheme is flexible enough and well documented, you can extend it to account for any changes in your viewpoint as you write your paper.

The same need for file organization applies to firms. Well-managed, carefully arranged files make it easy to obtain data for business decisions, whereas poorly managed files lead to chaos in information processing, high costs, poor performance, and little, if any, flexibility. Despite the use of excellent hardware and software, many organizations have inefficient information systems because of poor file management. In this section we describe the traditional methods that organizations have used to arrange data in computer files. We also discuss the problems with these methods.

FILE ORGANIZATION TERMS AND CONCEPTS

A computer system organizes data in a hierarchy that starts with bits and bytes and progresses to fields, records, files, and databases (see Figure 6-1). A bit represents the smallest unit of data a computer can handle. A group of bits, called a byte, represents a single character, which can be a letter, a number, or another symbol. A grouping of characters into a word, a group of words, or a complete number (such as a person's name or age) is called a **field.** A group of related fields, such as the student's name, the course taken, the date, and the grade, comprises a **record;** a group of records of the same type is called a **file.** For instance, the student records in Figure 6-1 could constitute a course file. A group of related files makes up a **database.** The student course file illustrated in Figure 6-1 could be grouped with files on students' personal histories and financial backgrounds to create a student database.

field A grouping of characters into a word, a group of words, or a complete number, such as a person's name or age.

record A group of related fields.

file A group of records of the same type.

database A group of related files.

FIGURE 6-1 The data hierarchy. A computer system organizes data in a hierarchy that starts with the bit, which represents either a 0 or a 1. Bits can be grouped to form a byte to represent one character, number, or symbol. Bytes can be grouped to form a field, and related fields can be grouped to form a record. Related records can be collected to form a file, and related files can be organized into a database.

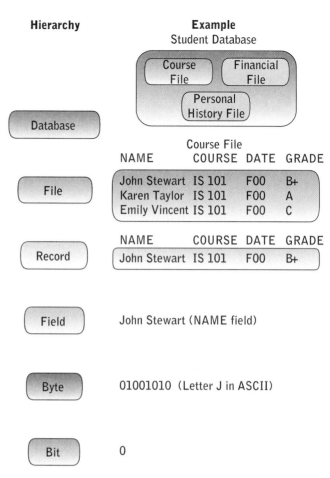

Hierarchy	Example Student Database
Database	Course File, Financial File, Personal History File

Course File

NAME	COURSE	DATE	GRADE
John Stewart	IS 101	F00	B+
Karen Taylor	IS 101	F00	A
Emily Vincent	IS 101	F00	C

File

NAME	COURSE	DATE	GRADE
John Stewart	IS 101	F00	B+

Record

Field — John Stewart (NAME field)

Byte — 01001010 (Letter J in ASCII)

Bit — 0

entity A person, place, thing, or event about which information must be kept.

attribute A piece of information describing a particular entity.

key field A field in a record that uniquely identifies instances of that record so that it can be retrieved, updated, or sorted.

sequential file organization A method of storing data records in which the records must be retrieved in the same physical sequence in which they are stored.

direct or random file organization A method of storing data records in a file so that they can be accessed in any sequence without regard to their actual physical order on the storage media.

A record describes an entity. An **entity** is a person, place, thing, or event on which we maintain information. An order is a typical entity in a sales order file, which maintains information on a firm's sales orders. Each characteristic or quality describing a particular entity is called an **attribute.** For example, order number, order date, order amount, item number, and item quantity would each be an attribute of the entity order. The specific values that these attributes can have can be found in the fields of the record describing the entity order (see Figure 6-2).

Every record in a file should contain at least one field that uniquely identifies instances of that record so that the record can be retrieved, updated, or sorted. This identifier field is called a **key field.** An example of a key field is the order number for the order record illustrated in Figure 6-2 or an employee number or social security number for a personnel record (containing employee data such as the employee's name, age, address, job title, and so forth).

ACCESSING RECORDS FROM COMPUTER FILES

Computer systems store files on secondary storage devices. Records can be arranged in several ways on storage media, and the arrangement determines the manner in which individual records can be accessed or retrieved. One way to organize records is sequentially. In **sequential file organization,** data records must be retrieved in the same physical sequence in which they are stored. In contrast, **direct** or **random file organization** allows users to access records in any sequence they desire, without regard to actual physical order on the storage media.

Sequential file organization is the only file organization method that can be used on magnetic tape. This file organization method is no longer popular, but some organizations still use it for batch processing applications in which they access and process each record sequentially. A typical application using sequential files is payroll, in which all employees in a firm must be paid one by one and issued a check. Direct or random file organization is associated with magnetic disk technology (although records can be stored sequentially on disk if desired). Most computer applications today use some method of direct file organization.

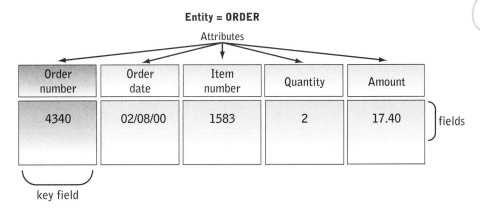

Entity = ORDER

Attributes

Order number	Order date	Item number	Quantity	Amount
4340	02/08/00	1583	2	17.40

fields

key field

FIGURE 6-2 Entities and attributes. This record describes the entity called ORDER and its attributes. The specific values for order number, order date, item number, quantity, and amount for this particular order are the fields for this record. Order number is the key field because each order is assigned a unique identification number.

The Indexed Sequential Access Method

Although records may be stored sequentially on direct access storage devices, individual records can be accessed directly using the **indexed sequential access method (ISAM).** This access method relies on an index of key fields to locate individual records. An **index** to a file is similar to the index of a book, as it lists the key field of each record and where that record is physically located in storage to expedite location of that record. Figure 6-3 shows how a series of indexes identifies the location of a specific record. Records are stored on disk in their key sequence. A cylinder index shows the highest value of the key field that can be found on a specific cylinder. A track index shows the highest value of the key field that can be found on

indexed sequential access method (ISAM) A file access method to directly access records organized sequentially using an index of key fields.

index A table or list that relates record keys to physical locations on direct access files.

FIGURE 6-3 The indexed sequential access method (ISAM). To find a record with a key field of 230, the cylinder index would be searched to find the correct cylinder (in this case, cylinder 2). The track index for cylinder 2 would then be searched to find the correct track. Because the highest key on track 2 of cylinder 2 is 238 and the highest key on track 1 of cylinder 2 is 208, track 2 must contain the record. Track 2 of cylinder 2 would then be read to find the record with key 230.

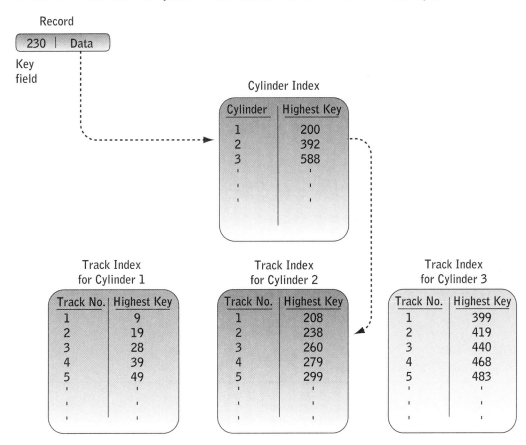

a specific track. (Chapter 4 described how data on disks are stored on concentric circular tracks. A *cylinder* is a set of tracks occupying the same position when the disks are stacked vertically on a shaft.) To locate a specific record, the cylinder index and then the track index are searched to locate the cylinder and track containing the record. The track itself is then sequentially read to find the record. If a file is very large, the cylinder index might be broken down into parts and a master index created to help locate each part of the cylinder index. ISAM is used in applications that require sequential processing of large numbers of records but that occasionally require direct access of individual records.

Direct File Access Method

direct file access method A method of accessing records by mathematically transforming the key fields into the specific addresses for the records.

The **direct file access method** is used with direct file organization. This method uses a key field to locate a record's physical address. However, the process is accomplished using a mathematical formula called a **transform algorithm** to translate the key field directly into the record's physical storage location on disk. The algorithm performs some mathematical computation on the record key, and the result of that calculation is the record's physical address. This process is illustrated in Figure 6-4.

transform algorithm A mathematical formula used to translate a record's key field directly into the record's physical storage location.

This access method is most appropriate for applications in which individual records must be located directly and rapidly for immediate processing only. A few records in the file may need to be retrieved at one time, and the required records are found in no particular sequence. An example might be an on-line hotel reservation system.

PROBLEMS WITH THE TRADITIONAL FILE ENVIRONMENT

Most organizations began information processing on a small scale, automating one application at a time. Systems tended to grow independently and not according to some grand plan. Each functional area tended to develop systems in isolation from other functional areas. Accounting, finance, manufacturing, human resources, and marketing all developed their own systems and data files. Figure 6-5 illustrates the traditional approach to information processing which many organizations still use.

Each application, of course, required its own files and its own computer programs to operate. For example, the human resources functional area might have a personnel master file, a payroll file, a medical insurance file, a pension file, a mailing list file, and so forth until tens,

FIGURE 6-4 The direct file access method. Records are not stored sequentially on the disk but are arranged according to the results of some mathematical computation. Here, the transform algorithm divides the value in the key field by the prime number closest to the maximum number of records in the file (in this case, the prime number is 997). The remainder designates the storage location for that particular record.

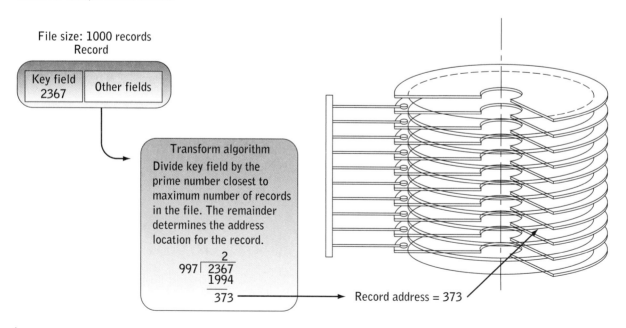

File size: 1000 records
Record

| Key field 2367 | Other fields |

Transform algorithm
Divide key field by the prime number closest to maximum number of records in the file. The remainder determines the address location for the record.

$$997\overline{)2367} \quad {\scriptstyle 2}$$
1994
373

Record address = 373

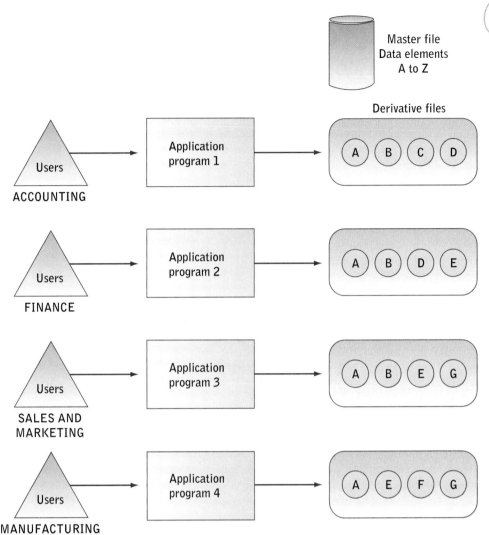

Master file
Data elements
A to Z

Derivative files

| Application program 1 | → | A B C D |

Users
ACCOUNTING

| Application program 2 | → | A B D E |

Users
FINANCE

| Application program 3 | → | A B E G |

Users
SALES AND
MARKETING

| Application program 4 | → | A E F G |

Users
MANUFACTURING

FIGURE 6-5 Traditional file processing. The use of a traditional approach to file processing encourages each functional area in a corporation to develop specialized applications. Each application requires a unique data file that is likely to be a subset of the master file. These subsets of the master file lead to data redundancy, processing inflexibility, and wasted storage resources.

perhaps hundreds, of files and programs existed. In the company as a whole, this process led to multiple master files created, maintained, and operated by separate divisions or departments.

As this process goes on for 5 or 10 years, the organization is saddled with hundreds of programs and applications, and no one who knows what they do, what data they use, or who is using the data. The organization is collecting the same information in far too many files. The resulting problems are data redundancy, program-data dependence, inflexibility, poor data security, and inability to share data among applications.

Data Redundancy and Confusion

Data redundancy is the presence of duplicate and often inconsistent data in multiple data files. Data redundancy occurs when different divisions, functional areas, and groups in an organization independently collect the same piece of information. For instance, within the commercial loans division of a bank, the marketing and credit information functions might collect the same customer information. Because it is collected and maintained in so many different places, the same data item may have different meanings or formats in different parts of the organization. Simple data items such as the fiscal year, employee identification, and product code can take on different meanings or formats as programmers and analysts work in isolation on different applications.

Program-Data Dependence

Program-data dependence is the tight relationship between data stored in files and the specific programs required to update and maintain those files. Every computer program has to describe the location and nature of the data with which it works. In a traditional file environment, any change in data organization or format requires a change in all programs that access the data.

data redundancy The presence of duplicate data in multiple data files.

program-data dependence The close relationship between data stored in files and the software programs that update and maintain those files. Any change in data organization or format requires a change in all the programs associated with those files.

Changes, for instance, in ZIP-code length require changes in programs. Such programming changes may cost millions of dollars to implement in programs that require the revised data.

Lack of Flexibility

A traditional file system can deliver routine scheduled reports after extensive programming efforts, but it cannot deliver ad hoc reports or respond to unanticipated information requirements in a timely fashion. The information required by ad hoc requests is somewhere in the system but too expensive to retrieve. Several programmers would have to work for weeks to put together the required data items in a new file.

Poor Security

Because there is little control or management of data, access to and dissemination of information may be out of control. Management may have no way of knowing who is accessing or even making changes to the organization's data.

Lack of Data-Sharing and Availability

The lack of control over access to data in this confused environment does not make it easy for people to obtain information. Because pieces of information in different files and different parts of the organization cannot be related to one another, it is virtually impossible for information to be shared or accessed in a timely manner.

6.2 The Database Environment

Database technology can cut through many of the problems a traditional file organization creates. A rigorous definition of a **database** is a collection of data organized to serve many applications efficiently by centralizing the data and minimizing redundant data. Rather than storing data in separate files for each application, data are stored physically to appear to users as being stored in only one location. A single database services multiple applications. For example, instead of a corporation storing employee data in separate information systems and separate files for personnel, payroll, and benefits, the corporation could create a single common human resources database. Figure 6-6 illustrates the database concept.

DATABASE MANAGEMENT SYSTEMS

A **database management system (DBMS)** is simply the software that permits an organization to centralize data, manage them efficiently, and provide access to the stored data by application programs. The DBMS acts as an interface between application programs and the physical data files. When the application program calls for a data item such as gross pay, the DBMS finds this item in the database and presents it to the application program. Using traditional data files the programmer would have to specify the size and format of each data element used in the program and then tell the computer where they were located. A DBMS eliminates most of the data definition statements found in traditional programs.

A database management system has three components:

- ○ A data definition language
- ○ A data manipulation language
- ○ A data dictionary

The **data definition language** is the formal language programmers use to specify the content and structure of the database. The data definition language defines each data element as it appears in the database before that data element is translated into the forms required by application programs.

Most DBMS have a specialized language called a **data manipulation language** that is used in conjunction with some conventional third- or fourth-generation programming languages to manipulate the data in the database. This language contains commands that permit end users and programming specialists to extract data from the database to satisfy information requests and develop applications. The most prominent data manipulation language today is

database (rigorous definition) A collection of data organized to service many applications at the same time and minimize redundancy by storing and managing data so that they appear to be in one location.

database management system (DBMS) Special software to create and maintain a database and enable individual business applications to extract the data they need without having to create separate files or data definitions in their computer programs.

data definition language The component of a database management system that defines each data element as it appears in the database.

data manipulation language A language associated with a database management system that end users and programmers use to manipulate data in the database.

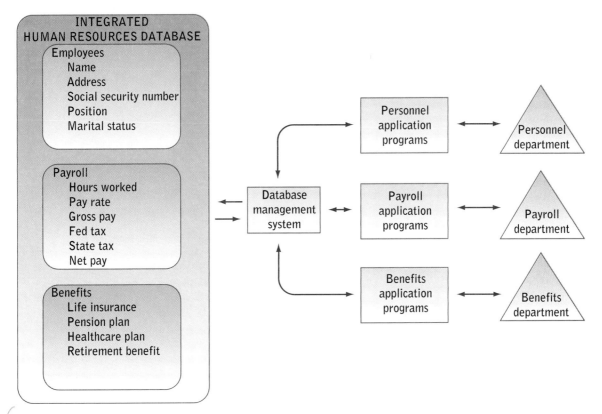

FIGURE 6-6 The contemporary database environment. A single human resources database serves multiple applications and also allows a corporation to easily draw together all the information for various applications. The database management system acts as the interface between the application programs and the data.

Structured Query Language, or SQL. Complex programming tasks cannot be performed efficiently with typical data manipulation languages. However, most mainframe DBMS are compatible with COBOL, FORTRAN, and other third-generation programming languages, permitting greater processing efficiency and flexibility.

The third element of a DBMS is a **data dictionary.** This is an automated or manual file that stores definitions of data elements and data characteristics such as usage, physical representation, ownership (who in the organization is responsible for maintaining the data), authorization, and security. Many data dictionaries can produce lists and reports of data use, groupings, program locations, and so on. Figure 6-7 illustrates a sample data dictionary report that shows the size, format, meaning, and uses of a data element in a human resources database. A **data element** represents a field. In addition to listing the standard name (AMT-PAY-BASE), the dictionary lists the names that reference this element in specific systems and identifies the individuals, business functions, programs, and reports that use this data element.

By creating an inventory of data contained in the database, the data dictionary serves as an important data management tool. For instance, business users could consult the dictionary to find out exactly what pieces of data are maintained for the sales or marketing function or even to determine all the information maintained by the entire enterprise. The dictionary could supply business users with the name, format, and specifications required to access data for reports. Technical staff could use the dictionary to determine what data elements and files must be changed if a program is changed.

Most data dictionaries are entirely passive; they simply report. More advanced types are active; changes in the dictionary can be automatically utilized by related programs. For instance, to change ZIP codes from five to nine digits, one could simply enter the change in the dictionary without having to modify and recompile all application programs using ZIP codes.

In an ideal database environment, the data in the database are defined only once and used for all applications whose data reside in the database, thereby eliminating data redundancy and

Structured Query Language (SQL) The standard data manipulation language for relational database management systems.

data dictionary An automated or manual tool for storing and organizing information about the data maintained in a database.

data element A field.

FIGURE 6-7 Sample dictionary report. The sample data dictionary report for a human resources database provides helpful information such as the size of the data element, which programs and reports use it, and which group in the organization is responsible for maintaining it. The report also shows some of the other names that the organization uses for this piece of data.

```
NAME:  AMT-PAY-BASE
FOCUS NAME:  BASEPAY
PC NAME:      SALARY

DESCRIPTION:  EMPLOYEE'S ANNUAL SALARY

SIZE: 9 BYTES
TYPE: N        (NUMERIC)
DATE CHANGED: 01/01/95
OWNERSHIP: COMPENSATION
UPDATE SECURITY:  SITE PERSONNEL
ACCESS SECURITY:  MANAGER, COMPENSATION PLANNING AND RESEARCH
                  MANAGER, JOB EVALUATION SYSTEMS
                  MANAGER, HUMAN RESOURCES PLANNING
                  MANAGER, SITE EQUAL OPPORTUNITY AFFAIRS
                  MANAGER, SITE BENEFITS
                  MANAGER, CLAIMS PAYING SYSTEMS
                  MANAGER, QUALIFIED PLANS
                  MANAGER, SITE EMPLOYMENT/EEO
BUSINESS FUNCTIONS USED BY:  COMPENSATION
                             HR PLANNING
                             EMPLOYMENT
                             INSURANCE
                             PENSION
                             ISP


PROGRAMS USING:  PI01000
                 PI02000
                 PI03000
                 PI04000
                 PI05000


REPORTS USING:  REPORT 124 (SALARY INCREASE TRACKING REPORT)
                REPORT 448 (GROUP INSURANCE AUDIT REPORT)
                REPORT 452 (SALARY REVIEW LISTING)
                PENSION REFERENCE LISTING
```

inconsistency. Application programs, which are written using a combination of the data manipulation language of the DBMS and a conventional programming language, request data elements from the database. Data elements called for by the application programs are found and delivered by the DBMS. The programmer does not have to specify in detail how or where the data are to be found.

A DBMS can reduce program-data dependence along with program development and maintenance costs. Access and availability of information can be increased because users and programmers can perform ad hoc queries of data in the database. The DBMS allows the organization to centrally manage data, its use, and security.

LOGICAL AND PHYSICAL VIEWS OF DATA

Perhaps the greatest difference between a DBMS and traditional file organization is that the DBMS separates the logical and physical views of the data, relieving the programmer or end user from the task of understanding where and how the data are actually stored.

The **logical view** presents data as they would be perceived by end users or business specialists, whereas the **physical view** shows how data are actually organized and structured on physical storage media. Suppose, for example, that a professor of information systems wanted to know at the beginning of the semester how students performed in the prerequisite computer literacy course (Computer Literacy 101) and the students' current majors. Using a database sup-

logical view A representation of data as they would appear to an application programmer or end user.

physical view The representation of data as they actually would be organized on physical storage media.

ported by the registrar, the professor would need something similar to the report shown in Figure 6-8.

Ideally, for such a simple report, the professor could sit at an office terminal connected to the registrar's database and write a small application program using the data manipulation language to create this report. The professor first would develop the desired logical view of the data (Figure 6-8) for the application program. The DBMS would then assemble the requested data elements, which might reside in several different files and disk locations. For instance, the student major information might be located in a file called *Student,* whereas the grade data might be located in a file called *Course.* Wherever they were located, the DBMS would pull these pieces of information together and present them to the professor according to the logical view requested.

The query using the data manipulation language constructed by the professor might resemble that shown in Figure 6-9. DBMS working on both mainframes and PCs permit this kind of interactive report creation.

6.3 Developing Databases

In order to create a database, one must understand the relationships among the data, the type of data that will be maintained in the database, and how the data will be used. We now describe alternative ways of organizing data and representing relationships among data in a database and the most important database design principles.

TYPES OF DATABASES

Contemporary DBMS use different database models to keep track of entities, attributes, and relationships. Each model has certain processing advantages and certain business advantages.

Relational Data Model

The most popular type of DBMS today for PCs as well as for larger computers and mainframes is the **relational data model.** The relational model represents all data in the database as simple two-dimensional tables called *relations.* The tables appear similar to flat files, but the information in more than one file can be easily extracted and combined. Sometimes the tables are referred to as files.

relational data model A type of logical database model that treats data as if they were stored in two-dimensional tables. It can relate data stored in one table to data in another as long as the two tables share a common data element.

Student Name	ID No.	Major	Grade in Computer Literacy 101
Lind	468	Finance	A-
Pinckus	332	Marketing	B+
Williams	097	Economics	C+
Laughlin	765	Finance	A
Orlando	324	Statistics	B

FIGURE 6-8 The report required by the professor. The report requires data elements that may come from different files but can easily be pulled together with a database management system if the data are organized into a database.

```
SELECT Stud_name, Stud.stud_id, Major, Grade
FROM Student, Course
WHERE Stud.stud_id = Course.stud_id
AND Course_id = "CL101"
```

FIGURE 6-9 The query used by the professor. This example shows how Structured Query Language (SQL) commands could be used to deliver the data required by the professor. These commands join two files, the student file (Student) and the course file (Course), and extract the specified pieces of information on each student from the combined file.

Figure 6-10 shows a supplier table, a part table, and an order table. In each table the rows are unique records and the columns are fields. Another term for a row or record in a relation is a **tuple.** Often a user needs information from a number of relations to produce a report. Here is the strength of the relational model: It can relate data in any one file or table to data in another file or table as long as both tables share a common data element.

To demonstrate, suppose we wanted to find in the relational database in Figure 6-10 the names and addresses of suppliers who could provide us with part number 137 or part number 152. We would need information from two tables: the supplier table and the part table. Note that these two files have a shared data element: SUPPLIER-NUMBER.

In a relational database, three basic operations are used to develop useful sets of data: select, project, and join. The *select* operation creates a subset consisting of all records in the file that meet stated criteria. *Select* creates, in other words, a subset of rows that meet certain criteria. In our example, we want to select records (rows) from the part table where the part number equals 137 or 152. The *join* operation combines relational tables to provide the user with more information than is available in individual tables. In our example we want to join the now shortened part table (only parts numbered 137 or 152 will be presented) and the supplier table into a single new result table.

The *project* operation creates a subset consisting of columns in a table, permitting the user to create new tables that contain only the information required. In our example, we want to extract from the new result table only the following columns: PART-NUMBER, SUPPLIER-NUMBER, SUPPLIER-NAME, and SUPPLIER-ADDRESS. Leading mainframe relational database management systems include IBM's DB2 and Oracle from the Oracle Corporation. DB2, Oracle, and Microsoft SQL Server are used as DBMS for midrange computers. Microsoft Access is a PC relational database management system.

FIGURE 6-10 The relational data model. Each table is a relation and each row or record is a tuple. Each column corresponds to a field. These relations can easily be combined and extracted to access data and produce reports, provided that any two share a common data element. In this example, the ORDER file shares the data element "PART-NUMBER" with the PART file. The PART and SUPPLIER files share the data element "SUPPLIER-NUMBER."

Table (Relation) — **Columns (Fields)**

ORDER

ORDER-NUMBER	ORDER-DATE	DELIVERY-DATE	PART-NUMBER	PART-AMOUNT	ORDER-TOTAL
1634	02/02/00	02/22/00	152	2	144.50
1635	02/12/00	02/29/00	137	3	79.70
1636	02/13/00	03/01/00	145	1	24.30

Rows (Records, Tuples)

PART

PART-NUMBER	PART-DESCRIPTION	UNIT-PRICE	SUPPLIER-NUMBER
137	Door latch	26.25	4058
145	Door handle	22.50	2038
152	Compressor	70.00	1125

SUPPLIER

SUPPLIER-NUMBER	SUPPLIER-NAME	SUPPLIER-ADDRESS
1125	CBM Inc.	44 Winslow, Gary IN 44950
2038	Ace Inc.	Rte. 101, Essex NJ 07763
4058	Bryant Corp.	51 Elm, Rochester NY 11349

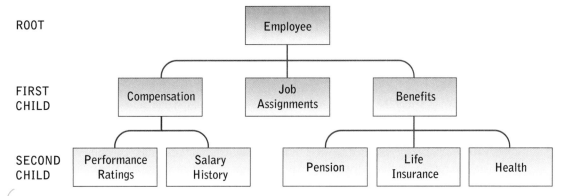

ROOT

FIRST CHILD

SECOND CHILD

FIGURE 6-11 A hierarchical database for a human resources system. The hierarchical database model looks like an organizational chart or a family tree. It has a single root segment (Employee) connected to lower level segments (Compensation, Job Assignments, and Benefits). Each subordinate segment, in turn, may connect to other subordinate segments. Here, Compensation connects to Performance Ratings and Salary History. Benefits connects to Pension, Life Insurance, and Health. Each subordinate segment is the child of the segment directly above it.

Hierarchical and Network Data Models

One can still find older database systems that are based on a hierarchical or network data model. The **hierarchical data model** presents data to users in a treelike structure. Within each record, data elements are organized into pieces of records called *segments*. To the user, each record looks like an organization chart with one top-level segment called the *root*. An upper segment is connected logically to a lower segment in a parent–child relationship. A parent segment can have more than one child, but a child can have only one parent.

Figure 6-11 shows a hierarchical structure that might be used for a human resources database. The root segment is Employee, which contains basic employee information such as name, address, and identification number. Immediately below it are three child segments: Compensation (containing salary and promotion data), Job Assignments (containing data about job positions and departments), and Benefits (containing data about beneficiaries and benefit options). The Compensation segment has two children below it: Performance Ratings (containing data about employees' job performance evaluations) and Salary History (containing historical data about employees' past salaries). Below the Benefits segment are child segments for Pension, Life Insurance, and Health, containing data about these benefit plans.

Whereas hierarchical structures depict one-to-many relationships, **network data models** depict data logically as many-to-many relationships. In other words, parents can have multiple children, and a child can have more than one parent. A typical many-to-many relationship for a network DBMS is the student–course relationship (see Figure 6-12). There are many courses in a university and many students. A student takes many courses and a course has many students.

hierarchical data model One type of logical database model that organizes data in a treelike structure. A record is subdivided into segments that are connected to each other in one-to-many parent–child relationships.

network data model An older logical database model that is useful for depicting many-to-many relationships.

FIGURE 6-12 The network data model. This illustration of a network data model showing the relationship the students in a university have to the courses they take represents an example of logical many-to-many relationships.

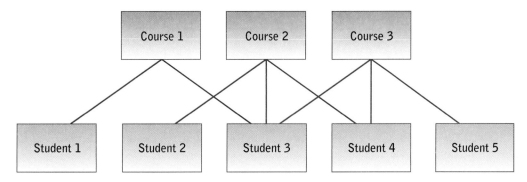

Hierarchical and network DBMS are considered outdated and are no longer used for building new database applications. They are less flexible than relational DBMS and do not support ad hoc, English language-like inquiries for information. All paths for accessing data must be specified in advance and cannot be changed without a major programming effort. For instance, if you queried the human resources database illustrated in Figure 6-11 to find out the names of the employees with the job title of administrative assistant, you would discover that there is no way that the system can find the answer in a reasonable amount of time. This path through the data was not specified in advance.

Relational DBMS, in contrast, have much more flexibility in providing data for ad hoc queries, combining information from different sources, and providing capability to add new data and records without disturbing existing programs and applications. However, these systems can be slowed down if they require many accesses to the data stored on disk to carry out the select, join, and project commands. Selecting one part number from among millions, one record at a time, can take a long time. Of course the database can be indexed and tuned to speed up prespecified queries.

Hierarchical DBMS can still be found in large legacy systems that require intensive high-volume transaction processing. A **legacy system** is a system that has been in existence for a long time and that continues to be used to avoid the high cost of replacing or redesigning it. Banks, insurance companies, and other high-volume users continue to use reliable hierarchical databases such as IBM's IMS (Information Management System), which was developed in 1969. Many organizations have converted to DB2, IBM's relational DBMS for new applications, while retaining IMS for traditional transaction processing. For example, Dallas-based Texas Instruments depends on IMS for its heavy processing requirements, including inventory, accounting, and manufacturing. As relational products acquire more muscle, firms will shift completely away from hierarchical DBMS, but this will happen over a long period of time.

Object-Oriented Databases

Conventional database management systems were designed for homogeneous data that can be easily structured into predefined data fields and records organized in rows or tables. But many applications today and in the future will require databases that can store and retrieve not only structured numbers and characters but also drawings, images, photographs, voice, and full-motion video. Conventional DBMS are not well suited to handling graphics-based or multimedia applications. For instance, design data in a Computer-Aided Design (CAD) database consist of complex relationships among many types of data. Manipulating these kinds of data in a relational system requires extensive programming to translate these complex data structures into tables and rows. However, an **object-oriented database management system** stores the data and procedures as objects that can be automatically retrieved and shared.

Object-oriented database management systems (OODBMS) are becoming popular because they can be used to manage the various multimedia components or Java applets used in Web applications, which typically integrate pieces of information from a variety of sources. OODBMS also are useful for storing data types such as recursive data. (An example would be parts within parts as found in manufacturing applications.) Finance and trading applications often use OODBMS because they require data models that must be easy to change to respond to new economic conditions. Siemens Building Technologies, Inc. is using the Objectivity OODBMS to store complex network configuration and historical information required for its building control system. The building control system manages heating, ventilation, and air conditioning information, including information for monitoring building humidity, security, and lighting.

Although object-oriented databases can store more complex types of information than relational DBMS, they are relatively slow compared with relational DBMS for processing large numbers of transactions. Hybrid **object-relational DBMS** systems are now available to provide capabilities of both object-oriented and relational DBMS. A hybrid approach can be accomplished in three different ways: by using tools that offer object-oriented access to relational DBMS, by using object-oriented extensions to existing relational DBMS, or by using a hybrid object-relational database management system.

legacy system A system that has been in existence for a long time, which is still used simply to avoid the high cost of replacing or redesigning it.

object-oriented DBMS An approach to data management that stores both data and the procedures acting on the data as objects that can be automatically retrieved and shared; the objects can contain multimedia.

object-relational DBMS A database management system that combines the capabilities of a relational DBMS and the capabilities of an object-oriented DBMS.

DESIGNING DATABASES

To create a database, one must go through two design exercises: a conceptual design and a physical design. The conceptual or logical design of a database is an abstract model of the database from a business perspective, whereas the physical design shows how the database is actually arranged on direct access storage devices. Logical design requires a detailed description of the business information needs of the actual end users of the database. Ideally, database design will be part of an overall organizational data planning effort (see Chapter 9).

The conceptual database design describes how the data elements in the database are to be grouped. The design process identifies relationships among data elements and the most efficient way of grouping data elements together to meet information requirements. The process also identifies redundant data elements and the groupings of data elements required for specific application programs. Groups of data are organized, refined, and streamlined until an overall logical view of the relationships among all the data elements in the database emerges.

Database designers document the conceptual data model with an **entity-relationship diagram,** illustrated in Figure 6-13. The boxes represent entities and the diamonds represent relationships. The 1 or M on either side of the diamond represents the relationship among entities as either one-to-one, one-to-many, or many-to-many. Figure 6-13 shows that the entity ORDER can have more than one PART and a PART can only have one SUPPLIER. Many parts can be provided by the same supplier. The attributes for each entity are listed next to the entity and the key field is underlined.

To use a relational database model effectively, complex groupings of data must be streamlined to eliminate redundant data elements and awkward many-to-many relationships. The process of creating small, stable data structures from complex groups of data is called **normalization.** Figures 6-14 and 6-15 illustrate this process. In the particular business modeled here, an order can have more than one part but each part is provided by only one supplier. If we built a relation called ORDER with all the fields included here, we would have to repeat

entity-relationship diagram A methodology for documenting databases illustrating the relationship between various entities in the database.

normalization The process of creating small stable data structures from complex groups of data when designing a relational database.

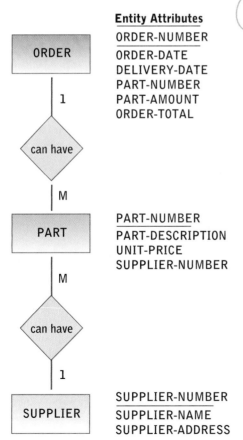

Entity Attributes

ORDER

ORDER-NUMBER
ORDER-DATE
DELIVERY-DATE
PART-NUMBER
PART-AMOUNT
ORDER-TOTAL

1

can have

M

PART

PART-NUMBER
PART-DESCRIPTION
UNIT-PRICE
SUPPLIER-NUMBER

M

can have

1

SUPPLIER

SUPPLIER-NUMBER
SUPPLIER-NAME
SUPPLIER-ADDRESS

FIGURE 6-13 An entity-relationship diagram. This diagram shows the relationships between the entities ORDER, PART, and SUPPLIER.

ORDER

ORDER-NUMBER	PART-AMOUNT	PART-NUMBER	PART-DESCRIPTION	UNIT-PRICE	SUPPLIER-NUMBER	SUPPLIER-NAME	SUPPLIER-ADDRESS	ORDER-DATE	DELIVERY-DATE	ORDER-TOTAL

FIGURE 6-14 An unnormalized relation for ORDER. In an unnormalized relation there are repeating groups. For example, there can be many parts and suppliers for each order. There is only a one-to-one correspondence between ORDER-NUMBER and ORDER-DATE, ORDER-TOTAL, and DELIVERY-DATE.

ORDER

ORDER-NUMBER	ORDER-DATE	DELIVERY-DATE	ORDER-TOTAL
Key			

ORDERED-PARTS

ORDER-NUMBER	PART-NUMBER	PART-AMOUNT
Key		

SUPPLIER

SUPPLIER-NUMBER	SUPPLIER-NAME	SUPPLIER-ADDRESS
Key		

PART

PART-NUMBER	PART-DESCRIPTION	UNIT-PRICE	SUPPLIER-NUMBER
Key			

FIGURE 6-15 A normalized relation for ORDER. After normalization, the original relation ORDER has been broken down into four smaller relations. The relation ORDER is left with only three attributes and the relation ORDERED-PARTS has a combined, or concatenated, key consisting of ORDER-NUMBER and PART-NUMBER.

the name, description, and price of each part on the order and the name and address of each part vendor. This relation contains what are called repeating groups because there can be many parts and suppliers for each order, and it actually describes multiple entities—parts and suppliers as well as orders. A more efficient way to arrange the data is to break down ORDER into smaller relations, each of which describes a single entity. If we go step by step and normalize the relation ORDER, we emerge with the relations illustrated in Figure 6-15.

If a database has been carefully considered, with a clear understanding of business information needs and usage, the database model will most likely be in some normalized form. Many real-world databases are not fully normalized because this may not be the most sensible way to meet business information requirements. Note that the relational database illustrated in Figure 6-10 is not fully normalized because there could be more than one part for each order. The designers chose to not use the four relations described in Figure 6-15 because most of the orders handled by this particular business are only for one part. The designers might have felt that for this particular business it was inefficient to maintain four different tables.

DISTRIBUTING DATABASES

Database design also considers how the data are to be distributed. Information systems can be designed with a centralized database that is used by a single central processor or by multiple processors in a client/server network. Alternatively, the database can be distributed. A **distributed database** is one that is stored in more than one physical location. Parts of the database are stored physically in one location, and other parts are stored and maintained in other locations. There are two main ways of distributing a database (see Figure 6-16). The central database (see Figure 6-16a) can be partitioned so that each remote processor has the necessary data to serve its local area. Changes in local files can be justified with the central database on a batch basis, often at night. Another strategy is to replicate the central database (Figure 6-16b) at all remote locations. For example, Lufthansa Airlines replaced its centralized mainframe database with a replicated database to make information more immediately available to flight dispatchers. Any change made to Lufthansa's Frankfort DBMS is automatically replicated in New York and Hong Kong. This strategy also requires updating of the central database on off hours.

Distributed systems reduce the vulnerability of a single, massive central site. They increase service and responsiveness to local users and often can run on smaller, less expensive computers.

distributed database A database that is stored in more than one physical location. Parts or copies of the database are physically stored in one location, and other parts or copies are stored and maintained in other locations.

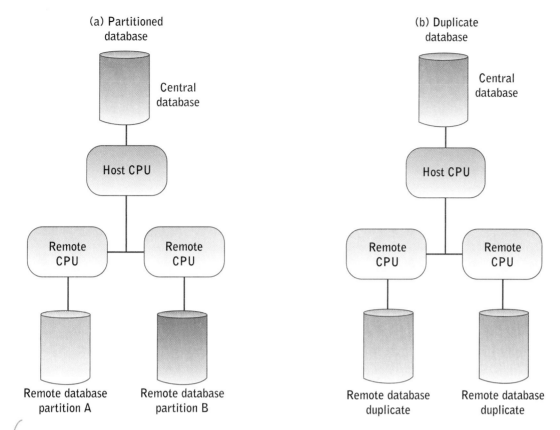

(a) Partitioned database

Central database

Host CPU

Remote CPU — Remote CPU

Remote database partition A | Remote database partition B

(b) Duplicate database

Central database

Host CPU

Remote CPU — Remote CPU

Remote database duplicate | Remote database duplicate

FIGURE 6-16 Distributed databases. There are alternative ways of distributing a database. The central database can be partitioned (a) so that each remote processor has the necessary data to serve its own local needs. The central database also can be duplicated (b) at all remote locations.

Distributed systems, however, are dependent on high-quality (and often expensive) telecommunications lines, which themselves are vulnerable. Moreover, local databases can sometimes depart from central data standards and definitions, and they pose security problems by widely distributing access to sensitive data. Database designers need to weigh these factors in their decisions.

6.4 Database Trends

Organizations are installing powerful data analysis tools and data warehouses to make better use of the information stored in their databases and are taking advantage of database technology linked to the World Wide Web. We now explore these developments.

MULTIDIMENSIONAL DATA ANALYSIS

Sometimes managers need to analyze data in ways that traditional database models cannot represent. For example, a company selling four different products—nuts, bolts, washers, and screws—in the East, West, and Central regions might want to know actual sales by product for each region and might also want to compare them with projected sales. This analysis requires a multidimensional view of data.

To provide this type of information, organizations can use either a specialized multidimensional database or a tool that creates multidimensional views of data in relational databases. Multidimensional analysis enables users to view the same data in different ways using multiple dimensions. Each aspect of information—product, pricing, cost, region, or time period—represents a different dimension. So a product manager could use a multidimensional data analysis tool to learn how many washers were sold in the East in June, how that compares with the previous month and the previous June, and how it compares with the sales forecast. Another term for multidimensional data analysis is **on-line analytical processing (OLAP).**

on-line analytical processing (OLAP) Capability for manipulating and analyzing large volumes of data from multiple perspectives.

FIGURE 6-17

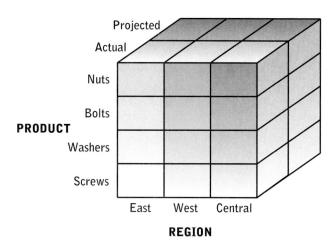

Multidimensional data model. The view that is showing is product versus region. If you rotate the cube 90 degrees, the face that will be showing is product versus actual and projected sales. If you rotate the cube 90 degrees again, you can see region versus actual and projected sales. Other views are possible. The ability to rotate the data cube is the main technique for multidimensional reporting. It is sometimes called "slice and dice."

Figure 6-17 shows a multidimensional model that could be created to represent products, regions, actual sales, and projected sales. A matrix of actual sales can be stacked on top of a matrix of projected sales to form a cube with six faces. If you rotate the cube 90 degrees one way, the face showing will be product versus actual and projected sales. If you rotate the cube 90 degrees again, you can see region versus actual and projected sales. If you rotate the cube 180 degrees from the original view, you can see projected sales and product versus region. Cubes can be nested within cubes to build complex views of data.

DATA WAREHOUSES

Decision makers need concise, reliable information about current operations, trends, and changes. What has been immediately available at most firms is current data only (historical data were available through special IS reports that took a long time to produce). Data often are fragmented in separate operational systems such as sales or payroll so that different managers make decisions from incomplete knowledge bases. Users and information system specialists may have to spend inordinate amounts of time locating and gathering data (Watson and Haley, 1998). Data warehousing addresses this problem by integrating key operational data from around the company in a form that is consistent, reliable, and easily available for reporting.

What Is a Data Warehouse?

A **data warehouse** is a database that stores current and historical data of potential interest to managers throughout the company. The data originate in many core operational systems and

data warehouse A database, with reporting and query tools, that stores current and historical data extracted from various operational systems and consolidated for management reporting and analysis.

The SAS MDDB Report Viewer offers a Web interface for viewing and manipulating multidimensional databases produced with SAS software using business dimensions such as time, geography, or product. Online analytical processing (OLAP) gives users quick, unlimited views of multiple relationships in large quantities of summarized data.

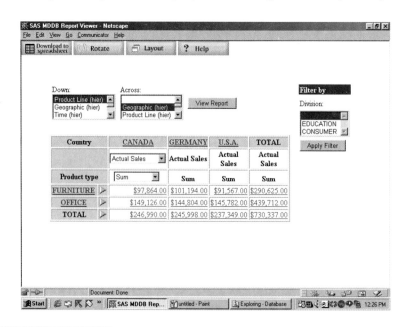

external sources and are copied into the data warehouse database as often as needed—hourly, daily, weekly, monthly. The data are standardized and consolidated so that they can be used across the enterprise for management analysis and decision making. The data are available for anyone to access as needed but cannot be altered. A data warehouse system provides a range of ad hoc and standardized query tools, analytical tools, and graphical reporting facilities, including tools for OLAP and datamining. These systems can perform high-level analyses of patterns or trends, but they can also drill into more detail where needed. Figure 6-18 illustrates the data warehouse concept.

Companies can build enterprise-wide data warehouses where a central data warehouse serves the entire organization, or they can create smaller, decentralized warehouses called data marts. A **data mart** is a subset of a data warehouse in which a summarized or highly focused portion of the organization's data is placed in a separate database for a specific population of users. For example, a company might develop marketing and sales data marts to deal with customer information. A data mart typically focuses on a single subject area or line of business, so it usually can be constructed more rapidly and at lower cost than an enterprise-wide data warehouse. However, complexity, costs, and management problems will rise if an organization creates too many data marts.

data mart A small data warehouse containing only a portion of the organization's data for a specified function or population of users.

Benefits of Data Warehouses

Data warehouses not only offer improved information, they make it easy for decision makers to obtain it. They even include the ability to model and remodel the data in the warehouse. It has been estimated that 70 percent of the world's business information resides on mainframe databases, many of which are for older legacy systems. Many of these legacy systems are critical production applications that support the company's core business processes. As long as these systems can efficiently process the necessary volume of transactions to keep the company running, firms are reluctant to replace them to avoid disrupting critical business functions and high system replacement costs. Many of these legacy systems use hierarchical DBMS or even older nondatabase files where information is difficult for users to access. Data warehouses

FIGURE 6-18 Components of a data warehouse. A data warehouse extracts current and historical data from operational systems inside the organization. These data are combined with data from external sources and reorganized into a central database designed for management reporting and analysis. The information directory provides users with information about the data available in the warehouse.

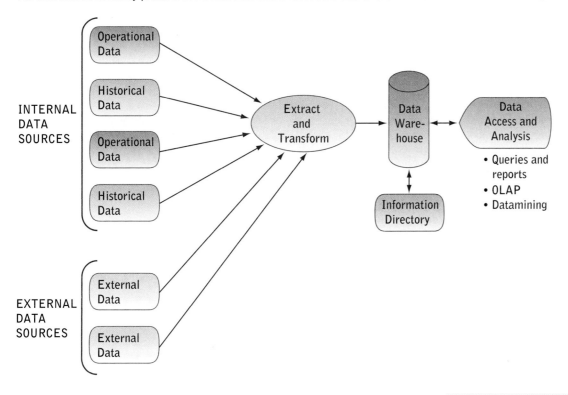

BREATHING NEW LIFE INTO LEGACY DATABASES

Legacy databases are tightly coupled to the systems for which they were created, making them inflexible and difficult to access when management wants to use them for other purposes. However, many organizations do not want to change those old systems because they work so well. So how are companies protecting their treasured legacy systems while giving management access to the data it needs? Let us look at three different solutions.

Owen & Minor Inc., the Richmond, Virginia, $3 billion surgical supplies company, had key production data stored on its mainframe in various hierarchical databases and older nondatabase files. "All these databases are independent," observed Don Stoller, director of information management, "which makes it hard to do queries." To bring the data together and create a multidimensional view, the company decided to build a data warehouse using an Oracle database. The company installed an easy-to-use query tool called Business Objects from Business Objects SA to provide an interface for users to access the database. In addition, they purchased software to extract data from the legacy production systems, transform it, and load it into the Oracle database.

To build the data warehouse quickly, Owen & Minor decided to bring in one function at a time, beginning with three years of sales data. The system was up and running with sales data within five months. Now, two years later, they have almost completed bringing in data from all nine of the planned business functions. The Oracle database contains more than three years of sales history data and takes up 120 gigabytes. Owen & Minor's next step is to develop a system it calls WISDOM (Web Intelligence Supporting Decisions from Owens & Minor). WISDOM will enable customers and suppliers to use the Web to access Owen's production data in the data warehouse, enabling them to be better informed and make better decisions.

Management at Aqua-Chem, the Milwaukee-based boiler manufacturer, also wanted to use legacy data to perform multidimensional financial analysis and also did not want to replace their legacy financial systems, which run on Computer Associates' CA-Datacom DBMS. "We liked the security, functionality, and reliability of the old system," explained Chuck Norris, Aqua-Chem's vice president and CIO. So Norris turned to on-line analytical processing (OLAP) and business intelligence tools. The company de-

veloped a financial data warehouse using Microsoft's SQL Server database management system. Manufacturing, sales, and other data were extracted, transformed, and transferred to the SQL Server database. Managers use OLAP software tools from Cognos Inc. to view, analyze, and even manipulate the data, while the old mainframe systems continue to do the basic transaction processing. Employees have easy access to the data through Aqua-Chem's intranet. One side benefit is that the company no longer generates and distributes dozens of paper-based management reports. Now everything is on-line; those who want hard paper just print what they want.

New York City's Board of Education faced a similar problem. With 1.1 million students, the school system generates and stores immense amounts of data, scattered among a number of isolated legacy systems and predatabase files. The Board will not eliminate those systems because they are still performing well. The city's 1,200 school principals, the superintendents, and the thousands of administrators need quick and easy access to this data if they are to achieve the performance goals being set by the Board of Education. Most were not using data and were making decisions off the cuff. The goal of Kamal Kumar, director of New York's office of students systems development, was to enable them to make information-based decisions.

The Board's systems were mainframe based. So Kumar built a data mart using a mainframe tool from Information Builders. It brings scattered data together and stores them in an IBM mainframe DB2 relational database. Because the schools use a different networking technology than the Board's network, Kumar found that the easiest way to make the information available to desktop computers at more than 1,200 sites was to provide access through the Web. Now appropriate personnel at any site in the system can get quick and easy access to the data they need.

TO THINK ABOUT: What factors do you think each of these three organizations addressed in devising technical solutions to the same management problem? Why did all three turn to the Internet or an intranet as a piece of the solution?

Sources: Alan Radding, "Bringing Legacy Databases Up to Date," Computerworld, July 12, 1999; and Bob Violino, "E-Business 100: The Leaders of E-Business," Information Week, December 13, 1999.

enable decision makers to access data as often as they need without affecting the performance of the underlying operational systems. Many organizations are making access to their data warehouses even easier by using Web technology. The Window on Technology describes how several companies used data warehouses, data marts and business intelligence tools to make better use of their legacy data for management decision making and analysis.

Organizations have used the information gleaned from data warehouses using OLAP and datamining to help them refocus their businesses. For example, MovieFone Inc. initially constructed a data warehouse to track historical calling patterns of people who phoned in for its free movie-listing service, to make sure it had sufficient phone lines set up to cover peak calling times. But MovieFone also found it could use these data combined with data from its sister Web site MovieLink to advise theater owners on how many screenings to allocate to popular films and to advise theater developers on hot new locations (Deck, 1999).

DATABASES AND THE WEB

Database technology plays an important role in making organizations' information resources available on the World Wide Web. We now explore the role of hypermedia databases in the Web and the growing use of Web sites to access information stored in conventional databases inside the firm.

The Web and Hypermedia Databases

Web sites store information as interconnected pages containing text, sound, video, and graphics using a hypermedia database. The **hypermedia database** approach to information management stores chunks of information in the form of nodes connected by links the user specifies (see Figure 6-19). The nodes can contain text, graphics, sound, full-motion video, or executable computer programs. Searching for information does not have to follow a predetermined organization scheme. Instead, one can branch instantly to related information in any kind of relationship the author establishes. The relationship between records is less structured than in a traditional DBMS.

The hypermedia database approach enables users to access topics on a Web site in whatever order they wish. For instance, from the Web page from the National Aeronautics and Space Administration (NASA) in the accompanying illustration, one could branch to other Web pages describing NASA's 1998 Education Catalog, ESE Education Strategy, Education Reports, For Kids Only, and ESE Web. The links from the on-screen page to the other related Web pages are highlighted in blue. We provide more detail on these and other features of Web sites in Chapter 8.

Linking Internal Databases to the Web

A series of middleware software products has been developed to help users gain access to organizations' legacy data through the Web. For example, a customer with a Web browser might want to search an online retailer's database for pricing information. Figure 6-20 illustrates how that customer might access the retailer's internal database over the Web. The user would first access the retailer's Web site over the Internet using Web browser software on his or her client PC. The user's Web browser software would request data from the organization's database, using HTML commands to communicate with the Web server. Because many back-end

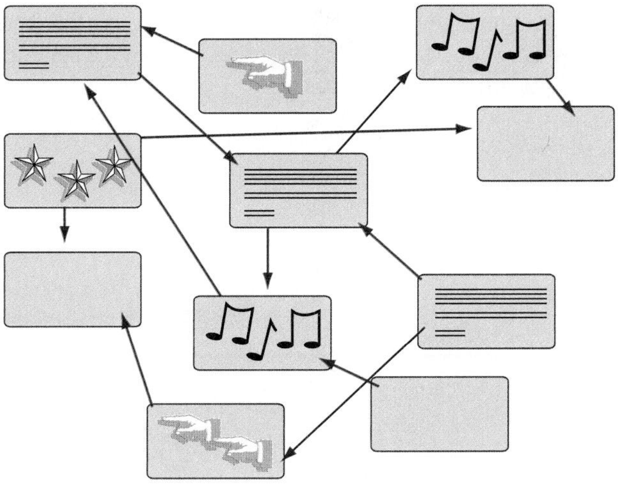

> **hypermedia database** An approach to data management that organizes data as a network of nodes linked in any pattern the user specifies; the nodes can contain text, graphics, sound, full-motion video, or executable programs.

FIGURE 6-19 A hypermedia database. In a hypermedia database, the user can choose his or her own path to move from node to node. Each node can contain text, graphics, sound, full-motion video, or executable programs.

By clicking on the words highlighted in blue, visitors to the National Aeronautical and Space Administration (NASA) Web site can be transported to other related Web pages. Web sites store information as interconnected pages containing text, sound, video, and graphics using a hypermedia approach to data management.

databases cannot interpret commands written in HTML, the Web server would pass these requests for data to special software that would translate HTML commands into SQL so that they could be processed by the DBMS working with the database. The DBMS receives the SQL requests and provides the requested data. The middleware would transfer the information from the organization's internal database back to the Web server for delivery in the form of a Web page to the user.

Figure 6-20 shows that the software working between the Web server and the DBMS could be an application server, a custom program, or a series of software scripts. An *application server* is a software program that handles all application operations between browser-based computers and a company's back-end business applications or databases. Common Gateway Interface (CGI) scripts are also used for this purpose. *Common Gateway Interface (CGI)* is a specification for transferring information between a World Wide Web server and a program designed to accept and return data. The program could be written in any programming language, including C, Perl, Java, or Visual Basic.

There are a number of advantages to using the Web to access an organization's internal databases. Web browser software is extremely easy to use, requiring much less training than even user-friendly database query tools. The Web interface requires no changes to the internal database. Companies leverage their investments in older systems because it costs much less to add a Web interface in front of a legacy system than to redesign and rebuild the system to improve user access. Accessing corporate databases through the Web is creating new efficiencies and opportunities, in some cases even changing the way business is being done, as described in the Window on Organizations. The Window on Management describes some of the benefits of providing the public with Web access to government databases.

FIGURE 6-20 Linking internal databases to the Web. Users can access an organization's internal database through the Web using their desktop PCs and Web browser software.

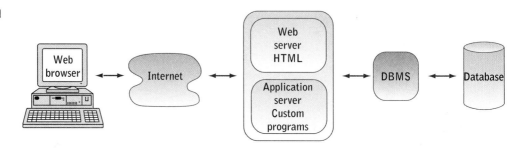

DATABASES POWER E-COMMERCE

Can enormous quantities of data rather than a large staff be the foundation for building a successful Web-based business? Only time will tell, but when the database stores data many other people want, it begins to look like a successful business model.

One database-driven business now on the Web is iGo.com, formerly 1-800-Batteries, perhaps the largest supplier of batteries and other parts for mobile electronic gear. Several years ago a young Stanford MBA, Ken Hawk, realized that finding the correct battery for portable electronic equipment could be daunting. With thousands of portable electronic articles and thousands of batteries to select from to run each item, he saw a business opportunity; he founded 1-800-Batteries, basing it on a giant cross-referenced database that runs on IBM's DB2 relational DBMS. One set of data is a listing of every laptop, personal digital assistant computer, portable telephone, camcorder, and all the other portable electronic items. Each of these items is cross-referenced to a list of the proper battery or batteries for that product. His database then cross-references each battery with one or more of more than 300 companies that are his battery sources. Hawk established the business before the Web explosion, and the company was originally based on a catalog and an 800 number. Following that model, his company grew to $13 million in sales in 1998.

Hawk expected to almost double his sales in 1999 because of his company's move to the Web. The company turned to the Web because Hawk believes "We are one of the few businesses where the experience on the Internet could be better than on the phone." He points out that describing a battery verbally takes a lot longer and is more difficult that seeing a picture of it on one's computer. In addition, of course, visitors to his Web site can find information on the battery's availability without having to phone the company. Hawk estimates that 98.5 percent of all queries to his Web database results in customers finding

what they need. Hawk has also built individualized Web interfaces for his large corporate customers, such as Dell Computer. To create his Web site, Hawk's company spent $2.2 million.

Eric Killorin also saw possibilities in matching people with a need to the right information without building a large staff. Killorin had always been interested in automobile memorabilia, particularly model cars. In 1993 he began publishing **Mobilia Magazine**, containing information for collectors of automobiles and car-related memorabilia. The magazine readership climbed quickly to 60,000, and in 1995 Killorin built a database and a Web site (http://www.mobilia.com/) to give the general public access. In that database he lists many car memorabilia, including 18,000 model cars. The listing for each model car contains the vehicle type, model, color, body style, and even whether the model includes a driver. Anyone can search the database for the specific car he or she wants. The search will respond by telling whether or not such a model exists, and if so, if there is one for sale. At Mobilia's Web site, visitors can also search for other automobile memorabilia, chat with other car aficionados, and even send queries to experts.

Both of these sites are popular. In both of these companies, the massive collection of data that is critical to a large interest community has become the basis of a potentially successful business. Moreover, in both of these cases, the large quantity of data, properly organized and made easily available, has replaced the need to build a large organization.

TO THINK ABOUT: How are these detailed databases related to both companies' business strategy? Suggest other electronic commerce businesses that could benefit from linking the Web to large databases.

Sources: Whit Andrews, "Detailed Database Can Be Key to E-Commerce Success," Internet World, June 14, 1999; Brian Caulfield, "A Site Where Batteries Are Included," Internet World, May 10, 1999; and http://www.mobilia.com/press/.

6.5 Management Requirements for Database Systems

Much more is required for the development of database systems than simply selecting a logical database model. Indeed, this selection may be among the last decisions. The database is an organizational discipline, a method, rather than a tool or technology. It requires organizational and conceptual change.

Without management support and understanding, database efforts fail. The critical elements in a database environment are (1) data administration, (2) data planning and modeling methodology, (3) database technology and management, and (4) users. This environment is depicted in Figure 6-21 and now will be described.

Visitors to the iGo.com Web site can immediately find online information about batteries and other parts for their computers or other portable electronic devices. The Web site is linked to a giant relational database housing information about each electronic device and the batteries and parts it uses.

Toshiba Portege 300CT

Product	Item #	Price	Qty
Laptop AC Adapters			
AC Adapter, AC, 15V, 2000mAH	27122	$89.00	
Auto / EM Power Cord, DC, 15V, 2000mAH	33464	$99.00	
Laptop Batteries			
Toshiba, Portege 300CT, Battery Pack, Lithium Ion, Extended Life Battery	27118	$179.00	
Laptop Rapid Chargers			
Charger, AC	27120	$279.00	
Storage			
Hard Drive, 4.0 GB, Internal	40344	$399.00	
Hard Drive, 6.4GB, Internal	40346	$499.00	
Hard Drive, 5.1 GB, Internal	40345	$449.00	

Window on Management

CANADIAN GOVERNMENT DATA ON THE WEB: A HOT ITEM

Why would the management of many Canadian companies agree to pay for Internet access to some of the data in the databases of four Canadian provincial governments? The answer appears to be that by paying a fee, these companies will be able to accomplish certain business goals more quickly and cheaply than if they continued to work the old fashioned ways. As a result, the governments of Nova Scotia, Newfoundland, Prince Edward Island, and New Brunswick have installed a new system called Atlantic Canada Online (ACOL), and its use by numerous Canadian companies indicates that the system is a success.

The ACOL system links Web sites to mainframes and servers in state agencies in these provinces so that the registered users can access selected government databases through the Web. The databases that these four governments have made available to the public are related to business registration and to property tax information. Many businesses, such as law firms and financial and real estate companies, need access to this data as part of their work. For example, lenders who use property as collateral for their loans will want to see the tax records and the business registration of the companies asking for the loans. Moreover, businesses need to be registered with the provincial governments. In the past all of this work had to be done by individuals actually going to the government offices to research the data or to register the business. In many cases they needed to go to more than one office because the data or process was located at the county level rather than at the provincial level. Nova Scotia, for example, has 18 counties,

and going from county office to county office would require a major manual effort. One of the largest users of ACOL is the Canadian Securities Registration System located in Richmond, British Columbia. According to Barb Heinrich, Canadian Securities' manager of national customer service, ACOL provides her company with faster access to information. The company uses ACOL to help its clients register property information with local authorities.

To use ACOL an individual or business pays a fee each time it uses the system. The fee for on-line document registration is $7 (Canadian), whereas a search costs $5 (Canadian). The fees actually go to Unisys Canada, the company that built and installed ACOL. Companies gain access by depositing funds with Unisys, and their account is charged for each usage. The fee goes to Unisys because Unisys invested $10 million (Canadian) while spending five years building ACOL. The provincial governments were able to open access to their vital data at no cost to themselves.

TO THINK ABOUT: What are the management benefits of making government information available through the Internet? What management, organization, and technology issues are created for the four provincial governments when they open their databases to the general public? How do you think they should handle those problems?

Sources: Jaikumar Vijayan, "Canadians Access Government Data Online," Computerworld, April 19, 1999; and http://www.atlantic online.ns.com.

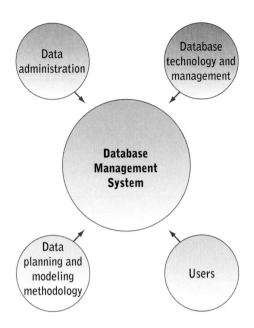

FIGURE 6-21 Key organizational elements in the database environment. For a database management system to flourish in any organization, data administration functions and data planning and modeling methodologies must be coordinated with database technology and management. Resources must be devoted to train end users to use databases properly.

DATA ADMINISTRATION

Database systems require that the organization recognize the strategic role of information and begin actively to manage and plan for information as a corporate resource. This means that the organization must develop a **data administration** function with the power to define information requirements for the entire company and with direct access to senior management. The chief information officer (CIO) becomes the primary advocate in the organization for database systems.

Data administration is responsible for the specific policies and procedures through which data can be managed as an organizational resource. These responsibilities include developing information policy, planning for data, overseeing logical database design and data dictionary development, and monitoring how information system specialists and end-user groups use data.

The fundamental principle of data administration is that all data are the property of the organization as a whole. Data cannot belong exclusively to any one business area or organizational unit. All data are to be made available to any group that requires them to fulfill its mission. An organization needs to formulate an **information policy** that specifies its rules for sharing, disseminating, acquiring, standardizing, classifying, and inventorying information throughout the organization. Information policy lays out specific procedures and accountabilities, specifying which organizational units share information, where information can be distributed, and who has responsibility for updating and maintaining the information. Although data administration is a very important organizational function, it has proved very challenging to implement.

DATA PLANNING AND MODELING METHODOLOGY

The organizational interests served by the DBMS are much broader than those in the traditional file environment; therefore, the organization requires enterprise-wide planning for data. Enterprise analysis, which addresses the information requirements of the entire organization (as opposed to the requirements of individual applications), is needed to develop databases. The purpose of enterprise analysis is to identify the key entities, attributes, and relationships that constitute the organization's data. These techniques are described in greater detail in Chapter 9.

DATABASE TECHNOLOGY, MANAGEMENT, AND USERS

Databases require new software and a new staff specially trained in DBMS techniques, as well as new management structures. Most corporations develop a database design and management group within the corporate information system division that is responsible for the more technical

data administration A special organizational function for managing the organization's data resources, concerned with information policy, data planning, maintenance of data dictionaries, and data quality standards.

information policy Formal rules governing the maintenance, distribution, and use of information in an organization.

CREATING COMPANYWIDE DATA STANDARDS

Your industrial supply company wants to create a data warehouse where management can obtain a single corporate-wide view of critical sales information to identify best-selling products in specific geographic areas, key customers, and sales trends. Your sales and product information are stored in several different systems: a divisional sales system running on a Unix server and a corporate sales system running on an IBM mainframe. You would like to create a single standard format that consolidates these data from both systems. The following format has been proposed:

Product ID	Product Description	Cost per Unit	Units Sold	Sales Region	Division	Customer-ID

The following are sample files from the two systems that would supply the data for the data warehouse:

Mechanical Parts Division Sales System

Prod. No	Product Description	Cost per Unit	Units Sold	Sales Region	Customer-ID
60231	4" Steel bearing	5.28	900,245	N.E.	Anderson
85773	SS assembly unit	12.45	992,111	Midwest	Kelly Industries

Corporate Sales System

Product_ID	Product Description	Unit Cost	Units Sold	Sales Territory	Division
60231	Bearing, 4"	5.28	900,245	Northeast	Parts
85773	SS assembly unit	12.02	992,111	M.W.	Parts

1. What business problems are created by not having these data in a single standard format?

2. How easy would it be to create a database with a single standard format that could store the data from both systems? Identify the problems that would have to be addressed.

3. Should the problems be solved by database specialists or general business managers? Explain.

4. Who should have the authority to finalize a single companywide format for this information in the data warehouse?

database administration
Refers to the more technical and operational aspects of managing data, including physical database design and maintenance.

and operational aspects of managing data. The functions it performs are called **database administration.** This group does the following:

○ Defines and organizes database structure and content

○ Develops security procedures to safeguard the database

○ Develops database documentation

○ Maintains the database management software

In close cooperation with users, the design group establishes the physical database, the logical relations among elements, and the access rules and procedures.

A database serves a wider community of users than traditional systems. Relational systems with fourth-generation query languages permit employees who are not computer specialists to access large databases. In addition, database users include trained computer specialists. To optimize access for nonspecialists, more resources must be devoted to training end users. Professional systems workers must be retrained in the DBMS language, DBMS application development procedures, and new software practices.

Database technology has provided many organizational benefits, but it allows firms to maintain large databases with detailed personal information that pose a threat to individual privacy. Chapter 14 provides a detailed discussion of this issue.

Selecting an appropriate data model and data management technology for the organization is a key management decision. Managers need to evaluate the costs and benefits of implementing a database environment and the capabilities of various DBMS or file management technologies. Management should ensure that organizational databases are designed to meet management information objectives and the organization's business needs.

Management

The organization's data model should reflect its key business processes and decision-making requirements. Data planning may need to be performed to ensure that the organization's data model delivers information efficiently for its business processes and enhances organizational performance. Designing a database is an organizational endeavor.

Organization

Many database and file management options are available for organizing and storing information. Key technology decisions should consider the efficiency of accessing information, flexibility in organizing information, the type of information to be stored and arranged, compatibility with the organization's data model, and compatibility with the organization's hardware and operating systems.

Technology

For Discussion

1. It has been said that you do not need database management software to create a database environment. Discuss.

2. To what extent should end users be involved in the selection of a database management system and database design?

SUMMARY

1. Compare traditional file organization and management techniques. In a traditional file environment, data records are organized using either a sequential file organization or a direct or random file organization. Records in a sequential file can be accessed sequentially or they can be accessed directly if the sequential file is on disk and uses an indexed sequential access method. Records on a file with direct file organization can be accessed directly without an index.

2. Explain the problems of the traditional file environment. By allowing different functional areas and groups in the organization to maintain their own files independently, the traditional file environment creates problems such as data redundancy and inconsistency, program-data dependence, inflexibility, poor security, and lack of data-sharing and availability.

3. Describe how a database management system organizes information. A database management system (DBMS) is the software that permits centralization of data and data management. A DBMS includes a data definition language, a data manipulation language, and a data dictionary capability. The most important feature of the DBMS is its ability to separate the logical and physical views of data. The user works with a logical view of data. The DBMS software translates user queries into

queries that can be applied to the physical view of the data. The DBMS retrieves information so that the user does not have to be concerned with its physical location. This feature separates programs from data and from the management of data.

4. Identify the principal types of databases and some principles of database design. The principal types of databases today are relational DBMS and object-oriented DBMS. Relational systems are very flexible for supporting ad hoc requests for information and for combining information from different sources. They support many-to-many relationships among entities and are efficient for storing alphanumeric data that can be organized into structured fields and records. Object-oriented DBMS can store graphics and other types of data in addition to conventional text data to support multimedia applications. Designing a database requires both a logical design and a physical design. The process of creating small, stable data structures from complex groups of data when designing a relational database is termed *normalization.* Database design considers whether a complete database or portions of the database can be distributed to more than one location to increase responsiveness and reduce vulnerability and costs. There are two major types of distributed databases: replicated databases and partitioned databases.

5. Discuss new database trends. New tools and technologies provide users with more powerful tools to analyze the information in databases and to take advantage of the information resources on the World Wide Web. Multidimensional data analysis, also known as on-line analytical processing (OLAP), represents relationships among data as a multidimensional structure, which can be visualized as cubes of data and cubes within cubes of data, allowing for sophisticated data analysis. Data can be conveniently analyzed across the enterprise using a data warehouse, in which current and historical data are extracted from many different operational systems and consolidated for management decision making. Hypermedia databases allow data to be stored in nodes linked together in any pattern the user establishes and are used for storing information at Web sites. Conventional databases can be linked to the Web to facilitate user access to the data.

6. Analyze the managerial and organizational requirements for creating a database environment. Developing a database environment requires much more than selecting technology. It requires a change in the corporation's attitude toward information. The organization must develop a data administration function and a data planning methodology. There is political resistance in organizations to many key database concepts, especially to sharing of information that has been controlled exclusively by one organizational group. There are difficult cost/benefit questions in database management. Often, to avoid raising difficult questions, database use begins and ends as a small effort isolated in the information systems department.

KEY TERMS

Attribute, 180

Data administration, 201

Data definition language, 184

Data dictionary, 185

Data element, 185

Data manipulation language, 184

Data mart, 195

Data redundancy, 183

Data warehouse, 194

Database, 179

Database (rigorous definition), 184

Database administration, 202

Database management system (DBMS), 184

Direct file access method, 182

Direct or random file organization, 180

Distributed database, 192

Entity, 180

Entity-relationship diagram, 191

Field, 179

File, 179

Hierarchical data model, 189

Hypermedia database, 197

Index, 181

Indexed sequential access method (ISAM), 181

Information policy, 201

Key field, 180

Legacy system, 190

Logical view, 186

Network data model, 189

Normalization, 191

Object-oriented DBMS, 190

Object-relational DBMS, 190

On-line analytical processing (OLAP), 193

Physical view, 186

Program-data dependence, 183

Record, 179

Relational data model, 187

Sequential file organization, 180

Structured Query Language (SQL), 185

Transform algorithm, 182

Tuple, 188

REVIEW QUESTIONS

1. Why is file management important for overall system performance?

2. Describe how indexes and key fields enable a program to access specific records in a file.

3. Define and describe the indexed sequential access method and the direct file access method.

4. List and describe some of the problems of the traditional file environment.

5. Define a database and a database management system.

6. Name and briefly describe the three components of a DBMS.

7. What is the difference between a logical and a physical view of data?

8. List some benefits of a DBMS.

9. Describe the principal types of databases and the advantages and disadvantages of each.

10. What is normalization? How is it related to the features of a well-designed relational database?

11. What is a distributed database, and what are the two main ways of distributing data?

12. Describe the capabilities of on-line analytical processing (OLAP) and multidimensional data analysis.

13. What is a data warehouse? How can it benefit organizations?

14. What is a hypermedia database? How does it differ from a traditional database? How is it used for the Web?

15. Describe how organizational databases can be accessed through the Web.

16. What are the four key elements of a database environment? Describe each briefly.

17. Describe and briefly comment on the major management challenges in building a database environment.

GROUP PROJECT

Review Figure 6-6, which provides an overview of a human resources database. Some additional information that might be maintained in such a database are an employee's date of hire, date of termination, number of children, date of birth, educational level, sex code, social security tax, Medicare tax, year-to-date gross pay and net pay, amount of life insurance coverage, healthcare plan payroll-deduction amount, life insurance plan payroll-deduction amount, and pension plan payroll-deduction amount.

Form a group with three or four of your classmates. Prepare two sample reports using the data in the database that might be of interest to either the employer or the employee. What pieces of information should be included on each report? In addition, prepare a data dictionary entry for one of the data elements in the database similar to the entry illustrated in Figure 6-7.

Your group's analysis should determine what business functions use this data element, which function has the primary responsibility for maintaining the data element, and which positions in the organization can access that data element. Present your findings to the class.

Tools for Interactive Learning

○ Internet Connection

The Internet Connection for this chapter will direct you to a series of Web sites where you can complete an exercise to evaluate various commercial database management system products. You can also use the Interactive Study Guide to test your knowledge of the topics in this chapter and get instant feedback where you need more practice.

○ Electronic Commerce Project

At the Laudon Web site for Chapter 6, you will find an Electronic Commerce project that uses the interactive software at the Thomson Communications Web site for searching an online database of communications industry firms in Australia and New Zealand.

○ CD-ROM

If you purchase and use the Multimedia Edition CD-ROM with this chapter, you can complete an interactive exercise asking you to select the appropriate database management system for a series of business problems. You can also find a video clip about Oracle, Acxiom, and data warehousing, an audio overview of the major themes of this chapter, and bullet text summarizing the key points of the chapter.

○ Application Exercise

At the Laudon Web site, you can find a database Application Exercise for this chapter, in which you can develop a relational database for a small business and create management reports from the database.

Somerfield is a giant retailer, one of the United Kingdom's largest supermarket chains. With 70,000 employees and annual sales of £6.5 billion, its 1,400 stores experience more than 15 million customer visits per week for a total of nearly 800 million separate customer sales in 1998. As recently as 1995 the chain had only 600 stores and was committed to being the primary center-of-town small retailer throughout the U.K. Even then it was turning to information technology to help it operate more efficiently, for example adopting Staffplanner, a computer-based staff scheduling system. Somerfield's giant growth leap took place in March 1998 when it merged with Kwik Save, another large U.K. food retailer. Since the merger the stores have continued to operate under their premerger names, but the two are becoming operationally united. Now the company is taking another large expansion step by joining with gasoline giant Elf to open small food and convenience shops in Elf's many U.K. gas stations.

Because it sells thousands of mostly low-priced products, a large retail supermarket operation produces an abundance of data. Like many other supermarkets, Somerfield collects point-of-sale transaction data one product at a time grouped by each customer basket. It also maintains data on its product stock by store, including stock quantities, stock purchasing, and stock wastage. All of these data, used properly, can be critical to achieving and retaining profitability because supermarket profit margins are razor thin and wastage rates are often very high. Adding or subtracting a penny or two to the value of each basket can have a dramatic effect on profits. Thus the issue for Somerfield was how to make all that data available to management in ways that could impact profitability.

If all these data were made easily available, what could management do with them to impact profitability? "From a store perspective," explained Somerfield systems manager Alan Steele, "you can see what was delivered during the week, as well as what it sold, reduced, or threw away on a daily basis." With access to these data, management would be able to analyze store sales patterns to understand the effects of putting certain products on promotion. Thus management would be

able to evaluate sales campaigns to understand how successful a particular campaign is or which products suffer a drop in sales as a result. In addition, using these data, individual stores would be able to determine the causes of their wastage and take action to reduce it. Moreover, Somerfield could use the data to improve its understanding of its customers. The company would know what each customer buys with what and when, what they don't buy, and so on. The data are precise enough to tell Somerfield what a customer bought, whether it was a four-pack of beer or a gallon of ice cream, what time they bought it, and how they paid for it. All of this information could be used to alert store and company management to the changing tastes of their customers. Management could also use the data to determine which products to link on store shelves and displays and which products to couple in sales.

The data could also be used to aid in the daily monitoring of all functions for individual products, individual stores, groups of products, and groups of stores. Company buyers need to be able to monitor the sales of every product and product group and to determine how those sales affect the costs and profits of the company. Management would be able to analyze results by demographic clusters of stores and evaluate the results of television advertising in specific regions. Management would also better be able to determine how the Somerfield and Kwik Save store groups are performing.

Like many other large companies, Somerfield's systems are older and were built one function, department, and division at a time. These systems were not developed according to a corporate plan. They were not built based on a company-wide information architecture. The data from different departments were often incompatible. Most of the data management wanted was available, but it was difficult to access and use. For managers to analyze the data, they had to turn to programmers who specialized in using SQL to create management reports, a slow, inflexible, and expensive process. The company also had IBM's QMF query and reporting tool on its mainframe, but that presented the same problem because managers could not do their own analysis of the

data. Instead they had to design the content of a report and then turn it over to a programmer to produce it for them.

Although much of the data were on Somerfield's mainframe, large amounts were stored in a variety of different locations, including people's PCs and network servers all over the place. There was no single source of information, and data could not be shared. The result, Steele said, was "that you'd ask somebody how many stores we had and you'd get various answers, depending on whom you spoke to." What Somerfield had to do was find a way first to bring that data together and then to enable the individual managers to access and manipulate the data quickly and easily, without the intervention of a computer professional.

To solve its data problems Somerfield turned to a data warehouse. "We wanted to consolidate information in one place, make it simple to access, and manage it better," explained Steele, "so everyone across the business could get a clear and consistent picture of data, however they chose to interrogate it." The information warehouse data are collected from the various sources and stored in two separate databases built on Oracle Database Server. The data are logically divided into two databases, one storing sales, store-stock movements, and wastage data and the other containing transaction and basket level data. The two databases contain two years of data, totaling more than 300 gigabytes.

Key to the success of any information warehouse is the user interface. In this case the managers can use Oracle Discover to make ad hoc queries. For more powerful requests, users can use Somerfield's custom application, which contains templates built using Sybase PowerBuilder. The interfaces include drill-down functionality. The interfaces have been successful. Users only need two to three hours of training to become independent.

Originally only 200 people at Somerfield's corporate headquarters in Bristol, England, were given access to the data. And of those, only 80 were allowed the use of Somerfield's more advanced custom interface. However, the users do come from key departments, including buying, marketing, merchandising, and IT. But Somerfield is looking to the future. Steele said that Somerfield intends to use the Internet and the Web to give store management access to the data. Further into the future, Somerfield is considering allowing key suppliers access to product sales and wastage data through the Internet.

Sources: Philip J. Gill, "Shopping for Integration," **Oracle Magazine**, July, 1999; "The Somerfield Case Study," Care Interactive Software, http://www.care-interactive.co.uk/somerfield.htm; and Paul Savage, IT Innovation, http://www.it-innovation.soton.ac.uk/success/.

CASE STUDY QUESTIONS

1. Analyze Somerfield from the viewpoint of the competitive forces and value chain models.

2. What problems did Somerfield have? What management, organization, and technology factors were responsible for those problems?

3. Did the data warehouse enhance the company's competitive position, and if so, how?

4. What management, organization, and technology factors had to be addressed in building the information warehouse? What management, organization, and technology factors will the company have to address as access to the information warehouse is spread to the stores and to suppliers?

CHAPTER 7

Telecommunications, Networks,

and the New Information Technology (IT) Infrastructure

Learning
Objectives

After completing this chapter, you will be able to:

1. Describe the basic components of a telecommunications system.

2. Calculate the capacity of telecommunications channels and evaluate transmission media.

3. Compare the various types of telecommunications networks and network services.

4. Describe the features of the new information technology (IT) infrastructure and important connectivity standards.

5. Identify principal telecommunications technologies for supporting electronic commerce and electronic business.

6. Analyze the management problems raised by the new information technology (IT) infrastructure and suggest solutions.

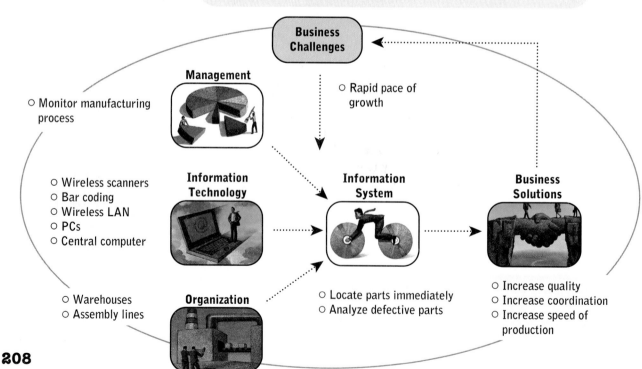

Business Challenges

○ Monitor manufacturing process

Management

○ Rapid pace of growth

○ Wireless scanners
○ Bar coding
○ Wireless LAN
○ PCs
○ Central computer

Information Technology

Information System

Business Solutions

○ Warehouses
○ Assembly lines

Organization

○ Locate parts immediately
○ Analyze defective parts

○ Increase quality
○ Increase coordination
○ Increase speed of production

BMW Reacts Instantly with Its Wireless Network

BMW Manufacturing Corporation, a unit of Bayerische Motoren Werke AG of Germany, turns out 225 cars each day in its South Carolina manufacturing facility and business is growing rapidly. Its Spartanburg, South Carolina, warehouse needs to make sure that parts are shipped swiftly to the nearby BMW plant that assembles automobiles so that the cars are available when they are needed.

Once an employee locates an item in the warehouse, he or she points a handheld scanner at the label on the box holding the part. The wireless scanner transmits information on the label about the type of part and the quantity in the box via a wireless local area network (LAN) to the company's inventory management system running on its central computer. The wire-less network links different computers without the physical constraints of wires. Personal computers, laptops, and handheld devices such as bar code scanners use radio-frequency transmission and receiving capabilities to communicate with each other. Warehouse workers like the fact that they don't have to spend countless hours manually entering the parts data.

Other employees, such as BMW logistics planners, accounting representatives, and shop floor supervisors can access the inventory management system to find out immediately what parts are available. They can also learn where the parts are located in the company's 2.1 million-square-foot plant and its off-site warehouse. For example, Mark Miller, BMW's Spartanburg body shop material supervisor, uses the system to keep tabs on parts. When a part first is received from a supplier, his team scans the inventory and takes it to a prescribed location. Miller can access the network from any location in the plant, determine when a part arrived, where it can be found, and when it is needed. Before BMW installed this wireless system, the only way Miller could find out if he had the parts he needed was by walking around the warehouse twice an hour.

Other BMW employees use the wireless network to monitor the assembly process. If a worker notices a crack in a taillight, he or she will scan the part number and remove the defective part from the assembly line. The information is transmitted to the plant's central computer where it can be accessed and analyzed by logistics planners to determine whether the problem occurred before or after the part left the supplier.

BMW had initially tried to use bar code scanning equipment that was physically connected to terminals on the plant floor. As the plant grew, however, the company had to install more terminals to provide seamless coverage, adding expense and inconvenience. The company then switched to a wireless LAN.

With the ability to monitor the manufacturing process in real time, BMW can react instantly to new orders, changes in suppliers, or production (shop floor, warehouse) problems, giving the company new speed and flexibility.

Sources: Nicole Harris, "All Together Now," *The Wall Street Journal Telecommunications Report,* September 20, 1999; and "Proxicom and Nether Systems Form Alliance to Jointly Develop Wireless E-Commerce Solutions," *CBS Market Watch,* February 10, 2000.

MANAGEMENT CHALLENGES

BMW, like many companies all over the world, is finding ways to benefit from using telecommunications technology to coordinate its internal activities and to communicate efficiently with customers, suppliers, and other external organizations. The ways in which networks and communications technology are being employed for electronic commerce and electronic business are multiplying, but they raise several management challenges:

1. **Managing LANs.** Although local area networks seem to be flexible and inexpensive ways of delivering computing power to new areas of the organization, they must be carefully administered and monitored. LANs are especially vulnerable to network disruption, loss of essential data, access by unauthorized users, and infection from computer viruses (see Chapter 13). Dealing with these problems requires special technical expertise that is not normally available in end-user departments and is in very short supply.

2. **Selecting telecommunications technologies for the new information technology (IT) infrastructure.** Internet technology can only provide limited connectivity. There are still major application areas where disparate hardware, software, and network components must be coordinated. Networks based on one standard may not be able to be linked to those based on another without additional equipment, expense, and management overhead. Networks that meet today's requirements may lack the connectivity for domestic or global expansion in the future. Managers may have trouble choosing the right telecommunications technologies for the firm's information technology (IT) infrastructure.

Most of the information systems we use today require networks and communications technology. Large and small companies from all over the world are using networked systems and the Internet to locate suppliers and buyers, to negotiate contracts with them, and to service their trades. Applications of networks are multiplying in research, organizational coordination, and control. Networked systems are fundamental to electronic commerce and electronic business.

Today's computing tasks are so closely tied to networks that some believe the network is the computer. This chapter describes the components of telecommunications systems, showing how they can be arranged to create various types of networks and network-based applications that can increase an organization's efficiency and competitiveness. It also describes the management challenges introduced by today's new information technology infrastructure and suggests solutions so organizations can maximize the benefits of communications technology.

7.1 The Telecommunications Revolution

Telecommunications is the communication of information by electronic means, usually over some distance. Previously, telecommunications meant voice transmission over telephone lines. Today, a great deal of telecommunications transmission is digital data transmission in which computers transmit data from one location to another. We are currently in the middle of a telecommunications revolution that is spreading communications technology and telecommunications services throughout the world.

telecommunications The communication of information by electronic means, usually over some distance.

THE MARRIAGE OF COMPUTERS AND COMMUNICATIONS

Telecommunications used to be a monopoly of either the state or a regulated private firm. In the United States, American Telephone and Telegraph (AT&T) provided virtually all telecommunications services. Telecommunications in Europe and in the rest of the world traditionally has been administered primarily by a state post, telephone, and telegraph authority (PTT). The United States monopoly ended in 1984 when the Justice Department forced AT&T to give up its monopoly and allow competing firms to sell telecommunications services and equipment. The 1996 Telecommunications Deregulation and Reform Act widened deregulation by freeing telephone companies, broadcasters, and cable companies to enter each other's markets. Other areas of the world are starting to open up their telecommunications services to competition as well.

Thousands of companies have sprung up to provide telecommunications products and services, including local and long-distance telephone services, cellular phones and wireless communication services, data networks, cable TV, communications satellites, and Internet services. Managers will be continually faced with decisions on how to incorporate these services and technologies into their information systems and business processes.

THE INFORMATION SUPERHIGHWAY

Deregulation and the marriage of computers and communications also has made it possible for the telephone companies to expand from traditional, voice communications into new information services, such as those providing transmission of news reports, stock reports, television programs, and movies. These efforts are laying the foundation for the **information superhighway,** a vast web of high-speed digital telecommunications networks delivering information, education, and entertainment services to offices and homes. The networks comprising the highway are national or worldwide in scope and accessible by the general public rather than restricted to use by members of a specific organization or set of organizations such as corporations. Some analysts believe the information superhighway will have as profound an impact on economic and social life in the twenty-first century as railroads and interstate highways did in the past.

information superhighway High-speed digital telecommunications networks that are national or worldwide in scope and accessible by the general public rather than restricted to specific organizations.

The information superhighway concept is broad and rich, providing new ways for organizations and individuals to obtain and distribute information that virtually eliminate the barriers of time and place. Uses of this new superhighway for electronic commerce and electronic business are quickly emerging. The most well known and easily the largest implementation of the information superhighway is the Internet.

Another aspect of the information superhighway is the national computing network proposed by the U.S. federal government. The Clinton administration is encouraging use of the Internet and other network resources to link universities, research centers, libraries, hospitals, and other institutions that need to exchange vast amounts of information while being accessible in homes and schools.

7.2 Components and Functions of a Telecommunications System

telecommunications system
A collection of compatible hardware and software arranged to communicate information from one location to another.

A **telecommunications system** is a collection of compatible hardware and software arranged to communicate information from one location to another. Figure 7-1 illustrates the hardware components of a typical telecommunications system. Telecommunications systems can transmit text, graphic images, voice, or video information. This section describes the major components of telecommunications systems. Subsequent sections describe how the components can be arranged into various types of networks.

TELECOMMUNICATIONS SYSTEM COMPONENTS

The following are essential components of a telecommunications system:

1. Computers to process information
2. Terminals or any input/output devices that send or receive data
3. Communications channels: the links by which data or voice are transmitted between sending and receiving devices in a network. Communications channels use various communications media, such as telephone lines, fiber-optic cables, coaxial cables, and wireless transmission.
4. Communications processors, such as modems, multiplexers, controllers, and front-end processors, which provide support functions for data transmission and reception

FIGURE 7-1 Components of a telecommunications system. This figure illustrates some of the hardware components that would be found in a typical telecommunications system. They include computers; terminals; communications channels; and communications processors such as modems, multiplexers, and the front-end processor. Special communications software controls input and output activities and manages other functions of the communications system.

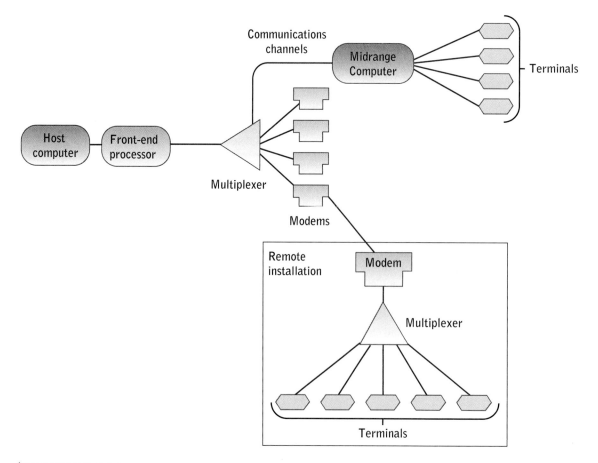

5. Communications software, which controls input and output activities and manages other functions of the communications network

FUNCTIONS OF TELECOMMUNICATIONS SYSTEMS

In order to send and receive information from one place to another, a telecommunications system must perform a number of separate functions. The system transmits information, establishes the interface between the sender and the receiver, routes messages along the most efficient paths, performs elementary processing of the information to ensure that the right message gets to the right receiver, performs editorial tasks on the data (such as checking for transmission errors and rearranging the format), and converts messages from one speed (say, the speed of a computer) into the speed of a communications line or from one format to another. Finally, the telecommunications system controls the flow of information. Many of these tasks are accomplished by computer.

A telecommunications network typically contains diverse hardware and software components that work together to transmit information. Different components in a network can communicate by adhering to a common set of rules that enable them to talk to each other. This set of rules and procedures governing transmission between two points in a network is called a **protocol.** Each device in a network must be able to interpret the other device's protocol. The principal functions of protocols in a telecommunications network are to identify each device in the communication path, to secure the attention of the other device, to verify correct receipt of the transmitted message, to verify that a message requires retransmission because it cannot be correctly interpreted, and to perform recovery when errors occur.

protocol A set of rules and procedures that govern transmission between the components in a network.

TYPES OF SIGNALS: ANALOG AND DIGITAL

Information travels through a telecommunications system in the form of electromagnetic signals. Signals are represented in two ways: analog and digital signals. An **analog signal** is represented by a continuous waveform that passes through a communications medium. Analog signals are used to handle voice communications and to reflect variations in pitch.

A **digital signal** is a discrete, rather than a continuous, waveform. It transmits data coded into two discrete states: 1-bits and 0-bits, which are represented as on–off electrical pulses. Most computers communicate with digital signals, as do many local telephone companies and some larger networks. However, if a traditional telephone network is set up to process analog signals, a digital signal cannot be processed without some alterations. All digital signals must be translated into analog signals before they can be transmitted in an analog system. The device that performs this translation is called a **modem.** (Modem is an abbreviation for MOdulation/DEModulation.) A modem translates a computer's digital signals into analog form for transmission over ordinary telephone lines, or it translates analog signals back into digital form for reception by a computer (see Figure 7-2).

analog signal A continuous waveform that passes through a communications medium; used primarily for voice communications.

digital signal A discrete waveform that transmits data coded into two discrete states as 1-bits and 0-bits, which are represented as on–off electrical pulses; used for data communications.

modem A device for translating digital signals into analog signals and vice versa.

COMMUNICATIONS CHANNELS

Communications **channels** are the means by which data are transmitted from one device in a network to another. A channel can use different kinds of telecommunications transmission media: twisted wire, coaxial cable, fiber optics, terrestrial microwave, satellite, and other wireless transmission. Each has advantages and limitations. High-speed transmission media are more expensive in general, but they can handle higher volume, which reduces the cost per bit. For instance, the cost per bit of data can be lower via satellite link than via leased telephone line if a firm uses the satellite link 100 percent of the time. There is also a wide range of speeds possible for any given medium depending on the software and hardware configuration.

channels The links by which data or voice are transmitted between sending and receiving devices in a network.

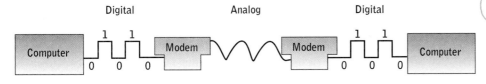

FIGURE 7-2 Functions of the modem. A modem is a device that translates digital signals from a computer into analog form so that they can be transmitted over analog telephone lines. The modem also is used to translate analog signals back into digital form for the receiving computer.

Twisted Wire

twisted wire A transmission medium consisting of pairs of twisted copper wires; used to transmit analog phone conversations but can be used for data transmission.

Twisted wire consists of strands of copper wire twisted in pairs and is the oldest transmission medium. Most of the telephone systems in a building rely on twisted wires installed for analog communication, but they can be used for digital communication as well. Although it is low in cost and already is in place, twisted wire is relatively slow for transmitting data, and high-speed transmission causes interference called *crosstalk*. However, new software and hardware have raised the twisted wire transmission capacity to make it useful for local and wide area computer networks as well as telephone systems.

Coaxial Cable

coaxial cable A transmission medium consisting of thickly insulated copper wire that transmits large volumes of data quickly.

Coaxial cable, like that used for cable television, consists of thickly insulated copper wire, which can transmit a larger volume of data than twisted wire. It often is used in place of twisted wire for important links in a telecommunications network because it is a faster, more interference-free transmission medium, with speeds of up to 200 megabits per second. However, coaxial cable is thick, is hard to wire in many buildings, and cannot support analog phone conversations. It must be moved when computers and other devices are moved.

Fiber Optics

fiber-optic cable A fast, light, durable transmission medium consisting of thin strands of clear glass fiber bound into cables. Data are transmitted as light pulses.

backbone Part of a network handling the major traffic and providing the primary path for traffic flowing to or from other networks.

Fiber-optic cable consists of thousands of strands of clear glass fiber, each the thickness of a human hair, which are bound into cables. Data are transformed into pulses of light, which are sent through the fiber-optic cable by a laser device at a rate from 500 kilobits to several billion bits per second. Fiber-optic cable is considerably faster, lighter, and more durable than wire media and is well suited to systems requiring transfers of large volumes of data. However, fiber-optic cable is difficult to work with, expensive, and hard to install. In most networks, fiber-optic cable is used as the high-speed **backbone,** whereas twisted wire and coaxial cable are used to connect the backbone to individual devices. A backbone is the part of a network that handles the major traffic. It acts as the primary path for traffic flowing to or from other networks.

Wireless Transmission

Wireless transmission that sends signals through air or space without any physical tether has become an increasingly popular alternative to tethered transmission channels such as twisted wire, coaxial cable, and fiber optics. Today, common technologies for wireless data transmission include microwave transmission, communication satellites, pagers, cellular telephones, personal communication services (PCSs), smart phones, personal digital assistants (PDAs), and mobile data networks.

The wireless transmission medium is the electromagnetic spectrum, as illustrated in Figure 7-3. Some types of wireless transmission, such as microwave or infrared, by nature occupy specific spectrum frequency ranges (measured in megahertz). Other types of wireless transmissions actually have functional uses, such as cellular telephones and paging devices, that have been assigned a specific range of frequencies by national regulatory agencies and international agreements. Each frequency range has its own strengths and weaknesses, and these help determine the specific function or data communications niche assigned to it.

microwave A high-volume, long-distance, point-to-point transmission in which high-frequency radio signals are transmitted through the atmosphere from one terrestrial transmission station to another.

satellite The transmission of data using orbiting satellites to serve as relay stations for transmitting microwave signals over very long distances.

Microwave systems, both terrestrial and celestial, transmit high-frequency radio signals through the atmosphere and are widely used for high-volume, long-distance, point-to-point communication. Microwave signals follow a straight line and do not bend with the curvature of the earth; therefore, long-distance terrestrial transmission systems require that transmission stations be positioned 25 to 30 miles apart, adding to the expense of microwave.

This problem can be solved by bouncing microwave signals off **satellites,** which serve as relay stations for microwave signals transmitted from terrestrial stations. Communication satellites are cost effective for transmitting large quantities of data over very long distances. Satellites are typically used for communications in large, geographically dispersed organizations that would be difficult to tie together through cabling media or terrestrial microwave. For instance, Amoco uses satellites for real-time data transfer of oil field exploration data gathered from searches of the ocean floor. Exploration ships transfer these data using geosynchronous satellites to central computing centers in the United States for use by researchers in Houston, Tulsa, and suburban Chicago. Figure 7-4 illustrates how this system works.

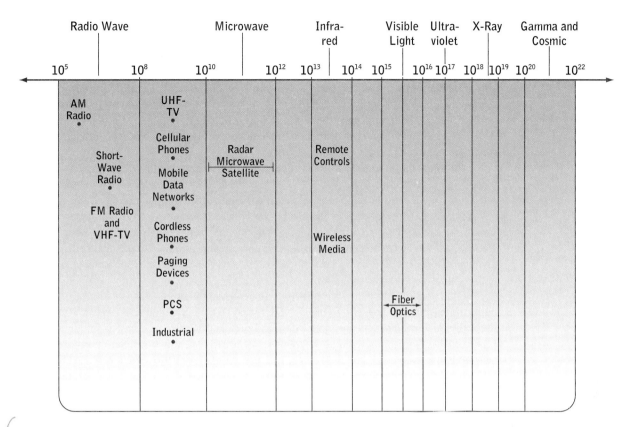

FIGURE 7-3 Frequency ranges for communications media and devices. Each telecommunications transmission medium or device occupies a different frequency range, measured in megahertz, on the electromagnetic spectrum.

Conventional communication satellites move in stationary orbits approximately 22,000 miles above the earth. A newer satellite medium, the low-orbit satellite, is beginning to be deployed. These satellites travel much closer to the earth and are able to pick up signals from weak transmitters. They also consume less power and cost less to launch than conventional satellites. With such wireless networks, businesspeople will be able to travel virtually anywhere in the world and have access to full communication capabilities including videoconferencing and the multimedia-rich Internet.

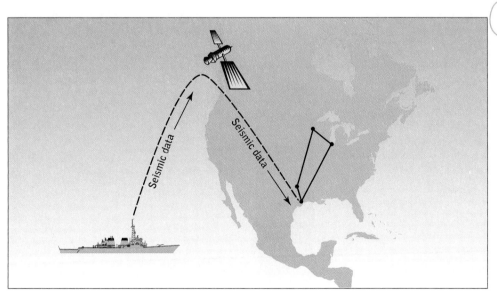

FIGURE 7-4 Amoco's satellite transmission system. Satellites help Amoco transfer seismic data between oil exploration ships and research centers in the United States.

paging system A wireless transmission technology in which the pager beeps when the user receives a message; used to transmit short alphanumeric messages.

cellular telephone A device that transmits voice or data, using radio waves to communicate with radio antennas placed within adjacent geographic areas called cells.

personal communication services (PCS) A digital cellular technology that uses lower power, higher frequency radio waves than does analog cellular technology.

smart phone Wireless phone with voice, text, and Internet capabilities.

microbrowser Web browser software that lets digital cellular phones or other wireless devices access Web pages formatted to send text or other information that is suitable for tiny screens.

personal digital assistants (PDA) Small, pen-based, handheld computers with built-in wireless telecommunications capable of entirely digital communications transmission.

mobile data networks Wireless networks that enable two-way transmission of data files cheaply and efficiently.

Other wireless transmission technologies are used in situations requiring remote access to corporate systems and mobile computing power. **Paging systems** have been used for several decades. Originally they simply beeped when the user received a message and the user telephoned an office to learn about the message. Today, paging devices can send and receive short alphanumeric messages that the user reads on the pager's screen. Paging is useful for communicating with mobile workers such as repair crews; paging also can provide an inexpensive way of communicating with workers in offices. For example, Computer Associates distributes two-way pagers with its CA Unicenter software, which allows computer network operators to monitor and respond to problems.

Cellular telephones use radio waves to communicate with radio antennas (towers) placed within adjacent geographic areas called cells. A telephone message is transmitted to the local cell by the cellular telephone and then is handed off from antenna to antenna—cell to cell—until it reaches the cell of its destination, where it is transmitted to the receiving telephone. As a cellular signal travels from one cell into another, a computer that monitors signals from the cells switches the conversation to a radio channel assigned to the next cell. The radio antenna cells normally cover eight-mile hexagonal cells, although their radius is smaller in densely populated localities.

Older cellular systems are analog and newer cellular systems are digital. **Personal communication services (PCS)** are one popular type of digital cellular service. PCS are entirely digital They can transmit both voice and data and operate in a higher frequency range (1,900 MHz) than analog cellular telephones. PCS cells are much smaller and more closely spaced than analog cells, and they can accommodate higher traffic demands.

In addition to handling voice transmission, newer models of digital cellular phones can handle voice mail, e-mail, and faxes, save addresses, access a private corporate network, and access information from the Internet. These **smart phones** are being equipped with **microbrowsers.** A microbrowser is Web browser software that lets digital cellular phones or other wireless devices access Web pages formatted to send text or other information that is suitable for tiny screens. (Yahoo and other Web sites are providing special text versions of their Web sites so that phone users can grab information such as weather reports, stock quotes, or airline schedules.) Some smart phone models offer larger screens and keypads to make Internet access easier.

Personal digital assistants (PDA) are small, pen-based, handheld computers capable of entirely digital communications transmission. Some have built-in wireless telecommunications capabilities as well as work-organization software. A well-known example is the Palm VII connected organizer. It can display and compose e-mail messages and can provide Internet access. The handheld device includes applications such as an electronic scheduler, address book, and expense tracker. It accepts data entered with a special stylus on an on-screen writing pad.

Wireless networks explicitly designed for two-way transmission of data files are called **mobile data networks.** These radio-based networks transmit data to and from handheld com-

The pdQ™ smartphone offers features of the Palm Computing(R) personal digital assistant as well as access to the Internet. Users can transfer and synchronize information between the pdQ™ smartphone and a personal computer.

puters. One type of mobile data network is based on a series of radio towers constructed specifically to transmit text and data. Ardis (owned by American Mobile Satellite Corp.) is a publicly available network that uses such media for national two-way data transmission. Otis Elevators uses the Ardis network to dispatch repair technicians around the United States from a single office in Connecticut and to receive their reports.

Wireless networks and transmission devices tend to be expensive, slower, and more error prone than transmission over wired networks, although the major digital cellular networks are upgrading the speed of their services to 100,000 to 170,000 bits per second. (Satellite systems such as Teledesic are also spending billions to provide data transmission speeds as high as 50 million bits per second for multimedia-heavy wireless Internet use.) Bandwidth and energy supply in wireless devices require careful management from both hardware and software standpoints (Imielinski and Badrinath, 1994). Security and privacy will be more difficult to maintain because wireless transmission can be intercepted easily (see Chapter 13).

Data cannot be transmitted seamlessly between different wireless networks if they use incompatible standards. For example, digital cellular service in the United States is provided by different operators using one of several competing digital cellular technologies (CDMA, GSM 1900, and TDMA IS-136), which are not compatible with each other. Many digital cellular handsets that use one of these technologies cannot operate in other countries outside North America, which operate at different frequencies with another set of standards.

Equipment makers are starting to develop some standards, including standards for small high-speed wireless networks to serve offices, campuses, or homes, that could provide high-speed data connections of up to 11 million bits per second. One standard under development, code named *Bluetooth,* allows high-speed communication among wireless phones, pagers, computers, and other handheld devices within any 10 meter area so that these devices could operate each other. For example, a person could highlight a telephone number on a Palm PDA and automatically activate a call on a digital telephone. Wireless digital cellular handset manufacturers have also agreed to adopt the Wireless Application Protocol (WAP) standard for microbrowser technology. We discuss other standards for networking in section 7.4.

Transmission Speed

The total amount of information that can be transmitted through any telecommunications channel is measured in bits per second (BPS). Sometimes this is referred to as the baud rate. A **baud** is a binary event representing a signal change from positive to negative or vice versa. The baud rate is not always the same as the bit rate. At higher speeds a single signal change can transmit more than one bit at a time, so the bit rate generally will surpass the baud rate.

One signal change, or cycle, is required to transmit one or several bits; therefore, the transmission capacity of each type of telecommunications medium is a function of its frequency. The number of cycles per second that can be sent through that medium is measured in hertz (see Chapter 4). The range of frequencies that can be accommodated on a particular telecommunications channel is called its **bandwidth.** The bandwidth is the difference between the highest and lowest frequencies that can be accommodated on a single channel. The greater the range of frequencies, the greater the bandwidth and the greater the channel's transmission capacity. Table 7-1 compares the transmission speed and relative costs of the major types of transmissions media.

COMMUNICATIONS PROCESSORS AND SOFTWARE

Communications processors, such as front-end processors, concentrators, controllers, multiplexers, and modems, support data transmission and reception in a telecommunications network. In a large computer system, the **front-end processor** is a special purpose computer dedicated to communications management and is attached to the main, or host, computer. The front-end processor performs communications processing such as error control, formatting, editing, controlling, routing, and speed and signal conversion.

A **concentrator** is a programmable telecommunications computer that collects and temporarily stores messages from terminals until enough messages are ready to be sent economically. The concentrator bursts signals to the host computer.

A **controller** is a specialized computer that supervises communications traffic between the CPU and peripheral devices such as terminals and printers. The controller manages messages

baud A change in signal from positive to negative or vice versa that is used as a measure of transmission speed.

bandwidth The transmission capacity of a communications channel as measured by the difference between the highest and lowest frequencies that can be transmitted by that channel.

front-end processor A special purpose computer dedicated to managing communications for the host computer in a network.

concentrator Telecommunications computer that collects and temporarily stores messages from terminals for batch transmission to the host computer.

controller A specialized computer that supervises communications traffic between the CPU and the peripheral devices in a telecommunications system.

Table 7-1 Typical Speeds and Costs of Telecommunications Transmission Media

Medium	Speed	Cost
Twisted wire	300 BPS–10 MBPS	Low
Microwave	256 KBPS–100 MBPS	
Satellite	256 KBPS–100 MBPS	
Coaxial cable	56 KBPS–200 MBPS	
Fiber-optic cable	500 KBPS–10 GBPS	High

BPS = bits per second

KBPS = kilobits per second

MBPS = megabits per second

GBPS = gigabits per second

from these devices and communicates them to the CPU. It also routes output from the CPU to the appropriate peripheral device.

A **multiplexer** is a device that enables a single communications channel to carry data transmissions from multiple sources simultaneously. The multiplexer divides the communications channel so that it can be shared by multiple transmission devices. The multiplexer may divide a high-speed channel into multiple channels of slower speed or may assign each transmission source a very small slice of time for using the high-speed channel.

Special telecommunications software residing in the host computer, front-end processor, and other processors in the network is required to control and support network activities. This software is responsible for functions such as network control, access control, transmission control, error detection/correction, and security. More detail on security software can be found in Chapter 13.

7.3 Communications Networks

A number of different ways exist to organize telecommunications components to form a network and hence provide multiple ways of classifying networks. Networks can be classified by their shape, or **topology.** Networks also can be classified by their geographic scope and the type of services provided. This section describes different ways of looking at networks. Sections 7.4 and 7.5 discuss the management and technical requirements of creating networks linking entire enterprises.

NETWORK TOPOLOGIES

One way of describing networks is by their shape, or topology. As illustrated in Figures 7-5 to 7-7, the three most common topologies are the star, bus, and ring.

The Star Network

The **star network** (see Figure 7-5) consists of a central host computer connected to a number of smaller computers or terminals. This topology is useful for applications where some processing must be centralized and some can be performed locally. One problem with the star network is its vulnerability. All communication between points in the network must pass through the central computer. Because the central computer is the traffic controller for the other computers and terminals in the network, communication in the network will come to a standstill if the host computer stops functioning.

The Bus Network

The **bus network** (see Figure 7-6) links a number of computers by a single circuit made of twisted wire, coaxial cable, or fiber-optic cable. All of the signals are broadcast in both direc-

multiplexer A device that enables a single communications channel to carry data transmissions from multiple sources simultaneously.

topology The shape or configuration of a network.

star network A network topology in which all computers and other devices are connected to a central host computer. All communications between network devices must pass through the host computer.

bus network Network topology linking a number of computers by a single circuit with all messages broadcast to the entire network.

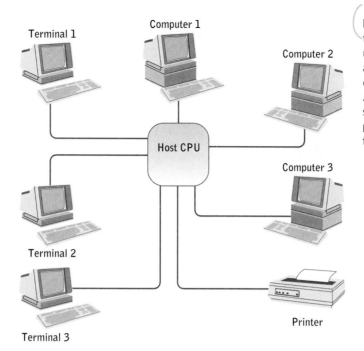

FIGURE 7-5 A star network topology. In a star network configuration, a central host computer acts as a traffic controller for all other components of the network. All communication between the smaller computers, terminals, and printers must first pass through the central computer.

tions to the entire network, and special software identifies which components receive each message (there is no central host computer to control the network). If one of the computers in the network fails, none of the other components in the network are affected. However, the channel in a bus network can handle only one message at a time, so performance can degrade if there is a high volume of network traffic. When two computers transmit messages simultaneously, a "collision" occurs, and the messages must be re-sent.

The Ring Network

Like the bus network, the **ring network** (see Figure 7-7) does not rely on a central host computer and will not necessarily break down if one of the component computers malfunctions. Each computer in the network can communicate directly with any other computer, and each processes its own applications independently. However, in ring topology, the connecting wire, cable, or optical fiber forms a closed loop. Data are passed along the ring from one computer to another and always flow in one direction. Both ring and bus topologies are used in LANs, which are discussed in the next section.

ring network A network topology in which all computers are linked by a closed loop in a manner that passes data in one direction from one computer to another.

PRIVATE BRANCH EXCHANGES, LOCAL AREA NETWORKS (LANS), AND WIDE AREA NETWORKS (WANS)

Networks may be classified by geographic scope into local networks and wide area networks. Wide area networks encompass a relatively wide geographic area, from several miles to thousands of miles, whereas local networks link local resources such as computers and terminals

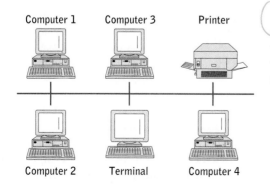

FIGURE 7-6 A bus network topology. This topology allows for all messages to be broadcast to the entire network through a single circuit. There is no central host, and messages can travel in both directions along the cable.

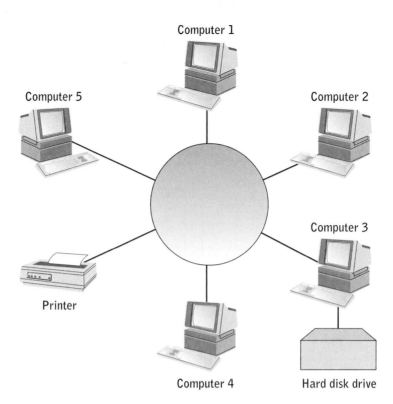

FIGURE 7-7 A ring network topology. In a ring network configuration, messages are transmitted from computer to computer, flowing in a single direction through a closed loop. Each computer operates independently so that if one fails, communication through the network is not interrupted.

Computer 1

Computer 5

Computer 2

Computer 3

Printer

Computer 4

Hard disk drive

in the same department or building of a firm. Local networks consist of private branch exchanges and local area networks.

Private Branch Exchanges

private branch exchange (PBX) A central switching system that handles a firm's voice and digital communications.

A **private branch exchange (PBX)** is a special-purpose computer designed for handling and switching office telephone calls at a company site. Today's PBXs can carry voice and data to create local networks. PBXs can store, transfer, hold, and redial telephone calls, and they also can be used to switch digital information among computers and office devices. Using a PBX, you can write a letter on a PC in your office, send it to the printer, then dial up the local copying machine and have multiple copies of your letter made.

The advantage of digital PBXs over other local networking options is that they do not require special wiring. A PC connected to a network by telephone can be plugged or unplugged anywhere in a building using the existing telephone lines. Commercial vendors support PBXs, so the organization does not need special expertise to manage them.

The geographic scope of PBXs is limited, usually to several hundred feet, although the PBX can be connected to other PBX networks or to packet switched networks (see the discussion of packet switching later in this section) to encompass a larger geographic area. The primary disadvantages of PBXs are that they are limited to telephone lines and they cannot easily handle very large volumes of data.

Local Area Networks

local area network (LAN) A telecommunications network that requires its own dedicated channels and that encompasses a limited distance, usually one building or several buildings in close proximity.

A **local area network (LAN)** encompasses a limited distance, usually one building or several buildings in close proximity. Most LANs connect devices located within a 2,000-foot radius, and they have been widely used to link PCs. LANs require their own communications channels.

LANs generally have higher transmission capacities than PBXs because they use bus or ring topologies and have a high bandwidth. They are recommended for applications transmitting high volumes of data and other functions requiring high transmission speeds including transmissions of video and graphics. LANs often are used to connect PCs in an office to shared printers and other resources or to link computers and computer-controlled machines in factories.

LANs are more expensive to install than PBXs and are more inflexible because they require new wiring each time a LAN is moved. One solution to this problem is to create a wireless LAN, such as that used by BMW described in the chapter opening vignette. LANs are usually controlled, maintained, and operated by end users. This means that the user must know a great deal about telecommunications applications and networking.

Figure 7-8 illustrates one model of a LAN. The server acts as a librarian, storing programs and data files for network users. The server determines who gets access to what and in what sequence. Servers may be powerful PCs with large hard-disk capacity, workstations, midrange computers, or mainframes, although specialized computers are available for this purpose.

The network gateway connects the LAN to public networks, such as the Internet, or to other corporate networks so that the LAN can exchange information with networks external to it. A **gateway** is generally a communications processor that can connect dissimilar networks by translating from one set of protocols to another. A **router** is used to route packets of data through several connected LANs or to a wide area network.

LAN technology consists of cabling (twisted wire, coaxial, or fiber-optic cable) or wireless technology that links individual computer devices, network interface cards (which are special adapters serving as interfaces to the cable), and software to control LAN activities. The LAN network interface card specifies the data transmission rate, the size of message units, the addressing information attached to each message, and network topology (Ethernet uses a bus topology, for example).

LAN capabilities also are defined by the **network operating system (NOS).** The network operating system can reside on every computer in the network, or it can reside on a single designated server for all the applications on the network. The NOS routes and manages communications on the network and coordinates network resources. Novell NetWare, Microsoft Windows 2000 Server and Windows 2000 Datacenter Server, and IBM's OS/2 Warp Server are popular network operating systems.

LANs may take the form of client/server networks, in which the server provides data and application programs to "client" computers on the network (see the Chapter 4 discussion of client/server computing), or they may use a peer-to-peer architecture. A **peer-to-peer** network treats all processors equally and is used primarily in small networks. Each computer on the network has direct access to each other's workstations and shared peripheral devices.

Wide Area Networks (WANs)

Wide area networks (WANs) span broad geographical distances, ranging from several miles to entire continents. WANs may consist of a combination of switched and dedicated lines,

gateway A communications processor that connects dissimilar networks by providing the translation from one set of protocols to another.

router Device that forwards packets of data from one LAN or wide area network to another.

network operating system (NOS) Special software that routes and manages communications on the network and coordinates network resources.

peer-to-peer Network architecture that gives equal power to all computers on the network; used primarily in small networks.

wide area network (WAN) Telecommunications network that spans a large geographical distance. May consist of a variety of cable, satellite, and microwave technologies.

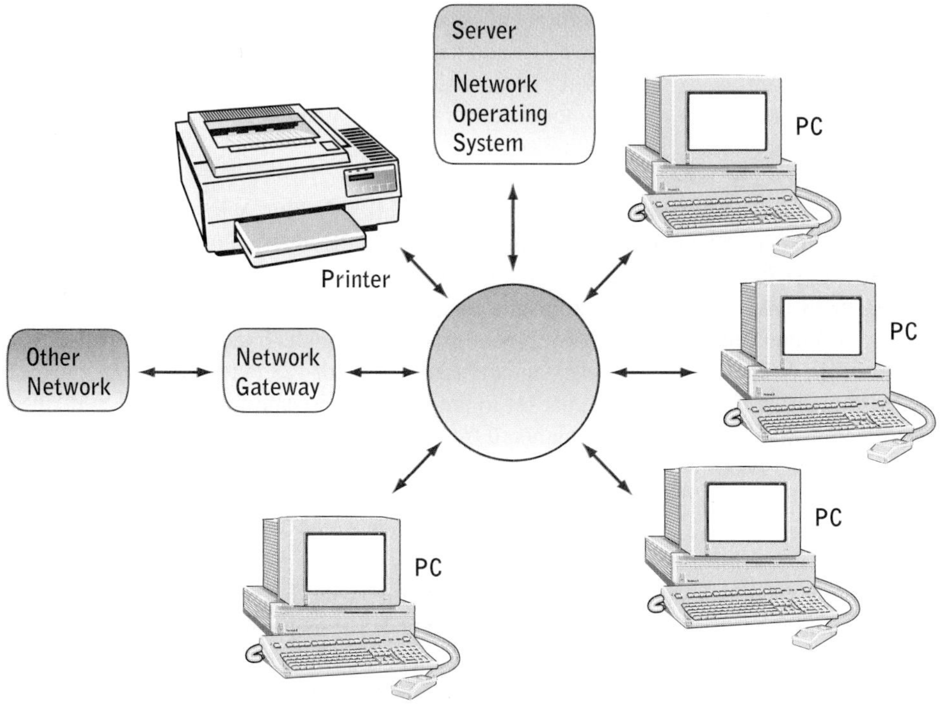

FIGURE 7-8 A local area network (LAN). A typical local area network connects computers and peripheral devices that are located close to each other, often in the same building.

switched lines Telephone lines that a person can access from a terminal to transmit data to another computer; the call is routed or switched through paths to the designated destination.

dedicated lines Telephone lines that are continuously available for transmission by a lessee. Typically conditioned to transmit data at high speeds for high-volume applications.

value-added network (VAN) Private, multipath, data-only, third-party-managed network that is used by multiple organizations on a subscription basis.

packet switching Technology that breaks blocks of text into small, fixed bundles of data and routes them in the most economical way through any available communications channel.

frame relay A shared network service technology that packages data into bundles for transmission but does not use error-correction routines. Cheaper and faster than packet switching.

microwave, and satellite communications. **Switched lines** are telephone lines that a person can access from his or her terminal to transmit data to another computer; the call is routed or switched through paths to the designated destination. **Dedicated lines,** or nonswitched lines, are continuously available for transmission, and the lessee typically pays a flat rate for total access to the line. The lines can be leased or purchased from common carriers or private communications media vendors. Most existing WANs are switched. Amoco's network for transmitting seismic data illustrated in Figure 7-4 is a WAN. Individual business firms may maintain their own wide area networks. The firm is responsible for telecommunications content and management. However, private wide area networks are expensive to maintain, and firms may not have the resources to manage their own wide area networks. In such instances, companies may choose to use commercial network services to communicate over vast distances.

NETWORK SERVICES

In addition to topology and geographic scope, networks can be classified by the types of service they provide.

Value-Added Networks (VANs)

Value-added networks are an alternative to firms designing and managing their own networks. **Value-added networks (VANs)** are private, multipath, data-only, third-party-managed networks that can provide economies in the cost of service and in network management because they are used by multiple organizations. The value-added network is set up by a firm that is responsible for managing the network. That firm sells subscriptions to other firms that wish to use the network. Subscribers pay only for the amount of data they transmit plus a subscription fee. The network may use twisted-pair lines, satellite links, and other communications channels leased by the value-added carrier.

The term *value added* refers to the extra value added to communications by the telecommunications and computing services these networks provide to clients. Customers do not have to invest in network equipment and software or perform their own error checking, editing, routing, and protocol conversion. Subscribers may achieve savings in line charges and transmission costs because the costs of using the network are shared among many users. The resulting costs may be lower than if the clients had leased their own lines or satellite services.

The leading international value-added networks provide casual or intermittent users international services on a dial-up basis and can provide a private network using dedicated circuits for customers requiring a full-time network. (Maintaining a private network may be most cost-effective for organizations with a high communications volume.) International VANs have representatives with language skills and knowledge of various countries' telecommunications administrations. The VANs already have leased lines from foreign telecommunications authorities or can arrange access to local networks and equipment abroad.

Other Network Services

Traditional analog telephone service is based on circuit-switching, where a direct connection must be maintained between two nodes in a network for the duration of the transmission session. **Packet switching** is a basic switching technique that can be used to achieve economies and higher speeds in long-distance transmission. VANs and the Internet use packet switching. Packet switching breaks up a lengthy block of text into small, fixed bundles of data called packets. (The X.25 packet switching standard uses packets of 128 bytes each.) The packets include information for directing the packet to the right address and for checking transmission errors along with the data. Data are gathered from many users, divided into small packets, and transmitted via various communications channels. Each packet travels independently through the network. Packets of data originating at one source can be routed through different paths in the network before being reassembled into the original message when they reach their destination. Figure 7-9 illustrates how packet switching works.

Frame relay is a shared network service that is faster and less expensive than packet switching and can achieve transmission speeds up to 1.544 megabits per second. Frame relay packages data into frames that are similar to packets, but it does not perform error correction. It works well on reliable lines that do not require frequent retransmissions because of errors.

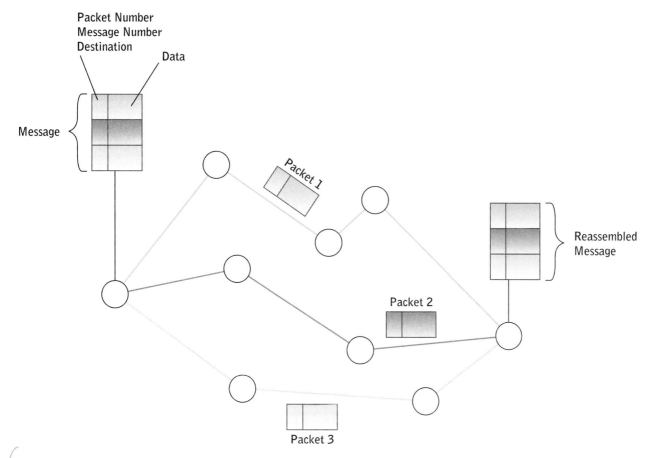

FIGURE 7-9 Packet switched networks and packet communications. Data are grouped into small packets, which are transmitted independently via various communication channels and reassembled at their final destination.

Most corporations today use separate networks for voice and data, each of which is supported by a different technology. A service called **asynchronous transfer mode (ATM)** may overcome some of these problems because it can seamlessly and dynamically switch voice, data, images, and video between users. ATM also promises to tie LANs and wide area networks together more easily. (LANs generally are based on lower speed protocols, whereas WANs operate at higher speeds.) ATM technology parcels information into uniform cells, each with 53 groups of 8 bytes, eliminating the need for protocol conversion. It can pass data between computers from different vendors and permits data to be transmitted at any speed the network handles. ATM can transmit up to 2.5 GBPS.

Integrated Services Digital Network (ISDN) is an international standard for dial-up network access that integrates voice, data, image, and video services in a single link. There are two levels of ISDN service: Basic Rate ISDN and Primary Rate ISDN. Each uses a group of B (bearer) channels to carry voice or data along with a D (delta) channel for signaling and control information. Basic Rate ISDN transmits data at a rate of 128 kilobits per second on an existing local telephone line. Organizations and individuals requiring simultaneous voice or data transmission over one physical line might choose this service. Primary Rate ISDN offers transmission capacities in the megabit range and is designed for large organizations that use telecommunications services.

Other high-capacity services include digital subscriber line (DSL) technologies, cable modems, and T1 lines. Like ISDN, **digital subscriber line (DSL)** technologies operate over existing copper telephone lines to carry voice, data, and video, but they have higher transmission capacities than ISDN. There are several categories of DSL. Asymmetric digital subscriber line (ADSL) supports a transmission rate of 1.5 to 9 megabits per second when receiving data

asynchronous transfer mode (ATM) A networking technology that parcels information into 8-byte cells, allowing data to be transmitted between computers from different vendors at any speed.

Integrated Services Digital Network (ISDN) International standard for transmitting voice, video, image, and data to support a wide range of service over the public telephone lines.

digital subscriber line (DSL) A group of technologies providing high-capacity transmission over existing copper telephone lines.

and up to 640 kilobits per second when sending data. Symmetric digital subscriber line (SDSL) supports the same transmission rate for sending and receiving data of up to 3 megabits per second. **Cable modems** are modems designed to operate over cable TV lines. They provide high-speed access to the Web or corporate intranets of up to 4 megabits per second. However, cable modems use a shared line so that transmission will slow down if there is a large number of local users sharing the cable line. A cable modem at present has better capabilities for receiving data than for sending data. A **T1 line** is a dedicated telephone connection comprising 24 channels that can support a data transmission rate of 1.544 megabits per second. Each of these 64-kilobit-per-second channels can be configured to carry voice or data traffic. These services often are used for high-capacity Internet connections. Table 7-2 summarizes these network services.

High-speed transmission technologies are sometimes referred to as **broadband.** The term broadband is also used to designate transmission media that can carry multiple channels simultaneously over a single communications medium.

NETWORK CONVERGENCE

Most companies maintain separate networks for voice, data, and video, but products are now available to create **converged networks,** which can deliver voice, data, and video in a single network infrastructure. These multiservice networks can potentially reduce networking costs by eliminating the need to provide support services and personnel for each different type of network. Multiservice networks can be attractive solutions for companies running multimedia applications, such as video collaboration, voice-data call centers, distance learning, or unified messaging, or for firms with high costs for voice services. The Window on Organizations shows how one organization used a multiservice network solution to enhance its competitive position.

7.4 Networks and the New Information Technology (IT) Infrastructure

Chapter 3 described the evolution of information technology (IT) infrastructures in organizations culminating in a new IT infrastructure capable of coordinating the activities of entire firms and even entire industries. By enabling companies to radically reduce their agency and transaction costs, this new IT infrastructure is creating a broad platform for electronic com-

cable modem Modem designed to operate over cable TV lines to provide high-speed access to the Web or corporate intranets.

T1 line A dedicated telephone connection comprising 24 channels that can support a total data transmission rate of 1.544 megabits per second. Each channel can be configured to carry voice or data traffic.

broadband High-speed transmission technology; also designates a communications medium that can transmit multiple channels of data simultaneously.

converged network Network with technology to enable voice and data to run over a single network.

Table 7-2 **Network Services**

Service	Description	Bandwidth
X.25	Packet switching standard that parcels data into packets of 128 bytes	Up to 1.544 MBPS
Frame Relay	Packages data into frames for high-speed transmission over reliable lines but does not use error-correction routines	Up to 1.544 MBPS
ATM (asynchronous transfer mode)	Parcels data into uniform cells to allow high-capacity transmission of voice, data, images, and video between different types of computers	25 MBPS–2.5 GBPS
ISDN	Digital dial-up network access standard that can integrate voice, data, and video services	Basic Rate ISDN: 128 KBPS Primary Rate ISDN: 1.5 MBPS
DSL (digital subscriber line)	Series of technologies for high-capacity transmission over copper wires	ADSL—up to 9 MBPS for receiving and up to 640 KBPS for sending data; SDSL—up to 3 MBPS for both sending and receiving
T1	Dedicated telephone connection with 24 channels for high-capacity transmission	1.544 MBPS
Cable Modem	Service for high-speed transmission of data over cable TV lines that are shared by many users	Up to 4 MBPS

CHOOSING AN INTERNET CONNECTION SERVICE

You run a graphic design company with 15 employees that does page layout and illustrations for magazine and book publishers in many different parts of the United States. You want to take advantage of network services to send files of your illustrations and layout work to your clients for review. The average size of each graphics file you transmit is 4 megabytes and an average of 25 of these files are sent to clients each day. Schedules are tight and productivity can be impacted if all of your network resources are tied up transmitting files. You are also on a very tight budget. The following network services are available in your area. At its current size, your business could use 1 dedicated telephone line with software that enables up to 20 employees to share Internet use.

Option	Transmission Capacity	Cost
Dial-up service with 56kbps analog modems for each employee	56KBPS	$40 per month for Internet service + basic $35 per month phone charge
ISDN line	128 KBPS	$100 per month + $300 installation fee
Cable modem	1-2 MBPS	$75 per month + $125 installation fee
Synchronous DSL	512 KBPS sending and receiving	$100 for DSL modem + $175 per month
T1 line	1.5 MBPS	$1200 per month

1. What is the average amount of time your business would spend daily transmitting files for each of these options?

2. Which of these options is most appropriate for your company? Why?

3. If your business expanded and you had 60 employees and 100 files to transmit daily, which option would you choose?

---

merce and other strategic business applications. Powerful networks provide the foundation of this new information technology (IT) infrastructure. We now describe the features of the new information technology (IT) infrastructure in detail.

ENTERPRISE NETWORKING AND INTERNETWORKING

Figure 7-10 illustrates the new information technology (IT) infrastructure. The new information technology (IT) infrastructure uses a mixture of computer hardware supplied by different vendors. Large, complex databases that need central storage are found on mainframes or specialized servers, whereas smaller databases and parts of large databases are loaded on PCs and workstations. Client/server computing often is used to distribute more processing power to the desktop. The desktop itself has been extended to a larger workspace that includes mobile personal information devices, programmable mobile phones, pagers, and other information appliances. This new information technology (IT) infrastructure also incorporates public infrastructures, such as the telephone system, the Internet, and public network services and electronic devices.

Through enterprise networking and internetworking, information flows smoothly between all of these devices within the organization and between the organization and its external environment. In **enterprise networking,** the organization's hardware, software, telecommunications, and data resources are arranged to put more computing power on the desktop and to create a company-wide network linking many smaller networks. The system is a network. In fact, for all but the smallest organizations the system is composed of multiple networks. A high-capacity backbone network connects many local area networks and devices.

The backbone may be connected to the networks of other organizations outside the firm, to the Internet, to the networks of public telecommunication service providers, or to other public networks. The linking of separate networks, each of which retains its own identity, into an interconnected network is called **internetworking.** Table 7-3 summarizes the key features of the new information technology (IT) infrastructure.

Vienna University in Austria illustrates enterprise networking and internetworking in the new information technology (IT) infrastructure. The university's network consists of 3,500 computers,

enterprise networking An arrangement of the organization's hardware, software, telecommunications, and data resources to put more computing power on the desktop and create a company-wide network linking many smaller networks.

internetworking The linking of separate networks, each of which retains its own identity, into an interconnected network.

BANCO DO BRASIL COMPETES WITH A MULTISERVICE WAN

Banco do Brasil is the largest bank in Brazil, with more than 4,300 branches in 2,700 locations in Brazil and 30 countries abroad. The bank handles more than 35 million transactions each day and services more than 15 million checking accounts. Competition in the Brazilian banking industry is fierce, and banks face high telecommunication costs. For example, a leased line in an urban area with a well-developed infrastructure, such as Sao Paulo, can cost U.S. $6,000 per month, and a single data-only telephone line between Latin American cities can cost up to U.S. $50,000 monthly. Banks are the heaviest users of Brazilian telecommunication services.

Leased lines in Brazil frequently experience trunk failures. Banco do Brasil created redundant infrastructures to ensure 24-hour availability of its transaction processing applications. Consequently, voice and data telecommunications costs were its single largest expense.

To remain competitive, Banco do Brasil started looking for ways to deliver innovative banking services and increase customer satisfaction while reducing costs. The bank set a goal of reducing customers' waiting time in bank branches by 65 percent as a means of both increasing customer satisfaction and reducing banking transaction costs. Each customer transaction completed at a bank branch teller's counter costs about U.S. $1.50. The bank also wanted to create a comprehensive set of electronic home banking, Internet banking, and call-center services and to deliver new financial products with the shortest time-to-market in its industry. It needed a fast multiservice network infrastructure to meet these objectives.

The bank selected Cisco System's IGX 8400 services wide area switch with Voice Network Switching (VNS) to provide the speed and intelligence to integrate voice, data, and video. The WAN uses 53 Cisco IGX 8400 switches connected using E3 ATM trunks to link three data centers in Brazil. Approximately 40 Cisco Catalyst 5500 series multilayer switches are also deployed at the bank's headquarters and 3,000 Cisco routers are installed in the bank's branches. Transactions and other network traffic are transported using Frame Relay over the IGX 8400 network backbone. With this multiservice network, Banco do Brasil can leverage its data network to provide voice services to every location without expenditures for additional voice channels between cities, significantly reducing telephone costs.

The bank's new Internet, home banking, and call-center services have changed the way it conducts its business. Today, 60 percent of its branches manage transactions electronically, compared to 20 percent in the past. The electronic services have reduced the number of customers waiting in line in branches and have slashed customer service costs from U.S. $1.50 to $.10 per transaction. The network has reduced transaction processing time while enhancing reliability.

In the year 2000, Banco do Brasil expects to have 30,000 automatic teller machines (ATMs) processing 6 times its previous transaction volume. Its new multiservice WAN will allow it to deliver new data, voice, and video applications with a high level of performance.

TO THINK ABOUT: What were the organizational benefits of Banco do Brasil's new WAN? What management, organization, and technology issues should be addressed when deciding whether to use a multiservice network?

Sources: Heliomar Lima, "Multiservice WAN Extends Banking Services to Every Corner of Brazil—and Beyond," **Packet Magazine** 11, no. 1 (First Quarter, 1999); and Amy K. Larsen, "Voice with Data," **Information Week**, February 1, 1999.

---

including an IBM Enterprise System/9000 mainframe, Unix workstations, and thousands of PCs. A backbone network uses Cisco routers to connect various university departments to the university's Computer Center, where traffic is routed to other universities in Vienna, to the Austrian Academic Network (ACOnet), Austria's national research network, and to the public Internet.

Other organizations are using the new information technology (IT) infrastructure to provide telecommuters and other employees with mobile computing capabilities and remote access to corporate information systems. The Window on Technology shows how three companies are benefiting from mobile computing.

THE ROLE OF STANDARDS

The new information technology (IT) infrastructure is most likely to increase productivity and competitive advantage when digitized information can move seamlessly through the organization's web of electronic networks, connecting different kinds of machines, people, sensors, databases, functional divisions, departments, and work groups. This ability of computers and computer-based devices to communicate with one another and "share" information in a meaningful way without human intervention is called **connectivity.** Internet technology and Java

connectivity A measure of how well computers and computer-based devices communicate and share information with one another without human intervention.

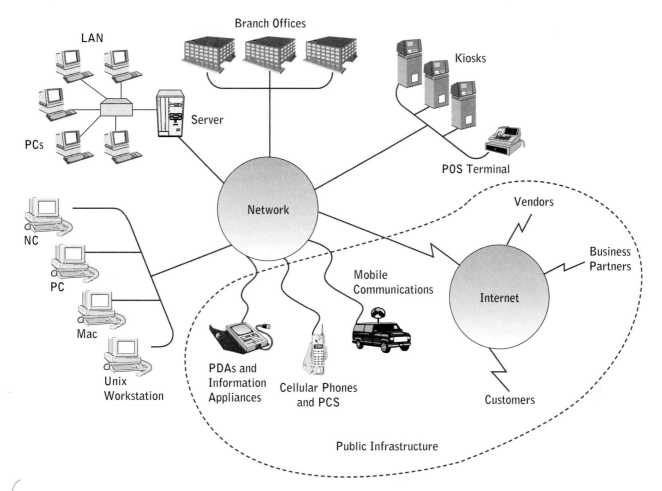

FIGURE 7-I 0 The new information technology (IT) infrastructure. The new IT infrastructure links desktop workstations, network computers, LANs, and server computers in an enterprise network so that information can flow freely between different parts of the organization. The enterprise network may be linked to kiosks, point-of-sale (POS) terminals, PDAs and information appliances, digital cellular telephones and PCS, and mobile computing devices as well as to the Internet using public infrastructures. Customers, suppliers, and business partners may also be linked to the organization through this new IT infrastructure.

software provide some of this connectivity, but the Internet cannot be used as a foundation for all of the organization's information systems. Most organizations still will require their own proprietary networks. They need to develop their own connectivity solutions to make different kinds of hardware, software, and communications systems work together.

Achieving connectivity requires standards for networking, operating systems, and user interfaces. Open systems promote connectivity because they enable disparate equipment and services to work together. **Open systems** are built on public, nonproprietary operating systems, user interfaces, application standards, and networking protocols. In open systems, software can operate on different hardware platforms and in that sense can be "portable." Java software, described in Chapter 5, can create an open system environment. The Unix operating system supports open systems because it can operate on many different kinds of computer hardware. However, there are different versions of Unix, and no one version has been accepted as an open systems standard. Linux also supports open systems.

Models of Connectivity for Networks

There are different models for achieving connectivity in telecommunications networks. The **Transmission Control Protocol/Internet Protocol (TCP/IP)** model was developed by the U.S. Department of Defense in 1972 and is used in the Internet. Its purpose was to help scientists link disparate computers. Figure 7-11 shows that TCP/IP has a five-layer reference model.

open systems Software systems that can operate on different hardware platforms because they are built on public nonproprietary operating systems, user interfaces, application standards, and networking protocols.

Transmission Control Protocol/Internet Protocol (TCP/IP) U.S. Department of Defense reference model for linking different types of computers and networks; used in the Internet.

Table 7-3 Elements of the New Information Technology (IT) Infrastructure

Feature	Description
Reliance on desktop and portable device computing	The "old" legacy infrastructures involved mainframe computers, controlled by a single Information Systems Department, using well integrated and defined software and telecommunications (often from the same vendor as the computer). Today's firms rely extensively on networked desktop computers supported by many vendors, communications firms, and software companies. The desktop itself has been extended to a larger "workspace" that includes mobile personal information devices from Palm PDAs to programmable mobile phones and pagers.
Rise of the Internet	The Internet and related technologies have become central components of the firm's IT infrastructure. The Internet and corporate intranets are becoming the main communication channel with customers, employees, vendors and distributors.
Growing use of public infrastructure	In the past there was a boundary between public and private infrastructures, such as the telephone system and corporate computing. Today the boundaries between public and private infrastructures are blurring as companies build systems using Internet services and trunk lines.
Reliance on third parties for technology services	In the past, firms generally built their own software and developed their own computing facilities. In many firms today, the IS Department acts as manager of packages and software services provided by third party vendors.

1. *Application:* Provides end-user functionality by translating the messages into the user/host software for screen presentation.

2. *Transmission Control Protocol (TCP):* Performs transport, breaking application data from the end user down into TCP packets called datagrams. Each packet consists of a header with the address of the sending host computer, information for putting the data back together, and information for making sure the packets do not become corrupted.

3. *Internet Protocol (IP):* The Internet Protocol receives datagrams from TCP and breaks the packets down further. An IP packet contains a header with address information and carries TCP information and data. IP routes the individual datagrams from the sender to the recipient. IP packets are not very reliable, but the TCP level can keep resending them until the correct IP packets get through.

FIGURE 7-11 The Transmission Control Protocol/Internet Protocol (TCP/IP) reference model. This figure illustrates the five layers of the TCP/IP reference model for communications.

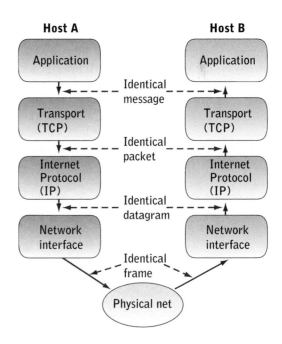

MOBILE COMPUTING BRINGS BUSINESSES INTO THE FUTURE

Mobile computing is revolutionizing how some corporations work. In response to the fiercely competitive economy, organizations have had to become more nimble, and that often means more mobile staffs and more mobile data collection and transmission. We examine how companies are benefiting from mobile technology.

Streamline is a six-year-old specialty delivery company located in Boston, Massachusetts. The company delivers not only packages, but also videos, dry cleaning, groceries, and even prepared meals. Dave Blakelock, the vice president of operations, believes his company is in the customer relations business rather than in the delivery business. "Our customers order every week," he says, "so we have to make sure we deliver the perfect order or the relationship will break down." To track and control deliveries, every item is bar coded and each of Streamline's 20 trucks has a scanner. Items are scanned when they arrive at the company warehouse, when they are loaded on the truck and again when they are delivered to the customer. One goal is to guarantee that the right items are delivered and that each order is complete.

Late in 1999, as the company was expanding into Washington, DC, it acquired a number of new devices that combine a handheld scanner and a Palm PDA with a telecommunications facility. The new devices transmit the data to the company as the driver scans the bar codes. The delivery is immediately checked for accuracy and any errors are instantly transmitted back to the driver who corrects the problem on the spot.

San Francisco-based Dine-One-One is a very different delivery company, delivering restaurant meals to customers that have placed their orders via telephone. In 1997, when Clement Lee purchased the company, its approximately 100 drivers were serving 150,000 customers and delivering meals from 210 restaurants. However, Lee found that all processes were paper based and manual. The drivers did have two-way radios, but the dispatcher could speak with only one driver at a time, and competition amongst the drivers to speak with the dispatcher wasted a great deal of the drivers' time. Lee decided to automate the whole process.

At the heart of the new process is an artificial intelligence system working in tandem with an on-board global position location system. Together they manage data on such key elements as the drivers' locations, their proximity to each restaurant, their average speed, and the food preparation time for each restaurant. The drivers all have very sophisticated wireless cell phones, which include a data modem, cursor keys, and a text message screen. Drivers use the phones to let the dispatching office know when they pick up orders and when they are delivered. The process is fully automated and has been very successful. In a five hour shift drivers now deliver two more orders than in the past, and the cost of taking a single phone order is only $1 compared to an industry average of $2.50. With its new technology, Dine-One-One is now going national. They have opened offices in Chicago and San Diego and are building a nationwide call center in Denver. Lee plans to add one new office per week either by opening a new one or by acquiring an existing service.

Many more companies are deploying handheld devices to help workers gather information in the field. For example, Navy Seahawk helicopter pilots use PalmPilot personal digital assistant (PDA) devices to gather flight data while they are flying or working on a fleet of ten Seahawk helicopters. The helicopters are constantly flying on missions including search and rescue. Before switching to the handheld computing devices, pilots had to spend an hour after every flight filling out paper forms and transferring that information to a PC.

TO THINK ABOUT: Explain how mobility was strategic for each of these three organizations. How did mobile computing technology support these strategies?

Source: Natalie Engler, "Mobile Benefits," *Information Week*, April 19, 1999; and Matt Hamblen, "Simple Tools Let Non-IT People Build Custom Apps," *Computerworld*, February 21, 2000.

---

4. *Network interface:* Handles addressing issues, usually in the operating system, as well as the interface between the initiating computer and the network.

5. *Physical net:* Defines basic electrical-transmission characteristic for sending the actual signal along communications networks.

Two computers using TCP/IP would be able to communicate even if they were based on different hardware and software platforms. Data sent from one computer to the other would pass downward through all five layers, starting with the sending computer's application layer and passing through the physical net. After the data reached the recipient host computer, they would travel up the layers. The TCP level would assemble the data into a format the receiving host computer could use. If the receiving computer found a damaged packet, it would ask the sending computer to retransmit it. This process would be reversed when the receiving computer responded.

Open Systems Interconnect (OSI) International reference model for linking different types of computers and networks.

The **Open Systems Interconnect (OSI)** model is an alternative model developed by the International Standards Organization for linking different types of computers and networks. It was designed to support global networks with large volumes of transaction processing. Like TCP/IP, OSI enables a computer connected to a network to communicate with any other computer on the same network or a different network, regardless of the hardware platform, by establishing communication rules that permit the exchange of information between dissimilar systems. OSI divides the telecommunications process into seven layers.

Section 7.2 described some of the connectivity standards being developed for wireless communication. Other connectivity-promoting standards have been developed for graphical user interfaces, electronic mail, packet switching, and electronic data interchange (see the next section). Any manager wishing to achieve some measure of connectivity in his or her organization should try to use these standards when designing networks, purchasing hardware and software, or developing information system applications.

ELECTRONIC COMMERCE AND ELECTRONIC BUSINESS TECHNOLOGIES

Baxter International, described in Chapter 2, realized the strategic significance of telecommunications. The company placed its own computer terminals in hospital supply rooms. Customers could dial up a local VAN and send their orders directly to the company. Other companies also are achieving strategic benefits by developing electronic commerce and electronic business applications based on the technologies available in the new information technology (IT) infrastructure.

Electronic mail (e-mail), voice mail, facsimile machines (fax), digital information services, teleconferencing, dataconferencing, videoconferencing, groupware, and electronic data interchange are key technologies for electronic commerce and electronic business because they provide network-based capabilities for communication, coordination, and speeding the flow of purchase and sale transactions.

Electronic Mail

We described the capabilities of electronic mail, or e-mail, in Chapter 5. E-mail eliminates telephone tag and costly long-distance telephone charges, and it expedites communication between different parts of an organization. Nestlé SA, the Swiss-based multinational food corporation, installed an electronic-mail system to connect its 60,000 employees in 80 countries. Nestlé's European units can use the electronic-mail system to share information about production schedules and inventory levels to ship excess products from one country to another.

Netscape Communicator includes e-mail functions such as attaching files, displaying messages, and providing logs of all incoming and outgoing messages. E-mail has become an important tool for organizational communication.

Many organizations operate their own internal electronic-mail systems, but communications companies such as GTE, MCI, and AT&T offer these services, as do commercial on-line information services such as America Online and Prodigy and public networks on the Internet (see Chapter 8). The chapter ending Case Study considers the privacy of e-mail messages from a different perspective, examining whether monitoring employee use of e-mail, the Internet, and other network facilities is ethical.

Voice Mail

A **voice mail** system digitizes the sender's spoken message, transmits it over a network, and stores the message on disk for later retrieval. When the recipient is ready to listen, the messages are reconverted to audio form. Various store-and-forward capabilities notify recipients that messages are waiting. Recipients have the option of saving these messages for future use, deleting them, or routing them to other parties.

voice mail A system for digitizing a spoken message and transmitting it over a network.

Facsimile Machines (Fax)

Facsimile (fax) machines can transmit documents containing both text and graphics over ordinary telephone lines. A sending fax machine scans and digitizes the document image. The digitized document is transmitted over a network and reproduced in hard copy form by a receiving fax machine. The process results in a duplicate, or facsimile, of the original.

facsimile (fax) A machine that digitizes and transmits documents with both text and graphics over telephone lines.

Digital Information Services

Powerful and far-reaching digital electronic services enable networked PC and workstation users to obtain information from outside the firm instantly without leaving their desks. Stock prices, periodicals, competitor data, industrial supplies catalogs, legal research, news articles, reference works, and weather forecasts are some of the information that can be accessed on-line. Many of these services provide capabilities for electronic mail, electronic bulletin boards, on-line discussion groups, shopping, and travel reservations as well as Internet access. Table 7-4 describes the leading commercial digital information services. The following chapter describes how organizations can access even more information resources using the Internet.

Teleconferencing, Dataconferencing, and Videoconferencing

People can meet electronically, even though they are hundreds or thousands of miles apart, using teleconferencing, dataconferencing, or videoconferencing. **Teleconferencing** allows a group of people to confer simultaneously via telephone or via electronic-mail group communication software. Teleconferencing that includes the ability of two or more people at distant locations to work on the same document or data simultaneously is called **dataconferencing.** With dataconferencing, users at distant locations are able to edit and modify data (text, such as word processing documents; numeric, such as spreadsheets; and graphic) files. Teleconferencing in which participants see each other over video screens is termed video teleconferencing, or **videoconferencing.**

teleconferencing The ability to confer with a group of people simultaneously using the telephone or electronic-mail group communication software.

dataconferencing Teleconferencing in which two or more users are able to edit and modify data files simultaneously.

videoconferencing Teleconferencing in which participants see each other on video screens.

Table 7-4 Commercial Digital Information Services

Provider	Type of Service
America Online	General interest/business information
Prodigy	General interest/business information
Microsoft Network	General interest/business information
Dow Jones News Retrieval	Business/financial information
Dialog	Business/scientific/technical information
Lexis	Legal research
Nexis	News/business information

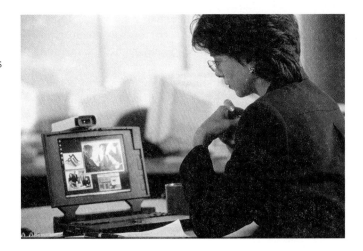

With PC desktop videoconferencing systems, users can see each other and simultaneously work on the same document. Organizations are using videoconferencing technology to improve coordination and to save travel time and costs.

These forms of electronic conferencing are growing in popularity because they save travel time and cost. Legal firms might use videoconferencing to take depositions and to convene meetings between lawyers in different branch offices. Videoconferencing can help companies promote remote collaboration from different locations or fill in personnel expertise gaps. Electronic conferencing is useful for supporting telecommuting, which enables home workers to meet with or collaborate with their counterparts working in the office or elsewhere.

Videoconferencing usually has required special videoconference rooms, videocameras, microphones, television monitors, and a computer equipped with a device called a codec that converts video images and analog sound waves into digital signals and compresses them for transfer over communications channels. Another codec on the receiving end reconverts the digital signals back into analog for display on the receiving monitor. PC-based, desktop videoconferencing systems in which users can see each other and simultaneously work on the same document are reducing videoconferencing costs so that more organizations can benefit from this technology.

Desktop videoconferencing systems typically provide a local window, in which you can see yourself, and a remote window to display the individual with whom you are communicating. Most desktop systems provide audio capabilities for two-way, real-time conversations and a whiteboard. The whiteboard is a shared drawing program that lets multiple users collaborate on projects by modifying images and text on-line. Software products such as Microsoft NetMeeting (a feature of the Windows 98 operating system) and CU-SeeMe (available in both

America Online gives subscribers access to extensive information resources, including news reports, travel, weather, education, financial services, and information on the World Wide Web. Companies and individuals can use such digital information services to obtain information instantly from their desktops.

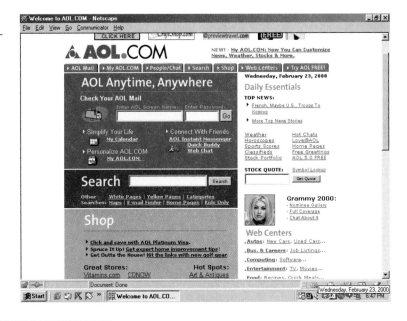

shareware and commercial versions) provide low-cost tools for desktop videoconferencing over the Internet.

Groupware

Chapter 5 described groupware's capabilities for supporting collaborative work. Individuals, teams, and work groups at different locations in the organization can use groupware to participate in discussion forums and work on shared documents and projects. More details on the use of groupware for collaborative work can be found in Chapter 11.

Electronic Data Interchange and Electronic Commerce

Electronic data interchange (EDI) is a key technology for electronic commerce because it allows the computer-to-computer exchange, between two organizations, of standard transaction documents such as invoices, bills of lading, or purchase orders. EDI lowers transaction costs because transactions can be automatically transmitted from one information system to another through a telecommunications network, eliminating the printing and handling of paper at one end and the inputting of data at the other. EDI also may provide strategic benefits by helping a firm lock in customers, making it easier for customers or distributors to order from them rather than from competitors. Chapter 2 also discussed how EDI can curb inventory costs by minimizing the amount of time components are in inventory.

EDI differs from electronic mail in that it transmits an actual structured transaction (with distinct fields such as the transaction date, transaction amount, sender's name, and recipient's name) as opposed to an unstructured text message such as a letter. Figure 7-12 illustrates how EDI works. Organizations can most fully benefit from EDI when they integrate the data supplied by EDI with applications such as accounts payable, inventory control, shipping, and production planning (Premkumar, Ramamurthy, and Nilakanta, 1994) and when they have carefully planned for the organizational changes surrounding new business processes. Management support and training in the new technology are essential (Raymond and Bergeron, 1996). Companies also must standardize the form of the transactions they use with other firms and comply with legal requirements for verifying that the transactions are authentic. Many organizations prefer to use private networks for EDI transactions, but they are increasingly turning to the Internet for this purpose (see Chapter 8).

> **electronic data interchange (EDI)** The direct computer-to-computer exchange, between two organizations, of standard business transaction documents.

7.5 Management Issues and Decisions

Telecommunications technology and networking are so deeply embedded in the core processes of businesses today that they require careful management and planning.

THE CHALLENGE OF MANAGING THE NEW INFORMATION TECHNOLOGY (IT) INFRASTRUCTURE

Implementing enterprise networking and the new information technology (IT) infrastructure has created problems as well as opportunities for organizations. Managers need to address

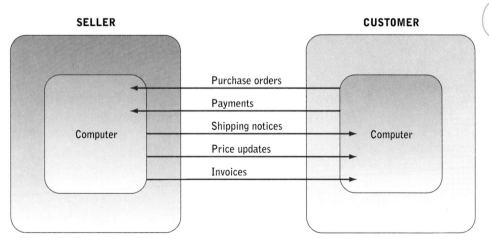

SELLER   **CUSTOMER**

Computer — Purchase orders — Payments — Shipping notices — Price updates — Invoices — Computer

FIGURE 7-1 2 Electronic data interchange (EDI). Companies can use EDI to automate electronic commerce transactions. Purchase orders and payments can be transmitted directly from the customer's computer to the seller's computer. The seller can transmit shipping notices, price changes, and invoices electronically back to the customer.

these problems as they design and build networking capabilities and telecommunications-based services for their organizations.

Problems Posed by the New Information Technology (IT) Infrastructure

The rapid, often unplanned, development of networks and distributed computing has created some problems. We already have described the connectivity problems that incompatible network components and standards create. Four additional problems stand out: loss of management control over information systems, the need for organizational change, the hidden costs of client/server computing, and the difficulty of ensuring network bandwidth, reliability and security (see Table 7-5).

Loss of Management Control   Managing information systems technology and corporate data are proving much more difficult in a distributed environment because of the lack of a single, central point where needed management can occur. Client/server computing and networks have empowered end users to become independent sources of computing power capable of collecting, storing, and disseminating data and software. Data and software no longer are confined to the mainframe and under the management of the traditional information systems department.

In the new IT infrastructure, it becomes increasingly difficult to determine where data are located and to ensure that the same piece of information, such as a product number, is used consistently throughout the organization (see Chapter 6). User-developed applications may combine incompatible pieces of hardware or software. However, observers worry that excess centralization and management of information resources will stifle end users' independence and creativity and reduce their ability to define their own information needs. The dilemma posed by enterprise networking is one of central-management control versus end-user creativity and productivity.

Organizational Change Requirements   Decentralization also results in changes in corporate culture and organizational structure. Enterprise-wide computing is an opportunity to reengineer the organization into a more effective unit, but it will only create problems or chaos if the underlying organizational issues are not fully addressed (Duchessi and Chengalur-Smith, 1998).

Hidden Costs of Client/Server Computing   Many companies have found that the savings they expected from client/server computing did not materialize because of unexpected costs. Hardware-acquisition savings resulting from significantly lower costs of MIPS on PCs often are offset by high annual operating costs for additional labor and time required for network and system management.

The most difficult to evaluate and control are the hidden costs that accompany a decentralized client/server system. Considerable time must be spent on tasks such as network maintenance; data backup; technical problem solving; and hardware, software, and software-update installations. The largest cost component for client/server systems is operations staff.

Network Reliability, Security and Bandwidth   Almost all corporate applications today are network-based, and electronic commerce places heavy demands on firms' networking resources. Companies embracing electronic commerce require information technology infra-

Table 7-5 Problems Posed by the New Information Technology (IT) Infrastructure

Connectivity problems

Loss of management control over systems

Organizational change requirements

Hidden costs of client/server computing

Network reliability, security, and bandwidth

structures that provide plentiful bandwidth and storage capacity for transmitting and maintaining all of the data generated by electronic commerce transactions.

Network technology remains immature and highly complex. The networks themselves have dense layers of interacting technology and the applications, too, are often intricately layered. Enterprise networking is highly sensitive to different versions of operating systems and network management software, and some applications require specific versions of each. It is difficult to make all of the components of large, heterogeneous networks work together as smoothly as management envisions. **Downtime**—periods of time in which the system is not operational—remains much more frequent in client/server systems than in established mainframe systems and should be considered carefully before taking essential applications off a mainframe.

Security is of paramount importance in organizations where information systems use networks extensively. Networks present end users, hackers, and thieves with many points of access and opportunities to steal or modify data in networks. Systems linked to the Internet are even more vulnerable because the Internet was designed to be open to everyone. We discuss these issues in greater detail in Chapter 13.

downtime Periods of time in which an information system is not operational.

Some Solutions

Organizations can meet the challenges posed by the new information technology (IT) infrastructure by planning for and managing the business and organizational changes; increasing end-user training; asserting data administration disciplines; and considering connectivity, bandwidth, and cost controls in their technology planning.

Managing the Change   To gain the full benefit of any new technology, organizations must carefully plan for and manage the change. Business processes may need to be redesigned to ensure that the organization fully benefits from the new technology (see Chapter 9). Firms will need to modify their information technology infrastructure and information architecture to support electronic commerce and distributed computing more fully. Management must address the organizational issues that arise from shifts in staffing, function, power, and organizational culture.

Education and Training   A well-developed training program can help end users overcome problems resulting from the lack of management support and understanding of networked computing (Westin et al., 1995; Bikson et al., 1985). Technical specialists will need training in Web site and client/server development and network support methods.

Data Administration Disciplines   The role of data administration (see Chapter 6) becomes even more important when networks link many different applications, business areas, and computing devices. Organizations must systematically identify where their data are located, which group is responsible for maintaining each piece of data, and which individuals and groups are allowed to access and use that data. They need to develop specific policies and procedures to ensure that their data are accurate, available only to authorized users, and properly backed up.

Planning for Connectivity, Bandwidth, and Reliability   Senior management must take a long-term view of the firm's information technology infrastructure, making sure that it has sufficient connectivity and bandwidth for its current and future information needs.

It is usually too expensive to achieve complete connectivity in most organizations. It is far more sensible to identify classes of connectivity problems and specific application groups (such as critical electronic commerce and electronic business applications) that can be enhanced through increased connectivity.

Although some connectivity problems can be solved by using intranets or the Internet, the firm will need to establish standards for other systems and applications that are enterprise-wide. Management can establish policies to keep networks and telecommunications services as homogeneous as possible, setting standards for data, voice, e-mail, and videoconferencing services along with hardware, software, and network operating systems.

Managers also need to develop strategies for dealing with steadily increasing loads placed on company networks, including activities across intranets and the Internet. The

MANAGING BANDWIDTH

"Bandwidth is to the networked economy what coal and steel were to the Industrial Age," observes Tom Jenkins, a senior consultant with TeleChoice Inc. Many other experts would agree. Networks are the foundation of electronic commerce and the digital economy, and managing a company's network resources is a central management concern. Without network infrastructures that offer fast, reliable access, companies would lose many on-line customers and jeopardize relationships with suppliers and business partners as well.

Managing bandwidth can be time consuming and complex. Although telecommunication transmission costs are rapidly dropping, total network bandwidth requirements are growing at a rate of more than 40 percent each year. If more people use networks or the firm implements data-intensive applications that require high-capacity transmission, a firm's network costs can easily spiral upward. For example, NCR Corporation's bandwidth costs are rising at an annual rate of 40 percent despite a drop in megabit per second charges.

Managers are looking for solutions to put a brake on escalating networking budgets. NCR is trying to control costs through a usage-based chargeback system for bandwidth accounting. The company is using software tools such as NetCountant software from Apogee Networks Inc. to collect statistics on network usage for each unit in its different lines of business. The company then charges each business unit for the bandwidth it has actually used. Users learn they can achieve savings by transferring large files over networks at night and running only the most critical bandwidth-consuming applications during the day.

Remote access, wide area networks, and Internet connections and servers create special bandwidth bottlenecks. Hoechst Marion Roussel, Inc. runs client applications of SAP R/3 enterprise system software at its 13 branch offices in Latin America. Only a few offices run the servers for the system. An employee in Santiago, Chile, would have to send data across a WAN to a server in Buenos Aires, Argentina. Bandwidth is relatively inexpensive, easily available at the company's LANs, and has transmission speeds of up to 155 megabits per second, but the connections to the WAN oper-

ate at a fraction of that speed, as little as 64 kilobits per second. An application that has to cross a LAN to link to a WAN is likely to slow to a crawl. For instance, an e-mail message with a 3-megabyte file attached would suspend operations on the 64-kilobits-per-second line for R/3 users.

Hoechst and other companies are dealing with this problem by using traffic-shaping devices that give one type of application on the network priority over another. Hoechst uses traffic shaping to ensure that critical R/3 applications are given the highest priority when they use low-speed international network connections. When Hoechst's WAN has no R/3 traffic, it then can run other applications. Traffic shaping saves Hoechst thousands of dollars a month. Without traffic-shaping devices, soaring bandwidth on the WAN connections would have raised the cost of international 64-kilobits-per-second lines from $4,000 to $10,000 per month.

Companies can also realize economies by carefully matching telecommunications services to their business needs. Yellow Corporation's Yellow Freight Systems unit in Overland Park, Kansas, has low-bandwidth requirements for most of is applications. The trucking company implemented a combination of frame relay and VSAT (very small aperture terminal) satellite connections for its 350 locations throughout the United States. VSAT is half the price of frame relay and each VSAT transmission station can handle up to 54 kilobits per second of digital transmission. Yellow Freight installed VSAT in 240 of its locations, reserving frame relay only for sites that can't support a satellite dish.

TO THINK ABOUT: Why is managing bandwidth an important management activity? What management, organization, and technology issues should be considered when planning for bandwidth in a company's telecommunications infrastructure?

Sources: Lenny Liebmann, "Bandwidth Fuels E-conomy," *Information Week*, May 10, 1999; Brian Riggs and Mary E. Thyfault, "Network Pressure," *Information Week*, August 16, 1999; and Craig Stedman, "Moving to Web Applications? Don't Forget Bandwidth," *Computerworld*, January 31, 2000.

Window on Management explores some of the strategies that companies have used to ensure fast, reliable network access.

TELECOMMUNICATIONS PLANNING FOR THE NEW INFORMATION TECHNOLOGY (IT) INFRASTRUCTURE

Many firms will need to develop a special telecommunications plan highlighting the role of networks and telecommunications technology services in their information technology (IT) infrastructures.

There are three steps to implementing a strategic telecommunications plan. Managers should begin with an audit of the firm's communications functions. What are the firm's voice, data, video, equipment, staffing, and management capabilities? What services are provided? What could be improved?

Next, managers should identify the long-range business plans of their firm. Their plan should include an analysis of how telecommunications will contribute to the specific five-year goals of the firm and enhance its competitive position. Managers need to ask how telecommunications can reduce agency costs by increasing the scale and scope of operations without additional management. They need to determine if telecommunications technology can help them differentiate products and services, or if it can improve the firm's cost structure by eliminating intermediaries such as distributors or by accelerating business processes.

Finally, managers should identify those critical areas where telecommunications applications could make a large difference in performance. In insurance, these may be systems that give field representatives quick access to policy and rate information; in retailing, inventory control and market penetration; and in industrial products, rapid, efficient distribution and transportation. They should then determine whether these applications require technology platforms that would require modifying the firm's IT infrastructure.

Implementing the Plan

Managers should take eight factors into account when designing networks and selecting telecommunications applications and services.

The first and most important factor is distance. Will most communication be local within a single business unit or will it encompass multiple business units at widely scattered locations? How much does the organization expect to communicate electronically with business units abroad or with faraway customers and suppliers?

Along with distance, managers must consider the range of services company networks must support, such as electronic mail, EDI, internally generated transactions, voice mail, videoconferencing, or imaging, and whether these services must be integrated in the same network. Will additional telecommunications services be required if the firm becomes heavily involved in electronic commerce?

A third factor to consider is security. The most secure means of long-distance communications is through lines that are owned by the organization. The next secure form of telecommunications is through leased, dedicated lines. VANs, ordinary telephone lines, wireless media, and the Internet are less secure.

A fourth factor to consider is multiple access. Will proposed applications need to be accessed by many users throughout the organization, or can access be limited to one or two node points in the network? If the application will be used by several thousand people in many different locations, a commonly available technology such as installed telephone wire is appropriate. However, if access is restricted to fewer than 100 high-intensity users in one building or campus, a high-bandwidth LAN may be recommended.

A fifth and most difficult factor to judge is utilization. There are two aspects of utilization that must be considered when developing a network: the frequency and the volume of communications. Together, these two factors determine the total load on the telecommunications system. On the one hand, high-frequency, high-volume communications suggest the need for high-speed LANs for local communication and leased lines for long-distance communication. On the other hand, low-frequency, low-volume communications may suggest dial-up, voice-grade telephone circuits operating through a traditional modem.

A sixth factor is cost. How much does each option cost? Total costs should include development, operations, maintenance, expansion, and overhead. Which cost components are fixed? Which are variable? Are there any hidden costs to anticipate? It is wise to recall the thruway effect. The easier it is to use a communications path, the more people want to use it. Most telecommunications planners estimate future needs on the high side yet still often underestimate the actual need. Underestimating the cost of telecommunications projects or uncontrollable telecommunications costs are principal causes of network failure.

Seventh, managers must consider the difficulties of installing the telecommunications system. Are the organization's buildings properly constructed to install fiber optics? In some instances, buildings have inadequate wiring channels underneath the floors, which makes installation of fiber-optic cable extremely difficult.

Table 7-6	Implementation Factors in Telecommunications Systems

Distance	Utilization
Range of services	Cost
Security	Installation
Multiple access	Connectivity

Eighth, management must consider how much connectivity would be required to make all of the components in a network communicate with each other or to tie together multiple networks. To what extent should telecommunications services be standardized throughout the firm? Will the firm be communicating with customers and suppliers using different technology platforms? We already have described some of the major connectivity standards. Internet technology could be used for this purpose. Table 7-6 summarizes these implementation factors.

MANAGEMENT WRAP-UP

Management

Managers need to be continuously involved in telecommunications decisions because so many important business processes are based on telecommunications and networks. Management should identify the business opportunities linked to telecommunications technology and establish the business criteria for selecting the firm's telecommunications platform. Some measure of management control should be maintained as computing power is distributed throughout the organization.

Organization

Telecommunications technology enables organizations to reduce transaction and coordination costs, thus promoting electronic commerce and electronic business. The organization's telecommunications infrastructure should support its business processes and business strategy.

Technology

Telecommunications technology is intertwined with all the other information technologies and deeply embedded in contemporary information systems. Networks are becoming more pervasive and powerful, and now have capabilities to transmit voice, data, and video over long distances. Key telecommunications technology decisions should consider network reliability, security, bandwidth, and connectivity and the role of networks and telecommunications services in the firm's information technology (IT) infrastructure.

For Discussion

1. Network design is a key business decision as well as a technology decision. Why?

2. If you were an international company with global operations, what criteria would you use to determine whether to use a value-added network (VAN) service or a private wide area network (WAN)?

SUMMARY

1. Describe the basic components of a telecommunications system. A telecommunications system is a set of compatible devices that are used to develop a network for communication from one location to another by electronic means. The essential components of a telecommunications system are computers, terminals, other input/output devices, communications channels, communications processors (such as modems, multiplexers, controllers, and front-end processors), and telecommunications software. Different components of a telecommunications network can communicate with each other with a common set of rules termed *protocols*. Data are transmitted throughout a telecommunications network using either analog signals or digital signals. A modem is a device that translates analog signals to digital signals and vice versa.

2. Calculate the capacity of telecommunications channels and evaluate transmission media. The capacity of a telecommunications channel is determined by the range of frequencies it can accommodate. The higher the range of frequencies, called *bandwidth,* the higher the capacity (measured in bits per second). The principal transmission media are twisted copper telephone wire; coaxial copper cable; fiber-optic cable; and wireless transmission using microwave, satellite, low-frequency radio waves, or infrared waves.

3. Compare the various types of telecommunications networks and network services. Networks can be classified by their shape or configuration, by their geographic scope, and by the type of services provided. The three common network topologies are the star network, the bus network, and the ring network. In a star network, all communications must pass through a central computer. The bus network links a number of devices to a single channel and broadcasts all of the signals to the entire network, with special software to identify which components receive each message. In a ring network, each computer in the network can communicate directly with any other computer but the channel is a closed loop. Data are passed along the ring from one computer to another.

Local area networks (LANs) and private branch exchanges (PBXs) are used to link offices and buildings in close proximity. Wide area networks (WANs) span a broad geographical distance, ranging from several miles to continents and are private networks that are independently managed. Value-added networks (VANs) also encompass a wide geographic area but are managed by a third party, which sells the services of the network to other companies. Other important network services include packet switching, frame relay, asynchronous transfer mode (ATM), ISDN, DSL, cable modem, and T1 lines.

4. Describe the features of the new information technology (IT) infrastructure and important connectivity standards. The new information technology (IT) infrastructure uses a mixture of computer hardware supplied by different vendors, including mainframes, PCs, and servers, which are networked to each other. More processing power resides on the desktop through client/server computing. Mobile personal information devices provide remote access to the desktop from outside the organization. The new information technology (IT) infrastructure also incorporates public infrastructures, such as the telephone system, the Internet, and public network services and electronic devices.

Connectivity is a measure of how well computers and computer-based devices can communicate with one another and "share" information in a meaningful way without human intervention. It is essential in enterprise networking in the new information technology infrastructure, where different hardware, software, and network components must work together to transfer information seamlessly from one part of the organization to another. TCP/IP and OSI are important reference models for achieving connectivity in networks. Each divides the communications process into layers. Unix is an operating system standard that can be used to create open systems as can the Linux operating system. Connectivity also can be achieved using Internet technology and Java.

5. Identify the principal telecommunications technologies for supporting electronic commerce and electronic business. The principal telecommunications technologies for electronic commerce and electronic business are electronic mail, voice mail, fax, digital information services, teleconferencing, dataconferencing, videoconferencing, electronic data interchange (EDI), and groupware. Electronic data interchange is the computer-to-computer exchange, between two organizations, of standard transaction documents such as invoices, bills of lading, and purchase orders.

6. Analyze the management problems raised by the new information technology (IT) infrastructure and suggest solutions. Problems posed by the new IT infrastructure include loss of management control over systems; the need to carefully manage organizational change; connectivity issues; difficulty of ensuring network reliability, security, and bandwidth; and controlling the hidden costs of client/server computing.

Solutions include planning for and managing the business and organizational changes associated with enterprise-wide computing; increasing end-user training; asserting data administration disciplines; and considering connectivity, bandwidth, and cost controls when planning the information technology infrastructure. Firms should develop strategic telecommunications plans to ensure that their telecommunications systems serve business objectives and operations. Important factors to consider are distance, range of services, security, access, utilization, cost, installation, and connectivity.

KEY TERMS

REVIEW QUESTIONS

1. What is the significance of telecommunications deregulation for managers and organizations?

2. What is a telecommunications system? What are the principal functions of all telecommunications systems?

3. Name and briefly describe each of the components of a telecommunications system.

4. Distinguish between an analog and a digital signal.

5. Name the different types of telecommunications transmission media and compare them in terms of speed and cost.

6. What is the relationship between bandwidth and a channel's transmission capacity?

7. Name and briefly describe the different kinds of communications processors.

8. Name and briefly describe the three principal network topologies.

9. Distinguish between a PBX and a LAN.

10. List and describe the various network services.

11. Define the following: modem, baud, wide area network (WAN), enterprise networking, and internetworking.

12. What are the features of the new information technology (IT) infrastructure?

13. Why is connectivity so important for enterprise networking and internetworking?

14. Name and describe the telecommunications applications that can support electronic commerce and electronic business.

15. Describe four problems posed by the new information technology (IT) infrastructure and some solutions to these problems.

16. What are the principal factors to consider when developing a telecommunications plan for the new information technology (IT) infrastructure?

GROUP PROJECT

With a group of two or three of your fellow students, describe in detail the ways that telecommunications technology can provide a firm with competitive advantage. Use the companies described in Chapter 2 or other chapters you have read so far to illustrate the points you make, or select examples of other companies using telecommunications from business or computer magazincs. Present your findings to the class.

Tools for Interactive Learning

○ Internet Connection

The Internet Connection for this chapter will take you to the Rosenbluth Travel Web site where you can complete an exercise to analyze how Rosenbluth International uses the Web and communications technology in its daily operations. You can also use the Interactive Study Guide to test your knowledge of the topics in the chapter and get instant feedback where you need more practice.

○ Electronic Commerce Project

At the Laudon Web Site for Chapter 7, you will find an Electronic Commerce project that will use the interactive software at the Goodyear Web site to assist customers in making tire purchases.

○ CD-ROM

If you purchase and use the Multimedia Edition CD-ROM with this chapter, you can perform an interactive exercise to select an appropriate network topology for a series of business scenarios and identify the main issue your selection presents to management. You also can find a video demonstrating the capabilities of personal communication services, an audio overview of the major themes in this chapter, and bullet text summarizing the key points in the chapter.

○ Application Exercise

At the Laudon Web site, you can find an Application Exercise for this chapter, in which you can use Web browser software for information retrieval.

Monitoring Employees on Networks: Unethical or Good Business?

In the past few years the Internet has grown almost at the speed of light, and it has rapidly become deeply embedded in our business and personal lives. One consequence is that employees are using their corporate facilities to surf the Net and to use e-mail for personal reasons, and such personal use can be disruptive and costly. Companies are now beginning to face these problems, which in turn raises serious ethical issues. Is it ethical for employees to use the Net at work for personal reasons, as they often were accustomed to doing with the telephone? Are employers obligated to bear the costs of the private use of their facilities by their employees? Is it ethical for employers to monitor private activities of employees as long as those employees are meeting their work goals? We begin by looking at the many ways employees are using the Net at work and the potential costs to the employers. Then we examine the ways corporations are addressing the problem.

When employers first became aware of employees using the Internet for personal purposes, the major concern was that employees would visit pornography sites that might offend other employees, perhaps even leading to lawsuits. Then concern grew that there would be too many visits to sports sites and retail outlets. However, the problem is far larger than a little bit of time on a few sites.

SurfWatch Software, of Los Gatos, California, which produces software to monitor Internet use, found in a survey of its customers that nearly 25 percent of employee on-line time is spent on nonwork-related surfing. A study by New York-based Media Metrix Inc., which meters Internet use, found that 22.8 million Americans used Web sites for personal business during working hours in one month (March 1999).

Investment monitoring and trading has now become the most popular nonwork-related Web activity performed by employees on the job, and these visits are apparently mushrooming. The Media Metrix study concluded that the amount of time employees spent visiting the top 10 financial Web sites increased 60 percent from December 1998 to March 1999 (just 3 months)! Jill Munden, a manager at Silicon Investor Inc., the largest Internet financial discussion forum, reports that 50 percent of the visits to her site come during regular working hours. "I can't imagine that this is not a problem in the workplace," she concludes.

New technology, particularly Web technology, makes it easy for people not only to trade, but also to research and monitor their own investments much as professionals have always done. Although many people are driven by hopes for the future, others are coming to view active investment activity as a way to generate immediate supplementary income.

E-mail use has also exploded as people the world over turn to it for speedy, convenient, and inexpensive business and personal communications. Not surprisingly, the use of e-mail for personal reasons at the workplace has also grown. Managements fear that racist, sexually explicit, or other potentially offensive material might create problems in the workplace and could even result in adverse publicity and harassment lawsuits brought by workers. Companies also fear the loss of trade secrets through e-mail. Personal use of e-mail can even clog the company's network so that the business work cannot be done. At Lockheed Martin Corp., an employee sent an e-mail message concerning an upcoming religious holiday to all of the company's 150,000 employees, which locked up the entire network for 6 hours.

A study by the American Management Association concludes that 27 percent of large U.S. companies are now monitoring employee e-mail in some way compared to only 15 percent in 1997. "Every time there's a story [about e-mail problems], the tendency is to become more aggressive on e-mail monitoring," explains Eric Rolfe Greenberg, the director of management studies at the American Management Association.

If employees are using company Internet facilities for personal reasons, how much can it cost? The most obvious cost is the loss of time and employee productivity when employees are focusing on personal rather than company business. Interestingly, to date the U.S. government has been unable to measure any economic effect of such wasted time. Personal Web time may just be a substitute for water-cooler gossip and discussions of sports and movies. However, studies might not show a loss of productivity if most people don't tell their bosses or co-workers what they are doing because it is either against company policy or it is at least overtly being nonproductive during working hours. If you want to calculate the cost to a company, multiply the estimated average amount employees are paid for an hour's work by the number of hours lost for the average employee, and then multiply the results by the number of employees involved. The number can be very large indeed.

An often-ignored but potentially critical cost is the effect personal Internet activities can have on the availability of the company's network bandwidth. If personal traffic is too high, it will interfere with the company's ability to carry on its business. The company may then have to expand its bandwidth, an expensive and time-consuming activity, or reduce the bandwidth drain by reducing or eliminating use of the Internet for personal business. Norcross, Georgia, civil-engineering firm Wolverton & Associate Inc. installed Telemate.Net monitoring software and found that broadcast.com was the third most visited site and consumed 4 percent of the company's bandwidth. Employees were using it to download music for themselves. E*trade, which soaked up another 3 percent of Wolverton's bandwidth, is just one of many on-line securities trading sites that employees were visiting. Douglas Dahlberg, Wolverton's IT manager, points out that bandwidth is critical to the company's operations because Wolverton engineers regularly send very large data-laden CAD files to their clients through e-mail.

Too much time on personal business, Internet or not, can mean lost revenue or overcharges to clients. Some employees may be charging time they spend trading stocks or pursuing other personal business to clients, thus overcharging the clients.

When employees access the Web using employer facilities, anything they do on the Web, including anything illegal, carries the company's name. Therefore, the employer can be traced and held liable. However, even if the company is found not to be liable, responding to lawsuits will likely cost the company tens of thousands of dollars at a minimum. In addition, lawsuits often result in adverse publicity for the company regardless of outcome. Even if lawsuits do not result, companies are often embarrassed by the publicity that can surround the on-line actions by a company's employees. Problems can arise not only from illegalities but also through very legal activities, such as employee participation in chat rooms society finds unacceptable. For example, employee participation in white power or anti-Semitic chat rooms can produce a public relations nightmare.

How has management been addressing these problems? Consultants in the technology field recommend that companies begin with a written corporate policy. However, studies show that relatively few companies have written Internet usage policies that specifically address such problems as on-line investing during work. A **Computerworld** survey of 102 network administrators found that 55 percent noticed employees visiting investment sites during working hours. Yet only 40 percent of their companies have written policies that prohibit such activities. And, in turn, only 25 percent of these specifically mention on-line trading in their policies.

What should the policies contain? They must include explicit ground rules that are written in clear, easily understood English. They should state, by position or level, who has the right to access what and under what circumstances they may access it. Naturally, the rules must be tailored to the specific organization because different companies may need to access different Web materials as part of their businesses. For example, although some companies may exclude anyone from visiting sites that have explicit sexual material, law firms or hospital employees may require access to such sites, and investment firms will need to allow many of their employees access to other investment sites.

Some companies want to ban all personal activities—zero tolerance. American Fast Freight policy, for example, bans any on-line activity "not specifically and exclusively work related." Ameritech Corp.'s policy stated that company equipment, including computers, "are to be used only to provide service to customers and for other business purposes." This policy ensured employees were focused on serving customers.

Many companies reject the zero tolerance approach because they believe they must allow employees to conduct some personal business during working hours. Bell South had once instituted a zero tol-

erance policy, but it softened that policy in the summer of 1998. Management had received many complaints from its employees. For example, some employees were afraid to give their business e-mail address for simple things like weekend soccer club notifications. Under Bell South's new policy, when employees log on they must read a warning about misuse of the Internet and e-mail and then click "OK" before they are allowed to continue. In this manner employees are repeatedly reminded to limit their personal activities. Employees also know by the warning screen that they might be monitored. Why did they soften their policy? According to Jerry Guthrie, Bell South's ethics officer, "We work long hours—we wanted to offer it as a benefit to employees."

Clear policy rules and guidelines can be very difficult to write. An individual act, such as a visit to a stockbroker to execute an order, may be acceptable, whereas repeated visits in order to monitor that stock might not be. Many find it impossible to draw a clear line between what is acceptable and what constitutes too much. For example, Boeing Corp. specifically allows employees to use the Internet, e-mail, and even fax machines for personal reasons, but the guidelines are vague, saying the use must be of "reasonable duration and frequency." Such indefinite terms may be difficult for employees and employers to apply fairly, and yet it is even more of a problem to achieve more precision. Some companies are even less specific, but at least they have all made it clear that anything the employee does for personal reasons cannot be considered private. Moreover, they usually indicate that employees may be disciplined for misuse of the company's facilities, which serves as an effective warning that employees will be monitored and will be held to a standard.

How valuable are policies and warnings? They do warn employees and so hopefully reduce misuse. At the same time they protect the company from any lawsuits by employees if the company does take action. In one instance Columbia/MCAHealthcare Corp. warned employees that "It is sometimes necessary for authorized personnel to access and monitor their contents," adding that "[i]n some situations the company may be required to publicly disclose e-mail messages, even those marked private." Some companies follow a potentially more effective strategy, combining policies and warnings with

filtering or monitoring software (discussed later).

Education should also play a key role. Lockheed Martin Corp., the giant aerospace company, goes much further. It requires all of its 150,000 employees to complete an extensive ethical training course on-line that includes material on the proper use of the company's Internet facilities.

One approach that some companies use is to block all employee access to specific sites. **Computerworld**'s survey of 102 network administrators found only 8 of the companies actually did block access to investment Web sites. Other solutions short of total blockage also exist. Content Technologies Inc., of Kirkland, Washington, produces software that prevents employees from opening executable files. This software allows people to visit the site but also effectively prevents them from placing orders. Not all agree that this approach is effective, however, because employees could pick up the phone to execute the trade, and that still costs employee time. Dahlberg solved his music-downloading problem by removing RealAudio music playing capability from all of Wolverton's systems.

Yet another approach used by many companies is to limit the Web sites employees can visit. SurfWatch software can be used by employers to allow visits to certain sites, such as investment sites, only during specific hours, such as during the lunch hour and before and after normal working hours.

Many companies are turning to software packages to monitor the Internet activities of their employees. Fearing uses of the Internet for other-than-business purposes, George Brandt, business manager of KBHK-TV, San Francisco, decided to use the Elron CommandView Internet Manager to monitor employee Internet usage. This software monitors Internet usage, records the data, and then allows managers to print detailed analyses of that usage. Managers can determine who visits what sites, how often an individual or a group visits a specific site, and how long those visits are. At first Brandt found extensive recreational surfing. Soon thereafter, however, once people were fully aware that they were being monitored, such usage clearly declined, and concurrently employee productivity increased.

Some companies may use monitoring software but prefer the personal approach for dealing with individual offenders.

When David Kroening, assistant director of technology and operations at New York law firm Epstein, Becker, and Green, PC, discovers a potential offender, he notifies the manager of the individual and asks that person to handle it. "It's more of a personal issue [than a technical one] now," he explains. Roy Crooks, director of information technology at Bard Manufacturing, Inc., uses monitoring software to find out who is creating a problem. Rather than turn the solution over to the offenders' managers, he attempts to solve the problems himself by talking with them personally.

A number of corporations are trying to limit on-line personal activity to an acceptable amount of time rather than trying to shut if off completely. This policy is a natural extension of one many employers followed well before the Internet explosion when they allowed employees to take care of personal business during working hours within limits. Cellular One developed a rule-of-thumb measure of how much time is reasonable. Employees spending more than half an hour on personal or recreational browsing will likely end up on a list of potential Internet abusers. The individuals who are judged as having abused the privilege can have their Internet access taken away. American Fast Freight established a policy that prohibited employees from visiting on-line investing sites during working hours but allows it during lunch and before and after work.

Some companies occasionally turn to the ultimate punishment: firing employees judged to be offenders. Some managers consider firing to send a strong, quick message to the remaining employees. The New York Times Company fired more than 20 employees from its Norfolk, Virginia, payroll center in early December 1999 for "inappropriate and offensive" e-mails. Other employees were sent disciplinary warning letters. An internal memo to employees explained that, "While the company does not routinely monitor the e-mail communications of employees, we do investigate when a violation of the company's e-mail policy is reported." Xerox Corp. fired 40 workers in 1999 for violating the company's Internet use policy. Some of them were dismissed because they had visited pornographic Web sites.

No solution is problem free. Instituting any policy can create a great deal of controversy and may even result in lawsuits, particularly if employees have not been clearly warned about new policies. Often, employers hear charges of unethical or improper spying from their staffs. Even warnings do not always work. Wolverton's Dahlberg warned the company's small staff of only 36 employees that they would be monitored before the company installed the monitoring software. But warnings "just mustn't sink in," said Dahlberg. "I can see every little Web page you read—and still there were problems."

Sources: Michael J. McCarthy, "Web Surfers Beware: The Company Tech May Be a Secret Agent," The Wall Street Journal, January 10, 2000; "U.S. Web Use Mostly at Work," Reuters, April 6, 2000; Lisa I. Fried, "Employers Crack Down on Personal Internet Use," New York Law Journal, January 3, 2000; Stacy Collett, "Net Managers Battle Online Trading Boom," Computerworld, July 5, 1999; Robert D. Hershey, Jr., "Some Abandon the Water Cooler for Stock Trading on the Internet," The New York Times, May 20, 1999; Michael J. McCarthy, "How One Firm Tracks Ethics Electronically," The Wall Street Journal, October 21, 1999; Michael J. McCarthy, "Now the Boss Knows Where You're Clicking," The Wall Street Journal, October 21, 1999; Michael J. McCarthy, "Virtual Morality: A New Workplace Quandary," The Wall Street Journal, October 21, 1999; Kathryn F. Munro, "Hands Off," Small Business Computing and Communications, June 1999; and Nick Wingfield, "More Companies Monitor Employees' E-Mail," The Wall Street Journal, December 2, 1999.

CASE STUDY QUESTIONS

1. Is it ethical for employers simply to check e-mail on a fishing expedition (that is, without having any specific reason to suspect that an employee has a problem that needs to be addressed)? Explain your answer.

2. If employees complain about an undue invasion of privacy, how can management determine if the employee's complaints are legitimate?

3. Write a rationale that would ban all employee personal use of the Internet including e-mail and the Web.

4. Evaluate as an effective tool a zero tolerance position (firing of employees any time an Internet access rule is broken). If you do not believe zero tolerance is an appropriate policy, under what circumstances would you support firing an employee for using the Internet or e-mail while on the job?

5. Write what you consider to be an effective e-mail and Web use policy for a company. Briefly describe the company and then explain your reasoning for its details.

CHAPTER 8

The Internet: Electronic Commerce and Electronic Business

Learning Objectives

After completing this chapter, you will be able to:

1. Describe how the Internet works and identify its major capabilities.

2. Identify benefits the Internet offers organizations.

3. Demonstrate how the Internet can be used for electronic commerce.

4. Demonstrate how Internet technology can be used to create private intraorganizational and interorganizational networks, and describe how these networks are used for electronic business.

5. Examine the challenges the Internet poses to businesses and society.

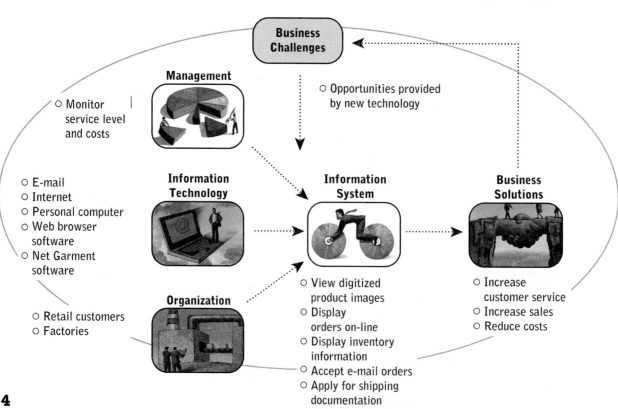

Business Challenges

Management

○ Opportunities provided by new technology

○ Monitor service level and costs

Information Technology

○ E-mail
○ Internet
○ Personal computer
○ Web browser software
○ Net Garment software

○ Retail customers
○ Factories

Organization

Information System

○ View digitized product images
○ Display orders on-line
○ Display inventory information
○ Accept e-mail orders
○ Apply for shipping documentation

Business Solutions

○ Increase customer service
○ Increase sales
○ Reduce costs

A Family Garment Business
Goes Global on the Internet

Lee Hung Fat Garment Factory Ltd. in Hong Kong supplies apparel such as leather jeans or denim jackets to about 60 companies in Europe, including Kaufhof Warenhaus AG in Germany and Woolworth's, a unit of Kingfisher PLC in Britain. The company employs about 2,000 workers in factories in China, Hong Kong, and Bangladesh and earns more than $40 million in revenue each year.

Using ordinary desktop PCs connected to the Internet, the company has linked into global supply chains and boosted efficiency. When the company was founded 35 years ago, overseas orders came by messenger from one of the big Hong Kong trading companies. Today, Lee Hung Fat receives garment specifications from its customers on a desktop computer terminal connected to the Internet. As a result, business processes that used to take five weeks to complete in the 1970s can be completed in one day today.

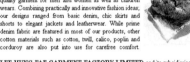

Lee Hung Fat turned to the Internet because so many of its customers were multinational companies that were using computers and networks to increase efficiency. The company also saw opportunities in using Internet technology to cut its own operating costs. After purchasing PCs in the early 1990s, the company installed NetGarment, a software system for the clothing industry. In 1996 the company began accepting customer orders via e-mail, and the following year it set up its own Web site.

Eddy Wong Fung-Ming, the company's operations director, can call up a customer order on his IBM desktop PC. With the click of a mouse, he can see details including production at company factories in China and Bangladesh, shipping schedules, and individual customer accounts. Each order can be simultaneously transmitted to any department involved in filling it, including the people responsible for making sure enough buttons are available.

Bills for telephone calls and faxes to factories and overseas customers used to cost Lee Hung Fat about $10,000 per month because the company sent about 2,000 faxes per day. The company still does some faxing, but it has switched to Internet e-mail for most of its communication, reducing its monthly bills by one-third. Mr. Wong can check his e-mail messages while he is on the golf course using a mobile telephone.

There are many other ways that using the Internet is saving money and manpower while bringing the company closer to its customers. Mr. Wong can apply over the Internet for required documentation to ship goods, a process that used to require an employee to visit the trade department and apply for an export license. Instead of sending mock-up samples of garments to buyers overseas by courier or through the mail, Mr. Wong can take a picture of the garment using a camera mounted on his PC and send the picture over the Internet. He can also scan a picture of the sample and send that to the customer, who can experiment with the cloth patterns or stitching and send back a new version. Samples are approved three or four times faster than before. Wong estimates that computers and Internet technology have saved the company between 15 percent and 20 percent in initial production costs alone.

Sources: Jonathan Weber, "The Net World Order," *The Industry Standard,* February 14, 2000; S. Karene Witcher, " Family Garment Business in Hong Kong Uses Internet to Gain Access to Global Customer Pool," *The Wall Street Journal,* November 24, 1999; and www.leehungfat.com.hk.

MANAGEMENT CHALLENGES

Like Lee Hung Fat Garment Factory, many companies are starting to use the Internet to communicate with both their customers and suppliers, creating new digital electronic commerce networks that bypass traditional distribution channels. They are using Internet technology to streamline their internal business processes as well. The Internet, the Web, and intranets can help companies achieve new levels of competitiveness and efficiency, but they raise the following management challenges:

1. **Internet computing requires a complete change of mindset.** To implement Internet technology for electronic commerce and electronic business successfully, companies may need to make organizational changes. They must examine and perhaps redesign an entire business process rather than implement new technology in existing business practices. Companies must consider a different organizational structure, changes in organizational culture, a different support structure for information systems, different procedures for managing employees and networked processing functions, and perhaps a different business strategy.

2. **Finding a successful Internet business model.** Companies are racing to put up Web sites in the hope of increasing earnings through electronic commerce. However, many electronic commerce sites have yet to turn a profit or to make a tangible difference in firms' sales and marketing efforts. Cost savings or access to new markets promised by the Web may not materialize. Companies need to think carefully about whether they can create a genuinely workable business model on the Internet and how the Internet relates to their overall business strategy.

The Internet has opened up many exciting possibilities for organizing and running a business that are transforming organizations and the use of information systems in everyday life. It is creating a universal technology platform for buying and selling goods and for driving important business processes inside the firm. Along with bringing many new benefits and opportunities, the Internet has created a new set of management challenges.

We describe these challenges so that organizations can understand the management, organization, and technology issues that must be addressed to benefit from the Internet, electronic commerce, and electronic business.

8.1 The Internet: Information Technology Infrastructure for Electronic Commerce and Electronic Business

The Internet is perhaps the most well-known, and the largest, implementation of internetworking, linking hundreds of thousands of individual networks all over the world. The Internet has a range of capabilities that organizations are using to exchange information internally or to communicate externally with other organizations. This giant network of networks has become the primary infrastructure for both electronic commerce and electronic business.

WHAT IS THE INTERNET?

The Internet began as a U.S. Department of Defense network to link scientists and university professors around the world. Even today individuals cannot connect directly to the Net, although anyone with a computer, a modem, and the willingness to pay a small monthly usage fee can access it through an Internet Service Provider. An **Internet Service Provider (ISP)** is a commercial organization with a permanent connection to the Internet that sells temporary connections to subscribers. Individuals also can access the Internet through such popular on-line services as Prodigy and America Online and through networks established by such giants as Microsoft and AT&T.

> **Internet Service Provider (ISP)** A commercial organization with a permanent connection to the Internet that sells temporary connections to subscribers.

Some of the most puzzling aspects of the Internet are that no one owns it and it has no formal management organization. As a creation of the Defense Department for sharing research data, this lack of centralization made it less vulnerable to wartime or terrorist attacks. To join the Internet, an existing network need only pay a small registration fee and agree to certain standards based on the TCP/IP (Transmission Control Protocol/Internet Protocol) reference model, which was described in Chapter 7. Costs are low because the Internet owns nothing and so has no costs to offset. Each organization, of course, pays for its own networks and its own telephone bills, but those costs usually exist independent of the Internet. Regional Internet companies have been established to which member networks forward all transmissions. These Internet companies route and forward all traffic, and the cost is still only that of a local telephone call. The result is that the costs of e-mail and other Internet connections tend to be far lower than equivalent voice, postal, or overnight delivery, making the Net a very inexpensive communications medium. It is also a very fast method of communication, with messages arriving anywhere in the world in a matter of seconds or a minute or two at most. We now briefly describe the most important Internet capabilities.

INTERNET TECHNOLOGY AND CAPABILITIES

The Internet is based on client/server technology. Individuals using the Net control what they do through client applications such as Web browser software. All the data, including e-mail messages and Web pages, are stored on servers. A client uses the Internet to request information from a particular Web server on a distant computer, and the server sends the requested information back to the client via the Internet.

Client platforms today include not only PCs and other computers but also a wide array of handheld devices and information appliances, some of which can even provide wireless Internet access. Table 8-1 lists some of the client devices, most of which were described in Chapters 4 and 7. Experts believe that the role of the PC or desktop computer as the Internet client is diminishing as people turn to these easy-to-use specialized information appliances to connect to the Internet.

Servers dedicated to the Internet or even to specific Internet services are the heart of the information on the Net. Each Internet service is implemented by one or more software programs. All of the services may run on a single server computer, as illustrated in Figure 8-1, or different services may be allocated to different machines. There may be only one disk storing the data for these services, or there may be multiple disks for each type, depending on the amount of information being stored.

Table 8-1 Examples of Internet Client Platforms

Device	Description	Example
PC	General purpose computing platform that can perform many different tasks, but can be unreliable or complex to use	Dell, Compaq, IBM PCs
Net PC	Network computer with minimal local storage and processing capability; designed to use software and services delivered over networks and the Internet	Sun Ray
Pager	Provides limited e-mail and Web browsing	Blackberry (blackberry.net)
Smart Phone	Device with a small screen and keyboard for browsing the Web and exchanging e-mail in addition to providing voice communication	Qualcomm pdQ™ smart phone
Game Machine	Game machine with a modem, keyboard, and capabilities to function as a Web access terminal	Sega Dreamcast (sega.com)
PDA	Wireless handheld personal digital assistant with e-mail and Internet service	Palm VII
E-mail machine	Tablet with keyboard that provides textual e-mail capabilities; requires linking to an e-mail service	MailStation (www.cidco.com)
Set top box	Provides Web surfing and e-mail capabilities using a television set and a wireless keyboard	WebTV (www.webtv.com)

Web server software receives requests for Web pages from the client and accesses the Web pages from the disk where they are stored. Web servers can also access other information from an organization's internal information system applications and their associated databases and return that information to the client in the form of Web pages if desired. Specialized middleware, including application servers and custom programs, is used to manage the interactions between the Web server and the organization's internal information systems for processing orders, tracking inventory, maintaining product catalogs, and other electronic commerce functions. For example, if a customer filled out an on-line form on a Web page to order a product such as a light fixture, the middleware would translate the request on the Web page into commands that could be used by the company's internal order processing system and customer database.

The most important Internet capabilities for business include e-mail, Usenet newsgroups, LISTSERVs, chatting, Telnet, FTP, gophers, and the World Wide Web. They can be used to retrieve and offer information. Table 8-2 lists these capabilities and describes the functions they support.

Internet Tools for Communication

Electronic Mail (E-Mail)   The Net has become the most important e-mail system in the world because it connects so many people worldwide, creating a productivity gain that observers have compared to Gutenberg's development of movable type in the fifteenth century. Organizations use it to facilitate communication between employees and offices and to communicate with customers and suppliers.

Researchers use this facility to share ideas, information, even documents. E-mail over the Net also has made possible many collaborative research and writing projects, even though the participants are thousands of miles apart. With proper software, the user will find it easy to attach documents and multimedia files when sending a message to someone or to broadcast a message to a predefined group. Figure 8-2 illustrates the components of an Internet e-mail address.

The portion of the address to the left of the @ symbol in Net e-mail addresses is the name or identifier of the specific individual or organization. To the right of the @ symbol is the domain name. The **domain name** is the unique name of a collection of computers connected to the Internet. The domain contains subdomains separated by a period. The domain that is far-

domain name The unique name of a collection of computers connected to the Internet.

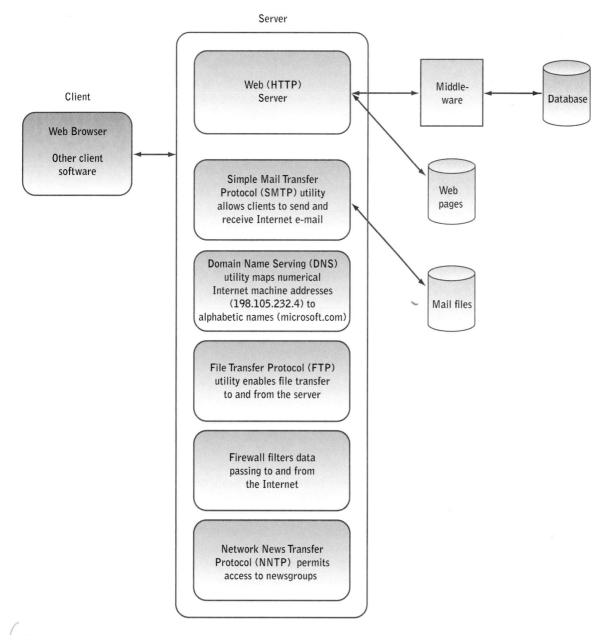

FIGURE 8-1 Client/server computing on the Internet. Client computers running Web browser and other software can access an array of services on servers via the Internet. The services may all run on a single server or on multiple specialized servers.

thest to the right is the top level domain, and each domain to the left helps further define the domain by network, department, and even specific computer. The top level domain name may be either a country indicator or a function indicator, such as *com* for a commercial organization or *gov* for a government institution. All e-mail addresses end with a country indicator except those in the United States, which ordinarily does not use one. In Figure 8-2, *it,* the top level domain, is a country indicator, indicating that the address is in Italy. *Edu* indicates that the address is an educational institution; *univpisa* (University of Pisa) indicates the specific location of the host computer.

Usenet Newsgroups (Forums) **Usenet** newsgroups are worldwide discussion groups in which people share information and ideas on a defined topic such as radiology or rock bands. Discussion takes place in large electronic bulletin boards where anyone can post messages for

Usenet Forums in which people share information and ideas on a defined topic through large electronic bulletin boards where anyone can post messages on the topic that others can see and to which they can respond.

Table 8-2 Major Internet Capabilities

Capability	Functions Supported
E-mail	Person-to-person messaging; document sharing
Usenet newsgroups	Discussion groups on electronic bulletin boards
LISTSERVs	Discussion groups using e-mail mailing list servers
Chatting	Interactive conversations
Telnet	Log on to one computer system and do work on another
FTP	Transfer files from computer to computer
Gophers	Locate information using a hierarchy of menus
World Wide Web	Retrieve, format, and display information (including text, audio, graphics, and video) using hypertext links

others to read. Almost 20,000 groups exist discussing almost all conceivable topics. Each Usenet site is financed and administered independently.

LISTSERV On-line discussion groups using e-mail broadcast from mailing list servers.

LISTSERV A second type of public forum, **LISTSERV,** allows discussions to be conducted through predefined groups but uses e-mail mailing list servers instead of bulletin boards for communications. If you find a LISTSERV topic you are interested in, you may subscribe. From then on, through your e-mail, you will receive all messages sent by others concerning that topic. You can, in turn, send a message to your LISTSERV and it will automatically be broadcast to the other subscribers. Tens of thousands of LISTSERV groups exist.

chatting Live, interactive conversations over a public network.

Chatting Chatting allows two or more people who are simultaneously connected to the Internet to hold live, interactive conversations. Chat groups are divided into channels, and each is assigned its own topic of conversation. The first generation of chat tools was for written conversations in which participants type their remarks using their keyboard and read responses on their computer screen. Systems featuring voice chat capabilities, such as those offered by HearMe and Excite, are now becoming popular.

instant messaging Chat service that allows participants to create their own private chat channels so that a person can be alerted whenever someone on his or her private list is on-line to initiate a chat session with that particular individual.

A new enhancement to chat service called **instant messaging** even allows participants to create their own private chat channels. The instant messaging system alerts a person whenever someone on his or her private list is on-line so that the person can initiate a chat session with that particular individual. There are several competing instant messaging systems including Yahoo Messenger and America Online's Instant Messenger. Some of these systems can provide voice-based instant messages so that a user can click on a "talk" button and have an on-line conversation with another person.

Chatting can be an effective business tool if people who benefit from interactive conversations set an appointed time to "meet" and "talk" on a particular topic. Many on-line retailers are enhancing their Web sites with chat services to attract visitors, to encourage repeat purchases, and to improve customer service.

FIGURE 8-2 Analysis of an Internet address. In English, the e-mail address of physicist and astronomer Galileo Galilei would be translated as "G. Galileo @ University of Pisa, educational institution, Italy." The domain name to the right of the @ symbol contains a country indicator, a function indicator, and the location of the host computer.

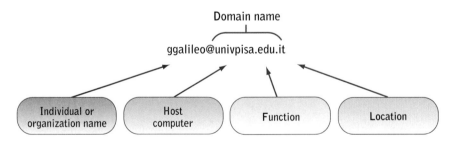

Telnet   **Telnet** allows someone to log on to one computer system while doing work on another. Telnet is the protocol that establishes an error-free, rapid link between the two computers, allowing you, for example, to log on to your business computer from a remote computer when you are on the road or working from home. You can also log on to use third-party computers that are accessible to the public, such as the catalog of the U.S. Library of Congress. Telnet uses the computer address you supply to locate the computer you want to reach and connect you to it.

Telnet Network tool that allows someone to log on to one computer system while doing work on another.

Information Retrieval on the Internet

Information retrieval is a second basic Internet function. Many hundreds of library catalogs are on-line through the Internet, including those of such giants as the Library of Congress, the University of California, and Harvard University. In addition, users are able to search many thousands of databases that have been opened to the public by corporations, governments, and nonprofit organizations. Individuals can gather information on almost any conceivable topic stored in these databases and libraries. Many use the Internet to locate and download some of the free, quality computer software that has been made available by developers on computers all over the world.

The Internet is a voluntary, decentralized effort with no central listing of participants or sites, much less a listing of the data located at those sites, so a major problem is finding what you need from among the storehouses of data found in databases and libraries. Here we introduce two important methods of accessing computers and locating files. We discuss additional information-retrieval methods in the next section on the World Wide Web.

FTP   **File transfer protocol (FTP)** is used to access a remote computer and retrieve files from it. FTP is quick and easy if you know the remote computer site where the file is stored. After you have logged on to the remote computer, you can move around directories that have been made accessible for FTP to search for the file(s) you want to retrieve. Once they are located, FTP makes transfer of the file to your own computer very easy.

file transfer protocol (FTP) Tool for retrieving and transferring files from a remote computer.

Gophers   Many files and digital information resources that are accessible through FTP also are available through gophers. A **gopher** is a computer client tool that enables the user to locate information stored on Internet gopher servers through a series of easy-to-use, hierarchical menus. The Internet has thousands of gopher server sites throughout the world. Each gopher site contains its own system of menus listing subject-matter topics, local files, and other relevant gopher sites. One gopher site might have as many as several thousand listings within its menus. When you use gopher software to search a specific topic and select a related item from a menu, the server automatically transfers you to the appropriate file on that server or to the selected server on which it is located. Once on that server, the process continues: You are presented with more menus of files and other gopher site servers that might interest you. You can move from site to site, narrowing your search as you go, locating information anywhere in the world. With descriptive menu listings linked to other gopher sites, you do not need to know in advance where relevant files are stored or the exact FTP address of a specific computer.

gopher A tool that enables the user to locate information stored on Internet servers through a series of easy-to-use, hierarchical menus.

THE WORLD WIDE WEB

The World Wide Web (the Web) is at the heart of the explosion in the business use of the Net. The Web is a system of universally accepted standards for storing, retrieving, formatting, and displaying information using a client/server architecture. It was developed to allow collaborators in remote sites to share their ideas on all aspects of a common project. If the Web was used for two independent projects and later relationships were found between the projects, information could flow smoothly between the projects without making major changes (Berners-Lee et al., 1994).

The Web combines text, hypermedia, graphics, and sound. It can handle all types of digital communication and makes it easy to link resources that are half-a-world apart. The Web uses graphical user interfaces for easy viewing. It is based on a standard hypertext language called Hypertext Markup Language (HTML), which formats documents and incorporates dynamic links to other documents and pictures stored in the same or remote computers. (We described HTML in Chapter 5.) Using these links, the user need only point at a highlighted key word or graphic, click on it, and immediately be transported to another document, probably on another computer somewhere else in the world. Users are free to jump from place to place following their own logic and interest.

Web browser software is programmed according to HTML standards (see Chapter 5). The standard is universally accepted, so anyone using a browser can access any of the millions of Web sites. Browsers use hypertext's point-and-click ability to navigate or *surf*—move from site to site on the Web—to another desired site. The browser also includes an arrow or back button to enable the user to retrace his or her steps, navigating back, site by site.

Those who offer information through the Web must establish a **home page**—a text and graphical screen display that usually welcomes the user and explains the organization that has established the page. For most organizations, the home page leads users to other pages, and all the pages of a company are known as its *Web site.* For a corporation to establish a presence on the Web, therefore, it must set up a Web site of one or more pages. Most Web pages offer a way to contact the organization. The individual in charge of an organization's Web site is called a **Webmaster.**

To access a Web site, the user must specify a **uniform resource locator (URL),** which points to the address of a specific resource on the Web. For instance, the URL for Prentice Hall, the publisher of this text, is

http://www.prenhall.com

Http stands for **hypertext transport protocol,** which is the communications standard used to transfer pages on the Web. Http defines how messages are formatted and transmitted and what actions Web servers and browsers should take in response to various commands. *Www.prenhall.com* is the domain name identifying the Web server storing the Web pages.

Searching for Information on the Web

Locating information on the Web is a critical function given the hundreds of millions of Web sites in existence. No comprehensive catalog of Web sites exists. The principal methods of locating information on the Web are Web site directories, search engines, and broadcast or "push" technology.

Several companies have created directories of Web sites and their addresses, which provide search tools for finding information. Yahoo! is an example. People or organizations submit sites of interest, which then are classified. To search the directory, you enter one or more key words and see a list of categories and sites displayed with those key words in the title.

Some search tools do not require Web sites to be preclassified and will search Web pages on their own automatically. Such tools, called **search engines,** can find Web sites that may be little known. They contain software that looks for Web pages containing one or more of the search terms; then they display matches ranked by a method that usually involves the location and frequency of the search terms. These search engines do not display information about every site on the Web, but they create indexes of the Web pages they visit. The search engine software then locates Web pages of interest by searching through the indexes. AltaVista, Lycos, and GO.com are examples of search engines. Some are more comprehensive or current than others depending on how their components are tuned, and some also classify Web sites by subject categories (see Figure 8-3). Specialized search tools are also available to help users locate specific types of information easily. For example, Google is tuned to find the home pages of companies and organizations. AltaVista provides capabilities for searching images, video, audio, discussion groups, products, and live, up-to-the-minute news feeds as well as conventional Web pages. AltaVista users can search in any language, including Chinese, Korean, Polish, or Russian.

Some Web sites for locating information, such as Yahoo! and AltaVista, have become so popular and easy to use that they also serve as portals for the Internet. A **portal** is a Web site or other service using Web browsers and search technology that provides an initial point of entry to the Web or to internal company data. Portals typically offer a broad array of resources or services such as e-mail, on-line shopping, news feeds, discussion forums, and tools for locating information; they can be custom tailored to the needs of a specific group of users. Specialized por-

home page A World Wide Web text and graphical screen display that welcomes the user and explains the organization that has established the page.

Webmaster The person in charge of an organization's Web site.

uniform resource locator (URL) The address of a specific resource on the Internet.

hypertext transport protocol (http) The communications standard used to transfer pages on the Web. Defines how messages are formatted and transmitted.

search engine A tool for locating specific sites or information on the Internet.

portal Web site or other service using Web browsers and search technology that provides an initial point of entry to the Web or to internal company data.

FIGURE 8-3 Example of a search engine. Altavista provides a powerful search engine for accessing Web information resources, including text, images, audio, and video and is a major Internet portal. Users can search for sites of interest by entering keywords or by exploring the directory of Web site categories.

tals such as AvantGo and Planetweb have been developed to steer users of Web-enabled wireless devices and information appliances to the information they are most likely to need.

Broadcast and "Push" Technology

Instead of spending hours surfing the Web, users can have the information they are interested in delivered automatically to their desktops through **"push" technology.** A computer broadcasts information of interest directly to the user, rather than having the user "pull" content from Web sites.

"Push" comes from server push, a term used to describe the streaming of Web page contents from a Web server to a Web browser. Special client software allows the user to specify the categories of information he or she wants to receive, such as news, sports, financial data, and so forth, and how often this information should be updated. The software runs in the background of the user's computer while the computer performs other tasks. When they find the kind of information requested, push programs serve it to the push client, notifying the user by sending e-mail, playing a sound, displaying an icon on the desktop, sending full articles or Web pages, or displaying headlines on a screen saver. The streams of information distributed through "push" technology are known as *channels* (see Figure 8-4). Microsoft's Internet Explorer and Netscape Communicator include push tools that automatically download Web pages, inform the user of updated content, and create channels of user-specified sites. Using "push" technology to transmit information to a select group of individuals is one example of **multicasting.** (LISTSERVs sending e-mail to members of specific mailing lists is another.)

"push" technology Method of obtaining relevant information on networks by having a computer broadcast information directly to the user based on prespecified interests.

multicasting Transmission of data to a selected group of recipients.

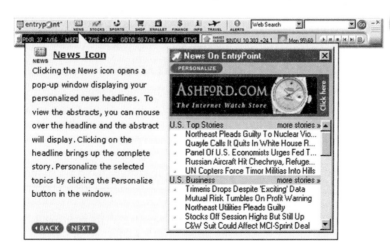

FIGURE 8-4 Delivering information through "push" technology. EntryPoint uses "push" technology to deliver timely, personalized news and information to users' desktops. The Web site also provides online shopping services geared to visitors' interests.

The audience for "push" technology is not limited to individual users. Companies are using push technology to set up their own channels to broadcast important information on their internal networks. For example, Mannesmann o.tel.o GmbH, one of the largest telecommunications providers in Germany, has developed an application using BackWeb's push delivery service that broadcasts new press releases about competitors' products as soon as the information appears on the Internet.

INTRANETS AND EXTRANETS

Organizations can use Internet networking standards and Web technology to create private networks called *intranets.* We introduced intranets in Chapter 1, explaining that an intranet is an internal organizational network that can provide access to data across the enterprise. It uses the existing company network infrastructure along with Internet connectivity standards and software developed for the World Wide Web. Intranets can create networked applications that can run on many different kinds of computers throughout the organization, including mobile hand-held computers and wireless remote access devices.

Intranet Technology

Although the Web is open to anyone, intranets are private and are protected from the public by **firewalls**—security systems with specialized software to prevent outsiders from invading private networks. The firewall consists of hardware and software placed between an organization's internal network and an external network, including the Internet. The firewall is programmed to intercept each message packet passing between the two networks, examine its characteristics, and reject unauthorized messages or access attempts. We provide more detail on firewalls in Chapter 13.

Intranets require no special hardware and can run over any existing network infrastructure. Intranet software technology is the same as that of the World Wide Web. Intranets use HTML to program Web pages and to establish dynamic, point-and-click hypertext links to other sites. The Web browser and Web server software used for intranets are the same as those on the Web. A simple intranet can be created by linking a client computer with a Web browser to a computer with Web server software via a TCP/IP network. A firewall keeps unwanted visitors out.

Extranets

Some firms are allowing people and organizations outside the firm to have limited access to their internal intranets. Private intranets that are extended to authorized users outside the company are called **extranets.** For example, authorized buyers could link to a portion of a company's intranet from the public Internet to obtain information about the cost and features of its products. The company can use firewalls to ensure that access to its internal data is limited and remains secure; firewalls can also authenticate users, making sure that only authorized people can access the site.

Extranets are especially useful for linking organizations with customers or business partners. They often are used for providing product-availability, pricing, and shipment data; electronic data interchange (EDI); or for collaborating with other companies on joint development or training efforts. Figure 8-5 illustrates one way that an extranet might be set up.

INTERNET BENEFITS TO ORGANIZATIONS

The Internet, intranets, and extranets are becoming the principal platforms for electronic commerce and electronic business because this technology provides so many benefits. The Internet's global connectivity, ease of use, low cost, and multimedia capabilities can be used to create interactive applications, services, and products. By using Internet technology, organizations can reduce communication and transaction costs, enhance coordination and collaboration, and accelerate the distribution of knowledge. Table 8-3 summarizes these benefits.

Connectivity and Global Reach

The value of the Internet lies in its ability to easily and inexpensively connect so many people from so many places all over the globe. Anyone who has an Internet address can log on to a

firewall Hardware and software placed between an organization's internal network and an external network to prevent outsiders from invading private networks.

extranet Private intranet that is accessible to select outsiders.

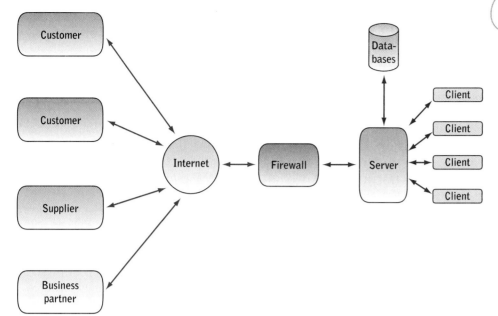

FIGURE 8-5 Model of an extranet. In this model of an extranet, select customers, suppliers, and business partners can access a company's private intranet from the public Internet. A firewall allows access only to authorized outsiders.

computer and reach any other computer on the network, regardless of location, computer type, or operating system.

The Internet's global connectivity and ease of use provides companies with access to businesses or individuals who normally would be outside their reach. Companies can link directly to suppliers, business partners, or individual customers at the same low cost, even if they are halfway around the globe. Businesses can find new outlets for their products and services abroad because the Internet facilitates cross-border transactions and information flows (Quelch and Klein, 1996). The Internet provides a low-cost medium for forming global alliances and virtual organizations. The Web provides a standard interface and inexpensive global access, which can be used to create interorganizational systems among almost any organizations (Isakowitz, Bieber, and Vitali, 1998).

The Internet has made it easier and less expensive for companies to coordinate their staffs when opening new markets or working in isolated places because they do not have to build their own networks. Small companies who normally would find the cost of operating, purchasing, or selling abroad too expensive will find the Internet especially valuable.

Reduced Communication Costs

Before the Net, organizations had to build their own wide area networks or subscribe to a value-added network (VAN) service. Employing the Internet, although far from cost free, is certainly more cost effective for many organizations than building a private network or paying VAN subscription fees. Thus, the Internet helps organizations reduce operational costs or minimize operational expenses while extending their activities.

Schlumberger Ltd., the New York and Paris oil-drilling equipment and electronics producer, operates in 85 countries, and in most of them employees are in remote locations. To

Table 8-3	**Internet Benefits to Organizations**

Connectivity and global reach

Reduced communication costs

Lower transaction costs

Reduced agency costs

Interactivity, flexibility, and customization

Accelerated distribution of knowledge

install its own network for so few people at each remote location would have been prohibitively expensive. Using the Net, Schlumberger engineers in Dubai (on the Persian Gulf) can check e-mail and stay in close contact with management at a very low cost. The field staff also are able to follow research projects as well as personnel within the United States. Schlumberger has found that since it converted to the Net from its own network, overall communications costs have dropped. E-mail reduces voice communication and overnight-delivery service charges (employees attach complete documents to their e-mail messages).

Hardware and software have been developed for **Internet telephony,** allowing companies to use the Internet for telephone voice transmission. (Internet telephony products sometimes are called IP telephony products.) For example the New York office of Kanematsu, Japan, was paying telephone bills of more than $10,000 per month primarily because of the expense of leasing a 64 kbps line between Tokyo and New York. The company wanted to connect its widely separated offices, which all use the same equipment, with voice and fax. In 1997, the company began using Internet telephony for its New York to Japan phone calls, installing Compaq ProLiant servers running Lucent Technologies' Internet Telephony Server Software. Kanematsu now pays only 17 cents per minute for calls that used to cost 50 cents per minute, saving $6,000 per month (Lewis, 1999). Although Internet telephony is still in its technical infancy, companies will increasingly turn to this service as its quality improves.

Internet technology can also reduce communication costs by allowing companies to create virtual private networks as low-cost alternatives to private WANs. A **virtual private network (VPN)** is a secure connection between two points across the Internet and is available through ISPs. The VPN provides many features of a private network at a much lower cost than using private leased telephone lines or frame-relay connections. Companies can save on long-distance communication costs because workers can access remote locations for the cost of making a local call to an ISP. Figure 8-6 illustrates how a VPN works using point-to-point tunneling protocol (PPTP), which is one of several competing protocols used to protect data transmitted over the public Internet. Companies are starting to use VPNs to reduce their wide area networking expenses. For example, the Forum Corporation, a Boston-based global training

Internet telephony The use of the Internet for telephone voice service.

virtual private network (VPN) A secure connection between two points across the Internet to transmit corporate data. Provides a low-cost alternative to a private network.

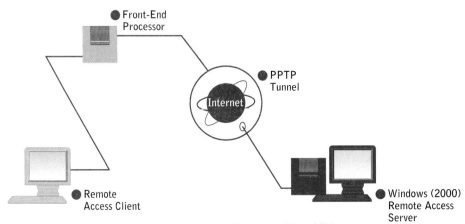

FIGURE 8-6 Point-to-point tunneling protocol in a virtual private network. Point-to-point tunneling protocol encodes information for transmission across the Internet using the Internet Protocol (IP). In a process called tunneling, PPTP wraps various protocols inside the IP so that non-IP data can travel securely through an IP network. By adding this "wrapper" around a network message to hide its content, organizations can create a private connection that travels through the public Internet. Source: "Point-to-point Tunneling Protocol," from Computerworld, August 2, 1999. Copyright 1999 Computerworld, Inc. Reprinted with the permission of Computerworld Magazine.

PPTP is necessary for creating Virtual Private Networks (VPN). A VPN is a private network of computers that uses the public Internet to connect private networks. PPTP was developed by Microsoft Corp. and several remote access vendor companies.

❶ The remote client makes a point-to-point connection to the front-end processor via a modem.

❷ The front-end processor connects to the remote access server, establishing a secure "tunnel" connection over the Internet. This connection then functions as the network backbone.

❸ The remote access server handles the account management and supports data encryption through IP, IPX, or NetBEUI protocols.

and consulting firm, saves $6,000 per month using a VPN instead of leased lines to link to its Hong Kong office (Wallace, 1999). We describe the benefits of VPNs for companies operating internationally in Chapter 15.

Lower Transaction Costs

Businesses have found that conducting transactions electronically can be done at a fraction of the cost of paper-based processes. For instance, the paper and human cost of producing and processing a purchase order might total $45, compared with $1.25 if processed electronically over the Internet. The average retail banking transaction costs $1.50, compared with 15 to 25 cents for an electronic version. Using Internet technology reduces these transaction costs even further. Here are some examples:

○ BeamScope Canada Inc. of Richmond Hill, Ontario, finds it can process Web orders for about 80 cents versus $5 to $15 for live orders. Customers appreciate the convenience of on-line shopping as well.

○ Each time Federal Express clients use FedEx's Web site to track the status of their packages instead of inquiring by telephone, FedEx saves $8, amounting to a $2 million savings in operating costs each year.

○ Oracle Corporation used to spend $350 per attendee on product-demonstration seminars. Holding these seminars on-line, presenting the material in text, video, and audio, and taking questions via e-mail costs $1.98 per attendee (Richtel, 1999).

Reduced Agency Costs

As organizations expand and globalization continues, the need to coordinate activities in remote locations is becoming more critical. The Internet reduces agency costs—the cost of managing employees and coordinating their work—by providing low-cost networks and inexpensive communication and collaboration tools that can be used on a global scale.

Schlumberger uses the Net for this purpose, as does networking giant Cisco Systems. Cisco uses the Internet intensively to link its corporate headquarters in San Jose, California, to more than 225 sales and support offices in 75 countries. Cisco employees use the corporate intranet to file expense reports, receiving training, and make changes to their health benefit plans. The company relies heavily on the Web and e-mail for employee communication and management review of employees.

Interactivity, Flexibility, and Customization

Internet tools can create interactive applications that can be customized for multiple purposes and audiences. Web pages have capabilities for interacting with viewers that cannot be found in traditional print media. Visitors attracted by alluring displays of text, graphics, video, and sound also can click on hot buttons to make selections, take actions, or pursue additional

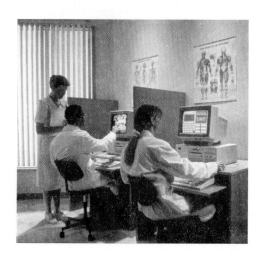

By enabling scientists, physicians, and other professionals to exchange information and ideas instantaneously, the Internet is accelerating the pace of scientific collaboration and the spread of knowledge.

dynamic page Web page with content that changes in response to information a visitor supplies to a Web site.

information. Companies can use e-mail, chat rooms, and electronic discussion groups to create ongoing dialogues with their customers, using the information they have gathered to tailor communication precisely to fit the needs of each individual. They can create **dynamic pages** that reflect each customer's interests, based on information the customer supplies to the Web site. The content of a dynamic page changes in response to user input at a Web site. Internet applications can be scaled up or down as the size of their audience changes because the technology works with the firm's existing network infrastructure.

Accelerated Distribution of Knowledge

In today's information economy, rapid access to knowledge is critical to the success of many companies. The Internet helps with this problem. Organizations are using e-mail and on-line databases to gain immediate access to information resources in key areas such as business, science, law, and government. With blinding speed, the Internet can link a lone researcher sitting at a computer screen to mountains of data (including graphics) all over the world, which would be otherwise too expensive and too difficult to tap. For example, scientists can obtain photographs taken by NASA space probes within an hour of the pictures being taken. It has become easy and inexpensive for corporations to obtain the latest U.S. Department of Commerce statistics, current weather data, and laws of legal entities worldwide.

In addition to accessing public knowledge resources on the Internet and the Web, companies can create internal Web sites as repositories of their own organizational knowledge. Multimedia Web pages can be used to organize this knowledge to give employees easy access to information and expertise. Web browser software provides a universal interface for accessing information resources from internal corporate databases as well as external information sources.

8.2 The Internet and Electronic Commerce

In earlier chapters, we described an array of information technologies that are transforming the way products are produced, marketed, shipped, and sold. Companies have been using their own WANs, VANs, EDI, e-mail, shared databases, digital image processing, bar coding, and interactive software to replace telephone calls and paper-based procedures for product design, marketing, ordering, delivery, payment, and customer support. Trading partners can directly communicate with each other, bypassing middlemen and inefficient multilayered procedures. The Internet provides a public and universally available set of technologies for these purposes.

Peter's Tasting Chart on the Wine.com Web site provides evaluations of wines according to dimensions of taste to help visitors make informed wine selections. By providing this information along with the ability to purchase wine on-line, Wine.com has created a successful new business model for wine retailing.

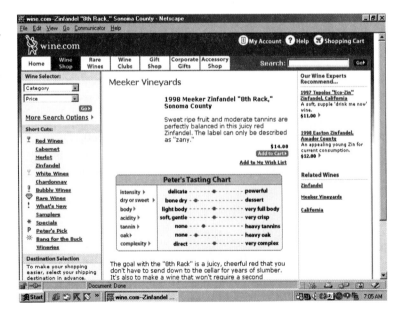

The Internet is rapidly becoming the infrastructure of choice for electronic commerce because it offers businesses an even easier way to link with other businesses and individuals at a very low cost. Web sites are available to consumers 24 hours a day. New marketing and sales channels can be created. Handling transactions electronically can reduce transaction costs and delivery time for some goods, especially those that are purely digital (such as software, text products, images, music, or videos). Consumers benefit by having instant access to information for comparing products, prices and services. It is estimated that more than $2 trillion in goods and services will be exchanged worldwide over the Internet by 2003.

INTERNET BUSINESS MODELS

Companies large and small are using the Internet to make product information, ordering, and customer support immediately available and to help buyers and sellers make contact. Some of these Internet electronic commerce initiatives represent automation of traditional paper-based business processes, whereas others are new business models. For example, Nashville Wraps uses the Web to advertise its traditional print catalog of packaging products, although orders must be placed by fax or telephone using the print catalog. Amazon.com represents a new type of business, as does Wine.com. Both are on-line storefronts that sell only over the Web. Another new business is WingspanBank.com, the virtual bank described in the Chapter 1 case study.

The Internet's rich communication capabilities have inspired new business models. eBay, described in the Chapter 1 opening vignette, is an on-line auction forum, using e-mail and other interactive features of the Web. People can make on-line bids for items such as computer equipment, antiques and collectibles, wine, jewelry, rock concert tickets, and electronics that are posted by sellers from around the world. The system accepts bids for items entered on the Internet, evaluates the bids, and notifies the highest bidder. EBay collects a small commission on each listing and sale. The chapter ending case study describes OnSale, which started out as another Internet auction site before merging with Egghead.com and its evolving business model.

Business-to-business auctions are proliferating as well. Bid.com in Toronto, which started out hosting consumer cyberauctions, now has Web-based auction services for business-to-business sales of items such as agricultural equipment. Many business-to-business companies have sprung up to help dispose of surplus inventory. On-line bidding, also known as **dynamic pricing,** is expected to grow rapidly, amounting to 40 percent of total on-line transactions by 2004 because buyers and sellers can interact so easily through the Internet to determine what an item is worth at any particular moment (Dalton, 1999).

The Internet has created on-line communities, where people with similar interests can exchange ideas from many different locations. Some of these virtual communities are providing

dynamic pricing Pricing of items based on real-time interactions between buyers and sellers that determine what an item is worth at any particular moment.

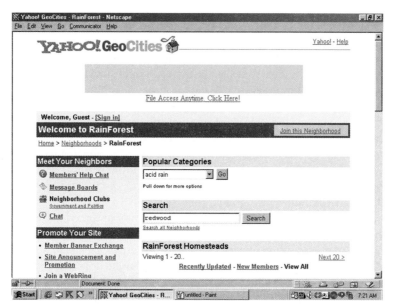

Geocities is an Internet business based on on-line communities for people sharing similar interests, such as sports, finance, film, or the environment. The company generates revenue from advertising banners on its Web pages and from providing ways for firms to target potential customers.

the foundation for new businesses. Tripod attracts college students and young college graduates by providing information about careers, health, personal finance, and travel; a resume-distribution service; and a facility to maintain a personal Web page. Members can link to on-line discussion groups on topics such as women's issues, work and money, or the arts or to other services on the Lycos Network of Web sites. Tripod's revenue comes from providing ways for corporate clients to target customers in the 18- to 30-year-old age group, including the placement of banner ads on its Web site. A **banner ad** is a graphic display on a Web page used for advertising. The banner is linked to the advertiser's Web site so that a person clicking on the banner will be transported to a Web page with more information about the advertiser's product. In addition to selling electronic advertising space, Tripod allows corporate customers to sell products on its Web site and receives a percentage of each transaction.

Even traditional retailing businesses are enhancing their Web sites with chat rooms, message boards, and community-building features as a means of encouraging customers to spend more time, return more frequently, and, hopefully, make more purchases on-line. For example, Gardener.com, which allows visitors to chat on-line about plants and flowers, found that registered members who chat are twice as likely to purchase at its Web site (Rafter, 1999).

Chapter 5 described application service providers that provide software that runs over the Web. *Virtual desktop* services that provide on-line calendars, calculators, address books, word processing and other office productivity software, as well as facilities to store users' data on remote servers, are proliferating. Table 8-4 describes other new businesses that deliver services over the Web along with additional Internet business models, which also are described at the Laudon Web site. Some replace internal organizational processes, some replace existing businesses, and some represent completely new kinds of businesses. All in one way or another add value: They provide the customer with a new product or service, they provide additional information or service along with a traditional product or service, or they provide a product or service at much lower cost than traditional means.

CUSTOMER-CENTERED RETAILING

The Internet provides companies with new channels of communication and interaction that can create closer and more cost-effective relationships with customers in sales, marketing, and customer support. For very little money, a business can provide highly detailed, customized information to a massive audience and can also collect huge amounts of information about each customer to help it sell more products and services (Evans and Wurster, 1999).

Direct Sales over the Web

Manufacturers can sell their products and services directly to retail customers, bypassing intermediaries such as distributors or retail outlets. Eliminating intermediaries in the distribution channel can significantly lower purchase transaction costs. Operators of virtual storefronts such as Amazon.com or Wine.com do not have expenditures for rent, sales staff, and the other operations associated with a traditional retail store. Airlines can sell tickets directly to passengers through their own Web sites or through travel sites such as Travelocity without paying commissions to travel agents.

To pay for all the steps in a traditional distribution channel, a product may have to be priced as high as 135 percent of its original cost to manufacture (Mougayar, 1998). Figure 8-7 illustrates how much savings can result from eliminating each of these layers in the distribution process. By selling directly to consumers or reducing the number of intermediaries, companies can achieve higher profits yet charge lower prices. The removal of organizations or business process layers responsible for intermediary steps in a value chain is called **disintermediation.**

The Internet is accelerating disintermediation in some industries and creating opportunities for new types of intermediaries in others. In certain industries, distributors with warehouses of goods, or intermediaries such as real estate agents, may be replaced by new intermediaries who specialize in helping Internet users efficiently obtain product and price information, locate on-line sources of goods and services, or manage or maximize the value of the information captured about them in electronic commerce transactions (Hagel III and

banner ad A graphic display on a Web page used for advertising. The banner is linked to the advertiser's Web site so that a person clicking on it will be transported to the advertiser's Web site.

disintermediation The removal of organizations or business process layers responsible for certain intermediary steps in a value chain.

Table 8-4 — Internet Business Models

Category	Description	Examples
Virtual storefront	Sells physical goods or services on-line instead of through a physical storefront or retail outlet. Delivery of nondigital goods and services takes place through traditional means.	Amazon.com Wine.com WingspanBank.com
Marketplace concentrator	Concentrates information about products and services from multiple providers at one central point. Purchasers can search, comparison-shop, and sometimes complete the sales transaction.	ShopNow.com DealerNet Industrial Marketplace InsureMarket
On-line exchange	Bid–ask system where multiple buyers can purchase from multiple sellers.	Asia Capacity Exchange E-Steel Energy Marketplace
Information broker	Provide product, pricing, and availability information. Some facilitate transactions, but their main value is the information they provide.	PartNet Travelocity
Transaction broker	Buyers can view rates and terms, but the primary business activity is to complete the transaction.	E*Trade Ameritrade
Auction	Provide electronic clearinghouse for products where price and availability are constantly changing, sometimes in response to customer actions.	eBay Ubid Bid.com
Reverse auction	Consumers submit a bid to multiple sellers to buy goods or services at a buyer-specified price.	Priceline.com Import-quote.com Yourprice.com
Aggregator	Groups of people who want to purchase a particular product sign up and then seek a volume discount from vendors.	Mercata.com Accompany.com
Digital product delivery	Sells and delivers software, multimedia, and other digital products over the Internet.	Build-a-Card PhotoDisc Beyond.com
Content provider	Creates revenue by providing content. The customer may pay to access the content, or revenue may be generated by selling advertising space or by having advertisers pay for placement in an organized listing in a searchable database.	Wall Street Journal Interactive Salon.com TheStreet.com
On-line service provider	Provides service and support for hardware and software users.	PCSupport.com @Backup

Singer, 1999). The information brokers listed in Table 8-4 are examples. In businesses impacted by the Internet, intermediaries will have to adjust their services to fit the new business model or create new services based on the model.

Interactive Marketing and Customer Personalization

Marketers can use the interactive features of Web pages to hold consumers' attention or to capture detailed information about their tastes and interests for one-to-one marketing (see Chapter 2). Web sites have become a bountiful source of detailed information about customer behavior, preferences, needs, and buying patterns that companies can use to tailor promotions, products, services, and pricing. Some customer information may be obtained by asking visitors to "register" on-line and provide information about themselves, but many companies are also

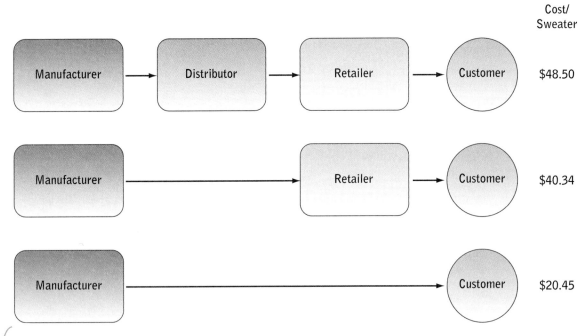

				Cost/Sweater
Manufacturer → Distributor → Retailer → Customer				$48.50
Manufacturer → Retailer → Customer				$40.34
Manufacturer → Customer				$20.45

FIGURE 8-7 The benefits of disintermediation to the consumer. The typical distribution channel has several intermediary layers, each of which adds to the final cost of a product, such as a sweater. Removing layers lowers the final cost to the consumer.

hit An entry into the log file of a Web server generated by each request to the server for a file.

collecting customer information using software tools that track the activities of Web site visitors. Companies can use special Web site auditing software capable of tracking the number of hits to their Web sites, the Web pages of greatest interest to visitors after they have entered the sites, and the path visitors followed as they clicked from Web page to Web page. (A **hit** is an entry into a Web server's log file generated by each request to the server for a file.) They can analyze this information about customer interests and behavior to develop profiles of existing and potential customers. Communications and product offerings can be tailored precisely to individual customers (Bakos, 1998).

For instance, TravelWeb, a Web site offering electronic information on more than 16,000 hotels in 138 countries and an on-line reservation capability, tracks the origin of each user and the screens and hypertext links he or she uses to learn about customer preferences. The Hyatt hotel chain found that Japanese users are most interested in the resort's golf facilities, which is valuable information for shaping market strategies and developing hospitality-related products.

Companies such as Amazon.com are using information generated by customers to create personalized Web pages. Amazon.com retains information on each customer's purchases. When a customer returns to the Amazon.com Web site, that person will be greeted with a Web page recommending books based on that person's purchase history or past purchases of other buyers with similar histories.

Many other Web sites are using personalization technologies to deliver Web pages with banner ads geared to the specific interests of the visitor. Chapter 14 describes additional technologies that gather the information on Web site visitors that makes such personalized advertising and customer interaction possible. It also describes tools to combine Web visitor data with customer data from other sources such as off-line purchases, customer service records, or product registrations to create detailed profiles of individuals. Critics worry that companies gathering so much personal information on Web site visitors pose a threat to individual privacy, especially when much of this information is gathered without the customer's knowledge. Chapter 14 provides a detailed discussion of Web site privacy issues raised by these practices.

MEASURING THE EFFECTIVENESS OF WEB ADVERTISING

You head an Internet company called Baby Boomers Online, which features articles of interest to people aged 40 to 60 years old on subjects such as travel, discount shopping, health, and financial planning, and links to Web sites selling related products and services. Your revenue comes from banner ads, which other companies place on your Web site for a fee. You would like to generate more revenue by raising your advertising rates. You can do this by increasing the quantity and quality of visitors to your site to justify charging more for ads placed there. One way to measure the success of ads placed on a Web site is by measuring the **click-through rate**, which is the percentage of ads that Web visitors viewed on a Web page and then clicked on to explore. Software on your Web server provided the displayed weekly report.

1. Calculate the click-through rate (expressed as a percentage) for each ad by dividing the number of ad clicks by the number of ad views. **Ad clicks** are the number of times a visitor clicks on a banner ad to access the advertiser's Web site. **Ad views** are the number of times visitors call up a page with a banner during a specific time period, such as a day or a week. Rank order the ads with the highest click-through rates.

2. What categories of ads are the most successful at your Web site? Least successful? Using this information, what kinds of companies should you be soliciting as advertisers on your site?

3. According to industry news sources, more than 27 percent of the visitors to the Travelocity Web site were 50 or older, as were more than 31 percent of the visitors to Priceline.com, which offers discount airline tickets. How can you use this information to increase click-throughs and revenues at your own Web site?

Web Usage for the Week Ending February 15, 2000

Ad Title	Ad Views	Ad Clicks	Click-Through Rate (%)
Soy Foods and Vitamins	321	19	
Budget Trips Inc.	674	228	
Budget Books Online	79	5	
No-Frills Getaways	945	311	
Computers for Less	118	5	
Boomer Financial Planners Inc.	63	16	

Companies can even use the Web and Internet capabilities such as electronic discussion groups, mailing lists, and e-mail to create ongoing dialogues with their customers. The Window on Technology describes how companies are using the Web to deliver customized advertisements, product offers, and personalized service.

The cost of customer surveys and focus groups is very high. Learning how customers feel or what they think about particular products or services through electronic visits to Web sites is much cheaper. Web sites providing product information also lower costs by shortening the sales cycle and reducing the amount of time sales staff must spend in customer education (Sterne, 1995). The Web shifts more marketing and selling activities to the customer because customers fill out their own on-line order forms (Hoffman, Novak, and Chatterjee, 1995).

Customer Self-Service

The Web and other network technologies are inspiring new approaches to customer service and support. Many companies are using their Web sites and e-mail to answer customer questions or to provide customers with helpful information. The Web provides a medium through which customers can interact with the company, at their convenience, and find information on their own that previously required a human customer-support expert. A few sites have added on-line chat capabilities so that visitors can have their questions answered immediately by a live customer support specialist if they desire.

Companies are realizing substantial cost savings from Web-based customer self-service applications. American, Northwest, and other major airlines have created Web sites where customers can review flight departure and arrival times, seating charts, and airport logistics, check frequent-flyer miles, and purchase tickets on-line. Chapter 1 described how UPS customers can use its Web site to track shipments, calculate shipping costs, determine time in transit, and

WEB CUSTOMERS: GETTING TO KNOW YOU

What is the key to successful selling on the Web? "Understanding how your customers feel is the ultimate driver of all online activity," claims Gary Bishop, the vice president for information technology with the American Heart Association (AHA) in Dallas, Texas (the site is used for fund raising). Many Web site companies share Bishop's thinking, and technology is supplying the tools to enable those sites to gain a far better understanding of their visitors and customers. E-retailers are using complex software to scrutinize customer behavior and tailor product offerings to each individual.

Gymboree Corp. of Burlingame, California, has 550 children's apparel retail stores nationwide and sells through its Web site as well. The goal of that site "is to provide service at least as good as customers get in our stores," according to Susan Neal, Gymboree's vice president of business development. How can Gymboree achieve such a challenging goal without a floor staff? It begins by using discounts and other incentives to coax visitors to register on the site, thus providing Gymboree with demographic data including the age and sex of the visitors' children. Although many people won't register because of security concerns, Neal says, "We're hoping that because Gymboree is a well-known brand name, they'll trust us to keep that information confidential." The company's database also contains a purchase history for each customer. Based on these data, when a customer returns to Gymboree.com, the software will suggest products relevant for the customer's children, even suggesting appropriately matching outfits. For instance, the Web site would deliver customized Web pages for parents of three-year-old girls and make product suggestions as they navigate through the site.

Gymboree uses E-Merchandising software from Blue Martini to combine and analyze all these data in order to make suitable product suggestions. In addition, the company sees a synergy between its Web site and its bricks-and-mortar stores and is planning to use its Web sales to boost store sales. By spotting best sellers in on-line sales, managers can make better decisions about which products to stock in its bricks-and-mortar stores.

Another approach to improving sales is to track visitors daily and to analyze that data to see what is and isn't working. Site-log analysis from Accrue Software Inc. lets Gateway Computer gauge relative performance of ads and special offers. It can use this information to judge the results of a facelift to its Web site. For instance, Gateway recently offered a $25 on-line rebate to those who purchased a PC, and data analysis showed that with the rebate offer people who visited went deeper into the site and stayed longer. However, Gateway Computer's vice president of Internet commerce, Chuck Geiger, wants information that is more content specific. "I want to know what's happening on the page. What are visitors entering into fields, submitted or not?" he asks. "What PC configurations are most popular? What other sites are they visiting?"

Geiger also asks, "Are people who come from Yahoo Finance more likely to buy than those who come from Yahooligans?" Like Gateway, many Web sites consider the entry point of site visitors and customers to be very valuable information. "There's a strong correlation between the choice of a search engine and a tendency to buy online," says Gabe Fried, e-commerce research manager for Toysmart.com. "Knowing which engines are most likely to produce sales for us, and knowing the terms parents are most likely to use when querying those [search engines], lets us conduct some pretty precise search engine campaigns," he adds. Toysmart.com uses software it has developed itself because it has not found commercial software that met its monitoring needs. It is clear that, like Toysmart.com, many companies will do whatever is necessary to obtain and analyze ever more detailed data on us as we surf our way through the Net.

TO THINK ABOUT: How does the Internet change relationships with customers and sales and marketing processes?

Sources: Dan Goodin, "Rearranging the Shelves for Each Customer," **The Industry Standard,** February 14, 2000; Beth Bacheldor, "Push for Performance," **Information Week,** September 20, 1999; Cynthia Morgan, "Playing for Keeps," **Computerworld,** August 2, 1999; Jeff Sweat and Rick Whiting, "Instant Marketing," **Information Week,** August 2, 1999; and Candee Wilde, "Personal Business," **Information Week,** August 9, 1999.

arrange for a package pickup. FedEx and other package delivery firms provide similar Web-based services.

New products are even integrating the Web with customer call centers, where customer service problems have been traditionally handled over the telephone. For example, visitors to Toshiba America's Web site can order on-line or place their orders through a sales representative or distributor. If the visitor wants to talk with a sales representative, the visitor can enter his or her telephone number, click on a "call me right now" button, and have the sales representative immediately call back on their telephone.

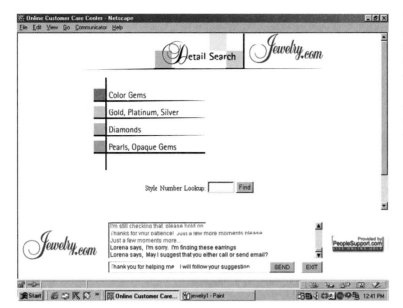

The Jewelry.com Web site provides on-line chat capabilities to answer visitors' questions and to help them find items they are looking for. Web sites can provide product information and online tools for contacting customer support representatives that enhance customer service.

Web sites where companies engage in ongoing dialogues with their customers can provide information for other purposes. For example, Dell Computer established a Dell newsgroup and other on-line services on the Net to receive and handle customer complaints and questions. They answer about 90 percent of the questions within 24 hours. Dell also does market research for free through these newsgroups rather than paying a professional for the same information.

BUSINESS-TO-BUSINESS ELECTRONIC COMMERCE: NEW EFFICIENCIES AND RELATIONSHIPS

The fastest growing area of electronic commerce is not retailing to individuals but the automation of purchase and sale transactions from business to business. For a number of years, companies have used proprietary electronic data interchange (EDI) systems for this purpose; now they are turning to the Web and extranets. By eliminating inefficient paper-based processes for locating suppliers, ordering supplies, or delivering goods, and by providing more opportunities for finding the lowest priced products and services, business-to-business Web sites can save participants anywhere from 18 percent to 45 percent (Cohen, 1999).

Corporate purchasing traditionally has been based on long-term relationships with one or two suppliers. The Internet makes information about alternative suppliers more accessible so that companies can find the best deal from a wide range of sources, including those overseas. A purchasing manager might also consult the Web when he or she needs to buy from an unfamiliar supplier or locate a new type of part. Identifying and researching potential trading partners is one of the most popular procurement activities on the Internet. Suppliers themselves can use the Web to research competitors' prices on-line. Organizations also can use the Web to solicit bids from suppliers on-line. Table 8-5 describes some examples of business-to-business electronic commerce.

For business-to-business electronic commerce, companies can use their own Web sites, like Cisco Systems, or they can conduct sales through Web sites set up as on-line marketplaces. On-line marketplaces represent some of the new Internet business models we introduced earlier in this chapter. The three principal business models for on-line marketplaces are marketplace concentrators, exchanges, and auctions.

Marketplace concentrators allow many different vendors to post on-line catalogs including their products and prices. The site provides customers with a standardized interface where they can order from multiple vendors. Industrial Marketplace is an example. This "industrial mall" brings together a large number of suppliers in one place, providing search tools so that buyers can quickly locate what they need. Industrial Marketplace earns revenue from

Table 8-5 · Business-to-Business Electronic Commerce

Business	Electronic Commerce Applications
Cisco Systems	This leading manufacturer of networking equipment conducts over 85 percent of its sales electronically through its Web site. Order taking, credit checking, production scheduling, technical support, and routine customer-support activities are handled on-line.
U.S. General Services Administration	The procurement arm of the U.S. federal government created an ordering system called GSA Advantage, which allows federal agencies to buy everything through its Web site. The Web site lists 220,000 products and accounts. By using the Web, agencies can see all of their purchasing options and make choices based on price and delivery.
W.W. Grainger	OrderZone.com provides on-line catalogs for a broad range of maintenance, repair, and operations goods from six major suppliers. Buyers can consolidate purchases from multiple vendors on a single purchase order.
General Electric Information Services	Operates a trading process network (TPN) where GE and other subscribing companies can solicit and accept bids from selected suppliers over the Internet. TPN is a secure Web site developed for internal GE use that now is available to other companies for customized bidding and automated purchasing. GE earns revenue by charging subscribers for the service and by collecting a fee from the seller if a transaction is completed.

fees paid by subscribing vendors. Another example is MetalSite, which is described in the Window on Organizations.

exchange Type of on-line marketplace where multiple buyers can purchase from multiple sellers using a bid–ask system.

Exchanges are on-line marketplaces where multiple buyers can purchase from multiple sellers using a bid–ask system. E-Steel, described in the Window on Organizations, is an example. Buyers log on and create inquiries, specifying details, terms, and suppliers for the steel they wish to purchase. Suppliers respond with specifications of their wares. Buyers can also search for certain types of steel, offer bids, and negotiate on-line with suppliers. On-line exchanges are available for many industries including chemicals and plastics, machine tools, energy, telecommunication capacity, paper products, and loans and mortgage products.

Figure 8-8 illustrates an on-line exchange for global logistics services. Companies such as Kmart, L.L. Bean, and Williams-Sonoma, which outsource their production to factories in the Far East or other locations around the world, might have to deal with up to 30 different logistics companies to transport their products from factory floors to their stores in the United

E-Steel is an online exchange for the global steel industry which allows buyers and sellers to initiate inquiries, search for products or inquiries, and negotiate the full details of a steel purchase transaction online. Online exchanges are becoming popular models for business-to-business electronic commerce in many industries.

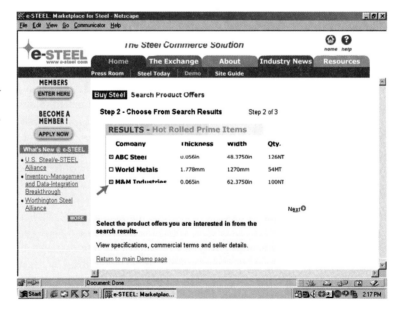

NETWORKS FOR STEELMAKERS

Steel is the second largest global industry, second only to energy. Yet steelmaking is an imperfect process, and to fill orders, steelmakers often produce more steel than they need. The leftover steel is eagerly gobbled up by hundreds of intermediaries whose job is to know the needs of potential buyers or to reprocess the steel for customers. With about 350 steel mills, minimills, and steel distributors in the United States, the buyers had to use the telephone to find what products were available, which was a frustrating and time-consuming process. After being kept on hold or only reaching an answering machine, more often than not these calls ended with no product available or the right product at the wrong price.

Weirton Steel Corp.'s chief information officer Patrick B. Stewart realized that other steel companies had the same need and, with financial support from Weirton, LTV Steel, and Steel Dynamics Inc., he established MetalSite.com. The idea was to use Internet technology to make it easier for the steel companies to dispose of their overproduction. Weirton, LTV, and Steel Dynamics each also agreed to sell 100,000 tons per month. With that start the buyers came, and the success of the site has attracted more steel producers and buyers.

The success of the site has revolutionized the whole steel overage business. The long hours spent trying to find steel have been replaced by a rapid search of MetalSite offerings. The site has also lowered the price of excess steel because steel buyers can log onto MetalSite, compare prices, and purchase the least expensive. Even the big automobile companies, the largest purchasers of steel, are now using such Web sites.

The steel producers are pleased as well, despite the increased pricing competition. Prior to the opening of MetalSite, the inventories of these companies were swelling because of low-priced competition from abroad. Now their inventories are dropping because of the lower prices and the ease with which consumers buy their products.

MetalSite has plans to become a full-service stop for the steel industry. "Our vision is to handle all aspects of buying and selling for this market," explained Stewart. For example, he plans to add a credit function so that buyers can apply for credit from cooperating banks right on-line.

E-Steel is another Web marketplace for the exchange of steel over the Internet. Unlike MetalSite, however, it does not own any of the products in its system and is not affiliated with any of the industry participants. (MetalSite currently sells only secondary steel from Weirton, LTV, and SDI.) E-Steel sells both prime and secondary carbon steel from both U.S. and foreign sources. Buyers make an offer on a selected product. The seller can award it or make a counter offer, which the buyer can accept or counter on his or her own. A feature called STEELDIRECT allows users to select a specific audience for each inquiry or posting. Messages can go to a single partner, a select group of partners, or the entire steel industry. Buyers can select the suppliers they wish to contact, while sellers can post existing inventory or future production capacity to preferred customers.

Both e-Steel and MetalSite make their money by charging a 1 to 2 percent transaction fee to the seller and by accepting advertising. Other sites for the metal industry are beginning to appear. These industry networks could revolutionize procurement processes.

TO THINK ABOUT: Why is Web technology so useful in creating these on-line marketplaces? How are these on-line marketplaces changing the way the steel industry conducts business?

Sources: Kris B. Manula, "U.S. Steel May Begin Web Sales Soon," Associated Press, February 24, 2000; Robert Guy Matthews, "Web Sites Made of Steel," The Wall Street Journal, September 16, 1999; Sarah L. Roberts-Witt, "MetalSite Listens and Learns," Internet World, June 14, 1999; and eMarketer, June 28, 1999.

States. To save time finding the best shipping rates or service, they can use the Celarix exchange, which enables these companies to compare various carrier rates and services.

Auctions, which we described earlier, provide on-line marketplaces where sellers offer items for which potential buyers submit bids; the items are sold to the highest bidder. In business-to-business electronic commerce, Imark.com is an auction site for used, capital machinery and equipment, whereas Farms.com specializes in auctions for cattle, genetics, feed, grain, hay, and real estate.

On-line marketplaces have some advantages over extranets for business-to-business transactions. Companies can link to many buyers without having to create point-to-point connections to each, and potentially they can find new customers. Many marketplaces have capabilities for integrating product information stored in disparate vendor systems. Companies purchasing products don't have to manage four or five different systems for buying from

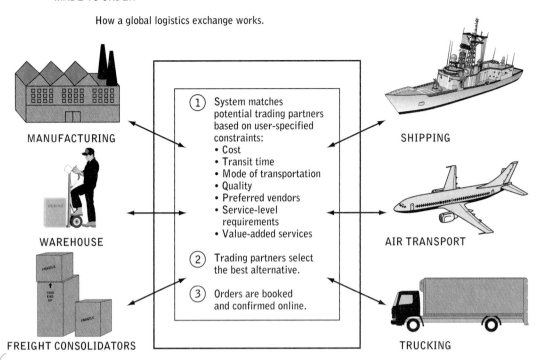

MADE TO ORDER

How a global logistics exchange works.

MANUFACTURING

WAREHOUSE

FREIGHT CONSOLIDATORS

① System matches potential trading partners based on user-specified constraints:
  • Cost
  • Transit time
  • Mode of transportation
  • Quality
  • Preferred vendors
  • Service-level requirements
  • Value-added services

② Trading partners select the best alternative.

③ Orders are booked and confirmed online.

SHIPPING

AIR TRANSPORT

TRUCKING

FIGURE 8-8 How a global logistics exchange works. Companies logging onto the Celarix Web site can immediately locate and place orders for alternative shipping services around the globe.
Source: "Made to Order," by Delia Craven from **Red Herring,** November 1999, p. 182. Reprinted by permission.

various suppliers and can save money by comparing prices and purchasing from a wide range of companies (Dalton, 1999).

Leading-Edge Electronic Commerce: Marshall Industries' Virtual Distribution System

Electronic commerce is changing the role of distributors, which traditionally served as intermediaries between manufacturers and customers. To survive, distributors may need to find other ways of providing value. Marshall Industries, the world's fourth-largest distributor of industrial electronic components and production supplies, reinvented itself by converting almost all of the processes it performs physically to a digital service on the Internet (El Sawy, Malhotra, Gosain, and Young, 1999). This is how its new "virtual" distribution environment works.

Marshall's customers and suppliers can access its intranet to obtain customized information. For example, high-tech suppliers can see information about their own accounts, such as sales reports, inventory levels, and design data. They also can accept or reject price quotes or order training materials. A personal knowledge-assistant process called Plugged-In allows customers to specify the product categories in which they are interested. They only receive information specific to their interests.

Visitors can view more than 100,000 pages of data sheets, up-to-date pricing, and inventory information from 150 major suppliers, and information on 170,000 part numbers. They quickly can locate products in Marshall's on-line catalog using a sophisticated search engine. The site links to the United Parcel Service (UPS) Website, where customers can track the status of their shipments. Sales representatives have secure intranet access so they can check sales and activity status only in their territory.

When a customer places an order, the system verifies price and quantity and initiates a real-time credit authorization and approval. As soon as the order is approved, the system sends an automated request to the warehouse for scheduling. The system then sends the customer an order acknowledgment accompanied by relevant shipping and logistics information from UPS. Messages about order status are automatically "pushed" to the customer. The system thus integrates the entire process of placing and receiving an order.

Other features of Marshall's Web site provide additional service and value. Visitors can access a free "Electronic Design Center" to test and run their designs over the Internet. For example, an engineer might use Marshall's Web site to test Texas Instruments' (TI) digital signal processors (DSPs) for the design of a new piece of multimedia hardware. (DSP chips improve the performance of some high-tech products such as computer hard disks, headphones, and power steering in cars.) At the site, the engineer can find technical specifications and even simulate designs using TI chips. The engineer would download sample code, modify the code to suit the product being built, test it on a "virtual chip" attached to the Web, and analyze its performance. If the engineer liked the results, Marshall could download his or her code, burn it into physical chips, and send back samples for designing prototypes. The entire process takes minutes.

Marshall's Web site provides after-sale training so that engineers do not have to attend special training classes or meetings in faraway locations. Marshall links to NetSeminar, a Web site where Marshall's customers can register for and receive educational programs developed for them by their suppliers using video, audio, and real-time chat capabilities.

ELECTRONIC COMMERCE SUPPORT SYSTEMS

Businesses pursuing electronic commerce over the Internet need capabilities for displaying product information, accepting payments, and taking orders. A business interested in setting up a system to support electronic commerce has three options: (1) using a Web server with a toolkit to build its own system, (2) purchasing a packaged electronic commerce server system, or (3) outsourcing the system to an e-commerce service provider. A number of merchant server or electronic commerce suite products are available. They typically provide a Web storefront, usually with some type of on-line catalog support, and a means for taking orders. Some of these systems link to financial networks to complete payment processing. Table 8-6 describes some of these products.

For companies that are not ready to operate their own electronic commerce sites, companies such as AT&T, MCI, and Yahoo! offer Web hosting services that process electronic commerce transactions for other organizations. A **Web hosting service** maintains a large Web server or series of servers and provides fee-paying subscribers with space to maintain their Web sites. The subscribing companies may create their own Web pages or have the hosting service or a Web design firm create them. Web hosting services offer solutions to small companies that do not have the resources to operate their own commerce servers, or companies that still are experimenting with electronic commerce.

Web hosting service Company with large Web servers to maintain the Web sites of fee-paying subscribers.

Integrating all of the processes associated with electronic commerce requires additional software and tools, such as software providing interfaces between Web servers and the

Table 8-6 Electronic Commerce Servers

Product	Description	Vendor
iCat Electronic Commerce Suite	Professional edition provides on-line catalog shopping and order placement for sophisticated Web sites; standard version available for small business storefronts.	iCat
Net.Commerce	Lower priced START version has a store creation wizard for catalog pricing, shipping, taxing, and secure payment processing with business-to-consumer and business-to-business capability; high-end PRO version for more advanced Web sites with intelligent catalog capability and tools to integrate the Web site with legacy systems and middleware.	IBM
Open Market Transact	Complete set of end-to-end transaction services including on-line customer authentication, on-line catalogs and search tools, order and payment processing, tax calculations, customer analysis and profiling, and customer service with multiple language capabilities.	Open Market
SellerXpert	Business-to-business application with industrial-strength catalog, search tools, credit checking, stock availability checking, and order management, including tax, shipping, and payment services; can be integrated with existing systems, EDI networks, and supply-chain systems.	Netscape

electronic payment system
The use of digital technologies such as electronic funds transfer, credit cards, smart cards, debit cards, and Internet-based payment systems to pay for products and services electronically.

company's core-transaction databases and electronic payment systems. **Electronic payment systems** use technologies such as electronic funds transfer, credit cards, smart cards, debit cards, and new Internet-based payment systems to pay for products and services electronically. Software to track and monitor Web site usage for marketing analysis also is desirable.

The process of paying for products and services purchased on the Internet is complex and merits additional discussion. Many security issues are involved, and there are many payment systems. We discuss secure electronic payment systems in detail in Chapter 13. Figure 8-9 provides an overview of the key information flows in electronic commerce.

8.3 Intranets and Electronic Business

Businesses are finding some of the greatest benefits of Internet technology come from applications that lower agency and coordination costs. Although companies have used internal networks for many years to manage and coordinate internal business processes, intranets quickly are becoming the technology of choice for electronic business.

HOW INTRANETS SUPPORT ELECTRONIC BUSINESS

Intranets are inexpensive, scalable to expand or contract as needs change, and accessible from most computing platforms. Whereas most companies, particularly the larger ones, must support a multiplicity of computer platforms that cannot communicate with each other, intranets provide instant connectivity, uniting all computers into a single, virtually seamless network system. Web software presents a uniform interface, which can be used to integrate many different processes and systems throughout the company. Companies can connect their intranet to company databases, enabling employees to take actions central to a company's operations. For instance, customer service representatives for U.S. West can access mainframe databases through the corporate intranet to turn on services such as call waiting or to check installation dates for new phone lines, all while the customer is on the telephone.

Intranets can help organizations create a rich, responsive information environment. Internal corporate applications based on the Web page model can be made interactive using a

FIGURE 8-9 Electronic commerce information flows. Individuals can purchase goods and services electronically from on-line retailers, who in turn can use electronic commerce technologies to link directly to their suppliers or distributers. Electronic payment systems are used in both business-to-consumer and business-to-business electronic commerce.

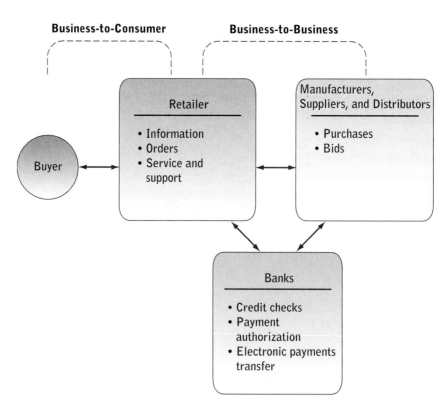

variety of media, text, audio, and video. A principal use of intranets has been to create on-line repositories of information that can be updated as often as required. Product catalogs, employee handbooks, telephone directories, or benefits information can be revised immediately as changes occur. This "event-driven" publishing allows organizations to respond more rapidly to changing conditions than traditional paper-based publishing, which requires a rigid production schedule. Made available via intranets, documents always can be up to date, while eliminating paper, printing, and distribution costs. For instance, Sun Healthcare, a chain of nursing and long-term care facilities headquartered in Albuquerque, New Mexico, saved $400,000 in printing and mailing costs when it put its corporate newsletter on an intranet. The newsletter is distributed to 69,000 employees in 49 states (Mullich, 1999).

Intranets have provided cost savings in other application areas as well. U.S. West saves $300,000 per year with an intranet application that automatically notifies service representatives of expiring service contracts. The intranet only cost $17,000 to build (Jahnke, 1998). Conservative studies of returns on investment (ROIs) from intranets show ROIs of 23 percent to 85 percent, and some companies have reported ROIs of more than 1,000 percent. More details on the business value of intranets can be found in Chapter 9.

For companies with an installed network infrastructure, intranets are very inexpensive to build and run. Programming Web pages is quick and easy with Web page authoring tools; employees can create Web pages of their own. The intranet provides a universal e-mail system, remote access, group collaboration tools, electronic library, application-sharing system, and company communications network. Some companies are using their intranets for virtual conferencing. Intranets are simple, cost-effective communication tools. Table 8-7 summarizes the organizational benefits of using intranets.

INTRANETS AND GROUP COLLABORATION

Intranets and other network technologies provide a rich set of tools for creating collaborative environments in which members of an organization can exchange ideas, share information, and work together on common projects and assignments regardless of their physical location. These tools include e-mail, fax, voice mail, teleconferencing, videoconferencing, dataconferencing, groupware, chat systems, and newsgroups. We already have described the capabilities of most of these tools.

Some companies are using intranets to create enterprise collaboration environments linking diverse groups, projects, and activities throughout the organization. The U.S. West Global Village intranet is a prominent example. Here are just a few of its capabilities:

○ A sales consultant in Chicago can check events throughout the company. He pulls up News of the Day, an internal newsletter.

○ A project manager can click on the lab page to inspect software being developed for a new service. He can test the software from his own computer.

○ Repair technicians can share a map showing damage to phone lines caused by ice storms and explore a strategy for repairing them.

Table 8-7 Organizational Benefits of Intranets

Connectivity: Accessible from most computing platforms

Can be tied to legacy systems and core transaction databases

Can create interactive applications with text, audio, and video

Scalable to larger or smaller computing platforms as requirements change

Easy to use, universal Web browser interface

Low start-up costs

Rich, responsive information environment

Reduced information distribution costs

○ An executive can log onto the intranet from her home after dinner to catch up on e-mail and check out the next day's schedule for her project team.

○ An engineer researching the design of a new network component can link to the public Internet via a gateway built into the Global Village home page. She surfs the Web to locate possible suppliers, then returns to the company intranet to inform her colleagues via e-mail about what she has found.

These intranet applications have enabled U.S. West to improve communications and streamline business processes, saving the company millions of dollars each year. Chapter 11 provides a detailed discussion of intranets in collaborative work.

INTRANET APPLICATIONS FOR ELECTRONIC BUSINESS

Intranets are springing up in all the major functional areas of the business, allowing organizations to manage more business processes electronically. Figure 8-10 illustrates some of the intranet applications that have been developed for finance and accounting, human resources, sales and marketing, and manufacturing and production.

Finance and Accounting

Many organizations have extensive TPS that collect operational data on financial activities, but their traditional management reporting systems, such as general ledger systems and spreadsheets, often cannot bring this detailed information together for decision making and performance measurement. Intranets can be very valuable for finance and accounting because they can provide an integrated view of financial and accounting information on-line in an easy-to-use format. Table 8-8 provides some examples.

Human Resources

Principal responsibilities of human resources departments include keeping employees informed of company issues and providing information about personnel records and employee benefits. Human resources can use intranets for on-line publishing of corporate policy manuals, job postings and internal job transfers, company telephone directories, and training classes. Employees can use an intranet to enroll in healthcare, employee savings, and other benefit plans if it is linked to the firm's human resources or benefits database, or to take on-line competency tests. Human resource departments can rapidly deliver information about up-

FIGURE 8-10 Functional applications of intranets. Intranet applications have been developed for each of the major functional areas of the business.

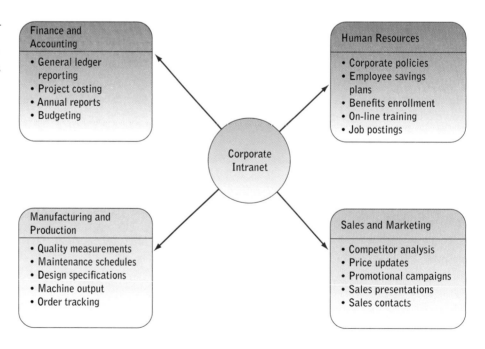

Table 8-8 **Intranets in Finance and Accounting**

Organization	Intranet Application
Charles Schwab	SMART reporting and analysis application provides managers with a comprehensive view of Schwab financial activities, including a risk-evaluation template that helps managers assess nine categories of risk. Schwab's intranet also delivers the FinWeb General Ledger reporting system on-line in an easy-to-digest format.
U.S. Department of Agriculture Rural Development	Intranet makes information about its loan and grant programs for rural and small communities available to its 7,200 employees. Employees can use Web browsers to find out which projects have been funded in specific local areas.
Pacific Northwest National Laboratory	Intranet Web Reporting System provides financial statistics for laboratory activities, including current costs charged to each project, number of hours spent on each project by individual employees, and how actual costs compare to projected costs. Lab employees can use Web browsers to perform ad hoc queries on financial data.

coming events or company developments to employees using newsgroups or e-mail broadcasts. Table 8-9 lists examples of how intranets are used in the area of human resources.

Sales and Marketing

Earlier we described how the Internet and the Web can be used for selling to individual customers and to other businesses. Internet technology also can be applied to the internal management of the sales and marketing function. One of the most popular applications for corporate intranets is to oversee and coordinate the activities of the sales force. Sales staff can dial in for updates on pricing, promotions, rebates, or customers, or obtain information about competitors. They can access presentations and sales documents and customize them for customers.

Haworth Inc. of Holland, Michigan, which makes office furniture, customized ERoom, a Web-based collaboration tool for sales force support. ERoom provides project-based collaboration sites where documents and threaded discussions can be stored. Haworth created "virtual workspaces" dedicated to sales reporting, sales strategy development, sales forecasting, field sales processes, and education and training. The system helps salespeople in many different countries work together on multinational accounts (Deckmyn, 1999).

Case Corp., a Racine, Wisconsin, manufacturer of earth-moving and farming equipment, supports its sales and marketing teams with intranet collaboration tools for contact management,

Table 8-9 **Intranets in Human Resources**

Organization	Intranet Application
Sandia National Laboratories	Tech Web intranet posts weekly newsletter and employee directory on-line. Employees can use the intranet for time and expense calculations and for project management.
Public Service & Gas Co. of New Jersey	Employees can use an intranet to access information on company savings plans, track historical performance, and reallocate funds in their 401K savings plans, taking advantage of asset-allocation models to make decisions. They also can use the intranet to choose a health plan, reviewing reports on HMO providers to guide their selection, and even select their physicians.
Sun Healthcare	Sunweb intranet provides virtual on-line tours of its facilities for new hires. Nurses and other employees can receive on-line training, including video clips. A three-dimensional cartoon figure called "Sunny" guides employees through intranet pages and explains the courses that are available.

discussion forums, document management, and calendars. Marketsmarter LLC develops customized intranet applications for marketing and sales personnel based on a proprietary process called PRAISE. (PRAISE stands for Purpose, Research, Analyze, Implement, Strategize, and Evaluate.) PRAISE applications facilitate sharing of information on competitors, potential product-development products, and research tasks, and include time-sensitive accountability to measure results (Sterne, 1998).

Manufacturing and Production

In manufacturing, information-management issues are highly complex, involving massive inventories, capturing and integrating real-time production data flows, changing relationships with suppliers, and monitoring volatile costs. The manufacturing function typically uses multiple types of data, including graphics as well as text, which are scattered in many disparate systems. Manufacturing information is often very time sensitive and difficult to retrieve because files must be continuously updated. Developing intranets that integrate manufacturing data under a uniform user interface is more complicated than in other functional areas.

Despite these difficulties, companies are launching intranet applications for manufacturing. Intranets coordinating the flow of information between lathes, controllers, inventory systems, and other components of a production system can make manufacturing information more accessible to different parts of the organization, increasing precision and lowering costs. Table 8-10 describes some of these uses.

COORDINATION AND SUPPLY CHAIN MANAGEMENT

Intranets and extranets also can be used to simplify and integrate business processes spanning more than one functional area. These cross-functional processes can be coordinated electronically, increasing organizational efficiency and responsiveness. One area of great interest to companies is the use of intranets and extranets to facilitate supply chain management.

Chapter 2 introduced the concept of supply chain management, which integrates procurement, production, and logistics processes to supply goods and services from their source to final delivery to the customer. The supply chain links material suppliers, distributors, retailers, and customers, as well as manufacturing facilities.

In the pre-Internet environment, supply chain coordination was hampered by the difficulties of making information flow smoothly between many different kinds of systems servicing different parts of the supply chain, such as purchasing, materials management, manu-

Table 8-10 Intranets in Manufacturing and Production

Organization	Intranet Application
Nortel Technologies	Intranet publishes three-dimensional models and animations for faster exploration of ideas, better feedback, and shorter development cycles. The application reduces miscommunication between process engineers and the shop floor because animations show how to fit different pieces together.
Sony Corporation	Intranet delivers financial information to manufacturing personnel so that workers can monitor the production line's profit-and-loss performance and adapt performance accordingly. The intranet also provides data on quality measurements, such as defects and rejects, as well as maintenance and training schedules.
Duke Power	Intranet provides on-line access to a computer-aided engineering tool for retrieving equipment designs and operating specifications that allows employees to view every important system in the plant at various levels of detail. Different subsets of systems can be formatted together to create a view of all the equipment in a particular room. Maintenance technicians, plant engineers, and operations personnel can use this tool with minimal training.
Rockwell International	Intranet improves process and quality of manufactured circuit boards and controllers by establishing home pages for its Milwaukee plant's computer-controlled machine tools that are updated every 60 seconds. Quality control managers can check the status of a machine by calling up its home page to learn how many pieces the machine output that day, what percentage of an order that output represents, and to what tolerances the machine is adhering.

facturing, and distribution. Internet technology provides the connectivity to overcome these barriers. Firms can use intranets to improve coordination among their internal supply chain processes, and they can use extranets to coordinate supply chain processes shared with their business partners (see Figure 8-11). Many of the industrial networks we introduced in Chapter 3, which link a company's systems with those of other companies in its industry, are based on extranets for streamlining supply chain management.

Chrysler developed an extranet for supply chain management called the Supplier Partner Information Network (SPIN). SPIN allows 3,500 of Chrysler's 12,000 suppliers selective access to portions of its intranet so they can access the most current data on design changes, parts shortages, packaging information, and invoice tracking. Chrysler believes that by streamlining product delivery and shortening the time to communicate process or design changes, SPIN has reduced the time to complete various business processes by 25 percent to 50 percent. Chrysler can use the information from SPIN to manage employees more efficiently. A critical parts tracking application permits reassignment of workers so that shortages do not hold up assembly lines. Chrysler added invoice tracking to SPIN so that staff spends less time fielding phone calls from suppliers inquiring about payments. SPIN has been revised to incorporate Chrysler's proprietary EDI system and "push" technology. SPIN can automatically notify suppliers of critical parts shortages.

Not all Internet-based supply chain applications are as ambitious as those of Chrysler, but they are changing the way businesses work internally and with each other. In addition to reducing costs, these supply chain management systems provide more responsive customer service, allowing the workings of the business to be driven more by customer demand. Earlier supply chain management systems were driven by production master schedules based on forecasts or best guesses of demand for products. With new flows of information made possible by intranets and extranets, supply chain management can follow a demand-driven model.

8.4 Management Challenges and Opportunities

Although the Internet offers a wealth of new opportunities for electronic commerce and electronic business, it also presents managers with a series of challenges. These challenges largely stem from the fact that Internet technology and its business functions are relatively new.

UNPROVEN BUSINESS MODELS

Not all companies make money on the Web. Industry.net, the comprehensive industrial mall that was run by IBM and Nets.Inc, is no longer in business. As of the writing of this chapter,

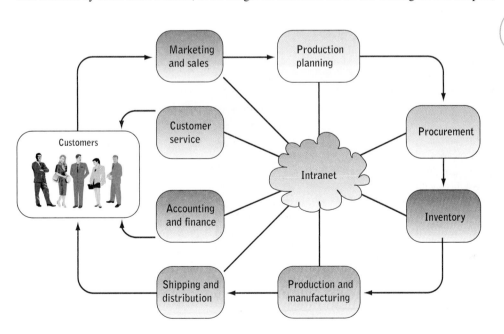

FIGURE 8-11 Intranet linking supply chain functions. Intranets can be used to integrate information from isolated business processes so that they can be coordinated for supply chain management.
Source: Kalakota, **Electronic Commerce**, p. 293. © 1997 by Addison-Wesley Publishing Company. Reprinted by permission of Addison Wesley Longman.

most "dot.com" companies whose revenues were based on electronic commerce sites had yet to turn a profit. Business models built around the Internet are new and largely unproven.

Challenges also confront businesses that are trying to use the Web to supplement or enhance a traditional business model. Many businesses are finding that it is not enough to "get on the Web." Businesses that are unclear about their on-line strategy can waste thousands and even millions of dollars building and maintaining a Web site that fails to deliver the desired results. Even successful Web sites can incur very high costs. The Window on Management describes the challenges that confronted one company that has been heralded as a model in Web retailing. At the moment, the greatest benefit of Internet technology for many firms may be the use of intranets to reduce internal operating costs.

BUSINESS PROCESS CHANGE REQUIREMENTS

Electronic commerce and electronic business require careful orchestration of the firm's divisions, production sites, and sales offices, as well as close relationships with customers, suppliers, banks, and other trading partners. Essential business processes must be redesigned and more closely integrated, especially those for supply chain management.

CHANNEL CONFLICTS

channel conflict Competition between two or more different distribution chains used to sell the products or services of the same company.

Using the Web for on-line sales and marketing may create **channel conflict** with the firm's traditional channels, especially for less information-intensive products that require physical intermediaries to reach buyers (Palmer and Griffith, 1998). The firm's sales force and distributors may fear that their revenues will decrease as customers make purchases directly from the Web or that they will be displaced by this new channel.

Channel conflict is an especially troublesome issue in business-to-business electronic commerce, where customers buy directly from manufacturers via the Web instead of through distributors or sales representatives. Milacron Inc. operates one of heavy industry's most extensive Web sites for selling machine tools to contract manufacturers. It is also benefiting from the customer information it collects on-line, which is forwarded to its research and development engineers for making product improvements. To minimize negative repercussions from channel conflict, Milacron is paying full commissions to its reps for on-line sales made in their territory, even if they have not done any work on the sale or met the buyer. By not penalizing sales representatives for on-line sales that bypass them, this policy also creates a single face for the customer. Other companies are devising other solutions, such as offering only a portion of their full product line on the Web. Using alternative channels created by the Internet requires very careful planning and management.

Recreational Equipment Inc. (REI) sells outdoor gear through its Web sites as well as through paper catalogs and a chain of retail stores. Although REI's Web site is profitable, it is a large sophisticated electronic commerce site that is very expensive to set up and to operate.

Window on Management

SELLING ON THE WEB IS MUCH HARDER THAN IT LOOKS

Is a bricks-and-mortar store really more expensive to operate than a Web site store? Not according to Dennis Madsen, the CEO of Recreational Equipment Inc. (REI), the famous seller of outdoor gear, headquartered in Kent, Washington. REI has bricks-and-mortar retail stores and hefty catalog sales. Its Web site is profitable and dominates its market, accounting for $1 out of every $100 spent on outdoor gear. If Web stores have much smaller staffs, dramatically lower real estate costs, and less inventory to finance than physical retail stores, why does Madsen think this way? Let's look closer at REI's experience in Web retailing.

Times have changed since the first retail Web sites could spend no more than $20,000 on start-up costs. Today start-up costs of $1 million for a major electronic commerce site are considered inexpensive. Web sites are no longer a novelty. Start-ups can no longer succeed by simply being there. Strategic planning is vital and doing it well easily can cost upwards of $100,000. Marketing is also critical. Most cannot simply "open their doors" and wait for people to enter. According to Send.com founder Mike Lannon, his company spent most of his $10 million start-up capital on off-line advertising.

Once its site had been set up, REI found all kinds of other costs unique to cyberspace commerce. It is true that Web site staffs are usually much smaller than retail stores. REI employs 300 people in its flagship Seattle store, compared to only 60 for its rei.com Web site. Nonetheless, payroll costs for rei.com surpass those of the Seattle store. "Technical people are a lot more expensive than part-time salesclerks," explains Matt Hyde, REI's vice president for on-line sales. And those costs are rising sharply because of the shortage of talented technical staff. Every few months Hyde reviews the latest industry salary studies and automatically raises the salaries of his skilled technical staff, which he feels he must do in order to hold on to them.

Physical stores may be redecorated every few years. However, Web sites are upgraded far more often. Because of fierce competition and low profit margins, Web technology is rapidly evolving and Web site owners must keep up. Hyde has updated rei.com's underlying IBM Web software 4 times in 4 years, and the latest upgrade cost $500,000. REI has also totally rebuilt its Web site several times in four years, not to mention other minor changes. Hyde esti-

mates that altogether rei.com has spent more than $15 million on upgrading and remodeling in 4 years.

Web sites all have other similar expenses. For example, Web sites are 24-hour operations. When something fails in the middle of the night, someone has to repair it immediately. In physical stores problems are seldom so critical even during business hours, except in rare cases of fires, floods, and other such disasters.

Some high Web costs differ depending on the business. Much of the REI business comes from catalog sales, and when Hyde was setting up the site, he planned to use the pictures from the catalog for display on the Web. However, he quickly found that film picture quality was far inferior to that of digital photographs when displayed on the Internet. So he had to spend tens of thousands of dollars to build several digital photography labs. Shipping is another expense that is higher for REI than for many traditional stores. Web customers expect immediate shipment, so REI had to find a way to meet that demand. REI's problem is that its thousands of items are produced by more than 1,000 small companies, most of whose staff had to be trained to ship at an acceptable speed. In addition REI's Web site sells throughout the world, so personnel must have expertise in tariffs, exchange rates, and customs regulations, something a bricks-and-mortar store does not need.

Although REI wants its Web site to support its other sales outlets as well as to produce small profits, Hyde says, "I still do not think we are going to make a big profit." He adds that with all the competition, "I don't think our customers would let us get away with [a big profit], and I don't think our competition would let us get away with it."

TO THINK ABOUT: What management, organization, and technology issues should be considered when setting up a Web storefront?

Sources: Leslie Kaufman, "Selling Backpacks on the Web Is Much Harder Than It Looks," *The New York Times*, May 24, 1999; Debra Malina, "The High Price of a Web Presence," *Computerworld*, July 19, 1999; David Passmore, "Scaling Large E-Commerce Infrastructure," *Packet Magazine*, Third Quarter, 1999; and Bob Tedeschi, "New York Times E-Commerce Report, *The New York Times*, November 1, 1999.

TECHNOLOGY HURDLES, BANDWIDTH, AND INTERNET 2

To make extensive use of the Internet, some companies need more expensive telecommunications connections, workstations, or high-speed computers that can handle the transmission of bandwidth-hungry graphics, and perhaps special computers dedicated as Web servers. Individuals and organizations in less-developed countries with poor telephone lines, limited hardware and software capacity, or government controls on communications will not be able to take full advantage of Internet resources (Goodman, Press, Ruth, and Rutkowski, 1994).

Bandwidth is another major technology issue. With the success of the Web, sound, graphics, and full-motion video are now important aspects of network computing. However, these all require immense quantities of data, greatly slowing down transmission and the downloading of Web pages. Some Web servers become overloaded with servicing requests and may be impossible to access during busy periods. The existing telecommunications infrastructure was not set up to handle large numbers of people using its services for hours at a time. (Current telephone systems were designed and priced under the assumption that 10 percent of all phones would be in use at any time and the average voice call would last 3 to 4 minutes. The average Internet session lasts 22 minutes, and many people stay connected for hours.) During peak periods of usage, Internet traffic slows to a crawl, and ISPs cannot keep up with the demand. The public Internet in its current form is not reliable enough for many business-critical applications.

Higher bandwidth alternatives are under development. Scientists at nearly 200 universities and scores of affiliated companies are working on a new version of the Internet, known as Internet2. **Internet2** is a research network with new protocols and transmission speeds that are much higher than the current Internet. The Internet2 infrastructure is based on a series of interconnected *gigapops,* which are regional high-speed points-of-presence that serve as aggregation points for traffic from participating institutions. (Several gigapops in operation at universities offer 622 megabit-per-second access to customer end points.) These gigapops in turn are connected to the National Science Foundation's high-performance Backbone Network infrastructure, which will soon operate at 2 gigabits per second. In addition to testing a more advanced version of the Internet Protocol and finding new ways to route broadcast messages, Internet2 is focusing on developing protocols for permitting different quality-of-service levels. Different types of packets can be assigned different levels of priority as they travel over the network. For example, packets for applications such as videoconferencing could be delivered instantaneously, whereas e-mail messages could be delivered when capacity was available. The new Internet will have the reliability and security features of private leased-line networks with much more bandwidth, enabling companies to distribute video, audio, three-dimensional animations, and data signals in broadcast fashion with minimal disruptions. Internet telephony will become a more viable option for corporate voice networks. Web sites will be able to offer applications such as distance learning, digital libraries, 180-degree, life-size video teleconferencing, and three-dimensional simulations that are much more interactive and data-intensive than today's without any degradation in performance. Instead of building private networks, companies will be able to obtain these capabilities on the public infrastructure.

Much of the work on Internet2 is being coordinated by a consortium of universities and companies called the University Corporation for Advanced Internet Development (UCAID). Another consortium, called Next Generation Internet (NGI) is also working on a high-capacity network that would connect research facilities across the United States to support next-generation applications in energy research, national security, and medical research. NGI is government sponsored and comprises research agencies such as the Defense Advanced Research Projects Agency (DARPA), the Department of Energy, the National Aeronautics and Space Administration (NASA), and the National Institute of Standards and Technology.

LEGAL ISSUES

Laws governing electronic commerce are just being written. Legislatures, courts, and international agreements are trying to settle such questions as the legality and enforcement of e-mail contracts including the role of electronic signatures, taxation of Internet-purchased goods, consumer privacy protection, and the application of copyright laws to electronically copied documents. Moreover, the Internet is global and is used by individuals and organizations in hundreds of different countries. If a product were offered for sale in Thailand via a server in Singapore and the purchaser lived in Hungary, whose law would apply? The legal and regulatory environment for electronic commerce is still evolving.

Internet2 Research network with new protocols and transmission speeds that provides an infrastructure for supporting high-bandwidth Internet applications.

Table 8-11 Using the Internet in Business: Top Questions for Managers

1. What value will the Internet and intranets provide the business? Will the benefits outweigh the costs? How can we measure success? Do we need to change our business strategy to incorporate this technology?

2. How will business processes have to be changed to use this technology for electronic commerce or electronic business? How much process integration is required?

3. What technical skills and employee training will be required to use Internet technology?

4. Do we have the appropriate information technology infrastructure and bandwidth for using the Internet and intranets?

5. How can we integrate Internet applications with existing applications and data?

6. How can we make sure our intranet is secure from entry by outsiders? How secure is the electronic payment system we are using for electronic commerce?

7. Are we doing enough to protect the privacy of customers we reach electronically?

SECURITY AND PRIVACY

Internet-based systems are even more vulnerable than those in private networks because the Internet was designed to be open to everyone. Many people have the skill and technology to intercept and spy on streams of electronic information as they flow through the Internet and all other open networks. Any information, including e-mail, passes through many computer systems on the Net before it reaches its destination. It can be monitored, captured, and stored at any of these points along the route. Valuable data that might be intercepted include credit card numbers and holders' names, private personnel data, marketing plans, sales contracts, product development and pricing data, and negotiations between companies. Concern about the security of electronic payments is one reason that electronic commerce has not grown more rapidly on the Net. We explore Internet security and the state of technology for secure electronic payments in greater detail in Chapter 13.

Hackers, vandals, and computer criminals have exploited Internet weaknesses to break into computer systems, causing harm by stealing passwords, obtaining sensitive information, eavesdropping electronically, or "jamming" corporate Web servers to make them inaccessible. Chapter 14 discusses computer crime and hacker problems as well as threats to individual privacy raised by the Internet. Using Web site monitoring software and other technology for tracking Web visitors, companies can gather information about individuals without their knowledge. In other instances, Web site visitors knowingly supply personal information such as their name, address, e-mail address, and special interests in exchange for access to sites without realizing how the organization owning the Web site may be using the information.

Effective use of the Internet, intranets, and extranets requires careful management planning. Table 8-11 lists what we believe are the top questions managers should ask when exploring the use of the Internet for electronic commerce and electronic business.

MANAGEMENT WRAP-UP

To obtain meaningful benefits from the Internet, managers need to determine how its technologies can support their business goals. Planning should carefully consider network costs, the costs and benefits of Internet computing, and new personnel requirements. Managers also should anticipate making organizational changes to take advantage of these technologies and plan to maintain some measure of management control over the process.

Management

Organization

The Internet can dramatically reduce transaction and agency costs and is fueling new business models. By using the Internet and other networks for electronic commerce, organizations can exchange purchase and sale transactions directly with customers and suppliers, eliminating inefficient intermediaries. Organizational processes can be streamlined by using the Internet and intranets to make communication and coordination more efficient. To take advantage of these opportunities, organizational processes must be redesigned.

Technology

Internet technology has created a universal computing platform that has become the primary infrastructure for electronic commerce and electronic business, using the TCP/IP network reference model and other standards for storing, retrieving, formatting, and displaying information. Web-based applications integrating voice, data, video, and audio are providing new products, services, and tools for communicating with employees and customers. Organizations can create intranets, which are internal networks based on Internet and Web technology, to reduce network costs and overcome connectivity problems. Key technology decisions should consider network reliability, security, bandwidth, and relationships to legacy systems, as well as the capabilities of Internet and other networking technologies.

For Discussion

1. The Internet is creating a business revolution and transforming the role of information systems in organizations. Do you agree with this statement? Why or why not?

2. What management, organization, and technology factors would you consider when deciding whether to build an intranet for your company?

SUMMARY

1. Describe how the Internet works and identify its major capabilities. The Internet is a worldwide network of networks that uses the client/server model of computing and the TCP/IP network reference model. Using the Net, any computer (or computing appliance) can communicate with any other computer connected to the Net throughout the world. The Internet has no central management. The Internet is used for communications, including e-mail, public forums on thousands of topics, and live, interactive conversations. It also is used for information retrieval from hundreds of libraries and many thousands of library, corporate, government, and nonprofit databases. It has developed into an effective way for individuals and organizations to offer information and products through a Web of graphical user interfaces and easy-to-use links worldwide. Major Internet capabilities include e-mail, Usenet, LISTSERV, chatting, Telnet, FTP, gophers, and the World Wide Web.

2. Identify the benefits the Internet offers organizations. Many organizations use the Net to reduce communications costs when they coordinate organizational activities and communicate with employees. Researchers and knowledge workers are finding the Internet a quick, low-cost way to gather and disperse knowledge. The global connectivity and low cost of the Internet helps organizations lower transaction and agency costs, allowing them to link directly to suppliers, customers, and business partners and to coordinate activities on a global scale with limited resources. The Web provides interactive multimedia capabilities that can be used to create new products and services and closer relationships with customers. Communication can be customized to specific audiences.

3. Demonstrate how the Internet can be used for electronic commerce. The Internet provides a universally available set of technologies for electronic commerce that can be used to create new channels for marketing, sales, and customer support and to eliminate intermediaries in buy and sell transactions. There are many different business models for electronic commerce on the Internet, including virtual storefronts, marketplace concentrators, information brokers, content providers, digital content delivery, on-line exchanges, auctions, and on-line service providers. Interactive capabilities such as the Web, e-mail, chatting and discussion groups can be used to build close relationships with customers in marketing and customer support.

4. Explain how Internet technology can be used to create private intraorganizational and interorganizational networks, and describe how these networks are used for electronic business. Private, internal corporate networks called intranets can be created using Internet connectivity standards, Web browsers, and Web servers. Extranets are private intranets that are extended to select organizations or individuals outside the firm. Intranets and extranets are forming the underpinnings of electronic business by providing a low-cost technology that can run on almost any computing platform. Organizations can use intranets to create collaboration environments for coordinating work and information sharing, and they can use intranets to make information flow between different functional areas of the firm. Extranets are used in business-to-business electronic commerce, joint development projects between organizations, and supply chain management.

5. Examine the challenges the Internet poses to businesses and society. Use of the Internet for electronic commerce and electronic business is in its infancy. Some of the new business models based on the Internet have not yet found proven ways to generate profits or reduce costs. Organizational change, including the redesign of business processes and new roles for employees, is often required; channel conflicts may erupt as the firm turns to the Internet as an alternative outlet for sales. Security, privacy, legal issues, network reliability, bandwidth, and integration of Internet-based applications with the firm's legacy systems pose additional challenges to Internet computing.

KEY TERMS

Banner ad, 260

Channel conflict, 276

Chatting, 250

Disintermediation, 260

Domain name, 248

Dynamic page, 258

Dynamic pricing, 259

Electronic payment
  system, 270

Exchange, 266

Extranet, 254

File transfer protocol
  (FTP), 251

Firewall, 254

Gopher, 251

Hit, 262

Home page, 252

Hypertext transport
  protocol (http), 252

Instant messaging, 250

Internet Service Provider
  (ISP), 247

Internet telephony, 256

Internet2, 278

LISTSERV, 250

Multicasting, 253

Portal, 252

"Push" technology, 253

Search engine, 252

Telnet, 251

Uniform resource locator
  (URL), 252

Usenet, 249

Virtual private network
  (VPN), 256

Web hosting service, 269

Webmaster, 252

REVIEW QUESTIONS

1. What is the Internet? List and describe its principal capabilities.

2. Why is the World Wide Web so useful for individuals and businesses?

3. Describe ways of locating information on the Web.

4. What are intranets and extranets? How do they differ from the Web?

5. Describe the benefits of the Internet to organizations.

6. How can the Internet facilitate electronic commerce and electronic business?

7. Describe six Internet business models for electronic commerce.

8. How can the Internet support sales and marketing to individual customers?

9. How can the Internet help provide customer service?

10. How can Internet technology support business-to-business electronic commerce?

11. Why are intranets so useful for electronic business?

12. How can intranets support organizational collaboration?

13. Describe the uses of intranets for electronic business in sales and marketing, human resources, finance and accounting, and manufacturing.

14. How can companies use extranets and Internet technology for supply chain management?

15. Describe the management challenges posed by electronic commerce and electronic business on the Internet.

16. What is channel conflict? Why is it a growing problem in electronic commerce?

GROUP PROJECT

Form a group with three or four of your classmates. Select two businesses that are competitors in the same industry and are using their Web sites for electronic commerce. Visit their Web sites. You might compare, for example, the Web sites for virtual banking created by Citibank and Wells Fargo Bank, or the Internet trading Web sites of E*Trade and Ameritrade. Prepare an evaluation of each business's Web site in terms of its functions, user-friendliness, and how well it supports the company's business strategy. Which Web site does a better job? Why? Can you make some recommendations to improve these Web sites?

Tools for Interactive Learning

○ Internet Connection

The Internet Connection for this chapter will take you to Wine.com and other Web sites where you can complete an exercise to evaluate virtual storefronts. You can also use the Interactive Study Guide to test your knowledge of the topics in this chapter and get instant feedback where you need more practice.

○ Electronic Commerce Project

At the Laudon Web site for Chapter 8, you can take a virtual tour of Electronic Commerce sites illustrating each of the Internet business models described in this chapter. Once you have finished the tour, you can start the comprehensive Electronic Commerce project in which you will select an Internet business model and develop an Internet strategy for a new business.

○ CD-ROM

If you purchase and use the Multimedia Edition CD-ROM with this chapter, you can complete an interactive exercise that requires you to select the appropriate Internet service for a series of problems. You can also find a video demonstrating the Internet services provided by Apple Computer, an audio overview of the major themes of this chapter, and bullet text summarizing the key points of the chapter.

○ Application Exercise

At the Laudon Web site, you can find an Application Exercise for this chapter requiring the use of Web browser, spreadsheet, and presentation software to research Web site development and hosting companies.

How low can retail prices go on the Internet? And how can companies survive selling at such low prices? We will examine the history of computer technology retailers Egghead.com (representing the merger of OnSale Inc. and Egghead.com) and Buy.com to help us better understand both Internet pricing and survival on the Web.

Before merging with Egghead.com in November 1999, OnSale began as a Web site for auctioning overstock, closeouts, and used computers and related products; it offered products from such computer leaders as IBM, Compaq, Dell, Hewlett Packard (HP), and Sun. The used equipment was refurbished and then tested thoroughly. New equipment was also available for auction because retailers and producers needed to liquidate excess inventory and outdated equipment. Much of the equipment offered was overstock that existed because producers and retailers had difficulty anticipating consumer demand and produced too much. Closeouts consisted of old models that were outdated because of the rapidity of computer technology improvements.

Customers were willing to purchase used and outdated computers because the computers were always much cheaper, making them affordable when budget was an issue. In many cases the purchaser did not need the power and technology of the newest models. Therefore, they were pleased not to have to pay high prices for technology they did not need.

The OnSale site was very successful for several years. The company had more than 650,000 registered bidders at the end of 1998, its third year in business. Significantly, 75 percent of its sales went to repeat customers. In that year it registered $250 million in sales according to S. Jerrold (Jerry) Kaplan, founder and CEO of OnSale. For a while sales were rising at 50 percent a month.

A fundamental part of OnSale's strategy was to use a number of techniques to stimulate interest in the bidding. Kaplan believed in constantly updating the Web site to keep it very attractive and competitive with other sites that function more like television or video games. Kaplan attempted regularly to change the offerings of the site, depending on what people seemed interested in. He also used Internet technology to stimulate bidding.

For example, OnSale used an automated e-mail system to notify the highest bidders when their bids were topped. The message also reminded the recipient of the deadline for a new bid.

Despite this well-thought-out strategy, OnSale ran into serious problems in 1998. OnSale was having increasing difficulty making money selling excess and refurbished computers. Because of increasing competition from new sites such as Surplus Direct, owned by Egghead.com, margins kept falling on the products the company was selling. Also parts for older equipment proved too often to be difficult to obtain. Moreover, 90 percent to 95 percent of potential OnSale customers could not find what they wanted because OnSale produced no machines to order.

Perhaps OnSale's biggest problem was the declining availability of excess and refurbished computers. Growing competition took some of the limited supply leaving less for OnSale. In addition, the number of leftovers shrank, partially because computer producers increasingly became more skilled in planning how much inventory they needed. However, the most important reason for the shrinking supplies was probably the very success of OnSale. Although the manufacturers had been happy to get rid of their used and overstock equipment, even at less than 10 cents on the dollar, by watching OnSale and others, the manufacturers realized they could recover closer to 50 percent if they were to auction or sell the items themselves. As a result, many manufacturers, including Compaq Computer and HP, began selling their own excess computers on their own Web sites. To add insult to injury, OnSale said that the growing supply constraints caused prices to rise, thus further reducing its profit margins.

OnSale had no choice but to develop a new strategy, which it announced on January 19, 1999. Without abandoning auctioning altogether, the company turned to selling new equipment. The centerpiece of its strategy was for OnSale to sell new products at its own cost, a price so low as to be very competitive. For example, OnSale sold 3Com Corp's Palm II handheld computer for $269.47, whereas 3Com sold the same item for $369. However, this strategy raised two obvious questions: How will the company cover its operating costs, and what will be the source of its profits? First, Onsale did not quite sell the computers and accessories at cost because it added a small fee of $10 per product. In addition, OnSale added the normal processing and shipping charges plus a 2.6 percent charge for credit card billing. Kaplan claimed that the tiny profit on each sale would amount to large profits because of high volume.

The company also planned to keep its costs very low by not retaining any inventory. Tech Data Corp. of Clearwater, Florida, the second-largest distributor of PCs in the world, manufactured the computers for them and shipped them directly to the customers. OnSale estimated this strategy would save as much as 10 percent over other on-line resellers and 30 percent over resellers selling through stores. OnSale saw advertising as another source of revenue. With consistently low prices, OnSale expected to draw a large number of regular customers, including many small businesses, enabling it to sell Web site advertising at favorable rates.

Kaplan pointed out that customers would always be able to find the computers they wanted, a great improvement over OnSale's past strategy. Kaplan expected that the strategy would add $100 million to sales revenue in 1999 without having a significant impact on operating costs. He said, "If we didn't do this, someone else would, so we decided to get there first and lead the market."

Noninsiders saw many problems with the strategy. A key issue was that OnSale was entering a very competitive business. Many companies were already selling computers at high discounts. In fact, Kaplan's company wouldn't always be offering the lowest price, even at cost, because some on-line companies were already selling some of their products below cost, as the following discussion of Buy.com will clarify. Other observers predicted this policy would further drive product prices down, forcing even lower margins. However, the biggest criticism from analysts was that it would be difficult for OnSale to make a profit with this strategy. "Anybody can sell products at cost and make a lot of revenue," explained Charles Finney, a securities analyst at the San Francisco brokerage firm of Volpe, Brown. "The question is how to make it profitable revenue. I could be selling 1 dollar bills for 85 cents."

Egghead.com has a very different history. It began in 1984 as Egghead Inc., a company dedicated to no-frills selling of computer software. Its more than 200 retail stores in 30 states gained a devoted following that made the company successful for a number of years. However, in time, sales began falling. Giant chains such as CompUSA began to offer lower prices, partly because they sold hardware as well as software, thus generating larger volumes and reducing their fixed cost per sale. In addition the new superstores did not maintain a highly qualified, high-priced staff as Egghead did. Moreover, new computers were reaching the market with more and more software included. In January 1997, the company established its first electronic commerce Web site, and within a few months it had closed all of its bricks-and-mortar stores. The Web seemed a natural place for Egghead because "Egghead had a very strong brand name, great vendor relationships, and a retail culture that would help us take advantage of the Internet opportunity," stated Egghead's chair and CEO, George Orban. Once on the Web, Egghead abandoned its software-only strategy and began selling computer peripherals and accessories, other consumer electronic products, and office products.

The move to the Web offered Egghead many advantages. Inventory costs dropped from about $100 million to only $14 million, and the company increased its offerings from about 2,000 products to about 40,000. Its real estate expenses fell sharply, and it no longer needed to pay more than 2,500 employees.

Although Egghead's name gave it a head start in moving to the Web, it still needed a way to attract new customers. To do so, it followed several strategies, including establishing affiliate programs with other sites. With the affiliate programs, other sites refer clients to Egghead, and those sites earn a commission for each product sold to referred clients. "Those relationships account for a substantial portion of our traffic," Orban said. In December 1998 the company processed 790,000 orders for 760,000 customers. By June 1999 analysts were predicting Egghead would have 3.7 million customers accounting for 6.3 million orders in 2003. In the first quarter of 1999 the company reported sales of

$13.7 million, double the sales of the previous quarter.

One of OnSale's and Egghead's main competitors is Buy.com, a privately held company founded in November 1997, in Aliso Viejo, California. Initially, the company was only in the business of selling computers and computer-related products over the Web, but it has since expanded and now sells books, music, and videos via the Web, all at close to wholesale prices. Buy.com guarantees its customers the best price on its products, and as a result, its sales price is occasionally even below cost.

To maintain the lowest price, Buy.com uses up-to-date Internet technology to automatically and constantly check its competitors' prices. If one of its prices is not lower than competitors', it immediately lowers its price to regain the lead position. Buy.com succeeded in generating high sales during 1998, its first year.

As a result of its success, Buy.com began to expand from a company selling only computer products to one selling many, many products. In November 1998 founder and CEO Scott Blum changed the company's name from BuyComp.com to Buy.com, an overarching name. It retains its BuyComp.com site for sales in the computer field. It also bought more than 2,000 Internet domain names starting with the word buy. This enabled the company to expand into many markets using a related name. The first to be launched starting early in 1999 were BuyBooks.com, BuyGames.com, BuySoft.com, BuyVideos.com, and BuyMusic.com. To support this expansion, Blum bought SpeedServe Inc., a unit of Ingram Entertainment, which is the largest distributor of videos and video games in the United States.

To keep its costs down, Buy.com is committed to simplified Web sites that are less expensive to develop and operate. For example, BuyBooks.com will not offer book reviews or a chat facility, as does Amazon.com. "We are going for someone who knows what they want and wants it at the best price," says Blum, who expects that buyers will browse sites such as Amazon.com and then go to BuyBooks.com to purchase the same products at a lower price.

To finance this expansion, Blum has received a lot of investments. In August 1998, Softbank Technology Ventures bought a 10 percent stake in Buy.com for $20 million. Two months later they were willing to pay twice that price for more

shares and invested $40 million more for another 10 percent.

How can Buy.com profit from this strategy? Like OnSale, Buy.com carries no inventory. Ingram Micro of Santa Ana, California, manufactures its computer products, filling Buy.com's orders the same day the order is taken. However, the key to the company's strategy is its ability to sell a lot of advertising on its Web sites. Buy.com expects its advertising rates to be driven by the fact that its low prices will attract a lot of people to the site. At the end of 1998, Buy.com's home page had 12 ads, each selling for $3,000 per month. Their strategy differs from OnSale in that Buy.com plans to have many sites, each carrying its share of advertising.

Some analysts have raised questions about Buy.com's strategy. "The first principle of Internet marketing is limited brand imprinting," explains Vern Keenan, an analyst with the e-commerce research firm Keenan Vision Inc. Amazon.com has built up enough trust to be a mainstream merchandiser, and it's very hard for a new brand to challenge that. However, Buy.com proved it is able to execute big ideas when, in July 1999, it announced a new on-line travel store, BuyTravel.com, in partnership with air travel giant United Airlines. The company site sells travel on all major airlines and also books hotels, cruises, and car rentals. Only time will tell if Blum can make his company a major success.

Web-based businesses are full of surprises, as observers discovered once again when, on July 14, 1999, OnSale announced it had agreed to purchase Egghead.com for about $400 million in stock. Kaplan and Orban said the reason for the merger was that they could combine their infrastructures and cut costs while combining their customer lists. Prior to the merger, the companies studied their customer bases and found that they had only a 15 percent overlap. Kaplan said, "The Internet is a space where market leaders are disproportionately rewarded. We are creating a clear market leader in the retailing of technology products on the Web." The merger was finalized on November 19, 1999, and the company launched a new Web site combining OnSale and Egghead.com's operations on November 22.

Kaplan and Orban do not believe a strategy of selling below cost is viable. "The idea is to be able to ride this out until rationality returns to pricing," explains Dalton Chandler, an analyst with Needham and Co. "With the cash reserves of $160 million that the 2 combined companies will have, they will be in a pretty good position to do that." Kaplan asks, "How long can we hold out?" and answers his own question, "as long as investors think we are a market leader."

Critics of the merger point out that both companies were losing money at the time. However some do see hope. Keenan believes, "Low-margin selling has a questionable future as a viable business. To be successful as a low-margin retailer, you need high volume," which is precisely the aim of the merger. Early results of the merger have been promising. During the fourth quarter of 1999, 325,000 new customers registered at Egghead.com to buy new goods or to bid in auctions of excess and closeout goods and services. Revenue for the fourth quarter of 1999 was $146.1 million, a 45% increase over the same quarter revenue a year earlier. A national advertising campaign helped build brand awareness for the new Web site, and Egghead.com emerged as one of the top e-commerce sites for the 1999 holiday season.

Sources: "Egghead.com Reports Fourth Quarter Results; Details Successful Merger Integration," **CBS Market Watch,** February 23, 2000; Tish Williams, "Good Old Egghead," **Upside Today,** July 7, 1999; Candee Wilde, "Egghead's Net Bet Pays Dividends," **Information Week,** June 7,1999 and "Smart and Smarter: Egghead Merges with OnSale," TheStandard.com, July 15, 1999; Chris Gaither, "Egghead's Smart Deal," **Wired,** July 14, 1999 and "OnSale Moves to Wholesale," **Wired,** January 19, 1999; Miguel Helft, "Online Rivals Egghead, OnSale to Merge," **Mercury News,** July 14, 1999; Sharon Machlis, "Survey: September Proves Robust for Online Retailers," **Computerworld,** October 11, 1999; Kathleen Ohlson, "Egghead.com, OnSale Merge," **Computerworld,** July 14, 1999; Stacy Collett, "United, Buy.com to Create Travel," **Computerworld,** July 20, 1999; Suzanne Galante and Cory Johnson, "Caught in a Squeeze," **The Industry Standard,** January 1, 1999; George Anders, "Web Seller Asks: How Low Can PC Prices Go?" **The Wall Street Journal,** January 4, 1999; Tom Diederich, "PC Vendor Promises to Get It for You Wholesale," **Computerworld,** January 19, 1999; Eric Auchard, "OnSale to Sell PCs at Cost, Make Money on Ads," Infoseek.go.com, January 20, 1999; Eric C. Fleming, "OnSale to Sell PCs at Cost," **PCWeek** (on-line), January 19, 1999; Larry Armstrong, "Anything You Can Sell, I Can Sell Cheaper," **Business Week,** December 14, 1998; "OnSale.Inc," Infoseek.go.com, January 25, 1999; Karen D. Schwartz, "Good Deals on Used Systems," **Information Week,** August 31, 1998; M. Duvall, "Buy.com Declares War on Competitor," **Inter@ctive Week,** November 19, 1998; and Stan Hibbard, Bruce Caldwell, and Clinton Wilder, "Season for Online Shopping Creates Retail Competition," **Information Week,** November 23, 1998.

CASE STUDY QUESTIONS

1. Analyze OnSale.com, Egghead.com, and Buy.com using the value chain and competitive forces models. Compare their positions based on those analyses.

2. Based on their plans to sell only through the Web, what are the special or unique problems these companies face in developing a business strategy?

3. Visit the Egghead.com and Buy.com Web sites and evaluate each in terms of how successfully you believe each meets its business objectives. Suggest ways the sites might be improved.

4. What management, organization, and technology problems do you think these companies faced in establishing their original and newer services?

5. With the existence of such companies as Egghead.com and Buy.com, what do you think will be the long-term effects of electronic commerce on prices, profits, and distribution? Do you think companies such as these two can continue to sell at or near cost? Why or why not? How viable are Egghead.com and Buy.com's business models? Explain.

CHAPTER 9

Redesigning the Organization with Information Systems

Learning Objectives

After completing this chapter, you will be able to:

1. Demonstrate how building new systems can produce organizational change.

2. Explain how the organization can develop information systems that fit its business plan.

3. Identify the core activities in the systems development process.

4. Analyze the organizational change requirements for building successful systems.

5. Describe models for determining the business value of information systems.

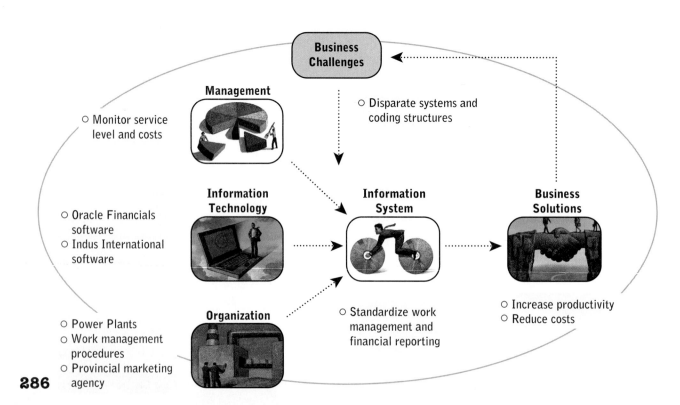

Business Challenges

Management
- Monitor service level and costs

Information Technology
- Oracle Financials software
- Indus International software

Organization
- Power Plants
- Work management procedures
- Provincial marketing agency

- Disparate systems and coding structures

Information System
- Standardize work management and financial reporting

Business Solutions
- Increase productivity
- Reduce costs

New Systems Light Up
Edmonton Power

Edmonton Power Generation, a subsidiary of EPCOR, generates 1,700 megawatts of power for the city of Alberta, Canada. The company manages production of electrical energy from coal and natural resources and sells energy to the Alberta provincial marketing agency. Before joining EPCOR, when it was still operated by the city of Edmonton, Edmonton Power Generation found that its systems for financial reporting and work management needed improvement.

Each of Edmonton Power's three power plants had a different inventory-cataloging system that required workers to go to a different plant to manually match new parts to the parts being used. Workers had to key information into multiple spreadsheets and databases, look through files to find work orders, figure out different codes, and consolidate data across systems.

Edmonton Power needed a system that would link information from work orders to its financial system. To create the new system, the company had to standardize work management and reporting practices for all of its power plants. The company selected software from Oracle Financials and from Indus International, which had a Solution Series with Asset and Work Management, Materials and Procurement, and Financial Integration for Oracle application products. In implementing the system, Edmonton Power had to convert and standardize data from its legacy systems for 70,600 assets, 26,830 stock items, and 116,253 work orders.

The new system simplifies many administrative tasks for Edmonton Power by consolidating and standardizing financial and work management data. Since the new system was installed, Edmonton's maintenance division alone experienced an 11 percent increase in the number of work orders completed and an 8 percent decrease in the number of work orders generated.

Sources: "Lights on Edmonton," *Profit Magazine,* November 1999; and "EPCOR Accepts EUB Decision on Power Purchase Arrangements," EPCOR Public Relations, January 4, 2000.

**MANAGEMENT
CHALLENGES**

Edmonton Power Generation's system illustrates the many factors at work in the development of a new information system. Building the new system entailed analyzing the company's problems with existing information systems, assessing people's information needs, selecting appropriate technology, and redesigning procedures and jobs. Management had to monitor the system-building effort and evaluate its benefits and costs. The new information system represented a process of planned organizational change. However, building information systems, especially those on a large scale, presents many challenges. Here are some to consider:

1. Major risks and uncertainties in systems development.
Information systems development has major risks and uncertainties that make it difficult for the systems to achieve their goals. One problem is the difficulty of establishing information requirements, both for individual end users and for the organization as a whole. The requirements may be too complex or too often subject to change. Another problem involves time and cost factors to develop an information system, which are very difficult to analyze, especially in large projects. A third problem is the difficulty of managing the organizational change associated with a new system. Although building a new information system is a process of planned organizational change, this does not mean that change can always be planned or controlled. Individuals and groups in organizations have varying interests, and they may resist changes in procedures, job relationships, and technologies. Although this chapter describes some ways of dealing with these risks and uncertainties, the issues remain major management challenges.

2. Determining benefits of a system when they are largely intangible. As the sophistication of systems grows, they produce fewer tangible and more intangible benefits. By definition, there is no solid method for pricing intangible benefits. Organizations could lose important opportunities if they use strictly financial criteria for determining information systems benefits. However, they could make very poor investment decisions if they overestimate intangible benefits.

This chapter describes how new information systems are conceived, built, and installed, with special attention to the issues of organizational design, business process reengineering, and organizational change. It describes the core systems development activities and the organizational change process of implementing a new information system. The chapter explains how to establish the business value of information systems (including those based on the Internet) and how to ensure that new systems are linked to the organization's business plan and information requirements.

9.1 Systems as Planned Organizational Change

This text has emphasized that an information system is a sociotechnical entity, an arrangement of both technical and social elements. The introduction of a new information system involves much more than new hardware and software. It also includes changes in jobs, skills, management, and organization. According to the sociotechnical philosophy, one cannot install new technology without considering the people who must work with it (Bostrom and Heinen, 1977). When we design a new information system, we are redesigning the organization.

One important thing to know about building a new information system is that the process is one kind of planned organizational change. System builders must understand how a system will affect the organization as a whole and focus particularly on organizational conflict and changes in the locus of decision making. Builders also must consider how the nature of work groups will change under the new system. Builders determine how much change is needed.

Systems can be technical successes but organizational failures if the social and political process of building the system fails. Analysts and designers are responsible for ensuring that key members of the organization participate in the design process and are permitted to influence the system's ultimate shape. These activities must be orchestrated carefully by information system builders (see Section 9.3).

LINKING INFORMATION SYSTEMS TO THE BUSINESS PLAN

Deciding which new systems to build should be an essential component of the organizational planning process. Organizations need to develop an information systems plan that supports their overall business plan and one in which strategic systems are incorporated into top-level planning (Grover, Teng, and Fiedler, 1998). Once specific projects have been selected within the overall context of a strategic plan for the business and the systems area, an **information systems plan** can be developed. The plan serves as a road map indicating the direction of systems development, the rationale, the current situation, the management strategy, the implementation plan, and the budget (see Table 9-1).

The plan contains a statement of corporate goals and specifies how information technology supports the attainment of those goals. The report shows how general goals will be achieved

information systems plan A road map indicating the direction of systems development, the rationale, the current situation, the management strategy, the implementation plan, and the budget.

Table 9-1 Information Systems Plan

1. **Purpose of the Plan**
   Overview of plan contents
   Changes in firm's current situation
   Firm's strategic plan
   Current business organization
   Key business processes
   Management strategy

2. **Strategic Business Plan**
   Current situation
   Current business organization
   Changing environments
   Major goals of the business plan

3. **Current Systems**
   Major systems supporting business functions and processes
   Major infrastructure capabilities
      Hardware
      Software
      Database
      Telecommunications
   Difficulties meeting business requirements
   Anticipated future demands

4. **New Developments**
   New system projects
      Project descriptions
      Business rationale

   New infrastructure capabilities required
      Hardware
      Software
      Database
      Telecommunications and Internet

5. **Management Strategy**
   Acquisition plans
   Milestones and timing
   Organizational realignment
   Internal reorganization
   Management controls
   Major training initiatives
   Personnel strategy

6. **Implementation Plan**
   Anticipated difficulties in implementation
   Progress reports

7. **Budget Requirements**
   Requirements
   Potential savings
   Financing
   Acquisition cycle

by specific systems projects. It lays out specific target dates and milestones that can be used later to monitor the plan's progress in terms of how many objectives were actually attained in the time frame specified in the plan. The plan indicates the key management decisions concerning hardware acquisition; telecommunications; centralization/decentralization of authority, data, and hardware; and required organizational change. Organizational changes are also usually described, including management and employee training requirements; recruiting efforts; changes in business processes; and changes in authority, structure, or management practice.

ESTABLISHING ORGANIZATIONAL INFORMATION REQUIREMENTS

In order to develop an effective information systems plan, the organization must have a clear understanding of both its long- and short-term information requirements. Two principal methodologies for establishing the essential information requirements of the organization as a whole are enterprise analysis and critical success factors.

Enterprise Analysis (Business Systems Planning)

enterprise analysis An analysis of organization-wide information requirements by looking at the entire organization in terms of organizational units, functions, processes, and data elements; helps identify the key entities and attributes in the organization's data.

Enterprise analysis (also called *business systems planning*) argues that the firm's information requirements can only be understood by looking at the entire organization in terms of organizational units, functions, processes, and data elements. Enterprise analysis can help identify the key entities and attributes of the organization's data. This method starts with the notion that the firm's or division's information requirements can be specified only with a thorough understanding of the entire organization. This method was developed by IBM in the 1960s explicitly for establishing the relationship among large system development projects (Zachman, 1982).

The central method used in the enterprise analysis approach is to ask a large sample of managers how they use information, where they get the information, what their environments are like, what their objectives are, how they make decisions, and what their data needs are. The results of this large survey of managers are aggregated into subunits, functions, processes, and data matrices. Data elements are organized into logical application groups—groups of data elements that support related sets of organizational processes. Figure 9-1 is an output of enterprise analysis conducted by the Social Security Administration as part of a massive systems redevelopment effort. It shows what information is required to support a particular process, which processes create the data, and which use them. The shaded boxes in the figure indicate a logical application group. In this case, actuarial estimates, agency plans, and budget data are created in the planning process, which suggests that an information system should be built to support planning.

The weakness of enterprise analysis is that it produces an enormous amount of data that is expensive to collect and difficult to analyze. Most of the interviews are conducted with senior or middle managers, and little effort is exerted to collect information from clerical workers and supervisory managers. Moreover, the questions frequently focus not on management's critical objectives and where information is needed, but rather on what existing information is used. The result is a tendency to automate whatever exists. But in many instances, entirely new approaches to how business is conducted are needed, and these needs are not addressed.

Strategic Analysis or Critical Success Factors

critical success factors (CSFs) A small number of easily identifiable operational goals shaped by the industry, the firm, the manager, and the broader environment that are believed to assure the success of an organization. Used to determine the information requirements of an organization.

The strategic analysis, or critical success factors, approach argues that an organization's information requirements are determined by a small number of **critical success factors (CSFs)** of managers. If these goals can be attained, the firm's or organization's success is assured (Rockart, 1979; Rockart and Treacy, 1982).

CSFs are shaped by the industry, the firm, the manager, and the broader environment. This broader focus, in comparison with that of previous methods, accounts for the description of this technique as strategic. An important premise of the strategic analysis approach is that there is a small number of objectives that managers can easily identify on which information systems can focus.

The principal method used in CSF analysis is personal interviews—three or four—with a number of top managers to identify their goals and the resulting CSFs. These personal CSFs are aggregated to develop a picture of the firm's CSFs. Then systems are built to deliver in-

LOGICAL APPLICATION GROUPS	PROCESSES \ DATA CLASSES	Actuarial estimates	Agency plans	Budget	Program regs./policy	Admin. regs./policy	Labor agreements	Data standards	Procedures	Automated systems documentation	Educational media	Public agreements	Intergovernmental agreements	Grants	External	Exchange control	Administrative accounts	Program expenditures	Audit reports	Organization/position	Employee identification	Recruitment/placement	Complaints/grievances	Training resources	Security	Equipment utilization	Space utilization	Supplies utilization	Workload schedules	Work measurement	Enumeration I.D.	Enumeration control	Earnings	Employer I.D.	Earnings control	Claims characteristics	Claims control	Decisions	Payment	Collection/waiver	Notice	Inquiries control	Quality appraisal
PLANNING	Develop agency plans	C	C	C	U	U									U																												
PLANNING	Administer agency budget	C	C	C	U	U						U	U	U		U	U	U		U	U					U	U	U		U		U			U		U			U		U	U
PLANNING	Formulate program policies	U	U		C				U						U				U				U															U					U
PLANNING	Formulate admin. policies		U		U	C	C		U						U				U	U			U																				
PLANNING	Formulate data policies		U	U		U		C	U	U															U	U	U	U															
PLANNING	Design work processes		U		U	U			C	C		U	U						U																			U					U
GENERAL MANAGEMENT	Manage public affairs		U		U	U			U		C	C	C																														
GENERAL MANAGEMENT	Manage intrgovt. affairs	U	U		U	U			U		U		C	C	C															U	U		U	U		U			U				
GENERAL MANAGEMENT	Exchange data				U				U			U	U	U	U	C	U	U												U													
GENERAL MANAGEMENT	Maintain admin. accounts			U		U			U			U	U				C				U					U	U	U								U			U				
GENERAL MANAGEMENT	Maintain prog. accounts			U	U				U			U	U					C														U			U		U	U	U	U		U	
GENERAL MANAGEMENT	Conduct audits				U	U			U	U							U	U	C		U								U														
GENERAL MANAGEMENT	Establish organizations			U		U			U											C	U								U	U													U
GENERAL MANAGEMENT	Manage human resources			U		U	U		U											C	C	C	C	C																			
GENERAL MANAGEMENT	Provide security				U	U		U	U	U															C	C	C	C		U													
GENERAL MANAGEMENT	Manage equipment			U		U		U	U	U															C	C	C	C															
GENERAL MANAGEMENT	Manage facilities			U		U			U																U	U	C																
GENERAL MANAGEMENT	Manage supplies			U		U			U																C	U	U	C															
GENERAL MANAGEMENT	Manage workloads	U		U	U	U			U							U										U	U	U	C	C		U			U		U					U	U
PROGRAM ADMIN.	Issue Social Security nos.								U				U		U																C	C											
PROGRAM ADMIN.	Maintain earnings								U				U	U	U																U		C	C	C	U							
PROGRAM ADMIN.	Collect claims information				U	U			U						U																U	U				C	C	U	U	U			
PROGRAM ADMIN.	Determine elig./entlmt.								U																						U	U	U			U		C	U	U			
PROGRAM ADMIN.	Compute payments				U				U									U													U		U			U		U	C	C			
PROGRAM ADMIN.	Administer debt mgmt.				U				U									U																					U	C			
SUPPORT	Generate notices								U						U																U		U			U		U	U	U	C		
SUPPORT	Respond to prog. inquiries				U				U		U																				U		U	U		U		U	U	U	U	C	
SUPPORT	Provide quality assessment				U	U			U	U																					U		U			U		U			U		C

KEY

C = creators of data U = users of data

FIGURE 9-1 Process/data class matrix. This chart depicts which data classes are required to support particular organizational processes and which processes are the creators and users of data.

formation on these CSFs. (See Table 9-2 for an example of CSFs. For the method of developing CSFs in an organization, see Figure 9-2.)

The strength of the CSF method is that it produces a smaller data set to analyze than does enterprise analysis. Only top managers are interviewed, and the questions focus on a small number of CSFs rather than a broad inquiry into what information is used or needed. This method can be tailored to each industry's structure, with different competitive strategies producing different information systems. Therefore, this method produces systems that are more custom-tailored to an organization.

A unique strength of the CSF method is that it takes into account the changing environment with which organizations and managers must deal. This method explicitly asks managers to look at the environment and consider how their analysis of it shapes their information needs. It is especially suitable for top management and for the development of DSS and ESS. Unlike enterprise analysis, the CSF method focuses organizational attention on how information should be handled.

Table 9-2	Critical Success Factors and Organizational Goals	
Example	**Goals**	**CSF**

Profit concern	Earnings/share
	Return on investment
	Market share
	New product
		Automotive industry
		  Styling
		  Quality dealer system
		  Cost control
		  Energy standards

Nonprofit	Excellent health care Meeting government regulations Future health needs	Regional integration with other hospitals Efficient use of resources Improved monitoring of regulations

Source: Rockart (1979).

The method's primary weakness is that the aggregation process and the analysis of the data are art forms. There is no particularly rigorous way in which individual CSFs can be aggregated into a clear company pattern. Also, there is often confusion among interviewees (and interviewers) between *individual* and *organizational* CSFs. They are not necessarily the same. What is critical to a manager may not be important for the organization. Moreover, this method is clearly biased toward top managers because they are the ones (generally the only ones) interviewed. Last, it should be noted that this method does not guarantee that requirements will

FIGURE 9-2 Using CSFs to develop systems. The CSF approach relies on interviews with key managers to identify their CSFs. Individual CSFs are aggregated to develop CSFs for the entire firm. Systems can then be built to deliver information on these CSFs.

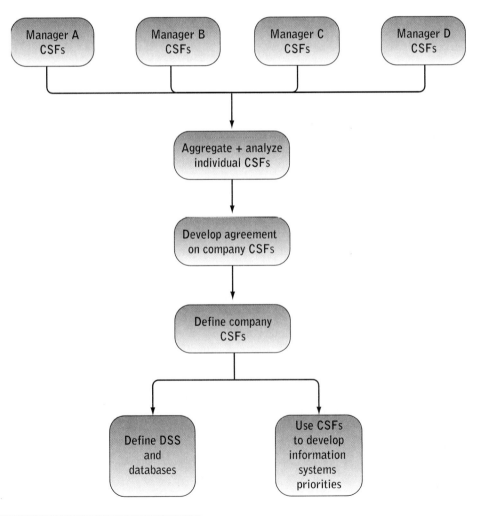

Table 9-3 **How Information Technology Can Transform Organizations**

Information Technology	Organizational Change
Global networks	International division of labor: The operations of a firm are no longer determined by location; the global reach of firms is extended; costs of global coordination decline. Transaction costs decline.
Enterprise networks	Collaborative work and teamwork: The organization of work can be coordinated across divisional boundaries; a customer and product orientation emerges; widely dispersed task forces become the dominant work group. The costs of management (agency costs) decline. Business processes are changed.
Distributed computing	Empowerment: Individuals and work groups now have the information and knowledge to act. Business processes are redesigned, streamlined. Management costs decline. Hierarchy and centralization decline.
Portable computing	Virtual organizations: Work is no longer tied to geographic location. Knowledge and information can be delivered anywhere they are needed, anytime. Work becomes portable. Organizational costs decline as real estate is less essential for business.
Graphical user interfaces	Accessibility: Everyone in the organization—even senior executives—can access information and knowledge; work flows can be automated, and all can contribute from remote locations. Organizational costs decline as work flows move from paper to digital image, documents, and voice.

accurately reflect the impact of a changing environment or changes in managers. Environments and managers change rapidly, and information systems must adjust accordingly.

SYSTEMS DEVELOPMENT AND ORGANIZATIONAL CHANGE

New information systems can be powerful instruments for organizational change, enabling organizations to redesign their structure, scope, power relationships, workflows, products, and services. Table 9-3 describes some of the ways that information technology is being used to transform organizations.

The Spectrum of Organizational Change

Information technology can promote various degrees of organizational change ranging from incremental to far-reaching. Figure 9-3 shows four kinds of structural organizational change

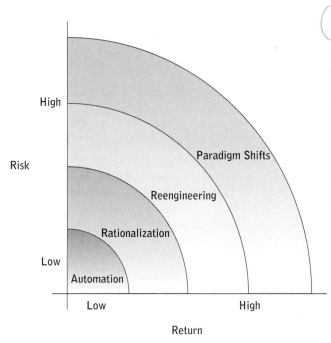

FIGURE 9-3 Organizational change carries risks and rewards. The most common forms of organizational change are automation and rationalization. These relatively slow moving and slow changing strategies present modest returns but little risk. Faster and more comprehensive change—such as reengineering and paradigm shifts—carry high rewards but offer a substantial chance of failure.

automation Using the computer to speed up the performance of existing tasks.

rationalization of procedures The streamlining of standard operating procedures, eliminating obvious bottlenecks, so that automation makes operating procedures more efficient.

business process reengineering The radical redesign of business processes, combining steps to cut waste and eliminating repetitive, paper-intensive tasks in order to improve cost, quality, and service, and to maximize the benefits of information technology.

that are enabled by information technology: (1) automation, (2) rationalization, (3) reengineering, and (4) paradigm shifts. Each carries different rewards and risks.

The most common form of IT-enabled organizational change is **automation.** The first applications of information technology involved assisting employees to perform their tasks more efficiently and effectively. Calculating paychecks and payroll registers, giving bank tellers instant access to customer deposit records, and developing a nationwide network of airline reservation terminals for airline reservation agents are all examples of early automation.

A deeper form of organizational change—one that developed quickly from early automation—is **rationalization of procedures.** Automation frequently reveals bottlenecks in production and makes the existing arrangement of procedures and structures painfully cumbersome. Rationalization of procedures involves the streamlining of standard operating procedures, which eliminates obvious bottlenecks, so that operating procedures become more efficient. For example, Edmonton Power's new system is effective not only because it uses state-of-the-art computer technology but also because its design allows it to operate more efficiently. The procedures of Edmonton Power, or of any organization, must be rationally structured to achieve this result. Edmonton Power had to have standard identification numbers for all parts in inventory and standard rules for matching work orders with accounts. Without a certain amount of rationalization in Edmonton Power's organization, its computer technology would have been useless.

A more powerful type of organizational change is **business process reengineering,** in which business processes are analyzed, simplified, and redesigned. Reengineering involves radically rethinking the flow of work and the business processes used to produce products and services with the intention of radically reducing the costs of business (see Table 9-4). Using information technology, organizations can rethink and streamline their business processes to improve speed, service, and quality. Business process reengineering reorganizes work flows, combining steps to cut waste and eliminating repetitive, paper-intensive tasks. (Sometimes the new design eliminates jobs as well.) It is much more ambitious than rationalization of procedures because it requires a new vision of how the process is to be organized.

Table 9-4 IT Capabilities and Their Organizational Impacts

Capability	Organizational Impact/Benefit
Transactional	IT can transform unstructured processes into routinized transactions.
Geographical	IT can transfer information with rapidity and ease across great distances, making processes independent of geography.
Automational	IT can replace or reduce human labor in a process.
Analytical	IT can bring complex analytical methods to bear on a process.
Informational	IT can bring vast amounts of detailed information into a process.
Sequential	IT can enable changes in the sequence of tasks in a process, often allowing multiple tasks to be worked on simultaneously.
Knowledge management	IT allows the capture and dissemination of knowledge and expertise to improve the process.
Tracking	IT allows the detailed tracking of task status, inputs, and outputs.
Disintermediation	IT can be used to connect two parties within a process who would otherwise communicate through an intermediary (internal or external).

Reprinted from "The New Industrial Engineering: Information Technology and Business Process Redesign," Thomas H. Davenport and James E. Short, *Sloan Management Review* 11, Summer 1990, by permission from the publisher. Copyright 1990 by Sloan Management Review Association. All rights reserved.

A widely cited example of business process reengineering is Ford Motor Company's *invoiceless processing*. Ford employed more than 500 people in its North American Accounts Payable organization. The accounts payable clerks spent most of their time resolving discrepancies between purchase orders, receiving documents, and invoices. Ford reengineered its accounts payable process, instituting a system wherein the purchasing department enters a purchase order into an on-line database that can be checked by the receiving department when the ordered items arrive. If the received goods match the purchase order, the system automatically generates a check for accounts payable to send to the vendor. There is no need for vendors to send invoices. After reengineering, Ford was able to reduce headcount in accounts payable by 75 percent and produce more accurate financial information (Hammer and Champy, 1993).

Rationalizing procedures and redesigning business processes are limited to specific parts of a business. New information systems can ultimately affect the design of the entire organization by transforming how the organization carries out its business or even the nature of the business itself. For instance, Schneider National, the largest carrier of full-truckload cargoes in North America, used new information systems to change its business model. Schneider created a new business managing the logistics for other companies. Its Schneider Brokerage Web Site allows shippers to select from thousands of approved carriers in the United States, Canada, and Mexico. Baxter International's stockless inventory system (described in Chapter 2) transformed Baxter into a working partner with hospitals and into a manager of its customers' supplies. This more radical form of business change is called a **paradigm shift.** A paradigm shift involves rethinking the nature of the business and the nature of the organization itself. The Window on Technology illustrates how Internet technology can be used for making these organizational changes. Paradigm shifts and reengineering often fail because extensive organizational change is so difficult to orchestrate (see Section 9.3). Why then do so many corporations entertain such radical change? Because the rewards are equally high (see Figure 9-3). In many instances firms seeking paradigm shifts and pursuing reengineering strategies achieve stunning, order-of-magnitude increases in their returns on investment (or productivity). Some of these success stories, and some failure stories, are cited throughout this book.

paradigm shift Radical reconceptualization of the nature of the business and the nature of the organization.

BUSINESS PROCESS REENGINEERING

Many companies today are focusing on building new information systems in which they can redesign business processes. Table 9-4 describes ways that information technology can streamline and consolidate business processes. If the business process is redesigned before computing power is applied, organizations potentially can obtain very large payoffs from their investments in information technology.

Mammoth Golf used the Internet to change its business model into a "click and mortar" retailer with both a physical store and a virtual storefront on the Web. Internet technology and the Web provide a flexible platform for redesigning work flows, products, and services.

REDESIGNING WITH THE INTERNET

Many companies are using Internet and Web technology to help them redesign their business processes or even change their business model. Here are two examples:

Four years ago, Mammoth Golf was a conventional bricks-and-mortar small retailer with a 2,000-square-foot showroom in the Baltimore suburbs. It had 14 employees and $5 million in revenue. Mammoth sold custom-built golf clubs, club components, and other gear in its store and through print catalogs. Since 1996, the company has moved more of its business onto the Internet and today it is a vastly different company. Mammoth still sells golf gear from its bricks-and-mortar showroom, but it has become a click-and-mortar retailer. The Web does not merely supplement its physical store—it has become a major sales channel.

Mammoth's business model and its technology infrastructure have changed to accommodate the crucial role played by the Internet. Mammoth's million-dollar Web site, www.mammothgolf.com, sells the store's full product line. The company now has 50 employees, a staff of technical specialists, 50 computers, and 9 Sun Microsystems servers. The servers run the same type of Oracle software that large Fortune 500 companies use to integrate transactions coming from the Web with internal systems.

At least 32,000 active buyers purchase through the site and more than a quarter of a million visitors come to window-shop. Customers with questions chat in real-time with on-line service representatives, who steer them to relevant Web pages or use push technology from FaceTime to provide them with information. Corporate customers can use an extranet to place regular orders for Mammoth.

About one-third of Mammoth's 1999 sales of $10 million were made on-line, and that percentage is growing. Owner Bill Allbright expects that 50 percent of revenues in the year 2000, which could amount to $50 million, will come from the Web. Business has grown so much that

Mammoth had to move to larger quarters and now occupies a 10,000-square-foot superstore.

Office Furniture U.S.A, based in Pelham, Alabama, built an extranet called Triple-Net in early 1998 that is used by its manufacturers, dealers, and employees. Before implementing Triple-Net, Office Furniture had many cumbersome work flow processes. For example, dealers who wanted to return damaged merchandise to a manufacturer had to send handwritten faxes to corporate headquarters. The hard-to-read faxes might languish on someone's desk for three weeks. Triple-Net automated the procedure for returning damaged merchandise, enabling Office Furniture's customer service center to handle return material authorizations more smoothly.

Using Triple-Net, orders that used to take customer service representatives up to five weeks to process can now be handled in three days or less. Sales representatives can obtain sales data with a few mouse clicks, whereas previously they had to pull it out of a file. Dealers can instantly receive reports about manufacturer items that might be out of stock. When a major Canadian furniture manufacturer lost power for a week, Triple-Net kept dealers up-to-date on the status of orders. In the past, they would have had to send faxes or make telephone calls to find out this information. Dealer productivity has risen because using Triple-Net eliminates the need to do duplicate sales order entry. Streamlining these business processes has saved Office Furniture $250,000 per year, 25 percent less than Triple-Net's total cost, according to firm CIO Gary Sweetapple.

TO THINK ABOUT: How are the companies described here using Internet technology for organizational design? What kinds of organizational changes are taking place?

Sources: Jane Hodges, "Putting It All Online," **Small Business Computing and Communications,** January 2000; and Joe Mullich, "Reinvent Your Intranet," **Datamation,** June 1999.

The home mortgage industry is a prime example in the United States of how major corporations have implemented business reengineering. The application process for a home mortgage currently takes about 6 to 8 weeks and costs about $3,000. The goal of many mortgage banks is to lower the cost to $1,000 and the time to obtain a mortgage to about 1 week. Leading mortgage banks such as BankBoston, Countrywide Funding Corporation, and BancOne Corporation have redesigned the mortgage application process.

The mortgage application process is divided into three stages: origination, servicing, and secondary marketing. Figure 9-4 illustrates how business process redesign has been used in each of these stages.

In the past, a mortgage applicant filled out a paper loan application. The bank entered the application into its computer system. Specialists such as credit analysts and underwriters from perhaps eight different departments accessed and evaluated the application individually. If the loan application was approved, the closing was scheduled. After the closing, bank specialists

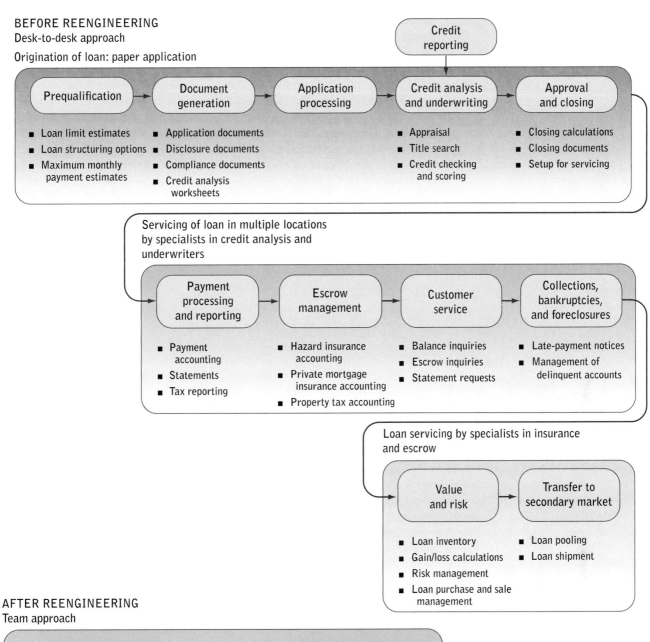

BEFORE REENGINEERING
Desk-to-desk approach

Origination of loan: paper application

Credit reporting

Prequalification → Document generation → Application processing → Credit analysis and underwriting → Approval and closing

- Loan limit estimates
- Loan structuring options
- Maximum monthly payment estimates

- Application documents
- Disclosure documents
- Compliance documents
- Credit analysis worksheets

- Appraisal
- Title search
- Credit checking and scoring

- Closing calculations
- Closing documents
- Setup for servicing

Servicing of loan in multiple locations by specialists in credit analysis and underwriters

Payment processing and reporting → Escrow management → Customer service → Collections, bankruptcies, and foreclosures

- Payment accounting
- Statements
- Tax reporting

- Hazard insurance accounting
- Private mortgage insurance accounting
- Property tax accounting

- Balance inquiries
- Escrow inquiries
- Statement requests

- Late-payment notices
- Management of delinquent accounts

Loan servicing by specialists in insurance and escrow

Value and risk → Transfer to secondary market

- Loan inventory
- Gain/loss calculations
- Risk management
- Loan purchase and sale management

- Loan pooling
- Loan shipment

AFTER REENGINEERING
Team approach

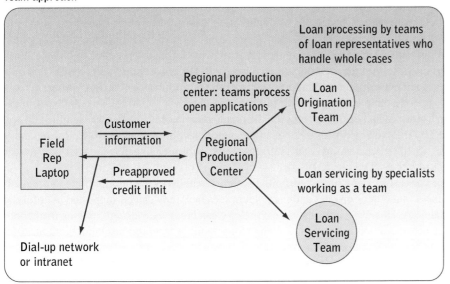

Loan processing by teams of loan representatives who handle whole cases

Regional production center: teams process open applications

Field Rep Laptop

Customer information →

← Preapproved credit limit →

Regional Production Center

→ Loan Origination Team

Loan servicing by specialists working as a team

→ Loan Servicing Team

Dial-up network or intranet

FIGURE 9-4 Redesigning mortgage processing in the United States. By redesigning their mortgage processing systems and the mortgage application process, mortgage banks will be able to reduce the costs of processing the average mortgage from $3,000 to $1,000 and reduce the time of approval from 6 weeks to 1 week or less. Some banks are even preapproving mortgages and locking interest rates the day the customer applies.

dealing with insurance or funds in escrow serviced the loan. This desk-to-desk assembly-line approach might take up to 17 days.

Leading banks have replaced the sequential desk-to-desk approach with a speedier "work cell," or team, approach. Now, loan originators in the field enter the mortgage application directly into laptop computers. Software checks the application transaction to make sure that all of the information is correct and complete. The loan originators transmit the loan applications using a dial-up network to regional production centers. Instead of working on the application individually, the credit analysts, loan underwriters, and other specialists convene electronically, working as a team, to approve the mortgage. Some banks provide customers with a nearly instant credit lock-in of a guaranteed mortgage so they can find a house that meets their budget immediately.

After closing, another team of specialists sets up the loan for servicing. The entire loan application process can take as little as two days. Loan information is easier to access than before, when the loan application could be in eight or nine different departments. Loan originators also can dial into the bank's network to obtain information on mortgage loan costs or to check the status of a loan for the customer.

In redesigning their approach to mortgage processing, mortgage banks have achieved remarkable efficiencies. They have not focused on redesigning a single business process; instead they have reexamined the entire set of logically connected processes required to obtain a mortgage. Instead of automating the previously used method of mortgage processing, the banks have completely rethought the entire mortgage application process.

Work Flow Management

work flow management The process of streamlining business procedures so that documents can be moved easily and efficiently from one location to another.

To streamline the paperwork in the mortgage application process, banks have turned to work flow and document management software. Using this software to store and process documents electronically, organizations can redesign their work flow so that documents can be worked on simultaneously or moved easily and efficiently from one location to another. The process of streamlining business procedures so that documents can be moved easily and efficiently is called **work flow management.** Work flow and document management software automates processes such as routing documents to different locations, securing approvals, scheduling, and generating reports. Two or more people can work simultaneously on the same document, facilitating quicker completion time. Work need not be delayed because a file is out or a document is in transit. And with a properly designed indexing system, users will be able to retrieve files in many different ways depending on the content of the document. Chapter 2 describes how Mercantile Mutual developed a document imaging system to obtain such benefits.

Steps in Effective Reengineering

To reengineer effectively, senior management needs to develop a broad strategic vision that calls for redesigned business processes. For example, Mitsubishi Heavy Industries management looked for breakthroughs to lower costs and accelerate product development that would enable the firm to regain market leadership in shipbuilding. The company redesigned its entire production process to replace expensive labor-intensive tasks with robotic machines and computer-aided design tools. Companies should identify a few core business processes to be redesigned and focus on those with the greatest potential payback (Davenport and Short, 1990).

Management must understand and measure the performance of existing processes as a baseline. If, for example, the objective of process redesign is to reduce time and cost in developing a new product or filling an order, the organization needs to measure the time and cost consumed by the existing process. For example, before reengineering, it cost C. R. England & Sons Inc. $5.10 to send an invoice; after processes were reengineered the cost per invoice dropped to 15 cents (Davidson, 1993).

The conventional method of designing systems establishes the information requirements of a business function or process and then determines how they can be supported by information technology. However, information technology can create new design options for various processes because it can be used to challenge longstanding assumptions about work arrangements that used to inhibit organizations. Table 9-5 provides examples of innovations that have overcome these assumptions using companies discussed in the text. Information technology should be allowed to influence process design from the start.

Table 9-5   New Process Design Options with Information Technology

Assumption	Technology	Options	Examples
Field personnel need offices to receive, store, and transmit information.	Wireless communications	Personnel can send and receive information from wherever they are.	Dine-One-One BMW
Information can appear only in one place at one time.	Shared databases	People can collaborate on the same project from scattered locations; information can be used simultaneously wherever it is needed.	U.S. West BancOne
People are needed to ascertain where things are located.	Automatic identification and tracking technology	Things can tell people where they are.	United Parcel Service Streamline
Businesses need reserve inventory to prevent stockouts.	Telecommunications networks and EDI	Just-in-time delivery and stock-less supply.	Wal-Mart Baxter International

Following these steps does not automatically guarantee that reengineering will always be successful. The organization's information technology (IT) infrastructure should have capabilities to support business process changes that span boundaries among functions, business units, or firms (Broadbent, Weill, and St. Clair, 1999). In point of fact, the majority of reengineering projects do not achieve breakthrough gains in business performance. Problems with reengineering are part of the larger problem of orchestrating organizational change, a problem that attends the introduction of all new innovations, including information systems. Managing change is neither simple nor intuitive. A reengineered business process or a new information system inevitably affects jobs, skill requirements, work flows, and reporting relationships (Teng, Jeong, and Grover, 1998). Fear of these changes breeds resistance, confusion, and even conscious efforts to undermine the change effort. We examine these organizational change issues more carefully in Section 9.3.

9.2 Overview of Systems Development

Whatever their scope and objectives, new information systems are an outgrowth of a process of organizational problem solving. A new information system is built as a solution to some type of problem or set of problems the organization perceives it is facing. The problem may be one in which managers and employees realize that the organization is not performing as well as expected, or it may come from the realization that the organization should take advantage of new opportunities to perform more successfully.

Review the diagrams at the beginning of each chapter of this text. They show an information system that is a solution to a particular set of business challenges or problems. The resulting information system is an outgrowth of a series of events called **systems development.** Systems development refers to all the activities that go into producing an information systems solution to an organizational problem or opportunity. Systems development is a structured kind of problem solving with distinct activities. These activities consist of systems analysis, systems design, programming, testing, conversion, and production and maintenance.

Figure 9-5 illustrates the systems development process. The systems development activities depicted here usually take place in sequential order. But some of the activities may need to be repeated or some may take place simultaneously depending on the approach to system building that is being used (see Chapter 10). Note also that each activity involves interaction with the organization. Members of the organization participate in these activities and the systems development process creates organizational changes.

SYSTEMS ANALYSIS

Systems analysis is the analysis of the problem that the organization will try to solve with an information system. It consists of defining the problem, identifying its causes,

systems development The activities that go into producing an information systems solution to an organizational problem or opportunity.

systems analysis The analysis of a problem that the organization will try to solve with an information system.

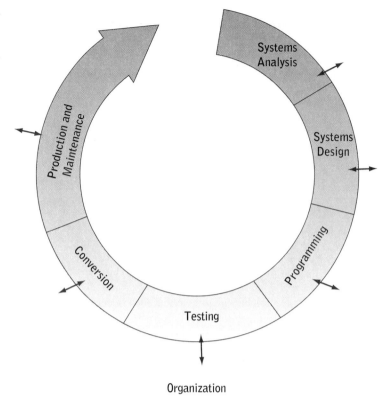

FIGURE 9-5 The systems development process. Each of the core systems development activities entails interaction with the organization.

specifying the solution, and identifying the information requirements that must be met by a system solution.

The systems analyst creates a road map of the existing organization and systems, identifying the primary owners and users of data in the organization. These stakeholders have a direct interest in the information affected by the new system. In addition to these organizational aspects, the analyst also briefly describes the existing hardware and software that serve the organization.

From this organizational analysis, the systems analyst details the problems of existing systems. By examining documents, work papers, and procedures; observing system operations; and interviewing key users of the systems, the analyst can identify the problem areas and objectives a solution would achieve. Often the solution requires building a new information system or improving an existing one.

Feasibility

In addition to suggesting a solution, systems analysis involves a **feasibility study** to determine whether that solution is feasible, or achievable, given the organization's resources and constraints. Three major areas of feasibility must be addressed:

feasibility study As part of the systems analysis process, the way to determine whether the solution is achievable given the organization's resources and constraints.

technical feasibility Determines whether a proposed solution can be implemented with the available hardware, software, and technical resources.

economic feasibility Determines whether the benefits of a proposed solution outweigh the costs.

operational feasibility Determines whether a proposed solution is desirable within the existing managerial and organizational framework.

1. **Technical feasibility:** Can the proposed solution can be implemented with the available hardware, software, and technical resources?

2. **Economic feasibility:** Do the benefits of the proposed solution outweigh the costs? We explore this topic in greater detail in Section 9.4, Understanding the Business Value of Information Systems.

3. **Operational feasibility:** Is the proposed solution desirable within the existing managerial and organizational framework?

Normally the systems analysis process identifies several alternative solutions that the organization can pursue. According to the process, the feasibility of each is then assessed. A written

Building successful information systems requires close cooperation among end users and information systems specialists throughout the systems development process.

systems proposal report describes the costs and benefits, advantages, and disadvantages of each alternative. It is up to management to determine which mix of costs, benefits, technical features, and organizational impacts represents the most desirable alternative.

Establishing Information Requirements

Perhaps the most difficult task of the systems analyst is to define the specific information requirements that must be met by the system solution selected. At the most basic level, the **information requirements** of a new system involve identifying who needs what information, where, when, and how. Requirements analysis carefully defines the objectives of the new or modified system and develops a detailed description of the functions that the new system must perform. Requirements must consider economic, technical, and time constraints, as well as the organization's goals, procedures, and decision processes. Faulty requirements analysis is a leading cause of systems failure and high systems development costs. A system designed around the wrong set of requirements will either have to be discarded because of poor performance or will need to be heavily revised. Therefore, the importance of requirements analysis cannot be overstated.

Developing requirements specifications may involve considerable research and revision. To derive information requirements, analysts may be forced to work and rework requirements

information requirements A detailed statement of the information needs that a new system must satisfy; identifies who needs what information, and when, where, and how the information is needed.

statements in cooperation with users. There are also alternative approaches to eliciting requirements that help minimize these problems (see Chapter 10).

In many instances, building a new system creates an opportunity to redefine how the organization conducts its daily business. Some problems do not require an information system solution but instead need an adjustment in management, additional training, or refinement of existing organizational procedures. If the problem is information related, systems analysis still may be required to diagnose the problem and arrive at the proper solution.

SYSTEMS DESIGN

systems design Details how a system will meet the information requirements as determined by the systems analysis.

Systems analysis describes what a system should do to meet information requirements, and **systems design** shows how the system will fulfill this objective. The design of an information system is the overall plan or model for that system. Like the blueprint of a building or house, it consists of all the specifications that give the system its form and structure.

The systems designer details the system specifications that will deliver the functions identified during systems analysis. These specifications should address all of the managerial, organizational, and technological components of the system solution. Table 9-6 lists the types of specifications that would be produced during systems design.

Logical and Physical Design

logical design Lays out the components of the information system and their relationship to each other as they would appear to users.

The design for an information system can be broken down into logical and physical design specifications. **Logical design** lays out the system's components and their relationship to each

Table 9-6	**Design Specifications**
Output	Controls
Medium	Input controls (characters, limit, reasonableness)
Content	Processing controls (consistency, record counts)
Timing	Output controls (totals, samples of output)
Input	Procedural controls (passwords, special forms)
Origins	Security
Flow	Access controls
Data entry	Catastrophe plans
User interface	Audit trails
Simplicity	Documentation
Efficiency	Operations documentation
Logic	Systems documents
Feedback	User documentation
Errors	Conversion
Database design	Transfer data files
Logical data relations	Initiate new procedures
Volume and speed requirements	Select testing method
File organization and design	Cut over to new system
Record specifications	Training
Processing	Select training techniques
Computations	Develop training modules
Program modules	Identify training facilities
Required reports	Organizational changes
Timing of outputs	Task redesign
Manual procedures	Job design
What activities	Process design
Who performs them	Office and organization structure design
When	Reporting relationships
How	
Where	

other as they would appear to users. It shows what the system solution will do as opposed to how it is actually implemented physically. It describes inputs and outputs, processing functions to be performed, business procedures, data models, and controls. (Controls specify standards for acceptable performance and methods for measuring actual performance in relation to these standards. They are described in detail in Chapter 13.)

Physical design is the process of translating the abstract logical model into the specific technical design for the new system. It produces the specifications for hardware, software, physical databases, input/output media, manual procedures, and specific controls. Physical design provides the remaining specifications that transform the abstract logical design plan into a functioning system of people and machines.

physical design The process of translating the abstract logical model into the specific technical design for the new system.

Like houses or buildings, information systems may have many possible designs. They may be centralized or distributed, on-line or batch, partially manual, or heavily automated. Each design represents a unique blend of all of the technical and organizational factors that shape an information system. What makes one design superior to others is the ease and efficiency it brings to users with a specific set of technical, organizational, financial, and time constraints.

The Role of End Users

User information requirements drive the entire system-building effort. Users must have sufficient control over the design process to ensure that the system reflects their business priorities and information needs, not the biases of the technical staff (Hunton and Beeler, 1997). Working on design increases users' understanding and acceptance of the system, reducing problems caused by power transfers, intergroup conflict, and unfamiliarity with new system functions and procedures. As we describe later in this chapter, insufficient user involvement in the design effort is a major cause of system failure.

The nature and level of user participation in design vary from system to system. There is less need for user involvement in designing systems with simple or straightforward requirements than in those with requirements that are elaborate, complex, or vaguely defined. Less structured systems need more user participation to define requirements and may necessitate many versions of design before specifications can be finalized. Different levels of user involvement in design are reflected in different systems development methods. Chapter 10 describes how user involvement varies with each development approach.

COMPLETING THE SYSTEMS DEVELOPMENT PROCESS

The remaining steps in the systems development process translate the solution specifications established during systems analysis and design into a fully operational information system. These concluding steps consist of programming, testing, conversion, production, and maintenance.

Programming

The process of translating design specifications into software for the computer constitutes a smaller portion of the systems development cycle than design and, perhaps, the testing activities. But it is here, in providing the actual instructions for the machine, that the heart of the system takes shape. During the **programming** stage, system specifications that were prepared during the design stage are translated into program code. On the basis of detailed design documents for files, transaction and report layouts, and other design details, specifications for each program in the system are prepared.

programming The process of translating the system specifications prepared during the design stage into program code.

Testing

Exhaustive and thorough **testing** must be conducted to ascertain whether the system produces the right results. Testing answers the question, "Will the system produce the desired results under known conditions?"

The amount of time needed to answer this question traditionally has been underrated in systems project planning (see Chapter 13). As much as 50 percent of the entire software development budget can be spent in testing. Testing is also time consuming: Test data must be

testing The exhaustive and thorough process that determines whether the system produces the desired results under known conditions.

unit testing The process of testing each program separately in the system. Sometimes called program testing.

system testing Tests the functioning of the information system as a whole in order to determine if discrete modules will function together as planned.

acceptance testing Provides the final certification that the system is ready to be used in a production setting.

test plan Prepared by the development team in conjunction with the users; it includes all of the preparations for the series of tests to be performed on the system.

conversion The process of changing from the old system to the new system.

parallel strategy A safe and conservative conversion approach where both the old system and its potential replacement are run together for a time until everyone is assured that the new one functions correctly.

FIGURE 9-6 A sample test plan to test a record change. When developing a test plan, it is imperative to include the various conditions to be tested, the requirements for each condition tested, and the expected results. Test plans require input from both end users and information system specialists.

carefully prepared, results reviewed, and corrections made in the system. In some instances parts of the system may have to be redesigned. The risks of glossing over this step are enormous.

Testing an information system can be broken down into three types of activities:

Unit testing, or program testing, consists of testing each program separately in the system. It is widely believed that the purpose of such testing is to guarantee that programs are error free, but this goal is realistically impossible. Testing should be viewed instead as a means of locating errors in programs, focusing on finding all the ways to make a program fail. Once they are pinpointed, problems can be corrected.

System testing tests the functioning of the information system as a whole. It tries to determine if discrete modules will function together as planned and whether discrepancies exist between the way the system actually works and the way it was conceived. Among the areas examined are performance time, capacity for file storage and handling peak loads, recovery and restart capabilities, and manual procedures.

Acceptance testing provides the final certification that the system is ready to be used in a production setting. Systems tests are evaluated by users and reviewed by management. When all parties are satisfied that the new system meets their standards, the system is formally accepted for installation.

It is essential that all aspects of testing be carefully thought out and that they be as comprehensive as possible. To ensure this, the development team works with users to devise a systematic test plan. The **test plan** includes all of the preparations for the series of tests previously described.

Figure 9-6 shows an example of a test plan. The general condition being tested is a record change. The documentation consists of a series of test-plan screens maintained on a database (perhaps a PC database) that is ideally suited to this kind of application.

Conversion

Conversion is the process of changing from the old system to the new system. It answers the question, "Will the new system work under real conditions?" Four main conversion strategies can be employed: the parallel strategy, the direct cutover strategy, the pilot study strategy, and the phased approach strategy.

In a **parallel strategy** both the old system and its potential replacement are run together for a time until everyone is assured that the new one functions correctly. This is the safest con-

Procedure	Address and Maintenance "Record Change Series"		Test Series 2		
	Prepared By:	Date:	Version:		
Test Ref.	Condition Tested	Special Requirements	Expected Results	Output On	Next Screen
2	Change records				
2.1	Change existing record	Key field	Not allowed		
2.2	Change nonexistent record	Other fields	"Invalid key" message		
2.3	Change deleted record	Deleted record must be available	"Deleted" message		
2.4	Make second record	Change 2.1 above	OK if valid	Transaction file	V45
2.5	Insert record		OK if valid	Transaction file	V45
2.6	Abort during change	Abort 2.5	No change	Transaction file	V45

version approach because, in the event of errors or processing disruptions, the old system can still be used as a backup. However, this approach is very expensive, and additional staff or resources may be required to run the extra system.

The **direct cutover** strategy replaces the old system entirely with the new system on an appointed day. At first glance, this strategy seems less costly than the parallel conversion strategy. However, it is a very risky approach that can potentially be more costly than parallel activities if serious problems with the new system are found. There is no other system to fall back on. Dislocations, disruptions, and the cost of corrections may be enormous.

The **pilot study** strategy introduces the new system to a limited area in the organization, such as a single department or operating unit. When this pilot version is complete and working smoothly, it is installed throughout the rest of the organization, either simultaneously or in stages.

The **phased approach** strategy introduces the new system in stages, either by functions or by organizational units. If, for example, the system is introduced by functions, a new payroll system might begin with hourly workers who are paid weekly, followed six months later by adding salaried employees (who are paid monthly) to the system. If the system is introduced by organizational units, corporate headquarters might be converted first, followed by outlying operating units four months later.

A formal **conversion plan** provides a schedule of all the activities required to install the new system. The most time-consuming activity is usually the conversion of data. Data from the old system must be transferred to the new system, either manually or through special conversion software programs. The converted data then must be verified carefully for accuracy and completeness.

Moving from an old system to a new one requires that end users be trained to use the new system. Detailed **documentation** showing how the system works from both a technical and an end-user standpoint is finalized during conversion time for use in training and everyday operations. Lack of proper training and documentation contributes to system failure, so this portion of the systems development process is very important.

Production and Maintenance

After the new system is installed and conversion is complete, the system is said to be in **production.** During this stage the system is reviewed by both users and technical specialists to determine how well it has met its original objectives and to decide whether any revisions or modifications are in order. Changes in hardware, software, documentation, or procedures to a production system to correct errors, meet new requirements, or improve processing efficiency are termed **maintenance.**

Studies of maintenance have examined the amount of time required for various maintenance tasks (Lientz and Swanson, 1980). Approximately 20 percent of the time is devoted to debugging or correcting emergency production problems; another 20 percent is concerned with changes in data, files, reports, hardware, or system software. But 60 percent of all maintenance work consists of making user enhancements, improving documentation, and recoding system components for greater processing efficiency. The amount of work in the third category of maintenance problems could be reduced significantly through better systems analysis and design practices. Table 9-7 summarizes the systems development activities.

Systems differ in terms of their size and technical complexity, and in terms of the organizational problems they are meant to solve. Because there are different kinds of systems, a number of methods have been developed to build systems. We describe these various methods in the next chapter.

9.3 System Implementation: Managing Change

The introduction or alteration of an information system has a powerful behavioral and organizational impact. It transforms the way various individuals and groups perform and interact. Changes in the way information is defined, accessed, and used to manage the organization's resources often lead to new distributions of authority and power. This internal organizational change breeds resistance and opposition and can lead to the demise of an otherwise good system.

---

direct cutover A risky conversion approach where the new system completely replaces the old one on an appointed day.

pilot study A strategy to introduce the new system to a limited area in the organization until it is proven to be fully functional; only then can the conversion to the new system across the entire organization take place.

phased approach Introduces the new system in stages, either by functions or by organizational units.

conversion plan Provides a schedule of all activities required to install a new system.

documentation Descriptions of how an information system works from either a technical or end-user standpoint.

production The stage after the new system is installed and the conversion is complete; during this time the system is reviewed by users and technical specialists to determine how well it has met its original goals.

maintenance Changes in hardware, software, documentation, or procedures to a production system to correct errors, meet new requirements, or improve processing efficiency.

Table 9-7	Systems Development
Core Activity	**Description**
Systems analysis	Identify problem(s)
	Specify solution
	Establish information requirements
Systems design	Create logical design specifications
	Create physical design specifications
	Manage technical realization of system
Programming	Translate design specifications into program code
Testing	Unit test
	Systems test
	Acceptance Test
Conversion	Plan conversion
	Prepare documentation
	Train users and technical staff
Production and maintenance	Operate the system
	Evaluate the system
	Modify the system

A very large percentage of information systems fail to deliver benefits or to solve the problems for which they were intended because the process of organizational change associated with system-building was not properly addressed. Successful system-building requires careful planning and change management. We now turn to the problem of change management by examining patterns of implementation.

IMPLEMENTATION SUCCESS AND FAILURE

implementation All of the organizational activities working toward the adoption, management, and routinization of an innovation.

change agent The individual acting as the catalyst during the change process to ensure successful organizational adaptation to a new system or innovation.

In the context of change management, **implementation** refers to all of the organizational activities working toward the adoption, management, and routinization of an innovation such as a new information system. In the implementation process, the systems analyst is a **change agent.** The analyst not only develops technical solutions but also redefines the configurations, interactions, job activities, and power relationships of various organizational groups. The analyst is the catalyst for the entire change process and is responsible for ensuring that the changes created by a new system are accepted by all parties involved. The change agent communicates with users, mediates between competing interest groups, and ensures that the organizational adjustments to changes are complete.

Whether system implementations are successful or not depends largely on managerial and organizational factors. The role of users, the degree of management support, the manner in which the systems project handles complexity and risk, and the management of the implementation process itself all have a profound impact on system outcome.

User Involvement and Influence

Heavy user involvement in the design and operation of information systems affords users opportunities to mold the system according to their priorities and business requirements. In addition, they are more likely to react positively to the completed system if they have been active participants in the change process.

user–designer communications gap The difference in backgrounds, interests, and priorities that impede communication and problem solving among end users and information systems specialists.

Communication problems between end users and designers are a major reason why user requirements are not properly incorporated into information systems and why users are driven out of the implementation process. Users and information system specialists tend to have different backgrounds, interests, and priorities and are often pursuing different goals. This is referred to as the **user–designer communications gap.** These differences are manifested in divergent organizational loyalties, approaches to problem solving, and vocabularies.

Table 9-8 The User–Designer Communications Gap

User Concerns	Designer Concerns
Will the system deliver the information I need for my work?	How much disk storage space will the master file consume?
How quickly can I access the data?	How many lines of program code will it take to perform this function?
How easily can I retrieve the data?	How can we cut down on CPU time when we run the system?
How much clerical support will I need to enter data into the system?	What is the most efficient way of storing this piece of data?
How will the operation of the system fit into my daily business schedule?	What database management system should we use?

Information system specialists, for example, often have a highly technical or machine orientation to problem solving. They look for elegant and sophisticated technical solutions in which hardware and software efficiency is optimized at the expense of ease of use or organizational effectiveness. Users, however, prefer systems that are oriented to solving business problems or facilitating organizational tasks. Often the orientations of both groups are so at odds that they appear to speak in different tongues. These differences are illustrated in Table 9-8, which depicts the typical concerns of end users and technical specialists (information system designers) regarding the development of a new information system.

Management Support

If an information systems project has management's backing and approval at various levels, it is more likely to be perceived positively by both users and the technical information services staff. Both groups will feel that their participation in the development process will receive high-level attention, priority, and reward. Management backing also ensures that a systems project will receive sufficient funding and resources to be successful. Furthermore, all of the changes in work habits and procedures and any organizational realignments associated with a new system depend on management backing to be enforced effectively.

Level of Complexity and Risk

Systems differ dramatically in their size, scope, level of complexity, and organizational and technical components. Some systems development projects are more likely to fail because they carry a much higher level of risk than others. Researchers have identified three key dimensions that influence the level of project risk (McFarlan, 1981).

Project Size   The larger the project—as indicated by the dollars spent, the size of the implementation staff, the time allocated for implementation, and the number of organizational units affected—the greater the risk because so many activities and processes must be managed and coordinated.

Project Structure   Projects that are more highly structured run a much lower risk than those whose user requirements are relatively undefined, fluid, and constantly changing. When requirements are clear and straightforward, outputs and processes can be easily defined. Users in highly structured projects tend to know exactly what they want and what the system should do; there is a much smaller possibility of them changing their minds.

Experience with Technology   The project risk will rise if the project team and the information system staff are unfamiliar with the hardware, system software, application software, networking technology, or database management system proposed for the project.

Table 9-9 Dimensions of Project Risk

Project Structure	Project Technology Level	Project Size	Degree of Risk
High	Low	Large	Low
High	Low	Small	Very low
High	High	Large	Medium
High	High	Small	Medium-low
Low	Low	Large	Low
Low	Low	Small	Very low
Low	High	Large	Very high
Low	High	Small	High

These dimensions of project risk will be present in different combinations for each implementation effort. Table 9-9 shows that eight different combinations are possible, each with a different degree of risk. The higher the level of risk, the more likely it is that the implementation effort will fail.

The Challenge of Business Process Reengineering (BPR) and Enterprise Resource Planning (ERP)

Given the challenges of innovation and implementation is it not surprising to find a very high failure rate among business process reengineering (BPR) and enterprise resource planning (ERP) projects, which typically require extensive organizational change and which may require replacing old technologies and legacy systems that are deeply rooted in many interrelated business processes (Lloyd, Dewar, and Pooley, 1999). A number of studies indicate that 70 percent of all business processing reengineering projects fail to deliver promised benefits (Hammer and Stanton, 1995; King, 1994). Likewise, 70 percent of all enterprise system projects fail to be fully implemented or to meet the goals of their users even after 3 years of work (Gillooly, 1998). The Window on Organizations describes some of the difficulties companies have encountered as they implemented enterprise systems.

Management of the Implementation Process

The conflicts and uncertainties inherent in any implementation effort will be magnified when an implementation project is poorly managed and organized. Under poor management basic elements of success may be omitted. Training to ensure that end users are comfortable with the new system and fully understand its potential uses is often sacrificed, in part because the budget is strained toward the end of a project. A systems development project without proper management will most likely suffer vast cost overruns, major time slippages, and technical performances that fall significantly below the estimated level.

How badly are projects managed? On average, private-sector projects are underestimated by one-half in terms of budget and time required to deliver the complete system promised in the system plan. A very large number of projects are delivered with missing functionality (promised for delivery in later versions). Government projects suffer about the same failure level, sometimes worse (Laudon, 1989; Helms and Weiss, 1986).

MANAGING IMPLEMENTATION

Not all aspects of the implementation process can be easily controlled or planned (Alter and Ginzberg, 1978). However, the chances for system success can be increased by anticipating potential implementation problems and applying appropriate corrective strategies. Strategies also have been devised for ensuring that users play an appropriate role throughout the implementation period and for managing the organizational change process. Various project man-

IMPLEMENTING ENTERPRISE SYSTEMS: EASIER SAID THAN DONE

Enterprise systems have given many companies new capabilities and efficiencies but they are notoriously difficult to implement. Enterprise resource planning (ERP) creates myriad interconnections among various business processes and data flows to make sure that information in one part of the business can be obtained by any other unit, which helps people eliminate redundant activities and make better management decisions. Massive organizational changes are required to make this happen. Information that was previously maintained by different systems and different departments or functional areas must be integrated and made available to the whole company. Business processes must be tightly integrated, jobs redefined, and new procedures created throughout the company. Employees are often unprepared for new procedures and roles.

Until the organization learns to coordinate its new business processes and technology, an ERP implementation can create operational disruptions. Crown Craft Inc., a $350 million manufacturer of home textile furnishings and accessories, experienced manufacturing disruptions and missed shipments when it first implemented its SAP R/3 enterprise system. Crown Craft believes that these problems led to a 24% drop in sales for the last quarter of 1999.

Toymaker Hasbro Inc. in Pawtucket, Rhode Island, struggled when it implemented SAP enterprise software in 1997 and 1998 because it did not have a detailed project plan. The company had not fully determined why the system was being implemented, what parts of the business would be affected, and how long the implementation process would take. Without a clear plan, Hasbro let users suggest many changes to the system that were not provided by the software package and that required extra resources and time to implement. Hasbro's project took 6 months longer than planned and cost $62 million instead of the $50 million originally budgeted.

Ottawa Truck of Ottawa, Kansas, implemented Baan's Baan IV ERP software package along with an Oracle database to replace a 15-year-old batch system that could not handle year 2000 dates. The company hoped that the enterprise system would also speed manufacturing, improve customer service, and reduce errors caused by manual processes. It had been manually assigning customer discounts based on purchasing volume, which occasionally created pricing discrepancies.

Unlike Hasbro, Ottawa Truck would not allow the software to be modified. But even with careful planning, the company set the budget for training too low. Training was originally designed to focus on the software skills workers needed to do their jobs. However, not knowing about the capabilities of the enterprise software and the requirements of the business created confusion when unexpected situations that were not considered standard procedures occurred, such as when a shipment was received without a requested part. When they discovered this, Ottawa Truck increased the training budget. The company now teaches all users about all the modules in the system and explains their role in executing business processes so that users can understand "why" the system works as it does as well as "how."

TO THINK ABOUT: What management, organizational, and technological factors explain why enterprise systems are so difficult to implement?

Sources: Alorie Gilbert and Jennifer Mateyaschuk, "A Question of Convenience," *Information Week*, February 21, 2000; Nick Wreden, "ERP Systems: Promise versus Performance," **Beyond Computing**, September 1999; and Jeff Sweat, "Learning Curve," **Information Week**, August 2, 1999.

agement, requirements gathering, and planning methodologies have been developed for specific categories of problems.

Increasing User Involvement

The level of user involvement should vary depending on both the development methodology used and the project's risk level. Tools to involve users—**external integration tools**—consist of ways to link the work of the implementation team to users at all organizational levels. For example, users can be made active members or leaders of systems development project teams or placed in charge of system training and installation.

external integration tools
Project management techniques that link the work of the implementation team to that of users at all organizational levels.

Overcoming User Resistance

Systems development is not an entirely rational process. Users leading design activities have used their position to further private interests and to gain power rather than to promote organizational objectives (Franz and Robey, 1984). Participation in implementation activities may not be enough to overcome the problem of user resistance. The implementation process demands organizational change. Such change may be resisted because different users may be affected by the system in different ways. Some users may welcome a new system because it brings changes they perceive as beneficial to them, whereas others may resist these changes because they believe the shifts are detrimental to their interests (Joshi, 1991).

If use of a system is voluntary, users may tend to avoid it. If use is mandatory, resistance will take the form of increased error rates, disruptions, turnover, and even sabotage. Implementation strategy must address the issue of **counterimplementation** (Keen, 1981). Counterimplementation is a deliberate strategy to thwart the implementation of an information system or an innovation in an organization.

Strategies to overcome user resistance include user participation (to elicit commitment as well as to improve design), user education (training), management coercion (edicts, policies), and user incentives. User resistance can be addressed through changes to the new system, such as improved human factors (user/system interface). Finally, users will be more cooperative if organizational problems are solved prior to introducing the new system.

Managing Technical Complexity

Projects with high levels of technology benefit from **internal integration tools.** The success of such projects depends on how well their technical complexity can be managed. Project leaders need both heavy technical and administrative experience. They must be able to anticipate problems and develop smooth working relationships among a predominantly technical team. Team members should be highly experienced. Team meetings should take place frequently, with routine distribution of meeting minutes concerning key design decisions. Essential technical skills or expertise not available internally should be secured from outside the organization.

Formal Planning and Control Tools

Large projects will benefit from appropriate use of **formal planning and control tools.** With project management techniques such as PERT (Program Evaluation and Review Technique) or Gantt charts, a detailed plan can be developed. (PERT lists the specific activities that make up a project, their duration, and the activities that must be completed before a specific activity can start. A Gantt chart, such as that illustrated in Figure 9-7, visually represents the sequence and timing of different tasks in a development project, as well as their resource requirements.) Tasks can be defined and resources budgeted.

These project management techniques can help managers identify bottlenecks and determine the impact problems will have on project completion times. Standard control techniques can be used to chart project progress against budgets and target dates, so that deviations can be spotted and the implementation team can make adjustments to meet their original schedule. Periodic formal status reports against the plan will show the extent of progress.

Controlling Risk Factors

One way implementation can be improved is by adjusting the project management strategy to the risk level inherent in each project. Thus, projects with little structure may involve users fully at all stages, whereas more formal projects may need to adjust user involvement according to the project phase. User participation may not be appropriate in some situations. For example, users may react negatively to a new design even though its overall benefits outweigh its drawbacks. Some individuals may stand to lose power as a result of design decisions (Robey and Markus, 1984), so that participation in design may actually exacerbate resentment and resistance.

Projects using complex, new technology are riskier and require more emphasis on internal integration tools. Large projects can reduce risk by increasing the use of formal planning and control tools.

DESIGNING FOR THE ORGANIZATION

The systems development process must explicitly address the ways in which the organization will change when the new system is installed. In addition to procedural changes, transforma-

---

counterimplementation A deliberate strategy to thwart the implementation of an information system or an innovation in an organization.

internal integration tools Project management technique that helps the implementation team operate as a cohesive unit.

formal planning tools Project management technique that structures and sequences tasks; budgeting time, money, and technical resources required to complete the tasks.

formal control tools Project management technique that helps monitor the progress toward completion of a task and fulfillment of goals.

HRIS COMBINED PLAN-HR	Da	Who	2000			2001												2002		
			Oct	Nov	Dec	Jan	Feb	Mar	Apr	May	Jun	Jul	Aug	Sep	Oct	Nov	Dec	Jan	Feb	Mar
DATA ADMINISTRATION SECURITY																				
QMF security review/setup	20	EF TP																		
Security orientation	2	EF JV																		
QMF security maintenance	35	TP GL																		
Data entry sec. profiles	4	EF TP																		
Data entry sec. views est.	12	EF TP																		
Data entry security profiles	65	EF TP																		
DATA DICTIONARY																				
Orientation sessions	1	EF																		
Data dictionary design	32	EF WV																		
DD prod. coordn-query	20	GL																		
DD prod. coordn-live	40	EF GL																		
Data dictionary cleanup	35	EF GL																		
Data dictionary maint.	35	EF GL																		
PROCEDURES REVISION DESIGN PREP																				
Work flows (old)	10	PK JL																		
Payroll data flows	31	JL PK																		
HRIS P/R model	11	PK JL																		
P/R interface orient. mtg.	6	PK JL																		
P/R interface coordn. I	15	PK																		
P/R interface coordn.	8	PK																		
Benefits interfaces (old)	5	JL																		
Ben. interfaces new flow	8	JL																		
Ben. communication strategy	3	PK JL																		
New work flow model	15	PK JL																		
Posn. data entry flows	14	WV JL																		
RESOURCE SUMMARY																				
Edith Farrell	5.0	EF	2	21	24	24	23	22	22	27	34	34	29	26	28	19	14			
Woody Holand	5.0	WH	5	17	20	19	12	10	14	10	2							4	3	
Charles Pierce	5.0	CP		5	11	20	13	9	10	7	6	8	4	4	4	4	4			
Ted Leurs	5.0	TL		12	17	17	19	17	14	12	15	16	2	1	1	1	1			
Toni Cox	5.0	TC	1	11	10	11	11	12	19	19	21	21	21	17	17	12	9			
Patricia Clark	5.0	PC	7	23	30	34	27	25	15	24	25	16	11	13	17	10	3	3	2	
Jane Lawton	5.0	JL	1	9	16	21	19	21	21	20	17	15	14	12	14	8	5			
David Holloway	5.0	DH	4	4	5	5	5	2	7	5	4	16	2							
Diane O'Neill	5.0	DO	6	14	17	16	13	11	9	4										
Joan Albert	5.0	JA	5	6			7	6	2	1				5	5	1				
Marie Marcus	5.0	MM	15	7	2	1	1													
Don Stevens	5.0	DS	4	4	5	4	5	1												
Casual	5.0	CASL		3	4	3			4	7	9	5	3	2						
Kathy Mendez	5.0	KM		1	5	16	19	22	19	20	18	20	11	2						
Anna Borden	5.0	AB				9	10	16	15	11	12	19	10	7	1					
Gail Loring	5.0	GL		3	6	5	9	10	17	18	17	10	13	10	10	7	17			
UNASSIGNED	0.0	X										9			236	225	230	14	13	3
Co-op	5.0	CO		6	4				2	3	4	4	2	4	16			216	178	9
Casual	5.0	CAUL								3	3	3								
TOTAL DAYS			49	147	176	196	194	174	193	195	190	181	140	125	358	288	284	237	196	12

FIGURE 9-7 Formal planning and control tools help to manage information systems projects successfully. The Gantt chart in this figure was produced by a commercially available project management software package. It shows the task, person-days, and initials of each responsible person, as well as the start and finish dates for each task. The resource summary provides a good manager with the total person-days for each month and for each person working on the project to successfully manage the project. The project described here is a data administration project.

tions in job functions, organizational structure, power relationships, and behavior will all have to be carefully planned.

This is true of Internet-based systems as well as traditional systems. Although Web sites and intranets may not require major changes in an organization's information technology infrastructure, they can create new business processes that require traditional functional areas such as marketing, sales, and customer service to collaborate more closely in new ways.

organizational impact analysis Study of the way a proposed system will affect organizational structure, attitudes, decision making, and operations.

Although systems analysis and design activities are supposed to include an organizational impact analysis, this area has traditionally been neglected. An **organizational impact analysis** explains how a proposed system will affect organizational structure, attitudes, decision making, and operations. To integrate information systems successfully with the organization, thorough and fully documented organizational impact assessments must be given more attention in the development effort.

Allowing for the Human Factor

The quality of information systems should be evaluated in terms of user criteria rather than just the technical criteria of the information systems staff. For example, a project objective might be that data entry clerks be able to learn the procedures and codes for four new on-line data entry screens in a half-day training session.

Areas where users interface with the system should be carefully designed with sensitivity to ergonomic issues. **Ergonomics** refers to the interaction of people and machines in the work environment. It considers the design of jobs, health issues, and the end-user interface of information systems. The impact of the application system on the work environment and job dimensions must be carefully assessed. One noteworthy study of 620 Social Security Administration claims representatives showed that the representatives with on-line access to claims data experienced greater stress than those with serial access to the data via teletype. Even though the on-line interface was more rapid and direct than teletype, it created much

ergonomics The interaction of people and machines in the work environment, including the design of jobs, health issues, and the end-user interface of information systems.

A well-designed user interface helps make a system easy to use, whereas one that is cluttered will add to users' frustrations. American Airlines redesigned its Web pages to make its Web site more inviting.

BEFORE

AFTER

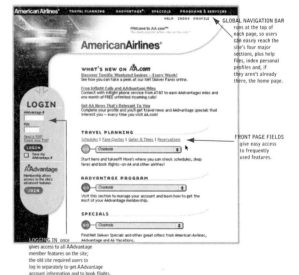

GLOBAL NAVIGATION BAR runs at the top of each page, so users can easily reach the site's four major sections, plus help files, index personal profiles and, if they aren't already there, the home page.

FRONT PAGE FIELDS give easy access to frequently used features.

LOGGING IN once gives access to all AAdvantage member features on the site; the old site required users to log in separately to get AAdvantage account information and to book flights.

more frustration. Claims representatives with on-line access could interface with a larger number of clients per day, which changed the dimensions of their jobs. The restructuring of work—involving tasks, quality of working life, and performance—had a more profound impact than the nature of the technology itself (Turner, 1984).

Management and organizational researchers have suggested a sociotechnical approach to information systems design and organizational change. **Sociotechnical design** aims to produce information systems that blend technical efficiency with sensitivity to organizational and human needs, leading to high job satisfaction (Mumford and Weir, 1979). The sociotechnical design process emphasizes participation by individuals most affected by a new system. The design plan establishes human objectives for the system that lead to increased job satisfaction. Designers set forth separate sets of technical and social design solutions. The social design plans explore different work group structures, allocation of tasks, and the design of individual jobs. The design solution that best fulfills both technical and social objectives is selected for the final design.

sociotechnical design Design to produce information systems that blend technical efficiency with sensitivity to organizational and human needs.

9.4 Understanding the Business Value of Information Systems

Information systems can have several different values for business firms. A consistently strong information technology infrastructure can, over the long term, play an important strategic role in the life of the firm. Looked at less grandly, information systems can permit firms simply to survive. The value of systems from a financial view comes down to one question: Does a particular information system investment produce sufficient returns to justify its costs? There are many issues to consider with this approach.

CAPITAL BUDGETING MODELS

Capital budgeting models are one of several techniques used to measure the value of investing in long-term capital investment projects. The process of analyzing and selecting various proposals for capital expenditures is called **capital budgeting.** Firms invest in capital projects in order to expand production to meet anticipated demand, or to modernize production equipment in order to reduce costs. Information systems are considered long-term capital investment projects.

capital budgeting The process of analyzing and selecting various proposals for capital expenditures.

Alternative methods are available to compare different projects with one another, and to make a decision about the investment. Three widely used methods are the cost–benefit ratio, the net present value, and the accounting rate of return on investment (ROI).

Cost–Benefit Ratio

A simple method for calculating the returns from a capital expenditure is to calculate the **cost–benefit ratio,** which is the ratio of benefits to costs. The formula is as follows:

$$\frac{\text{Total benefits}}{\text{Total costs}} = \text{Cost–benefit ratio}$$

cost–benefit ratio A method for calculating the returns from a capital expenditure by dividing the total benefits by total costs.

Table 9-10 lists some of the more common costs and benefits of systems. **Tangible benefits** can be quantified and assigned a monetary value. **Intangible benefits,** such as more efficient customer service or enhanced decision making, cannot be immediately quantified but may lead to quantifiable gains in the long run. Some firms establish a minimum cost–benefit ratio that must be attained by capital projects, looking primarily at tangible benefits.

tangible benefits Benefits that can be quantified and assigned monetary value; they include lower operational costs and increased cash-flows.

Net Present Value

Evaluating a capital project requires that the cost of an investment be compared with the net cash inflows that occur many years later as the investment produces returns. But these two kinds of cash inflows are not directly comparable because of the time value of money. Money you have been promised to receive three, four, and five years from now is not worth as much as money received today. Money received in the future has to be discounted by some appropriate

intangible benefits Benefits that are not easily quantified; they might include more efficient customer service or enhanced decision making.

| Table 9-10 | Costs and Benefits of Information Systems |

Costs	Benefits
Hardware	**Tangible Benefits (Cost savings)**
Telecommunications	Increased productivity
	Lower operational costs
Software	Reduced workforce
	Lower computer expenses
Services	Lower outside vendor costs
	Lower clerical and professional costs
Personnel	Reduced rate of growth in expenses
	Reduced facility costs
	Intangible Benefits
	Improved asset utilization
	Improved resource control
	Improved organizational planning
	Increased organizational flexibility
	More timely information
	More information
	Increased organizational learning
	Legal requirements attained
	Enhanced employee goodwill
	Increased job satisfaction
	Improved decision making
	Improved operations
	Higher client satisfaction
	Better corporate image

present value The value, in current dollars, of a payment or stream of payments to be received in the future.

percentage rate—usually the prevailing interest rate, or, sometimes, the cost of capital. **Present value** is the value in current dollars of a payment or stream of payments to be received in the future. It can be calculated by using the following formula:

$$\text{Payment} \times \frac{1 - (1 + \text{interest})^{-n}}{\text{Interest}} = \text{Present value}$$

Thus, in order to compare the investment (made in today's dollars) with future savings or earnings, you need to discount the earnings to their present value and then calculate the net present value of the investment. The **net present value** is the amount of money an investment is worth, taking into account its cost, earnings, and the time value of money. The formula for net present value is as follows:

net present value The amount of money an investment is worth, taking into account its cost, earnings, and the time value of money.

$$\text{Present value of expected cash flows} - \text{Initial investment cost} = \text{Net present value}$$

Accounting Rate of Return on Investment (ROI)

Firms make capital investments to earn a satisfactory rate of return. In the long run, the desired rate of return must equal or exceed the cost of borrowing money in the marketplace. The accounting rate of return on investment (ROI) calculates the rate of return from an investment by adjusting the cash inflows produced by the investment for depreciation. It gives an approximation of the accounting income earned by the project.

To find the ROI, first calculate the average net benefit. The formula for the average net benefit is as follows:

$$\frac{(\text{Total benefits} - \text{Total cost} - \text{Depreciation})}{\text{Useful life}} = \text{Net benefit}$$

This net benefit is divided by the total initial investment to arrive at ROI (rate of return on investment). The formula is

Window on Management

EXTRANET ROIS: FIGURING THE PAYBACK

Many businesses are building extranets to link to customers and suppliers because they are inexpensive to build and use while providing efficiencies in inventory management, order processing, and distributing information.

The problem is that measuring the payoff from extranets is more art than science. Because benefits are spread across multiple departments and companies, the return on investment must be measured not only within the company but also throughout business processes that span corporate boundaries.

One way to clarify the process of measuring extranet ROIs is to establish a few well-defined targets. Entex Information Services Inc., a $2.5 billion computer systems integrator based in Rye Brook, New York, started by identifying the business processes that were supposed to be improved by installing the extranet. Entex based its extranet ROI analysis on a study conducted by the consulting firm of KPMG Peat Marwick LLP that analyzed Entex's selling and distribution costs. Rob Laudadio, Entex's director of collaborative computing, first established baseline measurements for 12 activities highlighted in the consultant's report, including quote generation, order entry, and cash collection. He then planned an extranet that would increase productivity in those areas by eliminating manual or redundant tasks.

The KPMG analysis showed that 18 percent of the cost of Entex's sales organization was spent writing up price quotes for simple computer packages. Laudadio specified that the extranet was to include capabilities for quickly calling up frequently ordered configurations. After the extranet was completed, Entex could measure a 13 percent reduction across the organization in the cost of generating a quote. Entex expects a 161 percent ROI on extranet investments in the next 2 years.

To convince its customers to switch to extranet-based ordering, Laudadio prepared an analysis comparing the cost of executing a typical order; he determined that it would cost $12 to look up prices of components and another $10 to create an order spreadsheet to submit to Entex. He then calculated the costs of performing the same activities using the extranet. Price lookups would cost around $1 and order spreadsheets would be generated automatically on the extranet. The customer's average cost of placing an order would drop to $126 from $196 if they used the Entex extranet.

Experts also point out that extranets bring many business benefits such as improved customer service or reductions in the customer payment cycle that can't be easily quantified using traditional ROI accounting methods, and many companies build extranets because of these broader business benefits. Doug Bonzelaar, manager of business applications for Herman Miller Inc., a $2 billion furniture manufacturer in Holland, Michigan, judged the value of its extranet in terms of improved customer satisfaction. Miller's SupplyNet extranet has been transmitting orders to lumber companies and other materials suppliers since 1997. By replacing paper and EDI purchase orders with requests submitted on the Web and transmitted directly to suppliers' manufacturing control systems, SupplyNet reduced two-week lead times for making furniture to three days. Of 78,000 annual order deliveries, 99.7 percent are running on schedule. The extranet's impact on order fulfillment means more to the company than any financial metrics.

TO THINK ABOUT: To what extent is ROI a useful way to measure investments on extranets?

Sources: Jack M. Keen, "Build a Balanced Business Case," *Datamation,* January 2000; Noah Shachtman, "E-Business Demands a New Outlook on ROI," *Information Week,* October 18, 1999; and Andy Raskin, "The ROIght Stuff," *CIO Web Business Magazine,* February 1, 1999.

$$\frac{\text{Net benefit}}{\text{Total initial investment}} = \text{ROI}$$

The Window on Management illustrates the use of ROI in assessing the value of extranets.

Limitations of Financial Models

Financial models assume that all relevant alternatives have been examined, that all costs and benefits are known, and that these costs and benefits can be expressed in a common metric, specifically, money. However, financial models do not express the risks and uncertainty of their own cost and benefit estimates. Costs and benefits do not occur in the same time frame—costs tend to be up front and tangible, whereas benefits tend to be back-loaded and intangible. Inflation may affect costs and benefits differently. Technology—especially information technology—can change during the course of the project, causing estimates to vary greatly. Intangible benefits are difficult to quantify.

Herman Miller now sells furniture through its Web site and also uses Internet technology in an extranet for transmitting orders to suppliers. The extranet has helped reduce furniture lead times to as little as two days, improving customer service and increasing sales.

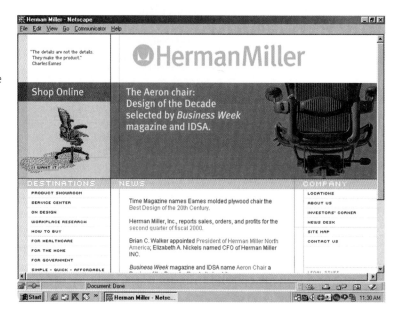

The difficulties of measuring intangible benefits give financial models an application bias: Transaction and clerical systems that displace labor and save space always produce more measurable, tangible benefits than management information systems, decision-support systems, or computer-supported collaborative work systems (see Chapter 11).

NONFINANCIAL AND STRATEGIC CONSIDERATIONS

Other methods of selecting and evaluating information system investments involve nonfinancial and strategic considerations. When the firm has several alternative investments to select from, it can employ portfolio analysis and scoring models. Several of these methods can be used in combination.

Portfolio Analysis

Rather than using capital budgeting, a second way of selecting among alternative projects is to consider the firm as having a portfolio of potential applications. Each application carries risks and benefits. The portfolio can be described as having a certain profile of risk and benefit to the firm (see Figure 9-8). Although there is no ideal profile for all firms, information-intensive industries (e.g., finance) should have a few high-risk, high-benefit projects to ensure that they stay current with technology. Firms in noninformation-intensive industries should focus on high-benefit, low-risk projects.

Some of the major risks in system-building are that benefits may not be obtained; system-building may exceed the organization's budget and time frame; or the system may not perform as expected. Risks are not necessarily bad. They are tolerable as long as the benefits are commensurate.

FIGURE 9-8 A system portfolio. Companies should examine their portfolio of projects in terms of potential benefits and likely risks. Certain kinds of projects should be avoided altogether and others developed rapidly. There is no ideal mix. Companies in different industries have different profiles.

	Project risk	
	High	Low
High Potential benefits to firm	Cautiously examine	Identify and develop
Low	Avoid	Routine projects

EVALUATING ERP SYSTEMS WITH A SCORING MODEL

Your company, Audio Direct, sells parts used in audio systems for cars and trucks and is growing very fast. Your management team has decided that the firm can speed up product delivery to customers and lower inventory and customer support costs by installing an enterprise resource planning (ERP) system. Two enterprise software vendors have responded to your request for proposal (RFP) and have submitted reports show-

ing which of your detailed list of requirements can be supported by their systems. Audio Direct attaches the most importance to capabilities for sales order processing, inventory management, and warehousing. The information systems staff prepared the following matrix comparing the vendors' capabilities for these functions. It shows the percentage of requirements for each function that each alternative ERP system can provide. It also shows the weight, or relative importance the company attaches to each of these functions.

Function	Weight	ERP System A (%)	ERP System A Score	ERP System B (%)	ERP System B Score
1.0 Order Processing					
1.1 On-line order entry	4	67		73	
1.2 On-line pricing	4	81		87	
1.3 Inventory check	4	72		81	
1.4 Customer credit check	3	66		59	
1.5 Invoicing	4	73		82	
Total Order Processing					
2.0 Inventory Management					
2.1 Production forecasting	3	72		76	
2.2 Production planning	4	79		81	
2.3 Inventory control	4	68		80	
2.4 Reports	3	71		69	
Total Inventory Management					
3.0 Warehousing					
3.1 Receiving	2	71		75	
3.2 Picking/packing	3	77		82	
3.3 Shipping	4	92		89	
Total Warehousing					
Grand Total					

1. Calculate each ERP vendor's score by multiplying the percentage of requirements met for each function by the weight for that function.

2. Calculate each ERP vendor's total score for each of the three major functions (order processing, inventory management, and warehousing). Then calculate the grand total for each vendor.

3. On the basis of vendor scores, which ERP vendor would you select?

4. Are there any other factors, including intangible benefits, that might affect your decision?

Once strategic analyses have determined the overall direction of system development, a **portfolio analysis** can be used to select alternatives. Obviously, one can begin by focusing on systems of high benefit and low risk. These promise early returns and low risks. Second, high-benefit, high-risk systems should be examined. Low-benefit, high-risk systems should be totally avoided, and low-benefit, low-risk systems should be reexamined for the possibility of rebuilding and replacing them with more desirable systems having higher benefits.

portfolio analysis An analysis of the portfolio of potential applications within a firm to determine the risks and benefits and select among alternatives for information systems.

Table 9-11 **Scoring Model Used to Choose Among Alternative Office Systems***

Criterion	Weight	AS/400		Unix		Windows 2000	
Percentage of user needs met	0.40	2	0.8	3	1.2	4	1.6
Cost of the initial purchase	0.20	1	0.2	3	0.6	4	0.8
Financing	0.10	1	0.1	3	0.3	4	0.4
Ease of maintenance	0.10	2	0.2	3	0.3	4	0.4
Chances of success	0.20	3	0.6	4	0.8	4	0.8
Final score			1.9		3.2		4.0

Scale: 1 = low, 5 = high.

*One of the major uses of scoring models is in identifying the criteria of selection and their relative weights. In this instance an office system based on Windows 2000 appears preferable.

Scoring Models

scoring models A quick method for deciding among alternative systems based on a system of ratings for selected objectives.

A quick, and sometimes compelling, method for arriving at a decision on alternative systems is a **scoring model.** Scoring models give alternative systems a single score based on the extent to which they meet selected objectives (Matlin, 1989; Buss, 1983).

In Table 9-11 the firm must decide among three alternative office systems: (1) an IBM, AS/400 client/server system with proprietary software; (2) a Unix-based client/server system using an Oracle database; and (3) a Windows 2000 client/server system using Lotus Notes. Column 1 lists the criteria that decision makers may apply to the systems. These criteria are usually the result of lengthy discussions among the decision-making group. Often the most important outcome of a scoring model is not the score but simply agreement on the criteria used to judge a system (Ginzberg, 1979; Nolan, 1982). Column 2 lists the weights that decision makers attach to each decision criterion. The scoring model helps to bring about agreement among participants concerning the rank of the criteria. Columns 3 to 5 use a 1-to-5 scale (lowest to highest) to express the judgments of participants on the relative merits of each system. For example, concerning the percentage of user needs that each system meets, a score of 1 for a system argues that this system when compared to others being considered will be low in meeting user needs.

As with all objective techniques, there are many qualitative judgments involved in using the scoring model. This model requires experts who understand the issues and the technology. It is appropriate to cycle through the scoring model several times, changing the criteria and weights, to see how sensitive the outcome is to reasonable changes in criteria. Scoring models are used most commonly to confirm, to rationalize, and to support decisions, rather than as the final arbiters of system selection.

MANAGEMENT WRAP-UP

Management

The key management issues in building systems are to stay in control of the process (to avoid runaway systems) and to lead the effort toward planned and sustained organizational change. Managers must link systems development to the firm's strategy and identify precisely which systems should be changed to achieve large-scale benefits for the organization as a whole. Understanding what process to improve from the firm perspective is more important than blindly reengineering whatever business process happens to need fixing or happens to yield a large return on investment (ROI). Many projects with huge ROIs have little impact on the business as a whole.

Building an information system is a process of planned organizational change. Many levels of organizational change are possible. Redesigning business processes is especially risky because it requires far-reaching changes that often are resisted by members of the organization. Eliciting management and user support and maintaining an appropriate level of user involvement throughout the system-building process is essential.

Organization

Selecting the right technology for a system solution that fits the problem's constraints and the organization's information technology infrastructure is a key business decision. Systems sometimes fail because the technology is too complex or sophisticated to be easily implemented. Managers and systems builders should be fully aware of the risks and rewards of various technologies as they make their technology selections.

Technology

For Discussion

1. It has been said that when we design an information system, we are redesigning the organization. What are the ramifications of this statement?

2. It has been said that the reason most systems fail is because system builders ignore organizational behavior problems. Why?

SUMMARY

1. Demonstrate how building new systems can produce organizational change. Building a new information system is a form of planned organizational change that involves many different people in the organization. Because information systems are sociotechnical entities, a change in information systems involves changes in work, management, and the organization. Four kinds of technology-enabled change are (1) automation, (2) rationalization of procedures, (3) business process reengineering, and (4) paradigm shift, with far-reaching changes carrying the greatest risks and rewards. Many organizations are attempting business process reengineering to redesign work flows and business processes in the hope of achieving dramatic productivity breakthroughs.

2. Explain how the organization can develop information systems that fit its business plan. Organizations should develop information systems plans that describe how information technology supports the attainment of their business goals. The plans indicate the direction of systems development, the rationale, implementation strategy, and budget. Enterprise analysis and critical success factors (CSFs) can be used to elicit organization-wide information requirements that must be addressed by the plans.

3. Identify the core activities in the systems development process. The core activities in systems development are systems analysis, systems design, programming, testing, conversion, production, and maintenance. Systems analysis is the study and analysis of problems of existing systems and the identification of requirements for their solution. Systems design provides the specifications for an information system solution, showing how its technical and organizational components fit together.

4. Analyze the organizational change requirements for building successful systems. From an organizational and behavioral standpoint, the major causes of information system failure are (1) insufficient or improper user participation in the systems development process, (2) lack of management support, (3) poor management of the implementation process, and (4) high levels of complexity and risk in systems development projects.

Implementation is the entire process of organizational change surrounding the introduction of a new information system. One can better understand system success and failure by examining different implementation patterns. Especially important is the relationship between participants in the implementation process, notably the interactions between system designers and users. The success of organizational change can be determined by how well information systems specialists, end users, and decision makers deal with key issues at various stages in implementation.

Management support and control of the implementation process are essential, as are mechanisms for dealing with the level of risk in each new systems project. The level of risk in a systems development project is determined by three key dimensions: (1) project size, (2) project structure, and (3) experience with technology. The risk level of each project will determine the appropriate mix of external integration tools, internal integration tools, formal planning tools, and formal control tools to be applied.

Appropriate strategies can be applied to ensure the correct level of user participation in the systems development process and to minimize user resistance. Information system design and the entire implementation process should be managed as planned organizational change. Sociotechnical design emphasizes the participation of the individuals most affected by a new system and aims for an optimal blend of social and technical design solutions.

5. Describe models for determining the business value of information systems. Capital budgeting models such as the cost–benefit ratio, net present value, and ROI are widely used financial models for determining the business value of information systems. Portfolio analysis and scoring models include nonfinancial considerations and can be used to evaluate alternative information systems projects.

KEY TERMS

REVIEW QUESTIONS

1. Why can a new information system be considered planned organizational change?
2. What are the major categories of an information systems plan?
3. How can enterprise analysis and critical success factors be used to establish organization-wide information system requirements?
4. Describe each of the four kinds of organizational change that can be promoted with information technology.
5. What is business process reengineering? What steps are required to make it effective?
6. What is the difference between systems analysis and systems design?
7. What is feasibility? Name and describe each of the three major areas of feasibility for information systems.
8. What are information requirements? Why are they difficult to determine correctly?
9. What is the difference between the logical design and the physical design of an information system?
10. Why is the testing stage of systems development so important? Name and describe the three stages of testing for an information system.
11. What is conversion? Why is it important to have a detailed conversion plan?
12. What role do programming, production, and maintenance play in systems development?
13. What is implementation? How is it related to information system success or failure?
14. Describe the ways that implementation can be managed to make the organizational change process more successful.
15. Name and describe the principal capital budgeting methods used to evaluate information systems projects. What are their limitations?
16. Describe how portfolio analysis and scoring models can be used to establish the worth of systems.

GROUP PROJECT

With three or four of your classmates, select a system described in this text that uses the Web. Examples might be Wingspan Bank in Chapter 1; iGo.com in Chapter 6; or MetalSite, E-Steel, REI, or Egghead.com in Chapter 8. Review the Web site for the system you select. Use what you have learned from the Web site and the text discussion in this book to prepare a report describing some of the design specifications for the system you select. Present your findings to the class.

Tools for Interactive Learning

○ Internet Connection

The Internet Connection for this chapter will direct you to a series of Web sites where you can complete an exercise to analyze the capabilities of various tools for work flow management and business process reengineering. You can also use the Interactive Study Guide to test your knowledge of the topics in this chapter and get instant feedback where you need more practice.

○ Electronic Commerce Project

At the Laudon Web site for Chapter 9, you will find an Electronic Commerce project that will use the interactive software at the Coder.com Web site to create a banner and then link to a related Web site to search for a Web hosting service.

○ CD-ROM

If you purchase and use the Multimedia Edition CD-ROM with this chapter, you can complete two interactive exercises. The first asks you to select the appropriate information technology solution to improve a series of business processes. The second exercise requires you to perform a systems analysis for a multidivisional corporation experiencing revenue slowdown. You can also find a video clip on Andersen Consulting's Smart Store and Retail Place illustrating the innovative use of technology to rethink the delivery of goods and services, an audio overview of the major themes of this chapter, and bullet text summarizing the key points of the chapter.

○ Application Exercise

At the Laudon Web site, you can find a spreadsheet Application Exercise for this chapter, which you can use to perform a capital budgeting analysis for a new information system.

When the doorbell rings, millions of people around the world are not surprised to hear "Avon Calling." Avon Products Inc., with world headquarters in New York, has been selling through house calls almost since its founding in 1885, and that approach continues to be its primary sales channel today. Despite its reliance on a method that many observers consider outmoded, the company had revenues of $5.3 billion in 1998 and employs 34,000 people. About 60 percent of Avon sales come from outside the United States, and sales are particularly strong in Asia, Latin America, and the U.K. Altogether Avon has an astounding total of 2.8 million independent sales representatives in 135 countries.

The company has many problems that it has begun to face. The overt sign of problems is that Avon's 1998 revenues climbed by only 3 percent over 1997. However, its real problems run much deeper, and to understand them we must examine the whole issue of the sales reps. Selling door-to-door is becoming increasingly difficult partly because more women are working and so fewer potential customers are at home. However, the issue is not only that more women are working, it is also about the fact that they have more options for purchasing Avon's and competitors' products. The sales reps face newer sales channels, even within Avon. The company has opened 50 retail stores within the United States, sells through catalogs, and even has a retail Web site where visitors can order Avon products on-line. Although the people who no longer purchase through sales reps simply may be buying Avon products through other channels, the company remains heavily dependent on its independent reps (Avon ladies account for 98 percent of company sales) and the changing conditions are hurting them.

Avon has an extremely high turnover of Avon sales reps, partially because of the problems in direct sales. However, the high turnover is caused by other things as well, including the slow, frustrating, and error-filled, paper-based order entry system that most of the reps must use. Most orders are telephoned into Avon's call centers distributed in various locations around the world. The call centers not only take orders, but they are supposed to solve order fulfillment problems as well. In addition they are charged with keeping sales representatives updated on product specials and sales incentives, and answering the reps' product questions. The call centers cannot cope with these responsibilities because many of them do not have access to current information on the sales representatives or even on Avon's products. For reps the problem is compounded by the fact that the call centers are so busy with their 4,000 calls per hour that each rep is only allowed to call in her orders on certain assigned days of the week.

When the orders are called in, at many of the call centers the staff records them on carbon paper forms and then mails them to Avon's headquarters where they are manually entered into Avon's old mainframe computer system. Two million orders are entered weekly this way. Many transcription errors occur (as much as 50 percent of orders are inaccurate) because the orders are spoken by the reps, recorded on paper by the call center staff, and then entered into a computer system by yet another person. Also, the order forms are long, causing further errors. To complicate the problem, Avon constantly changes its stock codes. "It is very difficult to do business with a paper-based company," concludes Sateesh Lele, Avon's chief information officer (CIO).

Avon's independent sales representatives have other problems as well. For one, Avon does not supply its reps with any kind of computer system to help them keep track of their clients or sales. "We're not an easy company to do business with," said Charles Perrin, Avon's former CEO. "We're still a paper-based company; we're not flexible enough; we don't offer the representative as much information as she should have in running her business."

Having such a high turnover is also very costly in terms of recruitment, training, and missed sales opportunities. Keeping good sales reps is so difficult that Avon's approximately 1,800 district sales managers spend almost all of their time recruiting and training new independent sales reps, leaving them very little time to work with current reps or to address more strategic issues. Even worse for the bottom line, when sales reps leave they may take their customers with them.

Avon has another major problem—it knows very little about its customers. As Cindy Faulknier, Avon's global director of customer service, sees the problem, "This company has never known who its customers are—and still doesn't." The sales reps do not want to share their customer information with the company. The reps have always feared that if they shared customer information with others, Avon would find a way to go straight to the customers and cut the reps out completely. From the perspective of Avon's management, customer information is necessary so that the company can market their products to the customers better. Customer information would also be vital in helping Avon with product development. Avon may have magnified the fears of the reps when it established its Avon.com Web site in February 1997 in order to take orders directly from its customers. As Adrian Dessi, senior director of Avon's direct marketing unit sees it, "Managing channel conflict is probably our number one concern right now."

Part of this problem stems from Avon's outdated information technology (IT) infrastructure. The company takes orders by telephone, fax, regular mail and e-mail, and over the Web, and these various sales channels are not united by shared systems. Moreover, the company's computer systems were developed independently all over the world and often a long time ago. Worldwide, "we wound up with 700 [disparate] local systems," said Perrin. The disparities are found in both Avon's hardware platforms and its application software. Much of the order processing and financial software is homegrown and outdated. Avon's U.S. order processing system is 20 years old, for example. Not surprisingly Avon's computer staff of 1,300 isn't any more up-to-date than its systems. Many of the staff are outdated because they have spent years working only on old mainframe applications and have had no client/server experience.

For the company as a whole, the lack of a standard hardware and database platform has been making it very difficult for the disparate systems to communicate with each other. Other issues that are not directly related to sales include the fact that the company has 35 major computer centers worldwide, which are expensive to maintain and add to the staffing and communications problems. In addition Avon is active in many countries with many different languages (the primary languages being English and Spanish) furthering communications problems.

Avon's management has outlined an ambitious plan to transform its business and add new products, new channels, and new technology. The company is sprucing up its catalog, expanding its business in jewelry and apparel, and replacing its entire information technology (IT) infrastructure. It hired Sateesh Lele as CIO in April 1999. Lele's experience was appropriate for this project. As the CIO at General Motors Corp. Europe, he had led GM in its major reengineering project, and he had previously led similar projects at two other smaller corporations. Lele has initiated the replacement of almost all of Avon's key back-office applications. He is considering a system for managing the company's sales reps and a customer relationship management (CRM) system.

New systems should provide electronic alternatives for field staff and representatives to communicate with Avon but still allow for orders and communication by traditional means. Avon would like better capabilities for tracking the activities of its sales reps, for obtaining feedback from sales reps, and for understanding its customers. The new systems should provide sales reps with tools to help them grow their own business, including tools for managing their customers and market information about consumer buying habits and sales trends in their own regions.

Management would like to make more use of the Internet without alienating door-to-door salespeople. Avon estimates that it saves between $1 and $3 for every order transmitted over its Web site which would amount to annual savings of be-

tween $650 million and $1 billion if all of its orders worldwide were handled through the Internet. Industry analysts believe that a high-profile Web site will help the company attract more technically savvy, upscale customers. The Web site will also help the company combat new competitors selling beauty products through the Web, including Gloss.com, Beauty.com, Eve.com, and Procter & Gamble's Reflect.com.

According to Andrea Jung, Avon's current CEO, the Web provides "an opportunity to get new customers who are currently not our shoppers." Jung has promised to keep 95 percent of Avon sales with the reps for at least the next 3 years. The company is encouraging sales representatives to set up their own Web pages linked to the Avon site. Customers could then place orders through the representatives' pages.

One challenge for any project is the attempt to automate the sales reps. In the United States, a country very advanced in Internet use, only about 30 percent of Avon's sales reps have Web access. It is far less advanced in some other key areas. For example only half of all independent sales reps in Latin America even have telephones, much less access to the Internet. Improving their communications will be a challenge. Avon is arranging discounted deals on computers and Internet service and is assisting reps in setting up their own Web pages.

Another issue Avon must face in its ambitious change project is finances. How much will the project cost? How much will it save? Are the costs even relevant given the nature of the changes required?

Sources: Claudia Graziano, "RFP: Know Thy Customer," Information Week, September 6, 1999; Erin White, "Ding-Dong, Avon Calling (On the Web, Not Your Door)," The Wall Street Journal, December 28, 1999; Stacy Collett, "Avon Calls for Revamp of Its Worldwide IT" Computerworld, July 12, 1999; and Gregory Dalton, "E-Business Moves to Center Stage," Information Week, September 27, 1999.

CASE STUDY QUESTIONS

1. Analyze Avon and its business model using the competitive forces and value chain models.

2. Analyze Avon's problems with its business model and its systems. What management, organization, and technology factors were responsible for these problems?

3. Propose a specific system solution for Avon. Your analysis should describe the objectives of the solution; the requirements to be met by the new system (or series of systems); and the technical, operational, and economic feasibility of your proposal. Include an overview of the systems you would recommend and explain how those systems would address the problems listed in your analysis. Your analysis should consider organizational and management issues to be addressed by the solution as well as technology issues.

4. If you were the systems analyst for this project, list five questions you would ask users during interviews to elicit the information you need for your systems study report.

CHAPTER 10

Approaches to Systems-Building

Learning Objectives

After completing this chapter, you will be able to:

1. Appraise system-building alternatives: the traditional systems lifecycle, prototyping, application software packages, end-user development, and outsourcing.

2. Compare the strengths and limitations of each approach.

3. Assess the solutions to the management problems these approaches create.

4. Describe the principal tools and methodologies used for systems development.

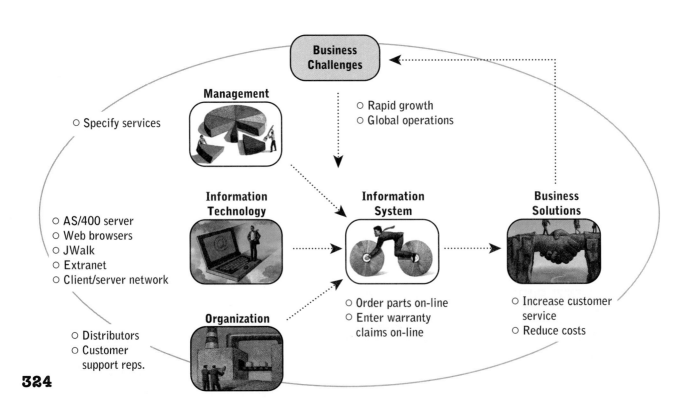

Business Challenges

Management
- Specify services
- Rapid growth
- Global operations

Information Technology
- AS/400 server
- Web browsers
- JWalk
- Extranet
- Client/server network

Information System
- Order parts on-line
- Enter warranty claims on-line

Business Solutions
- Increase customer service
- Reduce costs

Organization
- Distributors
- Customer support reps.

JLG Industries Gets a Lift
from Speedy Development

JLG Industries, Inc., in McConnellsburg, Pennsylvania, manufactures hydraulic lifts and has gotten its own lift from Web technology. The company has more than tripled its number of distributors from 600 to 2,000 and uses an extranet to share parts and warranty systems with them. The extranet replaced a private client/server system that the company had used since the mid-1990s, which was incapable of handling more than 75 users.

JLG needed a new system that was easier to maintain and that could be accessed easily by overseas customers who were beyond the reach of its private network. JLG needed applications that would enable users to access information on its corporate IBM AS/400 server using Web browser software.

However, its AS/400 applications were designed to work with a simple terminal-style text user interface. JLG found software called JWalk from Netherlands-based Seagull Software that could automate the process of creating Java applets that replicated the functions of the old-style terminal screens with graphical user interface controls. JWalk provides software development tools for building graphical client interfaces for new and existing applications that run on AS/400 hardware. JWalk includes an easy-to-use toolkit for customizing applet screens and eliminates the need to hire a team of Java programmers to develop a system from scratch.

The extranet costs only $2,000 per year to operate, compared to an annual cost of $80,000 to maintain JLG's old proprietary client/server system. JLG expects its extranet development project to pay for itself within 18 months. Now 50 percent of all parts orders and 85 percent of warranty claims come through the extranet. The company saves on customer support costs because it does not have to field many phone calls or answer mail correspondence yet can provide distributors with more rapid service. Before JLG had on-line capabilities, distributors that needed to make a warranty claim on a part had to send in a form by mail, wait for an authorization number, and then send back the part. By entering this transaction online, distributors can accomplish the same task within a few days.

Sources: David F. Carr, "Web Helps Manufacturer Improve Spare Parts, Warranty Operations," *Internet World,* May 3, 1999 and "SEAGULL Releases E-Business Upgrade to Industry-Leading JWalk," SEAGULL Public Relations, October 4, 1999.

Like JLG Industries, many organizations are examining alternative methods of building new information systems. Although they are designing and building some applications on their own, they also are turning to software packages, rapid application development tools, external consultants, and other strategies to reduce time, cost, and inefficiency. They also are experimenting with alternative tools to document, analyze, design, and implement systems. The availability of alternative systems-building approaches raises the following management challenges:

1. **Controlling information systems development outside the information systems department.** There may not be a way to establish standards and controls for systems development that is not managed by the information systems department, such as end-user development or outsourcing. Standards and controls that are too restrictive may not only generate user resistance but also may stifle end-user innovation. However, if controls are too weak, the firm may encounter serious problems with data integrity and connectivity. It is not always possible to find the right balance.

2. **Enforcing a standard methodology.** Although structured methodologies have been available for more than 25 years, very few organizations have been able to enforce them. It is impossible to use CASE or object-oriented methods effectively unless all participants in system-building adopt a common development methodology as well as common development tools. Methodologies are organizational disciplines.

This chapter examines the use of prototyping, application software packages, end-user development, and outsourcing as systems-building alternatives to the traditional systems lifecycle method of building an entire information system from scratch. It also looks at various systems development methodologies and tools. There is no one approach that can be used for all situations and types of systems. Each of these approaches has advantages and disadvantages, and each provides managers with a range of choices. We describe and compare the system-building approaches and methodologies so that managers know how to choose among them.

10.1 The Traditional Systems Lifecycle

systems lifecycle A traditional methodology for developing an information system that partitions the systems development process into formal stages that must be completed sequentially with a very formal division of labor between end users and information systems specialists.

The **systems lifecycle** is the oldest method for building information systems and is still used today for medium or large complex systems projects. This methodology assumes that an information system has a lifecycle similar to that of any living organism, with a beginning, middle, and end. The lifecycle for an information system has six stages: (1) project definition, (2) systems study, (3) design, (4) programming, (5) installation, and (6) postimplementation. Figure 10-1 illustrates these stages. Each stage consists of basic activities that must be performed before the next stage can begin.

The lifecycle methodology has a very formal division of labor between end users and information systems specialists. Technical specialists such as systems analysts and programmers are responsible for much of the systems analysis, design, and implementation work; end users are limited to providing information requirements and reviewing the technical staff's work. Formal sign-offs or agreements between end users and technical specialists are required as each stage is completed. Figure 10-1 also shows the product or output of each stage of the lifecycle that is the basis for such sign-offs. We now describe the stages of the lifecycle in detail.

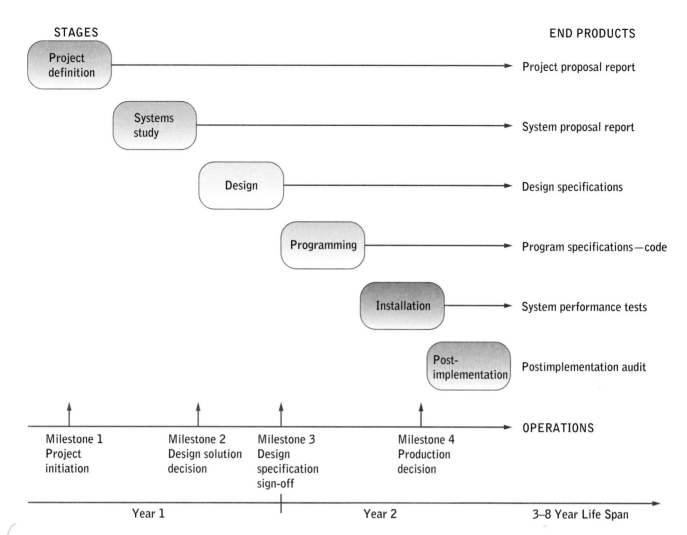

STAGES   END PRODUCTS

Project definition ————————————————————————————————→ Project proposal report

Systems study ————————————————————————————————→ System proposal report

Design ————————————————————————————————→ Design specifications

Programming ————————————————————————————————→ Program specifications—code

Installation ————————————————————————————————→ System performance tests

Post-implementation ——→ Postimplementation audit

↑   ↑   ↑   ↑
Milestone 1   Milestone 2   Milestone 3   Milestone 4   OPERATIONS
Project   Design solution   Design   Production
initiation   decision   specification   decision
                                          sign-off

| Year 1 | Year 2 | 3–8 Year Life Span |

FIGURE I 0-I The lifecycle methodology for systems development. The lifecycle methodology divides systems development into six formal stages with specific milestones and end products at each stage. A typical medium-size development project requires two years to deliver and has an expected life span of three to eight years.

STAGES OF THE SYSTEMS LIFECYCLE

The **project definition** stage tries to answer the questions, "Why do we need a new system project?" and "What do we want to accomplish?" This stage determines whether the organization has a problem and whether that problem can be solved by building a new information system or by modifying an existing one. If a system project is called for, this stage identifies its general objectives, specifies the project's scope, and develops a project plan that can be shown to management.

The **systems study** stage analyzes the problems of existing systems (manual or automated) in detail, identifies objectives to be attained by a solution to these problems, and describes alternative solutions. The systems study stage examines the feasibility of each solution alternative for review by management.

Systems study requires extensive information gathering and research; sifting through documents, reports, and work papers produced by existing systems; observing how these systems work; polling users with questionnaires; and conducting interviews. All of the information gathered during the systems study phase will be used to determine information system requirements. Finally, the systems study stage describes in detail the remaining lifecycle activities and the tasks for each phase.

project definition A stage in the systems lifecycle that determines whether the organization has a problem and whether the problem can be solved by launching a system project.

systems study A stage in the systems lifecycle that analyzes the problems of existing systems, defines the objectives a solution will attain, and evaluates various solution alternatives.

design A stage in the systems life-cycle that produces the logical and physical design specifications for the system solution.

programming A stage in the systems lifecycle that translates the design specifications produced during the design stage into software program code.

installation A stage in the systems lifecycle consisting of testing, training, and conversion; the final steps required to put a system into operation.

postimplementation The final stage of the systems lifecycle in which the system is used and evaluated while in production and is modified to make improvements or meet new requirements.

The **design** stage produces the logical and physical design specifications for the solution. The lifecycle emphasizes formal specifications and paperwork, so many of the design and documentation tools described in Section 10.3, such as data flow diagrams, program structure charts, or system flowcharts, are likely to be employed.

The **programming** stage translates the design specifications produced during the design stage into software program code. Systems analysts work with programmers to prepare specifications for each program in the system. Programmers write customized program code, typically using a conventional third-generation programming language such as COBOL or FORTRAN or a high-productivity, fourth-generation language. Large systems have many programs with hundreds of thousands of lines of program code, and entire teams of programmers may be required.

The **installation** stage consists of the final steps to put the new or modified system into operation: testing, training, and conversion. The software is tested to make sure it performs properly from both a technical and a functional business standpoint. (More detail on testing can be found in Chapter 13.) Business and technical specialists are trained to use the new system. A formal conversion plan provides a detailed schedule of all of the activities required to install the new system, and the old system is converted to the new one.

The **postimplementation** stage consists of using and evaluating the system after it is installed and is in production. Users and technical specialists go through a formal postimplementation audit that determines how well the new system has met its original objectives and whether any revisions or modifications are required. After the system has been fine-tuned it will need to be maintained while it is in production to correct errors, meet requirements, or improve processing efficiency. Over time, the system may require so much maintenance to remain efficient and meet user objectives that it will come to the end of its useful life span. Once the system's lifecycle comes to an end, a completely new system is called for and the cycle may begin again.

LIMITATIONS OF THE LIFECYCLE APPROACH

The systems lifecycle is still used for building large transaction processing systems (TPS) and management information systems (MIS) where requirements are highly structured and well defined (Ahituv and Neumann, 1984). It will also remain appropriate for complex technical systems such as space launches, air traffic control, and refinery operations. Such applications need a rigorous and formal requirements analysis, predefined specifications, and tight controls over the systems-building process.

However, the systems lifecycle approach is costly, time consuming, and inflexible. Volumes of new documents must be generated and steps repeated if requirements and specifications need to be revised. Because of the time and cost to repeat the sequence of lifecycle activities, the methodology encourages freezing of specifications early in the development process, discouraging change. The lifecycle method is ill-suited to decision-oriented applications where decision makers may need to experiment with concrete systems to clarify the kinds of decisions they wish to make. Formal specification of requirements may inhibit system-builders from exploring and discovering the problem structure (Fraser et al., 1994). Likewise, the lifecycle approach is not suitable for many small desktop systems, which tend to be less structured and more individualized.

10.2 Alternative System-Building Approaches

Alternative system-building approaches can solve some of the problems of the traditional systems lifecycle. These approaches include prototyping, application software packages, end-user development, and outsourcing.

PROTOTYPING

prototyping The process of building an experimental system quickly and inexpensively for demonstration and evaluation so users can better determine information requirements.

Prototyping consists of building an experimental system rapidly and inexpensively for end users to evaluate. By interacting with the prototype, users can get a better idea of their information requirements. The prototype endorsed by the users can be used as a template to create the final system.

The **prototype** is a working version of an information system or part of the system, but it is meant to be only a preliminary model. Once operational, the prototype will be further refined until it conforms precisely to users' requirements. Once the design has been finalized, the prototype can be converted to a polished production system.

The process of building a preliminary design, trying it out, refining it, and trying again has been called an **iterative** process of systems development because the steps required to build a system can be repeated over and over again. Prototyping is more explicitly iterative than the conventional lifecycle, and it actively promotes system design changes. It has been said that prototyping replaces unplanned rework with planned iteration, with each version more accurately reflecting users' requirements.

prototype The preliminary working version of an information system for demonstration and evaluation purposes.

iterative A process of repeating over and over again the steps to build a system.

Steps in Prototyping

Figure 10-2 shows a four-step model of the prototyping process, which consists of the following:

Step 1: *Identify the user's basic requirements.* The system designer (usually an information systems specialist) works with the user only long enough to capture his or her basic information needs.

Step 2: *Develop an initial prototype.* The system designer creates a working prototype quickly, using fourth-generation software, interactive multimedia, or computer-aided software engineering (CASE) tools described later in this chapter.

Step 3: *Use the prototype.* The user is encouraged to work with the system in order to determine how well the prototype meets his or her needs and to make suggestions for improving the prototype.

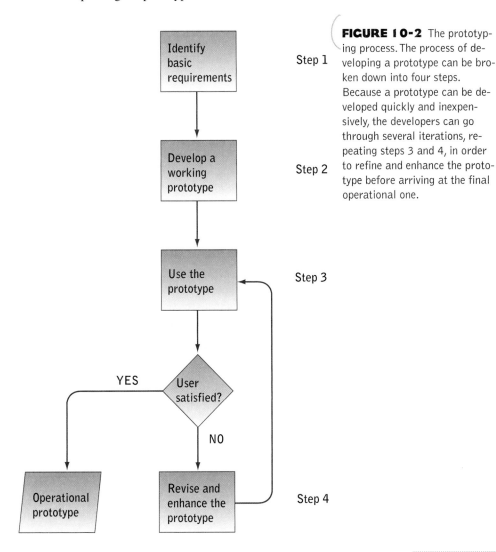

FIGURE 10-2 The prototyping process. The process of developing a prototype can be broken down into four steps. Because a prototype can be developed quickly and inexpensively, the developers can go through several iterations, repeating steps 3 and 4, in order to refine and enhance the prototype before arriving at the final operational one.

Step 4: *Revise and enhance the prototype.* The system builder notes all changes the user requests and refines the prototype accordingly. After the prototype has been revised, the cycle returns to step 3. Steps 3 and 4 are repeated until the user is satisfied.

When no more iterations are required, the approved prototype then becomes an operational prototype that furnishes the final specifications for the application. Sometimes the prototype itself is adopted as the production version of the system.

Advantages and Disadvantages of Prototyping

Prototyping is most useful when there is some uncertainty about requirements or design solutions. For example, a major securities firm requests consolidated information to analyze the performance of its account executives. But what should the measures of performance be? Can the information be extracted from the personnel system alone, or must data from client billings be incorporated as well? What items should be compared on reports? Initially users may not be able to see how the system will work.

Prototyping is especially valuable for the design of an information system's **end-user interface** (the part of the system that end users interact with, such as on-line display and data-entry screens, reports, or Web pages). The prototype enables users to react immediately to the parts of the system with which they will be dealing. Figure 10-3 illustrates the prototyping process for an on-line calendar for retail securities brokers. The first version of the screen was built according to user-supplied specifications for a calendar to track appointments and activities. But when users actually worked with the calendar screen, they suggested adding labels for the month and year to the screen and a box to indicate whether the appointment had been met or an activity completed. The brokers also found that they wanted to access information that was maintained in the system about clients with whom they had appointments. The system designer added a link enabling brokers to move directly from the calendar screen to client records.

Prototyping encourages intense end-user involvement throughout the systems development lifecycle (Cerveny et al., 1986) and thus is likely to produce systems that fulfill user requirements. However, rapid prototyping can gloss over essential steps in systems development. Once finished, if the prototype works reasonably well, management may not see the need for reprogramming, redesign, or full documentation and testing. Some of these hastily constructed systems may not easily accommodate large quantities of data or a large number of users in a production environment. Successful prototyping requires management and mechanisms for defining expectations, assigning resources, signaling problems, and measuring progress (Baskerville and Stage, 1996).

APPLICATION SOFTWARE PACKAGES

Another alternative strategy is to develop an information system by purchasing an application software package. As introduced in Chapter 5, an **application software package** is a set of prewritten, precoded application software programs that are commercially available for sale or lease. Application software packages may range from a simple task (e.g., printing address labels from a database on a PC) to more than 400 program modules with 500,000 lines of code for a complex mainframe system.

Packages have flourished because there are many applications that are common to all business organizations—for example, payroll, accounts receivable, general ledger, or inventory control. For such universal functions with standard procedures, a generalized system will fulfill the requirements of many organizations. Table 10-1 provides examples of applications for which packages are commercially available.

Advantages and Disadvantages of Software Packages

When an appropriate software package is available, it is often not necessary for a company to write its own programs; the prewritten, predesigned, pretested software package can fulfill most of the requirements and can be substituted instead. The package vendor has already done most of the design, programming, and testing, so the time frame and costs for developing a

end-user interface The part of an information system through which the end user interacts with the system, such as on-line screens and commands.

application software package A set of prewritten, precoded application software programs that are commercially available for sale or lease.

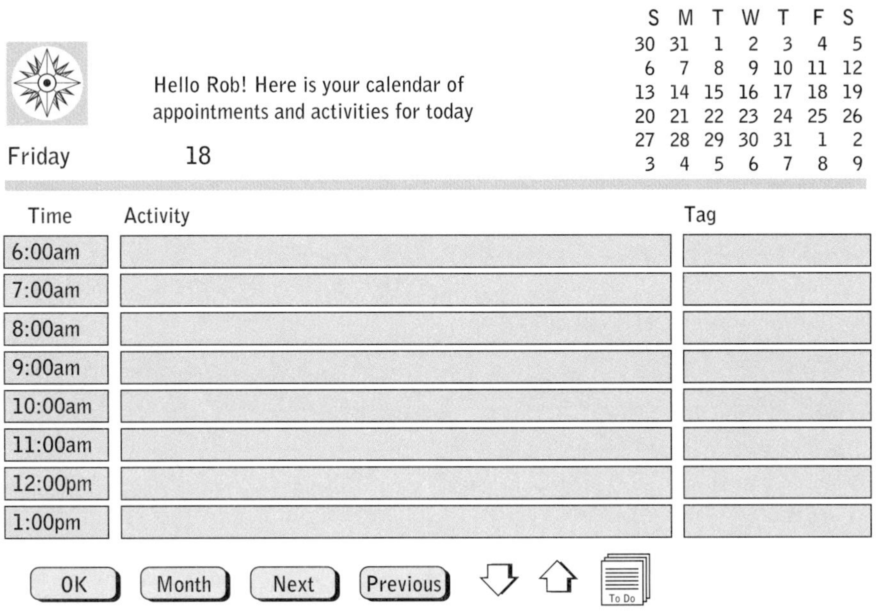

FIGURE 10-3 Prototyping a portfolio management application. This figure illustrates the process of prototyping one screen for the Financial Manager, a client and portfolio management application for securities brokers. Figure 10-3a shows an early version of the on-line appointment screen. Based on a client's special needs, Figure 10-3b has two enhancements: a "done" indicator to show whether the task has been completed and a link to reference information maintained by the system on the client with whom the broker has an appointment.

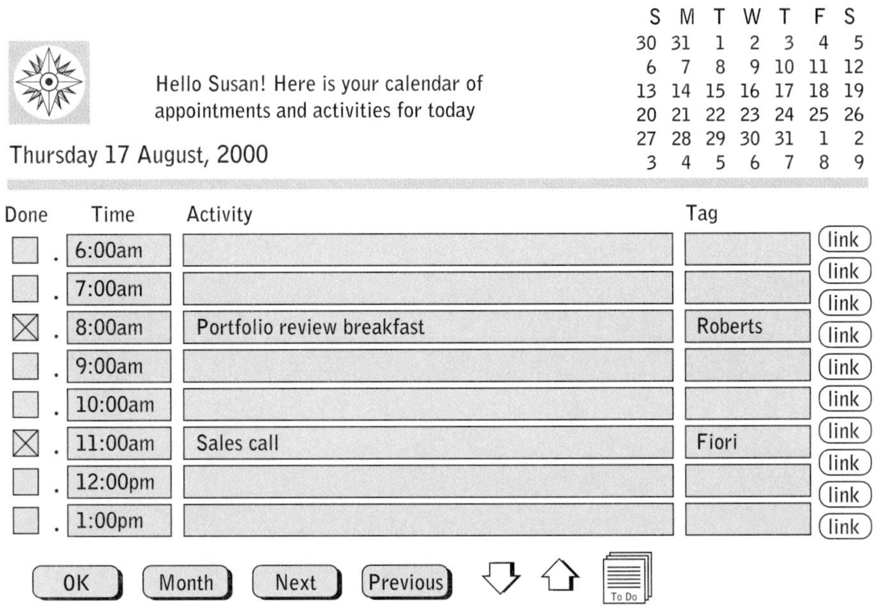

new system should be considerably reduced. Vendors provide much of the ongoing maintenance and support for the system, supplying enhancements to keep the system in line with ongoing technical and business developments.

To maximize market appeal, packages are geared to the most common requirements of all organizations. What happens if an organization has unique requirements that the package does not address? To varying degrees, package software developers anticipate this problem by providing features for customization that do not alter the basic software. **Customization** features allow a software package to be modified to meet an organization's unique requirements without destroying the integrity of the package software. For instance, the package may allocate parts of its files or databases to maintain an organization's own unique pieces of data. Some packages have a modular design that allows clients to select only the software functions with the processing they need from an array of options. An alternative way of satisfying

customization The modification of a software package to meet an organization's unique requirements without destroying the package software's integrity.

Table 10-1	Examples of Application Software Packages

Accounts receivable	Job costing
Bond and stock management	Library systems
Computer-aided design (CAD)	Life insurance
Document imaging	Mailing labels
E-mail	Mathematical/statistical modeling
Enterprise resource planning (ERP)	Order processing
Groupware	Payroll
Healthcare	Process control
Hotel management	Tax accounting
Internet telephone	Web browser
Inventory control	Word processing

organizational information requirements unmet by a software package is to supplement the package with another piece of software.

Ultimately, required customization and additional programming may become so expensive and time consuming that they eliminate many of the advantages of software packages. Figure 10-4 shows how package costs in relation to total implementation costs rise with the degree of customization. The initial purchase price of the package can be deceptive because of these hidden implementation costs. The Window on Management describes how one company grappled with these issues when it built its electronic commerce system.

Selecting Software Packages

Application software packages must be thoroughly evaluated before they can be used as the foundation of a new information system. The most important evaluation criteria are the functions provided by the package, flexibility, user-friendliness, hardware and software resources, database requirements, installation and maintenance effort, documentation, vendor quality, and cost. The package evaluation process often is based on a **Request for Proposal (RFP),** which is a detailed list of questions submitted to packaged software vendors.

Request for Proposal (RFP)
A detailed list of questions submitted to vendors of software or other services to determine how well the vendor's product can meet the organization's specific requirements.

FIGURE 10-4 The effects of customizing a software package on total implementation costs. As the modifications to a software package rise, so does the cost of implementing the package. Sometimes the savings promised by the package are whittled away by excessive changes. As the number of lines of program code changed approaches 5 percent of the total lines in the package, the costs of implementation rise fivefold.

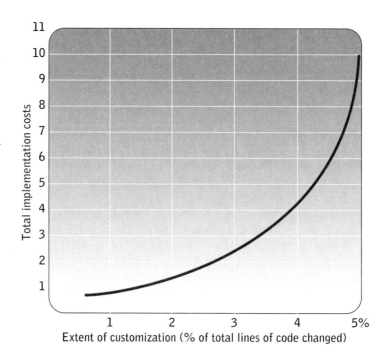

Window on Management

BUILD OR BUY AN ELECTRONIC COMMERCE SYSTEM? BUYONET INTERNATIONAL DECIDES

Buyonet International AB was set up in Gothenburg, Sweden, in 1997 to sell and deliver software on-line. The company initially planned to sell to Swedish and other Scandinavian users, but it has set its sights further. The Internet has no borders, so why not target mushrooming software markets in the United States and other parts of the world? The large and lucrative U.S. market was already being served by powerful competitors such as Beyond.com and Egghead.com, so Buyonet would need an extraordinarily robust and flexible electronic commerce system to meet these powerhouses head-on.

After examining off-the-shelf e-commerce products, Buyonet CEO Freddy Tengberg decided to build a system from scratch. Although this was a very ambitious and resource-consuming decision, Tengberg believed that Buyonet had unique yet important requirements that could not be met by an off-the-shelf product. For example, unlike other electronic software distributors, Buyonet allows customers to download the software first before paying for it. Once the customer has downloaded the software, Buyonet automatically checks that all of the pieces of the program have been successfully transferred to the customer's PC. The customer is then billed electronically. Once payment is received, Buyonet e-mails the customer a special password to activate the software. (Software downloaded from Buyonet can't be used until this password is supplied.) Buyonet's market research showed that individuals from some countries outside the United States would not pay for something they had not yet received.

Aiming for a global market, Buyonet needed a system that could support multiple languages and more than 20 different currencies. There was no commercially available electronic commerce software package or service that could fulfill these needs or Buyonet's plans for unique services such as a buyer bonus program.

Tengberg hired a team of contract programmers from Riga, Latvia, who developed a sophisticated and flexible system within four months. The team used C++ and Perl to write the software, which runs on Sun Microsystems Solaris Unix computers. The system provides a flexible platform for selling more than 120,000 different pieces of software, all of which reside on servers owned by Buyonet or its partners. The main system includes eight major modules for sales and database analysis, payment, delivery, antifraud,

reporting, special activities (such as promotional and affiliation programs), and Web site and systems maintenance. These modules are linked to a TcX DataKonsult AB My SQL database.

The system supports an array of payment options, including entering credit card numbers on-line through the Buyonet Web site, faxing the credit card information, or mailing in bank money orders or checks. Buyonet uses an ISDN link to National Westminster Bank PLC in London for instant payment processing. The customer can be notified whether his or her payment was accepted within 30 seconds.

Buyonet spent about $2 million on software development and $40,000 in hardware to create the system, much more than an off-the-shelf solution would cost. James McQuivey, a Forrester Research analyst for on-line retail strategies, believes that the advantages of proprietary electronic commerce systems such as Buyonet's are limited. Companies that built their own e-commerce systems must keep programmers on hand that have the special skills required to maintain them.

Buyonet has not yet been able to quantify the return on investment (ROI) for the system, but Tengberg believes Buyonet's custom system has lower transaction costs for order fulfillment and other processes than off-the-shelf software options and provides superior payment protection capabilities. Buyonet's proprietary "processing and protection technology is a factor in our success," he asserts. Many companies that license their electronic commerce software often have to pay a portion of the revenue from each sale transaction to the vendor. Buyonet can continue to make money on its sales transactions even if profit margins are shrinking. Moreover, the site has become immensely popular—the ninth best trading Web site in Europe according to Forrester Research.

TO THINK ABOUT: What were the benefits and drawbacks of Buyonet custom building its electronic commerce system? What management, organization, and technology issues should be addressed in deciding whether to build a custom system or use an application software package?

Sources: Lauren Gibbons Paul, "E for Two," *CIO Magazine,* February 15, 1999; and "Forrester Report Puts Buyonet on Cloud 9," August 27, 1999, www.buyonet.com.

When a system is developed using an application software package, systems analysis will include a package evaluation effort. Design activities will focus on matching requirements to package features. Instead of tailoring the system design specifications directly to user requirements, the design effort will consist of trying to mold user requirements to conform to the features of the package.

When a software package solution is selected, the organization no longer has total control over the system design process. At best, packages can meet only 70 percent of most

PRICING A SOFTWARE PACKAGE AND CALCULATING BENEFITS

Your rapidly growing pharmaceutical company has 24 sales representatives, annual sales of $20 million and an extensive inventory of products that it markets to hospitals and health care facilities. The sales department has used glossy brochures, printed catalogs, and electronic presentations to present information to customers about products, but you would like to be able to create custom catalogs and electronic presentations for customer sales calls that are tailored to different selling situations. You have found a sales software package called PowerSales that provides these capabilities and that can link automatically into the firm's enterprise resource planning (ERP) system to reflect changes in pricing, availability, and new products. The software also provides sales managers with forecasts and detailed reports of each sales call.

The package vendor has suggested the following pricing option.

Base software

One-time installation charge $115,000

Annual license charge $75,000

Custom content (one-time charges) for the entire sales force

Specific product promotions and product introduction $130,000

Product line overview presentations $65,000

Sales skills training $57,500

Your company plans to use the same content for two years. After determining the initial software configuration, the package vendor supplies a consultant to guide the customization process, working with the client to provide text, graphics, animation, audio, and video content for the system. The cost of the consultant is $2000 per day. You have been told that it would take about 50 days of consulting time to customize and complete the package implementation. Your firm would not need to purchase any new hardware to run the package, but you would need an information systems specialist at an annual full-time salary of $75,000 to spend 20 hours per month supporting the package.

1. What are the total costs of using this package for the first year? For two years?
2. The package vendor claims that after implementing the package, its customers have increased sales by an average of 10% over two years. How much increase in sales revenue should your company anticipate if you implement this package?
3. Calculate the cost/benefit ratio for using this package over a two-year period. Refer to the formula for the cost/benefit ratio in Chapter 9.
4. What additional information would be useful to guide your purchase decision?

organizations' requirements. If the package cannot adapt to the organization, the organization will have to adapt to the package and change its procedures.

END-USER DEVELOPMENT

end-user development The development of information systems by end users with little or no formal assistance from technical specialists.

In many organizations, end users are developing a growing percentage of information systems with little or no formal assistance from technical specialists. This phenomenon is called **end-user development.** End-user development has been made possible by the special fourth-generation software tools introduced in Chapter 5. With fourth-generation languages, graphics languages, and PC software tools, end users can access data, create reports, and develop entire information systems on their own, with little or no help from professional systems analysts or programmers. Many of these end-user developed systems can be created much more rapidly than with the traditional systems lifecycle. Figure 10-5 illustrates the concept of end-user development.

End-User Computing Tools: Strengths and Limitations

Many organizations have reported gains in application development productivity by using fourth-generation tools that in a few cases have reached 300 to 500 percent (Glass, 1999; Green, 1984–85; Harel and McLean, 1985). Fourth-generation tools have capabilities such as graphics, spreadsheets, modeling, and ad hoc information retrieval, that meet important business needs.

Unfortunately, fourth-generation tools still cannot replace conventional tools for some business applications because their capabilities remain limited. Fourth-generation software is relatively inefficient, processing individual transactions too slowly and at too high a cost to make these systems suitable for very large transaction processing systems. Slow response time and computer performance degradation often result when very large files are used.

Most fourth-generation tools likewise cannot easily handle applications with extensive procedural logic and updating requirements, such as systems used for optimal production

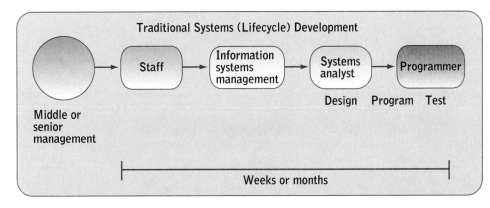

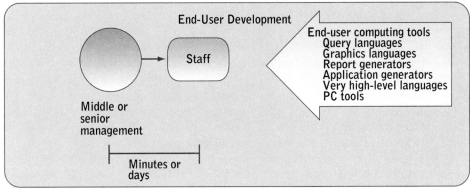

FIGURE 10-5 End-user versus systems lifecycle development. End users can access computerized information directly or develop information systems with little or no formal technical assistance. On the whole, end-user developed systems can be completed more rapidly than those developed through the conventional systems lifecycle.
From **Applications Development Without Programmers**, by James Martin, © 1982. Reprinted by permission of Prentice-Hall, Inc., Upper Saddle River, NJ.

scheduling or tracking daily trades of stocks, bonds, and other securities, that require complex processing and often the matching of multiple files.

Management Benefits and Problems

Without question, end-user development provides many benefits to organizations. These include the following:

○ Improved requirements determination as users specify their own business needs.

○ Increased user involvement and satisfaction. As users develop their systems themselves and control the system development process, they are more likely to use the system.

○ Reduced application backlog when users are no longer totally reliant on overburdened professional information systems specialists.

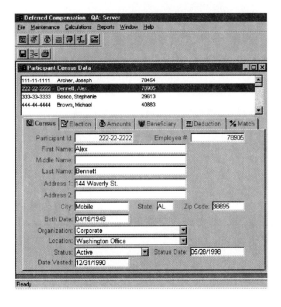

Emboss Technologies, which provides outsourcing services and consulting for employee benefits and executive compensation programs, developed an early version of an executive compensation system using PowerBuilder as a fourth-generation software tool. This screen lists individual participants in a deferred compensation plan.

At the same time, end-user computing poses organizational risks because it occurs outside of traditional mechanisms for information system management and control. Most organizations have not yet developed strategies to ensure that end-user-developed applications meet organizational objectives or meet quality assurance standards appropriate to their function. When systems are created rapidly, without a formal development methodology, testing and documentation may be inadequate.

Control over data can be lost in systems outside the traditional information systems department. When users create their own applications and files, it becomes increasingly difficult to determine where data are located and to ensure that the same piece of information (such as product number or annual earnings) is used consistently throughout the organization (see Chapters 6 and 7).

Managing End-User Development

A number of strategies have been suggested to help organizations maximize the benefits of end-user applications development while keeping it under management control (see Alavi, Nelson, and Weiss, 1987–88; Rockart and Flannery, 1983). Management should control the development of end-user applications by incorporating them into its strategic systems plans. Training and support should consider individual users' attitudes toward computers, educational levels, cognitive styles, and receptiveness to change (Harrison and Rainer, 1992). Management should also develop controls on critical end-user development, such as insisting on cost justification of end-user information system projects and establishing hardware, software, and quality standards for user-developed applications.

When end-user computing first became popular, organizations used information centers to promote standards for hardware and software so that end users did not introduce many disparate and incompatible technologies into the firm (Fuller and Swanson, 1992; see Chapter 7). **Information centers** are special facilities housing hardware, software, and technical specialists to supply end users with tools, training, and expert advice so they can create information system applications on their own or increase their productivity. The role of information centers is diminishing as end users become more computer literate, but organizations still need to closely monitor and manage end-user development, as described in the Window on Organizations.

OUTSOURCING

If a firm does not want to use its internal resources to build or operate information systems, it can hire an external organization that specializes in providing these services to do the work. The process of turning over an organization's computer center operations, telecommunications

information center A special facility within an organization that provides training and support for end-user computing.

WebWareLite by Today.com provides tools that allow non-technical users to take part in the creation and management of a Web site. After information system specialists define the look and feel of pages in a template, non-technical staff can create, manage, and instantly post content using Microsoft Word and edit that content on the page.

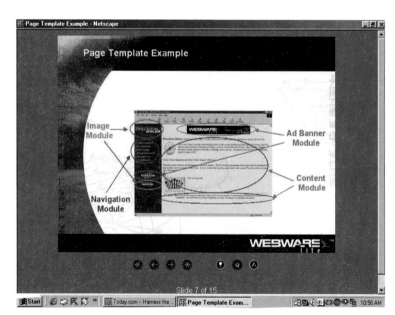

USERS CREATE THEIR OWN WEB CONTENT

Who should create and update content on corporate Web sites? If the end users know the business better than anyone else, why not them? The availability of many easy-to-use Web site development tools has made this an attractive option for many companies.

Providence Health Systems in Portland, Oregon, found that its Web sites contained too much outdated and inaccurate content, which had been placed on the Web sites by IT specialists. Because the content originated with and belonged to business groups, Providence Health Systems started letting end users in its business groups contribute content directly to its corporate intranet and intranet sites using Web content tools.

Businesses can choose from a wide array of software tools that make it easier for users to create, update, and manage Web sites without knowing the details of HTML programming. Providence Health selected Microsoft's FrontPage 98 for this purpose. The company had already standardized on the Microsoft Office software suite for desktop applications, and FrontPage had the same look and feel as the software tools the company's employees were used to working with. FrontPage could also provide the Web content and management capabilities the company needed at much less cost than more powerful high-end tools, and it has "wizard" tools to automate site creation that are useful for beginners. Providence Health allows some skilled users to work with more advanced tools if they can demonstrate their benefit.

Bank of America, which recently merged with NationsBank Corp., took a different track. The company selected Authoring Server Suite 3.0 from NetObjects for user Web publishing because it believed this tool could better handle different contributors to the same intranet sites. Employees contribute content from all over the world. The bank's Web development group did not want to manage and update hundreds of Web pages created by the merger. Bank of America does not allow all noninformation systems employees to publish on its intranet yet, but it does allow some units to contribute to their own corporate Web sites. For example, marketing groups in Atlanta and San Francisco have their own Web publishing. Their Web sites are so big that they require many people to work on them.

The major challenge in opening up Web site publishing to end users may not be technical. Management needs to realize that it can't just allow business groups to create and update corporate Web sites without some coordination and planning. Information systems specialists still need to make sure that the Web content created by end users meets corporate security requirements and that it maintains the same look and feel as the rest of the corporate intranet or public Web site. It might be useful, for example, to enforce some measure of company-wide standards for page layout and navigation between Web pages. Some organizations, for example, allow users to change only text content but not graphics and images. Managers should be held personally responsible for the content contributed by their subordinates.

At Providence Health, managers are required to approve end user requests to become Web publishers before they can receive training on FrontPage. The managers are also responsible for monitoring the content on their departments' sites and for eliminating questionable content.

TO THINK ABOUT: Should end users be allowed to create and publish content for corporate Web sites and intranets? What are the benefits? What are the drawbacks?

Sources: John C. Rotondo, "Business Tools," *Small Business Computing*, February 2000; Tim Ouellette, "Giving Users the Keys to Their Web Content," *Computerworld*, July 26, 1999; and Rich Broida, "Web Authoring Tools," *Home Office Computing*, June 1999.

---

networks, or applications development to external vendors is called **outsourcing.** Chapter 5 described one increasingly popular form of outsourcing, application service providers, which run software applications for subscribing companies.

Outsourcing has become popular because some organizations perceive it as a cost-effective measure that eliminates the need for maintaining their own computer center and information systems staff. The provider of outsourcing services benefits from economies of scale (the same knowledge, skills, and capacity can be shared with many different customers) and is likely to charge competitive prices for information systems services. Outsourcing allows a company with fluctuating needs for computer processing to pay for only what it uses rather than to build its own computer center, which would be underutilized when there is no peak load.

Some firms outsource because their internal information systems staff cannot keep pace with technological change or innovative business practices or because they want to free up scarce and costly talent for activities with higher payback. By outsourcing, companies hope to exploit the benefits of information technology in key business processes and improve the productivity of their information system resources.

outsourcing The practice of contracting computer center operations, telecommunications networks, or applications development to external vendors.

When to Use Outsourcing

Not all organizations benefit from outsourcing, and the disadvantages of outsourcing can create serious problems for organizations if they are not well understood and managed (Earl, 1996). When a firm allocates the responsibility for developing and operating its information systems to another organization, it can lose control over its information systems function. If the organization lacks the expertise to negotiate a sound contract, the firm's dependency on the vendor could result in high costs or loss of control over technological direction (Lacity, Willcocks, and Feeny, 1996). Trade secrets or proprietary information may leak out to competitors when a firm's information systems are run or developed by outsiders. This could be harmful if a firm allows an outsourcer to develop or to operate applications that give it some type of competitive advantage.

Despite such drawbacks, there are a number of circumstances in which outsourcing application development to an external vendor is advantageous.

○ *To reduce costs or offload some of the information systems department's work.* Applications such as payroll, for which the firm obtains little competitive advantage from excellence, or travel expense processing, where the predictability of uninterrupted information systems service is not very important, are strong candidates for outsourcing if the company's objective is to reduce costs or save internal information system resources for more important work. Firms should be more cautious about using outsiders to develop applications such as airline reservations or catalog shopping systems that represent critical business processes.

○ *When the firm's existing information system capabilities are limited, ineffective, or technically inferior.* Organizations might use an outsourcer to help them acquire capabilities in newer technologies such as object-oriented programming, Java, state-of-the-art electronic commerce applications, or enterprise systems.

○ *To improve the contribution of information technology to business performance.* Organizations are starting to turn to external vendors to help them develop critical or innovative business applications because these vendors have more expertise in technology, management, and business process reengineering. For instance, Rolls Royce Aerospace Group uses Electronic Data Systems (EDS) as consultants for systems integration and for business transformation projects relating to time-to-market, customer service, supply chain management, and manufacturing and engineering operations.

○ *To create new sources of revenue and profit from technology assets.* Companies are starting to enlist external vendors to help them create, develop, and market new technology-based products and services that can be licensed or sold to other companies. For instance, Swiss Bank Corporation (SBC) contracted with Perot Systems to help with its infrastructure transformation. Perot created a new division to provide state-of-the-art systems and network services to SBC and other global financial service companies (DiRomualdo and Gurbaxani, 1998).

Organizations need to manage the outsourcer as they would manage their own internal information systems. They should establish criteria for evaluating the outsourcing vendor. Firms should design outsourcing contracts carefully so that the outsourcing services can be adjusted if the nature of the business changes. The firm's relationship with the vendor specified in the outsourcing contract, decision rights, performance measures, and assessment of risks and rewards should be aligned with the strategic intent for outsourcing. The most successful outsourcing projects are ones where a climate of trust exists between both parties, and the outsourcing relationship should be structured to balance good feelings with proper controls (Sabherwal, 1999).

Table 10-2 compares the advantages and disadvantages of each of the system-building alternatives described in this chapter.

development methodology A collection of methods, one or more for every activity within every phase of a development project.

10.3 System-Building Methodologies and Tools

Various tools and development methodologies have been employed to help system builders document, analyze, design, and implement information systems. A **development methodology**

Table 10-2 Comparison of Systems-Development Approaches

Approach	Features	Advantages	Disadvantages
Systems lifecycle	Sequential step-by-step formal process Written specification and approvals Limited role of users	Necessary for large complex systems and projects	Slow and expensive Discourages changes Massive paperwork to manage
Prototyping	Requirements specified dynamically with experimental system Rapid, informal, and iterative process Users continually interact with the prototype	Rapid and relatively inexpensive Useful when requirements uncertain or when end-user interface is very important Promotes user participation	Inappropriate for large, complex systems Can gloss over steps in analysis, documentation, and testing
Application software package	Commercial software eliminates need for internally developed software programs	Design, programming, installation, and maintenance work reduced Can save time and cost when developing common business applications Reduces need for internal information systems resources	May not meet organization's unique requirements May not perform many business functions well Extensive customization raises development costs
End-user development	Systems created by end users using fourth-generation software tools Rapid and informal Minimal role of information systems specialists	Users control systems-building Saves development time and cost Reduces application backlog	Can lead to proliferation of uncontrolled information systems and data Systems do not always meet quality assurance standards
Outsourcing	Systems built and sometimes operated by external vendor	Can reduce or control costs Can produce systems when internal resources not available or technically deficient	Loss of control over the information systems function Dependence on the technical direction and prosperity of external vendors

is a collection of methods, one or more for every activity within every phase of a systems development project. Some development methodologies are suited to specific technologies, whereas others reflect different philosophies of systems development. The most widely used methodologies and tools include the traditional structured methodologies, object-oriented software development, computer-aided software engineering (CASE), and software reengineering.

STRUCTURED METHODOLOGIES

Structured methodologies have been used to document, analyze, and design information systems since the 1970s and remain an important methodological approach. **Structured** refers to the fact that the techniques are step-by-step, with each step building on the previous one. Structured methodologies are top-down, progressing from the highest, most abstract level to the lowest level of detail—from the general to the specific. For example, the highest level of a top-down description of a human resources system would show the main human resources functions: personnel, benefits, compensation, and Equal Employment Opportunity (EEO). Each of these would be broken down into the next layer. Benefits, for instance, might include pension, employee savings, healthcare, and insurance. Each of these layers in turn would be broken down until the lowest level of detail could be depicted.

The traditional structured methodologies are process-oriented rather than data-oriented. Although data descriptions are part of the methods, the methodologies focus on how the data are transformed rather than on the data themselves. These methodologies are largely linear; each phase must be completed before the next one can begin. Structured methodologies include structured analysis, structured design, and the use of flowcharts.

structured Refers to the fact that techniques are carefully drawn up, step by step, with each step building on a previous one.

Structured Analysis

structured analysis A method for defining system inputs, processes, and outputs and for partitioning systems into subsystems or modules that show a logical graphic model of information flow.

data flow diagram (DFD) A primary tool in structured analysis that graphically illustrates the system's component processes and the flow of data between them.

Structured analysis is widely used to define system inputs, processes, and outputs. It offers a logical graphic model of information flow, partitioning a system into modules that show manageable levels of detail. It rigorously specifies the processes or transformations that occur within each module and the interfaces that exist between them. Its primary tool is the **data flow diagram (DFD),** a graphic representation of a system's component processes and the flow of data between them.

Figure 10-6 shows a simple data flow diagram for a mail-in university course registration system. The rounded boxes represent processes, which portray the transformation of data. The square box represents an external entity, which is an originator or receiver of information located outside the boundaries of the system being modeled. The open rectangles represent data stores, which are either manual or automated inventories of data. The arrows represent data flows, which show the movement between processes, external entities, and data stores. They always contain packets of data with the name or content of each data flow listed beside the arrow.

This data flow diagram shows that students submit registration forms with their name, identification number, and the numbers of the courses they wish to take. In process 1.0 the system verifies that each course selected is still open by referencing the university's course file. The file distinguishes courses that are open from those that have been canceled or filled. Process 1.0 then determines which of the student's selections can be accepted or rejected. Process 2.0 enrolls the student in the courses for which he or she has been accepted. It updates the university's course file with the student's name and identification number and recalculates the class size. If maximum enrollment has been reached, the course number is flagged as closed. Process 2.0 also updates the university's student master file with information about new students or changes in address. Process 3.0 then sends each student applicant a confirmation-of-registration letter listing the courses for which he or she is registered and noting the course selections that could not be fulfilled.

FIGURE 10-6 Data flow diagram for mail-in university registration system. The system has three processes: Verify availability (1.0), Enroll student (2.0), and Confirm registration (3.0). The name and content of each of the data flows appear adjacent to each arrow. There is one external entity in this system: the student. There are two data stores: the student master file and the course file.

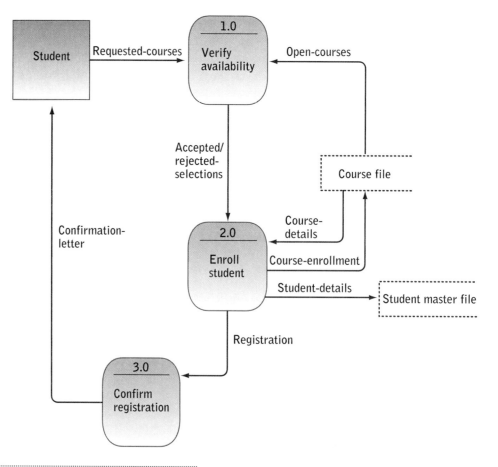

The diagrams can be used to depict higher level processes as well as lower level details. Through leveled data flow diagrams, a complex process can be broken down into successive levels of detail. An entire system can be divided into subsystems with a high-level data flow diagram. Each subsystem, in turn, can be divided into additional subsystems with second-level data flow diagrams, and the lower level subsystems can be broken down again until the lowest level of detail has been reached.

Another tool for structured analysis is a data dictionary, which contains information about individual pieces of data and data groupings within a system (see Chapter 6). The data dictionary defines the contents of data flows and data stores so that system builders understand exactly what pieces of data they contain. **Process specifications** describe the transformation occurring within the lowest level of the data flow diagrams. They express the logic for each process.

Structured Design

Structured design encompasses a set of design rules and techniques that promotes program clarity and simplicity, thereby reducing the time and effort required for coding, debugging, and maintenance. The main principle of structured design is that a system should be designed from the top down in hierarchical fashion and refined to greater levels of detail. The design should first consider the main function of a program or system, then break this function into subfunctions and decompose each subfunction until the lowest level of detail has been reached. The lowest level modules describe the actual processing that will occur. In this manner all high-level logic and the design model are developed before detailed program code is written. If structured analysis has been performed, the structured specification document can serve as input to the design process. Our earlier human resources top-down description provides a good overview example of structured design.

As the design is formulated, it is documented in a structure chart. The **structure chart** is a top-down chart, showing each level of design, its relationship to other levels, and its place in the overall design structure. Figure 10-7 shows a high-level structure chart for a payroll system. If a design has too many levels to fit onto one structure chart, it can be broken down further on more detailed structure charts. A structure chart may document one program, one system (a set of programs), or part of one program.

Structured Programming

Structured programming extends the principles governing structured design to the writing of programs to make software programs easy to understand and modify. It is based on the

process specifications
Describe the logic of the processes occurring within the lowest levels of the data flow diagrams.

structured design Software design discipline encompassing a set of design rules and techniques for designing a system from the top down in a hierarchical fashion.

structure chart System documentation showing each level of design, the relationship among the levels, and the overall place in the design structure; can document one program, one system, or part of one program.

structured programming A discipline for organizing and coding programs that simplifies the control paths so that the programs can be easily understood and modified; uses the basic control structures and modules that have only one entry point and one exit point.

FIGURE 10-7 High-level structure chart for a payroll system. This structure chart shows the highest or most abstract level of design for a payroll system, providing an overview of the entire system.

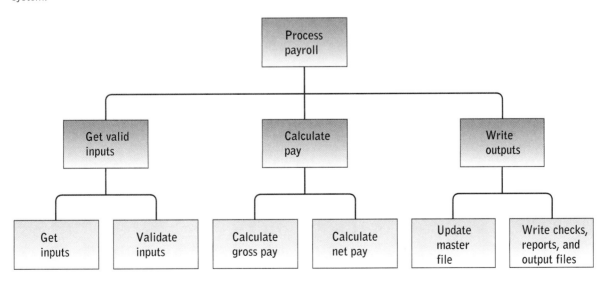

module A logical unit of a program that performs one or several functions.

sequence construct The sequential single steps or actions in the logic of a program that do not depend on the existence of any condition.

selection construct The logic pattern in programming where a stated condition determines which of two alternative actions can be taken.

iteration construct The logic pattern in programming where certain actions are repeated while a specified condition occurs or until a certain condition is met.

principle of modularization, which follows from top-down analysis and design. Each of the boxes in the structure chart represents a component **module** that is usually directly related to a bottom-level design module. It constitutes a logical unit that performs one or several functions. Ideally, modules should be independent of each other and should have only one entry to and exit from their parent modules. They should share data with as few other modules as possible. Each module should be kept to a manageable size. An individual should be able to read and understand the program code for the module and easily keep track of its functions.

Proponents of structured programming have shown that any program can be written using three basic control constructs, or instruction patterns: (1) simple sequence, (2) selection, and (3) iteration. These control constructs are illustrated in Figure 10-8.

The **sequence construct** executes statements in the order in which they appear, with control passing unconditionally from one statement to the next. The program will execute statement A and then statement B.

The **selection construct** tests a condition and executes one of two alternative instructions based on the results of the test. Condition R is tested. If R is true, statement C is executed. If R is false, statement D is executed. Control then passes to the next statement.

The **iteration construct** repeats a segment of code as long as a conditional test remains true. Condition S is tested. If S is true, statement E is executed and control returns to the test of S. If S is false, E is skipped and control passes to the next statement.

FIGURE 10-8 Basic control constructs. The three basic control constructs used in structured programming are sequence, selection, and iteration.

Sequence
   Action A
   Action B

Selection
   IF Condition R
     Action C
   ELSE
     Action D
   ENDIF

Iteration
   DO WHILE Condition S
     Action E
   ENDDO

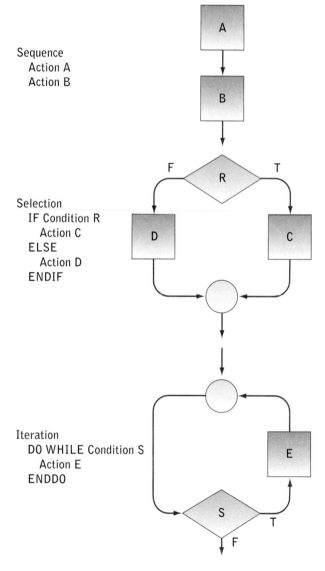

Flowcharts

Flowcharting is an old design tool that is still in use. **System flowcharts** detail the flow of data throughout an entire information system. Program flowcharts describe the processes taking place within an individual program in the system and the sequence in which they must be executed. Flowcharting is no longer recommended for program design because it does not provide top-down modular structure as effectively as other techniques. However, system flowcharts still may be used to document physical design specifications because they can show all inputs, major files, processing, and outputs for a system, and they can document manual procedures.

Using specialized symbols and flow lines, the system flowchart traces the flow of information and work in a system, the sequence of processing steps, and the physical media on which data are input, output, and stored. Figure 10-9 shows some of the basic symbols for system flowcharting. The plain rectangle is a general symbol. Flow lines are used to show the sequence of steps and the direction of information flow. Arrows are employed to show direction if it is not apparent in the diagram. Figure 10-10 illustrates a high-level system flowchart for a payroll system.

system flowchart A graphic design tool that depicts the physical media and sequence of processing steps used in an entire information system.

Limitations of Traditional Methods

Although traditional methods are valuable, they can be inflexible and time consuming. Completion of structured analysis is required before design can begin, and programming must

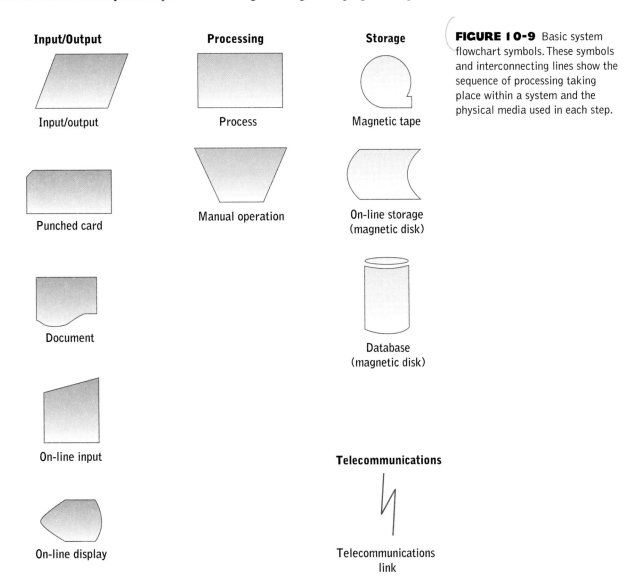

FIGURE 10-9 Basic system flowchart symbols. These symbols and interconnecting lines show the sequence of processing taking place within a system and the physical media used in each step.

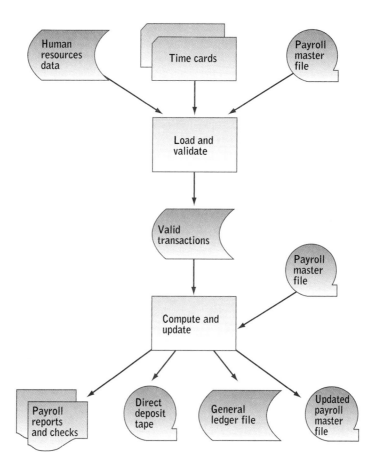

FIGURE 10-10 System flowchart for a payroll system. This is a high-level system flowchart for a batch payroll system. Only the most important processes and files are illustrated. Data are input from two sources: time cards and payroll-related data (such as salary increases) passed from the human resources system. The data are first edited and validated against the existing payroll master file before the payroll master is updated. The update process produces an updated payroll master file, various payroll reports (such as the payroll register and hours register), checks, a direct deposit tape, and a file of payment data that must be passed to the organization's general ledger system. The direct deposit tape is sent to the automated clearinghouse that serves the banks offering direct deposit services to employees.

await the completed deliverables from design. A change in specifications requires that first the analysis documents and then the design documents must be modified before the programs can be changed to reflect the new requirement. Structured methodologies are function oriented, focusing on the processes that transform the data rather than the data. System builders are turning to object-oriented software development, computer-aided software engineering (CASE), and software reengineering to deal with these issues.

OBJECT-ORIENTED SOFTWARE DEVELOPMENT

In Chapter 5, we explained that object-oriented programming combines data and the specific procedures that operate on those data into one object. Object-oriented programming is part of a larger approach to systems development called object-oriented software development. **Object-oriented software development** differs from traditional methodologies by shifting the focus from separately modeling business processes and data to combining data and procedures into unified objects. The system is viewed as a collection of classes and objects and includes the relationships among them. The objects are defined, programmed, documented, and saved as building blocks for future applications.

Objects are easily reusable, so object-oriented software development directly addresses the issue of reusability and can reduce the time and cost of writing software. Of course, no organization will see savings from reusability until it builds up a library of objects to draw on and understands which objects have broad use (Pancake, 1995). In theory, design and programming can begin as soon as requirements are completed through the use of iterations of rapid prototyping. Object-oriented frameworks have been developed to provide reusable semicomplete applications that the organization can further customize into finished applications (Fayad and Schmidt, 1997).

Although the demand for training in object-oriented techniques and programming tools is exploding, many organizations have not fully embraced object-oriented software development (Fayad and Tsai, 1995). No agreed-on object-oriented development methodology exists.

object-oriented software development An approach to software development that shifts the focus from modeling business processes and data to combining data and procedures to create objects.

Information systems specialists must learn a completely new way of modeling a system. Conversion to an object-oriented approach may require large-scale organizational investments, which management must balance against the anticipated payoffs.

COMPUTER-AIDED SOFTWARE ENGINEERING (CASE)

Computer-aided software engineering (CASE)—sometimes called computer-aided systems engineering—is the automation of step-by-step methodologies for software and systems development to reduce the amount of repetitive work the developer needs to do. Its adoption can free the developer for more creative problem-solving tasks. CASE tools also facilitate the creation of clear documentation and the coordination of team development efforts. Team members can share their work easily by accessing each other's files to review or modify what has been done. Some studies have found that systems developed with CASE and the newer methodologies are more reliable, and they require repairs less often (Dekleva, 1992). Modest productivity benefits can also be achieved if the tools are used properly. Many CASE tools are PC-based, with powerful graphical capabilities.

CASE tools provide automated graphics facilities for producing charts and diagrams, screen and report generators, data dictionaries, extensive reporting facilities, analysis and checking tools, code generators, and documentation generators. Most CASE tools are based on one or more of the popular structured methodologies. Some are starting to support object-oriented development. In general, CASE tools try to increase productivity and quality by doing the following:

○ Enforce a standard development methodology and design discipline.

○ Improve communication between users and technical specialists.

○ Organize and correlate design components and provide rapid access to them via a design repository.

○ Automate tedious and error-prone portions of analysis and design.

○ Automate code generation, testing, and control rollout.

computer-aided software engineering (CASE) The automation of step-by-step methodologies for software and systems development to reduce the amount of repetitive work the developer needs to do.

CASE Tools

Many CASE tools have been classified in terms of whether they support activities at the front end or the back end of the systems development process. Front-end CASE tools focus on capturing analysis and design information in the early stages of systems development, whereas back-end CASE tools address coding, testing, and maintenance activities. Back-end tools help convert specifications automatically into program code.

CASE tools automatically tie data elements to the processes where they are used. If a data flow diagram is changed from one process to another, the elements in the data dictionary would be altered automatically to reflect the change in the diagram. CASE tools thus support iterative design by automating revisions and changes and providing prototyping facilities.

A CASE information repository stores all the information defined by the analysts during the project. The repository includes data flow diagrams, structure charts, entity-relationship diagrams, data definitions, process specifications, screen and report formats, notes and comments, and test results.

CASE tools now have features to support client/server applications, object-oriented programming, and business process redesign. Methodologies and tool sets are being created to leverage organizational knowledge of business process reengineering (Nissen, 1998). Figure 10-11 illustrates the use of Scitor's Process 98, a flowcharting and process-analysis tool that lets developers diagram business processes with information such as resource requirements, costs, efficiencies, and delays. Developers can use this tool to visualize how processes are affected by internal and external factors.

The Challenge of Using CASE

To be used effectively, CASE tools require organizational discipline. Every member of a development project must adhere to a common set of naming conventions, standards, and development methodology. The best CASE tools enforce common methods and standards, which may discourage their use in situations where organizational discipline is lacking.

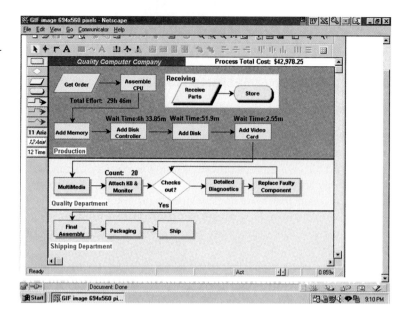

FIGURE 10-11 Scitor's Process 98 provides tools to map out business processes and to simulate the processes in real-time. The process models include time and cost information.

CASE is not a magic cure-all. It does not enable systems to be designed automatically or ensure that business requirements are met. Systems designers still have to understand what a firm's business needs are and how the business works. Systems analysis and design still depend on the analytical skills of the analyst/designer.

RAPID APPLICATION DEVELOPMENT (RAD)

rapid application development (RAD) Process for developing systems in a very short time period by using prototyping, fourth-generation tools, and close teamwork among users and systems specialists.

Using CASE tools, reusable software, object-oriented software tools, prototyping, and fourth-generation tools is helping system builders create working systems much more rapidly than they could using traditional structured approaches. The term **rapid application development (RAD)** is used to describe this process of creating workable systems in a very short period of time. RAD can include the use of visual programming and other tools for building graphical user interfaces, iterative prototyping of key system elements, the automation of program code generation, and close teamwork among end users and information systems specialists. Simple systems often can be assembled from prebuilt components. The process does not have to be sequential, and key parts of development can occur simultaneously. The Window on Technology shows some of the benefits of using RAD for Web application development.

joint application design (JAD) Process to accelerate the generation of information requirements by having end users and information systems specialists work together in intensive interactive design sessions.

Sometimes a technique called **JAD (joint application design)** is used to accelerate the generation of information requirements and to develop the initial systems design. JAD brings end users and information systems specialists together in an interactive session to discuss the system's design. Properly prepared and facilitated, JAD sessions can significantly speed the design phase while involving users at an intense level.

SOFTWARE REENGINEERING

software reengineering A methodology that addresses the problem of aging software by salvaging and upgrading it so that the users can avoid a long and expensive replacement project.

Software reengineering is a methodology that addresses the problem of aging software. A great deal of the software that organizations use was written without the benefit of a methodology such as structured analysis, design, and programming. Such software is difficult to maintain or update. However, the software serves the organization well enough to continue to be used, if only it could be more easily maintained. The purpose of software reengineering is to salvage such software by upgrading it so that users can avoid a long and expensive replacement project. In essence, developers use reengineering to extract design and programming intelligence from existing systems, thereby creating new systems without starting from scratch. Software reengineering involves three steps: (1) reverse engineering, (2) revision of design and program specifications, and (3) forward engineering.

RAD TOOLS PROPEL WEB DEVELOPMENT

In the Internet age, companies that can't develop electronic commerce and other Web-based applications quickly stand to lose important business opportunities. Fortunately, rapid application development (RAD) tools can help. Here are some examples.

Autobytel.com, a pioneer for automotive sales and services on the Web, relies on RAD tools to stay ahead of the competition. Consumers can search for cars and trucks by make, model, feature, and price and arrange to purchase a vehicle on-line from an affiliated auto dealer. The dealer delivers the vehicle, while Autobytel's system automatically forwards financing applications to affiliated banks. Autobytel's Web site requires frequent changes to its content and capabilities to keep one step ahead of competitors. Using RAD tools, Autobytel can complete most development projects in one to four weeks. Autobytel uses ColdFusion 4.0 from Allaire Corp. as its principal Web development tool. Internet developers use ColdFusion's built-in RAD tool called Studio to create applications with Web pages and tags linked to tables on a Microsoft SQL Server 7.0 database running on Compaq Windows NT servers. Using these tools, Autobytel built a new Web site for used-car auctions called wholesale.autobytel.com in 3 months in early 1999. The on-line auction site includes 200 Web pages and an automated process that advances the auctions from stage to stage.

Strategic Resource Solutions (SRS) Corporation, in Cary, North Carolina, needed to rapidly deploy a corporate intranet to keep pace with its breakneck growth. The firm helps design lighting and power systems and had mushroomed from 70 to 500 employees within 2 years. SRS wanted an intranet to provide its expanding workforce with immediate access to new sales information, facilities locations and addresses, benefits plan tracking, weekly news updates on industry deregulation, and contractor listings, all of which were housed in a Microsoft Access database. But the company only had two staff members available to build the intranet. Erik Polsky, SRS Webmaster, selected Gatsby Database Explorer to speed up the development process. Gatsby Database Explorer dynamically builds a Web interface to Microsoft Access databases without special HTML or Java programming. It is not as customizable as ColdFusion, but it is much simpler to use and appropriate for smaller firms or departmental intranets that use Microsoft Access databases. With the Gatsby interface, users can view, search, and edit databases over the Internet or through intranets. Using Gatsby, Polsky designed and built the SRS intranet in two weeks.

With RAD tools, Louisiana's Department of Natural Resources was able to put its SonRis2000 Web applications on-line in 18 months. Without RAD, development would have taken twice as long. SonRis2000 is a Web portal for free public access to documents, maps, diagrams, and other information about the state's oil and natural gas deposits. The system integrates an Oracle8 database and FileNet Inc. document imaging system, allowing users to search and retrieve documents comprising 50 million pages of information in departmental archives. The department developed the entire application using Oracle Designer, which provided a visual programming environment. Development is quicker because designers can build parts of the system by reusing standard program code found in libraries and templates.

TO THINK ABOUT: What are benefits of using RAD? What management, organization, and technology issues should be addressed when selecting a RAD tool?

Sources: Philip J. Gill, "Apps in a Hurry," *Information Week*, August 23, 1999; and Joe Mullich, "Out of the Box, Onto the Web," *Datamation*, August 1999.

Reverse engineering entails extracting the underlying business specifications from existing systems. Older, nonstructured systems do not have structured documentation of the business functions the system is intended to support. Nor do they have adequate documentation of either the system design or the programs. Reverse engineering tools read and analyze the program's existing code, file, and database descriptions and produce structured documentation of the system. The output shows design-level components, such as entities, attributes, and processes. With structured documentation to work from, the project team can then revise the design and specifications to meet current business requirements. In the final step, **forward engineering,** the revised specifications are used to generate new, structured code for a structured, and now maintainable, system. In Figure 10-12, you can follow the reengineering process.

Although software reengineering can reduce system development and maintenance costs, it is a very complex undertaking. Additional research and analysis are usually required to determine all of the business rules and data requirements for the new system (Aiken, Muntz, and Richards, 1994).

reverse engineering The process of converting existing programs, files, and database descriptions into corresponding design-level components that can then be used to create new applications.

forward engineering The final step in software reengineering, when the revised specifications are used to generate new, structured program code for a structured and maintainable system.

Gatsby Database Explorer generates a user-friendly interface to Microsoft Access databases that allows users to edit, view and search database content over an intranet or extranet. This RAD development tool enables companies to create rapid solutions without special programming.

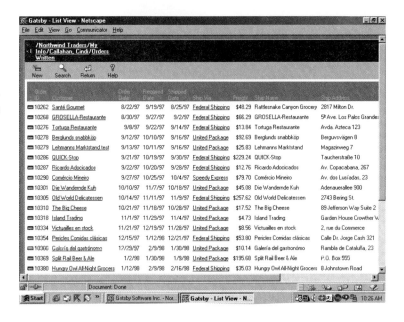

FIGURE 10-12 The reverse engineering process. Reverse engineering captures an existing system's functional capabilities and processing logic in a simplified form that can be revised and updated as the basis of a new replacement system. CASE tools can be used during forward engineering.

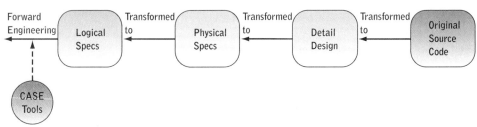

MANAGEMENT WRAP-UP

Management

Selection of a systems-building approach can have a large impact on the time, cost, and end product of systems development. Managers should be aware of the strengths and weaknesses of each systems-building approach and the types of problems for which each is best suited.

Organization

Organizational needs should drive the selection of a systems-building approach. The impact of application software packages and of outsourcing should be carefully evaluated before they are selected because these approaches give organizations less control over the systems-building process.

Technology

Various tools and methodologies are available to support the systems-building process. Key technology decisions should be based on the organization's familiarity with the methodology or technology and its compatibility with the organization's information requirements and information technology infrastructure. Organizational discipline is required to use these technologies effectively.

For Discussion

1. Why is selecting a systems development approach an important business decision? Who should participate in the selection process?

2. Some have said that the best way to reduce system development costs is to use application software packages or fourth-generation tools. Do you agree? Why or why not?

SUMMARY

1. Appraise system-building alternatives: the traditional systems lifecycle, prototyping, application software packages, end-user development, and outsourcing. The traditional systems lifecycle—the oldest method for building systems—breaks the development of an information system into six formal stages: (1) project definition, (2) systems study, (3) design, (4) programming, (5) installation, and (6) postimplementation. The stages must proceed sequentially and have defined outputs; each requires formal approval before the next stage can commence.

Prototyping consists of building an experimental system rapidly and inexpensively for end users to interact with and evaluate. The prototype is refined and enhanced until users are satisfied that it includes all of their requirements and can be used as a template to create the final system.

Developing an information system using an application software package eliminates the need for writing software programs when developing an information system. Using a software package cuts down on the amount of design, testing, installation, and maintenance work required to build a system.

End-user development is the development of information systems by end users, either alone or with minimal assistance from information systems specialists. End-user-developed systems can be created rapidly and informally using fourth-generation software tools.

Outsourcing consists of using an external vendor to build (or operate) a firm's information systems. The system may be custom built or may use a software package. In either case, the work is done by the vendor rather than by the organization's internal information systems staff.

2. Compare the strengths and limitations of each approach. The traditional system lifecycle is still useful for large projects that need formal specifications and tight management control over each stage of system-building. However, the traditional method is very rigid and costly for developing a system and is not well suited for unstructured, decision-oriented applications where requirements cannot be immediately visualized.

Prototyping encourages end-user involvement in systems development and iteration of design until specifications are captured accurately. The rapid creation of prototypes can result in systems that have not been completely tested or documented or that are technically inadequate for a production environment.

Application software packages are helpful if a firm does not have the internal information systems staff or financial resources to custom develop a system. To meet an organization's unique requirements, packages may require extensive modifications that can substantially raise development costs. A package may not be a feasible solution if implementation necessitates extensive customization and changes in the organization's procedures.

The primary benefits of end-user development are improved requirements determination, reduced application backlog, and increased end-user participation in, and control of, the systems development process. However, end-user development, in conjunction with distributed computing, has introduced new organizational risks by propagating information systems and data resources that do not necessarily meet quality assurance standards and that are not easily controlled by traditional means.

Outsourcing can save application development costs or allow firms to develop applications without an internal information systems staff; however, firms risk losing control over their information systems and becoming too dependent on external vendors.

3. Assess the solutions to the management problems these approaches create. Organizations can overcome some of the limitations of using software packages by performing a thorough requirements analysis and using rigorous package selection procedures to determine the extent to which a package will satisfy their requirements. The organization can customize the package or modify its procedures to ensure a better fit with the package.

Organizations can develop new policies and procedures concerning system development standards, training, data administration, and controls to manage end-user computing effectively. Organizations can benefit from outsourcing by only outsourcing part of their information systems, by thoroughly understanding which information systems functions are appropriate to outsource, by designing outsourcing contracts carefully, and by trying to build a working partnership with the outsourcing vendor.

4. Describe the principal tools and methodologies used for systems development. Structured analysis highlights the flow of data and the processes through which data are transformed. Its principal tool is the data flow diagram. Structured design and programming are software design disciplines that produce reliable, well-documented software with a simple, clear structure that is easy for others to understand and maintain. System flowcharts are useful for documenting the physical aspects of system design.

Computer-aided software engineering (CASE) automates methodologies for systems development. It promotes standards and improves coordination and consistency during systems development. CASE tools help system builders build a better model of a system and facilitate revision of design specifications to correct errors. Object-oriented software development can reduce the time and cost of writing software and of making maintenance changes because it models a system as a series of reusable objects that combine both data and procedures. Software reengineering helps system builders reconfigure aging software to conform to structured design principles, making it easier to maintain.

KEY TERMS

REVIEW QUESTIONS

1. What is the traditional systems lifecycle? Describe each of its steps.

2. What are the advantages and disadvantages of building an information system using the traditional systems lifecycle?

3. What do we mean by information system prototyping? What are its benefits and limitations?

4. List and describe the steps in the prototyping process.

5. What is an application software package? What are the advantages and disadvantages of developing information systems based on software packages?

6. What do we mean by end-user development? What are its advantages and disadvantages?

7. Name some policies and procedures for managing end-user development.

8. What is outsourcing? Under what circumstances should it be used for building information systems?

9. What is structured analysis? What is the role of the data flow diagram in structured analysis?

10. What are the principles of structured design? How is it related to structured programming?

11. Describe the use of system flowcharts.

12. What is the difference between object-oriented software development and traditional structured methodologies?

13. What is CASE? How can it help system builders?

14. What is rapid application development (RAD)? What system-building tools and methods can be used in RAD?

15. What are software reengineering and reverse engineering? How can they help system builders?

GROUP PROJECT

With a group of your classmates, obtain product information for two similar PC application software packages. You might compare Peachtree Accounting and QuickBooks for small business accounting or Quicken and Microsoft Money for personal finance. You can obtain some of this information from the Web and perhaps find demonstration versions of the packages on the vendor Web sites. Evaluate the strengths and limitations of the packages you select. Present your findings to the class.

Tools for Interactive Learning

○ Internet Connection

The Internet Connection for this chapter will direct you to SAP Web site where you can complete an exercise to evaluate the capabilities of this major enterprise software package and learn more about enterprise resource planning. You can also use the Interactive Study Guide to test your knowledge of the topics in this chapter and get instant feedback where you need more practice.

○ Electronic Commerce Project

At the Laudon Web site for Chapter 10, you can complete a comprehensive Electronic Commerce Project to assess the Total Cost of Ownership (TCO) of a Web site.

○ CD-ROM

If you purchase and use the Multimedia Edition CD-ROM with this chapter, you can complete two interactive exercises. The first asks you to construct a data flow diagram, and the second asks you to select an appropriate systems development approach for various business scenarios. You can also find a video clip illustrating how Andersen Consulting helped Subaru Isuzu Automotive develop a new information system, an audio overview of the major themes of this chapter, and bullet text summarizing the key points of the chapter.

○ Application Exercise

At the Laudon Web site, you can find a CASE tool Application Exercise for this chapter in which you can document a restaurant's major processing activities and prepare a data flow diagram.

AeroGroup International, the Edison, New Jersey, producer of Aerosoles shoes, began in 1987 when Jules Schneider purchased the $7 million junior footwear division of Kenneth Cole Productions. Schneider wanted to use this business to produce and sell shoes that were stylish, athletic, and comfortable, including loafers, sandals, and pumps. He wanted to sell them for as low as $40 a pair! Schneider and a partner in Italy had discovered a way to construct shoes using the soft, flexible method central to slipper manufacturing while giving them the durability of a shoe. Using this technology, AeroGroup's sales climbed to $150 million in 1998, representing an annual growth of more than 30 percent during its 11-year history. The corporate plan is to grow sales to $500 million by the year 2003.

In 1997 AeroGroup was facing many problems. The immediate issue was the flattening of growth in the footwear market. In addition, other companies had begun selling knock-offs that copy Aerosoles' patented shoe bottoms. The company was also facing serious management problems. In 1997, despite its rapid growth, Schneider remained the only senior executive in the company. Even worse, he was central to all decisions. For example, every pending order entered into AeroGroup's computer system had to be printed for Schneider to review so that he personally could decide which to fill. Schneider also had to sign off personally on all wholesale returns. Aside from the installation of an e-mail system, the firm's operational systems hadn't changed in five years. Because the sales force was only able to call in sales data nightly, sales information was always one day behind.

By 1997, AeroGroup's old computer system, called Footworks, could no longer handle the data from Aerosoles' vastly increased sales. In addition, the data from Aerosoles' systems were incomplete. Both the sales force and the factory complained about the lack of sales histories and projections. Although Footworks stored order and pricing data, it had no connection to the inventory and manufacturing systems. Often Footworks numbers differed from the numbers in the accounting systems, and management had no way to reconcile or verify the various sets of numbers. The company not only needed to modernize the computers to handle its current business,

but it also needed to increase resources so the company would be ready if the sales were to expand according to the plan and projections.

Schneider and his management team decided to investigate enterprise resource planning (ERP) software. A new ERP system would integrate finance, sales and marketing, and inventory modules to give the company control and produce reliable reports. Implementation of an ERP system also would offer the company a good opportunity to make major operational changes and would remove Schneider from responsibility for many of the day-to-day details.

The project became real on March 30, 1998, when AeroGroup sent out a Request for Proposal (RFP) for an ERP system. Rather than send the proposal to software companies, the 154-page document went to consulting firms that would help with the installation of the software. Included in the RFP was a request for profiles of the project manager and the other staff to be assigned to the Aerosoles project. Aerosoles CIO Jeffrey Zonenshine wanted to be able to screen the consulting staffs for experience in the footwear and similar industries as well as in the software package that would be selected.

When the Aerosoles staff received responses to its RFP, they undertook a function-by-function comparison of the various possible systems. Ultimately Aerosoles selected R/3 from SAP AG of Walldorf, Germany, as its ERP software. R/3 is an integrated, client/server, distributed system with a graphical user interface. It can operate on a wide range of mainframes, minicomputers, and servers and many different operating systems. The R/3 package includes integrated financial accounting, production planning, sales and distribution, cost-center accounting, order-costing, materials management, human resources, quality assurance, fixed assets management, plant maintenance, and project planning applications. R/3 can be configured to run on a single hardware platform, or it can be partitioned to run on separate machines (in whatever combination users choose) in order to minimize network traffic and place data where users need them the most.

The R/3 software package can be customized approximately 10 percent to handle multinational currencies and account-

ing practices. SAP has also developed modules of R/3 applications that are further customized for specific industries, including Apparel Footware Solution (AFS), which was specifically developed for the apparel and footwear industry.

Zonenshine also liked the fact that SAP had an implementation methodology called Accelerated SAP (ASAP), which had been developed in 1996. ASAP provides tools, templates, and questionnaires for companies to create a step-by-step road map that lets users clearly define each task. The templates incorporate "best practices" that show how things are done and help users figure out where to begin. ASAP was designed for smaller companies with revenues of less than $500 million, thus appropriate for AeroGroup. SAP claimed ASAP cuts the time of implementation in half. A study by AMR Research, Boston, was not quite that optimistic but still claimed a time saving of 25 to 50 percent. SAP also claimed that 34 percent of the organizations successfully installing R/3 had revenues less than $200 million, again a good fit for AeroGroup. However, AMR Research did point out that most of these organizations were in Europe, not the United States, where conditions are quite different.

R/3's main contender, JBA software, was designed to run only on IBM's AS/400 minicomputer and, therefore, did not offer Aerosoles the flexibility it wanted. When Aerosoles decided to adopt R/3, the company also selected Richard A. Eisner & Co. of New York City as the consulting firm on the project.

The reputation of ERP projects was that they usually drain corporate resources and funds. Moreover, ERP implementation is so complex that it has proven to be too difficult for many organizations. R/3 implementation had been abandoned by many organizations in the previous 18 months, including Alcoa, Dell Computer, and NEC Technologies.

Part of the issue is that ERP systems can bring massive organizational change. These systems consist of many functional modules that can span the whole organization and yet share a common database. Because departments are part of larger organizations, they are forced to share systems and act not as independent units but as part of a larger organization, requiring a whole new understanding of their own and their departments' work. Decisions must be for the betterment of the company, not for the betterment of individual units. All of this forces greater cooperation and teamwork. Ultimately, ERP implementation is not just a software project but an organizational change project and must be treated that way. Cooperation, teamwork, and planning for organizational change are difficult when senior management is too busy to give the project adequate attention.

Aerosoles' project began in the summer of 1998, and the team set February 1999 as the date to go live. The project budget was set at $3.2 million: $750,000 for software, $250,000 for hardware, and a $2 million fixed fee for Eisner's consulting. The price also included $200,000 that Aerosoles set aside for employee incentive bonuses. Forrester Research, in Cambridge, Massachusetts, estimated that for every dollar spent on SAP R/3 software, five more must be spent on training and systems integration because SAP ERP systems are so complicated to implement. It can take two to three years for even experienced technologists to understand all of the complexities and methodologies of SAP software, so consultants with genuine SAP expertise are very expensive and in short supply.

Aerosoles' executives and departmental managers who took on major responsibility for the project had to continue their ongoing business responsibilities as well, and this was during a time of growth and challenges for the company. A full project team meeting was held on July 21. Such meetings were clearly going to be almost impossible in the future because of travel schedules of many of the Aerosoles team. Much of the work would have to be done on the road, with distributions often taking place via e-mail. The material distributed at the meeting included detailed questionnaires, but Aerosoles didn't tailor the questionnaires as ASAP required because it didn't have time. The project team was broken into six subteams, focusing on specific functions such as warehousing and production. Each subteam set its own meeting schedules. Observers of the project expressed concern that because of the division into subteams whole-team meetings would not occur, fragmenting the project. Resulting problems might include not

identifying conflicts and interdependencies and not being able to see opportunities for positive functional and organizational change.

Problems occurred with AFS. It contained much new programming code that had not been used in actual production environments. Moreover, AFS was particularly difficult to develop because of the uniqueness and complexities of the footwear business. Some of the most complex design problems in any manufacturing sector are in footwear. The shoe and clothing production industries must keep track of thousands of items daily, many of which have a very short (months or only weeks) shelf life because of rapid changes in fashion. In addition many products are produced in small, technologically unsophisticated production facilities abroad, making the supply chain very complex and difficult to manage and control. Several years earlier, in order to persuade SAP to agree to develop AFS, a consortium was formed by Reebok and VF Corp., the largest apparel company in the United States, producing such brands as Vanity Fair, Lee, and Wrangler. The consortium agreed to underwrite the development costs and to be the source of the system's requirements. Later, Sara Lee Hosiery, Kurt Salmon Associates of Atlanta, and other companies, hearing about the consortium, agreed to join it as associate members without the ability to add functionality to the software.

During 1998, soft sales in clothing and shoe industries caused the stocks of a number of companies to fall. Many customers, including Florsheim, Warnaco, and even Reebok, withdrew their interest in the project. Eventually, during 1998, the consortium died of its own weight.

Despite the problems with the consortium, AFS was introduced in April 1998. Only two companies were using it by the beginning of 1999. One was the Greg Norman division of Reebok International. That division had $100 million in sales within a company of $3.6 billion in revenues—not a vote of confidence from Reebok. The other user was Justin Industries, a $440 million conglomerate, which used it at its Fort Worth, Texas, footwear unit. However, Justin predicted that problems with the software would have a significant negative impact on its

revenues. Even after SAP upgraded AFS with better order processing and inventory management capabilities, Reebok did not start using the new software to run its major sneaker operations in North America and Europe. The company decided to install the new release of AFS at its smaller operations first.

Aerosoles also had difficulties with ASAP and, like some other companies, stopped using it. Compounding that problem for Aerosoles, Zonenshine claimed that the Eisner consulting staff was not familiar with AFS despite their ample experience with R/3.

By early January 1999, the project had run into many problems, and AeroGroup abandoned AFS and R/3 and instead signed a contract to purchase the JBA package. The reason for abandoning AFS given by Morris and Zonenshine was that it was incomplete and too costly to be used to address Aerosoles' problems. The question is, what actually had gone wrong?

Sources: Craig Stedman, "SAP Plans Upgrade for Apparel/Footwear App," **Computerworld**, February 14, 2000; Larry Marion, "Autopsy of a Debacle," **Datamation**, February 1999; Deborah Ashbrand, "Peering Across the Abyss," **Datamation**, January 1999; "Riskier Business! The High Cost of ERP Implementations," **Datamation**, September 1998; "Risky Business: Bold R/3 Effort by Aerosoles," **Datamation**, July 1998; Michael Hammer, "Out of the Box," **Information Week**, February 8, 1999; and Tom Stein, "SAP Feels the Pinch," **Information Week**, January 11, 1999.

CASE STUDY QUESTIONS

1. Analyze Aerosoles using the value chain and competitive forces models.

2. Describe the problems facing Aerosoles that caused it to turn to ERP. Do you think ERP was an appropriate response to these problems? Explain your answer.

3. Do you think Aerosoles originally should have adopted R/3 and AFS? Explain your answer.

4. Describe the management, organizational, and technology problems faced by Aerosoles in the R/3 project.

5. What advantages and disadvantages of application software packages are illustrated by R/3 and AFS?

CHAPTER 11

Managing
Knowledge

Learning
Objectives

After completing this chapter, you will be able to:

1. Explain the importance of knowledge management in contemporary organizations.

2. Describe the applications that are most useful for distributing, creating, and sharing knowledge in the firm.

3. Evaluate the role of artificial intelligence in knowledge management.

4. Demonstrate how organizations can use expert systems and case-based reasoning to capture knowledge.

5. Demonstrate how organizations can use neural networks and other intelligent techniques to improve their knowledge base.

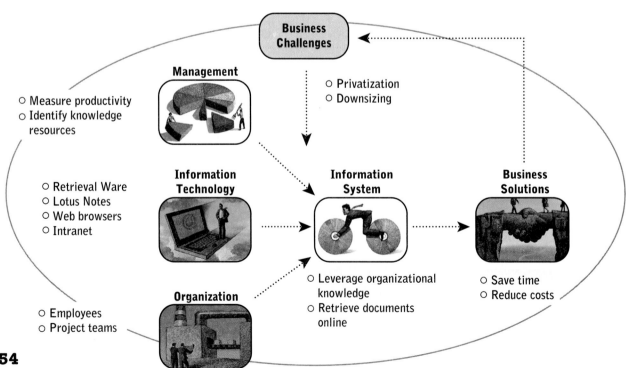

Business Challenges

- Privatization
- Downsizing

Management

- Measure productivity
- Identify knowledge resources

Information Technology

- Retrieval Ware
- Lotus Notes
- Web browsers
- Intranet

Organization

- Employees
- Project teams

Information System

- Leverage organizational knowledge
- Retrieve documents online

Business Solutions

- Save time
- Reduce costs

BG's Technology Bank Cashes
in on Knowledge Management

BG PLC, formerly known as British Gas, had been a state-run energy company. When it went private in 1997, it downsized its research arm, BG Technology, trimming staff from 1,800 to 600 employees. Yet BG Technology still had to provide the company and external customers with research and technology, despite its reduced size. As a leading international energy company, BG needed to put more emphasis on managing expertise, increasing innovation, and leveraging knowledge from one part of the business to another. One way to increase BG Technology's productivity and effectiveness was to make better use of the knowledge it had built up over the years.

BG Technology set up an intranet system known as the Technology Knowledge Bank, which enables staff members along with 16,500 workers at

BG PLC to use their Web browsers instantly to retrieve research documents from various sources on topics such as gas exploration and environmental protection. The system includes documents produced by project teams during the course of their work, more than 10,000 scanned and indexed pages from more than 6 years of research reports, access to databases for specific technologies produced for BG customers, and information on competitors. It features a search engine that recognizes concepts instead of only key words and searches for information across teams and communities. The company selected RetrievalWare from Excalibur Technologies Corp. to help users search and retrieve information from a wide variety of sources, including relational databases, local file systems, scanned documents, Lotus Notes applications, and the Web. Excalibur RetrievalWare can handle documents stored in Lotus Notes groupware systems that can only be accessed and changed by authorized users as well as large volumes of data and users.

Technology Bank is being enhanced to include data from external sources, advanced analytic tools, and capabilities to alert BG automatically to business opportunities or potential new business partners. The system has become so useful that BG Technology plans to generate revenue by selling the application to other firms. Mark Taylor, one of BG's technology managers who must communicate BG Technology's research and development work to the rest of the company, claims that using Technology Bank saves him a half-day of work every week.

Sources: Dominique Deckmyn, "U.K. Firm Hopes to Cash in on Knowledge Management," *Computerworld,* June 28, 1999; and "Case Study—Knowledge Management: BG Technology," Excalibur Technologies Corporation, www.excalib.com/customers/cases.

CHAPTER OUTLINE

BG's Technology Bank is one example of how systems can be used to leverage organizational knowledge by making it more easily available. Collaborating and communicating with practitioners and experts and sharing ideas and information have become essential requirements in business, science, and government. In an information economy, capturing and distributing intelligence and knowledge and enhancing group collaboration have become vital to organizational innovation and survival. Special systems can be used for managing organizational knowledge, but they raise the following management challenges:

1. **Designing information systems that genuinely enhance the productivity of knowledge workers.** Information systems that truly enhance the productivity of knowledge workers may be difficult to build because the manner in which information technology can enhance higher level tasks such as those performed by managers and professionals (i.e., scientists or engineers) is not always clearly understood. Some aspects of organizational knowledge cannot be captured easily or codified, or the information that organizations finally manage to capture may become outdated as environments change (Malhotra, 1998). High-level knowledge workers may resist the introduction of any new technology, or they may resist knowledge work systems because they believe such systems diminish personal control and creativity.

2. **Creating robust expert systems.** Expert systems must be changed every time there is a change in the organizational environment. Each time there is a change in the rules experts use, systems must be reprogrammed. It is difficult to provide expert systems with the flexibility of human experts. Many thousands of businesses have undertaken experimental projects in expert systems, but only a small percentage have created expert systems that actually can be used on a production basis.

This chapter examines information system applications specifically designed to help organizations create, capture, and distribute knowledge and information. First, we examine information systems for supporting information and knowledge work. Then we look at the ways that organizations can use artificial intelligence technologies for capturing and storing knowledge and expertise.

11.1 Knowledge Management in the Organization

Chapter 1 described the emergence of the information economy, in which the major source of wealth and prosperity is the production and distribution of information and knowledge. For example, 55 percent of the U.S. labor force consists of knowledge and information workers, and 60 percent of the gross domestic product of the United States comes from the knowledge and information sectors, such as finance and publishing. Knowledge-intensive technology is vital to these information-intense sectors, but it also plays a major role in traditional industrial sectors, such as the automobile and mining industries.

In an information economy, knowledge and core competencies—the two or three things that an organization does best—are key organizational assets. Producing unique products or services or producing them at a lower cost than competitors depends on superior knowledge of the production process and superior design. Knowing how to do things effectively and efficiently in ways that other organizations cannot duplicate is a primary source of profit. Some management theorists believe that these knowledge assets are as important, if not more important, than physical and financial assets in ensuring the firm's competitiveness and survival. Management of organizational knowledge may be especially important in flattened or network organizations where layers of management have been eliminated to help members of teams and task forces maintain ties to other specialists in their field (Favela, 1997).

As knowledge becomes a central productive and strategic asset, organizational success increasingly depends on the ability to gather, produce, maintain, and disseminate knowledge. Developing procedures and routines to optimize the creation, flow, learning, protection, and sharing of knowledge and information in the firm becomes a central management responsibility. The process of systematically and actively managing and leveraging the stores of knowledge in an organization is called **knowledge management.** Information systems can play a valuable role in knowledge management by helping the organization optimize its flow of information and capture its knowledge base.

knowledge management The process of systematically and actively managing and leveraging the stores of knowledge in an organization.

Companies cannot take advantage of their knowledge resources if they have inefficient processes for capturing and distributing knowledge, or if they fail to appreciate the value of the knowledge they possess. Some corporations, such as BG Technology described in the chapter opening vignette and others discussed in this chapter, have created explicit knowledge management programs for protecting and distributing knowledge resources that they have identified and for discovering new sources of knowledge. These programs are often headed by a **chief knowledge officer (CKO).** The chief knowledge officer is a senior executive who is responsible for the firm's knowledge management program. The CKO helps design programs and systems to find new sources of knowledge or to make better use of existing knowledge in organizational and management processes (Earl and Scott, 1999).

chief knowledge officer (CKO) Senior executive in charge of the organization's knowledge management program.

INFRASTRUCTURE AND SYSTEMS FOR KNOWLEDGE MANAGEMENT

Knowledge management requires an information technology (IT) infrastructure with appropriate networks and databases that facilitate the collection and sharing of organizational knowledge assets as well as powerful hardware and software tools to make the information accessible and meaningful. Information systems that support knowledge management make use of this infrastructure.

All the major types of information systems described in this text facilitate the flow of information and have organizational knowledge embedded in them. However, office systems, knowledge work systems (KWS), group collaboration systems, and artificial intelligence applications are especially useful for knowledge management because they focus on supporting information and knowledge work and on defining and capturing the organization's knowledge base. This knowledge base may include (1) structured internal knowledge, such as product manuals or research reports; (2) external knowledge, such as competitive intelligence; and (3) informal internal knowledge, often called **tacit knowledge,** which resides in the minds of individual employees but has not been documented in structured form (Davenport, DeLong, and Beers, 1998).

tacit knowledge Expertise and experience of organizational members that has not been formally documented.

Figure 11-1 illustrates the information technology (IT) infrastructure and information systems for supporting knowledge management. Office systems help disseminate and coordinate the flow of information in the organization. KWS support the activities of highly skilled knowledge workers and professionals as they create new knowledge and try to integrate it into the firm. Group collaboration and support systems support the creation and sharing of knowledge among people working in groups. Artificial intelligence systems provide organizations and managers with codified knowledge that can be reused by others in the organization. These systems require an information technology (IT) infrastructure that makes heavy use of powerful processors, networks, databases, software, and Internet tools.

KNOWLEDGE WORK AND PRODUCTIVITY

In information economies, organizational productivity depends on increasing the productivity of information and knowledge workers. Consequently, companies have made massive investments in technology to support information work. Information technology now accounts for

FIGURE 11-1 Knowledge management requires an information technology (IT) infrastructure that facilitates the collection and sharing of knowledge as well as software for distributing information and making it more meaningful. The information systems illustrated here give close-in support to information workers at many levels in the organization

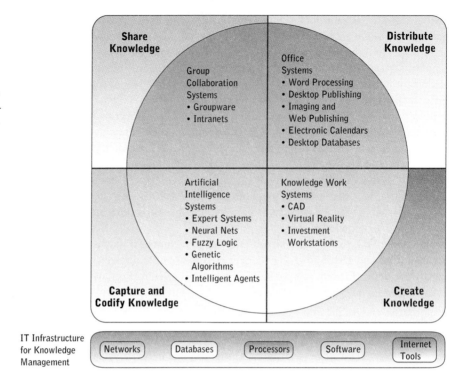

Share Knowledge

Distribute Knowledge

Group Collaboration Systems
• Groupware
• Intranets

Office Systems
• Word Processing
• Desktop Publishing
• Imaging and Web Publishing
• Electronic Calendars
• Desktop Databases

Artificial Intelligence Systems
• Expert Systems
• Neural Nets
• Fuzzy Logic
• Genetic Algorithms
• Intelligent Agents

Knowledge Work Systems
• CAD
• Virtual Reality
• Investment Workstations

Capture and Codify Knowledge

Create Knowledge

IT Infrastructure for Knowledge Management

Networks Databases Processors Software Internet Tools

over 40 percent of total business expenditures on capital equipment in the United States. Much of that information technology investment has poured into offices and the service sector.

Although information technology has increased productivity in manufacturing, the extent to which computers have enhanced the productivity of information workers remains under debate. Some experts believe that investment in information technology has not led to any appreciable growth in productivity among office workers. Corporate downsizings and cost-reduction measures have increased worker efficiency but have not yet led to sustained enhancements signifying genuine productivity gains (Roach, 2000, 1996 and 1998). Cell phones, home fax machines, laptop computers, and other appliances allow highly-paid knowledge workers to get more work done by working longer hours and by bringing their work home with them. To improve productivity, people would have to get more work done in a specified unit of work time, not just work longer. Others suggest that information technology investments are starting to generate a productivity payback. Brynjolfsson and Hitt's examination of information systems spending at 380 large firms during a 5-year period found that return on investment (ROI) averaged more than 50 percent per year for computers of all sizes (Brynjolfsson and Hitt, 1993). Productivity growth has been higher during the past decade than during the 1980s, when white-collar productivity only rose .28 percent each year. The debate centers on whether these gains arc short term or represent fundamental changes in service-sector productivity that can be attributed to computers.

Productivity changes among information workers are difficult to measure because of the problems of identifying suitable units of output for information work (Panko, 1991). How does one measure the output of a law office? Should one measure productivity by examining the number of forms completed per employee (a measure of physical unit productivity) or by examining the amount of revenue produced per employee (a measure of financial unit productivity) in an information- and knowledge-intense industry? How does one track gains from investments resulting from changes in management, business processes, or increased employee training (Strassmann, 1999)? In addition, different types of organizations derive different levels of productivity benefit from information technology (Brynjolfsson and Hitt, 1998).

In addition to reducing costs, computers may increase the quality of products and services for consumers. These intangible benefits are difficult to measure and, consequently, are not addressed by conventional productivity measures. Moreover, because of competition, the value created by computers may primarily flow to customers rather than to the companies making the investments (Brynjolfsson, 1996). Scholars are now looking at other ways to measure productivity from computers, including increases in corporate profits.

Introduction of information technology does not automatically guarantee productivity. Desktop computers, e-mail, and fax applications actually can generate more drafts, memos, spreadsheets, and messages—increasing bureaucratic red tape and paperwork. Firms are more likely to produce high returns on information technology investments if they rethink their procedures, processes, and business goals.

11.2 Information and Knowledge Work Systems

Information work is work that consists primarily of creating or processing information. It is carried out by information workers who usually are divided into two subcategories: **data workers,** who primarily process and disseminate information; and **knowledge workers,** who primarily create knowledge and information.

Examples of data workers include secretaries, sales personnel, bookkeepers, and draftspeople. Researchers, designers, architects, writers, and judges are examples of knowledge workers. Data workers usually can be distinguished from knowledge workers because knowledge workers usually have higher levels of education and memberships in professional organizations. In addition, knowledge workers exercise independent judgment as a routine aspect of their work. Data and knowledge workers have different information requirements and different systems to support them.

information work Work that primarily consists of creating or processing information.

data workers People such as secretaries or bookkeepers who process and disseminate the organization's information and paperwork.

knowledge workers People such as engineers, scientists, or architects who design products or services or create knowledge for the organization.

DISTRIBUTING KNOWLEDGE: OFFICE AND DOCUMENT MANAGEMENT SYSTEMS

Most data work and a great deal of knowledge work takes place in offices, including most of the work done by managers. The office plays a major role in coordinating the flow of information throughout the entire organization. The office has three basic functions (see Figure 11-2):

○ Managing and coordinating the work of data and knowledge workers

○ Connecting the work of the local information workers with all levels and functions of the organization

○ Connecting the organization to the external world, including customers, suppliers, government regulators, and external auditors.

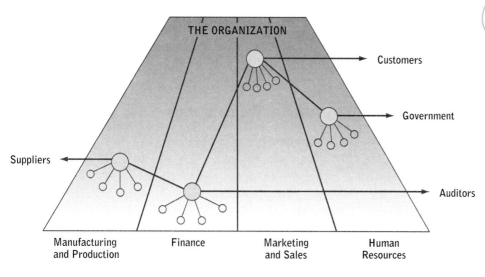

FIGURE 11-2 The three major roles of offices. Offices perform three major roles. (1) They coordinate the work of local professionals and information workers. (2) They coordinate work in the organization across levels and functions. (3) They couple the organization to the external environment.

Office workers span a very broad range: professionals, managers, salespeople, and clerical workers working alone or in groups. Their major activities include the following:

○ Managing documents, including document creation, storage, retrieval, and dissemination

○ Scheduling for individuals and groups

○ Communicating, including initiating, receiving, and managing voice, digital, and document-based communications for individuals and groups

○ Managing data, such as on employees, customers, and vendors.

office systems Computer systems, such as word processing, voice mail, and imaging, that are designed to increase the productivity of information workers in the office.

These activities can be supported by office systems (see Table 11-1). **Office systems** are any application of information technology that intends to increase productivity of information workers in the office. Fifteen years ago, office systems handled only the creation, processing, and management of documents. Today professional knowledge and information work remains highly document-centered. However, digital image processing—words and documents—is also at the core of systems, as are high-speed digital communications services. Because office work involves many people jointly engaged in projects, contemporary office systems have powerful group assistance tools like networked digital calendars. An ideal office environment would be based on a seamless network of digital machines linking professional, clerical, and managerial work groups and running a variety of types of software.

Although word processing and desktop publishing address the creation and presentation of documents, they only exacerbate the existing paper avalanche problem. Work flow problems arising from paper handling are enormous. It has been estimated that up to 85 percent of corporate information is stored on paper. Locating and updating information in that format is a great source of organizational inefficiency.

document imaging systems Systems that convert documents and images into digital form so they can be stored and accessed by the computer.

One way to reduce problems stemming from paper work flow is to use document imaging systems. **Document imaging systems** are systems that convert documents and images into digital form so they can be stored and accessed by a computer. Such systems store, retrieve, and manipulate a digitized image of a document, allowing the document itself to be discarded. The system must contain a scanner that converts the document image into a bit-mapped image and stores the image as a graphic. If the document is not in active use, it usually is stored on an optical disk system. Optical disks, kept on-line in a **jukebox** (a device for storing and retrieving many optical disks), require up to a minute to retrieve the document automatically.

jukebox A device for storing and retrieving many optical disks.

An imaging system also requires indexes that allow users to identify and retrieve documents when needed. Index data are entered so that a document can be retrieved in a variety of ways, depending on the application. For example, the index may contain the document scan date, the customer name and number, the document type, and some subject information. Finally, the system must include retrieval equipment, which are primarily workstations capable of handling graphics, although printers usually are included. Figure 11-3 illustrates the components of a typical imaging system. Mercantile Mutual's imaging system in Chapter 2 illustrates the kinds of benefits imaging technology can provide.

Traditional document-management systems can be expensive, requiring proprietary client/server networks, special client software, and storage capabilities. Intranets provide a

Table 11-1 Typical Office Systems

Office Activity	Technology
Managing documents	Word processing; desktop publishing; document imaging; Web publishing; work flow managers
Scheduling	Electronic calendars; groupware, intranets
Communicating	E-mail; voice mail; digital answering systems; groupware; intranets
Managing data	Desktop databases; spreadsheets; user-friendly interfaces to mainframe databases

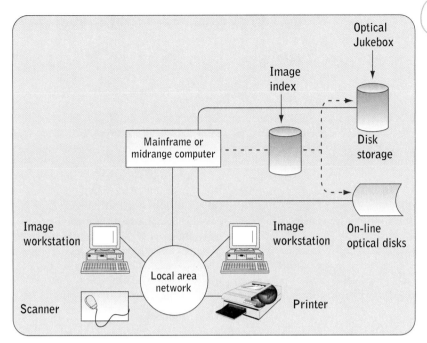

FIGURE 11-3 Components of an imaging system. A typical imaging system stores and processes digitized images of documents using scanners, an optical disk system, an image index, workstations, and printers. A midrange or small mainframe computer may be required to control the activities of a large imaging system.

low-cost and universally available platform for basic document publishing, and many companies are using them for this purpose. Employees can publish information using Web-page authoring tools and post it to an intranet Web server where it can be shared and accessed throughout the company with standard Web browsers. These Weblike "documents" can be multimedia objects combining text, graphics, audio, and video along with hyperlinks. After a document has been posted to the server, it can be indexed for quick access and linked to other documents (see Figure 11-4).

For more sophisticated document-management functions, such as controlling changes to documents, maintaining histories of activity and changes in the managed documents, and the ability to search documents on either content or index terms, commercial Web-based systems such as those from IntraNet Solutions or Open Text are available. Vendors such as FileNet and Documentum have enhanced their traditional document-management systems with Web capabilities.

The Window on Management describes the benefits of the Web-based system from BidCom, Inc., for work flow management, document control, and project management in the architectural, engineering, and construction industries.

To achieve the high productivity gains promised by imaging technology, organizations must redesign their work flow. In the past, the existence of only one copy of a document largely shaped work flow. Work had to be performed serially; two people could not work on the same document at the same time. Significant staff time was devoted to filing and retrieving documents. After a document has been stored electronically, work flow management can change the traditional methods of working with documents (see Chapter 9).

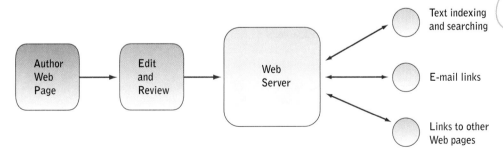

FIGURE 11-4 Web publishing and document management. An author can post information on an intranet Web server, where it can be accessed through a variety of mechanisms.

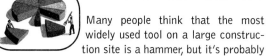

MANAGING BUILDING PROJECTS WITH THE INTERNET

Many people think that the most widely used tool on a large construction site is a hammer, but it's probably a fax machine. A complex construction project requires the coordination of many different groups and hundreds of thousands of blueprints and other design documents. Many different CAD/CAM and document management systems have been developed to deal with this problem. Now such tools are available on the Web, allowing project managers to exchange documents and work on-line wherever they are using Web browser software.

BidCom, a San Francisco–based application service provider founded in 1995, is hoping to revolutionize the architecture and construction industries by allowing managers to coordinate project work flow and documents from a Web-based system called in-Site. Architects, project owners, or general contractors can purchase time and space on the BidCom system, paying for setup and monthly fees, which are based on the number of system users and level of service required by the project. The project owner or general contractor creates a specific profile for each user based on his or her role in the project, which determines what documents and portions of the system the user can access and update.

Users can post CAD drawings of project plans and even use a "markup layer" to redline drawings of the subsystems for which they are responsible. They can also post budgets, contracts, schedules, material safety data sheets, design descriptions, announcements, forms, field reports, daily di-

aries, and government safety regulations, as well as project team directories and proceedings of project meetings or construction permits. All of these documents can be tracked easily individually or by type of document. The system can identify different versions of each document if the documents have to be revised.

BidCom uses the Oracle8 database management system, running on Windows 2000 Web servers at various locations. Oracle Application Server serves the Web pages built by the database, which can be accessed and read by users equipped with Netscape or Internet Explorer Web browsers over the Internet. In-Site also uses the Oracle8 Lite database management system, which runs on small wireless devices. Construction supervisors can input data into the system using wireless personal digital assistants, or engineers can be contacted through the system using pagers. Recently, in-Site has been enhanced with capabilities for a photo gallery, local weather reports from AccuWeather, and global project management.

Swinerton and Walberg Builders, an old San Francisco construction management and general contracting firm, used in-Site in a project to renovate the headquarters of discount broker Charles Schwab & Co. in downtown San Francisco. Swinerton and Walberg were in charge of coordinating 100 people and 30 vendors responsible for air-handling, communication, and electrical systems. In-Site helped manage the paper flow between the vendors, saving money and clerical time. Willie Brown, mayor of San Francisco, credits BidCom with creating project management efficiencies that shaved four months off the completion time for the San Francisco Giants' new stadium. BidCom also helped the city reduce both the budget and lifecycle of its Embarcadero light-rail project.

TO THINK ABOUT: What are the management benefits of using Web-based document and project management systems? Are there any drawbacks?

Sources: Bob Tedeschi, "Construction Heads Into the Internet Age," **The New York Times,** February 21, 2000; Michael Miley, "Hard Hats and Laptops," **Oracle Magazine,** January/February 1999; and Delia Craven, "Click and Mortar," **Red Herring,** November 1999.

CREATING KNOWLEDGE: KNOWLEDGE WORK SYSTEMS

Knowledge work is that portion of information work that creates new knowledge and information. For example, knowledge workers create new products or find ways to improve existing ones. Knowledge work is segmented into many highly specialized fields, and each field has a different collection of **knowledge work systems (KWS)** that are specialized to support workers in that field. Knowledge workers perform three key roles that are critical to the organization and to the managers who work within the organization:

knowledge work systems (KWS) Information systems that aid knowledge workers in the creation and integration of new knowledge in the organization.

○ Keeping the organization up-to-date in knowledge as it develops in the external world in technology, science, social thought, and the arts

○ Serving as internal consultants regarding the areas of their knowledge, the changes taking place, and the opportunities

○ Acting as change agents evaluating, initiating, and promoting change projects.

Knowledge workers and data workers have somewhat different information systems support needs. Most knowledge workers rely on office systems such as word processors, voice mail, and calendars, but they also require more specialized knowledge work systems. Knowledge work systems are specifically designed to promote the creation of knowledge and to ensure that new knowledge and technical expertise are properly integrated into the business.

Requirements of Knowledge Work Systems

Knowledge work systems have characteristics that reflect the special needs of knowledge workers. First, knowledge work systems must give knowledge workers the specialized tools they need, such as powerful graphics, analytical tools, and communications and document-management tools. These systems require much computing power in order to handle rapidly the sophisticated graphics or complex calculations necessary to such knowledge workers as scientific researchers, product designers, and financial analysts. Because knowledge workers are so focused on knowledge in the external world, these systems also must give the worker quick and easy access to external databases.

A user-friendly interface is very important to a knowledge worker's system. User-friendly interfaces save time by allowing the user to perform needed tasks and get to required information without having to spend a lot of time learning how to use the computer. Saving time is more important for knowledge workers than for most other employees because knowledge workers are highly paid; wasting a knowledge worker's time is simply too expensive. Figure 11-5 summarizes the requirements of knowledge work systems.

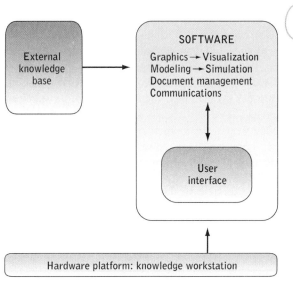

FIGURE 11-5 Requirements of knowledge work systems. Knowledge work systems require strong links to external knowledge bases in addition to specialized hardware and software.

Knowledge workstations often are designed and optimized for the specific tasks to be performed, so a design engineer will require a different workstation than a lawyer. Design engineers need graphics with enough power to handle 3-D computer-aided design (CAD) systems. However, financial analysts are more interested in having access to myriad external databases and in optical disk technology so they can access massive amounts of financial data very quickly.

Examples of Knowledge Work Systems

Major knowledge work applications include computer-aided design (CAD) systems, virtual reality systems for simulation and modeling, and financial workstations. **Computer-aided design (CAD)** automates the creation and revision of designs, using computers and sophisticated graphics software. Using a more traditional physical design methodology, each design modification requires a mold to be made and a prototype to be physically tested. That process must be repeated many times, which is very expensive and time-consuming. Using a CAD workstation, the designer only needs to make a physical prototype toward the end of the design process because the design can be easily tested and changed on the computer. The ability of CAD software to provide design specifications for the tooling and the manufacturing process also saves a great deal of time and money while producing a manufacturing process with far fewer problems. For example, The Maddox Design Group of Atlanta, Georgia, uses MicroArchitect CAD software from IdeaGraphix for architectural design. Designers can quickly put the architectural background in, pop in doors and windows, and then do the engineering layout. The software can generate door and window schedules, time accounting reports, and projected costs. Additional descriptions of CAD systems can be found in Chapter 2.

Virtual reality systems have visualization, rendering, and simulation capabilities that go far beyond those of conventional CAD systems. They use interactive graphics software to create computer-generated simulations that are so close to reality that users almost believe they are participating in a real-world situation. In many virtual reality systems, the user dons special clothing, headgear, and equipment, depending on the application. The clothing contains sensors that record the user's movements and immediately transmit the information back to the computer. For instance, to walk through a virtual reality simulation of a house, you would need garb that monitors the movement of your feet, hands, and head. You also would need goggles that contain video screens and sometimes audio attachments and feeling gloves so that you can be immersed in the computer feedback.

Virtual reality is starting to provide benefits in educational, scientific, and business work. For example, Michael Kwartler, director of the Environmental Simulation Center in Manhattan, built a three-dimensional model of a SoHo neighborhood in lower Manhattan for a developer seeking to build a hotel in that location. Kwartler's group won community support for the project by allowing neighborhood residents to work with the model and fly around to look at things from different angles (Teicholz, 1999). Surgeons at Boston's Brigham and Women's Hospital are using a virtual reality system in which a 3-D representation of the brain using CT and MRI scans is superimposed on live video. With this version of X-ray vision, surgeons can pinpoint the location of a tumor in the brain with 0.5 millimeter accuracy (Ditlea, 1998).

Virtual reality applications are being developed for the Web using a standard called **Virtual Reality Modeling Language (VRML).** VRML is a set of specifications for interactive, 3-D modeling on the World Wide Web that can organize multiple media types, including animation, images, and audio, to put users in a simulated real-world environment where they can manipulate 3-D objects. VRML is platform-independent, operates over a desktop computer, and requires little bandwidth. Users can download a 3-D virtual world designed using VRML from a server over the Internet using their Web browser. (Recent versions of Netscape Communicator and Microsoft Internet Explorer are VRML compliant.)

Lockheed Martin Missile & Space is using VRML in a 3-D training environment to show employees how to operate large pieces of machinery. DuPont, the Wilmington, Delaware, chemical company, created a VRML application called HyperPlant, which allows users to access 3-D data over the Internet with Netscape Web browsers. Engineers can go through 3-D models as if they were physically walking through a plant, viewing objects at eye

---

computer-aided design (CAD) Information system that automates the creation and revision of designs using sophisticated graphics software.

virtual reality systems Interactive graphics software and hardware that create computer-generated simulations that provide sensations that emulate real-world activities.

Virtual Reality Modeling Language (VRML) A set of specifications for interactive 3-D modeling on the World Wide Web.

Women can create a VRML "personal model" that approximates their physical proportions to help them visualize how they will look in clothing sold at the Lands End Web site. The digitized image can be rotated to show how the outfits will look from all angles and users can click to change the clothes' color.

level. This level of detail reduces the number of mistakes they make during construction of oil rigs, oil plants, and other structures.

The Sharper Image (www.sharperimage.com) 3-D Enhanced Catalog for Web site visitors with high-speed Internet connections and powerful processors provides images of products in three dimensions. Visitors can rotate digitized images of many products to examine them from any angle. The user could zoom in to see specific details and manipulate the object to see how the lid opens or how it folds for storage (Lewis, 1999).

The financial industry is using specialized **investment workstations** to leverage the knowledge and time of its brokers, traders, and portfolio managers. Firms such as Merrill Lynch and Paine Webber have installed investment workstations that integrate a wide range of data from both internal and external sources, including contact management data, real-time and historical market data, and research reports (Stirland, 1998). Previously, financial professionals had to spend considerable time accessing data from separate systems and piecing together the information they needed. By providing one-stop information faster and with fewer errors, the workstations streamline the entire investment process from stock selection to updating client records. Table 11-2 summarizes the major types of knowledge work systems.

investment workstation
Powerful desktop computer for financial specialists, which is optimized to access and manipulate massive amounts of financial data.

SHARING KNOWLEDGE: GROUP COLLABORATION SYSTEMS AND INTRANET KNOWLEDGE ENVIRONMENTS

Although many knowledge and information work applications have been designed for individuals working alone, organizations have an increasing need to support people working in

Table 11-2 **Knowledge Work Systems**

Knowledge Work System	Function in Organization
CAD/CAM (Computer-aided design/ computer-aided manufacturing)	Provides engineers, designers, and factory managers with precise control over industrial design and manufacturing
Virtual reality systems	Provide drug designers, architects, engineers, and medical workers with precise, photorealistic simulations of objects
Investment workstations	High-end PCs used in financial sector to analyze trading situations instantaneously and facilitate portfolio management

groups. Chapters 5, 7, and 8 introduced key technologies that can be used for group coordination and collaboration: e-mail, teleconferencing, dataconferencing, videoconferencing, groupware, and intranets. Groupware and intranets are especially valuable for this purpose.

Groupware

groupware Software that recognizes the significance of groups in offices by providing functions and services that support the collaborative activities of work groups.

Until recently, **groupware** (which we introduced in Chapter 5) was the primary tool for creating collaborative work environments. Groupware is built around three key principles: communication, collaboration, and coordination. It allows groups to work together on documents, schedule meetings, route electronic forms, access shared folders, develop shared databases, and send e-mail. Table 11-3 lists the capabilities of major commercial groupware products that make them such powerful platforms for capturing information and experiences, coordinating common tasks, and distributing work through time and place.

Information-intensive companies such as consulting firms, law firms, and financial management companies have found groupware a valuable tool for leveraging their knowledge assets. The Window on Organizations shows how several companies have benefited from using groupware for this purpose.

Intranet Knowledge Environments

Chapter 8 described how some organizations are using intranets and Internet technologies for group collaboration, including e-mail, discussion groups, and multimedia Web documents. Some of these intranets are providing the foundation for knowledge environments in which information from a variety of sources and media, including text, sound, video, and even digital slides, can be shared, displayed, and accessed across an enterprise through a simple common interface. BG's Technology Knowledge Bank, described in the chapter opening vignette, is an example. Examples of other intranet knowledge environments can be found in Table 11-4. These comprehensive intranets can transform decades-old processes, allowing people to disseminate information, share best practices, communicate, conduct research, and collaborate in ways that were never before possible.

Intranet knowledge environments are so rich and vast that many organizations have built specialized corporate portals to help individuals navigate through various knowledge resources. These portals direct individuals to digital knowledge objects and information system applications, helping them make sense of the volume of information that is available and also showing how organizational knowledge resources are interconnected. Figure 11-6 illustrates what a corporate intranet portal might look like.

Table 11-3 Knowledge Management Capabilities of Groupware

Capability	Description
Publishing	Posting documents as well as simultaneous work on the same document by multiple users along with a mechanism to track changes to these documents
Replication	Maintaining and updating identical data on multiple PCs and servers
Discussion tracking	Organizing discussions by many users on different topics
Document management	Storing information from various types of software in a database
Work flow management	Moving and tracking documents created by groups
Security	Preventing unauthorized access to data
Portability	Availablilty of the software for mobile use to access the corporate network from the road
Application development	Developing custom software applications with the software

LEVERAGING KNOWLEDGE ASSETS WITH GROUPWARE

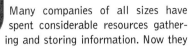

Many companies of all sizes have spent considerable resources gathering and storing information. Now they realize they have to manage and share it. Groupware has become an important tool for corporate knowledge management as companies try to share stores of data from disparate sources and locations.

Atlas Venture, a Boston venture-capital firm managing $850 million in funds, raises money from investors and then invests in start-up high-tech and life science firms. It must manage a staggering amount of data for each of its deals, and information for each project is generated by many different employees in offices across several time zones. Atlas Venture implemented Microsoft Exchange to manage its deal-flow system. It created "public" folders within Exchange where employees can share information that needs to be instantly updated and viewed by many people at the same time. The system logs transcripts of telephone calls, legal documents, and forms showing the source, status, and origin of each deal. Using Exchange, firm members can pool all their information in real time and avoid duplicated efforts.

Swiss Bank Corporation (SBC) is a leading international investment and asset management bank that provides investment services, portfolio management, and financial planning to private individuals as well as services for large financial institutions. The business processes at its Private Banking division, which works with private individuals, are very information intensive. The division had been manually locating and accessing research data and analyses for developing client financial plans using hard copy reports clipped in volumes of binders. It had to mail this information to consultants in remote locations. The Private Banking division wanted to improve and streamline the overall knowledge management process so that it could improve plan delivery for individuals and reduce risks associated with inaccurate information.

Working with consultants, Swiss Bank's Private Banking division implemented an application called Financial Information Tool (FIT) based on LiveLink groupware from the OpenText corporation. Each Swiss Bank financial advisor can access FIT using a standard Web browser. An adviser can access client data from SBC's client database through LiveLink or use the system to locate and assign tasks to other specialists and consultants with expertise helpful to the client. Swiss Bank has hundreds of consultants in North America, Europe, and the Far East, but they can collaborate on LiveLink as a virtual project team. The adviser can also use LiveLink search services to retrieve existing account information, similar financial plans, research reports, and current tax laws from the corporate knowledge base. The system can attach these documents to the project for other participants to use. All project members can use the system for on-line discussions. LiveLink has powerful security features that only allow authorized users to view and update information, and it has capabilities for managing work flow and business processes. For example, the system could route documents through a defined process-review by an inheritance tax specialist or get an approval from senior management. Swiss Bank created a set of standard work flows for consultants to use, ensuring adherence to corporate guidelines. Consultants and senior managers can monitor tasks, activities, and work flows throughout the course of a project. All of the information captured by the system can be stored in the company's knowledge base for future reference.

Care Canada, the Canadian arm of the worldwide relief organization, manages many projects and must communicate with organizations in 60 countries. It established an intranet to share information on its various projects but found that so many employees made contributions that the information became impossible to manage without some sort of controllable structure. The organization implemented LiveLink groupware to manage its Web publishing. LiveLink helped Care Canada organize its information in "folders" based on its various projects, which were subcategorized by countries or other factors. Every folder has its own administrator and authorized set of viewers, who are automatically notified of changes by e-mail. Employees can use LiveLink's search engine, which works like the ones for the Internet, to tap into internal company knowledge on the intranet.

TO THINK ABOUT: How did groupware help these companies manage their knowledge resources? It has been said that the main challenges in using groupware are managerial and organizational rather than technical. Do you agree? Explain.

Sources: Aaron Ricadela, "Group Efforts," *Information Week*, August 30, 1999; Charles Waltner, "Control the Flow," *Information Week*, June 21, 1999; and "Customer Case Study: Swiss Bank Corporation," www.Opentext.com.

Table 11-4 Examples of Intranets for Knowledge Management

Organization	Intranet Capabilities
Ford Motor Company	Intranet delivers information about news, people, processes, products, and competition to 95,000 professional employees. Employees can access on-line libraries and a Web Center of Excellence with information on best practices, standards, and recommendations. Engineers can access images on the intranet from wherever they are in the world instead of waiting for project documentation to arrive by mail.
Shell Oil Company	Knowledge management system (KMS) provides a communications and collaboration environment where employees can learn about and share information about best practices. Includes information from internal sources and from external sources such as universities, consultants, other companies, and research literature. A Lotus Domino groupware application allows employees to carry on dialogues through the company intranet. The author of a best practice in the repository might use this tool to talk with colleagues about his or her experiences.
Booz Allen Hamilton	Knowledge Online intranet provides an on-line repository of consultants' knowledge and experience, including a searchable database organized around the firm's best specialties and best practices; other intellectual capital such as research reports, presentations, graphs, images, and interactive training material; and links to resumes and job histories.

The collaborative and knowledge-sharing features of intranets, combined with their low cost, have made them attractive alternatives to proprietary groupware for collaborative work, especially among small and medium-size businesses. For simple tasks, such as sharing documents or document publishing, an intranet generally is less expensive to build and maintain than applications based on commercial groupware products, which require proprietary software and client/server networks.

FIGURE 11-6 A corporate portal for a knowledge environment. The portal provides a single point of access to the firm's knowledge resources; it helps the firm coordinate information and people.

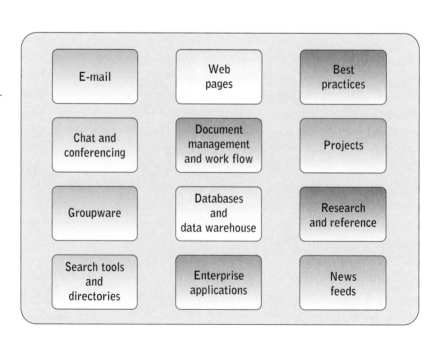

MEASURING PRODUCTIVITY FROM A KNOWLEDGE INTRANET

You head a growing electronic commerce consulting company with over 150 employees in an expanding but fiercely competitive field. You need to recruit many junior consultants every year to replace employees who have left the firm and to fill new positions. In the past, your firm trained new employees by first sending them to a one-month training program. After completing the program they could work full-time on projects. This process has proved very expensive and a drain on company resources. Junior consultants cannot work on any projects to generate client billings for the firm until they have finished the training program. In January 2000 your firm installed an intranet which provides the following:

- An online training class in company practices and methods.
- Repository of "best practices," model proposals with search capabilities.
- Directory of employees, the projects they have worked on, and their special expertise.

You have started to compile a table showing training time and costs before and after installing the intranet. Training time goes down as the company gains experience using the intranet.

	1999	2000	2001
Time to train a new consultant	20 days	14 days	12 days
Daily training cost per consultant	$2000	$1400	$1000
Additional billings revenue per consultant	0		

1. If your intranet trains new consultants more quickly and each trained consultant can start billing clients $1700 per day for work on projects, how much should this new intranet increase revenue from client billings generated by newly-trained consultants in 2000 and 2001? Your firm hires and trains an average of 40 new consultants each year.

2. Using only these metrics how much knowledge worker productivity has your intranet created since the intranet was installed?

3. What other capabilities would you add to the intranet to make your consultants even more productive? How could you measure productivity increases from these capabilities?

For applications requiring extensive coordination and management, groupware software has important capabilities that intranets cannot yet provide. Groupware is more flexible when documents must be changed, updated, or edited on the fly. It can track revisions to a document as it moves through a collaborative editing process. Internal groupware-based networks are more secure than intranets. Web sites are more likely to crash or to have their servers overloaded when there are many requests for data. High-end groupware software such as Lotus Notes or OpenText LiveLink is thus more appropriate for applications requiring production and publication of documents by many authors, frequent updating and document tracking, and high security and replication. Lotus Notes and other groupware products have been enhanced so they can be integrated with the Internet or private intranets.

Intranet technology works best as a central repository with a small number of authors and relatively static information that does not require frequent updating, although intranet tools for group collaboration are improving. Netscape Communications' Communicator software bundles a Web browser with messaging and collaboration tools, including e-mail, newsgroup discussions, a group scheduling and calendaring tool, and point-to-point conferencing. Web technology is most useful for publishing information across multiple types of computer platforms and for displaying knowledge as multimedia objects linked to other knowledge objects in hyperlinks.

Commercial software tools called teamware make intranets more useful for working in teams. **Teamware** consists of intranet-based applications for building a work team, sharing ideas and documents, brainstorming, scheduling, and archiving decisions made or rejected by project team members for future use. Teamware is similar to groupware, but it is customized for team work. Instinctive Technology's eRoom and Lotus Quickplace are examples of commercial teamware products.

teamware Group collaboration software that is customized for teamwork.

Group collaboration technologies alone cannot promote information sharing if team members do not feel it is in their interest to share, especially in organizations that encourage competition among employees. This technology can best enhance the work of a group if the applications are properly designed to fit the organization's needs and work practices and if management encourages a collaborative atmosphere (Alavi, 1999).

11.3 Artificial Intelligence

Organizations are using artificial intelligence technology to capture individual and collective knowledge and to codify and extend their knowledge base.

WHAT IS ARTIFICIAL INTELLIGENCE?

artificial intelligence (AI)
The effort to develop computer-based systems that can behave like humans, with the ability to learn languages, accomplish physical tasks, use a perceptual apparatus, and emulate human expertise and decision making.

Artificial intelligence (AI) is the effort to develop computer-based systems (both hardware and software) that behave like humans. Such systems would be able to learn natural languages, accomplish coordinated physical tasks (robotics), use a perceptual apparatus that informs their physical behavior and language (visual and oral perception systems), and emulate human expertise and decision making (expert systems). Such systems also would exhibit logic, reasoning, intuition, and the just-plain-common-sense qualities that we associate with human beings. Figure 11-7 illustrates the elements of the artificial intelligence family. Another important element is intelligent machines, the physical hardware that performs these tasks.

Successful artificial intelligence systems are based on human expertise, knowledge, and selected reasoning patterns, but they do not exhibit the intelligence of human beings. Existing artificial intelligence systems do not come up with new and novel solutions to problems. Existing systems extend the powers of experts but in no way substitute for them or capture much of their intelligence. Briefly, existing systems lack the common sense and generality of naturally intelligent human beings.

Human intelligence is vastly complex and much broader than computer intelligence. A key factor that distinguishes human beings from other animals is their ability to develop associations and to use metaphors and analogies such as *like* and *as*. Using metaphor and analogy, humans create new rules, apply old rules to new situations, and, at times, act intuitively and/or instinctively without rules. Much of what we call common sense or generality in humans resides in the ability to create metaphors and analogies.

Human intelligence also includes a unique ability to impose a conceptual apparatus on the surrounding world. Metaconcepts such as cause-and-effect and time, and concepts of a lower order such as breakfast, dinner, and lunch are all imposed by human beings on the world around them. Thinking in terms of these concepts and acting on them are central characteristics of intelligent human behavior.

WHY BUSINESS IS INTERESTED IN ARTIFICIAL INTELLIGENCE

Although artificial intelligence applications are much more limited than human intelligence, they are of great interest to business for the following reasons:

- To preserve expertise that might be lost through the retirement, resignation, or death of an acknowledged expert

- To store information in an active form—to create an organizational knowledge base—that many employees can examine, much like an electronic textbook or manual, so that others may learn rules of thumb not found in textbooks

- To create a mechanism that is not subject to human feelings such as fatigue and worry. This may be especially useful when jobs are environmentally, physically, or mentally dangerous to humans. These systems also may be useful advisers in times of crisis.

FIGURE 11-7 The artificial intelligence family. The field of AI currently includes many initiatives: natural language, robotics, perceptive systems, expert systems, and intelligent machines.

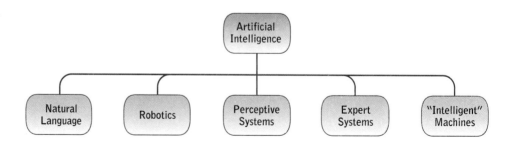

○ To eliminate routine and unsatisfying jobs held by people

○ To enhance an organization's knowledge base by suggesting solutions to specific problems that are too massive and complex to be analyzed by human beings in a short period of time

CAPTURING KNOWLEDGE: EXPERT SYSTEMS

In limited areas of expertise, such as diagnosing a car's ignition system or classifying biological specimens, the rules of thumb used by real-world experts can be understood, codified, and placed in a machine. Information systems that solve problems by capturing knowledge for a very specific and limited domain of human expertise are called **expert systems.** An expert system can assist decision making by asking relevant questions and explaining the reasons for adopting certain actions.

expert system Knowledge-intensive computer program that captures the expertise of a human in limited domains of knowledge.

Expert systems lack the breadth of knowledge and the understanding of fundamental principles of a human expert. They are quite narrow, shallow, and brittle. They typically perform very limited tasks that can be performed by professionals in a few minutes or hours. Problems that cannot be solved by human experts in the same short period of time are far too difficult for an expert system. However, by capturing human expertise in limited areas, expert systems can provide benefits, helping organizations make high-quality decisions with fewer people.

How Expert Systems Work

Human knowledge must be modeled or represented in a way that a computer can process. The model of human knowledge used by expert systems is called the **knowledge base.** Two ways of representing human knowledge and expertise are rules and knowledge frames.

knowledge base Model of human knowledge that is used by expert systems.

A standard structured programming construct (see Chapter 10) is the IF–THEN construct, in which a condition is evaluated. If the condition is true, an action is taken. For instance

IF INCOME > $45,000 (condition)
THEN PRINT NAME AND ADDRESS (action)

A series of these rules can be a knowledge base. Any reader who has written computer programs knows that virtually all traditional computer programs contain IF–THEN statements. The difference between a traditional program and a **rule-based expert system** program is one of degree and magnitude. AI programs can easily have 200 to 10,000 rules, far more than traditional programs, which may have 50 to 100 IF–THEN statements. Moreover, in an AI program the rules tend to be interconnected and nested to a far greater degree than in traditional programs, as shown in Figure 11-8. Hence the complexity of the rules in a rule-based expert system is considerable.

rule-based expert system An AI program that has a large number of interconnected and nested IF–THEN statements, or rules, that are the basis for the knowledge in the system.

Could you represent the knowledge in the *Encyclopedia Britannica* this way? Probably not, because the **rule base** would be too large, and not all the knowledge in the encyclopedia can be represented in the form of IF–THEN rules. In general, expert systems can be efficiently used only in those situations in which the domain of knowledge is highly restricted (such as in granting credit) and involves no more than a few thousand rules.

rule base The collection of knowledge in an AI system that is represented in the form of IF–THEN rules.

Knowledge frames can be used to represent knowledge by organizing information into chunks of interrelated characteristics. The relationships are based on shared characteristics rather than a hierarchy. This approach is grounded in the belief that humans use frames, or concepts, to make rapid sense out of perceptions. For instance, when a person is told, "Look for a tank and shoot when you see one," experts believe that humans invoke a concept, or frame, of what a tank should look like. Anything that does not fit this concept of a tank is ignored. In a similar fashion, AI researchers can organize a vast array of information into frames. The computer then is instructed to search the database of frames and list connections to other frames of interest. The user can follow the pathways pointed to by the system.

knowledge frames A method of organizing expert system knowledge into chunks; the relationships are based on shared characteristics determined by the user.

Figure 11-9 shows part of a knowledge base organized by frames. A "CAR" is defined by characteristics or slots in a frame as a vehicle with four wheels, a gas or diesel motor, and

FIGURE 11-8 Rules in an AI program. An expert system contains a number of rules to be followed when used. The rules themselves are interconnected; the number of outcomes is known in advance and is limited; there are multiple paths to the same outcome; and the system can consider multiple rules at a single time. The rules illustrated are for simple credit-granting expert systems.

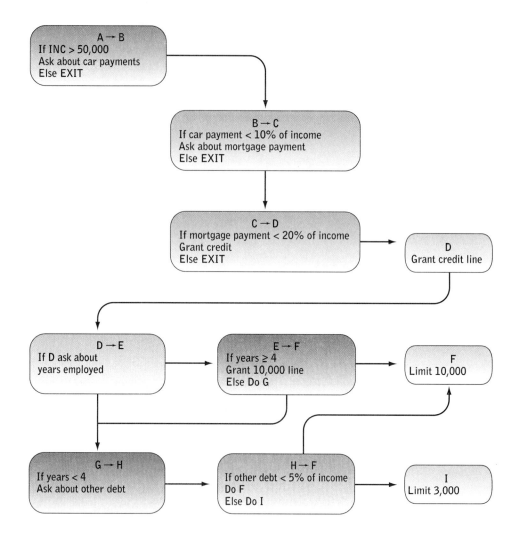

FIGURE 11-9 Frames to model knowledge. Knowledge and information can be organized into frames. Frames capture the relevant characteristics of the objects of interest. This approach is based on the belief that humans use "frames" or concepts to narrow the range of possibilities when scanning incoming information to make rapid sense out of perceptions.

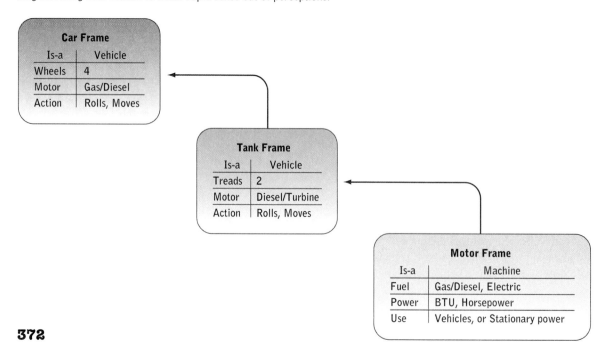

an action such as rolling or moving. This frame could be related to almost any other object in the database that shares any of these characteristics, such as the tank frame.

The **AI shell** is the programming environment of an expert system. In the early years of expert systems, computer scientists used specialized artificial intelligence programming languages such as LISP or Prolog that could process lists of rules efficiently. Today a growing number of expert systems use AI shells that are user-friendly development environments. AI shells can quickly generate user-interface screens, capture the knowledge base, and manage the strategies for searching the rule base.

The strategy used to search through the rule base is called the **inference engine.** Two strategies are commonly used: forward chaining and backward chaining (see Figure 11-10).

In **forward chaining** the inference engine begins with the information entered by the user and searches the rule base to arrive at a conclusion. The strategy is to fire, or carry out, the action of the rule when a condition is true. In Figure 11-10, beginning on the left, if the user enters a client with income greater than $100,000, the engine will fire all rules in sequence from left to right. If the user then enters information indicating that the same client owns real estate, another pass of the rule base will occur and more rules will fire. Processing continues until no more rules can be fired.

In **backward chaining** the strategy for searching the rule base starts with a hypothesis and proceeds by asking the user questions about selected facts until the hypothesis is either confirmed or disproved. In our example in Figure 11-10, ask the question, "Should we add this person to the prospect database?" Begin on the right of the diagram and work toward the left. You can see that the person should be added to the database if a sales representative is sent, term insurance is granted, or a financial advisor visits the client.

Building an Expert System

Building an expert system is similar to building other information systems, although building expert systems is an iterative process with each phase possibly requiring several iterations before a full system is developed. Typically the environment in which an expert system operates is continually changing so that the expert system must also continually change. Some expert

AI shell The programming environment of an expert system.

inference engine The strategy used to search through the rule base in an expert system; can be forward or backward chaining.

forward chaining A strategy for searching the rule base in an expert system that begins with the information entered by the user and searches the rule base to arrive at a conclusion.

backward chaining A strategy for searching the rule base in an expert system that acts like a problem solver by beginning with a hypothesis and seeking out more information until the hypothesis is either proved or disproved.

FIGURE 11-10 Inference engines in expert systems. An inference engine works by searching through the rules and "firing" those rules that are triggered by facts gathered and entered by the user. Basically, a collection of rules is similar to a series of nested "IF" statements in a traditional software program; however, the magnitude of the statements and degree of nesting are much greater in an expert system.

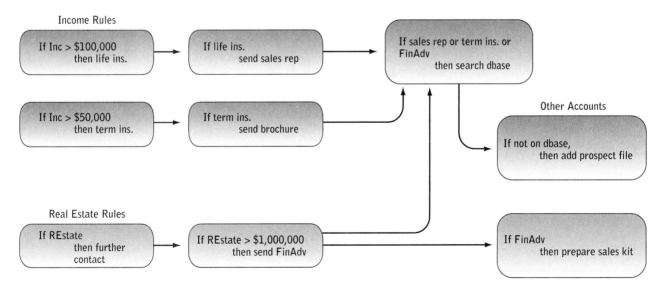

systems, especially large ones, are so complex that in a few years the maintenance costs will equal the development costs.

An AI development team is composed of one or more experts who have a thorough command of the knowledge base, and one or more knowledge engineers, who can translate the knowledge (as described by the expert) into a set of rules or frames. A **knowledge engineer** is similar to a traditional systems analyst but has special expertise in eliciting information and expertise from other professionals.

The team members must select a problem appropriate for an expert system. The project will balance potential savings from the proposed system against the cost. The team members will develop a prototype system to test assumptions about how to encode the knowledge of experts. Next, they will develop a full-scale system, focusing mainly on the addition of a very large number of rules. The complexity of the entire system grows with the number of rules, so the comprehensibility of the system may be threatened. Generally, the system will be pruned to achieve simplicity and power. The system is tested by a range of experts within the organization against the performance criteria established earlier. Once tested, the system will be integrated into the data flow and work patterns of the organization.

Examples of Successful Expert Systems

There is no accepted definition of a successful expert system. What is successful to an academic ("It works!") may not be successful to a corporation ("It costs a million dollars!"). The following are examples of expert systems that provide organizations with an array of benefits, including reduced errors, reduced cost, reduced training time, improved decisions, and improved quality and service.

Countrywide Funding Corp. in Pasadena, California, is a loan-underwriting firm with about 400 underwriters in 150 offices around the country. The company developed a PC-based expert system in 1992 to make preliminary creditworthiness decisions on loan requests. The company had experienced rapid, continuing growth and wanted the system to help ensure consistent, high-quality loan decisions. CLUES (Countrywide's Loan Underwriting Expert System) has about 400 rules. Countrywide tested the system by sending every loan application handled by a human underwriter to CLUES as well. The system was refined until it agreed with the underwriter in 95 percent of the cases.

Countrywide will not rely on CLUES to reject loans, because the expert system cannot be programmed to handle exceptional situations such as those involving a self-employed per-

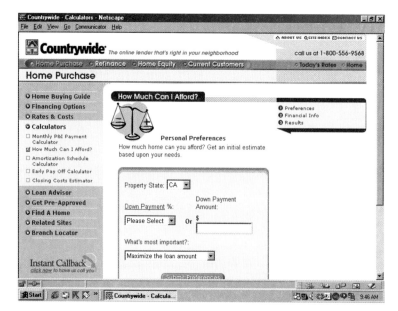

Countrywide Funding Corporation developed an expert system called CLUES to evaluate the creditworthiness of loan applicants. Countrywide is using the rules in this system to answer inquiries from visitors to its Web site who want to know if they can qualify for a loan.

knowledge engineer A specialist who elicits information and expertise from other professionals and translates it into a set of rules or frames for an expert system.

son or complex financial schemes. An underwriter reviews all rejected loans and makes the final decision. CLUES has other benefits. Traditionally, an underwriter could handle six or seven applications a day. Using CLUES, the same underwriter can evaluate at least 16 per day (Nash, 1993). Countrywide now is using the rules in its expert system to answer e-mail inquiries from visitors to its Web site who want to know if they qualify for a loan (Cole-Gomolski, 1998).

The Digital Equipment Corporation (DEC) and Carnegie-Mellon University developed XCON in the late 1970s to configure VAX computers on a daily basis. The system configured customer orders and guided the assembly of those orders at the customer site. XCON was used for major functions such as sales and marketing, manufacturing and production, and field service, and played a strategic role at DEC (Sviokla, June 1990; Barker and O'Connor, 1989). It is estimated that XCON and related systems saved DEC approximately $40 million per year. XCON started out with 250 rules but expanded to about 10,000.

The United Nations developed an expert system to help calculate employees' salaries, taking into account numerous and complex rules for calculating entitlements such as benefits based on location of work and employees' contracts. The knowledge base for the system is on-line and is capable of applying entitlements automatically in payroll calculations. The system also reassesses circumstances when a change to an employee's status is approved and generates the appropriate salary for the next payroll (Baum, 1996).

Problems with Expert Systems

Although expert systems lack the robust and general intelligence of human beings, they can provide benefits to organizations if their limitations are well understood. Only certain classes of problems can be solved using expert systems. Virtually all successful expert systems deal with problems of classification in which there are relatively few alternative outcomes and in which these possible outcomes are all known in advance. Many expert systems require large, lengthy, and expensive development efforts. Hiring or training more experts may be less expensive than building an expert system.

The knowledge base of expert systems is fragile and brittle; they cannot learn or change over time. In fast-moving fields such as medicine or the computer sciences, keeping the knowledge base up to date is critical. Digital Equipment Corporation stopped using XCON because its product line was constantly changing and it was too difficult to keep updating the system to capture these changes. Expert systems can only represent limited forms of knowledge. IF–THEN knowledge exists primarily in textbooks. There are no adequate representations for deep causal models or temporal trends. No expert system, for instance, can write a textbook on information systems or engage in other creative activities not explicitly foreseen by system designers. Many experts cannot express their knowledge using an IF–THEN format. Expert systems cannot yet replicate knowledge that is intuitive, based on analogy and on a sense of things.

Contrary to early promises, expert systems are most effective in automating lower level clerical functions. They can provide electronic checklists for lower level employees in service bureaucracies such as banking, insurance, sales, and welfare agencies. The applicability of expert systems to managerial problems is very limited. Managerial problems generally involve drawing facts and interpretations from divergent sources, evaluating the facts, and comparing one interpretation of the facts with another, and are not limited to simple classification. Expert systems based on the prior knowledge of a few known alternatives are unsuitable for the problems managers face on a daily basis.

ORGANIZATIONAL INTELLIGENCE: CASE-BASED REASONING

Expert systems primarily capture the knowledge of individual experts, but organizations also have collective knowledge and expertise that they have built up over the years. This organizational knowledge can be captured and stored using case-based reasoning. In **case-based reasoning (CBR),** descriptions of past experiences of human specialists, represented as cases, are stored in a database for later retrieval when the user encounters a new case with similar parameters. The

case-based reasoning (CBR) Artificial intelligence technology that represents knowledge as a database of cases and solutions.

system searches for stored cases with problem characteristics similar to the new one, finds the closest fit, and applies the solutions of the old case to the new case. Successful solutions are tagged to the new case and both are stored together with the other cases in the knowledge base. Unsuccessful solutions also are appended to the case database along with explanations as to why the solutions did not work (see Figure 11-11).

Expert systems work by applying a set of IF–THEN–ELSE rules against a knowledge base, both of which are extracted from human experts. Case-based reasoning, in contrast, represents knowledge as a series of cases, and this knowledge base is continuously expanded and refined by users. For example, let us examine Compaq Computer of Houston, Texas, a company that operates in a highly competitive, customer service-oriented business environment that is flooded daily with customer phone calls crying for help. Keeping those customers satisfied requires Compaq to spend millions of dollars annually to maintain large, technically skilled, customer-support staffs. When customers call with problems, they describe the problems to the customer-service staff and then wait while customer service transfers the calls to appropriate technicians. The customers then describe the problem all over again while the technicians try to come up with answers—all in all, a most frustrating experience. To improve

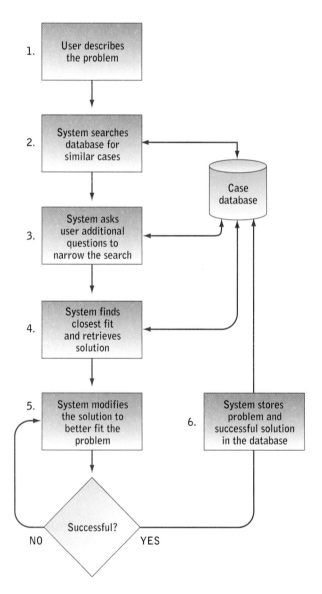

FIGURE 11-11 How case-based reasoning works. Case-based reasoning represents knowledge as a database of past cases and their solutions. The system uses a six-step process to generate solutions to new problems encountered by the user.

customer service and rein in costs, Compaq began giving away expensive case-based reasoning software to customers purchasing their Pagemarq printer.

The software knowledge base is a series of several hundred actual cases of Pagemarq printer problems—actual war stories about smudged copies, printer memory problems, jammed printers—all the typical problems people face with laser printers. Trained CBR staff entered case descriptions in textual format into the CBR system. They entered key words necessary to categorize the problem, such as smudge, smear, lines, streaks, and paper jam. They also entered a series of questions that might be needed to allow the software to further narrow the problem. Finally, solutions also were attached to each case.

With the Compaq-supplied CBR system running on their computer, owners no longer need to call Compaq's service department for most problems. Instead, they run the software and describe the problem to the software. The system swiftly searches actual cases, discarding unrelated ones, selecting related ones. If it becomes necessary to further narrow the search results, the software will ask the user for more information. In the end, one or more cases relevant to the specific problem are displayed along with their solutions. Now, customers can solve most of their own problems quickly without a telephone call, and Compaq saves $10 million to $20 million annually in customer-support costs.

New commercial software products, such as Inference's CasePoint WebServer, allow customers to access a case database through the Web. Using case-based reasoning, the server asks customers to answer a series of questions to narrow down the problems. CasePoint then extracts solutions from the database and passes them on to customers. Audio-product manufacturer Kenwood USA used this tool to put its manuals and technical-support solutions on the Web.

11.4 Other Intelligent Techniques

Organizations are using other intelligent computing techniques to extend their knowledge base by providing solutions to problems that are too massive or complex to be handled by people with limited resources. Neural networks, fuzzy logic, genetic algorithms, and intelligent agents are developing into promising business applications.

NEURAL NETWORKS

There has been an exciting resurgence of interest in bottom-up approaches to artificial intelligence in which machines are designed to imitate the physical thought process of the biological brain. Figure 11-12 shows two neurons from a leech's brain. The soma, or nerve cell at the center, acts like a switch, stimulating other neurons and being stimulated in turn. Emanating from the neuron is an axon, which is an electrically active link to the dendrites of other neurons. Axons and dendrites are the "wires" that electrically connect neurons to one another. The junction of the two is called a synapse. This simple biological model is the metaphor for the development of neural networks. A **neural network** consists of hardware or software that attempts to emulate the processing patterns of the biological brain.

The human brain has about 100 billion (10^{11}) neurons, each of which has about 1,000 dendrites, which form 100,000 billion (10^{14}) synapses. The brain's neurons operate in parallel, and the human brain can accomplish about 10^{16}, or ten million billion, interconnections per second. This far exceeds the capacity of any known machine or any machine planned or ever likely to be built with current technology.

However, complex networks of neurons have been simulated on computers. Figure 11-13 shows an artificial neural network with two neurons. The resistors in the circuits are variable and can be used to teach the network. When the network makes a mistake (i.e., chooses the wrong pathway through the network and arrives at a false conclusion), resistance can be raised on some circuits, forcing other neurons to fire. If this learning process continues for thousands of cycles, the machine learns the correct response. The neurons are highly interconnected and operate in parallel.

neural network Hardware or software that attempts to emulate the processing patterns of the biological brain.

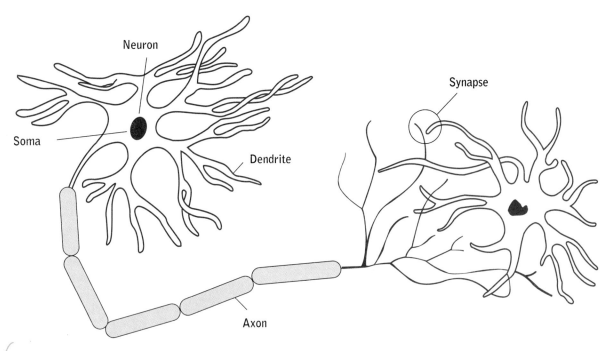

FIGURE 11-12 Biological neurons of a leech. Simple biological models, like the neurons of a leech, have influenced the development of artificial or computational neural networks in which the biological cells are replaced by transistors or entire processors.
Source: Defense Advance Research Projects Agency (DARPA), 1988. Unclassified.

A neural net has many sensing and processing nodes that continuously interact with each other. Figure 11-14 represents a neural network comprising an input layer, an output layer, and a hidden processing layer. The network is fed a training set of data for which the inputs produce a known set of outputs or conclusions. This helps the computer learn the correct solution by example. As the computer is fed more data, each case is compared with the known outcome. If it differs, a correction is calculated and applied to the nodes in the hidden processing layer. These steps are repeated until a condition, such as corrections being less than a certain amount, is reached. The neural network in Figure 11-14 has "learned" how to identify a good credit risk.

FIGURE 11-13 Artificial neural network with two neurons. In artificial neurons, the biological neurons become processing elements (switches), the axons and dendrites become wires, and the synapses become variable resistors that carry weighted inputs (currents) that represent data.
Source: DARPA, 1988. Unclassified.

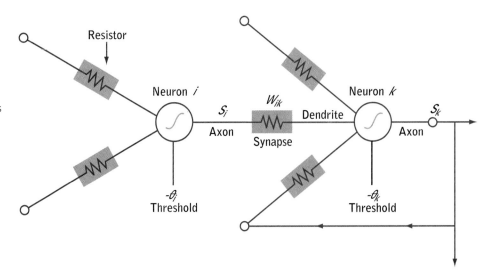

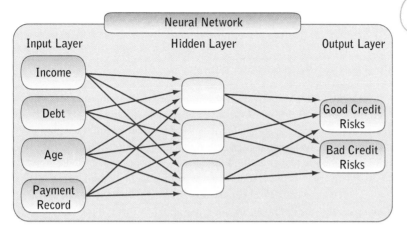

FIGURE 11-14 A neural network uses rules it "learns" from patterns in data to construct a hidden layer of logic. The hidden layer processes inputs and classifies them based on the experience of the model.
Source: Herb Edelstein, "Technology How-To: Mining Data Warehouses," InformationWeek, January 8, 1996. Copyright © 1996 CMP Media, Inc., 600 Community Drive, Manhasset, NY 11030. Reprinted with permission.

The Difference Between Neural Networks and Expert Systems

What is different about neural networks? Expert systems seek to emulate or model a human expert's way of solving problems, but neural network builders claim that they do not model human intelligence, do not program solutions, and do not aim to solve specific problems per se. Instead, neural network designers seek to put intelligence into the hardware in the form of a generalized capability to learn. In contrast, the expert system is highly specific to a given problem and cannot be retrained easily.

Take a simple problem like identifying a cat. An expert system approach would interview hundreds of people to understand how humans recognize cats, resulting in a large set of rules, or frames, programmed into an expert system. In contrast, a trainable neural network would be brought to a test site, connected to a television, and started on the process of learning. Every time a cat was not correctly perceived, the system's interconnections would be adjusted. When cats were correctly perceived, the system would be left alone and another object scanned.

Neural network applications are emerging in medicine, science, and business to address problems in pattern classification, prediction and financial analysis, and control and optimization. Papnet is a neural net-based system that distinguishes between normal and abnormal cells when examining Pap smears for cervical cancer that has far greater accuracy than visual examinations by technicians. The computer is not able to make a final decision, so a technician will review any selected abnormal cells. Using Papnet, a technician requires one-fifth the time to review a smear while attaining perhaps 10 times the accuracy of the existing manual method.

Neural networks are being used by the financial industry to discern patterns in vast pools of data that might help investment firms predict the performance of equities, corporate bond ratings, or corporate bankruptcies. VISA International Inc. is using a neural network to help detect credit card fraud by monitoring all VISA transactions for sudden changes in the buying patterns of cardholders.

Unlike expert systems, which typically provide explanations for their solutions, neural networks cannot always explain why they arrived at a particular solution. Moreover, they cannot always guarantee a completely certain solution, arrive at the same solution again with the same input data, or always guarantee the best solution (Trippi and Turban, 1989–1990). They are very sensitive and may not perform well if their training covers too little or too much data. In most current applications, neural networks are best used as aids to human decision makers instead of substitutes for them.

FUZZY LOGIC

Traditional computer programs require precision: on–off, yes–no, right–wrong. However, we human beings do not experience the world this way. We might all agree that +120 degrees is hot and −40 degrees is cold; but is 75 degrees hot, warm, comfortable, or cool? The answer depends on many factors: the wind, the humidity, the individual experiencing the temperature, one's clothing, and one's expectations. Many of our activities also are inexact. A tractor trailer driver would find it nearly impossible to back a rig into a space precisely specified to less than an inch on all sides.

fuzzy logic Rule-based AI that tolerates imprecision by using non-specific terms called membership functions to solve problems.

Fuzzy logic, a relatively new, rule-based development in AI, tolerates imprecision and even uses it to solve problems that previously we could not have solved. Fuzzy logic consists of a variety of concepts and techniques for representing and inferring knowledge that is imprecise, uncertain, or unreliable. Fuzzy logic can create rules that use approximate or subjective values and incomplete or ambiguous data. By expressing logic with some carefully defined imprecision, fuzzy logic is closer to the way people actually think than traditional IF–THEN rules.

Ford Motor Co. developed a fuzzy logic application that backs a simulated tractor trailer into a parking space. The application uses the following three rules:

> IF the truck is *near* jackknifing, THEN *reduce* the steering angle.
> IF the truck is *far away* from the dock, THEN steer *toward* the dock.
> IF the truck is *near* the dock, THEN point the trailer *directly* at the dock.

This logic makes sense to us as human beings, for it represents how we think as we back that truck into its berth.

How does the computer make sense of this programming? The answer is relatively simple. The terms (known as *membership functions*) are imprecisely defined so that, for example, in Figure 11-15, *cool* is between 50 degrees and 70 degrees, although the temperature is most clearly cool between about 60 degrees and 67 degrees. Note that *cool* is overlapped by *cold* or *norm.* To control the room environment using this logic, the programmer would develop similarly imprecise definitions for humidity and other factors such as outdoor wind and temperature. The rules might include one that says: *"If the temperature is cool or cold and the humidity is low while the outdoor wind is high and the outdoor temperature is low, raise the heat and humidity in the room."* The computer would combine the membership function readings in a weighted manner and, using all the rules, raise and lower the temperature and humidity.

Fuzzy logic is widely used in Japan and is gaining popularity in the United States. Its popularity has occurred partially because managers find they can use it to reduce costs and shorten development time. Fuzzy logic code requires fewer IF–THEN rules, making it simpler

FIGURE 11-15 Implementing fuzzy logic rules in hardware. The membership functions for the input called temperature are in the logic of the thermostat to control the room temperature. Membership functions help translate linguistic expressions such as "warm" into numbers that the computer can manipulate.
Source: James M. Sibigtroth, "Implementing Fuzzy Expert Rules in Hardware," **AI Expert,** April 1992. © 1992 Miller Freeman, Inc. Reprinted with permission.

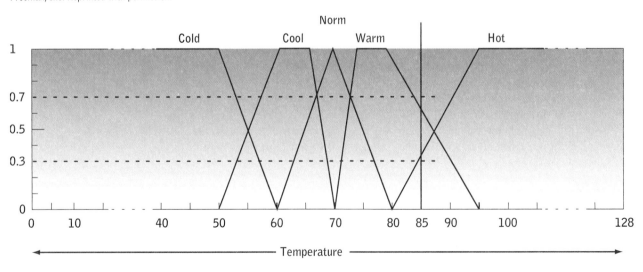

than traditional program code. The rules required in the previous trucking example, plus its term definitions, might require hundreds of IF–THEN statements to implement in traditional logic. Compact code requires less computer capacity, allowing Sanyo Fisher USA to implement camcorder controls without adding expensive memory to their product.

Fuzzy logic also allows us to solve problems not previously solvable, thus improving product quality. In Japan, Sendai's subway system uses fuzzy logic controls to accelerate so smoothly that standing passengers need not hold on. Mitsubishi Heavy Industries in Tokyo has been able to reduce the power consumption of its air conditioners by 20 percent by implementing control programs in fuzzy logic. The auto-focus device in our cameras is only possible because of fuzzy logic. Williams-Sonoma sells an "intelligent" rice steamer made in Japan that uses fuzzy logic. A variable heat setting detects the amount of grain, cooks the food at the preferred temperature, and keeps food warm for up to 12 hours.

Management also has found fuzzy logic useful for decision making and organizational control. A Wall Street firm had a system developed that selects companies for potential acquisition using the language stock traders understand. Recently a system has been developed to detect possible fraud in medical claims submitted by healthcare providers anywhere in the United States.

GENETIC ALGORITHMS

Genetic algorithms (also referred to as adaptive computation) refer to a variety of problem-solving techniques that are conceptually based on the method that living organisms use to adapt to their environment—the process of evolution. They are programmed to work the way populations solve problems—by changing and reorganizing their component parts using processes such as reproduction, mutation, and natural selection. Thus, genetic algorithms promote the evolution of solutions to particular problems, controlling the generation, variation, adaptation, and selection of possible solutions using genetically based processes. As solutions alter and combine, the worst ones are discarded and the better ones survive to go on to produce even better solutions. Genetic algorithms breed programs that solve problems even when no person can fully understand their structure (Holland, 1992).

A genetic algorithm works by representing information as a string of 0s and 1s. A possible solution can be represented by a long string of these digits. The genetic algorithm provides methods of searching all possible combinations of digits to identify the right string representing the best possible structure for the problem.

In one method, the programmer first randomly generates a population of strings consisting of combinations of binary digits (see Figure 11-16). Each string corresponds to one of the variables in the problem. One applies a test for fitness, ranking the strings in the population according to their level of desirability as possible solutions. After the initial population is evaluated for fitness, the algorithm produces the next generation of strings, consisting of strings that survived the fitness test plus offspring strings produced from mating pairs of strings, and tests their fitness. The process continues until a solution is reached.

Solutions to certain types of problems in areas of optimization, product design, and the monitoring of industrial systems are especially appropriate for genetic algorithms. Many business problems require optimization because they deal with issues such as minimization of costs, maximization of profits, efficient scheduling, and use of resources. If these situations are very dynamic and complex, involving hundreds of variables or hundreds of formulas, genetic algorithms can expedite the solution because they can evaluate many different solution alternatives quickly to find the best one. For example, General Electric engineers used genetic algorithms to help optimize the design for jet turbine aircraft engines, where each design change required changes in up to 100 variables. Coors Brewing Company and the U.S. Navy used genetic algorithms to help them with scheduling problems (Burtka, 1993).

Hybrid AI Systems

Genetic algorithms, fuzzy logic, neural networks, and expert systems can be integrated into a single application to take advantage of the best features of these technologies. Such systems are called **hybrid AI systems.** Hybrid applications in business are growing. In Japan, Hitachi, Mitsubishi, Ricoh, Sanyo, and others are starting to incorporate hybrid AI in products such as

genetic algorithms Problem-solving methods that promote the evolution of solutions to specified problems using the model of living organisms adapting to their environment.

hybrid AI systems Integration of multiple AI technologies into a single application to take advantage of the best features of these technologies.

FIGURE 11-16 The components of a genetic algorithm. This example illustrates an initial population of "chromosomes," each representing a different solution. The genetic algorithm uses an iterative process to refine the initial solutions so that the better ones, those with the higher fitness, are more likely to emerge as the best solution.
Source: From "Intelligent Decision Support Methods" by Vasant Dhar and Roger Stein, p. 65 © 1997. Reprinted by permission of Prentice-Hall, Inc. Upper Saddle River, NJ.

A population of chromosomes		Decoding of chromosomes			Evaluation of chromosomes
		Color	Speed	Intelligence	Fitness
1 0 1 1 0 1	1	White	Medium	Dumb	40
0 1 0 1 0 1	2	Black	Slow	Dumb	43
1 1 0 1 1 0	3	White	Slow	Very Dumb	22
0 0 0 1 0 1	4	Black	Fast	Dumb	71
1 0 1 0 0 0	5	White	Medium	Very Smart	53

home appliances, factory machinery, and office equipment. Matsushita has developed a "neurofuzzy" washing machine that combines fuzzy logic with neural networks. Nikko Securities has been working on a neurofuzzy system to forecast convertible-bond ratings.

INTELLIGENT AGENTS

Intelligent agents are software programs that work in the background to carry out specific, repetitive, and predictable tasks for an individual user, business process, or software application. The agent uses a built-in or learned knowledge base to accomplish tasks or make decisions on the user's behalf. Intelligent agents can be programmed to make decisions based on the user's personal preferences—for example, to delete junk e-mail, schedule appointments, or travel over interconnected networks to find the cheapest airfare to California. The agent can be likened to a personal digital assistant collaborating with the user in the same work environment. It can help the user by performing tasks on the user's behalf, training or teaching the user, hiding the complexity of difficult tasks, helping the user collaborate with other users, or monitoring events and procedures (Maes, 1994).

intelligent agent Software program that uses a built-in or learned knowledge base to carry out specific, repetitive, and predictable tasks for an individual user, business process, or software application.

My Simon uses intelligent agent technology to search virtual retailers for price and availability of products specified by the user. Displayed here are the results for a search of prices and sources for purchasing a digital camera.

WHEN THE GOING GETS TOUGH, THE BOTS GO SHOPPING

Think of the Internet as the world's largest shopping mall. Then think of how you would get around the mall and find items that you need. There is no mall directory or road map. Search engines can help, but what if you also want to comparison shop for the vendors with the best prices or service? Many consumers have found that search-and-comparison tools such as bots, also known as shopping agents, are the perfect way to bargain hunt. "I don't have time to go to a bunch of sites," says Tim Smith, a marketer with the Stencil Group in San Francisco. "Shopping bots give me quick and dirty access," and they save time and money.

Bots give equal treatment to large and small storefronts, forcing retailers of every size to keep their prices competitive. Smaller, unknown vendors that do not have well-known brand names can especially benefit. "The consumer may know 3 bookstores but we know 50," says Brian Rolfe, corporate communications director at MySimon, a leading shopping bot. MySimon listings include both large vendors and mom-and-pop stores, giving the consumer a wide array of options.

Shopping bots are multiplying—by the end of 1999 there were about 400. But not everyone is happy with bot technology. After spending millions on marketing for their Web sites, merchants worry that bots will take away the advantages of brand identity, steer consumers toward lower-priced competitors, and consume valuable bandwidth searching their site that otherwise could be allocated to customers.

Bots are also less useful for business-to-business electronic commerce where multiparty exchanges are commonplace. For example, a chemical company might start out bidding on premium-quality benzene. If the high-quality product proved too expensive, the company might decide to purchase lower-quality benzene at a lower price, ship it to a refinery, and then have it transported to its own facilities. Rapidly combining the bids of various benzene companies, refineries, and transporters to estimate the price that a chemical company would pay is still considered to be too complex a task for bot technology to handle.

The newest shopping bots are more respectful of bandwidth. They search merchant sites during off-hours, keep their own local databases of product listings, and give merchants the options of sending them data directly on their product prices and availability rather than having bots search their Web sites for this information. These bots also provide information on customer service, delivery options, and warranties as well as on prices. For example, BizRate rates businesses on factors such as customer service, ease of ordering, on-time delivery, privacy protection, and shipping and return policies as well as on prices.

Professor Hal Varian of the University of California at Berkeley and specialist on the information economy, notes that shopping bots could eventually lead to higher prices. Vendors are likely to use bots to monitor the prices of their competitors. If they saw competitors lowering their prices they would automatically follow suit. But if competitors raised their prices, they would automatically raise theirs as well. Once the on-line marketplace boils down to a few vendors, there could actually be a general drifting toward higher prices. Varian points to the airline industry, where this "fast-follow" mentality has lead to steadily rising fares for business travelers.

TO THINK ABOUT: What are the advantages and disadvantages of using shopping bots for merchants and for consumers?

Sources: Karen Solomon, "To Bot or Not to Bot," and "Revenge of the Bots," **The Industry Standard,** November 15, 1999; Steve G. Steinberg, "The Trouble with Bots," **The Industry Standard,** September 20, 1999; and Alex Gove, "Bot and Sold," **Red Herring,** August 1999.

There are many intelligent agent applications today in operating systems, application software, e-mail systems, mobile computing software, and network tools. For example, the Wizards found in Microsoft Office software tools have built-in capabilities to show users how to accomplish various tasks, such as formatting documents or creating graphs, and to anticipate when users need assistance.

Of special interest to business are intelligent agents that cruise networks, including the Internet, in search of information. They are used in electronic commerce applications to help consumers find products they want and to assist them in comparing prices and other features. Because these mobile agents are personalized, semiautonomous, and continuously running, they can help automate several of the most time-consuming stages of the buying process and thus reduce transaction costs. Agents can help people interested in making a purchase filter and retrieve information about products of interest, evaluate competing products according to criteria they have established, and negotiate with vendors for price and delivery terms (Maes, Guttman, and Moukas, 1999). The Window on Technology describes some of the advantages and disadvantages of using bots, agent technology for shopping the Internet.

Table 11-5	Examples of Electronic Commerce Agents

Agent	Description
MySimon	Real-time shopping bot that searches more than 1,000 affiliated and unaffiliated merchants in 90 categories. Collects a 3 to 10 percent finders fee on sales.
Junglee	Shopping bot used in Amazon.com's Shop the Web comparison shopping service.
Jango	ProductFinder shopping bot searches 500 unaffiliated merchants in 40 categories.
W3Shopping.com	Uses Inktomi's C2B shopping bot technology to list 380 affiliated and unaffiliated merchants in 14 categories.
AuctionBot	Allows sellers to set up their own auctions where buyers and sellers can place bids according to the protocols and parameters that have been established for the auction. Using AuctionBot, sellers create auctions by selecting the type of auction and parameters (such as clearing time or number of sellers) they wish to use. AuctionBot then manages the buyer bidding according to the specified parameters.

Agents can also help buyers identify items they might need to buy, including repetitive purchases such as out-of-stock supplies or purchases that can be predicted based on earlier purchasing habits. Yahoo! and Excite, two of the major Web search services, now offer "shopping agents" for a few merchandise categories, such as music, books, electronics, and toys. To use these agents, the consumer enters the desired product into an on-line shopping form. Using this information, the shopping agent searches the Web for product pricing and availability. It returns a list of sites that sell the item along with pricing information and a purchase link. Table 11-5 compares various types of electronic commerce agents.

Agent-based electronic commerce will become even more widespread as agent and Web technology become more powerful and flexible. Increased use of XML (extensible markup language), Java, and distributed objects (see Chapter 5) will allow software agents and other automated processes to access and interact with Web-based information more easily (Glushko, Tenenbaum, and Meltzer, 1999; Wong, Paciorek, and Moore, 1999). More sophisticated programming techniques for training agents will enable agents to identify problems they cannot solve and communicate where additional input is needed from users to achieve a solution (Bauer, Dengler, Paul, and Meyer, 2000).

MANAGEMENT WRAP-UP

Management

Leveraging and managing organizational knowledge have become core management responsibilities. Managers need to identify the knowledge assets of their organizations and make sure that appropriate systems and processes are in place to maximize their use.

Organization

Systems for knowledge and information work and artificial intelligence can enhance organizational processes in a number of ways. They can facilitate communication, collaboration, and coordination, bring more analytical power to bear in the development of solutions, or reduce the amount of human intervention in organizational processes.

An array of technologies is available to support knowledge management, including artificial intelligence technologies and tools for knowledge and information work and group collaboration. Managers should understand the costs, benefits, and capabilities of each technology and the knowledge management problems for which each is best suited.

Technology

For Discussion

1. Discuss some of the ways that knowledge management provides organizations with strategic advantage. How strategic are knowledge management systems?

2. How much can the use of artificial intelligence change the management process?

SUMMARY

1. Explain the importance of knowledge management in contemporary organizations. Knowledge management is the process of systematically and actively managing and leveraging the stores of knowledge in an organization. Knowledge is a central productive and strategic asset in an information economy. Information systems can play a valuable role in knowledge management, helping the organization optimize its flow of information and capture its knowledge base. Office systems, knowledge work systems (KWS), group collaboration systems, and artificial intelligence applications are especially useful for knowledge management because they focus on supporting information and knowledge work and on defining and codifying the organization's knowledge base.

2. Describe the applications that are most useful for distributing, creating, and sharing knowledge in the firm. Offices coordinate information work in the organization, link the work of diverse groups in the organization, and couple the organization to its external environment. Office systems support these functions by automating document management, communications, scheduling, and data management. Word processing, desktop publishing, Web publishing, and digital imaging systems support document management activities. Electronic-mail systems and groupware support communications activities. Electronic calendar applications and groupware support scheduling activities. Desktop data-management systems support data management activities.

Knowledge work systems (KWS) support the creation of knowledge and its integration into the organization. KWS require easy access to an external knowledge base; powerful computer hardware that can support software with intensive graphics, analysis, document management, and communications capabilities; and a friendly user interface. KWS often run on workstations that are customized for the work they must perform. Computer-aided design (CAD) systems and virtual reality systems, which create interactive simulations that behave like the real world, require graphics and powerful modeling capabilities. KWS for financial professionals provide access to external databases and the ability to analyze massive amounts of financial data very quickly.

Groupware is special software to support information-intensive activities in which people work collaboratively in groups. Intranets can perform many group collaboration and support functions and allow organizations to use Web publishing capabilities for document management.

3. Evaluate the role of artificial intelligence in knowledge management. Artificial intelligence is the development of computer-based systems that behave like humans. There are five members of the artificial intelligence family tree: natural language, robotics, perceptive systems, expert systems, and intelligent machines. Artificial intelligence lacks the flexibility, breadth, and generality of human intelligence, but it can be used to capture and codify organizational knowledge.

4. Demonstrate how organizations can use expert systems and case-based reasoning to capture knowledge. Expert systems are knowledge-intensive computer programs that solve problems, which previously required human expertise. The systems capture a limited domain of human knowledge using rules or frames. The strategy to search through the knowledge base, called the inference engine, can use either forward or backward chaining. Expert systems are most useful for problems of classification or diagnosis. Case-based reasoning represents organizational knowledge as a database of cases that can be continually expanded and refined. When the user encounters a new case, the system searches for similar cases, finds the closest fit, and applies the solutions of the old case to the new case. The new case is stored with successful solutions in the case database.

5. Demonstrate how organizations can use neural networks and other intelligent techniques to improve their knowledge base. Neural networks consist of hardware and software that attempt to mimic the thought processes of the human brain. Neural networks are notable for their ability to learn without programming and to recognize patterns that cannot be described easily by humans. They are being used in science, medicine, and business primarily to discriminate patterns in massive amounts of data.

Fuzzy logic is a software technology that expresses logic with some carefully defined imprecision so that it is closer to the way people actually think than traditional IF–THEN rules.

Fuzzy logic has been used for controlling physical devices and is starting to be used for limited decision-making applications.

Genetic algorithms develop solutions to particular problems using genetically based processes such as fitness, crossover, and mutation. Genetic algorithms are beginning to be applied to problems involving optimization, product design, and monitoring industrial systems.

Intelligent agents are software programs with built-in or learned knowledge bases that carry out specific, repetitive, and predictable tasks for an individual user, business process, or software application. Intelligent agents can be programmed to search for information or conduct transactions on networks, including the Internet.

KEY TERMS

AI shell, 373	Document imaging systems, 360	Intelligent agent, 382	Neural network, 377
Artificial intelligence (AI), 370	Expert system, 371	Investment workstation, 365	Office systems, 360
Backward chaining, 373	Forward chaining, 373	Jukebox, 360	Rule base, 371
Case-based reasoning (CBR), 375	Fuzzy logic, 380	Knowledge base, 371	Rule-based expert system, 371
Chief knowledge officer (CKO), 357	Genetic algorithms, 381	Knowledge engineer, 374	Tacit knowledge, 357
Computer-aided design (CAD), 364	Groupware, 366	Knowledge frames, 371	Teamware, 369
	Hybrid AI systems, 381	Knowledge management, 357	Virtual Reality Modeling Language (VRML), 364
Data workers, 359	Inference engine, 373	Knowledge workers, 359	Virtual reality systems, 364
	Information work, 359	Knowledge work systems (KWS), 363	

REVIEW QUESTIONS

1. What is knowledge management? List and briefly describe the information systems that support it and the kind of information technology (IT) infrastructure it requires.

2. What is the relationship between information work and productivity in contemporary organizations?

3. Describe the roles of the office in organizations. What are the major activities that take place in offices?

4. What are the principal types of information systems that support information worker activities in the office?

5. What are the generic requirements of knowledge work systems? Why?

6. Describe how the following systems support knowledge work: computer-aided design (CAD), virtual reality, investment workstations.

7. How does groupware support information work? Describe its capabilities and Internet and intranet capabilities for collaborative work.

8. What is artificial intelligence? Why is it of interest to business?

9. What is the difference between artificial intelligence and natural or human intelligence?

10. Define an expert system and describe how it can help organizations use their knowledge assets.

11. Define and describe the role of the following in expert systems: rule base, frames, inference engine.

12. What is case-based reasoning? How does it differ from an expert system?

13. Describe three problems of expert systems.

14. Describe a neural network. At what kinds of tasks would a neural network excel?

15. Define and describe fuzzy logic. For what kinds of applications is it suited?

16. What are genetic algorithms? How can they help organizations solve problems? For what kinds of problems are they suited?

17. What are intelligent agents? How can they be used to benefit businesses?

GROUP PROJECT

With a group of classmates, select two groupware products such as Lotus Notes and OpenText LiveLink and compare their features and capabilities. To prepare your analysis, use articles from computer magazines and the Web sites for the groupware vendors. Present your findings to the class.

Tools for Interactive Learning

○ Internet Connection

The Internet Connection for this chapter will take you to the National Aeronautics and Space Administration (NASA) Web site, where you can complete an exercise showing how this Web site can be used by knowledge workers. You can also use the Interactive Study Guide to test your knowledge of the topics in this chapter and get instant feedback where you need more practice.

○ Electronic Commerce Project

At the Laudon Web site for Chapter 11, you will find an Electronic Commerce project that will direct you to Web sites where you can compare the capabilities of two shopping bots for the Web.

○ CD-ROM

If you purchase and use the Multimedia Edition CD-ROM with this chapter, you will find two interactive exercises. The first asks you to choose the proper software tools for solving a series of knowledge management problems. The second asks you to select an appropriate AI technology to solve another series of problems. You can also find a video clip illustrating the benefits of Lotus Notes groupware, an audio overview of the major themes of this chapter, and bullet text summarizing the key points of the chapter.

○ Application Exercise

At the Laudon Web site, you can find an Application Exercise for this chapter requiring the use of an expert system development tool to create a small expert system for retirement planning.

Cluster Competitiveness is a small but rapidly growing consulting firm located in Barcelona but operating throughout Europe and in North America. It recently opened a second office in Varese, Italy. The company consults in a very specialized area: the development of industry-specific geographic clusters, such as the leather tanning cluster in northern Italy or the high-tech cluster in Silicon Valley near San Jose, California. A cluster is an informal association of firms, which are usually in the same geographic area, which pursue deliberate practices of collaboration and innovation to increase their competitiveness in regional, national, and international markets. Cluster Competitiveness is a relatively new company; it was founded in 1993 by Emiliano Duch. The company's business model is based on a fast-growth strategy and on finding ways to prosper in a niche market.

Cluster Competitiveness is one of a small number of consulting firms for geographic clustering. To help explain the geographic cluster concept, let us examine the Tucson, Arizona, optics cluster, one of Cluster Competitiveness's clients. The Tucson cluster includes more than 170 small, high-tech optics companies. By gathering together in one local area even though many are competitors, they have much to gain. They draw on a common supply and support infrastructure, which will develop with so many companies to serve. For many reasons clusters also make it easier for their companies to attract both entrepreneurial and other dynamic people who naturally are drawn to them. Clusters tend to generate the kind of independent, specialized, educational facilities that these people need. In addition the cluster makes possible the living and social milieu that educated and technically skilled employees want surrounding them. Finally, companies that are part of clusters are constantly learning and gaining from each other. In particular the smaller, newer companies learn from the larger ones. Moreover, all the companies working in a cluster generate a synergy that can benefit all. For example, Bob Breault, the chair of Tucson's Breault Research Organization Inc., explains that his company is not able to go global alone because it is too small. "But," he continues, "we go to Thailand or Scotland as a group and say, 'Hey, I've got a billion bucks,'" in com-

bined revenues and the potential customers listen. Breault also claims that cooperation is important: the cluster groups share a kind of cooperation that would not develop without the close geographic proximity. "I got a call yesterday from a fierce competitor—but a friend—in the cluster," Breault relates, "and he's setting me up next Monday morning for a contract that doesn't fit his bill but fits mine, and we'll do it together."

What do consultants specializing in geographic clustering offer their customers? One way to describe their business is to realize they are actually promoting economic development by either helping a geographic area establish a cluster appropriate to the area or by helping an existing cluster become stronger and more effective. The problem for Duch and other cluster consulting firms is that their clients—governments and small to medium-size businesses—cannot pay the high consulting fees that big corporations do. In general, business consulting is a high-powered field that can be very lucrative. Most university graduates who are planning to be consultants prefer to accept positions in the big consulting firms where their starting pay will be much higher than Duch can afford. Because Cluster Competitiveness cannot compete with the big firms in salaries, they usually are unable to lure away experienced senior consultants from other firms. In fact, the big firms are easily able to lure away Cluster Competitiveness's employees once they are trained and experienced. However, despite these problems, Duch is happy with the career he has chosen.

The problem Duch faced was how to attract and hold affordable consultants when he could not compete financially with the big firms. He solved the problem by analyzing and following the model of apprenticeship that was central to European economies for several centuries before 1800. In those days highly skilled masters in many trades took in young apprentices for a limited period of time, usually seven years. During those years the master would benefit from the low-cost labor of the apprentice, and in exchange the master trained his apprentices. For the master the downside of this approach was that at the end of the seven years the apprentices would be skilled and would leave to establish their own businesses. Duch decided that he could design a system that followed

the apprenticeship model—he would hire and train young, lower paid consultants in return for their labor. The consultants he could hire were not the most sought after, but they were still quite talented and capable. However, his approach had to enable his young consultants to be effective right from the start because he knew he would not have seven years of their service. Instead, he knew, in only about two years his apprentices would begin to receive more lucrative offers from higher paying firms. Duch would have to make Cluster Competitiveness succeed by finding ways to make a junior staff immediately productive without a lengthy training period.

The system Duch developed begins with the recognition that junior staff assume a great deal of responsibility and leadership right from the beginning. The system provides for only very minimal supervision from more experienced (more than one year) staff. To accomplish this Duch turned to computer systems. At the heart of the new system is his vision that all consultants must be equally capable of serving a client at the highest level, and that they must be able to do so from any geographic location. Duch required that all information of value be stored in the company database, that nothing of value be kept on paper. During the autumn of 1997, to enforce this rule, he ordered that Cluster Competitiveness's offices be swept clean of all paper once a week. He even went so far as to require that the consultants' laptops be cleaned of data when they returned from business trips, thus forcing the consultants quickly to transfer anything of importance to the corporate database. In addition the company's library only exists on-line and not on paper. Even company news is stored on the server, as are consultant "war stories," although in a separate database. As part of this approach, the Varese office has no computer server of its own. Rather, its consulting data is added to the database in the Barcelona office. In these ways Duch created a digital repository of the whole business that was equally accessible to all of his staff.

The company does allow a small amount of paper in the office. A normal assignment may last four-to-five months, and during that time the client case team has the "right" to fill one file drawer and one file box with paper. However, when the project is completed, with only very rare exceptions, all the paper files are thrown out. Duch's philosophy is that if anything being thrown out is ever needed again, it can be requested, and if it is no longer available, it is outdated anyway.

The cluster-building methodology followed by Cluster Competitiveness is the reason companies, clusters, and governments hire the company, and it too is stored on-line. It actually exists as a tutorial that contains 27 training steps to prepare a consultant for a client engagement. It even encompasses such seemingly minor issues as holding a reception for clients (consultants are advised to serve canapés so that attendees will be able to talk without having to handle clumsy food). The company also offers in-house training for a brief period, but only until the new hire is assigned to a project. Once assigned, the new hire can access all client and project information on-line via the company's intranet, which is accessible anywhere through an Internet connection.

To solve its underlying problem the company does use other technology as well. Quite naturally Cluster Competitiveness relies on e-mail, which consultants can access either through their laptops or through the cell phones they are issued. Consultants all use Microsoft Project to plan and schedule meetings, interviews, presentations, and other events. Cluster Competitiveness also has developed Poeta, a software application based on Microsoft's Access and Outlook applications. With Poeta consultants track all of the relationships of all participants with each project. The Access database stores all business contacts, including not only meetings and telephone calls, but also e-mails and traditional mailings. The consultants' personal agendas are recorded in Outlook. Poeta simplifies the administrative and logistic part of a case,

leaving much more time for the consultants to think about the analytic parts.

Personal contact within the firm is not totally eliminated and in fact is quite important. Consultants do not have their own separate offices at Cluster Competitiveness, so when they are in the home office, they are grouped together. The entire staff of Cluster Competitiveness gathers together for three hours every two weeks at the Fortnightly All Together Meeting (FOAM). At FOAM the consultants trade stories and share their experiences both about their clients and about Cluster Competitiveness. The company also holds two off-site gatherings per year to enable everyone to share experiences. Finally, consultants consult with each other when they think it necessary for their work, and, of course, the senior consultants (usually those with about a year's experience) do watch out some for the junior consultants.

The whole approach has clearly benefited Cluster Competitiveness. The company is a success and is growing fast. With the company knowledge accessible to all, people on the same project can cooperate easily with each other, and consultants on a project can learn from previous or from other concurrent projects. Because all valuable project information is stored in an open company database, when a consultant does leave Cluster Competitiveness, the company does not lose nearly as much as it might have otherwise. Moreover, new hires can use all of the company's collective knowledge to quickly bring themselves up-to-speed, enabling Duch to hire many more new consultants each year. "If we had to teach apprentices," Duch claims, "we could add at most two or three consultants a year." Instead, he feels he can hire many more, increasing his staff by 50 percent if necessary. Clients too benefit from the system because they are

given direct, but limited, access to the company's digital database.

Duch used metrics to measure the effects his approach has had on Cluster Competitiveness during their first four years. He tracked the cost of training a consultant up to the level of case leader, the number of consultants who can be trained simultaneously, and the number of client billings generated by each consultant. With this new method, the company's measured training capacity has risen 100 percent in four years, and the number of billings for each consultant has more than doubled.

Sources: Gary Abramson, "Operation Brain-Trap," **CIO Enterprise Magazine,** November 15, 1999; "Cluster Power," **CIO Enterprise Magazine,** August 15, 1998; and M. Christina Martinez-Fernandez, "Industry Clusters: Competitive Advantage through Innovation," **Industry Cluster Studies** Number 1 (July 1998).

CASE STUDY QUESTIONS

1. Analyze Cluster Competitiveness using the competitive forces and value chain models.

2. How significant a strategic advantage does knowledge management provide for Cluster Competitiveness? What role does information technology play in the company's knowledge management program?

3. Explain the management, organization, and technology issues that had to be addressed when designing Cluster Competitiveness's knowledge management program and information systems.

CHAPTER 12

Enhancing Management Decision Making

Learning Objectives

After completing this chapter, you will be able to:

1. Differentiate a decision-support system (DSS) and a group decision-support system (GDSS).

2. Describe the components of decision-support systems and group decision-support systems.

3. Demonstrate how decision-support systems and group decision-support systems can enhance decision making.

4. Describe the capabilities of executive support systems (ESS).

5. Assess the benefits of executive support systems.

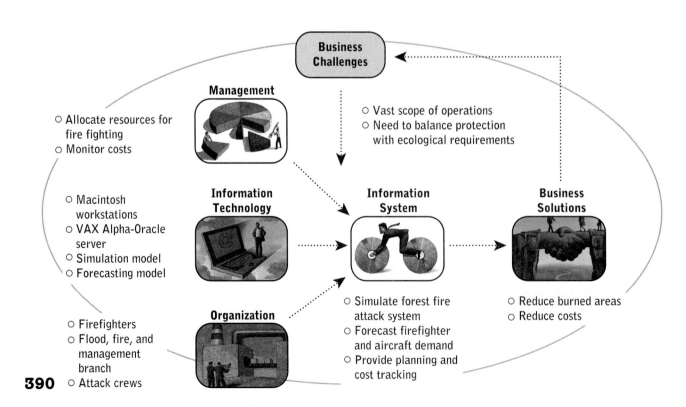

Business Challenges

Management
- Allocate resources for fire fighting
- Monitor costs

- Vast scope of operations
- Need to balance protection with ecological requirements

Information Technology
- Macintosh workstations
- VAX Alpha-Oracle server
- Simulation model
- Forecasting model

Information System
- Simulate forest fire attack system
- Forecast firefighter and aircraft demand
- Provide planning and cost tracking

Business Solutions
- Reduce burned areas
- Reduce costs

Organization
- Firefighters
- Flood, fire, and management branch
- Attack crews

Ontario Fights Fires with a DSS

The Ontario Ministry of Natural Resources (OMNR) is responsible for forest fire management on nearly 800 square kilometers of public land in the Canadian province of Ontario. Although fires pose threats to public safety, timber production, and recreational activities, they also are a natural component of Ontario's forest ecosystem. Forest fire management is complicated by the need to balance protection of vast areas of terrain with the recognition that fire cannot and should not be excluded from all forest areas. OMNR tries to contain fires while they are small to reduce the number of large destructive fires that burn out of control and cost hundreds of thousands or even millions of dollars to extinguish.

The OMNR's Aviation, Flood, and Fire Management Branch (AFFMB) administers the forest fire management program. Forest fire managers realized that they could do a better job if they used formal decision-analysis tools in their job. Working with information systems specialists, OMNR built a series of decision-support systems (DSS) to help with forest fire management. One of its first projects was a DSS to simulate the attack system for fighting fires. Initial attack crews travel to each fire by helicopter or truck and use power pumps, hoses, and hand tools to establish a control line around the fire. Air tankers will often be dispatched ahead of them to fight the fire until they arrive. The DSS provides a simulation model of the initial attack system in which specified air tankers, transport helicopters, and firefighters battle fires and evaluate various attack system alternatives. OMNR used what it learned from the system to support a request for funds to upgrade its aging aircraft fleet.

AFFMB staff developed a firefighter and aircraft demand forecasting model that is used when new fires break out while large escaped fires are taxing suppression resources to their limits. Once a fire flap becomes entrenched, the OMNR must assess firefighter and aircraft requirements for combating existing escaped fires, new escaped fires, and new initial attack fires. Crews can be quickly recycled from one fire to another, and OMNR can borrow additional resources from other agencies. The forecasting model is based on a spreadsheet and helps evaluate manpower planning strategies in anticipation of fire flaps.

The AFFMB's Daily Fire Operations Support System (DFOSS) provides easy-to-use tools to capture and manage daily weather, fire, and lightning data as

CHAPTER OUTLINE

well as capabilities for daily planning, weather analysis, fire behavior, fire occurrence prediction, and cost tracking. It can also generate a wide range of maps and reports. DFOSS is a client/server application that runs on over 100 Macintosh workstations located in 30 different fire department offices and is linked to a VAX/Alpha-Oracle server.

Investing in information systems and firefighting equipment helped OMNR fight fires more effectively. In 1998-99 the ministry contained the total area burned in the province to almost 50% less than the ten-year average, saving $4.5 million.

Sources: David L. Martell, Al Tithecott, and Paul C. Ward, "Fighting Fire with OR," *OR/MS Today*, April 1999; and Ontario Ministry of Natural Resources, "1999-2000 Business Plan," December 21, 1999, www.mnr.gov.on.ca.

MANAGEMENT CHALLENGES

The Ontario Ministry of Natural Resources systems for forest fire management are examples of decision-support systems (DSS). Such systems have powerful analytical capabilities to support managers during the process of arriving at a decision. Other systems in this category are group decision-support systems (GDSS), which support decision making in groups, and executive support systems (ESS), which provide information for making strategic-level decisions. These systems can enhance organizational performance, but they raise the following management challenges:

1. **Building information systems that can actually fulfill executive information requirements.** Even with the use of critical success factors and other information requirements determination methods, it may still be difficult to establish information requirements for ESS and DSS serving senior management. Chapter 3 described why certain aspects of senior management decision making cannot be supported by information systems because the decisions are too unstructured and fluid. Even if a problem can be addressed by an information system, senior management may not fully understand its actual information needs. For instance, senior managers may not agree on the firm's critical success factors, or the critical success factors they describe may be inappropriate or outdated if the firm is confronting a crisis requiring a major strategic change.

2. **Integrating DSS and ESS with existing systems in the business.** Even if system builders do know the information requirements for DSS or ESS, it may not be possible to fulfill them using data from the firm's existing information systems. Various MIS or TPS may define important pieces of data, such as the time period covered by the fiscal year, in different ways. It may not be possible to reconcile data from incompatible internal systems for analysis by managers even through data cleansing and data warehousing. A significant amount of organizational change may be required before the firm can build and install effective DSS and ESS.

Most information systems described throughout this text help people make decisions in one way or another, but DSS, GDSS, and ESS are part of a special category of information systems that are explicitly designed to enhance managerial decision making. This chapter describes the characteristics of each of these types of information systems and shows how each enhances the managerial decision-making process.

DSS, GDSS, and ESS can support decision making in a number of ways. They can automate certain decision procedures (for example, determining the highest price that can be charged for a product to maintain market share). They can provide information about different aspects of the decision situation and the decision process, such as what opportunities or problems triggered the decision process, what solution alternatives were generated or explored, and how the decision was reached. Finally, they can stimulate innovation in decision making by helping managers question existing decision procedures or explore different solution designs (Dutta, Wierenga, and Dalebout, 1997).

12.1 Decision-Support Systems (DSS)

As noted in Chapter 2, a **decision-support system (DSS)** assists management decision making by combining data, sophisticated analytical models and tools, and user-friendly software into a single powerful system that can support semistructured or unstructured decision making. A DSS provides users with a flexible set of tools and capabilities for analyzing important blocks of data.

decision-support system (DSS) Computer system at the management level of an organization that combines data, analytical tools, and models to support semistructured and unstructured decision making.

MIS AND DSS

Some of the earliest applications for supporting management decision making were *management information systems (MIS),* which we introduced in Chapter 2. MIS primarily provide information on the firm's performance to help managers monitor and control the business. They typically produce fixed, regularly scheduled reports based on data extracted and summarized from the organization's underlying transaction processing systems (TPS). The format of these reports is often specified in advance. A typical MIS report might show a summary of monthly sales for each of the major sales territories of a company. Sometimes MIS reports are exception reports, highlighting only exceptional conditions, such as when the sales quotas for a specific territory fall below an anticipated level or employees who have exceeded their spending limit in a dental care plan. Traditional MIS produced primarily hard copy reports. Today these reports might be available on-line through an intranet, and more MIS reports can be generated on demand. Table 12-1 provides some examples of MIS applications.

DSS provide new sets of capabilities for nonroutine decisions and user control. An MIS provides managers with reports based on routine flows of data and assists in the general control of the organization, whereas a DSS emphasizes change, flexibility, and a rapid response. DSS are tightly focused on a specific decision or classes of decisions such as routing, queueing, evaluating, predicting, and so forth. In philosophy, a DSS promises end-user control of data, tools, and sessions. With a DSS less effort is needed to link users to structured information flows, and a correspondingly greater emphasis is placed on models, assumptions, ad hoc

Table 12-1 Examples of MIS Applications

Organization	MIS Application
California Pizza Kitchen	Inventory Express application "remembers" each restaurant's ordering patterns, and compares the amount of ingredients used per menu item to predefined portion measurements established by management. The system identifies restaurants with out-of-line portions and notifies their management so that corrective action can be taken.
PharMark	Extranet MIS identifies patients with drug-use patterns that place them at risk for adverse outcomes.
Black & Veatch	Intranet MIS tracks construction costs for its various projects across the United States.
Taco Bell	TACO (Total Automation of Company Operations) system provides information on food cost, labor cost, and period-to-date costs for each restaurant.

queries, and display graphics. Both the DSS and MIS rely on professional analysis and design. However, whereas an MIS usually follows a traditional systems development methodology, freezing information requirements before design and throughout the lifecycle, a DSS is consciously iterative and never frozen.

Chapter 3 introduced the distinction between structured, semistructured, and unstructured decisions. Structured problems are repetitive and routine, for which known algorithms provide solutions. Unstructured problems are novel and nonroutine, for which there are no algorithms for solutions. One can discuss, decide, and ruminate about unstructured problems, but they are not solved like one finds an answer to an equation. Semistructured problems fall between structured and unstructured problems. Although MIS primarily address structured problems, DSS support semistructured and unstructured problem analysis.

Chapter 3 also introduced Simon's description of decision making, which consists of four stages: intelligence, design, choice, and implementation. Decision-support systems are intended to help design and evaluate alternatives, and monitor the adoption or implementation process.

TYPES OF DECISION-SUPPORT SYSTEMS

The earliest DSS tended to draw on small subsets of corporate data and were extremely model driven. Recent advances in computer processing and database technology have expanded the definition of a DSS to include systems that can support decision making by analyzing vast quantities of data.

Today there are two basic types of decision-support systems, model driven and data driven (Dhar and Stein, 1997). Early DSS developed in the late 1970s and 1980s were model driven. **Model-driven DSS** were primarily stand-alone systems isolated from major organizational information systems that used some type of model to perform "what-if" and other kinds of analyses. Such systems were often developed by end-user divisions or groups not under central IS control. Their analysis capabilities were based on a strong theory or model combined with a good user interface that made the model easy to use. The voyage-estimating DSS described in Chapter 2 is an example of a model-driven DSS.

The second type of DSS is a **data-driven DSS.** These systems analyze large pools of data found in major organizational systems. They support decision making by allowing users to extract useful information that previously was buried in large quantities of data. Often data from transaction processing systems (TPS) are collected in data warehouses for this purpose. On-line analytical processing (OLAP) and datamining can then be used to analyze the data. Companies are starting to build data-driven DSS to mine customer data gathered from their Web sites as well (Wilder, 1999).

Traditional database queries answer such questions as, "How many units of product number 403 were shipped in November 1999?" OLAP, or multidimensional analysis, supports much more complex requests for information, such as, "Compare sales of product 403 relative to plan by quarter and sales region for the past 2 years." We described OLAP and multidimensional data analysis in Chapter 6. With OLAP and query-oriented data analysis, users need to have a good idea about the information for which they are looking.

Datamining is more discovery driven. **Datamining** provides insights into corporate data that cannot be obtained with OLAP by finding hidden patterns and relationships in large databases and inferring rules from them to predict future behavior. The patterns and rules then can be used to guide decision making and forecast the effect of those decisions. The types of information that can be yielded from datamining include associations, sequences, classifications, clusters, and forecasts.

Associations are occurrences linked to a single event. For instance, a study of supermarket purchasing patterns might reveal that when corn chips are purchased, a cola drink is purchased 65 percent of the time, but when there is a promotion, cola is purchased 85 percent of the time. With this information, managers can make better decisions because they have learned the profitability of a promotion.

In *sequences,* events are linked over time. One might find, for example, that if a house is purchased, then a new refrigerator will be purchased within two weeks 65 percent of the time, and an oven will be bought within one month of the home purchase 45 percent of the time.

model-driven DSS Primarily stand-alone system that uses some type of model to perform "what-if" and other kinds of analyses.

data-driven DSS A system that supports decision making by allowing users to extract and analyze useful information that was previously buried in large databases.

datamining Technology for finding hidden patterns and relationships in large databases and inferring rules from them to predict future behavior.

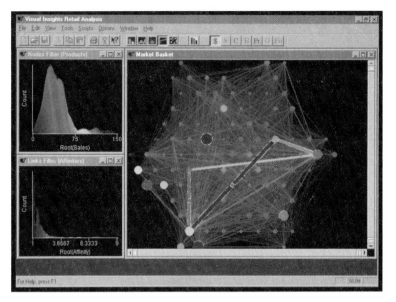

Lucent Technologies Visual Insights software can help businesses detect patterns in their data. Each dot in this example represents items purchased at one supermarket, with lines drawn between the purchases of individual shoppers. The software shows links between different purchase items, such as cookies and milk.

Classification recognizes patterns that describe the group to which an item belongs by examining existing items that have been classified and by inferring a set of rules. For example, businesses such as credit card or telephone companies worry about the loss of steady customers. Classification can help discover the characteristics of customers who are likely to leave and can provide a model to help managers predict who they are so that they can devise special campaigns to retain such customers.

Clustering works in a manner similar to classification when no groups have yet been defined. A datamining tool will discover different groupings within data, such as finding affinity groups for bank cards or partitioning a database into groups of customers based on demographics and types of personal investments.

Although these applications involve predictions, *forecasting* uses predictions in a different way. It uses a series of existing values to forecast what other values will be. For example, forecasting might find patterns in data to help managers estimate the future value of continuous variables such as sales figures.

Datamining uses statistical analysis tools as well as neural networks, fuzzy logic, genetic algorithms, or rule-based and other intelligent techniques (described in Chapter 11).

As noted in Chapter 3, it is a mistake to think that only individuals in large organizations make decisions. In fact, most decisions are made collectively. Chapter 3 describes the rational, bureaucratic, political, and "garbage can" models of organizational decision making. Frequently, decisions must be coordinated with several groups before being finalized. In large organizations, decision making is inherently a group process, and a DSS can be designed to facilitate group decision making. Section 12.2 deals with this issue.

COMPONENTS OF DSS

Figure 12-1 illustrates the components of a DSS. They include a database of data used for query and analysis; a software system with models, datamining, and other analytical tools; and a user interface.

The **DSS database** is a collection of current or historical data from a number of applications or groups. It may be a small database residing on a PC that contains a subset of corporate data that has been downloaded and possibly combined with external data. Alternatively, the DSS database may be a massive data warehouse that is continuously updated by major organizational TPS. The data in DSS databases are generally extracts or copies of production databases so that using the DSS does not interfere with critical operational systems.

The **DSS software system** contains the software tools that are used for data analysis. It may contain various OLAP tools, datamining tools, or a collection of mathematical and analytical models that easily can be made accessible to the DSS user. A **model** is an abstract

DSS database A collection of current or historical data from a number of applications or groups. Can be a small PC database or a massive data warehouse.

DSS software system Collection of software tools that are used for data analysis, such as OLAP tools, datamining tools, or a collection of mathematical and analytical models.

model An abstract representation that illustrates the components or relationships of a phenomenon.

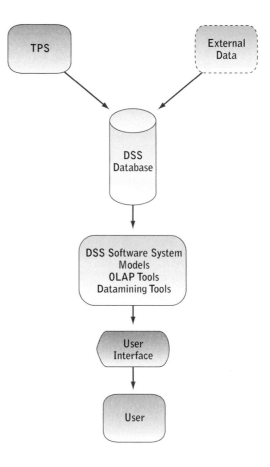

FIGURE 12-1 Overview of a decision-support system (DSS). The main components of the DSS are the DSS database, the DSS software system, and the user interface. The DSS database may be a small database residing on a PC or a massive data warehouse.

representation that illustrates the components or relationships of a phenomenon. A model can be a physical model (such as a model airplane), a mathematical model (such as an equation), or a verbal model (such as a description of a procedure for writing an order). Each decision-support system is built for a specific set of purposes and will make different collections of models available depending on those purposes.

Perhaps the most common models are libraries of statistical models. Such libraries usually contain the full range of expected statistical functions including means, medians, deviations, and scatter plots. The software has the ability to project future outcomes by analyzing a series of data. Statistical modeling software can be used to help establish relationships, such as relating product sales to differences in age, income, or other factors between communities. Optimization models, often using linear programming, determine optimal resource allocation to maximize or minimize specified variables such as cost or time. A classic use of optimization models is to determine the proper mix of products within a given market to maximize profits.

Forecasting models often are used to forecast sales. The user of this type of model might supply a range of historical data to project future conditions and the sales that might result from those conditions. The decision maker could vary those future conditions (entering, for example, a rise in raw materials costs or the entry of a new, low-priced competitor in the market) to determine how these new conditions might affect sales. Companies often use this software to predict the actions of competitors. Model libraries exist for specific functions, such as financial and risk analysis models.

Among the most widely used models are **sensitivity analysis** models that ask "what-if" questions repeatedly to determine the impact of changes in one or more factors on outcomes. "What-if" analysis—working forward from known or assumed conditions—allows the user to vary certain values to test results in order to better predict outcomes if changes occur in those values. "What happens if" we raise the price by 5 percent or increase the advertising budget by $100,000? What happens if we keep the price and advertising budget the same? Desktop spreadsheet software, such as Microsoft Excel or Lotus 1-2-3, often is used for this purpose

sensitivity analysis Models that ask "what-if" questions repeatedly to determine the impact of changes in one or more factors on outcomes.

FIGURE 12-2 Sensitivity analysis. This table displays the results of a sensitivity analysis of the effect of changing the sales price of a necktie and the cost per unit on the product's breakeven point. It answers the question "What happens to the breakeven point if the sales price and the cost to make each unit increase or decrease?"

Total fixed costs	19000
Variable cost per unit	3
Average sales price	17
Contribution margin	14
Breakeven point	1357

		Variable Cost per Unit				
Sales	1357	2	3	4	5	6
Price	14	1583	1727	1900	2111	2375
	15	1462	1583	1727	1900	2111
	16	1357	1462	1583	1727	1900
	17	1267	1357	1462	1583	1727
	18	1188	1267	1357	1462	1583

(see Figure 12-2). Backward sensitivity analysis software is used for goal seeking: If I want to sell one million product units next year, how much must I reduce the price of the product?

The DSS user interface permits easy interaction between users of the system and the DSS software tools. A graphic, easy-to-use, flexible user interface supports the dialogue between the user and the DSS. The DSS users are usually corporate executives or managers, persons with well-developed working styles and individual preferences. They may have little or no computer experience and no patience for learning to use a complex tool, so the interface must be relatively intuitive. In addition, what works for one may not work for another. Many executives, offered only one way of working (a way not to their liking), simply will not use the system. To mimic a typical way of working, a good user interface should allow the manager to move back and forth between activities at will. Building successful DSS requires a high level of user participation and, often, the use of prototyping to ensure these requirements are met.

EXAMPLES OF DSS APPLICATIONS

There are many ways in which DSS can be used to support decision making. Table 12.2 lists examples of DSS in well-known organizations. To illustrate the range of capabilities of a DSS, we describe some successful DSS applications. Pioneer Natural Resources' business simulation system, the Ontario Ministry of Natural Resources forest fire management systems (described in the chapter opening vignette), and the San Miguel Corporation's logistics management system (described in the Window on Organizations) are examples of model-driven DSS. Farmers Insurance Group and KeyCorp are examples of data-driven DSS. We also examine

Table 12-2 **Examples of Decision-Support Systems**

Organization	DSS Application
American Airlines	Price and route selection
Equico Capital Corporation	Investment evaluation
General Accident Insurance	Customer buying patterns and fraud detection
Bank of America	Customer profiles
Frito-Lay, Inc.	Price, advertising, and promotion selection
Burlington Coat Factory	Store location and inventory mix
National Gypsum	Corporate planning and forecasting
Southern Railway	Train dispatching and routing
Texas Oil and Gas Corporation	Evaluation of potential drilling sites
United Airlines	Flight scheduling, passenger demand forecasting
U.S. Department of Defense	Defense contract analysis

MAKING A CAPITAL BUDGETING DECISION

Your firm, Wilmington Tool and Die Corporation, is considering purchasing four new CAD workstations for a total of $220,000 to improve productivity by translating designs for new dies more efficiently into finished products with fewer defects. You believe that this investment would increase the firm's after-tax income by $60,000 per year over a five-year period by reducing production costs. At the end of five years, the equipment would be replaced. Management believes the workstations would have no salvage value because their technology becomes quickly outdated. (The amount the firm would recover when it sells the used equipment is called the salvage value of the equipment.)

You would like to evaluate this expenditure to see if it is a good investment. To be considered worthwhile a capital expenditure must produce at least the same rate of return on the money invested as if the amount of the investment were invested somewhere else, such as at a bank, at a certain rate of interest specified by the firm.

Review the discussion of capital budgeting methods for information system investments in Chapter 9. The following spreadsheet shows the results of using the net present value method for Wilmington's investment in the new CAD equipment. The total cash flow is the sum of the additional income produced by the investment plus any salvage value of the equipment.

To arrive at the return from the investment in today's dollars, one must first calculate the present value of the total cash flow from this new equipment discounted at the prevailing interest rate for borrowing money. The initial purchase price of the equipment in today's dollars is then subtracted from the present value of the total cash flow from the investment to arrive at the net present value of the investment. If the net present value for the investment is positive, it is a worthwhile investment. If it is negative, the investment should be rejected.

The following spreadsheet shows the results of your calculations assuming that interest rates are 8% and that the investment is producing $60,000 each year in additional income for the firm. Since investments are highly sensitive to changes in interest rates and economic conditions, you have added a sensitivity analysis to see whether the equipment makes a good investment under a wide range of situations. The data table shows the impact on net present value if the interest rate and the annual income from using the new equipment are lower or higher than the original assumptions.

1. Should the company make this investment or should it be rejected? Explain your answer.

2. What other actions can management take to ensure a positive return on the investment?

Assumptions

Interest rate	8.0%
Salvage value	0
Annual additional income	60,000

Wilmington Tool & Die Company Capital Budgeting Analysis

	2000	2001	2002	2003	2004
Annual additional income	60,000	60,000	60,000	60,000	60,000
Salvage value					0
Annual cash flow	60,000	60,000	60,000	60,000	60,000
Total cash flow	300,000				
Present value	239,563				
Cost of investment	220,000				
Net present value	19,563				

			Interest rates		
19563	6.0%	7.0%	8.0%	9.0%	10.0%
40000	(51,505)	(55,992)	(60,292)	(64,414)	(68,369)
45000	(30,444)	(35,491)	(40,328)	(44,966)	(49,415)
50000	(9,382)	(14,990)	(20,364)	(25,517)	(30,461)
55000	11,680	5,511	(401)	(6,069)	(11,507)
Annual additional income 60000	32,742	26,012	19,563	13,379	7,447
65000	53,804	46,513	39,526	32,827	26,401
70000	74,865	67,014	59,490	52,276	45,355

some applications of geographic information systems (GIS), a special category of DSS for visualizing data geographically.

Pioneer Natural Resources

In the oil and gas industry, there are many variables associated with running an energy company, including development and production costs and the ratio of gas and oil in a field. The number and complex relationship among these variables makes it difficult for managers to determine the cost-effectiveness of their business decisions. Pioneer Natural Resources (PNR) in Las Colinas, Texas, decided to create a DSS that could provide more precise information for those decisions.

In 1995, PNR executives started identifying all of the management variables and diagrammed all of the business processes in their company to create a model that could show the impact on the business when one or more of those variables changed. The company built a prototype DSS using Powersim, a simulation development tool from Powersim Corporation in Herndon, Virginia. PNR executives first tested the prototype to simulate PNR's volatile Gulf Coast division, which had very long production timelines.

The company primarily uses Powersim to create a model for scenario planning and "what-if" analyses. For example, by modeling different scenarios with Powersim, PNR management can determine how much more to pay a service company to put a well into production earlier yet still earn a profit. Powersim runs on a Windows-based PC and uses Microsoft Excel spreadsheet software and Access database software for the input and output of business variables.

The company believes that each of its 5 divisions could potentially raise revenues by 25 to 40 percent using Powersim to model scenarios and adjust business variables. In addition, the simulation technology provides management with more control by helping managers determine the specific actions necessary to arrive at a desired business result or model the result of each business decision under consideration (Baldwin, 1998).

The Window on Organizations describes a series of model-driven DSS for supply chain management.

Farmers Insurance Group

Farmers Insurance Group, a Los Angeles-based provider of automobile and homeowner insurance in 38 states, wanted to analyze customer information to develop more competitive rates. When the company used IBM's Decision-Edge software to mine data related to sports car owners, it found that a large group of sports car owners are between 30 and 50 years of age, married, own two cars, and do not have a high risk of accidents. Farmers used these findings to adjust its premium rates. The company is trying to use datamining to identify a group of customers that have not yet been identified by its competitors so that it can attract them with a discount and gain a competitive edge (Davis, 1999).

KeyCorp

KeyCorp, the Cleveland-based retail bank, mines data on 3.3 million households and 7 million customers in its data warehouse to find ways of marketing to customers more effectively and to discover cross-selling opportunities. KeyCorp uses IBM's Decision-Edge for Relationship Marketing and for Finance running on an IBM system 390 mainframe and Exchange Application's VALEX software for selecting customers for direct-mail marketing campaigns. Using the information provided by its data-driven DSS to select direct-mail candidates, KeyCorp increased its direct-mail response rates from an average of 1 or 2 percent to a rate of between 5 and 10 percent. The system also showed that nine of the bank's offerings were unprofitable. KeyCorp eliminated these products, simplifying the selling process and improving profits. KeyCorp also uses its data on 7 million customers for one-to-one marketing and is evaluating datamining tools to profile customers for cross-selling, loyalty, retention, and acquisition programs (McCune, 1999).

Geographic Information Systems (GIS)

Geographic information systems (GIS) are a special category of DSS that can analyze and display data for planning and decision making using digitized maps. The software can assemble, store, manipulate, and display geographically referenced information, tying data to points,

geographic information systems (GIS) Systems with software that can analyze and display data using digitized maps to enhance planning and decision making.

DSS HELP MANAGE SAN MIGUEL CORPORATION'S SUPPLY CHAIN

Logistics plays a vital role in the operations of the San Miguel Corporation (SMC), which distributes more than 300 products such as beer, liquor, mineral waters, dairy products, and feedgrains to every corner of the Philippine archipelago. Because of the complexity and difficulty of delivering goods in the Philippines, distribution costs represent a large component of total product costs. SMC's profitability depends on proper management of its logistics function.

SMC purchases and stores raw materials, which are then processed and stored with other finished products in numerous facilities and vehicles until final delivery to the customer. San Miguel Philippines alone uses 50 seacraft and more than 300 tractor trailers to move cases of beer from its breweries to 140 sales offices. Hundreds of route trucks then deliver this beer to supermarkets, grocery stores, and other beer outlets. San Miguel has built a series of DSS to efficiently manage this supply chain for beer and other products.

Raw material accounts for about 10 percent of SMC's total assets. DSS help the company reduce the amount of money tied up in inventory by finding the optimum safety stock for malt, hops, chemicals, dairy, and cheese curd. If inventory levels are too low, the amount of "safety stock" a company needs to avoid running out may be insufficient. If inventory levels are too high, the company will spend more than it needs to purchase and warehouse stock. The DSS balances ordering, carrying, and stock-out costs while considering delivery frequency constraints and minimum order quantity. The DSS called for maintaining a safety stock for items such as malts, hops, and chemicals, which have low expediting costs and high unit costs, that was lower than San Miguel's original target of 60 days, saving the company $180,000 in 1 year.

SMC uses a Production Load Allocation System to determine the quantity of products to produce for each bottling line and period and how bottling line production output should be assigned to warehouses. San Miguel assigns warehouses to serve specific bottling plants and sales territories. However, during peak months of sales, the company must transfer finished goods across organizational boundaries to counter imbalances in capacity and demand. The DSS generates optimal production allocation plans based on either minimizing cost or maximizing profit. San Miguel's finished beer products are transported from 3 plants to 14 warehouses and distributed to retailers using about 200 route trucks. The company uses three different types of distribution routes: conventional routes, distributors, and presell/delivery routes. Because the company does not know what level of sales for each customer to anticipate for conventional routes, its trucks may return almost full after they have completed their routes or they may have to return to the warehouse in a few hours for another pickup. Distributors, however, pick up the products directly from the warehouses in exchange for discounted prices, and they often do this in territories covered by conventional delivery routes. In presell delivery routes, sales are conducted separately from actual deliveries. Account specialists called presellers sell the products and third party logistics providers deliver the goods on a per case basis. San Miguel used a DSS to help it move more of its delivery business to presell delivery routes and reduce conventional deliveries. The DSS was able to provide management with information on how to divide the area into territories, the number of presell account specialists and delivery teams to meet customer requirements, and how to assign SMC's current distributors to areas where they could maintain their current incomes. A pilot run of the project indicated that San Miguel could reduce the number of routes serving sales districts in metro Manila alone by 43 percent.

TO THINK ABOUT: How can using the DSS described here promote San Miguel's business strategy? How did these DSS change the way San Miguel ran its business?

Sources: Elise del Rosario, "Logistical Nightmare," OR/MS Today, April 1999; and David Orenstein, "Business Quick Study: Inventory Allocation," Computerworld, November 8, 1999.

---

lines, and areas on a map. GIS thus can be used to support decisions that require knowledge about the geographic distribution of people or other resources in scientific research, resource management, and development planning. For example, GIS might be used to help state and local governments calculate emergency response times to natural disasters or to help banks identify the best locations for installing new branches or ATM terminals. GIS tools have become affordable even for small businesses and some can be used on the Web.

GIS have modeling capabilities that allow managers to change data and automatically revise business scenarios to find better solutions. Johanna Dairies of Union, New Jersey, used GIS software to display its customers on a map and then design efficient delivery routes that saved the company $100,000 annually for each route that was eliminated. Sonny's Bar-B-Q, the Gainesville, Florida-based restaurant chain, used GIS with federal and local census data on median age, household income, total population, and population distribution to help manage-

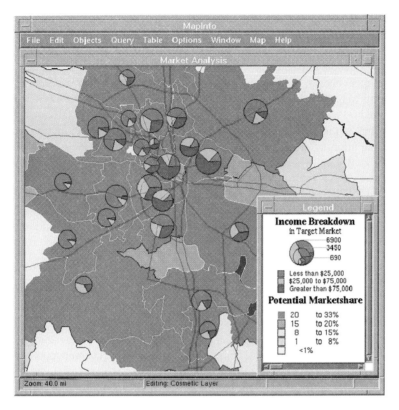

Geographic information systems (GIS) software presents and analyzes data geographically, tying business data to points, lines, and areas on a map. This map can help decision makers with market analysis, using pie charts and color variation of territories to display potential market share and income breakdown in the target market.

ment decide where to open new restaurants. The company's growth plan specifies that it will only expand into regions where barbecue food is very popular and where the number of barbecue restaurants is very small. Sonny's restaurants must be at least seven miles away from each other. Quaker Oats has used GIS to display and analyze sales and customer data by store locations. This information helps the company determine the best product mix for each retail store that carries Quaker Oats products and design advertising campaigns targeted specifically to each store's customers.

WEB-BASED DSS

DSS based on the Web and the Internet are being developed to support decision making, providing on-line access to various databases and information pools along with software for data analysis. Some of these DSS are targeted toward management, but some have been developed to attract customers by providing information and tools to assist their decision making as they select products and services. Companies are finding that deciding which products and services to purchase has become increasingly information intensive. People use more information from

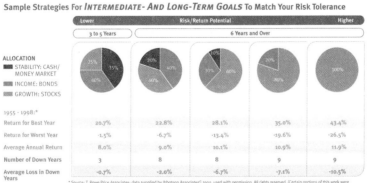

The T. Rowe Price Web site features a series of online tools to help visitors make decisions about retirement planning options. DSS based on the Web can provide information from multiple sources and analytical tools to help potential customers select products and services.

customer decision-support
system (CDSS) System to support the decision-making process of
an existing or potential customer.

multiple sources to make purchasing decisions (such as purchasing a car or computer) before they interact with the product or sales staff. **Customer decision-support systems (CDSS)** support the decision-making process of an existing or potential customer.

People interested in purchasing a product or service can use Internet search engines, intelligent agents, on-line catalogs, Web directories, newsgroup discussions, e-mail, and other tools to help them locate the information they need to help make their decision. Information brokers, such as Travelocity, described in Chapter 8, are additional sources of summarized, structured information for specific products or industries and may provide models for evaluating information. Companies also have developed specific customer Web sites where all the information, models, or other analytical tools for evaluating alternatives are concentrated in one location. Table 12.3 lists some examples.

Web-based DSS have become especially popular in the financial services area because so many people are trying to manage their own assets and retirement savings. The Window on Technology illustrates some of the new Web-based DSS for providing financial advice on retirement planning to individual investors.

12.2 Group Decision-Support Systems (GDSS)

Early DSS focused largely on supporting individual decision making. However, because so much work is accomplished in groups within organizations, system developers and scholars began to focus on how computers can support group and organizational decision making. A new category of systems developed known as group decision-support systems (GDSS).

WHAT IS A GDSS?

group decision-support
system (GDSS) An interactive,
computer-based system that facilitates solutions to unstructured
problems by a set of decision makers working together as a group.

A **group decision-support system (GDSS)** is an interactive, computer-based system that facilitates solutions to unstructured problems by a set of decision makers working together as a group (DeSanctis and Gallupe, 1987).

Groupware and Web-based tools for videoconferencing and electronic meetings described earlier in this text can support some group decision processes, but their focus is primarily on communication. This section focuses on the tools and technologies geared explicitly toward group decision making. GDSS were developed in response to a growing concern over the quality and effectiveness of meetings. The underlying problems in group decision making have been the explosion of decision-maker meetings, the growing length of those

Table 12-3 Web-Based DSS

DSS	Description
General Electric Plastics	Web site provides a searchable repository of product-specification information that can be updated weekly. Visitors can use on-line continuous-simulation models that automatically generate graphs and diagrams in response to customer inputs. (For example, a simulation model might show how a particular plastic would behave at very high temperatures.) An e-mail capability allows visitors to forward technical questions to engineers, who then contact the visitor.
Fidelity Investments	Web site features an on-line, interactive decision-support application to help clients make decisions about investment savings plans and investment portfolio allocations. The application allows visitors to experiment with numerous "what-if" scenarios to design investment savings plans for retirement or a child's college education. If the user enters information about his or her finances, time horizon, and tolerance for risk, the system will suggest appropriate portfolios of mutual funds. The application performs the required number-crunching and displays the changing return on investment as the user alters these assumptions.
Pedestal Capital	Bond Network Web site provides data on potential investments and financial models that visitors can use to evaluate alternative investments in mortgage portfolios. It features analytical software tools that can perform in a few minutes a number of tasks that often take hours with a spreadsheet. For instance, if a potential buyer wants to determine the level of prepayments that can be expected of a portfolio, he or she goes to the Web, accesses Bond Network, and clicks on one of the displayed menu options. The numbers are analyzed and the answer appears in a few seconds.

RETIREMENT PLANNING GOES ON-LINE

The growing popularity of 401k plans has put millions of Americans in charge of their own assets for retirement. (A 401k plan allows employees to use a percentage of their wages to make pretax contributions to a retirement plan, thereby reducing their taxable wages. Employers can match some or all employee contributions.) Yet less than 20 percent of the 38 million individuals with 401k plans consult with professional investment advisers. The result is that many people are looking for affordable advice. A number of Web-based companies have been created to roll out low-cost advice on-line.

Employers who sponsor 401k programs contract with plan providers, such as Fidelity Investments, the Vanguard Group, State Street, and Merrill Lynch, to manage employees' funds and to provide them with investment education. These plan providers run seminars for employees, distribute literature on investments, and are starting to provide advice on the Web.

When people first visit a Web-based advice service, they fill out a questionnaire concerning their expected income potential, other investments, expected retirement age, expected retirement income, and tolerance for risk. The data they provide on-line are combined with data provided by their employer, such as their current 401k investments, income, and 401k plan contribution amount per paycheck. The Web site software then matches the employee with an appropriate portfolio. The system might recommend a high-risk growth portfolio to a 25-year-old programmer and a conservative one to a 57-year-old office manager. The on-line service can also tell the individual whether he or she is on track to meet retirement goals. If not, the system will recommend strategies to compensate, such as working longer, saving more, or moving into a riskier portfolio. The user inputs the changes each time the "what-if" analysis needs to be repeated. No two on-line retirement calculators are likely to produce identical results because of differences in the type, complexity, and the number of questions each calculator asks and the underlying assumptions used in their calculation formulas.

The investment advice provided by these services is generally based on information supplied by human financial analysts. The service offered by Financial Engines is considered radically different because it uses an automated advice system called Advisor that is powered by forecasting models. Advisor uses a complex series of mathematical software models based on the inner workings of financial markets and a database of the historical returns of more than 15,500 securities. Advisor uses simulation technology to compute the probable long-term value of an investment portfolio, taking into account inflation, fluctuations in interest rates, equity returns, and dividends. Instead of making investment recommendations, Advisor shows users the likely outcomes of investment decisions, including which investments are most likely to meet their goals. After an individual inputs personal data into the system, Advisor runs that person's 401k investments through tens of thousands of possible economic scenarios and calculates the probability that the individual's portfolio will meet his or her retirement goals. Advisor also shows the maximum amount of money that the individual could expect to lose during the next 12 months. After completing its forecast, Advisor computes an optimal portfolio of funds that is most likely to meet the plan participant's goals for a specified degree of risk. If the individual is dissatisfied with the results, risk level, savings rate, retirement age, or financial goal can be adjusted to see how chances improve. The system displays probabilities graphically using a simple weather icon. As an economic forecast improves, clouds are gradually replaced by sun. Financial Engines offers its service directly to employers and also to 401k plan providers such as Merrill Lynch and Hewitt Associates.

TO THINK ABOUT: What kind of DSS are described here? How can using such DSS benefit businesses as well as individuals? What are the disadvantages of using these services for retirement planning?

Sources: Bridget O'Brian, "Calculating Retirement? It's No Simple Equation," *The Wall Street Journal*, February 7, 2000; Michael Menduno, "Retirement Plans Go Online," *The Industry Standard*, August 2–9, 1999; and Mara DER Hovanesian "Online Advice Draws Quality Concerns," *The Wall Street Journal*, January 31, 2000.

---

meetings, and the increased number of attendees. Estimates on the amount of a manager's time spent in meetings range from 35 to 70 percent.

Meeting facilitators, organizational development professionals, and information systems scholars have been focusing on this issue and have identified a number of discrete meeting elements that need to be addressed (Grobowski et al., 1990; Kraemer and King, 1988; Nunamaker et al., 1991). Among these elements are the following:

1. *Improved preplanning,* to make meetings more effective and efficient.

2. *Increased participation,* so that all attendees will be able to contribute fully even if the number of attendees is large. Free riding (attending the meeting but not contributing) must also be addressed.

3. *Open, collaborative meeting atmosphere,* in which attendees from various organizational levels feel able to contribute freely. The lower level attendees must be able to participate without fear of being judged by their management; higher status participants must be able to participate without having their presence or ideas dominate the meeting and result in unwanted conformity.

4. *Criticism-free idea generation,* enabling attendees to contribute without undue fear of feeling personally criticized.

5. *Evaluation objectivity,* creating an atmosphere in which an idea will be evaluated on its merits rather than on the basis of the source of the idea.

6. *Idea organization and evaluation,* which require keeping the focus on the meeting objectives, finding efficient ways to organize the many ideas that can be generated in a brainstorming session, and evaluating those ideas not only on their merits but also within appropriate time constraints.

7. *Setting priorities and making decisions,* which require finding ways to encompass the thinking of all the attendees in making these judgments.

8. *Documentation of meetings,* so that attendees will have as complete and organized a record of the meeting as may be needed to continue the work of the project.

9. *Access to external information,* which will allow significant, factual disagreements to be settled in a timely fashion, thus enabling the meeting to continue productively.

10. *Preservation of "organizational memory,"* so that those who do not attend the meeting can also work on the project. **Organizational memory** is the stored information from an organization's history that can be used for decision making and other purposes. Often a project will include teams at different locations who will need to understand the content of a meeting at only one of the affected sites.

organizational memory
Stored information from an organization's history.

One response to the problems of group decision making has been the adoption of new methods of organizing and running meetings. Techniques such as facilitated meetings, brainstorming, and criticism-free idea generation have become popular and are now accepted as standards. Another response has been the application of technology to the problems resulting in the emergence of group decision-support systems.

CHARACTERISTICS OF GDSS

How can information technology help groups arrive at decisions? Scholars have identified at least three basic elements of a GDSS: hardware, software tools, and people. *Hardware* refers to the conference facility itself, including the room, the tables, and the chairs. Such a facility must be physically laid out in a manner that supports group collaboration. It also must include some electronic hardware, such as electronic display boards, as well as audiovisual, computer, and networking equipment.

A wide range of *software tools,* including tools for organizing ideas, gathering information, ranking and setting priorities, and other aspects of collaborative work are being used to support decision-making meetings. We describe these tools in the next section. *People* refers not only to the participants but also to a trained facilitator and often to a staff that supports the hardware and software. Together these elements have led to the creation of a range of different kinds of GDSS, from simple electronic boardrooms to elaborate collaboration laboratories. In a collaboration laboratory, individuals work on their own desktop PCs or workstations. Their input is integrated on a file server and is viewable on a common screen at the front of the room; in most systems the integrated input is also viewable on the individual participant's screen. See Figure 12-3 for an illustration of an actual GDSS collaborative meeting room.

GDSS SOFTWARE TOOLS

Some features of groupware tools for collaborative work described in Chapters 5 and 11 can be used to support group decision making. There also are specific GDSS software tools for supporting group meetings. These tools were originally developed for meetings in which all participants are in the same room, but they also can be used for networked meetings in which participants are in different locations. Specific GDSS software tools include the following:

FIGURE 12-3 Illustration of the Gjensidige Insurance collaborative meeting room. There is one microphone for every two seats and a speaker system on the wall. This equipment is used for same-time meetings between Gjensidige's offices in Oslo and Trondheim.
Source: © 1996–1997. All rights reserved. Ventana Corporation.

○ *Electronic questionnaires* aid the organizers in premeeting planning by identifying issues of concern and by helping to ensure that key planning information is not overlooked.

○ *Electronic brainstorming tools* allow individuals simultaneously and anonymously to contribute ideas on the topics of the meeting.

○ *Idea organizers* facilitate the organized integration and synthesis of ideas generated during brainstorming.

○ *Questionnaire tools* support the facilitators and group leaders as they gather information before and during the process of setting priorities.

○ *Tools for voting or setting priorities* make available a range of methods from simple voting, to ranking in order, to a range of weighted techniques for setting priorities or voting (see Figure 12-4).

○ *Stakeholder identification and analysis tools* use structured approaches to evaluate the impact of an emerging proposal on the organization and to identify stakeholders and evaluate the potential impact of those stakeholders on the proposed project.

○ *Policy formation tools* provide structured support for developing agreement on the wording of policy statements.

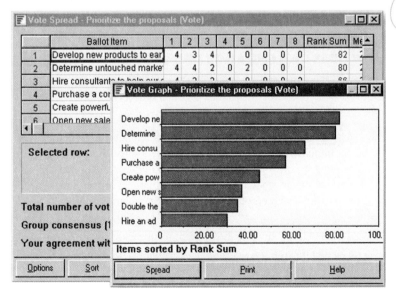

FIGURE 12-4 GDSS software tools. The Ventana Corporation's Group Systems electronic meeting software helps people create, share, record, organize, and evaluate ideas in meetings, between offices, or around the world.

○ *Group dictionaries* document group agreement on definitions of words and terms central to the project.

Additional tools are available, such as group outlining and writing tools, software that stores and reads project files, and software that allows the attendees to view internal operational data stored by the organization's production computer systems.

Overview of a GDSS Meeting

electronic meeting system (EMS) A collaborative GDSS that uses information technology to make group meetings more productive by facilitating communication as well as decision making. Supports meetings at the same place and time or at different places and times.

An **electronic meeting system (EMS)** is a type of collaborative GDSS that uses information technology to make group meetings more productive by facilitating communication as well as decision making. It supports any activity in which people come together, whether at the same place at the same time or in different places at different times (Dennis et al., 1988; Nunamaker et al., 1991). IBM has a number of EMSs installed at various sites. Each attendee has a workstation. The workstations are networked and are connected to the facilitator's console, which serves as both the facilitator's workstation and control panel and the meeting's file server. All data that the attendees forward from their workstations to the group are collected and saved on the file server. The facilitator is able to project computer images onto the projection screen at the front of the room. The facilitator also has an overhead projector available. Whiteboards are visible on either side of the projection screen. Many electronic meeting rooms are arranged in a semicircle and are tiered in legislative style to accommodate a large number of attendees.

The facilitator controls the use of tools during the meeting, often selecting from a large tool box that is part of the organization's GDSS. Tool selection is part of the premeeting planning process. Which tools are selected depends on the subject matter, the goals of the meeting, and the facilitation methodology the facilitator will use.

Attendees have full control of their own desktop computers. An attendee is able to view the agenda (and other planning documents), look at the integrated screen (or screens as the session progresses), use ordinary desktop PC tools (such as a word processor or a spreadsheet), tap into available production data, or work on the screen associated with the current meeting step and tool (such as a brainstorming screen). However, no one can view anyone else's screens so participants' work is confidential until it is released to the file server for integration with the work of others. All input to the file server is anonymous. At each step everyone's input to the file server (brainstorming ideas, idea evaluation and criticism, comments, voting, etc.) can be seen by all attendees on the integrated screens, but no information is available to identify the source of specific inputs. Attendees enter their data simultaneously rather than in round-robin fashion as is done in meetings that have little or no electronic systems support.

Figure 12-5 shows the sequence of activities at a typical EMS meeting. For each activity it also indicates the type of tools used and the output of those tools. During the meeting all input to the integrated screens is saved on the file server. As a result, when the meeting is completed, a full record of the meeting (both raw material and resultant output) is available to the attendees and can be made available to anyone else with a need for access.

HOW GDSS CAN ENHANCE GROUP DECISION MAKING

GDSS are being used more widely, so we are able to understand some of their benefits and evaluate some of the tools. We look again at how a GDSS affects the 10 group meeting issues raised earlier.

1. *Improved preplanning.* Electronic questionnaires, supplemented by word processors, outlining software, and other desktop PC software, can structure planning, thereby improving it. The availability of the planning information at the actual meeting also can serve to enhance the quality of the meeting. Experts seem to feel that these tools add significance and emphasis to meeting preplanning.

2. *Increased participation.* Studies show that in traditional decision-making meetings without GDSS support the optimal meeting size is three to five attendees. Beyond that size, the meeting process begins to break down. Using GDSS software, studies show the meeting size can increase while productivity also increases. One reason for this is that attendees contribute simultaneously rather than one at a time, which makes more

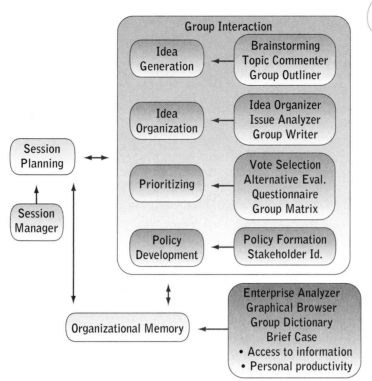

FIGURE 12-5 Group system tools. The sequence of activities and collaborative support tools used in an electronic meeting system (EMS) facilitates communication among attendees and generates a full record of the meeting. Source: From Nunamaker et al., "Electronic Meeting Systems to Support Group Work" in **Communications of the ACM,** July 1991. Reprinted by permission.

efficient use of the meeting time. Interviews of GDSS meeting attendees indicate that the quality of participation is higher than in traditional meetings.

3. *Open, collaborative meeting atmosphere.* A GDSS contributes to a collaborative atmosphere in several ways. First, anonymity of input is essentially guaranteed. Individuals need not fear being judged by their boss for contributing a possibly offbeat idea. Second, anonymity reduces or eliminates the deadening effect that often occurs when high-status individuals contribute. And third, the numbing pressures of social cues are reduced or eliminated.

4. *Criticism-free idea generation.* Anonymity ensures that attendees can contribute without fear of being criticized personally or of having their ideas rejected because of the identity of the contributor. Several studies show that interactive GDSS meetings generate more ideas and more satisfaction with those ideas than verbally interactive meetings (Nunamaker et al., 1991). GDSS can help reduce unproductive interpersonal conflict (Miranda and Bostrum, 1993–1994).

5. *Evaluation objectivity.* Anonymity prevents criticism of the source of ideas, thus supporting an atmosphere in which attendees focus on evaluating the ideas themselves. The same anonymity allows participants to detach from their own ideas so they are able to view them from a critical perspective. Evidence suggests that evaluation in an anonymous atmosphere increases the free flow of critical feedback and even stimulates the generation of new ideas during the evaluation process.

6. *Idea organization and evaluation.* GDSS software tools used for this purpose are structured and are based on methodology. They usually allow individuals to organize and then submit their results to the group (still anonymously). The group then iteratively modifies and develops the organized ideas until a document is completed. Attendees generally have viewed this approach as productive.

7. *Setting priorities and making decisions.* Anonymity helps lower level participants have their positions taken into consideration along with the higher level attendees.

8. *Documentation of meetings.* Evidence at IBM indicates that postmeeting use of the data is crucial. Attendees use the data to continue their dialogues after the meetings, to

discuss the ideas with those who did not attend, and even to make presentations (Grobowski et al., 1990). Some tools enable the user to zoom in to more details on specific information.

9. *Access to external information.* Often a great deal of meeting time is devoted to factual disagreements. More experience with GDSS will indicate whether GDSS technology reduces this problem.

10. *Preservation of "organizational memory."* Specific tools have been developed to facilitate access to the data generated during a GDSS meeting, allowing nonattendees to locate needed information after the meeting. The documentation of a meeting by one group at one site also has been used successfully as input to another meeting on the same project at another site. GDSS could be further enhanced to integrate meeting memory with other organizational memory and supply this information to other parts of the organization (Schwabe, 1999).

Studies to date suggest that GDSS meetings can be more productive, make more efficient use of time, and produce the desired results in fewer meetings, although these results are not dramatically better than face-to-face meetings. GDSS seem most useful for tasks involving idea generation, complex problems, and large groups (Fjermestad and Hiltz, 1998–1999). One problem with understanding the value of GDSS is their complexity. A GDSS can be configured in an almost infinite variety of ways. In addition, the effectiveness of the tools will partially depend the facilitator's effectiveness and role in the meeting (Miranda and Bostrom, 1999), the quality of the planning, the cooperation of the attendees, and the appropriateness of tools selected for different types of meetings. GDSS can enable groups to exchange more information, but they can't always help participants process the information effectively or reach better decisions (Dennis, 1996). Nor can group brainstorming, even using electronic means, produce consistently better results than working alone (Pinsonneault et al., 1999).

Researchers have noted that the design of an electronic meeting system and its technology is only one of a number of contingencies that affect the outcome of group meetings. Other factors, including the nature of the group, the task, the manner in which the problem is presented to the group, and the organizational context (including the organization's culture and environment) also affect the process of group meetings and meeting outcomes (Dennis et al., 1999; Fjermestad, 1998; Caouette and O'Connor, 1998; Dennis et al., 1988; Dennis, 1996; Nunamaker et al., 1991; Watson, Ho, and Raman, 1994). New types of group support systems with easy-to-use, Web-based interfaces and multimedia capabilities may provide additional benefits.

12.3 Executive Support Systems (ESS)

We have described how DSS and GDSS help managers make unstructured and semistructured decisions. **Executive support systems (ESS)** also help managers with unstructured problems; they focus on the information needs of senior management. Combining data from internal and external sources, ESS create a generalized computing and communications environment that can be focused and applied to a changing array of problems. ESS help senior executives monitor organizational performance, track activities of competitors, spot problems, identify opportunities, and forecast trends.

THE ROLE OF ESS IN THE ORGANIZATION

Before ESS, it was common for executives to receive numerous fixed-format reports, often hundreds of pages every month (or even every week). By the late 1980s, analysts found ways to bring together data from throughout the organization and allow the manager to select, access, and tailor them easily as needed. Today, an ESS is apt to include a range of easy-to-use desktop analytical tools and on-line data displays. Use of the systems has migrated down several organizational levels so that the executive and any subordinates are able to look at the same data in the same way.

Today's systems try to avoid the problem of data overload so common in paper reports because the data can be filtered or viewed in graphic format (if the user so chooses). ESS sys-

executive support system (ESS) Information system at the strategic level of an organization designed to address unstructured decision making through advanced graphics and communications.

Window on Management

GATHERING BUSINESS INTELLIGENCE: HOW USEFUL IS THE INTERNET?

The software industry continues to provide new products to help gather and manage information, products that can be vital to the success of business organizations. Millipore Corp., the $700 million manufacturer of purification systems headquartered in Bedford, Massachusetts, has 13 plants and 31 offices around the world. To give its executives convenient access to information, the company has built an "executive dashboard," which is modeled on such popular Web portals as Yahoo! and Lycos. The dashboard runs on the company intranet and gives managers a personalized home page that is a single entry point to internal and external business data. However, managers must never forget that software cannot make decisions for them. Moreover the computer cannot be the sole source of information management uses in making decisions. Many executives balance the use of computer technology with personal contacts in gathering needed business intelligence.

Don Middleberg, who heads his own New York City public relations firm, Middleberg Associates Inc., says "being on-line and looking at sites takes at least 15 hours a week just for my own education." He also finds e-mail valuable, particularly messages from his staff informing him of articles he should read or new Web sites to visit. Yet, he says, "despite all the high tech available, I most value personal relationships. There's no substitute for friends and contacts in the business for industry scuttlebutt."

Lee M. Kennedy, international operations business planner for St. Paul, Minnesota's 3M Corp., is another executive who relies on many sources for his information. In 1996, when 3M wanted to establish a Romanian corporation, he felt he had to see conditions in the country himself. While he was there, he participated in a wide range of talks, including meeting with American commerce officials and with Romania's ambassador to the United States. As a skilled surfer, Kennedy also relies on the Internet, regularly "visiting" countries where 3M is considering expansion. Kennedy reads a great deal, and the Net is his source for a number of publications including London's **Financial Times** and economic information from the Central Intelligence Agency. He also subscribes to the **International Herald Tribune** on the Net, which he claims is "probably the closest thing I know to a global newspaper."

Even Mark Adams, the CEO of Web-based Intralinks Inc., mixes the sources of his business intelligence. Intralinks provides deal-management services for global capital markets, and Adams uses the Net to gather a lot of information. "We have access to American Banker Online," which "keeps us up on industry news," he says. Moreover, he subscribes to their alert service, which gives him rapid notification of relevant developments. He subscribes to **The Wall Street Journal** and **The New York Times** on the Net to keep updated on potential mergers. Nonetheless, Adams spends 25 to 30 percent of his day talking to clients, and those talks are the source of much of the most critical information he needs. "There's nothing better than talking to [clients such as] Bill Hartmann, a director at Citibank, to see how the market is going, how the merger is going, and how it will affect our business."

TO THINK ABOUT: What are the advantages of gathering needed business information via the Internet rather than in person? In turn, what are the advantages of gathering it in person?

Sources: Gary Abramson, "The Thrill of the Hunt," **CIO Enterprise Magazine**, January 14, 1999; and Philip J. Gill, "Cost Drivers," **Profit Magazine**, August 1999.

---

tems have the ability to **drill down,** moving from a piece of summary data to lower and lower levels of detail. The ability to drill down is useful not only to senior executives but to employees at lower levels of the organization who need to analyze data. OLAP tools for analyzing large databases provide this capability.

> **drill down** The ability to move from summary data down to lower and lower levels of detail.

One limitation in an ESS is that it uses data from systems designed for very different purposes. Often data that are critical to the senior executive are simply not there. For example, sales data coming from an order-entry transaction processing system may not be linked to marketing information, a linkage the executive would find useful. External data now are much more available in many ESS systems. Executives need a wide range of external data, from current stock market news to competitor information, industry trends, and even projected legislative action. Through their ESS, many managers have access to news services, financial market databases, economic information, and whatever other public data they may require. Managers can also use the Internet for this purpose. The Window on Management looks at the role of information from the Internet and computerized systems in management decision making.

ESS today include tools for modeling and analysis. For example, many ESS use Excel or other spreadsheets as the heart of their analytical tool base. With only a minimum of experience, most managers find they can use these common software packages to create graphic comparisons of data by time, region, product, price range, and so on. Costlier systems include more sophisticated specialty analytical software. (Whereas DSS use such tools primarily for modeling and analysis in a fairly narrow range of decision situations, ESS use them primarily to provide status information about organizational performance.) Some ESS are being developed for use with the Web, such as Millipore's executive dashboard described in the Window on Management.

DEVELOPING ESS

ESS are executive systems, and executives create special systems development problems (we introduced this topic in Chapter 3). Because executives' needs change so rapidly, most executive support systems are developed through prototyping. A major difficulty for developers is that high-level executives expect success the first time. Developers must be certain that the system will work before they demonstrate it to the user. In addition, the initial system prototype must be one that the executive can learn very rapidly. Finally, if executives find that the ESS offers no added value, they will reject it.

One area that merits special attention is the determination of executive information requirements. ESS need to have some facility for environmental scanning. A key information requirement of managers at the strategic level is the capability to detect signals of problems in the organizational environment that indicate strategic threats and opportunities (Walls et al., 1992). The ESS needs to be designed so that both external and internal sources of information can be used for environmental scanning purposes. The critical success factor methodology for determining information requirements (see Chapter 9) is recommended for this purpose.

ESS potentially could give top executives the capability of examining other managers' work without their knowledge, so there may be some resistance to ESS at lower levels of the organization. Implementation of ESS should be carefully managed to neutralize such opposition (see Chapter 9).

Cost justification presents a different type of problem with an ESS. Because much of an executive's work is unstructured, how does one quantify benefits for a system that primarily supports such unstructured work? An ESS often is justified in advance by the intuitive feeling that it will pay for itself (Watson et al., 1991). If ESS benefits can ever be quantified, it is only after the system is operational.

BENEFITS OF ESS

How do executive support systems benefit managers? As we stated earlier, it is difficult at best to cost-justify an executive support system. Nonetheless, interest in these systems is growing, so it is essential to examine some of the potential benefits scholars have identified.

Much of the value of ESS is found in their flexibility. These systems put data and tools in the hands of executives without addressing specific problems or imposing solutions. Executives are free to shape the problems as necessary, using the system as an extension of their own thinking processes. These are not decision-making systems; they are tools to aid executives in making decisions.

The most visible benefit of ESS is their ability to analyze, compare, and highlight trends. The easy use of graphics allows the user to look at more data in less time with greater clarity and insight than paper-based systems can provide. In the past, executives obtained the same information by taking up days and weeks of their staffs' valuable time. By using ESS, those staffs and the executives themselves have more time available for the creative analysis and decision making in their jobs. ESS capabilities for drilling down and highlighting trends also may enhance the quality of such analysis and can speed up decision making (Leidner and Elam, 1993–1994).

Executives are using ESS to monitor performance more successfully in their own areas of responsibility. Some are using these systems to monitor key performance indicators. The timeliness and availability of the data result in needed actions being identified and taken earlier. Problems can be handled before they become too damaging; opportunities also can be identified earlier.

Executive support systems can and do change the workings of organizations. Immediate access to so much data allows executives to better monitor activities of lower units reporting

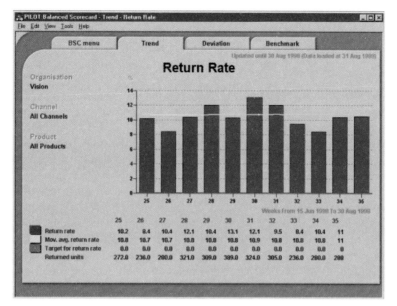

Pilot Software's Balanced Scorecard is a strategic enterprise-wide application that provides managers with a comprehensive picture of their business performance by analyzing key performance indicators for growth and success. The "big picture" view of the business which it provides can help executives improve internal business processes, increase efficiency, and achieve strategic and tactical objectives.

to them. That very monitoring ability often allows decision making to be decentralized and to take place at lower operating levels. Executives are often willing to push decision making further down into the organization as long as they can be assured that all is going well. ESS can enable them to get that assurance. A well-designed ESS could dramatically improve management performance and increase upper management's span of control.

EXAMPLES OF ESS

To illustrate the ways in which an ESS can enhance management decision making, we now describe three executive support systems, two for private industry and one for the public sector. These systems were developed for very different reasons and serve their organizations in different ways.

Sutter Home Winery: ESS for Business Intelligence

Unlike other businesses, Sutter Home Winery cannot analyze its sales data to determine consumer buying patterns. The Twenty-first Amendment to the U.S. Constitution ended Prohibition, but it also created laws forbidding producers of alcoholic beverages from selling directly to retailers. Because of this restriction, Sutter can only find out how much and what types of products its distributors sell, and such information is often a month old. Sutter needs more data about who buys its wines and who buys its competitors' wines. In order to comply with the law, this $200 million producer of wine and food products must collect customer information in other ways.

Sutter's management compensates by using information systems to combine internal sales data with business intelligence from external sources, including data from the Internet and point-of-sale data about consumer purchasing from market data-collection firms such as A. C. Nielsen or Information Resources. A variety of tools and technologies transform a motley collection of information into valuable insights that can be used to guide long-term planning and forecasting by senior management.

Sutter's salespeople, who work with distributors and retailers, provide information about what products are selling best and why, along with competitors' activities in pricing and promotional campaigns. They enter this information into a Lotus Notes database that can be accessed by sales managers and by management at corporate headquarters, including the company president. Occasionally, the company adds data from focus groups and market research, especially when it is launching a new product. The data are organized and analyzed using AS/400 and PC databases, spreadsheets, groupware, and OLAP decision-support tools such as Cognos' PowerPlay. Sutter executives use this information for short- and long-term sales forecasts, marketing campaigns, and capital investment plans.

Sutter has assigned an employee to monitor Web sites that are industry-specific or related to the company's products and distribute reports two or three times a week to winery staff and senior managers. Business intelligence from the Internet has proven a useful and timely source of industry news (Wreden, 1997).

Royal Bank of Canada

Royal Bank of Canada, headquartered in Toronto, is one of the 5 largest lending institutions in North America, with assets of more than $146 billion (U.S.). Its Risk Management division is responsible for analysis and control of the risk exposure of the bank's global credit portfolio. Its financial managers need information about the level of risk it is exposed to by clients, countries, or sectors. Obtaining this information used to be a cumbersome process, requiring programmers to create and run special batch reports on the mainframe that might take two days or more to produce.

Royal Bank used rapid application development tools from Information Builders to create a PC-based executive information system called the Portfolio Query System (PQS) that presents credit risk information directly to managers in a graphical format. The system uses data from Royal Bank's mainframe database but provides an intuitive interface with easy-to-use drill down, navigation, sorting, reporting, and printing capabilities.

PQS is widely used in many Royal Bank locations. Managers can view and analyze credit portfolio data using many different criteria, including market segment, line of business, management responsibility, assigned risk ratings, customer residency, and industry. The data can be presented as either graphical or tabular displays that allow for more than 15 criteria (Information Builders, 1998).

The U.S. General Services Administration

The General Services Administration (GSA) manages the vast real estate holdings of the U.S. government. In a period of tight federal budget restraints and as part of Vice President Al Gore's "reinventing government" initiatives, the organization needed to find ways to optimize the use of the government's multibillion-dollar inventory of 16,000 properties worldwide. Yet GSA managers facing this challenge had no system that would support them by making easily available to them the four gigabytes of data stored in their computers. The data were available only in old-fashioned printed reports and through slow, expensive custom programming. Analysis of the data was nearly impossible. GSA's response was GAMIS (Glenn Asset Management Information System), an executive support system based primarily on Lotus Notes that puts the needed data and analysis at the fingertips of the GSA nontechnical managers.

The main purpose of the system was to give management quick and easy views of the organization's assets. Managers now can easily use ad hoc queries, perform "what-if" analysis, and receive the results on screen, in graphics format when desired. After indicating a specific office building, for example, the user will be offered 13 choices of data on that building, such as who occupies it, its financials, information on the congressional district it is in (if it is in the United States), and even a scanned photograph of the building. The data can be accessed via geographic information system (GIS) software from MapInfo Corp. Through this software interface, the user begins with a national map and drills down into regional and city maps that show details on location and type of property. With another click of the mouse, the user can pull up all the data on a particular piece of property. Users can limit the data at the outset, specifying, for example, that they want to look only at Justice Department properties with more than 50,000 square feet of floor space. All data are available to about 100 GSA employees in Washington, and about 50 employees in each of 10 regions have access to all data for their own region. Washington employees also have available a database of commercial properties with rental space available.

With GAMIS, nontechnical managers can access and analyze gigabytes of information that were formerly available only via printouts and custom programming. The system has received high marks from many officials, including John Glenn, then Democratic senator from Ohio and long a vocal critic of the GSA's antiquated computer system. When Glenn saw the system demonstrated, he was reported to have been so impressed that the GSA named the system after him. Observers also have praised the system because it was built from off-the-shelf software, making it quick and inexpensive to develop, providing high returns with minimum investments (Anthes, 1994).

Management is responsible for determining where management support systems can make their greatest contribution to organizational performance and for allocating the resources to build them. At the same time, management needs to work closely with system builders to make sure that the systems effectively capture their information requirements and decision processes.

Management

Management support systems can improve organizational performance by speeding up decision making or improving the quality of management decisions themselves. However, some of these decision processes may not be clearly understood. A management support system will be most effective when system builders have a clear idea of its objectives, the nature of the decisions to be supported, and how the system will actually support decision making.

Organization

Systems to support management decision making can be developed with a range of technologies, including the use of large databases, modeling tools, graphics tools, datamining and analysis tools, and electronic meeting technology. Identifying the right technology for the decision or decision process to be supported is a key technology decision.

Technology

For Discussion

1. As a manager or user of information systems, what would you need to know to participate in the design and use of a DSS or an ESS? Why?

2. If businesses used DSS, GDSS, and ESS more widely, would they make better decisions? Explain.

SUMMARY

1. Differentiate a decision-support system (DSS) and a group decision-support system (GDSS). A decision-support system (DSS) is an interactive system under user control that combines data, sophisticated analytical models and tools, and user-friendly software into a single powerful system that can support semistructured or unstructured decision making. There are two kinds of DSS: model-driven DSS and data-driven DSS. DSS targeted toward customers as well as managers are becoming available on the Web. A group decision-support system (GDSS) is an interactive computer-based system to facilitate the solution of unstructured problems by a set of decision makers working together as a group rather than individually.

2. Describe the components of decision-support systems and group decision-support systems. The components of a DSS are the DSS database, the DSS software system, and the user interface. The DSS database is a collection of current or historical data from a number of applications or groups that can be used for analysis. The DSS software system consists of OLAP and datamining tools or mathematical and analytical

models that are used for analyzing the data in the database. The user interface allows users to interact with the DSS software tools directly.

Group decision-support systems (GDSS) have hardware, software, and people components. Hardware components consist of the conference room facilities, including seating arrangements and computer and other electronic hardware. Software components include tools for organizing ideas, gathering information, ranking and setting priorities, and documenting meeting sessions. People components include participants, a trained facilitator, and staff to support the hardware and software.

3. Demonstrate how decision-support systems and group decision-support systems can enhance decision making. Both DSS and GDSS support steps in the process of arriving at decisions. A DSS provides results of model-based or data-driven analysis that help managers design and evaluate alternatives and monitor the progress of the solution that was adopted. A GDSS helps decision makers meeting together to arrive at a decision efficiently and is especially useful for increasing the productivity of meetings with more than four or five people. However, the effectiveness of GDSS is contingent on the nature of the group, the task, and the context of the meeting.

4. Describe the capabilities of executive support systems (ESS). Executive support systems help managers with unstructured problems that occur at the strategic level of management. ESS provide data from both internal and external sources and provide a generalized computing and communications environment that can be focused and applied to a changing array of problems. ESS help senior executives spot problems, identify opportunities, and forecast trends. These systems can filter out extraneous details for high-level overviews, or they can drill down to provide senior managers with detailed transaction data if required.

5. Assess the benefits of executive support systems. ESS help senior managers analyze, compare, and highlight trends so that they more easily may monitor organizational performance or identify strategic problems and opportunities. ESS may increase the span of control of senior management and allow decision making to be decentralized and to take place at lower operating levels.

KEY TERMS

Customer decision-support system (CDSS), 402

Data-driven DSS, 394

Datamining, 394

Decision-support system (DSS), 393

Drill down, 409

DSS database, 395

DSS software system, 395

Electronic meeting system (EMS), 406

Executive support system (ESS), 408

Geographic information systems (GIS), 399

Group decision-support system (GDSS), 402

Model, 395

Model-driven DSS, 394

Organizational memory, 404

Sensitivity analysis, 396

REVIEW QUESTIONS

1. What is a decision-support system (DSS)? How does it differ from a management information system (MIS)?

2. How can a DSS support unstructured or semistructured decision making?

3. What is the difference between a data-driven DSS and a model-driven DSS? Give examples.

4. What are the three basic components of a DSS? Briefly describe each.

5. What is a customer decision-support system? How can the Internet be used for this purpose?

6. What is a group decision-support system (GDSS)? How does it differ from a DSS?

7. What are the three underlying problems in group decision making that led to the development of GDSS?

8. Describe the three elements of a GDSS.

9. Name and describe five GDSS software tools.

10. What is an electronic meeting system (EMS)? Describe its capabilities.

11. For each of the three underlying problems in group decision making referred to in question 7, describe one or two ways GDSS can contribute to a solution.

12. Define and describe the capabilities of an executive support system.

13. How can the Internet be used to enhance executive support systems?

14. In what ways is building executive support systems different from building traditional MIS systems?

15. What are the benefits of ESS? How do these systems enhance managerial decision making?

GROUP PROJECT

With three or four of your classmates, identify several groups in your university that could benefit from a GDSS. Design a GDSS for one of those groups, describing its hardware, software, and people elements. Present your findings to the class.

Tools for Interactive Learning

○ Internet Connection

The Internet Connection for this chapter will take you to a series of Web sites where you can complete an exercise to evaluate two Web-based DSS. You can also use the Interactive Study Guide to test your knowledge of the topics in this chapter and get instant feedback where you need more practice.

○ Electronic Commerce Project

At the Laudon Web site for Chapter 12, you will find an Electronic Commerce project that will use the interactive software at the Fidelity Investments Web site for investment portfolio analysis.

○ CD-ROM

If you purchase and use the Multimedia Edition CD-ROM with this chapter, you can complete an interactive exercise asking you to design a group decision-support system (GDSS). You can also find a video clip illustrating the use of Intel videoconferencing technology, an audio overview of the major themes of this chapter, and bullet text summarizing the key points of the chapter.

○ Application Exercise

At the Laudon Web site for this chapter, you can find a spreadsheet Application Exercise for a breakeven analysis.

American Airlines is one of the largest airlines in the United States, with the 1999 revenues of AMR Corp., its parent company, approaching $20 billion. American, headquartered in Fort Worth, Texas, has long been considered a leader in the use of information technology, gaining that reputation with its development of SABRE, its computerized airline reservation system, in the early 1960s. SABRE gave American a clear strategic advantage for a number of years, and over time it came to be used by other airlines as well as by travel agents (providing American with additional income). However, American Airlines has not been a company that sits on its IT laurels. The group that developed SABRE became The Sabre Group, a separate company from American Airlines but a subsidiary of AMR Corp., and Sabre has continued to do the systems development for American Airlines. Over the years Sabre enhanced and improved the SABRE system while also developing numerous other new, critical systems for American, such as its pricing, scheduling, and yield management systems. It also developed systems for other airlines and even for nonairline transportation companies.

During the 1980s the competitive environment of the airline industry changed drastically because the U.S. government deregulated the industry by removing most nonsafety related regulations governing airline routes and flights. Suddenly, for the first time in decades, airlines were free to make their own competitive route and scheduling decisions. Existing airlines quickly sought to expand into routes in territories dominated by their competitors. They also opened new routes and abandoned existing unprofitable routes that previously had been government mandated. Start-up airlines appeared and identified all kinds of opportunities. They opened new routes where they believed a potential demand existed. They began service on existing routes in an attempt to steal some of the business of older airlines, often competing through lower prices based on diminished services. Thus, airline deregulation resulted in a fiercely competitive environment for all the existing airlines. American's management team realized that it must become more nimble in order to survive. To do that it had to be able to forecast more quickly and accurately the financial impact of any company decision to

add or subtract flights from its schedule. It also needed to be able to forecast the impact on American of other carriers' decisions to add or change routes that are in competition with its own service.

In this new competitive environment, several large airlines did fail. Pan American Airways, the great pioneer in overseas passenger flights, was the most conspicuous example of an airline that finally had to shut down. These developments made it clear to the American Airlines management team, including CEO and chair Bob Crandall, that accurate and speedy forecasting was urgent if the company wished to remain successful. Unfortunately, forecasting systems in those days consisted only of PC spreadsheets and calculators. Using such low-level technology, American analysts had to work for days merely to estimate the effects of a change in only one single flight. Forecasting the financial effects of a large schedule change was well beyond the abilities of American's planning department. American soon moved to develop a powerful mainframe-based forecasting system that it named Integrated Forecasting System (IFS).

The 1989 collapse of another major competitor, Eastern Airlines, gave American the opportunity to test its new system. During those years airlines were very busy building hub systems, and toward the end of the decade, American had decided it needed to build a new hub somewhere in the southeastern United States. Atlanta, Georgia, emerged as the leading candidate for the location before the Eastern bankruptcy became public. However, the Eastern collapse opened up another possibility because Eastern Airlines had dominated the profitable New York–Florida routes. Now American had to consider Miami, Florida, as another possible hub location. Management at American quickly turned to its newly completed IFS for supporting data to help the management team make a decision as to which would be the best site for their new hub. The problem for the IFS was that this decision was infinitely more complex than that of making a change in the schedule of a single flight. A new hub meant a dramatic change in many flights and routes, and the new IFS would have to forecast the results of all these massive changes. Moreover, it would have to do it for two separate locations. The planning department put IFS to its first big test, and it

passed with flying colors.

To complete the whole task IFS only had to work a total of eight hours. The system output indicated that Miami would be more advantageous financially, and Crandall quickly presented that plan to his board of directors who then approved it. According to Brad Jensen, vice president of application development for Sabre Technology Solutions, the Miami hub has generated hundreds of millions of dollars in profit in the years since that decision.

The new IFS system did have a major problem—it had to handle an immense amount of data. The system draws on 60 source data files, supplying both internal and public data. The files provide such varied information as passenger demand, fares, aircraft seating capacities, unit costs per flying hour, and even competitor flight schedules. To try to understand the quantity of data, consider that American has about 4,000 flights daily, and that the company must track at one time approximately 400,000 flight combinations (that is, pairs of cities that are or might be linked by flights). Moreover, the success of IFS on the hub questions generated another problem for American. The demand for the use of the system rose rapidly. However, users were unwilling to wait eight hours to get a response to their questions. In order to speedily handle such an enormous amount of data while responding to the greatly increased number of requests, the Sabre team decided the system would have to be moved to a parallel-processing architecture. A project to accomplish this goal was estimated to cost an immense $16 million. Fortunately, Crandall supported the project because the SABRE reservation system had been so successful. In fact, according to reports, when Crandall first was told of the proposal, including the cost, he jumped out of his chair yelling, "I want the system." Sabre management also was strongly in support of the project. Thomas M. Cook, president of Sabre Technology Solutions, remembers that, "There was a realization among the senior management at both companies that in order to have significant breakthroughs, you have to take significant risk."

The development team made two critical decisions in 1991. The first was to convert to a client/server platform that would not only provide a parallel-processing environment but would place control of the upgraded system on the desktops of the users. Thus, the users would be able to initiate and manage their own forecasts right from their own PCs. The second decision was to adopt a new and, at that time, relatively unproven technology, object-oriented programming. On reflection a third decision has been seen as critical to the success of the project. The development team decided it must work closely with the end users, American's capacity planning department, and so the team was housed on the same floor as the planners. The result was a very close working relationship between the two sides and a successful project. Adding to the project's success was the commitment by senior American executives to attend weekly project meetings, thereby lending not only their strong and visible support to the project but their design and usage insights as well.

The project was completed in 1996, and American found itself with a much faster and more powerful IFS. Sabre continued to improve the system so that the queries it can handle today are much more complex even than were those in 1996. It now forecasts within 3 minutes the company's market share for its 4 million services worldwide as well as 400,000 city pairs. With the new client/server system, planners can actually get answers to hundreds of questions about a potential single flight change, whereas, previously, the mainframe IFS could only handle two or three questions. American planners are now able to do much more planning, do it more effectively, and yet do it with a reduced staff. American's planners use IFS constantly to find ways to cut costs and increase revenues. The planners analyze the financial impact of adding or deleting flights, adding service to a new city or dropping an existing service, or changing the size of an aircraft for a specific flight or route. They even use it to project the fi-

nancial impact of schedule changes made by American's competitors. One interesting example of a result of IFS projections was American's decision to replace some jet planes with propeller planes. Despite the fear of many that the change would result in a loss of passengers, the system showed that American could redeploy the jets by adding flights to longer, more profitable routes. American's cost-per-mile declined while profits rose. All-in-all American planners and management have gained a much deeper and more complete understanding of its customers, its competition, and the marketplace. Moreover, management claims American's profits have gone up about $500 million as a result of the first 2 years of using IFS.

Although American Airlines has benefited greatly from AMR's ownership of Sabre, that relationship is about to change. Over the years Sabre has developed many systems for other companies, including selling versions of IFS to the London subway system and to the French railways. However, Sabre's close ties to American Airlines have been seen by other airlines as a problem. According to James Poage, senior vice president of worldwide marketing for Sabre, the problem "we faced in the past is [other airlines would] say 'Because of your relationship with American Airlines, is our information secure?' " Because of this fear Sabre garnered no significant airline outsourcing contracts during 1998 and 1999. As a result, and with the goal of increasing the potential for Sabre, AMR announced on December 14, 1999, that it is spinning Sabre off, making it a fully independent technology company. Sabre president and CEO William J. Hannigan explained the expected result, saying "With our independence, it's more clear that success for Sabre won't mean enrichment for American. That's real important to those

carriers. Soon AMR will be able to sell its systems to any company and will be free to develop for any airline."

Sources: Scott McCartney, "Airlines Find a Bag of High-Tech Tricks to Keep Income Aloft," **The Wall Street Journal**, January 20, 2000; Stacy Collett, "Update: Sabre to Sell Software Once Controlled by American Airlines," **Computerworld**, December 14, 1999; Polly Schneider, "Clear Skies Forecast," **CIO Magazine**, February 1, 1999; Lauren Gibbons Paul, "From Harrowing to Heroism," **CIO Magazine**, September 1, 1998; and Linda Rosencrance, "AMR to Spin Off Sabre," **Computerworld**, December 12, 1999.

CASE STUDY QUESTIONS

1. Evaluate American Airlines using the value chain and competitive forces models.

2. How is forecasting related to American Airlines' business strategy?

3. How did IFS help American Airlines pursue its business strategy? What kind of DSS is IFS?

4. What management, technology, and organization problems did the IFS project present to American Airlines? To Sabre?

5. What were the advantages and disadvantages for American Airlines of having its information technology development being done by Sabre, a sister company, rather than by American Airlines itself? How do you think the spinoff of Sabre will affect the competitive position of American Airlines in the short run? In the long run?

CHAPTER 13

Information Systems Security and Control

Learning Objectives

After completing this chapter, you will be able to:

1. Demonstrate why information systems are so vulnerable to destruction, error, abuse, and system quality problems.

2. Compare general controls and application controls for information systems, including controls to safeguard use of the Internet.

3. Select the factors that must be considered when developing the controls for information systems.

4. Describe the technologies used for Internet security and the major types of secure electronic payment systems for e-commerce.

5. Describe the most important software quality assurance techniques.

6. Demonstrate the importance of auditing information systems and safeguarding data quality.

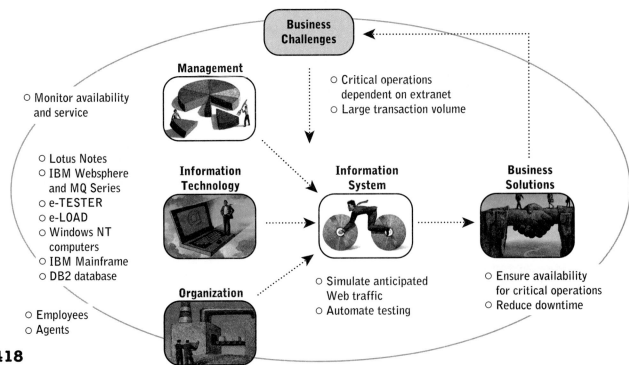

Business Challenges

Management

○ Monitor availability and service

- Critical operations dependent on extranet
- Large transaction volume

Information Technology

○ Lotus Notes
○ IBM Websphere and MQ Series
○ e-TESTER
○ e-LOAD
○ Windows NT computers
○ IBM Mainframe
○ DB2 database

Information System

Business Solutions

○ Employees
○ Agents

Organization

○ Simulate anticipated Web traffic
○ Automate testing

○ Ensure availability for critical operations
○ Reduce downtime

Manulife Stress Tests Its Web Site

Hardly a week goes by without an outage at a major electronic commerce site, including giants such as Amazon.com, eBay, Ameritrade, and E*Trade. According to some experts, it is a wonder such mission-critical Web sites and those of other companies don't crash all the time. Behind each large Web site are hundreds of computers, thousands of miles of network cable, and hundreds of software programs, creating numerous points of vulnerability. Many Web site outages have been caused by large surges in the number of legitimate visitors and by hackers overwhelming the sites with requests for services and the inability of the site to handle those surges in traffic. In other words, performance failures often accompany a Web site's success. And if a Web site can't quickly respond to visitor requests, customers can easily go elsewhere.

Manulife, a Toronto-based firm providing financial protection products and investment management services, was concerned about this problem as it built a large and complex extranet. The firm operates in 15 countries around the world, with about 28,000 employees and agents managing almost $100 billion. Manulife's extranet was designed to allow members and participants to use the Web to inquire about account balances, make interaccount transfers, and issue investment instructions. The application had multiple layers, including IBM's Websphere and MQSeries, and Lotus Notes, all funneling into a DB2 relational database running on an IBM mainframe.

Early demand projections indicated that 2,000 people might be using the extranet at any given time. Traditional manual testing methods could not provide a high enough volume of users to test the system as it would actually have to operate. Manulife's extranet development team decided to solve this problem by adopting automated stress-testing tools that are specifically designed to simulate anticipated Web traffic. The objective of stress-testing is to create enough transaction volume on a system to measure its capacity and performance and see if it will stand up to real-world demands.

Manulife selected the e-TESTER and e-LOAD products from RSW Software Inc. in Boston. E-TESTER creates test scripts describing typical user interactions with the system, and e-LOAD generates Web site traffic based on test

CHAPTER OUTLINE

profiles. Both products work in Manulife's system development environment, and both allow nontechnical staff to test daily content or program code changes. Manulife's project met its deadline and produced an extranet that could handle the peak projected load demand.

Even with only 2,000 users, the RSW testing system required about 7 Windows NT computers with high-speed processors to generate the volume of traffic for test purposes that Manulife's extranet would have to handle in the real world. The question is, what do companies do to test Web sites that anticipate 200,000 or 1 million concurrent users? Can automated stress-testing tools scale to test this level of activity?

Sources: Linda Hayes, "Stress for Sale, " *Datamation,* March 2000; "Virtual Stress Testing," *Datamation,* August 1999; and Matt Richtel, "Keeping E-Commerce On Line," *The New York Times,* June 21, 1999.

MANAGEMENT CHALLENGES

The experience of Manulife illustrates the need for careful testing of information systems to make sure that they are reliable, accurate, and secure. Software failures, as well as hardware failures, communication disruptions, natural disasters, employee errors, and use by unauthorized people, can prevent information systems from running properly or running at all. As you read this chapter, you should be aware of the following management challenges.

1. Designing systems that are neither overcontrolled nor undercontrolled. The biggest threat to information systems is posed by authorized users, not outside intruders. Most security breaches and damage to information systems come from organizational insiders. If a system requires too many passwords and authorizations to access information, the system will go unused. However, there is a growing need to create secure systems based on distributed multiuser networks and the Internet. Controls that are effective but that do not prevent authorized individuals from easily using a system are difficult to design.

2. Applying quality assurance standards in large systems projects. This chapter explains why the goal of zero defects in large, complex pieces of software is impossible to achieve. If the seriousness of remaining bugs cannot be ascertained, what constitutes acceptable—if not perfect—software performance? And even if meticulous design and exhaustive testing could eliminate all defects, software projects have time and budget constraints that often prevent management from devoting as much time to thorough testing as it should. Under such circumstances it will be difficult for managers to define a standard for software quality and to enforce it.

Computer systems play such a critical role in business, government, and daily life that organizations must take special steps to protect their information systems and to ensure that they are accurate and reliable. This chapter describes how information systems can be controlled and made secure so that they serve the purposes for which they are intended.

Auction and Brokerage Sites Stand to Lose the Most

Estimated Financial Loss Due to a Site Outage*

Type of Loss	Brokerage Site	Auction Site
Direct revenues loss	$204,000	$341,652
Compensatory loss	0	$943,521
Inventory costs	0	0
Depreciation expenses	$4,110	$6,279
Lost future revenues	$4,810,320	$1,024,955
Worker downtime loss	$117,729	$46,097
Contract labor cost	$24,000	$52,180
Delay-to-market cost	$60,000	$358,734
Total financial impact	$5,220,159	$2,773,416

*Based on an eight-hour brokerage site outage during the trading day and a 22-hour auction site outage.

Source: Cahners In-Stat Group.

FIGURE 13-1 Financial impact of Web site outages. Firms that need Web sites constantly available for electronic commerce face heavy losses for every business day that the sites are not working. **Source:** "Technology Spotlight: The Financial Impact of Site Outages," **The Industry Standard,** October 4, 1999. Reprinted by permission of The Industry Standard; www.thestandard.com

13.1 System Vulnerability and Abuse

Before computer automation, data about individuals or organizations were maintained and secured as paper records dispersed in separate business or organizational units. Information systems concentrate data in computer files that potentially can be accessed easily by large numbers of people and by groups outside the organization. Consequently, automated data are more susceptible to destruction, fraud, error, and misuse.

When computer systems fail to run or work as required, firms that depend heavily on computers experience a serious loss of business function. The longer computer systems are down, the more serious the consequences for the firm. Figure 13-1 describes the estimated financial losses caused by Web site outages for brokerage and auction sites. Some firms relying on computers to process their critical business transactions might experience a total loss of business function if they lose computer capability for more than a few days.

WHY SYSTEMS ARE VULNERABLE

When large amounts of data are stored in electronic form they are vulnerable to many more kinds of threats than when they exist in manual form. Table 13-1 lists the most common threats against computerized information systems. They can stem from technical, organizational, and environmental factors compounded by poor management decisions.

Computerized systems are especially vulnerable to such threats for the following reasons:

- A complex information system cannot be replicated manually.
- Computerized procedures seem to be invisible and are not easily understood or audited.
- Although the chances of disaster in automated systems are no greater than in manual systems, the effect of a disaster can be much more extensive. In some cases all of a system's records can be destroyed and lost forever.

Table 13-1 Threats to Computerized Information Systems

Hardware failure	Fire
Software failure	Electrical problems
Personnel actions	User errors
Terminal access penetration	Program changes
Theft of data, services, equipment	Telecommunications problems

○ On-line information systems are directly accessible by many individuals. Legitimate users may gain easy access to portions of computer data that they are not authorized to view. Unauthorized individuals can also gain access to such systems.

Advances in telecommunications and computer software have magnified these vulnerabilities. Through telecommunications networks, information systems in different locations can be interconnected. The potential for unauthorized access, abuse, or fraud is not limited to a single location but can occur at any access point in the network.

Additionally, more complex and diverse hardware, software, organizational, and personnel arrangements are required for telecommunications networks, creating new areas and opportunities for penetration and manipulation. Wireless networks using radio-based technology are even more vulnerable to penetration because radio frequency bands are easy to scan. The Internet poses special problems because it was explicitly designed to be accessed easily by people on different computer systems. The vulnerabilities of telecommunications networks are illustrated in Figure 13-2.

Hackers and Computer Viruses

The explosive growth of Internet use by businesses and individuals has been accompanied by rising reports of Internet security breaches. The main concern comes from unwanted intruders, or hackers, who use the latest technology and their skills to break into supposedly secure computers or to disable them. A **hacker** is a person who gains unauthorized access to a computer network for profit, criminal mischief, or personal pleasure. The potential damage from intruders is frightening. The Window on Organizations describes problems hackers create for organizations that use the Internet.

Alarm has risen over hackers propagating **computer viruses,** rogue software programs that spread rampantly from system to system, clogging computer memory or destroying programs or data. Many thousands of viruses are known to exist, and 200 or more

hacker A person who gains unauthorized access to a computer network for profit, criminal mischief, or personal pleasure.

computer virus Rogue software programs that are difficult to detect and that spread rapidly through computer systems, destroying data or disrupting processing and memory systems.

FIGURE 13-2 Telecommunications network vulnerabilities. Telecommunications networks are highly vulnerable to natural failure of hardware and software and to misuse by programmers, computer operators, maintenance staff, and end users. It is possible to tap communications lines and illegally intercept data. High-speed transmission over twisted wire communications channels causes interference called crosstalk. Radiation can disrupt a network at various points as well.

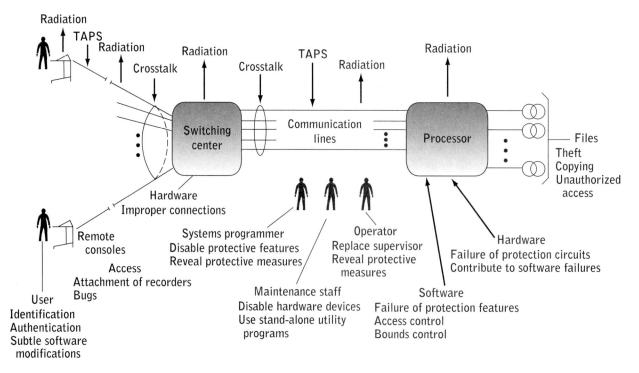

INTERNET HACKERS ON THE RISE

In early January 2000, a mysterious intruder tried to extort $100,000 from CD Universe, an Internet music retailer, claiming to have copied more than 300,000 credit card files that CD Universe had collected on its customers. The credit card numbers in these files could be used by other people to charge purchases on-line or by telephone. CD Universe refused to pay the blackmail, and the cyber-extortionist released some of the credit card files on the Internet, claiming that he had used other credit card numbers to obtain money for himself.

An e-mail trail traced the extortionist to Latvia, Bulgaria, or Russia. The extortionist had been operating a Web site, called Maxus Credit Card Pipeline, where a visitor could obtain a valid credit card number, name, and address from the site's massive database. Before the Maxus site was shut down, a traffic counter indicated that several thousand visitors had downloaded more than 25,000 credit card numbers since December 25, 1999. The extortionist claimed he had found a way to subvert ICVerify, a credit card verification program sold by Cybercash Inc. CD Universe employs ICVerify but the company was not ready to conclude that the blackmailer had obtained the credit card information by manipulating the software. The credit card extortionist claimed he hacked into a chain of shops in 1998 and obtained the ICVerify program with configuration files for transferring money.

During the second week of February 2000, a wave of hacker attacks temporarily disabled a series of major e-commerce sites, including Yahoo, Amazon.com, Buy.com, E*Trade, and ZDNet. These "denial of service" attacks were not designed to penetrate the Web sites but to disable them by inundating them with phony requests for data, overloading the sites' servers and preventing legitimate traffic from getting through. The Web sites were shut down for several hours, but no systems were compromised, no customer data were stolen, and financial losses from the outages were minor. The FBI launched a nationwide investigation to find the hackers and many companies started looking for new ways to fortify their Web site security.

These incidents highlight a mounting problem with Internet hackers plaguing both government and business organizations. U.S. military security analysts have been uncovering and deterring computer hackers who continually find new ways to attack open Pentagon networks on the Internet. It is unclear whether the hacker probes actually originated overseas or were merely routed through the overseas Web sites as a way of covering the hackers' tracks.

In the past, nearly 80 percent of documented security breaches came from within organizations. It now appears that the number of attacks from outside hackers is catching up with the number of breaches from insiders.

Don Erwin, an information security strategy specialist at Dow Chemical Company in Midland, Michigan, noted that many companies have opened themselves up to attack by installing firewalls without allocating the resources to manage them effectively. Firewalls must be managed professionally and audited regularly, and effective security requires training, management support, and an adequate budget. Marcus Ranum, a security tools developer who is known as the "father of the firewall," observed that many companies don't update their firewall software to guard against known vulnerabilities. Richard Power, editorial director of the Computer Security Institute, said security management accounts for less than 3 percent of information technology budgets, with an average of only 1 security staff member assigned for every 1000 users.

TO THINK ABOUT: How can hacker attacks from the Internet harm organizations? What management, organization, and technology issues should be considered when developing an Internet security plan?

Sources: Elinor Abreu, "The Hack Attack," **The Industry Standard**, February 21, 2000; David P. Hamilton with David S. Cloud, "The Internet Under Siege: Stalking the Hackers," **The Wall Street Journal**, February 10, 2000; John Markoff, "Thief Reveals Credit Card Data When Web Extortion Plot Fails," **The New York Times**, January 10, 2000; and Ann Harrison, "Cyberattacks on the Rise," Computerworld, March 8, 1999.

---

new viruses are created each month. Table 13-2 describes the characteristics of the most common viruses.

In addition to spreading via computer networks, viruses can invade computerized information systems from "infected" diskettes from an outside source, through infected machines, from files of software downloaded via the Internet, or from files attached to e-mail. The potential for massive damage and loss from future computer viruses remains a serious threat.

Organizations can use antivirus software and screening procedures to reduce the chances of infection. **Antivirus software** is special software designed to check computer systems and disks for the presence of various computer viruses. Often the software can eliminate the virus from the infected area. However, most antivirus software is only effective against viruses already known when the software is written. To protect their systems, management must continually update their antivirus software.

antivirus software Software designed to detect, and often eliminate, computer viruses from an information system.

Table 13-2 Examples of Computer Viruses

Virus Name	Description
Concept, Melissa	Macro viruses that exist inside executable programs called macros, which provide functions within programs such as Microsoft Word. Can be spread when Word documents are attached to e-mail. Can copy from one document to another and delete files.
Form	Makes a clicking sound with each keystroke but only on the eighteenth day of the month. May corrupt data on the floppy disks it infects.
Explore.exe	"Worm" type virus that arrives attached to e-mail. When launched, it tries to e-mail itself to other PCs and destroy certain Microsoft Office and programmer files.
Monkey	Makes the hard disk look like it has failed because Windows will not run.
Chernobyl	Erases a computer's hard drive and ROM BIOS (Basic Input/Output System).
Junkie	A "multipartite" virus that can infect files as well as the boot sector of the hard drive (the section of a PC hard drive that the PC first reads when it boots up). May cause memory conflicts.

CONCERNS FOR SYSTEM BUILDERS AND USERS

The heightened vulnerability of automated data has created special concerns for the builders and users of information systems. These concerns include disaster, security, and administrative error.

Disaster

Computer hardware, programs, data files, and other equipment can be destroyed by fires, power failures, or other disasters. It may take many years and millions of dollars to reconstruct destroyed data files and computer programs, and some may not be able to be replaced. If an organization needs them to function on a day-to-day basis, it will no longer be able to operate. This is why companies such as VISA USA Inc. and National Trust employ elaborate emergency backup facilities. VISA USA Inc. has duplicate mainframes, duplicate network pathways, duplicate terminals, and duplicate power supplies. VISA even uses a duplicate computer center in McLean, Virginia, to handle half of its transactions and to serve as an emergency backup to its primary data center in San Mateo, California. National Trust, a large bank in Ontario, Canada, uses uninterruptable power supply technology provided by International Power Machines (IPM) because electrical power at its Mississauga location fluctuates frequently.

Antivirus software products such as Norton AntiVirus2000, illustrated here, identify viruses that have infected a system and provide tools for eradicating them. Companies can detect and eliminate many computer viruses in their systems by using antivirus software regularly.

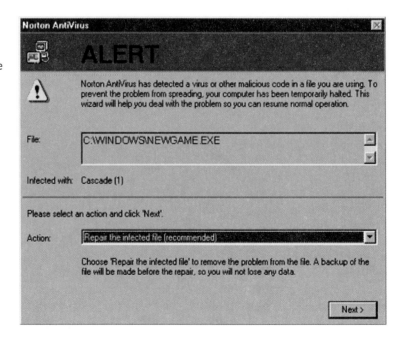

Fault-tolerant computer systems contain extra hardware, software, and power supply components that can back the system up and keep it running to prevent system failure. Fault-tolerant computers contain extra memory chips, processors, and disk storage devices. They can use special software routines or self-checking logic built into their circuitry to detect hardware failures and automatically switch to a backup device. Parts from these computers can be removed and repaired without disruption to the computer system.

Firms use fault-tolerant technology for critical applications with heavy on-line transaction processing requirements. In **on-line transaction processing,** transactions entered on-line are immediately processed by the computer. Multitudinous changes to databases, reporting, or requests for information occur each instant.

Rather than build their own backup facilities, many firms contract with disaster recovery firms, such as Comdisco Disaster Recovery Services in Rosemont, Illinois, and Sungard Recovery Services headquartered in Wayne, Pennsylvania. These disaster recovery firms provide *hot sites* housing spare computers at locations around the country where subscribing firms can run their critical applications in an emergency. Disaster recovery services offer backup for client/server systems as well as traditional mainframe applications. The Window on Management explores some of the issues that organizations need to address as they create disaster recovery plans.

Security

Security refers to the policies, procedures, and technical measures used to prevent unauthorized access, alteration, theft, and physical damage to information systems. Security can be promoted with an array of techniques and tools to safeguard computer hardware, software, communications networks, and data. We already have discussed disaster protection measures. Other tools and techniques for promoting security are discussed in subsequent sections.

Errors

Computers also can serve as instruments of error, severely disrupting or destroying an organization's record keeping and operations. For instance, on February 25, 1991, during Operation Desert Storm, a Patriot missile defense system operating at Dharan, Saudi Arabia, failed to track and intercept an incoming Scud missile because of a software error in the system's weapons control computer. The Scud hit an army barracks, killing 28 Americans. Errors in automated systems can occur at many points in the processing cycle: through data entry, program error, computer operations, and hardware. Figure 13-3 illustrates all of the points in a typical processing cycle where errors can occur.

SYSTEM QUALITY PROBLEMS: SOFTWARE AND DATA

In addition to disasters, viruses, and security breaches, defective software and data pose a constant threat to information systems, causing untold losses in productivity. An undiscovered error in a company's credit software or erroneous financial data can result in millions of dollars of losses. Several years ago, a hidden software problem in AT&T's long distance system brought down that system, bringing the New York–based financial exchanges to a halt and interfering with billions of dollars of business around the country for a number of hours. Modern passenger and commercial vehicles are increasingly dependent on computer programs for critical functions. A hidden software defect in a braking system could result in the loss of lives.

Bugs and Defects

A major problem with software is the presence of hidden **bugs** or program code defects. Studies have shown that it is virtually impossible to eliminate all bugs from large programs. The main source of bugs is the complexity of decision-making code. Even a relatively small program of several hundred lines will contain tens of decisions leading to hundreds or even thousands of different paths. Important programs within most corporations are usually much larger, containing tens of thousands or even millions of lines of code, each with many times more choices and paths than the smaller programs. Such complexity is difficult to document and design—designers sometimes document some reactions inappropriately or fail to consider other possibilities. Studies show that about 60 percent of errors discovered during testing are

---

fault-tolerant computer systems Systems that contain extra hardware, software, and power supply components that can back a system up and keep it running to prevent system failure.

on-line transaction processing Transaction processing mode in which transactions entered on-line are immediately processed by the computer.

security Policies, procedures, and technical measures used to prevent unauthorized access, alteration, theft, or physical damage to information systems.

bugs Program code defects or errors.

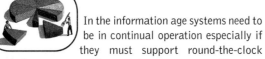

DISASTER RECOVERY IN THE INFORMATION AGE

In the information age systems need to be in continual operation especially if they must support round-the-clock electronic commerce. The cost to a company without an emergency plan can be high, even calamitous. According to a 1999 study of "The Cost of Lost Data" by Pepperdine University professor David Smith, U.S. companies spent $11.8 billion to recover data during the previous year. Disaster recovery and crisis management are becoming more challenging, reflecting the rapidly growing complexity of information systems technology and pressures to keep electronic commerce systems available 24 hours a day.

When Landstar Corp.'s roof collapsed from heavy rain, flooding its data center, the Florida transportation company was able to recover within four days because of its disaster recovery system. The company had backed up its data onto tapes every night and moved the tapes to a fireproof vault 26 miles away. This is the approach followed by many corporations. But is four days fast enough anymore? According to a recent report from Gartner Group Inc., in our current competitive environment, customers are no longer satisfied with their suppliers or service partners being down for four days. Competitive companies will need to be able to recover within 24 hours by the year 2003, the report concludes.

Faster recovery from disaster is available. Comdisco Corp., a specialist in backup and recovery, offers a system that promises recovery within four hours. It includes a preconfigured disk drive stored at one of Comdisco's recovery sites along with the backed-up data. When a customer experiences a disaster, the programs and data can be quickly loaded onto the already prepared drive, and the customer is back in business. Comdisco even offers access to the data via its virtual private networks (VPN). As with other recovery sites, customers can also use Comdisco's computers until their own are back in operation. The problem with this approach is that it is very expensive and time consuming. Management will have to be convinced that such a high cost is necessary.

Yet another crucial problem is that various critical applications run on different platforms and use different operating systems. This is particularly true in companies that have multiple locations (most companies, these days). The problem management faces is the ability to back up all their companies' applications easily. Computer Associates offers ArcServe and Unicenter TNG, which are capable of backing up from many platforms. The software uses one interface for all platforms, making it easy to learn and to use. In addition, the system enables the organization to manage its backups from one central location. When data problems occur, the administrator is even able to restore data remotely.

Following the right procedures during a disaster is just as important as having the technology available to keep systems running. Charles Schwab, the Web-based financial services giant, established specific crisis management procedures to keep its Web site up and running even when threatened by downtime and other technical problems. IT managers make sure that each person knows his or her role during a crisis and follows a defined set of procedures when a crisis strikes. When one of Schwab's IBM mainframes malfunctioned during the July 14, 1999, trading day, members of its Internet team first ran mainframe diagnostic tests. When these tests did not reveal anything, they checked to see what programs were running or if a staff member did anything unusual. Eleven minutes after the first sign of trouble, the team had solved the problem by recycling some regions of the mainframe. Within 15 minutes the team brought Schwab's Web site performance back to normal.

TO THINK ABOUT: What are the management benefits of a disaster recovery plan? The costs? What management, organization, and technology issues should be addressed in a disaster recovery plan?

Sources: David Essex, "Data Resurrection," **Computerworld**, March 6, 2000; Jennifer Mateyaschuk, "Backup Plans Become Critical," **Information Week**, January 11, 1999; Brian Walsh, "RFP: Heading for Disaster?" **TechSearch**, January 11, 1999; and Jenny C. McCune, "Why You Need a Business Recovery Plan," **Beyond Computing**, March, 1999.

the result of specifications in the design documentation that were missing, ambiguous, erroneous, or in conflict.

Zero defects, a goal of the total quality management movement, cannot be achieved in large programs. Complete testing simply is not possible. Fully testing programs that contain thousands of choices and millions of paths would require thousands of years. Eliminating software bugs is an exercise in diminishing returns because it takes proportionately longer testing to detect and eliminate obscure residual bugs (Littlewood and Strigini, 1993). Even with rigorous testing, one could not know for sure that a piece of software was dependable until the product proved itself after much operational use. The message? We cannot eliminate all bugs, and we cannot know with certainty the seriousness of the bugs that do remain. Still, we must test for what we can eliminate.

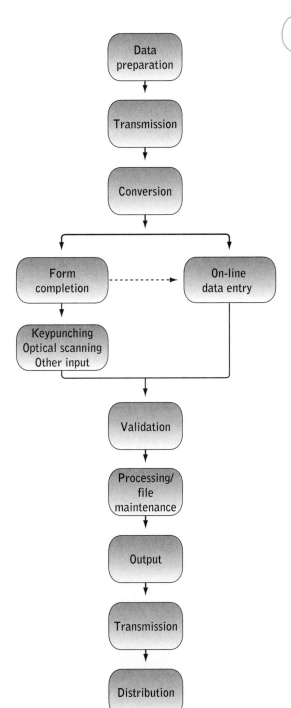

FIGURE 13-3 Points in the processing cycle where errors can occur. Each of the points illustrated in this figure represents a control point where special automated and/or manual procedures should be established to reduce the risk of errors during processing.

The Maintenance Nightmare

Another reason that systems are unreliable is that computer software traditionally has been a nightmare to maintain. Maintenance, the process of modifying a system in production use, is the most expensive phase of the systems development process. In most organizations nearly half of information systems' staff time is spent in the maintenance of existing systems.

Why are maintenance costs so high? One major reason is organizational change. The firm may experience large internal changes in structure or leadership, or change may come from its surrounding environment. These organizational changes affect information requirements. Another reason appears to be software complexity, as measured by the number and size of interrelated software programs and subprograms and the complexity of the flow of program logic between them (Banker, Datar, Kemerer, and Zweig, 1993). A third common cause of long-term maintenance problems is faulty systems analysis and design, especially information requirements analysis. Some studies of large TPS systems by TRW, Inc., have found that a majority of system errors—64 percent—result from early analysis errors (Mazzucchelli, 1985).

Figure 13-4 illustrates the cost of correcting errors based on the experience of consultants reported in the literature. If errors are detected early, during analysis and design, the cost to the systems development effort is small. But if they are not discovered until after programming, testing, or conversion has been completed, the costs can soar astronomically. A minor logic error, for example, that could take 1 hour to correct during the analysis and design stage, could take 10, 40, and 90 times as long to correct during programming, conversion, and postimplementation, respectively.

Data Quality Problems

The most common source of information system failure is poor data quality. Data that are inaccurate, untimely, or inconsistent with other sources of information can create serious operational and financial problems for businesses. When bad data go unnoticed, they can lead to bad decisions, product recalls, and even financial losses (Redman, 1998). Companies cannot pursue aggressive marketing and customer relationship management strategies unless they have high-quality data about their customers. For example, Sears Roebuck, described in the Chapter 2 case study, could not effectively pursue cross-selling among its customers because each of its businesses, including retail, home services, credit, and the Web site, had their own information systems with unreliable and conflicting data. Sears needed to develop a massive data warehouse that consolidated and cleansed the data from all of these systems in order to create a single customer list (Wallace, 1999).

Data quality problems plague the public sector as well. A study of the FBI's computerized criminal record systems found a total of 54.1 percent of the records in the National Crime Information Center System to be inaccurate, ambiguous, or incomplete, and 74.3 percent of the records in the FBI's semiautomated Identification Division system exhibited significant quality problems. A summary analysis of the FBI's automated Wanted Persons File also found that 11.2 percent of the warrants were invalid. A study by the FBI itself found that 6 percent of the warrants in state files were invalid and that 12,000 invalid warrants were sent out nationally each day.

The FBI has taken some steps to correct these problems, but low levels of data quality in these systems have disturbing implications. In addition to their use in law enforcement, computerized criminal history records are increasingly being used to screen employees in both the public and private sectors. Many of these records are incomplete and show arrests but no court disposition; that is, they show charges without proof of conviction or guilt. Many individuals may be denied employment unjustifiably because these records overstate their criminality. These criminal record systems are not limited to violent felons. They contain the records

FIGURE 13-4 The cost of errors over the systems development cycle. The most common, most severe, and most expensive system errors develop in the early design stages. They involve faulty requirements analysis. Errors in program logic or syntax are much less common, less severe, and less costly to repair than design errors.
Source: Alberts, 1976.

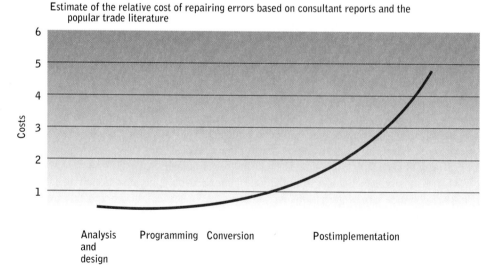

Estimate of the relative cost of repairing errors based on consultant reports and the popular trade literature

of 36 million people, about one-third of the labor force. Inaccurate and potentially damaging information is being maintained on many law-abiding citizens. The level of data quality in these systems threatens citizens' constitutional rights to due process and impairs the efficiency and effectiveness of any law enforcement programs in which these records are used (Laudon, 1986a). Chapter 14 provides more detail on other data quality problems.

Poor data quality may stem from errors during data input or from a faulty information system and database design (Wand and Wang, 1996; Strong, Lee, and Wang, 1997). In the following sections we examine how organizations deal with data and software quality problems as well as other threats to information systems.

13.2 Creating a Control Environment

To minimize errors, disaster, computer crime, and breaches of security, special policies and procedures must be incorporated into the design and implementation of information systems. The combination of manual and automated measures that safeguard information systems and ensure that they perform according to management standards is called controls. **Controls** consist of all the methods, policies, and organizational procedures that ensure the safety of the organization's assets, the accuracy and reliability of its accounting records, and operational adherence to management standards.

In the past, the control of information systems was treated as an afterthought, addressed only toward the end of implementation, just before the system was installed. Today, however, organizations are so critically dependent on information systems that vulnerabilities and control issues must be identified as early as possible. The control of an information system must be an integral part of its design. Users and builders of systems must pay close attention to controls throughout the system's life span.

Computer systems are controlled by a combination of general controls and application controls. **General controls** are those that control the design, security, and use of computer programs and the security of data files in general throughout the organization. On the whole, general controls apply to all computerized applications and consist of a combination of system software and manual procedures that create an overall control environment. **Application controls** are specific controls unique to each computerized application, such as payroll, accounts receivable, and order processing. They consist of controls applied from the user's functional area of a particular system and from programmed procedures.

GENERAL CONTROLS

General controls are overall controls that ensure the effective operation of programmed procedures. They apply to all application areas. General controls include the following:

- ○ Controls over the system implementation process
- ○ Software controls
- ○ Physical hardware controls
- ○ Computer operations controls
- ○ Data security controls
- ○ Administrative disciplines, standards, and procedures

Implementation Controls

Implementation controls audit the systems development process at various points to ensure that the process is properly controlled and managed. The systems development audit should look for the presence of formal review points at various stages of development that enable users and management to approve or disapprove the implementation.

The systems development audit also should examine the level of user involvement at each stage of implementation and check for the use of a formal cost/benefit methodology in establishing system feasibility. The audit should look for the use of controls and quality assurance techniques for program development, conversion, and testing and for complete and thorough system, user, and operations documentation.

controls All of the methods, policies, and procedures that ensure protection of the organization's assets, accuracy and reliability of its records, and operational adherence to management standards.

general controls Overall controls that establish a framework for controlling the design, security, and use of computer programs throughout an organization.

application controls Specific controls unique to each computerized application.

implementation controls The audit of the systems development process at various points to make sure that it is properly controlled and managed.

Software Controls

software controls Controls to ensure the security and reliability of software.

Controls are essential for the various categories of software used in computer systems. **Software controls** monitor the use of system software and prevent unauthorized access of software programs, system software, and computer programs. System software is an important area to control because it performs overall control functions for the programs that directly process data and data files.

Hardware Controls

hardware controls Controls to ensure the physical security and correct performance of computer hardware.

Hardware controls ensure that computer hardware is physically secure, and they check for equipment malfunctions. Computer hardware should be physically secured so that it can be accessed only by authorized individuals. Computer equipment should be specially protected against fires and extremes of temperature and humidity. Organizations that are critically dependent on their computers also must make provisions for emergency backup in case of power failure.

Many kinds of computer hardware contain mechanisms that check for equipment malfunctions. Parity checks detect equipment malfunctions responsible for altering bits within bytes during processing. Validity checks monitor the structure of on–off bits within bytes to make sure that it is valid for the character set of a particular computer machine. "Echo checks" verify that a hardware device is performance ready. Chapter 4 discusses computer hardware in detail.

Computer Operations Controls

computer operations controls Procedures to ensure that programmed procedures are consistently and correctly applied to data storage and processing.

Computer operations controls apply to the work of the computer department and help ensure that programmed procedures are consistently and correctly applied to the storage and processing of data. They include controls over the setup of computer processing jobs, operations software and computer operations, and backup and recovery procedures for processing that ends abnormally.

Instructions for running computer jobs should be fully documented, reviewed, and approved by a responsible official. Controls over operations software include manual procedures designed to both prevent and detect error. Specific instructions for backup and recovery can be developed so that in the event of a hardware or software failure, the recovery process for production programs, system software, and data files does not create erroneous changes in the system.

Data Security Controls

data security controls Controls to ensure that data files on either disk or tape are not subject to unauthorized access, change, or destruction.

Data security controls ensure that valuable business data files on either disk or tape are not subject to unauthorized access, change, or destruction. Such controls are required for data files when they are in use and when they are held for storage.

When data can be input on-line through a terminal, entry of unauthorized input must be prevented. For example, a credit note could be altered to match a sales invoice on file. In such situations, security can be developed on several levels:

❍ Terminals can be physically restricted so that they are available only to authorized individuals.

❍ System software can include the use of passwords assigned only to authorized individuals. No one can log on to the system without a valid password.

❍ Additional sets of passwords and security restrictions can be developed for specific systems and applications. For example, data security software can limit access to specific files, such as the files for the accounts receivable system. It can restrict the type of access so that only individuals authorized to update these specific files will have the ability to do so. All others will only be able to read the files or will be denied access altogether.

Many systems that allow on-line inquiry and reporting must have data files secured. Figure 13-5 illustrates the security allowed for two sets of users of an on-line personnel database with sensitive information such as employees' salaries, benefits, and medical histories. One set of users consists of all employees who perform clerical functions such as inputting employee data into the system. All individuals with this type of profile can update the system but cannot read or update sensitive fields such as salary, medical history, or earnings data. Another

SECURITY PROFILE 1

User: Personnel Dept. Clerk

Location: Division 1

Employee Identification
Codes with This Profile: 00753, 27834, 37665, 44116

Data Field Restrictions	Type of Access
All employee data for Division 1 only	Read and Update
• Medical history data	None
• Salary	None
• Pensionable earnings	None

SECURITY PROFILE 2

User: Divisional Personnel Manager

Location: Division 1

Employee Identification
Codes with This Profile: 27321

Data Field Restrictions	Type of Access
All employee data for Division 1 only	Read Only

FIGURE 13-5 Security profiles for a personnel system. These two examples represent two security profiles or data security patterns that might be found in a personnel system. Depending on the security profile, a user would have certain restrictions on access to various systems, locations, or data in an organization.

profile applies to a divisional manager, who cannot update the system but who can read all employee data fields for his or her division, including medical history and salary. These profiles would be established and maintained by a data security system. The data security system illustrated in Figure 13-5 provides very fine-grained security restrictions, such as allowing authorized users to inquire about all employee information except for that in confidential fields such as salary or medical history.

Administrative Controls

Administrative controls are formalized standards, rules, procedures, and control disciplines to ensure that the organization's general and application controls are properly executed and enforced. The most important administrative controls are (1) segregation of functions, (2) written policies and procedures, and (3) supervision.

Segregation of functions means that job functions should be designed to minimize the risk of errors or fraudulent manipulation of the organization's assets. The individuals responsible for operating systems should not be the same ones who can initiate transactions that change the assets held in these systems. In a typical arrangement, the organization's information systems department is responsible for data and program files, and end users are responsible for initiating transactions such as payments or checks.

Written policies and procedures establish formal standards for controlling information system operations. Procedures must be formalized in writing and authorized by the appropriate level of management. Accountabilities and responsibilities must be clearly specified.

Supervision of personnel involved in control procedures ensures that the controls for an information system are performing as intended. Without adequate supervision, the best-designed set of controls may be bypassed, short-circuited, or neglected.

Weakness in each of these general controls can have a widespread effect on programmed procedures and data throughout the organization. Table 13-3 summarizes the effect of weaknesses in major general control areas.

administrative controls Formalized standards, rules, procedures, and disciplines to ensure that the organization's controls are properly executed and enforced.

segregation of functions The principle of internal control to divide responsibilities and assign tasks among people so that job functions do not overlap, to minimize the risk of errors and fraudulent manipulation of the organization's assets.

Table 13-3 Effect of Weakness in General Controls

Weakness	Impact
Implementation controls	New systems or systems that have been modified will have errors or fail to function as required.
Software controls (program security)	Unauthorized changes can be made in processing. The organization may not be sure which programs or systems have been changed.
Software controls (system software)	These controls may not have a direct effect on individual applications. Other general controls depend heavily on system software, so a weakness in this area impairs the other general controls.
Physical hardware controls	Hardware may have serious malfunctions or may break down altogether, introducing numerous errors or destroying computerized records.
Computer operations controls	Random errors may occur in a system. (Most processing will be correct, but occasionally it may not be.)
Data file security controls	Unauthorized changes can be made in data stored in computer systems or unauthorized individuals can access sensitive information.
Administrative controls	All of the other controls may not be properly executed or enforced.

APPLICATION CONTROLS

Application controls are specific controls within each separate computer application, such as payroll or order processing. They include automated and manual procedures that ensure that only authorized data are completely and accurately processed by that application. The controls for each application should encompass the whole sequence of processing.

Not all of the application controls discussed here are used in every information system. Some systems require more of these controls than others depending on the importance of the data and the nature of the application. Application controls can be classified as (1) input controls, (2) processing controls, and (3) output controls.

Input Controls

input controls The procedures to check data for accuracy and completeness when they enter the system.

Input controls check data for accuracy and completeness when they enter the system. There are specific input controls for input authorization, data conversion, data editing, and error handling. Input must be properly authorized, recorded, and monitored as source documents flow to the computer. For example, formal procedures can be set up to authorize only select members of the sales department to prepare sales transactions for an order entry system. Input must be properly converted into computer transactions, with no errors as it is transcribed from one form to another. Transcription errors can be eliminated or reduced by keying input transactions directly into computer terminals or by using some form of source data automation.

control totals A type of input control that requires counting transactions or quantity fields prior to processing for comparison and reconciliation after processing.

Control totals can be established beforehand for input transactions. These totals can range from a simple document count to totals for quantity fields such as total sales amount (for a batch of transactions). Computer programs count the totals from transactions input.

edit checks Routines performed to verify input data and correct errors prior to processing.

Edit checks include various programmed routines that can be performed to edit input data for errors before they are processed. Transactions that do not meet edit criteria will be rejected. The edit routines can produce lists of errors to be corrected later. Important types of edit techniques are summarized in Table 13-4.

Processing Controls

processing controls The routines for establishing that data are complete and accurate during updating.

Processing controls establish that data are complete and accurate during updating. The major processing controls are run control totals, computer matching, and programmed edit checks.

run control totals The procedures for controlling completeness of computer updating by generating control totals that reconcile totals before and after processing.

Run control totals reconcile the input control totals with the totals of items that have updated the file. Updating can be controlled by generating control totals during processing. The totals, such as total transactions processed or totals for critical quantities, can be compared manually or by computer. Discrepancies are noted for investigation.

Table 13-4 Important Edit Techniques

Edit Technique	Description	Example
Reasonableness checks	To be accepted, data must fall within certain limits set in advance, or they will be rejected.	If an order transaction is for 20,000 units and the largest order on record was 50 units, the transaction will be rejected.
Format checks	Characteristics of the contents (letter/digit), length, and sign of individual data fields are checked by the system.	A nine-position Social Security number should not contain any alphabetic characters.
Existence checks	The computer compares input reference data to tables or master files to make sure that valid codes are being used.	An employee can have a Fair Labor Standards Act code of only 1, 2, 3, 4, or 5. All other values for this field will be rejected.
Dependency checks	The computer checks whether a logical relationship is maintained between data for the same transaction. When it is not, the transaction is rejected.	A car loan initiation transaction should show a logical relationship between the size of the loan, the number of loan repayments, and the size of each installment.

Computer matching matches the input data with information held on master or suspense files, with unmatched items noted for investigation. Most matching occurs during input, but under some circumstances it may be required to ensure completeness of updating. For example, a matching program might match employee time cards with a payroll master file and report missing or duplicate time cards.

Most edit checking occurs when data are input. However, certain applications require some type of reasonableness or dependency check during updating. For example, consistency checks might be used by a utility company to compare a customer's electric bill with previous bills. If the bill was 500 percent higher this month compared to last month, the bill would not be processed until the meter was rechecked.

computer matching The processing control that matches input data to information held on master files.

Output Controls

Output controls ensure that the results of computer processing are accurate, complete, and properly distributed. Typical output controls include the following:

output controls Measures that ensure that the results of computer processing are accurate, complete, and properly distributed.

- ○ Balancing output totals with input and processing totals
- ○ Reviews of the computer processing logs to determine that all of the correct computer jobs executed properly for processing
- ○ Formal procedures and documentation specifying authorized recipients of output reports, checks, or other critical documents

INTERNET SECURITY AND ELECTRONIC COMMERCE

Linking to the Internet or transmitting information via intranets and extranets require special security measures. Large public networks, including the Internet, are more vulnerable because they are virtually open to anyone and because they are so huge that when abuses do occur, they can have an enormously widespread impact. When the Internet becomes part of the corporate network, the organization's information systems can be vulnerable to actions from outsiders. Computers that are constantly connected to the Internet via cable modem or DSL line are more open to penetration by outsiders because they are more likely to use a fixed Internet address where they can be more easily identified by outsiders. Chapter 8 describes the use of *firewalls* to prevent unauthorized users from accessing private networks. As growing numbers of businesses and individuals expose their networks continually to Internet traffic, firewalls are becoming a necessity.

A firewall is generally placed between internal LANs and WANs and external networks such as the Internet. The firewall controls access to the organization's internal networks by acting like a gatekeeper that examines each user's credentials before users are allowed access to

Check Point's FireWall-1 software provides a user-friendly graphical interface for defining security rules. FireWall-1 includes tools to monitor and control what goes into and out of an organization's network.

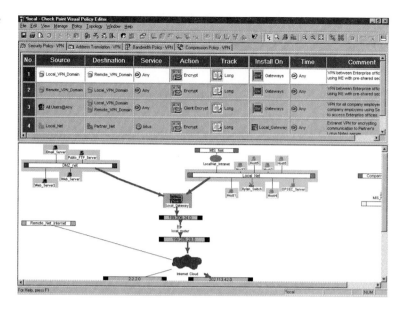

the network. The firewall identifies names, Internet Protocol (IP) addresses, applications, and other characteristics of incoming traffic. It checks this information against the access rules that have been programmed into the system by the network administrator. The firewall prevents unauthorized communication into and out of the network, allowing the organization to enforce a security policy on traffic flowing between its network and the Internet (Oppliger, 1997).

There are essentially two major types of firewall technologies: proxies and stateful inspection. *Proxies* stop data originating outside the organization at the firewall, inspect them, and pass a proxy to the other side of the firewall. If a user outside the company wants to communicate with a user inside the organization, the outside user first "talks" to the proxy application and the proxy application communicates with the firm's internal computer. Likewise, a computer user inside the organization goes through the proxy to "talk" to computers on the outside. Because the actual message doesn't pass through the firewall, proxies are considered more secure than stateful inspection. However, they have to do a lot of work and can consume system resources, degrading network performance. The Raptor Firewall product is primarily a proxy-based firewall.

In *stateful inspection,* the firewall scans each packet of incoming data, checking its source, destination addresses, or services. It sets up state tables to track information over multiple packets. User-defined access rules must identify every type of packet that the organization does not want to admit. Although stateful inspection consumes fewer network resources than proxies, it is theoretically not as secure because some data pass through the firewall. Cisco Systems' firewall product is an example of a stateful inspection firewall. Hybrid firewall products are being developed. For instance, Check Point is primarily a stateful inspection product but it has incorporated some proxy capabilities for communication.

To create a good firewall, someone must write and maintain the internal rules identifying the people, applications, or addresses that are allowed or rejected in very fine detail. Firewalls can deter, but not completely prevent, network penetration from outsiders and should be viewed as one element in an overall security plan. In order to deal effectively with Internet security, broader corporate policies and procedures, user responsibilities, and security awareness training may be required (Segev, Porra, and Roldan, 1998).

Security and Electronic Commerce

Security of electronic communications is a major control issue for companies engaged in electronic commerce. It is essential that commerce-related data of buyers and sellers be kept private when they are transmitted electronically. The data being transmitted also must be protected against being purposefully altered by someone other than the sender, so that, for example, stock market execution orders or product orders accurately represent the wishes of the buyer and seller.

Many organizations rely on encryption to protect sensitive information transmitted over networks. **Encryption** is the coding and scrambling of messages to prevent unauthorized access to or understanding of the data being transmitted. A message can be encrypted by applying a secret numerical code called an encryption key so that it is transmitted as a scrambled set of characters. (The key consists of a large group of letters, numbers, and symbols.) In order to be read, the message must be decrypted (unscrambled) with a matching key. A number of encryption standards exist. SSL (Secure Sockets Layer) and S-HTTP (Secure Hypertext Transport Protocol) are protocols for secure information transfer over the Internet. They allow client and server computers to manage encryption and decryption activities as they communicate with each other during a secure Web session.

There are several alternative methods of encryption, but "public key" encryption is becoming popular. Public key encryption, illustrated in Figure 13-6, uses two different keys, one private and one public. The keys are mathematically related so that data encrypted with one key only can be decrypted using the other key. To send and receive messages, communicators first create separate pairs of private and public keys. The public key is kept in a directory and the private key must be kept secret. The sender encrypts a message with the recipient's public key. On receiving the message, the recipient uses his or her private key to decrypt it.

Encryption is especially useful to shield messages on the Internet and other public networks because they are less secure than private networks. Encryption helps protect transmission of payment data, such as credit card information, and addresses problems of authentication and message integrity. **Authentication** refers to the ability of each party to know that the other parties are who they claim to be. In the nonelectronic world, we use our signatures. Bank-by-mail systems avoid the need for signatures on checks they issue for their customers by using well-protected private networks where the source of the request for payment is recorded and can be proven. **Message integrity** is the ability to be certain that the message that is sent arrives without being copied or changed.

Experts are working on standards for certified digital signatures. A **digital signature** is a digital code attached to an electronically transmitted message that is used to verify the origins and contents of a message. It provides a way to associate a message with the sender, performing a function similar to a written signature. A recipient of data can use the digital signature to verify who sent the data and that the data were not altered after being "signed."

Authentication can be reinforced by attaching a **digital certificate** to an electronic message. A digital certificate system uses a trusted third party known as a certificate authority (CA) to verify a user's identity. The CA system can be run as a function inside an organization or by an outside company such as VeriSign Inc. in Mountain View, California. The CA verifies a digital certificate user's identity off-line by telephone, postal mail, or in person. This information is put into a CA server, which generates an encrypted digital certificate containing owner identification information and a copy of the owner's public key. The certificate authenticates that the public key belongs to the designated owner. The CA makes its own public key available publicly either in print or perhaps on the Internet. The recipient of an encrypted message uses the CA's public key to decode the digital certificate attached to the message, verifies it was

encryption The coding and scrambling of messages to prevent their being read or accessed without authorization.

authentication The ability of each party in a transaction to ascertain the identity of the other party.

message integrity The ability to ascertain that a transmitted message has not been copied or altered.

digital signature A digital code attached to an electronically transmitted message that uniquely identifies its contents and the sender.

digital certificate An attachment to an electronic message that verifies the identity of the sender and provides the receiver with the means to encode a reply.

FIGURE 13-6 Public key encryption. A public key encryption system can be viewed as a series of public and private keys that lock data when they are transmitted and unlock the data when they are received. The sender locates the recipient's public key in a directory and uses it to encrypt a message. The message is sent in encrypted form over the Internet or a private network. When the encrypted message arrives, the recipient uses his or her private key to decrypt the data and read the message.

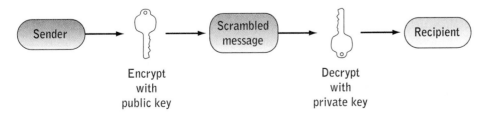

issued by the CA, and then obtains the sender's public key and identification information contained in the certificate. Using this information, the recipient can send an encrypted reply. The digital certificate system would enable, for example, a credit card user and merchant to validate that their digital certificates were issued by an authorized and trusted third party before they exchange data.

Much on-line commerce continues to be handled through private EDI networks usually run over VANs. VANs (value-added networks) are relatively secure and reliable. However, because they have to be privately maintained and run on high-speed private lines, VANs are expensive, easily costing a company $100,000 per month. They also are inflexible because they are connected only to a limited number of sites and companies. As a result, the Internet is emerging as the network technology of choice. EDI transactions on the Internet run from one-half to one-tenth the cost of VAN-based transactions (Knowles, 1997).

Secure Electronic Payment Systems

Special systems have been developed to handle ways of paying for goods electronically on the Internet. They include systems for credit card payments, digital cash, digital wallets, smart cards, electronic checks, and electronic billing systems.

The more sophisticated electronic commerce merchant server software has capabilities for processing credit card purchases on the Web. Businesses can also contract with services such as PC Authorize, WebAuthorize, and ICVerify to process their credit card transactions. These services accept merchant transactions containing customer credit card information, authenticate the credit card to make sure that it is valid and that funds are available, and arrange for the bank that issued the credit card to deposit money for the amount of the purchase in the merchant's bank account.

Digital wallets make paying for purchases over the Web more efficient by eliminating the need for shoppers to repeatedly enter their address and credit card information each time they buy something. A **digital wallet** stores credit card, electronic cash, and owner identification information and provides that information at an electronic commerce site's "checkout counter." The electronic wallet enters the shopper's name, credit card number, and shipping information automatically when invoked to complete the purchase. Amazon.com's 1-Click shopping, which enables a consumer to automatically fill in shipping and credit card information by clicking one button, uses electronic wallet technology. 1-Click is proprietary and only works at Amazon.com, but there are electronic wallet systems such as Microsoft Passport, Gator, and America Online's Quick Checkout that can be used at many different electronic commerce sites.

Many credit card payment systems use the Secure Sockets Layer (SSL) protocol (which is included in standard Web browser software) for encrypting the credit card payment data. However, SSL does not verify that the purchaser is the owner of the card being used for payment. VISA International, MasterCard International, American Express, and other major credit card companies and banks have adopted a more secure protocol called the **Secure Electronic Transaction (SET)** protocol for encrypting credit card payment data over the Internet and other open networks. Figure 13-7 illustrates how SET works. A user acquires a digital certificate and digital wallet from his or her bank, which acts like an intermediary in an e-commerce transaction. The wallet and certificate specify the identity of the user and the credit card being used. When the user shops at a Web site that uses the SET payment method, the merchant's servers send a signal over the Internet that invokes the user's SET wallet. The digital wallet encrypts the payment information and sends it to the merchant. The merchant verifies that the information is a SET packet and adds its digital certificate to the message. The merchant then encrypts this information and passes it on to a payment clearinghouse and to a certificate authority, which verifies the transaction as belonging to the sender. The clearinghouse approves or denies the transaction based on credit standing and passes that information over the Internet to the merchant and back to the user's wallet. The approved transaction is sent to the merchant's bank, which arranges for the fund transfer from the user's to the merchant's account, and the user's credit card account is charged for the transaction amount. The merchant ships the merchandise to the purchaser.

Micropayment systems have been developed for purchases that cost less than $10, which would be too small for credit card payments. If one needed to pay an Internet service

digital wallet Software that stores credit card, electronic cash, owner identification, and address information and provides these data automatically during electronic commerce purchase transactions.

Secure Electronic Transaction (SET) A standard for securing credit card transactions over the Internet and other networks.

micropayments Payments for very small sums of money, often $1.00 or less.

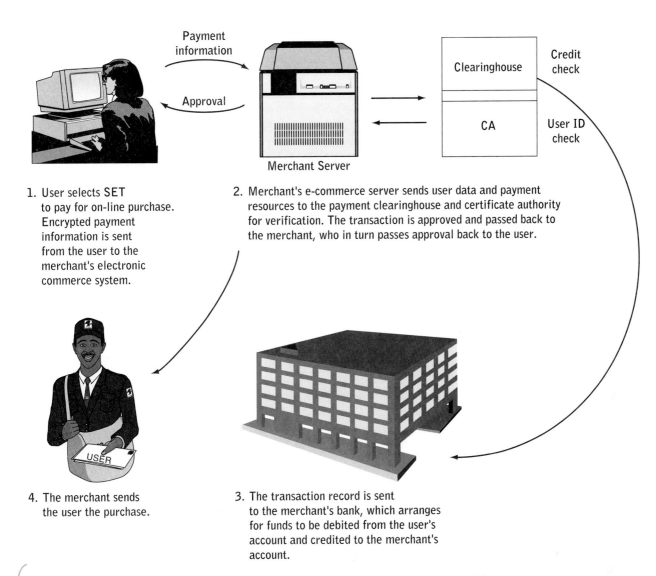

1. User selects SET to pay for on-line purchase. Encrypted payment information is sent from the user to the merchant's electronic commerce system.

2. Merchant's e-commerce server sends user data and payment resources to the payment clearinghouse and certificate authority for verification. The transaction is approved and passed back to the merchant, who in turn passes approval back to the user.

4. The merchant sends the user the purchase.

3. The transaction record is sent to the merchant's bank, which arranges for funds to be debited from the user's account and credited to the merchant's account.

FIGURE 13-7 How SET (Secure Electronic Transaction protocol) works. The SET standard for secure credit card transactions supports both sellers and buyers.

$1.50 to search for a specific piece of information or several dollars to reprint an article, electronic cash or smart cards would be useful for this purpose. **Electronic cash** or **e-cash** is currency represented in electronic form that is moving outside the normal network of money (paper currency, coins, checks, credit cards) and, for now, is not under the purview of the Federal Reserve within the United States. Users are supplied with client software for their PCs and can exchange money with another e-cash user over the Internet. The consumer presents identification to a bank and sets up an electronic cash account with a bank. When the customer makes an on-line purchase, the e-cash software creates a "coin" in an amount specified by the user and sends it to the bank wrapped in a virtual envelope. The bank withdraws the amount requested from the user's account, puts a validating stamp on the envelope to validate the coin's value, and returns it to the user. When the user receives the envelope back, he or she can spend the coin by sending it to an on-line merchant. Digicash, CyberCash and e-Coin.net offer micropayment services. Although e-cash can be very useful for micropayments, consumers have found it confusing to use, and a number of e-cash systems have not proven successful.

Smart cards, which were introduced in Chapter 4, offer an alternative system for processing micropayments because the smart card's microchip can contain electronic cash as well as other information. The Mondex smart card contains electronic cash and can be used to transfer funds to merchants in physical storefronts and to merchants on the Internet. Mondex cards

electronic cash (e-cash)
Currency represented in electronic form that moves outside the normal network of money, preserving the anonymity of its users.

Gator is a digital wallet system which stores personal information in an encrypted file on the user's computer. When the user encounters a registration or order form on the Web, Gator pops up and fills in the form with one or just a few clicks.

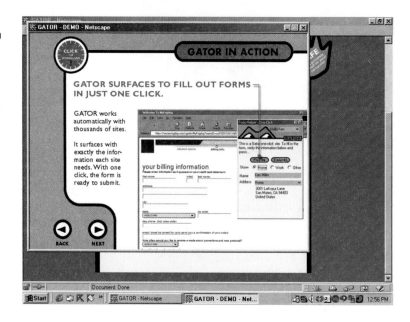

can accept electronic cash transferred from users' bank accounts over the Web. The card requires the use of a special card reading and writing device whenever the card needs to be "recharged" with cash or whenever the card needs to transfer cash to either an on-line or off-line merchant. Internet users must attach a Mondex reader to their PC to use the card. To pay for a Web purchase, the user swipes the smart card through the card reader.

On-line merchants and financial service companies offer bill presentment and payment services over the Web as well as over proprietary networks. These services support payment for on-line and physical store purchases of goods or services after the purchase has taken place. They notify purchasers about bills that are due, present the bills, and process the payments. Some of these services, such as CheckFree, consolidate subscribers' bills from various sources so that they can all be paid at one time.

Payment systems, such as NetChex, that use electronic checks are also available. These checks are encrypted with a digital signature that can be verified and used for payments in electronic commerce. Electronic check systems are especially useful in business-to-business electronic commerce. Table 13-5 summarizes the features of these payment systems.

The Window on Technology describes how companies are using encryption, firewalls, and other technologies to create secure infrastructures for electronic commerce.

Table 13-5 Electronic Payment Systems

Payment System	Description	Commercial Example
Credit card-SET	Protocol providing security for credit card payments on the Internet that protects information transmitted among users, merchant sites, and processing banks	MasterCard, VISA using SET
Electronic cash (e-cash)	Digital currency that can be used for micropayments	CyberCash, e-Coin
Digital (electronic) wallet	Software that stores credit card and other information to facilitate payment for goods on the Web	Passport, Gator, AOL Quick Checkout
Electronic check	Check with an encrypted digital signature	NetChex
Smart card	Microchip that stores electronic cash to use for on-line and off-line micropayments	Mondex
Electronic bill payment	Supports electronic payment for online and physical store purchases of goods or services after the purchase has taken place	CheckFree

BUILDING A SECURITY INFRASTRUCTURE FOR ELECTRONIC COMMERCE

Electronic commerce poses a security paradox because it requires companies to be more open yet more closed at the same time. To benefit from electronic commerce and the Internet, companies need to be open to outsiders, such as customers and trading partners, yet they must be closed to hackers and other intruders. Businesses are trying to create a security culture and infrastructure that allows them to straddle this fine line.

First Union Corporation, the sixth largest bank in the United States, is rapidly moving into on-line banking. Customers can open and close accounts, transfer funds, and apply for loans and mortgages on-line. It is one of the first banks to introduce an on-line stock trading service. Security is so important that First Union's IT security chief is at the same level as its CIO on the company organization chart, and its budget for information systems security alone is more than $5 million. When First Union considers mergers or acquisitions, it reviews the security measures at the other company even before examining the other company's finances.

First Union uses a wide array of security tools to protect its information assets. Multiple internal and external firewalls protect the bank's networks and Internet connections from both external and internal intruders. Secure virtual private networks (VPNs) connect the bank to its business partners. The bank is trying to use encryption for virtually all external communication, including e-mail. To provide additional security for its Internet offerings and funds transfer services, First Union is using authentication tokens from Vasco Data Security International, which generates one-time passwords.

First Union built security-compliance software tools for all of its hardware and software platforms. These tools evaluate the level of security of specified systems or network components against a company standard so that security personnel can determine if systems are meeting First Union's compliance goals. The bank's security programs take into account the level of risk of a system. For example, a system supporting funds transfer would have a high risk level and, therefore, require a high level of security.

First Union provides ongoing security training for employees through videos, manuals, and the Web. The bank posts security updates on its intranet, and information systems managers and administrators can download security standards for specific computing platforms from its Web site. Managers must attend information systems security training sessions several times a year.

Libbey Inc., a glass manufacturer and china and tableware distributor based in Toledo, Ohio, became concerned about its security exposure as its presence grew on the Web. Libbey has about 300 users authorized for Web access and wanted to isolate its internal network from external Internet users except for a few well-defined points. Phil Reed, Libbey's network administrator, helped install the company's network for its 1,100 employees in 1996. When he began testing for new vulnerabilities, he found numerous security holes. Reed immediately started searching for a firewall and installed FireWall-1 from CheckPoint Software Technologies. Reed found CheckPoint's user interface for defining access rules easy to use. Reed could also pick and choose the products from CheckPoint's suite that best fit his security plan.

Initially, Libbey's firewall ran on a 166 MegaHertz Pentium computer running the Windows NT operating system. Reed observed that the firewall was starting to require more resources than could be provided by its computer hardware platform. Libbey's firewall has to handle 85,000 to 100,000 accesses per day, most of which are from internal company users surfing the Web for business reasons.

Primus Telecommunications Group turned to Pilot Network Services Inc. for a distributed security architecture to improve the security of its global network. Primus connected its computer center to Pilot's Heuristic Defense Infrastructure, a network system that monitors e-mail and other data traveling over a network, detects e-mail-borne viruses, and identifies unauthorized network access. By enhancing security through the Pilot system, Primus expects to improve its Internet access, business-to-business electronic commerce, and Web hosting services it offers to other businesses.

TO THINK ABOUT: What management, organization, and technology issues should be considered when developing a security infrastructure for electronic commerce?

Sources: Brian Riggs, "Stronger Security for Global Networks," *Information Week*, January 10, 2000; Bob Violino and Amy K. Larsen, "Security: An E-Biz Asset," *Information Week*, February 15, 1999; and Gerald Lazar, "A Net for the Net," *Datamation*, January 1999.

DEVELOPING A CONTROL STRUCTURE: COSTS AND BENEFITS

Information systems can make exhaustive use of all the control mechanisms previously discussed. But they may be so expensive to build and so complicated to use that the system is economically or operationally unfeasible. Some cost/benefit analysis must be performed to determine which control mechanisms provide the most effective safeguards without sacrificing operational efficiency or cost.

One of the criteria that determines how much control is built into a system is the importance of its data. Major financial and accounting systems, such as a payroll system or one that tracks purchases and sales on the stock exchange, must have higher standards of control than a tickler system to track dental patients and remind them that their six-month checkup is due. For instance, Swissair invested in additional hardware and software to increase its network reliability because it was running critical reservation and ticketing applications.

The cost effectiveness of controls also will be influenced by the efficiency, complexity, and expense of each control technique. For example, complete one-for-one checking may be time consuming and operationally impossible for a system that processes hundreds of thousands of utilities payments daily. But it might be possible to use this technique to verify only critical data such as dollar amounts and account numbers, while ignoring names and addresses.

A third consideration is the level of risk if a specific activity or process is not properly controlled. System builders can undertake a **risk assessment** to determine the likely frequency of a problem and the potential damage if it were to occur. For example, if an event is likely to occur no more than once a year, with a maximum of $1,000 loss to the organization, it would not be feasible to spend $20,000 on the design and maintenance of a control to protect against that event. However, if that same event could occur at least once a day, with a potential loss of more than $300,000 a year, $100,000 spent on a control might be entirely appropriate.

Table 13-6 illustrates sample results of a risk assessment for an on-line order processing system that processes 30,000 orders per day. The probability of a power failure occurring in a one-year period is 30 percent. Loss of order transactions while power is down could range from $5,000 to $200,000 for each occurrence, depending on how long processing was halted. The probability of embezzlement occurring over a yearly period is about 5 percent, with potential losses ranging from $1,000 to $50,000 for each occurrence. User errors have a 98 percent chance of occurring over a yearly period, with losses ranging from $200 to $40,000 for each occurrence. The average loss for each event can be weighted by multiplying it by the probability of its occurrence annually to determine the expected annual loss. Once the risks have been assessed, system builders can concentrate on the control points with the greatest vulnerability and potential loss. In this case, controls should focus on ways to minimize the risk of power failures and user errors. Increasing management awareness of the full range of actions they can take to reduce risks can substantially reduce system losses (Straub and Welke, 1998).

In some situations, organizations may not know the precise probability of threats occurring to their information systems, and they may not be able to quantify the impact of such events. In these instances, management may choose to describe risks and their likely impact in a qualitative manner (Rainer, Snyder, and Carr, 1991).

To decide which controls to use, information system builders must examine various control techniques in relation to each other and to their relative cost effectiveness. A weak control at one point may be offset by a strong control at another. It may not be cost effective to build tight controls at every point in the processing cycle if the areas of greatest risk are secure or if

risk assessment Determining the potential frequency of the occurrence of a problem and the potential damage if the problem were to occur. Used to determine the cost/benefit of a control.

Table 13-6 On-Line Order Processing Risk Assessment

Exposure	Probability of Occurrence (%)	Loss Range/ Average ($)	Expected Annual Loss ($)
Power failure	30	5,000–200,000 (102,500)	30,750
Embezzlement	5	1,000–50,000 (25,500)	1,275
User error	98	200–40,000 (20,100)	19,698

This chart shows the results of a risk assessment of three selected areas of an on-line order processing system. The likelihood of each exposure occurring over a one-year period is expressed as a percentage. The third column shows the highest and lowest possible loss that could be expected each time the exposure occurred and an average loss calculated by adding the highest and lowest figures together and dividing by two. The expected annual loss for each exposure can be determined by multiplying the average loss by its probability of occurrence.

ANALYZING SECURITY VULNERABILITIES

A survey of your firm's information technology infrastructure has produced the following security analysis statistics:

Security Vulnerabilities by Type of Computing Platform

Platform	Number of Computers	High Risk	Medium Risk	Low Risk	Total Vulnerabilities
Windows 2000 Server (corporate applications)	1	11	37	19	
Windows 2000 Workstation (high-level administrators)	3	56	242	87	
Linux (e-mail and printing services)	1	3	154	98	
Sun Solaris (Unix) (E-commerce and Web servers)	2	12	299	78	
Windows 95/98 User desktops and laptops with office productivity tools that can also be linked to the corporate network running corporate applications and intranet	195	14	16	1237	

High risk vulnerabilities include non-authorized users accessing applications, guessable passwords, user name matching the password, active user accounts with missing passwords, and the existence of unauthorized programs in application systems.

Medium risk vulnerabilities include the ability of users to shut down the system without being logged on, passwords and screen saver settings that were not established for PCs, and outdated versions of software still being stored on hard drives.

Low risk vulnerabilities include the inability of users to change their passwords, user passwords that have never been changed, and passwords that were smaller than the minimum size specified by the company.

1. Calculate the total number of vulnerabilities for each platform. What is the potential impact of the security problems identified for each computing platform on the organization?

2. If you only have one information systems specialist in charge of security, which platforms should you address first in trying to eliminate these vulnerabilities? Second? Third? Last? Why?

3. Identify the types of control problems illustrated by these vulnerabilities and explain the measures that should be taken to solve them.

4. What does your firm risk by ignoring the security vulnerabilities identified?

compensating controls exist elsewhere. The combination of all of the controls developed for a particular application will determine its overall control structure.

THE ROLE OF AUDITING IN THE CONTROL PROCESS

How does management know that information systems controls are effective? To answer this question, organizations must conduct comprehensive and systematic audits. An **MIS audit** identifies all of the controls that govern individual information systems and assesses their effectiveness. To accomplish this, the auditor must acquire a thorough understanding of operations, physical facilities, telecommunications, control systems, data security objectives, organizational structure, personnel, manual procedures, and individual applications.

The auditor usually interviews key individuals who use and operate a specific information system concerning their activities and procedures. Application controls, overall integrity controls, and control disciplines are examined. The auditor should trace the flow of sample transactions through the system and perform tests using, if appropriate, automated audit software.

The audit lists and ranks all control weaknesses and estimates the probability of their occurrence. It then assesses the financial and organizational impact of each threat. Figure 13-8 is a sample auditor's listing of control weaknesses for a loan system. It includes a section for notifying management of such weaknesses and for management's response. Management is expected to devise a plan for countering significant weaknesses in controls.

MIS audit Identifies all the controls that govern individual information systems and assesses their effectiveness.

Auditors can analyze the quality of data in a system by conducting a survey of data files for accuracy.

13.3 Ensuring System Quality

Organizations can improve system quality by using software quality assurance techniques and by improving the quality of their data.

SOFTWARE QUALITY ASSURANCE

Solutions to software quality problems include using an appropriate systems development methodology, proper resource allocation during systems development, metrics, attention to testing, and quality tools.

FIGURE 13-8 Sample auditor's list of control weaknesses. This chart is a sample page from a list of control weaknesses that an auditor might find in a loan system in a local commercial bank. This form helps auditors record and evaluate control weaknesses and shows the results of discussing those weaknesses with management, as well as any corrective actions taken by management.

Function: Personal Loans _____   Prepared by: _____ J. Ericson _____   Received by: _____ T. Barrow _____
Location: Peoria, Ill. _____   Preparation date: __ June 16, 2000 _____   Review date: _____ June 28, 2000 _____

Nature of Weakness and Impact	Chance for Substantial Error		Effect on Audit Procedures	Notification to Management	
	Yes/ No	Justification	Required Amendment	Date of Report	Management Response
Loan repayment records are not reconciled to borrower's records during processing.	Yes	Without a detection control, errors in individual client balances may remain undetected.	Confirm a sample of loans.	5/10/00	Interest Rate Compare Report provides this control.
There are no regular audits of computer-generated data (interest charges).	Yes	Without a regular audit or reasonableness check, widespread miscalculations could result before errors are detected.		5/10/00	Periodic audits of loans will be instituted.
Programs can be put into production libraries to meet target deadlines without final approval from the Standards and Controls group.	No	All programs require management authorization. The Standards and Controls group controls access to all production systems, and assigns such cases to a temporary production status.			

Methodologies

Chapter 10 described widely used systems development methodologies. The primary function of a development methodology is to provide discipline to the entire development process. A good development methodology establishes organization-wide standards for requirements gathering, design, programming, and testing. To produce quality software, organizations must select an appropriate methodology and then enforce its use. The methodology should call for systems requirement and specification documents that are complete, detailed, accurate, and documented in a format the user community can understand before they approve it. Specifications also must include agreed-on measures of system quality so that the system can be evaluated objectively while it is being developed and once it is completed.

Resource Allocation During Systems Development

Views on **resource allocation** during systems development have changed significantly over the years. Resource allocation determines the way the costs, time, and personnel are assigned to different phases of the project. In earlier times, developers focused on programming, and only about 1 percent of the time and costs of a project were devoted to systems analysis (determining specifications). More time should be spent in specifications and systems analysis, decreasing the proportion of programming time and reducing the need for so much maintenance time. Documenting requirements so that they can be understood from their origin through development, specification, and continuing use can also reduce errors as well as time and costs (Domges and Pohl, 1998). Current literature suggests that about one-quarter of a project's time and cost should be expended in specifications and analysis, with perhaps 50 percent of its resources being allocated to design and programming. Installation and postimplementation ideally should require only one-quarter of the project's resources. Investments in software quality initiatives early in a project are likely to provide the greatest payback (Slaughter, Harter, and Krishnan, 1998).

resource allocation The determination of how costs, time, and personnel are assigned to different phases of a systems development project.

Software Metrics

Software metrics can play a vital role in increasing system quality. **Software metrics** are objective assessments of the system in the form of quantified measurements. Ongoing use of metrics allows the IS department and the user jointly to measure the performance of the system and identify problems as they occur. Examples of software metrics include the number of transactions that can be processed in a specified unit of time, on-line response time, the number of payroll checks printed per hour, and the number of known bugs per hundred lines of code. Unfortunately, most manifestations of quality are not so easy to define in metric terms. In those cases developers must find indirect measurements. For example, an objective measurement of a system's ease of use might be the number of calls for help the IS staff receives per month from system users.

For metrics to be successful, they must be carefully designed, formal, and objective. They must measure significant aspects of the system. In addition, metrics are of no value unless they are used consistently and users agree to the measurements in advance.

software metrics The objective assessments of the software used in a system in the form of quantified measurements.

Testing

Early, regular, and thorough testing will contribute significantly to system quality. In general, software testing is often misunderstood. Many view testing as a way to prove the correctness of work they have done. In fact, we know that all sizable software is riddled with errors, and we must test to uncover these errors.

Testing begins at the design phase. Because no coding yet exists, the test normally used is a **walkthrough**—a review of a specification or design document by a small group of people carefully selected based on the skills needed for the particular objectives being tested. Once coding begins, coding walkthroughs also can be used to review program code. However, code must be tested by computer runs. When errors are discovered, the source is found and eliminated through a process called **debugging.**

Chapter 9 described the stages of testing required to put an information system in operation—program testing, system testing, and acceptance testing. Testing will be successful only if planned properly.

walkthrough Review of a specification or design document by a small group of people carefully selected based on the skills needed for the particular objectives being tested.

debugging The process of discovering and eliminating the errors and defects—the bugs—in program code.

Quality Tools

Finally, system quality can be significantly enhanced by the use of quality tools. Many tools have been developed to address every aspect of the systems development process. Information systems professionals are using project management software to manage their projects. Products exist to document specifications and system design in text and graphic forms. Programming tools include data dictionaries, libraries to manage program modules, and tools that actually produce program code (see Chapters 5 and 10). Many types of tools exist to aid in the debugging process. The most recent set of tools automates much of the preparation for comprehensive testing.

DATA QUALITY AUDITS

data quality audit Survey of files and samples of files for accuracy and completeness of data in an information system.

Information system quality also can be improved by identifying and correcting faulty data, making error detection a more explicit organizational goal (Klein, Goodhue, and Davis, 1997). The analysis of data quality often begins with a **data quality audit,** which is a structured survey of the accuracy and level of completeness of the data in an information system. Data quality audits are accomplished by the following methods:

○ Surveying end users for their perceptions of data quality

○ Surveying entire data files

○ Surveying samples from data files

Unless regular data quality audits are undertaken, organizations have no way of knowing to what extent their information systems contain inaccurate, incomplete, or ambiguous information. Unfortunately, many organizations are not giving data quality the priority it deserves (Tayi and Ballou, 1998). Some organizations, such as the Social Security Administration, have established data quality audit procedures. These procedures control payment and process quality by auditing a 20,000-case sample of beneficiary records each month. The FBI, however, did not conduct a comprehensive audit of its record systems until 1984. With few data quality controls, the FBI criminal record systems were found to have serious problems.

MANAGEMENT WRAP-UP

Management

Management is responsible for developing the control structure and quality standards for the organization. Key management decisions include establishing standards for systems accuracy and reliability, determining an appropriate level of control for organizational functions, and establishing a disaster recovery plan.

Organization

The characteristics of the organization play a large role in determining its approach to quality assurance and control issues. Some organizations are more quality and control conscious than others. Their cultures and business processes support high standards of quality and performance. Creating high levels of security and quality in information systems can entail a lengthy process of organizational change.

Technology

A number of technologies and methodologies are available for promoting system quality and security. Technologies such as antivirus and data security software, firewalls, and programmed procedures can be used to create a control environment, whereas software metrics, systems development methodologies, and automated tools for systems development can be used to improve software quality. Organizational discipline is required to use these technologies effectively.

1. It has been said that controls and security should be among the first areas to be addressed in the design of an information system. Do you agree? Why or why not?

2. How much software testing is "enough"? What management, organization, and technology issues should you consider in answering this question?

SUMMARY

1. Demonstrate why information systems are so vulnerable to destruction, error, abuse, and system quality problems. With data concentrated into electronic form and many procedures invisible through automation, computerized information systems are vulnerable to destruction, misuse, error, fraud, and hardware or software failures. The effect of disaster in a computerized system can be greater than in manual systems because all of the records for a particular function or organization can be destroyed or lost. On-line systems and those utilizing the Internet are especially vulnerable because data and files can be immediately and directly accessed through computer terminals or at many points in the network. Computer viruses can spread rampantly from system to system, clogging computer memory or destroying programs and data. Software presents problems because of the high costs of correcting errors and because software bugs may be impossible to eliminate. Data quality can also severely impact system quality and performance.

2. Compare general controls and application controls for information systems, including controls to safeguard use of the Internet. Controls consist of all the methods, policies, and organizational procedures that ensure the safety of the organization's assets, the accuracy and reliability of its accounting records, and adherence to management standards. There are two main categories of controls: general controls and application controls.

General controls handle the overall design, security, and use of computer programs and files for the organization as a whole. They include physical hardware controls, system software controls, data file security controls, computer operations controls, controls over the system implementation process, and administrative disciplines.

Application controls are those unique to specific computerized applications. They focus on the completeness and accuracy of input, updating and maintenance, and the validity of the information in the system. Application controls consist of (1) input controls, (2) processing controls, and (3) output controls.

3. Select the factors that must be considered when developing the controls for information systems. To determine which controls are required, designers and users of systems must identify all of the control points and control weaknesses and perform risk assessment. They must also perform a cost/benefit analysis of controls and design controls that can effectively safeguard systems without making them unusable.

4. Describe the technologies used for Internet security and the major types of secure electronic payment systems for e-commerce. Firewalls help safeguard private networks from unauthorized access when organizations use intranets or link to the Internet. Encryption is a widely used technology for securing electronic payment systems by coding and scrambling messages to prevent them from being understood.

Secure electronic payment systems for the Internet include credit card payment systems based on SSL and SET protocols, electronic cash (e-cash and smart cards for micropayments), electronic checks, electronic billing systems, and digital wallets.

5. Describe the most important software quality assurance techniques. The quality and reliability of software can be improved by using a standard development methodology, software metrics, thorough testing procedures, quality tools, and by reallocating resources to put more emphasis on the analysis and design stages of systems development.

6. Demonstrate the importance of auditing information systems and safeguarding data quality. Comprehensive and systematic MIS auditing can help organizations determine the effectiveness of the controls in their information systems. Regular data quality audits should be conducted to help organizations ensure a high level of completeness and accuracy of the data stored in their systems.

KEY TERMS

Administrative controls, 431

Antivirus software, 423

Application controls, 429

Authentication, 435

Bugs, 425

Computer matching, 433

Computer operations
   controls, 430

Computer virus, 422

Control totals, 432

Controls, 429

Data quality audit, 444

Data security controls, 430

Debugging, 443

Digital certificate, 435

Digital signature, 435

Digital wallet, 436

Edit checks, 432

Electronic cash (e-cash), 437

Encryption, 435

Fault-tolerant computer
   systems, 425

General controls, 429

Hacker, 422

Hardware controls, 430

Implementation controls, 429

Input controls, 432

Message integrity, 435

Micropayments, 436

MIS audit, 441

On-line transaction
   processing, 425

REVIEW QUESTIONS

1. Why are computer systems more vulnerable than manual systems to destruction, fraud, error, and misuse? Name some of the key areas where systems are most vulnerable.

2. List some features of on-line information systems that make them difficult to control.

3. What are fault-tolerant computer systems? When should they be used?

4. How can bad software and data quality affect system performance and reliability? Describe two software quality problems.

5. What are controls? Distinguish between general controls and application controls.

6. Name and describe the principal general controls for computerized systems.

7. List and describe the principal application controls.

8. How does MIS auditing enhance the control process?

9. What is the function of risk assessment?

10. Name and describe four software quality assurance techniques.

11. Why are data quality audits essential?

12. What is security? List and describe controls that promote security for computer hardware, computer networks, computer software, and computerized data.

13. What special security measures must be taken by organizations linking to the Internet?

14. Describe the role of firewalls and encryption systems in promoting security.

15. List and describe the major types of electronic payment systems for Internet electronic commerce.

GROUP PROJECT

Form a group with two or three other students. Select a system described in one of the chapter ending cases. Write a description of the system, its functions, and its value to the organization. Then write a description of both the general and application controls that should be used to protect the organization. Present your findings to the class.

Tools for Interactive Learning

○ Internet Connection

The Internet Connection for this chapter will take you to a series of Web sites where you can complete an exercise to evaluate various secure electronic payment systems for the Internet. You can also use the Interactive Study Guide to test your knowledge of the topics in this chapter and get instant feedback where you need more practice.

○ Electronic Commerce Project

At the Laudon Web Site for Chapter 13, you will find an Electronic Commerce project that uses the interactive software at the Holistix.net Web site to remotely test an e-commerce Web site's transactions, response time, and availability.

○ CD-ROM

If you purchase and use the Multimedia Edition CD-ROM with this chapter, you can complete an interactive exercise asking you to identify the security and control problems faced by a company and select appropriate solutions. You can also find a video clip illustrating the Comdisco disaster recovery service, an audio overview of the major themes of this chapter, and bullet text summarizing the key points of the chapter.

○ Application Exercise

At the Laudon Web site for this chapter, you can find a spreadsheet Application Exercise in which you can perform a security risk assessment.

The Federal Aviation Administration (FAA), through its air traffic controllers, controls all commercial planes in the United States. With many thousands of flights daily, the air space of the United States is very crowded, and without the air traffic controllers, airplane crashes would probably occur daily. The controllers give permission for landings and take offs, they approve flight paths, and they monitor all airplanes in flight. The air traffic controllers have a simple goal—flight safety. With so many airplanes, computer systems are vital to the success of the controllers. The issue in the minds of most observers and many travelers concerns how well the FAA manages its computer systems.

The FAA has more than 250 separate computer systems to manage. Before a flight, pilots file their flight plans, which are then entered into a computer. Once in the air, each plane continually transmits data to computers, including its flight number, location, and altitude. The computers also continually receive data from radar stations around the country and data from weather computers. The systems keep track of all planes in U.S. air space, displaying their locations on a screen. These systems also have specialty functions, such as issuing warnings when two planes are flying too close to one another or when planes are flying too low. In today's world, controllers could not manage airplane traffic without these computers.

Controller applications are divided into two major types of systems. The airport control systems at all commercial airports control all aircraft when they are within 20 to 30 miles of the airport. The others, the Air Route Traffic Control (en-route) systems, operate at 20 centers around the country and control the high-altitude planes that are flying between their points-of-origin and their destinations.

What is the condition of current FAA computer systems? Many of the computers are very old, particularly those used at the Air Route Traffic Control centers. Some even go back to the 1950s and are still using vacuum tubes. Most of the "newer" ones are from the 1960s and 1970s. Of the 20 en-route control sites, only New York, Chicago, Washington, Fort Worth, and Cleveland have modern ES/9121 mainframes. The other 15 sites have large IBM 3083 computers that are at least 15 years old and haven't even

been produced or sold by IBM for 10 years. In fact, according to IBM, fewer than 100 of the 3083s are still in operation. "This is old equipment," explains Craig Lowder, IBM spokesperson, "and it is well past its natural life cycle."

The old computers present many problems. Despite their huge size, these mainframes have less power than today's desktops. Spare parts are hard to obtain. IBM no longer makes many replacement parts for 3083s. One such part, the thermal conduction module, is necessary to keep the computers from overheating. As of February 1998 only 7 spares existed in the world. Another problem is that fewer and fewer technicians are available to keep these computers running. Because they are so old, these computers suffer many breakdowns. For example, from September 1994 to September 1995, 11 major breakdowns occurred. Small outages occur nearly every day at one site or another. To make matters worse, the FAA employs 5,000 fewer computer technicians today than it did 7 or 8 years ago despite the growing number of failures as the equipment ages. In addition to the age of the hardware, much of the software is 30 years old. Outdated software often cannot be updated because of the computers' age. Newer, more sophisticated software could make air travel much safer.

Backup systems do exist, but they do not have many of the more sophisticated functions, such as the warnings when airplanes are too close or too low. Also, many are just as old as the front-line systems. In addition, the controllers' training in these systems is limited. When the backups also fail, the controllers must work directly with pilots, using slips of paper to keep track of each flight—an impossible task given the number of flights. Also, when the backups fail, many flights are not allowed to take off at the affected airports, and flights scheduled to land at those airports must be put in holding patterns or diverted to other airports. This situation costs airlines hundreds of millions of dollars yearly, and it costs passengers major delays and inconvenience.

Air traffic controllers suffer major stress under the best of circumstances. Many feel that the workload on controllers is too heavy, partially because of all the manual processing the old systems require. However, when systems fail, "It's total

chaos," says Chicago controller Ken Kluge. Peter Neumann, a specialist in computer reliability and safety, described it this way: "Controllers are under enormous pressure, and anything that goes slightly wrong makes their job inordinately harder."

The FAA, recognizing it had potential problems, began planning for upgrading in 1983. The project, labeled AAS (Advanced Automation System), called for a complete overhaul of its computers, software, radar units, and communications network. Its original goals were to lower operating costs, to improve systems reliability and efficiency, and to make flying safer. In 1988 the AAS contract was awarded to IBM. The projected was budgeted at $4.8 billion, and completion was targeted for 1994.

The project did not go well. In December 1990, IBM announced that the project was 19 months behind schedule. By late 1992, IBM announced that the project was 33 months late, and it estimated that the cost had risen to $5.1 billion. The project was scaled back, but in December 1993, the estimated cost of the now smaller project rose to $5.9 billion. In April 1994 an independent study commissioned by the FAA concluded that the project design had "a high risk of failure."

In June 1994, the FAA announced further major changes. The contract was shifted from IBM to Lockheed Martin Corp. In addition, major parts of the project were dropped, including a project to combine the two major controller systems and another to replace the hardware and software that controls aircraft near the airports. The plan to replace control tower equipment at the 150 largest airports was downsized to include only the 70 largest airports. The estimated cost of the slimmed-down project was $6 billion, and the planned completion date was postponed to the year 2000.

Evaluations of the new project were mixed. An analyst for a congressional aviation oversight committee summarized the new system as "basically just a replacement of the radar screen for air traffic controllers." However, Frederico Peña, the U.S. Secretary of Transportation, stated the project "is now back on track and will deliver important safety improvements that will carry aviation into the next century."

Meanwhile, signs of system aging were multiplying. For example, in June 1995 a computer outage at Washington Air Route

Traffic Control Center lasted 41 hours, and one in Chicago a year later lasted 122 hours. In August 1998 the Nashua, New Hampshire, center, which is responsible for all of New England and part of New York, went down for 37 minutes. Even before this outage, there were many complaints of frozen radar screens and minor outages. For instance, in October 1996, there was a minor outage in Phoenix in which the power-conditioning system triggered an electrical surge that brought the terminal's radar control system down. Its effects lasted several minutes longer while the computer recaptured the flight-path data.

In 1996 the National Transportation Safety Board (NTSB) issued a report that referred to the many FAA computer failures in recent months that had resulted in reliance on the backup system. The report listed a series of problems, including the special features not found in the backup control systems. It cited frequent hardware failures because of reliance on mainframes that are so old.

In September 1996 a new project, the Standard Terminal Automation Replacement System (STARS), was announced. This announcement marked the end of AAS. Estimates of the cost of AAS range from $7.6 billion to $23 billion, and yet it failed to improve much of the FAA's IT infrastructure. STARS is supposed to bring together flight-plan data, air-traffic automation systems, terminal-control facilities, and radar systems around the United States. The prime contractor this time is Raytheon Co. of Lexington, Massachusetts.

STARS is targeted to replace the 20-year-old systems used by air traffic controllers that control flights near the airports. Its goals are to improve safety and reduce flight delays. It is to be installed at 317 airports and military bases, and installation was to begin at Boston's Logan Airport in 1998. The project, scheduled to be completed in 2007, is estimated to cost about $11 billion through 2003. The new system will have four computers at each site: one primary, one backup, and a second pair that mirrors the first (redundancy).

The FAA started much too late addressing the year 2000 problem in its systems. During February 1998 IBM announced that it would not make its 3083s Y2K-compliant. In response, the FAA quickly announced that it would reprogram its 3083s at a cost of $91 million. This announcement was met with serious

doubt. In October 1998, in a letter from IBM to Lockheed Martin Air Traffic Management, the contractor for these FAA systems, IBM stated that, "The appropriate skills and tools do not exist to conduct a complete year 2000 test assessment" of the 3083 computers. It added, "IBM believes it is imperative that the FAA replace the equipment" before the year 2000.

To be doubly sure its computers would work properly, the FAA announced in February 1998 that it would simultaneously work to replace its 3083s before January 1, 2000, at a cost of about $100 million. Although replacement of the 40 computers may be a possible solution, as of the beginning of 1999 the FAA had budgeted no money for replacement (the cost was estimated as high as $200 million). Even the FAA official in charge of the enroute systems stated in January 1999 that, "it would be an extraordinary feat" to replace approximately forty 3083s by the year 2000.

When January 1, 2000, arrived the FAA reported only a handful of minor outages, far fewer than on an average day. However, hundreds of flights were delayed across the U.S. East Coast when the main computer at the FAA air traffic control center in Leesburg, Virginia, experienced problems transferring data on January 6 and a computer malfunctioned at the FAA center in Nashua, New Hampshire. The FAA quickly solved these problems, noting that they were not Y2K related. Technicians who install and maintain the FAA's equipment weren't so sure. According to Mike Perrone, a national assistant of Professional Airways Systems Specialists (PASS), the FAA technicians' union, the FAA had ordered PASS technicians to install a last-minute software patch to fix a potential Y2K problem at its host computers at the air traffic control centers across the country. PASS wondered if there was a connection between the FAA's computer problems and the patch, despite the FAA's assurance that all of its systems were Y2K compliant.

Why did the FAA have so many problems upgrading its computers and addressing the Y2K problem? One specific issue is the lack of an FAA systems architecture. The FAA did develop a logical architecture called the National Airspace System (NAS). This architecture document describes the FAA's services and functions and outlines the systems needed for both air traffic management

and navigation systems. It even includes a systems plan through the year 2015. Thus, it gives a high-level overview of the business functions and the systems needed to serve them, including the interconnection between the various systems. However, the FAA did not translate this plan into the required physical or technical architecture. The FAA's air traffic control development work is assigned to 1 of 10 teams, and the lack of a technical architecture left all 10 teams to determine their own specific standards for developing the software, hardware, communications, data management, security, and performance characteristics.

Let's look at the results of the lack of standards. Of the 10 development teams, 7 have no technical architecture at all. The other three developed their own architectures, and they are all different. One result is the systems that feed the main computers use several different communications protocols and data formats. Of the three teams with standards, one architecture specifies Ethernet, whereas another specifies Fiber Distributed Data Interface (the two are incompatible). Two of the architectures specify writing programs in C and C++, whereas the third specifies Ada. Altogether the 10 teams developed 54 air traffic control system applications using 53 different languages. Incompatibility is one result. Staffs are forced to spend time (and money) creating complex interfaces, which also must be supported. These translation programs increase the possibility of data errors. Moreover, the use of multiple standards greatly increases staff training costs. The February 1998 GAO report said that the result of the lack of a FAA uniform architecture is that, "the FAA permits and perpetuates" inconsistency and incompatibilities. It stresses that any organization must implement a technical architecture before it replaces an old computer system.

The FAA agreed that the report reflected a problem, but they pointed out that the FAA does have an informal architecture control system in place. "We don't envision having a complete document of technical specifications that we would publish," stated Steven Zaidman, the FAA's director of system architecture. He added, "We're light-years ahead of where we were. We have learned from our past failures."

Congressional observers have severely criticized the culture of the FAA, characterizing its employees as unwilling to face up to its problems. Rona B. Stillman, the GAO's chief scientist for computers, stated that the "FAA has a culture ... that is averse to change and has entrenched autonomous organizations that tend not to respond to change." David Schaefer, the counsel to the U.S. House Aviation Subcommittee, said, "The FAA will say they've worked out their problems, but it turns out it's not enough."

One issue appears to be the organization of the information systems function within the agency. As previously described, with 10 independent development organizations, the FAA lacks needed central control. Regionalized management appears not to work well. According to the GAO, "The FAA certainly could use stronger central direction to ride herd over the regions to ensure technological consistency." The 1997 GAO report concluded, "No FAA organizational entity is responsible for developing and maintaining the technical Air Traffic Control architecture." In its opinion, this leaves the agency "at risk of making ill-informed decisions on critical multimillion-dollar, even billion-dollar, air-traffic-control systems." The same report, in referring to the failure of the AAS project, determined that the "FAA did not recognize the technical complexity of the effort, realistically estimate the resources required, adequately oversee its contractors' activities, or effectively control system requirements."

The IT Management Reform Act of 1996, known also as the Clinger-Cohen Act, mandates major information technology (IT) reforms in government agencies,

including a requirement that federal agencies have CIOs. The FAA has no such centralized management because it successfully lobbied to have itself exempted from the act.

One other problem cited by several labor representatives of the controllers' union is the communications gap between the FAA management and the users of the air traffic control systems. That the gap exists perhaps is no surprise. Problems developed between management and controllers in the 1970s and became a disaster when the controllers went out on strike in 1981 (the Patco union strike). Ultimately, President Reagan dismissed more than 11,000 controllers. The current communications gap is evident when management claims positive results on the STARS project and the controllers apparently disagree. Controllers often have spoken out in meetings, saying that STARS is cumbersome, that the controls are complex, and the terminal displays are unclear.

Sources: Linda Rosencrance, "Update: Technicians: Are FAA Computer Problems Y2K-Related?" Computerworld, January 7, 2000; Alan Sipress, "FAA Glitch Grounds Planes," The Washington Post, January 6, 2000; Sami Lais, "Update: FAA Reports Only Minor Outages," Computerworld, January 1, 2000; Patrick Thibodeau, "IBM Says FAA Air Traffic Computers Should Be Retired," Computerworld, January 15, 1999, and "Air Traffic Controllers Say Old Computers Hobble, FAA," Computerworld, June 22, 1998; Matthew L. Wald, "Warning Issued on Air Traffic Computers," The New York Times, January 12, 1999; Thomas Hoffman, "On a Wing and a Prayer . . .," Computerworld, February 2, 1999 and "Feds Slam FAA for Millennium Mess," Computerworld, February 9, 1998; Matt Hamblen, "IBM, Others Question FAA's 2000 Progress," Computerworld, July 24, 1998, "FAA: Systems Are a Go for 2000," Computerworld, July 24, 1998, and "FAA's IT Management Slammed," Computerworld, February 10, 1997; Jeff Cole, "FAA, Air Groups Agree on Traffic Plan," The Wall Street Journal, April 23, 1998; Mary Mosquera, "FAA Faces Year 2000 Emergency, Report Says," TechWeb, February 4, 1998; Jeff Sweat, "FAA: We're Y2K OK," Information Week, October 5, 1998; Bruce D. Nordwall, "FAA Structural Problems Impede ATC Upgrades," Aviation Week and Space Technology, February 10, 1997; Gary Anthes, "Ancient Systems Put Scare in Air," and "Revamp Flies Off Course," Computerworld, August 5, 1996; "$1B Award to Fix Air Traffic System," Computerworld, September 23, 1996; and George Leopold, "FAA Sets Massive Systems Overhaul, But Will It Fly?" TechWeb News, October 28, 1996.

CASE STUDY QUESTIONS

1. List and explain the control weaknesses in the FAA and its air traffic control systems.

2. What management, organization, and technology factors were responsible for the FAA's control weaknesses?

3. How effectively did the FAA deal with its control weaknesses? Evaluate the importance of the AAS and STARS projects for the FAA, for the air traffic controllers, and for the flying public.

4. Design a complete set of controls for the FAA to deal effectively with its control problems and the management of the FAA's information systems projects.

CHAPTER 14

Ethical and Social Impact of Information Systems

Learning Objectives

After completing this chapter, you will be able to:

1. Analyze the relationship among ethical, social, and political issues raised by information systems.

2. Identify the main moral dimensions of an information society and apply them to specific situations.

3. Apply an ethical analysis to difficult situations.

4. Examine specific ethical principles for conduct.

5. Design corporate policies for ethical conduct.

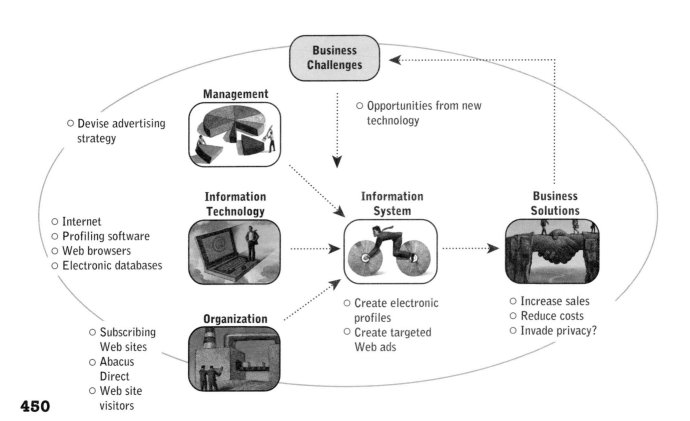

Business Challenges

Management
○ Devise advertising strategy

○ Opportunities from new technology

Information Technology
○ Internet
○ Profiling software
○ Web browsers
○ Electronic databases

Organization
○ Subscribing Web sites
○ Abacus Direct
○ Web site visitors

Information System
○ Create electronic profiles
○ Create targeted Web ads

Business Solutions
○ Increase sales
○ Reduce costs
○ Invade privacy?

Linking Consumer Data On-line and Off-line:

A New Threat to Privacy?

If you move your mouse over an ad on the Web, there's a good chance that you'll see "ad.doubleclick.net" at the bottom of your browser window. An Internet advertising broker called DoubleClick (www.doubleclick.net) placed that ad there using proprietary targeting technology. DoubleClick monitors the activities of visitors to hundreds of cooperating Web sites, including Quicken and Travelocity. These Web sites allow DoubleClick to track the activity of their visitors in exchange for revenue from advertisements based on the visitor information DoubleClick gathers. DoubleClick uses this information to identify potential buyers for ads from other companies. For example, DoubleClick could use this information to identify photography enthusiasts who might be interested in digital cameras.

DoubleClick's proprietary software reads the Internet (IP) addresses of visitors to its subscribing companies' Web sites and matches them against a database of 70,000 Internet domain names that include a line-of-business code. Although DoubleClick does not know a Web site visitor's name, street address, or phone number, it does know the Internet address of the visitor's computer, its operating system, its Web browser, its Internet service provider, and the activities of the visitor at the Web sites it tracks. DoubleClick uses this information to create a dossier for each on-line visitor attached to an identification (ID) number. The first time an on-line surfer visits one of the cooperating DoubleClick sites, the DoubleClick server running that site assigns the visitor an ID number and stores it on the visitor's computer. Whenever that person visits any of the Double Click sites, the DoubleClick server picks up the ID number and gathers information about the visit. Over time, DoubleClick can build up a detailed dossier of a person's spending and computing habits on the Web. DoubleClick has amassed profiles on 10 million anonymous Web visitors.

DoubleClick recently purchased market research firm Abacus Direct, and this targeted advertising could grow even more powerful. Abacus Direct, based in Broomfield, Colorado, manages the Abacus Alliance database holding nearly 3 billion transactions that 80 million households have completed using 1,100 catalogs. Abacus records customer purchases to help catalog companies predict future purchases and to target publications and marketing campaigns more precisely. DoubleClick could use the Abacus data to make sure that ads to individual Web users are customized.

Integrating data collected by both companies raises challenges and concerns. DoubleClick would have to be able to match traffic patterns and anonymous information about browsers and Internet addresses to specific names and addresses in the database of catalog shoppers. But privacy advocates worry that if such on-line and off-line data could be successfully combined, the result would be a massive database of personal information about consumers that could threaten individual privacy. The combined database could contain profiles with an individual's name, address, catalog buying habits, and details of their activities at every Web site they visited that is part of DoubleClick's network, giving marketers much information about an individual's on-line and off-line behavior. Privacy groups such as the Electronic Privacy Information Center believe consumers should have more control over the information that is gathered about them by organizations and how it is used. DoubleClick and Abacus stated that they are concerned about consumer privacy and give people the option of removing themselves from their databases. In response to a probe by the Federal Trade Commission, a lawsuit by the State of Michigan, and a torrent of criticism from privacy advocates, DoubleClick stated in early March 2000 that it would not connect the Abacus data with the data it collects on Web activities until the government and industry groups set privacy standards. DoubleClick also announced it would hire a chief privacy officer and that it had hired Price Waterhouse Coopers LLP to conduct regular privacy audits to ensure that its practices were in accord with its principles.

Sources: Andrea Petersen, "DoubleClick Reverses Course after Privacy Outcry," *The Wall Street Journal,* March 3, 2000; Diane Anderson and Keith Perne, "Marketing the DoubleClick Way," *The Industry Standard,* March 13, 2000; and Nelson Wang, "$1B Ad Targeting Deal Alarms Privacy Groups," *Internet World,* June 21, 1999.

MANAGEMENT CHALLENGES

Technology can be a double-edged sword. It can be the source of many benefits. One great achievement of contemporary computer systems is the ease with which digital information can be analyzed, transmitted, and shared among many people. But at the same time, this powerful capability creates new opportunities for breaking the law or taking benefits away from others. Balancing the convenience and privacy implications of creating electronic dossiers on consumers is one of the compelling ethical issues raised by contemporary information systems. As you read this chapter, you should be aware of the following management challenges:

1. Understanding the moral risks of new technology. Rapid technological change means that the choices facing individuals also rapidly change, and the balance of risk and reward and the probabilities of apprehension for wrongful acts change as well. Protecting individual privacy has become a serious ethical issue precisely for this reason, in addition to other issues described in this chapter. In this environment it is important for management to conduct an ethical and social impact analysis of new technologies. One might take each of the moral dimensions described in this chapter and briefly speculate on how a new technology will impact each dimension. There may not always be right answers for how to behave, but there should be management awareness of the moral risks of new technology.

2. Establishing corporate ethics policies that include information systems issues. As managers you will be responsible for developing, enforcing, and explaining corporate ethics policies. Historically, corporate management has paid much more attention to financial integrity and personnel policies than to the information systems area. But from what you will know after reading this chapter, it is clear that your corporation should have an ethics policy in the information systems area, covering such issues as privacy, property, accountability, system quality, and quality of life. The challenge will be in educating non-IS managers about the need for these policies, as well as educating your workforce.

Protecting personal privacy on the Internet and establishing information rights represent two of the new ethical issues raised by the widespread use of information systems. Others include protecting intellectual property rights, establishing accountability for the consequences of information systems, setting standards to safeguard system quality that protect the safety of the individual and society, and preserving values and institutions considered essential to the quality of life in an information society. This chapter describes these issues and suggests guidelines for dealing with these questions.

14.1 Understanding Ethical and Social Issues Related to Systems

Ethics refers to the principles of right and wrong that individuals, acting as free moral agents, use to make choices to guide their behavior. Information technology and information systems raise new ethical questions for both individuals and societies because they create opportunities for intense social change and, thus, threaten existing distributions of power, money, rights, and obligations. Like other technologies, such as steam engines, electricity, telephone, and radio, information technology can be used to achieve social progress, but it can also be used to commit crimes and threaten cherished social values. The development of information technology will produce benefits for many and costs for others. When using information systems, it is essential to ask, What is the ethical and socially responsible course of action?

ethics Principles of right and wrong that can be used by individuals acting as free moral agents to make choices to guide their behavior.

A MODEL FOR THINKING ABOUT ETHICAL, SOCIAL, AND POLITICAL ISSUES

Ethical, social, and political issues are closely linked. The ethical dilemma you may face as a manager of information systems typically is reflected in social and political debate. One way to think about these relationships is illustrated in Figure 14-1. Imagine society as a more or less calm pond on a summer day, a delicate ecosystem in partial equilibrium with individuals and with social and political institutions. Individuals know how to act in this pond because social institutions (family, education, organizations) have developed well-honed rules of behavior, and these are backed by laws developed in the political sector that prescribe behavior and promise sanctions for violations. Now toss a rock into the center of the pond. But imagine instead of a rock that the disturbing force is a powerful shock of new information technology and systems hitting a society more or less at rest. What happens? Ripples, of course.

Suddenly individual actors are confronted with new situations often not covered by the old rules. Social institutions cannot respond overnight to these ripples—it may take years to

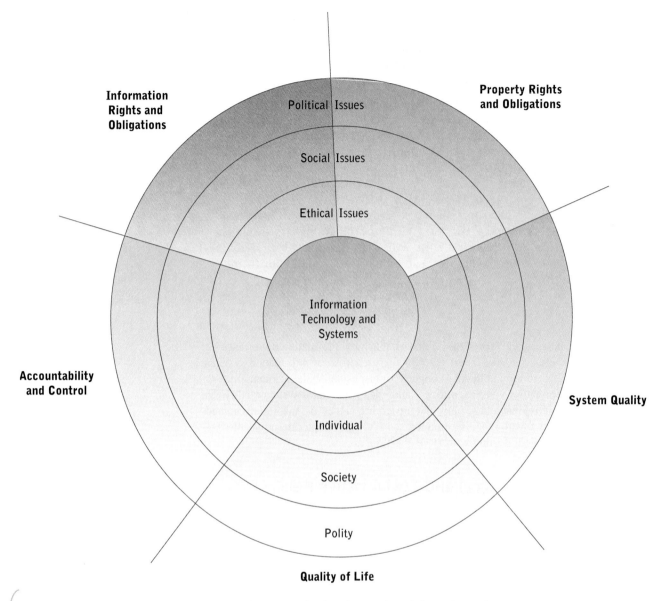

FIGURE 14-1 The relationship between ethical, social, and political issues in an information society. The introduction of new information technology has a ripple effect, raising new ethical, social, and political issues that must be dealt with on the individual, social, and political levels. These issues have five moral dimensions: information rights and obligations, property rights and obligations, system quality, quality of life, and accountability and control.

develop etiquette, expectations, social responsibility, "politically correct" attitudes, or approved rules. Political institutions also require time before developing new laws and often require the demonstration of real harm before they act. In the meantime, you may have to act. You may be forced to act in a "gray area" where moral judgments about what constitutes ethical uses of systems have not yet solidified (Gattiker and Kelley, 1999).

We can use this model to illustrate the dynamics that connect ethical, social, and political issues. This model is also useful for identifying the main moral dimensions of the "information society," which cut across various levels of action—individual, social, and political.

FIVE MORAL DIMENSIONS OF THE INFORMATION AGE

A review of the literature on ethical, social, and political issues surrounding systems identifies five moral dimensions of the information age that we introduce here and explore in greater detail in Section 14.3. The five moral dimensions are as follows:

○ **Information rights and obligations:** What **information rights** do individuals and organizations possess with respect to information about themselves? What can they protect? What obligations do individuals and organizations have concerning this information?

information rights The rights that individuals and organizations have with respect to information that pertains to themselves.

○ **Property rights:** How will traditional intellectual property rights be protected in a digital society in which tracing and accounting for ownership is difficult and ignoring such property rights is so easy?

○ **Accountability and control:** Who can and will be held accountable and liable for the harm done to individuals, collective information, and property rights?

○ **System quality:** What standards of data and system quality should we demand to protect individual rights and the safety of society?

○ **Quality of life:** What values should be preserved in an information- and knowledge-based society? What institutions should we protect from violation? What cultural values and practices are supported by the new information technology?

Before we analyze these dimensions let us briefly review the major technology and system trends that have heightened concern about these issues.

KEY TECHNOLOGY TRENDS THAT RAISE ETHICAL ISSUES

Ethical issues long preceded information technology—they are the abiding concerns of free societies everywhere. Nevertheless, information technology has heightened ethical concerns, put stress on existing social arrangements, and made existing laws obsolete or severely crippled. There are four key technological trends responsible for these ethical stresses and they are summarized in Table 14-1.

The doubling of computing power every 18 months has made it possible for most organizations to use information systems for their core production processes. As a result, our dependence on systems and our vulnerability to system errors and poor data quality have increased. Social rules and laws have not yet adjusted to this dependence. Standards for ensuring the accuracy and reliability of information systems (see Chapter 13) are not universally accepted or enforced.

Advances in data storage techniques and rapidly declining storage costs are responsible for the multiplying databases on individuals—employees, customers, and potential customers—maintained by private and public organizations. These advances in data storage have made the routine violation of individual privacy both cheap and effective. Already massive data storage systems are cheap enough for regional and even local retailing firms to use in identifying customers. For example, Amazon.com is building a massive data warehouse with over 3 terabytes of customer sales data and Web site visitor data that could grow 1000-fold in the next few years (Whiting, 2000).

Advances in datamining techniques for large databases are a third technological trend that heightens ethical concerns because they enable companies to find out detailed personal information about individuals. With contemporary information systems technology, companies can assemble and combine the myriad pieces of information stored on an individual by computers much more easily than in the past. Think of all the ways you generate computer information about yourself—credit card purchases, telephone calls, magazine subscriptions, video

Table 14-1 **Technology Trends That Raise Ethical Issues**

Trend	Impact
Computing power doubles every 18 months	More organizations depend on computer systems for critical operations
Rapidly declining data storage costs	Organizations can easily maintain detailed databases on individuals
Datamining advances	Companies can analyze vast quantities of data gathered on individuals to develop detailed profiles of individual behavior
Networking advances	Copying data from one location to another and accessing personal data from remote locations are easier

Credit card purchases can make personal information available to market researchers, telephone marketers, and direct mail companies. Advances in information technology facilitate the invasion of privacy.

profiling The use of computers to combine data from multiple sources and create electronic dossiers of detailed information on individuals.

rentals, mail-order purchases, banking records, and local, state, and federal government records (including court and police records). Put together and mined properly, this information could reveal not only your credit information but also your driving habits, your tastes, your associations, and your political interests.

Companies with products to sell purchase relevant information from these sources to help them finely target their marketing campaigns. Chapter 2 describes how companies can use datamining on very large pools of data from multiple sources to rapidly identify buying patterns of customers and suggest individual responses. The use of computers to combine data from multiple sources and create electronic dossiers of detailed information on individuals is called **profiling.** DoubleClick, described in the chapter opening vignette, amasses data on Web visitors and uses profiling to help companies target their Web ads precisely.

Last, advances in networking, including the Internet, promise to reduce greatly the costs of moving and accessing large quantities of data and allow the possibility of mining large pools of data remotely using small desktop machines, which will invite an invasion of privacy on a scale and precision heretofore unimaginable.

The development of global, digital-superhighway, communication networks widely available to individuals and businesses poses many ethical and social concerns. Who will take responsibility for the flow of information over these networks? Will you be able to trace and verify information collected about yourself? What will these networks do to the traditional relationships between family, work, and leisure? How will traditional job designs be altered when millions of "employees" become subcontractors using mobile offices for which they themselves must pay?

In the next section we consider some ethical principles and analytical techniques for dealing with these kinds of ethical and social concerns.

14.2 Ethics in an Information Society

Ethics is a concern of humans who have freedom of choice. Ethics is about individual choice: When faced with alternative courses of action, what is the correct moral choice? What are the main features of "ethical choice"?

BASIC CONCEPTS: RESPONSIBILITY, ACCOUNTABILITY, AND LIABILITY

responsibility Accepting the potential costs, duties, and obligations for the decisions one makes.

Ethical choices are decisions made by individuals who are responsible for the consequences of their actions. Responsibility is a key element of ethical action. **Responsibility** means that you accept the potential costs, duties, and obligations for the decisions you make. **Accountability** is a feature of systems and social institutions: It means that mechanisms are in place to determine who took responsible action, who is responsible. Systems and institutions in which it is impossible to find out who took what action are inherently incapable of ethical analysis or ethical action. Liability extends the concept of responsibility further to the area of laws. **Liability** is a feature of political systems in which a body of law is in place that permits individuals to recover the damages done to them by other actors, systems, or organizations. **Due process** is a related feature of law-governed societies and is a process in which laws are known and understood and there is an ability to appeal to higher authorities to ensure that the laws were applied correctly.

These basic concepts form the underpinning of an ethical analysis of information systems and those who manage them. First, as discussed in Chapter 3, information technologies are filtered through social institutions, organizations, and individuals. Systems do not have "impacts" by themselves. Whatever information system impacts exist are products of institutional, organizational, and individual actions and behaviors. Second, responsibility for the consequences of technology falls clearly on the institutions, organizations, and individual managers who choose to use the technology. Using information technology in a "socially responsible" manner means that you can and will be held accountable for the consequences of your actions. Third, in an ethical, political society, individuals and others can recover damages done to them through a set of laws characterized by due process.

accountability The mechanisms for assessing responsibility for decisions made and actions taken.

liability The existence of laws that permit individuals to recover the damages done to them by other individuals, systems, or organizations.

due process A process in which laws are well known and understood, and there is an ability to appeal to higher authorities to ensure that laws are applied correctly.

ETHICAL ANALYSIS

When confronted with a situation that seems to present ethical issues, how should you analyze and reason about the situation? Following is a five-step process that should help:

○ **Identify and describe clearly the facts.** Find out who did what to whom, and where, when, and how. In many instances, you will be surprised at the errors in the initially reported facts, and often you will find that simply getting the facts straight helps define the solution. It also helps to get the opposing parties involved in an ethical dilemma to agree on the facts.

○ **Define the conflict or dilemma and identify the higher-order values involved.** Ethical, social, and political issues always reference higher values. The parties to a dispute all claim to be pursuing higher values (e.g., freedom, privacy, protection of property, and the free enterprise system). Typically, an ethical issue involves a dilemma: two diametrically opposed courses of action that support worthwhile values. For example, the chapter opening vignette and ending case study illustrate two competing values: the need for companies to use marketing to become more efficient and the need to protect individual privacy.

○ **Identify the stakeholders.** Every ethical, social, and political issue has stakeholders: players in the game who have an interest in the outcome, who have invested in the situation, and who usually have vocal opinions. Find out the identity of these groups and individuals and what they want. This will be useful later when designing a solution.

○ **Identify the options that you can reasonably take.** You may find that none of the options satisfy all the interests involved, but some options do a better job than others. Sometimes arriving at a "good" or ethical solution that represents the best interests of the firm or society at large may not always be a "balancing" of consequences to stakeholders (Smith and Hasnas, 1999).

○ **Identify the potential consequences of your options.** Some options may be ethically correct but disastrous from other points of view. Other options may work in one instance but not in other similar instances. Always ask yourself, "What if I choose this option consistently over time?"

Once your analysis is complete, what ethical principles or rules should you use to make a decision? What higher order values should inform your judgment?

CANDIDATE ETHICAL PRINCIPLES

Although you are the only one who can decide which among many ethical principles you will follow, and how you will prioritize them, it is helpful to consider some ethical principles with deep roots in many cultures that have survived throughout history.

Immanuel Kant's Categorical Imperative A principle that states that if an action is not right for everyone to take, it is not right for anyone.

Descartes' rule of change A principle that states that if an action cannot be taken repeatedly, then it is not right to be taken at any time.

Utilitarian Principle Principle that assumes one can put values in rank order and understand the consequences of various courses of action.

Risk Aversion Principle Principle that one should take the action that produces the least harm or incurs the least cost.

ethical "no free lunch" rule Assumption that all tangible and intangible objects are owned by someone else unless there is a specific declaration otherwise and that the creator wants compensation for this work.

1. Do unto others as you would have them do unto you (the Golden Rule). Putting yourself into the place of others, and thinking of yourself as the object of the decision, can help you think about "fairness" in decision making.

2. If an action is not right for everyone to take, then it is not right for anyone (**Immanuel Kant's Categorical Imperative**). Ask yourself, "If everyone did this, could the organization, or society, survive?"

3. If an action cannot be taken repeatedly, then it is not right to take at all (**Descartes' rule of change**). This is the slippery-slope rule: An action may bring about a small change now that is acceptable, but if the action is repeated, it would bring unacceptable changes in the long run. In the vernacular, it might be stated as "once started down a slippery path you may not be able to stop."

4. Take the action that achieves the higher or greater value (the **Utilitarian Principle**). This rule assumes you can prioritize values in a rank order and understand the consequences of various courses of action.

5. Take the action that produces the least harm, or incurs the least potential cost (**Risk Aversion Principle**). Some actions have extremely high failure costs with very low probability (e.g., building a nuclear generating facility in an urban area) or extremely high failure costs of moderate probability (speeding and automobile accidents). Avoid these high failure cost actions; pay greater attention to high failure cost potential with moderate to high probability.

6. Assume that virtually all tangible and intangible objects are owned by someone else unless there is a specific declaration otherwise. (This is the **ethical "no free lunch" rule.**) If something someone else has created is useful to you, it has value and you should assume the creator wants compensation for this work.

Unfortunately, these ethical rules have too many logical and substantive exceptions to be absolute guides to action. Nevertheless, actions that do not observe these rules deserve some very close attention and a great deal of caution because the appearance of unethical behavior may do as much harm to you and your company as actual unethical behavior.

PROFESSIONAL CODES OF CONDUCT

When groups of people claim to be professionals, they accept special rights and obligations because of their special claims to knowledge, wisdom, and respect. Professional codes of conduct are promulgated by associations of professionals such as the American Medical Association (AMA), the American Bar Association (ABA), the Association of Information Technology Professionals (AITP), and the Association of Computing Machinery (ACM). These professional groups take responsibility for the partial regulation of their professions by determining entrance qualifications and competence. Codes of ethics are promises by professions to regulate themselves in the general interest of society. For example, avoiding harm to others, honoring property rights (including intellectual property), and respecting privacy are among the General Moral Imperatives of the ACM's Code of Ethics and Professional Conduct (ACM, 1993).

Extensions to these moral imperatives state that ACM professionals should consider the health, privacy, and general welfare of the public in the performance of their work and that professionals should express their professional opinion to their employer regarding any adverse consequences to the public (see Oz, 1994).

SOME REAL-WORLD ETHICAL DILEMMAS

The recent ethical problems described in this section illustrate a wide range of issues. Some of these issues are obvious, ethical dilemmas in which one set of interests is pitted against another. Others represent some type of breach of ethics. In either instance, there are rarely any easy solutions.

○ **Downsizing with technology at the telephone company.** Many of the large telephone companies in the United States are using information technology to reduce the size of their workforce. For example, AT&T is using voice recognition software to reduce the need for human operators by allowing computers to recognize a customer's responses to a series of computerized questions. AT&T planned for the new technology to eliminate 3,000 to 6,000 operator jobs nationwide, 200 to 400 management positions, and 31 offices in 21 states.

○ **Electronic profiling at the airport.** The Federal Aviation Administration instituted an electronic profiling system to identify potential terrorists. The system collects data about people from multiple sources and uses datamining and artificial intelligence to create a profile on all purchasers of airline tickets that identifies the risks each might present. The American Civil Liberties Union (ACLU) believes this type of profiling is discriminatory because it singles out people of Middle Eastern descent (Nash, 1998).

○ **Employee monitoring on the Internet.** Bell Mobility Cellular in Toronto fired a worker for spending too much time at work on the Internet. That company and many others monitor what their employees are doing on the Internet to prevent them from wasting company resources for nonbusiness activities (Machlis, 1997). Many firms also claim the right to monitor the electronic mail of their employees because they own the facilities, intend their use for business purposes only, and create the facility for a business purpose (see the Chapter 7 Case Study).

In each instance, you can find competing values at work, and there is support on both sides of the issue. A company may argue, for example, that it has a right to use information systems to increase productivity and reduce the size of its workforce to lower costs and stay in business. Employees displaced by information systems may argue that employers have some responsibility for their welfare. A close analysis of the facts can sometimes produce compromised solutions that give each side "half a loaf." Try to apply some of the principles of ethical analysis described to each of these cases. What is the right thing to do?

MANAGEMENT DECISION PROBLEM

WHAT TO DO ABOUT EMPLOYEE WEB USAGE

As the head of a small insurance company with six employees, you are concerned about how effectively your company is using its networking and human resources. Budgets are tight, and you are struggling to meet payrolls because employees are reporting many overtime hours. You do not believe that the employees have a sufficiently heavy work load to warrant working longer hours and are looking into the amount of time they spend on the Internet. Each employee uses a computer with Internet access on the job. You requested the following weekly report of employee Web usage from your company Web server.

1. Calculate the total amount of time each employee spent on the Web for the week and the total amount of time that company computers were used for this purpose. Rank the employees in the order of the amount of time each spent on-line.

2. Do your findings and the contents of the report indicate any ethical problems employees are creating? Is the company creating an ethical problem by monitoring its employees' use of the Internet?

3. Use the guidelines for ethical analysis presented in this chapter to develop a solution to the problems you have identified.

Web Usage Report for the Week Ending January 14, 2000

User Name	Minutes On-line	URL Visited
Kelleher, Claire	45	www.doubleclick.net
Kelleher, Claire	57	www.yahoo.com
Kelleher, Claire	96	www.insuremarket.com
McMahon, Patricia	83	www.e-music.com
Milligan, Robert	112	www.shopping.com
Milligan, Robert	43	www.travelocity.com
Olivera, Ernesto	40	www.internetnews.com
Talbot, Helen	125	www.e*trade.com
Talbot, Helen	27	www.wine.com
Talbot, Helen	35	www.yahoo.com
Talbot, Helen	73	www.ebay.com
Wright, Steven	23	www.geocities.com
Wright, Steven	15	www.autobytel.com

14.3 The Moral Dimensions of Information Systems

In this section, we take a closer look at the five moral dimensions of information systems first described in Figure 14-1. In each dimension we identify the ethical, social, and political levels of analysis and use real-world examples to illustrate the values involved, the stakeholders, and the options chosen.

INFORMATION RIGHTS: PRIVACY AND FREEDOM IN THE INTERNET AGE

privacy The claim of individuals to be left alone, free from surveillance or interference from other individuals, organizations, or the state.

Privacy is the claim of individuals to be left alone, free from surveillance or interference from other individuals or organizations including the state. Claims to privacy are also involved at the workplace: Millions of employees are subject to electronic and other forms of high-tech surveillance. Information technology and systems threaten individual claims to privacy by making the invasion of privacy cheap, profitable, and effective.

The claim to privacy is protected in the U.S., Canadian, and German constitutions in a variety of ways and in other countries through various statutes. In the United States, the claim to privacy is protected primarily by the First Amendment guarantees of freedom of speech and association and the Fourth Amendment protections against unreasonable search and seizure of one's personal documents or home, and the guarantee of due process.

Due process has become a key concept in defining privacy. Due process requires that a set of rules or laws exist that clearly define how information about individuals will be treated, and what appeal mechanisms are available. Perhaps the best statement of due process in record-keeping is given in the Fair Information Practices Doctrine developed in the early 1970s.

Fair Information Practices (FIP) A set of principles originally set forth in 1973 that governs the collection and use of information about individuals; it forms the basis of most U.S. and European privacy laws.

Most American and European privacy law is based on a regime called Fair Information Practices (FIP) first set forth in a report written in 1973 by a federal government advisory committee (U.S. Department of Health, Education, and Welfare, 1973). **Fair Information Practices (FIP)** is a set of principles governing the collection and use of information about individuals. The five FIP principles are identified in Table 14-2.

FIP principles are based on the notion of a "mutuality of interest" among the record-holder and the individual. The individual has an interest in engaging in a transaction, and the recordkeeper—usually a business or government agency—requires information about the individual to support the transaction. Once gathered, the individual maintains an interest in the record, and the record may not be used to support other activities without the individual's consent.

Fair Information Practices form the basis of the federal statutes listed in Table 14-3 that set forth the conditions for handling information about individuals in such areas as credit reporting, education, financial records, newspaper records, cable communications, electronic communications, and even video rentals. The Privacy Act of 1974 is the most important of these laws, regulating the federal government's collection, use, and disclosure of information. Most federal privacy laws apply only to the federal government. Only credit, banking, cable, and video rental industries have been regulated by federal privacy law.

In the United States, privacy law is enforced by individuals who must sue agencies or companies in court to recover damages. European countries and Canada define privacy in a similar manner to that in the United States, but they have chosen to enforce their privacy laws by creating privacy commissions or data protection agencies to pursue complaints brought by citizens.

Table 14-2 Fair Information Practices Principles

1. There should be no personal record systems whose existence is secret.
2. Individuals have rights of access, inspection, review, and amendment to systems that contain information about them.
3. There must be no use of personal information for purposes other than those for which it was gathered without prior consent.
4. Managers of systems are responsible and can be held accountable and liable for the damage done by systems for their reliability and security.
5. Governments have the right to intervene in the information relationships among private parties.

Table 14-3   Federal Privacy Laws in the United States

1. General Federal Privacy Laws	2. Privacy Laws Affecting Private Institutions
Freedom of Information Act, 1968 as Amended (5 USC 552)	Fair Credit Reporting Act of 1970
Privacy Act of 1974 as Amended (5 USC 552a)	Family Educational Rights and Privacy Act of 1978
Electronic Communications Privacy Act of 1986	Right to Financial Privacy Act of 1978
Computer Security Act of 1987	Privacy Protection Act of 1980
Computer Matching and Privacy Protection Act of 1988	Cable Communications Policy Act of 1984
	Electronic Communications Privacy Act of 1986
	Video Privacy Protection Act of 1988
	Communications Privacy and Consumer Empowerment Act of 1997
	Data Privacy Act of 1997
	Consumer Internet Privacy Protection Act of 1999

The European Directive on Data Protection

In Europe, privacy protection is much more stringent than in the United States. On October 25, 1998, the European Directive on Data Protection came into effect, broadening privacy protection in the European Union (EU) nations. The Directive requires companies to inform people when they collect information about them and disclose how it will be stored and used. Customers must provide their informed consent before any company can legally use data about them, and they have the right to access that information, correct it, and request that no further data be collected. EU member nations must translate these principles into their own laws and cannot transfer personal data to countries such as the United States that don't have similar privacy protection regulations (see Chapter 15).

Internet Challenges to Privacy

The Internet introduces technology that poses new challenges to the protection of individual privacy that existing Fair Information Practices principles are inadequate to address. Information sent over this vast network of networks may pass through many different computer systems before it reaches its final destination. Each of these systems is capable of monitoring, capturing, and storing communications that pass through it.

It is possible to record many on-line activities, including which on-line newsgroups or files a person has accessed, which Web sites he or she has visited, and what items that person has inspected or purchased over the Web. This information can be collected by both a subscriber's own Internet service provider and the system operators of remote Web sites that a subscriber visits. Tools to monitor visits to the World Wide Web have become popular because they help organizations determine who is visiting their Web sites and how to better target their offerings. (Some firms also monitor the Internet usage of their employees to see how they are using company network resources.) Web retailers now have access to software that lets them watch the on-line shopping behavior of individuals and groups while they are visiting a Web site and making purchases (Dalton, 1999). The commercial demand for this personal information is virtually insatiable.

Web sites can learn the identity of their visitors if the visitors voluntarily register at the site to purchase a product or service or to obtain a free service, such as information. Web sites can also capture information about visitors without their knowledge using "cookie" technology. **Cookies** are tiny files deposited on a computer hard drive when a user visits certain Web sites. Cookies identify the visitor's Web browser software and track visits to the Web site. When the visitor returns to a site that has stored a cookie, the Web site software will search the visitor's computer, find the cookie, and "know" what that person has done in the past. It may also update the cookie, depending on the activity during the visit. In this way, the site can customize its contents for each visitor's interests. For example, if you purchase a book on the Amazon.com Web site and return later from the same browser, the site will welcome you by

cookie Tiny file deposited on a computer hard drive when an individual visits certain Web sites. Used to identify the visitor and track visits to the Web site.

Don't I Know You?

How Web servers identify their visitors.

1 The server reads the PC's browser to determine the user's operating system, browser name and version number, IP address, and other information, sometimes including the user's e-mail address.

2 The server uses the browser information to transmit tiny bits of personalized data called cookies, which the user's browser receives and stores on the PC's hard drive.

3 When the user revisits the Web site, the server requests the contents of any cookie previously provided by that site.

4 The Web server reads the cookie, identifies the user, then calls up its data on the visitor.

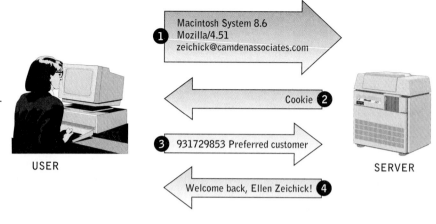

USER   SERVER

1 Macintosh System 8.6
Mozilla/4.51
zeichick@camdenassociates.com

2 Cookie

3 931729853 Preferred customer

4 Welcome back, Ellen Zeichick!

FIGURE 14-2 How cookies identify Web visitors. Cookies are written by a Web site on a visitor's hard drive. When the visitor returns to that Web site, the Web server requests the ID number from the cookie and uses it to access the data stored by that server on that visitor. The Web site uses these data to display personalized information.
Source: "Personalization Explained," by Alan Zeichick, from **Red Herring**, September, 1999, p. 130. Reprinted by permission.

name and recommend other books of interest based on your past purchases. DoubleClick, described in the chapter opening vignette, uses cookies to build its dossiers with details of online purchases and behavior of Web site visitors. Figure 14-2 illustrates how cookies work.

If you are a regular Web user, search your hard drive for files named "cookie.txt" and you are likely to find some. The site may use the data from its cookies for itself, or it may sell that data to other companies. Web sites using "cookie" technology cannot directly obtain visitors' names and addresses. However, if a person has registered at any other site, some of that information will be stored in a cookie. Examine the cookies on your own computer and you will see how much personal data is there. Often, scattered within the cookies, you will find your real name, your user name, your bank, your stockbroker, and perhaps your account numbers. These cookies are not secured in any way, and Web site owners can surreptitiously search them for personal data stored there. Thus if one site stores your name, another will find it. The result is that many sites know a great deal more about you than you might suspect or desire.

Web sites are starting to post their privacy policies for visitors to review. The TRUSTe seal designates Web sites that have agreed to adhere to TRUSTe's established privacy principles of disclosure, choice, access, and security.

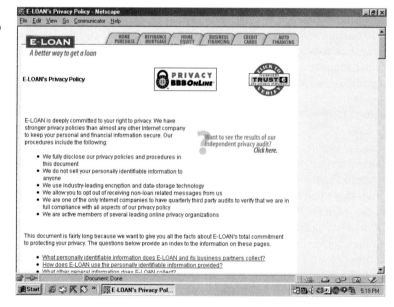

Organizations can collect e-mail addresses to send out thousands and even hundreds of thousands of unsolicited e-mail and electronic messages. This practice is called **spamming,** and it is growing because it only costs a few cents to send thousands of messages advertising one's wares to Internet users.

spamming The practice of sending unsolicited e-mail and other electronic communication.

At present, Web site visitors can't easily find out how the information collected about them from their visits to Web sites is being used. Only a small percentage of Web sites openly post their privacy policies or offer consumers a choice about how their personal data are to be used (Reagle and Cranor, 1999; Lohr, 1999). To encourage self-regulation in the Internet industry, the U.S. Department of Commerce has issued guidelines for Fair Information Practices in on-line business. Industry groups such as the Online Privacy Alliance (OPA), consisting of more than 100 global corporations and associations, have also issued guidelines for self-regulation. Privacy-enhancing technologies for protecting user privacy during interactions with Web sites are being developed (Reiter and Rubin, 1999; Goldschlag, Reed, and Syverson, 1999; Gabber et al., 1999). Additional legislation and government oversight may be required to make sure that privacy in the Internet age is properly safeguarded. The chapter ending case study explores the issue of Web site privacy in greater detail.

Ethical Issues

The ethical privacy issue in this information age is as follows: Under what conditions should I (you) invade the privacy of others? What legitimates intruding into others' lives through unobtrusive surveillance, through market research, or by whatever means? Do we have to inform people that we are eavesdropping? Do we have to inform people that we are using credit history information for employment screening purposes?

Social Issues

The social issue of privacy concerns the development of "expectations of privacy" or privacy norms, as well as public attitudes. In what areas of life should we as a society encourage people to think they are in "private territory" as opposed to public view? For instance, should we as a society encourage people to develop expectations of privacy when using electronic mail, cellular telephones, bulletin boards, the postal system, the workplace, the street? Should expectations of privacy be extended to criminal conspirators?

Political Issues

The political issue of privacy concerns the development of statutes that govern the relations between recordkeepers and individuals. Should we permit the FBI to prevent the commercial development of encrypted telephone transmissions so they can eavesdrop at will (Denning et al., 1993)? Should a law be passed to require direct-marketing firms to obtain the consent of individuals before using their names in mass marketing (a consensus database)? Should e-mail privacy—regardless of who owns the equipment—be protected by law? In general, large organizations of all kinds—public and private—are reluctant to remit the advantages that come from the unfettered flow of information on individuals. Civil libertarians and other private groups have been the strongest voices supporting restraints on large organizations' information-gathering activities.

PROPERTY RIGHTS: INTELLECTUAL PROPERTY

Contemporary information systems have severely challenged existing law and social practices that protect private intellectual property. **Intellectual property** is considered to be intangible property created by individuals or corporations. Information technology has made it difficult to protect intellectual property because computerized information can be copied or distributed so easily on networks. Intellectual property is subject to a variety of protections under three different legal traditions: trade secret, copyright, and patent law (Graham, 1984).

intellectual property Intangible property created by individuals or corporations that is subject to protections under trade secret, copyright, and patent law.

Trade Secrets

Any intellectual work product—a formula, device, pattern, or compilation of data—used for a business purpose can be classified as a **trade secret** provided it is not based on information in the public domain. Protections for trade secrets vary from state to state. In general, trade

trade secret Any intellectual work or product used for a business purpose that can be classified as belonging to that business, provided it is not based on information in the public domain.

secret laws grant a monopoly on the ideas behind a work product, but they can be a very tenuous monopoly.

Software that contains novel or unique elements, procedures, or compilations can be included as a trade secret. Trade secret law protects the actual ideas in a work product, not only their manifestation. To make this claim, the creator or owner must take care to bind employees and customers with nondisclosure agreements and to prevent the secret from falling into the public domain.

The limitation of trade secret protection is that although virtually all software programs of any complexity contain unique elements of some sort, it is difficult to prevent the ideas in the work from falling into the public domain when the software is widely distributed.

Copyright

copyright A statutory grant that protects creators of intellectual property against copying of their work by others for any purpose for 28 years.

Copyright is a statutory grant that protects creators of intellectual property from having their work copied by others for any purpose for 28 years. Since the first Federal Copyright Act of 1790 and the creation of the Copyright Office to register copyrights and enforce copyright law, Congress has extended copyright protection to books, periodicals, lectures, plays, musical compositions, maps, drawings, artwork of any kind, and motion pictures. The congressional intent behind copyright laws has been to encourage creativity and authorship by ensuring that creative people receive the financial and other benefits of their work. Most industrial nations have their own copyright laws, and there are several international conventions and bilateral agreements through which nations coordinate and enforce their laws.

In the mid-1960s the Copyright Office began registering software programs, and in 1980 Congress passed the Computer Software Copyright Act, which clearly provides protection for source and object code and for copies of the original sold in commerce, and sets forth the rights of the purchaser to use the software while the creator retains legal title.

Copyright protection is clear-cut: It protects against copying entire programs or their parts. Damages and relief are readily obtained for infringement. The drawback to copyright protection is that the underlying ideas behind a work are not protected, only their manifestation in a work. A competitor can use your software, understand how it works, and build new software that follows the same concepts without infringing on a copyright.

"Look and feel" copyright infringement lawsuits are precisely about the distinction between an idea and its expression. For instance, in the early 1990s Apple Computer sued Microsoft Corporation and Hewlett-Packard Inc. for infringement of the expression of Apple's Macintosh interface. Among other claims, Apple claimed that the defendants copied the expression of overlapping windows. The defendants counterclaimed that the idea of overlapping windows can only be expressed in a single way and, therefore, was not protectable under the "merger" doctrine of copyright law. When ideas and their expression merge, the expression cannot be copyrighted. In general, courts appear to be following the reasoning of a 1989 case—*Brown Bag Software* vs. *Symantec Corp.*—in which the court dissected the elements of software alleged to be infringing. The court found that neither similar concept, function, general functional features (e.g., drop-down menus), nor colors are protectable by copyright law (*Brown Bag* vs. *Symantec Corp.*, 1992).

Patents

patent A legal document that grants the owner an exclusive monopoly on the ideas behind an invention for 17 years; designed to ensure that inventors of new machines or methods are rewarded for their labor while making widespread use of their inventions.

A **patent** grants the owner an exclusive monopoly on the ideas behind an invention for 17 years. The congressional intent behind patent law was to ensure that inventors of new machines, devices, or methods receive the full financial and other rewards of their labor while allowing widespread use of the invention by providing detailed diagrams for those wishing to use the idea under license from the patent's owner. The granting of a patent is determined by the Patent Office and relies on court rulings.

The key concepts in patent law are originality, novelty, and invention. The Patent Office did not accept applications for software patents routinely until a 1981 Supreme Court decision that held that computer programs could be a part of a patentable process. Since that time hundreds of patents have been granted and thousands await consideration.

The strength of patent protection is that it grants a monopoly on the underlying concepts and ideas of software. The difficulty is passing stringent criteria of nonobviousness (e.g., the work must reflect some special understanding and contribution), originality, and novelty. Years of waiting to receive protection may be necessary.

ELECTRONIC BANDITS

The wife of a Microsoft Corporation employee thought it was strange that two small print shops in Westminister, California's Vietnamese district were grinding out user manuals for Windows 95. She notified Microsoft, which then asked local law enforcement authorities to investigate. The Westminister Police Department found that the print shops were part of a large network of Asian gangs in southern California that produced and sold counterfeit Microsoft products.

With the right equipment, counterfeiters can make Windows 98 for about $10 and sell it for $55 to $70 per copy. Tools of the trade include stampers, which are dinner-plate-size master disks that can each produce 140,000 to 150,000 CD-ROMs, and equipment to reproduce Microsoft-like cardboard boxes, warranty cards, end-user license agreements, and even the foil hologram used to mark authentic Microsoft products. The California counterfeiters received financing from China and Taiwan. The crime rings used their profits from selling illegally copied software to finance other criminal activities, including narcotics, prostitution, and extortion.

In another incident, a regional court in Aachen, Germany, sentenced a 39- year-old Texan in June 1999 to 4 years in prison for software piracy. Authorities had confiscated illegally reproduced software and related products worth DM 120 million (Deutsche Marks), or U.S. $64.14 million, from a truck and warehouses near Aachen and Cologne. The confiscated items included hundreds of thousands of CD-ROMs, user manuals, registration cards, and certificates of authenticity for Microsoft Office, Windows NT, Windows 95, and Corel software products. The counterfeit software had been produced in England, and the defendant was trying to sell it in Germany. The German sentence might have been longer, but the court acknowledged that the defendant faces further prosecution in the United Kingdom.

These arrests are not isolated events. Software piracy is exploding all over the world, fueled by the Internet. According to a recent study of global software piracy conducted by the Business Software Alliance (BSA) and the Software & Information Industry Association (SIIA), 38 percent of all new business software applications installed worldwide in 1998 were pirated. Revenue losses to the global software industry resulting from piracy amounted to $11 billion. SIIA and BSA represent software developers all over the world in their efforts to expand trade opportunities and combat software piracy.

In Russia, the Philippines, Indonesia, Vietnam, and El Salvador, as much as 90 percent of the software in use may have been copied illegally. More than 2 million Web sites offer, link to, or reference "warez," the Internet code word for illegal copies of software. The proliferation of Internet auction sites has exacerbated the problem—about 60 percent of the software offered on popular U.S. and European auction sites has been estimated to be counterfeit.

Users, as well as software developers, are hurt by software piracy because they pay higher prices to offset the losses. If piracy could be curbed, many software firms would have the resources to invest more in research and development to improve their products. Large software companies can survive piracy, but many small firms cannot afford to lose 30 to 50 percent of their revenue.

TO THINK ABOUT: If an employee finds someone in the firm who is copying software, what should he or she do? Are there any circumstances in which software copying should be allowed?

Sources: Mary Lisbeth D'Amico, "German Court Gives Texan Software Pirate Jail Term," *Computerworld*, June 15, 1999; Kim S. Nash, "Software Gangsters," *Computerworld*, May 3, 1999; and "Worldwide Business Software Piracy Losses Estimated at Nearly $11 Billion in 1998," Software Information Industry Association, May 25, 1999.

Challenges to Intellectual Property Rights

Contemporary information technologies, especially software, pose a severe challenge to existing intellectual property regimes and, therefore, create significant ethical, social, and political issues. Digital media differ from books, periodicals, and other media in terms of ease of replication; ease of transmission; ease of alteration; difficulty classifying a software work as a program, book, or even music; compactness (making theft easy); and difficulties in establishing uniqueness.

The proliferation of electronic networks, including the Internet, has made it even more difficult to protect intellectual property. Before widespread use of networks, copies of software, books, magazine articles, or films had to be stored on physical media, such as paper, computer disks, or videotape, creating some hurdles to distribution. Using networks, information can be more widely reproduced and distributed (Johnson, 1997). The Window on Technology explores the growing problem of international software piracy.

With the World Wide Web in particular, one can easily copy and distribute virtually anything to thousands and even millions of people around the world, even if they are using different types of computer systems. Information can be illicitly copied from one place and distributed through other systems and networks even though these parties do not willingly participate in the infringement. For example, the music industry is worried because individuals can illegally copy MP3 music files to Web sites where they can be downloaded by others who do not know that the MP3 files are not licensed for copying or distribution (Ghajar et al., 1999). The Internet was designed to transmit information freely around the world, including copyrighted information. Intellectual property that can be copied easily is likely to be copied (Cavazos, 1996; Chabrow, 1996).

The manner in which information is obtained and presented on the Web further challenges intellectual property protections (Okerson, 1996). Web pages can be constructed from bits of text, graphics, sound, or video that may come from many different sources. Each item may belong to a different entity, creating complicated issues of ownership and compensation (see Figure 14-3). Web sites can also use a capability called "framing" to let one site construct an on-screen border around content obtained by linking to another Web site. The first site's border and logo stay on screen, making the content of the new Web site appear to be "offered" by the previous Web site.

Mechanisms are being developed to sell and distribute books, articles, and other intellectual property on the Internet, but publishers continue to look for copyright violations because intellectual property can now be copied so easily.

FIGURE 14-3 Who owns the pieces? Anatomy of a Web page. Web pages are often constructed with elements from many different sources, clouding issues of ownership and intellectual property protection.

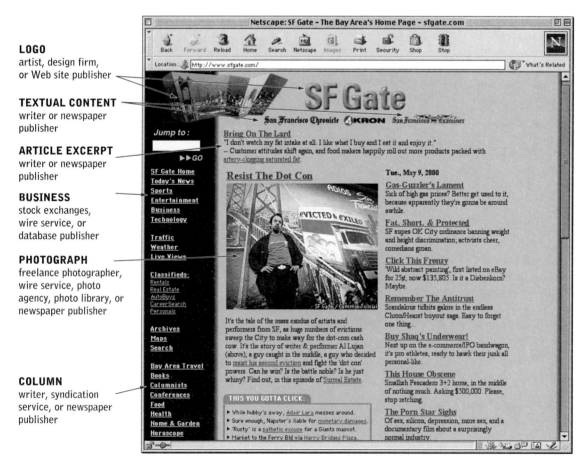

LOGO
artist, design firm, or Web site publisher

TEXTUAL CONTENT
writer or newspaper publisher

ARTICLE EXCERPT
writer or newspaper publisher

BUSINESS
stock exchanges, wire service, or database publisher

PHOTOGRAPH
freelance photographer, wire service, photo agency, photo library, or newspaper publisher

COLUMN
writer, syndication service, or newspaper publisher

Ethical Issues

The central ethical issue posed to individuals concerns copying software: Should I (you) copy for my own use a piece of software protected by trade secret, copyright, and/or patent law? In the information age, it is so easy to obtain perfect, functional copies of software that the software companies themselves have abandoned software protection schemes to increase market penetration, and enforcement of the law is so rare. However, if everyone copied software, very little new software would be produced because creators could not benefit from the results of their work.

Social Issues

There are several property-related social issues raised by new information technology. Most experts agree that the current intellectual property laws are breaking down in the information age. The vast majority of Americans report in surveys that they routinely violate some minor laws—everything from speeding to taking paper clips from work to copying software. The ease with which software can be copied contributes to making us a society of lawbreakers. These routine thefts threaten significantly to reduce the speed with which new information technologies can and will be introduced and, thereby, threaten further advances in productivity and social well being.

Political Issues

The main property-related political issue concerns the creation of new property protection measures to protect investments made by creators of new software. Microsoft and 1,400 other software and information content firms are represented by the Software and Information Industry Association (SIIA), which lobbies for new laws and enforcement of existing laws to protect intellectual property around the world. SIIA was formed on January 1, 1999, from the merger of the Software Publishers Association (SPA) and the Information Industry Association (IIA). The SIIA runs an antipiracy hotline for individuals to report piracy activities and educational programs to help organizations combat software piracy. The SIIA has developed model Employee Usage Guidelines for software as described in Table 14-4.

Allied against SIIA are a host of groups and millions of individuals who believe that antipiracy laws cannot be enforced in the digital age and that software should be free or be paid for on a voluntary basis (shareware software). According to these groups, the greater social benefit results from the free distribution of software.

ACCOUNTABILITY, LIABILITY, AND CONTROL

Along with privacy and property laws, new information technologies are challenging existing liability law and social practices for holding individuals and institutions accountable. If a person is injured by a machine controlled, in part, by software, who should be held accountable and, therefore, held liable? Should a public bulletin board or an electronic service such as Prodigy or America Online permit the transmission of pornographic or offensive material (as broadcasters), or should they be held harmless against any liability for what users transmit (as is true of common carriers such as the telephone system)? What about the Internet? If you outsource your information processing, can you hold the external vendor liable for injuries done to your customers? Some real-world examples may shed light on these questions.

Some Recent Liability Problems

On March 13, 1993, a blizzard hit the East Coast of the United States, knocking out an Electronic Data Systems Inc. (EDS) computer center in Clifton, New Jersey. The center operated 5,200 ATM machines in 12 different networks across the country involving more than 1 million cardholders. In the two weeks required to recover operations, EDS informed its customers to use alternative ATM networks operated by other banks or computer centers, and offered to cover more than $50 million in cash withdrawals. Because the alternative networks did not have access to the actual customer account balances, EDS was at substantial risk of fraud. Cash withdrawals were limited to $100 per day per customer to reduce the exposure. Most service was restored by March 26. Although EDS had a disaster-recovery plan, it did not have a

Table 14-4 Employee Usage Guidelines for [Organization]

Purpose

Software will be used only in accordance with its license agreement. Unless otherwise provided in the license, any duplication of copyrighted software, except for backup and archival purposes by software manager or designated department, is a violation of copyright law. In addition to violating copyright law, unauthorized duplication of software is contrary to [organization's] standards of conduct. The following points are to be followed to comply with software license agreements:

1. All users must use all software in accordance with its license agreements and the [organization's] software policy. All users acknowledge that they do not own this software or its related documentation, and unless expressly authorized by the software publisher, may not make additional copies except for archival purposes.

2. [Organization] will not tolerate the use of any unauthorized copies of software or fonts in our organization. Any person illegally reproducing software can be subject to civil and criminal penalties including fines and imprisonment. All users must not condone illegal copying of software under any circumstances and anyone who makes, uses, or otherwise acquires unauthorized software will be appropriately disciplined.

3. No user will give software or fonts to any outsiders including clients, customers, and others. Under no circumstances will software be used within [organization] that has been brought in from any unauthorized location under [organization's] policy, including, but not limited to, the Internet, the home, friends, and colleagues.

4. Any user who determines that there may be a misuse of software within the organization will notify the Certified Software Manager, department manager, or legal counsel.

5. All software used by the organization on organization-owned computers will be purchased through appropriate procedures.

I have read [organization's] software code of ethics. I am fully aware of our software compliance policies and agree to abide by them. I understand that violation of any above policies may result in my termination.

_____

Employee Signature

_____

Date

Published by the SPA Anti-Piracy. You are given permission to duplicate and modify this policy statement as long as attribution to the original document comes from the SPA Anti-Piracy.

---

dedicated backup facility. Who is liable for any economic harm caused to individuals or businesses who could not access their full account balances in this period (Joes, 1993)?

In April 1990, a computer system at Shell Pipeline Corporation failed to detect a human operator error. As a result, 93,000 barrels of crude oil were shipped to the wrong trader. The error cost $2 million because the trader sold oil that should not have been delivered to him. A court ruled later that Shell Pipeline was liable for the loss of the oil because the error was caused by a human operator who entered erroneous information into the system. Shell was held liable for not developing a system that would prevent the possibility of misdeliveries (King, 1992). Whom would you have held liable—Shell Pipeline? The trader for not being more careful about deliveries? The human operator who made the error?

These cases point out the difficulties faced by information systems executives who ultimately are responsible for the harm done by systems developed by their staffs. In general, insofar as computer software is part of a machine, and the machine injures someone physically or economically, the producer of the software and the operator can be held liable for damages. Insofar as the software acts more like a book, storing and displaying information, courts have been reluctant to hold authors, publishers, and booksellers liable for contents (the exception being instances of fraud or defamation), and hence courts have been wary of holding software authors liable for "booklike" software.

In general, it is very difficult (if not impossible) to hold software producers liable for their software products when those products are considered like books, regardless of the physical or economic harm that results. Historically, print publishers, books, and periodicals have not been held liable because of fears that liability claims would interfere with First Amendment rights guaranteeing freedom of expression.

What about "software as service"? ATMs are a service provided to bank customers. Should this service fail, customers will be inconvenienced and perhaps harmed economically if they cannot access their funds in a timely manner. Should liability protections be extended to software publishers and operators of defective financial, accounting, simulation, or marketing systems?

Software is very different from books. Software users may develop expectations of infallibility about software; software is less easily inspected than a book and more difficult to compare with other software products for quality; software claims actually to perform a task rather than describe a task like a book; and people come to depend on services essentially based on software. Given the centrality of software to everyday life, the chances are excellent that liability law will extend its reach to include software even when it merely provides an information service.

Telephone systems have not been held liable for the messages transmitted because they are regulated "common carriers." In return for their right to provide telephone service, carriers must provide access to all, at reasonable rates, and achieve acceptable reliability. But broadcasters and cable television systems are subject to a wide variety of federal and local constraints on content and facilities. Organizations can be held liable for offensive content on their Web sites or e-mail, and on-line services such as Prodigy or America Online might be held liable for postings by their users (Sipior and Ward, 1999).

Ethical Issues

The central liability-related ethical issue raised by new information technologies is whether individuals and organizations who create, produce, and sell systems (both hardware and software) are morally responsible for the consequences of their use (see Johnson and Mulvey, 1995). If so, under what conditions? What liabilities (and responsibilities) should the user assume, and what should the provider assume? The Window on Organizations raises some of these issues as it explores the proliferation of sites dispensing medical information on the Internet.

Social Issues

The central liability-related social issue concerns the expectations that society should allow to develop around service-providing information systems. Should individuals (and organizations) be encouraged to develop their own backup devices to cover likely or easily anticipated system failures, or should organizations be held strictly liable for system services they provide? If organizations are held strictly liable, what impact will this have on the development of new system services? Can society permit networks and bulletin boards to post libelous, inaccurate, and misleading information that will harm many persons? Or should information service companies become self-regulating and self-censoring?

Political Issues

The leading liability-related political issue is the debate between information providers of all kinds (from software developers to network service providers), who want to be relieved of liability as much as possible (thereby maximizing their profits), and service users (individuals, organizations, communities) who want organizations to be held responsible for providing high-quality system services (thereby maximizing the quality of service). Service providers argue they will withdraw from the marketplace if they are held liable, whereas service users argue that only by holding providers liable can we guarantee a high level of service and compensate injured parties. Should legislation impose liability or restrict liability

MEDICINE AT THE CLICK OF A MOUSE

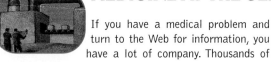

If you have a medical problem and turn to the Web for information, you have a lot of company. Thousands of medical-related Web sites exist, and millions of people turn to them regularly. One estimate reveals that more than 25 million people from the United States alone sought medical information on the Web in 1999. How do you know to which sites you should go? How accurate is the information you receive? And what ethical issues are involved in their offering medical information?

Selecting a trustworthy medical Web site may not seem difficult. The U.S. National Institute of Health has Web sites as does Dr. C. Everett Koop, the former U.S. Surgeon General and maybe the most highly respected medical figure in the United States. Many other respected medical organizations have sites, including hospitals, doctors, and medical journals. Corporations such as pharmaceutical houses and drug store chains also have a strong Web presence. Even such respected sources of information as the **Encyclopedia Britannica** will answer medical questions. There are thousands of other sites, and some specialize in specific illnesses (from AIDS to headaches).

However, finding a trustworthy site is very difficult. The **Journal of the American Medical Association** recently said, "When it comes to medical information, the Internet too often resembles a cocktail conversation rather than a tool for effective healthcare communication and decision making." The **Journal** adds, "The problem is not too little information but too much, vast chunks of it incomplete, misleading, or inaccurate." Experts, specialists, authorities, professionals, alternative therapy promoters, interested lay people, charlatans, and hucksters have all set up sites. So it really is a case of "Let the reader beware."

A University of Minnesota study of 371 Web sites reported in the August 1999 edition of **Cancer** concluded that the Internet is filled with fundamental, life-threatening errors. Its researchers looked at information offered on Ewing sarcoma, an uncommon bone cancer that particularly strikes children and young adults. Whereas the University team says the disease is relatively curable with a survival rate of 70 to 75 percent, some sites, including the **Encyclopedia Britannica**, claimed a mortality rate of about 95 percent. Such misinformation can not only be dev-

astating to the readers, but, the report says, those finding this information "may even be driven to consider refusing therapy if they are convinced that conventional medical science (even 'radical' therapy) yields such a dismal prognosis." One problem, the study concluded, was that about one-third of the sites contained no indication that independent experts had reviewed and declared accurate the information on the site. Peer review is a long-accepted central tenet for the publication of medical information.

Many of the sites use language that the layperson cannot understand. Others present information that may be biased by the commercial interests of the site owners or sponsors, such as pharmaceutical houses. For example, a breast cancer site by Health Talk Interactive Inc. featured a panel discussion on new therapies with lengthy discussion of the drug Herceptin, which is made by Genentech Inc., the site's sponsor. In several articles in late 1999, **The New York Times** reported on conflicts of interest and ethical problems related to Dr. Koop's site, DrKoop.com. For example, the **Times** reported that Dr. Koop made a commission on products and services he sold, a practice Dr. Koop abandoned on August 27, 1999. DrKoop.com also obtains revenue from its Community Partners Program, a listing of hospitals and health centers that are "the most innovative and advanced" in the country. These 31 organizations pay between $100,000 and $150,000 to be included on the list. DrKoop.com attracts 2.5 million unique visitors each month, providing an attractive audience for targeted content and marketing campaigns.

TO THINK ABOUT: What are the advantages and disadvantages of Web sites offering medical information? How can a Web site be ethical when so much medical information is disputed within the medical field?

Sources: Marilyn Chase, "Do Sponsors Survey Health Web Sites?" **The Wall Street Journal,** February 8, 2000; Larry Stevens, "Rx for Success," **The Industry Standard,** January 24, 2000; Jane E. Brody, "Of Fact, Fiction and Medical Web Sites," **The New York Times,** August 31, 1999; Jane E. Brody, "Point-and-Click Medicine: A Hazard to Your Health," **The New York Times,** August 31, 1999; and Holcomb B. Noble, "Hailed as a Surgeon General, Koop Criticized on Web Ethics," **The New York Times,** September 4, 1999.

on service providers? This fundamental cleavage is at the heart of numerous political and judicial conflicts.

SYSTEM QUALITY: DATA QUALITY AND SYSTEM ERRORS

The debate over liability and accountability for unintentional consequences of system use raises a related but independent moral dimension: What is an acceptable, technologically feasible level of system quality (see Chapter 13)? At what point should system managers say, "Stop testing, we've done all we can to perfect this software. Ship it!" Individuals and organizations may be held responsible for avoidable and foreseeable consequences, which they have a duty to perceive and correct. And the gray area is that some system errors are foreseeable and correctable only at very great expense, an expense so great that pursuing this level of perfection is not feasible economically—no one could afford the product. For example, although software companies try to debug their products before releasing them to the marketplace, they knowingly ship buggy products because the time and cost of fixing all minor errors would prevent these products from ever being released (Rigdon, 1995). What if the product was not offered in the marketplace? Would social welfare as a whole not advance and perhaps even decline? Carrying this further, just what is the responsibility of a producer of computer services? Should they withdraw the product that can never be perfected, warn the user, or forget about the risk (let the buyer beware)?

Three principal sources of poor system performance are software bugs and errors, hardware or facility failures caused by natural or other causes, and poor input data quality. Chapter 13 discusses why zero defects in software code of any complexity cannot be achieved and why the seriousness of remaining bugs cannot be estimated. Hence, there is a technological barrier to perfect software, and users must be aware of the potential for catastrophic failure. The software industry has not yet arrived at testing standards for producing software of acceptable but not perfect performance (Collins et al., 1994).

Although software bugs and facility catastrophe are likely to be widely reported in the press, by far the most common source of business system failure is data quality. Few companies routinely measure the quality of their data but studies of individual organizations report data error rates ranging from 0.5 to 30 percent (Redman, 1998).

Ethical Issues

The central quality-related ethical issue information systems raise is at what point should I (you) release software or services for consumption by others? At what point can you conclude that your software or service achieves an economically and technologically adequate level of quality? What are you obliged to know about the quality of your software, its procedures for testing, and its operational characteristics?

Social Issues

The leading quality-related social issue once again deals with expectations: As a society, do we want to encourage people to believe that systems are infallible, that data errors are impossible? Do we instead want a society where people are openly skeptical and questioning of the output of machines, where people are at least informed of the risk? By heightening awareness of system failure, do we inhibit the development of all systems, which in the end contribute to social well being?

Political Issues

The leading quality-related political issue concerns the laws of responsibility and accountability. Should Congress establish or direct the National Institute of Science and Technology (NIST) to develop quality standards (software, hardware, data quality) and impose those standards on industry? Or should industry associations be encouraged to develop industry-wide standards of quality? Or should Congress wait for the marketplace to punish poor system quality, recognizing that in some instances this will not work (e.g., if all retail grocers maintain poor quality systems, then customers have no alternatives)?

QUALITY OF LIFE: EQUITY, ACCESS, BOUNDARIES

The negative social costs of introducing information technologies and systems are beginning to mount along with the power of the technology. Many of these negative social consequences are not violations of individual rights, nor are they property crimes. Nevertheless, these negative consequences can be extremely harmful to individuals, societies, and political institutions. Computers and information technologies potentially can destroy valuable elements of our culture and society even while they bring us benefits. If there is a balance of positive and negative consequences of using information systems, whom do we hold responsible for the negative consequences? Next, we briefly examine some of the negative social consequences of systems, considering individual, social, and political responses.

Balancing Power Center Versus Periphery

An early fear of the computer age was that huge, centralized mainframe computers would centralize power at corporate headquarters and in the nation's capital, resulting in a Big Brother society as suggested in George Orwell's novel, *1984*. The shift toward highly decentralized computing, coupled with an ideology of "empowerment" of thousands of workers, and the decentralization of decision making to lower organizational levels, have reduced fears of power centralization in institutions. Yet much of the empowerment described in popular business magazines is trivial. Lower level employees may be empowered to make minor decisions, but the key policy decisions may be as centralized as in the past.

Rapidity of Change: Reduced Response Time to Competition

Information systems have helped to create much more efficient national and international markets. Today's efficient global marketplace has reduced social buffers that previously permitted businesses many years to adjust to competition. "Time-based competition" has an ugly side: The business you work for may not have enough time to respond to global competitors and may be wiped out in a year, along with your job. We stand the risk of developing a "just-in-time society" with "just-in-time jobs" and "just-in-time" workplaces, families, and vacations.

Maintaining Boundaries: Family, Work, Leisure

Parts of this book were produced on trains and planes as well as on family "vacations" and what otherwise might have been "family" time. The danger of ubiquitous computing, telecommuting, nomad computing, and the "do anything anywhere" computing environment is that it might actually come true. If so, the traditional boundaries that separate work from family and leisure will weaken. Although authors have traditionally worked just about anywhere (typewriters have been portable for nearly a century), the advent of information systems, coupled with the growth of knowledge-work occupations, means that more and more people work when traditionally they would have been playing or communicating with family and friends. The "work umbrella" now extends far beyond the eight-hour day.

Weakening these institutions poses clear-cut risks (Hafner, 2000). Family and friends historically have provided powerful support mechanisms for individuals, and they act as balance points in a society by preserving "private life," providing a place for one to collect one's thoughts, think in ways contrary to one's employer, and dream.

Dependence and Vulnerability

Today, our businesses, governments, schools, and private associations such as churches are incredibly dependent on information systems and are, therefore, highly vulnerable if these sys-

While some people may enjoy the convenience of working at home, the "do anything anywhere" computing environment can blur the traditional boundaries between work and family time.

tems should fail. With information systems now as ubiquitous as the telephone system, it is startling to remember that there are no regulatory or standard-setting forces in place for them as there are for telephone, electrical, radio, television, or other public-utility technologies. The absence of standards and the criticality of some system applications will probably call forth demands for national standards and perhaps regulatory oversight.

Computer Crime and Abuse

Many new technologies in the industrial era have created new opportunities for committing crime. Technologies including computers create new valuable items to steal, new ways to steal them, and new ways to harm others. **Computer crime** is the commission of illegal acts through the use of a computer or against a computer system. Computers or computer systems can be the object of the crime (destroying a company's computer center or a company's computer files) as well as the instrument of a crime (stealing computer lists by illegally gaining access to a computer system using a home computer). Simply accessing a computer system without authorization, or intent to do harm, even by accident is now a federal crime. **Computer abuse** is the commission of acts involving a computer that may not be illegal but are considered unethical.

> **computer crime** The commission of illegal acts using a computer or against a computer system.

> **computer abuse** The commission of acts involving a computer that may not be illegal but are considered unethical.

No one knows the magnitude of the computer crime problem—how many systems are invaded, how many people engage in the practice, or what is the total economic damage, but it is estimated to cost more than $1 billion in the United States alone. Many companies are reluctant to report computer crimes because they may involve employees. The most economically damaging kinds of computer crime are introducing viruses, disruption of computer systems, and theft of services. "Hacker" is the pejorative term for a person who uses computers in illegal ways. Hacker attacks are on the rise, posing new threats to organizations linked to the Internet (see Chapter 13).

Computer viruses (see Chapter 13) have grown exponentially during the past decade. More than 20,000 viruses have been documented, many causing huge losses because of lost data or crippled computers. Although many firms now use antivirus software, the proliferation of computer networks will increase the probability of infections.

Following are some illustrative computer crimes:

○ An 11-member group of hackers dubbed "The Phonemasters" by the FBI gained access to telephone networks of companies including British Telecommunications, AT&T Corporation, MCI, Southwestern Bell, and Sprint. They were able to access credit-reporting databases belonging to Equifax and TRW Inc., as well as databases owned by Lexis-Nexis and Dun & Bradstreet information services. Members of the ring sold credit reports, criminal records, and other data they pilfered from the databases, causing $1.85 million in losses. The FBI apprehended group members Calvin Cantrell, Corey Lindsley, and John Bosanac, and they were sentenced to jail terms of two to four years in federal prison. Other members remain at large (Simons, 1999).

○ Timothy Lloyd, a former chief computer network administrator at Omega Engineering Inc. in Bridgeport, New Jersey, was charged with planting a "logic bomb" that deleted all of the firm's software programs on July 30, 1996. A "logic bomb" is a malicious program that is set to trigger at a specified time. The company suffered $10 million in damages. Lloyd recently had been dismissed from his job. Federal prosecutors also charged Lloyd with stealing about $50,000 of computer equipment, which included a backup tape that could have allowed Omega to recover its lost files (Chen, 1998).

○ On December 16, 1999, two California men were charged with a conspiracy to commit securities fraud. Arash Aziz-Golshani and Hootan Melamed were alleged to have sent bogus messages over the Internet to pump up the price of stock in an obscure bankrupt company. The share price rose from 13 cents to more than $15 in only two trading days in November 1999, creating profit of $364,000 for the alleged perpetrators and a third man (Morgenson, 1999).

In general, it is employees—insiders—who have inflicted the most injurious computer crimes because they have the knowledge, access, and frequently a job-related motive to commit such crimes.

Congress responded to the threat of computer crime in 1986 with the Computer Fraud and Abuse Act. This act makes it illegal to access a computer system without authorization. Most states have similar laws, and nations in Europe have similar legislation. Other existing legislation covering wiretapping, fraud, and conspiracy by any means, regardless of the technology employed, is adequate to cover computer crimes committed thus far.

The Internet's ease of use and accessibility have created new opportunities for computer crime and abuse. Table 14-5 describes some common areas in which the Internet has been used for illegal or malicious purposes.

Employment: Trickle-Down Technology and Reengineering Job Loss

Reengineering work (see Chapter 9) is typically hailed in the information systems community as a major benefit of new information technology. It is much less frequently noted that redesigning business processes could potentially cause millions of middle-level managers and clerical workers to lose their jobs. One economist has raised the possibility that we will create a society run by a small "high tech elite of corporate professionals . . . in a nation of the permanently unemployed" (Rifkin, 1993).

Other economists are much more sanguine about the potential job losses. They believe relieving bright, educated workers from reengineered jobs will result in these workers moving to better jobs in fast-growth industries. Left out of this equation are blue-collar workers, and older, less well educated middle managers. It is not clear that these groups can be retrained easily for high-quality (high-paying) jobs. Careful planning and sensitivity to employee needs can help companies redesign work to minimize job losses.

Equity and Access: Increasing Racial and Social Class Cleavages

Does everyone have an equal opportunity to participate in the digital age? Will the social, economic, and cultural gaps that exist in America and other societies be reduced by information systems technology? Or will the cleavages be increased, permitting the "better off" to become even better off relative to others? These questions have not yet been fully answered because the impact of systems technology on various groups in society is not well studied. What is known is that information, knowledge, computers, and access to these resources through educational institutions and public libraries are inequitably distributed along racial and social class lines, as are many other information resources. Figure 14-4 illustrates the differences in U.S. home computer ownership based on income and ethnicity. Left uncorrected, we could end up creating a society of information haves, computer literate and skilled, versus a large group of information have-nots, computer illiterate and unskilled.

The Clinton administration and public interest groups want to narrow this "digital divide" by making digital information services—including the Internet—available to "virtually everyone" just as basic telephone service is now. An amendment to the Telecommunications

Table 14-5 Internet Crime and Abuse

Problem	Description
Hacking	Hackers exploit weaknesses in Web site security to obtain access to proprietary data such as customer information and passwords. They may use "Trojan horses" posing as legitimate software to obtain information from the host computer.
Jamming	Jammers use software routines to tie up the computer hosting a Web site so that legitimate visitors can't access the site.
Malicious software	Cyber vandals use data flowing through the Internet to transmit computer viruses, which can disable computers that they "infect" (see Chapter 13).
Sniffing	Sniffing, a form of electronic eavesdropping, involves placing a piece of software to intercept information passing from a user to the computer hosting a Web site. This information can include credit card numbers and other confidential data.
Spoofing	Spoofers fraudulently misrepresent themselves as other organizations, setting up false Web sites where they collect confidential information from unsuspecting visitors to the site.

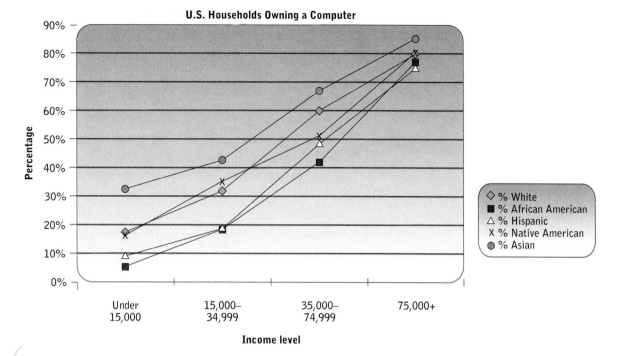

FIGURE 14-4 The widening digital divide. Households at the lowest income levels are up to 9 times less likely to have a computer at home than those with incomes of $75,000 or higher. Home computer ownership among African-American and Hipsanic households is also lower than among other ethnic groups.

Source: U.S. Department of Commerce. National Telecommunications and Information Association, "Falling Through the Net: Defining the Digital Divide," July 8, 1999.

Act of 1996, which widened telecommunications deregulation, stipulates subsidies for schools and libraries so that people of all backgrounds have access to the tools of information technology (Sanger, 1999; Lohr, 1996). This is only a partial solution to the problem.

Health Risks: RSI, CVS, and Technostress

The most important occupational disease today is **repetitive stress injury (RSI).** RSI occurs when muscle groups are forced through repetitive actions often with high-impact loads (such as tennis) or tens of thousands of repetitions under low-impact loads (such as working at a computer keyboard). RSI presents a serious problem for business and management, as described in the Window on Management.

The single largest source of RSI is computer keyboards. Around 50 million Americans use computers at work. The most common kind of computer-related RSI is **carpal tunnel syndrome (CTS),** in which pressure on the median nerve through the wrist's bony structure called a "carpal tunnel" produces pain. The pressure is caused by constant repetition of keystrokes: In a single shift, a word processor may perform 23,000 keystrokes. Symptoms of CTS include numbness, shooting pain, inability to grasp objects, and tingling. Millions of workers have been diagnosed with CTS.

RSI is avoidable. Designing workstations for a neutral wrist position (using a wrist rest to support the wrist), proper monitor stands, and footrests all contribute to proper posture and reduced RSI. New, ergonomically correct keyboards are also an option, although their effectiveness has yet to be clearly established. These measures should be backed by frequent rest breaks, rotation of employees to different jobs, and voice or scanner data entry.

RSI is not the only occupational illness computers cause. Back and neck pain, leg stress, and foot pain also result from poor ergonomic designs of workstations.

Computer vision syndrome (CVS) refers to any eye strain condition related to computer display screen use. Its symptoms, usually temporary, include headaches, blurred vision, and dry and irritated eyes.

repetitive stress injury (RSI) Occupational disease that occurs when muscle groups are forced through repetitive actions with high-impact loads or thousands of repetitions with low-impact loads.

carpal tunnel syndrome (CTS) Type of RSI in which pressure on the median nerve through the wrist's bony carpal tunnel structure produces pain.

computer vision syndrome (CVS) Eye strain condition related to computer display screen use; symptoms include headaches, blurred vision, and dry, irritated eyes.

SURVIVING RSI

Imagine that your exciting career working on the Internet is suddenly ended because of repetitive stress injury (RSI). Or, imagine being a Web entrepreneur but finding the costs of preventing and treating RSI too high to continue. As the Web has exploded in size, RSI has mushroomed into a major hazard that the Internet industry must face.

How serious is the problem? The experience of Debra Lieberman, an occupational therapist with Washington, DC's National Rehabilitation Hospital, seems to be typical. "About 65 to 70 percent [of my patients] and growing are computer workers," she estimates. Other therapists are finding that more and more of their RSI patients come from the Internet industry. We need to address three questions: Why the Internet? Can RSI threaten a career? What can management do about it?

Why are Internet employees especially susceptible to RSI? First, the field is heavily dependent on Web site design, programming, and content development of the site. Moreover, Web-based employees spend hours laboriously keying in responses to site visitors. Despite these problems, people are attracted to the Internet and the Web. The work is new, challenging, and exciting. Internet workers are often highly motivated, absorbed in their work, and eager to devote long hours to the job without rest and/or extra pay. Because they also tend to be young, these workers may more often ignore risks.

Can RSI threaten a career? RSI is a debilitating injury. It develops from repetitive motion without opportunities for rest and for stretching one's muscles. Before computers took over, many people spent long hours working on typewriters, but typewriters did not lead to RSI. Pressing typewriter keys required enough effort to help build muscle strength. Typists moved their arms at the end of each line in order to return the carriage. Numerous breaks were required to replace the typing paper, the carbon paper, and the ribbon. Today typing is repetitive with no natural breaks. RSI can be so painful that sufferers cannot lift their coffee cup or brush their hair. The problem faced by Karyn Young, a program manager in IBM's Internet Division, is common. "There were times," she said, "I thought I was going to have

to go on disability." She added that "I seriously considered other careers." She stuck with it only because she said she would have been "heartbroken" to leave the Internet field.

Management must face the RSI issue if only because its costs are high. According to Rob deViere, a program instructor at the federal Occupational Safety and Health Administration (OSHA), a single workplace injury costs about $16,000. OSHA estimates the cost of lost work days and workers compensation claims to be nearing $20 billion a year.

What can management do? Effective solutions are available. Many companies, such as Internet giant America Online, have established ergonomics programs to prevent RSI. Employees are given ergonomically correct workstations, including adjustable chairs and keyboard trays, and training on how to adjust and position them. In addition all employees are given stretch bands and exercise programs so they can do strengthening exercises during work. They are given numerous regular breaks and are automatically reminded to take them. These preventive measures are relatively inexpensive compared with the bills for lost workdays, medical treatments, and increased insurance premiums.

The problem for many Internet companies is that needed equipment, training, and exercise time is expensive. Most Internet companies are small start-ups with tiny budgets. They cannot afford expensive equipment, training, and lost time. So they are caught in a bind because they also cannot afford the injuries. Even the entrepreneurs themselves are sometimes sidelined by RSI. For small struggling companies no clear answer exists. Entrepreneurs must include RSI in their planning and consider long and hard how they will survive.

TO THINK ABOUT: What are the responsibilities of the management of Internet companies in relation to RSI? How would you factor in the ethical issue presented by RSI if you were the entrepreneur of a small, startup Web company? What management, organization, and technology issues would you address?

Sources: Lisa Harman-Greenawalt, "What's Ailing Net Workers," *Internet World*, May 3 1999; and Melissa J. Perenson, "Straighten Up!" *Small Business Computing*, October 1999.

---

technostress Stress induced by computer use; symptoms include aggravation, hostility toward humans, impatience, and enervation.

The newest computer-related malady is **technostress,** which is stress induced by computer use. Its symptoms include aggravation, hostility toward humans, impatience, and fatigue. The problem according to experts is that humans working continuously with computers come to expect other humans and human institutions to behave like computers, providing instant responses, attentiveness, and an absence of emotion. Computer-intense workers are aggravated when put on hold during a phone call or becoming incensed or alarmed when their PCs take a few seconds longer to perform a task. Technostress is thought to be related to high levels of job turnover in the computer industry, high levels of early retirement from computer-intense occupations, and elevated levels of drug and alcohol abuse.

Repetitive stress injury (RSI) is the leading occupational disease today. The single largest cause of RSI is computer keyboard work.

The incidence of technostress is not known but is thought to be in the millions in the United States and growing rapidly. Computer-related jobs now top the list of stressful occupations based on health statistics in several industrialized countries.

To date the role of radiation from computer display screens in occupational disease has not been proved. Video display terminals (VDTs) emit nonionizing electric and magnetic fields at low frequencies. These rays enter the body and have unknown effects on enzymes, molecules, chromosomes, and cell membranes. Long-term studies are investigating low-level electromagnetic fields and birth defects, stress, low birth weight, and other diseases. All manufacturers have reduced display screen emissions since the early 1980s, and European countries such as Sweden have adopted stiff radiation emission standards.

The computer has become a part of our lives—personally as well as socially, culturally, and politically. It is unlikely the issues and our choices will become easier as information technology continues to transform our world. The growth of the Internet and the information economy suggests that all the ethical and social issues we have described will be heightened further as we move into the first digital century.

MANAGEMENT ACTIONS: A CORPORATE CODE OF ETHICS

Some corporations have developed far-reaching corporate IS codes of ethics—Federal Express, IBM, American Express, and Merck and Co. are just a few. Most firms, however, have not developed these codes of ethics, leaving their employees unsure about expected correct behavior. There is some dispute concerning a general code of ethics versus a specific information systems code of ethics. As managers, you should strive to develop an IS-specific set of ethical standards for each of the five moral dimensions:

○ **Information rights and obligations.** A code should cover topics such as employee e-mail privacy, workplace monitoring, treatment of corporate information, and policies on customer information.

○ **Property rights and obligations.** A code should cover topics such as software licenses, ownership of firm data and facilities, ownership of software created by employees on company hardware, and software copyrights. Specific guidelines for contractual relationships with third parties should be covered as well.

○ **Accountability and control.** The code should specify a single individual responsible for all information systems. Other staff members reporting to this individual should be responsible for individual rights, the protection of property rights, system quality, and quality of life (e.g., job design, ergonomics, employee satisfaction). Responsibilities for control of systems, audits, and management should be clearly defined. The potential liabilities of systems officers and the corporation should be detailed in a separate document.

○ **System quality.** The code should describe the general levels of data quality and system error that can be tolerated with detailed specifications left to specific projects. The code should require that all systems attempt to estimate data quality and system error probabilities.

○ **Quality of life.** The code should state that the purpose of systems is to improve the quality of life for customers and for employees by achieving high levels of product quality, customer service, employee satisfaction, and human dignity through proper ergonomics, job and work-flow design, and human resource development.

MANAGEMENT WRAP-UP

Management

Managers are ethical rule makers for their organizations (Green, 1994). They are charged with creating the policies and procedures to establish ethical conduct, including the ethical use of information systems. Managers are also responsible for identifying, analyzing, and resolving the ethical dilemmas that invariably crop up as they balance conflicting needs and interests.

Organization

Rapid changes fueled by information technology are creating new situations where existing laws or rules of conduct may not be relevant. New "gray areas" are emerging in which ethical standards have not yet been codified into law. A new system of ethics for the information age is required to guide individual and organizational choices and actions.

Technology

Information technology is introducing changes that create new ethical issues for societies to debate and resolve. Increasing computing power, storage, and networking capabilities—including the Internet—can expand the reach of individual and organizational actions and magnify their impact. The ease and anonymity with which information can be communicated, copied, and manipulated in on-line environments are challenging traditional rules of right and wrong behavior.

For Discussion

1. Should producers of software-based services such as ATMs be held liable for economic injuries suffered when their systems fail?

2. Should companies be responsible for unemployment caused by their information systems? Why or why not?

SUMMARY

1. **Analyze the relationship among ethical, social, and political issues raised by information systems.** Ethical, social, and political issues are closely related in an information society. Ethical issues confront individuals who must choose a course of action, often in a situation in which two or more ethical principles are in conflict (a dilemma). Social issues spring from ethical issues. Societies must develop expectations in individuals about the correct course of action, and social issues then become debates about the kinds of situations and expectations that societies should develop so that individuals behave correctly. Political issues spring from social conflict and are largely concerned with laws that prescribe behavior; to avoid social conflict laws help promote situations in which individuals behave correctly.

2. **Identify the main moral dimensions of an information society and apply them to specific situations.** There are five main moral dimensions that tie together ethical, social, and political issues in an information society. These moral dimensions are information rights and obligations, property rights, accountability and control, system quality, and quality of life.

3. **Apply an ethical analysis to difficult situations.** An ethical analysis is a five-step methodology for analyzing a situation. The method involves identifying the facts, values, stakeholders, options, and consequences of actions. Once the ethical analysis has been performed, you can begin to consider what ethical principle you should apply to a situation to arrive at a judgment.

4. **Examine specific ethical principles for conduct.** Six ethical principles are available to judge your own conduct (and that of others). These principles are derived independently from several cultural, religious, and intellectual traditions. They are not hard-and-fast rules and may not apply in all situations. The principles are the Golden Rule, Immanuel Kant's Categorical Imperative, Descartes' rule of change, the Utilitarian Principle, the Risk Aversion Principle, and the ethical "no free lunch" rule.

5. **Design corporate policies for ethical conduct.** For each of the five moral dimensions, corporations should develop an ethics policy statement to assist individuals and to encourage appropriate decision making. The policy areas are as follows. (a) Individual information rights: Spell out corporate privacy and due process policies. (b) Property rights: Clarify how the corporation will treat property rights of software owners. (c) Accountability and control: Clarify who is responsible and accountable for information. (d) System quality: Identify methodologies and quality standards to be achieved. (e) Quality of life: Identify corporate policies on family, computer crime, decision making, vulnerability, job loss, and health risks.

KEY TERMS

Accountability, 457	Copyright, 464	Immanuel Kant's Categorical	Repetitive stress injury
Carpal tunnel syndrome	Descartes' rule of change, 458	Imperative, 458	(RSI), 475
(CTS), 475	Due process, 457	Intellectual property, 463	Responsibility, 456
Computer abuse, 473	Ethical "no free lunch"	Liability, 457	Risk Aversion Principle, 458
Computer crime, 473	rule, 458	Patent, 464	Spamming, 463
Computer vision syndrome	Ethics, 453	Privacy, 460	Technostress, 476
(CVS), 475	Fair Information Practices	Profiling, 456	Trade secret, 463
Cookie, 461	(FIP), 460		Utilitarian Principle, 458

REVIEW QUESTIONS

1. In what ways are ethical, social, and political issues connected? Give some examples.
2. What are the key technological trends that heighten ethical concerns?
3. What are the differences between responsibility, accountability, and liability?
4. What are the five steps in an ethical analysis?
5. Identify six ethical principles.
6. What is a professional code of conduct?
7. What are meant by "privacy" and "Fair Information Practices"?
8. How is the Internet challenging the protection of individual privacy?

9. What are the three different regimes that protect intellectual property rights? What challenges to intellectual property rights are posed by the Internet?
10. Why is it so difficult to hold software services liable for failure or injury?
11. What is the most common cause of system quality problems?
12. Name and describe four "quality of life" impacts of computers and information systems.
13. What is *technostress*, and how would you identify it?
14. Name three management actions that could reduce RSI.

GROUP PROJECT

With three or four of your classmates, develop a corporate ethics code on privacy that addresses both employee privacy and the privacy of customers and users of the corporate Web site. Be sure to consider e-mail privacy and employer monitoring of worksites, as well as corporate use of information about employees concerning their off-the-job behavior (e.g., lifestyle, marital arrangements, and so forth). Present your ethics code to the class.

Tools for Interactive Learning

○ Internet Connection

The Internet Connection for this chapter will direct you to a series of Web sites where you can learn more about the privacy issues raised by the use of the Internet and the Web. You can complete an exercise to analyze the privacy implications of existing technologies for tracking Web site visitors. You can also use the Interactive Study Guide to test your knowledge of the topics in this chapter and get instant feedback where you need more practice.

○ Electronic Commerce Project

At the Laudon Web site for Chapter 14, you will find an Electronic Commerce project that uses the interactive software at the Deja.com Web site to explore the use of Internet discussion groups for targeted marketing.

○ CD-ROM

If you purchase and use the Multimedia Edition CD-ROM with this chapter, you can complete an interactive exercise asking you to perform an ethical analysis of problems encountered by a business. You can also find a video clip on software piracy, an audio overview of the major themes of this chapter, and bullet text summarizing the key points of the chapter.

○ Application Exercise

At the Laudon Web site you can find an Application Exercise for this chapter requiring you to use Web browser and electronic presentation software to research and present a comparison of alternative database development systems for a nonprofit organization.

The Internet has quickly become one of the most important sources of personal data. Obviously, we openly volunteer personal information such as our names, addresses, and e-mail addresses when we register to gain access to a Web site, or when we subscribe to an on-line newsletter. If you bank through the Net or invest through an on-line brokerage firm, you must provide a great deal of personal data. Although you give this information freely, you rarely have any control over what the site will do with it. However, many sites are gathering much more personal information without our ever being aware of it. Web sites can obtain basic personal data when you visit them even though that site does not yet know your identity. When you stop by a Web site, the owners can instantly obtain your Internet address, your browser type, your operating system, and the site from which you arrived. That isolated data may seem perfectly harmless, but it is only the beginning.

In addition to "cookies," which we described earlier in this chapter, Web site owners and others have devised other surreptitious methods of gathering personal data when we are on-line. In February 1999 the public learned that Intel's new Pentium III chips carried a serial number that could be read remotely through the Web and then used to tie the owner directly to activities on that computer. Thus Intel could trace your movements and activities on the Internet. A month later Microsoft Corp. admitted that it had a database of unique serial numbers for each user who had registered a copy of Windows 98. That number could be used to identify the owner of any documents that are sent traveling through the Net. Both Intel and Microsoft claimed their identification numbers were for use only by their technicians to aid in supporting customers. Following the unexpected publicity, both companies quickly announced changes in their policies and said they had eliminated these identifiers. Nevertheless, these two cases alerted the general public to the ease of establishing a system to trace the movements, activities, and ideas of Internet users.

Other methods of learning about your personal habits have been devised. One-to-One from BroadVision Inc., linked with Andromedia's Aria eCommerce 3.0, are examples of software packages that are now being used to observe and record individual on-line visitors' behavior. Their purpose is to understand the behavioral patterns of individuals and groups in order to effectively market to them. To appreciate how these tools electronically "watch" a Web site visitor, imagine being in a supermarket or clothing store where someone surreptitiously trailed you with a notebook recording your every move. Do you find this an acceptable method of data gathering?

Once these data are collected, they are often merged with other personal data about the individual. (The chapter opening vignette described how DoubleClick might try to combine its data about Internet consumers with off-line data about catalog shoppers collected by Abacus Direct.) Many companies sell data in order to obtain income. For some companies the sale of personal data is their primary business. Acxiom Corp. has collected data on 176 million individuals, and this data is for sale. "They follow you more closely than the U.S. government," says Anthony Picardi, a software analyst at International Data Corp.

Public institutions, such as hospitals, schools, and law enforcement agencies, also collect massive amounts of data on their clients (patients, students, and citizens). Medical data in particular are becoming more and more centralized into huge databases. Joe Pellegrino, manager of database administration at New York Presbyterian Hospital, claims, "There's no question this is leading to a national universal medical database." Many companies would be interested in purchasing these data, and so they too might end up on the auction block. Many of these institutions are private and, without government regulation, are free to sell their data. Moreover, these organizations are occasionally privatized, merged, or closed, and so their data could end up in the hands of someone else who would sell them.

Why this lucrative trade in personal data? Obviously, one reason is to increase sales. Many businesses use the information to locate good sales prospects or to target repeat customers with new offers of items to purchase. Web sites even use their own data to direct visitors to other sites in ex-change for a fee. Insurance companies, lawyers, bail bondspersons, manufacturers of home security equipment, and even funeral parlors want personal data on recent crime victims in the hope of finding new clients.

Increasing sales is not the only reason for interest in these data, however. Organizations can use data on your Web travels to draw implications about you, and those implications may be wrong and harmful. For example, employers could use these data to help them determine whom they want to hire. Job applicants may find that trouble they had in elementary school has followed them throughout their lives. Or the employer may find that an applicant has visited a number of sites relating to AIDS. The candidate may then be denied employment based on the conclusion that the candidate has AIDS even though the person may have visited those sites for many reasons, such as curiosity, research (for work or school), or to help a friend. Compounding this problem, data errors are likely to abound. Data can be inaccurate, false, and out-of-date, and still be sold repeatedly or used in ways that harms the individual.

Because personal data can help as well as harm, its collection presents many people with a dilemma. "There's no question that this technology could be hugely invasive," explains Christine Varney, who was the Internet expert for the FTC until August 1997 and now heads the Online Privacy Alliance. "But," she continues, "it could also be enormously empowering by allowing individuals to make their own choices and by saving us all time and money." Studies do show that most users want some protection from the indiscriminate use of their personal data, but users are willing to supply information as long as they benefit from the disclosure and are fully informed about how the data will be used.

Many individuals and organizations are addressing the Internet privacy issue. Self-regulation (that is, regulation by the industry rather than by the government) is a major approach favored by some of the leading Internet companies. Online Privacy Alliance, the organization headed by Christine Varney, is a trade association of about 100 companies including America Online Inc., Yahoo, Microsoft,

Hewlett-Packard, IBM, and the Direct Marketing Association. The alliance recommends four guidelines that it urges all companies on the Internet to adopt:

○ Notify visitors of data collection practices

○ Give visitors the choice of exiting the site that is collecting personal data

○ Give visitors access to their own personal data

○ Assure visitors that their personal data are secure

A major goal of the alliance is to persuade the government and U.S. citizens that little government Internet privacy regulation is needed because the industry can adequately regulate itself. Varney believes, "we can have a market-driven approach to privacy on the Internet."

TRUSTe is another industry organization promoting self-regulation. It issues a seal of approval that qualifying Web sites can display. To obtain permission to display its seal of approval, a Web site must agree to comply with TRUSTe's consumer privacy guidelines. A company would be in violation if it used personal information it gathered in ways about which the customer was not explicitly informed. Hundreds of companies now display the TRUSTe seal of approval. However, many question its value. When TRUSTe members such as Real Networks, Alexa Internet (a subsidiary of Amazon.com), Microsoft, and six health care Web sites were found to have violated the terms of their TRUSTe seal of approval, TRUSTe refused to take any action against them. When the Microsoft collection of private data was disclosed, TRUSTe refused to revoke its seal of approval. TRUSTe professed that the storing of the serial number was unrelated to Microsoft's Web site.

Some companies, including Disney, IBM, and Microsoft, have announced they will not work with advertisers who don't have a baseline privacy policy for their Web sites. In April 1999 IBM announced it would not advertise on any U.S. or Canadian Web site that does not post clear privacy policies. However, IBM's position has been called weak because the company only requires that the sites post a policy; it makes no requirements about the content of the policy. IBM's position, if

stronger, could be a powerful incentive for some sites because IBM is the number one Web site advertiser, spending about $60 million in 1999.

Some companies take Web site privacy very seriously. A few pay for outside audits to determine if they are protecting the privacy of their visitors/customers. For example E-loan, a Web site company based in Dublin, California, hired Pricewaterhouse Coopers for a month-long $200,000 privacy audit in order to be able to assure its customers that they were protected. After the original audit, Chris Larsen, E-loan's CEO, decided to establish ongoing quarterly audits despite the expense. His reasons are complex, including both concerns about state and federal financial regulatory agencies and a desire to give customers confidence that their loan data will not be shared with other organizations. Some companies are taking action because they fear being sued and conclude that a good privacy policy will cost less than successful lawsuits.

The main reasons companies don't establish or enforce privacy policies are cost and revenue loss. It can be expensive to hire auditors or experts who can help the company establish and enforce a privacy policy. In addition, enforcing such policies often requires redesign of the Web site and its databases. Moreover, companies can sell private information and thereby generate a good income.

Privacy advocates have developed a Web site visitors' bill of rights that can be used to measure the success of existing efforts to protect Web privacy. The bill of rights is based on two principles: Visitors must control their own data, and sites must disclose their privacy policies. The bill of rights states that site visitors must have the right to prevent use of the information beyond the clear purpose of the site unless the visitor is explicitly notified and is given the opportunity to prohibit such expanded use. Visitors must have the right to prevent the Web site from distributing the information on the visitor outside the Web site's own organization unless the visitor has explicitly given permission. In addition, visitors must also have the right to correct existing errors in their personal data, including the right to modify outdated information.

The FTC issued a report in June 1998 that concluded that self-regulation was

not working. The study found that only 14 percent of the 1,400 Web sites surveyed informed their visitors about what they would do with the personal information they collected. Even fewer sites offered their visitors a choice about how the site could use the information.

Addressing these concerns in November 1999, a group of leading Internet advertising and data-profiling companies, including DoubleClick and CMGI, agreed to develop voluntary privacy-protection guidelines that would notify consumers about their data collection practices and allow them to "opt out" of the profiling technology. These data-profiling companies are also encouraging other Web sites that work with them to clearly advise customers that they are using the data-profiling services.

One "problem is that you now have the Government taking its lead from industry on the privacy issue," declared Marc Rotenberg, the executive director of Electronic Privacy Information Center, a Washington, DC, civil liberties advocacy group. Rotenberg also believes that posted privacy policies actually protect the site operators rather than the visitors because the site operators are then free to do as they wish. "It becomes a privacy policy as a disclaimer," says Rotenberg. His organization is supporting technical changes to the Internet that would allow individuals to surf the Net anonymously.

The FTC already has rules that require companies to enforce any privacy policies that they publicly post. Critics claim that the problem with this FTC requirement is that the FTC does not enforce its own rules. The commission has several times warned companies that have sold or exchanged data after public promises not to do so, and it has even worked with them to stop the practice. In early 2000, the FTC launched an investigation of DoubleClick and Amazon.com's data collection practices and started expanding its activities for monitoring Internet commerce. The FTC is proposing rules for financial institutions to safeguard customer information which might also be applicable to other related online businesses. In February 2000 a bipartisan group of lawmakers established a Congressional Privacy Caucus to push for tougher privacy protection laws and a number of states are proposing even stricter privacy laws.

Sources: Keith Perine, "The Privacy Police," **The Industry Standard,** February 21, 2000; Keith Perine, "Get Ready for Regulation," **The Industry Standard,** March 13, 2000; Michelle V. Rafter, "Trust or Bust?" **The Industry Standard,** March 13, 2000; Steve Lohr, "Internet Companies Set Policies to Help Protect Consumer Privacy," **The New York Times,** November 5, 1999; "Seizing the Initiative on Privacy," **The New York Times,** October 11, 1999; Jon G. Auerbach, "To Get IBM Ad, Sites Must Post Privacy Policies," **The Wall Street Journal,** April 30, 1999; Edward C. Baig, Marcia Stepanek, and Neil Gross, "Privacy," **Business Week,** April 5, 1999; Gregory Dalton, "Online Data's FineLine," **Information Week,** March 29, 1999; Alex Lash, "Privacy, Practically Speaking," **The Industry Standard,** August 2–9, 1999; and James Linderman, "The Right to Website Privacy," **Beyond Computing,** July/August 1999.

CASE STUDY QUESTIONS

1. Is Web site privacy a serious problem? Why or why not?

2. What are the gains for the Web-based businesses if they collect, use, sell, and otherwise disseminate information on their visitors or use it in ways not explicitly approved by the visitor? The losses (costs)?

3. Apply an ethical analysis to the question of Web site visitors' privacy rights.

4. Should Web sites be allowed to collect information on their visitors that is not voluntarily provided?

5. How should Web site privacy be promoted? What role should the government play? What role should private business play?

6. How appropriate are the FTC and Online Privacy Alliance's privacy guidelines? Do you think they meet the goals of the privacy advocates' bill of rights? Explain your answer.

CHAPTER 15

Managing International Information Systems

Learning
Objectives

After completing this chapter, you will be able to:

1. Identify the major factors behind the growing internationalization of business.

2. Compare global strategies for developing business.

3. Demonstrate how information systems support different global strategies.

4. Plan the development of international information systems.

5. Evaluate the main technical alternatives in developing global systems.

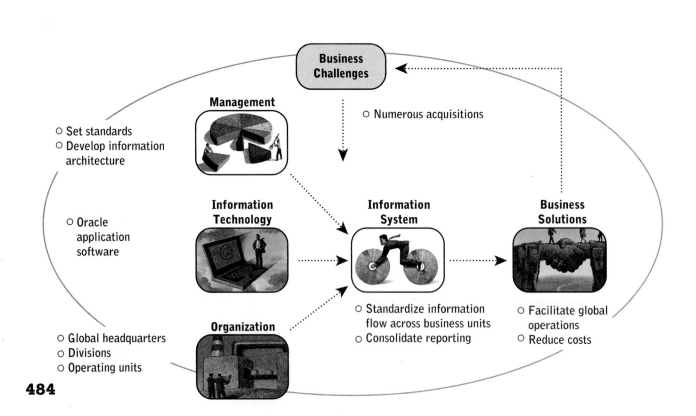

Business Challenges

Management
- Set standards
- Develop information architecture

○ Numerous acquisitions

Information Technology
- Oracle application software

Information System

Business Solutions

Organization
- Global headquarters
- Divisions
- Operating units

- Standardize information flow across business units
- Consolidate reporting

- Facilitate global operations
- Reduce costs

Information Systems Help AMETEK
Pull Together Worldwide

AMETEK Inc. manufactures a wide variety of electric motors and electronic instruments in more than 350 product categories, including process instruments such as pressure gauges, process monitors, and analyzers; heavy-vehicle instruments such as speedometers and tachometers; aircraft engine and air frame sensors; and air-moving motors for vacuum cleaners and other household appliances. The company was founded in 1930 and now has 7,500 employees working in operating units in Canada, Mexico, the United Kingdom, Denmark, France, Italy, Germany, the Czech Republic, Singapore, Taiwan, and China as well as the United States. Much of AMETEK's recent growth has come from acquisitions, and the company has purchased 8 companies since 1997.

AMETEK needs to integrate the products and business operations of every company it acquires into one of its divisions. But because its business units have so many different products and manufacturing styles, the company has been saddled with a patchwork of disparate information systems that has hindered coordination and prevented information from being shared across business units. For example, AMETEK's various business units had trouble sharing work-in-process information regarding an order that multiple sites needed to fill, and the company could not coordinate day-to-day purchasing across different business units. AMETEK needed a way to consolidate reporting and provide numbers and data for quick business decisions.

The company looked for a single enterprise resource planning (ERP) system that it could implement across all of its business units. Managers and representatives of user departments selected Oracle integrated application software for each of AMETEK's divisions, including Oracle Database Server, Oracle Financials, Oracle Manufacturing, Oracle Supply Chain, and Oracle Distribution. Using standard software has helped consolidate and integrate business units. For example, AMETEK's Process and Analytical Instruments Division was able to use Oracle Financial applications to consolidate the financial operations and financial reporting for all three units in one centralized location. The Oracle software also helped AMETEK coordinate supply chain activities among units, create reports in multiple currencies, and provide managers with consolidated profit and loss statements.

With standard systems, AMETEK operates easily across national boundaries. In order to consolidate its Calibration Products business unit, AMETEK had to combine four different business units that were acquired at different times in Denmark, the United Kingdom, and the United States, and that each use different software. With the Oracle software, AMETEK can view these business entities as a single unit.

Sources: Dawn Barrs, "Pulling IT Together," *Profit Magazine,* August 1999; and "Company Profile: AMETEK Specialty Metal Products," *International Journal of Powder Metallurgy,* January/February 1999.

MANAGEMENT CHALLENGES

AMETEK is one of many business firms moving toward global forms of organization that transcend national boundaries. AMETEK could not make this move unless it reorganized its information systems and standardized some of them so that the same information could be used by disparate business units in different countries. Such changes are not always easy to make, and they raise the following management challenges:

1. **Lines of business and global strategy.** Firms must decide whether some or all of their lines of business should be managed on a global basis. There are some lines of business in which local variations are slight, and the possibility exists to reap large rewards by organizing globally. PCs and power tools may fit this pattern, as well as industrial raw materials. Other consumer goods may be quite different by country or region. It is likely that firms with many lines of business will have to maintain a very mixed organizational structure.

2. **The difficulties of managing change in a multicultural firm.** Although engineering change in a single corporation in a single nation can be difficult, costly, and long term, bringing about significant change in very large scale global corporations can be daunting. Both the agreement on "core business processes" in a transnational context and the decision for common systems require either extraordinary insight, a lengthy process of consensus building, or the exercise of sheer power.

The changes AMETEK seeks are some of the changes in international information systems infrastructure—the basic systems needed to coordinate worldwide trade and other activities—that organizations need to consider if they want to operate globally. This chapter explores how to organize, manage, and control the development of international information systems.

15.1 The Growth of International Information Systems

We already have described two powerful worldwide changes driven by advances in information technology that have transformed the business environment and posed new challenges for management. One is the transformation of industrial economies and societies into knowledge- and information-based economies. The other is the emergence of a global economy and global world order.

The new world order will sweep away many national corporations, national industries, and national economies controlled by domestic politicians. Much of the Fortune 500—the 500 largest U.S. corporations—will disappear in the next 50 years, mirroring past behavior of large firms since 1900. Many firms will be replaced by fast-moving, networked corporations that transcend national boundaries. The growth of international trade has radically altered domestic economies around the globe. About $1 trillion worth of goods, services, and financial instruments—one-fifth of the annual U.S. gross national product—changes hands each day in global trade.

Consider a laptop computer as an example: The CPU is likely to have been designed and built in the United States; the DRAM (or dynamic random access memory, which makes up the majority of primary storage in a computer) was designed in the United States but built in Malaysia; the screen was designed and assembled in Japan, using American patents; the keyboard is from Taiwan; and it was all assembled in Japan, where the case also was made. Management of the project, located in Silicon Valley, California, along with marketing, sales, and finance, coordinated all the activities from financing and production to shipping and sales efforts. None of this would be possible without powerful international information and telecommunication systems—an international information systems infrastructure.

To be effective, managers need a global perspective on business and an understanding of the support systems needed to conduct business on an international scale.

DEVELOPING THE INTERNATIONAL INFORMATION SYSTEMS INFRASTRUCTURE

This chapter describes how to go about building an **international information systems infrastructure** suitable for your international strategy. An international information systems infrastructure consists of the basic information systems required by organizations to coordinate worldwide trade and other activities. Figure 15-1 illustrates the reasoning we will follow

international information systems infrastructure The basic information systems required by organizations to coordinate worldwide trade and other activities.

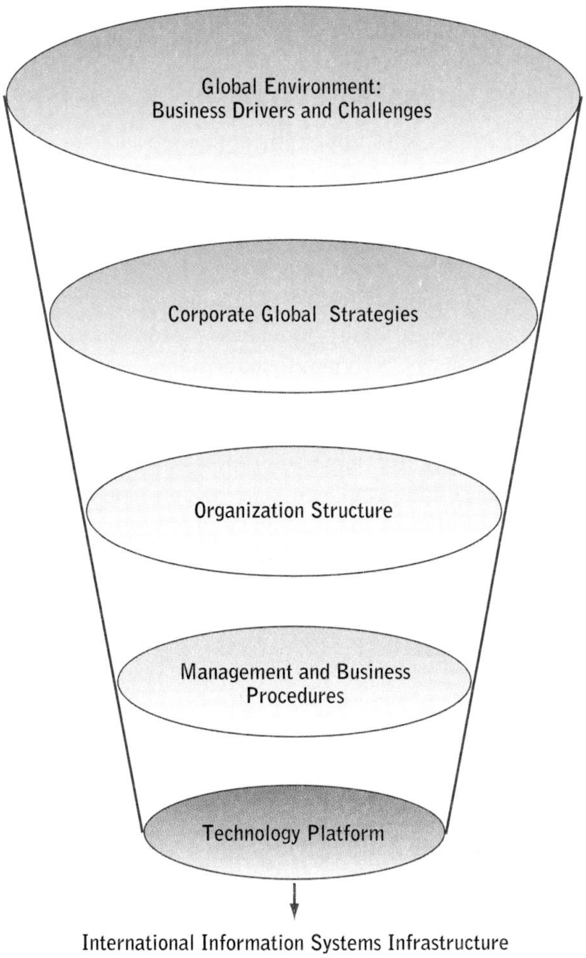

FIGURE 15-1 International information systems infrastructure. The major dimensions for developing an international information systems infrastructure are the global environment, the corporate global strategies, the structure of the organization, the management and business procedures, and the technology platform.

Global Environment: Business Drivers and Challenges

Corporate Global Strategies

Organization Structure

Management and Business Procedures

Technology Platform

International Information Systems Infrastructure

throughout the chapter and depicts the major dimensions of an international information systems infrastructure.

The basic strategy to follow when building an international system is to understand the global environment in which your firm is operating. This means understanding the overall market forces, or business drivers, that are pushing your industry toward global competition. A **business driver** is a force in the environment to which businesses must respond and that influences the direction of the business. Likewise, examine carefully the inhibitors or negative factors that create management challenges—factors that could scuttle the development of a global business. Once you have examined the global environment, you will need to consider a corporate strategy for competing in that environment. How will your firm respond? You could ignore the global market and focus on domestic competition only, sell to the globe from a domestic base, or organize production and distribution around the globe. There are many in-between choices.

After you have developed a strategy, consider how to structure your organization so it can pursue the strategy. How will you accomplish a division of labor across a global environment? Where will production, administration, accounting, marketing, and human resource functions be located? Who will handle the systems function?

Next, consider the management issues in implementing your strategy and making the organization design come alive. Key here will be the design of business procedures. How can you discover and manage user requirements? How can you induce change in local units to conform to international requirements? How can you reengineer on a global scale, and how can you coordinate systems development?

The last issue to consider is the technology platform. Although changing technology is a key driving factor leading toward global markets, you need to have a corporate strategy and structure before you can rationally choose the right technology.

After you have completed this process of reasoning, you will be well on your way toward an appropriate international information systems infrastructure capable of achieving your corporate goals. Let us begin by looking at the overall global environment.

THE GLOBAL ENVIRONMENT: BUSINESS DRIVERS AND CHALLENGES

Table 15-1 illustrates the business drivers in the global environment that are leading all industries toward global markets and competition.

The global business drivers can be divided into two groups: general cultural factors and specific business factors. There are easily recognized general cultural factors driving internationalization since World War II. Information, communication, and transportation technologies have created a global village in which communication (by telephone, television, radio, or computer network) around the globe is no more difficult and not much more expensive than communication down the block. Moving goods and services to and from geographically dispersed locations has fallen dramatically in cost.

The development of global communications has created a global village in a second sense: There is now a **global culture** created by television and other globally shared media such as movies that permits different cultures and peoples to develop common expectations about right and wrong, desirable and undesirable, heroic and cowardly. The collapse of the

business driver A force in the environment to which businesses must respond and that influences the direction of business.

global culture The development of common expectations, shared artifacts, and social norms among different cultures and peoples.

Table 15-1	The Global Business Drivers	
General Cultural Factors		**Specific Business Factors**
Global communication and transportation technologies		Global markets
Development of global culture		Global production and operations
Emergence of global social norms		Global coordination
Political stability		Global workforce
Global knowledge base		Global economies of scale

Businesses need an international information systems infrastructure to coordinate the activities of their sales, manufacturing, and warehouse units worldwide.

Eastern bloc has sped up the growth of a world culture enormously, increased support for capitalism and business, and reduced the level of cultural conflict considerably.

A last factor to consider is the growth of a global knowledge base. At the end of World War II, knowledge, education, science, and industrial skills were highly concentrated in North America, Europe, and Japan, with the rest of the world euphemistically called the Third World. This is no longer true. Latin America, China, Southern Asia, and Eastern Europe have developed powerful educational, industrial, and scientific centers, resulting in a much more democratically and widely dispersed knowledge base.

These general cultural factors leading toward internationalization result in specific business globalization factors that affect most industries. The growth of powerful communications technologies and the emergence of world cultures create the condition for global markets—global consumers interested in consuming similar products that are culturally approved. Coca-Cola, American sneakers (made in Korea but designed in Los Angeles), and CNN News (a television show) can now be sold in Latin America, Africa, and Asia.

Responding to this demand, global production and operations have emerged with precise on-line coordination between far-flung production facilities and central headquarters thousands of miles away. At Sealand Transportation, a major global shipping company based in Newark, New Jersey, shipping managers in Newark can watch the loading of ships in Rotterdam on-line, check trim and ballast, and trace packages to specific ship locations as the activity proceeds. This is all possible through an international satellite link.

The new global markets and pressure toward global production and operation have called forth whole new capabilities for global coordination of all factors of production. Not only production but also accounting, marketing and sales, human resources, and systems development (all the major business functions) can be coordinated on a global scale. Frito Lay, for instance, can develop a marketing sales force automation system in the United States and, once provided, may try the same techniques and technologies in Spain. Micromarketing—marketing to very small geographic and social units—no longer means marketing to neighborhoods in the United States, but to neighborhoods throughout the world! These new levels of global coordination permit for the first time in history the location of business activity according to comparative advantage. Design should be located where it is best accomplished, as should marketing, production, and finance.

Finally, global markets, production, and administration create the conditions for powerful, sustained global economies of scale. Production driven by worldwide global demand can be concentrated where it can be best accomplished, fixed resources can be allocated over larger production runs, and production runs in larger plants can be scheduled efficiently and estimated precisely. Lower cost factors of production can be exploited wherever they emerge. The result is a powerful strategic advantage to firms that can organize globally. These general and specific business drivers have greatly enlarged world trade and commerce.

Not all industries are similarly affected by these trends. Clearly, manufacturing has been much more affected than services that still tend to be domestic and highly inefficient.

Table 15-2 Challenges and Obstacles to Global Business Systems		
General	**Specific**
Cultural particularism: regionalism, nationalism, language differences	Standards: different EDI, e-mail, telecommunications standards
Social expectations: brand-name expectations, work hours	Reliability: phone networks not uniformly reliable
Political laws: transborder data and privacy laws, commercial regulations	Speed: different data transfer speeds, many slower than United States
	Personnel: shortage of skilled consultants

However, the localism of services is breaking down in telecommunications, entertainment, transportation, financial services, and general business services including law. Clearly, those firms within an industry that understand the internationalization of the industry and respond appropriately will reap enormous gains in productivity and stability.

Business Challenges

Although the possibilities of globalization for business success are significant, fundamental forces are operating to inhibit a global economy and to disrupt international business. Table 15-2 lists the most common and powerful challenges to the development of global systems.

At a cultural level, **particularism,** making judgments and taking action on the basis of narrow or personal characteristics, in all its forms (religious, nationalistic, ethnic, regionalism, geopolitical position) rejects the very concept of a shared global culture and rejects the penetration of domestic markets by foreign goods and services. Differences among cultures produce differences in social expectations, politics, and ultimately legal rules. In certain countries, such as the United States, consumers expect domestic name-brand products to be produced domestically and are disappointed to learn that much of what they thought of as domestically produced is in fact foreign made.

Different cultures produce different political regimes. Among the different countries of the world, there are different laws governing the movement of information, information privacy of citizens, origins of software and hardware in systems, and radio and satellite telecommunications. Even the hours of business and the terms of business trade vary greatly across political cultures. These different legal regimes complicate global business and must be considered when building global systems.

For instance, European countries have very strict laws concerning **transborder data flow** and privacy. Transborder data flow is defined as the movement of information across international boundaries in any form. Some European countries prohibit the processing of financial information outside their boundaries or the movement of personal information to foreign countries. The European Union Data Protection Directive, which went into effect in October 1998, restricts the flow of any information to countries (such as the United States) that do not meet strict European information laws on personal information. Financial services, travel, and healthcare companies could be directly affected. For example, information on an airline passenger's food preferences collected in one of the European Union countries might not be able to be forwarded to the United States, given its privacy laws. In response, most multinational firms develop information systems within each European country to avoid the cost and uncertainty of moving information across national boundaries.

Cultural and political differences profoundly affect organizations' standard operating procedures. A host of specific barriers arise from the general cultural differences—everything from different reliability of phone networks to the shortage of skilled consultants (see Steinbart and Nath, 1992). The Window on Organizations illustrates how such differences can affect efforts to implement electronic commerce globally.

National laws and traditions have created disparate accounting practices in various countries, which impact the ways profits and losses are analyzed. German companies generally do not recognize the profit from a venture until the project is completely finished and they

particularism Making judgments and taking actions on the basis of narrow or personal characteristics.

transborder data flow The movement of information across international boundaries in any form.

BLOCKING THE PATH TO BORDERLESS COMMERCE

Many experts believe that Europe is likely to experience an electronic commerce boom during the next five years. However, it may not be easy for companies from the United States or other areas of the world to capitalize on Europe's e-revolution. Cultural and linguistic differences, high prices for telecommunications services and Internet access, corporate conservatism, and European Union trading and privacy legislation present hurdles. Merrill Lynch European analyst Peter Bradshaw believes it is two-and-one-half times more difficult to do business in Europe than in the United States.

Many U.S. sellers may not want to incur extra costs, delays, and risks to sell their products in Europe because European regulations governing commercial transactions are not identical to those in the United States. For example, under European Union regulations, a consumer could return a product for any or no reason, even if the product was perfect and the company selling it made full disclosure of all elements required by rule. That concept does not exist in the United States.

An exemption from European Union rules allows automakers to dictate retail prices and to bar dealers from competing with each other, thus barring on-line auto sales. To protect small mom-and-pop stores, German regulations prohibit most price discounting on consumer goods except for 2 two-week periods each year. This law prevents airlines from offering last-minute low ticket prices to fill empty seats. Reverse auctions such as Priceline.com, where consumers name a price they are willing to pay for airline tickets, hotel rooms, cars, and other items, likewise are not allowed to operate. And on-line auctions such as eBay run up against laws requiring the physical display of goods to be sold at auction.

Europeans are more reluctant than Americans to purchase goods and services on-line, especially southern Europeans, who seem to be tied to personal relationships with local shopkeepers. Some of this resistance to on-line buying is crumbling, and the International Data Corporation predicts that 35 percent of Western European consumers will be using the Internet by 2002. Nevertheless, change comes slowly and many Europeans want to see clearcut reasons for buying on-line before they start Internet shopping. Many Europeans also lack the financial tools for Internet shopping. Only one in seven Germans or Italians owns a credit card.

Many U.S. companies expect to use English to sell to Europeans and think that most Europeans who use the Internet can understand English. Yet European consumers prefer to use their native language when doing business over the Internet. Many Europeans see the Internet as an extension of American culture. Companies seeking European customers are advised to translate a portion of their Web sites into most European languages and to register their Web sites in international indexes if they want to attract non–English-speaking visitors. Smaller enterprises in the United States cannot afford to localize their Web sites or set up distribution and marketing networks for many different countries. They can, however, translate the most important material on their Web sites into several European languages and find a European partner to help with local distribution, payment, and services.

TO THINK ABOUT: What political and organizational issues should firms consider when setting up a Web site to sell products and services in other countries?

Sources: Bernhard Warner, "Coming to America," *The Industry Standard*, March 13, 2000; Dermot McGrath, "When 'E' Stands for Europe," **Computerworld**, September 5, 1999; and Neal E. Boudette, "In Europe, Surfing a Web of Red Tape," **The Wall Street Journal**, October 29, 1999.

---

have been paid. Conversely, British firms begin posting profits before a project is completed when they are reasonably certain they will get the money.

These accounting practices are tightly intertwined with each country's legal system, business philosophy, and tax code. British, U.S., and Dutch firms share a predominantly Anglo-Saxon outlook that separates tax calculations from reports to shareholders to focus on showing shareholders how fast profits are growing. Continental European accounting practices are less oriented toward impressing investors, focusing rather on demonstrating compliance with strict rules and minimizing tax liabilities. These diverging accounting practices make it difficult for large international companies with units in different countries to evaluate their performance.

Cultural differences can also affect the way organizations use information technology. For example, Japanese firms fax extensively but have been reluctant to take advantage of the capabilities of e-mail. One explanation is that the Japanese view e-mail as poorly suited for much intragroup communication and for depiction of the complex symbols used in the Japanese written language (Straub, 1994).

Language remains a significant barrier. Although English has become a kind of standard business language, this is truer at higher levels of companies and not throughout the middle and lower ranks. Software may have to be built with local language interfaces before a new information system can be successfully implemented.

Currency fluctuations can play havoc with planning models and projections. A product that appears profitable in Mexico or Japan may actually produce a loss because of changes in foreign exchange rates. Some of these problems will diminish if the euro becomes more widely used.

These inhibiting factors must be taken into account when you are designing and building an international infrastructure for your business. For example, companies trying to implement "lean production" systems spanning national boundaries typically underestimate the time, expense, and logistical difficulties of making goods and information flow freely across different countries (Levy, 1997).

STATE OF THE ART

One might think, given the opportunities for achieving competitive advantages as outlined previously and the interest in future applications, that most international companies have rationally developed marvelous international systems architectures. Nothing could be further from the truth. Most companies have inherited patchwork international systems from the distant past, often based on concepts of information processing developed in the 1960s—batch-oriented reporting from independent foreign divisions to corporate headquarters with little on-line control and communication. Corporations in this situation increasingly will face powerful competitive challenges in the marketplace from firms that have rationally designed truly international systems. Still other companies have recently built technology platforms for an international infrastructure but have nowhere to go because they lack a global strategy.

As it turns out, there are significant difficulties in building appropriate international infrastructures. The difficulties involve planning a system appropriate to the firm's global strategy, structuring the organization of systems and business units, solving implementation issues, and choosing the right technical platform. Let us examine these problems in greater detail.

15.2 Organizing International Information Systems

There are three organizational issues facing corporations seeking a global position: choosing a strategy, organizing the business, and organizing the systems management area. The first two are closely connected, so we will discuss them together.

GLOBAL STRATEGIES AND BUSINESS ORGANIZATION

Four main global strategies form the basis for global firms' organizational structure. These are domestic exporter, multinational, franchiser, and transnational. Each of these strategies is pursued with a specific business organizational structure (see Table 15-3). For simplicity's sake, we describe three kinds of organizational structure or governance: centralized (in the home country), decentralized (to local foreign units), and coordinated (all units participate as equals). There are other types of governance patterns observed in specific companies (e.g., au-

Table 15-3   Global Business Strategy and Structure

Business Function	Domestic Exporter	Multinational	Franchiser	Transnational
	Strategy			
Production	Centralized	Dispersed	Coordinated	Coordinated
Finance/accounting	Centralized	Centralized	Centralized	Coordinated
Sales/marketing	Mixed	Dispersed	Coordinated	Coordinated
Human resources	Centralized	Centralized	Coordinated	Coordinated
Strategic management	Centralized	Centralized	Centralized	Coordinated

thoritarian dominance by one unit, a confederacy of equals, a federal structure balancing power among strategic units, and so forth; see Keen, 1991).

The **domestic exporter** strategy is characterized by heavy centralization of corporate activities in the home country of origin. Nearly all international companies begin this way, and some move on to other forms. Production, finance/accounting, sales/marketing, human resources, and strategic management are set up to optimize resources in the home country. International sales are sometimes dispersed using agency agreements or subsidiaries, but even here foreign marketing is totally reliant on the domestic home base for marketing themes and strategies. Caterpillar Corporation and other heavy capital-equipment manufacturers fall into this category of firm.

domestic exporter A strategy characterized by heavy centralization of corporate activities in the home country of origin.

The **multinational** strategy concentrates financial management and control from a central home base, and decentralizes production, sales, and marketing operations to units in other countries. The products and services on sale in different countries are adapted to suit local market conditions. The organization becomes a far-flung confederation of production and marketing facilities in different countries. Many financial service firms, along with a host of manufacturers such as General Motors, DaimlerChrysler, and Intel, fit this pattern.

multinational A global strategy that concentrates financial management and control from a central home base and decentralizes production, sales, and marketing operations to units in other countries.

Franchisers are an interesting mix of old and new. The product is created, designed, financed, and initially produced in the home country, but for product-specific reasons must rely heavily on foreign personnel for further production, marketing, and human resources. Food franchisers such as McDonald's, Mrs. Fields Cookies, and Kentucky Fried Chicken fit this pattern. McDonald's created a new form of fast-food chain in the United States and continues to rely largely on the United States for inspiration of new products, strategic management, and financing. Nevertheless, because the product must be produced locally (it is perishable), extensive coordination and dispersion of production, local marketing, and local recruitment of personnel are required. Generally, foreign franchisees are clones of the mother country units, but fully coordinated worldwide production that could optimize factors of production is not possible. For instance, potatoes and beef can generally not be bought where they are cheapest on world markets but must be produced reasonably close to the area of consumption.

franchiser A firm where a product is created, designed, financed, and initially produced in the home country, but for product-specific reasons must rely heavily on foreign personnel for further production, marketing, and human resources.

Transnational firms are the stateless, truly globally managed firms that may represent a larger part of international business in the future. Transnational firms have no single national headquarters but instead have many regional headquarters and perhaps a world headquarters. In a **transnational** strategy, nearly all the value-adding activities are managed from a global perspective without reference to national borders, optimizing sources of supply and demand wherever they appear, and taking advantage of any local competitive advantages. Transnational firms take the globe, not the home country, as their management frame of reference. The governance of these firms has been likened to a federal structure in which there is a strong central management core of decision making, but considerable dispersal of power and financial muscle throughout the global divisions. Few companies have actually attained transnational status, but Citigroup, Sony, Ford, and others are attempting this transition.

transnational Truly globally managed firms that have no national headquarters; value-added activities are managed from a global perspective without reference to national borders, optimizing sources of supply and demand and taking advantage of any local competitive advantage.

Information technology and improvements in global telecommunications are giving international firms more flexibility to shape their global strategies. Protectionism and a need to serve local markets better encourage companies to disperse production facilities and at least become multinational. At the same time, the drive to achieve economies of scale and take advantage of short-term local advantage moves transnationals toward a global management perspective and a concentration of power and authority. Hence, there are forces of decentralization and dispersal, as well as forces of centralization and global coordination (Ives and Jarvenpaa, 1991).

GLOBAL SYSTEMS TO FIT THE STRATEGY

The configuration, management, and development of systems tend to follow the global strategy chosen (Roche, 1992; Ives and Jarvenpaa, 1991). Figure 15-2 depicts typical arrangements. By systems we mean the full range of activities involved in building information systems: conception and alignment with the strategic business plan, systems development, and ongoing operation. For the sake of simplicity, we consider four types of systems configuration. *Centralized systems* are those in which systems development and operation occur totally at the domestic home base. *Duplicated systems* are those in which development occurs at the home

FIGURE 15-2 Global strategy and systems configurations. The large Xs show the dominant patterns, and the small Xs show the emerging patterns. For instance, domestic exporters rely predominantly on centralized systems, but there is continual pressure and some development of decentralized systems in local marketing regions.

SYSTEM CONFIGURATION	STRATEGY			
	Domestic Exporter	Multinational	Franchiser	Transnational
Centralized	X			
Duplicated			X	
Decentralized	x	X	x	
Networked		x		X

base but operations are handed over to autonomous units in foreign locations. *Decentralized systems* are those in which each foreign unit designs its own unique solutions and systems. *Networked systems* are those in which systems development and operations occur in an integrated and coordinated fashion across all units. As can be seen in Figure 15-2, domestic exporters tend to have highly centralized systems in which a single domestic systems development staff develops worldwide applications. Multinationals offer a direct and striking contrast: Here foreign units devise their own systems solutions based on local needs with few if any applications in common with headquarters (the exceptions being financial reporting and some telecommunications applications). Franchisers have the simplest systems structure: Like the products they sell, franchisers develop a single system usually at the home base and then replicate it around the world. Each unit, no matter where it is located, has identical applications. Last, the most ambitious form of systems development is found in the transnational: Networked systems are those in which there is a solid, singular global environment for developing and operating systems. This usually presupposes a powerful telecommunications backbone, a culture of shared applications development, and a shared management culture that crosses cultural barriers. The networked systems structure is the most apparent in financial services where the homogeneity of the product—money and money instruments—seems to overcome cultural barriers.

REORGANIZING THE BUSINESS

How should a firm organize itself for doing business on an international scale? To develop a global company and an information systems support structure, a firm needs to follow these principles:

1. Organize value-adding activities along lines of comparative advantage. For instance, marketing/sales functions should be located where they can best be performed, for least cost and maximum impact; likewise with production, finance, human resources, and information systems.

2. Develop and operate systems units at each level of corporate activity—regional, national, and international. To serve local needs, there should be host country systems units of some magnitude. Regional systems units should handle telecommunications and systems development across national boundaries that take place within major geographic regions (European, Asian, American). Transnational systems units should be established to create the linkages across major regional areas and coordinate the devel-

Table 15-4 Management Challenges in Developing Global Systems

Agreeing on common user requirements

Introducing changes in business procedures

Coordinating applications development

Coordinating software releases

Encouraging local users to support global systems

opment and operation of international telecommunications and systems development (Roche, 1992).

3. Establish at world headquarters a single office responsible for development of international systems, a global chief information officer (CIO) position.

Many successful companies have devised organizational systems structures along these principles. The success of these companies relies not only on the proper organization of activities, but also on a key ingredient—a management team that understands the risks and benefits of international systems and that can devise strategies for overcoming the risks. We turn to these management topics next.

15.3 Managing Global Systems

Table 15-4 lists the principal management problems posed by developing international systems. It is interesting to note that these problems are the chief difficulties managers experience in developing ordinary domestic systems as well! But they are enormously complicated in the international environment.

A TYPICAL SCENARIO: DISORGANIZATION ON A GLOBAL SCALE

Let us look at a common scenario. A traditional multinational consumer-goods company based in the United States and operating in Europe would like to expand into Asian markets and knows that it must develop a transnational strategy and a supportive information systems structure. Like most multinationals it has dispersed production and marketing to regional and national centers while maintaining a world headquarters and strategic management in the United States. Historically, it has allowed each of the subsidiary foreign divisions to develop its own systems. The only centrally coordinated system is financial controls and reporting. The central systems group in the United States focuses only on domestic functions and production. The result is a hodgepodge of hardware, software, and telecommunications. The e-mail systems between Europe and the United States are incompatible. Each production facility may use a different manufacturing resources planning system and different marketing, sales, and human resource systems. The technology platforms are wildly different: Europe is using mostly Unix-based file servers and IBM PC clones on desktops. Communications between different sites are poor because of the high cost and low quality of European intercountry communications. The U.S. group is moving from an IBM mainframe environment centralized at headquarters to a highly distributed network architecture based on a national value-added network, with local sites developing their own local area networks. The central systems group at headquarters recently was decimated and dispersed to the U.S. local sites in the hope of better serving local needs and reducing costs.

What do you recommend to the senior management leaders of this company, who now want to pursue a transnational strategy and develop an information systems infrastructure to support a highly coordinated global systems environment? Consider the problems you face by reexamining Table 15-4. The foreign divisions will resist efforts to agree on common user requirements; they have never thought about much other than their own units' needs. The systems groups in American local sites, which have been enlarged recently and told to focus on local needs, will not easily accept guidance from anyone recommending a transnational strategy. It will be difficult to convince local managers anywhere in the world that they should change their business procedures to align with other units in the world, especially if this might interfere with their local performance. After all, local managers are rewarded in this company for meeting local objectives of their division or plant. Finally, it will be difficult to coordinate development of projects around the world in the absence of a powerful telecommunications network and, therefore, difficult to encourage local users to take on ownership in the systems developed.

STRATEGY: DIVIDE, CONQUER, APPEASE

Figure 15-3 lays out the main dimensions of a solution. First, consider that not all systems should be coordinated on a transnational basis; only some core systems are truly worth sharing from a cost and feasibility point of view. **Core systems** are systems that support functions that are absolutely critical to the entire organization. Other systems should be partially coordinated because they share key elements, but they do not have to be totally common across national boundaries. For such systems, a good deal of local variation is possible and desirable. A final group of systems are peripheral, truly provincial, and needed only to suit local requirements.

Define the Core Business Processes

How do you identify core systems? The first step is to define a short list of critical core business processes. Business processes were defined in Chapter 3, which you should review. Briefly, business processes are sets of logically related tasks such as shipping out correct orders to customers or delivering innovative products to the market. Each business process typically involves many functional areas, communicating and coordinating work, information, and knowledge.

The way to identify these core business processes is to conduct a work-flow analysis. How are customer orders taken, what happens to them once they are taken, who fills the orders, how are they shipped to the customers? What about suppliers? Do they have access to manufacturing resource planning systems so that supply is automatic? You should be able to

core systems Systems that support functions that are absolutely critical to the entire organization.

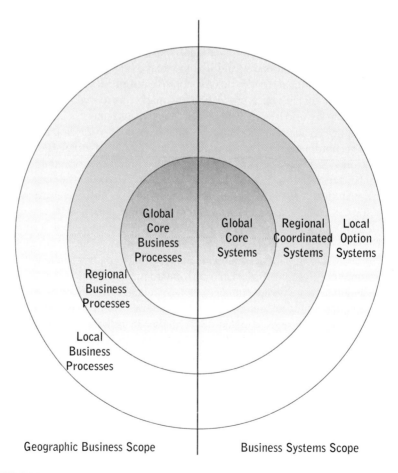

FIGURE 15-3 Agency and other coordination costs increase as the firm moves from local option systems toward regional and global systems. However, transaction costs of participating in global markets probably decrease as firms develop global systems. A sensible strategy is to reduce agency costs by developing only a few core global systems that are vital for global operations, leaving other systems in the hands of regional and local units.
Source: From Managing Information Technology in Multinational Corporations by Edward M. Roche, © 1993. Adapted by permission of Prentice-Hall, Inc., Upper Saddle River, NJ.

identify and set priorities in a short list of about 10 business processes that are absolutely critical for the firm.

Next, can you identify centers of excellence for these processes? Is the customer order fulfillment superior in the United States, manufacturing process control superior in Germany, and human resources superior in Asia? You should be able to identify some areas of the company, for some lines of business, where a division or unit stands out in the performance of one or several business functions.

When you understand the business processes of a firm, you can rank-order them. You then can decide which processes should be core applications, centrally coordinated, designed, and implemented around the globe, and which should be regional and local. At the same time, by identifying the critical business processes, the really important ones, you will have gone a long way toward defining a vision of the future to which you should be working.

Identify the Core Systems to Coordinate Centrally

By identifying the critical core business processes, you begin to see opportunities for transnational systems. The second strategic step is to conquer the core systems and define these systems as truly transnational. The financial and political costs of defining and implementing transnational systems are extremely high. Therefore, keep the list to an absolute minimum; let experience be your guide and err on the side of minimalism. By identifying a small group of systems as absolutely critical, you divide opposition to a transnational strategy. At the same time, you can appease those who oppose the central worldwide coordination implied by transnational systems by permitting peripheral systems development to progress unabated, with the exception of some technical platform requirements.

Choose an Approach: Incremental, Grand Design, Evolutionary

The third step is to choose an approach. Avoid piecemeal approaches. These surely will fail for lack of visibility, opposition from all who stand to lose from transnational development, and lack of power to convince senior management that the transnational systems are worth it. Likewise, avoid grand design approaches that try to do everything at once. These also tend to fail because of an inability to focus resources. Nothing gets done properly, and opposition to organizational change is needlessly strengthened because the effort requires huge resources. An alternative approach is to evolve transnational applications from existing applications with a precise and clear vision of the transnational capabilities the organization should have in five years.

Make the Benefits Clear

What is in it for the company? One of the worst situations and one that should be avoided is building global systems for the sake of building global systems. From the beginning, it is crucial that senior management at headquarters and foreign division managers clearly understand the benefits the company as well as individual units will reap. Although each system offers unique benefits to a particular budget, the overall contribution of global systems lies in four areas.

Global systems—truly integrated, distributed, and transnational systems—contribute to superior management and coordination. A simple price tag cannot be put on the value of this contribution, and the benefit will not show up in any capital budgeting model. The benefit lies in the ability to switch suppliers on a moment's notice from one region to another in a crisis, the ability to move production in response to natural disasters, and the ability to use excess capacity in one region to meet raging demand in another.

A second major contribution is vast improvement in production, operation, and supply and distribution. Imagine a global value chain, with global suppliers and a global distribution network. For the first time, senior managers can locate value-adding activities in regions where they are most economically performed.

Third, global systems mean global customers and global marketing. Fixed costs around the world can be amortized over a much larger customer base. This will unleash new economies of scale at production facilities.

Last, global systems mean the ability to optimize the use of corporate funds over a much larger capital base. This means, for instance, that capital in a surplus region can be moved efficiently to expand production of capital-starved regions; that cash can be managed efficiently within the company and put to use effectively.

These strategies will not by themselves create global systems. You will have to implement what you strategize and this is a whole new challenge.

IMPLEMENTATION TACTICS: COOPTATION

The overall tactic for dealing with resistant local units in a transnational company is cooptation. **Cooptation** is defined as bringing the opposition into the process of designing and implementing the solution without giving up control over the direction and nature of the change. As much as possible, raw power should be avoided. Minimally, however, local units must agree on a short list of transnational systems, and raw power may be required to solidify the idea that transnational systems of some sort are truly required.

How should cooptation proceed? Several alternatives are possible. One possibility is to permit each country unit the opportunity to develop one transnational application first in its home territory, and then throughout the world. In this manner, each major country systems group is given a piece of the action in developing the transnational system, and local units feel a sense of ownership in the transnational effort. However, this assumes that all participants have the ability to develop high-quality systems, and that, say, the German team can successfully implement systems in France and Italy. This will not always be the case. Also, the transnational effort will have low visibility.

A second tactic is to develop new transnational centers of excellence, or a single center of excellence. There may be several centers around the globe that focus on specific business processes. These centers draw heavily from local national units, are based on multinational teams, and must report to worldwide management—their first line of responsibility is to the core applications. Centers of excellence perform the initial identification and specification of the business process, define the information requirements, perform the business and systems analysis, and accomplish all design and testing. Implementation, however, and pilot testing occur in World Pilot Regions where new applications are installed and tested first. Later, they are rolled out to other parts of the globe. This phased rollout strategy is precisely how national applications are successfully developed.

THE MANAGEMENT SOLUTION

We now can reconsider how to handle the most vexing problems facing managers developing the transnational information system infrastructures that were described in Table 15-4.

- ○ *Agreeing on common user requirements:* Establishing a short list of the core business processes and core support systems will begin a process of rational comparison across the many divisions of the company. It will also help develop a common language for discussing the business, and naturally lead to an understanding of common elements (as well as the unique qualities that must remain local).

- ○ *Introducing changes in business procedures:* Your success as a change agent will depend on your legitimacy, your actual raw power, and your ability to involve users in the change design process. **Legitimacy** is defined as the extent to which your authority is accepted on grounds of competence, vision, or other qualities. The selection of a viable change strategy, which we have defined as evolutionary but with a vision, should assist you in convincing others that change is feasible and desirable. Securing support from senior management, involving people in change, and assuring them that change is in the best interests of the company and their local units, is a key tactic.

- ○ *Coordinating applications development:* Choice of change strategy is critical for this problem. At the global level there is far too much complexity to attempt a grand design strategy of change. It is far easier to coordinate change by taking small incremental steps toward a larger vision. Imagine a five-year plan of action rather than a two-year plan of action, and reduce the set of transnational systems to a bare minimum to reduce coordination costs.

- ○ *Coordinating software releases:* Firms can institute procedures to ensure that all operating units convert to new software updates at the same time so that everyone's software is compatible.

cooptation Bringing the opposition into the process of designing and implementing the solution without giving up control over the direction and nature of the change.

legitimacy The extent to which one's authority is accepted on grounds of competence, vision, or other qualities.

○ *Encouraging local users to support global systems:* The key to this problem is to involve users in the creation of the design without giving up control over the development of the project to parochial interests. Recruiting a wide range of local individuals to transnational centers of excellence helps send the message that all significant groups are involved in the design and will have an influence.

Even with the proper organizational structure and appropriate management choices, it is still possible to stumble over technological issues. Choices of technology, platforms, networks, hardware, and software are the final elements in building transnational information system infrastructures.

15.4 Technology Issues and Opportunities

Information technology is itself a powerful business driver for encouraging the development of global systems, but it creates significant challenges for managers. Global systems presuppose that business firms develop a solid information technology (IT) infrastructure and are willing to upgrade facilities continually.

MAIN TECHNICAL ISSUES

Hardware, software, and telecommunications pose special technical challenges in an international setting. The major hardware challenge is finding some way to standardize the firm's computer hardware platform when there is so much variation from operating unit to operating unit and from country to country. Managers need to think carefully about where to locate the firm's computer centers and how to select hardware suppliers. The major global software challenge is finding applications that are user friendly and that truly enhance the productivity of international work teams. The major telecommunications challenge is making data flow seamlessly across networks shaped by disparate national standards. Overcoming these challenges requires systems integration and connectivity on a global basis.

Hardware and Systems Integration

The development of transnational information system infrastructures based on the concept of core systems raises questions about how the new core systems will fit in with the existing suite of applications developed around the globe by different divisions, different people, and for different kinds of computing hardware. The goal is to develop global, distributed, and integrated systems. Briefly, these are the same problems faced by any large domestic systems development effort. However, the problems are more complex because of the international environment. For instance, in the United States, IBM mainframe and midrange operating systems have played the predominant role in building core systems for large organizations, whereas in Europe, Unix was much more commonly used for large systems. How can the two be integrated in a common transnational system?

The appropriate solution often will depend on the history of the company's systems and the extent of commitment to proprietary systems. For instance, finance and insurance firms typically have relied almost exclusively on IBM proprietary equipment and architectures, and it would be extremely difficult and costly to abandon that equipment and software. Newer firms and manufacturing firms generally find it easier to adopt open Unix systems for international systems. As pointed out in previous chapters, open Unix-based systems could be more cost effective in the long run because they support connectivity.

After a hardware platform is chosen, the question of standards must be addressed. Just because all sites use the same hardware does not guarantee common, integrated systems. Some central authority in the firm must establish data, as well as other technical standards, with which sites are to comply. For instance, technical accounting terms such as the beginning and end of the fiscal year must be standardized (review our earlier discussion of the cultural challenges to building global businesses) as well as the acceptable interfaces between systems, communication speeds and architectures, and network software.

Connectivity

The heart of the international systems problem is telecommunications—linking together the systems and people of a global firm into a single integrated network just like the phone sys-

Table 15-5 Problems of International Networks

Costs and tariffs	Regulatory constraints
Network management	Changing user requirements
Installation delays	Disparate standards
Poor quality of international service	Network capacity

tem but capable of voice, data, and image transmissions. However, integrated global networks are extremely difficult to create (see Table 15-5). For example, many countries cannot fulfill basic business telecommunications needs such as obtaining reliable circuits, coordinating among different carriers and the regional telecommunications authority, obtaining bills in a common currency standard, and obtaining standard agreements for the level of telecommunications service provided.

Despite moves toward economic unity, Europe remains a hodgepodge of disparate national technical standards and service levels. The problem is especially critical for banks or airlines that must move massive volumes of data around the world. Although most circuits leased by multinational corporations are fault free more than 99.8 percent of the time, line quality and service vary widely from the north to the south of Europe. Network service is much more unreliable in southern Europe.

Existing European standards for networking and EDI (electronic data interchange) are very industry specific and country specific. Most European banks use the SWIFT (Society for Worldwide Interbank Financial Telecommunications) protocol for international funds transfer, whereas automobile companies and food producers often use industry-specific or country-specific versions of standard protocols for EDI. Complicating matters further, the United States's standard for EDI is ANSI (American National Standards Institute) X.12. The Open Systems Interconnect (OSI) reference model for linking networks is more popular in Europe than it is in the United States. Various industry groups have standardized on other networking architectures, such as Transmission Control Protocol/Internet Protocol (TCP/IP) or IBM's proprietary Systems Network Architecture (SNA). Even standards for cellular phone systems vary from country to country.

Firms have several options for providing international connectivity: They can build their own international private network, rely on a network service based on the public switched networks throughout the world, or use the Internet and intranets.

One possibility is for the firm to put together its own private network based on leased lines from each country's PTT (post, telegraph, and telephone authorities). Each country, however, has different restrictions on data exchange, technical standards, and acceptable vendors of equipment. These problems are magnified in certain parts of the world. Despite such limitations, in Europe and the United States, reliance on PTTs still makes sense while these public networks expand services to compete with private providers.

The second major alternative to building one's own network is to use one of several expanding network services. With deregulation of telecommunications around the globe, private providers have sprung up to service business customers' data needs, along with some voice and image communication.

Already common in the United States, IVANs (International Value-Added Network Services) are expanding in Europe and Asia. These private firms offer value-added telecommunications capacity, usually rented from local PTTs or international satellite authorities, and then resell it to corporate users. IVANs add value by providing protocol conversion, operating mailboxes and mail systems, and offering integrated billing that permits a firm to track its data communications costs. Currently, these systems are limited to data transmissions, but in the future they will expand to voice and image.

The third alternative, which is becoming increasingly attractive, is to create global intranets or extranets to use the Internet for international communication. However, the Internet is not yet a worldwide tool because many countries lack the communications infrastructure for extensive Internet use. These countries face high costs, government control, or government monitoring.

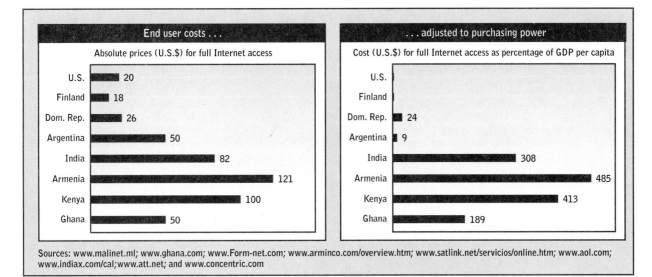

End user costs . . .	. . . adjusted to purchasing power
Absolute prices (U.S.$) for full Internet access	**Cost (U.S.$) for full Internet access as percentage of GDP per capita**

Country	Absolute prices (U.S.$)	Cost as % of GDP per capita
U.S.	20	
Finland	18	
Dom. Rep.	26	24
Argentina	50	9
India	82	308
Armenia	121	485
Kenya	100	413
Ghana	50	189

Sources: www.malinet.ml; www.ghana.com; www.Form-net.com; www.arminco.com/overview.htm; www.satlink.net/servicios/online.htm; www.aol.com; www.indiax.com/cal;www.att.net; and www.concentric.com

FIGURE 15-4 End-user costs for full Internet access. The cost of accessing the Internet is much higher in developing countries than in the United States and Western Europe. These disparities are even greater when users' purchasing power is taken into account.
Source: From "The Internet in Developing Countries," by Ben Petrazzini and Mugo Kibati in **Communications of the ACM** 42, no. 6, June 1999. . Reprinted by permission.

Western Europe faces both high transmission costs and lack of common technology because it is not politically unified and because European telecommunications systems are still in the process of shedding their government monopolies. The lack of an infrastructure and the high costs of installing one are even more widespread in the rest of the world. The International Telecommunications Union estimates that only 500 million of the world's 1.5 billion households have basic telephone services (Wysocki, 2000). In South Africa only 10 percent of the population has telephone lines, and Internet users must pay for each minute they spend on-line (Manson, 1998). Low penetration of PCs and widespread illiteracy limit demand for Internet service in India (Burkhardt, Goodman, Mehta, and Press, 1999). Where an infrastructure exists, as in China and Pakistan, it is often outdated, lacks digital circuits, and has very noisy lines. Figure 15-4 illustrates some of these global disparities in the cost and pricing of Internet service. The purchasing power of most people in developing countries makes access to Internet services very expensive (Petrazzini and Kibati, 1999).

The Window on Management explores the question of Internet availability in greater detail as an important issue for managers developing an international Web strategy.

Many countries monitor transmissions. The governments in China and Singapore monitor Internet traffic and block Web sites considered morally or politically offensive (Rosenthal, 1999; Blanning, 1999). Corporations may be discouraged from using this medium. Companies planning international operations through the Internet still will have many hurdles.

Software

Compatible hardware and communications provide a platform but not the total solution. Also critical to global core infrastructure is software. The development of core systems poses unique challenges for software: How will the old systems interface with the new? Entirely new interfaces must be built and tested if old systems are kept in local areas (which is common). These interfaces can be costly and messy to build. If new software, including enterprise systems, must be developed and installed, another challenge is to build software that can be realistically used by multiple business units from different countries, given that these business units are accustomed to their unique procedures and definitions of data (Soh, Kien, and Tay-Yap, 2000).

Aside from integrating the new with the old systems, there are problems of human interface design and functionality of systems. For instance, to be truly useful for enhancing productivity of a global workforce, software interfaces must be understood easily and mastered

DEVELOPING AN INTERNATIONAL WEB STRATEGY

The Internet now links 200 countries, but is it ready to be a world tool for conducting business? Managers trying to develop a Web strategy to reach customers, suppliers, and distributors need to think about certain realities. Only one-third of the households throughout the globe have telephones, let alone personal computers. It is estimated that only 1.5 to 2.5 percent of the world's 6 billion people can access the Internet, and most of them live in wealthy industrial nations. Even there, the level of Internet access varies widely. For example, Germany has no flat rate for local telephone calls, so 20 hours of off-peak Internet access could amount to $75 per month with an additional $40 for telephone charges. Countries with more advanced telecommunications infrastructures such as Finland generally have faster and more reliable Internet access than countries such as Greece.

Internet use should grow and prices should drop as European telecommunications deregulation continues and governments promote Internet use in schools and workplaces. But it is very important for businesses to understand the variable Internet presence in different countries when they target their Web efforts. Germany and northern Europe would be more lucrative Web targets at present, and continental Europe will become more attractive a few years from now. Asia, Hong Kong, Singapore, and Malaysia have very rich technology and international business infrastructures, and Japan, Korea, and Taiwan are also active in global business. Among Latin American countries, telecommunications services are growing most rapidly in Brazil.

Internet access in the countries served by Avis Europe PLC was sufficient for the company to develop an extranet to allow licensees in 35 countries in Asia, Africa, and central Europe to connect to its mainframe Wizard car rental reservation system. In the past, small licensees in countries such as Russia and Kenya had to communicate with Avis Europe's headquarters in England using fax or telex because they did not conduct enough business to warrant the cost of linking to the corporate wide area network. Now licensees can use their PC Web browser and a dial-up Internet service from a local provider for this communication.

In addition to Internet access, global Web strategies need to consider timing and coordination issues. Dell Computer Corporation coordinates its Web priorities with its business priorities, rolling out new country-specific Web stores at the same time that it launches manufacturing and marketing operations in a particular area. Most of Dell's on-line business is in the United States, but about one-fifth of Dell's Web sales now come from other countries.

Goodyear Tire & Rubber's public Web site first had country-specific information for five Latin American countries, but had to wait some months before posting similar information for Europe. The company wanted to make sure that its non-U.S. Web content matched corporate Web standards for look and feel as well as technology. For example, the Web site put up by its German units had to be modified to look like the corporate site.

TO THINK ABOUT: What management, organization, and technology issues should be addressed when developing a global Web strategy?

Sources: Sari Kalin, "The Worldlier Wider Web," **CIO Web Business Magazine,** March 1, 1999; and John Tagliabue, "Foie Gras and Chips, Anyone?" **The New York Times,** March 27, 1999.

Goodyear Tire and Rubber Company provides country-specific information on its Web site using corporate guidelines for technology and interfaces. Companies need to consider these issues as well as Internet availability when designing an international Web strategy.

WholeTree.com provides technology and services for developing multilingual Web sites. Web sites and software interfaces for global systems may have to be translated to accommodate users in East Asia and other parts of the world.

quickly. Graphical user interfaces are ideal for this but presuppose a common language—often English. When international systems involve knowledge workers only, English may be the assumed international standard. But as international systems penetrate deeper into management and clerical groups, a common language may not be assumed and human interfaces must be built to accommodate different languages and even conventions.

What are the most important software applications? Although most international systems focus on basic transaction and MIS systems, there is an increasing emphasis on international collaborative work groups. EDI (electronic data interchange) is a common global transaction processing application used by manufacturing and distribution firms to connect units of the same company, as well as customers and suppliers on a global basis. Groupware systems and other products supporting shared data files, notes, and electronic mail are much more important to knowledge- and data-based firms such as advertising firms, research-based firms in medicine and engineering, and graphics and publishing firms. Increasingly, the Internet will be used for such purposes.

NEW TECHNICAL OPPORTUNITIES AND THE INTERNET

Technical advances described in Chapter 7, such as ISDN and digital subscriber line (DSL) services, should continue to fall in price and gain in power, facilitating the creation and operation of global networks. Communicate and compute anytime, anywhere networks based on satellite systems, digital cellular phones, and personal communications services will make it even easier to coordinate work and information in many parts of the globe that cannot be reached by existing ground-based systems. Thus, a salesperson in China could send an order-confirmation request to the home office in London effortlessly and expect an instant reply.

Companies are using Internet technology to construct virtual private networks (VPNs) to reduce wide area networking costs and staffing requirements. Instead of using private, leased telephone lines or frame-relay connections, the company outsources the VPN to an Internet service provider. The VPN comprises WAN links, security products, and routers, providing a secure and encrypted connection between two points across the Internet to transmit corporate data. These VPNs from Internet service providers can provide many features of a private network to firms operating internationally.

However, VPNs may not provide the same level of quick and predictable response as private networks, especially during times of the day when Internet traffic is very congested. VPNs may not be able to support large numbers of remote users.

Throughout this text we have shown how the Internet facilitates global coordination, communication, and electronic business. As Internet technology becomes more widespread outside the United States, it will expand opportunities for electronic commerce and international

Mercantil.com is a portal for promoting business in Latin America. It includes news stories, descriptions of business opportunities, a directory of businesses, and search capabilities to locate businesses and products of interest to visitors.

trade. The global connectivity and low cost of Internet technology will further remove obstacles such as geography and time zones for companies seeking to expand operations and sell their wares abroad. Small companies may especially benefit (Quelch and Klein, 1996).

The Window on Technology describes some software tools and services that can help companies promote global electronic commerce.

MANAGEMENT DECISION PROBLEM

PLANNING A GLOBAL WEB SITE

Your company manufactures and sells tennis racquets and would like to start selling its products to countries outside the United States. You are in charge of developing a global Web strategy. Based on these statistics, what countries would you target first with your Web site? (Gross Domestic Product [GDP] per capita is a measure of relative purchasing power.)

Country	Total Population (in millions)	Percent On-line	Total On-line Population (in millions)	GDP Per Capita
Brazil	172	4.0%		$6,100
China	1,247	.05%		$3,600
Germany	82	15.0%		$22,100
Italy	57	8.4%		$20,800
Japan	126	14.4%		$23,100
Sweden	9	43.3%		$19,700

1. Calculate the total number of people in each country who have Internet access.
2. Based on these statistics alone, what countries would you target first for selling your products? Why?
3. Using what you have learned in this chapter, what other considerations should you address in your Web strategy? What additional information would be helpful to make sure your Web sales effort is successful? Where could you find this information?
4. What features would you put on your Web site to attract buyers from the countries you target?

TOOLS FOR GLOBALIZING E-COMMERCE

The Web is the quick and easy way for companies to globalize their businesses in the minds of many people, and those people are probably correct. Nonetheless, Web globalization can be slow and costly and it can present many pitfalls. Let us examine a few of the pitfalls and then look at some tools and services being offered.

Although some companies can compete globally with English-only Web sites, many others require that their sites display in local languages. Translation of those sites into other languages can be slow and very costly. Moreover, any changes to the home language site will require that related changes be made to the foreign language sites, so that the translation issues never end. The problem can really be immense if the amount of information carried on the sites is large. Eastman Kodak Co.'s site, Kodak.com, for example, contains 30,000 to 40,000 content pages. Translation can be daunting if only because it can involve many types of materials, including technical documents, marketing materials, market research, sales information, product literature, price lists, and even competitor information. Moreover, application server and content management software was initially developed for the monolingual U.S. market and often doesn't work smoothly with non-English character sets.

Telecommunications is usually a major issue also. Compared to the United States, Internet access elsewhere can be far more costly when users are charged by the on-line minute. Leased-lines outside cost about 10 times what they do inside the United States. Even the availability of adequate resources, reliability, and channel conflicts are larger problems in most of the world than in the United States. Fortunately, help for many of these problems is finally becoming available.

Chipshot.com is an e-commerce site selling golf equipment in the United States. In mid-1999 it decided to create a Japanese version of its site because of the popularity of golf in that country. To accomplish this, Chipshot's vice president of technology, Rajeev Goel, turned to WorldServer from Idiom Technologies. WorldServer starts by automatically translating the English-language Web site into Extensible Markup Language (XML). Then the software produces an idiomatic Japanese translation for a human to approve. Changes are made without programmers ever touching the code, and then the software creates the Web site automatically. One advantage of WorldServer is that Asian character languages require double bytes for each character, which the software package handles automatically. Also, the software automatically converts the currency between dollars and yen on a daily basis. WorldServer was run on Idiom's computer so that there were no installation and maintenance costs or problems. Chipshot can use the software to enter other markets when it is ready. Chipshot spent about $100,000 to enter the Japanese market, and this figure included not only the translation but also labor, marketing costs, and monthly fees paid to Idiom. In addition the cost included a Japanese market consultant to check the translation and advise on the cultural issues.

Chipshot is looking for the best ISP to provide it with speedy fiber links to Japan. A number of companies such as Digital Island and Qwest are now providing technical answers for faster, more reliable Web site access in many different countries, such as hosted servers, mirror sites, and even optimized global distribution networks. These organizations will even install and maintain their customers' servers and take care of tape-backup rotation.

One word of warning, however. Companies must be certain they understand the technical problem before deciding on a solution. Kodak solved its translation problem by adopting WorldPoint's PassPort software to help it create region-specific versions of Kodak.com in 16 countries. But its Web site performance internationally was very slow. Kodak initially considered establishing additional mirrored sites to speed Web response time. However, it discovered that mirrored sites would have solved nothing because the problem resided with their slow backbone.

TO THINK ABOUT: What are the organization and management problems Chipshot faced when deciding to use the Web to globalize its business? What technical problems not discussed in this Window will Chipshot encounter because of Web globalization? To what extent can the tools and services described here help companies with global Web sites?

Sources: Natalie Engler, "Global E-Commerce," *Information Week*, October 4, 1999; and James C. Luh, "Few Tools for Automating," *Internet World*, July 15, 1999.

MANAGEMENT WRAP-UP

Managers are responsible for devising an appropriate organizational and technology infrastructure for international business. Choosing a global business strategy, identifying core business processes, organizing the firm to conduct business on an international scale, and selecting an international information systems infrastructure are key management decisions.

Management

Organization

Cultural, political, and language diversity magnifies differences in organizational culture and standard operating procedures when companies operate internationally in various countries. These differences create barriers to the development of global information systems that transcend national boundaries.

Technology

The main technology decision in building international systems is finding a set of workable standards in hardware, software, and networking for the firm's international information technology infrastructure. The Internet and intranets will increasingly be used to provide global connectivity and to serve as a foundation for global systems, but many companies will still need proprietary systems for certain functions, and therefore international standards.

For Discussion

1. If you were a manager in a company that operates in many countries, what criteria would you use to determine whether an application should be developed as a global application or as a local application?

2. Describe ways the Internet can be used in international information systems.

SUMMARY

1. Identify the major factors behind the growing internationalization of business. There are general cultural factors and specific business factors to consider. The growth of cheap international communication and transportation has created a world culture with stable expectations or norms. Political stability and a growing global knowledge base that is widely shared also contribute to the world culture. These general factors create the conditions for global markets, global production, coordination, distribution, and global economies of scale.

2. Compare global strategies for developing business. There are four basic international strategies: domestic exporter, multinational, franchiser, and transnational. In a transnational strategy, all factors of production are coordinated on a global scale. However, the choice of strategy is a function of the type of business and product.

3. Demonstrate how information systems support different global strategies. There is a connection between firm strategy and information systems design. Transnational firms must develop networked system configurations and permit considerable decentralization of development and operations. Franchisers almost always duplicate systems across many countries and use centralized financial controls. Multinationals typically rely on decentralized independence among foreign units with some movement toward development of networks. Domestic exporters typically are centralized in domestic headquarters with some decentralized operations permitted.

4. Plan the development of international information systems. Implementing a global system requires an implementation strategy. Typically, global systems have evolved without a conscious plan. The remedy is to define a small subset of core business processes and focus on building systems that could support these processes. Tactically, you will have to coopt widely dispersed foreign units to participate in the development and operation of these systems, being careful to maintain overall control.

5. Evaluate the main technical alternatives in developing global systems. The main hardware and telecommunications issues are systems integration and connectivity. The choices for integration are to go either with a proprietary architecture or with an open systems technology such as Unix. Global networks are extremely difficult to build and operate. Some measure of connectivity may be achieved by relying on local PTT authorities to provide connections, building a system oneself, relying on private providers to supply communications capacity, or using the Internet and intranets. Companies can use Internet services to create virtual private networks (VPNs) as low-cost alternatives to global private networks. The main software issues concern building interfaces to existing systems and providing much needed group support software.

KEY TERMS

Business driver, 488	Franchiser, 493	Legitimacy, 498	Transborder data flow, 490
Cooptation, 498	Global culture, 488	Multinational, 493	Transnational, 493
Core systems, 496	International information	Particularism, 490	
Domestic exporter, 493	systems infrastructure, 487		

REVIEW QUESTIONS

1. What are the five major factors to consider when building an international information systems infrastructure?
2. Describe the five general cultural factors leading toward growth in global business and the four specific business factors. Describe the interconnection among these factors.
3. What is meant by a global culture?
4. What are the major challenges to the development of global systems?
5. Why have firms not planned for the development of international systems?
6. Describe the four main strategies for global business and organizational structure.
7. Describe the four different system configurations that can be used to support different global strategies.
8. What are the major management issues in developing international systems?
9. What are three principles to follow when organizing the firm for global business?
10. What are three steps of a management strategy for developing and implementing global systems?
11. What is meant by cooptation, and how can it be used in building global systems?
12. Describe the main technical issues facing global systems.
13. Describe three new technologies that can help firms develop global systems.

GROUP PROJECT

With a group of students, identify an area of information technology and explore how this technology might be useful for supporting global business strategies. For instance, you might choose an area such as digital telecommunications (e.g., electronic mail, wireless communications, value-added networks) or collaborative work group software or new standards in operating systems, EDI, or the Internet. It will be necessary to choose a business scenario to discuss the technology. You might choose, for instance, an automobile parts franchise or a clothing franchise such as the Limited Express as example businesses. What applications would you make global, what core business processes would you choose, and how would the technology be helpful?

Tools for Interactive Learning

○ Internet Connection

The Internet Connection for this chapter will take you to a series of Web sites where you can complete an exercise to evaluate the capabilities of various global package tracking and delivery services. You can also use the Interactive Study Guide to test your knowledge of the topics in this chapter and get instant feedback where you need more practice.

○ Electronic Commerce Project

At the Laudon Web site for Chapter 15, you will find an Electronic Commerce project that uses the interactive software at a series of Web sites for international marketing and pricing.

○ CD-ROM

If you purchase and use the Multimedia Edition CD-ROM with this chapter, you can complete an interactive exercise asking you to design a global network for a multinational corporation. You can also find a video clip illustrating the United Parcel Service International Shipping and Processing System (ISPS), an audio overview of the major themes of this chapter, and bullet text summarizing the key points of the chapter.

○ Application Exercise

At the Laudon Web site, you can find an Application Exercise for this chapter, which requires the use of database and Web page building software to develop a job database application for a global consulting firm.

The Kelly girl was a famous business icon in the post–World War II United States. Kelly Services, Inc., of Troy, Michigan (originally known as Kelly Girl Service), was founded by William Russell Kelly in Detroit in 1946. It was the first company to establish a service that supplied companies with temporary office help. The concept spread slowly at first, and it was not until 1954 that Kelly opened an office outside of Michigan; that office was in Louisville, Kentucky. Then the company spread rapidly so that by 1965 the company had 169 offices in 44 states. In 1972 the company opened its first European office in Paris, and in 2000 it has more than 1,600 offices in 20 countries including Great Britain, Sweden, Russia, Italy, and Australia. Sales have grown to more than $4 billion in 1999. Today the company has about 750,000 temporary employees servicing more than 200,000 customers. Kelly's own full-time staff numbers around 6,500. Although the company originally provided only clerical help, today, in addition to skilled office workers, it supplies information technology specialists, lawyers, accountants, engineers, and scientists as well as other professionals.

Originally the company used three-by-five-inch cards to keep track of its temps and to match the temps with customers, but as the company grew, manual procedures were no longer feasible, and computerization had to begin in local offices. In time the nature of the business also evolved. In the early days temporary services were localized: Local businesses obtained temporary help from their local temp offices, which explains why the local offices carried out the early computerization. However, by the 1980s and 1990s many of Kelly's customers had grown so large and geographically spread out that one local office could no longer service the customers' needs. Kelly was forced to abandon its local computerization approach and to begin building centralized systems. As a result of the globalization of both Kelly and its customers, Kelly's IT had to make major changes.

According to a recent interview with Tommi White, executive vice president and chief administrative and technology officer at Kelly Services, the U.S. offices had been using front- and back-office systems that were 15 to 20 years old, many of which were developed in-house. Kelly's North American operation ran an in-house-developed billing and accounts receivable system along with a general ledger application based on a software package that was out of date. Naturally, offices outside the United States ran their own independent systems. Moreover, Kelly had not even established corporate-wide hardware, software, or application standards, a common situation in the corporate world in the 1980s. Although this chaotic approach had been acceptable in earlier years, in today's business world Kelly needed to be able to service many of its customers from any of its offices anywhere in the world. The company made the decision to establish common IT standards for all of its offices, and to replace many local systems with newer, more appropriate corporate-wide systems.

White described Kelly's business problem, saying, "We have to have the right person, with the right skills, the right culture fit, able to stay the right length of time." In addition, she added, "We need to know where people are and where they'll be next, and we need to be able to do that without bar coding them." In order to keep track of the company's temp workers, Kelly's new systems obviously have to be very different from most logistics systems because, as White so vividly points out, Kelly's products are people and people are not stored or shipped in bar-coded boxes. Kelly had to develop its own new front-office system, a system that would automatically match Kelly temps with the needs of Kelly customers. The new system would include a tickler function that stored past customer usage of Kelly temps and automatically notified Kelly when certain conditions were met, such as a recurring seasonal busy period. The system would automatically locate appropriate temps who might be available for an assignment at that customer's site. White believes that "If we give the system more intelligence, it lets Kelly supervisors manage the relationships with the customer 's needs and the employee's career in mind."

Kelly management realized that its customers also needed easier access to Kelly so that they could conveniently make their temp requirements known. By the end of 1999 Kelly had built a Web interface to its new front-office system. Now Kelly customers can use the Web to request temporary help. The new front-office system with its Web interface is now global, operating in about 1,800 offices around the world. According to Jim Bradley, Kelly's vice president of field automation, "Our clients see a set of consistently delivered business services and practices, regardless of the office they deal with." He sees benefits for Kelly offices as well, adding, "If we can save each office an hour of processing time each day, it doesn't take a rocket scientist to multiply that hour by the number of offices by the number of working days in a year."

As important to Kelly as its front-office systems were its back-office systems, which also needed renewal. With about 25 percent of Kelly's revenue coming through its international divisions, the company had to consolidate its operations in all countries under a standard chart of accounts. In addition, White said, "We felt that it was important to move our technology forward to establish a global-standard concept . . . not only to finance but to human resources, administration, [and] service delivery. . . ." She points out that all customers throughout the world expect "consistent practices, metrics, and measurement."

Above all, globalization and consistency has meant information consolidation to Kelly. Its new back-office systems include transaction-level data warehousing that facilitates consolidated billing and information reporting. Kelly Services now has a consistent chart of accounts and a consistent data model for collecting invoice information. As White explains, "Our industry is moving from a marketplace of individual retail accounts to national and global accounts." She adds that Kelly's "high-end" accounts actually required Kelly to make changes because those key customers are consolidating suppliers and demand consolidated information. When Kelly provided consolidated reports to its big customers using its legacy systems, the data first had to be collected automatically from many hundreds of local systems. Then the central system merged the local data and produced consolidated reports. In some cases, this consolidation still had to be done manually. With the new systems Kelly now has "a seamless flow of data," according to White, and so Kelly can supply complete, accurate reports to its customers. Management at Kelly also directly benefits from the new systems because it is able for the first time to trust the consistency of the data it is seeing.

To meet its back-office needs, the team decided to purchase Oracle's Back Office systems. Although the implementation is not scheduled to be completed until 2002, much of the system is already in place and being used. To install the systems, the Kelly team decided to set up separate projects for each country, and then prioritized the countries based on their perceived needs and the Kelly resources available. Installation began with pilot projects in Australia and the Netherlands. The team chose the Netherlands because its small operation gave the installation team the opportunity to learn about the software they were installing. They selected Australia because it seemed the best place to test two particular modules of concern, Oracle Projects and Receivables. The pilot installations were completed in January 1999.

According to White, "The hardest part of the project [has been] trying to convince businesspeople of exactly how much a deployment such as this will change the way they conduct business." She felt a strong leadership team was vital because Kelly has "people who are used to operating very independently of the corporate office." To overcome any resistance both within and outside the United States, White used a carrot-and-stick approach. On the carrot side, the team educated the people at its various offices around the world on the strategic direction of the company and on the contribution the new centralized software would make in taking the company in that direction. On the stick side, the team made it clear that the various offices simply had no other acceptable alternative.

When asked to give advice to other companies on this type of project, White's response was "Get a commitment on global standards from the senior management team—particularly the CFO [chief financial officer], human resources, and operations executives." She pointed out that their support will be vital when something goes wrong. She emphasized the word "when," making it clear that an international project of this magnitude will always have things go wrong.

Sources: Ken Siegmann, "Work Force," **Profit Magazine**, November 1999; Mary E. Thyfault, "IT Puts the Right People in the Right Place," **Information Week**, September 27, 1999; "Corporate Information: 50 Years," Kelly Services, Inc., www.kelleyservices.com; "Kelly Services, Inc.," **The Standard**, http://www.thestandard.com; and Sandy Taylor, "Application Life-Cycle Management," **Information Week**, May 17, 1999.

CASE STUDY QUESTIONS

1. What were the business needs driving Kelly when it undertook its front- and back-office projects?

2. Describe the types of organizational changes that had to take place for the projects to succeed. What do you think might have been the greatest threats to the success of the projects?

3. What organization, management, and technical issues did the project team have to face within the United States? In the countries outside the United States?

CASE STUDY 1: Barwon Water (A): Creating and Exploiting an IT Infrastructure

Joel B. Barolsky, Paul Richardson, and Peter Weill, University of Melbourne (Australia)

This case study, written by Paul Richardson and Peter Weill, is an abridged version of the case "Geelong and District Water Board—Information Technology Management." The original case was awarded the Australian Computer Society prize for "Best IT Case Study." The Melbourne Business School gratefully acknowledges the cooperation of Barwon Water in the preparation of this case study, and its consent to the use and publication of the material contained therein.

Joe Adamski, the Geelong and District Water Board's (GDWB) Executive Manager Information Systems, clicked his mouse on the phone messages menu option. Two messages caught his attention—the first was from an IT manager from a large Sydney-based insurance company confirming an appointment to "visit the GDWB and to assess what the insurance company could learn from GDWB's IT experience." The second was from the general manager of a Queensland-based water board asking whether Adamski and his team could assist, on a consultancy basis, in their IT strategy formulation and implementation. Adamski immediately called the GDWB's Chief Executive Officer, Geoff Vines.

> Geoff, that Queensland water board I was telling you about wants us to come over to give them a hand. They've got quite an interesting set up over there and it would be a good challenge and some extra income for our people. What's more, they aren't as stretched for cash as some of the Victorian boards and I'm sure we could make a fair return for our involvement. What's the current position on us doing outside consulting work?

> It's a bit difficult to give you a direct answer, Joe. We've got to achieve some sort of balance. We still have a long way to go with our in-house information system developments and we aren't short of new projects. We must also remember that we aren't in the consultancy business. Its really not a cut and dried issue. I think we'll

raise it at the next Executive Group meeting and we'll see what the others think.

> Okay, I'll stall the Queenslanders for the moment. By the by, we've got another corporate visitor coming down to see our set up. Its the third this month so far. Its quite an irony—all these corporate whiz kids coming to learn from a public sector organisation. At the rate they're coming, I think we should start charging them a fee.

ORGANISATIONAL BACKGROUND

Barwon Water is the new name[1] for the Geelong and District Water Board (GDWB) which was constituted as a statutory authority of the State of Victoria on 1st July 1984 following amalgamation of the Geelong Waterworks and Sewerage Trust (GWST) and a number of other smaller regional water boards. GDWB operated under the Water Act 1989 which gave it the responsibility for the collection and distribution of water and the treatment and disposal of wastewater within the Geelong region and the management of a 20 kilometre section of the Barwon River. GDWB served an area of more than 3,900 square kilometres. In 1991, the permanent population serviced by GDWB exceeded 190,000 people, this number grew significantly in the holiday periods due to an influx of tourists.

The GDWB financed all its capital expenditure and operational expenditure through revenue received from its customers and through additional borrowings. Any profits generated were reinvested in the organisation or used to pay off long term debt. For the financial year 1990/91 GDWB invested over $35.3 million in capital works and spent over $25 million in operating expenditure.

The GDWB was headed by a Governing Board with a State Government-appointed chairperson and eight elected (by the residents of the community) members who each sat for a three year term. Any member of the community could be nominated for Governing Board membership. Managerial

and administrative responsibilities were delegated to the GDWB's Executive Group which consisted of the CEO and Executive Managers from each of the five operating divisions, namely Finance, Corporate Services, Engineering Development, Information Systems and Engineering Operations. From 1981 to 1991, the number of GDWB employees across all divisions rose from 304 to 454 (see Exhibit 1).

The GDWB's Head Office, situated on Ryrie Street in the heart of Geelong's central business district, housed most of GDWB's customer service, public relations, finance, administration, personnel, engineering, IS and other managerial staff. Complementing these activities, the GDWB operated five regional offices located at Ocean Grove, Portarlington, Torquay, Drysdale and Anglesea. A 24 hour emergency contact service was maintained at GDWB's South Geelong complex. Duty officers were on call to respond to problems such as burst water mains, property service faults, meter stop tap repairs and wastewater overflows. Additional customer services were provided by field workers such as meter readers, maintenance workers and plumbing inspectors.

Commenting on GDWB's competitive environment, Wal Whiteside, the GDWB Governing Board Chairperson, stated:

> Although the organisation operates in a monopolistic situation there are still considerable pressures on us to perform efficiently. Firstly, and most importantly, our objective is to be self funding—our customers wouldn't tolerate indiscriminate rate increases as a result of our inefficiencies and we can't go cap in hand to the State Government. Secondly, the amalgamation trend of water boards is continuing and the stronger GDWB is the less likely we would be a target of a takeover. And thirdly, in a sense we do compare ourselves with private sector organisations and in some ways with other water boards. One must be careful, however, with direct comparisons because there are so many variables

Exhibit 1 **Number of Employees as of 30 June 1991**

Staff Type	IS	FIN	C/S	DEV	OPS	CEO	Total
Professional	8	6	11	29	14	1	69
Technical	3	-	5	37	21	-	66
Administrative	2	31	23	7	12	3	78
General	-	-	10	5	32	-	47
Wages	-	-	16	17	161	-	194
Total	13	37	65	95	240	4	454

*Includes 9 temporary employees.

KEY PROBLEM AREAS

Reflecting on the development of GDWB up until the mid-1980's, Vines, an engineer by training with extensive experience in the water industry and in the military, stated:

GDWB had always had a strong 'engineering' orientation and tended to be a little aloof and insensitive to its customers' needs. We provided services in the way we thought best and our customers just had to accept it—they had no choice. Over time our customers had become better educated and their expectations of service levels had risen. They had become more demanding of us and we didn't really respond with an improvement in the ways we serviced them. If our customers had to wait three weeks for an encumbrance certificate, it was perceived to be their problem not ours. From an internal operations perspective we ran things reasonably efficiently but we still felt that substantial improvements could be made—especially in key areas like asset management, staff productivity, operations planning and in the way we stored and managed our corporate data.

One of these key operational problems related to difficulties in collectively identifying one of GDWB's largest assets—its underground pipes, drains, pumps, sewers and other facilities. Most of these facilities were installed at least two or three meters below the surface and therefore it was almost impossible to gain immediate physical access to them. The exact specifications of each particular asset could only be ascertained through a thorough analysis of the original installation documentation and other geophysical surveys and maps of the area.

The limitations on identifying these underground facilities meant that most of the maintenance work conducted by GDWB was based on reactive responses to leaks and other faults in the systems. It was difficult to introduce a coordinated preventative maintenance program because it was not possible to accurately predict when a particular pipe or piece of equipment was nearing the end of its expected life span. The information on the layout and types of piping and drainage systems for each block of land was available on hard copy but it was infeasible to manually review and analyse all this data for the entire GDWB region.

In an effort to maintain consistent and complete records GDWB ensured that only a limited number of hardcopies of this underground facility information were kept. This significantly reduced the productivity of the engineering and operations staff, especially in remote areas where they had to request this information from the central record keeping systems. Backlogs and inaccuracies in filing also impacted efforts to repair, upgrade or install new piping, pumps and other equipment. On numerous occasions changes would be made to one set of plans without the same changes being recorded on the other copies of the same plans.

Limited access to the underground equipment also hindered GDWB's ability to place a realistic replacement or book value on these assets. Senior management in consultation with GDWB's auditors would make an estimate, based on the previous year's valuation, of the total value of the underground assets. It was not practical to physically identify and value each individual asset and to give each item a unique asset number. Moreover, the valuation task was compounded in that some piping and equipment had been installed for only one week whilst other assets had been in the ground for periods exceeding 150 years. This significantly impacted depreciation calculations and provisions for maintenance and renewal.

With over 100,000 rateable properties in its area of responsibility, the GDWB maintained a centralised paper filing system containing more than a billion pages of related property information. The documents, most of which were of different sizes, quality and age, were divided into 95,000 different files and sorted chronologically within each file. Access to the documents was made difficult as larger documents were cumbersome to copy and older documents were beginning to disintegrate. Having just one physical storage area significantly increased the potential exposure to fire and other risks and limited the wider distribution and sharing of the information. In the early 1980s, it was commonplace for a customer request for a statement of encumbrances placed at one of the GDWB's regional offices to take in excess of four weeks. The delays usually centred on finding the appropriate documents at the Property Services' central files, making the necessary copies and transferring the documents back to the regional offices.

Property inquiries primarily came from owners, plumbers, architects or builders who were either renovating, selling or buying a particular property, and usually related to:

○ making copies of the original plumbing and drainage plans of individual properties,

- seeking information on the exact location of water and sewerage pipes,
- seeking information of prior building approvals, letters, notices outstanding and other documentation.

STRATEGIC REVIEW

In November 1985, the Governing Board adopted a proposal from Vines that an external review of management and operations should take place. Vines stated:

> In the mid-eighties, the situation was such that I felt it was important that GDWB take one step back and take stock of the way it conducted its business. There was a growing concern that the GDWB's operating environment was changing and we weren't changing with it. We had to ensure that the organisation was adapting sufficiently to mirror these external developments. We also needed to address some key internal productivity and operational problems. To be more customer oriented our people must have easy access to data wherever it is needed in the organisation. I felt that in some ways GDWB was being left behind and that we needed to take a fresh look of all our operations before we planned the next step forward. I had a sense of what had to be done but in order to convince the Governing Board I thought it would be best to get an independent assessment and set of recommendations.

The PA Consulting Group were commissioned to conduct the review with the objectives of identifying areas of weakness and strength and offering recommendations as to how to effect improvements. Following the advice of the consultancy, the organisation restructured itself along function groupings within the divisions to allow for the "increasing sophistication of GDWB's technology, works and responsibilities . . . and to facilitate greater customer orientation in GDWB's operations."

PA Consulting also suggested that the organisation adopt a more disciplined and systematic approach to strategic planning. A Corporate Planning Group (CPG) was established, lead by the CEO, and a formal planning process was initiated. In March 1991, GDWB's first comprehensive corporate planning document was accepted and included the GDWB's stated charter and mission, its corporate objectives, and the strategies necessary including key actions and performance targets for the achievement of these objectives.

THE INFORMATION SYSTEMS DIVISION

The consultant's report recommended that GDWB create a new division for its computing services and that a person be recruited to manage this new area who would report directly to the CEO. In May 1987, the Information Systems Division was created with the specific objectives of "satisfying GDWB's Information System needs through the provision of integrated and flexible corporate computer systems and communication network."

Vines believed GDWB needed a stand-alone information services group that could be used as a resource centre for all users and that could add value to the work conducted by each functional group within GDWB:

> From the 1970's to the mid-1980's, IS did not have a specific integrated plan or mission. What's more, it was not perceived by most people as being vitally important in servicing GDWB's needs and objectives. The culture had not been moulded into seeing a role for computers beyond finance and admin. We didn't really have the skills and experience to effectively use information technology to break free from some of the problems that we were facing.

In April 1987, Joe Adamski was employed to fill the new position of IS Manager. Adamski, an Applied Science graduate from Geelong's Deakin University, had worked for 12 years in the IS development area in the telecommunications industry prior to joining the GDWB. Adamski spent the first six months is his new position acquainting himself with the functions and operations of GDWB. This involved developing an understanding of the existing computer systems, ascertaining user problems and information needs and establishing contacts at both managerial and operational levels across all divisions. Adamski explained:

> My ability to delve into problems and gain access to every functional area within GDWB was greatly enhanced by the fact that I reported directly to Geoff Vines. This gave me the clout and status I needed, especially as I came in from outside the organisation. What was also really important was that Geoff gave me, and continued to give me, his full support and commitment.

At the time of Adamski's arrival, only a small part of the GDWB's work systems were computerised. GDWB operated a "low-end" IBM System 38 primarily to run financial and other accounting software and some word processing applications. The System 38 also ran an in-house developed rate collection system which kept basic information on ratepayers including property details and consumption records. The System 38 was accessed by 19 "dumb" terminals and had limited printing facilities. None of GDWB's regional offices had terminal access to the central computer systems. In addition to the System 38, GDWB had established a terminal link to Deakin University's DEC 20 computer to support the technical and laboratory services.

A computerised correspondence registry was established in an effort to improve the efficiency of dealing with all correspondence including that received from customers. The system registered and traced all incoming correspondence and provided various management reports. Four stand-alone PCs were also in use, running some individual word processing packages as well as spreadsheet, basic CAD and data base applications. Computer maintenance, support and development was allocated to the Finance Division. Adamski noted:

> The computer set-up when I joined was pretty outdated and inefficient. For example, the secretarial staff at Head Office were using the System 38's word processing facility and had to collect their dot matrix print-outs from the computer room situated on the ground floor of the five storey building. In the technical area, some water supply network analysis data was available through the use of the DEC 20 system, however, hard copy output had to be collected from the University which was over five kilometres away. Most of the design engineers were using old drafting tables with rulers, erasers and pencils as their only drafting tools.

Recognising that some users required immediate solutions to problems they were facing, GDWB purchased additional terminals, peripherals and stand-alone microcomputers for the various areas to be in greatest need. As Adamski recalls, these additional purchases further compounded some of GDWB's computer-related problems:

> We had a situation where we had at least four different Computer Aided Design packages in use in different departments and we couldn't transfer data between them. There was a duplication of peripheral equipment with no sharing of printers, plotters and other output devices.

PLANNING THE NEW ROLE FOR IT

Vines believes that GDWB was not vastly different from most other Australian organisations at that time which were starting to grapple with increasing informational complexity:

> It was clearly evident that the way we were using, storing and handling our information was pretty archaic and it was having a detrimental impact on our performance. I felt that we needed to be more pro-active in the way we managed information at GDWB. We needed to use the opportunities that IT offered as a means to realise our corporate objectives and to significantly improve the way we operated, both internally and externally. I wanted to get ahead of the game—to take a quantum leap forward rather than flounder on at the back of the pack. Access to any GDWB information from wherever it is needed is a critical part of this vision.

The Planning Process

In July 1988, Adamski initiated a long-term computing strategy planning process with the establishment of a special planning project team. The project team was guided in its activities by a Steering Committee which included the project team members, Adamski and the Executive Managers from the Engineering Development and Engineering Operations Divisions. The team's terms of reference were:

> The development of a long-term strategy for technical computing and a strategy for its implementation taking into account the current IT portfolio.

> The establishment of information flows and data management ie. identify the data utilised throughout GDWB.

An assessment of the overall size of the implementation of the strategy and to identify:
- ○ Likely hardware and software needs,
- ○ Broad user expectations in respect of ease of user access and information content,
- ○ The degree of change involved in practices in order to support the project implementation,
- ○ The available resource skills and training requirements,
- ○ The time resources and potential cost boundaries.

The planning process encompassed six distinct phases:

1. Extensive interviews with managers and staff from throughout GDWB to discuss their information and computing needs.

2. Broad data flow requirements for each department were specified and a detailed data interflow table prepared. This involved identifying all the actual data items transferred (such as plans, charts, documents, correspondence, technical reports, financial data, technical specifications, etc.) the source, owners and originators of the data and all the potential users and destinations of the data.

3. Detailed information systems and technology requirements were specified.

4. The Project Team visited a number of external organisations as well as hardware and software vendors to evaluate possible solutions and system alternatives.

5. An outline of software, resources and possible applications was sent to each department and user group for comments and evaluation. The feedback received was then used to further refine the final set of recommendations.

6. A draft report was prepared and forwarded to the Executive Group for discussion and finally to the Governing Board for approval.

The project team completed their assignment in November 1988. As Hart elaborated:

> One of the biggest challenges in the planning process was ascertaining from users what their systems requirements actually were. Most of them weren't aware of what IT could deliver in terms of providing

solutions to problems or as a means of supporting or improving the work that they did. We ended up presenting various alternatives to them and then asked for feedback.

The Proposed Solutions

The project team developed a comprehensive corporate computing strategy that would provide, as Adamski put it, the "quantum leap forward in GDWB's IT portfolio." The preamble to the strategy was a statement of the computing policy which provided the linking pin between GDWB's stated corporate objectives and the plans and activities of the IS Division. It was envisaged that the policy should guide decision making for the IS Division.

Central to the computing strategy was that there should be as much integration and flexibility as possible in all GDWB's technical and administrative systems. Adamski stated:

> Linked to this strategy was the notion that we should strive for an "open systems" approach with all our applications. This meant that each system had to have publicly specifiable interfaces so that each system could talk to each other. From the users' perspective an open systems approach meant that all the different applications looked pretty much the same and it was simple and easy to cross-over from one to the other. It also meant that if we weren't happy with one particular product within the portfolio or we wanted to add a new one we could do it without too much disruption to the whole system.

> A key decision was made that we should build on our existing IT investments. With this in mind we had to make sure that the new systems were able to use the data and communicate with the System 38. We wanted only one hardware platform using only one operating system and only one relational data base management system (RDBMS). We also wanted only one homogenous network that was able to cater to a number of protocols and interfaces such as the network system for the microcomputers, workstations and the Internet connection. There also had to be a high degree of compatibility and interaction with all the data files and applications that were proposed.

Exhibit 2 **Proposed Hardware Installations**

- ○ Central processor(s) to run the FIS, CADD and WIMS systems.
- ○ 25 Workstations to provide access to FIS, CADD and other applications.
- ○ A Wide Area Network, including a special high-speed data link throughout the Board's Head Office and at the South Geelong complex. This would:
  - ○ facilitate the free transfer of data and information,
  - ○ allow all levels of computers to 'talk to each other' and in some cases 'emulate each other' ie. allow system support staff to simulate a user's application environment,
  - ○ enable a variety of output devices to be accessed by users across the network.
- ○ A centralised file server with over 2 Gigabytes of memory to store digital mapping related databases, the WIMS system, modelling data, wordprocessor archiving and other programs.
- ○ An image processing system to scan existing documents and plans onto optical laser disks.
- ○ Additional microcomputers for wordprocessing, desktop publishing and specific departmental applications.
- ○ Additional output devices including four A4 laser printers and specialised plotters.
- ○ Other items such as digitisers to allow for data capture and digital data loggers for recording analog information such as water levels.

Working within the basic "foundation" guidelines they had set and in view of the findings of their computing requirements study, the Technical Computing Project Team recommended the implementation of five major new initiatives:

Document Imaging Processing System (DIPS) that would be used for scanning, storing and managing all documents on each property within the GDWB region which were being kept in the 95,000 separate paper files. This system would also be used for the storage, backup and retrieval of 25,000 engineering plans and drawings.

Facilities Information System (FIS) that would provide for the storage, management and on-going maintenance of all graphic (map related) and non-graphic information relating to water and wastewater services, property information, cadastral boundaries and easements throughout GDWB's region.

Computer Aided Design and Drafting (CADD) system that would allow the creation of drawings and designs that could be edited and manipulated as screen images and then stored on disk.

Word Processing and Office Automation (WP/OA) systems providing users the ability to prepare quality documentation integrating graphics, spreadsheets, mail merge and data bases, as well as other utilities such as electronic mail and phone message handling.

Relational Database Management System and 4th Generation Language as a base foundation and for the development of new applications. Some of the RDBMS applications included:

- ○ A Drawing and Retrieval Management System (DRMS) to control the development, release and revision of all CADD projects and files,
- ○ A Water Information Management System (WIMS) used for the storage and management of hydrographic engineering and laboratory data, both current and historical.

In addition to specifying the above initiatives, the project team outlined the hardware that was necessary to run the new systems (see Exhibit 2).

GOVERNING BOARD APPROVAL

Throughout the planning period Adamski held numerous consultations with the CEO and the Executive Group to discuss, among other items, the operational implications of the proposed IS strategy, the feasibility and acceptability of the various proposals and the linkages to other corporate objectives. By mid-February 1989 the corporate computing strategy planning process was completed and Adamski presented the key recommendations to GDWB later that month. In his presentation, Adamski stated that the infrastructure cost of implementing the strategy was estimated to be about $1.5 million for Stage 1 and a further $2.5 million for Stages 2 and 3. He estimated

that the project would take up to the end of 1995 for full commissioning, excluding FIS data capture. Adamski added that the capital expenditure of the IS strategy would be included in GDWB's 10-Year Capital Works Programme. Commenting on the Governing Board decision process, Vines said:

Joe and his staff started to get their message to the Governing Board, through me and through other means, even prior to the February meeting. At the meeting Joe was very careful to develop trust and a sense of confidence. He avoided using jargon, he used graphics to explain difficult concepts and he justified each program with specific quantifiable and non-quantifiable benefits. He stressed the importance of establishing a flexible base on which we could develop future corporate systems. After a fair bit of discussion and clarification of key points, the Governing Board endorsed the strategy and the commitment of the expenditure. It was also decided to add the key recommendations of the computing strategy to GDWB's corporate planning documentation.

From my perspective, the proposed IS strategy took into account the critical functions in the organisation that needed to be supported, such as customer services, asset management and asset creation. These were fundamental components of GDWB's corporate objectives and the computer strategy provided a means to realise these objectives and provide both short and long term benefits. There were some immediate short-term benefits like securing property services data that had no back up and productivity gains in design and electronic mail. From a long-term perspective, I believe you can never really do an accurate rate of return calculation and base your decision solely on that. If you did you probably would never make such a large capital investment in IS. We did try to cost-justify all the new systems as best we could but we stressed that implementing IS strategy should be seen as providing long-term benefits for the entire organisation that were not immediately measurable and would come to fruition many years later. Until all the information was captured and loaded on the IS facilities from the manual systems, the full benefits could not be realised. Throughout my discussions with GDWB and the Executive Group I made sure that this point came through and was understood.

THE TENDERING PROCESS

The tender document was divided into five sections, namely the FIS digital mapping system, CADD system, RDBMS and 4GL, DIPS system, and microcomputing software and hardware for network communications. Suppliers responded with "total" integrated solutions encompassing hardware and software products from themselves and other vendors where they did not have a suitable product of their own. Following evaluation of the initial tenderers, three "total solution" suppliers, namely Hewlett Packard, Intergraph and Sun Microsystems, were selected and given six weeks to prepare for benchmarking.

Based on their solid performance during benchmarking and their perceived ability to manage their sub-vendors, GDWB appointed Sun Microsystems to be the main hardware supplier and to be the "prime contractor" for the implementation of the whole project. Commenting on their selection as prime contractor, a representative from Sun Microsystems, Fraser Gardiner, stated:

As prime contractor we signed one contract with the GDWB worth about $1.8 million for supply of the total solution including project implementation, and then Sun negotiated separate contracts with all the other vendors.

IMPLEMENTATION

In April 1990, the implementation of the IS strategy commenced with the delivery of the Sun file servers and workstations and installation of one network throughout GDWB. Reflecting on the installation, Fraser Gardiner of Sun Microsystems said that from a technical point of view things went relatively smoothly:

GDWB had the expertise and skills to know how to make the most from the equipment. We weren't in our usual role of 'educating the client'—they knew what they wanted and were aware of the capabilities of the systems. They also wanted to make sure that they developed the in-house expertise to ensure success of the implementation and on-going systems support. This self-sufficiency helped them in the long run and it also helped us.

Whilst Sun was intricately involved in the implementation of the systems, the IS Division staff provided the leadership in systems integration and application development in creating the "complete" system. Adamski said that up until the end of 1990, the IS Division was primarily concerned about getting the equipment installed, making sure the key systems were operational and that the data capture process had started. He said that they placed most of their initial attention on the networking and communications, the linkages to the System 38, the FIS system, the CADD systems and the document imaging.

In consultation with the other Executive Managers, Adamski arranged the required changes in staffing and in physical office arrangements to commence the data capture and scanning for the DIPS system and for the FIS.

In May 1990, the pilot study to assess the feasibility of implementing a full FIS was completed and concluded that the system could be cost justified. This cost justification was based on a rough assessment of both the measurable and intangible benefits of developing the system. GDWB approved the project and the expenditure of $3 million over the following five years to capture the data necessary to make the FIS fully operational. It was estimated that it would take three years for the project team of eight staff to complete FIS data capture in the urban areas, and a further two years to cover rural areas. In October of that year, GDWB agreed to the expenditure of $1.81 million for Stage 2 of the implementation of the IS Strategy. Stage 1 was completed two months later. Vines said:

I tried not to get personally involved in the implementation but I made sure that I kept a close eye on what was going on. We didn't fire anybody as a direct result of the new systems but jobs were changed. There was some resistance to the new technology—most of it was borne out of unfamiliarity and fear of not having the appropriate skills. Some people were very committed in doing things 'their way'. When some of these people started to perceive tangible productivity benefits their perspective's started to change. We tried to counsel people as best we could and encourage them to experiment with the new systems. Most eventually converted but there were still some objectors. What really helped the process along, was that Joe and his staff made sure that the users were properly trained and acclimatised to the new ways of doing things. Joe viewed the users across the organisation as his 'customers' and it was his intention to maximise their satisfaction.

Adamski stated that while they were implementing the new systems it was important for the IS Division not to lose sight of its key objectives and role within the organisation:

We had to make sure that we didn't get carried away with the new whiz-bang technology and reduce our support and maintenance of the older, more conventional systems. For example, GDWB went onto a user pays tariff system[2] and we had to make significant changes to our rating system to accommodate this.

In May 1992, GDWB's computer facilities included 4 Sun file servers, 80 Sun workstations, 100 Microcomputers, 40 Terminals, and the IBM System 38 Model 700. At this time, the IS Division had implemented the following systems:

Document Imaging Processing System (DIPS). Approximately 60% of the 95,000 property files and all the engineering plans and drawings had been scanned, touched-up (if required) and stored using DIPS. The DIPS system had a sophisticated indexing system that facilitated easy real-time retrieval of all property documentation by designated users across GDWB's entire computer network.

Facilities Information System (FIS). The FIS system provided a computerised "seamless" geographic map covering the entire GDWB region. FIS data capture involved recording all maps in digitised form and attaching an X and Y coordinate to each digitised point using the standard Australian Mapping Grid system. Once each point on a map was precisely addressed and identified, specific attributes were attached to the map—e.g., sewer pipe details, property details, water consumption, vertical heights above sea level, etc. These attributes are used as indexes for access by other programs.

The FIS allowed the storage of all maps on one standard scale and size without the need for duplication. It enabled fast and standard access and printing of plans and maps by all departments and facilitated improved control in updating existing maps and creating new plans. The system allowed cross-referencing to financial, rating and consumption data (through indexing). It also enabled each underground facility to be numbered, catalogued and identified as an asset with its associated data being integrated into other asset management systems. The FIS enabled users to select the amount of detail they required for display. For example users could selectively display just water pipes, sewerage, cadastrals, future plans, or any combination of these. Using a high resolution workstation monitor users could zoom in or out of particular geographical areas—at the broadest level showing the whole of southern Victoria and at the most detailed, the individual plumbing and drainage plan of one particular property (through cross-referencing to the DIPS system).

Some problems had been encountered in data capture in that the original plans and installation documentation used as the base data for the FIS were incomplete. This meant additional surveying work had to be commissioned.

Computer Aided Design and Drafting (CADD). CADD was fully operational and provided an integrated programmable 3-D environment for a range of design and drafting applications, including digital terrain modelling, electronic field data recording, design of site layouts, automated reticulation design, and survey set out.

Word Processing and Office Automation (WP/OA). All Head Office secretarial staff had access to and were trained in the WP/OA systems. The WP system allowed users to integrate images from the DIPS and FIS systems into their documents.

Relational Database Management System and 4th Generation Language. The RDMBS had been installed and specific applications developed included the Drawing and Retrieval Management System (DRMS) and the Water Information Management System (WIMS).

OUTCOMES

Adamski recalls that the reaction from GDWB staff to the whole corporate computing strategy initially ranged from scepticism to outright hostility, however as the value of the outcomes became apparent this situation changed:

> By the end of 1991, I would say that there had been a general reversal in attitude. Managers started to queue outside my office asking if we could develop specific business applications for them. They had begun to appreciate what the technology could do and most often they suddenly perceived a whole range of opportunities and different ways in which they could operate. Putting together the IS Division budget is now a difficult balancing act with a whole range of options and demands from users. I now ask the users to justify the benefits to be derived from new application proposals and I help out with the cost side. Cost/benefit justification usually drives the decisions as well as the "fit" with the existing IS and other corporate objectives.

Vines believes one of the most important strategic outcomes of the changes has been the way in which decision-making at all levels of the organisation had been enhanced:

> This improvement is largely due to the fact that people have now got ready access to information they have never had before, whenever they need it. This information is especially useful in enhancing our ability to forward plan. We must remember though that we are still in the implementation and data capturing stage with most of the larger systems. In the areas that have come on-line there has been a definite improvement in productivity and in customer service. The CADD system, for example, is greatly enhancing our ability to design and plan new facilities. The turnaround time, the accuracy of the plans and the creativity of the designers has been improved dramatically. The flow and reporting of financial information has also speeded up and we now complete our final accounts up to two months earlier than we used to. In many departments there has been a change in work practices—some of the mundane activities are handled by the computer allowing more productive work to be carried out, like spending more time with customers. Our asset management and control also started to improve. There was greater integrity in the information kept and having just one central shared record meant that updating with new data or changes to existing data was far more efficient.

A number of GDWB staff indicated that the new systems had enhanced their ability to fulfil their work responsibilities:

○ A customer service officer at GDWB's Drysdale regional office stated that the Document Imaging System had enabled her to respond to customer requests for encumbrance statements within a matter of minutes instead of weeks. She said that the new DIPS system had "flow on" benefits that weren't fully recognised. She cited the case where architects were able to charge their clients less because they had more ready access to information from the GDWB.

○ A maintenance manager from the South Geelong complex declared that the FIS system had enabled his department to predict when pipes and drains should be replaced before they actually ruptured or broke down by examining their installation dates and the types of materials used. He said this process over time started to shift the emphasis of his department's maintenance work from being reactive to being more preventative. He added that the system also enabled him to easily identify and contact the residents that would be affected by work that GDWB were going to do in a particular area. He said that the FIS enabled him to plot out with his mouse a particular area of a map on his screen. It would then "pick up" all the relevant properties in the area and identify the names and addresses of the current ratepayers residing in those properties.

Adamski said that one of the flow-on benefits from the FIS system in particular was that GDWB had the potential of selling the information stored on the system to authorities such as municipal councils, the Geelong Regional Commission and other utilities such as Telecom, the State Electricity Commission and the Gas and Fuel Corporation. He added that they had also considered marketing the information to private organisations such as building managers, architects and property developers.

In April 1992, Adamski prepared a report on the current projects and the expected completion dates for the IS Division. One new area that was receiving widespread interest was the development of a four dimension Digital Terrain Modelling system. The system would enable GDWB's designers to mark the general path of a road or a pipeline on a digitised map and then have the system calculate the "best" path through the particular terrain and provide all the gradients and other specifications needed to build it.

THE FUTURE

Commenting on the future prospects for GDWB's IS Division, Adamski said:

There are some very complex applications that we are developing but we now have the skills, the tools and the infrastructure to develop them cost effectively and to ensure that they deliver results. Choosing a UNIX platform with client/server processing and a strong networking backbone gave us the flexibility and integration that we will need in the future. It's a lot easier now to cost-justify requests for new applications. The challenges ahead lie in three areas. Firstly, it's going to be difficult to consistently satisfy all our users' needs in that their expectations will be increasing all the time and they will become more demanding. Requests for new applications and new equipment keep on coming in. We have to recognise these demands and at the same time keep investing and maintaining our infrastructure. Secondly, we still have some way to go in developing a total corporate management information system. There are still

some "islands of data" floating around and the challenge is to get it all integrated. And thirdly, as the most senior IS manager at GDWB I have to make sure that we retain our key IS staff and we compensate them adequately, both monetarily and in providing them stimulating and demanding work.

Vines added:

One of the reasons there was some initial resistance to change to the computing strategy was the feeling that IS was driving change, rather than the business driving change. The development of IS at GDWB has been part of a clearly articulated, well thought through plan derived from GDWB's business objectives.

Vines highlighted that the result will be access to important information whenever it is needed. We have to continue to support and optimise the use of IS and ensure that the IS strategy can meet any changes in GDWB's business strategy. Without any doubt, the development of the computing resources has had a major impact on the organisation. Vines concluded:

Other organisations approaching us for advice and assistance is a complement to our achievements. Whilst its good for our corporate image and makes us feel good about ourselves, we have to balance the demand for these outside consulting services with our in-house needs and developments.[3]

This case is intended to be read in conjunction with "Barwon Water (B)" by Paul Richardson and Peter Weill.

This case was written for the purposes of class discussion, rather than to illustrate either effective or ineffective handling of a managerial situation.

© 1999 Joel B. Barolsky, Paul Richardson and Peter Weill (7 Jan 1999).

Distributed by Melbourne Case Study Services at the Melbourne Business School, The University of Melbourne, 200 Leicester Street, Carlton 3053, Australia. Contact email: m.larosa@mbs.unimelb.edu.au Telephone +61 3 9349 8121. All rights reserved to the contributors.

[1] The name was changed from Geelong and District Water Board to Barwon Water in February 1994.

[2] In 1991, the GDWB changed from a 'rate-based' system whereby consumers were charged for water based on an estimated value of their individual properties, to a 'user-pays' system which allowed for charges for water to be based on the actual amount of water consumed plus a connection fee. The GDWB was one of the first water boards in Australia to introduce this new charging system.

[3] The inspiration for preparing this case study came from a class assignment completed by Ms Lisa Musgrave as part of her assessment on the Business Value of Information Technology subject on the Melbourne Business School MBA program.

Barwon Water (B): Creating and Exploiting an IT Infrastructure

The Geelong and District Water Board changed its name to Barwon Water in February, 1994, and then merged with Otway Water on July 1, 1997. After the merger, Barwon Water had 120,000 water and sewage assessments, approximately 22.5% of the Victorian non-metropolitan total, making it the largest regional water authority in the State.

Barwon Water's existing Information Technology (IT) infrastructure, such as financial and mapping systems, was able to accommodate the merger. An ongoing challenge is the development and enhancement of the IT infrastructure to meet the changing business needs.

As well as providing information to internal business users, Barwon Water has a strategy—partly driven by the Victorian Government—of providing electronic access to its customers. Electronic Commerce provides a new set of strategic opportunities and IT infrastructure requirements for Barwon Water.

Joe Adamski glanced towards the deep blue water of Geelong's port, sparkling under the midday sun. In his mind he could easily visualise the scene a little further around the coast—away from the sheltered water of Corio and Port Phillip bays. On a summer's day like this the town of Torquay, indeed the whole Surf Coast, would be swarming with visitors from nearby Melbourne[1] who would make the one hour drive to enjoy the area's excellent surf beaches. When he was a student living and studying in Geelong, Adamski would have been out there too—bobbing in the swell at the world renowned Bells Beach just a breaking wave or two from Torquay.

These days, however, Adamski tended to think of the summer crowds more in terms of their load on the region's water resources and their faith that the tap water was safe to drink and sewage was treated and discharged in an environmentally responsible manner. Adamski is now responsible for Strategic Planning and Information Technology at Barwon Water—the largest non-metropolitan water utility in Victoria.

Adamski read the fax he had just received. It was from a water utility in Western Australia asking if Adamski's group could do some consulting work for them—solving a flood plain management problem using Barwon Water's IT systems. In the four years since July 1995, his team had earned several hundreds of thousands of dollars on external consulting projects such as this. He knew his team would be keen to work on this project after hours or over a weekend. And they certainly had the knowledge, facilities and processes—along with ISO 9001 quality certification to back it up.

Adamski sipped from a glass of water and looked back out his window, "I think its time that we put together a formal policy on external consulting work," he thought.

RECENT DEVELOPMENTS AT BARWON WATER

Business Environment

The Geelong and District Water Board changed its name to Barwon Water in February 1994. The name change reflected the change in the organisation's governance structure with the appointment by the State Government of a professional, skills-based Board to replace community-elected members. This initiative was part of a broader Government strategy to commercially focus state-owned utilities and strive for greater efficiencies and productivity across the public service.

Four months after the name change, the Chief Executive, the late Mr. Geoff Vines retired and was replaced by Dennis Brockenshire. A senior manager with the State Electricity Commission, Brockenshire had considerable business and engineering experience relating to large-scale supply systems serving a large customer base.

A major organisational restructure in early 1995 saw Adamski take over responsibility for strategic planning as well as information systems. Adamski felt this restructure ensured that Information Technology (IT) developments would be closely aligned with broader business objectives and strategies. As part of the restructure, new business units were formed with the managers of these units made accountable for both revenue and cost items (refer to Exhibit 1).

In December 1996, the Minister for Agriculture and Resources, the Hon. Pat McNamara requested that a number of water authorities investigate the benefits that would result from amalgamation, with a view to reducing the total number of authorities in the state. In response, Barwon Water undertook extensive modelling studies with Otway Water to determine the extent of customer benefits and business impacts of a merger of the two authorities. These studies showed a merger could realise substantial savings through increased business efficiency with substantial benefits to customers.

Barwon Water merged with Otway Water on July 1, 1997. After the merger, Barwon Water had 120,000 water and sewage assessments, approximately 22.5% of the Victorian non-metropolitan total, making it the largest regional water authority in the State.

Benefits of the merger were passed on to the customer. The average reduction on 1996/97 (pre-merger) water and sewerage charges was 20 percent. In the first year of the merger, taking a typical residential customer using 175 kilometres of water and connected to sewerage, the resulting annual savings were: Lorne $239.50, Airey's Inlet $182.00 and Colac $110.00. Further savings will be delivered to customers in the Otway region as full parity pricing with Barwon region customers by July 2000 for Colac, Apollo Bay and Lorne and July 2002 for Airey's Inlet.

Barwon Water's Vision is to "continue to be the leading provider of quality customer services in the water industry." Barwon Water's core business is the delivery of clean and safe water and the collection and disposal of waste in an environmentally sensitive manner.

Information Technology Environment

A comparison of the IT infrastructure in 1988 and 1998 is shown in Exhibit 2. The 1998 IT architecture has evolved from the original plan, as Adamski notes:

> Most people are still using UNIX as their back end because of reliability, but on the desktop we are finding many of the new solutions are based on [Microsoft] NT because this is what [external] developers are using. So as the applications we have used over the past 10 years are beginning to age, consideration will be given to NT applications. The architecture must continue to develop to meet the applications specified by the key users.

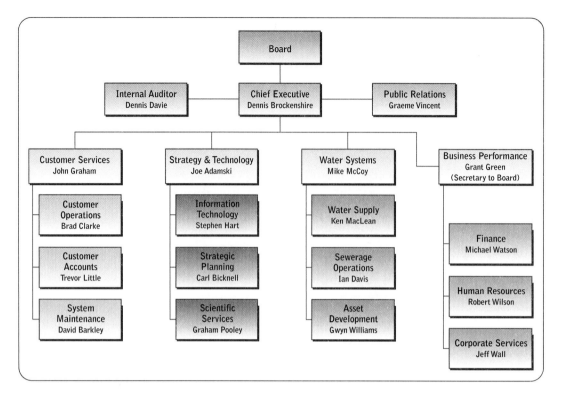

EXHIBIT 1 Barwon Water Organisational Chart

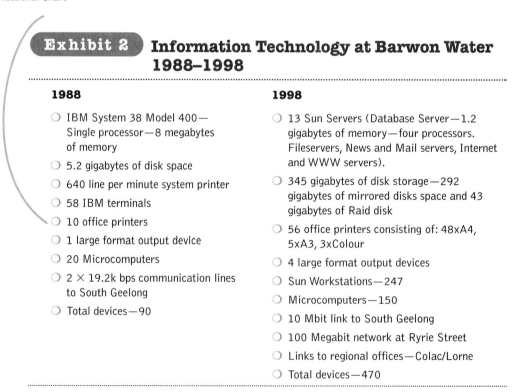

Exhibit 2 **Information Technology at Barwon Water 1988–1998**

1988	1998
○ IBM System 38 Model 400—Single processor—8 megabytes of memory	○ 13 Sun Servers (Database Server—1.2 gigabytes of memory—four processors. Fileservers, News and Mail servers, Internet and WWW servers).
○ 5.2 gigabytes of disk space	○ 345 gigabytes of disk storage—292 gigabytes of mirrored disks space and 43 gigabytes of Raid disk
○ 640 line per minute system printer	
○ 58 IBM terminals	○ 56 office printers consisting of: 48xA4, 5xA3, 3xColour
○ 10 office printers	
○ 1 large format output device	○ 4 large format output devices
○ 20 Microcomputers	○ Sun Workstations—247
○ 2 × 19.2k bps communication lines to South Geelong	○ Microcomputers—150
○ Total devices—90	○ 10 Mbit link to South Geelong
	○ 100 Megabit network at Ryrie Street
	○ Links to regional offices—Colac/Lorne
	○ Total devices—470

Barwon Water intends to keep using UNIX systems on the server side, and high powered workstations because of its reliability. However, the popularity of NT has required a rethink of the desktop strategy.

Because of the significant investment in about 300 Unix workstations, Barwon Water has installed a product called Wincentre that enables the UNIX workstations to mimic a PC and thus run NT. Users

who need the functionality of a UNIX workstation will still have one, however other users (e.g., those doing word processing) will be provided with an NT workstation. The proliferation of different end user equipment—UNIX stations through to desktop PC's and laptops—is a departure from the original infrastructure plan but shows the original plan's flexibility.

Business Value of the IT Investment

A number of efficiency gains were realised with the utilisation of the IT infrastructure. For example, the productivity of the engineering design staff increased by 20 to 50% for most drawings and 90% for redrawings. The distributed computing design also reduced design cycles by enabling staff to share files and work on a common file to avoid duplicated effort.

Overall staff numbers with Barwon Water had dropped to around 440 by mid-1995 and about 320 at the time of Barwon's merger with Otway Water. Numbers increased by approximately 50 at the time of the merger and by the end of 1998 numbers were down to 325.

Adamski said that while the total reduction in staff numbers could not be directly attributed to the new systems, there were several areas where staff had been redeployed as a result. In particular the former survey area allowed 9 employees to be redeployed or reduced through natural attrition resulting in annual savings of about $450,000pa. Another 4 employees were redeployed from Customer Operations and Property Services resulting in annual savings of about $200,000pa. He said that in many cases the systems "freed-up" front-line service personnel to devote more time to customer service.

Customer service also was improved by mapping business processes and examining where steps could be eliminated or replaced by new IT applications. For example a paperless encumbrance certificate system was developed so that a solicitor handling a property matter could interact with Barwon Water via fax without the need to visit a Barwon Water office. All documents sent to and from Barwon Water and those transferred within the organisation were accomplished electronically with no need for hardcopy. Processing times for these applications were reduced from an average of 10 days to a few hours.

Barwon Water continued to receive acclaim for its innovative IT systems. In 1994, it was awarded the Geelong Business Excellence Award in the Innovation Systems Development of Technology category. It also was nominated for an award for innovation by the Washington-based Smithsonian Institute.

To learn from the major IT investments and document the benefits, the internal auditor conducted a post-implementation review of the Property and Facilities Information System (ProFIS) for the audit committee. The internal auditor found the ProFIS project had a NPV of $151,800 on a total investment of approximately $2.9m.

Impact of Merger on IT Systems

During the period 1992-1995, Barwon Water's Information Systems (IS) department focused on the large task of capturing all the relevant mapping, customer and facilities data for its key systems.

When Barwon Water merged with the former Otway Water, a decision needed to be made as to whether their assets also should be captured on the new system or whether the existing (paper-based) systems should remain. Adamski comments:

> We did a cost benefit analysis and found there were benefits in capturing the Otway data on our system. One of the difficulties was that the records were very inaccurate—they didn't precisely reflect what the assets really were and where they were located. This required surveying work to correct the information.

Similar data integrity issues were discovered in the property records. When Barwon Water sent out its first accounts to customers in the Otway region, some people queried why they had a bill:

> We haven't had a bill in 2½ years; why are we getting one now?

Differences in the Barwon and Otway billing schemes were accommodated by the IT systems. While both water authorities charged according to a "user pays" system, Otway's system was based on "user pays" for water and fixed sewer charge whereas Barwon's reflected water and sewer.

Maintaining the IT Infrastructure

With the major infrastructure developments in place, attention has shifted to more of a support and systems integration

---

Exhibit 3 Planned Major Hardware and Software Investments

1998/99	$	1999/00 and 2000/01	$
Disk Storage	280,000	Disaster Recovery	250,000
Optical Fibre to South Geelong and Associated Network Switches	200,000	Desktop Upgrades	560,000
Backup Devices	80,000	Financial System Upgrades	250,000
ProFIS Upgrade including Y2K	245,000	ProFIS Software/Licences	200,000
Memory for Database Server	20,000	Workflow Licences	200,000
NT Application Server	20,000	Disk Storage (e.g., Telemetry Data)	300,000
Microcomputer/Wincentre packages/licences	42,000	Security—Firewall	50,000
Mail/Calendar Upgrade	50,000	Memory	100,000
Quarterly Billing	270,000	NT Operating System	200,000
		Client Software—Business Systems	600,000
Total	1,207,000	Network Upgrade/Extension	200,000
		Total	2,910,000

role. Major planned investments for the years 1998-2001 are shown in Exhibit 3.

The IT group, which had peaked to about 15 people, was down to 11 and external consultants were used to handle specific activities. The increasing emphasis in support is reflected in the hiring of a help-desk person who fields about 200-300 calls per week from users. The calls are typically about Microsoft Word and desktop maintenance issues such as putting PCs together or replacing broken monitors. Help desk statistics are monitored and patterns—say with a specific product—are identified.

As Barwon Water focuses increasingly on efficiency, more emphasis is placed on considering benchmarking functions, says Adamski:

> We continually need to benchmark IT delivery and we should look every now and again at optimal use of internal and external resources when considering options. But I think if you are in a client server environment, it becomes increasingly difficult to outsource—especially when you're already running a very tight set up. We've spoken to external IT providers and they've come in, looked around and said it would be difficult because they need people on site. Furthermore, the knowledge required and the dependence on expertise within the organisation is high and if they didn't pick up that expertise they would be struggling to deliver the service at the same cost.

A major challenge is to make small incremental investments that enhance the infrastructure to meet the needs of business units. Commenting on Barwon Water's Information Technology infrastructure, Brockenshire stated:

> Barwon Water has made and continues to make a significant investment in IT. The organisation has spent in the region of $7 to $10 million in building its IT infrastructure and has recurrent costs of 3% of total expenditure. I want to make sure we get an appropriate return for this investment. It is critical IT delivers real business benefits. Since I've come into this role, I have insisted that my line managers justify any new IT investment on the grounds of the business value it will create.

Adamski comments:

> There is always this disbelief—why is IT always so much? Our new investments are around 5% of our capital works, which is within the industry range of IT expenditure. In the last three years, the CE has ensured costs and benefits are clearly defined. In each case if we can prove that what we are doing is cost-effective, the CE and Board have been strongly supportive.
>
> The key things are business efficiency and customer service. So anything we can improve in these areas we can make the investment.
>
> For example, in the past twelve months, we put up a case for expenditure for information systems—initially it was about $2.5 million. We cut it back by saying we won't have as much redundancy in the system—the implication being that if we had a major disaster it could take up to two weeks to recover. We also took out additional work on our firewall and came up with an innovative way of improving front desk operations without having to buy faster workstations. Those three cuts alone brought the expenditure down to $1.8 million.
>
> Just recently the Chairman looked at what we had done and asked: "Why are you potentially jeopardising customer service and business continuity?" He is keen for us to reduce the down-time if we have a major disaster to about two working days—so that means he is understanding of IT and its impact on our business.

Implicit in the process of justifying expenditure is the partition of IT facilities into shared infrastructure capability and user expenditure. Shared IT infrastructure capability is specified and justified by the IT group. Adamski describes the process:

> We have shifted the emphasis for IT justification such that users are now becoming much more responsible for IT expenditure. They still send requests saying "We need upgrades to 10 workstations" and I just send it back with a note: "You justify it and I will provide it." When it comes time to decide capital works expenditure, I put together a report which clearly shows how the infrastructure has to be enhanced. All other expenditure and justification is done by the user community.

For example, the telemetry system is not year 2000 compliant and needs to be replaced. An overall telemetry strategy was developed by a team under the leadership of the Manager Strategic Planning Branch and a technology solution recommended. A project manager from the user group was appointed to develop, justify and implement the system. Adamski notes:

> The telemetry case is an example of the advantage of having both IT and strategy report to one person. Telemetry capability is a strategic choice for Barwon Water. We were able to understand the strategic issue and generate an appropriate IT solution.

FUTURE ISSUES AT BARWON WATER

On completion of the Otway region data capture, Barwon Water will have essentially all the data it requires to do business online. The focus is shifting to providing tools to enable access to information whenever and wherever it is needed to run the business. Data warehousing is being considered as a means to provide all business units with the data they need in the form they require. This principal will extend to corporate governance: directors are on-line and will be capable of getting information directly from Barwon Water's systems.

As well as providing the information to internal business users, Barwon Water has a strategy—in line with the Victorian Government—of providing electronic access to its customers. Says Adamski:

> The Government is striving to deliver information for customers online. We have actually got that technology now, but my concern is whether our customers are ready to take advantage of it. For example, we have many different payment mechanisms available now: pay at the bank, post office, credit card by mail or phone, send in a cheque and so on, but you still get people walking into this office. So if you go to the next step and say you can pay through the Web, then it is easy for us to enable it. But as to whether it takes off . . . I think you are almost looking toward the next generation.

As well as using a Web payment option, there also was the possibility of using the "Maxi" system. This State Government-supported system provides bill paying and other services to customers via public "kiosks", telephone and the WWW. Several utilities, councils and government departments (eg. VicRoads) are already using the system. Adamski notes:

> We have spoken to kiosk suppliers, but at this stage we don't see any benefits because we can actually do the same sorts of things with our system without using kiosks. Also, there is a question as to how much kiosks will be used out in the marketplace. But with an investment of tens of thousands of dollars required per kiosk, there is a real issue of costs to install these. Unless you do it with other service organisations, it becomes a very expensive way of providing online services.

Nonetheless, Adamski sees ample opportunity for cooperation with other organisations in the region. In a 1994 article[2], Adamski outlined his vision for a regional computer centre for the greater Geelong area:

> Barwon Water covers over 8,000 square kilometres. Within this region, there has recently been an amalgamation of a number of councils. These organisations serve the same customers as ourselves. We have articulated the benefits of using common databases, mapping and other information to serve these customers. Benefits include a service one-stop shopfront where customers could pay rates, water

tariffs and apply for property approvals. The systems we now have at Barwon Water would be a good starting point in building this regional concept. Data is one of our region's most valuable assets and there is no point in duplicating it.

This vision is slowly being realised. The City of Greater Geelong has since implemented an online planning scheme running on Barwon Water's servers but operated and maintained by the City of Greater Geelong. Through this system, changes to planning schemes are immediately available to Barwon Water. The City of Greater Geelong has access to Barwon Water's property information, and several applications have been developed by Barwon Water to help the City better use this information. For example, the City's planning permit applications process has been streamlined. Adamski says:

> So with the GIS there is, I think, some hope of having a regional concept for this area which would give the whole region a competitive advantage. There are many organisations which have expressed an interest in working with us. On top of that, we have many day-to-day queries wanting access to data. For example we are using our IT infrastructure to do flood plain management for a number of consultants undertaking work for several councils in Melbourne and VicRoads in Gippsland. They supply the data or we capture it and

do the analysis in partnership with the consultants.

We are not chasing any of this work; its all word of mouth and we have to knock a lot back. In addition, we are still receiving requests from other organisations which want to see our systems—in the last three weeks we have had six or seven organisations visit. My employees are enjoying it and are enthusiastic about the thought of marketing ourselves to even a greater extent in the future.

CASE STUDY QUESTIONS

1. Describe the Barwon Water Board and the environment in which it operates. What problems did the Board encounter before 1988? What management, organization, and technology factors contributed to those problems?

2. Describe Barwon Water's information technology (IT) infrastructure and information system applications before 1988?

3. Analyze and compare Barwon's efforts to upgrade its information technology (IT) infrastructure in 1988 and 1998.

4. How did Barwon Water justify its information technology (IT) infrastructure investments? What were the benefits?

5. How well did Barwon's IT infrastructure and systems support the merger with Otway Water? How well can it support future business needs?

Barwon Water (B) is intended to be read in conjunction with "Creating and Exploiting an IT Infrastructure (A)" by Joel B. Barolsky, Paul Richardson and Peter Weill.
The Melbourne Business School gratefully acknowledges the cooperation of Barwon Water in the preparation of this case study, and its consent to the use and publication of the material contained therein.

This case was written for the purposes of class discussion, rather than to illustrate either effective or ineffective handling of a managerial situation.
© 1999 Paul Richardson, Peter Weill and Joel B. Barolsky (28 May 1999).
Distributed by Melbourne Case Study Services at the Melbourne Business School, The University of Melbourne, 200 Leicester Street,

Carlton 3053, Australia. Contact email: m.larosa@mbs.unimelb.edu.au Telephone +61 3 9349 8121. All rights reserved to the contributors.
[1] Melbourne (population ~3.4 million) is the capital city of the State of Victoria.
[2] "IT manager leads corporate plan to Water," MIS, April 1994, pages 41-46.

CASE STUDY 2: Ginormous Life Insurance Company

Len Fertuck, University of Toronto (Canada)

Ginormous Life is an insurance company with a long tradition. The company has four divisions that each operate their own computers. The IS group provides analysis, design, and programming services to all of the divisions. The divisions are actuarial, marketing, operations, and investment. All divisions are located at the corporate headquarters building. Marketing also has field offices in 20 cities across the country.

○ **The Actuarial Division** is responsible for the design and pricing of new kinds of policies. They use purchased industry data and weekly summaries of data obtained from the Operations Division. They have their own DEC VAX minicomputer, running the UNIX operating system, to store data files. They do most of their analysis on PCs and Sun workstations, either on spreadsheets or with a specialized interactive language called APL.

○ **The Marketing Division** is responsible for selling policies to new customers and for follow-up of existing customers in case they need changes to their current insurance. All sales orders are sent to the Operations Division for data entry and billing. They use purchased external data for market research and weekly copies of data from operations for follow-ups. They have their own IBM AS/400 minicomputer with dumb terminals for clerks to enter sales data. There are also many PCs used to analyze market data using statistical packages like SAS.

○ **The Operations Division** is responsible for processing all mission-critical financial transactions including payroll. They record all new policies, send regular bills to customers, evaluate and pay all claims, and cancel lapsed policies. They have all their data and programs on two IBM ES/9000 mainframes running under the OS/390 operating system. The programs are often large and complex because they must service not only the 15 products currently being sold but also the 75 old kinds of policies that are no longer being sold but still have existing policy holders. Clerks use dumb terminals to enter and update

data. Applications written in the last five years have used an SQL relational database to store data, but most programs are still written in COBOL. The average age of the transaction processing programs is about ten years.

○ **The Investment Division** is responsible for investing premiums until they are needed to pay claims. Their data consist primarily of internal portfolio data and research data obtained by direct links to data services. They have a DEC minicomputer to store their data. The internal data are received by a weekly download of cash flows from the Operations Division. External data are obtained as needed. They use PCs to analyze data obtained either from the mini or from commercial data services.

A controlling interest in Ginormous Life has recently been purchased by Financial Behemoth Corp. The management of Financial Behemoth has decided that the firm's efficiency and profitability must be improved. Their first move has been to put Dan D. Mann, a hotshot information systems specialist from Financial Behemoth, in charge of the Information Systems Division. He has been given the objective of modernizing and streamlining the computer facilities without any increase in budget.

In the first week on the job, Dan discovered that only seven junior members of the staff of 200 information systems specialists know anything about CASE tools, End-User Computing, or LANs. They have no experience in implementing PC systems. There is no evidence of any formal decision-support systems or executive information systems in the organization. New applications in the last five years have been implemented in COBOL on DB2, a relational database product purchased from IBM. Over two-thirds of applications are still based on COBOL flat files. One of the benefits of using DB2 is that it is now possible to deliver reports quickly based on ad hoc queries. This is creating a snowballing demand for conversion of more systems to a relational database so that other managers can get similar service.

There have been some problems with the older systems. Maintenance is difficult and costly because almost every change to the data structure of applications in opera-

tions requires corresponding changes to applications in the other divisions. There has been a growing demand in other divisions for faster access to operations data. For instance the Investment Division claims that they could make more profitable investments if they had continuous access to the cash position in operations. Marketing complains that they get calls from clients about claims and cannot answer them because they do not have current access to the status of the claim. Management wants current access to a wide variety of data in summary form so they can get a better understanding of the business. The IS group says that it would be difficult to provide access to data in operations because of security considerations. It is difficult to ensure that users do not make unauthorized changes to the COBOL files.

The IS group complains that they cannot deliver all the applications that users want because they are short-staffed. They spend 90 percent of their time maintaining the existing systems. The programmers are mostly old and experienced and employee turnover is unusually low, so there is not likely to be much room for improvement by further training in programming. Employees often remark that the company is a very pleasant and benevolent place to work. At least they did until rumors of deregulation and foreign competition started to sweep the industry.

Dan foresees that there will be an increasing need for computer capacity as more and more applications are converted to on-line transaction processing and more users begin to make ad hoc queries. Dan is also wondering if intranets or the Internet should become part of any new software.

Dan began to look for ways to solve the many problems of the Information Systems Division. He solicited proposals from various vendors and consultants in the computer industry. After a preliminary review of the proposals, Dan was left with three broad options suggested by IBM, Oracle Corp., and Datamotion, a local consulting firm. The proposals are briefly described below.

IBM proposes an integrated solution using IBM hardware and software. The main elements of the proposal are:

○ **Data and applications will remain on a mainframe.** The IBM ES/9000 series of hardware running their OS/390 operating system will provide mainframe services. Mainframe hardware capacity will have to be approximately doubled by adding two more ES/9000 series machines. The four machines will run under OS/390 with Parallel Sysplex clustering technology that allows for future growth. The Parallel Sysplex system can be scaled by connecting up to 32 servers to work in parallel and be treated as a single system for scheduling and system management. The OS/390 operating system can also run UNIX applications.

○ **AS/400 minicomputers running under the OS/400 operating system** will replace DEC minicomputers.

○ **RS/6000 workstations running AIX—** a flavor of the UNIX operating system—can be used for actuarial computations. All hardware will be interconnected with IBM's proprietary SNA network architecture. PCs will run under the OS/2 operating system and the IBM LAN Server to support both Microsoft Windows applications and locally designed applications that communicate with mainframe databases.

○ **A DB2 relational database will store all data on-line.** Users will be able to access any data they need through their terminals or through PCs that communicate with the mainframe.

○ **Legacy systems will be converted using reengineering tools,** like Design Recovery and Maintenance Workbench from Intersolv, Inc. These will have the advantage that they will continue to use the COBOL code that the existing programmers are familiar with. New work will be done using CASE tools with code generators that produce COBOL code.

○ **Proven technology.** The IBM systems are widely used by many customers and vendors. Many mission-critical application programs are available on the market that address a wide variety of business needs.

Oracle Corp. proposed that all systems be converted to use their Oracle database product and its associated screen and report generators. They said that such a conversion would have the following advantages:

○ **Over 90 hardware platforms are supported.** This means that the company is no longer bound to stay with a single hardware vendor. Oracle databases

and application programs can be easily moved from one manufacturer's machine to another manufacturer's machine by a relatively simple export and import operation as long as applications are created with Oracle tools. Thus the most economical hardware platform can be used for the application. Oracle will also access data stored in an IBM DB2 database.

○ **Integrated CASE tools and application generators.** Oracle has its own design and development tools called Designer/2000 and Developer/2000. Applications designed with Designer/2000 can be automatically created for a wide variety of terminals or for the World Wide Web. The same design can be implemented in Windows, on a Macintosh, or on X-Windows in UNIX. Applications are created using graphic tools that eliminate the need for a language like COBOL. The designer works entirely with visual prototyping specifications.

○ **Vertically integrated applications.** Oracle sells a number of common applications, like accounting programs, that can be used as building blocks in developing a complete system. These applications could eliminate the need to redevelop some applications.

○ **Distributed network support.** A wide variety of common network protocols like SNA, DecNet, Novell, and TCP/IP are supported. Different parts of the database can be distributed to different machines on the network and accessed or updated by any application. All data are stored on-line for instant access. The data can be stored on one machine and the applications can be run on a different machine, including a PC or workstation, to provide a client/server environment. The ability to distribute a database allows a large database on an expensive mainframe to be distributed to a number of cheaper minicomputers.

Datamotion proposed a data warehouse approach using software tools from Information Builders Inc. Existing applications would be linked using EDA, a middleware data warehouse server that acts as a bridge between the existing data files and the users performing enquiries. New applications would be developed using an application tool called Cactus. The advantages of this approach are:

○ **Data Location Transparency.** EDA Hub Server provides a single connection point from which applications can

access multiple data sources anywhere in the enterprise. In addition, users can join data between any supported EDA databases—locally, cross-server, or cross-platform. Users can easily access remote data sources for enhanced decision-making capabilities.

○ **The EDA server can reach most non-relational databases** and file systems through its SQL translation engine. EDA also supports 3GL, 4GL, static SQL, CICS, IMS/TM, and proprietary database stored procedure processing.

○ **Extensive network and operating system support.** EDA supports 14 major network protocols and provides protocol translation between dissimilar networks. EDA also runs on 35 different processing platforms. EDA servers support optimized SQL against any RDBMS. And the EDA server can automatically generate the dialect of SQL optimal for the targeted data source. It is available on Windows 3.x, Windows 95/98, Windows NT, OS/2, MVS, UNIX, CICS, VM, OpenVMS, Tandem, and AS/400.

○ **Comprehensive Internet Support.** With EDA's Internet services, users can issue requests from a standard Web browser to any EDA-supported data source and receive answer sets formatted as HTML pages.

○ **Cactus promotes modern development methods.** Cactus allows the developer to partition an application, keeping presentation logic, business logic, and data access logic separate. This partitioning of functionality can occur across a large number of enterprise platforms to allow greater flexibility in achieving scalability, performance, and maintenance. Cactus provides all the tools needed to deal with every aspect of developing, testing, packaging, and deploying client/server traditional applications or Web-based applications.

Dan is not sure which approach to take for the future of Ginormous Life. Whichever route he follows, the technology will have an enormous impact on the kinds of applications his staff will be able to produce in the future and the way in which they will produce them. While industry trends toward downsizing and distribution of systems may eventually prove to be more efficient, Dan's staff does not have much experience with the new technologies that would be required. He is uncertain about whether there will be a sufficient payoff to justify the organizational turmoil that will result from a major change in direction. Ideally he would like to move quickly to a modern client/server system with minimal disturbance to existing staff and development methods, but he fears that both of these are not simultaneously possible.

Source: Reprinted by permission of Len Fertuck, University of Toronto, Canada.

CASE STUDY QUESTIONS

Dan must prepare a strategy for the renewal of the Information Systems Division over the next three years. As his assistant, prepare an outline, in point form, containing the following items:

1. A list of factors or issues that must be considered in selecting a technology platform for the firm.

2. Weights for each factor obtained by dividing up 100 points among the factors in proportion to their importance.

3. A score from 0 to 10 of how each of the three proposals performs on each factor.

4. A grand score for each proposal obtained by summing the product of the proposal score times the factor weight for each proposal.

5. The technology that you would recommend that Dan adopt and the reason for choosing the particular technology that you recommend.

6. The order in which each component of the technology should be introduced and the reason for selecting the order.

International Case Study

CASE STUDY 3: From Analysis to Evaluation— the Example of Cuparla

Gerhard Schwabe, University of Koblenz—Landau (Germany)

ANALYSIS AND DESIGN

Just like in other towns, members of the Stuttgart City Council have a large workload: In addition to their primary profession (e.g. as an engineer at Daimler Benz) they devote more than 40 hours a week to local politics. This extra work has to be done under fairly unfavorable conditions. Only council sessions and party meetings take place in the city hall; the deputies of the local council do not have an office in the city hall to prepare or coordinate their work. This means, for example, that they have to read and file all official documents at home. In a city with more than 500,000 inhabitants they receive a very large number of documents. Furthermore, council members feel that they could be better informed by the administration and better use could be made of their time. Therefore Hohenheim University and partners' launched the Cuparla project to improve the information access and collaboration of council members.

A detailed analysis of their work revealed the following characteristics of council work:

○ Since council members are very mobile support has to be available to them any time and in any place.

○ Council members collaborate and behave differently in different contexts: While they act informally and rather open in the context of their own party, they behave more controlled and formal in official council sessions.

○ A closer investigation of council work reveals a low degree of process structure. Every council member has the right of initiative and can inform and involve other members and members of the administration in any order.

○ Council members rarely are power computer users. Computer support for them has to be very straightforward and intuitive to use.

When designing computer support we initially had to decide on the basic orientation of our software. We soon abandoned a workflow model as there are merely a few steps and there is little order in the collaboration of local politicians. Imposing a new structure into this situation would have been too restrictive for the council members. We then turned to pure document orientation, imposing no structure at all on the council members' work. We created a single large database with all the documents any member of the city council ever needs. However, working with this database turned out to be too complex for the council members. In addition, they need to control the access to certain documents at all stages of the decision-making process. For example, a party may not want to reveal a proposal to other parties before it has officially been brought up in the city council. Controlling access to each document individually and changing the access control list was not feasible.

Therefore, the working context was chosen as a basis of our design. Each working context of a council member can be symbol-

ized by a "room." A private office corresponds to the council member working at home; there is a party room, where he collaborates with his party colleagues, and a committee room symbolises the place for committee meetings. In addition, there is a room for working groups, a private post office and a library for filed information. All rooms hence have an electronic equivalent in the Cuparla software. When a council member opens the Cuparla software, he sees all the rooms from the entrance hall (Figure 1).

The council member creates a document in one room (e.g. his private office) and then shares it with other council members in other rooms. If he moves a document into the room of his party, he shares it with his party colleagues; if he hands it on to the administration, he shares it with the mayors, administration officials, and all council members.

The interface of the electronic rooms resembles the setup of the original rooms. Figure 2 shows the example of the room for a parliamentary party. On the left hand side of the screen there are document locations, whereas, on the right hand side, the documents of the selected location are presented. Documents that are currently worked on are displayed on the "desk." These documents have the connotation that they need to be worked on without an additional outside trigger. If a document is in the files, it belongs to a topic that is still on the political agenda. However, a trigger is necessary to move it off of the shelf. If a topic is not on the political agenda any more, all documents belonging to it are moved to the archive.

FIGURE I Entrance Hall

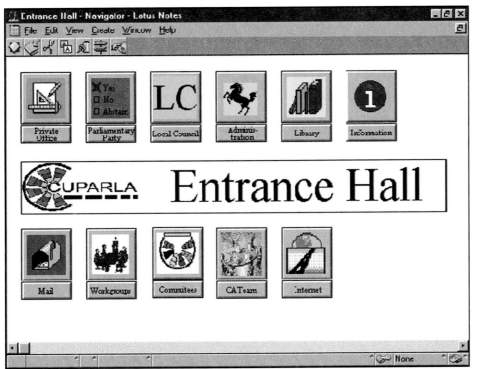

The other locations support the collaboration within the party. The conference desk contains all documents for the next (weekly) party meeting. Any council member of the party can put documents there. When a council member gets prepared for the meeting, he or she merely has to check the conference desk for relevant information. The mailbox for the chairman contains all documents that the chairman needs to decide on. In contrast to his E-mail account all members have access to the mailbox. Double work is avoided as every council member is aware of the chairman's agenda. The mailbox of the assistant contains tasks for the party assistants, the mailbox for the secretary assignments for the secretary (e.g. a draft for a letter). The inbox contains documents that have been moved from other rooms into this room.

Thus, in the electronic room all locations correspond to the current manual situation. Council members do not have to relearn their work. Instead, they collaborate in the shared environment they are accustomed to with shared expectations about the other peoples' behaviour. Feedback from the pilot users indicates that this approach is appropriate.

Some specific design features make the software easy to use. The software on purpose does not have a fancy 3D-interface that has the same look as a real room.

Buttons (in the entrance hall) and lists (in the rooms) are much easier to use and do not distract the user from the essential parts. Each location (e.g. the desk) has a little arrow. If a user clicks on this arrow, a document is moved to the location. This operation is much easier for a beginner than proceeding by "drag and drop."

Furthermore, software design is not restricted to building an electronic equivalent of a manual situation. If one wants to truly benefit from the opportunities of electronic collaboration support systems, one has to include new tools that are not possible in the manual setting. For example, additional cross location and room search features are needed to make it easy for the council member to retrieve information. The challenge of interface design is to give the user a starting point that is close to the situation he is used to. A next step is to provide the user with options to improve and adjust his working behavior to the opportunities offered by the use of a computer.

ORGANIZATIONAL IMPLEMENTATION

Bulding the appropriate software is only one success factor for a groupware project. Organizational implementation typically is at least as difficult. Groupware often has a free rider problem: All want to

gain the benefit and nobody wants to do the work. Furthermore many features are only beneficial if all participate actively. For example, if a significant part of a council faction insists on using paper documents for their work, providing and sharing electronic documents actually means additional work for the others. This can easily lead to the situation that groupware usage never really gets started. To "bootstrap" usage we started with the (socially) simple activities and ended with the (socially) complex activities (Figure 3).

In the first step we provided the basic council information in digital form. The city council has the power to demand this initial organizational learning process from the administration. Once there is sufficient information the individual council member can already benefit from the system without relying on the usage of his fellow councillors. The usage conventions are therefore socially simple. As better information is a competitive advantage for a council member, there was an incentive for the individual effort required to learn the system. Communication support (E-Mail, Fax) is a more complex process, because its success depends on reliable usage patterns by all communication partners. The usage patterns are straightforward and easy to learn. We therefore implemented them in a second phase. Coordination

FIGURE 2 Parliamentary Party
Room

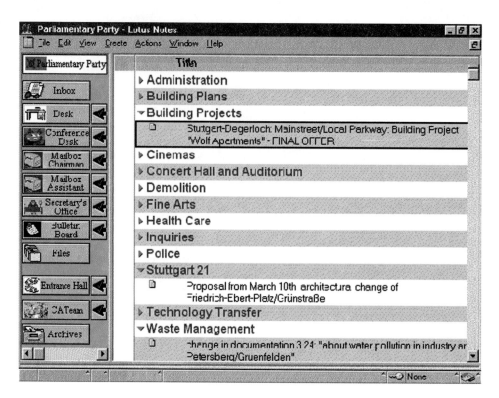

activities (sharing to-do-lists, sharing calendars) and cooperation activities (sharing documents and room locations, electronic meetings) depend on the observance of socially complex usage conventions by all group members. For example, the council member had to learn that her activities had effects on the documents and containers of all others and that "surprises" typically resulted from ill-coordinated activities of several group members. The council has to go through an intensive organiza-tional learning process to benefit from the features. For example, the party's business processes had to be reorganized.

We offered collaboration and coordination support in the same phase to the council members. Their appropriation depended on the party's culture: a hierarchically organized party preferred to use the coordination features and requested to turn off many collaborative feature. In another party most councillors had equal rights. This party preferred the collaborative features.

ECONOMIC BENEFITS

The ultimate success of any IS-project is not only determined by the quality of the developed technology but also by its economic benefits. Thus, the economic benefit of Cuparla was evaluated in the first quarter of 1998 after about 4 months of use by the whole city council (pilot users had been using the system for more than a year). Evaluating the economic benefits of an innovative software is notoriously difficult. Reasons for that include:

FIGURE 3 Steps of groupware
implementation

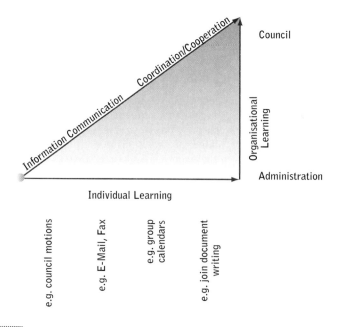

1. It is difficult to attribute costs to a single project. For example, the city of Stuttgart had to wire part of their city hall for Cuparla –is this a cost of the project? And how about the servers bought for Cuparla and co-used for other purposes? And the cost for the information that was collected for the city council and is now being used in the administration's intranet?

2. Many benefits cannot be quantified in monetary terms. For instance, how much is it worth if the council members make better informed decisions? Or, how much is it worth if council membership becomes more attractive?

3. What is the appropriate level of aggregation for economic benefits? Should it be the cost and benefit for the individual council member? Or the parties? Or the whole city council? Or even the whole city of Stuttgart? Or should the improved processes be measured?

The evaluation of Cuparla was therefore not based on purely monetary terms; rather evaluation results were aggregated on five sets of criteria (cost, time, quality, flexibility and human situation) and four levels of aggregation (individual, group, process, organization) resulting in a 4*5 matrix (Figure 4).

The trick is to attribute the effects only to the lowest possible level, e.g. if one can attribute the cost of an individual PC to an individual council member, it counts only there and not on the group level. On the other hand, a server probably can only be attributed to the group of all council members and so on. We will now briefly go through the major effects:

Costs: Both on the individual and the group level costs have gone up significantly (notebooks, ISDN, printer, server etc.). There is a potential for cost savings if the council members forgo the delivery of paper copies of the documents. There have been some additional costs on the process level, but not as much as on the two levels below. There may have been direct cost savings by the provision of electronic documents in the council-related business processes, but we were not able to identify them. As the administration was reluctant to really reorganize its internal business processes, many potential cost savings could not be realized. As all costs could be attributed to the levels business process, group or individual, we noted a cost neutrality for the level "organization" (the costs for provisionally wiring the city hall were negligible)

Time: During the pilot phase, the system did not save time for the councilors; to the contrary, the individual councilors had to work longer in order to learn how to use the Cuparla system. However, the councilors also indicated that they used their time more productively, i.e., the overtime was well invested. Thus, we decided to summarize the effects on the individual level as "neutral." Cuparla had also not yet led to faster or more efficient decisions in the council or its subgroups. Therefore the effects are graded 'unchanged'. The council members see a potential here, but the speed of decisions is not only a matter of work efficiency but also has a political dimension and politics does not change that fast. Some business processes were rated as being faster, particularly the processes at the interface between council and administration (e.g. the process of writing the meeting minutes). There was no effect on the organization as a whole, i.e. the city of Stuttgart was not faster at reacting to external challenges and opportunities.

Quality: The council members reported a remarkable improvement of quality of their work. The council members feel that the quality of their decisions has been improved by the much better access to information. The work of the parties has benefited from the e-mail and the collaboration features of Cuparla as well as the computer support of strategic party meetings. As the interface between different subprocesses of council work has fewer media changes and the (partially erroneous) duplication of information has been reduced, the council members and members of the administration also reported an improved quality of their business processes. The creation of an organization-wide database of council-related information even contributed to a somewhat better work in the whole administration.

Flexibility: Improved individual flexibility was the most important benefit of Cuparla. This holds true for spatial, temporal and interpersonal flexibility. People can work and access other people any place and any time they want. On the group level Cuparla has enhanced the flexibility within parties as it has become easier to coordinate the actions of the council members. There have not been any significant changes to the flexibility on the process or organizational level.

Human situation: Cuparla has made council membership more attractive because it has become easier to

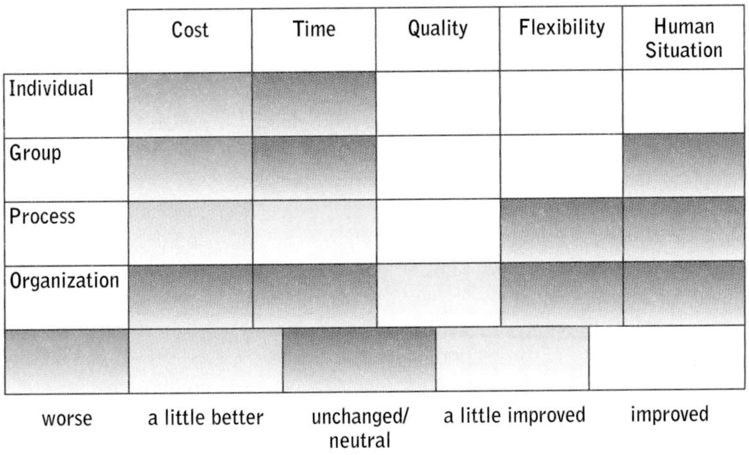

	Cost	Time	Quality	Flexibility	Human Situation
Individual					
Group					
Process					
Organization					

worse   a little better   unchanged/neutral   a little improved   improved

FIGURE 4 Aggregated evaluation of Cuparla (March 1998)

reconcile one's primary job, council work and private life. Furthermore Cuparla is regarded as an opportunity for the council member's individual development. There were no significant changes to the human situation on the group, process or organizational level.

As mentioned above, these effects were measured after a relatively short period of usage. By the time of writing this case study, (January 2000), Cuparla has become an indispensable part of council work. When the system was down for a week in the beginning of 2000 because of router problems, the council members were so annoyed that the local newspaper reported their unanimous complaint in a committee meeting.

Additional English literature:

Schwabe, G.; Krcmar, H.: "Digital Material in a Political Work Context—the Case of Cuparla." Appears in the Proceedings of the European Conference on Information Systems ECIS 2000 in Vienna.

Schwabe, G.; Krcmar, H.: "Piloting a Sociotechnical Innovation." Appears in the Proceedings of the European Conference on Information Systems ECIS 2000 in Vienna.

Schwabe, G.: "Understanding and Supporting Knowledge Management and Organizational Memory in a City Council." In: Hawaii International Conference on System Sciences 1999 (HICSS99), CD-ROM, 12 pages.

Schwabe, G.; Krcmar, H.: "Electronic Meeting Support for Councils." Appears in: Journal of AI and Society 1999.

CASE STUDY QUESTIONS

1. Analyze the management, organization, and technology issues that had to be addressed by the Cuparla project.

2. Analyze the interface and design of the Cuparla system. What problems does it solve? What organizational processes does it support? How effective is it?

3. How successful was the Cuparla project? Describe the implementation issues, costs and benefits.

Source: From "Analysis to Interface Design—The Example of Cuparia," by Gerhard Schwabe, Stephen Wilczek, and Helmut Krcmar. Reprinted by permission.

*The project partners were Hohenheim University (Coordinator), Datenzentrale Baden-Württemberg and GroupVision Softwaresysteme GmbH. The project was funded as part of its R&D program by DeTeBerkom GmbH, a 100% subsidiary of German Telekom.

International Case Study

CASE STUDY 4: Citibank Asia Pacific: Managing Information Technology Consolidation, Change, and New Challenges

Christina Soh and Neo Boon Siong, Information Management Research Center (IMARC), Nanyang Business School, Nanyang Technological University (Singapore)

I. CITICORP

Citicorp in 1991 recorded a net loss of $457 million[1], suspended the dividend on its common stock, and saw the price of that stock fall to a long-time low before rebounding after year end. Nevertheless, and despite the magnitude of our problems, 1991 for Citicorp was in key respects a transitional, turnaround year.

John Reed, Citicorp's chairman acknowledged Citicorp's problems in his letter to stockholders in the 1991 annual report. The bank had been struggling with a large third world loan portfolio, as well as significant problems with its commercial property loans, and with its financing of highly leveraged transactions in the U.S. The bank needed more equity but third world debt costs prevented Citicorp from increasing its equity through retention of earnings.

The severe storms that Citicorp had been subjected to prompted significant changes. To combat the slowdown in revenue growth, and the rise in consumer and credit write-offs, Citicorp aggressively reduced expenses in order to improve the operating margin, issued stock to improve their capital ratio, and made structural changes at the senior executive level which were aimed at providing more focused direction to the business. John Reed articulated three requirements for being a "great bank in the 1990s"—meeting customer needs, having financial strength, and "marshalling human and **technological** resources **...more imaginatively and cost-effectively** than one's competitors." (emphasis added).

In the midst of this organizational turbulence, one of Citicorp's undisputed strengths was its global presence. It is unrivalled in its network of banks in more than 90 countries. Its overseas consumer banking operations in particular, were showing healthy growth. Global consumer banking includes mortgage and insurance business and non-U.S. credit card business. Citicorp only entered the field of consumer banking in the mid-70s. John Reed's vision was to pursue growth in the consumer banking area, and to pursue it through global expansion and leveraging information technology.

The primary vision in consumer banking is "Citibanking"—combining relationship banking with technology that enables Citibank to serve its customers anywhere anytime with the high standard of service that they receive in their home countries. In the early 1990s, this involved technology-enabled innovations such as: having a one-stop account opening with paperless relationship opening, instant card and check issuance, and instant account availability; having a customer relationship database that supports cross-product relationships; creation of hybrid and customized product; and relationship pricing that more closely matches the value to the customer. The Citicard is the "key" to Citibanking services such as checking, money market, and bankcard accounts. Consumer banking products are distributed through bank branches, Citicard centre, and Citiphone banking, which gives 24-hour, 7-day-a-week service. The global services available to customers were augmented in 1991 when Citibank joined the CIRRUS ATM network, allowing Citicard holders access to cash around the world.

Today, the Internet provides another channel for delivery of Citibank services and products, and the Citibanking strategy now includes ensuring that the bank is "one mile, one phone call, or one click" away from anyone on earth.[2] The multiple delivery channels has also led Citibank to emphasize consistency of experience for all customers by establishing design standards to ensure that every Citibank access point is instantly recognizable.[3] The Citibanking concept has also evolved to include building lifelong relationships by providing product sets to match customers' needs at each stage of their financial lives[4]—"offering all the banking products needed as young people complete their education, enter the workforce, establish a household, rear a family, and eventually retire . . ."[5]

The results of operating and structural changes made in the early 1990s, as well as the impact of the growing Asian consumer market, contributed to the turnaround at Citicorp, where the 1992 net earning was $772 million. This earned it an A minus credit rating from Standard and Poor, which also upgraded the bank's outlook from negative to stable. Citicorp share price also moved up to $36.88 during 1993, from a low of $23 in 1990. In early 1994, the bank was also given permission by the U.S. regulatory agency to resume issuing dividends. By the end of 1997, the share price had risen to $126, and net income in 1998 was $5.8b.[6]

In 1998, Citicorp merged with Travelers to form Citigroup. Each brings to Citigroup complementary products and services—Citicorp's strengths are in consumer and corporate banking, and Traveler's strengths are in insurance, securities and investment banking. Their combined customer list is 100m and the "stretch target" is one billion customers by 2010.[7] In 1999, Citigroup had almost $10b in net incomes worldwide, and its stock has risen 63%.[8]

II. CITIBANK IN ASIA PACIFIC

Citicorp has been in Asia since 1902 when it set up finance houses in a number of Asian ports, such as Shanghai and Singapore. It has built up an understanding of the local markets in which it operates. Citicorp's major competitors in terms of established presence throughout Asia are Hong Kong and Shanghai Bank, and Standard Chartered Bank, but neither has the global reach that Citicorp offers.

Citibank began pursuing consumer banking in earnest in 1986, and since then Asian accounts have increased from 1 million to 6 million in 1997. Asian consumer deposits grew six-fold to $13.6 billion between 1983 and 1992, while loans grew seventeenfold to $10.8 billion over the same period.[9] This growth is a reflection of the region's high gross savings rate (about 35%), and high GNP growth. Critics had suggested that Citicorp may run into credit problems because Asians had little experience with personal debt. Although revenue decreased between 1996 and 1997 due to the Asian financial crisis, there has been strong growth in the customer deposits and accounts.[10] In 1998, accounts increased 19%, and customer deposits 18%.[11] Since then accounts and customer deposits have grown by more than 20% across the Asia Pacific region,[12] continuing to fuel the growth in consumer banking in Citibank.

Citibank made significant innovations in packaging financial services for the relatively rich customer, and has managed to cream the Asian market. They pioneered the concept of consumer credit in Asia, with then innovative offerings such as round-the-clock phone banking and automated teller cards. Interestingly, some innovations such as phone-banking, were motivated by local regulations that severely restricted the number of branches that it may operate. More recent innovations include International Personal Banking, which offers a broad and flexible range of investment opportunities, time deposits, overdraft facilities and the ability to trade and deposit in any of 18 international currencies. This is to tap the fast growing offshore banking component of Asian consumer banking.[13]

III. PREVIOUS TECHNOLOGY INFRASTRUCTURE

In the early 1990s, each of Citibank's Asia Pacific countries belong to one of three automation platforms—MVS, AS/400, or UNIX—and has one of two consumer banking applications—COSMOS CORE. COSMOS was the earlier set of applications, and was fairly typical of most U.S. banks' offshore banking applications. It was written in COBOL in order to provide flexibility in complying with varying regulatory reporting formats, and it provided back-room support for standard areas such as current accounts, general ledger, and some loans processing. Subsequently, Citibank began to replace COSMOS with CORE, which was to provide an all encompassing system to run on IBM's minicomputers, the AS/400s. CORE was used in a number of countries with smaller operations, like Indonesia. It was not suitable for countries, such as India, where IBM did not have a presence, and in countries with high volumes, like Hong Kong. Both COSMOS and CORE were subject to many country-specific modifications over time, as the local banks responded to varying regulatory and business requirements. The wholesale banking division also used COSMOS, and it ran on large IBM mainframes. Over time, the wholesale banking version of COSMOS has also proliferated. The result is significant differences in each country's basic banking software.

The underlying philosophy of customizing to meet local customer needs resulted in each country having its own IT infrastructure and unique applications. While it worked adequately in the past, the local markets approach did not allow Citibank to integrate its products, services, and information to serve its highly sophisticated, mobile and increasingly demanding global customers. Further, there are substantial economies of scale that may be gained from standardizing and consolidating bank products and processing across the diverse countries of the Asia Pacific region. The key to achieving these goals lay in re-architecting the technology infrastructure that enables the consumer banking business.

IV. REGIONAL CARD CENTRE AS PROTOTYPE OF THE NEW STRATEGY

A significant piece of Citibank's Asian Pacific IT infrastructure that provided the prototype for subsequent consolidation in consumer banking is the Regional Card Centre. The RCC was set up in Singapore in 1989 to support start-up credit card businesses in South East Asia. Country managers whose credit card data processing was to be centralized demanded exacting performance standards from the centre because of its direct impact on their operating performance. Ajit Kanagasundram, who used to run the data centre for Citibank Singapore, was given the mandate to set up and run the centre. He explained the rationale for the centre:

> The purpose of the RCC was to jump-start the credit card businesses in Citibank countries in South East Asia. Setting up the processing infrastructure before offering credit card services in each country would take too long and be too costly for start-up businesses. The time constraint to make the RCC operational also dictated our approach, which was to get the operational software requirements from a couple of lead businesses, in this case, Citibank HongKong and Singapore. Trying to get requirements from all countries would be too time consuming and result in

missed market opportunities. Further, 80% of credit card operational requirements are stipulated by the card associations and were common across countries. We recruited a few staff experienced in credit card operations, used our own production experience, plus onsite consultants to modify the package software, CARDPAC, and got the RCC operational in 8 months.

By 1990, we had reduced the processing cost per credit card by 45% and we were given the mandate to extend our operations to cover the Middle East and North Asia, excluding Hong Kong. By 1994, in the midst of heightened cost consciousness because of corporate financial troubles, our cost per card was down to 32% of the 1989 cost. None of the country managers asked for decentralization of the credit card operations—who wants cost per card to triple overnight?

In 1993, Citibank beat out other regional rivals to become the issuer of affinity Visa and Mastercard for Passages, a joint frequent-flyer program of 15 Asian airlines. Citibank credits its ability to launch and support the cards regionally, enabled by the RCC, as being a key factor for being selected. By 1999, the RCC was processing credit cards for 27 countries—12 countries in Asia, 7 in Central Europe and the Middle East, and 8 in Latin America. The cost economies offered by the RCC made it obvious for countries to join it rather than go on their own. Average costs in 1999 are 40% less than they were 3 years earlier, and it is projected that the marginal cost of adding 5 million cards will be a third of the current average costs. The creation of "starter kits" also means that new countries can be added with relative ease and at far less expense. The decreasing costs of telecommunications and the cost savings from standardizing hardware, software and procedures enable RCC to reap ever increasing economies of scale as each new country joins its fold, and as businesses of member countries grow.

The RCC concept combines both centralization and decentralization ideas to meet specific local business needs and low costs of processing at the same time. The business strategy, marketing, credit evaluation, and customer service for credit cards continue to be decentralized in each country to cater to local market conditions and needs. The front-end data capture and printing of customer statements are also decentralized to each country. What is centralized is the back-end transaction processing and data repository. The control and active management of credit card businesses continue to be with country managers and the business gains are reflected in the financial performance of each country. The RCC provides the technology infrastructure for lowering operational costs, diffusing best practices, and attracting the needed technical talent.

The RCC experience provided the experiential base for subsequent re-architecting of the technology of the consumer bank. The experience and expertise that RCC had built up would be re-positioned to serve the processing requirements of the Asia-Pacific Consumer Bank.

V. RE-ARCHITECTING THE IT INFRASTRUCTURE

The appointment of George DiNardo, as the new Chief Technology Officer signalled the bank's strategic intent to develop a new technology infrastructure for capitalizing the opportunities from rapid economic growth in Asian countries which is expected to continue well into the 21st century. Recipient of **Information Week's** CIO of the Year Award for 1988, DiNardo had been with Mellon Bank in Pittsburgh from 1969 to 1991, and was its executive vice president of their information systems function from 1985 to 1991. Prior to joining Citicorp, he was a consulting partner for Coopers and Lybrand, and Professor of Information Systems at a leading university. He crisply summed up his job portfolio at Citicorp:

My job is to introduce the most advanced technology possible in Asia and I spent 35 years doing that for other banks, Bankers Trust and Mellon Bank. I am truly a bank businessman and a technologist ... I have also been given the responsibility for all re-engineering efforts in Citibank Asia.

According to George DiNardo, the Citibanking vision requires that "a customer going anywhere in the world is able to transact the same way wherever he goes. It is moving to (the concept of) Citibank recognizes you, and relationship manages you. If you have $100,000 with Citibank, you have certain services free, and it will be the same wherever you go.

It's the ability to use the ATM wherever you are."

Moving towards this level of global banking requires that a Citibank branch anywhere in the world have access to the customer's addresses, customary services, and relationships anywhere else in the world. It would have been costly to achieve this with the current decentralized computing structure, where each country in the Asia Pacific has its own host computer and where each country has a different technology platform. It would also be difficult to ensure simultaneous roll-out across countries of new products. Hence, the foundational changes to computing at Citibank Asia Pacific begin with the centralization of processing, and having a uniform backroom platform. The bank standardized on an IBM MVS platform. DiNardo explained the logic of centralization for Citibank Asia:

The old days of having the computer centre next to you are gone. Where should your computer centre be—remote! Now, with fibre, put your console, command centre in your main office, and your big box is remote. Our command centre is here in Singapore . . . The telecommunications are improving enough that we can centralize. The economies of large IBM are important to banking. I have promised that if we regionalize on a new single system, we will get a saving. It will cost $50m to do this, but we will break even in year two, and we should have a $50m running rate cost reduction at the end of year four. We will put the largest IBM box we can get in a centre in Singapore. I have promised a 10-20% computing reduction every year. How am I going to do that? You buy the biggest building, so you can pull any computer in anytime, backup for 100% uptime, 99.9% on-time completion of batch jobs. Therefore you don't need backup all over Asia. You put in all the other countries account processing, and transmit all the rest.

Initially, the major saving will come from avoiding the building of another computer centre in Hong Kong. Savings arise also from having all processing in one site, with only one other hot backup site, as compared to having processing distributed in fourteen countries, with each country having its own backup. Citibank will be leveraging off the networks that are already in place as a result of the regional card centre. Another significant source of savings comes from the centralization of software development.

Citibank is aiming for uniformity in its back-room processing software. Citibank replaced individual country systems that have evolved over time with a $20 million integrated back-office banking applications package from Systematics. The strength of the Systematics package is that is has evolved significantly through its sale to more than 400 banks, and therefore offers many functions and features. It uses a traditional design based on the MVS/CICS/COBOL platform, and has been proven to support high volumes. According to DiNardo, the idea is to not reinvent the wheel by writing yet another in-house back-office processing system, but to take this package and "turn the 2000 Citibank systems professionals loose on innovation . . . its delivery and panache that counts . . . to create reusable modules to be called in through Systematics user exits. Systematics have promised to keep the exits constant through time." The plan also calls for eventual conversion of all other programs to the Systematics format, for example, using the same approach to data modelling, COBOL programming, and naming conventions.

A new Asia-Pacific data center running an IBM ES/9000 model 821 mainframe was set up in Singapore's Science Park on the western part of the island in October 1994. The hot-site backup running an IBM ES/9000 model 500 was located in Singapore's Chai Chee Industrial Park on the eastern part of the island.

The conversion of the Asia Pacific countries to Systematics was completed by the end of 1997. Work then began on Y2k certification. Citibank has one of the more stringent Y2k certification processes in the world, and is estimated to have spent $600m globally over three years on Y2k certification.[14] However, a senior executive noted that Y2k certification was easier and probably less costly in Citibank Asia Pacific because the backend systems had been centralized and standardized prior to the certification process.

VI. BUILDING COMMON FRONTEND SYSTEMS

Running in parallel with the IT infrastructure changes was a re-engineering effort. Peter Mills, then Director of Business Improvement noted that the goal was to:

create common business processes that may result in common frontend systems that are compatible with our back-end platforms. As part of the re-architecting of Citibank's technology infrastructure, we initiated several process re-engineering projects to develop new process templates for Asia-Pacific. For example, we will use the redesigned Australian mortgage process and the new Taiwan auto business process as templates for other countries.

A common thread that emerged from both the re-engineering and infrastructural change efforts is the idea of incorporating best practice. In the area of software development, the emphasis on adopting best practice among the Citibank countries is a guard against the common trap of settling for the lowest common denominator in the process of standardization. The commitment to develop a re-engineering template incorporating the best redesigned processes from each country, for use in developing common systems is another embodiment of this idea. DiNardo explained what is being practised in Citibank Asia Pacific:

The purchase of the Systematics package provides the bank with increased functionality and standardized processing without significant systems development effort. In-house development effort will be focused on strategic products such as those for currency trading, Citiplus, and the SABRE front-end teller and platform systems. The approach to future systems development will no longer be one of letting 'a hundred flowers bloom.' There will no longer be systems development or enhancement only for individual countries. Any country requiring any change needs to convince at least two other countries to support it. Any changes made would then be made for all Citibank countries in Asia. Several countries have now been identified as likely centers of excellence for front-end software development: Taiwan for auto loans processing, Australia for mortgage products, HongKong for personal finance products, India, Philippines and Singapore will become centers for application software development, design, and the generation of high quality code at competitive cost.

The re-engineering of business processes in Singapore provides a glimpse of how Citibank intends to introduce best practices in banking products and service delivery, which would be built into common front-end systems. Citibank has been in Singapore for more than 90 years. It started out as a wholesale bank. The consumer bank business was started later in the 1960s. Being a foreign bank, it is allowed to set up only 3 branches in Singapore. Nonetheless, Citibank has done very well in Singapore. Customer accounts have more than tripled since 1989, largely due to the successful introduction of Citibank's Visa card business. There has been an accompanying ten-fold increase in profit in the same period.

The increase in account volume however, has been accomplished without any major increase in staff or changes in processes. Staff, processes and infrastructure that were originally designed to support about 50,000 accounts, are strained when they have to support an account volume of about 250,000. This has contributed to a drop in customers' perception of service levels. Annual surveys conducted indicated that customer satisfaction has dropped from a high of 90% in 1987 to a low of 65% in 1993. Some departments are experiencing high overtime and employee turnover. A cultural assessment study conducted by consultants confirmed that some employees did not feel valued and trusted. Frontline operations were also paper intensive and perceived to have significant opportunities for improvements. In addition, there was the need to achieve the vision of Citibanking, which required cross-product integration as a basis for relationship banking.

The project was carried out in three phases, 1) building the case for action, 2) design, and 3) implementation. In the first two phases, the consultants worked closely with four Citibankers who were assigned full time to the re-engineering project. After six months, the team had completed phase two and had come up with a list of 28 recommended process changes. Three core processes were identified for change—delivery of services to the customer, marketing and transaction processing. The delivery process included account opening and servicing, credit, and customer problem resolution. The team found that it was encumbered with many hand-offs, a "maker-checker" mindset where transactions had to be checked by someone other than the originating employee, and unclear accountability for problem resolution. The transaction processing process was basically the back-end processing for the transactions originating in the branches. The major observation here was that the processing was fragmented by product or system. The marketing processes were currently also product focused, and there was limited understanding of customer segments and individual customers.

The vision that the team presented included a streamlined front-end delivery process with clear accountability and quick turnaround on customer problem resolution, a unified approach to transaction processing, and segment-focused, cross-product marketing. They felt that the most radical change required would be that of the organizational culture. One aspect of culture manifested in the many "maker-checker" was a legacy of the days when the bank was a wholesale bank, and each transaction value was very high while volume was relatively low. In the retail bank business, the high volume and low individual value of transactions required a different mindset. Other aspects of Citibank culture that would needed to change included the emphasis and the incentive system that rewarded product innovation and individuality. The process changes required a culture that focused more on relationships with customers and on team efforts.

The team also set detailed targets for each of the core processes. Among the many set for the delivery processes, examples are a rise in the percentage of customers who were highly satisfied from 64% to 80%, an increase in the percentage of customers served within 5 minutes from 71% to 80%, and improved transaction processing accuracy from 2 errors per 5000 transactions to 1 error per 5000 transactions. Detailed targets for productivity and cost improvements were also set. These targets were in effect also a list of measures that would be used to evaluate each process on a recurring basis.

In phase three, three implementation teams—service delivery, operations, and product development and marketing—involving many more employees were formed. Each team was headed by the vice-president in charge of the function. The role of the consultants in phase three was scaled back. Some resistance was encountered to the recommended changes. George DiNardo and Peter Mills addressed the problem of resistance by having discussions with key stakeholders of the processes to be re-

engineered, and by focusing on a number of projects. Before the end of the first year, the consultants had been phased out. The Citibank implementation teams were driving their own implementation.

A major part of implementation was to develop and implement the information systems needed to support the reengineered processes. One resulting new system is SABRE (Strategic Asia Pacific Branch Retail Environment). SABRE consists of two complementary subsystems: SABRE I is at the teller level, and provides automated support for signature verification, paperless teller transactions, and Citicard transactions. SABRE II includes the phone banking systems, together with facilities for telemarketing and cross-product marketing at the branches. The bank developed the SABRE system in-house, because it considers this to be a strategic product. SABRE I has been a great success and is considered to be best of breed. Today, the SABRE platform itself is of strategic importance as a vehicle to deliver Citibanking to customers, and to enable cross selling of multiple products to customers.

VII. MANAGING CHANGE

The changes to the IT architecture and business processes are not trivial. George DiNardo, as Chief Technology Officer, was a catalyst for change and his ability to communicate convincingly with senior officers of the bank in corporate headquarters and in Asia was an important asset. He brought a different perspective to technology management, starting from the premise that the IT infrastructure had to be standardized to obtain the maximum benefit for the bank. Countries wanting to be different will have to justify it, quite a change from the days when country managers decided the types of technology they wanted for each country.

The RCC experience provides a useful model for the current consumer bank consolidation. The in-depth technical expertise gained from running a regional data centre would be directly relevant to the new infrastructure that Citibank is putting in place for Consumer Banking. Not surprisingly, Ajit was asked to set up and run the data centre for the new Asian Pacific Consumer Banking technology infrastructure. However, the new infrastructure is more than just scaling up to process more transactions. The business of Citibanking in Global Consumer Banking is more diverse and complex than cards, and

requires the internalization of many business parameters in developing software to support back-end banking operations. Correspondingly, the business impact is also far greater. Citibank, as an American bank operating in Asia, is subjected to restrictions on the number of branches allowed in each country. The reliance on an electronic interface with customers and for an electronic channel for delivery of banking services is significantly higher than many local banks. Citibank sees the new technological infrastructure as a key enabler for flexibility in its product and service offerings throughout Asia at a competitive cost.

The conversion to a new technology infrastructure at Citibank Asia Pacific meant some loss of control over computing for the Citibank country managers. DiNardo felt that there had not been serious opposition to the changes, although country managers were understandably "nervous" about the sweeping changes. He stated:

> It's an idea whose time has come. The Asia Pacific high profit margin must be maintained! They all know this. They know the value of what we're doing. Computer costs will be down for them, it will affect their bottom line. There is no longer any desire for the sophisticated manager to have his/her own mainframe computer. They know that I have done it 700 times already. No one objects to the logic of the idea. We will insist on a post implementation audit. The country managers in Asia did see that to survive the next 10 years something like this is necessary. It's all about customer service.

However, it is the level of service and support from the center that country managers are concerned about. The standardization and centralization strategy obviously restricted flexibility in country operations. It was adopted consciously and the gain in integrated customer service and economies of scale is substantial. Nonetheless, the issue of responsiveness to local needs is unlikely to go away, and there are concerns about how priorities for enhancements will be handled if there are not enough resources and capacity to meet requests in a timely manner. In 1999, George DiNardo retired from Citibank. Without his forceful personality to enforce standardization, countries' requests for customization will be more difficult to resist.

VIII. NEW CHALLENGES: MERGER AND THE INTERNET

By 1998, when Citicorp merged with Travelers, Citibank Asia Pacific had largely completed its centralization of back-end processing for consumer banking. The other regions began a little later, but had also been centralizing their IT infrastructure for several years. At the time of the merger, Citicorp was three quarters of the way through a huge back-office restructuring effort, under Mary Taylor, head of Citibank's operations and technology division. She took re-structuring one step further, pulling together the operations and technology for the Corporate and Consumer sides of the bank. Today, Citibank's data centers have gone from 66 to 12 worldwide. Ms Taylor notes that:

> The consumer bank handles huge volumes of transactions that are of much smaller value. The corporate bank handles fewer transactions but with large dollar value. There are real synergies you can take advantage of because you can add more transactions without really impacting capacity.[15]

Outside of the U.S., the main data centers are now in Dublin, London, Singapore, Hong Kong and Sydney, and together serve over a hundred countries.

The merger with the Travelers Group posed another set of challenges to the bank's infrastructure. The merger offered the opportunity of providing a financial services supermarket to customers. However, to do so requires integration of information systems, customer databases, product lines, and multiple transaction types.[16] The integration options that are open to Citigroup are broadly: "total integration of platforms, servers, risk management and front and back-office operations—or instead establish a data warehouse for customer information, accessed by object-oriented middleware."[17] The latter option is more expedient and avoids the need for risky reengineering of business processes. However, total system integration offers more effective cross selling of products and risk management. The decisions made are likely to have implications for the IT infrastructure in the Asia Pacific given the bank's desire for increasing standardization globally.

The other global trend that affects Citibank Asia Pacific is the rise of Internet banking. E-banking offers some unique op-

portunities and threats to established banks. For example, Internet transactions costs about one-tenth of traditional bank counter transactions, according to William Lo, Chief Executive of Citibank Hong Kong's consumer banking operations.[18] Citibank, with its long tradition of technology-enabled banking initiatives appears well placed to take advantage of the Internet. However, it has not been smooth sailing.

Citigroup has spent about $400m on e-banking, more than other large banks.[19] In 1999, Citigroup recorded a $172m net loss in e-banking.[20] Citigroup's biggest consumer banking initiatives are either in test phase, or have only been soft-launched. Citi f/i, (f/i stands for financial interactive) rolled out quietly in mid-1999, and will not be widely marketed yet.[21] There are those who believe that Internet banking will take off when the most common devices for connecting to the Web are mobile phones. This may be particularly true in Asia where mobile phone ownership is much higher than PC ownership. In 1999, a trial service began in Singapore with carrier Mobile One to let users perform retail banking functions using cell phones. The long-term goal is to allow customers to switch easily among banking, credit card, insurance and brokerage services using the cell phone.[22]

In contrast to retail e-banking initiatives, Citibank's corporate e-banking initiatives appear to be more well received. In 1999, Citibank launched a well-regarded small-business site—Bizzed.com, which is expected to make a profit in two years.[23] In May 1999, Citibank also launched a B to B E-commerce system—Citibank Commerce—that lets customers order products, monitor order status, complete settlement and reconciliation processes. Interestingly, it was first made available in the Asia pacific region.[24] It targets 8000 Citibank corporate customers in the Asia Pacific region, and will be introduced to the US, Europe and Latin America later in 2000.[25] The service has its competitors even in the region. For example, the Singapore government and Visa International recently launched an online business-to-business trading network for companies and financial institutions in Singapore, called the Commerce Exchange.

The rise of Internet banking also has strong implications for the bank's IT infrastructure. Citicorp is converting its technology platforms to make them more web-compatible. For example, its internal data networks are being converted worldwide to

TCP/IP, with the help of AT&T. E-Citi, Citigroup's Internet banking innovation group, is developing middleware that links the mainframe environment to the Web architecture.[26] At present, most of the core products will remain on mainframes, but they will increasingly be linked to web-based front-ends. Internet based direct banking initiatives are already using different core banking systems. Sanchez, a client-server based core banking system, is being used to support Citi f/i. Citibank is also considering Sanchez as "part of an ongoing effort to standardize operations and processes across the bank's various consumer businesses."[27] To that end, all four of Citibank's four regional consumer banking operations have the option to independently acquire Sanchez for their core retail banking system. Sanchez's potential advantages compared to mainframe core retail banking systems such as Systematics, are responsiveness to time-to-market demands, and channel integration requirements. Questions about scalability of client-server systems to meet traditional retail banking volumes however remain.

While Citibank Asia Pacific has managed the transition to centralized back-end processing, it continues to face new challenges from global trends in bank mergers and Internet banking. Virtual banks without brick and mortar compete with established banks and have the advantage of lower overheads, greater agility and speed of response to the market. Non-bank companies like AOL and Microsoft are also offering financial services, and compete on the pervasiveness of their customer reach, as well as the large set of potentially complementary products and services. Sunil Sreenivasan, Chief Executive of Citibank Singapore and clearly recognizes the implications for Citibank:

> In the future, the list of competitors in financial services will include unfamiliar names such as telcos, power companies and dot-com companies. What is frightening to us traditionalists is that we will have to canniblize our own products in order to avoid others cannibalizing those very same products. Or put it more extremely, we may in certain respects need to commit suicide in order to survive.[28]

Clearly, the competitive environment will be very different in the future. Will the economics of large-scale, centralized computing hold sway? To what extent will the major infrastructural changes made in the 1990s be a help or a hindrance to the next wave of changes brought on by the changing business environment?

Source: From Boon Siong Neo and Christina Soh, Information Management Research Center (IMARC), Nanyang Business School, Nanyang Technological University, Singapore. Reprinted by permission.

[1] All financial figures are in US$ unless otherwise stated.

[2] "Legacy Systems Under Strain," US Banker, May 1998, p 103-107.

[3] Brand, A., Weill, P., Soh, C. and Periasamy, "Citibank—Asia Pacific: Positioning IT as a Strategic Resource," Melbourne Business School Case Study, 1999.

[4] Ibid.

[5] Citigroup Annual Report 1998, p 9.

[6] Ibid.

[7] Clark, D., "Megadeal Challenges Citicorp to Meld Systems Successfully," American Banker Online, April 9, 1998. http://www.americanbanker

[8] Flanigan, J., "Citigroup as Barometer and Business Model," LA Times, January 23, 2000, http://www.latimes.com:80/

[9] "Thinking Globally, Acting Locally," The China Business Review, May-June, 1993, pp. 23-25.

[10] Brand, A., Weill, P., Soh, C. and Periasamy, "Citibank—Asia Pacific: Positioning IT as a Strategic Resource," Melbourne Business School Case Study, 1999.

[11] Citicorp Annual Report 1998, p 13.

[12] Citigroup press release, April 19, 1999. http://www.citi.com/citigroup/pr/news/pr95.htm

[13] TimesNet Asia, http://web3.asia1.com.sg/timesnet/data/ab/docs/ab1406.html

[14] Clark, D., "Megadeal Challenges Citicorp to Meld Systems Successfully," American Banker Online, April 9, 1998. http://www.americanbanker.

[15] Power, C., "Citibank Exec Finishing a Systems Harnessing," American Banker, October 27, 1998. http://www.americanbanker.

[16] Schmerken, I., "The Big Gamble: Mergers and Technology," WST Online Magazine, July 1998. http://www.wstonline.com/mfwt

[17] Helland, E., "Can Citigroup Reign in Citicorp's Decentralized IT Strategy?", WST Online Magazine, July 1998. http://www.wstonline.com/mfwt

[18] Bickers, C., "Net Returns," Far Eastern Economic Review Interactive Edition, May 6, 1999.

[19] Beckett, P. "Citigroup Struggles to Gain Momentum in New Business," The Wall Street Journal, January 21, 2000.

[20] Flanigan, J., "Citigroup as Barometer and Business Model," LA Times, January 23, 2000, http://www.latimes.com:80/

[21] "E-Citi's Soft Launch Raises Eyebrows," Future Banker, November 1999, http://www.thebankingchannel.com/fb/fbnov99-5

[22] Violino, B., "Banking on E-Business" Information Week Online, May 3 1999. http://www.informationweek.com/

[23] Beckett, P. "Citigroup Struggles to Gain Momentum in New Business," The Wall Street Journal, January 21, 2000.

[24] Violino, B., "Banking on E-Business" Information Week Online, May 3 1999. http://www.informationweek.com/

[25] "Cyberspace Race," CitiCOmerce.com: In the News, http://www.citibank.com/singapore

[26] Violino, B., "Banking on E-Business," Information Week Online, May 3 1999. http://www.informationweek.com/

[27] Costanzo, C., "Software Deal May Signal End of Citi's Mainframes," American Banker Online, July 16, 1999. http://www.americanbanker.

[28] Sunil Sreenivasan, "Banking in a Brave New World," The Business Times, February 2, 2000.

CASE STUDY QUESTIONS

1. What business strategy has Citicorp been pursuing in Asia?

2. Evaluate Citibank's Asia-Pacific information technology (IT) infrastructure and systems in light of this strategy. How well do they support it?

3. How well do Citibank's infrastructural changes made in the 1990's support the merger with Travelers Group and Citigroup's efforts to deal with the impact of the Internet on the banking and financial services industries? What management, organization, and technology issues will Citibank need to address?

International Case Study

CASE STUDY 5: Dell Direct in Europe: Delighting the Customer with Every Order

Andrew Boynton, Donald A. Marchand, and Janet Shaner,
International Institute for Management Development (Switzerland)

Monday. 2:00. Dell® representatives from marketing, sales, manufacturing, engineering, and service hustled to the conference room for their weekly business review meeting. The team meets weekly to identify proactively new opportunities and resolve problems. For example, the previous week's meeting focused on the transition management plan for the new Intel chip. Dell had to execute the new chip introduction flawlessly. Everything had to be coordinated to ship product right the first time.

On this Monday, Jan Gesmar-Larsen, president of Dell Europe, attended the meeting to raise a special concern.

Ladies and Gentlemen, yet another of our leading competitors has announced that it is going direct. For now we lead the industry, but we can't stand still. Today I challenge you to question everything about our direct model. Can our competitors copy it? Can we sustain the process improvements that have reduced costs and improved velocity? Will customers continue to buy direct and use the Internet? What opportunities do we have to grow the business? Where is our market going and how should Dell play?

These are important strategic questions. We need everyone's input and creativity to keep Dell on top. I want your feedback at next week's business review meeting. We have to work together to stay ahead of our competition.

DELL EUROPE: BUILDING THE CUSTOMER RELATIONSHIP

Michael Dell's mission for Dell is:

To be the most successful company in the world at delivering the best customer experience in the markets we serve.

From 1995–1999, Dell grew at 51% annually in sales and 77% annually in net income. For the year ended January 1999,

Exhibit 1

Dell Financial Performance
(Year end 29 January 1999, $ million)

	1995	1996	1997	1998	1999	Five year CAGR
Sales	3,475	5,296	7,759	12,327	18,243	51%
Operating Income	249	377	714	1,316	2,046	69%
Net Income	149	272	518	944	1,460	77%
Total Assets	1,594	2,148	2,993	4,268	6,877	44%
Shareholder's Equity	652	973	806	1,293	2,321	37%
Operating Margin %	7.2%	7.1%	9.2%	10.7%	11.2%	
Net ROS %	4.3%	5.1%	6.7%	7.7%	8.0%	
ROA %	9%	13%	17%	22%	21%	
ROE %	23%	28%	64%	73%	63%	

Geographical Sales Distribution (1999)

	Sales	% of Sales
Americas	12,405	68%
Europe	4,743	26%
Asia-Pacific and Japan	1,095	6%
Consolidated	18,243	100%

Source: Dell Computer Corporation, 1999 Annual Report.

Dell achieved 21% return on assets and 8% return on sales. (Refer to Exhibit 1 for Dell financial performance and Exhibit 2 for industry comparisons.)

In Europe, the Middle East and Africa (EMEA), Dell sells direct in 18 countries from a manufacturing and support base in Limerick, Ireland. Dell Europe had increased its overall European unit market share to 9.8% at the end of Q1 FY00, compared to Compaq (18.5%), IBM (9.6%), and Siemens (6.3%).

Product Line Focused on Desktops, Laptops, Servers

These outstanding financial results were generated from a focused product line. Dell custom tailors its Dell Dimension™, Optiplex®, and Dell Precision™ WorkStation desktop computers, its Latitude® and Inspiron® notebook computers, its PowerVault™ storage systems, and its PowerEdge™ servers to meet exact customer specifications.

Dell's competitive advantage is in selling the latest technology direct to customers, building it to customer order, and delivering the highest quality product most quickly at the lowest cost. The Dell product offering includes the complete package from order to delivery.

Exhibit 2

Competitor Financial Comparisons
($ million)

Financial Results	Dell	Compaq	Hewlett-Packard	Gateway
Year End	29 Jan 1999	31 Dec 1998	31 Oct 1998	31 Dec 1998
Sales	18,243	31,169	47,061	7,468
EBIT	2,046	(2,662)	3,841	494
EBIT/Sales	11.2%	(8.5%)	8.2%	6.6%
EBIT Return on Assets	29.8%	(11.5%)	11.4%	17.1%
Inventory Turnover	56	12	4	28
Cash Flow from Operations	2,436	644	5,442	908
Cash Flow as % of Sales	13%	2%	12%	12%

Source: Corporate Annual Reports.

Every customer wants service, support, and reliability. They want a product that works.[1]

Customer Segmentation Based on Unique Customer Needs

Dell Europe segments its customers into five groups: global customers, large corporate businesses, the preferred account division (medium-sized businesses), public sector (government, local government, health, education and defense), and home and small businesses. (In contrast, Dell US segments its customer base into twelve groups.) Dell creates new customer segments when the sales volume grows large enough to support them without creating a "layered bureaucracy."

> It's a customer-oriented company. Michael drives that. Seventy percent of the people outside of the factory touch the customer directly.[2]

Global Customers

Global customers are large and medium-sized businesses that need the same equipment and the same image on every computer screen around the world. Specifically, global customers demand consistent products, consistent prices, consistent service, and global account managers who can make things happen in other sales territories.

Selling direct gives Dell a big advantage in winning and retaining business with these customers because Dell has the capability to respond seamlessly worldwide. Dell's account team matches the customer's organisation structure. For example, if a customer makes central buying decisions, the account team is centralised. If a customer makes regional buying decisions, each region is serviced by a key account representative and coordinated by the global account manager. Account reps are supported by Dell's engineering team which works closely with the customer's information team to get the equipment operating to customer specifications.

Large Businesses (> 5,000 employees)

Dell salespeople build relationships with the information technology (IT) departments in large companies to provide products built for each customer's needs. Corporate customers often visit Dell's production facility to see the direct model in action. Dell's Premier Pages™ (individually customised Internet pages) and services like

asset tagging, leasing, and Dell Plus, where Dell can integrate customer-specific hardware and pre-load images and software in an ISO environment, are of vital importance to these accounts.

Preferred Account Division (PAD), (500–5,000 employees)

PAD customers are medium-sized businesses, and Dell's sales force focuses on customer acquisition and specific customer projects. Customers leverage telephone and Internet-based sales and support more extensively than large customers, but they can also receive the same value added services such as Dell Plus, Premier Pages, or Business Care Plus. Traditionally these businesses would have purchased competitors' products through local dealers, giving Dell a unique competitive advantage in the product range and in the customer service it provided.

Public Sector

The public sector division focuses on servicing the needs of government, local government, health, education and defense. Public sector business is largely determined by the submission of a tender document and is extremely price sensitive. Again, customers in this category use the telephone and Premier pages, but the larger government accounts do meet their account managers frequently. Within public sector, individual teams concentrate on government, local government, health, education, and defense as the requirements are different for each segment.

Small Businesses and Home Users (< 500 employees)

Smaller customers want value for money, presale advice, product-repair service, and help-desk support. Dell's services include its Internet site (available 24 hours a day, 7 days a week, covering 17 countries, in multiple languages) where customers can compare prices, see the latest products, and purchase systems in seconds. Customers can also track their order status and get service support.

Alternatively, customers (depending on their location) can order directly over the telephone from call centres in Dublin, Ireland; Montpellier, France; Copenhagen, Denmark; Amsterdam, The Netherlands; and Längen, Germany. A customer call first goes to "Qualifying," where trained representatives gather customer information and then direct the call to the appropriate sales representative according to

customer size. The qualifier transfers the call, and the salesperson answers with, for example, "Hello, Mrs. Hilliard, what can I help you with today?" The sales representative can access the complete history of the customer's account including details about previous information requests, orders, and service issues. On a new sales call, each rep uses a predefined eight-minute sales script to ensure that each customer is ordering the right product for his or her needs. A customer may be responding to a targeted advertisement for a specific system package or to a positive review featured in a magazine, but it is the responsibility of the rep to direct the customer to the right product configuration to fit his exact needs.

> It's all about driving revenue. We do this by targeted print and direct mail campaigns to stimulate individual customer demand. Then we follow through by spending time with customers on the phone to identify their unique needs and selling them the right product.[3]

Sales representatives are measured on sales volume and product mix. They track up-to-the-minute goal progress from pie charts on their computer screens. Customer questions can be answered easily from Dell help screens. Ultimately, Dell's database makes every rep knowledgeable and professional in communications with customers.

Teams Mirror the Supply/Demand Chain

Dell hires people who have a constructive attitude, are flexible, can grow with the company, and can adapt in a rapidly changing environment. For sales personnel, it is important to select people who like to be rewarded for performance. Dell's flat structure is organised functionally, but each customer segment has its own product engineering, marketing, sales and service group to design and support products for its unique needs. Both successes and failures are shared freely within the organisation, and functional areas communicate across customer lines instead of acting as silos hoarding information.

Teams are encouraged to innovate, try new ideas, take risks, and drive change to make the best product for the customer. They are constantly looking for new product opportunities and new ways to stay ahead of the competition.

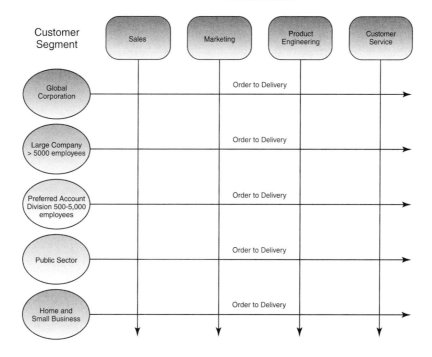

Functional Area

If I have an idea on how to improve the operation, I suggest it to my supervisor, we work out the economics, and then decide to do it or not. My supervisor wants to hear my ideas.[4]

At the same time, Dell encourages its people to identify mistakes and propose solutions. Failures offer opportunities to learn instead of to "shoot messengers."

BUILDING THE CUSTOMER ORDER

Build to order sums up everything about Dell.[5]
Every order has a home before we build it.[6]

Irish Production Facilities

Dell manufactures its European products in one of three plants in Limerick, Ireland. Ireland has an advanced telecommunication infrastructure, strong governmental support, and world-class suppliers. In addition, the local university in Limerick produces top-quality graduates specialising in computer science and engineering. The Irish population have a young profile (50% under age 25) and are highly educated, and the country wants to grow.

Dell purchased its first production facility in Limerick from Atari and hired experienced computer executives who wanted to do things right.

We didn't want to make the same fundamental errors experienced in other companies. Dell offered the opportunity to correct and improve upon previous manufacturing experiences.[7]

Assembling the Product Direct to Order

The foundation for Dell's business model is the customer, and the physical link between the customer and manufacturing is the order. The company builds to order—lot size one—instead of to forecast. The only inventory on the plant floor is product in "staging," waiting for the rest of the order to come off the assembly line so the order can be shipped complete. Low inventory levels reduce Dell's costs and increase its efficiency, thus driving profits. It also means that Dell can always introduce the latest technology fast and does not have obsolete inventory to get rid of.

Dell processes customer orders the way a baker makes bread: **Today's bread today.** For Dell, that means: **Today's orders today.** Dell downloads orders throughout the day, schedules them through the production line, produces them, and loads the finished product directly onto trucks. The trucks loaded with computers designated for the customer's country go via the hub to collect monitors, speakers, and other peripheral parts, and then the complete order is delivered to the customer's door within four days in Europe.

Supplier and Delivery Partners Hold Inventory for Just-in-Time Assembly

In Europe, Dell maintains over 200 suppliers for over 2,000 component parts. For each component, Dell selects a few high-performing companies (i.e., Intel processors, Sony monitors, and Logitech mouses) and builds strategic alliances with them. Dell shares order and inventory information freely with them through integrated computer systems and personal communication. Dell's suppliers store inventory in one of two Limerick hubs located within five kilometres of Dell's factories.

Suppliers maintain pre-defined stock levels based on Dell's sales forecasts and buffer requirements of approximately 8 to 10 days. Suppliers own the inventory until it is shipped to Dell. When demand exceeds forecast or when specific problems arise, Dell asks its suppliers to "row in and cooperate" to keep production flowing.

Suppliers find that the real-time information sharing allows them to manage inventory more effectively. In addition, Dell is often the first to communicate a component quality problem because it ships within five days of assembly and can get reports of issues in the field directly from customers.

For delivery, Dell works with companies such as Walsh Western and UPS. The Dell-approved carriers' systems are linked to Dell's customer service system and automatically update the shipping status based on the Dell order number and the shipping label barcode. When a customer calls Dell's customer care department or checks the order status on the Internet, Dell can tell the customer where his order is, no matter which supplier has physical possession of the product at the time.

KEEPING THE CUSTOMER AFTER THE SALE

Calling Technical Support

All customers who need service call Dell's service hotline. A Dell technical service representative answers, pulls up the customer's order on the computer, and tries to diagnose and solve the problem (90% are solved over the phone.) The Internet, Intranet, online help screens and diagrams of the customer's equipment help reps do their job professionally and effectively.

Dell works with Wang and Unisys to provide actual repair service for the remaining 10% of calls. Dell notifies these companies when service is required, and a Wang or Unisys engineer is dispatched within the contractual service period. At the same time, necessary parts are dispatched from Dell regional logistics centres. Dell maintains responsibility for the quality and speed of customer service. When the customer's problem is solved, the Wang or Unisys engineer calls Dell's service hotline to close the loop on the customer record.

The effectiveness of Dell's support service shows in customer repurchase rates. Customers who have no service problems buy from Dell again 86% of the time. This drops to 46% when customers have unresolved service problems. However, the re-purchase rate for customers who experience problems but have them resolved is 96%!

Performance Measurements Reinforce the Service Mission

Employee bonus and profit sharing incentives are tied to quality metrics such as on-time delivery and after-sales service. In addition, each employee has financial measurements tailored to his/her specific responsibilities including asset velocity, "cost per box," sales/product mix, days inventory in the field, and days receivable and payable. Employees monitor their impact on these metrics on an ongoing basis. For example, the marketing department calculates the ROI[8] for each advertisement and mailing, and purchasing managers figure out the cost of unsold inventory.

> We spent 15 months educating people about return on invested capital, convincing them they could impact our future.[9]

THE CHALLENGE: CAN DELL "AMAZON" OR BE "AMAZONED"?

One week following the Monday meeting, Gesmar-Larsen again was leading the business review meeting. New developments were occurring weekly. Headlines included:

> "Dell and Amazon.com Announce Online Agreement"
> "Dell Launches Gigabuys.com Online Superstore"
> "IBM and Dell Unveil $16 billion IT Swap Deal"

Larsen started the meeting.

> Ladies and gentlemen, as I said last week, everyone is trying to copy our direct model. We must find ways to stay ahead. Just to give you an example, I read an article over the weekend describing a new verb, "to Amazon," as in "to Amazon a market." The article commented that more and more industries present opportunities to sell direct, especially over the Internet.[10] I want Dell to "Amazon" markets and not be "Amazoned."

Since that meeting another new verb has been introduced into the language: "to Dell." The Wall Street Journal Europe reported that the chairman of Benchmarking Partners Inc. told a business executive Internet think-tank meeting recently that "You want to be the Deller rather than the Dellee of your industry."

CASE STUDY QUESTIONS

1. Analyze Dell Computer Corporation using the competitive forces and value chain models.

2. What is Dell's business model and business strategy? How do its information systems support its strategy? How is this strategy implemented in Europe?

3. Identify and describe some of the business processes that provide Dell with competitive advantage.

4. Is Dell's competitive advantage sustainable? Explain your answer.

*This case was prepared by Research Associate Janet Shaner under the supervision of Professors Andrew Boynton and Donald A. Marchand as a basis for class discussion rather than to illustrate either effective or ineffective handling of a business situation. Copyright © 1999 by **IMD**—International Institute for Management Development, Lausanne, Switzerland. Not to be used or reproduced without written permission directly from **IMD**. Dell Computer Corporation's copyrighted material used herein is the exclusive property of Dell with all rights reserved. Dell and the Dell logo, OptiPlex, Latitude, Inspiron are registered trademarks and Dell Dimension, Dell Precision, PowerEdge and PowerVault and Premier Pages are trademarks of Dell Computer Corporation.

[1] Gerry Clarke, European strategic distribution manager, Dell Products Europe.
[2] Nike Pike, vice president, service marketing, Dell Products Europe.
[3] Dell customer service representative.
[4] Dell process engineer.
[5] Gerry Clarke.
[6] Annette Condon, product public relations manager, Dell UK and Ireland.
[7] Gerry Clarke.
[8] ROI = return on investment. Net profit/total assets.
[9] (CFO Thomas Meredith,) McWilliams, Gary. "Whirlwind on the Web." **Business Week.** 7 April 1997: 53.
[10] Corcoran, Elizabeth. "Amazoned!" **Forbes Global Business & Finance.** 22 March 1999: 25.

References

CHAPTER 1

Ackoff, R. L. "Management Misinformation System." *Management Science* 14, no. 4 (December 1967), B140–B116.

Allen, Brandt R., and **Andrew C. Boynton.** "Information Architecture: In Search of Efficient Flexibility." *MIS Quarterly* 15, no. 4 (December 1991).

Anthony, R. N. *Planning and Control Systems: A Framework for Analysis.* Cambridge, MA: Harvard University Press (1965).

Applegate, Lynda, and **Janice Gogan.** "Electronic Commerce: Trends and Opportunities." Harvard Business School, 9-196-006 (October 6, 1995).

Applegate, Lynda M., Clyde W. Holsapple, Ravi Kalakota, Franz J. Radermacher, and **Andrew B. Whinston.** "Electronic Commerce: Building Blocks of New Business Opportunity." *Journal of Organizational Computing and Electronic Commerce* 6, no. 1 (1996).

Bakos, J. Yannis. "A Strategic Analysis of Electronic Marketplaces." *MIS Quarterly* 15, no. 3 (September 1991).

Barrett, Stephanie S. "Strategic Alternatives and Interorganizational System Implementations: An Overview." *Journal of Management Information Systems* (Winter 1986–1987).

Benjamin, Robert, and **Rolf Wigand.** "Electronic Markets and Virtual Value Chains on the Information Superhighway." *Sloan Management Review* (Winter 1995).

Brynjolfsson, E. T., T. W. Malone, V. Gurbaxani, and **A. Kambil.** "Does Information Technology Lead to Smaller Firms?" *Management Science* 40, no. 12 (1994).

Davis, Gordon B., and **Margrethe H. Olson.** *Management Information Systems: Conceptual Foundations, Structure, and Development,* 2nd ed. New York: McGraw-Hill (1985).

Deans, Candace P., and **Michael J. Kane.** *International Dimensions of Information Systems and Technology.* Boston, MA: PWS-Kent (1992).

DeSanctis, Geraldine and **Peter Monge.** "Communication Processes for Virtual Organizations." *Organization Science* 10, no. 6 (November–December 1999).

Engler, Natalie. "Small but Nimble." *Information Week* (January 18, 1999).

Fedorowicz, Jane, and **Benn Konsynski.** "Organization Support Systems: Bridging Business and Decision Processes." *Journal of Management Information Systems* 8, no. 4 (Spring 1992).

Feeny, David E., and **Leslie P. Willcocks.** "Core IS Capabilities for Exploiting Information Technology." *Sloan Management Review* 39, no. 3 (Spring 1998).

Gallupe, R. Brent. "Images of Information Systems in the Early 21st Century." *Communications of the Association for Information Systems* 3, no. 3 (February 2000).

Gilmore, James H., and **B. Joseph Pine, II.** "The Four Faces of Mass Customization." *Harvard Business Review* (January–February 1997).

Gorry, G. A., and **M. S. Scott Morton.** "A Framework for Management Information Systems." *Sloan Management Review* 13, no. 1 (1971).

Hardwick, Martin, and **Richard Bolton.** "The Industrial Virtual Enterprise." *Communications of the ACM* 40, no. 9 (September 1997).

Johnston, Russell, and **Michael J. Vitale.** "Creating Competitive Advantage with Interorganizational Information Systems." *MIS Quarterly* 12, no. 2 (June 1988).

Joy, Bill. "Design for the Digital Revolution." *Fortune* (March 6, 2000).

Keen, Peter G. W. *Shaping the Future: Business Design Through Information Technology.* Cambridge, MA: Harvard Business School Press (1991).

King, John. "Centralized vs. Decentralized Computing: Organizational Considerations and Management Options." *Computing Surveys* (October 1984).

Kling, Rob, and **William H. Dutton.** "The Computer Package: Dynamic Complexity." In *Computers and Politics,* edited by James Danziger, William H. Dutton, Rob Kling, and Kenneth Kraemer. New York: Columbia University Press (1982).

Laudon, Kenneth C. "A General Model for Understanding the Relationship Between Information Technology and Organizations." Working paper, Center for Research on Information Systems, New York University (1989).

Leonard-Barton, Dorothy. *Wellsprings of Knowledge.* Boston, MA: Harvard Business School Press (1995).

Liker, Jeffrey K., David B. Roitman, and **Ethel Roskies.** "Changing Everything All at Once: Work Life and Technological Change." *Sloan Management Review* (Summer 1987).

Malone, T. W., and **J. F. Rockart.** "Computers, Networks, and the Corporation." *Scientific American* 265, no. 3 (September 1991).

Malone, Thomas W., JoAnne Yates, and **Robert I. Benjamin.** "Electronic Markets and Electronic Hierarchies." *Communications of the ACM* (June 1987).

——— . "The Logic of Electronic Markets." *Harvard Business Review* (May–June 1989).

McFarlan, F. Warren, James L. McKenney, and Philip Pyburn. "The Information Archipelago—Plotting a Course." *Harvard Business Review* (January–February 1983).

———. "Governing the New World." *Harvard Business Review* (July–August 1983).

McKenney, James L., and F. Warren McFarlan. "The Information Archipelago—Maps and Bridges." *Harvard Business Review* (September–October 1982).

Orlikowski, Wanda J., and Jack J. Baroudi. "Studying Information Technology in Organizations: Research Approaches and Assumptions." *Information Systems Research* 2, no. 1 (March 1991).

Quinn, James Brian. "Strategic Outsourcing: Leveraging Knowledge Capabilities." *Sloan Management Review* 40, no. 4 (Summer 1999).

Rayport, J. F., and J. J. Sviokla. "Managing in the Marketspace." *Harvard Business Review* (November–December 1994).

Roche, Edward M. "Planning for Competitive Use of Information Technology in Multinational Corporations." AIB UK Region, Brighton Polytechnic, Brighton, UK, Conference Paper (March 1992). Edward M. Roche, W. Paul Stillman School of Business, Seton Hall University.

Rockart, John F., and James E. Short. "IT in the 1990s: Managing Organizational Interdependence." *Sloan Management Review* 30, no. 2 (Winter 1989).

Scott Morton, Michael, ed. *The Corporation in the 1990s*. New York: Oxford University Press (1991).

Tornatsky, Louis G., J. D. Eveland, Myles G. Boylan, W. A. Hertzner, E. C. Johnson, D. Roitman, and J. Schneider. "The Process of Technological Innovation: Reviewing the Literature." Washington, DC: National Science Foundation (1983).

Tuomi, Ilkka. "Data Is More Than Knowledge." *Journal of Management Information Systems* 16, no. 3 (Winter 1999–2000).

Weill, Peter, and Marianne Broadbent. *Leveraging the New Infrastructure*. Cambridge, MA: Harvard Business School Press (1998).

———. "Management by Maxim: How Business and IT Managers Can Create IT Infrastructures," *Sloan Management Review* (Spring 1997).

CHAPTER 2

Allen, Brandt R., and Andrew C. Boynton. "Information Architecture: In Search of Efficient Flexibility." *MIS Quarterly* 15, no. 4 (December 1991).

Anthony, R. N. *Planning and Control Systems: A Framework for Analysis*. Cambridge, MA: Harvard University Press (1965).

Bakos, J. Yannis, and Michael E. Treacy. "Information Technology and Corporate Strategy: A Research Perspective." *MIS Quarterly* (June 1986).

Beath, Cynthia Mathis, and Blake Ives. "Competitive Information Systems in Support of Pricing." *MIS Quarterly* (March 1986).

Bensaou, M. "Portfolios of Buyer-Supplier Relationships. " *Sloan Management Review* 40, no. 4 (Summer 1999).

Berry, Leonard L., and A. Parasuraman. "Listening to the Customer—the Concept of a Service-Quality Information System." *Sloan Management Review* (Spring 1997).

Bower, Joseph L., and Thomas M. Hout. "Fast-Cycle Capability for Competitive Power." *Harvard Business Review* (November–December 1988).

Caldwell, Bruce. "A Cure for Hospital Woes." *Information Week* (September 9, 1991).

Cash, J. I., and Benn R. Konsynski. "IS Redraws Competitive Boundaries." *Harvard Business Review* (March–April 1985).

Chan, Yolande E., Sid L. Huff, Donald W. Barclay, and Duncan G. Copeland. "Business Strategic Orientation, Information Systems Strategic Orientation, and Strategic Alignment." *Information Systems Research* 8, no. 2 (June 1997).

Clemons, Eric K. "Evaluation of Strategic Investments in Information Technology." *Communications of the ACM* (January 1991).

Clemons, Eric K., and Bruce W. Weber. "Segmentation, Differentiation, and Flexible Pricing: Experience with Information Technology and Segment-Tailored Strategies." *Journal of Management Information Systems* 11, no. 2 (Fall 1994).

Clemons, Eric K., and Michael Row. "McKesson Drug Co.: Case Study of a Strategic Information System." *Journal of Management Information Systems* (Summer 1988).

———. "Sustaining IT Advantage: The Role of Structural Differences." *MIS Quarterly* 15, no. 3 (September 1991).

———. "Limits to Interfirm Coordination Through IT." *Journal of Management Information Systems* 10, no. 1 (Summer 1993).

Copeland, Duncan G., and James L. McKenney. "Airline Reservations Systems: Lessons from History." *MIS Quarterly* 12, no. 3 (September 1988).

Culnan, Mary J. "Transaction Processing Applications as Organizational Message Systems: Implications for the Intelligent Organization." Working paper no. 88-10, Twenty-second Hawaii International Conference on Systems Sciences (January 1989).

Deutsch, Claudia. "Six Sigma Enlightenment." *The New York Times* (December 7, 1998).

Eardley, Alan, David Avison, and Philip Powell. "Developing Information Systems to Support Flexible Strategy." *Journal of Organizational Computing and Electronic Commerce* 7, no. 1 (1997).

Evans, Philip and Thomas S. Wurster. *Blown to Bits: How the New Economics of Information Transforms Strategy*. Boston, MA: Harvard Business School Press (2000).

———. "Strategy and the New Economics of Information." *Harvard Business Review* (September–October 1997).

Feeny, David E., and Blake Ives. "In Search of Sustainability: Reaping Long-Term Advantage from Investments in Information Technology." *Journal of Management Information Systems* (Summer 1990).

Fisher, Marshall L. "What Is the Right Supply Chain for Your Product?" *Harvard Business Review* (March–April 1997).

Glazer, Rashi. "Winning in Smart Markets." *Sloan Management Review* 40, no. 4 (Summer 1999)

Henderson, John C., and John J. Sifonis. "The Value of Strategic IS Planning: Understanding Consistency, Validity, and IS Markets." *MIS Quarterly* 12, no. 2 (June 1988).

Hopper, Max. "Rattling SABRE—New Ways to Compete on Information." *Harvard Business Review* (May–June 1990).

Houdeshel, George, and Hugh J. Watson. "The Management Information and Decision Support (MIDS) System at Lockheed Georgia." *MIS Quarterly* 11, no. 1 (March 1987).

Huber, George P. "Organizational Information Systems: Determinants of Their Performance and Behavior." *Management Science* 28, no. 2 (1984).

Johnston, Russell, and Michael R. Vitale. "Creating Competitive Advantage with Interorganizational Information Systems." *MIS Quarterly* 12, no. 2 (June 1988).

Kambil, Ajit, and James E. Short. "Electronic Integration and Business Network Redesign: A Roles-Linkage Perspective." *Journal of Management Information Systems* 10, no. 4 (Spring 1994).

Kane, Karen. "L. L. Bean Delivers the Goods." *Fast Company* (August/September 1997).

Keen, Peter G. W. *Competing in Time: Using Telecommunications for Competitive Advantage.* Cambridge, MA: Ballinger Publishing Company (1986).

——— . *Shaping the Future: Business Design Through Information Technology.* Cambridge, MA: Harvard Business School Press (1991).

Keen, Peter G. W., and M. S. Morton. *Decision Support Systems: An Organizational Perspective.* Reading, MA: Addison-Wesley (1978).

Kettinger, William J., Varun Grover, Subashish Guhan, and Albert H. Segors. "Strategic Information Systems Revisited: A Study in Sustainability and Performance." *MIS Quarterly* 18, no. 1 (March 1994).

King, John. "Centralized vs. Decentralized Computing: Organizational Considerations and Management Options." *Computing Surveys* (October 1984).

Konsynski, Benn R., and F. Warren McFarlan. "Information Partnerships—Shared Data, Shared Scale." *Harvard Business Review* (September–October 1990).

Lederer, Albert L., Dinesh A. Mirchandani, and Kenneth Sims. "The Link Between Information Strategy and Electronic Commerce." *Journal of Organizational Computing and Electronic Commerce* 7, no. 1 (1997).

Lee, Hau L., V. Padmanabhan, and Seugin Whang. "The Bullwhip Effect in Supply Chains." *Sloan Management Review* (Spring 1997).

Levy, David. "Lean Production in an International Supply Chain." *Sloan Management Review* (Winter 1997).

McFarlan, F. Warren. "Information Technology Changes the Way You Compete." *Harvard Business Review* (May–June 1984).

Main, Thomas J., and James E. Short. "Managing the Merger: Building Partnership Through IT Planning at the New Baxter." *MIS Quarterly* 13, no. 4 (December 1989).

Mata, Franciso J., William L. Fuerst, and Jay B. Barney. "Information Technology and Sustained Competitive Advantage: A Resource-Based Analysis." *MIS Quarterly* 19, no. 4 (December 1995).

Porter, Michael. *Competitive Strategy.* New York: Free Press (1980).

——— . *Competitive Advantage.* New York: Free Press (1985).

——— . "How Information Can Help You Compete." *Harvard Business Review* (August–September 1985a).

Rangan, V. Kasturi, and Marie Bell. "Dell Online." Harvard Business School Case 9-598-116 (1998).

Rebello, Joseph. "State Street Boston's Allure for Investors Starts to Fade." *The Wall Street Journal* (January 4, 1995).

Rockart, John F., and Michael E. Treacy. "The CEO Goes On-line." *Harvard Business Review* (January–February 1982).

Shapiro, Carl, and Hal R. Varian. *Information Rules.* Boston, MA: Harvard Business School Press (1999).

Short, James E., and N. Venkatraman. "Beyond Business Process Redesign: Redefining Baxter's Business Network." *Sloan Management Review* (Fall 1992).

Sprague, Ralph H., Jr., and Eric D. Carlson. *Building Effective Decision Support Systems.* Englewood Cliffs, NJ: Prentice Hall (1982).

Wiseman, Charles. *Strategic Information Systems.* Homewood, IL: Richard D. Irwin (1988).

CHAPTER 3

Allison, Graham T. *Essence of Decision—Explaining the Cuban Missile Crisis.* Boston: Little Brown (1971).

Alter, Steven, and Michael Ginzberg. "Managing Uncertainty in MIS Implementation." *Sloan Management Review* 20, no. 1 (Fall 1978).

Anthony, R. N. *Planning and Control Systems: A Framework for Analysis.* Cambridge, MA: Harvard University Press (1965).

Argyris, Chris. *Interpersonal Competence and Organizational Effectiveness.* Homewood, IL: Dorsey Press (1962).

Attewell, Paul, and James Rule. "Computing and Organizations: What We Know and What We Don't Know." *Communications of the ACM* 27, no. 12 (December 1984).

Beer, Michael, Russell A. Eisenstat, and Bert Spector. "Why Change Programs Don't Produce Change." *Harvard Business Review* (November–December 1990).

Bikson, T. K., and J. D. Eveland. "Integrating New Tools into Information Work." The Rand Corporation (1992). RAND/RP-106.

Blau, Peter, and W. Richard Scott. *Formal Organizations.* San Francisco: Chandler Press (1962).

Bradsher, Keith. "Carmakers to Buy Parts on Internet." *The New York Times* (February 26, 2000).

Brancheau, James C., Brian D. Janz, and James C. Wetherbe. "Key Issues in Information Systems Management: 1994–1995 SIM Delphi Results." *MIS Quarterly* 20, no. 2 (June 1996).

Cohen, Michael, James March, and Johan Olsen. "A Garbage Can Model of Organizational Choice." *Administrative Science Quarterly* 17 (1972).

Davenport, Tom. "Putting the Enterprise into Enterprise Systems." *Harvard Business Review* (July–August 1998).

Davenport, Thomas H., and Keri Pearlson. "Two Cheers for the Virtual Office." *Sloan Management Review* 39, no. 4 (Summer 1998).

Drucker, Peter. "The Coming of the New Organization." *Harvard Business Review* (January–February 1988).

Earl, Michael J., and Jeffrey L. Sampler. "Market Management to Transform the IT Organization." *Sloan Management Review* 39, no. 4 (Summer 1998).

El Sawy, Omar A. "Implementation by Cultural Infusion: An Approach for Managing the Introduction of Information Technologies." *MIS Quarterly* (June 1985).

Etzioni, Amitai. *A Comparative Analysis of Complex Organizations.* New York: Free Press (1975).

Fayol, Henri. *Administration industrielle et generale.* Paris: Dunods (1950, first published in 1916).

Freeman, John, Glenn R. Carroll, and Michael T. Hannan. "The Liability of Newness: Age Dependence in Organizational Death Rates." *American Sociological Review* 48 (1983).

Fritz, Mary Beth Watson, Sridhar Narasimhan, and Hyeun-Suk Rhee. "Communication and Coordination in the Virtual Office." *Journal of Management Information Systems* 14, no. 4 (Spring 1998).

Fulk, Janet, and Geraldine DeSanctis. "Electronic Communication and Changing Organizational Forms." *Organization Science* 6, no. 4 (July–August 1995).

Garvin, David A. "The Processes of Organization and Management." *Sloan Management Review* 39, no. 4 (Summer 1998).

Gorry, G. Anthony, and Michael S. Scott Morton. "A Framework for Management Information Systems." *Sloan Management Review* 13, no. 1 (Fall 1971).

Gurbaxani, V., and S. Whang, "The Impact of Information Systems on Organizations and Markets." *Communications of the ACM* 34, no. 1 (January 1991).

Hinds, Pamela, and Sara Kiesler. "Communication Across Boundaries: Work, Structure, and Use of Communication Technologies in a Large Organization." *Organization Science* 6, no. 4 (July–August 1995).

Hitt, Lorin M. "Information Technology and Firm Boundaries: Evidence from Panel Data." *Information Systems Research* 10, no. 2 (June 1999).

Hitt, Lorin M., and Erik Brynjolfsson. "Information Technology and Internal Firm Organization: An Exploratory Analysis." *Journal of Management Information Systems* 14, no. 2 (Fall 1997).

Huber, George P. "Cognitive Style as a Basis for MIS and DSS Designs: Much Ado About Nothing?" *Management Science* 29 (May 1983).

Huber, George. "Organizational Learning: The Contributing Processes and Literature." *Organization Science,* 2 (1991), pp. 88–115.

——— . "The Nature and Design of Post-Industrial Organizations." *Management Science* 30, no. 8 (August 1984).

Isenberg, Daniel J. "How Senior Managers Think." *Harvard Business Review* (November–December 1984).

Jensen, M., and W. Mekling. "Theory of the Firm: Managerial Behavior, Agency Costs, and Ownership Structure." *Journal of Financial Economics* 3 (1976).

Jensen, M. C., and W. H. Meckling. "Specific and General Knowledge and Organizational Science." In *Contract Economics,* edited by L. Wetin and J. Wijkander. Oxford: Basil Blackwell (1992).

Johnston, David Cay. "A Kinder, Smarter Tax System for Kansas." *The New York Times* (June 22, 1998).

Kanter, Rosabeth Moss. "The New Managerial Work." *Harvard Business Review* (November–December 1989).

Keen, P. G. W. "Information Systems and Organizational Change." *Communications of the ACM* 24, no. 1 (January 1981).

Keen, Peter G. W. *The Process Edge.* Boston, MA: Harvard Business School Press (1997).

King, W. R. "Creating a Strategic Capabilities Architecture." *Information Systems Management* 12, no. 1 (Winter 1995).

King, J. L., V. Gurbaxani, K. L. Kraemer, F. W. McFarlan, K. S. Raman, and C. S. Yap. "Institutional Factors in Information Technology Innovation." *Information Systems Research* 5, no. 2 (June 1994).

Kling, Rob. "Social Analyses of Computing: Theoretical Perspectives in Recent Empirical Research." *Computing Survey* 12, no. 1 (March 1980).

Kling, Rob, and William H. Dutton. "The Computer Package: Dynamic Complexity." In *Computers and Politics,* edited by James Danziger, William Dutton, Rob Kling, and Kenneth Kraemer. New York: Columbia University Press (1982).

Kolb, D. A., and A. L. Frohman. "An Organization Development Approach to Consulting." *Sloan Management Review* 12, no. 1 (Fall 1970).

Kotter, John T. "What Effective General Managers Really Do." *Harvard Business Review* (November–December 1982).

Kraemer, Kenneth, John King, Debora Dunkle, and Joe Lane. *Managing Information Systems.* Los Angeles: Jossey-Bass (1989).

Kraut, Robert, Charles Steinfield, Alice P. Chan, Brian Butler, and Anne Hoag. "Coordination and Virtualization: The Role of Electronic Networks and Personal Relationships." *Organization Science* 10, no. 6 (November–December 1999).

Kumar, Kuldeep and Jos Van Hillegersberg. "ERP Experiences and Revolution." *Communications of the ACM* 43, no. 4 (April 2000).

Laudon, Kenneth C. *Computers and Bureaucratic Reform.* New York: Wiley (1974).

——— . *Dossier Society: Value Choices in the Design of National Information Systems.* New York: Columbia University Press (1986).

——— . "Environmental and Institutional Models of Systems Development." *Communications of the ACM* 28, no. 7 (July 1985).

——— . "A General Model of the Relationship Between Information Technology and Organizations." Center for Research on Information Systems, New York University. Working paper, National Science Foundation (1989).

——— . "The Promise and Potential of Enterprise Systems and Industrial Networks." Working paper, The Concours Group. Copyright Kenneth C. Laudon (1999).

Lawrence, Paul, and Jay Lorsch. *Organization and Environment.* Cambridge, MA: Harvard University Press (1969).

Leavitt, Harold J. "Applying Organizational Change in Industry: Structural, Technological, and Humanistic Approaches." In *Handbook of Organizations,* edited by James G. March. Chicago: Rand McNally (1965).

Leavitt, Harold J., and Thomas L. Whisler. "Management in the 1980s." *Harvard Business Review* (November–December 1958).

Lee, Ho-Geun. "Do Electronic Marketplaces Lower the Price of Goods?" *Communications of the ACM* 41, no. 1 (January 1998).

Lindblom, C. E. "The Science of Muddling Through." *Public Administration Review* 19 (1959).

Machlup, Fritz. *The Production and Distribution of Knowledge in the United States.* Princeton, NJ: Princeton University Press (1962).

McKenney, James L., and Peter G. W. Keen. "How Managers' Minds Work." *Harvard Business Review* (May–June 1974).

Maier, Jerry L., R. Kelly Rainer, Jr., and Charles A. Snyder. "Environmental Scanning for Information Technology: An Empirical Investigation." *Journal of Management Information Systems* 14, no. 2 (Fall 1997).

Malcolm, Andrew H. "How the Oil Spilled and Spread: Delay and Confusion Off Alaska." *The New York Times* (April 16, 1989).

Malone, Thomas W. "Is Empowerment Just a Fad? Control, Decision Making, and IT." *Sloan Management Review* (Winter 1997).

March, James G., and Herbert A. Simon. *Organizations.* New York: Wiley (1958).

March, James G., and G. Sevon. "Gossip, Information, and Decision Making." In *Advances in Information Processing in*

Lange, Danny B. "An Object-Oriented Design Approach for Developing Hypermedia Information Systems." *Journal of Organizational Computing and Electronic Commerce* 6, no. 2 (1996).

March, Salvatore T., and Young-Gul Kim. "Information Resource Management: A Metadata Perspective." *Journal of Management Information Systems* 5, no. 3 (Winter 1988–1989).

McFadden, Fred R., Jeffrey A. Hoffer and Mary B. Prescott. *Modern Database Management,* 5th ed. Upper Saddle River, NJ: Prentice Hall (1999).

Silberschatz, Avi, Michael Stonebraker, and Jeff Ullman, eds. "Database Systems: Achievements and Opportunities." *Communications of the ACM* 34, no. 10 (October 1991).

Smith, John B., and Stephen F. Weiss. "Hypertext." *Communications of the ACM* 31, no. 7 (July 1988).

Watson, Hugh J., and Barbara J. Haley. "Managerial Considerations." *Communications of the ACM* 41, no. 9 (September 1998).

CHAPTER 7

Bikson, Tora K., Cathleen Stasz, and Donald A. Monkin. "Computer-Mediated Work: Individual and Organizational Impact on One Corporate Headquarters." Rand Corporation (1985).

Chatterjee, Samir. "Requirements for Success in Gigabit Networking." *Communications of the ACM* 40, no. 7 (July 1997).

Chatterjee, Samir and Suzanne Pawlowski. "All-Optical Networks." *Communications of the ACM* 42, no. 6 (June 1999).

Duchessi, Peter, and InduShobha Chengalur-Smith. "Client/Server Benefits, Problems, Best Practices." *Communications of the ACM* 41, no. 5 (May 1998).

Gefen, David, and Detmar W. Straub. "Gender Differences in the Perception and Use of E-Mail: An Extension to the Technology Acceptance Model." *MIS Quarterly* 21, no. 4 (December 1997).

Grover, Varun, and Martin D. Goslar. "Initiation, Adoption, and Implementation of Telecommunications Technologies in U.S. Organizations." *Journal of Management Information Systems* 10, no. 1 (Summer 1993).

Hansen, James V., and Ned C. Hill. "Control and Audit of Electronic Data Interchange." *MIS Quarterly* 13, no. 4 (December 1989).

Harris, Nicole. "All Together Now." *The Wall Street Journal* (September 20, 1999).

Hart, Paul J., and Carol Stoak Saunders. "Emerging Electronic Partnerships: Antecedents and Dimensions of EDI Use from the Supplier's Perspective." *Journal of Management Information Systems* 14, no. 4 (Spring 1998).

Hill, G. Christian. "First Voice, Now Data." *The Wall Street Journal* (September 20, 1999).

Huff, Sid, Malcolm C. Munro, and Barbara H. Martin. "Growth Stages of End User Computing." *Communications of the ACM* (May 1988).

Imielinski, Tomasz, and B. R. Badrinath. "Mobile Wireless Computing: Challenges in Data Management." *Communications of the ACM* 37, no. 10 (October 1994).

Keen, Peter G. W. *Competing in Time.* Cambridge, MA: Ballinger Publishing Company (1986).

Kim, B. G., and P. Wang. "ATM Network: Goals and Challenges." *Communications of the ACM* 38, no. 2 (February 1995).

Laudon, Kenneth C. "From PCs to Managerial Workstations." In Matthias Jarke, *Managers, Micros, and Mainframes.* New York: John Wiley (1986).

Lee, Ho Geun, Theodore Clark, and Kar Yan Tam. "Research Report: Can EDI Benefit Adopters?" *Information Systems Research* 10, no. 2 (June 1999).

Massetti, Brenda, and Robert W. Zmud. "Measuring the Extent of EDI Usage in Complex Organizations: Strategies and Illustrative Examples." *MIS Quarterly* 20, no. 3 (September 1996).

Mueller, Milton. "Universal Service and the Telecommunications Act: Myth Made Law." *Communications of the ACM* 40, no. 3 (March 1997).

Nakamura, Kiyoh, Toshihiro Ide, and Yukio Kiyokane. "Roles of Multimedia Technology in Telework." *Journal of Organizational Computing and Electronic Commerce* 6, no. 4 (1996).

Ngwenyama, Ojelanki, and Allen S. Lee. "Communication Richness in Electronic Mail: Critical Social Theory and the Contextuality of Meaning." *MIS Quarterly* 21, no. 2 (June 1997).

"Plans and Policies for Client/Server Technology." *I/S Analyzer* 30, no. 4 (April 1992).

Pottie, G. J. and W. J Kaiser. "Wireless Integrated Network Sensors." *Communications of the ACM* 43, no. 5 (May 2000).

Premkumar, G., K. Ramamurthy, and Sree Nilakanta. "Implementation of Electronic Data Interchange: An Innovation Diffusion Perspective." *Journal of Management Information Systems* 11, no. 2 (Fall 1994).

Raymond, Louis, and Francois Bergeron. "EDI Success in Small- and Medium-sized Enterprises: A Field Study." *Journal of Organizational Computing and Electronic Commerce* 6, no. 2 (1996).

Richardson, Gary L., Brad M. Jackson, and Gary W. Dickson. "A Principles-Based Enterprise Architecture: Lessons from Texaco and Star Enterprise." *MIS Quarterly* 14, no. 4 (December 1990).

Roche, Edward M. *Telecommunications and Business Strategy.* Chicago: The Dryden Press (1991).

Sharda, Nalin. "Multimedia Networks: Fundamentals and Future Directions." *Communications of the Association for Information Systems* (February 1999).

Sinha, Alok. "Client-Server Computing." *Communications of the ACM* 35, no. 7 (July 1992).

Teo, Hock-Hai, Bernard C. Y. Tan, and Kwok-Kee Wei. "Organizational Transformation Using Electronic Data Interchange: The Case of TradeNet in Singapore." *Journal of Management Information Systems* 13, no. 4 (Spring 1997).

Thompson, Marjorie Sarbough, and Martha S. Feldman. "Electronic Mail and Organizational Communication." *Organization Science* 9, no. 6 (November–December 1998).

Torkzadeh, Gholamreza, and Weidong Xia. "Managing Telecommunications Strategy by Steering Committee." *MIS Quarterly* 16, no. 2 (June 1992).

Varshney, Upkar. "Networking Support for Mobile Computing." *Communications of the Association for Information Systems* 1 (January 1999).

Vetter, Ronald J. "ATM Concepts, Architectures, and Protocols." *Communications of the ACM* 38, no. 2 (February 1995).

Waldo, Jim. "The Jini Architecture for Network-centric Computing." *Communications of the ACM* 42, no. 7 (July 1999).

Westin, Alan F., Heather A. Schweder, Michael A. Baker, and **Sheila Lehman.** *The Changing Workplace.* New York: Knowledge Industries (1995).

Whitman, Michael E., Anthony M. Townsend, and **Robert J. Aalberts.** "Considerations for Effective Telecommunications-Use Policy." *Communications of the ACM* 42, no. 6 (June 1999).

CHAPTER 8

Applegate, Lynda, and **Janice Gogan.** "Paving the Information Superhighway: Introduction to the Internet," *Harvard Business School* 9-195-202 (August 1995).

Armstrong, Arthur, and **John Hagel, III.** "The Real Value of On-line Communities." *Harvard Business Review* (May–June 1996).

Bakos, Yannis. "The Emerging Role of Electronic Marketplaces and the Internet." *Communications of the ACM* 41, no. 8 (August 1998).

Baron, John P., Michael J. Shaw, and **Andrew D. Bailey, Jr.** "Web-based E-catalog Systems in B2B Procurement." *Communications of the ACM* 43, no.5 (May 2000).

Barua, Anitesh, Sury Ravindran, and **Andrew B. Whinston.** "Efficient Selection of Suppliers over the Internet." *Journal of Management Information Systems* 13, no. 4 (Spring 1997).

Berners-Lee, Tim, Robert Cailliau, Ari Luotonen, Henrik Frystyk Nielsen, and **Arthur Secret.** "The World-Wide Web." *Communications of the ACM* 37, no. 8 (August 1994).

Borriello, Gaetano and **Roy Want.** "Embedded Computation Meets the World Wide Web." *Communications of the ACM* 43, no. 5 (May 2000).

Choi, Soon-Yong, Dale O. Stahl, and **Andrew B. Whinston.** *The Economics of Electronic Commerce.* Indianapolis, IN: Macmillan Technical Publishing (1997).

Cohen, Jackie. "Taking Care of Business," *The Industry Standard,* September 13, 1999.

Corcoran, Cate T. "The Auction Economy." *Red Herring* (August 1999).

Crede, Andreas. "Electronic Commerce and the Banking Industry: The Requirement and Opportunities for New Payment Systems Using the Internet." *JCMC* 1, no. 3 (December 1995).

Cronin, Mary. *The Internet Strategy Handbook.* Boston, MA: Harvard Business School Press (1996).

Dalton, Gregory. "Going, Going, Gone!" *Information Week* (October 4, 1999).

Downes, Larry, and **Chunka Mui.** *Unleashing the Killer App: Digital Strategies for Market Dominance.* Boston, MA: Harvard Business School Press (1998).

El Sawy, Omar A., Arvind Malhotra, Sanjay Gosain, and **Kerry M. Young.** "IT-Intensive Value Innovation in the Electronic Economy: Insights from Marshall Industries." *MIS Quarterly* 23, no. 3, (September 1999).

Elofson, Greg, and **William N. Robinson.** "Creating a Custom Mass Production Channel on the Internet." *Communications of the ACM* 41, no. 3 (March 1998).

Evans, Philip, and **Thomas S. Wurster.** "Getting Real about Virtual Commerce." *Harvard Business Review* (November–December 1999).

Garner, Rochelle. "Internet2 . . . and Counting." *CIO Magazine* (September 1, 1999).

Ghosh, Shikhar. "Making Business Sense of the Internet." *Harvard Business Review* (March–April 1998).

Goodman, S. E., L. I. Press, S. R. Ruth, and **A. M. Rutkowski.** "The Global Diffusion of the Internet: Patterns and Problems." *Communications of the ACM* 37, no. 8 (August 1994.)

Grover, Varun, and **Pradipkumar Ramanlal.** "Six Myths of Information and Markets: Information Technology Networks, Electronic Commerce, and the Battle for Consumer Surplus." *MIS Quarterly* 23, no. 4 (December 1999).

Gulati, Ranjay, and **Jason Garino.** "Get the Right Mix of Bricks and Clicks." *Harvard Business Review* (May–June, 2000).

Hagel, John, III, and **Marc Singer.** *Net Worth.* Boston, MA: Harvard Business School Press (1999).

——— . "Unbundling the Corporation." *Harvard Business Review* (March–April 1999).

Hardman, Vicky, Martina Angela Sasse, and **Isidor Kouvelas.** "Successful Multiparty Audio Communication over the Internet." *Communications of the ACM* 41, no. 5 (May 1998).

Hoffman, Donna L., Thomas P. Novak, and **Patrali Chatterjee.** "Commercial Scenarios for the Web: Opportunities and Challenges." *JCMC* 1, no. 3 (December 1995).

Hoffman, Donna L., William D. Kalsbeek, and **Thomas P. Novak.** "Internet and Web Use in the U.S." *Communications of the ACM* 39, no. 12 (December 1996).

Isakowitz, Tomas, Michael Bieber, and **Fabio Vitali.** "Web Information Systems." *Communications of the ACM* 41, no. 7 (July 1998).

Jahnke, Art. "It Takes a Village." *CIO WebBusiness* (February 1, 1998).

Kalakota, Ravi, and **Andrew B. Whinston.** *Electronic Commerce: A Manager's Guide.* Reading MA: Addison-Wesley (1997).

——— . *Frontiers of Electronic Commerce.* Reading, MA: Addison-Wesley (1996).

Kaplan, Steven, and **Mohanbir Sawhney.** "E-Hubs: the New B2B Marketplaces." *Harvard Business Review* (May–June 2000).

Kanan, P. K., Ai-Mei Chang, and **Andrew B. Whinston.** "Marketing Information on the I-Way." *Communications of the ACM* 41, no. 3 (March 1998).

Kautz, Henry, Bart Selman, and **Mehul Shah.** "ReferralWeb: Combining Social Networks and Collaborative Filtering." *Communications of the ACM* 40, no. 3 (March 1997).

Kendall, Kenneth E., and **Julie E. Kendall.** "Information Delivery Systems: An Exploration of Web Push and Pull Technologies." *Communications of the Association for Information Systems* 1 (April 1999).

Kuo, Geng-Sheng and **Jing-Pei Lin.** "New Design Concepts for an Intelligent Internet." *Communications of the ACM* 41, no. 11 (November 1998).

Lee, Ho Geun. "Do Electronic Marketplaces Lower the Price of Goods?" *Communications of the ACM* 41, no. 1 (January 1998).

Lee, Ho Geun, and **Theodore H. Clark.** "Market Process Reengineering Through Electronic Market Systems: Opportunities and Challenges." *Journal of Management Information Systems* 13, no. 3 (Winter 1997).

Lewis, Nicole. "Internet Telephony: The Business Connection." *Beyond Computing* (July/August 1999).

Lohse, Gerald L., and **Peter Spiller.** "Electronic Shopping." *Communications of the ACM* 41, no. 7 (July 1998).

Mougayar, Walid. *Opening Digital Markets,* 2nd ed. New York: McGraw-Hill (1998).

O'Leary, Daniel E., Daniel Koukka, and Robert Plant. "Artificial Intelligence and Virtual Organizations." *Communications of the ACM* 40, no. 1 (January 1997).

McWilliam, Gil. "Building Stronger Brands through Online Communities." *Sloan Management Review* 41, no. 3 (Spring 2000).

Mullich, Joe. "Reinvent Your Intranet." *Datamation* (June 1999).

Palmer, Jonathan W., and David A. Griffith. "An Emerging Model of Web Site Design for Marketing." *Communications of the ACM* 41, no. 3 (March 1998).

Quelch, John A., and Lisa R. Klein. "The Internet and International Marketing." *Sloan Management Review* (Spring 1996).

Rafter, Michelle V. "Can We Talk?" *The Industry Standard* (February 15, 1999).

Richtel, Matt. "The Next Waves of Electronic Commerce." *The New York Times* (December 19, 1999).

Sarkar, Mitra Barun, Brian Butler, and Charles Steinfield. "Intermediaries and Cybermediaries: A Continuing Role for Mediating Players in the Electronic Marketplace." *JCMC* 1, no. 3 (December 1995).

Singh, Surendra N., and Nikunj P. Dalal. "Web Home Pages as Advertisements." *Communications of the ACM* 42, no. 8 (August 1999).

Steinfield, Charles. "The Impact of Electronic Commerce on Buyer-Seller Relationships." *JCMC* 1, no. 3 (December 1995).

Sterne, Jim. "Customer Interface." *CIO WebBusiness* (February 1, 1998).

———. *World Wide Web Marketing.* New York: John Wiley (1995).

Venkatraman, N. "Five Steps to a Dot-Com Strategy: How to Find Your Footing on the Web." *Sloan Management Review* 41, no. 3 (Spring 2000).

Wigand, Rolf T., and Robert Benjamin. "Electronic Commerce: Effects on Electronic Markets." *JCMC* 1, no. 3 (December 1995).

CHAPTER 9

Alter, Steven, and Michael Ginzberg. "Managing Uncertainty in MIS Implementation." *Sloan Management Review* 20 (Fall 1978).

Armstrong, Curtis P., and V. Sambamurthy. "Information Technology Assimilation in Firms: The Influence of Senior Leadership and IT Infrastructures." *Information Systems Research* 10, no. 4 (December 1999).

Attewell, Paul. "Technology Diffusion and Organizational Learning: The Case of Business Computing." *Organization Science,* no. 3 (1992).

Barua, Anitesh, Sophie C. H. Lee, and Andrew B. Whinston. "The Calculus of Reengineering." *Information Systems Research* 7, no. 4 (December 1996).

Beath, Cynthia Mathis, and Wanda J. Orlikowski. "The Contradictory Structure of Systems Development Methodologies: Deconstructing the IS-User Relationship in Information Engineering." *Information Systems Research* 5, no. 4 (December 1994).

Bostrom, R. P., and J. S. Heinen. "MIS Problems and Failures: A Socio-Technical Perspective. Part I: The Causes." *MIS Quarterly* 1 (September 1977); "Part II: The Application of Socio-Technical Theory." *MIS Quarterly* 1 (December 1977).

Broadbent, Marianne, Peter Weill, and Don St. Clair. "The Implications of Information Technology Infrastructure for Business Process Redesign." *MIS Quarterly* 23, no. 2 (June 1999).

Brier, Tom, Jerry Luftman, and Raymond Papp. " Enablers and Inhibitors of Business—IT Alignment." *Communications of the Association for Information Systems* 1 (March 1999).

Bullen, Christine, and John F. Rockart. "A Primer on Critical Success Factors." Cambridge, MA: Center for Information Systems Research, Sloan School of Management (1981).

Buss, Martin D. J. "How to Rank Computer Projects." *Harvard Business Review* (January 1983).

Clement, Andrew, and Peter Van den Besselaar. "A Retrospective Look at PD Projects." *Communications of the ACM* 36, no. 4 (June 1993).

Davenport, Thomas H. *Mission Critical: Realizing the Promise of Enterprise Systems.* Boston, MA: Harvard Business School Press, (2000).

Davenport, Thomas H., and James E. Short. "The New Industrial Engineering: Information Technology and Business Process Redesign." *Sloan Management Review* 31, no. 4 (Summer 1990).

Davidson, W. H. "Beyond Engineering: The Three Phases of Business Transformation." *IBM Systems Journal* 32, no. 1 (1993).

Davis, Fred R. "Perceived Usefulness, Ease of Use, and User Acceptance of Information Technology." *MIS Quarterly* 13, no. 3 (September 1989).

Davis, Gordon B. "Determining Management Information Needs: A Comparison of Methods." *MIS Quarterly* 1 (June 1977).

———. "Information Analysis for Information System Development." In *Systems Analysis and Design: A Foundation for the 1980's,* edited by W. W. Cotterman, J. D. Cougar, N. L. Enger, and F. Harold. New York: Wiley (1981).

———. "Strategies for Information Requirements Determination." *IBM Systems Journal* 1 (1982).

Desmarais, Michel C., Richard Leclair, Jean-Yves Fiset, and Hichem Talbi. "Cost-Justifying Electronic Performance Support Systems." *Communications of the ACM* 40, no. 7 (July 1997).

Doll, William J. "Avenues for Top Management Involvement in Successful MIS Development." *MIS Quarterly* (March 1985).

Dos Santos, Brian. "Justifying Investments in New Information Technologies." *Journal of Management Information Systems* 7, no. 4 (Spring 1991).

Ein-Dor, Philip, and Eli Segev. "Organizational Context and the Success of Management Information Systems." *Management Science* 24 (June 1978).

———. "Strategic Planning for Management Information Systems." *Management Science* 24, no. 15 (1978).

El Sawy, Omar, and Burt Nanus. "Toward the Design of Robust Information Systems." *Journal of Management Information Systems* 5, no. 4 (Spring 1989).

Emery, James C. "Cost/Benefit Analysis of Information Systems." Chicago: Society for Management Information Systems Workshop Report No. 1 (1971).

Fichman, Robert G., and Scott A. Moses. "An Incremental Process for Software Implementation." *Sloan Management Review* 40, no. 2 (Winter 1999).

Franz, Charles, and **Daniel Robey.** "An Investigation of User-Led System Design: Rational and Political Perspectives." *Communications of the ACM* 27 (December 1984).

Gardner, Julia. "Strengthening the Focus on Users' Working Practices." *Communications of the ACM* 42, no. 5 (May 1999).

Giaglis, George. "Focus Issue on Legacy Information Systems and Business Process Change: On the Integrated Design and Evaluation of Business Processes and Information Systems." *Communications of the AIS* 2, (July 1999).

Ginzberg, Michael J. "Early Diagnosis of MIS Implementation Failure: Promising Results and Unanswered Questions." *Management Science* 27 (April 1981).

Gogan, Janis L., Jane Fedorowicz, and **Ashok Rao.** "Assessing Risks in Two Projects: A Strategic Opportunity and a Necessary Evil." *Communications of the Association for Information Systems* 1 (May 1999).

Grover, Varun. "IS Investment Priorities in Contemporary Organizations." *Communications of the ACM* 41, no. 2 (February 1998).

Hammer, Michael. "Reengineering Work: Don't Automate, Obliterate." *Harvard Business Review* (July–August 1990).

Hammer, Michael, and **James Champy.** *Reengineering the Corporation.* New York: HarperCollins Publishers (1993).

Hammer, Michael, and **Steven A. Stanton.** *The Reengineering Revolution.* New York: HarperCollins (1995).

Helms, Glenn L., and **Ira R. Weiss.** "The Cost of Internally Developed Applications: Analysis of Problems and Cost Control Methods." *Journal of Management Information Systems* (Fall 1986).

Huizing, Ard, Esther Koster, and **Wim Bouman.** "Balance in Business Process Reengineering: An Empirical Study of Fit and Performance." *Journal of Management Information Systems* 14, no. 1 (Summer 1997).

Hunton, James E., and **Jesse D. Beeler.** "Effects of User Participation in Systems Development: A Longitudinal Field Study." *MIS Quarterly* 21, no. 4 (December 1997).

Jesser, Ryan, Rodney Smith, Mark Stupeck, and **William F. Wright.** "Information Technology Process Reengineering and Performance Measurement." *Communications of the Association for Information Systems* 1 (February 1999).

Joshi, Kailash. "A Model of Users' Perspective on Change: The Case of Information Systems Technology Implementation." *MIS Quarterly* 15, no. 2 (June 1991).

Karat, John. "Evolving the Scope of User-Centered Design." *Communications of the ACM* 40, no. 7 (July 1997).

Keen, Peter W. "Information Systems and Organizational Change." *Communications of the ACM* 24 (January 1981).

Keil, Mark, Paul E. Cule, Kalle Lyytinen, and **Roy C. Schmidt.** "A Framework for Identifying Software Project Risks." *Communications of the ACM* 41, 11 (November 1998).

Keil, Mark, and **Ramiro Montealegre.** "Cutting Your Losses: Extricating Your Organization When a Big Project Goes Awry." *Sloan Management Review* 41, no. 3 (Spring 2000).

Keil, Mark, Richard Mixon, Timo Saarinen, and **Virpi Tuunairen.** "Understanding Runaway IT Projects." *Journal of Management Information Systems* 11, no. 3 (Winter 1994–1995).

Kelly, Sue, Nicola Gibson, Christopher P. Holland, and **Ben Light.** "Focus Issue on Legacy Information Systems and Business Process Change: A Business Perspective of Legacy Information Systems." *Communications of the AIS* 2 (July 1999).

Kendall, Kenneth E., and **Julie E. Kendall.** *Systems Analysis and Design,* 4th ed. Upper Saddle River, NJ: Prentice Hall (1999).

King, Julia. "Reengineering Slammed." *Computerworld* (June 13, 1994).

Kolb, D. A., and **A. L. Frohman.** "An Organization Development Approach to Consulting." *Sloan Management Review* 12 (Fall 1970).

Laudon, Kenneth C. "CIOs Beware: Very Large Scale Systems." Center for Research on Information Systems, New York University Stern School of Business, working paper (1989).

Lederer, Albert, and **Jayesh Prasad.** "Nine Management Guidelines for Better Cost Estimating." *Communications of the ACM* 35, no. 2 (February 1992).

Lientz, Bennett P., and **E. Burton Swanson.** *Software Maintenance Management.* Reading, MA: Addison-Wesley (1980).

Lucas, Henry C., Jr. *Implementation: The Key to Successful Information Systems.* New York: Columbia University Press (1981).

Markus, M. Lynne, Conelis Tanis, and **Paul C. van Fenema.** "Multisite ERP Implementations." *Communications of the ACM* 43, no. 3 (April 2000).

Markus, M. Lynne, and **Mark Keil.** "If We Build It, They Will Come: Designing Information Systems That People Want to Use." *Sloan Management Review* (Summer 1994).

Markus, M. Lynne, and **Robert I. Benjamin.** "Change Agentry— The Next IS Frontier." *MIS Quarterly* 20, no. 4 (December 1996).

Markus, M. Lynne, and **Robert I. Benjamin.** "The Magic Bullet Theory of IT-Enabled Transformation." *Sloan Management Review* (Winter 1997).

Matlin, Gerald. "What Is the Value of Investment in Information Systems?" *MIS Quarterly* 13, no. 3 (September 1989).

McFarlan, F. Warren. "Portfolio Approach to Information Systems." *Harvard Business Review* (September–October 1981).

McKeen, James D., and **Tor Guimaraes.** "Successful Strategies for User Participation in Systems Development." *Journal of Management Information Systems* 14, no. 2 (Fall 1997).

Mumford, Enid, and **Mary Weir.** *Computer Systems in Work Design: The ETHICS Method.* New York: John Wiley (1979).

Nolan, Richard L. "Managing Information Systems by Committee." *Harvard Business Review* (July–August 1982).

Orlikowski, Wanda J., and **J. Debra Hofman.** "An Improvisational Change Model for Change Management: The Case of Groupware Technologies." *Sloan Management Review* (Winter 1997).

Parker, M. M. "Enterprise Information Analysis: Cost-Benefit Analysis and the Data-Managed System." *IBM Systems Journal* 21 (1982).

Rai, Arun, Ravi Patnayakuni, and **Nainika Patnayakuni.** "Technology Investment and Business Performance." *Communications of the ACM* 40, no. 7 (July 1997).

Randall, Dave, John Hughes, Jon O'Brien, Tom Rodden, Mark Rouncefield, Ian Sommerville, and **Peter Tolmie.** "Focus Issue on Legacy Information Systems and Business Process Change: Banking on the Old Technology: Understanding the Organizational Context of 'Legacy' Issues." *Communications of the AIS* 2, (July 1999).

Robey, Daniel, and **M. Lynne Markus.** "Rituals in Information System Design." *MIS Quarterly* (March 1984).

Rockart, John F. "Chief Executives Define Their Own Data Needs." *Harvard Business Review* (March–April 1979).

Rockart, John F., and Michael E. Treacy. "The CEO Goes On-Line." *Harvard Business Review* (January–February 1982).

Scheer, August-Wilhelm, and Frank Habermann. "Making ERP a Success." *Communications of the ACM* 43, no. 3 (April 2000).

Schneiderman, Ben. "Universal Usability." *Communications of the ACM* 43, no. 5 (May 2000).

Segars, Albert H., and Varun Grover. "Profiles of Strategic Information Systems Planning." *Information Systems Research* 10, no. 3 (September 1999).

Shank, Michael E., Andrew C. Boynton, and Robert W. Zmud. "Critical Success Factor Analysis as a Methodology for MIS Planning." *MIS Quarterly* (June 1985).

Sia, Siew Kien, and Boon Siong Neo. "Reengineering Effectiveness and the Redesign of Organizational Control: A Case Study of the Inland Revenue Authority in Singapore." *Journal of Management Information Systems* 14, no. 1 (Summer 1997).

Swanson, E. Burton. *Information System Implementation.* Homewood, IL: Richard D. Irwin (1988).

Teng, James T. C., Seung Ryul Jeong, and Varun Grover. "Profiling Successful Reengineering Projects." *Communications of the ACM* 41, no. 6 (June 1998).

Tornatsky, Louis G., J. D. Eveland, M. G. Boylan, W. A. Hetzner, E. C. Johnson, D. Roitman, and J. Schneider. *The Process of Technological Innovation: Reviewing the Literature.* Washington, DC: National Science Foundation (1983).

Truex, Duane P., Richard Baskerville, and Heinz Klein. "Growing Systems in Emergent Organizations." *Communications of the ACM* 42, no. 8 (August 1999).

Turner, Jon A. "Computer-Mediated Work: The Interplay Between Technology and Structured Jobs." *Communications of the ACM* 27 (December 1984).

Venkatraman, N. "Beyond Outsourcing: Managing IT Resources as a Value Center." *Sloan Management Review* (Spring 1997).

Vessey, Iris, and Sue Conger. "Learning to Specify Information Requirements: The Relationship Between Application and Methodology." *Journal of Management Information Systems* 10, no. 2 (Fall 1993).

Vitalari, Nicholas P. "Knowledge as a Basis for Expertise in Systems Analysis: Empirical Study." *MIS Quarterly* (September 1985).

Wastell, David G. "Learning Dysfunctions in Information Systems Development: Overcoming the Social Defenses with Transitional Objects." *MIS Quarterly* 23, no. 1 (December 1999).

Watad, Mahmoud M., and Frank J. DiSanzo. "Case Study: The Synergism of Telecommuting and Office Automation." *Sloan Management Review* 41, no. 2 (Winter 2000).

Yin, Robert K. "Life Histories of Innovations: How New Practices Become Routinized." *Public Administration Review* (January–February 1981).

Zachman, J. A. "Business Systems Planning and Business Information Control Study: A Comparison." *IBM Systems Journal* 21 (1982).

CHAPTER 10

Ahituv, Niv, and Seev Neumann. "A Flexible Approach to Information System Development." *MIS Quarterly* (June 1984).

Aiken, Peter, Alice Muntz, and Russ Richards. "DOD Legacy Systems: Reverse Engineering Data Requirements." *Communications of the ACM* 37, no. 5 (May 1994).

Alavi, Maryam. "An Assessment of the Prototyping Approach to Information System Development." *Communications of the ACM* 27 (June 1984).

Alavi, Maryam, R. Ryan Nelson, and Ira R. Weiss. "Strategies for End-User Computing: An Integrative Framework." *Journal of Management Information Systems* 4, no. 3 (Winter 1987–1988).

Anderson, Evan A. "Choice Models for the Evaluation and Selection of Software Packages." *Journal of Management Information Systems* 6, no. 4 (Spring 1990).

Baskerville, Richard L., and Jan Stage. "Controlling Prototype Development through Risk Analysis." *MIS Quarterly* 20, no. 4 (December 1996).

Brooks, Frederick P. "The Mythical Man-Month." *Datamation* (December 1974).

Cline, Marshall, and Mike Girou. "Enduring Business Themes." *Communications of the ACM* 43, no. 5 (May 2000).

Lee, Jae Nam, and Young-Gul Kim. "Effect of Partnership Quality on IS Outsourcing Success." *Journal of Management Information Systems* 15, no. 4 (Spring 1999).

Hirscheim, Rudy and Mary Lacity. "The Myths and Realities of Information Technology Insourcing." *Communications of the ACM* 43, no. 2 (February 2000).

Martin, J., and C. McClure. "Buying Software Off the Rack." *Harvard Business Review* (November–December 1983).

Martin, James. *Application Development Without Programmers.* Englewood Cliffs, NJ: Prentice Hall (1982).

Martin, James, and Carma McClure. *Structured Techniques: The Basis of CASE.* Englewood Cliffs, NJ: Prentice Hall (1988).

Mason, R. E. A., and T. T. Carey. "Prototyping Interactive Information Systems." *Communications of the ACM* 26 (May 1983).

Matos, Victor M., and Paul J. Jalics. "An Experimental Analysis of the Performance of Fourth-Generation Tools on PCs." *Communications of the ACM* 32, no. 11 (November 1989).

Mazzucchelli, Louis. "Structured Analysis Can Streamline Software Design." *Computerworld* (December 9, 1985).

McIntyre, Scott C., and Lexis F. Higgins. "Object-Oriented Analysis and Design: Methodology and Application." *Journal of Management Information Systems* 5, no. 1 (Summer 1988).

Nerson, Jean-Marc. "Applying Object-Oriented Analysis and Design." *Communications of the ACM* 35, no. 9 (September 1992).

Nissen, Mark E. "Redesigning Reengineering Through Measurement-Driven Inference." *MIS Quarterly* 22, no. 4 (December 1998).

Pancake, Cherri M. "The Promise and the Cost of Object Technology: A Five-Year Forecast." *Communications of the ACM* 38, no. 10 (October 1995).

Rivard, Suzanne, and Sid L. Huff. "Factors of Success for End-User Computing." *Communications of the ACM* 31, no. 5 (May 1988).

Rockart, John F., and Lauren S. Flannery. "The Management of End-User Computing." *Communications of the ACM* 26, no. 10 (October 1983).

Sabherwahl, Rajiv. "The Role of Trust in IS Outsourcing Development Projects." *Communications of the ACM* 42, no. 2 (February 1999).

Schmidt, Douglas C., and Mohamed E. Fayad. "Lessons Learned Building Reusable OO Frameworks for Distributed Software." *Communications of the ACM* 40, no. 10 (October 1997).

Sharma, Srinarayan, and **Arun Rai.** "CASE Deployment in IS Organizations." *Communications of the ACM* 43, no. 1 (January 2000).

Sprott, David. "Componentizing the Enterprise Application Packages." *Communications of the ACM* 43, no. 3 (April 2000).

Vessey, Iris, and **Sue A. Conger.** "Requirements Specification: Learning Object, Process, and Data Methodologies." *Communications of the ACM* 37, no. 5 (May 1994).

Willis, T. Hillman, and **Debbie B. Tesch.** "An Assessment of Systems Development Methodologies." *Journal of Information Technology Management* 2, no. 2 (1991).

Yourdon, Edward, and **L. L. Constantine.** *Structured Design.* New York: Yourdon Press (1978).

CHAPTER 11

Alavi, Maryam, and **Dorothy Leidner.** "Knowledge Management Systems: Issues, Challenges, and Benefits." *Communications of the Association for Information Systems* 1 (February 1999).

Allen, Bradley P. "CASE-Based Reasoning: Business Applications." *Communications of the ACM* 37, no. 3 (March 1994).

Asakawa, Kazuo, and **Hideyuki Takagi.** "Neural Networks in Japan." *Communications of the ACM* 37, no. 3 (March 1994).

Badler, Norman I., Martha S. Palmer, and **Rama Bindiganavale.** "Animation Control for Real-time Virtual Humans." *Communications of the ACM* 42, no. 8 (August 1999).

Balasubramanian, V., and **Alf Bashian.** "Document Management and Web Technologies: Alice Marries the Mad Hatter." *Communications of the ACM* 41, no. 7 (July 1998).

Barker, Virginia E., and **Dennis E. O'Connor.** "Expert Systems for Configuration at Digital: XCON and Beyond." *Communications of the ACM* (March 1989).

Baum, David. "U.N. Automates Payroll with AI System." *Datamation* (November 1996).

Beer, Randall D., Roger D. Quinn, Hillel J. Chiel, and **Roy E. Ritzman.** "Biologically Inspired Approaches to Robots." *Communications of the ACM* 40, no. 3 (March 1997).

Blanning, Robert W., David R. King, James R. Marsden, and **Ann C. Seror.** "Intelligent Models of Human Organizations: The State of the Art." *Journal of Organizational Computing* 2, no. 2 (1992).

Brutzman, Don. "The Virtual Reality Modeling Language and Java." *Communications of the ACM* 41, no. 6 (June 1998).

Brynjolfsson, Erik. "The Contribution of Information Technology to Consumer Welfare." *Information Systems Research* 7, no. 3 (September 1996).

———. "The Productivity Paradox of Information Technology." *Communications of the ACM* 36, no. 12 (December 1993).

Brynjolfsson, Erik, and **Lorin M. Hitt.** "Information Technology and Organizational Design: Evidence from Micro Data." (January 1998).

Brynjolfsson, Erik, and **Lorin M. Hitt.** "Beyond the Productivity Paradox." *Communications of the ACM* 41, no. 8 (August 1998).

———. "New Evidence on the Returns to Information Systems." MIT Sloan School of Management (October 1993).

Burtka, Michael. "Generic Algorithms." *The Stern Information Systems Review* 1, no. 1 (Spring 1993).

Busch, Elizabeth, Matti Hamalainen, Clyde W. Holsapple, Yongmoo Suh, and **Andrew B. Whinston.** "Issues and Obstacles in the Development of Team Support Systems." *Journal of Organizational Computing* 1, no. 2 (April–June 1991).

Churchland, Paul M., and **Patricia Smith Churchland.** "Could a Machine Think?" *Scientific American* (January 1990).

Cole, Kevin, Olivier Fischer, and **Phyllis Saltzman.** "Just-in-Time Knowledge Delivery." *Communications of the ACM* 40, no. 7 (July 1997).

Cole-Gomolski, Barbara. "Customer Service with a :-)" *Computerworld* (March 30, 1998).

Cross, Rob, and **Lloyd Baird.** "Technology Is Not Enough: Improving Performance by Building Organizational Memory." *Sloan Management Review* 41, no. 3 (Spring 2000).

Davenport, Thomas H., David W. DeLong, and **Michael C. Beers.** "Successful Knowledge Management Projects." *Sloan Management Review* 39, no. 2 (Winter 1998).

Davenport, Thomas H., and **Lawrence Prusak.** *Working Knowledge: How Organizations Manage What They Know.* Boston, MA: Harvard Business School Press (1997).

Dhar, Vasant. "Plausibility and Scope of Expert Systems in Management." *Journal of Management Information Systems* (Summer 1987).

Dhar, Vasant, and **Roger Stein.** *Intelligent Decision Support Methods: The Science of Knowledge Work.* Upper Saddle River, NJ: Prentice Hall (1997).

Earl, Michael J., and **Ian A. Scott.** "What Is a Chief Knowledge Officer?" *Sloan Management Review* 40, no. 2 (Winter 1999).

El Najdawi, M. K., and **Anthony C. Stylianou.** "Expert Support Systems: Integrating AI Technologies." *Communications of the ACM* 36, no. 12 (December 1993).

Favela, Jesus. "Capture and Dissemination of Specialized Knowledge in Network Organizations." *Journal of Organizational Computing and Electronic Commerce* 7, nos. 2 and 3 (1997).

Feigenbaum, Edward A. "The Art of Artificial Intelligence: Themes and Case Studies in Knowledge Engineering." *Proceedings of the IJCAI* (1977).

Gelernter, David. "The Metamorphosis of Information Management." *Scientific American* (August 1989).

Giuliao, Vincent E. "The Mechanization of Office Work." *Scientific American* (September 1982).

Glushko, Robert J., Jay M. Tenenbaum, and **Bart Meltzer.** "An XML Framework for Agent-Based E-Commerce." *Communications of the ACM* 42, no. 3 (March 1999).

Goldberg, David E. "Genetic and Evolutionary Algorithms Come of Age." *Communications of the ACM* 37, no. 3 (March 1994).

Grant, Robert M. "Prospering in Dynamically Competitive Environments: Organizational Capability as Knowledge Integration." *Organization Science* 7, no. 4 (July–August 1996).

Gregor, Shirley, and **Izak Benbasat.** "Explanations from Intelligent Systems: Theoretical Foundations and Implications for Practice." *MIS Quarterly* 23, no. 4 (December 1999).

Hansen, Morton T., Nitin Nohria, and **Thomas Tierney.** "What's Your Strategy for Knowledge Management?" *Harvard Business Review* (March–April 1999).

Hayes-Roth, Frederick. "Knowledge-Based Expert Systems." *Spectrum IEEE* (October 1987).

Hayes-Roth, Frederick, and **Neil Jacobstein.** "The State of Knowledge-Based Systems." *Communications of the ACM* 37, no. 3 (March 1994).

Hinton, Gregory. "How Neural Networks Learn from Experience." *Scientific American* (September 1992).

Holland, John H. "Genetic Algorithms." *Scientific American* (July 1992).

Johansen, Robert. "Groupware: Future Directions and Wild Cards." *Journal of Organizational Computing* 1, no. 2 (April–June 1991).

Kanade, Takeo, Michael L. Reed, and Lee E. Weiss. "New Technologies and Applications in Robotics." *Communications of the ACM* 37, no. 3 (March 1994).

Kock, Ned, and Robert J. McQueen. "An Action Research Study of Effects of Asynchronous Groupware Support on Productivity and Outcome Quality in Process Redesign Groups." *Journal of Organizational Computing and Electronic Commerce* 8, no. 2 (1998).

Lee, Soonchul. "The Impact of Office Information Systems on Power and Influence." *Journal of Management Information Systems* 8, no. 2 (Fall 1991).

Leonard-Barton, Dorothy, and John J. Sviokla. "Putting Expert Systems to Work." *Harvard Business Review* (March–April 1988).

Lou, Hao, and Richard W. Scannell. "Acceptance of Groupware: The Relationships Among Use, Satisfaction, and Outcomes." *Journal of Organizational Computing and Electronic Commerce* 6, no. 2 (1996).

Maes, Patti. "Agents that Reduce Work and Information Overload." *Communications of the ACM* 38, no. 7 (July 1994).

Maes, Patti, Robert H. Guttman, and Alexandros G. Moukas. "Agents that Buy and Sell." *Communications of the ACM* 42, no. 3 (March 1999).

Malhotra, Yogesh. "Toward a Knowledge Ecology for Organizational White-Waters." Keynote Presentations for the Knowledge Ecology Fair '98 (1998).

McCarthy, John. "Generality in Artificial Intelligence." *Communications of the ACM* (December 1987).

Munakata, Toshinori, and Yashvant Jani. "Fuzzy Systems: An Overview." *Communications of the ACM* 37, no. 3 (March 1994).

Nash, Jim. "State of the Market, Art, Union, and Technology." *AI Expert* (January 1993).

O'Leary, Daniel, Daniel Kuokka, and Robert Plant. "Artificial Intelligence and Virtual Organizations." *Communications of the ACM* 40, no. 1 (January 1997).

Orlikowski, Wanda J. "Learning from Notes: Organizational Issues in Groupware Implementation." Sloan Working Paper, no. 3428. Cambridge, MA: Sloan School of Management, Massachusetts Institute of Technology (1992).

Panko, Raymond R. "Is Office Productivity Stagnant?" *MIS Quarterly* 15, no. 2 (June 1991).

Porat, Marc. "The Information Economy: Definition and Measurement." Washington, DC: U.S. Department of Commerce, Office of Telecommunications (May 1977).

Press, Lawrence. "Lotus Notes (Groupware) in Context." *Journal of Organizational Computing* 2, nos. 3 and 4 (1992b).

Roach, Stephen S. "Industrialization of the Information Economy." New York: Morgan Stanley and Co. (1984).

——— . "Making Technology Work." New York: Morgan Stanley and Co. (1993).

——— . "Services Under Siege—The Restructuring Imperative." *Harvard Business Review* (September–October 1991).

——— . "Technology and the Service Sector." *Technological Forecasting and Social Change* 34, no. 4 (December 1988).

——— . "The Hollow Ring of the Productivity Revival." *Harvard Business Review* (November–December 1996).

——— . "Working Better or Just Harder?" *The New York Times* (February 14, 2000).

Ruhleder, Karen, and John Leslie King. "Computer Support for Work Across Space, Time, and Social Worlds." *Journal of Organizational Computing* 1, no. 4 (1991).

Rumelhart, David E., Bernard Widrow, and Michael A. Lehr. "The Basic Ideas in Neural Networks." *Communications of the ACM* 37, no. 3 (March 1994).

Salisbury, J. Kenneth, Jr. "Making Graphics Physically Tangible." *Communications of the ACM* 42, no. 8 (August 1999).

Schultze, Ulrike, and Betty Vandenbosch. "Information Overload in a Groupware Environment: Now You See It, Now You Don't." *Journal of Organizational Computing and Electronic Commerce* 8, no. 2 (1998).

Selker, Ted. "Coach: A Teaching Agent that Learns." *Communications of the ACM* 37, no. 7 (July 1994).

Sibigtroth, James M. "Implementing Fuzzy Expert Rules in Hardware." *AI Expert* (April 1992).

Sproull, Lee, and Sara Kiesler. *Connections: New Ways of Working in the Networked Organization.* Cambridge, MA: MIT Press (1992).

Starbuck, William H. "Learning by Knowledge-Intensive Firms." *Journal of Management Studies* 29, no. 6 (November 1992).

Stirland, Sarah. "Armed with Insight." *Wall Street and Technology* 16, no. 8 (August 1998).

Storey, Veda C., and Robert C. Goldstein. "Knowledge-Based Approaches to Database Design," *MIS Quarterly* 17, no. 1 (March 1993).

Stylianou, Anthony C., Gregory R. Madey, and Robert D. Smith. "Selection Criteria for Expert System Shells: A Socio-Technical Framework." *Communications of the ACM* 35, no. 10 (October 1992).

Sukhatme, Gaurav S., and Maja J. Mataric. "Embedding Robots into the Internet." *Communications of the ACM* 43, no. 5 (May 2000).

Sviokla, John J. "An Examination of the Impact of Expert Systems on the Firm: The Case of XCON." *MIS Quarterly* 14, no. 5 (June 1990).

——— . "Expert Systems and Their Impact on the Firm: The Effects of PlanPower Use on the Information Processing Capacity of the Financial Collaborative." *Journal of Management Information Systems* 6, no. 3 (Winter 1989–1990).

Trippi, Robert, and Efraim Turban. "The Impact of Parallel and Neural Computing on Managerial Decision Making." *Journal of Management Information Systems* 6, no. 3 (Winter 1989–1990).

Turban, Efraim, and Paul R. Watkins. "Integrating Expert Systems and Decision Support Systems." *MIS Quarterly* (June 1986).

Vandenbosch, Betty, and Michael J. Ginzberg. "Lotus Notes and Collaboration: Plus ca change . . ." *Journal of Management Information Systems* 13, no. 3 (Winter 1997).

Weitzel, John R., and Larry Kerschberg. "Developing Knowledge Based Systems: Reorganizing the System Development Life Cycle." *Communications of the ACM* (April 1989).

Wijnhoven, Fons. "Designing Organizational Memories: Concept and Method." *Journal of Organizational Computing and Electronic Commerce* 8, no. 1 (1998).

Widrow, Bernard, David E. Rumelhart, and Michael A. Lehr. "Neural Networks: Applications in Industry, Business, and Science." *Communications of the ACM* 37, no. 3 (March 1994).

Wong, David, Noemi Paciorek, and Dana Moore. "Java-Based Mobile Agents." *Communications of the ACM* 42, no. 3 (March 1999).

Zack, Michael H. "Managing Codified Knowledge." *Sloan Management Review* 40, no. 4 (Summer 1999).

Zadeh, Lotfi A. "The Calculus of Fuzzy If/Then Rules." *AI Expert* (March 1992).

——— . "Fuzzy Logic, Neural Networks, and Soft Computing." *Communications of the ACM* 37, no. 3 (March 1994).

CHAPTER 12

Ackerman, Mark S., and Christine A. Halverson. "Reexamining Organizational Memory." *Communications of the ACM* 43, no. 1 (January 2000).

Alavi, Maryam, and Erich A. Joachimsthaler. "Revisiting DSS Implementation Research: A Meta-Analysis of the Literature and Suggestions for Researchers." *MIS Quarterly* 16, no. 1 (March 1992).

Anthes, Gary H. "Notes System Sends Federal Property Data Nationwide." *Computerworld* (August 8, 1994).

Brachman, Ronald J., Tom Khabaza, Willi Kloesgen, Gregory Piatetsky-Shapiro, and Evangelos Simoudis. "Mining Business Databases." *Communications of the ACM* 39, no. 11 (November 1996).

Caouette, Margarette J., and Bridget N. O'Connor. "The Impact of Group Support Systems on Corporate Teams' Stages of Development." *Journal of Organizational Computing and Electronic Commerce* 8, no. 1 (1998).

Chidambaram, Laku. "Relational Development in Computer-Supported Groups." *MIS Quarterly* 20, no. 2 (June 1996).

Dennis, Alan R. "Information Exchange and Use in Group Decision Making: You Can Lead a Group to Information, but You Can't Make It Think." *MIS Quarterly* 20, no. 4 (December 1996).

Dennis, Alan R., Craig K. Tyran, Douglas R. Vogel, and Jay Nunamaker, Jr. "Group Support Systems for Strategic Planning." *Journal of Management Information Systems* 14, no. 1 (Summer 1997).

Dennis, Alan R., Jay E. Aronson, William G. Henriger, and Edward D. Walker III. "Structuring Time and Task in Electronic Brainstorming." *MIS Quarterly* 23, no. 1 (March 1999).

Dennis, Alan R., Jay F. Nunamaker, Jr., and Douglas R. Vogel. "A Comparison of Laboratory and Field Research in the Study of Electronic Meeting Systems." *Journal of Management Information Systems* 7, no. 3 (Winter 1990–1991).

Dennis, Alan R., Joey F. George, Len M. Jessup, Jay F. Nunamaker, and Douglas R. Vogel. "Information Technology to Support Electronic Meetings." *MIS Quarterly* 12, no. 4 (December 1988).

Dennis, Alan R., Sridar K. Pootheri, and Vijaya L. Natarajan. "Lessons from Early Adopters of Web Groupware." *Journal of Management Information Systems* 14, no. 4 (Spring 1998).

DeSanctis, Geraldine, and R. Brent Gallupe. "A Foundation for the Study of Group Decision Support Systems." *Management Science* 33, no. 5 (May 1987).

Dutta, Soumitra, Berend Wierenga, and Arco Dalebout. "Designing Management Support Systems Using an Integrative Perspective." *Communications of the ACM* 40, no. 6 (June 1997).

Edelstein, Herb. "Technology How To: Mining Data Warehouses." *Information Week* (January 8, 1996).

El Sawy, Omar. "Personal Information Systems for Strategic Scanning in Turbulent Environments." *MIS Quarterly* 9, no. 1 (March 1985).

El Sherif, Hisham, and Omar A. El Sawy. "Issue-Based Decision Support Systems for the Egyptian Cabinet." *MIS Quarterly* 12, no. 4 (December 1988).

Etzioni, Oren. "The World-Wide Web: Quagmire or Gold Mine?" *Communications of the ACM* 39, no. 11 (November 1996).

Fjermestad, Jerry. "An Integrated Framework for Group Support Systems." *Journal of Organizational Computing and Electronic Commerce* 8, no. 2 (1998).

Fjermestad, Jerry, and Starr Roxanne Hiltz. "An Assessment of Group Support Systems Experimental Research: Methodology and Results." *Journal of Management Information Systems* 15, no. 3 (Winter 1998–1999).

Forgionne, Guiseppe. "Management Support System Effectiveness: Further Empirical Evidence." *Journal of the Association for Information Systems* 1 (May 2000).

Gallupe, R. Brent, Geraldine DeSanctis, and Gary W. Dickson. "Computer-Based Support for Group Problem-Finding: An Experimental Investigation." *MIS Quarterly* 12, no. 2 (June 1988).

George, Joey. "Organizational Decision Support Systems." *Journal of Management Information Systems* 8, no. 3 (Winter 1991–1992).

Ginzberg, Michael J., W. R. Reitman, and E. A. Stohr, eds. *Decision Support Systems.* New York: North Holland Publishing Co. (1982).

Grobowski, Ron, Chris McGoff, Doug Vogel, Ben Martz, and Jay Nunamaker. "Implementing Electronic Meeting Systems at IBM: Lessons Learned and Success Factors." *MIS Quarterly* 14, no. 4 (December 1990).

Henderson, John C., and David A. Schilling. "Design and Implementation of Decision Support Systems in the Public Sector." *MIS Quarterly* (June 1985).

Ho, T. H., and K. S. Raman. "The Effect of GDSS on Small Group Meetings." *Journal of Management Information Systems* 8, no. 2 (Fall 1991).

Hogue, Jack T. "Decision Support Systems and the Traditional Computer Information System Function: An Examination of Relationships During DSS Application Development." *Journal of Management Information Systems* (Summer 1985).

Hogue, Jack T. "A Framework for the Examination of Management Involvement in Decision Support Systems." *Journal of Management Information Systems* 4, no. 1 (Summer 1987).

Houdeshel, George, and Hugh J. Watson. "The Management Information and Decision Support (MIDS) System at Lockheed, Georgia." *MIS Quarterly* 11, no. 2 (March 1987).

Jessup, Leonard M., Terry Connolly, and Jolene Galegher. "The Effects of Anonymity on GDSS Group Process with an Idea-Generating Task." *MIS Quarterly* 14, no. 3 (September 1990).

Jones, Jack William, Carol Saunders, and Raymond McLeod, Jr., "Media Usage and Velocity in Executive Information Acquisition: An Exploratory Study." *European Journal of Information Systems* 2 (1993).

Kalakota, Ravi, Jan Stallaert, and Andrew B. Whinston. "Worldwide Real-Time Decision Support Systems for Electronic Commerce Applications." *Journal of Organizational Computing and Electronic Commerce* 6, no. 1 (1996).

Keen, Peter G. W., and M. S. Scott Morton. *Decision Support Systems: An Organizational Perspective.* Reading, MA: Addison-Wesley (1982).

King, John. "Successful Implementation of Large-Scale Decision Support Systems: Computerized Models in U.S. Economic Policy Making." *Systems Objectives Solutions* (November 1983).

Kraemer, Kenneth L., and John Leslie King. "Computer-Based Systems for Cooperative Work and Group Decision Making." *ACM Computing Surveys* 20, no. 2 (June 1988).

Laudon, Kenneth C. *Communications Technology and Democratic Participation.* New York: Praeger (1977).

Leidner, Dorothy E., and Joyce Elam. "Executive Information Systems: Their Impact on Executive Decision Making." *Journal of Management Information Systems* (Winter 1993–1994).

Leidner, Dorothy E., and Joyce Elam. "The Impact of Executive Information Systems on Organizational Design, Intelligence, and Decision Making." *Organization Science* 6, no. 6 (November–December 1995).

Lewe, Henrik, and Helmut Krcmar. "A Computer-Supported Cooperative Work Research Laboratory." *Journal of Management Information Systems* 8, no. 3 (Winter 1991–1992).

Miranda, Shaila M., and Robert P. Bostrum. "The Impact of Group Support Systems on Group Conflict and Conflict Management." *Journal of Management Information Systems* 10, no. 3 (Winter 1993–1994).

———. Meeting Facilitation: Process Versus Content Interventions." *Journal of Management Information Systems* 15, no. 4 (Spring 1999).

Nidumolu, Sarma R., Seymour E. Goodman, Douglas R. Vogel, and Ann K. Danowitz. "Information Technology for Local Administration Support: The Governorates Project in Egypt." *MIS Quarterly* 20, no. 2 (June 1996).

Niederman, Fred, Catherine M. Beise, and Peggy M. Beranek. "Issues and Concerns about Computer-Supported Meetings: The Facilitator's Perspective." *MIS Quarterly* 20, no. 1 (March 1996).

Nunamaker, J. F., Alan R. Dennis, Joseph S. Valacich, Douglas R. Vogel, and Joey F. George. "Electronic Meeting Systems to Support Group Work." *Communications of the ACM* 34, no. 7 (July 1991).

Nunamaker, Jay, Robert O. Briggs, Daniel D. Mittleman, Douglas R. Vogel, and Pierre A. Balthazard. "Lessons from a Dozen Years of Group Support Systems Research: A Discussion of Lab and Field Findings." *Journal of Management Information Systems* 13, no. 3 (Winter 1997).

O'Keefe, Robert M., and Tim McEachern. "Web-based Customer Decision Support Systems." *Communications of the ACM* 41, no. 3 (March 1998).

Pinsonneault, Alain, Henri Barki, R. Brent Gallupe, and Norberto Hoppen. "Electronic Brainstorming: The Illusion of Productivity." *Information Systems Research* 10, no. 2 (July 1999).

Rockart, John F., and David W. DeLong. *Executive Support Systems: The Emergence of Top Management Computer Use.* Homewood, IL: Dow-Jones Irwin (1988).

Schwabe, Gerhard. "Providing for Organizational Memory in Computer-Supported Meetings." *Journal of Organizational Computing and Electronic Commerce* 9, no. 2 and 3 (1999).

Sharda, Ramesh, and David M. Steiger. "Inductive Model Analysis Systems: Enhancing Model Analysis in Decision Support Systems." *Information Systems Research* 7, no. 3 (September 1996).

Silver, Mark S. "Decision Support Systems: Directed and Nondirected Change." *Information Systems Research* 1, no. 1 (March 1990).

Sprague, R. H., and E. D. Carlson. *Building Effective Decision Support Systems.* Englewood Cliffs, NJ: Prentice Hall (1982).

Todd, Peter, and Izak Benbasat. "Evaluating the Impact of DSS, Cognitive Effort, and Incentives on Strategy Selection. *Information Systems Research* 10, no. 4 (December 1999).

"The New Role for 'Executive Information Systems.' " *I/S Analyzer* (January 1992).

Turban, Efraim, and Jay E. Aronson. *Decision Support Systems and Intelligent Systems: Management Support Systems,* 5th ed. Upper Saddle River, NJ: Prentice Hall (1998).

Tyran, Craig K., Alan R. Dennis, Douglas R. Vogel, and J. F. Nunamaker, Jr. "The Application of Electronic Meeting Technology to Support Senior Management." *MIS Quarterly* 16, no. 3 (September 1992).

Vedder, Richard G., Michael T. Vanacek, C. Stephen Guynes, and James J. Cappel. "CEO and CIO Perspectives on Competitive Intelligence." *Communications of the ACM* 42, no. 8 (August 1999).

Vogel, Douglas R., Jay F. Nunamaker, William Benjamin Martz, Jr., Ronald Grobowski, and Christopher McGoff. "Electronic Meeting System Experience at IBM." *Journal of Management Information Systems* 6, no. 3 (Winter 1989–1990).

Volonino, Linda, and Hugh J. Watson. "The Strategic Business Objectives Method for EIS Development." *Journal of Management Information Systems* 7, no. 3 (Winter 1990–1991).

Walls, Joseph G., George R. Widmeyer, and Omar A. El Sawy. "Building an Information System Design Theory for Vigilant EIS." *Information Systems Research* 3, no. 1 (March 1992).

Watson, Hugh J., Astrid Lipp, Pamela Z. Jackson, Abdelhafid Dahmani, and William B. Fredenberger. "Organizational Support for Decision Support Systems." *Journal of Management Information Systems* 5, no. 4 (Spring 1989).

Watson, Hugh J., R. Kelly Rainer, Jr., and Chang E. Koh. "Executive Information Systems: A Framework for Development and a Survey of Current Practices." *MIS Quarterly* 15, no. 1 (March 1991).

Watson, Richard T., Geraldine DeSanctis, and Marshall Scott Poole. "Using a GDSS to Facilitate Group Consensus: Some Intended and Unintended Consequences." *MIS Quarterly* 12, no. 3 (September 1988).

Watson, Richard T., Teck-Hua Ho, and K. S. Raman. "Culture: A Fourth Dimension of Group Support Systems." *Communications of the ACM* 37, no. 10 (October 1994).

Wilder, Clinton. "Tapping the Pipeline." *Information Week* (March 15, 1999).

Wreden, Nick. "Business Intelligence: Turning on Success," *Beyond Computing* (September 1997).

CHAPTER 13

Abdel-Hamid, Tarek K., Kishore Sengupta, and Clint Swett. "The Impact of Goals on Software Project Management: An

Experimental Investigation." *MIS Quarterly 23,* no. 4 (December 1999).

Alberts, David S. "The Economics of Software Quality Assurance." Washington, DC: National Computer Conference, 1976 Proceedings.

Banker, Rajiv D., Robert J. Kaufmann, and **Rachna Kumar.** "An Empirical Test of Object-Based Output Measurement Metrics in a Computer-Aided Software Engineering (CASE) Environment." *Journal of Management Information Systems* 8, no. 3 (Winter 1991–1992).

Banker, Rajiv D., Srikant M. Datar, Chris F. Kemerer, and **Dani Zweig.** "Software Complexity and Maintenance Costs." *Communications of the ACM* 36, no. 11 (November 1993).

Banker, Rajiv D., and **Chris F. Kemerer.** "Performance Evaluation Metrics in Information Systems Development: A Principal-Agent Model." *Information Systems Research* 3, no. 4 (December 1992).

Boehm, Barry W. "Understanding and Controlling Software Costs." *IEEE Transactions on Software Engineering* 14, no. 10 (October 1988).

Corbato, Fernando J. "On Building Systems that Will Fail." *Communications of the ACM* 34, no. 9 (September 1991).

Chin, Shu-Kai. "High-Confidence Design for Security." *Communications of the ACM* 42, no. 7 (July 1999).

Dekleva, Sasa M. "The Influence of Information Systems Development Approach on Maintenance." *MIS Quarterly* 16, no. 3 (September 1992).

DeMarco, Tom. *Structured Analysis and System Specification.* New York: Yourdon Press (1978).

Dijkstra, E. "Structured Programming." In *Classics in Software Engineering,* edited by Edward Nash Yourdon. New York: Yourdon Press (1979).

Domges, Rolf, and **Klaus Pohl.** "Adapting Traceability Environments to Project-Specific Needs." *Communications of the ACM* 41, no. 12 (December 1998).

Durst, Robert, Terrence Champion, Brian Witten, Eric Miller, and Luigi Spagnuolo. "Testing and Evaluating Computer Intrusion Detection Systems." *Communications of the ACM* 42, no. 7 (July 1999).

Dutta, Soumitra, Luk N. Van Wassenhove, and **Selvan Kulandaiswamy.** "Benchmarking European Software Management Practices." *Communications of the ACM* 41, no. 6 (June 1998).

Fraser, Martin D., and **Vijay K. Vaishnavi.** "A Formal Specifications Maturity Model." *Communications of the ACM* 40, no. 12 (December 1997).

Forrest, Stephanie, Steven A. Hofmeyr, and **Anil Somayaji.** "Computer Immunology." *Communications of the ACM* 40, no. 10 (October 1997).

Gane, Chris, and **Trish Sarson.** *Structured Systems Analysis: Tools and Techniques.* Englewood Cliffs, NJ: Prentice Hall (1979).

Ghosh, Anup K., and **Jeffrey M. Voas.** "Inoculating Software for Survivability." *Communications of the ACM* 42, no. 7 (July 1999).

Goan, Terrance. "A Cop on the Beat: Collecting and Appraising Intrusion Evidence." *Communications of the ACM* 42, no. 7 (July 1999).

Jajoda, Sushil, Catherine D. McCollum, and **Paul Ammann.** "Trusted Recovery." *Communications of the ACM* 42, no. 7 (July 1999).

Jarzabek, Stan, and **Riri Huang.** "The Case for User-Centered CASE Tools." *Communications of the ACM* 41, no. 8 (August 1998).

Johnson, Philip M. "Reengineering Inspection." *Communications of the ACM* 41, no. 2 (February 1998).

Kaplan, David, Ramayya Krishnan, Rema Padman, and **James Peters.** "Assessing Data Quality in Accounting Information Systems." *Communications of the ACM* 41, no. 2 (February 1998).

Kemerer, Chris F. "Progress, Obstacles, and Opportunities in Software Engineering Economics." *Communications of the ACM* 41, no. 8 (August 1998).

Klein, Barbara D., Dale L. Goodhue, and **Gordon B. Davis.** "Can Humans Detect Errors in Data?" *MIS Quarterly* 21, no. 2 (June 1997).

Knowles, Ann. "EDI Experiments with the Net." *Software Magazine* (January 1997).

Laudon, Kenneth C. "Data Quality and Due Process in Large Interorganizational Record Systems." *Communications of the ACM* 29 (January 1986a).

———. *Dossier Society: Value Choices in the Design of National Information Systems.* New York: Columbia University Press (1986b).

Lientz, Bennett P., and **E. Burton Swanson.** *Software Maintenance Management.* Reading, MA: Addison-Wesley (1980).

Littlewood, Bev, and **Lorenzo Strigini.** "The Risks of Software." *Scientific American* 267, no. 5 (November 1992).

———. "Validation of Ultra-high Dependability for Software-based Systems." *Communications of the ACM* 36, no. 11 (November 1993).

Loch, Karen D., Houston H. Carr, and **Merrill E. Warkentin.** "Threats to Information Systems: Today's Reality, Yesterday's Understanding." *MIS Quarterly* 16, no. 2 (June 1992).

Mazzucchelli, Louis. "Structured Analysis Can Streamline Software Design." *Computerworld* (December 9, 1985).

Needham, Roger M. "Denial of Service: An Example." *Communications of the ACM* 37, no. 11 (November 1994).

Nerson, Jean-Marc. "Applying Object-Oriented Analysis and Design." *Communications of the ACM* 35, no. 9 (September 1992).

Neumann, Peter G. "Risks Considered Global(ly)." *Communications of the ACM* 35, no. 1 (January 1993).

Oppliger, Rolf. "Internet Security, Firewalls, and Beyond." *Communications of the ACM* 40, no.7 (May 1997).

Orr, Kenneth. "Data Quality and Systems Theory." *Communications of the ACM* 41, no. 2 (February 1998).

Parsons, Jeffrey, and **Yair Wand.** "Using Objects for Systems Analysis." *Communications of the ACM* 40, no. 12 (December 1997).

Rainer, Rex Kelley, Jr., Charles A. Snyder, and **Houston H. Carr.** "Risk Analysis for Information Technology." *Journal of Management Information Systems* 8, no. 1 (Summer 1991).

Ravichandran, T., and **Arun Rai.** "Total Quality Management in Information Systems Development." *Journal of Management Information Systems* 16, no. 3 (Winter 1999–2000).

Redman, Thomas. "The Impact of Poor Data Quality on the Typical Enterprise." *Communications of the ACM* 41, no. 2 (February 1998).

Segev, Arie, Janna Porra, and **Malu Roldan.** "Internet Security and the Case of Bank of America." *Communications of the ACM* 41, no. 10 (October 1998).

Slaughter, Sandra A., Donald E. Harter, and Mayuram S. Krishnan. "Evaluating the Cost of Software Quality." *Communications of the ACM* 41, no. 8 (August 1998).

Stillerman, Matthew, Carla Marceau, and Maureen Stillman. "Intrusion Detection for Distributed Applications." *Communications of the ACM* 42, no. 7 (July 1999).

Straub, Detmar W., and Richard J. Welke. "Coping with Systems Risk: Security Planning Models for Management Decision Making." *MIS Quarterly* 22, no. 4 (December 1998).

Strong, Diane M., Yang W. Lee, and Richard Y. Wang. "Data Quality in Context." *Communications of the ACM* 40, no. 5 (May 1997).

Swanson, Kent, Dave McComb, Jill Smith, and Don McCubbrey. "The Application Software Factory: Applying Total Quality Techniques to Systems Development." *MIS Quarterly* 15, no. 4 (December 1991).

Tayi, Giri Kumar, and Donald P. Ballou. "Examining Data Quality." *Communications of the ACM* 41, no. 2 (February 1998).

United States General Accounting Office. "Patriot Missile Defense: Software Problem Led to System Failure at Dharan, Saudi Arabia." GAO/IMTEC-92-26 (February 1992).

Wand, Yair, and Richard Y. Wang. "Anchoring Data Quality Dimensions in Ontological Foundations." *Communications of the ACM* 39, no. 11 (November 1996).

Wang, Richard. "A Product Perspective on Total Data Quality Management." *Communications of the ACM* 41, no. 2 (February 1998).

Wang, Richard Y., Yang W. Lee, Leo L. Pipino, and Diane M. Strong. "Manage Your Information as a Product." *Sloan Management Review* 39, no. 4 (Summer 1998).

Weber, Ron. *EDP Auditing: Conceptual Foundations and Practice,* 2nd ed. New York: McGraw-Hill (1988).

CHAPTER 14

Association of Computing Machinery. "ACM's Code of Ethics and Professional Conduct." *Communications of the ACM* 36, no. 12 (December 1993).

Baig, Edward C., Marcia Stepanek, and Neill Gross. "Privacy." *Business Week* (April 5, 1999).

Berdichevsky, Daniel, and Erik Neunschwander. "Toward an Ethics of Persuasive Technology." *Communications of the ACM* 42, no. 5 (May 1999).

Bjerklie, David. "Does E-Mail Mean Everyone's Mail?" *Information Week* (January 3, 1994).

Bowen, Jonathan. "The Ethics of Safety-Critical Systems." *Communications of the ACM* 43, no. 3 (April 2000).

Brod, Craig. *Techno Stress—The Human Cost of the Computer Revolution.* Reading MA: Addison-Wesley (1982).

Brown Bag Software vs. Symantec Corp. 960 F2D 1465 (Ninth Circuit, 1992).

Cavazos, Edward A. "The Legal Risks of Setting up Shop in Cyberspace." *Journal of Organizational Computing* 6, no. 1 (1996).

Chabrow, Eric R. "The Internet: Copyrights." *Information Week* (March 25, 1996).

Chen, David W. "Man Charged with Sabotage of Computers." *The New York Times* (February 18, 1998).

Cheng, Hsing K., Ronald R. Sims, and Hildy Teegen. "To Purchase or to Pirate Software: An Empirical Study." *Journal of Management Information Systems* 13, no. 4 (Spring 1997).

Clarke, Roger. "Internet Privacy Concerns Confirm the Case for Intervention." *Communications of the ACM* 42, no. 2 (February 1999).

Collins, W. Robert, Keith W. Miller, Bethany J. Spielman, and Phillip Wherry. "How Good Is Good Enough? An Ethical Analysis of Software Construction and Use." *Communications of the ACM* 37, no. 1 (January 1994).

Computer Systems Policy Project. "Perspectives on the National Information Infrastructure." (January 12, 1993).

Couger, J. Daniel. "Preparing IS Students to Deal with Ethical Issues." *MIS Quarterly* 13, no. 2 (June 1989).

Cranor, Lorrie Faith, and Brian A. LaMacchia. "Spam!" *Communications of the ACM* 41, no. 8 (August 1998).

Dalton, Gregory. "Online Data's Fine Line." *Information Week* (March 29, 1999).

Dejoie, Roy, George Fowler, and David Paradice, eds. *Ethical Issues in Information Systems.* Boston: Boyd & Fraser (1991).

Denning, Dorothy E., et al., "To Tap or Not to Tap." *Communications of the ACM* 36, no. 3 (March 1993).

Diamond, Edwin, and Stephen Bates. "Law and Order Comes to Cyberspace." *Technology Review* (October 1995).

Gattiker, Urs E., and Helen Kelley. "Morality and Computers: Attitudes and Differences in Judgments." *Information Systems Research* 10, no. 3 (September 1999).

Ghajar, Bobby A., Lisa M. Martens, and Chris Jandacek. "Policing the Pirates." *The Industry Standard* (October 4, 1999).

Gopal, Ram D., and G. Lawrence Sanders. "Preventive and Deterrent Controls for Software Piracy." *Journal of Management Information Systems* 13, no. 4 (Spring 1997).

Graham, Robert L. "The Legal Protection of Computer Software." *Communications of the ACM* (May 1984).

Green, R. H. *The Ethical Manager.* New York: Macmillan (1994).

Harrington, Susan J. "The Effect of Codes of Ethics and Personal Denial of Responsibility on Computer Abuse Judgments and Intentions." *MIS Quarterly* 20, no. 2 (September 1996).

Hafner, Katie. " For the Well Connected, All the World's an Office." *The New York Times Circuits* (March 30, 2000).

Huff, Chuck, and C. Dianne Martin. "Computing Consequences: A Framework for Teaching Ethical Computing." *Communications of the ACM* 38, no. 12 (December 1995).

Joes, Kathryn. "EDS Set to Restore Cash-Machine Network." *The New York Times* (March 26, 1993).

Johnson, Deborah G. "Ethics Online." *Communications of the ACM* 40, no. 1 (January 1997).

Johnson, Deborah G., and John M. Mulvey. "Accountability and Computer Decision Systems." *Communications of the ACM* 38, no. 12 (December 1995).

King, Julia. "It's CYA Time." *Computerworld* (March 30, 1992).

Kling, Rob. "When Organizations Are Perpetrators: The Conditions of Computer Abuse and Computer Crime." In *Computerization & Controversy: Value Conflicts & Social Choices,* edited by Charles Dunlop and Rob Kling. New York: Academic Press (1991).

Laudon, Kenneth C. "Ethical Concepts and Information Technology." *Communications of the ACM* 38, no. 12 (December 1995).

Lohr, Steve. "A Nation Ponders Its Growing Digital Divide." *The New York Times* (October 21, 1996).

Markoff, John. "Growing Compatibility Issue: Computers and User Privacy." *The New York Times* (March 3, 1999).

———. "In the Data Storage Race, Disks Are Outpacing Chips." *The New York Times* (February 23, 1998).

Mason, Richard O. "Applying Ethics to Information Technology Issues." *Communications of the ACM* 38, no. 12 (December 1995).

Mason, Richard O. "Four Ethical Issues in the Information Age." *MIS Quarterly* 10, no. 1 (March 1986).

Memon, Nasir, and **Ping Wah Wong.** "Protecting Digital Media Content." *Communications of the ACM* 41, no. 7 (July 1998).

Milberg, Sandra J., Sandra J. Burke, H. Jeff Smith, and **Ernest A. Kallman.** "Values, Personal Information Privacy, and Regulatory Approaches." *Communications of the ACM* 38, no. 12 (December 1995).

Mykytyn, Kathleen, Peter P. Mykytyn, Jr., and **Craig W. Slinkman.** "Expert Systems: A Question of Liability." *MIS Quarterly* 14, no. 1 (March 1990).

Neumann, Peter G. "Inside RISKS: Computers, Ethics, and Values." *Communications of the ACM* 34, no. 7 (July 1991).

———. "Inside RISKS: Fraud by Computer." *Communications of the ACM* 35, no. 8 (August 1992).

National Telecommunications & Information Administration, U.S. Department of Commerce. "Falling Through the Net: Defining the Digital Divide." July 8, 1999.

Nissenbaum, Helen. "Computing and Accountability." *Communications of the ACM* 37, no. 1 (January 1994).

Okerson, Ann. "Who Owns Digital Works?" *Scientific American* (July 1996).

Oz, Effy. "Ethical Standards for Information Systems Professionals." *MIS Quarterly* 16, no. 4 (December 1992).

———. *Ethics for the Information Age.* Dubuque, Iowa: W. C. Brown (1994).

Reagle, Joseph, and **Lorrie Faith Cranor.** "The Platform for Privacy Preferences." *Communications of the ACM* 42, no. 2 (February 1999).

Redman, Thomas C. "The Impact of Poor Data Quality on the Typical Enterprise." *Communications of the ACM* 41, no. 2 (February 1998).

Rifkin, Jeremy. "Watch Out for Trickle-Down Technology." *The New York Times* (March 16, 1993).

Rigdon, Joan E. "Frequent Glitches in New Software Bug Users." *The Wall Street Journal* (January 18, 1995).

Rotenberg, Marc. "Communications Privacy: Implications for Network Design." *Communications of the ACM* 36, no. 8 (August 1993).

———. "Inside RISKS: Protecting Privacy." *Communications of the ACM* 35, no. 4 (April 1992).

Samuelson, Pamela. "Computer Programs and Copyright's Fair Use Doctrine." *Communications of the ACM* 36, no. 9 (September 1993).

———. "Copyright's Fair Use Doctrine and Digital Data." *Communications of the ACM* 37, no. 1 (January 1994).

———. "Liability for Defective Electronic Information." *Communications of the ACM* 36, no. 1 (January 1993).

———. "Self-Plagiarism or Fair Use?" *Communications of the ACM* 37, no. 8 (August 1994).

———. "The Ups and Downs of Look and Feel." *Communications of the ACM* 36, no. 4 (April 1993).

Sipior, Janice C., and **Burke T. Ward.** "The Dark Side of Employee E-mail." *Communications of the ACM* 42, no. 7 (July 1999).

———. "The Ethical and Legal Quandary of E-mail Privacy." *Communications of the ACM* 38, no. 12 (December 1995).

Smith, H. Jeff. "Privacy Policies and Practices: Inside the Organizational Maze." *Communications of the ACM* 36, no. 12 (December 1993).

Smith, H. Jeff, and **John Hasnas.** "Ethics and Information Systems: The Corporate Domain." *MIS Quarterly* 23, no. 1 (March 1999).

Smith, H. Jeff, Sandra J. Milberg, and **Sandra J. Burke.** "Information Privacy: Measuring Individuals' Concerns about Organizational Practices." *MIS Quarterly* 20, no. 2 (June 1996).

Straub, Detmar W., Jr., and **Rosann Webb Collins.** "Key Information Liability Issues Facing Managers: Software Piracy, Proprietary Databases, and Individual Rights to Privacy." *MIS Quarterly* 14, no. 2 (June 1990).

Straub, Detmar W., Jr., and **William D. Nance.** "Discovering and Disciplining Computer Abuse in Organizations: A Field Study." *MIS Quarterly* 14, no. 1 (March 1990).

The Telecommunications Policy Roundtable. "Renewing the Commitment to a Public Interest Telecommunications Policy." *Communications of the ACM* 37, no. 1 (January 1994).

Thong, James Y. L., and **Chee-Sing Yap.** "Testing an Ethical Decision-Making Theory." *Journal of Management Information Systems* 15, no. 1 (Summer 1998).

Tuttle, Brad, Adrian Harrell, and **Paul Harrison.** "Moral Hazard, Ethical Considerations, and the Decision to Implement an Information System." *Journal of Management Information Systems* 13, no. 4 (Spring 1997).

United States Department of Health, Education, and Welfare. *Records, Computers, and the Rights of Citizens.* Cambridge: MIT Press (1973).

Wang, Huaiqing, Matthew K. O. Lee, and **Chen Wang.** "Consumer Privacy Concerns about Internet Marketing." *Communications of the ACM* 41, no. 3 (March 1998).

Whiting, Rich. "Mind Your Business." *Information Week* (March 6, 2000).

Wilder, Clinton. "Feds Allege Internet Scam." *Information Week* (June 10, 1996).

Zviran, Moshe, and **William J. Haga.** "Password Security: An Empirical Study." *Journal of Management Information Systems* 15, no. 4 (Spring 1999).

CHAPTER 15

Agarwal, P. K. "Building India's National Internet Backbone." *Communications of the ACM* 42, no. 6 (June 1999).

Blanning, Robert W. "Establishing a Corporate Presence on the Internet in Singapore." *Journal of Organizational Computing and Electronic Commerce* 9, no. 1 (1999).

Burkhardt, Grey E., Seymour E. Goodman, Arun Mehta, and **Larry Press.** "The Internet in India: Better Times Ahead?" *Communications of the ACM* 41, no. 11 (November 1998).

Chismar, William G., and **Laku Chidambaram.** "Telecommunications and the Structuring of U.S. Multinational Corporations." *International Information Systems* 1, no. 4 (October 1992).

Cox, Butler. *Globalization: The IT Challenge.* Sunnyvale, CA: Amdahl Executive Institute (1991).

Deans, Candace P., and **Michael J. Kane.** *International Dimensions of Information Systems and Technology.* Boston, MA: PWS-Kent (1992).

Deans, Candace P., Kirk R. Karwan, Martin D. Goslar, David A. Ricks, and **Brian Toyne.** "Key International Issues in U.S.-Based Multinational Corporations." *Journal of Management Information Systems* 7, no. 4 (Spring 1991).

Dutta, Amitava. "Telecommunications Infrastructure in Developing Nations." *International Information Systems* 1, no. 3 (July 1992).

Holland, Christopher, Geoff Lockett, and **Ian Blackman.** "Electronic Data Interchange Implementation: A Comparison of U.S. and European Cases." *International Information Systems* 1, no. 4 (October 1992).

Ives, Blake, and **Sirkka Jarvenpaa.** "Applications of Global Information Technology: Key Issues for Management." *MIS Quarterly* 15, no. 1 (March 1991).

———. "Global Business Drivers: Aligning Information Technology to Global Business Strategy." *IBM Systems Journal* 32, no. 1 (1993).

———. "Global Information Technology: Some Lessons from Practice." *International Information Systems* 1, no. 3 (July 1992).

Jarvenpaa, Sirkka L., Kathleen Knoll, and **Dorothy Leidner.** "Is Anybody Out There? Antecedents of Trust in Global Virtual Teams." *Journal of Management Information Systems* 14, no. 4 (Spring 1998).

Karin, Jahangir, and **Benn R. Konsynski.** "Globalization and Information Management Strategies." *Journal of Management Information Systems* 7 (Spring 1991).

Keen, Peter. *Shaping the Future.* Cambridge, MA: Harvard Business School Press (1991).

Kibati, Mugo, and **Donyaprueth Krairit.** "Building India's National Internet Backbone." *Communications of the ACM* 42, no. 6 (June 1999).

King, William R., and **Vikram Sethi.** "An Empirical Analysis of the Organization of Transnational Information Systems." *Journal of Management Information Systems* 15, no. 4 (Spring 1999).

Levy, David. "Lean Production in an International Supply Chain." *Sloan Management Review* (Winter 1997).

Mannheim, Marvin L. "Global Information Technology: Issues and Strategic Opportunities." *International Information Systems* 1, no. 1 (January 1992).

Neumann, Seev. "Issues and Opportunities in International Information Systems." *International Information Systems* 1, no. 4 (October 1992).

Palvia, Shailendra, Prashant Palvia, and **Ronald Zigli,** eds. *The Global Issues of Information Technology Management.* Harrisburg, PA: Idea Group Publishing (1992).

Petrazzini, Ben, and **Mugo Kibati.** "The Internet in Developing Countries." *Communications of the ACM* 42, no. 6 (June 1999).

Quelch, John A., and **Lisa R. Klein.** "The Internet and International Marketing." *Sloan Management Review* (Spring 1996).

Roche, Edward M. *Managing Information Technology in Multinational Corporations.* New York: Macmillan (1992).

Rosenthal, Elisabeth. "Web Sites Bloom in China and Are Weeded." *The New York Times* (December 23, 1999).

Soh, Christina, Sia Siew Kien, and **Joanne Tay-Yap.** "Cultural Fits and Misfits: Is ERP a Universal Solution?" *Communications of the ACM* 43, no. 4 (April 2000).

Steinbart, Paul John, and **Ravinder Nath.** "Problems and Issues in the Management of International Data Networks." *MIS Quarterly* 16, no. 1 (March 1992).

Straub, Detmar W. "The Effect of Culture on IT Diffusion: E-Mail and FAX in Japan and the U.S." *Information Systems Research* 5, no. 1 (March 1994).

Tan, Zixiang (Alex), Milton Mueller, and **Will Foster.** "China's New Internet Regulations: Two Steps Forward, One Step Backward." *Communications of the ACM* 40, no. 12 (December 1997).

Tan, Zixiang, William Foster, and **Seymour Goodman.** "China's State-Coordinated Internet Infrastructure." *Communications of the ACM* 42, no. 6 (June 1999).

Tractinsky, Noam, and **Sirkka L. Jarvenpaa.** "Information Systems Design Decisions in a Global Versus Domestic Context." *MIS Quarterly* 19, no. 4 (December 1995).

Walsham, Geoffrey, and **Sundeys Sahay.** "GIS and District Level Administration in India: Problems and Opportunities." *MIS Quarterly* 23, no. 1 (March 1999).

Watson, Richard T., Gigi G. Kelly, Robert D. Galliers, and **James C. Brancheau.** "Key Issues in Information Systems Management: An International Perspective." *Journal of Management Information Systems* 13, no. 4 (Spring 1997).

Wong, Poh-Kam. "Leveraging the Global Information Revolution for Economic Development: Singapore's Evolving Information Industry Strategy." *Information Systems Research* 9, no. 4 (December 1998).

Wysocki, Bernard. "The Big Bang." *The Wall Street Journal* (January 1, 2000).

Indexes

Name Index

Organization Index

International Organizations Index

Subject Index

Photo and Screen-Shot Credits

Chapter 9

Chapter 10

Chapter 11

Chapter 12

Chapter 13

Chapter 14

Chapter 15

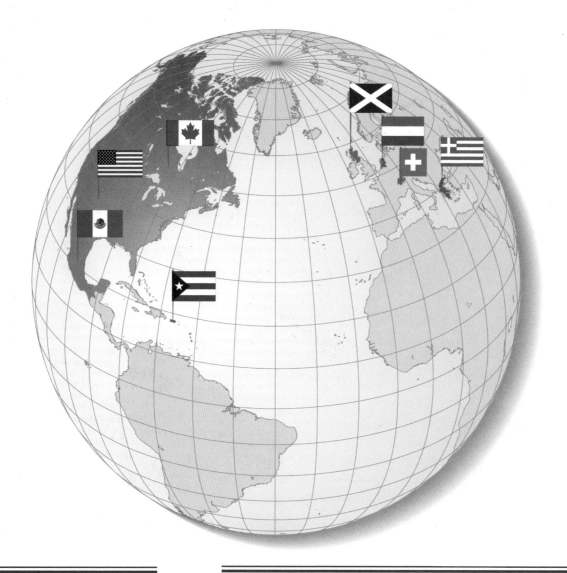

Contributors

 AUSTRALIA

Joel B. Barolsky, University of Melbourne
Paul Richardson, University of Melbourne
Peter Weill, University of Melbourne

 CANADA

Len Fertuck, University of Toronto

 GERMANY

Helmut Krcmar, University of Hohenheim
Gerhard Schwabe, University of Hohenheim
Stephen Wilczek, University of Hohenheim

SINGAPORE

Boon Siong Neo, Nanyang Technological
University
Christina Soh, Nanyang Technological
University

 SWITZERLAND

Andrew Boynton, International
Institute for Management Development
Donald A. Marchand, International
Institute for Management Development
Janet Shaner, International
Institute for Management Development

Consultants

 AUSTRALIA

Robert MacGregor, University of
Wollongong
Alan Underwood, Queensland
University of Technology
Peter Weill, University of Melbourne

 CANADA

Wynne W. Chin, University of Calgary
Len Fertuck, University of Toronto
Robert C. Goldstein, University of
British Columbia
Rebecca Grant, University of Victoria
Kevin Leonard, Wilfrid Laurier University
Anne B. Pidduck, University of Waterloo

 GREECE

Anastasios V. Katos, University of
Macedonia

 HONG KONG

Enoch Tse, Hong Kong Baptist University

 INDIA

Sanjiv D. Vaidya, Indian Institute of
Management, Calcutta

 ISRAEL

Phillip Ein-Dor, Tel-Aviv University
Peretz Shoval, Ben Gurion University

 MEXICO

Noe Urzua Bustamante, Universidad
Tecnológica de México

NETHERLANDS

E.O. de Brock, University of Groningen
Theo Thiadens, University of Twente
Charles Van Der Mast, Delft University
of Technology

 PUERTO RICO, Commonwealth
of the United States

Brunilda Marrero, University of Puerto
Rico

SWEDEN

Mats Daniels, Uppsala University

SWITZERLAND

Andrew C. Boynton, International
Institute for Management Development